THE WORK AND FAMILY HANDBOOK

Multi-Disciplinary Perspectives, Methods, and Approaches

THE WORK AND FAMILY HANDBOOK

Multi-Disciplinary Perspectives, Methods, and Approaches

Edited by

Marcie Pitt-Catsouphes
Boston College

Ellen Ernst Kossek
Michigan State University

Stephen Sweet
Ithaca College

LEA LAWRENCE ERLBAUM ASSOCIATES, PUBLISHERS
2006   Mahwah, New Jersey   London

Senior Acquisitions Editor:	Anne Duffy
Editorial Assistant:	Rebecca Larsen
Cover Design:	Kathryn Houghtaling Lacey
Full-Service Compositor:	TechBooks
Text and Cover Printer:	Hamilton Printing Company

This book was typeset in 10/12 pt. Times Roman, Italic, Bold, and Bold Italic.
The heads were typeset in Helvetica, Helvetica Italic, Helvetica Bold, Helvetica Bold Italic.

Lawrence Erlbaum Associates, Inc., Publishers
10 Industrial Avenue
Mahwah, New Jersey 07430
www.erlbaum.com

Library of Congress Cataloging-in-Publication Data

The work and family handbook : multi-disciplinary perspectives, methods, and approaches /
edited by Marcie Pitt-Catsouphes, Ellen Ernst Kossek, Stephen Sweet.
     p. cm.
  Includes bibliographical references and index.
  ISBN 0-8058-5025-2 (cloth : alk. paper) ISBN 0-8058-5026-0 (pbk : alk. paper)
1. Work and family. 2. Work and family—United States. 3. Work and family—Research.
I. Pitt-Catsouphes, Marcie. II. Kossek, Ellen Ernst. III. Sweet, Stephen A.
  HD4904.25.W6626 2006
  306.3′6—dc22

                                     2005023365

Printed in the United States of America
10 9 8 7 6 5 4 3 2 1

I dedicate this book to my husband Corvis and sons Marcus and Jayme, who have always encouraged me to find meaning and joy at home and at work.

—Marcie Pitt-Catsouphes
Boston, Massachusetts

I would like to dedicate this book to my grandmothers Elaine Ernst and Elinor Robinson, for whom my name is a merged hybrid. Both my grandmothers were bright, remarkable, and educated women who lived rich work and nonwork lives, given the constraints of their generation.

—Ellen Ernst Kossek
East Lansing, Michigan

I dedicate this book to my parents Alfred Sweet and Melissa Sweet. Aside from this sociologist, they found the energy to raise five other children, including a taxidermist, a manager, a mechanic, a bookstore owner, and a teacher. They know the challenges of bridging work and family, and I learned much from witnessing their efforts.

—Stephen Sweet
Ithaca, New York

Contents

III: METHODOLOGICAL APPROACHES

Foreword

Beyond the Myth of Separate Worlds

Rosabeth Moss Kanter
Harvard Business School

Love and work: these basic human needs are the foundation for the huge edifice of society. Yet the connections between them are still not fully understood nor managed effectively in the public realm.

Interpersonal relationships and material sustenance are fundamentals of human existence. One is the realm of reproduction and human development; the other, the domain for the production of goods and services. Both are necessary, yet they are not always in synch. Taken together, loving and working use time and define temporal rhythms, provide identity and meaning, create social standing, and shape values, politics, and public policies. From something as simple and basic as these human drives spring complex social arrangements and institutions that locate people in time and space—the nature of families, reflected in laws as well as personal choices; and the patterns of work, reflected in organizational policies as well as the demands of occupations.

The thread that runs between work and family is carried by each individual. It is held by everyone who splits each day between homes and workplaces; who juggles demands of spouses, lovers, children, bosses, colleagues, or clients deciding how much attention to allocate to each; who cashes paychecks or welfare checks and makes financial plans. At the same time, the opportunities open to people to have a viable family life while working, or to have satisfying work while carrying out responsibilities to family members, are heavily influenced by decisions made by legislators, policy-makers, public opinion, and rule-shapers. Government is definitely in the bedroom as well as the boardroom, whether people like it or not.

The topic of work and family is thus both micro and macro in scope. It has implications for individuals in their personal lives and managers or public policy-makers in their official capacities. And its study embraces every social science and nearly every professional discipline.

That is a relatively recent revelation. For a long time it was assumed that each institution took care of itself separately, and separate, specialized professions dealt with problems and pathologies of each, embedded in independent professional schools: e.g., social work for those dealing with families, MBA programs for those dealing with work. Gradually, there has been recognition that the boundaries are permeable, that issues spillover from one realm to the other. It is difficult to understand what is happening in the home or to children without knowing about their parents' work situations, and it is difficult to motivate and retain employees without being attentive to the fact that their relationships outside of work affect their capacity to do their job.

It's about time we finish burying what I call "the myth of separate worlds."

Challenging the myth of separate worlds was important to me personally and professionally at the start of my own career, because it was one of the things that seemed to confine women and men to stereotyped roles: women as unpaid family workers, men as breadwinners too absorbed at work to have meaningful relationships with their families. As a young scholar interested in organizations and communities, and as a sociologist interested in alternative institutions, I was enticed into research dialogues about both the changing nature of work systems and the changing nature of family systems.

It was clear then that these topics were addressed by different literatures and scholars that rarely spoke to one another. There were exceptions in outstanding researchers such as Rhona Rapoport in the U.K. and Lotte Bailyn in the U.S. who had done seminal work bringing them together, but they were few. I decided to make an attempt at integration. I wrote a review and policy statement for the Russell Sage Foundation, published in 1977 as *Work and Family in the United States*.

The "myth of separate worlds" was under attack, but the battle had just been joined. It was clear from a reading of history that this myth arose in industrial era, corresponding to male-female role differentiation, and very convenient for large bureaucratic companies (such as the one I wrote about in *Men and Women of the Corporation*, also published in 1977) that could demand nearly all their male managers' time or get two executives for the price of one (via the corporate wife role).

That was the right moment to look behind the myth. Scholars start to see things clearly at points of inflection, when challenges to institutions put institutional patterns, assumptions, and ideologies in relief. There were numerous social changes that awakened interest in the connections between work and family. The quest for equal opportunity for women, corresponding to a rise in women in the paid work force, brought family issues to forefront. The baby boom generation that began to enter the paid work force in droves in the 1970s brought a different set of values from their "organization man"/"feminine mystique" suburban parents. And work itself was beginning to change, as the industrial era was passing into a post-industrial information age with a new kind of company—one that blurred all sorts of boundaries, eventually becoming the 24/7 Internet Age—and a new kind of work, so-called "knowledge work," that is less observable, more portable, and more demanding of mental energy.

Also beginning in the 1970s, there was public examination of problems in both work and family, through commissions and conferences at the highest levels of national government. America faced a productivity problem, which then turned into a competitiveness problem starting with the rise of Japanese manufacturing companies beating the U.S. on its own territory, from autos to copiers. Training and motivating workers and ensuring the quality of their work life (which sometimes also meant just life) became urgent. Numerous changes in families were also a concern, with rise of single-parent households, dysfunctional family systems among segments of the poor, and children ill-prepared for school achievement (a problem employers grasped, as reflected in their zeal to improve public education starting with the *Nation at Risk* report in the 1980s).

Work and family became a prominent topic of policy debates in the 1980s, especially as corporations grappled with the changes in the composition of their work force, and "human resources" replaced the traditional personnel department, signaling a shift of emphasis. But change was much slower than I thought it would be. For example, there were numerous studies, first in Germany and then in the U.S., of the benefits to workplace productivity of flexible work hours, or "flex-time," yet companies were exceedingly slow to let go of control of the structure of the work day.

Today there are numerous signs of change: a child care industry, an after-school movement, and increased benefits for working parents, among many other developments. "Work/life balance" is the new buzz-phrase.

Social change is neither smooth nor uni-directional. Unexpected twists and unresolved issues make roadmaps hard to create. Gay marriage or civil unions is one political issue that surfaced in the 2004 presidential election, though many larger corporations long ago extended partner benefits to gay couples. It is also not clear that all constituencies want or need the same things. Witness various contradictory developments. On the one hand, "anti-parent" and "child-free" movements argue against special privileges for working parents; and, on the other hand, a rise in women above the age of 35 taking fertility treatments, on the other hand, to give birth at older ages when they are established in their careers and employers have been expecting them to undertake greater responsibilities at work. Similarly, many middle-class families cannot survive without two incomes, forcing both spouses to work at either marginal or dual jobs; while some educated women with affluent husbands are abandoning paid careers for which they underwent expensive training and attained advanced degrees, in order to stay home with their children.

As with any set of complex social changes, such phenomena need to be identified, named, conceptualized, deconstructed, segmented, researched, and discussed. Policies and programs need to be evaluated, with hypotheses and frameworks that help answer questions about results. What are the outcomes of changes and social experiments and new arrangements? And for whom? Parents? Children? People with new life-styles? Employers? Co-workers? Managers? The economy?

And how do these issues show up outside of the industrialized world, in developing countries where people are moving beyond subsistence in small villages to become employees in a paid work force? A researcher at Harvard's School of Public Policy has argued that the best thing corporations can do to solve global health problems is to provide employment with flexible hours and child care.

With so many questions, we should all be grateful that there are now many insightful academics searching for answers.

In short, there is much to be learned from the scholars in this book who take the risk of working on the boundaries, at the intersection of two major social institutions. Some researchers look at the work-family issue from the micro perspective of individuals, some from the macro vantage point of the economy and social policy, some from an intermediate managerial perspective about how organizations can respond. All levels of analysis shed new light on dynamic relationships with significant implications for scholars and practitioners alike.

Taken as a whole, this book helps us stand back and watch the unfolding process of social change. Work life and family life have both changed dramatically in recent times. Which leads, which lags? Does the design of organizations reflect changes in people's lives, or does it propel changes by opening new possibilities or restricting opportunities? Do people compose their lives around the possibilities that their work permits, or do they push organizations to accommodate to their needs?

The papers in this book push knowledge a step further. This will ultimately contribute to better conversations across the social sciences, as the economy and society are viewed together. My hope is that people and their needs will be better reflected in managerial actions and public policy, and that both working and loving will become more fulfilling as a result. People have to make a living, and they have to make a life.

—Rosabeth Moss Kanter holds the Ernest L. Arbuckle Chair as Professor of Business Administration at Harvard Business School. She is the author or co-author of 16 books, including her most recent book *Confidence: How Winning Streaks & Losing Streaks Begin & End* (Crown). She is the recipient of numerous honors, including 21 honorary doctoral degrees and the Academy of Management's Distinguished Career Award for Scholarly Contributions.

Acknowledgments

The preparation of this handbook reflects the vision and commitment of a large group of colleagues, family members, and friends who believe that it is important to move the work-family field forward in a purposeful manner. As editors, we have received significant support from many individuals and institutions. We would like to thank them with sincerity and deep appreciation.

It is most appropriate for us to first thank the creative and forward-thinking individuals who have served on the Editorial Board of the *Work-Family Encyclopedia*, a publication of the Sloan Work and Family Research Network http://www.bc.edu/bc_org/avp/wfnetwork/rft/index.html (Marcie Pitt-Catsouphes and Ellen Ernst Kossek, founding co-editors). In 2002, the members of the Editorial Board had the foresight to anticipate the need for a handbook that could capture the multi-disciplinary nature of the work-family area of study. These individuals recognized that faculty who incorporate work-family content into their courses could use a resource that would present information about the range of scholarly perspectives and the diversity of methods used by work-family academics. This handbook would not be a reality without the urging and thinking by Mark Auslander, Leslie Hammer, Jacqueline Lerner, Sharon Lobel, Patricia Raskin, Teresa Rothhausen-Vange, and Cynthia Thompson.

The work-family area of study has many leading thinkers, most of whom are more than fully engaged in their own investigations, teaching, and writing. We cannot adequately express how grateful we are that 63 scholars saw the development of this handbook as a priority and devoted the time necessary to write their chapters, consider the comments and suggestions made by the reviewers, and prepare the final versions of their work. We introduce you to these insightful and talented individuals in the biography pages that follow.

A large group of scholars also reviewed the chapters. Reviewing is often an invisible and thankless task, but essential for the quality of the product. Therefore, we would like to thank the following individuals: Marietta Baba, Rosalind Barnett, James T. Bond, Wayne Cascio, Nan Crouter, Charles Darrah, Francine M. Deutsch, Chai Feldblum, Naomi Gerstel, Lonnie Golden, Leslie Hammer, Mona Harrington, MaryAnne Hyland, Susan Jackson, Erin Kelly, Tom Kochan, Suzan Lewis, Shelley MacDermid, Stephen Marks, Margaret Neal, Cheryl Peters Barbara Schneider, Janet Smithson, Mary Still, Jennifer Swanberg, Raymond Swisher, Cynthia Thompson, Amy Wharton, Ben Wolkinson, and Carrie Yodanis.

Each of our "home-base" institutions has made it possible for this editorial team to function effectively and efficiently. Marcie Pitt-Catsouphes would like to thank Ted Gaiser, Beth Clark, and their colleagues at the Boston College Academic Technology Services. Ellen Kossek would like to thank the School of Labor and Industrial Relations for providing research time to work on this document as part of her normal appointment. Stephen Sweet is indebted to the support of his department's administrative assistant Vikki Hammond as well as his undergraduate student assistant Michael Proctor.

We would like to thank Anne Duffy, Senior Editor at Lawrence Erlbaum Associates, and her editorial assistant Kristin Duch for providing us with timely assistance and ongoing encouragement to work on this volume.

Finally, we offer our appreciation to our spouses and children, who forgave our absences while we were "off to work on the handbook." Marcie thanks her husband Corvis and sons Marcus and Jayme. Ellen thanks her husband Sandy and children Andrew, Sarah, Haley, and Dylan. Stephen thanks his wife Jai and children Arjun and Nisha. These individuals remind us every day about what matters most in life.

About the Contributors

THE EDITORS

Marcie Pitt-Catsouphes is Associate Professor at the Boston College Graduate School of Social Work. Her work has been published in journals including *Community, Work and Family,* the *ANNALS of Political and Social Science,* and *Nonprofit Management & Leadership.* Dr. Pitt-Catsouphes is a co-principal investigator of the study, "Understanding the First Job: Nurturing Families," funded by the Alfred P. Sloan Foundation and the principal investigator of the Sloan Work and Family Research Network.

Ellen Ernst Kossek (PhD Yale) is Professor at Michigan State University. She is elected to the Board of Governors of the National Academy of Management, and is a Fellow of the American Psychological Association and the Society of Industrial and Organizational Psychology. She recently co-edited *Managing Work and Life Integration: Organizational, Cultural and Individual Perspectives* (LEA). A prize-winning author, she has published dozens of articles in such journals as the *Academy of Management Journal*, *Personnel Psychology*, *Journal of Applied Psychology (JAP)*, and *Journal of Organizational Behavior (JOB)*. She currently serves on the editorial boards of *JOB*, *JAP*, *Human Resource Management Journal*, and the *Journal of Applied Behavioral Science*. Dr. Kossek is a co-principal investigator on an Alfred P. Sloan-funded study on managing professionals in new work forms (http://flex-work.lir.msu.edu/).

Stephen Sweet is Assistant Professor of Sociology at Ithaca College. His studies of work and family have appeared in a variety of publications, including the *New Directions in Life Course Research, Journal of Vocational Behavior, Journal of Marriage and the Family, Innovative Higher Education, Journal of College Student Development,* and *Community, Work and Family.* Dr. Sweet is a co-principal investigator on an Alfred P. Sloan Foundation-funded project to study the effects of job insecurity on families.

THE AUTHORS

Tammy D. Allen is Associate Professor of Psychology at the University of South Florida. She received her PhD in Industrial and Organizational Psychology from the University of Tennessee. Her research interests include work and family issues, employee well-being, mentoring relationships, career development, and organizational citizenship behavior. She is a member of the editorial boards of *Journal of Applied Psychology*, *Personnel Psychology*, *Journal of Vocational Behavior*, *Journal of Organizational Behavior*, and *Journal of Occupational Health Psychology*.

Robin Appleberry is a Teaching Fellow in the Federal Legislation Clinic at Georgetown Law, where she supervises law students providing pro bono legislative lawyering for Workplace Flexibility 2010. Robin is a graduate of Yale University (BA, 1996) and the University of California at Berkeley (JD, 2001) and will receive her LLM from Georgetown in 2005. Through her work before and after law school, Robin has sustained a deep commitment to advancing women's health, civil and human rights, and work-life balance through the law.

Lotte Bailyn is the T. Wilson (1953) Professor of Management at MIT's Sloan School of Management and Co-Director of the MIT Workplace Center. Her research deals with the intersection between work and family life, and explores management systems and workplace practices meant to reconcile the demands of both. She is the author of *Breaking the Mold: Women, Men, and Time in the New Corporate World* and co-author of *Beyond Work-Family Balance: Advancing Gender Equity and Workplace Performance*.

Rosalind Chait Barnett, PhD, is Senior Scientist and Executive Director of the Community, Families & Work Program at Brandeis University's Women's Studies Research Center. She has published widely on work, family, and gender. Alone and with others, she has published over 90 articles, 20 chapters, and 7 books. Her newest book, with co-author Caryl Rivers, is *Same Difference: How Gender Myths Are Hurting Our Relationships, Our Children, and Our Jobs* (Basic Books, 2004).

Laura L. Beauvais is Professor of Management at the University of Rhode Island in Kingston, Rhode Island. She received her PhD in Industrial/Organizational Psychology from the University of Tennessee in 1987. Her research interests include the management of work/professional/family roles among employees, self-concept-based motivation processes, moral development among business students, and organizational change. She teaches graduate and undergraduate courses in organizational behavior, organizational design and change, human resources management, leadership, and women in business.

James (Terry) Bond is Vice President for Research at the Families and Work Institute, a nonprofit research organization. He has primary responsibility for the Institute's *National Study of the Changing Workforce*. Before joining the Families and Work Institute, he was Deputy Director of the National Center for Children in Poverty at Columbia University, founding Director of the NCJW Center for the Child, and Director of Research at the High/Scope Educational Research Foundation.

Ann Bookman is Executive Director of the MIT Workplace Center. She is a social anthropologist who has authored publications in the areas of women's work, work and family issues, unionization, and child and family policy. Her new book, *Starting in Our Own Backyards: How Working Families Can Build Community and Survive the New Economy*, extends the discourse on work-family integration to include issues of community organizations, community involvement, and civil society.

Eileen Boris, an interdisciplinary historian, is the Hull Professor of Women's Studies and Director of the Center for the Study of Women and Social Justice at the University of California,

Santa Barbara. She specializes in gender, race, labor, and the welfare state. A prize-winning author, she currently is writing a history of the long-term care workforce, called *Neither Nurses, Nor Maids: Housekeepers, Health Aides, and Personal Attendants in the Home Workplace.*

Thomas Bradbury, Professor of Psychology at UCLA, uses observational and longitudinal methods to study marriage and family development. He is the editor of *The Psychology of Marriage* (with Frank Fincham) and *The Developmental Course of Marital Dysfunction*, and with Benjamin Karney, he has twice received the Reuben Hill Award for Research and Theory from the National Council on Family Relations.

Julia Brannen is Professor of Sociology of the Family in the Institute of Education, University of London. She has researched and written about work-family issues in Britain and Europe, including children and young people. She has a particular interest in methodology and is a co-founder and co-editor of the *International Journal of Social Research Methodology: Theory and Practice*. Her most recent book is *Working and Caring over the Twentieth Century.*

Kathleen Christensen founded and directs the Program on the Workplace, Workforce and Working Families at the Alfred P. Sloan Foundation in New York City. Dr. Christensen has published extensively on the changing nature of work and its relationship to the family. Her books include *Contingent Work: American Employment Relations in Transition, Turbulence in the American Workplace,* and *Women and Home-Based Work: The Unspoken Contract.* She has been awarded fellowships from the Danforth Foundation, National Endowment for the Humanities, Mellon Foundation, and Rockefeller Foundation, and received the 2004 Work Life Legacy Award from the Families and Work Institute.

Ann C. Crouter is Professor of Human Development and Director of the Center for Work and Family Research at the Pennsylvania State University. Her interests revolve around the connections between parents' work circumstances, family dynamics, and the development and adjustment of children and youth. She currently co-directs two longitudinal studies of dual-earner families and collaborates on a large, multi-method, longitudinal study of young children growing up in rural, low-income families in Pennsylvania and North Carolina.

Charles N. Darrah is Professor of Anthropology at San Jose State University. He is a cultural anthropologist whose research has focused on work, families, and technology. He is a co-founder of the Silicon Valley Cultures Project at San Jose State University (www.sjsu.edu/depts/anthropology/svcp/). His 1997 book, *Learning and Work: An Exploration in Industrial Ethnography*, is based on fieldwork in two manufacturing plants. Darrah and his colleagues, J. A. English-Lueck and J. M. Freeman, are collaborating on a book, *Busy-Bodies: Busyness and the American Dream.*

Francine M. Deutsch is Professor of Psychology at Mount Holyoke College. Author of *Halving It All: How Equally Shared Parenting Works*, her research focuses on the inequities in the division of domestic labor between men and women. Her articles have been published in *Journal of Personality and Social Psychology, Journal of Family Issues, Social Psychology and Personality Bulletin, Sex Roles, Psychology of Women Quarterly*, and *Journal of Comparative Family Studies.*

Robert Drago is Professor of Labor Studies and Women's Studies at the Pennsylvania State University, a Professorial Fellow at the University of Melbourne, moderates the work/family newsgroup on the Internet, and is a co-founder of the Take Care Net. Holding a PhD in

Economics from the University of Massachusetts, he has written over 50 articles and three books. His recent research for the Alfred P. Sloan Foundation addresses biases against caregiving and work-family policies.

Chai Rachel Feldblum is Professor of Law at Georgetown University Law Center and Director of Workplace Flexibility 2010, an Alfred P. Sloan Foundation Initiative. A graduate of Harvard Law School and a law clerk to Judge Frank Coffin and Justice Harry Blackmun, Professor Feldblum was the lead lawyer responsible for negotiating the Americans with Disabilities Act. Since 1988, Professor Feldblum has been actively involved in shaping legislative and regulatory initiatives on civil rights, health care, and employment policy.

Alyssa Friede is a graduate student in Industrial/Organizational Psychology at Michigan State University. Her research is focused on the psychology of work-life balance, with a particular interest in the influence of personality, coping, and decision-making. Alyssa worked with Professors Ellen Ernst Kossek and Mary Dean Lee on an Alfred P. Sloan Foundation grant examining reduced-load work among professionals and managers. She recently completed a book chapter with Ann Marie Ryan on personality and work-life balance.

Ellen Galinsky is President and Co-Founder of the Families and Work Institute. She is the author of over 25 books and reports, including *Ask the Children*. She has published more than 100 articles in academic journals, books, and magazines. She co-directs the most comprehensive studies of the workforce—the *National Study of the Changing Workforce*—and of employers, the *National Study of Employers*. She staffs the Conference Board's Work Life Leadership Council and directs their annual work life conference.

Karen C. Gareis, PhD, is Senior Research Associate and Program Director of the Community, Families & Work Program at Brandeis University's Women's Studies Research Center. Her research interests include work-family issues, gender, and social support. She currently directs two studies for Dr. R. C. Barnett, both funded by the Alfred P. Sloan Foundation: one on maternal work schedules and child and family well-being, and the other, on how employed parents of school-age children coordinate family schedules.

Naomi Gerstel is Professor at the University of Massachusetts. She has published on the gender gap in caregiving, racial differences in kin support, privileges embedded in the Family Medical Leave Act, a comparison of U.S. and European child care, sibling ties, and the labor unions' response to family policies. Her current ongoing research consists of two projects: one on the racialized gender gap in care to relatives and friends, and the other, on time spent on the job.

Lonnie Golden is Associate Professor of Economics and Labor Studies at Pennsylvania State University Abington College. His research focuses on the labor market, particularly working hours, work schedule flexibility, overtime law, overwork, work-life balance, behavioral labor supply, and productivity in the jobless recovery. He has co-edited the books, *Working Time: International Trends, Theory and Policy Perspectives*, and *Nonstandard Work: The Nature and Challenge of Changing Employment Arrangements*.

Anthony P. Graesch is a doctoral candidate in the UCLA Department of Anthropology and a graduate research fellow at the UCLA Center on Everyday Lives of Families. He studies the congruency between modern-day family life and culturally construed ideals of normative family behavior as encoded in the design of Los Angeles houses. He also examines and has published on indigenous western North American household organization and post-contact cultural change from an archaeological perspective.

Maria das Dores Guerreiro is Professora in the Department of Sociology at the Instituto Superior de Ciências do Trabalho e da Empresa (ISCTE) and a researcher at CIES. She is the editor of *Sociologia, Problemas e Práticas*. Her research interest areas are in family and work relations, gender, generations, sociology of the family, and social policies. She is author and co-author of several publications on these subjects.

Leslie B. Hammer is Associate Professor in the Department of Psychology, Portland State University. Her forthcoming book with Margaret Neal, *Working Couples Caring for Children and Aging Parents*, is based on a national, longitudinal study funded by the Alfred P. Sloan Foundation. She has written articles and book chapters in the area of work and family, and also serves on the founding editorial board of the Sloan Work and Family Research Network's on-Line *Work and Family Encyclopedia*.

Brad Harrington is the Executive Director of the Center for Work & Family (CWF) and a faculty member in Organization Studies in the Carroll School of Management at Boston College. He holds a doctorate in Human Resource Development from Boston University. Previously, Brad was an executive in organization development with Hewlett-Packard Company for 20 years. He is currently writing a book on career management and work/life integration with Professor Douglas T. Hall of Boston University.

Mona Harrington, who holds degrees in political science and law from Harvard, is Program Director at the MIT Workplace Center where she chairs a project for the formation of a Massachusetts Work-Family Council. She is also a writer who examines connections between American political culture and social policy. Her latest book, *Care and Equality: Inventing a New Family Politics*, calls for a national conversation about new ways to connect families, care, women, and work.

Ashley Harvey has a master's degree in human development and family studies from Colorado State University. She is a doctoral candidate in the Department of Child Development and Family Studies at Purdue University and is a licensed marriage and family therapist. Her research focus is gender equity in dual-earner families. She is currently serving as the interview editor for the *Journal of Feminist Family Therapy*.

MaryAnne Hyland is Assistant Professor of Human Resource Management at Adelphi University. Her research interests include work/life balance and flexible work arrangements. She has published her research in *Journal of Applied Psychology*, *Journal of Applied Social Psychology*, *Managerial Auditing Journal*, and *Personnel Psychology*. MaryAnne completed her PhD in human resource management at Rutgers University.

Susan E. Jackson is Professor of Human Resource Management and Director of the PhD Program in Industrial Relations and Human Resources at Rutgers University. Her primary research interests include strategic human resource management, work team functioning, and workforce diversity. She is a Fellow and active member of the American Psychological Association, the Society for Industrial and Organizational Psychology, and the Academy of Management.

Jacquelyn B. James is the Director of Research at the Boston College Center for Work & Family. Dr. James received her PhD in developmental psychology at Boston University. Prior to her present role, she was associate director of the Murray Research Center at Harvard University. Currently, she is co-authoring a book titled, *Charting New Life Stage: The Third Age*, about the opportunities and challenges in the early retirement years.

Erin L. Kelly is Assistant Professor of Sociology at the University of Minnesota and an affiliate of the university's Life Course Center and Center for Labor Policy. Her research on the development and diffusion of employers' family policies has appeared in *The American Journal of Sociology*. She is also interested in the consequences of workplace policies and practices for organizations, for caregivers' careers, and for workers' health and well-being.

Thomas A. Kochan is the George M. Bunker Professor of Management at MIT's Sloan School of Management and Co-Director of the MIT Workplace Center. He has done research on a variety of topics related to industrial relations and human resource management in the public and private sector. Professor Kochan is a Past President of the International Industrial Relations Association and the Industrial Relations Research Association (IRRA). In 1996, he received the Heneman Career Achievement Award from the Human Resources Division of the Academy of Management.

Susan J. Lambert is Associate Professor in the School of Social Service Administration at the University of Chicago. Lambert's research focuses on the "work side" of work-life issues. Her most current research examines the extent to which opportunities available in today's corporations trickle down to jobs at lower-organizational levels. Her research seeks to identify the mechanisms by which employers pass variations in consumer demand onto workers to absorb, thus introducing greater instability into workers' lives.

Carolyn Herbst Lewis is a doctoral student in the Department of History and the Women's Studies Program at the University of California, Santa Barbara. She has an MA in American History from Ohio University. Currently, she is completing her dissertation, "Coitus Perfectus: The Medical Construction of Heterosexuality in the Mid-Twentieth Century United States." Her writings have appeared in *The Journal of the History of Sexuality and Women's America: Refocusing the Past*.

Suzan Lewis is Professor of Organisational and Work-Life Psychology at Manchester Metropolitan University, U.K. Her research on work-life integration focuses on workplace practice, culture, and change and she has led many national and international research projects on these topics. Her publications include *The Work Family Challenge: Rethinking Employment,* and *Work-Life Integration: Case Studies of Workplace Change.* She is a founding editor of the international journal, *Community, Work and Family.*

Shelley M. MacDermid is Professor in the Department of Child Development and Family Studies at Purdue University, where she also directs the Center for Families. In May 2000, she became co-director of a new Military Family Research Institute, also at Purdue. Dr. MacDermid earned an MBA in Management and a PhD in Human Development and Family Studies from The Pennsylvania State University. Her research focuses on relationships between job conditions and family life, with special interests in organizational size, adult development, and organizational policies.

Stephen R. Marks is Professor of Sociology at the University of Maine. His approach to work-family balance is embedded in an interest in overall role balance. His work has alerted researchers to the options that people have in organizing their multiple roles as a pattern or system. He has shown that hierarchical self- and role-systems are neither inevitable nor necessary, and when people expand the reach of their role systems in an evenhanded way, there are often salutary consequences for their well-being. His interest in family diversity is rooted in the recognition that socially constructed categories—especially race, class, gender, sexual orientation, and age—may privilege some people and disadvantage others as they attempt to balance their multiple roles.

Angela Mittmann is an advanced graduate student in clinical psychology at UCLA. Her research focuses on the association between workplace stress and working parents' communication patterns with family, particularly emotion-focused communication and marital communication. She is also focused on understanding individual differences that moderate such work-family association.

Phyllis Moen is the McKnight Presidential Chair in Sociology from the University of Minnesota. Her recent co-authored book, *The Career Mystique: Cracks in the American Dream,* addresses the fundamental mismatch between the ways work and retirement are organized and the realities of a changing workforce and an uncertain global economy. Dr. Moen has published widely on the topics of gender, aging, the life course, work, retirement, and social policy. She also founded the Bronfenbrenner Life Course Center at Cornell University and was lead investigator at the Cornell Careers Institute, an Alfred P. Sloan Center for the Study of Working Families.

David L. Morgan is University Professor at Portland State University. He is well known for his work on focus groups and qualitative research. More recently, he has concentrated on research designs that combine qualitative and quantitative methods, and is currently completing a book on this topic.

Margaret B. Neal is Director of the Institute on Aging and Professor of Community Health, College of Urban and Public Affairs, and former director of the Survey Research Laboratory, Portland State University, Portland, Oregon. Her research interests include work-family integration and how the public and private sectors can assist employed caregivers to elders. Her latest book, co-authored with Leslie Hammer, is based on an Alfred P. Sloan Foundation-funded study involving qualitative and quantitative data and concerns working, sandwiched-generation couples.

Megan L. Notter is a graduate student at Oregon State University. Her research interests include domestic violence and child outcomes, intervention, program evaluation, and family policy.

Elinor Ochs is Professor of Anthropology and Director of the UCLA Sloan Center on the Everyday Lives of Families. She examines language socialization and discursive practices of typical and impaired individuals across codes, situations, institutions, and communities throughout the life span. She was named MacArthur Fellow, American Academy of Arts and Sciences Fellow, Guggenheim Fellow, Lewis Henry Morgan Lecturer, and received a Helsinki University Rector's medal of Distinctive Scholarship and Honorary Doctorate from Linkoping University.

Russell Ormiston is a PhD candidate at the School of Labor and Industrial Relations at Michigan State University.

Cheryl L. Peters is a PhD candidate in the Department of Human Development and Family Sciences at Oregon State University. Her research interests include intergenerational relationships, work-family issues, and retirement decisions of the baby boom generation.

Amy E. Pirretti, a doctoral student in Human Development and Family Studies at Penn State, received her BA in Psychology from the University of Kansas and MS in Industrial Relations and Human Resources from Penn State. Currently, she is a research assistant on a large project that examines the development of children growing up in low-income, rural communities. This research includes a focus on parents' work circumstances and their implications for parents and children.

Rena Repetti is Professor in the Department of Psychology at UCLA. She received her PhD in 1985 from Yale University. Repetti studies stress and coping processes in the family. Her work points to the dynamic interplay between an individual's efforts to cope with daily stressors and patterns of family interaction. For example, Repetti has shown how stress at work can have both a short-term and a long-term impact on the parent-child relationship.

Pete Richardson (Emory, 2002) is a postdoctoral fellow at the Center for the Ethnography of Everyday Life at the University of Michigan. He is now engaged in fieldwork centered on an auto parts plant in the Detroit area. His work experience includes time as a commercial fisherman in Alaska, bookseller, and bouncer. His interests include the fields of psychological, philosophical, and social anthropology, the anthropologies of work and nature, and western and labor histories.

Martha Farnsworth Riche is with the Center for the Study of Economy and Society, Cornell University. She served as Director of the U.S. Census Bureau between 1994 and 1998. Through Farnsworth Riche Associates, Dr. Riche consults, writes, and lectures on demographic changes and their effects on policies, programs, and products. A Fellow of the American Statistical Association, she is the author of numerous articles, papers, and publications in academic and business journals and is a frequent speaker before university, business, and policy audiences.

Natalia Sarkisian is Assistant Professor in the Department of Sociology, Boston College. Her PhD dissertation research at the University of Massachusetts Amherst, funded by a Social Science Research Council Dissertation Fellowship, explores the differences and similarities between Whites and Blacks in social support. She has recently published on employment and the gender gap in help to parents in the *Journal of Marriage and Family* and on kin support and race in the *American Sociological Review*.

Barbara Schneider is Professor of Sociology at the University of Chicago. She co-directs, with Linda Waite, the Alfred P. Sloan Center on Parents, Children, and Work. Author of numerous books and articles, Schneider's major interests are in families, adolescents, and transitions to adulthood. Several of her books, including *Ambitious Generation* and *Becoming Adult*, use the experience sampling method. Her most recent co-authored book is *Being Together, Working Apart: Dual-Career Families and the Work-Life Balance*.

Janet Smithson is a research fellow in the department of Psychology, Manchester Metropolitan University, U.K. She is project manager of an eight-country European project on transitions to parenthood in the context of changing organizations. Other research interests include youth and transitions to adulthood, experiences of insecure work and the effects on work-life choices, environmental effects of work-life choices, discourse and conversation analytic approaches to gender, and organizational talk.

Mary C. Still is a faculty fellow at the University of California Hastings College of the Law. She was an Alfred P. Sloan predoctoral fellow at the Cornell Couples & Careers Institute for five years. Still's research interests are in the areas of organizational change, gender in the workplace, social networks, and innovation. She has published in *Social Forces, Sociological Theory, The Journal of Industrial and Corporate Change*, and *Evolution and Human Behavior*.

Jennifer E. Swanberg, Assistant Professor at the College of Social Work, University of Kentucky, conducts research on the relationships between work, family and organizational effectiveness, especially among understudied populations including low-wage workers, victims of intimate partner violence, and employed informal caregivers. She has published in *Work, Family and Community* and *Nonprofit Management & Leadership*, and has articles forthcoming in *Journal of Economic and Family Issues, Family Issues*, and *Journal of Occupational Health Psychology*.

Raymond Swisher is Assistant Professor of Policy Analysis and Management at Cornell University. His current research focuses on the effects of social contexts on well-being across the life course. One project examines the influence of neighborhood poverty and violence on adolescent well-being, violence, and educational attainment. Other research examines how workplace and neighborhood contexts shape dual-earner families' efforts to manage work and family demands.

Cynthia A. Thompson is Professor of Management in the Zicklin School of Business at Baruch College, City University of New York. Her research focuses on the integration of work and life and, in particular, the extent to which supportive work-family cultures affect employee attitudes and behavior. Her work has been published in the *Journal of Applied Psychology, Journal of Vocational Behavior, Journal of Managerial Issues, Sex Roles*, and *Community, Work and Family*, among others.

Amy S. Wharton is Professor of Sociology at Washington State University. Her research interests include gender inequality, work, and organizations. With Mary Blair-Loy, she is studying work-family programs in a large international financial services firm. Papers based on this research have been published in *Social Forces, Work and Occupations*, and *Sociological Perspectives*. Wharton is also interested in the effects of organizations' "core ideologies" on their commitment to work-family policies over time.

Joan C. Williams, prize-winning author and Distinguished Professor of Law at University of California, Hastings College of the Law, is Director of the Center for WorkLife Law and Co-Director of the Project on Attorney Retention. She has published more than 50 scholarly articles and a book, *Unbending Gender: Why Work and Family Conflict and What to Do About It*. She has been widely quoted in the press, in publications as diverse as *Business Week*, the *New York Times, Parenting Magazine*, and *O*.

Benjamin W. Wolkinson is Professor of Labor Relations at the School of Labor and Industrial Relations at Michigan State University. He is a member of the National Academy of Arbitrators and serves as an arbitrator for many employers and labor unions in Michigan and Ohio. His books include *Arab Employment in Israel: The Quest for Equal Employment Opportunity*,

Employment Law: The Workplace Rights of Employees and Employers, and *Blacks, Unions and the EEOC*.

Anisa M. Zvonkovic is Professor of Human Development and Family Studies at Texas Tech University. She received her MS and PhD degrees in Human Development and Family Studies from the Pennsylvania State University. Her research focuses on work and family issues from a close relationships and feminist perspective. She currently studies the personal lives of workers whose jobs require extensive travel.

THE WORK AND FAMILY HANDBOOK

*Multi-Disciplinary Perspectives,
Methods, and Approaches*

PART I: Families and Jobs in the 21st Century

1

Charting New Territory: Advancing Multi-Disciplinary Perspectives, Methods, and Approaches in the Study of Work and Family

Marcie Pitt-Catsouphes
Boston College

Ellen Ernst Kossek
Michigan State University

Stephen Sweet
Ithaca College

For the past 30 years, there has been a sustained surge in academic interest in work-family issues. However, despite the increase in scholarly studies about work-family relationships and the explosive growth in work-family publications, until now there has not been any single handbook that compiled the work of scholars across the disciplines and also compared and contrasted their approaches to the study of work-family phenomena. This handbook, the culmination of efforts of 63 leading work and family researchers, fills that gap and offers an overview of the major insights, challenges, and opportunities present in the work-family field. But, what exactly is the "work-family" field, when did it emerge, and why?

Kathleen Christensen, author of the last chapter in this handbook, has often remarked that the work-family field may be the only field of study best known by a hyphen—the hyphen that is placed between the words "work" and "family." As editors of this handbook, we have come to believe that the hyphen is important, because it symbolizes the field's focus on the connections between *work* experiences and *family* issues. These connections have been conceptualized as "relationships," "interactions," and "interface." As Rosabeth Moss Kanter cogently observes in her Foreword to this volume, if work and family are considered as "separate spheres" in policy and cultural action, our understanding of both institutions suffers.

In general, work-family research focuses on two overarching concerns. One stream of studies primarily focuses on the different ways that work can affect the family, the other on how family responsibilities impact work. It is instructive to consider a few examples.

Some researchers who have studied the ways that *work impacts family lives* have explored how job demands (and associated factors such as organizational structures, the design of work roles, and workplace cultures) affect employees and their management of family responsibilities (e.g., see Appelbaum, Berg, & Kalleberg, 2000; Bailyn & Harrington, 2004; Batt & Valcour, 2003; Berg, Kalleberg, & Appelbaum, 2003; Blair-Loy & Wharton, 2002; O'Driscoll et al., Cooper, 2003; Viega, Baldridge, & Eddleston, 2004). Extensive research has also been devoted to the relationships between work hours, work schedules, and different aspects of well-being (e.g., Bihan & Martin, 2004; Cousins & Tang, 2004; Jacobs & Gerson, 2004; Jansen, Kant, Kristensen, & Nijhuis, 2003; Strazdins, Korda, Lim, Broom, & D'Souza, 2004; van Rijswijk, Bekker, Rutte, & Croon, 2004), with some of these studies considering whether time devoted to work might otherwise be devoted to family rituals (such as evening meals), carework (essential to the needs of children, spouses, aging parents), or self care (such as medical care, exercise, and stress management) (e.g., Crouter, Bumpus, Head, & McHale, 2001). It is important to note that other scholars have examined whether *work can enhance individual well-being and family life*. For example, some have studied relationships between family well-being and economic compensation, whereas other scholars have studied how the intrinsic rewards of jobs and work roles shape family development, health, and well-being (for examples of such studies, see Barnett & Gareis, chapter 10 in this volume; Grzywacz & Marks, 2000; Nordenmark, 2002; Voydanoff, 2004).

On the other hand, the work-family equation can also be inverted to consider the ways that families support the workplace as well as circumstances in which family obligations distract workers from employers' priorities (Kanter, 1977a). Some studies, for instance, have investigated how family demands and needs can impinge on labor force attachment and worker productivity (e.g., Moen & Sweet, 2003). Others have considered the family-to-work interaction from a different viewpoint—how positive aspects of family life can spill over into the workplace, thereby benefiting businesses (for examples of studies examining the family-to-work interface, see Bayraktar & Salman, 2003; Creamer & Associates, 2001; Crouter, 1984; Ferber & Hoffman, 1997; Powers, 2001; Sweet & Moen, 2004). Academics in this stream of research understand that if families do not perform their roles, such as reproduction and socialization of the next generation of workers, employers and the society-at-large will inevitably suffer (Kanter, Foreword, this volume).

Thus, it has been the concern of work-family scholarship to juxtapose our knowledge of how workplaces operate with our understandings of how families function. The academic work conducted over the past three decades has revealed the connections between these institutions and has linked the scholarly work of what has traditionally been perceived as separate areas of study. We are presently witnessing the successes of academics' efforts to create a new field of study with a distinct body knowledge that has been developed by a multi-disciplinary community of academics.

In this chapter, we offer an overview of the development of the new work-family field, its multi-disciplinary shape, and prevailing themes of inquiry. We discuss how work-family scholarship emerged during a time when there was a confluence of demographic, economic, and cultural shifts. We note that scholarship during the early years of the work-family area of study typically reflected the confines of existing disciplinary boundaries and divisions of labor within academe. These traditional structures made it difficult for scholars to move forward with multi-disciplinary perspectives. In many respects, the current work-family field is now challenging rigid academic institutional arrangements in an effort to forge bridges between disciplinary perspectives. It is to this larger goal that this handbook is devoted.

WORK-FAMILY ISSUES TAKE ROOT

Historians persuasively argue that work-family concerns are not necessarily "new" experiences, as people have always had to coordinate their family responsibilities with their economic pursuits (e.g., Eileen Boris and Carolyn Lewis's chapter 4, this volume). Indeed, academic commentary and policy discourse about work-family experiences have deep roots in different social science disciplines, suggesting that work-family challenges were also visible in early times.

For example, Friedrich Engels discussed the relationships between economic arrangements and the family, paying particular attention to the ways that the new industrial order ravaged family lives and communities in Europe (Engels, 1936 [1845]). Industrialization also drew attention to work-family issues in the United States. During the transitional years when America moved from being a primarily agrarian society to an industrialized economy, some companies established employer-supported programs including child-care centers and hospitals that became part of the industrial welfare system (Brandes, 1976). By the late 19th century, the first family responsive public social policy, the Civil War Pensioners Fund, was implemented, to address the needs of widows and children left destitute in the wake of the Civil War (Skocpol, 1992). In the early 20th century, demographic shifts in America (including urbanization and immigration) coupled with progressive era philosophies, motivated scholars such as Jane Addams (1999 [1912]), W. I. Thomas (1928), and W. E. B. DuBois (1998 [1899]) to chronicle how families were (or failed to be) integrated into an expanding economy.

By the 1940s, central features of the New Deal addressed workplace responsibilities and government commitment to working families. Indeed, the Social Security Act and the Fair Labor Standards Act regulated workplace responsibilities in consideration of life-course factors that outlast short-term contractual relations between employers and employees. The work of many postwar scholars reflected the culture and norms of that time, often focusing on work and family themes. At the time, many of these arguments had a conservative bent, such as Talcott Parsons' (1942) assertion of the functionality of sexual divisions of labor, a theoretical framework that added social-scientific legitimacy to the entrenchment of the traditional husband-breadwinner, wife-homemaker middle class roles of the time. Subsequently, feminist writers began to articulate critical assessments of these arrangements, which in turn advanced work-family scholarship. For example, in her classic book, *The Feminine Mystique* (1963), Betty Friedan argued that societal acceptance of a segmented division of family caregiving and breadwinning—aligned along gender lines—served to further entrap women and perpetuate discrimination against them. These examples illustrate that work-family issues have been embedded in academic, policy, and cultural debates well in advance of the recognition of work-family as an area of expertise.

Despite the historical evidence of long-standing interest in work-family issues, many simultaneous transformations in the fabric of society occurred at the end of the 20th century that elevated the level and "volume" of the discourse about work and family. There were changes in the structure of families, the composition of the workforce, and the demographic characteristics of our society (see, for example, chapter 6 by Farnsworth Riche and chapter 3 by Marks, this volume). Furthermore, technological and organizational changes altered the ways that jobs were performed (e.g., see Wharton chapter 2, this volume and Valcour & Hunter, 2005). And, significantly, the growing presence and engagement of women in key leadership positions within universities, business, and government helped to position work-family experiences as central concerns for research, practice, and policy-making. In the 1990s, work-family issues increasingly resonated with discussions at the workplace and debates among public policymakers.

It has taken some time for cultural and structural institutions to catch up to these societal shifts, resulting in lags both in policy and programmatic responses. Observers have noted that existing laws, employer policies, and work processes and practices often fail to meet the needs of contemporary working families (see, for example, Kelly chapter 5; Still & Williams chapter 15, this volume). Many academics have described the discontinuities between the needs of families and today's institutional structures as being "mismatched." For example, cultural norms and expectations about the so-called ideal employee have been predicated on assumptions that workers can be available for work "on demand" and can be present at the workplace as needed. This notion of the ideal worker is based on a separate but related assumption that employees have another adult family member at home on a full-time basis who can take care of the family caregiving and home management responsibilities. However, such taken-for-granted notions about the ideal worker do not reflect the realities of contemporary employees. As noted by several of the authors who have contributed to this handbook, most families are no longer structured with one full-time breadwinner and one full-time homemaker; therefore, employees with family responsibilities rarely have the flexibility to be at the workplace for unlimited periods of time or for unscheduled hours. Although some employers and policymakers have attempted to rework workplace practices and public policies in an effort to alleviate mismatches (see Bond & Galinsky, chapter 19) in general, the incompatibilities remain (Bianchi, Casper, & King, 2005).

The continued visibility of mismatches between the needs of working families and societal structures has kept the connections (and the "dis-connects") between work and family visible, and has sustained broad-based interest in work-family issues. For instance, the *Wall Street Journal* and other newspapers have created journalistic niches focused on work-family experiences. Following the lead of *Working Mother* magazine, which conducted its first annual competition to identify the 100 best companies for working mothers in 1986, a number of industry journals and community papers now sponsor competitions to identify and showcase family-friendly workplaces. Even the business-oriented radio program, "Marketplace," produced by Public Radio International, has created a work-family beat.

A large number of business leaders, union officials, and organizational consultants also became engaged in different facets of the work-family agenda toward the end of the 20th century. Some companies crafted signature work/life initiatives. IBM, for example, forged into new territory with global surveys of its employees around the world (Hill, Yang, Hawkins, & Ferris, 2004). Businesses leaders also helped to establish a number of different professional groups that supported their efforts to further develop work/life policies and programs. Some of these associations, such as the Work & Family Roundtable, created membership structures comprised of company representatives, whereas other groups, such as the Alliance of Work-Life Progress (AWLP), invited individuals from a range of stakeholder groups, including unions and consulting firms, to join. AWLP further contributed to the institutionalization of work-family initiatives at the workplace through its certificate program, which offers a series of courses and workshops. Unions and union-supported organizations, such as the Labor Project for Working Families, were visibly active in the development of services and supports at the workplace, such as dependent care program, and provided leadership for public policy innovations (Labor Project for Working Families, 2004). Work-family issues also garnered attention in the political arena. Interest in working families not only became embedded in the rhetoric of national elections, but also was woven into state and local political activities (see, for example, Working Families Party, 2004).

CREATING A MULTI-DISCIPLINARY FIELD OF STUDY

While pundits, practitioners, advocates, and policy-makers were busy exploring different work-family frontiers, academics also began to forge new paths leading to increasingly sophisticated understandings of work-family phenomena. By the mid-1990s, scholars' interest in work-family issues had developed into a loosely coupled area of study. Today, a large number of academics see work-family issues as an important focal point for their teaching, research, and writing.

Many who have attempted to chronicle the contemporary history of the work-family field point to the publication of Rosabeth Moss Kanter's 1977 monograph, *Work and Family in the United States: A Critical Review and Agenda for Research and Policy*, as an important marker of the beginning of concerted academic study of work-family issues in the United States. Interestingly, this publication was part of the Russell Sage Foundation's series, "Social Science Frontiers: Occasional Publications Reviewing *New Fields* for Social Science Development" [emphasis added]. At the time, it was unclear whether the work-family area of study would, in fact, develop the institutionalized structures needed to identify it as a field.

During the early years of the work-family area of study, it was common for scholars trained in different disciplines to focus on different aspects of work-family issues, bring different schools of thought to the framing of research questions, and adopt different methods to examine current work and family experiences. At that time, for example, psychologists would typically have read different journals than their colleagues trained in economics and each would likely have gone to different conferences. Even within disciplines, the efforts to move work-family research agendas forward did not proceed in any coordinated fashion. For instance, it took some time before sociologists who focused on "family sociology" regularly consulted the work of those who focused on "sociology of work." The divides that tended to separate academics in different disciplines created significant challenges to the work-family researchers who wanted to study phenomena that do not fit neatly within disciplinary boundaries. However, as the connections were established among the disciplines, the contours of the new field began to take shape.

Considering why work-family emerged when it did is a question appropriate for an analysis using a "sociology of knowledge" orientation, the branch of sociology that studies the social processes involved in the production of knowledge (Jary & Jary, 1991). Sociology of knowledge focuses attention on the cultural experiences, dynamic social interactions, and structural institutions that form the context of knowledge-building. This field examines how social contexts relate to the socially dynamic development, acquisition, and transmission of knowledge and understanding (Swidler & Arditi, 1994; DiMaggio & Powell, 1983; Ritzer, 1992). For the purposes of this chapter, we have used a sociology of knowledge framework to examine some of the indicators that the work-family area of study has become an scholarly field with its own structured activities, socialization processes, products, and norms that reflect a unique academic subculture.

One sign of the emergence of the work-family field of study is work-family scholars' engagement in rituals that define them as members of a loosely coupled community (see Pitt-Catsouphes, 2005). The annual conferences of many disciplines and professions—ranging from economics to management to family relations—now regularly include panels or even tracks of sessions devoted to work-family research. Over the past two decades, the number of presentations that focus on work-family issues at these conferences has increased. For instance, the Gender and Diversity in Organizations division and the Careers division of the National Academy of Management have steadily accepted more work-family research papers. Importantly, organizations such as the Business and Professional Women's Foundation, the Alfred P. Sloan Foundation, and Brandeis University have sponsored multi-disciplinary work-family scholarly conferences that bring together scholars from different disciplines.

The concept of membership in an academic work-family community has also been reinforced by communication networks such as the Workfam listserv, which was founded and continues to be coordinated by Robert Drago of the Penn State University, as well as the Sloan Work and Family Research Network (www.bc.edu/wfnetwork). In 2005, more than 1200 individuals interested in work-family research were members of the Sloan Work and Family Research Network's virtual community (approximately three-fourths of whom are academics), giving them access to resources and communication that promote connections within the community.

Work-family academics have also begun to develop strategies, such as approaches to teaching, designed to pass on knowledge and the "work-family research culture" to the next generation of scholars and practitioners. Many universities across the country and around the world, including the Harvard Business School and the Sloan School of Management at MIT, currently offer courses that address work-family issues. These faculty members are making conscious efforts to transmit knowledge about work-family issues to their students. Some of these academics have also created mechanisms for sharing their course syllabi and ideas for teaching activities with colleagues in the work-family academic community who are located at other universities. Web posting has become an effective way for faculty to share teaching experiences and ideas (see http://wfnetwork.bc.edu/activities.php and http://flex-work.lir.msu.edu/). The existence of socialization strategies like these suggests that the work-family field has become institutionalized.

It is particularly important to note that literature which discusses work-family issues is now being archived as a unique category of research. During the early 1990s, some work-family scholars lamented that it was difficult to get their manuscripts about work-family topics accepted for publication in peer-reviewed academic journals. Work-family issues are no longer perceived as being a stumbling block, and some journals even favor a manuscript's prospects for publication if it contributes to the work-family knowledge base (see analysis by Drago & Kashian, 2003). There has been a remarkable growth in the venues for, and acceptance of, scholarly research on the intersection of work and family. In recent decades, there has been steady increase in the number of work-family articles cited in four widely used academic literature databases: socioabs (a library database that includes sociology and many demography journals), econlit (a library database that includes economics and some business journals), psychinfo (a library database that includes psychology, psychiatric, and many social work journals), and historical abstracts. The number of articles depicted in Fig. 1.1 were calculated after conducting a Boolean keyword search using synonyms of the terms "work" [work(ers) or job(s)] and "family" [family(ies), parent(s), mother(s), father(s), or child(ren)] in select years.

By 2000, there had been a threefold increase in the number of history articles that focused on work and family concerns, when compared to the number of these articles in 1970. In psychology there were seven times as many over the course of those three decades, and in sociology there were 12 times as many. Our database search did not identify a single work-family publication in the econlit database in 1970, but there were more than 500 in 2000. There are similar trends in the increase of work-family publications occurring across

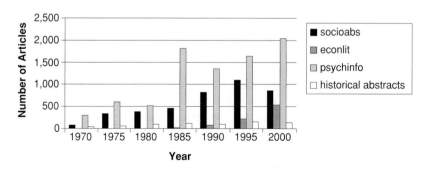

FIG. 1.1.   Trends in journal articles that focus on work and family concerns.

many of the other disciplines as well. A 2004 analysis of the Online Work-Family Literature Database maintained by the Sloan Work and Family Research Network (a database containing the citations and annotations of more than 6,500 scholarly work-family publications) found that the journals that had published the greatest number of work-family research articles entered into the database represented many different disciplines. The "top" journals included *Journal of Family Issues*; *Work and Occupations*; *Community, Work & Family*; *Journal of Family & Economic Issues*; *Gender & Society*; *Sex Roles*; *Human Relations*; *Industrial Labor Relations*; *Social Forces*; *Monthly Labor Review*; *Academy of Management Journal*; *Journal of Occupational & Organizational Psychology*; *American Journal of Sociology*; and *Qualitative Sociology*.

One notable event in the emergence of the work-family field occurred in 1994, when Suzan Lewis and Carolyn Kagan at Manchester Metropolitan University in England founded the journal *Community, Work and Family*. This journal was a milestone not only because it was the first (and remains the only) peer-reviewed journal devoted to work-family issues, but also because the editors created the journal to address many of the challenges that had confronted work-family scholars. From the beginning, Lewis and Kagan made an effort to bring global perspectives to the discussion of work-family issues. The authors of articles published in *Community, Work and Family* have chronicled and analyzed the work-family experiences of people living in Africa, Asia, Australia, Europe, North America, and South America.

Finally, we note that a shared academic culture is beginning to develop among work-family researchers. As part of this culture, scholars routinely test sets of commonly held assumptions and beliefs, such as assumptions about the interface between the work and family domains of life (see MacDermid & Harvey, chapter 27). In addition, academics have begun to clarify norms and expectations with regard to the rigor and quality of work-family studies. Beginning in 2000, academics began to collaborate with Shelley MacDermid of Purdue University, who founded the Rosabeth Moss Kanter Award for Excellence in Work-Family Research. Each year, 30 to 40 scholars review the contents of the previous year's issues of nearly 40 peer-reviewed journals that publish work-family articles in an effort to identify the "best of the best" research publications. These scholars are not only producing their own research, but they are also articulating standards of excellence for future studies.

The efforts of work-family academics to establish a work-family field of study have not gone unnoticed by funding agencies. For 10 years, different researchers have benefited from the resources provided by corporations as well as private foundations. In the United States, the Alfred P. Sloan Foundation has provided noteworthy support to work-family research, including the establishment of seven university-based work-family research centers (see Christensen, chapter 34). In 2004, the National Institute on Child and Human Development (part of the federal National Institutes on Health in the United States) announced a new initiative that will support efforts to examine health and other outcomes associated with work-family interventions. The resources provided by funding organizations and agencies have been critical, not only to support research initiative, but also to sustain and further institutionalize the work-family field.

Our hopes are that eventually this handbook will be viewed as another milestone in the "coming of age" of work-family studies as a recognized field that attempts to link rigorous, multi-disciplinary scholarship to enlightened *praxis*, or the professional application of scholarly knowledge. Although there are other edited books of work and family theory and scholarship that have appeared (e.g., Zedeck, 1992; Kossek & Lambert, 2005b: Bianchi, Casper, & King, 2005), to our knowledge it is the first formal handbook on work-family to be published.

ANALYTIC REFLECTIONS OF THE WORK-FAMILY HANDBOOK

When we stepped forward to coordinate the development of a handbook that could be widely used by work-family scholars and their students, we realized that it would be particularly important to position the disciplinary mosaic that has contributed to the richness and the rigor of the work-family area of study. By doing so, we hoped to craft a volume that discussed the focus and the unique characteristics of diverse types of scholarship that have contributed to the work-family field.

Collectively, the chapters in this *Handbook* address four fundamental work-family questions:

- How do academics discuss key work and family constructs?
- What conceptual frameworks do different disciplines use to examine work-family experiences and how do these frameworks shape the types of questions asked about work-family connections?
- What methodological approaches do researchers use to document and test linkages between work and family?
- How can scholarly inquiry contribute to social change at the workplace and in public policies that enhances individuals' work and family lives?

Reading "across the chapters," it is possible to triangulate information that can be used to answer these questions. We summarize some of our observations below.

Key Work-Family Constructs: For some time, the work-family field has stumbled over basic language about key constructs that anchor the work-family field. It is appropriate to begin our analytic commentary with a note about the considerable controversy with regard to the use of the term "work-family." Two primary concerns have been voiced. Some work-family leaders contend that the word "family" in the term "work-family" continues to conjure up images of an ideal-type family that consists of a married couple family with a stay-at-home mother and a breadwinner father who have dependent children. As many of the authors in this volume discuss, this ideal-type is not consistent with the diversity of family structures that exist. Therefore, the use of the term "work-family" may have the unintended consequence of giving inadequate acknowledgment of—and research attention to—the experiences of different types of families. Other scholars, as well as a majority of workplace practitioners, also feel that the field should broadly consider all the work and the nonwork domains of life, not just work and family. For instance, many people are highly involved in community life or religious activities. In an effort to consider people's experiences from a "whole life" perspective and to define the field as being interested in the experiences of working people who may not perceive themselves as being part of a family (or at least part of a family that resembles a two-parent/single earner family), some have adopted the term "work/life" for the field. These advocates suggest that the work/life term is more inclusive and would be relevant to the experiences of diverse working people, such as single people or gay/lesbian couples (see Marks, chapter 3). Of course, the term work/life has its limitations as well. Work is, obviously, part of life so the juxtaposition of work and life may suggest an artificial separation. Furthermore, the scope of the construct of "life" is so broad that, for the purposes of research, it loses analytic sharpness. Having made a decision to focus on the intersection of two of life's domains—work and family—we have, therefore, used the term "work-family" for this handbook. We are pleased that many of the authors who have contributed to this volume carefully remind readers that the referent "family" is meant to suggest diverse family forms.

Readers will also find many of the chapters in this book use the concept of "work-family balance," an almost taken-for-granted metaphor. Some have interpreted the concept to mean that "balance" results from spending "roughly equal" or "enough" time at work and at home. By implication, being "out-of-balance" implies that "too much" time spent on one of these sets of responsibilities would come at the expense of being able to fulfill the other set. There is evidence, some of which is discussed by authors who have contributed to this hand-book, that does demonstrate that there can be a zero-sum aspect to the way we spend our time. But, other chapters offer important critiques of this metaphor. For instance, Rosalind Barnett and Karen Gareis (chapter 10) show that work and family roles are not necessarily in competition and that, on the whole, the addition of paid work roles enhances women's lives. Importantly, Charles Darrah (chapter 17) informs us that working couples seldom think of their lives in terms of being able to "balance things"; rather, they view their daily lives as being forever fractionalized by competing tasks that constitute the "busyness" of life. Given these different perspectives, it is not surprising that there has been significant scholarly discussion about the appropriate term for the positive outcomes associated with work-family interface. While some researchers continue to use the term "work-family balance," others have opted for "work-family or work/life integration," and yet others have begun to use the term "harmonization" (Rapoport, Bailyn, Fletcher, & Pruit, 2002; Bailyn & Harrington, 2004; Kossek & Lambert, 2005a, b; Lewis & Cooper, 2005).

Scholars have long been aware that the definition of core concepts guides the development of their studies and shapes the nature of their research questions, sometimes in unanticipated ways. For example, the authors of many of the chapters included in this handbook discuss "jobs" and "job demands" as tasks performed by individual workers for specified durations. In contrast, Stephen Sweet and Phyllis Moen (chapter 9) ask readers to adopt the concept "career pathways" and to consider how the entries into jobs (and exits from them) are shaped by decisions made at earlier points in the life course. Thus, their focus is less on jobs than on the forces that shape the development of individuals into the types of people who can (or cannot) hold these jobs.

In summary, the lack of consensus about work-family has introduced many challenges, but it has also spurred the further development of theory and measures.

Work-Family Frameworks: The side-by-side positioning of the chapters in this volume not only facilitates comparisons between the chapters, but it also helps readers to focus on the divergences and convergences in the conceptual frameworks adopted by scholars trained in different disciplines. As editors, we knew at the outset that no single prevailing perspective adequately responds to all of the diverse research questions which have been posed about the root causes, the specific nature, and range of outcomes connected to work-family experiences. The answers to these questions, in large part, depend on how the issue is framed. Therefore, in a purposeful manner, we invited authors with a range of disciplinary orientations to contribute chapters to this handbook so that it could archive accumulated knowledge. But, more important, our hopes were to juxtapose different scholarly orientations to reveal the strengths and limitations of different intellectual traditions.

We want to explicitly acknowledge there can be as much diversity *within* each discipline as there is between disciplines. For example, this handbook includes several chapters prepared by psychologists, including one with expertise in experimental psychology (see Deutsch, chapter 11), one in developmental and clinical psychology (see Barnett & Gareis, chapter 10), and several in industrial organizational psychology (see Thompson, Beauvais, & Allen, chapter 14 and Kossek & Friede, chapter 29). Even though these authors share some common areas of disciplinary training, they have used different frameworks to explore different types of research questions. Furthermore, many social sciences and professional schools—including sociology, economics, and social work—embrace both the "macro" and the "micro." Within each discipline, the macro and micro perspectives typically reflect very different theoretical foundations (see discussion in Pitt-Catsouphes & Swanberg, chapter 16).

For illustrative purposes, it may be useful to compare the frameworks typically adopted by scholars from two different disciplines: history and anthropology. Historians who conduct work-family research typically examine archival information to gain new insights about the patterns, trends, and interpretations of work-family experiences by different groups of people living in designated areas during specific, past time periods (see Boris & Lewis, chapter 4). Their perspectives not only introduce us to some of the work-family experiences of previous generations, but their findings can also facilitate a better understanding of today's situations as they are contextualized in the specific social, economic, and political circumstances of our time. Although the work of historians can intersect with those anthropologists who focus on past as well as current cultures, anthropologists often conduct in-person observations of unfolding practices and rituals in which individuals and families engage (at home or at work) to gain a deep understanding of the interpretation and the enactment of belief systems, values, and expectations (see Richardson, chapter 8; Darrah, chapter 17, and Ochs, Graesch, Mittman, Bradbury, & Repetti, chapter 18). We hope that our readers will begin to make comparisons such as these between the chapters of this handbook so that the important different types of contributions of the disciplines become more salient.

Interestingly, our analytic reading of the chapters uncovered as much common ground among the disciplines as differences. We would like to bring some of these to your attention as well.

The concern of human development is sufficiently compelling that academics from many different disciplines adopt aspects of the life course perspective. As explained by sociologists Sweet & Moen (chapter 9), the life course perspective positions the experiences associated with life stages in different contexts: in the life of the person, in the life of the family, and in historical time. Child and family studies scholars as well as developmental psychologists are also often interested in studying the experiences of family members at different life stages, paying particular attention to the effect of a range of work factors on the family relationships and outcomes as experienced by different types of families (see Zvonkovic, Notter, & Peters, chapter 7).

Many work-family researchers use frameworks that place work-family experiences in different social contexts. Although there are many disciplinary variants of theories about social contexts, several of them echo a social ecology or person-in-environment point of view (see Pitt-Catsouphes & Swanberg, chapter 16). Industrial organizational psychologists and other organizational studies researchers often consider how the "employee" as a "person" responds to the workplace "environment." The person-in-environment framework is often adapted to examine the formal and informal aspects of the workplace environment and the impact on employees' work-family experiences (see Thompson, Beauvais, & Allen, chapter 14 as well as Bond & Galinsky, chapter 19). The person-in-environment framework also helps to inform the work of economists, for example, who focus on resources (such as money and time) that individuals and families access in different environments, including at the workplace, at home, and in the community (see Drago & Golden, chapter 13). Finally, academics who focus on the macro societal context draw attention to the impact of institutional and societal changes—such as the rise of capitalism—on work-family issues (see Wharton, chapter 2).

Another common thread, which follows the lead of demographers, is that academics trained in virtually every discipline ground their studies in the demographics that are related to work opportunities and/or family structures (e.g., see Farnsworth Riche, chapter 6; Wharton, chapter 2; and Marks, chapter 3). Demographers focus specific attention to the study of the characteristics of populations and often identify trends and changes in those characteristics over time. The simple observation that the composition of society is changing in terms of age, fertility, and geographic location opens vistas of questions that span disciplinary boundaries. A very quick scan of work-family literature will demonstrate the impact that changing demographics have had on the field.

Finally, we observed that all the authors in this volume shared in common a pragmatic focus, and they oriented their questions and analyses to issues that are of critical importance to the functioning of workplaces and families. However, there is significant variation in the outcomes of interest to scholars from different disciplines. Those affiliated with organizational studies and management, for example, usually focus attention on outcomes that are related (directly or indirectly) to the bottom line and to business effectiveness (see Hyland & Jackson, chapter 25; Kossek & Friede, chapter 29; Harrington & James, chapter 32). As one would expect, scholars in the area of child and family studies are particularly interested in the quality of relationships and developmental outcomes of work-family situations (see Zvonkovic, Notter, & Peters, chapter 7). An important development in the field is the presence of academics who are interested in both organizational and work-family outcomes; this is at the heart of the "dual agenda" articulated by Bailyn, Bookman, Harrington, and Kochan (chapter 31).

Methods: As evidenced by the chapters in this handbook, the work-family field is not only multi-disciplinary; it is also multi-methodological. In fact, one of the beneficial outcomes of the multi-disciplinarity of the work-family field is that researchers have begun to share their methodological expertise. We have not been able to locate any academic literature published to date that discusses the range of methodologies used by researchers in the work-family field. Therefore, it is important to note that work-family researchers have begun to "experiment" with a number of different methods. For instance, sociologists and psychologists are as likely as economists and demographers to engage in time diary studies (see Schneider, chapter 22). Researchers in such diverse areas as organizational studies, policy studies, and child and family studies have used focus groups as a way to develop a deep understanding of people's experiences and their interpretations of those experiences (see Smithson, chapter 20). Those trained in disciplines such as sociology and professional fields such as social work and management have found that case studies can help them to explore the relationships between work-family experiences as they unfold in different social contexts (see Lewis, das Dores Guerreiro, & Brannen, chapter 23). Academics from virtually every social science discipline have begun to explore new analytic techniques, such as hierarchal linear modeling (HLM), to consider the relationships between work-family experiences at different analytic levels, such as individual experiences as they are "nested" in family experiences (see Swisher, chapter 26). Due to the intensive nature of longitudinal research, a smaller proportion of work-family studies have been designed to gather information over long periods of time; however, researchers from several disciplines and fields, including child and family studies, psychology, and sociology, have used longitudinal studies to understand the trajectories and changing dynamics of work and family over time (see Crouter & Pirretti, chapter 21). Although historians such as Boris and Lewis (chapter 4) have perfected research strategies that identify and then analyze archival information, this approach to data collection and data interpretation has been adopted by other disciplines and fields including policy studies, management, and social work (see Lambert, chapter 24). The movement toward a sharing of methodological approaches across disciplines is evident in the increasing numbers of studies that have adopted mixed methods for gathering information about work-family experiences (see Neale, Hammer, & Morgan, chapter 28). It is perhaps to be expected that academics from different disciplines are also beginning to conduct secondary analyses of the same datasets, such as the National the Changing Workforce (Bond & Galinsky, chapter 19).

Toward Change: Our analysis of this fourth component of the work-family field brings us back to our discussion of some of the societal changes that precipitated interest in work-family issues in the first place. Among work-family researchers, there is a widely shared belief that additional change is possible that could enhance the well-being of working families.

Several of the authors who have written chapters for this handbook discuss the equity and social justice implications of specific work-family circumstances. Sociologists, for instance, have contributed extensively to understanding how inequalities may shape and have differential impact on working people at home and at work. Some sociologists have also begun to examine how simultaneous membership in different social groups, such as gender, race and class, can affect work-family experiences (see Gerstel & Sarkisian, chapter 12). Economists interested in equity explore the differential access that individuals and groups have to a range of resources and opportunities and the consequences of these differences (see Drago & Golden, chapter 13). And values related to social justice are at the core of analytic frameworks adopted by social workers who pay particular attention to the differences in opportunities as well as well-being of specific population groups (see Lambert, chapter 24; Pitt-Catsouphes & Swanberg, chapter 16).

Given the proclivities of work-family researchers to remain vigilant for change opportunities, it is not surprising that scholars have examined the possibilities for change at the workplace as well as in society-at-large. Academics such as Harrington and James (chapter 32), Kossek and Friede (chapter 29), and Bailyn, Bookman, Harrington, and Kochan (chapter 31) not only discuss a vision for change but also detail strategies that can facilitate positive action. Other academics who study law, analyze policies, and examine workplace practices have provided insight about options for changes in public policy (see Still & Williams, chapter 15; Feldblum & Appleberry, chapter 30; Wolkinson & Ormiston, chapter 33).

In some ways, our analysis across the chapters has come full circle. While noting some of the differences voiced by the authors, we are impressed to see that there is also a remarkable overlap in the literatures cited in each chapter, the concepts used, and issues addressed. This supports our contention that the work-family field has developed into a multi-disciplinary endeavor. We wish to echo the observations of Thompson, Beauvais, and Allen about the extent of overlap between those in their field, industrial organizational psychology, and other disciplines. In chapter 14 they state, "Work-family research by I/O psychologists also overlaps with research by sociologists, developmental psychologist, social psychologists, anthropologists, economists, and social workers, as can be seen in the diversity of authors in this handbook." As the field further develops, scholars will need to be even more cognizant of, and willing to consider, the insights offered by various perspectives. Similarly, we will need to become more familiar with and use a greater variety of methodologies to gain new knowledge and understanding.

THE WORK-FAMILY HANDBOOK: A RESOURCE
FOR THE WORK-FAMILY FIELD

Being aware of the extent of scholarly interest in work-family issues, we decided to develop a handbook that could serve as a resource for researchers, teachers, and students who are interested in multi-disciplinary perspectives of a diverse range of work-family issues and experiences. It has been a gratifying experience to have engaged so many of the leading work-family experts in this effort to publish the first *Work-Family Handbook*. In its entirety, this handbook offers readers a broad overview of important components of the state of knowledge in the work-family field.

The idea for creating this handbook emerged from a group of scholars who were members of the Editorial Board of the *Work-Family Encyclopedia*, a peer-reviewed collection of scholarly literature overview articles prepared for faculty and students interested in the work-family area of study (http://wfnetwork.bc.edu/encyclopedia.php?mode=nav). The Editorial

Board was aware that a number of edited work-family volumes had already been published (e.g., Goldsmith, 1989; Zedeck, 1992; Frediksen-Goldsen & Scharlach, 2000; Kossek & Lambert, 2005a; Bianchi, Casper, & King, 2005). However, no single publication discussed the diverse nature of experiences people have at home and at work, analyzed the work-family area of study from different disciplinary points of view, compared and contrasted different methodological approaches that have been used to build the work-family knowledge base, *and* linked research to work and family policy and to practice. We have organized the handbook into four sections that reflect these goals for this volume.

We devoted Section I to critical discussions about the diversity of working families and different types of work situations that are present in the new economy of the 21st century. As editors, we felt that it was essential to include chapters at the very beginning of the handbook that could help our readers carefully examine and raise questions about statements made about "average" work-family phenomena. We recognize that popular culture and mainstream media tend to focus on "central tendencies" (such as "average" work hours) and on the experiences of families who seem to resemble a particular family archetype. Simply put, the collective contributions represented in this volume suggest that it is problematic to propose any work-family initiative, to study, or to advocate for the typical family. This fundamental observation is critical to the framing of research questions, the structuring of study designs, and to the dissemination of information to leaders at the workplace and in public policy arenas.

In Section I, titled "Families and Jobs in the 21st Century," readers will find articles that address two important issues, changes in work and the workforce and changes in families, which are related to significant societal changes as well as to the development of the work-family field. In "Understanding Diversity of Work in the 21st Century and Its Impact on the Work-Family Area of Study," Amy S. Wharton provides a window into several dimensions of diversity at the workplace. Throughout the chapter, Wharton encourages us to think carefully about the operational definitions of two constructs: "work" and "diversity." Reflecting sociological perspectives of stratification, Wharton focuses on three diversity variables: gender, race, and class. This provocative chapter considers some of the factors that affect diversity in the workplace, including underlying ideologies that shape our ideas about "who" should be at the workplace and what should they do, characteristics of jobs themselves, and even geography. Wharton deepens our understanding of diversity in several important ways. For example, rather than considering gender, race, and class as if they were mutually exclusive categories, Wharton's discussion explores the diversity within each of these categories of diversity, such as gender within race. This chapter also offers insights about the limitations of our understanding about diversity and work-family. As Wharton notes, although there is abundant literature about workforce diversity, there is surprisingly little literature about the work-family experiences of diverse employees groups. Her comments about "the relative invisibility of family status and relation in studies of workplace diversity—with the exception of those focused on gender and women" suggest that this is a fertile area for new research.

Stephen Marks's "Understanding Diversity of Families in the 21st Century and Its Impact on the Work-Family Area of Study" grounds us in diversity embedded in the "family" side of the "work-family" discussion. Marks opens his discussion with an anecdote that effectively challenges assumptions about the meanings we attach to the word "diversity." He continues this theme in the chapter as he ponders the meaning and interpretation of the notion of "the average family." Marks considers numerous dimensions of family diversity, including household composition, sexual orientation, race/ethnicity, age, gender, immigrant status, and income. Although he carefully points out "master trends" related to the diversity of American families, Marks also focuses our attention on some of the less visible aspects of diversity and links the hierarchies of diversity, such as class and age, with privileges and disadvantages. Marks also devotes several sections of his chapter to an examination of the diversity within particular family groups. For example, he considers the implications of social class among gay/lesbian families and presents an argument for understanding the class privilege among more highly educated gay/lesbian parents who tend to have more access to family-friendly policies and programs than other workers may. Finally, Marks opens an important line of inquiry about the relationships between family diversity and discrimination. He questions, "to what extent does occupational discrimination erode a person's sense of work-family balance?" This chapter presents a compelling case for the need to update our research questions, analyses, and interpretations of family diversity so that we capture the nuances which texture the experiences of working families.

Section II introduces readers to a variety of perspectives that have been applied to the study of work and the family. We designed this section to support ongoing efforts within the academy to foster multi-disciplinary perspectives about work and the family and to facilitate a deeper understanding of these different points of view. Readers will find contributions by a demographer, family studies scholars, anthropologists, psychologists, sociologists, organizational analysts, legal scholars, and scholars of social work. Each of these perspectives reflects different intellectual schools of thought; however, the authors of these chapters illustrate how many academics are actively attempting to connect their perspectives to those of other fields. As editors of this handbook, we believe that the very nature of work-family research necessitates making this bridge across disciplines. We have included descriptive summaries of each of these chapters in the Introduction to Section II.

Section III, "Methodological Approaches," provides overviews of some of the dominant methods used by work-family social scientists and highlights how researchers have used these methods to examine the connections between the family and the workplace. These chapters give readers a sense of the challenges as well as the rewards of studying families and jobs through ethnographies, videographies, surveys, focus groups, longitudinal studies, experience sampling methods, case studies, organizational archives, and the use of analytic approaches such as hierarchical linear modeling. It is our hope that researchers will be able to appreciate the strengths of each methodology and will consider strategically using different methods to create a more complete assessment of work and family experiences. The Introduction to Section III offers readers additional information about each chapter in this section.

Finally, the chapters in Section IV discuss alternatives for advancing future policy and organizational change based on scholarship. As discussed in many of the chapters in this handbook, current job structures, career ladders, and governmental/legal policies are mismatched with respect to the needs of contemporary working families or their employers (see comments by Christensen in chapter 34). The chapters in Section IV focus on different approaches for making effective arguments or cases for institutional change, such as presenting different rationales or business cases for organizational reform, considering opportunities for legislative and regulator reform, partnering with business leaders to articulate standards for quality work-life initiatives, collaborating with groups at the workplace to introduce innovative interventions, and negotiating equitable resolutions in employer and family conflicts. The Sloan Foundation Program Officer, Kathleen Christensen, offers a concluding chapter in which she discusses the opportunities and constraints of multi-disciplinary perspectives. She suggests that the future successes of the work-family research community will, in part, reflect the extent to which scholars, practitioners, and policymakers can transcend traditional boundaries and work collaboratively to articulate an agenda for the advancement of the work and family field.

We believe that scholars have an important and unique role in the efforts that will be made to address the work-family concerns of today and tomorrow. Recognizing that work-family studies now constitute a distinct academic field, we hope that this handbook is a useful resource to academics and their students.

REFERENCES

Addams, J. (1999 [1912]). *Twenty years at Hull-House*. New York: Signet Classics.

Appelbaum, E., Berg, P., & Kalleberg, A. (2000). Balancing work and family: Effects of high performance work systems and high-commitment workplaces. In E. Appelbaum (Ed.), *Balancing acts: Easing the burden & improving the options for working families* (pp. 115–124). Washington, DC: Economic Policy Institute.

Bailyn, L., & Harrington, M. (2004). Redesigning work for work-family integration. *Community, Work & Family, 7*(2), 197–202.

Batt, R., & Valcour, P. M. (2003). Human resource practices as predictors of work-family outcomes and employee turnover. *Industrial Relations, 42*(2), 189–220.

Bayraktar, M., & Salman, M. (2003). The impact of family life on work efficiency: A study of employed women from different occupational statuses in a metropolitan area in Turkey. *International Journal of Consumer Studies, 27*(1), 80–86.

Berg, P., Kalleberg, A., & Appelbaum, E. (2003). Balancing work and family: The role of high-commitment environments. *Industrial Relations, 42*(2), 168–188.

Bianchi, S., Casper, L., & King , R. (Eds.). (2005). *Workforce/workplace mismatch? Work, family, health, and well being*. Mahwah, NJ: Lawrence Erlbaum Associates.

Bihan, B. L., & Martin, C. (2004). Atypical working hours: Consequences for childcare arrangements. *Social Policy & Administration, 38*(6), 565–590.

Blair-Loy, M. & Wharton, A. (2002). Employees' use of work-family policies and the workplace social context. *Social Forces, 80*(3), 813–845.

Brandes, S. D. (1976). *American welfare capitalism, 1889–1940*. Chicago: University of Chicago Press.

Cousins, C., & Tang, N. (2004). Working time and work and family conflict in the Netherlands, Sweden and the UK. *Work, Employment & Society, 18*(3), 531–549.

Creamer, E., & Associates. (2001). *Working equal: Academic couples as collaborators*. New York: RoutledgeFalmer.

Crouter, A. (November 1984). Spillover from family to work: The neglected side of the work-family interface. *Human Relations, 37*(6), 425–442.

Crouter, A., Bumpus, M., Head, M., & McHale, S. (2001). Implications of overwork and overload for the quality of men's family relationships. *Journal of Marriage and Family, 63*(2), 404–416.

DiMaggio, D., & Powell, W. (1983). The iron cage revisited. *American Sociological Review, 48*, 147–160.

Drago, R., & Kashian, R. (2003). Mapping the terrain of work/family journals. *Journal of Family Issues, 24*(4), 488–512.

DuBois, W. E. B. (1998 [1899]). *The Philadelphia Negro: A social study*. Philadelphia: University of Pennsylvania Press.

Engels, F. (1936 [1845]). *The condition of the working-class in England in 1844*. New York: Allen & Unwin.

Ferber, M., & Hoffman, E. S. (1997). Are academic partners at a disadvantage? In M. Ferber & J. W. Loeb (Eds.), *Academic couples: Problems and promises*. Chicago: University of Illinois Press.

Frediksen-Goldsen, K., & Scharlach, A. (Eds.). (2000). *Families and work: New directions in the twenty-first century*. New York: Oxford University Press.

Friedan, B. (1963). *The feminine mystique*. New York: Norton.

Goldsmith, E. (1989). *Work and family: Theory research and applications*. Thousand Oaks, CA: Sage.

Greenhaus, J. H. (1988). The intersection of work and family roles: Individual, interpersonal and organizational issues. In E. Goldsmith (Ed.), *Work and family: Theory, research and applications* (pp. 23–44). Thousand Oaks, CA: Sage.

Grzywacz, J., & Marks, N. (2000). Reconceptualizing the work-family interface: An ecological perspective on the correlates of positive and negative spillover between work and family. *Journal of Occupational Health Psychology, 5*(1), 111–126.

Hill, J. E., Yang, C., Hawkins, A. J., & Ferris, M. (2004). A cross-cultural test of the work-family interface in 48 countries. *Journal of Marriage and Family, 66*(5), 1300–1316.

Jacobs, J., & Gerson, K. (2004). *The time divide: Work, family and gender inequality*. Cambridge, MA: Harvard University Press.

Jansen, N., Kant, I., Kristensen, T., & Nijhuis, F. (2003). Antecedents and consequences of work-family conflict: A prospective cohort study. *Journal of Occupational and Environmental Medicine, 45*(5), 479–491.

Jary, D., & Jary, J. (1991). *The HarperCollins sociology dictionary*. New York: HarperCollins.

Kanter, R. (1977a). *Work and family in the United States: A critical review and agenda for research and policy*. New York: Russell Sage Foundation.

Kanter, R. (1977b). *Men and women of the corporation*. New York: Basic Books.

Kossek, E., & Lambert, S. (2005a). Introduction. "Work-family scholarship": Voice and context. In E. Kossek and S. Lambert (Eds.), *Work and life integration: organizational, cultural, and individual Perspectives* (pp. i–xx). Mahwah, NJ: Lawrence Erlbaum Associates.

Kossek, E., & Lambert, S. (2005b). *Work and life integration: Organizational, cultural, and individual perspectives.* Mahwah, NJ: Lawrence Erlbaum Associates.

Labor Project for Working Families. (2004). http://www.laborproject.org/.

Lewis, S., & Cooper, C. (2005). *Work-life integration: Case studies of organizational change.* Chichester, UK: Wiley.

Moen, P., & Sweet, S. (2003). Time clocks: Couples' work hour strategies. In P. Moen (Ed.), *It's about time: Career strains, strategies, and successes* (pp. 17–34). Ithaca: Cornell University Press.

Nordenmark, M. (2002). Multiple social roles—a resource or a burden: Is it possible for men and women to combine work with family life in a satisfactory way? *Gender, Work, and Organizations, 9*(2), 125–145.

O'Driscoll, M., Poelmans, S., Spector, P., Kalliath, T., Allen, T., Cooper, C., & Sanchez, J. (2003). Family-responsive interventions, perceived organizational and supervisor support, work-family conflict, and psychological role strain. *International Journal of Stress Management, 10*(4), 326–344.

Parsons, T. (1942). Age and sex in the social structure of the United States. *Essays in sociological theory* (pp. 89–103). New York: The Free Press.

Pitt-Catsouphes, M. (February 2005). Building a virtual research and teaching community: The Sloan Work and Family Research Network. *Community, Work and Family, 9*(1), 93–105.

Powers, E. (2001). New estimates of child disability on maternal employment. *American Economic Review, 91*(2), 135–139.

Rapoport, R., Bailyn, L., Fletcher, J., & Pruit, J. (2002). *Beyond work-family balance: Advancing gender equity and workplace performance.* San Francisco, CA: Jossey Bass.

Ritzer, G. (1992). *Sociological theory.* New York: McGraw-Hill.

Skocpol, T. (1992). *Protecting soldiers and mothers: The political origins of social policy in the United States.* Cambridge, MA: Harvard University Press.

Sloan Work and Family Research Network. www.bc.edu/wfnetwork.

Strazdins, L., Korda, R., Lim, L., Broom, D., & D'Souza, R. (2004). Around-the-clock: Parent work schedules and children's well-being in a 24 hour economy. *Social Science & Medicine, 59*(7), 1517–1527.

Sweet, S., & Moen, P. (2004). Intimate academics: Coworking couples in two universities. *Innovative Higher Education, 28*(4), 252–274.

Swidler, A., & Arditi, J. (1994). The new sociology of knowledge. *Annual Review of Sociology, 20*, 305–329.

Thomas, W. I. (1928). *The child in America.* Chicago: University of Chicago Press.

Valcour, P. M., & Hunter, L. (2005). Technology, organizations, and work-life integration. In E. Kossek & S. Lambert (Eds.), *Work and life integration: Organizational, cultural, and individual perspectives* (pp. 61–84). Mahwah, NJ: Lawrence Erlbaum Associates.

Van Rijswijk, K., Bekker, M., Rutte, C., & Croon, M. (2004). The relationships among part-time work, work-family interface, and well-being. *Journal of Occupational Health Psychology, 9*(4), 286–296.

Viega, J., Baldridge, D., & Eddleston, K. (2004). Toward understanding employee reluctance to participate in family-friendly programs. *Human Resource Management Review, 14*(3), 337–352.

Voydanoff, P. (2004). The effects of work demands and resources on work-to-family conflict and facilitation. *Journal of Marriage and Family, 66*, 398–412.

Working Families Party. (12/8/04). About the working families party. Downloaded 12-29-04 from http://www. workingfamiliesparty.org/about.html.

Zedeck, S. (1992). *Work, family and organizations.* San Francisco: Jossey-Bass.

2

Understanding Diversity of Work in the 21st Century and Its Impact on the Work-Family Area of Study

Amy S. Wharton
Washington State University

The growth and development of work-family research closely parallel trends in the institutions of work and family. Work-family scholarship has documented changes in these institutions and the relations between them, and this scholarship has helped to shape these changes. This chapter focuses on the institution of work, exploring how the evolution of this institution, particularly in the United States, has shaped work-family scholarship.

My aim in this chapter is twofold. The first is to trace the complex interdependencies between sociological approaches to work and work-family scholarship as these developed historically. The second aim is more forward-looking, as I attempt to identify areas where greater dialogue between work-family researchers and sociologists of work would be fruitful. Recent years have seen an outpouring of scholarship on work and family that is broadly interdisciplinary and often prescriptively oriented. Work-family researchers have produced many useful studies of workers' needs and desires and advocated for policies designed to address them. Sociologists of work, on the other hand, have often focused their attention on the workplace itself—its organization, structures, and practices. These research trajectories have developed relatively independently. By focusing attention in this chapter on the contributions of sociologists of work, I hope to encourage more conversation between these two areas.

Gender is an important part of this discussion. As many have shown, work, family, and gender have been intertwined historically. As the organization of work and family life have changed, so too have women's and men's lives. In addition, beliefs about gender—about what men and women are and should be—are conditioned by these institutions. Gender enters into discussions of work and family not simply as an *object* of knowledge, however; gender is also implicated in the *production* of that knowledge. Rising sociological interest in work and family coincided with women's increasing presence in social scientific disciplines. Among sociologists, early interest in gender and work was fueled largely by feminists. Over time, this interest has broadened and fundamentally reshaped the ways sociologists view the workplace. The chapter is divided into two main parts, each loosely focused on a different historical era. The first offers a look at the links between the institution of work and sociological conceptions of work and family through the lens of industrialization. Industrialization—as a process shaping the structure and organization of work, the composition of the labor force, and beliefs about workers and the workplace—has had a profound influence on conceptions of work, family, and gender. Among industrialization's most important legacies is the gender system of "domesticity" (Williams, 2000).

Although the legacies of industrialization endure, new work arrangements based on service have thoroughly transformed the U.S. economy and initiated other changes that are still ongoing. In the second part of the chapter, I examine these changes, focusing on trends affecting workers and work organization in the late 20th and early 21st centuries. Diversity—in labor force demographics, service content and organization, and work structures and employment relations—is one of the most important characteristics of this emerging 21st-century workplace. Understanding the implications of work diversity for work and family life are the main challenges for work-family scholars in the years ahead.

THE LEGACIES OF INDUSTRIALIZATION

In the 18th and early 19th centuries, America was a predominantly rural society and most people were involved in agriculture (Cowan, 1983; Haraven, 1990). In these settings, work and family life were highly intertwined, as were the roles of women and men. The work of providing for oneself and family took place in and around the household and required the labor of all members, including women, men, and children. Although responsibilities were typically divided along gender lines, there was no clear separation between women's work and men's work, or between what was later called "housework" and breadwinning. These relations changed during the 19th century as industrialization took hold.

The Emergence of Domesticity and the Emergence of the "Modern" Workplace

The beginning of the 20th century saw the convergence of two key forces that would shape conceptions of work, work-family relations, and work-family scholarship for the next three quarters of a century. The first was the masculinization of the paid labor force and the corresponding construction of the home as the place of women and children. The second was the growth of the "modern" workplace.

The Emergence of Domesticity

Although women and children were heavily involved in paid labor during the earliest stages of industrialization, they were gradually replaced by an adult male labor force. By 1900, men comprised roughly 80% of the U.S. labor force (Padavic & Reskin, 2002). Most of these men worked in manufacturing jobs or in agriculture; smaller numbers were in the professions or among the small, but growing ranks of white-collar workers. These working men were a diverse lot; some were married and others single; many were immigrants and others native-born; they lived in cities and rural areas. What tied them together, however, was their status as men in a labor force that had become more and more closely associated with masculinity.

Women's share of the early 20th-century labor force was much smaller and had shown a decline since the previous decades. Employed women tended to be single; if married, their husbands were likely to be low-paid and their households poor. African American women and other women of color were more likely to work for pay than women of European descent (Padavic & Reskin, 2002). Though women who could afford to stay at home did so, this does not mean that their lives were easier than men's or preceding generations of women. If anything, industrialization had made women's work at home more difficult. As Cowan (1983, pp. 63–64) explained:

As the nineteenth century wore on, in almost every aspect of household work, industrialization served to eliminate the work that men (and children) had once been assigned to do, while at the same time leaving the work of women either untouched or even augmented.

Cowan (1983) attributed this to several factors, including the absence of men as helpers at home, new conceptions of children and childhood that came with expanded notions of mothers' responsibilities, and changes in household technologies that saved labor but increased the time required to complete tasks.

Williams (2000, p. 20) conceived of these social arrangements, with men defined as "ideal workers" and women as mothers and caregivers, as essential features of the system of "domesticity." Domesticity, she argued, is comprised of three elements: "Employers' entitlement to demand an ideal worker with immunity from family work"; "husbands' right, and their duty, to live up to this work ideal"; and the view that mothers' lives "should be framed around caregiving."

In addition to a strictly demarcated gender division of labor, domesticity involved a set of cultural beliefs that defined women and men as categorically different, possessing talents and skills best suited to different domains. In this view, men were "naturally" better equipped for paid work, whereas women's essential natures received fullest expression at home, surrounded by children. Domesticity thus attached gendered meanings not only to individual characteristics, but also to institutions and entire realms of human expression (Williams, 2000).

The Emergence of the "Modern" Workplace

Much has been written about domesticity and the "doctrine of separate spheres" that accompanied it (Cancian, 1987, 1989). Yet, they were not the only features of industrialization that contributed to a growing separation between work and family. The organization of work was also changing in fundamental ways. The most important of these involved the rise of mass production and the growth of large, bureaucratic, hierarchically organized firms (Perrow, 2002; Jacoby, 1985). Accompanying these changes was a view of work and work organization as increasingly subject to impersonal forces, such as market competition, technology, and capitalism. These forces shaped work directly in the form of organizational structures and technological innovations, and they led to the creation of new roles in industry for those trained to apply "scientific" techniques to ever more expanding areas of the workplace, including the social relations of work and the management of workers (Mayo, 1936; Taylor, 1911).

Efforts by employers, managers, engineers, and other white-collar professionals to extend their control over workers and work organization resulted in even greater separation between work and family life (Kanter, 1977a). They helped construct a view of work as governed by principles separate and distinct from those organizing life outside the workplace. In addition, in more direct ways, they attempted to minimize the effects of outside influences on the workplace. For example, antinepotism laws sought to prevent family ties from interfering with organizational authority and discipline. For more affluent white-collar workers, zoning laws and the growth of suburbs created a real geographic separation between work and home, further severing ties between these realms (Kanter, 1977a).

Early Conceptions of Work-Family Relations and the Legacies of Industrialization

As a set of cultural beliefs, domesticity conceived of paid work as separate and distinct from family life. These ideas became an important centerpiece of work-family scholarship in the decades surrounding World War II. This literature transformed domesticity from a description of the world into the prescriptive theoretical language of functionalism. Not only did this contribute to sociologists' general incapacity to conceive of and explore work-family connections, but it also reinforced a particular approach to understanding work.

Talcott Parsons and the tradition of structural functionalism, for which he became known, is among the most influential American social theorists of the World War II era. Parsons and his colleagues (Parsons, 1964; Parsons & Bales, 1955) viewed domesticity as especially well-suited to an industrial economy and derived what they saw as general principles of social organization from this observation. In particular, Parsons used the social norms that expected men to work for pay as the family breadwinner and women to care for children and maintain the home as the foundation for his conceptions of role differentiation and male and female "sex roles." The male sex role, according to Parsons, was oriented toward instrumental action, while the female sex role was expressively oriented. Parsons associated this distinction with occupational roles and family roles, respectively. Moreover, he argued that a division of labor whereby men have responsibility for the instrumental tasks associated with being a wage-earner and women are responsible for the expressive tasks of caring for children and providing emotional support enhanced both family solidarity and industrial society as a whole.

Parsons (1964, p. 79) saw the occupational system as "organized primarily in terms of universalistic criteria of performance and status within functionally specialized fields." By emphasizing its impersonality and rationality, Parsons' conception of work was consistent with other sociological treatments of industrial capitalism extending back at least to Weber and Marx. Although the details differed in important ways, each contributed to a view of work as fundamentally distinct from other areas of life. For American sociologists in the first half of the 20th century, however, Parsons' views were especially influential. Not only did he call attention to the distinctiveness of work, but also went further by explicitly contrasting the "instrumental" principles of work organization to the "expressive" realm of family life.

Parsons' views on these matters have been extensively criticized, and his conception of sex roles in particular has few adherents today. At the same time, we should not underestimate his more long-lasting influence on sociological treatments of work, family, and gender. Parsons provided modern sociologists with a conception of work and family as fundamentally separate areas of life, paralleling distinctions along gender lines. As Kanter (1977a) observed, these views helped to inscribe domesticity's conception of work and family as separate worlds within sociology, thus limiting social scientists' ability to take seriously the deep interconnections between these realms.

In the latter third of the 20th century, these ideas came under increased scrutiny. Several factors contributed to this rethinking. First, work itself had changed. The post-World War II industrial economy gave way to one based on service. The demographic composition of the workforce had also begun to be transformed. The numerical dominance of adult White males was declining as women of many racial and ethnic backgrounds, non-White men, and immigrants entered the labor force in large numbers (Johnston & Packer, 1987). Families were also changing (see chapter 5). In addition, the social sciences had become more feminized *and* more feminist. This transformation produced critiques of existing paradigms, new ways of understanding social life, and ultimately a resurgence of interest and scholarship on work and family.

Challenges to Domesticity

Wage-Earning Women and the Erosion of Male Breadwinning

The term "breadwinner" arose during the early part of the 19th century, as industrialization was beginning and cultural norms were beginning to draw a distinction between women's and men's spheres (Williams, 2000; Bernard, 1992). In a recent study, Townsend (2002) found that dominant cultural values continue to stress employment and breadwinning as key elements of fatherhood and masculinity. This suggests that the part of domesticity that emphasizes men's roles as providers still resonates. At the same time, as Townsend (2002) noted, cultural norms do not necessarily reflect people's experiences. In the case of male breadwinning, this disjuncture is especially apparent. Men's ability to be breadwinners eroded steadily during the last half of the 20th century.

The gap between the cultural norms and lived experience has always been more acute for poor and working-class, and nonwhite families than others. Rates of labor force participation historically have been higher for women in these groups. African American women in particular have had higher rates of labor force participation than women of other racial and ethnic groups (Levy, 1998). This pattern partly reflects racial differences in men's ability to earn a living wage. Although the size of these differences has fluctuated over time, African American men's lower rates of labor force participation, higher rates of unemployment, and lower average wages relative to White men have persisted for generations (Levy, 1998). Because men's ability to be breadwinners depends on the opportunity to earn enough money to support themselves and a family, domesticity has been more elusive for African Americans than Whites.

In the past few decades, however, almost all groups of men—not just African American men—have seen their earning power eroded, increasing the labor force participation rates of women in all racial and ethnic groups. Wages for workers other than managers and professionals increased steadily from the 1950s to the early 1970s, fluctuated over the next few years, and then, around 1977, began to decline (Mishel, Bernstein, & Schmitt, 2001). Wages for these workers did not begin to rise until the mid-1990s.

Disaggregating these trends by gender shows that, from the late 1970s to the early 1990s, female workers' earnings rose faster than men's earnings (U.S. Department of Labor, 2004) (Fig. 2.1). As men's wages stagnated, it became more and more difficult for them to support their wives and children. This economic reality helped to push many married women into the paid labor force. Although women's paychecks were not equal to those of men, women's salaries helped considerably to ease the economic burdens on families. Indeed, households with two wage-earners continue to earn substantially more than households with only one employed adult (Casper & Bianchi, 2002).

These changes in the gender composition of the workforce are well-documented and explored in detail in chapter 10. The vast majority of women and men today work for pay, and majorities of both sexes are employed full-time (Fig. 2.2). Men and women work for pay even when they are parents; rates of labor force participation for both sexes during the primary child-bearing years (i.e., 25–45) are over 70%. In 2002, 60.5% of women with a child under age 3 were employed (U.S. Department of Labor, 2004) (Fig. 2.3). Paid employment is typical for women and men in all racial groups: 61.8% of African American women, 59.3% of White women, 59.1% of Asian American women, and 57.6% of Hispanic women 16 years of age and older worked for pay in 2002, as did majorities of men in each group (U.S. Department of Labor, 2004) (Fig. 2.4).

Bridging Separate Worlds

Work and family have never been truly separate worlds. Work-family scholars, including historians, economists, legal scholars, and sociologists, have provided vivid accounts of the shift from preindustrial to industrial capitalism (see, for example, Williams, 2000; Kanter, 1977a; Cowan, 1983; Jones, 1987). In addition to their detailed descriptions of work and family life in preindustrial and industrial times, this research has revealed the many ways in which work and family life have been intertwined—even during the industrial era. Despite this knowledge, these interconnections were not at the forefront of sociological approaches to work

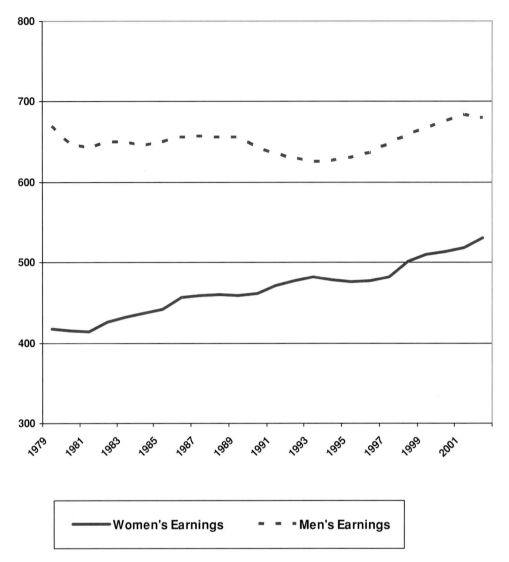

FIG. 2.1.   Median usual weekly earnings of full-time wage and salary workers in constant (2002) dollars by sex, 1979–2002 annual averages.
Source: Women in the labor force: A databook. U.S. Department of Labor, Februray 2004.

during the 1970s. Even as women's paid employment began to be systematically explored, many sociologists tended to embrace a separate worlds conception of work and family life.

The labor force participation of women has generated an enormous body of research in the social sciences throughout the industrialized world (van der Lippe & van Dijk, 2001). The feminist movement provided the early impetus for much of this research. One of the most important expressions of the 1960s and 1970s feminist movement in colleges and universities was its critique of academic disciplines, like sociology and other social sciences, for ignoring women (Smith, 1974). Research on work, occupations, and organizations was singled out as being especially inattentive to women. Documenting women's experiences in the paid labor force was seen as one way to compensate for this previous neglect (Wharton, 2000).

This early scholarship on women and work impressively surveyed women's work involvement and raised awareness of gender inequality in the paid workplace. These efforts owe their

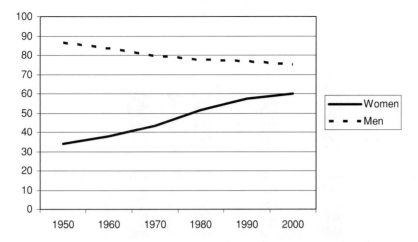

FIG. 2.2.   Rates of female and male labor force participation for people 16 years of age and over, 1950–2000.
Source: U.S. Department of Labor. Bureau Labor Statistics Data (http:// www.bls.gov/data) Data extracted on August 30, 2004.

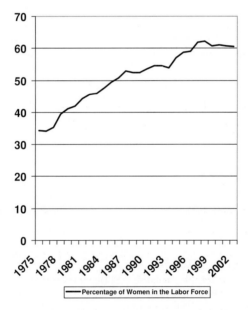

FIG. 2.3.   Employment status of women with youngest child under age 3, 1975–2002.
Source: Women in the labor force: A databook. U.S. Department of Labor, February 2004.

success to feminist scholars, who forced their disciplines to take women workers seriously. Looking back, however, it is instructive to examine this literature in terms of what it overlooked as well as what it highlighted. Although there are important exceptions to this pattern (e.g., Kanter, 1977a), early feminist scholarship on women and work inadvertently helped to reinforce, rather than challenge, the separate worlds view of work and family. Frameworks that had been used to understand work and workers at least since industrialization—if not before—were applied to women's work experiences. These frameworks, as noted earlier, reflected a view of work as driven largely by impersonal organizational and structural forces, thereby conceiving

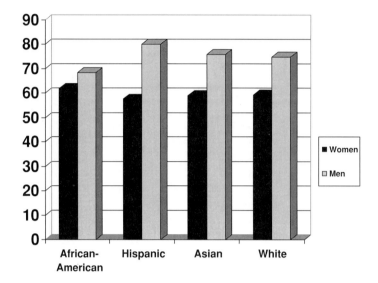

FIG. 2.4.   Rates of Labor force participation for those age 16 and over by sex, race, and Hispanic origin, 2002.
Source: Women in the labor force: A databook. U.S. Department of Labor, February 2004.

of it as separate and distinct from other areas of life. Women's large-scale movement into the workplace created opportunities for their work experiences to be analyzed on these same terms.

This industrial-era view of work was also extended outside the paid workplace and used to understand women's work in the family. Virtually all sociological research on work at that time focused on paid work; unpaid work done by women in the home had received virtually no attention. Indeed, sociologists rarely treated households as places of work, viewing them instead as realms of "expressive activity" in the tradition of sociologist Talcott Parsons. Feminist scholars attempted to show that housework could be understood in the same terms as paid work.

Feminist scholarship on housework and homemakers called attention to the productive, but unpaid, work performed in the home, and it also highlighted the precarious economic position of full-time housewives. Although "wages for housework" did not become a major feminist demand, feminist efforts to calculate the economic value of homemaking showed that women in this "occupation" worked long hours and performed services that would command a substantial wage in the paid labor market (Bergmann, 1986). Because homemakers are unpaid, however, their contributions to the household were unrecognized. Feminist economists like Bergmann (1986) showed how current policies designed to protect wage-earners, such as Social Security, offer little protection to displaced full-time homemakers.

These studies represented real contributions to the sociological understanding of work, including unpaid work. They also helped to focus attention on women workers and their concerns by drawing parallels with the study and experiences of employed men. Yet, by relying on frameworks that had been developed to study men's paid work in the context of an industrial economy, early feminist studies of women's work tended to reinforce the separate worlds view of work and family. This changed, however, as sociologists began attending more closely to the rapidly expanding service economy.

A view of work and family as separate worlds is difficult to sustain in a service economy. This is partly due to the intrinsic interconnections between services offered to consumers in the market and those historically provided by and for family members in the home. Shifting production from the household to the market was not new. For example, during industrialization,

"households ceased to manufacture cloth and began to buy it; they similarly ceased to manufacture candles, and instead, purchased kerosene; they ceased to chop wood and, instead, began
to purchase the products of the meat packers in Chicago (Cowan, 1983, p. 41). The massive
shift of services out of the household and into the market economy that took place during the
second half of the 20th century, however, was unparalleled. The preparing and serving of food,
caring for children and the elderly, and cleaning are but a few of such jobs that moved from
home to the paid workplace. In recent years, the kinds of services that used to be performed
in families that can now be purchased have expanded even more.

At the broadest level, these activities are linked together by their ties to social reproduction,
defined as "the array of activities and relationships involved in maintaining people both on a
daily basis and intergenerationally" (Glenn, 1992, p. 1). Many service jobs involve reproductive
labor that has moved out of the household and into the market economy. These jobs, filled
primarily by women in the paid labor market, are substitutes for the caregiving tasks historically
performed by women in the home (England & Folbre, 2000; Abel & Nelson, 1990). In both
settings, they involve activities performed directly for others' benefit or well-being.

As sociologists of work began to focus on service jobs more generally and caregiving more
specifically, connections between work and family life became harder to ignore. The separate
worlds view of work and family—at least as it applied to some aspects of employment—was
undermined to an even greater degree. Feminist scholars throughout the social sciences began
to address issues that implicitly or explicitly drew connections between work and family. For
example, some focused on issues of caregiving (e.g., Abel & Nelson, 1990). Others began to
focus on sexuality as a link between work and family life. Even more influential was Hochschild's
(1983) attempt to link spheres of work and nonwork by focusing on the ways people in both
spheres were expected to manage their emotions.

In contrast to Parsons, who separated the instrumental from the affective, and in contrast to
early feminists, who focused only on the instrumental aspects of household work and caring,
these research traditions united these two aspects. In this way, they moved at least some
areas of sociological research on work away from a separate worlds model. Although these
developments were important, their impact was greater in some areas than others. Studies
of women's work and research on service jobs were much more likely to acknowledge work-
family connections than research focused on men or on other areas of paid work. This changed,
however, with the rise of a more far-reaching rethinking of work as a gendered institution.

Work as a Gendered Institution

The erosion of men's wages, the increased employment of women in service jobs, and the
growing influence of feminist scholarship in studies of women's work all helped to undermine
domesticity. Although less influential in shaping the work and family lives of real women and
men, domesticity continued to inform many areas of sociological research on the workplace.
In particular, even as many sociologists agreed that work and family were not separate worlds,
the workplace tended to be seen as intrinsically gender-neutral.

Rosabeth Moss Kanter's 1977 classic, *Men and Women of the Corporation*, was especially
important in this regard. Kanter (1977b) argued that many gender differences in work-related
behaviors and attitudes stemmed from women's and men's different structural positions in
organizations. She was skeptical of views that attributed these gender differences to differences
in characteristics that women and men brought with them to the labor market. Instead, Kanter
suggested that ways of behaving on the job were shaped by the organization of work itself.

On one hand, Kanter's (1977b) contention that women's and men's behavior at work was
a function of the structures in which they were placed was an important counterpoint to the
separate worlds view that regarded women and men as intrinsically or essentially different.

At the same time, gender scholars disputed Kanter's (1977b) belief that work structures themselves were gender-neutral and had similar consequences for women and men (e.g., Williams, 1989, 1995). This critique was accompanied by other research on issues such as sex segregation and the male–female wage gap that called attention to the systemic nature of gender inequality in the workplace (e.g., Bielby & Baron, 1984; Baron & Bielby, 1985). These studies showed that the disadvantages women faced relative to men were built into the structure and organization of work and thus could not be attributed simply to differences in the individual characteristics of male and female workers. This line of research shifted the focus from "*women's* work" to issues of *gender* and gender inequality (see also Huber, 1998 and Chafetz, 1998 for discussions of this transition).

Acker (1992) drew on these ideas to develop her conception of work as a "gendered institution." In her words, to say that an institution is gendered means "that gender is present in the processes, practices, images and ideologies, and distributions of power in the various sectors of social life. Taken as more or less functioning wholes, the institutional structures of the United States and other societies are organized along the lines of gender.... [These institutions] have been historically developed by men, currently dominated by men, and symbolically interpreted from the standpoint of men in leading positions, both in the present and historically" (p. 567). This way of thinking about gender directs attention to the organization, structure, and practices of social institutions, and it emphasizes the ways that these entrenched, powerful, and relatively taken-for-granted aspects of the social order produce and reproduce gender distinctions and inequality.

According to Acker (1990), jobs are one of the vehicles through which gender distinctions and inequalities enter into and help constitute the workplace: "The concept [of] 'a job' is ... implicitly a gendered concept.... [It] already contains the gender-based division of labor and the separation between the public and private sphere. The concept of a 'job' assumes a particular gendered organization of domestic life and social reproduction" (p. 149). Jobs, for example, may be understood as activities performed for pay, as opposed to activities that do not provide wages, such as caring for one's children or maintaining a household. A job perhaps connotes an activity performed out of necessity rather than one performed out of love. "Finding a job" typically implies a process of seeking paid employment outside the home. These understandings presume a society that distinguishes between paid and unpaid labor and one in which activities performed in the home and for the family are outside the sphere of work.

Drawing on the notion of work as a "gendered institution," researchers have examined the ways in which gender has been incorporated into the workplace. This research is premised on the belief that many work practices and structures privilege masculinity (Williams, 2000; Britton, 2000; Maier, 1999). In Steinberg's (1992, p. 576) words: "Masculine values are at the foundation of informal and formal organizational structures ... Images of masculinity and assumptions about the gendered division of labor organize institutional practices and expectations about work performance...." As Williams (2000) described, masculine norms in the workplace have made it difficult for women to succeed—especially at the highest levels, and they have had particularly negative consequences for those women (and men) whose lives involve caring for children.

A gendered institutions view has helped to demonstrate that the processes shaping work structure and organization—both historically and in the present—cannot be understood apart from the construction of gender distinctions and inequalities in the society as a whole. Hence, as feminist scholars have addressed issues raised by a gendered institutions approach, they have helped to reframe understandings of fundamental social processes, including the social processes that organize the workplace (Nelson & Bridges, 1999; Steinberg, 1992). In reshaping the way sociologists conceive of work, a gendered institutions view has challenged the industrial-era view of work structures and practices as inherently gender-neutral.

CHANGES IN THE POSTINDUSTRIAL ECONOMY IN THE LATE 20TH CENTURY: FROM DOMESTICITY TO DIVERSITY

Although sociologists studying work at the beginning of the 21st century disagree over many issues, they share the belief that the United States is undergoing a period of economic and organizational restructuring and uncertainty (Cornfield, Campbell, & McCammon, 2001). Smith (2001, p. 7) used the metaphor of a "divide" to capture the vantage point of workers, employers, and the public as a new economic and social landscape appears on the horizon. Because this landscape is more diverse than ever, understanding its contours is particularly challenging.

Sociologists of work thus confront a different world than their counterparts who explored the implications of the industrial era. Yet, they also bring different conceptual and theoretical perspectives to bear on their investigations. Most important, most would reject the industrial-era view of work as separate and distinct from other realms of life; they are skeptical of perspectives that analyze workplace hierarchies and practices as governed by impersonal, economic, or market forces disconnected from social relationships; and they acknowledge that work is structured and rewarded according to ascriptive characteristics, like gender and race, as well as the characteristics representing achievement.

The implications for the future of work-family scholarship are twofold. First, the recognition that workers and jobs look qualitatively different from and more diverse than those previously means that there is much to learn about the nature of work-family relations in the 21st century. At the same time, sociologists of work are perhaps better equipped to understand these issues than in the past. Whether this potential is realized, however, depends on forging closer ties between work-family scholarship and the new sociology of work. Although there is some overlap between these literatures, they remain relatively self-contained. This point is illustrated below, as I examine three key research areas in the sociology of work and discuss their implications for work-family scholarship.

First, the labor force has become more demographically diverse, along several dimensions. Growing diversity *among men* and *among women* has challenged the gender system from which domesticity was derived and helped to reinforce. Second, while the rise of a service economy provided a basis for challenging the separate worlds view of work and family, more recent research on the service sector provides a more nuanced look at these issues. Finally, new forms of work organization, such as nonstandard employment contracts and nonstandard schedules, have reshuffled relations between work and family. These changes are creating both dilemmas and opportunities for workers as they confront more diverse types of employment.

Workforce Diversity and Work-Family Research

The composition of the workforce and the organization of work have changed dramatically since the middle of the 20th century. The U.S. workforce has always been diverse, but has become more so in recent years. White men's share of the labor force is declining, as the proportions of workers who are women and minorities rises (Tsui & Gutek, 1999). In 1947, for example, two thirds of the labor force were White males (Levy, 1998), as compared to an estimated 40 percent in 2006 (Fullerton, 1997). These increases in gender, racial, and ethnic diversity have been accompanied by greater diversity in workers' family and living arrangements. This includes higher proportions of workers living in nonfamily households or in households headed by women (Levy, 1998; Casper & Bianchi, 2002). Diversity along these dimensions intersects with and cross-cuts occupational distributions and income levels, creating a workforce whose composition is quite different from the immediate post-World War II era.

The growing diversity of the American workplace has generated tremendous interest from scholars and practitioners (Tsui & Gutek, 1999; Chemers, Oskamp, & Costanzo, 1995; Williams & O'Reilly, 1998). Most of these studies focus on the implications of gender, racial, and ethnic diversity for the social relations of work, or they examine the relations between demographic diversity and income inequality. Despite the considerable amount of diversity research, only some forms of diversity have figured prominently in work-family scholarship, and studies of workplace diversity rarely address work-family issues.

Gender has long been an organizing principle of work-family research, and women's experiences specifically have received much attention. This emphasis on gender in general and women in particular is understandable; work and family are gendered institutions that differentially structure the lives of women and men. The work-family literature contains fewer studies that examine racial, ethnic, or social class differences, however, or that systematically analyze the interconnections between gender and these aspects of diversity.

Workforce diversity research—particularly studies designed to address racial, ethnic, class, or even age stratification in the labor market—contains its own set of blinders, however, as researchers interested in these issues often overlook work-family connections. For example, in their review of research on jobs and labor markets, Reskin and Charles (1999, p. 395) found that "Researchers almost invariably consider workers' family status when their object is to explain sex differences in labor market outcomes and ignore it when their focus is on men or on race differences in labor market outcomes. Moreover, research that includes women is likely to be about gender whereas some studies of jobs or labor markets continue to exclude women." Women workers, these researchers suggest, thus are much more likely than men to be studied in the context of their family situations, while studies designed to explore race or ethnicity at work (especially those that do not also address gender issues) often ignore workers' family status.

Reskin and Charles's (1999) primary aim was to critique labor market research for failing to examine gender, race, and ethnicity and the interactions between them. Their critique also indirectly highlighted the relative invisibility of family status and relations in studies of workplace diversity—with the exception of those focused on gender and women. The inattention to work-family connections in research on race, ethnicity, and social class in the labor market suggests that the separate worlds view of work and family has not completely disappeared.

In addition to raising these issues, Reskin and Charles (1999) lamented the "balkanization" of the scholarly literatures on gender and race or ethnicity. A form of balkanization can also be seen in the research on work versus work-family. A rich portrait of the work and family situations and concerns of workers from diverse backgrounds and jobs can be culled from the broader sociological literature, though an explicit interest in work-family ties may not be the primary motivation for this research. For example, Hay's (2003) study of the effects of welfare reform yields much about poor women's work and family concerns, although this is not the author's primary focus. Similarly, in her study of Chicago's working poor, Newman (1999) explored the work *and family* lives of low-waged women and men.

In contrast, among those with self-described interests in work-family relations, the concerns of more advantaged women and men, such as managers and professionals, figure prominently. In part, this reflects middle-class workers' greater power to express their needs and concerns and shape public debate (Blair-Loy & Wharton, 2002). Middle-class workers are also more likely than others to have access to work-family policies, thus accounting for their prominence in studies of policy use and effectiveness (Chivers, Wharton, & Blair-Loy, 2004; Osterman et al., 2001).

This focus is not inherently problematic; there are valid substantive reasons for focusing on middle-class workers. For example, managers' and professionals' working hours have increased in recent years, and a large minority now works 50 hours a week or more in addition to commuting time (Jacobs & Gerson, 1997). Managers' and professionals' long work weeks are partly due to distinctive features of their jobs. Because productivity is often difficult to measure, hours spent at work may be used as a proxy for work output. In addition, firms demand that managers and professionals demonstrate commitment by working long hours and by making work the central focus of their lives (Kanter, 1977b; Fried, 1998). These circumstances make managerial and professional work an important setting for work-family research.

At the same time, it would be unfortunate if the study of work and family became synonymous with the study of women and gender among the middle class (while studies focused on racial, ethnic, or class differences among workers ignored work-family relations). For work-family scholars, the challenge ahead is to make work-family scholarship a better reflection of the demographically diverse workforce that has become so important in recent years. Creating avenues for interaction among different scholarly areas and traditions is not an easy task. Overcoming these barriers may offer fruitful opportunities for theoretical development and insight, however. Two examples illustrate the potential of and need for such research.

The emerging literature on the globalization of care work is an example of research that has successfully linked the concerns of work-family scholars with those interested in racial and ethnic inequality. This literature represents a coming together of two lines of research. One contains studies of domestic workers, informed by the literatures on gender, race, ethnicity, and immigration (e.g., Hondagneu-Sotelo, 2001; Romero, 1992; Ehrenreich, 2001). A second line of research draws from the work-family literature, particularly studies of time pressures among managers and professionals (e.g., Hochschild, 1997). Although gender issues and links between paid and unpaid care work figure into both literatures, each tends to highlight only one aspect of this issue: The paid care work of female nannies is the focus of the literature on domestic work, whereas their female employers figure less prominently. The work-family literature reverses this balance by emphasizing the work-family dilemmas of middle-class women and their families, while their paid care workers play a less central role.

In their recent anthology on women's global migration patterns, Ehrenreich and Hochschild (2002) began the conversation between these two areas. For example, they argued that "The lifestyles of the First World are made possible by a global transfer of services associated with a wife's traditional role—child care, homemaking, and sex—from poor countries to rich ones" (p. 4). In making this case, however, they also call attention to the growing divide between the affluent and the poor in the service economies of the industrialized world. Although research that systematically addresses these linkages is just beginning, Ehrenreich and Hochschild (2002) forcefully illuminated the work-family connections of two groups whose lives are being brought together by global economic trends. Furthermore, they showed that the global economic forces that are reshaping paid work and the labor force have had far-reaching implications for the family lives of service providers as well as those who pay their salaries.

Racial, ethnic, class, and gender divisions can also be seen in care work that is done outside the home. As Jacobs and Gerson (2004) showed, the number of live-in nannies has been declining since 1940, and most children of working parents are cared for outside the home in child-care centers. Child-care workers are one part of the low-wage service sector labor force, referred to by Macdonald and Sirianni (1996, p. 3) as the "emotional proletariat." This group of workers includes those in frontline, interactive service jobs where the work is insecure, low-paid, and highly routinized. Unlike the research on nannies and domestics discussed earlier, the literature on paid care work offers an example where more could be done to connect the concerns of work-family scholars with those interested in diversity and inequality.

Referring to low-level service jobs, Macdonald and Sirianni (1996, p. 15) claimed that "These occupations are so stratified that worker characteristics such as race and gender determine not only who is considered desirable or even eligible to fill certain jobs, but also who will want to fill certain jobs and how the job itself is to be performed. In no other area of wage labor are the personal characteristics of the workers so strongly associated with the nature of the work." The expansion of these types of jobs is one aspect of service-sector growth more generally and is thus among those factors that helped to both "push" and "pull" women into the labor force (Mishel, Bernstein, & Boushey, 2003). At the same time, the high levels of stratification among women and among men in this sector have exacerbated race and class inequalities within each group.

While work-family research has examined issues such as the availability and use of child-care or elder-care services, these studies have had less to say about the work-family concerns of the employees who provide them. Similarly, research on stratification and inequality within the service sector has confined most of its attention to people's work situations. We need to know more about the work and family lives of service providers.

Demographic diversity is an important characteristic of the 21st century labor force. For work-family researchers, attention to diversity can and should produce more than a proliferation of studies on different segments of the labor force. Instead, the challenge for work-family research is to acknowledge the complexity of diversity, while remaining attentive to broader principles that structure work-family relations. The examples discussed above show how this can be achieved and where more needs to be accomplished.

The Growth and Diversification of the Service Economy

Manufacturing industries, such as auto, electronics, and steel, were the economic backbone of industrial society. These goods-producing industries expanded their share of employment until the 1950s, but have declined every decade since that time (Levy, 1998). The percentage of the population employed in agriculture has declined even more dramatically; this sector now employs just under 3% of the labor force. By contrast, service-producing industries, such as hospitality or real estate, have been increasing their share of employment over time, now employing roughly three out of every four workers. The rise of services can also be seen in the types of occupations people hold. Although the majority of service jobs are located in service industries, these occupations can be found in almost every employment sector. These trends document that the United States has become a "service" economy.

In contrast to the kinds of products generated by a goods-producing economy, such as cars or machinery, the products of a postindustrial economy are services. Services diverge in important ways from manufacturing, imposing different demands on workers and new concerns for employers. Bowen and Cummings (1990, pp. 4–5) located the distinctiveness of services in three defining attributes: they are "intangible," consisting of "experiences that are rendered," as compared to "objects that are possessed"; they are produced and consumed simultaneously; and services depend on customer involvement both in their production and delivery. As a result of these characteristics, many service jobs require "emotional labor," defined as the "management of feeling to create a publicly observable facial and bodily display" (Hochschild, 1983, p. 7).

Services have come to play an increasingly important role in virtually all industrial-ized economies, and women have been central to this process (van der Lippe & Van Dijk, 2002; Levy, 1998). According to Gornick, Meyers, and Ross (1998, p. 35): "Many labor economists describe the influx of women into paid work as the single most influential change in the labor markets of industrialized countries in the postwar period." By far the biggest change in the female labor force since the 1960s has been the entrance of married women with children (Goldscheider & Waite, 1991; Reskin & Padavic, 1994; Johnston & Packer, 1987). The expanding service sector accounted for a significant share of this increase (Levy, 1998).

Service Work, the Care Sector, and the Price of Motherhood

The growth of the service sector and the related increase in women's labor force participation fundamentally transformed the institutions of work and family, and it reshaped work-family scholarship by undermining the separate worlds view of these institutions. As this chapter has shown, while not disappearing entirely in the last half of the 20th century, the system of domesticity was undermined in some respects (Williams, 2000). This "first generation" of research on the service sector bridged work and family by focusing on women's movement across spheres and the intrinsic connections between the jobs women performed for pay and those they performed in the home. The consolidation and continued expansion of the service sector in the 21st century creates even more opportunities and challenges for work-family research.

Most research on work organization in the United States focuses on production rather than service work (Frenkel et al., 1999). These authors attribute this to several factors, including assumptions about this sector's resistance to innovation and change, its lower levels of unionization, and the preponderance of low-paid, low-status service jobs filled by women. Although the latter characteristic attracted the interest of gender and work-family scholars early on (and continues to do so), the service sector in general has received much more systematic attention from researchers of all kinds in recent years. Studies of "the care sector" and its workers represent one way in which research on the service economy has been conceptually refined—and done so in ways that shed light on work-family relations and the status of "domesticity" in the 21st century.

As England and Folbre (2000, pp. 37–38) noted, "'services' have always been distinguished simply by their lack of a material output that could be counted or weighed," rather than by any reference to a job's "personal or emotional content." Reliance on such a broad definition has obscured important differences among service occupations. In particular, England and Folbre (2000, p. 37) called attention to "the care sector" of the economy (see also Meyer, 2000). This sector includes jobs whose performance depends heavily on personal contact between the worker and the customer or client and involve workers showing concern for others. The care sector thus includes professions such as teachers or nurses, but also includes many low-paying and more routinized jobs where workers are involved in caring for children, the sick, students, or the elderly.

In their studies of care work and the care sector, England and Folbre (1999, 2000) provided a framework for examining the fate of domesticity in the 21st century. Recall that one aspect of this system, as Williams (2000) depicted it, is the expectation that women have the obligation to provide more care than men. This expectation may have weakened as women have entered the labor force but has not entirely disappeared. At the same time, women's lesser economic dependence on men and other changes in a patriarchal family system have disrupted the supply, delivery, and cost of care (England & Folbre, 2000). Patriarchal family arrangements and women's economic dependence on men helped guarantee a low-cost supply of care, in part because women had few alternatives. Although women are still expected to provide more care than men, the terms on which they meet this obligation have changed dramatically.

In particular, the very nature of care creates dilemmas for its supply in a society that does not value these services. For example, as England and Folbre (2000, p. 47) argued, pressures to increase productivity and cut costs in the care sector are likely to have negative consequences on the quality of services. Although paid care work is not, in principle, of lower quality than care work formerly provided by women in the home, it is often a far from perfect substitute. In England and Folbre's (2000, p. 47) words: "The supply of caring labor to the market economy resembles the supply of unpriced natural resources such as air and water. None of these resources appear to have much value until their quality deteriorates to the point that they threaten to become scarce. By that time, however, it may be too late to replenish them."

One of the most important aspects of this research is its close attention to the "value" of care and the individual and social costs of undervaluing this labor (England & Folbre, 1999; Crittenden, 2001). Several studies have found that jobs requiring care pay less than otherwise comparable occupations where this is not required (England & Folbre, 1999; England et al., 1994; Kilbourne et al., 1994; England, 1992). Others have shown that mothers in particular earn lower average wages than others, regardless of whether they are in a caring occupation (Crittenden, 2001; Budig & England, 2001; Waldfogel, 1997). This care penalty has direct economic consequences for those who provide care—whether paid or unpaid, and it may have broader societal consequences in terms of its effects on people's willingness to perform this work.

New Employment Relationships and Diverse Work Structures

Like research on the organization of work more generally, studies of new forms of work organization began with a focus on production jobs in manufacturing industries, later being extended to the service sector (Kalleberg, 2001; Smith, 1997). This large and growing literature focuses on issues related to flexible capitalism, alternative types of work arrangements, and new employment contracts (Smith, 1997, 2001; Osterman, 1999; Capelli, 1999; Vallas, 1999). Two issues are especially relevant for work-family research: (a) the increase in "nonstandard" employment contracts (e.g, temporary, part-time, contingent) and nonstandard work schedules; and (b) the emergence of new forms of work organization.

The Growth of Nonstandard Employment Contracts and the "24/7" Economy

Several observers have characterized U.S. employment relations as shifting from permanent, long-term ties between workers and employers to short-term, temporary ties (Kalleberg, 2001). According to Pfeffer and Baron (1988), this shift reflects changes in both employers' and workers' needs and desires for greater flexibility. The primary outcome of this shift has been a dramatic increase in the "contingent" workforce (Kalleberg, 2001; Kalleberg & Schmidt, 1996). This segment of workers contains all who are not working regular, full-time jobs, such as those employed part-time (voluntary or involuntary), in temporary jobs, or working on a contractual basis. In 2001, just under one third of employed women and one quarter of employed men worked under a nonstandard employment contract (Mishel, Bernstein, & Boushey, 2003).

Related to these developments is the rise of what Presser (1998, 2003) has called the "24/7" economy. In particular, she noted that the numbers of people working nonstandard schedules (e.g., evenings, nights, and/or weekends) is on the rise. Roughly one quarter of dual-earner married couples are "split-shift" couples. Among those with children under 3, the number rises to one third; among young, recently married dual-earner couples, one of every two is a split-shift couple (Presser, 1998).

Nonstandard employment arrangements—including both nonstandard contracts and nonstandard schedules—are more common in some industries than others. Part-time and temporary jobs in particular are more common in the service sector (Kalleberg & Schmidt, 1996). Workers with nonstandard schedules are also most likely to be found in the service sector—especially in personal service jobs (Presser, 1998). Nonstandard workers are generally more likely to be found in lower-paying occupations and industries (Presser, 2003; Mishel, Bernstein, & Boushey, 2003). Compared with other employees, workers with nonstandard employment contracts have fewer opportunities for promotion and are generally less satisfied with their jobs than workers on standard contracts (Mishel, Bernstein, & Boushey, 2003). Working a nonstandard schedule has been linked to a variety of negative physical and psychological problems, such as sleep disorders, stress, and depression (Fenwick & Tausig, 2001; Peterson, 1985).

The increases in these employment arrangements raise several issues for work-family researchers. A central research question has been whether nonstandard work arrangements—either in the form of contingent jobs or nonstandard work schedules—provide workers with greater or fewer options for balancing work and family life. Some see the growth of nonstandard employment contracts as providing workers—particularly women—with the flexibility they need to integrate job and family demands. Part-time jobs are the type of nonstandard work most often viewed as an option for people seeking greater balance in their lives (Mishel, Bernstein, & Boushey, 2003). In her study of mothers working the night shift, Garey (1999, p. 139) found that some viewed this as a way to be "'working mothers' who are 'stay-at-home' moms."

At the same time, there is little systematic evidence that women (or men) who need or want greater work-life balance are more likely than others to have nonstandard employment contracts or schedules, or that these arrangements are truly beneficial in facilitating greater work-family balance. Women with nonstandard employment contracts are only slightly more likely to have children than other women, and men with nonstandard employment contracts are less likely to have children than other men (Mishel, Bernstein, & Boushey, 2003). Moreover, many of these workers would prefer regular, full-time employment (Mischel, Bernstein, & Boushey, 2003; Kalleberg & Schmidt, 1996). As Kalleberg and Schmidt (1996, p. 256) explained, the view "that employers created contingent work schedules in response to employee demand should not be overstated."

Research on workers with nonstandard schedules yields similar conclusions in terms of their effects on work-family relations. As Presser (1998) explained, while women are more likely than men to cite family concerns as a reason for working a nonstandard schedule, both women and men are much more likely to work nonstandard schedules for involuntary rather than voluntary reasons. Moreover, evidence suggests that the consequences of working a nonstandard schedule for workers' family lives and relationships are mixed at best (Presser, 1998, 2003). For example, split-shift couples have higher divorce rates and lower levels of marital quality than otherwise comparable couples working standard schedules (Presser, 1998). However, fathers in split-shift couples do more household work than other men and are the primary caregivers of their children when mothers are working (Presser, 1998). These findings suggest that split-shift arrangements may be beneficial for children and families in some limited respects, but much more research is needed in this area.

The growing number of people with nonstandard employment contracts, who often work alongside more permanent, core workers, has created the beginnings of a two-tiered labor force (Kalleberg, 2001). Along similar lines, Presser (1998) anticipated growing diversity in work schedules, especially among women. These divisions create work forces with very different interests vis-à-vis their employers' involvement in work and family life. For example, workers on nonstandard contracts are only weakly connected to firms and the workplace benefits they provide. In contrast, employees on standard contracts face even more intensive demands on their loyalty and commitment.

The standard employment contract providing relatively permanent, full-time work has always been more available to white men than other groups. These work arrangements, with their implied exchange of loyalty and hard work on employees' part for secure employment and the prospect of mobility and wage growth on the part of employers, are consistent with domesticity's "ideal worker" norm. Women—especially those with children—were never viewed as ideal workers in the same way as men, and thus have always been less likely to obtain the jobs and rewards associated with stable, permanent work. Although nonstandard work schedules have increased for both genders, women with young children are expected to obtain a disproportionate share of new jobs organized in this way (Presser, 1998). As global competition forces large employers to restructure their workplaces and service employers continue to look for ways to cut their labor costs, workers most likely to need jobs that are compatible with raising families and work-family benefits have less access to these job characteristics and rewards than other workers.

Although workers' access to "good" jobs has always differed, the workforce has grown more divided in recent years (Morris & Western, 1999; Mishel, Bernstein, & Boushey, 2003). As Levy (1998) noted, one difference from the past is that "the winners" in today's economy have a much greater influence on economic policies than in the past. Although the divisions noted above are only one part of this polarization, they are important insofar as they signal a fundamental restructuring of work and employment. Even as employers, workers, and the public express greater concern about work-family balance, workers' access to jobs that make such accommodation possible grows increasingly more divided.

The High Commitment Workplace

The growth of nonstandard employment contracts has increased the numbers of workers without access to stable, permanent jobs and the 24/7 economy has expanded the numbers of people working nonstandard schedules. Those most affected by these changes have been workers at the lower end of the wage distribution. Even those who obtain stable employment with a regular daytime schedule, however, are experiencing changes in their organizations and their career prospects (Kalleberg, 2001). This has been especially true for managers and professionals, those most subject to the "ideal worker" norm of domesticity. The 21st century firm is, on the one hand, relinquishing hierarchical bureaucracy for more "empowering and commitment-inducing systems of management. On the other hand, jobs and firms are becoming decoupled, with workers experiencing unprecedented career insecurity" (DiMaggio, 2001, p. 26). Two decades of mergers, acquisitions, downsizing, deregulation, and "investor capitalism" (Useem, 1996) have led to record layoffs of white-collar workers and created demoralization and longer, more stressful work hours for remaining employees. Yet, corporations need to motivate their highly skilled professional and managerial employees to meet the demands of the fast-changing and competitive global economy (Powell, 2001). Firms that succeed in a global economy have, among other strategies, tried to elicit creative collaboration from their most highly skilled employees (Harrison, 1994). But, at the same time, downsizing and the flattening of firm hierarchies have reduced managers' job security and eroded their organizational commitment (Powell, 2001; Osterman, 1996).

In the midst of mergers, layoffs, and long hours, how can firms retain their best employees and inspire the committed effort required in a competitive and complex global market? One response has been to adopt policies and programs designed to help employees balance work and family responsibilities. Consistent with this view, Osterman's (1995) study of 875 American establishments finds that establishments trying to implement "high commitment" work systems are more likely than other firms to adopt work-family policies (see also Berg, Kalleberg, & Appelbaum, 2003; Gittelman, Horrigan, & Joyce, 1998).

Commitment, in Osterman's (1995, p. 686) terms, represents "the employees' willingness to engage themselves and offer their ideas and knowledge with a degree of authenticity that, by its very nature, is not enforceable and which therefore requires substantial element of volunteerism on the part of the workforce." Work-family policies are assumed to help induce these behaviors by signaling that employers are invested in their employees. Researchers suggest that these policies, as well as access to other kinds of benefits and opportunities, help sustain employees' beliefs that their long work hours and intensified work efforts are appreciated and rewarded by employers (Osterman, 2000; Gittelman, Horrigan, & Joyce, 1998; Konrad & Mangel, 2000).

These new work systems, like nonstandard employment contracts, are often described as creating more opportunities for flexibility at work and more recognition from employers of workers' interest in balancing work and family. Work-family specialists, government officials, and human resource managers have developed a "business case" for work-family policies that describes these programs as helping employers recruit, retain, and motivate a committed and productive workforce (Friedman & Greenhaus, 2000; Grover & Crooker, 1995; Kelly, 1999). Work-family scholars have tended to embrace these claims, motivated by an interest in work-family policy adoption and implementation.

As the growing sociological literature on organizational restructuring and new work practices reveals, however, there are gaps between how high commitment work systems and other arrangements operate in theory and their effects in practice (Smith, 2001; Osterman, 2000). In particular, some contend that that there has been a general deterioration of commitment among managers and professionals (Fraser, 2001). This argument is that, despite the popular rhetoric about family-friendly workplaces, various corporate policies, linked in part to globalization, have recently worsened the quality of managers' and professionals' work and family lives. In their study of an international financial services firm, Blair-Loy and Wharton (2004) found that corporate work conditions and intense job demands make it hard for many employees of both genders to take advantage of work-life policies, and these processes could be contributing to the deteriorating work lives studied by previous researchers.

These findings point to possible contradictions in the high commitment model of employment: It simultaneously increases work demands *and* provides extensive benefits ostensibly designed for greater work-life balance. To the extent that the demands of work interfere with employees' ability to use work-family policies, however, employees' commitment to the firm is likely to decline. This will make it more difficult to sustain the "win-win" scenario promoted by advocates of high commitment work systems (Osterman, 2000).

Hence, although "high commitment" work practices and generous work-family benefits are presumed to be part of the same package of workplace restructuring, we need to know more about the links between them as well as the effects of both on workers and their families. This aim would be furthered by greater dialogue between researchers interested in organizational restructuring and those interested in work-family policies. In general, work-family policies receive scant attention in sociological discussions of organizational restructuring, while studies of work-family policies rarely link these policies to broader changes occurring at work (but for exceptions to these patterns, see Berg, Kalleberg, & Appelbaum, 2003; Osterman, 1995; & Kelly, 1999).

CONCLUSION

The rise of industrial capitalism had two significant impacts on the institution of work and conceptions of work-family relations. The first was the division of work and family into "separate spheres"; the second concerned the growth of modern management and the corresponding view of work as governed by the impersonal forces of capitalism and the market. Neither view survives intact today: The workplace has changed as have sociological views of work, family, and the relations between them.

The 21st century thus presents challenges and opportunities for researchers interested in work and family. The challenges stem from the need to understand recent changes in the workplace, including the increased demographic diversity of workers, the continuing expansion and diversification of service work, and the broader efforts underway to restructure organizations and the employment contract. These trends may represent something other than a continuation of earlier processes; they may signal the beginnings of a radically new economic landscape. At the same time, researchers' capacity to understand these changes and their implications for work and family life may be greater than ever. Work and family have changed in fundamental ways, but so too have the frameworks for making sense of these of these important institutions. The goal now should be to apply these frameworks in ways that promote dialogue between researchers with work-family concerns at the top of their agenda and those seeking to make sense of broader changes in the organization of work in the 21st century.

REFERENCES

Abel, E. K., & Nelson, M. K. (Eds.). (1990). *Circles of care: Work and identity in women's lives.* Albany: State University of New York Press.

Acker, J. (1990). Hierarchies, jobs, and bodies: A theory of gendered organizations. *Gender & Society, 4,* 139–158.

Acker, J. (1992). Gendered institutions. *Contemporary Sociology, 21,* 565–569.

Baron, J. N., & Bielby, W. T. (1985). Organizational barriers to gender equality. In A. Rossi (Ed.), *Gender and the life course* (pp. 233–251). Hawthorne, NY: DeGruyter.

Bell, D. (1973). *The coming of post-industrial society.* New York: Basic Books.

Berg, P., Kalleberg, A. L., & Appelbaum, E. (2003). Balancing work and family: The role of high commitment environments. *Industrial Relations, 42,* 168–188.

Bergmann, B. (1986). *The economic emergence of women.* New York: Basic Books.

Bernard, J. (1992). The good-provider role: Its rise and fall. In M. S. Kimmel & M. A. Messner (Eds.), *Men's lives* (pp. 203–221). New York: Macmillan.

Bielby, W. T., & Baron, J. N. (1984). A woman's place is with other women: Sex segregation within organizations. In B. F. Reskin (Ed.), *Sex segregation in the workplace: Trends, explanations, remedies* (pp. 27–55). Washington, DC: National Academy Press.

Bielby, W. T., & Baron, J. N. (1986). Men and women at work: Sex segregation and statistical discrimination. *American Journal of Sociology, 91,* 759–799.

Blair-Loy, M., & Wharton, A. S. (2002). Employees' use of family-responsive policies and the workplace social context. *Social Forces, 80,* 813–845.

Blair-Loy, M., & Wharton, A. S. (2004). Organizational commitment and constraints on work-family policy use: Corporate flexibility policies in a global firm. *Sociological Perspectives, 47,* 243–267

Bowen, D. E., & Cummings, T. G. (1990). Suppose we took service seriously? In D. E. Bowen, R. B. Chase, & T. G. Cummings & Associates (Eds.), *Service management effectiveness* (pp. 1–14). San Francisco: Jossey-Bass.

Britton, D. M. (2000). The epistemology of the gendered organization. *Gender & Society, 14,* 418–434.

Budig, M. J., & England, P. (2001). The wage penalty for motherhood. *American Sociological Review, 66,* 204–225.

Cancian, F. (1987). *Love in America: Gender and self-development.* Cambridge, England: Cambridge University Press.

Cancian, F. (1989). Love and the rise of capitalism. In B. J. Risman & P. Schwartz (Eds.), *Gender in intimate relationships* (pp. 12–25). Belmont, CA: Wadsworth.

Capelli, P. (1999). *The new deal at work: Managing the market-driven workforce.* Boston, MA: Harvard Business School Press.

Casper, L. M., & Bianchi, S. M. (2002). *Continuity and change in the American family.* Thousand Oaks, CA: Sage.

Chafetz, J. S. (1998). From sex/gender roles to gender stratification: From victim blame to system blame. In K. A. Myers, C. D. Anderson, & B. J. Risman (Eds.), *Feminist foundations: Toward transforming sociology* (pp. 159–164). Thousand Oaks, CA: Sage.

Chatman, J. A., Polzer, J., Barsade, S., & Neale, M. (1998). Being different yet feeling similar: The influence of demographic composition and organizational culture on work processes and outcomes. *Administrative Science Quarterly, 43,* 749–780.

Chemers, M. M., Oskamp, S., & Costanzo, M. A. (Eds.) (1995). *Diversity in organizations: New perspectives for a changing workplace.* Thousand Oaks, CA: Sage.

Chivers, S., Wharton, A. S., & Blair-Loy, M. (2004). Low-waged workers in a "family-friendly" corporation: Call center employees' use of formal and informal work-family policies. Unpublished paper. Washington State University.

Cornfield, D. B., Campbell, K. E., & McCammon, H. J. (Eds.). (2001). *Working in restructured workplaces: Challenges and new directions in the sociology of work.* Thousand Oaks, CA: Sage.

Cowan, R. S. (1983). *More work for mother.* New York: Basic Books.

Crittenden, A. (2001). *The price of motherhood.* New York: Henry Holt.

DeVault, M. L. (1991). *Feeding the family: The social organization of caring as gendered work.* Chicago: University of Chicago Press.

DiMaggio, P. (2001). Introduction: Making sense of the contemporary firm and prefiguring its future. In P. DiMaggio (Ed.), *The twenty-first century firm: Changing economic organization in international perspective* (pp. 3–30). Princeton and Oxford: Princeton University Press.

Ehrenreich, B. (2001). *Nickel and dimed.* New York: Metropolitan Books.

Ehrenreich, B., & Hochschild, A. R. (2002). Introduction. In B. Ehrenreich & A. R. Hochschild (Eds.), *Global woman: Nannies, maids, and sex workers in the new economy* (pp. 1–15). New York: Metropolitan Books.

England, P. (1982). The failure of human capital theory to explain occupational sex segregation. *Journal of Human Resources, 17,* 358–370.

England, P. (1992). *Comparable worth: Theories and evidence.* New York: DeGruyter.

England, P., & Folbre, N. (1999). The cost of caring. *Annals of the American Academy of Political and Social Science, 561,* 39–51.

England, P., & Folbre, N. (2000). Capitalism and the erosion of care. In J. Madrick (Ed.), *Unconventional wisdom: Alternative perspectives on the new economy* (pp. 29–48). New York: Century Foundation Press.

England, P., Herbert, M., Kilbourne, B., Reid, L., & Megdal, L. (1994). The gendered valuation of occupations and skills: Earnings in 1980 census occupations. *Social Forces, 73*: 65–100.

Fenwick, R., & Tausig, M. (2001). Scheduling stress: Family and health outcomes of shift work and schedule control. *American Behavioral Scientist, 44,* 1179–1199.

Fligstein, N. (2001). *The architecture of markets: An economic sociology of twenty-first century capitalist societies.* Princeton and Oxford: Princeton University Press.

Fraser, J. A. (2001). *White collar sweatshop: The deterioration of work and its rewards in corporate America.* New York and London: Norton.

Frenkel, S. J., Korczynski, M., Shire, K. A., & Tam, M. (1999). *On the front line: Organization of work in the information economy.* Ithaca, NY: Cornell University Press.

Fried, M. (1998). *Taking time: Parental leave policy and corporate culture.* Philadelphia: Temple University Press.

Friedman, S. D., & Greenhaus, J. H. (2000). *Work and family: Allies or enemies?* New York: Oxford University Press.

Fullerton, H. N. (1997). Labor force 2006: Slowing down and changing composition. *Monthly Labor Review, November,* 23–38.

Garey, A. I. (1999). *Weaving work and motherhood.* Philadelphia: Temple University Press.

Gittleman, M., Horrigan, M., & Joyce, M. (1998). "Flexible" workplace practices: Evidence from a nationally representative survey. *Industrial and Labor Relations Review, 52,* 99–115.

Glenn, E. N. (1992). From servitude to service work: Historical continuities in the racial division of paid reproductive labor. *Signs, 18,* 1–43.

Goldscheider, F. K., & Waite, L. J. (1991). *New families, no families?: The transformation of the American home.* Berkeley: University of California Press.

Gordon, J. M. (1996). *Fat and mean: The corporate squeeze of working Americans and the myth of managerial downsizing.* New York: Free Press.

Gornick, J., Meyers, M., & Ross, K. E. (1998). Public policies and the employment of mothers: A cross-national study. *Social Science Quarterly, 79,* 35–54.

Grover, S. L., & Crooker, K. J. (1995). Who appreciates family-responsive human resource policies: The impact of family-friendly policies on the organizational attachment of parents and non-parents. *Personnel Psychology, 48,* 271–288.

Hareven, T. K. (1990). A complex relationship: Family strategies and the processes of economic and social change. In R. Friedland & A. F. Robertson (Eds.), *Beyond the marketplace: Rethinking economy and society* (pp. 215–244). New York: DeGruyter.

Harrison, B. (1994). *Lean and mean: The changing landscape of corporate power in an age of flexibility.* New York: Basic Books.

Hays, S. (2003). *Flat broke with children: Women in the age of welfare reform.* New York: Oxford University press.

Hochschild, A. R. (1983). *The managed heart: The commercialization of human feeling.* Berkeley: University of California Press.

Hochschild, A. R. (1989). *The second shift: Working parents and the revolution at home.* New York: Viking Penguin.

Hochschild, A. (1997). *The time bind.* New York: Metropolitan Books.

Hodson, R., & Sullivan, T. A. (1995). *The social organization of work* (2nd ed.). Belmont, CA: Wadsworth.

Hondagneu-Sotelo, P. (2001). *Domestica: Immigrant workers cleaning and caring in the shadows of affluence.* Berkeley: University of California Press.

Huber, J. (1998). Trends in gender stratification, 1970–1985. In K. A. Myers, C. D. Anderson, & B. J. Risman (Eds.), *Feminist foundations: Toward transforming sociology* (pp. 83–101). Thousand Oaks, CA: Sage.

Jacobs, J. A., & Gerson, K. (1997). *The endless day or the flexible office? Working time, work-family conflict, and gender equity in the modern workplace.* Report to the Alfred E. Sloan Foundation.

Jacobs, J. A., & Gerson, K. (2004). *The time divide.* Cambridge, MA: Harvard University Press.

Jacoby, S. M. (1985). *Employing bureaucracy: Managers, unions and the transformation of work in American industry, 1900–1945.* New York: Columbia University Press.

Jepperson, R. L. (1991). Institutions, institutional effects, and institutionalism. In W. W. Powell & P. J. DiMaggio (Eds.), *The new institutionalism in organizational analysis* (pp. 143–163). Chicago: University of Chicago Press.

Johnston, W. B., & Packer, A. E. (1987). *Workforce 2000.* Indianapolis, IN: The Hudson Institute.

Jones, J. (1987). *Labor of love, labor of sorrow: Black women, work, and the family from slavery to the present.* New York: Vintage.

Kalleberg, A. L. (2001). The advent of the flexible workplace: Implications for theory and research. In D. B. Cornfield, K. E. Campbell, & H. J. McCammon (Eds.), *Working in restructured workplaces: Challenges and new directions for the sociology of work* (pp. 437–453). Thousand Oaks, CA: Sage.

Kalleberg, A. L., & Schmidt, K. (1996). Contingent employment in organizations In A. L. Kalleberg, D. Knoke, P. V. Marsden, & J. L. Spaeth (Eds.), *Organizations in America* (pp. 253–275). Thousand Oaks, CA: Sage.

Kanter, R. M. (1977a) *Work and family in the United States: A critical review and agenda for research and policy.* New York: Russell Sage Foundation.

Kanter, R. M. (1977b) *Men and women of the corporation.* New York: Basic Books.

Kelly, E. (1999). Theorizing corporate family policies: How advocates built the "business case" for "family-friendly" programs. *Research in the Sociology of Work, 7,* 1169–1202.

Kilbourne, B., England, P., & Beron, K. (1994). Effects of individual, occupational, and industrial characteristics on earning: Intersections of race and gender. *Social Forces, 72,* 1149–1176.

Konrad, A., & Mangel, R. (2000). The impact of work-life programs on firm productivity. *Strategic Management Journal, 21,* 1225–1237.

Levy, F. (1998). *The new dollars and dreams.* New York: Russell Sage Foundation.

Lippe, T. van der, & van Dijk, L. (Eds.). (2001). *Women's employment in a comparative perspective.* New York: DeGruyter.

Lippe, T. van der, & van Dijk, L. (Eds.). (2002). Comparative research on women's employment. *Annual Review of Sociology, 28,* 221–41.

Macdonald, C. L., & Sirianni, C. (1996). The service society and the changing experience of work. In C. L. Macdonald & C. Sirianni (Eds.), *Working in the service society* (pp. 1–26). Philadelphia: Temple University Press.

Maier, M. (1999). On the gendered substructure of organization: Dimensions and dilemmas of corporate masculinity. In G. N. Powell (Ed.), *Handbook of gender and work* (pp. 69–93). Thousand Oaks, CA: Sage.

Mayo, E. (1936). *The human problems of an industrial civilization.* New York: Macmillan.

Meyer, M. H. (Ed.). (2000). *Care work.* New York: Routledge.

Mishel, L., Bernstein, J., & Boushey, H. (2003). *The state of working America, 2002–2003.* Ithaca, NY: ILR Press.

Mishel, L., Bernstein, J., & Schmitt, J. (2001). *The state of working America 2000–2001.* Ithaca, NY: Cornell University Press.

Morris, M., & Western, B. (1999). Inequality in earnings at the close of the twentieth century. *Annual Review of Sociology, 25,* 623–657.

Nelson, R. L., & Bridges, W. P. (1999). *Legalizing gender inequality.* New York: Cambridge University Press.

Newman, K. S. (1999). *No shame in my game: The working poor in the inner city.* New York: Alfred A. Knopf, Inc. and the Russell Sage Foundation.

Osterman, P. (1995). Work/family programs and the employment relationship. *Administrative Science Quarterly, 40,* 681–700.

Osterman, P. (Ed.). (1996). *Broken ladders: Managerial careers in the new economy.* New York: Oxford University Press.

Osterman, P. (1999). *Securing prosperity. The American labor market: How it has changed and what to do about it.* Princeton, NJ: Princeton University Press.

Osterman, P. (2000). Work reorganization in an era of restructuring: Trends in diffusion and effects on employee welfare. *Industrial and Labor Relations Review, 53,* 179–196.

Padavic, I., & Reskin, B. (2002). *Women and men at work.* Thousand Oaks, CA: Pine Forge Press.

Parsons, T. (1964). *Essays in sociological theory.* New York: The Free Press.

Parsons, T., & Bales, R. F. (1955). *Family, socialization and interaction process.* New York: The Free Press.

Perrow, C. (2002). *Organizing America: Wealth, power, and the origins of corporate capitalism.* Princeton: Princeton University Press.

Peterson, M. (1985). Attitudinal differences among work shifts: What do they reflect? *Academy of Management Journal, 28,* 723–732.

Pfeffer, J., & Baron, J. N. (1998). Taking the workers back out: Recent trends in the structuring of employment. In B. M. Staw & L. L., Cummings (Eds.), *Research in organizational behavior*, Vol. 10 (pp. 257–303). Greenwich, CN: JAI Press.

Powell, W. W. (2001). The capitalist firm in the twenty-first century: Emerging patterns in western enterprise. In P. DiMaggio (Ed.), *The twenty-first century firm: Changing economic organization in international perspective* (pp. 33–68). Princeton and Oxford: Princeton University Press.

Presser, H. B. (1998). Toward a 24 hour economy: The U.S. experience and implications for family. In D. Vannoy & P. J. Dubeck (Eds.), *Challenges for work and family in the twenty-first century* (pp. 39–48). New York: DeGruyter.

Presser, H. B. (2003). *Working in a 24/7 economy: Challenges for American families*. New York: Russell Sage.

Reskin, B. F., & Charles, C. Z. (1999). Now you see 'em, now you don't: Race, ethnicity, and gender in labor market research. In I. Brown (Ed.), *Latinas and African-American women at work* (pp. 380–407). New York: Russell Sage.

Reskin, B., & Padavic, I. (1994). *Women and men at work*. Thousand Oaks, CA: Pine Forge Press.

Romero, M. (1992). *Maid in the U.S.A.* New York: Routledge.

Smith, D. (1974). Women's perspective as a radical critique of sociology. *Sociological Inquiry, 44,* 7–13.

Smith, V. (1997). New forms of work organization. *Annual Review of Sociology, 23,* 315–339.

Smith, V. (2001). *Crossing the great divide: Worker risk and opportunity in the new economy.* Ithaca, NY: ILR Press.

Steinberg, R. J. (1992.) Gender on the agenda: Male advantage in organizations. *Contemporary Sociology, 21*: 576–581.

Taylor, F. (1911). *The principales of scientific management.* New York: Harper & Brothers.

Townsend, N. (2002). *The package deal: Marriage, work, and fatherhood in men's lives.* Philadelphia: Temple University Press.

Tsui, A. S., Egan, T. D., & O'Reilly, III, C. A. (1992). Being different: Relational demography and organizational attachment. *Administrative Science Quarterly, 37,* 549–579.

Tsui, A. S., & Gutek, B. A. (1999). *Demographic differences in organizations.* New York: Lexington.

U.S. Department of Labor. (2004). Women in the labor force: A databook. Washington, DC: U.S. Government Printing Office.

U.S. Department of Labor. (2004). Bureau of Labor Statistics (http://www.bls.gov/data). Data extracted on August 30, 2004.

Useem, M. (1996). Investor capitalism: How money managers are changing the face of corporate America. New York: Basic Books.

Vallas, S. (1999). Re-thinking post-Fordism: The meaning of workplace flexibility. *Sociological Theory, 17,* 68–101.

Waldfogel, J. (1997). The effects of children on women's wages. *American Journal of Sociology, 62,* 209–217.

Wharton, A. S. (2000). Feminism and the study of work: From 'women's work' to gendered institutions. *Annals of the American Academy of Political and Social Sciences* (September): 167–182.

Wharton, A. S., & Blair-Loy, M. (2002). The "overtime culture" in a global corporation: A cross-national study of finance professionals' interest in working part-time. *Work & Occupations, 29,* 32–63.

Williams, C. (1989). *Gender differences at work: Women and men in nontraditional occupations.* Berkeley: University of California Press.

Williams, C. (1995). *Still a man's world.* Berkeley: University of California Press.

Williams, C. L., Giuffre, P. A., & Dellinger, K. (1999). Sexuality in the workplace. *Annual Review of Sociology, 25,* 73–93.

Williams, J. (2000). *Unbending gender: Why work and family conflict and what to do about it.* New York: Oxford University Press.

Williams, K. Y., & O'Reilly III, C. A. (1998). Demography and diversity in organizations: A review of 40 years of research. *Research in Organizational Behavior, 20,* 77–140.

3

Understanding Diversity of Families in the 21st Century and Its Impact on the Work-Family Area of Study

Stephen R. Marks
University of Maine

Ian Wheeler-Nicholson (2000) recalls a childhood regularly punctuated by moves to a new town. It seemed that by every summer's end, family-life-as-usual would bring Ian to a new elementary school. He knew that any "new kid" was always at a disadvantage, especially one who was not rich, big, tough, nor athletic enough to seize control, and he had therefore learned to keep to himself so as not to attract attention. When one day his mother cryptically warned him not to tell anyone where his father is, just before he was to start yet another school, Ian's apprehensiveness rose higher than usual. That year he began to put things together. Another boy got called a "faggot" and beaten up for the crime of hanging out too much with girls and enjoying art. A girl was branded a "lesbo" because she was already developing breasts, and she was quite good at athletics. Ian's usual policy of smiling and saying nothing when people talked to him was a much-needed protective cover. Through his relative silence, Ian recalls:

> I had stumbled on my mother's very own solution to the problem of leading a covert homosexual life. In later years, she would tell me that the main reason for our constant moves was that, in each place, eventually a nosy neighbor or co-worker would begin to suspect the truth about my mother or her partner. *My mother was always afraid of losing her job*, and there was the looming threat of violence. And so we became an itinerant family. (Wheeler-Nicholson, 2000, p. 111, italics added)

I offer this snippet of Ian's story because it defies the popular imagination, in which there resides an "average American family person" who must juggle the demands of spouse, children, job, friends, recreational interests, and so on. This mind's-eye family has found its way into family studies and other social sciences, and it has influenced studies of the work-family interface as well. It is the family referenced by the appeal to "family values," the family of political election rhetoric. Its adult members are married, White and heterosexual, and they have children living with them at home. Nowadays, the image of this traditional family has been updated: Instead of father working and mother at home, both partners have paid work, but one of them—the wife—works less than full-time in order to look after the children and take care of the home.

41

Ian's family, like millions of others, does not fit either the older or the updated versions of this traditional family image. Our typical models of the work-family interface are not fully adequate to the facts of daily life for people like Ian's mother and her partner Veronica. To be sure, like all workers and parents, these women had work schedules that fit the needs of their family either poorly or well, and the specific attributes of their jobs either promoted a better work-family balance or a worse one. But quite aside from these important job qualities, Ian's mother and Veronica were obviously struggling with a "stressor" that made a bigger impact on their work-family "interface" than any other, one that also spilled over onto Ian's life: As a lesbian couple raising a child, they were far too different from the "average American family" image, and that difference could have cost them their jobs and their family security.

WHAT IS FAMILY DIVERSITY?

This chapter highlights some features of family diversity in the 21st century. My focus is necessarily selective rather than a state-of-the-art treatment. Scholarship on family diversity has been mushrooming, and it is not possible in a single chapter to thoroughly survey the area (a recent book-length compendium may be found in Demo, Allen, & Fine, 2000).

In focusing on contemporary and emerging families as "diverse," I want to signal two different senses of the term "diversity." First, it points to the simple fact of variety. In this vein, we often spotlight the compositional variety of households—for example, two-parent families, single-parent families, "blended" families, extended families, couples (married or cohabiting), and people living alone (often networked with other households through kinship or "chosen" family). Beyond household composition, a focus on variety often seizes on the fact that different families are systematically linked to different life chances, depending on where the family is located on a society's most salient hierarchies—race–ethnicity, social class, gender, sexual orientation, and age. These hierarchies are often seen to "intersect" as a "matrix of domination" (Andersen & Collins, 1998), such that some families may enjoy double or triple privileges while others must struggle with multiple disadvantages. Of course, some individuals may be privileged in some categories and disadvantaged in others. For example, a wealthy lesbian African American couple may enjoy social class privileges, but they may run into multiple barriers not encountered by males, heterosexuals, and European Americans. In this chapter, I will consider a range of issues suggested both by the variety of household types and by the fact of differential location on society's major hierarchies.

A second meaning of the term "diversity" springs from the abiding sense that there is some "standard North American family" (Smith, 1993) or "average family," and that we ought to recognize points of difference from this standard or average. Ian's story (above) easily grabs our attention because it jolts us outside of this imagined standard. Here, my argument is that the "average family" is most accurately seen as an ideological trope that hides rather than reflects empirical diversity. White, middle-class, heterosexual families with children may be prominent because of their relative hegemony, but they are anything but average in the statistical sense, and they will become less and less so as the 21st century unfolds. Therefore, to break out of the "average family" image is to make more room in the center of our theory and research for those who had previously been relegated to the periphery as "minority groups." The minority status of these people is rapidly fading with their swelling populations, and it is incumbent on work and family scholars to see them clearly.

Plan of the Chapter

This chapter is organized into three major sections. The first section identifies five master trends that are shifting American families away from the traditional "average family" image. First, I consider the distribution of the population into various household types, taking particular notice of the historical decline of some types (e.g., households composed of two parents and at least one child) and the historical ascendancy of others (e.g., single-parent and single individual households). Second, I focus on the shifting racial-ethnic balance of the population, calling specific attention to the growing percentages of Hispanic and Asian Americans. Third, I consider how patterns of immigration are adding enormous complexity to how we reckon the racial-ethnic mix in this country. The fourth pattern is the decline of heteronormativity. Here, I take special care to describe this process as something that not simply affects lesbians and gay men but also the inner workings of heterosexual households. Fifth, I consider the aging of the U.S. population and some of the challenges that this implies for families and for work-family scholars.

The second section is a consideration of how social class differences generate some of the most important factors of family diversity that bear on the work-family interface. In particular, I spotlight the importance of family income, differences in socialization patterns among the middle and working classes, and issues faced by some of the more vulnerable categories of the population—immigrants, low-income people, single parents, and lesbian and gay couples and families. In the third major section, I piggyback on some recent advances in the sociology of health to suggest how work and family scholars might focus more attention on patterns of prejudice and discrimination and their impact. Specifically, if we want a more fine-grained understanding of everyday obstacles within the lives of disadvantaged categories of the population, we will need to design our studies in ways that capture some of the unique stressors that these people encounter.

SOME PROCESSES OF SOCIETAL TRANSFORMATION

The Transformation of American Households

The first master trend concerns an increase in the percentages of Americans living in some types of households and a decrease of those living in other types. Single-parent households— both mother–child and father–child—are on the rise, as are households consisting of a single individual. Plainly, it is now inaccurate to visualize an average household as a group consisting of a mother, a father, and one or more children. Table 3.1 shows the distribution of people across household categories, comparing 1970 with 2000 percentages. Consider that in the 2000 census, married couples living with one or more children comprised only 24% of all American households, down from 40% of the total in 1970. Put simply, less than one out of four households now fits the traditional family image, even less than the 26% of households occupied by a single person.

To be sure, an additional 29% of households in 2000 consisted of a married couple living alone. Many of the younger of these couples will eventually have children and will then join

TABLE 3.1
Households by Type—1970 and 2000

Year	Total Households	Married With Children	Married Without Children	One Person	Single Parent	Other Blood Relatives	Unmarried Couples: (Opposite Sex)
2000	104,705,000	24.1%	28.7%	25.5%	8.9%	7.0%	4.5%
1970	63,401,000	40.3%	30.3%	17.1%	5.2%	5.5%	1.0%

Source: American Association for Single People. 2000 Census—AASP report.

the ranks of those living in a traditional household, unless or until they separate or divorce. And many of the older couples have already raised children, who have since moved out to form their own households. These older couples (or some of them) at one point did live in a traditional nuclear family. It is no doubt true that the vast majority of American people have lived in a household with both their mother and father for at least a small portion of their lives, just as the vast majority have later formed new families consisting of a spouse and child or children, and so they too fit the traditional image at least for a short period. In that sense, it is misleading to look at the distribution of households at only one point in time.

In another sense, however, the snapshot view of how people are distributed in households is a good way to gauge the full variety of needs that work-family scholars ought to address. People with dependent children have a different set of needs than people who live alone, as children's activities and school schedules in particular are a daily fact of parents' lives in ways that have no relevance for households with no dependent children. In turn, single-parent needs may also differ in important ways from those within two-parent households. For example, single parents may find their job options and work schedules far more constrained than do the adults within two-parent households, as the former must often take on the entire burden of coordinating with children's schedules.

The Racial–Ethnic Transformation

The second master trend is that White families have become a shrinking proportion of American families, as people of color (including self-identified Hispanics) comprise an increasingly larger percentage of the population. Table 3.2 draws on population projections for each of the five racial–ethnic groups tracked by the census, focusing on the 2000 baseline and looking ahead to 2050.

The table shows with dramatic clarity the continuing racial–ethnic transformation that will shrink the proportion of non-Hispanic White people while the numbers of Asian Americans and Hispanic Americans will approximately double their year 2000 percentages. No one can know the full impact of this transformation, but perhaps a reasonable assumption is that if non-Hispanic Whites retain their lopsided share of American wealth, privilege, and power, racial–ethnic category will remain a central organizing component of American consciousness. And, as the white minority grows smaller, political pressures that challenge its hegemony will grow increasingly vehement.

TABLE 3.2

Percent of Total Population by Race—2000 and Projections for 2020 and 2050

	2000	2020	2050
Hispanic (of any race)	12.6	17.8	24.4
Asian	3.8	5.4	8.0
Black—Non-Hispanic	12.7	13.5	14.6
White—Non-Hispanic	69.4	61.3	50.1
All other races[1]	2.5	3.5	5.3

[1] Includes American Indian and Alaska Native, Native Hawaiian, Other Pacific Islander, and two or more races.

Source: U.S. Census Bureau, 2004, "U.S. Interim Projections by Age, Sex, Race, and Hispanic Origin."

Immigration Complicates the Categories

The third master trend is that immigration patterns are complicating the racial–ethnic trans-formation in at least two ways. First, unlike previous waves of immigration that brought pre-dominantly White Europeans to our shores, the current wave consists largely of non-European Hispanics and people of color. In 2002, Europeans comprised just 14% of the foreign-born U.S. population, while Hispanics comprised 52.2%, Asians 25.5%, and Carribeans 9.6% (Schmidley, 2003). Second, the increasing diversity within each overall category of the "new" immigrant—Asian, Black, and Hispanic—defies any easy generalizations that hold up across the category, as people from different nations of origin bring their different backgrounds and traditions to the new land.

Hispanics.   I begin here with the regions and nations of origin that have been contributing the largest share of the Hispanic population in the United States. Table 3.3 shows Hispanic population estimates for 1990 and 2000, and it indicates the rate of growth in that time period, drawing on the Mumford Center's use of Current Population Report data to produce more detailed information about those Hispanics who were listed only as "Other Hispanics" in the 2000 census data collection procedures (see Logan, 2001b).

Most notable in Table 3.3 is the emergent shift toward "new Latinos" as the fastest-growing Hispanic groups. Although people of Mexican, Puerto Rican, and Cuban origin are still the largest Hispanic groups, new Latinos are now more numerous than Puerto Ricans and Cubans combined. Research on Hispanic families is still in its infancy. Most of it has focused on Mexicans, and even here, scholars have barely begun to document the probable variety that is out there. Nevertheless, some generalizations may be advanced, and I take them up in the section on social class.

Asians.   As with Hispanics, the recent wave of Asian immigrants has diversified the category. Table 3.4, compiled by the Mumford Center (Logan, 2001a), indicates an overall population growth of Asian Americans of 69% between 1990 and 2000. People of Chinese or Filipino origin remain the largest contributors to the Asian population, but Indians have surged into third place, having increased at nearly twice the growth rate of Chinese or Filipinos in the 10-year period. Vietnamese have become the second fastest growing category, having doubled their numbers over the same period.

TABLE 3.3
Hispanic Population Growth by Region and Selected Nations of Origin

	1990	*2000*	*Increase*
HISPANIC TOTAL	21,900,089	35,305,818	61%
Mexican	13,576,346	23,060,224	70%
Puerto Rican	2,705,979	3,640,460	35%
Cuban	1,067,416	1,315,346	23%
New Latino groups	3,019,780	6,153,989	104%
Dominican	537,120	1,121,257	109%
Central American	1,387,331	2,863,063	106%
South American	1,095,329	2,169,669	98%

Source: Adapted from Logan, J. L. (2001b). The new Latinos: Who they are, where they are. Lewis Mumford Center for Comparative Urban and Regional Research.

TABLE 3.4
Asian Population in the U.S., 1990 and 2000

Population	1990		2000		Population Growth
All Asians	7,273,662		12,275,972		69%
	Number	Percent	Number	Percent	
Chinese	1,645,472	22.6	2,734,841	22.3	66%
Filipinos	1,406,770	19.3	2,364,815	19.3	68%
Japanese	847,562	11.7	1,148,932	9.4	36%
Indians	815,447	11.2	1,899,599	15.5	133%
Koreans	798,849	11.0	1,228,427	10.0	54%
Vietnamese	614,547	8.4	1,223,736	10.0	99%
Other	1,145,015	15.7	1,306,330	13.5	14%

Source: Logan, J. L. (2001a). From many shores: Asians in Census 2000. Lewis Mumford Center for Comparative Urban and Regional Research, University at Albany, October 6, 2001.

Like Hispanics, Asian Americans from different nations of origin have fared differently in terms of their life chances in the United States. Although Asian American median household income suggests a relatively privileged standing, we will see that social class variations render the "model minority" image of Asians inadequate to capture the variety of Asian experience here.

Blacks.   The overall rate of Black population growth has been far more moderate than that of either Hispanics or Asians, but immigration patterns are again creating some important diversification. Here, I follow current practice of distinguishing between African Americans (Blacks who were born here but claim a nonspecific African heritage), Africans (recent immigrants principally from West or East Africa), and Afro-Caribbeans (e.g., Jamaicans and Haitians). The Mumford Center noted that between 1990 and 2000, recent arrivals from sub-Saharan Africa and from the Caribbean accounted for nearly 25% of the growth of the Black population (Logan & Deane, 2003). The report adds, "although not an often-recognized part of the American ethnic mosaic, both of these groups are emerging as large and fast-growing populations; Afro-Caribbeans now outnumber and are growing faster than such well-established ethnic minorities as Cubans and Koreans" (Logan & Deane, 2003). As with Hispanics and Asians, we will see that social class differences among the three major subcategories of Black people are considerable. These differences at times become politically explosive, as when the Black Republican candidate for a U.S. Senate seat in Illinois took issue in 2004 with the Black Democratic candidate's claim of an African American heritage (the latter has a Kenyan father and a White, American-born mother): "My ancestors toiled in slavery in this country," the Republican proclaimed; "my consciousness, who I am as a person, has been shaped by my struggle, deeply emotional and deeply painful, with the reality of that heritage" (Swarns, 2004). Although the explicit focus here is on racial–ethnic identity claims, the implicit issue is opportunity for upward mobility through the social class system.

The Decline of Heteronormativity

The fourth master trend is that the foundations of heteronormativity are slowly eroding and will continue to do so as the century unfolds. Along with the demographic changes noted above, this is a social and cultural transformation that is generating a sea of change within family life. As noted by Oswald, Blume, and Marks (2005), heteronormativity is an ideological composite of several elements. It is, of course, a notion about "natural" versus unnatural sexuality, and as gay and lesbian families become more visible, their presence will increasingly challenge narrow images of what is natural. But heteronormativity is also a prescription for "normal" gender expression and family formation, and its impact affects heterosexual couples as well as gays and lesbians. At its core are two interrelated beliefs: First, males and females are held to be "opposite sexes" who are drawn together by natural forces of sexual attraction; and second, "natural" family patterns are held to spring from these attractions and to take shape in ways that simply reflect these differing (and opposite) gender sensibilities of men and women.

This heteronormative ideological system is being challenged on two fronts. First, a new wave of gay activism exploded across the American landscape late in 2003, triggered by decisions handed down by the Supreme Judicial Court in Massachusetts and culminating in 2004 in the first legally married lesbian and gay Americans in that state. In San Francisco, the spectacle of hundreds of gay and lesbian couples lining up outside City Hall to take their marriage vows (later invalidated by California's highest court) was a nightly phenomenon on network television news. Perhaps their sheer ordinariness was the biggest story. They seemed to be an utterly conventional cross-section of the American middle class—elderly, middle-aged, young, fresh-from-a-business-meeting or job at the bank, fat, thin, and attired in every imaginable style from staidly conservative to high fashion to punk.

Predictably, these developments have set off a new round of culture wars. Traditionalists have marshaled support for an amendment to the U.S. constitution that would define marriage as an arrangement solely between a man and a woman, and many state legislatures have recently made this definition the law of their respective states. Whatever the outcome, the fight for gay rights will not quietly go away. Even if the traditionalists ultimately prevail in limiting civil marriage to heterosexuals, they may have to accept strong same-sex domestic partnership provisions in exchange, and then the outcome may well be the same: Lesbian and gay couples will have found a recognized and protected place at the table of American families, a place that may no longer be threatened by the vagaries of unfriendly state laws.

The other challenge to heteronormativity is found squarely within heterosexual relationships. Until the last third of the 20th century, the notion of males and females as opposites had led to a rigid set of gender prescriptions. Males were seen as "instrumental" specialists who are good at such things as work and politics, while females excel at nurturing other people, particularly in the form of homemaking activities and family caregiving (Parsons, 1964). In the past 35 years, however, the rigidity of these prescriptions has been met with an ever-increasing set of challenges, and the genders have grown more and more alike. Men have been challenged to become more involved in housework and child care, and they have done so, albeit modestly (Coltrane, 2000). Women have fought for full participation in education, athletics, occupations, and politics, with a considerable degree of success. Labor force participation rates for U.S. women with an infant under age 1 have risen from 31% percent in 1976 to a high of 59% in 1998 (Downs, 2003). Since then, the rate has dropped slightly to 55% in 2000 and in 2002, but the year 2000 decline occurred only among White, married women over age 30 with some college education (O'Connell, 2001)—arguably the most economically privileged category of women in the United States.

For families, this convergence of the genders has generated some far-reaching changes that bear greatly on the emerging work-family interface. First, heterosexual women desiring marriage have delayed their first marriages: Age at first marriage averaged 21 in 1970, and by 2000 it rose to nearly 25. There is widespread consensus that this delay is part and parcel of the expanding educational and occupational opportunities for women. The National Center for Health Statistics reported that in this 30-year period, "the number of women completing college has nearly doubled and the number in the labor force has gone up by almost 40 percent" (Matthews & Hamilton, 2002). As women come to have attractive socioeconomic alternatives to marriage, there is no longer such a compelling economic urgency to marry, and women can afford to be more scrutinizing in their choice of a partner and in the timing of a union.

Second, if and when they do marry, women increasingly expect to have paid work until some time in their later mid-life or into their senior years, with only brief interruptions if any. It is now a commonplace assumption among most heterosexual married couples that two regular paychecks—his and hers—will be financially necessary to maintain their preferred level of income. The resulting pattern of daily couple life has made it more difficult to sustain the notion of the genders as opposites, especially when both partners have full-time jobs or careers. "Good partners" come to be seen as people who do their fair share of income-earning, housework, and (if the couple has children) child care, regardless of gender. Schwartz's *Peer Marriage* (1994) may be seen as a postmodern primer for such couples—people oriented to gender sameness instead of oppositeness.

To be sure, vigorous forces of traditionalism will remain, as evidenced by the popularity of John Gray's books (e.g., 1992), which proclaim that men and women come from different planets. The General Social Survey is arguably the most representative sample of United States attitudes, and we can draw on some items in the 2002 survey (Davis & Smith, 2002) to illustrate the persistence of family traditionalism. Nearly 39% of Americans say they "agree" that "it is much better for everyone involved if the man is the achiever outside the home and the woman takes care of the home and family" (the other response choices are "disagree" and "neither agree nor disagree"). The same percentage agrees with the statement, "All in all, family life suffers when the woman has a full-time job." And a 1996 item asked which of "two types of relationships would the respondent prefer?: 1. A relationship where the man has the main responsibility for providing the household income and the woman has the main responsibility for taking care of the home and family, or 2. A relationship where the man and woman equally share responsibility for providing the household income and taking care of the home and family?" Nearly 30% chose the traditional family type (Davis & Smith, 1996).

The resulting "culture wars" between those who remain eager to create gendered domains of everyday life and those who see such differences as an anachronism will probably linger, but the GSS trends show that the more postmodern pattern is the ascendant one. If 39% of Americans still agree with the image of man-the-"achiever" and woman-the-homebody, this traditional preference is down dramatically from the 66% who agreed with the same item in 1977 (Davis & Smith, 2002). The fact is that as men and women's activities grow increasingly similar to each other, their overall sensibilities and their perceptions of what they need and what they want will more and more converge. Coltrane (1991) uncovered a tendency among active, role-sharing fathers to eschew friendships with other men who are not as involved as they are in child care. These men are more likely to compare themselves to women than to more traditional men, and at work they sometimes choose to hide their child-involvement from male coworkers who might judge them to be insufficiently career-motivated.

The children of these gender-convergent couples are likely to gravitate as adults to their parents' role-sharing pattern. Risman (1998) found that children from "fair families" fully absorb their parents' liberal gender ideology. Although they alter it in school, once they are exposed to their peers' creation of the genders as opposites, Risman suggested that as adults they are likely to revert to the postgendered pattern that was their initial family baseline.

As women and men who rear children together become more alike and less like opposites, and as their children eventually replicate what they have grown up with, the consequences for the work-family interface will be considerable. The pressure on workplaces to adapt not simply to the family needs of their female workers but also to those of their male workers will accelerate. As fathers continue their long, slow march toward greater family involvement, mothers will see less need to scale down their work involvement or to settle for lower pay. Neither men nor women will continue to tolerate the "motherhood wage penalty," which has persisted despite the fact that women now work longer into their pregnancies and return to work sooner after giving birth (Avellar & Smock, 2003).

The crux of the matter is that gender discrimination at work has long participated in the *creation* of gender difference by making it more valuable for men to prioritize work and for women to prioritize family, thus generating two different kinds of people. As men and women increasingly undo their differences at home, they will grow less tolerant of the forces that render them into opposites at work. Employers will then be forced to undo the motherhood wage penalty, and they will either become more family-friendly or they will lose their competitive edge when they recruit their employees.

The Graying of America

The final master trend is the aging of the American population. Table 3.5 shows the proportion of older people in U.S. Census data for 1970 and 2000, and it includes current projections for 2020 and 2050. The progression over these four time points demonstrates a rather dramatic trend toward an aging population, culminating by mid-century in people age 65 or older comprising 20.7% of the population, up from 12.4% in the 2000 census. In absolute numbers, this will mean that more than 86 million of the projected 419 million total population of the United States will be older people. Moreover, additional projections provided by the U.S. Administration on Aging (AoA) suggest that these older people will have a considerably longer life expectancy. For example, a 65-year-old male in 2050 will be expected to live another 20.3 years, compared to the 15.5 more years he would have lived in 1995. And, an 85-year-old female who was projected in 1995 to live an additional 6.5 years would have a life expectancy of 9.4 years in 2050.

For work-family issues and for society as a whole, there are a number of consequences of this growing number of older Americans. Concerning paid work, the current trend of more elders (especially women) lengthening their stay in the labor force will no doubt accelerate, as longevity rates increase. The AoA (2003) reported that by 2005, 16% of women between age 65 and 74 will be in the labor force, an increase of 18% over the 1994 level. And 4.3% of women age 75 and higher will be in the labor force, an increase of 22% over the 1994 level. Looking forward, the American economy will be under pressure to accommodate this swelling population of elderly workers.

Concerning living arrangements, the vast majority of elders remain noninstitutionalized, and the AoA (2003) reported that in 2002 most of these people lived either in a separate household with their spouse (53.6%) or alone (30%). By gender, however, most men age 65 or older (73%) lived with a spouse, compared to only 41% of women, reflecting the fact that most husbands predecease their wives. The fact that elderly people typically live alone (with or without a spouse) should not suggest that they remain totally nondependent. For elderly couples, wives will remain the primary caregivers of husbands who become ill or disabled,

TABLE 3.5

Percent of Older People in the U.S. Population—1970, 2000, 2020, and 2050

	1970	*2000*	*2020*	*2050*
Age 65 and over	9.8	12.4	16.3	20.7
Age 85 and over	0.7	1.5	2.2	5.0

Source: U.S. Census Bureau, 2004, U.S. Interim Projections by Age, Sex, Race, and Hispanic Origin.

and given the increased labor force participation of elderly women, the stresses of balancing work with family needs may become considerable.

Of course, the other family caregiving resource for the elderly is their adult children, and a useful report compiled by the National Center on Caregiving (2003) notes that "the average caregiver is age 46, female, married and working outside the home...." Many of these women are exemplars of what has been dubbed the "sandwich generation"—people who are dealing with their own dependent children while at the same time attending to the needs of aging parents. And whether sandwiched between two generations or not, fully 33% of women caring for their elders must cut back their work hours, pass up a promotion or new work opportunity (29%), and/or switch from full- to part-time (20%). Approximately one out of every six quit their jobs entirely (National Center on Caregiving, 2003). The resulting loss of income coupled with the time involved in elder care may give rise to considerable stress and worry, especially for single women and for women whose spouses or partners are doing very little of this care work. Caregiving, however, is not simply a stressor, as it may also be a powerful gratifier. Walker and Allen's (1991) study cautions against the caregiving-as-burden perspective, showing that for many of the adult daughters who provided regular care for their widowed mothers, the relationship provided far more gratifications than burdens, and this was so for both mothers and daughters. In any case, the challenge of working out these relationships will grow increasingly commonplace as the baby boom generation moves into its middle years, swelling the number of people sandwiched between two generations.

SOCIAL CLASS DIVISION

Accompanying the five master trends discussed in the previous section is a sixth one, more continuous with the past than a transformation of it: Social class differences among families of the 21st century will continue to result in some adults and their children having much better life chances than others. Indeed, the importance of the racial–ethnic transformation discussed in the previous section may inhere in the persistent social class disadvantages of the swelling populations of Hispanics and people of color. For example, what conclusion do we draw from the fact that while 27.3% of the nation's 72 million children in 2002 lived with a single parent, the number falls to 16.1% for White children while it rises to 48.3% for Black children (U.S. Census Bureau, 2003)? Below I will review several of the well-known advantages of a child growing up in a two-parent family, and I will argue that these benefits may have far more to do with social class advantages than with who resides in the household (e.g., one or two parents) or with what their racial–ethnic category is.

Social Class, Income, and the Work-Family Interface

Family income is a crude but widely accepted proxy for social class position, and I begin with some income variations among the overall racial–ethnic categories discussed earlier. Table 3.6 (DeNavas-Walt, Cleveland, & Webster, 2003) shows the "real" median household income in 2002 for the four major racial ethnic categories.

The table shows clearly the considerable differences across racial–ethnic categories. Within category, however, there are important social class variations. Among Hispanics, all subcategories remain far behind the average U.S. median income, but Puerto Ricans "remain the most economically disadvantaged of all major Latino groups" (Baca Zinn & Wells, 2000, p. 257), while Cubans remain the most economically privileged. In addition, family patterns are not always the same among Latinos as they are for European Americans, and the work-family interface may therefore function differently for these two categories across the same social

TABLE 3.6

Real Median Household Income by Racial–Ethnic Category: 2002*

Asian alone	$50,604
White alone (not Hispanic)	$47,199
All races	$43,760
Hispanic Origin (of any race)	$35,447
Black alone	$31,408

*These "real" income averages include the cost and benefits of taxes, capital gains and losses, employer-provided health benefits, noncash transfers (e.g., food stamps), and annualized home equity. Excluded from the table are the 2.4% of the population who indicated two or more races in the 2000 Census.

Source: U.S. Census Bureau, Current Population Survey, 2003 Annual Social and Economic Supplement.

class. For example, studies of Mexicans have indicated that even within the middle class, kinship networks may remain more vigorous than among "Anglo" families. Baca Zinn and Wells (2000, p. 266) noted that "Mexican children are socialized into a context of 'thick' social relations," in contrast to the more isolated patterns of interaction within the European American middle class, and that when the former enter the school system, they may be ill-equipped to deal with its more individualistic and competitive structures of relationships. As we will see later in this section, family-derived cultural capital may have a considerable impact on status attainment, as children move through school and enter the domain of work.

Asian subcategories are likewise associated with differential life chances. Among first- and second-generation Asian Americans in 1998–2000, the average Indian adult had the equivalent of a college education, compared to a high school education for the average Vietnamese (Logan, 2001a). Predictably, these differences in education carry over into other socioeconomic characteristics. The average personal income of Asian Indians in this period ($31,732) was twice the average Vietnamese ($15,758), and the 17.1% poverty rate of Vietnamese was nearly twice the rate (8.7%) for Indians (Logan, 2001).

Social class variations among Black subcategories are equally striking. While Table 3.6 showed that Blacks have by far the lowest overall economic standing, immigrants from Africa and from the Caribbean are far more advantaged than African Americans, and their median household income is considerably higher than Hispanics as well, although still much lower than either Asians or non-Hispanic Whites. Africans and Afro-Caribbeans have more years of education, much of which is typically acquired prior to their arrival here, and their unemployment and poverty rates are much lower than those of African Americans (see Logan & Deane, 2003).

The Special Vulnerability of Low-Income Immigrants

The National Immigration Law Center's (2004) "Facts about Immigrants" reported some useful social-class related information about the 30 million-plus U.S. immigrants, drawing on the Census as well as other sources. In 2000, approximately 11% of the population consisted of immigrants, who comprised some 15% of the total labor force. These people are economically vulnerable in disproportionate numbers. For example, "almost 43 percent of immigrants work at jobs paying less than $7.50 an hour, compared to 28 percent of all workers" (National Immigration Law Center, 2004). Fix, Zimmerman, and Passel (2001) noted that although immigrant employment rates benefited from the economic boom toward the end of the 1990s, the median wages of natives "rose more than 50 percent faster than immigrants."

Poverty rates are thus considerably higher for immigrant families than for natives. The Center for Immigration Studies (Camarota, 2001) reported that in 1999, "16.8 percent of immigrants compared to 11.2 percent of natives lived in poverty," but this rate jumps to 23.5 percent for the most recent wave of immigrants, those who entered in the 1990s. It follows that the native-born children of immigrant parents likewise have higher poverty rates than the children of native parents. Specifically, "among persons under age 21 living in poverty, 24.2 percent are the children of immigrants" (Camarota, 2001). As a consequence, these children are "more likely to [have no health insurance] (22 percent versus 10 percent); more likely to have no usual source of medical care (14 percent versus 4 percent); and more likely not to have a steady source of food (37 percent versus 27 percent)" (Capps, 2001). Of course, the situation is not indelibly fixed, as immigrant families tend to fare better with each successive generation. English fluency, coupled with high rates of intermarriage and the identification of oneself as a hyphenated American, suggest "a potential" for upward mobility (Frey, 1999).

Looking more closely at some elements of vulnerability for immigrant families, Sweatshop Watch (2004) pointed out that "the overwhelming majority of garment workers in the U.S. are immigrant women" and added that "the Department of Labor estimates that more than half of the country's 22,000 sewing shops violate minimum wage and overtime laws." In a 2001 interview, the author of *Sweatshop Warriors* (Louie, 2001) reported that "Latina/os represent 60 percent and Asians 35 percent of workers in all garment factories in the United States which the government classifies as sweatshops. Latina/os represent 53 percent and Asians 25 percent of workers in sweatshop restaurants. Eighty percent of farmworkers in the U.S. are of Mexican descent" (Multinational Monitor, 2001).

How Social Class Differences Affect Children

Although the 20% of U.S. children born to immigrants are especially vulnerable, social class origins are consequential for all children. The impact of social class has been explored by many work-family researchers. Some of these efforts have focused on how children are differentially prepared for educational achievement, depending on the social class position of the parents. The logic of explanation is that family resources—both money capital and cultural capital—provide the ticket to success at school, and this success (or lack of it) is the direct prelude to occupationally driven status attainment. Ample money resources place families in wealthy neighborhoods, which give children access to schools with well-paid teachers and abundant educational resources. School achievement is then a springboard for recruitment into occupations.

Quantitative studies have linked parents' income (a proxy for social class) directly to greater levels of cognitive stimulation provided to their children—a prelude first to success at school and then at work. Votruba-Drzal (2003) found that additional increments of income have the biggest impact on cognitive stimulation within families that are at the lowest level of income—obviously the most vulnerable of all families. Cognitive stimulation was measured at the preschool level by such items as how often someone reads to the child and helps him or her learn the alphabet, and at the elementary school level by additional items such as taking the child to a museum or theater. In addition, Votruba-Drzal found that mothers' educational level was also positively related to cognitive stimulation in the home. She noted that because additional income may make it possible for a mother to purchase additional education for herself, perhaps thereby leading to still greater cognitive stimulation for her children, the effect of additional income may actually have been underestimated in the study. This is a consequence of including maternal education and family income simultaneously in the regression equations: "Any influence of income that is mediated by control variables [in this case, maternal education]...will be attributed to the control variable itself and not income. In this respect, these analyses do not capture the totality of income's influence" (2003, p. 353).

Votruba-Drzal's findings partly replicate those of Entwisle and Alexander (2000) in their Beginning School Study in Baltimore. These researchers found several factors that contribute to educational advantage for the children in some families and disadvantage in others. Most important was a family's economic status, in keeping with Vortruba-Drzal's findings just cited. Also important were parents' expectations—both their opinions and their activities—concerning their children's school performance.

Social Class and Single-Parent Families

In the same Baltimore study, Entwisle and Alexander (2000, p. 333) also found that children in single-parent families fared worse when they started school than children in two-parent families. They added, however, that "children live in many kinds of 'one-parent' homes," and they discovered that single mother–grandmother households gave children entering the first grade a considerable school advantage over those children who lived alone with a single mother. These children "had better work habits," "even a little better than those of the children in mother-father settings" (2000, p. 326).

The complexities of issues of poverty, single parenthood, and household composition become especially transparent in the Baltimore study. Children need adult encouragement and involvement to do well in school. When single mothers live alone with their children, poverty may drive these women into paid work for long hours each day, and the children may get less parental involvement. Add an involved grandparent to the family mix, however, and the children's education may benefit, even more so in some instances than if the child had been living in a two-parent family. The grandparent's influence on the child in some respects may become a proxy for the cognitive stimulation that added income and/or a second parent might otherwise have made possible. This situation is not at all uncommon. The Census Bureau reported that in 2002, more than 13% of all single-parented children had at least one grandparent living in their household in addition to their parent. This figure understates the extent of grandparental influence, because some grandparents may not live in the same household as their children and grandchildren but may be near enough to provide an ongoing, even daily, influence on their grandchildren. In addition, Collins (2000) alerted us to the phenomenon of "othermothers"—networks of women who are not necessarily kin but who likewise may become an integral part of the lives of a mother's children.

In light of the variety of support systems that single parents may have access to, perhaps the recent governmental marriage-promotion campaign is well-intentioned but misguided. What children need for school achievement and for solid development in general is consistent adult encouragement, more so than they need fathers. If, along with mothers, fathers provide that encouragement, the child may indeed thrive. If someone else provides it instead, the child may thrive as well. What single mothers and single fathers need are real resources for themselves and their children: jobs that pay them a living wage, health care, child-care help, and good public services including schools and reliable transportation facilities.

Another look at the stresses on low-income families is a qualitative study by Dodson and Dickert (2004), again focusing mainly on single-mother households and the limited options that mothers in many such families have. The study also provides an understanding of the intergenerational transmission of social class, focusing on one pathway through which the lower end of the social stratification system may get reproduced. These researchers explored the involvement of daughters as "mini-moms" in low-income households. When women with young children must take low-wage jobs after being pushed off of welfare, they may not be able to afford day-care charges or have access to adult kin such as a grandmother who would serve as a caregiver. Under these circumstances, a mother's best option may be to depend on her oldest daughter to care for her much younger children while she is at work. The authors suggest that while these mini-moms may develop high levels of responsibility and parenting skills at a tender age, they sometimes do so at the expense of developing their education and job training. Without marketable skills and higher education, and with parenting skills being their most highly developed asset as they enter adulthood, early parenthood may then appear as their best option. The cycle of poverty is thus renewed intergenerationally. This is a remarkable account of how the lower end of the social stratification system gets reproduced through a family process in which parenting skills are cultivated and occupational skills (via education) are underplayed.

In this analysis, we can focus on the specific work-family pathway (mothers' hours at paid work spills over on daughters' school time and on other lost opportunities), but we might also recognize that the identified work-family spillover pattern is merely the midpoint of a more complex set of pathways. The starting point of the set—the independent variable—might be framed in any number of ways, and exactly what it is that "causes" this chain of circumstances is open to debate and creative interpretation. Garey and Arendell (2001) cautioned that "mother-blame"—holding mothers responsible for any and every child outcome that is held to be problematic—has a long legacy in social science. To move beyond it in this example, we need to consider the macro context that renders child-care solutions by "mini-moms" a rational choice for many low-income mothers. The causal pathway would then begin with political decisions that change the distribution of welfare, resulting in low-income mothers being forced into low-wage jobs with inflexible hours and poor benefits, all of which may result in young daughters being pressed into service as caregivers for their younger siblings while their mothers are at work.

Social Class and Work-to-Family Influences

Some social class-oriented approaches focus more directly on work-to-family influences, often adopting an implicit or explicit intergenerational transmission perspective. In large part due to the pioneering work of Kohn (1969; see also Kohn & Schooler, 1982), attention focused on how different jobs generate the personality tendencies that are required to perform them. In turn, job-driven personality tendencies then get transmitted to one's children via parenting "values."

Because middle-class jobs require different skills and proclivities than working-class jobs, parenting values accordingly vary by social class. Kohn found that middle-class professional jobs characterized by substantive complexity and by the requirement of independent thinking resulted in worker dispositions that were likewise oriented to complexity and to intellectual flexibility. These dispositions were then reenacted as values that guided childrearing. Working-class jobs with less substantive complexity and with a greater premium on conformity to the rigid requirements of supervisors will generate more compliant and obedient personalities, who will then adopt parenting values premised on the notion that children need to learn to conform to authority.

Kohn's line of analysis was extremely useful, as it got us thinking about how the specifics of job activities may generate spillover effects in the home sphere that vary by social class. In one of the best studies within this genre, Parcel and Menaghan (1994) found a positive relationship between the complexity of employed mothers' work and the quality of their home environments, the latter measured by such variables as intellectual stimulation and maternal warmth and responsiveness. The greater the job complexity and the opportunities for self-direction, the "higher" the home quality.

Menaghan's work stopped short of being a direct test of Kohn's thesis, because there is no attempt either to uncover the specific parenting values of these mothers or to uncover the extent to which these values are in fact transmitted to their children. Indeed, Kohn's thesis about social class and conformity was never offered as a theory of intergenerational transmission of different values for different social classes. That is, it is one thing to demonstrate that workers acquire certain parental values that vary by social class, in accordance with the substantive complexity of jobs. Kohn clearly established this link. It is another thing, however, to show that parents make specific efforts to transmit these values, or that their children actually wind up internalizing them. Kohn himself expressed some reservations about there being any appreciable similarity between the values of parents and the values of their children (see Kohn & Schooler, 1983, p. 309), and he makes no attempt to discover if children's levels of behavioral conformity or autonomy in some way follow from their parents' values for them.

Recent ethnographic work by Lareau (2003) launched an implicit challenge to the Kohn thesis at precisely its weakest link—the connection between what parents do at work and the values they actually teach their children at home. Kohn had assumed that having a middle-class job requiring autonomous thought and action would culminate in a process of cultivating the value of autonomy in their children. Lareau did find markedly different socialization patterns in middle-class families from those she observed in working-class and in poor families, but the differences did not entirely fit Kohn's assumed pattern. Indeed, it was the 9- and 10-year-olds from the working-class and poor families who appeared to be supreme exemplars of autonomy. Their parents reared them in accordance with a philosophy of "natural growth," which is oriented to "keeping children safe, enforcing discipline, and, when they deem it necessary, regulating their behavior in specific areas. Within these boundaries, working-class and poor children are allowed to grow and to thrive" (Lareau, 2003, pp. 66–67). They are given "an autonomous world, apart from adults, in which they are free to try out new experiences and develop important competencies.... They learn how to manage their own time. They learn how to strategize" (p. 67).

In contrast, Lareau's middle-class parents embrace a philosophy of "concerted cultivation," through which children "are treated as a project to be developed" (p. 67). Here, children's pace of life is frenetic, exhausting, overscheduled, and overseen by the ever-watchful eyes of adults, who take their children from one adult-supervised activity to the next. The children rarely have significant portions of leisure time in which they are responsible for organizing their own activity, and when they do, they complain of being "bored"—something that Lareau never heard from children in working-class and poor families.

What middle-class children do learn, with the help of their carefully cultivated reasoning skills and their direct observations of their parents' constant interventions in institutions on their behalf, is that their own needs and interests are paramount. They emerge from their childhoods with the conviction that middle-class institutions ought to be responsive to them, and when they are not, one has every right to negotiate with them and the people who staff them so that they will better serve their individual needs. The contrast is clear: The children of working-class and poor parents learn a stance of constraint, as they navigate through the complex world of middle-class institutions beginning with the schools, and they channel their extensive autonomy-training into their free time. The middle-class children learn entitlement (see Marks, 2000, for an autobiographical narrative about the learning of entitlement). When they find their way into the world of work, they will come armed with the understanding that they will be treated as equals by any superordinates as well as by their peers. They will then apply their reasoning skills and their experience at using their agency to develop themselves *within* adult-run organizations and institutions and to consolidate their advantages, which they will once again transmit to their own children (see Cookson, Jr., & Persell, 1985, for an account of how upper-class families use elite boarding schools as central socializing agents that arrange and organize a still higher level of class advantage than Lareau's middle-class families secure for their children).

Here we have a remarkable treatment of family-to-work intergenerational transmission effects, all patterned by social class and fully illustrated through painstaking ethnographic detail. Lareau's explanatory framework is essentially a socialization argument. Parents from different social classes teach children different pathways through organizations and institutions, starting with the schools, and children's enactment of these differential approaches affect their success first at school and later in the domain of work. This is a social class-trumps-race approach, as Lareau is clear that the socialized outcomes within middle-class Black families in her sample bear a much greater resemblance to those in middle-class White families than to those in working-class and poor Black families.

Social Class and Lesbian and Gay Families

I end this section by exploring how social class affects lesbian and gay families, which have sometimes been heralded as modeling a more equitable approach to balancing work and family life. In Dunne's (1996, 2000a, 2000b) study of 60 lesbians in Britain, participants held fiercely to the importance of financial "co-independence" within an intimate relationship, and they credited their sexuality with being an important factor in making this possible. In the words of one respondent, "You almost have to be gay . . . I couldn't hold down a marriage . . . I couldn't run a house, a family and do the job that I do. . . . In the heterosexual relationships that I know, the man wants to be looked after, come home, dinner there" (Dunne, 2000a, p. 139). Dunne notes that while the majority of British heterosexual women do not earn enough income to keep them financially independent of their husbands or the State, fully 86% of her sample are in this empowering situation.

Dunne (2000a, 2000b) probes these issues further in a follow-up study of 37 lesbian couples living together with dependent children, most of whom were conceived through donor insemination and were still in their preschool years at the time of the interviews. Unlike heterosexual married birth mothers in Britain, who rarely contribute a substantial proportion of the family income, fully 50% of the lesbian birth mothers in this study earn at least half of the total household income. Respondents who managed to integrate employment identities with mothering identities did so in a variety of ways, such as taking turns being the primary earner or having both partners be half-time earners. In this way partners retain their financial co-independence without having to sacrifice their family time, and the couple can avoid the breadwinner–homemaker split experienced by most heterosexual married couples. Within some couples the higher-earning woman actually negotiated a reduction of hours and therefore pay, apparently willing to exchange a lowered standard of living for more child-care and family time.

Dunne offered a compelling vision of a more balanced work-family interface when both partners retain strong footholds in both domains, and in that respect, she demonstrated for lesbians the same egalitarian model that Schwartz (1994) and Risman (1998) demonstrated for "peer" and "postgender" heterosexual couples. Notice, however, that this accomplishment may be something of a social class privilege that cuts across whatever sexual orientation a couple has. Dunne conceded that her lesbian respondents tend to be "educationally and/or occupationally advantaged" (2000b, p. 14). Schwartz's (1994, p. 6) peer couples likewise appear to be highly educated, and the husbands in these marriages had jobs with "some flexibility and controllable hours." And Risman (1998) indicated that most couples in her "fair families" study were highly educated. All the husbands and most of the wives in Risman's sample had jobs in which working conditions were flexible, thereby providing both partners the latitude to devote time to child-related activities—school, doctor appointments, or whatever.

Such family-friendly jobs are not available to most workers. Those who have them are likely to be highly educated professionals who have the power to negotiate more family-friendly work practices. Perhaps, then, Dunne makes too much of lesbians' freedom from the traditional gendered breadwinner/homemaker arrangement, and too little of the privileges that higher social class position confer on those who have them. Carrington's (1999) study of 52 lesbigay (his preferred designator) couples in the San Francisco Bay area is more alert to these variations of privilege. By closely tracking domesticity as a daily production process, encompassing feeding work, housework, kinwork, and consumption work, Carrington found little evidence among these 26 lesbian and 26 gay male couples of the domestic equality that is so heralded by lesbigay public ideology. Only 25% of his couples maintained a "rough parity" in their contribution to domestic work, and the biggest drivers of this accomplishment were jobs and money.

Carrington noted that wealthy lesbigay egalitarians were able to purchase a variety of their domestic needs from restaurants and from service workers at home, with the result that neither partner had an overload of domestic responsibilities. Other egalitarians were found among couples—both male and female—in which both partners worked in female-identified professions such as nursing, primary and secondary education, and social work. For these couples, the decisive factor was time as well as money. Their work-week rarely exceeded 40 hours, and although their paychecks were often modest, their jobs offered paid vacations, paid sick days and holidays, and a variety of other family-friendly practices. When both partners had this kind of job, they avoided the tendency of one partner becoming overwrought by career responsibilities and the other curtailing his or her job life in order to maintain the domestic front for both of them. When only one partner had this kind of job and the other had a more time-consuming position, the couple again gravitated to the split responsibilities that mirror the traditional heterosexual provider/homemaker split, even if both jobs were defined as full-time.

The majority of Carrington's families evolved into this kind of split, "encouraging the family member with the greatest economic opportunity to pursue paid work vigorously" (p. 188). The other partner then took on the lion's share of domesticity, either curtailing paid work obligations if total family income made that possible, or using the opportunities of flexible, family-friendly work schedules to maintain domesticity, often gravitating to this family role without having consciously chosen it.

As only five of Carrington's 52 lesbigay families had children residing with them, there was not enough of a subsample to look for distinguishing characteristics of such families. Had this kind of analysis been possible, perhaps Carrington, like Dunne, would have turned up a more evenly divided work-family balance than he did for most of his childless couples. If so, it could be that the lesbigay couples who opt for children are disproportionately found amongst those who already enjoy family-friendly jobs. The greater deliberateness required for lesbians to have children may extend into their planning for how they are going to manage child care together, and it is likely that their respective paid work requirements factor more consciously into their plans.

The fact remains, however, that in Carrington's sample, social class and the job-derived income that drives it means everything. Following Dizard and Gadlin's (1990) analysis of heterosexual families, Carrington argued that family and the domesticity that constitutes it is something that must get actively produced. When both partners lack the time and money resources that stem from social class privilege, the best that many couples can muster is a rather minimal production of family: "As resources accumulate, participants begin to think in familial terms about their lesbian-and-gay-defined household lives. They have more resources required to create more elaborate domestic regimens, and more stable families" (1999, p. 111). Again, however, this elaboration is a perquisite of social class privilege that is not enjoyed by a majority of Americans, either heterosexual or gay.

PREJUDICE, DISCRIMINATION, AND THE WORK-FAMILY
INTERFACE: A NEW RESEARCH PROGRAM

In this section I attempt to open a new line of inquiry, focusing on the impact of workplace prejudice and discrimination on individual and family well-being. This kind of analysis does not put attention on the impact of work hours, schedule fit, types of benefits, and other official job conditions that are specific to a given job. Obviously, job conditions matter, as they may have a powerful impact on individuals and their families, as Gerson and Jacobs (2001) have shown. Here, however, following previous analysis (Marks & Leslie, 2000), my concern is with some macrolevel structural variables that may cut across jobs and their attributes. Specifically, I focus on how membership in dominant versus nondominant social categories may differentially affect individuals' experiences and create ripple affects for their family processes. This difference by category is obviously true across jobs, as access to the "better" ones is restricted to relatively privileged social categories. But even within the same job and with the same benefits, doors may open for some people that are felt by others to be closed. People of color, women, people perceived to be gender deviants, lesbians and gay men, people who claim or are perceived as a nondominant ethnicity—these and other categorical differences may mark a person as "different" or "less than" at their workplace. Instead of being perceived solely in terms of their job performance, that performance may get refracted through the lens of their "difference," and then their treatment by their superordinates and by their coworkers may reflect that perceived difference.

Although this basic insight about categorical diversity may have profound implications for work-family studies on both theoretical and the methodological levels, these implications have yet to be seriously explored. Marks and Leslie (2000) suggested that in quantitative studies, the significance of social categories such as race may not be fully uncovered by simply sampling more than one racial–ethnic group, then dummy-coding the racial identification of the respondent, and finally running the hypotheses using race as either a control or a moderator variable. We argued that in addition to simple codes for racial category, researchers need to include more fine-grained measures of phenomena that are historically specific to the category. In the matter of race, for example, we need to conceptually specify the reasons why race might be important enough to influence other variables, and then operationalize these reasons in meaningful and creative ways. Given the legacy of racialized advantage and disadvantage in this country, variables that identify instances of prejudice and discrimination are obvious candidates for inclusion in our studies. Racial–ethnic identity salience—measured as a metric variable rather than using a dummy code—is another such candidate, especially given its potential for mollifying the impact of prejudice and discrimination.

Discrimination, Racial Category, and Racial Ethnic Identity

Turner (2003) recently noted that differences in exposure to social stress on the basis of different social statuses—race–ethnicity, gender, social class, and so on—may be far more important to variations in health outcomes than has typically been assumed. Although Turner's point will not come as much of a surprise to family scholars, who have long been alert to the impact of social stress on family-related outcomes, one major stressor that has not yet received much attention from family scholars is prejudice and discrimination. In a landmark paper, Kessler, Mickelson, and Williams (1999) drew on a national sample of 3,032 respondents between the ages of 25 and 74 to explore two kinds of discrimination: *major events*, which included specific instances of workplace discrimination (not being hired for a job, not being given a promotion, or having been fired from a job), and more routine, *day-to-day discrimination* (e.g., "people act as if you are inferior"; "people act as if you are not smart"). Respondents were also queried about the reasons for the perceived discrimination. Race–ethnicity, gender, appearance, and age were the most commonly reported reasons, while sexual orientation and several other reasons were also coded but less often cited (for an updated and extremely useful list of the scale items for major discrimination, day-to-day discrimination, and reasons why people think they received discriminatory treatment, see the appendix in Turner & Avison, 2003).

The results of this national survey were stunning. Fully 33.5% reported experiencing one or more major discrimination events, and 60.9% reported experiencing day-to-day discrimination. Non-Hispanic Whites perceived far less discrimination—both "major" and "day-to-day"—than either non-Hispanic Blacks or "others." And, the racialized disadvantage of identifying as non-Hispanic Black or some "other" race was further confirmed in the finding that these respondents reported with much greater frequency than Whites that their race was the reason for the discrimination. Although the link between perceived discrimination and mental health was inconsistently predicted by disadvantaged social status, the researchers concluded that "perceived discrimination needs to be treated much more seriously . . . in future studies of stress and mental health" (p. 208).

These new strategies for measuring discriminatory treatment have great promise for enriching our approach to work-family scholarship, and it is well worth reviewing additional exemplars of epidemiological studies. These studies have perhaps overfocused on predicting depression, but because this research has grown increasingly sophisticated, work-family scholars might benefit from using it as a model, substituting more family-related outcomes for depression. Moreover, as Whitbeck, McMorris, Hoyt, Stubben, and LaFromboise (2002) have noted, depressive affect has been closely linked to a variety of childhood family phenomena, such as having had a history of childhood neglect and/or sexual or physical abuse, and having had inconsistent parental discipline and limit setting.

In a California study of 3,012 Mexican origin respondents, Finch, Kolody, and Vega (2000) found "a clear, direct relationship between perceived discrimination and depressive symptomatology" (p. 309). Discrimination was measured by a three-item scale that asked respondents how often people dislike them, treat them unfairly, or treat friends unfairly because they are Mexican or of Mexican origin. In this study the perception of discrimination is unfortunately decontextualized, unlike the several work-related discrimination items in Kessler et al. (1999), and we are thus unable to determine where the perceived discrimination occurred. Presumably, a good deal of it occurred at a workplace, a point that work-family scholars would obviously seize upon in redesigning this study. The outcome measure—depression—is likewise of lesser interest to work-family scholars than other more family-relevant variables.

Whitbeck's et al. (2002) study of 287 American Indians is another impressive attempt to measure the impact of prejudice and discrimination as a stressor variable, and it draws on a creative measure of Indian identity to add complexity to the research design. In addition, it carefully links adult depressive symptoms to childhood family history variables. Prejudice and discrimination were measured by a 10 item scale with four response choices from "never" to "always." The items ask respondents if someone "said something derogatory . . . because you are Native American"; if a store owner or sales clerk or other worker "treated you in a disrespectful way because you are Native American; if "someone ignored or excluded you from some activity because you were Native American," and so on (p. 414). The results are striking: Even with a variety of controls in the final model, "perceived discrimination was a powerful indicator of depressive symptoms among the American Indian adults" (p. 411). However, traditional identity-strengthening practices such as going to a powwow made it less likely that a person would have depressive symptoms. An interaction term revealed that those who had above-average levels of traditional Indian practices were most buffered from the impact of discrimination.

These central findings from Whitbeck et al. (2002) parallel later research by Sellers, Caldwell, Schmeelk-Cone, and Zimmerman (2003), who found that young African Americans for whom race was a highly central identity were relatively protected from the negative impact of perceived discrimination on psychological distress. They also parallel a recent study of Filipino Americans by Mossakowski (2003), who found that although perceived discrimination is associated with depressive symptoms, having a strong Filipino identity buffers that hazard. All three of these studies take racial/ethnic membership seriously, exploring both the vulnerabilities that result from being a subjugated group and the advantages that accrue to that group from identity-strengthening processes (For another attempt to assess the strength of racial/ethnic identity, but framed generically enough for researchers to use the scale for any and every racial/ethnic group, see Noh, Beiser, Kaspar, Hou, & Rummens, 1999). For purposes of work and family analyses, perhaps the most important drawback of the three studies cited here (along with Finch et al., 2000) is that most of their discrimination items remain decontextualized; there is little attempt to uncover the domain (whether the workplace or some other locale) where the discrimination occurred.

Other recent research, drawing on an African American and European American sample in the Detroit area, was able to disentangle the contribution of poverty from the contribution of race, exploring variations in psychological distress and life satisfaction. Schulz et al. (2000) found that perceptions of "unfair treatment" and living below the poverty line were the critical independent variables that drove the variations in the outcomes they explored. The "unfair treatment" items are essentially versions of the "major" discrimination and "day-to-day" discrimination items used in Kessler, Mickelson, and Williams (1999), but in this study only three of the major discrimination items were used. Respondents were asked if they had ever been unfairly fired from a job or denied a promotion, not hired for a job for unfair reasons, or unfairly stopped or mistreated by the police. The findings of this study are complex, and they are outside the scope of our purposes for this volume. It is obvious, however, that two of the "unfair treatment" measures tap directly into instances of workplace discrimination in ways that ought to be of great interest to work-family scholars. Although the explored outcomes— psychological distress and life satisfaction—are of less import to us than more family-specific outcomes, this is a research model that is eminently adaptable to work-family studies.

As a final exemplar of recent epidemiological explorations of perceived discrimination and health and well-being, Forman's (2003) study of 1,199 African Americans is remarkable for its attention to both individual and institutional discrimination. Because its measures are exclusively oriented to workplace discrimination, it should be of particular interest to work and family researchers. Drawing on two different data sets, Forman explored the impact of "racial segmentation"—the perception that one's racial group is being targeted for a certain kind of job. For example, in the National Survey of Black Americans, respondents were asked two questions: (a) "In the place where you work, do Black people tend to get certain kinds of jobs?" and (b) "Is your job one that Black people tend to get more than whites?" (p. 338).

Forman's results indicated that "African Americans who perceive their current job to be a 'Black job' have lower levels of life satisfaction and higher levels of psychological distress than their counterparts who do not perceive their jobs in this light" (p. 345), and this linkage persisted even after controlling for reports of individual job discrimination and for other occupational characteristics. In addition, Forman found that this linkage was "particularly powerful for the African American middle class" (p. 345), in keeping with relative deprivation theory. That is, a paradox of the civil rights movement is that in its aftermath, although African Americans experienced an increase in available middle-class positions that were now open to them, levels of discontent often increased instead of lessened for people who entered these positions. This is because in comparison to the opportunities they perceive white workers to have, these "[Black jobs] afford minorities little opportunity to supervise production, to supervise largely white staffs, or to implement important organizational policies" (p. 334). African Americans are thus more prone to feel alienated despite the fact that their incomes may have risen.

Work and family researchers interested in family diversity should draw considerable inspiration from Forman's work and from the other exemplars cited here. It should be easy enough to link these discrimination measures to outcomes that are more central to our ongoing concerns. For example, to what extent does occupational discrimination erode a person's sense of work-family balance? How is a marriage affected by a person's perception of occupational discrimination—both the individual and the institutional variants of discrimination? Do married people who perceive discrimination keep their spouses insulated from the knowledge of that discrimination, and is there a gender difference in the likelihood of disclosure to the spouse? What are the consequences for the marital relationship of disclosure versus lack of disclosure, and are there different consequences by gender? In the face of discrimination at the workplace, who, if anyone, is more likely to withdraw from family relationships, and who, if anyone, is likely to draw closer to them in pursuit of some needed emotional sustenance? Are episodes of family violence more or less likely to occur in the aftermath of episodes of occupational discrimination? Does the strength of one's racial–ethnic identity in some way moderate the linkages between occupational discrimination and family relationship variables?

I offer the foregoing questions as mere "teases," hoping to inspire work and family scholars to launch new inquiries about the impact of social stratification in general and its consequences for occupational discrimination in particular. In turn, the possible linkages between occupational discrimination and family-specific phenomena are of course endless, limited only by the reach of our research imaginations.

In addition to more research on racial stratification and its impact, we need to expand our research on other forms of social stratification. Occupational discrimination may occur not only on the basis of race but also on the basis of gender, sexuality, age, social class, and so on, and may generate spillover effects for innumerable family-specific phenomena. Moreover, occupational discrimination is not the only conduit along which social stratification systems may make their impact on the work-family interface. We have seen in several different studies how racial–ethnic identity may serve as a buffer between occupational discrimination and mental health, but racial–ethnic and other identities that people bring with them to work may generate main effects as well as moderating effects.

Sexual Diversity at the Workplace

Consider, for example, the complex dynamics of lesbian and gay workers coming out at their workplace. Alan Bell (1995, p. 260) noted that as a gay man, in most of his jobs he has been "a minority of one":

> At about half these positions I've felt comfortable enough to disclose myself to the few co-workers I believed I could trust. But only in my current assignment, with the Los Angeles Department of City Planning, have I felt almost literally free—certainly not the same kind of freedom enjoyed by straights who live in a world designed for them—but a freedom nevertheless, the most amount of freedom I could imagine possible in an environment where heterosexuals are the majority.

In the Planning Department, Bell eventually discovered that three of his coworkers were also gay, a critical mass that made a difference. Hassan, fully "out" and ever-ready to widen the circle of knowers about him, was at times an inspiration—especially to Alex and Alan, who initially were more given to reserve if not downright secretiveness. Hassan explained his open style as partly a political strategy: "If I act like a big flaming faggot, maybe other people won't feel as uncomfortable about being openly gay" (Bell, 1995, p. 266). Hassan, Alan, and Michael, all were instrumental in Alex coming out at work:

> Later, [Alex] said that each of us, in our own way, had been a role model for him. Michael had taught him how to dress and introduced him to the coolest [gay] clubs. I had counseled him about his career. Hassan had shown him how to be outrageously out. A role model himself these days, Alex volunteers for a community education program, visiting area high schools and junior colleges to speak to students about what it's like to be gay. (Bell, 1995, p. 266)

Bell's workplace evinces a quality of support for gay workers that is the opposite of a situation in which a stigmatized minority must contend with occupational discrimination. In sharp contrast, when Meagan Rosser (2000) approached her boss for some leave time to visit her mother's partner Charlotte, who was then dying of cancer, her boss's initial response was: "I don't know how I feel about this, Meagan. I mean, maybe if it was one of your *parents....*" Meagan protested that Charlotte *was* her parent, and although her boss relented, note the discriminatory hurdle Meagan had to jump over first. Consider how Bell and his gay coworkers are comparatively free to develop as keen of a sense of gay identity as they wish, with presumably salutary spillover effects on their families and relationships. Consider, too, the impact of these men on their heterosexually identified coworkers, who receive daily reminders that gay workers are merely workers like themselves, reminders that are perhaps shared in turn with their own family members. When lesbian and gay workers in Los Angeles organized on behalf of stronger domestic partnership provisions and better enforcement of nondiscrimination laws, Bell mentioned his involvement to some of his straight coworkers. Soon after, he was approached by two of them who wanted to join the fledgling organization, in solidarity with and support of their gay coworkers. Bell's workplace was clearly one that nurtured rather than stigmatized its minority members.

CONCLUSION

This is an age of increasing family diversity. It is a time when the institution of marriage—that venerated traditional cornerstone of family formation—is being stretched, scrutinized, debated, and fought about in the courts. It is a time when the racial–ethnic composition of the nation's families is undergoing a period of rapid transformation that will ultimately culminate in European Americans becoming a statistical minority. It is an age of globalization in which virtually nothing remains that is purely local. Work and family life is affected as much by events in the Middle East and within major multinational corporations as it is by local community developments. Under these circumstances, the best that we can do is to strain to be inclusive. Instead of bemoaning the loss of this or that traditional understanding of what a family is, our heritage is best served by going the extra mile to embrace the variety that is out there.

I end this essay by echoing the view put forth recently by Fineman (2004), who seeks to close up some of the distance between public responsibility and "private" lives. Fineman noted that domestic policies in this country have always been too narrowly legalistic. If the state defines you as a legitimate family, it will offer you some subsidies, and then only if you default in your "private" capacity to meet your own and your family's needs. Fineman argued that it is caregiving relationship, not sexual affiliation, which should be the focal point of public policy. This view implies an end to all discrimination based on sexual orientation as well as an eagerness to recognize and support all the families within which people live, including those that stretch across more than one household. In order to create the smoothest integration between work and family life, we need domestic partner benefits at least as much as we need marriage. And we need living wages, national health care, and guaranteed family and medical leave when necessary, all organized around caregiving relationships rather than around narrow definitions of "the" family.

REFERENCES

Administration on Aging. (2003). A profile of Older Americans: 2003. U.S. Department of Health and Human Services. http://research.aarp.org/general/profile_2003.pdf.

American Association for Single People. (retrieved August 14, 2004). 2000 Census—AASP report. http://www.unmarriedamerica.org/Census%202000/households-type-trends-family%20diversity.htm.

Andersen, M., & Collins, P. H. (Eds.). (1998). *Race, class, and gender: An anthology* (3rd ed.). Belmont, CA: Wadsworth.

Avellar, S., & Smock, P. J. (2003). Has the price of motherhood declined over time? A cross-cohort comparison of the motherhood wage penalty. *Journal of Marriage and Family, 65*, 597–607.

Baca Zinn, M., & Wells, B. (2000). Diversity within Latino families: New lessons for family social science. In D. H. Demo, K. R. Allen, & M. A. Fine (Eds.), *Handbook of family diversity* (pp. 252–273). New York: Oxford University Press.

Bell, A. (1995). Alex, Hassan, and Michael. In J. Preston (Ed., with M. Lowenthal), *Friends and lovers: Gay men write about the families they create me* (pp. 293–303). Berkeley: University of California Press.

Camarota, S. A. (2001). Immigrants in the United States—2000: A snapshot of America's foreign-born population. Center for Immigration Studies. http://www.cis.org/articles/2001/back101.pdf.

Carrington, C. (1999). *No place like home: Relationships and family life among lesbians and gay men*. Chicago: University of Chicago Press.

Capps, R. (2001). Hardship among children of immigrants: Findings from the 1999 National Survey of America's Families. Urban Institute. http://www.urban.org/UploadedPDF/anf_b29.pdf.

Collins, P. H. (2000). *Black feminist thought: Knowledge, consciousness, and the politics of empowerment* (2nd ed.). New York: Routledge.

Coltrane, S. (1991). Social networks and men's family roles. *Men's Studies Review, 8*, 8–15.

Coltrane, S. (2000). Research on household labor: Modeling and measuring the social embeddedness of routine family work. *Journal of Marriage and the Family, 62*, 1208–1233.

Cookson, P. W., & Persell, C. H. (1985). *Preparing for power: America's elite boarding schools*. New York: Basic Books.

Davis, J. A., & Smith, T. W. (2002, 1996, 1977). *General social surveys, 2002, 1996, 1977*. Principal investigator, J. A. Davis; Director and Co-principal investigator, T. W. Smith; Co-principal investigator, P. V. Marsden, NORC ed. Chicago: National Opinion Research Center, producer, 2002, Storrs, CT. The Roper Center for Public Opinion Research, University of Connecticut, distributor.

Demo, D. H., Allen, K. R., & Fine, M. A. (Eds.). (2000). *Handbook of family diversity*. New York: Oxford University Press.

DeNavas-Walt, C., Cleveland, R., & Webster, B. H., Jr. (2003). Income in the United States: 2002. U.S. Census Bureau, Current Population Reports, P60-221, Washington, DC: U.S. Government Printing Office.

Dizard, J., & Gadlin, H. (1990). *The minimal family*. Amherst: University of Massachusetts Press.

Dodson, L., & Dickert, G. (2004). Girls' family labor in low-income households: A decade of qualitative research. *Journal of Marriage and the Family, 66*, 318–332.

Downs, B. (2003). Fertility of American women: June 2002. U.S. Census Bureau: Current Population Reports.

Dunne, G. A. (1996). *Lesbian lifestyles: Women's work and the politics of sexuality*. Toronto: University of Toronto Press.

Dunne, G. A. (2000a). Lesbians as authentic workers? Institutional heterosexuality and the reproduction of gender inequalities. *Sexualities, 3*, 133–148.

Dunne, G. A. (2000b). Opting into motherhood: Lesbians blurring the the boundaries and transforming the meaning of motherhood. *Gender & Society, 14*, 11–35.

Entwisle, D. R., & Alexander, K. L. (2000). Diversity in family structure: Effects on schooling. In D. H. Demo, K. R. Allen, & M. A. Fine (Eds.), *Handbook of family diversity* (pp. 316–337). New York: Oxford University Press.

Finch, B. K., Kolody, B. K., & Vega, W. A. (2000). Perceived discrimination and depression among Mexican-origin adults in California. *Journal of Health and Social Behavior, 41*, 295–313.

Fineman, M. A. (2004). The autonomy myth: A theory of dependency. New York: New Press.

Fix, M., Zimmerman, W., & Passel, J. S. (2001). The integration of immigrant families in the U.S. Washington, DC: The Urban Institute. http://www.urban.org/UploadedPDF/immig_integration.pdf.

Forman, T. A. (2003). The social psychological costs of racial segmentation in the workplace: A study of African Americans' well-being. *Journal of Health and Social Behavior, 44*, 332–352.

Frey, W. H. (1999). The United States population: Where the new immigrants are. *Electronic Journal of the U.S. Information Agency*, Vol. 4, No. 2. http://usinfo.state.gov/journals/itsv/0699/ijse/toc.htm.

Garey, A. I., & Arendell, T. (2001). Children, work, and family: Some thoughts on "mother-blame." In R. Hertz & N. L. Marshall (Eds.), *Working families: The transformation of the American home* (pp. 293–303). Berkeley: University of California Press.

Gerson, K., & Jacobs, J. A. (2001). Changing the structure and culture of work: Work and family conflict, work flexibility, and gender equity in the modern workplace. In R. Hertz & N. L. Marshall (Eds.), *Working families: The transformation of the American home* (pp. 207–226). Berkeley: University of California Press.

Gray, J. (1992). *Men are from Mars, women are from Venus: A practical guide for improving communication and getting what you want in your relationships.* New York: HarperCollins.

Kessler, R. C., Mickelson, K. D., & Williams, D. R. (1999). The prevalence, distribution, and mental health correlates of perceived discrimination in the United States. *Journal of Health and Social Behavior, 40*, 208–230.

Kohn, M. L. (1969). *Class and conformity: A study in values.* Homewood, IL: Dorsey.

Kohn, M. L., & Schooler, C. (1982). Job conditions and personality: A longitudinal assessment of their reciprocal effects. *American Journal of Sociology, 87*, 1257–1284.

Kohn, M. L., & Schooler, C. (1983). Work and personality: An inquiry into the impact of social stratification. Norwood, NJ: Ablex.

Lareau, A. (2003). Unequal childhoods: Class, race, and family life. Berkeley: University of California Press.

Logan, J. L. (2001a). From many shores: Asians in Census 2000. Lewis Mumford Center for Comparative Urban and Regional Research. http://mumford1.dyndns.org/cen2000/AsianPop/AsianReport/AsianDownload.pdf.

Logan, J. L. (2001b). The new Latinos: Who they are, where they are. University at Albany: Lewis Mumford Center for Comparative Urban and Regional Research. http://www.hccwpa.org/Census_and_Data/HCC_New_Latino2.htm.

Logan, J. L., & Deane, G. (2003). Black diversity in metropolitan America. University at Albany: Lewis Mumford Center for Comparative Urban and Regional Research. http://mumford1.dyndns.org/cen2000/BlackWhite/BlackDiversityReport/black-diversity01.htm.

Louie, Miriam Ching Yoon. (2001). *Sweatshop warriors: Immigrant women workers take on the global factory.* Cambridge, MA: South End Press.

Marks, S. R. (2000). Teasing out the lessons of the 1960s: Family diversity and family privilege. *Journal of Marriage and the Family, 62*, 609–622.

Marks, S. R., & Leslie, L. A. (2000). Family diversity and intersecting categories: Toward a richer approach to multiple roles. In D. H. Demo, K. R. Allen, & M. A. Fine (Eds.), *Handbook of family diversity* (pp. 402–423). New York: Oxford University Press.

Matthews, T. J., & Hamilton, B. E. (2002). Mean age of mother, 1970–2000. National Vital Statistics Reports, V. 51 no. 1. Hyattsville, MD: National Center for Health Statistics, 2002.

Mossakowski, K. N. (2003). Coping with perceived discrimination: Does ethnic identity protect mental health? *Journal of Health and Social Behavior, 44*, 318–331.

Multinational Monitor. (2001). Migrating from exploitation to dignity: Immigrant women workers and the struggle for justice. Volume 22, Number 10, retrieved September 16, 2004. http://multinationalmonitor.org/mm2001/01october/oct01interviewlouie.html.

National Center on Caregiving. (2003). Women and caregiving: Facts and figures. http://www.caregiver.org/caregiver/jsp/content_node.jsp?nodeid=892.

National Immigration Law Center. (July 2004). Facts about immigrants. http://www.nilc.org/immspbs/research/pbimmfacts_0704.pdf.

Noh, S., Beiser, M., Kaspar, V., Hou, F., & Rummens, J. (1999). Perceived racial discrimination, depression, and coping: A study of Southeast Asian refugees in Canada. *Journal of Health and Social Behavior, 40*, 193–207.

O'Connell, M. (2001). Labor force participation for mothers with infants declines for first time, Census Bureau reports. www.census.gov/Press-Release/www/releases/ archives/fertility/000329.html.

Oswald, R. F., Blume, L. B., & Marks, S. R. (2005). Decentering heteronormativity: A model for family studies. In V. L. Bengston, A. C. Acock, K. R. Allen, P. Dilworth Anderson, & D. M. Klein (Eds.), *Sourcebook of family theory and research* (pp. 143–154). Thousand Oaks, CA: Sage Publications.

Parcel, T. L., & Menaghan, E. G. (1994). *Parents' jobs and children's lives.* New York: DeGruyter.

Parsons, T. (1964). *Social structure and personality.* New York: Macmillan.

Risman, B. (1998). *Gender vertigo.* New Haven: Yale University Press.

Rosser, M. (2000). Charlotte. In N. Howey & E. Samuels (Eds.), *Out of the ordinary: Essays on growing up with gay, lesbian, and transgender parents* (pp. 151–162). New York: St. Martin's Press.

Schmidley, D. (2003). *The foreign-born population in the United States: March, 2002.* Current Population Reports P20-539, U.S. Census Bureau, Washington, DC. http://www.census.gov/prod/2003pubs/p20-539.pdf.

Schulz, A., Williams, D., Israel, B., Becker, A., Parker, E., James, S. A., & Jackson, J. (2000). Unfair treatment, neighborhood effects, and mental health in the Detroit metropolitan area. *Journal of Health and Social Behavior, 41*, 314–332.

Schwartz, P. (1994). *Peer marriage: How love between equals really works.* New York: Free Press.

Sellers, R. M., Caldwell, C. H., Schmeelk-Cone, K. H., & Zimmerman, M. A. (2003). Racial identity, racial discrimination, perceived stress, and psychological distress among African American young adults. *Journal of Health and Social Behavior, 43*, 302–317.

Smith, D. (1993). The standard North American family: SNAF as an ideological code. *Journal of Family Issues, 14*, 50–65.

Swarns, R. L. (retrieved August 29, 2004). "African-American" becomes a term for debate. *New York Times.*

Sweatshop Watch. (retrieved September 16, 2004). The garment industry. Oakland, CA. http://swatch.igc.org/swatch/industry/.

Turner, R. J. (2003). The pursuit of socially modifiable contingencies in mental health. *Journal of Health and Social Behavior, 44*, 1–17.

Turner, R. J., & Avison, W. R. (2003). Status variations in stress exposure: Implications for the interpretation of research on race, socioeconomic status, and gender. *Journal of Health and Social Behavior, 44*, 488–505.

U.S. Census Bureau. (2000). *Population projections of the United States by age, sex, race, Hispanic origin, and nativity: 1999 to 2100.* Population Projections Program, Population Division, Washington, DC.

U.S. Census Bureau. (June 12, 2003). Children's living arrangements and characteristics: March 2002. Population Division, Fertility & Family Statistics Branch. www.census.gov/population/socdemo/hh-fam/cps2002/tabC4-all.pdf.

U.S. Census Bureau. (2004). U.S. interim projections by age, sex, race, and Hispanic origin. www.census.gov/ipc/www/usinterimproj/.

Votruba-Drzal, E. (2003). Income changes and cognitive stimulation in young children's home learning environments. *Journal of Marriage and Family, 65*, 341–355.

Walker, A. J., & Allen, K. R. (1991). Relationships between caregiving daughters and their elderly mothers. *The Gerontologist, 31*, 389–396.

Wheeler-Nicholson, I. (2000). Smile and say nothing. In N. Howey & E. Samuels (Eds.), *Out of the ordinary: Essays on growing up with gay, lesbian, and transgender parents* (pp. 103–112). New York: St. Martin's Press.

Whitbeck, L. B., McMorris, B. J., Hoyt, D. R., Stubben, J. D., & LaFromboise, T. (2002). Perceived discrimination, traditional practices, and depressive symptoms among American Indians in the upper Midwest. *Journal of Health and Social Behavior, 43*, 400–418.

PART II: DISCIPLINARY APPROACHES AND THEORETICAL PERSPECTIVES

Introduction: The Insights Gained From Integrating Disciplines

Ellen Ernst Kossek
Michigan State University

Stephen Sweet
Ithaca College

Marcie Pitt-Catsouphes
Boston College

A young woman who has been employed at the local factory for several years with an excellent attendance and performance record decides to quit work shortly after the birth of her and her husband's second child. She had returned to work for a few months after her 6-week maternity leave and it seemed as if things were working fine, but then she gave her 2 weeks' notice to her supervisor. Senior management noted that that the young woman's behavior was similar to that of many other working parents at the plant and they were becoming worried about the lost productivity. They decided to consult a variety of researchers from the local university.

The psychologist stated that the working parents were probably experiencing role conflict between the demands of work and those of the family. The sociologist added that traditional societal and marital gender expectations were causing women to work a second domestic shift when they got home from their jobs. The economist surmised that the wages the plant was offering were not sufficiently generous to offset the cost of paying for quality child care. The demographer observed that workforce data suggest that if a working mother has more than one child under 3 years old and is also part of the sandwich generation providing elder care, she is likely to temporarily leave the labor force. The historian stated that the factory has retained employment approaches not much different from those first adopted a century ago, and these traditional production methods have made it difficult to alter workplace structures to provide flexible work hours. This perspective was echoed by the anthropologist, who noted the strong factory cultural norms reinforcing segmentation of the workplace for at least 10 hours a day from personal life.

As this opening vignette suggests, there are many lenses that can be used to understand the nexus of work and family. Although there has been an increase in the work-family nexus as a focal point for study, scholars from diverse disciplines have framed their research questions in different ways, adopted different methods to examine current work and family experiences, and used different approaches to study the intersection of work and family. As researchers, we tend to approach work and family from the disciplinary perspectives we were taught as a doctoral students. These perspectives then direct us to certain horizons of inquiry, and conversely, sometimes shield our visions from alternate interpretations of data and sometimes even the importance of asking certain types of questions. Although social scientists often attempt to approach their investigations with scholarly objectivity, more likely our own disciplinary perspectives frame what we "see" in work-family phenomena. We believe the next generation of work-family research will benefit from more cross-disciplinary interaction. Wisdom for understanding the antecedents, processes, and outcomes from the interaction between work and family is not limited to one discipline. We have been surprised by how little cross-disciplinary dialogue has gone on between disciplines in terms of citing published studies in another discipline's journals or developing research teams and collaborating authors that integrate voices from different fields to analyze a particular work and family issue.

To promote greater understanding of what each discipline brings to the work-family scholarly table, we asked the writers in Section II of this volume to focus on the assumptions, research questions and areas of interest, theories, key constructs, and selected insights that have resulted from their specific discipline. Each chapter is designed to give the reader a sense of the unique ways that researchers from the different disciplines look at the world of work-family. They amplify the "contributions" that each discipline makes to our understanding of work-family issues. We asked authors, leaders in their respective disciplines, to illustrate their perspectives using their own research, but also to integrate the research of others to exemplify their understanding of how their particular disciplinary perspective shapes the types of questions and answers generated from considering relationships between work and family domains. What follows is not a comprehensive overview of all perspectives (for example, we do not provide a chapter on "postmodern" perspectives per se), but rather an overview of many disciplinary camps.

As historians, Eileen Boris and Carolyn Herbst Lewis observe that integrating work and family, while commonly portrayed as a new problem, is not new at all. Casting our vision as far back as colonial America, they show that most women have worked and cared. However, what has changed, in remarkable ways, are the expectations of working families, the demands of their jobs, and what our culture expects of home relative to the workplace. They believe that future solutions to what we now call the work and family dilemma, for families, society, and the state, will be rooted in the historical record. From the early twentieth century, Boris and Lewis argue that social policies have reinforced male breadwinning and female caregiving, leading to relief programs and protective legislation structured around the male breadwinner/female caregiver model.

While Boris and Lewis use history as a lens for studying work and family, Erin Kelly focuses on U.S. policy on work and family, juxtaposing it in international comp arisons. This comparative approach to the study of welfare states and on family policies enables us to better understand the limitations of U.S. family leaves, child-care policies, and regulations about working time as well as alternate arrangements (and their potential costs). Kelly notes that many of the limited policies in existence oftentimes fail to meet the needs of working families or are not enforced. The unpaid Family and Medical Leave Act is one case in point. Kelly's approach of comparing the policies adopted in different countries offers great strengths not only in highlighting the shortcomings in any individual society, but also how to document the ways work-family policies affect women's employment and children's well-being.

Martha Farnsworth Riche, who served as U.S. Census Bureau Director under President Clinton, discusses how demography, the science of the study of populations, informs work-family research. By drawing on the basic task of counting people, assessing their characteristics, and placing them, either where they live or where they work, demography brings geographic as well as social and economic dimensions to the study of work and family. For example, such connections might allow other disciplines to analyze the relationship between such important factors as transportation and/or housing and work issues, or early childhood education and maternal employment. Notwithstanding the growing elder-care responsibilities continuing to be placed on older workers, Farnsworth Riche highlights contemporary demographic patterns suggesting declining birth rates. She believes that over time, American employers may decide that it would be worthwhile to make an investment to address work-family issues that would support more women in the labor market. If such actions are not taken, a likely prospect is a continued trend toward lower fertility or delayed childbirth, and subsequent impacts on the structure of the labor force and our communities.

Anisa Zvonkovic, Megan Notter, and Cheryl Peters offer a family studies perspective on work and family, which analyzes the human development and relationships over the life course in social and other contexts. An interdisciplinary field by definition, some of the main theories in family studies emanate from the ecological perspective, the family life course perspective, social constructionism, feminist perspectives, and general systems theory related to family stress and interventions. They show how interdisciplinary discourse can be used to to understand the concept of time as a unifying construct to explore research from a family studies perspective. The belief that families are time-deprived is reflective of the "social problems" thrust of this domain. They review how family members spend their time and examine what families do in terms of their daily activities and how they understand their work and family lives. Cognizant of variations across family structure, social class, the life course (as children are added to families and as children mature), and time cycles and calendars, the authors also discuss how different family members experience their everyday lives in work and in interaction with each other.

Pete Richardson discusses the anthropology of the workplace and the family. A main theme of his chapter is how family, or relatedness, is found in the workplace and invoked as an idiom within moral discourses concerning right action in working. He argues that attention must also be paid to how the workplace enters and structures the family and the home. He contends that the main question for research and practice is not how do we adapt the workplace to the family, but how do we understand the multitude of heterogeneous ways in which the family and the workplace are already bound together and interpenetrating. Once the separation of work and family is recognized to be historically conditioned and strategically placed in opposition as cultural socialization, then the more important anthropological question becomes: Why this particular constellation and assumed relationships between work and family rather than another?

Stephen Sweet and Phyllis Moen provide insights using a life course perspective on work and family. Their chapter's emphasis is on the concept of *career* to provide a window into dynamic links between individuals, families, employers, and other institutions. Work and family transitions and trajectories are seen as shaped by the weight of existing institutional and cultural arrangements that frame work and family life. By analyzing lives lived in context, they show how individual decisions are made in consideration with relational ties to children, spouses, and parents. These decisions play out over time, creating biographies that emerge as individuals make strategic decisions on how to manage their work and family responsibilities. By documenting careers, Sweet and Moen demonstrate that some of the most important questions concern effective pathways of entering, exiting, and scaling back work roles for family needs, something that contemporary cultural and structural forces largely fail to accommodate.

Drawing from psychological and sociological traditions, Rosalind Barnett and Karen Gareis ask readers to reconsider the whole concept of the "role" and general assumption that multiple roles (such as work and family roles) necessarily create negative consequences. They note that although most traditional work-family research is based on the assumption that work and family is associated with distress and conflict due to incompatible role pressures between work and the family, research in another domain suggests a more positive relationship due to the benefits of multiple roles, health, and quality-of-life outcomes. They review the major empirical findings from these competing views, and propose strategies for reconciling the differences between these perspectives, role conflict and role enhancement, and for bridging the theoretical divide.

Francine Deutsch brings us into the world of experimental social psychology, a perspective in work and family that focuses on the intra- and interpersonal processes that drive decisions, perceptions, and psychological outcomes in social life. The adoption of experimental designs that test cause-and-effect relationships has proven to be an innovative approach to documenting the mechanisms by which the gendered world of work and family is maintained. She reviews four main social psychological theories of relevance: attachment theory, self-determination theory, social role theory, and norm focus theory. These theories can be used to develop more gender-balanced relationships between work and home.

As sociologists, Naomi Gerstel and Natalia Sarkisian remind us about the importance of considering gender, class and race influences on work and family, and how in doing so we broaden the way work and family researchers have overemphasized the nuclear family and underemphasized single parents and extended kin. Emphasizing the work, both paid and unpaid, that families do, they focus on the relationship between paid and unpaid labor across gender, race, and class. They examine three types of unpaid family work: (a) housework, (b) parenting, and (c) kin work. They argue that the historical legacy of work and family relationships continues to shape the relationship of paid and unpaid family labor in the 21st century. These include the persistent inequalities in the relationship of paid work to housework, parenting, and kin work. They critique existing policy solutions for maintaining the status quo and reconceptualizations of employer support of work and life integration.

Economists Robert Drago and Lonnie Golden contend that of all disciplines that research issues relevant to work-family, the economics field probably holds the most untapped potential. It can most directly make the "business case" and "public goods" argument that work-family issues remain insufficiently resolved. However, because work-family conflict and imbalance continue to be framed most often as individual, private concerns only, it remains at the margins of what could be a promising area of inquiry. Economic models have evolved somewhat, mainly to capture the "work" aspect of work-family, by recognizing that unpaid work takes time and energy from paid work and leisure time. Work-family issues remained in the background of economics until the massive entry of women and mothers into the labor market in the latter half of the 20th century. They note in particular that little attention has attended to unpaid child care and the motivations to perform such tasks, but this is certainly an area of inquiry that fits well in the perspective of economists.

Cynthia Thompson, Laura Beauvais, and Tammy Allen review the industrial/organizational psychology perspective, which largely focuses on the work side of the work-family interface and the individual employee rather than the employee's family, workgroup, or community. They often measure employee attitudes and behavior as they affect the workplace. Thompson and colleagues believe that current research seems to support the beneficial effects of work-life policies, programs, and supportive work-family cultures on work and family balance. However, it is limited by not grounding work-family policies in the strategic planning of the organization. They suggest future research focus on demonstrating the connections between work-life policies and human resource activities such as employee recruitment, retention, and performance management.

Mary Still and Joan Williams provide a legal perspective on family issues at work, examining how new and existing labor laws hurt or ease work/family conflicts. They review legal trends in the courts as a result of workers suing their employers and discuss the underlying process of stereotyping and cognitive bias that can turn employer actions against workers with family or caregiver conflicts into litigation.

Marcie Pitt-Catsouphes and Jennifer Swanberg connect social work perspectives to work-family research and practice and explain the person-in-environment conceptual framework that is salient in much of their literature. They believe that the value added by social work emanates from the value orientation of the social work profession, which is anchored in explicit commitments to social justice, social equity, and the well-being of individuals, families, groups, and communities. By emphasizing populations that are either marginalized, vulnerable, or have limited access to resources and opportunities, the social work field can provide insights into the family experiences of population groups that may encounter particular challenges with regard to the management of work-family responsibilities. They focus on three levels of research and intervention with regard to work-family issues: the micro, meso, and macro levels.

In closing, it is important to note, that although we asked each author to highlight the unique contributions of his or her respective discipline, attentive readers will also observe considerable repetition of citation of core studies and concerns in work and family. Repeated concerns are raised about care work, time strains, role conflicts, gendered arrangements, economic strains, and a variety of other issues. The ways these concerns are framed and analyzed are sometimes subtly—and other times profoundly—influenced by the disciplinary perspectives adopted. Attentive readers will also observe that some studies are repeatedly cited irrespective of the discipline that spawned the research. We see this as the future of work and family research. As we build a community of scholarship, we see it as one that not only transcends traditional boundaries but one that also builds to a cohesive agenda for the advancement of knowledge, methodological rigor, as well as political and organizational change.

4

CAREGIVING AND WAGE-EARNING: A HISTORICAL PERSPECTIVE ON WORK AND FAMILY

Eileen Boris
Carolyn Herbst Lewis
University of California, Santa Barbara

At the beginning of the 21st century, a gap persists between public policies and women's responsibilities. The organization of most workplaces and the division of labor within most families assume a full-time homemaker even though nearly 80% of mothers in the United States are in the labor force (Costello, Wright, & Stone, 2002, p. 263). Nearly alone among Western democracies, the United States offers little public assistance to families faced with the dual responsibilities of caregiving and wage-earning (Gornick & Meyers, 2004). Why is it that to meet the needs of the household, American families of all types must rely on private and market-based solutions to supplement family labor, predominantly of mothers, rather than turn to public solutions for child care, elder care, and home maintenance? Why is it that men still perform considerably less household work than women or that more prosperous women solve their "double day" by hiring other women as domestics, nannies, and personal attendants (Ehrenreich, 2002)?

Historians provide a long view on current social arrangements, highlighting the structural and ideological forces behind their development. A historical perspective not only explains where we have been, but also reveals alternative ways of organizing work and family by class, race/ethnicity, religion, region, and other factors. Our task in this chapter is twofold: first, to present a basic narrative of both the strategies of ordinary people and the policies of elites on combining work and family over the last three centuries and, second, to introduce the rich literature generated by historians. From this vibrant but disparate scholarship, we develop three models for combining work and family that we name the household economy model, the male breadwinner/female caregiver model, and the dual breadwinner/female caregiver model. With less than half of mothers living with their spouses in 2000, this third model has taken the form of wage-earning lone motherhood (Costello, Wright, & Stone, 2002, p. 57).

While the household economy model appeared first in the colonial era, followed by the emergence of the male breadwinner/female caregiver model in the mid-19th century, and finally the dual breadwinner/female caregiver model in the 20th, we suggest that these models have often overlapped rather than progressed along a clear-cut chronology. Factors such as class, race/ethnicity, region, immigration status, and the nature of the task to be performed have affected the structure of work and family life. For example, the household economy model associated with preindustrial and subsistence organization of work in the 18th and early 19th centuries persisted in agricultural and rural areas into the early 20th century. With urbanization, the household economy morphed into a family economy system practiced by immigrants, African American migrants, and other members of an emerging working class. Meanwhile, in the mid-19th century the male breadwinner/female caregiver, embodied in the cult of domesticity, became the ideal for the urban, White middle class. Yet even though female domesticity was the ideal, most women contributed to the well-being of the family either through unwaged family labor or employment in the home and other workplaces.

The history of how ordinary people have balanced their work and family obligations is also the history of how policymakers, elites, and activists have responded to these strategies. This is especially true with the expansion of state regulation and public assistance at the end of the 19th century. At that time, the mother who must earn and the father who deserted became objects of reform; her wage-earning and his failure to support constituted social problems. The origins of the nation's public/private welfare state—a state that bases pensions, health care, and most other social services on the employment relationship and makes available a safety net of direct services and monies only to those marked as poor, pathological, or otherwise at risk (Boris & Michel, 2001; Klein, 2003)—began as a response to the difficulties that the urban, often immigrant, working-class family had in caring for children while earning adequate income (Boris, 2005a).

In the midst of the Great Depression, the New Deal encoded the male breadwinner/female caregiver into proposals for social security (Kessler-Harris, 2001), but in such a manner as to disadvantage African Americans, Latina/os, and Asian immigrants as well as poor, unmarried mothers, no matter their race or ethnicity (Boris, 1995). The rise of married women's labor force participation after World War II, whether to make ends meet or fulfill individual aspirations, increasingly placed work and family issues on the national political agenda. So did the jump in single motherhood, whether through divorce or out-of-wedlock pregnancy (Weiner, 1985).

The dual breadwinner/female caregiver model developed in this context. Since the 1940s, feminists in the trade unions and their supporters in government fought for social supports like flexible hours and maternity leave to enable women to care for their families by earning a wage. The new feminism of the 1960s and 1970s saw many of their proposals become public policy, though the actual division of labor between the sexes, in which women still disproportionately undertook family work, belied the presumption of gender neutrality encoded in law (Cobble, 2004). Much of the work and family agenda of those years sought to permit women to leave the home for employment by relieving but not eliminating their dual responsibilities as caregiver and breadwinner. By the 1990s, however, some feminists sought to revalue carework. While more privileged women "opted out" of the workforce to return to full-time motherhood, others fought welfare reform that would force poor women to leave their children to work off benefits through various "workfare" programs or labor at minimum-wage jobs (Mink, 1998; Michel, 2000). Some proposed upgrading paid carework through enhanced training and living wages. Family-friendly workplaces remained few; the structure of work as much as the paucity of public supports contributed to what had emerged as a persistent work and family dilemma by the beginning of the 21st century (Heymann, 2000).

Much of women's history has addressed the relationship of home to work, grappling with the impact of gender conventions on the lives of women by race and class (Boris & Kleinberg, 2003). But, this topic rarely has been the main subject of monographs, which cover specific aspects, like child care (Michel, 1999), or groups of women, like the enslaved (Morgan, 2004). With few exceptions, the literature replicates policy debates by focusing on women's roles rather than questioning the terms of the discussion. The equality/difference fault line within feminism also has shaped interpretations of a host of work and family concerns, depending on whether a historian judges treating women the same as men as advancing women's rights. As historical sociologists Ann S. Orloff and Renee Monson (2002, p. 69) concluded in one of the few essays to consider men's place in the family, "to the extent that state social policies address men as fathers—which is quite limited—they are expected to contribute cash rather than care; but, for the most part, the 'privacy' of family life in the liberal [welfare state] ... means that men and women are left free—from state interference or support—to construct their households as they will, but only as they can afford." Here we consider men as well as women and political economy as well as discourse.

MODEL I: THE HOUSEHOLD ECONOMY

During the colonial and Early Republican periods of American history, work and family life were organized primarily according to the household economy model. Under this system, all inhabitants of an individual household—husband, wife, children, servants or slaves, extended kin, and other residents, like boarders—labored together to produce the goods necessary for household maintenance. The sites of work and home overlapped, so much so that they were virtually indistinguishable from one another. So, too, was women's reproductive and productive labor. While the details and division of work varied by class, period, and location, the essentials remained the same (Mintz & Kellogg, 1988).

In the colonial Northeast, among Anglo or White families, women may have ventured into the fields to help with planting and men may have sat down to spin during the winter months, but, for the most part, men's and women's labors divided along gender lines. Men took responsibility for most tasks that occurred outside of the family dwelling, either undertaking heavy farm work or laboring in the family workshop or store. Women performed much of their labor within the immediate proximity of the home, whether they were the wives of farmers or artisans. They canned, preserved, and stored fruits, vegetables, jellies, and meats. They prepared meals. Many kept chickens and kitchen gardens. They manufactured garments and bedding as well as laundered and mended them. They were responsible for daily and seasonal cleaning along with the supervision of young children (Ulrich, 1980, 1990; Boydston, 1990).

Women also joined with neighbors to assist at childbirths, sick beds, weddings, and funerals. This guaranteed aid during their own times of need. They also bartered their time and skills for other items, such as eggs or fine cloth. Although some women worked as professional midwives, many others simply offered mutual support (Ulrich, 1990; Borst, 1995). Thus, colonial women's productive and reproductive labors were indistinguishable from one another, a pattern that replicated itself into the 19th century and persisted into the 20th as the frontier of settlement shifted and as agricultural communities remained only partially incorporated into the market economy (Faragher, 1986; Fink, 1992; Garceau, 1997; Sharpless, 1999; Walker, 2000).

Although men and women shared equally in the maintenance of the colonial household, wives were not the social, political, or economic equals of their husbands. With some variations in time, place, and circumstance, most women could not own property, which led to loss of custody of children upon the rare occasion of divorce. They certainly could not vote and they were not expected to hold public office. Men were the heads of both individual households and their communities. Thus, the household economy was no "glorious" moment in the American past, in which women's labors ensured women's equality (Norton, 1980, 1984; Boydston, 1990; Ulrich, 1980).

Nevertheless, women's work was highly valued. The skewed sex ratio of colonial settlements meant that, at one point, men outnumbered women six to one (Greene, 1988). A man who could secure a wife could expect to dramatically improve his economic productivity as well as his quality of life (Boydston, 1990; Shammas, 1990). The success of the household economy depended on the efforts of all family members, particularly husbands and their wives. The work—both productive and reproductive—that women did within their homes was critical. As historian Jeanne Boydston (1990, p. 5) has argued, "Not only did women work, but they were *recognized* as workers, and the value of that labor—both to their households and to their communities—was openly and repeatedly acknowledged." Even in 18th-century towns and urban markets, where families began to depend on the wages of husbands and the domestic consumption of wives, a recognition of women's fundamental contribution to the household economy persisted.

The Household Economy in the 19th Century

But the framework of the household economy model was not confined solely to the American colonial period. Historians have identified other times and places in which the household economy functioned as the primary means of organizing work and family life. Well into the 19th century in Hispanic village communities of New Mexico and Colorado, for example, women controlled food production, even its exchange; some specialized in the crafts, yet all engaged in housework and child care (Deutsch, 1987).

Life in rural farm communities also remained remarkably unchanged in the early 19th century, despite the urbanization and industrialization that would transform other areas of the country (Clark, 1990). The gender division of labor of colonial America persisted: While men shouldered the brunt of the heaviest physical labor, women maintained responsibility for more household-oriented tasks. However, in rural farm areas, women were also likely to join their husbands in the fields on a regular or seasonal basis. The example of dairy production in the early to mid-19th century illuminates this process. The inflexibility of this work—"cows had to be milked twice a day, milk had to be skimmed after it had separated but before it soured, and cream had to be churned within a certain range of temperatures" (Osterud, 1987, p. 94)—generated flexibility in terms of who would perform which duty. Women's regular participation in farming suggested a blurring of the gendered division of labor, yet certain jobs remained gender-specific, despite variations in time and place. Men in some areas of New England, for example, participated in butter churning as dairy production increased in the 19th century, but in upstate New York, churning remained "women's work," as did most tasks associated with hearth and family care (Osterud, 1987; Jensen, 1986). When women took to the fields or milked a cow, they did so in addition to their domestic duties.

Nineteenth-century farm women increasingly divided their time not only between household and farm work. With the aid of their older daughters or the daughters of their neighbors and the assistance of servants, hired help, and slaves before emancipation, they also could combine unpaid family labor with income generating activities (Jensen, 1986; Clark, 1990; Dublin, 1994). Women took in spinning, laundry, and mending and worked in their neighbors' fields. In rural Massachusetts and New Hampshire, farm women engaged in industrial outwork, binding shoes, weaving cloth, and braiding hats (Dublin, 1994). They also earned wages producing goods to be sold at market. The wages farm wives earned selling homemade soap, candles, rugs, and featherbeds enabled their families to purchase the goods, materials, and services that could not be made within the home (Jensen, 1986; Clark, 1990). In the rural outskirts of Philadelphia and in upstate New York during the mid- to late 19th century, the butter trade became the primary form of domestic production for White farm women as the urban population became dependent on rural farms for dairy products (few families living within the city limits would have owned a cow) (Jensen, 1986; Osterud, 1987).

The Household Economy of African American Families

For African American women, the household economy model served as the primary mode of organizing work and family throughout the 19th and into the early 20th centuries. Under slavery, they toiled as part of the White master's household. Their backbreaking labor in Southern tobacco, cotton and rice fields, as well as their work in family kitchens, dairies, and homes, freed White women from many of the burdensome tasks of household production and domestic maintenance (Weiner, 1998; Kierner, 1998). However, the size of a plantation and its labor force influenced the duties of the White "mistress," who usually controlled the keys to the larder and storeroom and engaged in preparatory activities, like cutting cloth for enslaved women to sew into garments. Mistresses also produced goods themselves, nursed the sick, and sometimes even managed the farm (Clinton, 1982; Fox-Genovese, 1988). Poorer White women even worked in the fields (Bynum, 1992).

The reproductive work of enslaved women was also critical to the success of the White plantation household. African American women not only reproduced the slave labor force, but they also served as wet nurses and caregivers to White children (Weiner, 1998; Morgan, 2004). Their labor for the plantation jeopardized labor for their families. Enslaved women struggled for relief from field work during pregnancy, and some plantations assigned the pregnant and nursing mothers, along with the elderly and young girls, to a female "trash" gang with lighter tasks. Mothers sometimes brought infants to the fields for nursing, but the demands of planting and harvesting took their toil in an upsurge of infant deaths during such seasons. Large plantations often had nurseries, where elders and older children watched over the babies and toddlers (White, 1985; Schwartz, 1996). Thus, enslaved women bore the burden of women's reproductive and productive roles within the Southern household economy (White, 1985; Fox-Genovese, 1988; Stevenson, 1996; Weiner, 1998; Kierner, 1998). The Civil War disrupted this order of things, with White women of the slaveholding class having to become, according to historian Drew Gilpin Faust (1996), "mothers of invention."

After emancipation, African Americans sought social, political, and economic independence that would enable them to care for their families on their own terms. The realities of the nation's race system, particularly the development of Jim Crow in the late 19th-century South, made securing this independence difficult. In the rural South, the once enslaved and their descendents became entangled in a sharecropping system in which they lived and farmed land often owned by former masters, who received a disproportionate share of the income from the sale of crops. After calculating for the costs of seed, equipment, and supplies, a tenant could end up with no cash for a year's effort. Debt peonage grew as the landowners frequently also owned local stores. While the entire family needed to labor for household survival, a struggle developed between sharecroppers and their landlords over who would control the labor of wives and children. Following emancipation, landlords who tried to replicate the gang labor of the plantation, with its indiscriminate deployment of mothers and their children, found tenants sneaking away just as the crop came in, and were forced to move toward sharecropping. Thus, the sharecrop system developed out of the need of landlords for labor power and the desire of the freed people to decide for themselves when and under what conditions wives and children would work in the fields or whether children could attend school (Foner, 1988; Schwalm, 1997; Frankel, 1999).

Freed women sought a strategic balance between work and family responsibilities. Wives "divided their time among domestic responsibilities, field work, and petty money-making activities" (Jones, 1985, p. 80). Although all family members labored together in the fields, gender increasingly coded their work. For example, on cotton farms, men ploughed, while women hoed and picked (Jones, 1985). Although their activities might be similar to work performed under enslavement, the social context differed significantly. As slaves, women's time and energy to care for their own children and homes not only had been curtailed, but the results of their labor—the reproduction of the slave family—also belonged to owners. As freedwomen, they now labored on behalf of their own families (Jones, 1985). When women spent their days in the fields, at night they engaged in household chores. When older children or elderly kin were not available to babysit, women took their youngest children with them, who joined in the tasks. While husbands might work for additional wages on other farms, women supplemented the family's income by taking in laundry, serving as midwives, or, less frequently in the rural South, performing domestic labor in White homes (Jones, 1985). Indeed, domestic service became the chief occupation of urban African American women, including married ones. While washerwomen labored out of their homes, and in cities like Atlanta could watch over their own and neighborhood children, other servants had to fight against living-in and for day work; rarely could children accompany them to workplaces. While they could bring home food and additional items given or borrowed from employers, often they had to leave their own families to care for the household and children of others, not returning until their half day off on Sunday (Clark-Lewis, 1994; Hunter, 1997).

The Household Economy Among the Urban Working Class

The persistence of the household economy in organizing farm women's work and family responsibilities into the early 20th century might be expected, but its appearance in urban, industrial settings may be surprising. Immigrant families living and working in the modernizing nation relied on the wage and household labors of all members for family survival. In some factories and mills, beginning with the Rhode Island system in the 1790s and continuing into the late 19th century, entire families contracted to work together, with the male head assuming responsibility for collecting their wages (Coontz, 1988). Even when workplaces varied, family members pooled wages to afford rent, food, clothing, and various necessities. Child labor made the difference between getting by and getting ahead. Yet many wives, especially among second-generation immigrant families in the late 19th century, did not work for wages outside of the home (Coontz, 1988; Glenn, 1990). These women took in boarders and piecework, but their primary labor revolved around preparing meals, making and mending clothes, caring for infants and small children, and perhaps even growing a kitchen garden (Kleinberg, 1989). As with the household economies of the colonial Northeast, their efforts within the home were critical.

The experience of Asian immigrants in the early 20th century further illustrates the persistence of the household economy. Between 1920 and 1960, restrictions based on race and class severely curtailed Asian immigration to the United States. Men generally arrived first, then sent for their wives and children when circumstances and the law allowed. Chinese and Japanese women told immigration officials that they intended to "keep house" for their husbands as members of the respectable, merchant middle class (Gee, 2003; Yung, 1995). But the arrival of wives and children meant more often hands to labor in the family laundry, restaurant, or grocery. "During the period from about 1920 to the mid-1960s [when immigration restrictions eased], the typical immigrant and first-generation family functioned as a productive unit in which all members, including children, worked without wages in a family business. The business was profitable only because it was labor-intensive and members put in extremely long hours," historical sociologist Evelyn Nakano Glenn (1983, p. 82) has concluded. Tasks in the household economy here too divided by sex; women bore responsibility for domestic duties along with their participation in the family business.

As the next section reveals, the urban, White, middle class began reorganizing itself along a male breadwinner/female caregiver model as early as the 1820s and 1830s. Yet the above examples make clear that race, class, and ethnicity, as well as region and occupation, significantly impacted the reproductive and productive labor choices available to women. As a result, the two models for organizing work and family responsibilities continued to overlap well into the 20th century. For the rural, the immigrant, and certain sectors of the working class, the household economy model persisted as the primary mode of balancing work and family.

MODEL II: THE MALE BREADWINNER/FEMALE CAREGIVER

In the first half of the 19th century, the United States experienced a dramatic reorganization of home and work (Cott, 1977; Kessler-Harris, 1982; Boydston, 1990). Aided by innovations in transportation and banking, factories replaced the home and the artisan's shop as the site of production for a variety of goods, such as shoes and textiles. A consumer revolution further contributed to the emergence of a new class of workers that labored in the banks, shops, and offices that managed the new industrial market economy (Boydston, 1990).

Appearing first in the urban, industrial areas of the Northeast, this new "middle class" in the 1830s and 1840s developed a male breadwinner/female caregiver model that relied on a sharper distinction between men's and women's labors and familial responsibilities. Men would become the economic provider for the family. Employed as bankers, lawyers, manufacturing managers, and clerks, the men of the middle class went out into "the world of nineteenth century business, where 'cunning, intrigue, falsehood, slander, [and] vituperative violence' reigned" in order to bring home the wages that would support their families in an increasingly cash-dependent economy. The ability to support a family through wage-earning thus marked a new standard of manhood. Men's reward for breadwinning was the ability to retreat into the sanctity of the home at the end of a long day (Boydston, 1990, p. 143; Ryan, 1983).

The link between work and wages coupled with the glorification of the home as the site of men's restoration and leisure had a dramatic impact on the status of women's household labors. Because women's work within the home did not yield a wage, it came to be viewed as nonproductive. Although women certainly produced a great many things within the home, the items they made and the services they performed became redefined as caring for their families, rather than providing for them (Boydston, 1990).

This redefinition of women's household labor reinforced what historians have identified as the "cult of domesticity," which many historians claim appeared around the same time that work became linked to wages (Cott, 1977), though Boydston (1990) located the devaluation of women's labors as before industrialization. According to this ideology, "Home was 'an oasis in the desert,' a 'sanctuary' where 'sympathy, honor, virtue are assembled,' where 'disinterested love is ready to sacrifice everything at the altar of affection'" (Cott, 1977, p. 64). The creator of this sanctuary and the source of affective sacrifice were the wife and mother. But a woman could not be simultaneously the "angel in the household" and a drudge toiling to provide for family needs. Hence, the cult of domesticity necessitated the redefinition of women's household labors as care rather than work. In regions marked by extensive slave labor, this reinterpretation of White women's domestic duties occurred much earlier (Kierner, 1998), but for nonslaveholding White women of the middling classes, the cult of domesticity transformed the meaning of household labor in the early 19th century. Household tasks such as scrubbing floors, hanging laundry, changing bedding, sewing garments, making meals, and churning butter became "pastoralized" into idyllic images of nurturing activities that women carried out of duty and love (Boydston, 1990). Household work turned invisible.

"Helping Out": Wage Earning Versus Breadwinning

Any work that women performed that many have yielded wages also became hidden within the household. Taking in single men as boarders was a common practice in both urban middle- and working-class homes. In addition to the cost of renting a room or a bed, a boarder also paid for laundry, mending, and meals. While women earned wages for these services, this income did not elevate them or their labors to the status of breadwinning (Strasser, 1982). Their wages were supplementary, not equal, to those of husbands. Similarly, wives of artisans and merchants frequently assisted in the family business, but their unpaid labor, while critical to the family's success, certainly was not understood as breadwinning (Branson, 2001). These women were simply "helping out." Other urban women sent their children out to scavenge the streets for items to turn into household items; this too was never judged as work (Stansell, 1986).

Wage work that women engaged in outside the home was considered temporary and circumstantial. The new factories employed young, unmarried women, who were not expected to become permanent wage earners. Instead, wage work represented a transitional phase in their lives between childhood and marriage. The paternalistic rules and guidelines that regulated young workers' labor and leisure demonstrated that these women were not to be mistaken for members of a proletariat. Once they were wed, they would leave paid employment and assume the role of full-time homemaker (Kessler-Harris, 1982; Weiner, 1985).

The cult of domesticity both ignored and disparaged those women who were permanent wage earners and thus unable to live up to its tenets. Although only 5% of married women were counted in the labor force in the mid-19th century, many more of the homebound sewed garments, bound shoes, and braided hats in between household tasks and child care (Kessler-Harris, 1982). As with the household economy model, their wages were just as critical to the maintenance of families as were those of husbands. Nevertheless, their work was not given the same value. Husbands alone assumed the status of breadwinners. The wages that men brought into the home fulfilled their obligation to the household. Yet even as women worked for wages in factories, fields, and at their kitchen tables, they also remained responsible for the many household tasks necessary to feed, clothe, and otherwise tend to families (Kessler-Harris, 1982; Cowan, 1983; Coontz, 1988; González, 1999). Contributions as wage earners were secondary to responsibilities as caregivers. By 1900, according to new calculations that include home-based labor, nearly half of women aged 15 to 64 and 40% of wives generated income, though much of this came from unpaid work on family farms and shops or from boarders (Bose, 2001, pp. 40–41).

Protecting Mothers: Policymakers, Social Housekeepers, and the Wage-Earning Woman

Even though the experiences of the urban, White, middle class lay behind the male breadwinner/female caregiver model, the gender ideology it depended on applied to all women (Cott, 1977). This becomes abundantly clear when we consider efforts of reformers in the late 19th and early 20th centuries to "Americanize" European and Mexican immigrants as well as Native Americans into female domesticity and male breadwinning (Mink, 1994; Anderson, 1996; Jacobs, 1999; Mihesuah, 1993). In this period, educated middle-class women increasingly sought a vocation outside the home and forged one through social reform. They justified participation in activities that removed them from their families and delayed or avoided marriage. Claims to "public housekeeping" legitimized middle-class women's work without calling into question their femininity, respectability, or even commitment to the "mother-care tradition" (Berry, 1993; Muncy, 1991; Sklar, 1993).

The same could not be said for the wage labor of working class and poor women. Of the 6 million of such women in 1900, 40% were immigrants and another 20% were African American (Kessler-Harris, 2001). Reformers worried about the respectability of single native-born "women adrift," that is, away from the family, as well as the ability of immigrant mothers to nurture children if forced, by destitution, out to work (Weiner, 1985). Campaigns for state minimum wages, maximum hours, restrictions on night work, and other "protective" labor legislation reflected concern over the debilitating physical and mental effects of wage work on women's reproductive functions, though historians disagree on whether these laws intensified occupational segregation by racialized gender or improved the working conditions of those least able to organize against employers on their own (Kessler-Harris, 1990; Sklar, 1993; Hart, 1994). Most historians would agree that reform efforts did not confirm women's right to wage labor as a legitimate alternative to full-time housekeeping, but they distinguish between the discourse and motives of women reformers, variously named social feminists, industrial feminists, or maternalists, compared to the domestic ideology of the Supreme Court (Lipschultz, 1991; Ladd-Taylor, 1994). In the landmark 1908 case, *Muller v. Oregon*, the United States Supreme Court ruled that it was not only constitutional to limit the hours that women were permitted to work, but it was also appropriate and necessary to do so. As Justice David Brewer wrote for the majority: "That woman's physical structure and the performance of maternal functions place her at a disadvantage in the struggle for subsistence is obvious . . . and, as healthy mothers are essential to vigorous offspring, the physical well-being of a woman becomes an object of public interest and care in order to preserve the strength and vigor of the race." Women's role as the mother of future generation put them in a special "class" of workers in need of protection and supervision. Wage work would be secondary to the care they gave their families.

While the "typical" female wage worker at the turn of the 20th century was young, White, and single, the number of employed married women doubled between 1900 and 1930 (Berry, 1993). In order to reconcile this increase with the male breadwinner/female caregiver model, many reformers and policymakers asserted that women worked only as "a final defense against destitution" (Weiner, 1985, p. 85). Women's wage labor became evidence of failed masculinity, of men's inability or unwillingness to support their families; municipal courts ordered men to fulfill their duty as the provider or face prison (Weiner, 1985, Willrich, 2001). Questioning the respectability, femininity, and parenting capabilities of wage-earning mothers, reformers unapologetically entered the homes of working-class women, especially immigrants, to police housekeeping and childrearing habits, often as a condition for receiving public aid or private charity (Muncy, 1991; Mink, 1994).

Child Care

Given their family responsibilities, the labor patterns of wage-earning mothers differed significantly from those of single women. The development of compulsory public education and the establishment of child labor laws especially affected the timing of mothers' wage work (Weiner, 1985). Mothers often delayed entry or reentry into the workforce until small children started school. Those who could not put off earning wages found other ways to balance child care with employment. In 1920, one quarter to one third of married women labored at home, with the aid of their children, taking in laundry, keeping boarders, or manufacturing garments (Weiner, 1985). While the form of such labor resembled earlier outwork, it lacked recognition as real work and served as the epitome of exploitative labor in a maturing industrial economy (Boris, 1994).

For others, child care remained a critical issue (Glenn, 1990; Berry, 1993). "Maternal invention" led to children picking cotton alongside mothers, playing on the cement floors of canneries, and lying at the feet of machine operators, who would steal a minute to nurse. Mothers worked split shifts or night shifts. They left the young with slightly older siblings or other family members, with neighbors, and locked in rooms; they also sent them to orphanages (Michel, 1999). Some middle-class women reformers established day nurseries for the children of poor wage-earning mothers (Berry, 1993; Kessler-Harris, 2001).

Under assault by educational and social welfare professionals, day nurseries were reluctant to encourage maternal wage earning and adverse to government intervention into their affairs; they lost ground to the movement for mothers' pensions. Pensions represented a form of state provision for social reproduction that enabled mothers to care for their children at home. In practice, they were underfunded; their administration, intrusive, given only to those judged as worthy, which led to discrimination against the unwed, divorced, or non-White. Their meagerness actually encouraged part-time work, which reinforced women's position in the low-waged labor market. Mothers' pensions of the 1910s and 1920s evolved into Aid to Dependent Children (ADC) under Social Security in 1935 (Mink, 1994; Goodwin, 1997; Michel, 1999).

The Institutionalization of the Male Breadwinner/Female Caregiver Model

During the Great Depression, the tensions surrounding wage-earning mothers were thrown into stark relief. Among the most immediate of official and unofficial responses to the employment crisis was an effort to limit households to a single wage earner (Kessler-Harris, 1990, 2001). While some married women and their supporters claimed that such women had just as much right to work as anyone else, many others judged the married who had other means of support—that is, an employed husband—a drain on the economy. They were unfairly taking jobs from men and women who needed to work to provide for families (Kessler-Harris, 1990; Berry, 1993; Rose, 1999). This called into question the distinction between wage earning and providership (Kessler-Harris, 1990, 2001). While men's wages continued to be understood as essential, women's wages long had been linked with frivolous extras. While most married women, especially African Americans, labored before and during the Great Depression for family survival (Jones, 1985), the specter of the middle-class women who worked out of choice, rather than need, haunted employment policies and relief programs throughout the decade. Thus, Section 213 of the 1932 Economy Act, known as the "married person clause," led to the dismissal of women if the government also employed their spouse; it took until 1937 for Congress to repeal this measure, which passed with the intention of making more jobs available to male household heads (Scharf, 1980). Teachers continued to face dismissal upon marriage into the 1950s, but here fears of exposing children to pregnancy also entered into discriminatory rules (Kessler-Harris, 1990, pp. 57–80).

The New Deal institutionalized the nation's commitment to the male breadwinner/female caregiver model as the appropriate relationship between men and women, work and home (Boris, 2005a). Relief programs, like the Works Progress Administration (WPA), reinforced gender and racial hierarchies; they employed men over women and Whites over other groups. In her analysis of Atlanta, historian Georgina Hickey underscored how the New Deal "favored welfare work for men as family breadwinners, direct assistance for mothers, and work relief for women only when the gendered wage economy dictated" (Hickey, 2003, p. 13). Other historians have documented how the WPA offered work relief to only one family member and laid off women first during funding cutbacks (Faue, 1991; Rose, 1994).

The system of welfare initiated under the New Deal linked wage work to benefits so that "some people (generally women) would get benefits by virtue of their family positions and others (mainly men) by virtue of their paid employment" (Kessler-Harris, 2001, p. 4). Old age pensions, unemployment insurance, and various relief measures assumed a male breadwinner/female caregiver norm for American families (Mettler, 1998). Social Security, the National Industrial Relations (or Wagner) Act, and the Fair Labor Standards Act covered only industries engaged in interstate commerce, excluding those that typically employed a predominately female workforce, such as office work. Moreover, by excluding agricultural and service industries dominated by men and women of color, both social security and labor law privileged White male industrial workers and their dependents (Mink, 1994).

The 1939 amendments to Social Security created survivor's benefits for widows deemed worthy by virtue of the eligibility of their deceased spouses, relegating other poor lone mothers to ADC because they lacked a relationship to covered men or were never married. Similarly, elderly women who lacked coverage through their own work history or their husbands could not qualify for Social Security or old age insurance and had to turn to Old Age Assistance, the program administered by the states that by the 1950s was less generous. ADC developed into a means-tested and stigmatized program, also run by the states, which varied tremendously in requirements and amount of aid (Gordon, 1994; Kessler-Harris, 1995, 2001; Mettler, 1998). Mink (1994, p. 137) has emphasized how these amendments "fastened women's social rights to dependent motherhood." Still, the formulators of ADC assumed that "worthy" widows would earn something toward their upkeep. Indeed, ADC, unlike survivor's benefits, originally provided monies only for children and lacked any grant for caregivers (Gordon, 1994).

The attempt to ban industrial homework under the National Recovery Administration (NRA) illuminates dominant gender discourses. Policymakers argued that homework undercut wages and took work away from factories, which, by extension, meant from men. But while the ban claimed to protect women, it eliminated an income-generating strategy that families had been relying on for more than a century (Boris, 1985). Although people with disabilities, their caregivers, and older, longtime homeworkers could gain an exemption, to permit mothers would defeat the whole purpose of the ban, as it was "mothers and their offspring—considered potential child laborers—[who] were precisely the group that [the ban] . . . would save from the exploitation of homework and would restore to a 'normal' family life—that is, one with a male breadwinner, a housewife, and children" (Boris, 1985, p. 749).

The lack of suitable child-care options continued to plague employed mothers. For example, in 1930, while most families relied on informal caretakers, there were only 40 day-care facilities for African American children in the entire country (Berry, 1993, p. 105). Although the New Deal offered some new child-care programs, it failed to implement a nationwide system of public day care. It created centers for the purpose of providing employment for out-of-work janitors, teachers, and nurses (Michel, 1999; Berry, 1993) rather than to encourage mothers to work outside the home. Only the unemployed could send their children to these centers, which meant that the children of parents who found a job lost their space (Berry, 1993).

During World War II, the federal government increased child-care funding for wage-earning mothers. Nevertheless, while the female labor force peaked at 19 million in 1944, the maximum capacity for federally funded child-care centers never surpassed 130,000 (Michel, 1999, p. 142). Whether because of their personal preference for private or familial care, the racism imbedded in the system, the lack of available services, or the stigma attached to government-sponsored day care as a relief measure, most working mothers continued to find other forms of child care. Still, the war period also witnessed experimentation in the organization of wage work and family labor that did not rely on mothers. Kaiser Shipyards in Portland, Oregon, for example, housed model child-care centers, with the government picking up the cost by reimbursing the Kaiser Corporation. Other factories experimented with shopping, laundry, and meal services to ease the double day of employed mothers (Michel, 1999; Kesselman, 1990; Anderson, 1981).

By war's end, the male breadwinner/female caregiver model that had initially appeared as the idealized relationship between work and home had become institutionalized in public policy, no less than in cultural expectations. Despite women's wartime labors, their right to a job remained conditional, confirmed by definitions of full employment that classified housewives as outside the labor force and thus ineligible for federal jobs programs and unaccounted in official employment statistics (Kessler-Harris, 2001, p. 19). The GI Bill—with its education, housing, and additional benefits—mostly privileged men; by excluding discharged gays and lesbians from its largesse, it also shored up the heterosexual male breadwinner/female caregiver family at the moment when a dual breadwinner/female caregiver model was emerging in practice, if not as a cultural ideal (Canady, 2003).

MODEL III: THE DUAL BREADWINNER/FEMALE CAREGIVER

Social policies during World War II encouraged mothers to enter the labor force and even work overtime while fulfilling their familial or domestic obligations (Anderson, 1981; Milkman, 1987; Gabin, 1990; Michel, 1999). That public expenditure for child care, health care, and maternity leave failed to cover all who qualified for such resources underscored the power of market ideology and the weakness of the U.S. welfare state (O'Connor, Orloff, & Shaver, 1999). Except during wartime, solutions for combining work and family either were private, located within families or informally among neighbors, or amounted to cash transactions. None of these strategies deviated from the past, but the numbers of families who had to substitute paid caregivers for mother work grew in the half century after the war (Abel, 2000).

In *The Feminine Mystique* of 1963, Betty Friedan portrayed the early post-World War II years as a retreat into domesticity, but historians now recognize the 1950s as a period when a new consumer economy, higher standard of living, and rising prices led mothers into the labor force, if only part-time and after children entered school (Friedan, 1963; Meyerowitz, 1994; Cohen, 2003). The wage-earner mother of our own day represents not so much a break with 1950s America as an intensification of patterns already evident in the early postwar years (Coontz, 1992). In seeking to explain the present, historians have focused more on the public discourse and social policies of the last 50 years than on the coping strategies of families, leaving that topic to sociology and other disciplines.

Again, we see overlapping models for combining work and family. The male breadwinner/female caregiver remained the ideal, especially for White women whom cultural arbiters told to trade off the ability to purchase goods for staying home with their children (Solinger, 1999). Men's responsibility for family provision persisted, although they gained praise in the popular media and from women for caregiving, whether in the form of 1950s family "togetherness" or from helping with women's domestic tasks (Weiss, 2000; May, 1988). They benefited from tax write-offs, especially income splitting with a wife outside of the labor force (Kessler-Harris, 2001). These ideals remained racialized, with Whites as the norm, and thus African Americans appeared deviant and deficient because their men failed to earn enough to support children (Mittelstadt, 2005; O'Connor, 2001; Orloff & Monson, 2002).

Necessity or Right, Sameness or Difference? Policy Debates Over the Working Mother

Reigning gender constructions certainly influenced defenders of mothers on the job. They finessed women's right to work, the choice question, by framing their defense in the language of needs. A necessity argument conceded women's presence in the labor force, while to prevent the return of economic depression and win the Cold War, purchasing power and womanpower arguments made it her patriotic duty to do so (Boris & Michel, 2001; Hartmann, 1994). Only during the 1960s did rights arguments come to dominate discussions of women and employment (Kessler-Harris, 2001). By the 1990s, going out to work was justified as enabling women to better engage in intensive mothering when they returned home (Hays, 1996).

With half of employed women married and a third of the married wage earners with children under 18 in 1953 (U.S. House, 1953, p. 32), the U.S. Women's Bureau readily embraced the necessity argument in seeking to improve the income, benefits, hours, and working conditions of women wage earners. So did mass production, service, and white-collar unions. These saw women's work in terms of family obligations (Kessler-Harris, 2001). With the maternal role primary, the Bureau promoted part-time work as a solution to the double day and offered lessons in home management. But it also supported expansion of day care. For most male-dominated craft unions, in contrast, the necessity argument coexisted with a continued embrace of family wage ideology that sought higher wages for men to support their families (Cobble, 2004; Deslippe, 2000; Laughlin, 2000).

Until the late 1960s, recognition of female difference, that is, women's ability to have children and undertake the cultural and social assignment of carework, shaped policy initiatives. Thus, labor feminists focused on obtaining maternity leave, child care, and a shorter workday, while demanding higher wages, end to discrimination based on marital status, and greater participation in their unions and at the workplace. As historian Dorothy Sue Cobble (2004, p. 13) explained, "Working-class women tended to see themselves as worker *and* mother, breadwinner *and* homemaker." They sought equal rights but also special accommodations to make equality possible; they refused "to privilege breadwinning over caregiving" or equate equality with "assimilation to the male sphere" (Cobble, 2004, p. 120). The President's Commission on the Status of Women, created by John F. Kennedy in 1961, embraced the dual agenda of labor feminists; its task was to recommend ways to overcome discrimination "in government and private employment on the basis of sex" but also "enable women to continue their roles as wives and mothers while making a maximum contribution to the world around them" (Harrison, 1988, p. 225).

During the Cold War, the nation was caught between the desire to harness all available "manpower," which demanded maternal wage earning, even if part-time, and the desire to meet what psychologists claimed was the best interest of children, which required a stay-at-home mother (National Manpower Council, 1957). Though unstated, this discussion was primarily about White women, their contributions, and the potential disruption to their families. The place of Black women, it was assumed, always had been out to work. Black families engaged in "other mothering," a practice of child care through extended community networks of blood and fictive kin (Hill Collins, 1994). However, most commentators ignored Black mothers before the civil rights and welfare rights movements demanded equal access to social benefits (particularly Aid to Families with Dependent Children or welfare) and the *Moynihan Report* transformed Black mothers into pathological man-devourers (Feldstein, 2000; Mink, 1999).

The public agenda ignored how women from other racial–ethnic groups managed to combine work and family. Migrant Mexican farmworkers, for example, breastfed less than other groups of women; they found it difficult to juggle reproductive and productive labor (de la Torre, 1993). As they increasingly entered light manufacturing and service industries, Chicanas continued to rely on *commadrazgo*, "ties of blood and fictive kinship," for child care and domestic labor. These ties involved reciprocity, including the care of elderly mothers (Anderson, 1996; Ruiz, 1998, p. 4). However, Mexicanas felt less ambivalence about full-time employment than Chicanas, whom sociologist Denise Segura (2000, p. 199) found, desired "to realize the prevailing social construction of motherhood that exalts child rearing over paid employment" and thus sought part-time jobs if they could not afford to leave the labor force entirely. Cuban and other recent immigrants turned to the household economy strategies of the past, including taking manufacturing into the home (Boris, 1984). Asian Americans still engaged in family businesses that allowed for the combination of domestic duties and income generation, or labored in neighborhood garment shops or restaurants that permitted them to bring children to the workplace. No matter their social class, Asian American women also continued to draw upon elder kin when going out to work (Parreñas, 2003). But, for working-class Chinese garment makers in New York City, who fought a successful campaign for their own day-care center, "the prolonged absence of the husbands due to long hours of work also led many women . . . to play dual roles as major 'rice winners' and care providers in the family," according to historian Xiaolan Bao (2003, p. 289). Filipinas immigrants, in contrast, left children in their home countries to be cared for by others, while they tended to the elderly, disabled, and the young in the United States (Parreñas, 2001).

Reproductive Rights at Work: From Maternity to Family and Medical Leave

The lack of social support for the dual breadwinner/female caregiver model is apparent in the history of state policy, especially laws and programs addressing childbearing and child care. With arguments embracing the health of the mother, the welfare of the infant, and the economic maintenance of the woman worker, the Woman's Bureau began campaigning for paid maternity leave in the late 1940s out of the realization that the United States was nearly alone in offering no such federally funded system (Women's Bureau, 1952). A 1946 amendment to the Federal Railroad Unemployment Insurance Act included pregnancy and related disabilities in its sickness insurance, but covered few women, given the gender composition of the industry (Boris, 2001). Subsequent attempts to include maternity benefits as part of the disability allowances under Social Security proved unsuccessful.

Indeed, state unemployment compensation laws excluded pregnant women (Mettler, 1998, p. 156), while Connecticut, Massachusetts, Missouri, New York, Vermont, and Washington actually prohibited the pregnant from employment for specified times, usually 4 weeks before and after childbirth, without any compensation. Such prohibitions did not oblige reemployment (Women's Bureau, 1960). Women covered by the civil service could draw upon sickness and annual leave for "job protection and income" when "absent from work because of pregnancy." Public employment by the late 1950s also provided unpaid additional leave (National Manpower Council, 1957, p. 339). However creative, such a use of already existing leave reduced the number of paid work days that expectant women had relative to other workers.

The private sector offered some maternity leave, usually secured by union contract. Benefits could include hospitalization and obstetrical costs, cash allowances, retention of seniority, and job security up to a year. Such plans usually came with a waiting period of at least 9 months before eligibility. But their inadequacy led the Bureau to call for more "social protection . . . for employed married women and working mothers" (Blackwelder, 1997, p. 141). Having benefits did not always mean being able to use them. Representing a predominantly female workforce, the International Ladies Garment Worker Union, for instance, reported "less than 1 percent of the total disbursements from local funds have been for maternity benefits." In fact, "most locals do not include such protection" (Women's Bureau, 1952, p. 13).

By 1958, the Women's Bureau (1960, p. 28) observed: "women drop out of the work force when their first—or perhaps their second—baby is born," though those in manufacturing were more likely to return to work after a maternity leave than women in retail and service industries, who actually had left employment sooner and received slightly higher cash benefits. Only 30% of all married women remained on the job after having children (Women's Bureau, 1960, pp. 2–3). Without universal application, private schemes that developed in the postwar years left out those laboring women in the unorganized sectors of the economy, particularly domestic service and agricultural labor. As with public benefits, African American and other women of color found their pregnancy and confinement devalued—uncovered by law or employment contract (Vogel, 1993).

With the addition of "sex" to Title VII of the 1964 Civil Rights Act, nondiscrimination in employment extended to women as well as men. Among the hundreds of initial complaints filed with the agency formed to administer the law, the Equal Employment Opportunity Commission

(EEOC), were charges of pregnancy discrimination, led by women from the International Union of Electrical Workers. They charged that "management forced pregnant women to quit, took away their seniority, or refused them sickness and accident benefits" (Hartmann, 1998, p. 44). Though the EEOC first ruled that a company could exclude "from its long-term salary continuation program those disabilities which result from pregnancy" and comply with Title VII, it reversed itself in 1972 guidelines that defined disability stemming from pregnancy "as a temporary disability 'for all job-related purposes.'" Termination or refusal to hire on the basis of pregnancy violated Title VII, it judged, and "an employment policy which provided 'insufficient or no leave,' and which resulted in the firing of pregnant employees, might constitute a violation" (Vogel, 1993, pp. 65–66).

The Supreme Court, however, was unpersuaded. In 1974 it upheld exclusion of "normal" pregnancy under California's worker disability plan. The majority denied any discrepancy with the goal of "equal protection" because, as Justice Potter Stewart explained, "the program divides potential recipients into two groups—pregnant women and non-pregnant people" (*Geduldig v. Aiello*, 1974, p. 497 n.20). Sex discrimination occurred only by handling men and women differently, not the pregnant and the nonpregnant, the Court reaffirmed in *General Electric Company v. Gilbert* (1976). Feminists responded by organizing the Campaign to End Discrimination Against Pregnant Workers, which led to passage of the Pregnancy Discrimination Act (PDA) of 1978. Pregnancy would be treated not as a disability per se but in terms of its functional comparability with other conditions that impacted on employment (Boris & Michel, 2001; Vogel, 1993, p. 72). After the PDA, the Communications Workers of America were able to negotiate paid pregnancy leave and nonpaid child-care leave with the Bell system, while the airlines finally permitted flight attendants to apply sick leave to pregnancy rather than terminating them (Cobble, 2004, p. 217).

State laws still offered the pregnant special treatment, deviating from the equality principle behind the PDA. Some feminists argued that such recognition of female difference could actually enhance equality in the workplace. When receptionist Lillian Garland, an African American woman, lost her job at California Federal Savings and Loan after taking disability leave during a difficult pregnancy in 1982, she sued under California's Fair Employment and Housing Act that guaranteed job security following such a leave. In the resulting case, *California Federal Savings and Loan Association's v. Guerra* (1987), the Coalition for Reproductive Equality in the Workplace (CREW)—composed of labor organizations, feminist Betty Friedan, and California NOW—argued that lack of coverage interfered with women's, as opposed to men's, procreative choice, for men but not women could both earn wages and have children. Even as they advocated for federal parental leave and called for California to extend similar benefits to all disabled employees, no matter their sex or ailment, National NOW and the Women's Rights Project of the American Civil Liberties Union sided with the employers on the basis of a strict equality standard. "We don't think women are weak and in need of special assistance," they claimed (Cobble, 2004, p. 218). The Supreme Court went with those who would compensate for women's childbearing through special treatment; it rejected employer attempts to deploy the PDA to strike down state maternity laws as violating the guarantee of equal rights (Vogel, 1993).

Courts were more likely to protect White women's reproductive capacity than their right to work. With World War I, government agencies issued regulations against exposure of women to hazardous materials out of the same kind of reasoning that had propelled the Brandeis brief in *Muller*—the health of future generations. During World War II, women's "integration" into manufacturing "largely meant acceptance of existing [workplace safety] standards" that were inadequate for either sex (Helper, 2000, p. 82). After the war, General Motors and other companies formulated their own fetal protection policies, restricting fertile women from exposure to lead. Some firms, like American Cyanamid, encouraged women who wished to keep better-paying, albeit more dangerous, jobs, to undergo sterilization. Such policies narrowly conceived reproduction as biological, without considering the social acts of caregiving that feminists sought to protect. Furthermore, they sought to mitigate against extensive workers' compensation and other occupational health claims. Trade unions, however, protested fetal protection policies during the next quarter century, with the United Automobile Workers bringing suit in 1984. In its 1991 decision against battery manufacturer Johnson Controls, the Supreme Court ruled fetal protection policies unconstitutional, but did not mandate that companies mitigate workplace dangers for both sexes. Workplace poisons, after all, also curtailed male fertility and damaged sperm (Helper, 2000; Kenney, 1992). In finding the company discriminatory, Justice Blackman asserted, "It is no more appropriate for the courts than it is for individual employers to decide whether a woman's reproductive role is more important to herself and her family than her economic role" (Daniels, 1993, p. 90).

Few women on the U. S. mainland, no matter their race or class, agreed to sterilization as a condition of employment or to ease their own double day, though Puerto Rican women on the island had undergone "la operación" for decades from lack of other options to combine reproductive labor with employment. Poor women of color, especially Native Americans, had to struggle against sterilization abuse and for the right to have children, whether or not employed. Forced sterilizations of African American women, uncovered by the Southern Poverty Law Center, persisted into the 1970s. The Chicana Welfare Rights Organization initiated an unsuccessful lawsuit in 1977 against the Los Angeles County Medical Center, which had sterilized women without explaining the procedure in Spanish. At that time the Department of Health, Education, and Welfare would pay the costs for sterilization, but hospitals sometimes ignored its consent guidelines. Into the 1990s, states punished women who had children while already on welfare by refusing to provide funds for an additional child or demanding use of hormonal contraceptives as a condition for receiving aid. (Smith, 2002; Roberts, 1997; Espino, 2000; Briggs, 2002). The lack of reproductive rights for poor women reflected a dominant culture that also harshly evaluated their mothering as defective (Solinger, 2001).

Historians' assessment of protective labor legislation, like state maternity leave, replicate the division between special treatment and equal treatment adherents in the feminist legal community 30 years ago. Alice Kessler-Harris attributed the slow adoption of maternity leave to a gendered imagination that assumed women were impermanent workers; that the cost of childbirth belonged to husbands, not employers; and that mothers ought to stay home caring for children. Protective leaves, unlike policies that facilitate women's rights as wage earners, she claimed reinforced traditional divisions of labor and left poor and working-class women with the necessity to earn without the ability to care for their children. Emphasizing women's right to work and the necessity for economic independence for full citizenship, Kessler-Harris judged efforts by trade union women, the Women's Bureau, and the President's Commission "as much restraint as encouragement for freedom of choice" (Kessler-Harris, 2001, p. 233).

In contrast, Dorothy Sue Cobble stressed how labor feminists reformulated "the gender spheres by revaluing those things deemed female." They too wanted greater economic independence and opportunity, but they argued that "the work traditionally associated with women, whether paid or unpaid, was just as skilled, essential, and worthy of attribute as the work of men" (Cobble, 2004, p. 224). Their support for maternity leave reflected not traditional gender constructions so much as a revaluing of female "difference." Feminist critics of recent welfare "reform" also have argued for supporting women's right to care (Mink, 1999).

Originally introduced in 1985, the Family and Medical Leave Act (FMLA) marked the dominance of the equality side in these debates by speaking of parents rather than mothers. One goal was "to prevent and remedy various forms of sex discrimination in employment stemming from the pervasive and intractable stereotype that family care is primarily women's work and is women's primary responsibility" (Brief of Women's History Scholars, 2002).

It finally became law in 1993 as one of the first acts of President Bill Clinton, after being vetoed twice by his Republican predecessor. Applicable to only companies with 50 or more employees, its provisions were far less generous than those long offered by other welfare states; it initially permitted men and women only 3 months of unpaid leave for birth, adoption, or care of an ill family member, though the leave taker was guaranteed her or his job and health benefits. Between 1993 and 1999, 20 million workers, 40% of whom were men, took advantage of its provisions. However, only litigation secured the rights of men and state employees to obtain parental and medical leave. Congress expanded coverage by extending the act to smaller businesses, but, without replacing income, FMLA could aid only those able to afford a leave (Wallen, 2002; Freedman, 2002, p. 192; *Nevada Department of Human Resources v. Hibbs* 2003). Mothers who took leave or went part-time, however, faced being placed on "the mommy track," a secondary tier of employment with limited promotion and lesser earnings. Leave-taking fathers, too, faced barriers to advancement as they appeared less serious or committed to their jobs (Crittenden, 2001; Dowd, 2000).

Child Care Redux

Government-funded child care during World War II stopped in most places within a year of de-mobilization. However, mothers, providers, and advocates organized protests in Philadelphia, New York City, Washington, DC, Cleveland, and elsewhere to retain state-funded child care. A New York City coalition of activists, some calling for a universal entitlement and others seeking to service needy families, won municipal funding for some 100 centers supervised by a Division of Day Care within the city's Department of Welfare. In California, child care previously available to war workers also became means tested, offered only to families with limited economic resources. But its centers became permanent in 1957 (Stoltzfus, 2003; Michel, 1999; Rose, 1999). This outcome of a multiyear campaign involving parents and child-care workers illuminates the growing public/private structuring of the welfare state in America, where the best benefits come to those working in the private sector, usually in unionized jobs, or for large corporations, but the needy could qualify for some state services (Boris & Michel, 2001). The struggle to maintain publicly financed child care highlights the precariousness of the right to earn for mothers; rather than a universal provision, public child care became available only to the deficient, whose poverty and other inadequacies generated, in the minds of their detractors, a dependency on the state (Michel, 1999).

In the context of Cold War mobilization, the Women's Bureau had stressed the need for facilities to lighten the burdens on wage-earning mothers; it regarded day care as the service upon which such women most depended and consistently called for increased access. During the 1950s and 1960s, it joined the U.S. Children's Bureau first to promote private solutions and then government ones to improve the availability and quality of day care. Beginning in the late 1940s, it spearheaded a coalition of trade unionists, child-care advocates, and middle-class women's organizations to reform the tax code. Congress finally passed their proposal to permit deduction of child-care expenses among low-income wage-earning women as part of an overall 1954 tax revision (Stoltzfus, 2003; Michel, 1999). A congressional act was needed because the United States Board of Tax Appeals in 1939 had rejected the deductibility of child care, classifying this expense as a personal choice and analogizing it to clothing and medicine, rather than business lunches (McCaffery, 1997, pp. 111–114). This tax break marked an important shift: While legislators still believed that mothers belonged at home, they fashioned policies to encourage poor women to go out to work, thus valuing the motherwork of only the more privileged, even viewing child care as an alternative to welfare (Michel, 1999).

During the last quarter of the century, child care was on the national agenda but suffered from what historian Sonya Michel (1999, p. 237) has called "a divided constituency" that stemmed from its diverse forms: for-profit and nonprofit centers, licensed family day care in private homes, church or employer-organized centers, schools, relatives, and nannies. Numbers of child-care slots expanded but failed to match the rise in women's labor force participation. Of children under 5 with employed mothers in 1990, for example, 38% were in child-care centers, 20% in family day care, and 33% in home care with either a nonrelative or family member. In the 1960s, antipoverty programs directly funded some child care, while from the mid-1970s a broadened child-care credit aided the more prosperous while encouraging the growth of private-sector solutions. Labeling federal funding a step toward "Sovietizing" the family, Richard Nixon vetoed the Comprehensive Child Development Act of 1971, which would have increased the supply of quality day-care centers through federal subsidizing middle-class access as well as paying for low-income families. Instead, state subsidy of child care remained tied to welfare; Title XX, added to Social Security in 1974, replaced War on Poverty funding for centers for low-income populations. Child-care provision became entangled with the politics of workfare, as funds were to go to women in job training programs or who were moving from welfare to employment. Under Reagan, however, these funds were cut, as Title XX became a block grant, exacerbating the difficulties of poor women to care for their families away from public assistance (Michel, 1999).

Whose Carework? The Crisis in Wage-Earning Lone Motherhood

By the late 1960s, the expanding labor force participation of middle-class mothers made public assistance to poor single mothers politically untenable (Boris, 2005b). The "opting out" of the double burden of employment and family labor by some professional women 30 years later exposed motherhood as a class privilege, as historian Rickie Solinger (2001) characterized limiting the "choice" to mother to the affluent. Women with resources bought goods and services to lessen or replace their own domestic labor. These ranged from purchasing new technologies and precooked foods and sending out laundry to the hiring of all sorts of personal attendants, from dog walkers to gardeners and housecleaners. Sandwiched between their children and elderly parents, some juggled nurseries and nursing homes. Others brought in home care workers, while those unable to afford care purchased through the private market sometimes left or reduced employment to look after impaired family. In a few states, notably California, Medicare funded the poorest to work as home care providers for their own relatives (Strasser, 1982; Boris & Klein, 2005). But, social workers never allocated adequate hours out of the assumption that family members would care for love rather than for money.

The perceived racialization of welfare, no matter actual demographics, brought with it "employable mother" and work requirements beginning with Louisiana in 1943 and intensifying in subsequent decades (Goodwin, 1995). Additional "man in the house" rules, such as Georgia's of 1949, reinforced male breadwinning and responsibility for the family by requiring stepfathers or any cohabiting man to support children and mothers to request courts to enforce payments from absent fathers. Additional suitable home and employable mother rules in 1952 and 1953 halted the equitable coverage of African Americans that had developed during the previous decade (Reese, 2001).

From 1956, amendments to Social Security encouraged wage earning for mothers on ADC, a shift in philosophy that worried retired Social Security commissioner Arthur Altemeyer as undermining a mother's "right to assistance even if she refused to go to work" (Berkowitz, 1995, pp. 106–107). Extension of ADC to families with unemployed fathers in 1961 further justified "work" or job training as a condition for receiving welfare; additional legislation, as we have noted, funded child care to enable women on welfare to "work." ADC became AFDC, Aid to Families with Dependent Children, in 1962. The Work Incentive Program (WIN) of 1967 further encouraged employment by offering an income disregard—"the thirty plus one-third" rule that allowed recipients to earn more without losing benefits. With this carrot came a stick: States could end assistance to parents and children over 16 if they refused participation in training or "work" programs. The 1971 amendments, in turn, mandated the employment of mothers with children older than 6 if child care was available (Boris, 2005b).

The replacement of AFDC with TANF (Temporary Assistance for Needy Families) in 1996 forced recipients to take any job, even one below minimum wage, kicking them out of higher education as well as making them leave the home. It also limited social assistance to no more than 5 years in a lifetime and continued the attempt to garnish the wages of poor men to reimburse the state for assisting the mothers of their children. From a liberal strategy to increase women's independence, employment had become a conservative weapon to punish female sexuality and reinforce the low-wage labor force. While poor women always have labored, after the end of welfare they lacked any social safety net (Mink, 1998). Providing for their families became even more difficult.

CONCLUSION

Policymakers may express nostalgia for a bygone era in which men's and women's roles were clearly defined around male breadwinning and female caregiving, but that past only existed for a small group of privileged women and even then the labor of care extended beyond the intensive mothering that some now celebrate. Women have always worked; what has changed is the economic, political, and social meaning given to their productive and reproductive labors. While policies and attitudes have shifted, women have remained responsible for the bulk of family labor even if they more often purchase goods and services to fulfill their obligations to home, children, kin, and partners. In doing so, they are merely following the path taken by rural women 200 years ago who embraced the commercial revolution and gladly substituted the store-bought for the home produced. They also are replicating the behavior of the better-off, who long relied on the labor of lower-class women to clean, cook, and care for children.

By considering the historical relationship between work and family through the lens of three overlapping models—the household economy, the male breadwinner/female caregiver, and the dual breadwinner/female caregiver—this chapter demonstrates the remarkably consistency that has characterized women's experiences. It also highlights variations in women's lives based on class, race/ethnicity, time, and place. Taking a long view of the organization of work and family reveals that women have always needed to balance workplace demands with family duties. State intervention has occurred only for those who failed to meet their work and family obligations through the family or the market, serving as a safety net at best and as a disciplining force at worse. From the early 20th century, social policies have reinforced male breadwinning and female caregiving, leading to relief programs and protective legislation structured around the male breadwinner/female caregiver model. With the development of the private/public welfare state by mid-century, the fiscal crisis of the state, and the rise of non-white applicants for public goods, lawmakers became reluctant to fund child care or adequate relief programs. This has served to reinforce racist and elitist definitions of what it means to be a "good mother" by judging the carework of single mothers inadequate if they required state aid.

But, while the state has offered little help, women themselves have displayed great ingenuity in simultaneously undertaking productive and reproductive labor. They have joined with neighbors to share the work, whether in assisting in childbirth or watching the sick or minding each other's children. They have enlisted household and family members and earned income to buy time from less agreeable tasks. They have brought piecework into the home and turned their domestic space into the site of family businesses. They have protested and organized to gain from employers or the state shorter hours, maternity leave, child care, and other benefits necessary to combine employment with carework. In short, they have made their own histories.

This chapter also leaves space for further inquiry. What other coping strategies have women used? How does the experience of the wage earning lone mother complicate the historical picture as well as the present situation? How will the increasing numbers of stay-at-home fathers impact the gendered meaning of breadwinning and caregiving? One thing is certain: Future solutions to what we now call the work and family dilemma, for families, society, and the state, will be rooted in the historical record, even in their response to a shifting political economy.

REFERENCES

Abel, E. (2000). *Hearts of wisdom: American women caring for kin, 1850–1940*. Cambridge, MA: Harvard University Press.

Anderson, K. (1981). *Wartime women: Sex roles, family relations, and the status of women during World War II*. Westport, CT: Greenwood.

Anderson, K. (1996). *Changing woman: A history of racial ethnic women in modern America*. New York: Oxford University Press.

Bao, X. (2003). Politicizing motherhood: Chinese garment workers' campaign for daycare centers in New York City, 1977–1982. In S. Hume & G. M. Nomura (Eds.), *Asian/Pacific Islander American women: A historical anthology* (pp. 286–300). New York: New York University Press.

Berkowitz, E. (1995). *Mr. social security: The life of Wilbur J. Cohen*. Lawrence: University Press of Kansas.

Berry, M. F. (1993). *The politics of parenthood: Child care, women's rights, and the myth of the good mother*. New York: Viking Penguin.

Blackwelder, J. K. (1997). *Now hiring: The feminization of work in the United States, 1900–1995*. College Station: Texas A&M Press.

Boris, E. (1985). Regulating industrial homework: The triumph of "sacred motherhood." *Journal of American History, 71*, 745–763.

Boris, E. (1994). *Home to work: Motherhood and the politics of industrial homework in the United States*. New York: Cambridge University Press.

Boris, E. (1995). The racialized gendered state: Constructions of citizenship in the United States. *Social Politics, Summer,* 160–80.

Boris, E. (2001). Pregnant workers and the road not taken: Paid leave and the social democratic alternative in 1940s America. Institute for Women's Policy Research, *Conference Proceedings: The Status of Women: Facing the Facts, Forging the Future,* June 8–9 (pp. 156–159). Washington, DC: Institute for Women's Policy Research.

Boris, E. (2005a). Changing work and family lives: A historical perspective. In C. Beem & J. Heymann (Eds.), *Unfinished work: Building equality and democracy in an era of working families* (pp. 36–62). New York: New Press.

Boris, E. (2005b). Contested rights: The great society between home and work. In S. Milkis & J. Mileur (Eds.), *The great society and the right revolution* (pp. 115–144). Amherst: University of Massachusetts Press.

Boris, E., & Klein, J. (2005). Organizing home care. Unpublished paper in authors' possession.

Boris, E., & Kleinberg, S. J. (2003). Mothers and other workers: (Re) conceiving labor, maternalism, and the state. *Journal of Women's History, 15,* 90–117.

Boris, E., & Michel, S. (2001). Social citizenship and women's right to work in postwar America. In P. Grimshaw, K. Holmes & M. Lake (Eds.), *Women's rights and human rights: International historical perspectives* (pp. 199–219). New York: Palgrave.

Borst, C. (1995). *Catching babies: The professionalization of childbirth, 1870–1920*. Cambridge, MA: Harvard University Press.

Bose, C. E. (2001). *Women in 1900: Gateway to the political economy of the twentieth century*. Philadelphia: Temple University Press.

Boydston, J. (1990). *Home and work: Housework, wages, and the ideology of labor in the early republic*. New York and Oxford: Oxford University Press.

Branson, S. (2001). Women and the family economy in the early republic: The case of Elizabeth Meredith. In J. M. Hawes & E. I. Nybakken (Eds.), *Family and society in American history* (pp. 72–94). Urbana and Chicago: University of Illinois Press.

Brief of Women's History Scholars Alice Kessler-Harris, Linda Kerber et al., In Support of Respondents, Department of Human Resources v. Hibbs. (2002). New York: Record Press.

Briggs, L. (2002). *Reproducing empire: Race, sex, science, and U. S. imperialism in Puerto Rico*. Berkeley: University of California Press.

Bynum, V. E. (1992). *Unruly women: The politics of social and sexual control in the old South*. Chapel Hill: University of North Carolina Press.

California Federal Savings & Loan Association v. Guerra, 479 U.S. 272 (1987).

Canady, M. (2003). Building a straight state: Sexuality and social citizenship under the 1944 G.I. Bill. *Journal of American History, 90*, 235–257.

Clark, C. (1990). *The roots of rural capitalism: Western Massachusetts, 1780–1860*. Ithaca, NY and London: Cornell University Press.

Clark-Lewis, E. (1994). *Living in, living out: African American domestics in Washington, D.C., 1910–1940*. Washington, DC: Smithsonian Institution Press.

Clinton, C. (1982). *The plantation mistress: Woman's world in the old South*. New York: Pantheon.

Cobble, D. S. (2004). *The other women's movement: Workplace justice and social rights in modern America*. Princeton, NJ: Princeton University Press.

Cohen, L. (2003). *A consumers' republic: The politics of mass consumption in postwar America*. New York: Knopf.

Coontz, S. (1988). *The social origins of private life: A history of American families, 1600–1900*. London and New York: Verso.

Coontz, S. (1992). *The way we never were: American families and the nostalgia trap*. New York: Basic Books.

Coontz, S. (1999). Working-class families, 1870–1890. In S. Coontz (Ed.), *American families: A multicultural reader* (pp. 94–127). New York and London: Routledge. New York: Basic Books.

Costello, C. B., Wright, V. R., & Stone, A. J. (2002). *The American woman, 2003–2004: Daughters of a revolution—young women today*. New York: Palgrave.

Cott, N. (1977). *The bonds of womanhood: "Woman's sphere" in New England, 1780–1835*. New Haven, CT: Yale University Press.

Cowan, R. S. (1983). *More work for mother: The ironies of household technology from the open hearth to the microwave*. New York: Basic Books.

Crittenden, A. (2001). *The price of motherhood: Why the most important job in the world is still the least valued*. New York: Metropolitan Books.

Daniels, C. R. (1993). *At women's expense: State power and the politics of fetal rights*. Cambridge, MA: Harvard University Press.

de la Torre, A. (1993). Hard choices and changing roles among Mexican migrant *campesinas*. In A. de la Torre & B. M. Pesquera (Eds.), *Building with our hands: New directions in Chicana studies*. (pp. 168–180). Berkeley: University of California Press.

Deslippe, D. A. (2000). *"Rights, not roses": Unions and the rise of working-class feminism, 1945-80*. Urbana: University of Illinois Press.

Deutsch, S. (1987). *No separate refuge: Culture, class, and gender on an Anglo-Hispanic frontier in the American southwest, 1880–1940*. New York: Oxford University Press.

Dowd, N. E. (2000). *Redefining fatherhood*. New York: New York University Press.

Dublin, T. (1994). *Transforming women's work: New England lives in the industrial revolution*. Ithaca, NY and London: Cornell University Press.

Ehrenreich, B. (2002). Maid to order. In B. Ehrenreich & A. Russell Hochschild (Eds.), *Global woman: Nannies, maids, and sex workers in the new economy* (pp. 85–103). New York: Metropolitan Books.

Espino, V. (2000). "Women sterilized as gives birth": Forced sterilization and Chicana resistance in the 1970s. In V. Ruiz (Ed.), *Las Obreras* (pp. 65–81). Los Angeles: UCLA Chicano Studies Research Center.

Faragher, J. M. (1986). *Sugar creek: Life on the Illinois prairie*. New Haven, CT: Yale University Press.

Faue, E. (1991).*Community of suffering and struggle: Women, men, and the labor movement in Minneapolis, 1915–1945*. Chapel Hill: University of North Carolina Press.

Faust, D. G. (1996). *Mothers of invention: Women of the slaveholding South in the American Civil War*. Chapel Hill: University of North Carolina Press.

Feldstein, R. (2000). *Motherhood in black and white: Race and sex in American liberalism, 1930–1965*. Ithaca, NY: Cornell University Press.

Fink, D. (1992). *Agrarian women: Wives and mothers in rural Nebraska, 1880–1940*. Chapel Hill: University of North Carolina Press.

Foner, E. (1988). *Reconstruction: America's unfinished revolution, 1863–1977*. New York: Harper & Row.

Fox-Genovese, E. (1988). *Within the plantation household: Black and white women of the old South*. Chapel Hill: University of North Carolina Press.

Frankel, N. (1999). *Freedom's women: Black women and families in Civil War era Mississippi*. Bloomington: Indiana University Press.

Freedman, E. B. (2002). *No turning back: The history of feminism and the future of women*. New York: Ballantine.

Friedan, B. (1963). *The feminine mystique*. New York: Norton.

Gabin, N. F. (1990). *Feminism in the labor movement: Women and the United Auto Workers, 1935–1975*. Ithaca, NY: Cornell University Press.

Garceau, D. (1997). *The important things of life: Women, work, and family in Sweetwater County, Wyoming, 1880–1929*. Lincoln: University of Nebraska Press.

Geduling v. Aiello, 417 U.S. 484 (1974).

Gee, J. (2003). Housewives, men's villages, and sexual respectability: Gender and the interrogation of Asian women at the Angel Island immigration station. In S. Hume & G. M. Nomura (Eds.), *Asian/Pacific Islander American women: A historical anthology* (pp. 90–105). New York: New York University Press.

General Electric v. Gilbert, 429 U.S. 125 (1976).

Glenn, E. Nakano. (1999). Split household, small producer, and dual wage earner: An analysis of Chinese-American family strategies. In S. Coontz (Ed.), *American families: A multicultural reader* (pp. 74–93). New York and London: Routledge.

Glenn, S. A. (1990). *Daughters of the shtetl: Life and labor in the immigrant generation*. Ithaca, NY and London: Cornell University Press.

González, D. J. (1999). *Refusing the favor: The Spanish-Mexican women of Santa Fe, 1820–1880*. New York: Oxford University Press.

Goodwin, J. L. (1995). "Employable mothers" and "suitable work": A reevaluation of welfare and wage earning for women in the twentieth-century United States. *Journal of Social History. 29*, 253–274.

Goodwin, J. L. (1997). *Gender and the politics of welfare reform: Mothers' pensions in Chicago, 1911–1929*. Chicago: University of Chicago Press.

Gordon, L. (1994). *Pitied but not entitled: Single mothers and the history of welfare*. New York: Free Press.

Gornick, J. C. & Meyers, M. K. (2004). *Families that work: Policies for reconciling parenthood and employment*. New York: Russell Sage.

Greene, J. P. (1988). *Pursuits of happiness: The social development of early modern British colonies and the formation of American culture*. Chapel Hill: University of North Carolina Press.

Harrison, C. (1988). *On account of sex: The politics of women's issues, 1945–1968*. Berkeley: University of California Press.

Hart, V. (1994). *Bound by our Constitution: Women, workers, and the minimum wage*. Princeton, NJ: Princeton University Press.

Hartmann, S. (1994). Women's employment and the domestic ideal in the early cold war years. In J. Meyerowitz (Ed.), *Not June Cleaver* (pp. 84–100). Philadelphia: Temple University Press.

Hartmann, S. M. (1998). *The other feminists: Activists in the liberal establishment*. New Haven, CT: Yale University Press.

Hays, S. (1996). *The cultural contradictions of motherhood*. New Haven, CT: Yale University Press.

Helper, A. L. (2000). *Women in labor: Mothers, medicine, and occupational health in the United States, 1890–1980*. Columbus: Ohio State University Press.

Heymann, J. (2000). *The widening gap: Why America's working families are in jeopardy and what can be done about it*. New York: Basic Books.

Hickey, G. (2003). "The lowest form of work relief": Authority, gender, and the state in Atlanta's WPA sewing rooms. In E. C. Green (Ed.), *The New Deal and beyond: Social welfare in the South since 1930* (pp. 3–29). Athens: University of Georgia Press.

Hill Collins, P. (1994). Shifting the center: Race, class, and feminist theorizing about motherhood. In E. Nakano Glenn, G. Chang, & L. Rennie Forcey (Eds.), *Mothering: Ideology, experience, and agency* (pp. 45–65). New York: Routledge.

Hunter, T. W. (1997). *To 'joy my freedom: Southern black women's lives and labors after the Civil War*. Cambridge, MA: Harvard University Press.

Jacobs, M. D. (1999). *Engendered encounters: Feminism and Pueblo cultures, 1879–1934*. Lincoln and London: University of Nebraska Press.

Jensen, J. (1986). *Loosening the bonds: Mid-Atlantic farm women, 1750–1850*. New Haven, CT: Yale University Press.

Jones, J. (1985). *Labor of love, labor of sorrow: Black women, work, and the family from slavery to the present*. New York: Basic Books.

Kenney, S. J. (1992). *For whose protection? Reproductive hazards and exclusionary policies in the United States and Britain*. Ann Arbor: University of Michigan Press.

Kesselman, A. (1990). *Fleeting opportunities: Women shipyard workers in Portland and Vancouver during World War II and reconversion*. Albany: State University of New York Press.

Kessler-Harris, A. (1982). *Out to work: A history of wage-earning women in the United States*. New York: Oxford University Press.

Kessler-Harris, A. (1990). *A woman's wage: Historical meanings and social consequences*. Lexington: University Press of Kentucky.

Kessler-Harris, A. (1995). Designing women and old fools: The construction of the social security amendments of 1939. In L. K. Kerber, A. Kessler-Harris, & K. Kish Sklar, (Eds.), *U.S. history as women's history: New feminist essays* (pp. 87–106). Chapel Hill: University of North Carolina Press.

Kessler-Harris, A. (2001). *In pursuit of equity: Women, men, and the quest for economic citizenship in 20th-century America*. New York: Oxford University Press.

Kierner, C. A. (1998). *Beyond the household: Women's place in the early South, 1700–1835*. Ithaca, NY: Cornell University Press.

Kleinberg, S. J. (1989). *The shadow of the mills: Working-class families in Pittsburgh, 1870–1907*. Pittsburgh: University of Pittsburgh Press.

Klein, J. (2003). *For all these right: Business, Labor, and the Shaping of America's Public-Private Welfare State*. Princeton, NJ: Prinecton University Press.

Ladd-Taylor, M. (1994). *Mother-work: Women, child welfare and the state, 1890–1930*. Urbana: University of Illinois Press.

Laughlin, K. (2000). *Woman's work and public policy: A history of the women's bureau, U.S. department of labor. 1945–1970*. Boston: Northeastern University Press.

Lipschultz, S. (1991). Social feminism and legal discourse, 1908–1923. In M. Albertson Fineman & N. Sweet Thomadsen (Eds.), *At the boundaries of law: Feminism and legal theory* (pp. 209–225). New York: Routledge.

May, E. Tyler. (1988). *Homeward bound*. New York: Basic Books.

McCaffery, E. (1997). *Taxing women*. Chicago: University of Chicago Press.

Mettler, S. (1998). *Dividing citizens: Gender and federalism in New Deal public policy*. Ithaca, NY: Cornell University Press.

Meyerowitz, J., ed. (1994). *Not June Cleaver: Women and gender in postwar America, 1945–1960*. Philadelphia: Temple University Press.

Michel, S. (1999). *Children's interests/mothers' rights: The shaping of America's child care policy*. New Haven, CT: Yale University Press.

Michel, S. (2000). Claiming the right to care. In M. Harrington Meyer (Ed.), *Care work: Gender, labor and the welfare state* (pp. 37–44). New York: Routledge.

Mihesuah, D. A. (1993). *Cultivating the rosebuds: The education of women at the Cherokee female seminary, 1851–1909*. Urbana: University of Illinois Press.

Milkman, R. (1987). *Gender at work: The dynamics of job segregation by sex during World War II*. Urbana: University of Illinois Press.

Mink, G. (1994). *The wages of motherhood: Inequality in the welfare state, 1917–1942*. Ithaca, NY: Cornell University Press.

Mink, G. (1998). *Welfare's end*. Ithaca, NY: Cornell University Press.

Mink, G., (Ed.) (1999). *Whose welfare?* Ithaca, NY: Cornell University Press.

Mintz, S. & Kellogg, S. (1988). *Domestic revolutions: A social history of American family life*. New York: Free Press.

Mittelstadt, J. (2005). *From welfare to workfare: The unintended consequences of labor reform, 1945–1965*. Chapel Hill: University of North Carolina Press.

Morgan, J. L. (2004). *Laboring women: Reproduction and gender in New World slavery*. Philadelphia: University of Pennsylvania Press.

Muller v. Oregon, 208 U.S. 412 (1908).

Muncy, R. (1991). *Creating a female dominion in American reform, 1890–1935*. New York: Oxford University Press.

National Manpower Council. (1957). *Womanpower*. New York: Columbia University Press.

Nevada Department of Human Resources v. Hibbs, 538 U.S. 721 (2003).

Norton, M. B. (1980). *Liberty's daughters: The Revolutionary experience of American woman, 1750–1800*. Boston: Little, Brown.

Norton, M. B. (1984). The evolution of white women's experience in Early America. *The American Historical Review, 89*, 593–619.

O'Connor, A. (2001). *Poverty knowledge: Social science, social policy, and the poor in twentieth-century U.S. history*. Princeton, NJ: Prinecton University Press.

O'Connor, J. S., Orloff, A. S., & Shaver, S. (1999). *States, markets, families: Gender, liberalism and social policy in Australia, Canada, Great Britain, and the United States*. New York: Cambridge University Press.

Orloff, A. S. (2001). Ending the entitlements of poor single mothers: Changing social policies, women's employment, and caregiving in the contemporary United States. In N. J. Hirschmann & U. Liebert (Eds.), *Women & welfare: Theory and practice in the United States and Europe* (pp. 133–159). New Brunswick: Rutgers University Press.

Orloff, A. S., & Monson, R. (2002). Citizens, workers, or fathers? Men in the history of U. S. social policy. In B. Hobson (Ed.), *Making men into fathers: Men, masculinities and the social politics of fatherhood*. (pp. 61–91). New York: Cambridge University Press.

Osterud, N. G. (1987). "She helped me hay it as good as a man": Relations among women and men in an agricultural community. In C. Groneman & M. B. Norton (Eds.), *"To toil the livelong day": America's women at work, 1780–1980* (pp. 87–97). Ithaca, NY: Cornell University Press.

Parreñas, R. S. (2001). *Servants of globalization: Women, migration, and domestic work*. Stanford, CA: Stanford University Press.

Parreñas, R. S. (2003). Asian immigrant women and global restructuring, 1970s–1990s. In S. Hume & G. M. Nomura (Eds.), *Asian/Pacific Islander American women: A historical anthology* (pp. 271–285). New York: New York University Press.

Peiss, K. (1986). *Cheap amusements: Working women and leisure in turn-of-the-century New York*. Philadelphia: Temple University Press.

Reese, E. (2001). The politics of motherhood: The restriction of poor mothers' welfare rights in the United States, 1949–1960. *Social Politics: International Studies in Gender, State, and Society, 8*, 65–112.

Roberts, D. (1997). *Killing the black body: Race, reproduction, and the meaning of liberty*. New York: Pantheon.

Rose, E. (1999). *A mother's job: The history of day care, 1890–1960*. New York: Oxford University Press.

Rose, N. E. (1994). *Put to work: Relief programs in the Great Depression*. New York: Monthly Review Press.

Ruiz, V. (1998). *From out of the shadows: Mexican women in twentieth-century America*. New York: Oxford University Press.

Ryan, M. P. (1983). *Cradle of the middle class: The family in Oneida County, New York, 1790–1865*. New York: Cambridge University Press.

Scharf, L. (1980). *To work and to wed: Female employment, feminism, and the Great Depression*. Westport, CT: Greenwood Press.

Schwalm, L. A. (1997). *A hard fight for we: Women's transition from slavery to freedom in South Carolina*. Urbana: University of Illinois Press.

Schwartz, M. J. (1996). "At noon, oh how I ran": Breastfeeding and weaning on plantation and farm in antebellum Virginia and Alabama. In P. Morton (Ed.), *Discovering the women in slavery: Emancipating perspectives on the American past* (pp. 241–259). Athens: University of Georgia Press.

Segura, D. (2000). Ambivalence or continuity?: Motherhood and employment among Chicanas and Mexican immigrant women workers. In V. Ruiz (Eds.), *Las oberas: Chicana politics of work and family* (pp. 181–209). Los Angeles: UCLA Chicano Studies Research Center.

Shammas, C. (1990). *The pre-industrial consumer in England and America*. Oxford, England: Clarendon Press.

Sharpless, R. (1999). *Fertile ground, narrow choices: Women on Texas cotton farms, 1900–1940*. Chapel Hill: University of North Carolina Press.

Sklar, K. Kish. (1993). The historical foundations of women's power in the creation of the American welfare state, 1830–1930. In S. Koven & S. Michel (Eds.), *Mothers of a new world: Maternalist politics and the origins of welfare states* (pp. 43–93). New York: Routledge.

Smith, A. (2002). Better dead than pregnant: The colonization of native women's reproductive health. In J. Sillman & A. Bhattacharjee (Eds.), *Policing the national body: Race, gender, and criminalization* (pp. 123–46). Boston: South End Press.

Solinger, R. (1999). Dependency and choice: The two faces of Eve. In G. Mink (Ed.), *Whose welfare?* (pp. 7–35). Ithaca, NY: Cornell university Press.

Solinger, R. (2001). *Beggars and choosers: How the politics of choice shapes adoption, abortion, and welfare in the United States*. New York: Hill & Wang.

Stansell, C. (1986). *City of women: Sex and class in New York, 1789–1860*. New York: Knopf.

Stevenson, B. E. (1996). *Life in black and white: Family and community in the slave South*. New York: Oxford University Press.

Stoltzfus, E. (2003). *Citizen, mother, worker: Debating public responsibility for child care after the second world war*. Chapel Hill: University of North Carolina Press.

Strasser, S. (1982). *Never done: A history of American housework*. New York: Pantheon Books.

Ulrich, L. Thatcher. (1980). *Good wives: Image and reality in the lives of women in northern New England, 1650–1750*. New York: Vintage Books.

Ulrich, L. Thatcher. (1990). *A midwife's tale: The life of Martha Ballard, based on her diary, 1785–1812*. New York: Vintage Books.

U.S. House of Representatives. (1953). *General Revenue Revision: Hearings before the U.S. Cong., Committee on Ways and Means, 83rd Cong., 1st sess. June 16, pt.1.*

Vogel, L. (1993). *Mothers on the job: Maternity policy in the U.S. workplace*. New Brunswick, NJ: Rutgers University Press.

Walker, M. (2000). *All we knew was to farm: Rural women in the upcountry South, 1919–1941*. Baltimore: Johns Hopkins University Press.

Wallen, J. (2002). *Balancing work and family: The role of the workplace*. Boston: Allyn & Bacon.

Weiner, L. Y. (1985). *From working girl to working mother: The female labor force in the United States, 1820–1980*. Chapel Hill: University of North Carolina Press.

Weiner, M. F. (1998). *Mistresses and slaves: Plantation women in South Carolina, 1830–1880*. Urbana: University of Illinois Press.

Weiss, J. (2000). *To have and to hold: Marriage, the baby boom and social change*. Chicago: University of Chicago Press.

White, D. G. (1985). *Ar'n't I a woman? Female slaves in the plantation South*. New York: W.W. Norton.

Willrich, M. (2001). Home slackers: Men, the state, and welfare in modern America. *Journal of American History, 87*, 460–489.

Women's Bureau, U.S. Department of Labor. (1952). Maternity protection of employed women. *Women's Bureau Bulletin*, No. 240. Washington, DC: GPO.

Women's Bureau, U.S. Department of Labor. (1960). Maternity benefit provisions for employed women. *Women's Bureau Bulletin*, No. 272. Washington, DC: GPO.

Yung, J. (1995). *Unbound feet: A social history of Chinese women in San Francisco*. Berkeley: University of California Press.

5

Work-Family Policies: The United States in International Perspective

Erin L. Kelly
University of Minnesota

Compared to other industrialized nations, the United States has quite meager public policies and programs for working families and a relatively well-developed set of employer-based benefits for working families. To take just one example, U.S. law does not guarantee new mothers or fathers any paid family leave, while the countries of the European Union all provide paid leaves of at least 14 weeks for mothers and additional parental leave time (usually partially paid) for either mothers or fathers. American students who learn about the public policies that are available to working parents in other countries often joke that they would like to move to Sweden. This joke expresses the Americans' envy, but also their sense that public policies to support working families are foreign, exotic, and not likely to appear in the United States anytime soon. This intuition is probably correct, but the limited action in the public policy realm does not mean there is nothing going on in the United States. In fact, the development of employers' "family-friendly" policies is intimately related to American public policies for working families.

Because the United States seems so different from other countries, there have been two separate scholarly conversations about work-family policies—one focused on other countries' public policies and one focused on U.S. employers' work-family policies. Public policy scholars have documented how little the United States does in comparative perspective (e.g., Gornick & Meyers, 2003; Kamerman & Kahn, 1991; Waldfogel, 2001). This literature is explicitly comparative and explicitly focused on public policies to support working families. Organizational scholars, who study corporations, nonprofit organizations, and the public sector, have examined these employers' work-family policies and programs as "fringe benefits" or organizational innovations. This literature tries to explain what organizational and economic factors lead some employers to provide these policies and programs when other employers do not (e.g., Goodstein, 1994; Ingram & Simmons, 1995; Knoke, 1996; Osterman, 1995). Public policy scholars have often ignored the employer-based system or discounted these policies because they are not available to all workers. Organizational scholars, on the other hand, have generally ignored the influence of public policy on the development of employers' family policies. This is partly because organizational scholars tend to use cross-sectional data on U.S. firms; where there is no variation in the policy environment, one cannot determine the effects of public policies on employers' decisions. It is only when organizational scholars examine employers' work-family policies across time (e.g., Kelly & Dobbin, 1999; Kelly, 2003) or across space (e.g., Guthrie & Roth, 1999; Den Dulk et al., 1999) that researchers can examine the link between public and corporate work-family policies. In this chapter, I draw on these two literatures to argue that we can better understand the U.S. experience—both the limited public supports for working families and the system of employer-based work-family policies—by placing it in an international context.

The chapter unfolds as follows: I first describe family leaves, child-care policies, and regulations about working time in the United States and selected industrialized countries. Next, I introduce the comparative research on welfare states and on family policies in particular. Then, I review new research on whether and how work-family policies affect women's employment and children's well-being, before turning to my concluding comments on this field of research. In a single chapter, some topics and some countries must be neglected. Because most of this literature focuses on work-family policies for employed parents, I do not provide details on policies designed to help workers care for sick relatives or elderly parents. Also, because most of this literature focuses on work-family policies in Western Europe and North America, I do not describe policies in Eastern Europe, Africa, or Central or South America. I do summarize key aspects of work-family policies in Japan, Singapore, and Korea in an attempt to broaden the international comparisons somewhat.

WORK-FAMILY POLICIES IN VARIOUS COUNTRIES

Many industrialized countries provide a rich package of public policies designed to support working families and mothers' employment, in particular. These work-family policies include family leaves that allow mothers and fathers time off from work to care for their young children and publicly supported child care programs where working parents can be confident that their children are in safe, healthy, and educational settings. Other public policies that affect caregivers' efforts to combine work and family responsibilities include laws about work hours (including the treatment of part-time workers), tax policies, and the rules of public pension systems (see also Moen & Rochling, 2005). I discuss these work-family policies in the United States and selected other countries here.

Family Leave Policies in the U.S.

In the United States, some—but not all—employees are guaranteed access to unpaid family leaves through the federal Family and Medical Leave Act (FMLA). The FMLA was passed and signed into law by President Clinton in 1993, after almost a decade of debate in Congress and two vetoes by President George H. W. Bush (Elving, 1995). This law requires certain employers to allow qualified employees to take up to 12 weeks of unpaid leave to care for family members—including the employee's baby, newly adopted child, or seriously ill relative—or to recover from the worker's own serious illness. The most common reason for taking FMLA leaves is to recover from one's own serious illness, with caring for a newborn or newly adopted child in second place, caring for a seriously ill parent in third place, and smaller numbers of workers caring for a seriously ill child or spouse (Cantor et al., 2001, chapter 2.1.2). The FMLA was a great victory for advocates because, for the first time, it created job security for employees who need to take some time off for family caregiving and it recognized men's caregiving as well as women's.

However, there are significant limitations to the FMLA, including the large number of workers who are not covered by the law, the fact that FMLA leave is unpaid, and the apparent ease with which employers can violate the law. Establishments with 50 workers at one site or within a 75-mile radius of the site are covered by the FMLA. Only employees working at least 1,250 hours over the past year for a covered employer are eligible for leaves under the FMLA. Official estimates suggest that only 11% of U.S. work establishments are covered by the FMLA, though these establishments employ 58% of the workforce (Cantor et al., 2001, chapter 3.1). Covered and eligible workers tend to have higher educations and higher family incomes than workers who are not able to use FMLA leaves (Cantor et al., 2001, chapter 3.2.2), even though it is less privileged workers who are more likely to report *needing* a family leave (Gerstel & McGonagle, 1999). Fifteen U.S. states cover smaller employers and thereby broaden access to legally protected family leaves in those states (Gornick & Meyers, 2003, p. 115).

The lack of pay during family leaves discourages some workers from taking time off, pushes other workers to cut their leaves short, and makes it less likely that men will use family leaves. Many employees are unable to afford much time off without pay. Using a nationally representative survey of workers, Cantor et al. (2001) estimated that 3.5 million U.S. workers who needed a family leave in the last 18 months did not take any time off. Of those "leave-needers," 78% reported that they were unable to afford an unpaid family leave (Cantor et al., 2001, chapter 2.2.4). Additionally, among those who did take a family leave, 37% reported that they cut their leave shorter than they would have wished because of financial concerns (Cantor et al., 2001, chapter 4.2). Short maternity leaves have been associated with lower mental health in the first 6 months after birth (McGovern et al., 2003) and higher risk of depression and anxiety, especially when coupled with other risk factors (Hyde et al., 1995). Unpaid parental leaves also make it less likely that men will take time off to care for a new baby, a sick child, or an elderly parent. It makes economic sense for the spouse who earns less to forego her or his earnings and for the higher-earning spouse to stay at work (Gornick & Meyers, 2003; Becker, 1991). Because it is still the case that about 75% of married women in U.S. dual-earner households earn less than their spouses (Winkler, 1998), there are economic—as well as cultural and biological—reasons that men are less likely than women to use unpaid family leaves.

Another part of the economic story behind women's greater use of family leaves is women's greater access to paid leave time. Although the FMLA does not provide paid family leaves, other laws and employer-based benefits combine to provide some women with partially paid maternity leaves. The Pregnancy Discrimination Act of 1978 requires that employers that provide temporary disability insurance cover pregnancy as a disability; to do otherwise constitutes sex discrimination (Kelly & Dobbin, 1999). Workers who have temporary disability insurance receive partial pay while they are physically unable to work. Generally, women who have just given birth are counted as unable to work for 6 to 8 weeks, giving these women—but not new fathers or adoptive parents—a partially paid family leave. Five states (California, Hawaii, New Jersey, New York, Rhode Island) and Puerto Rico require employers to provide temporary disability insurance. Therefore, employers in those states must provide temporary disability pay to women on maternity leave. In other states, temporary disability insurance is an optional benefit provided by some—but not all—U.S. employers.[1]

California is the only U.S. state that provides paid family leaves to mothers, fathers, and those caring for sick relatives (Milkman & Appelbaum, 2004). This program is generous compared to current U.S. policies, but quite limited in its benefits in international perspective. California's Paid Family Leave program, which went into effect in July 2004, provides eligible workers with 6 weeks of leave time paid at 55% of their normal wages (with a cap of $728 per week; Employment Development Department, California, 2005). It is available to employees of almost all firms, but the law does not create job protection for employees at firms with fewer than 50 employees. This means it is possible for workers in small organizations to get 6 weeks' paid "leave" but lose their jobs. Furthermore, the program is completely funded by employees through a payroll tax of approximately $30 per year for the average earner ($12 per year for minimum-wage workers). Employers do not contribute to the paid family leave insurance fund nor is it supported with general tax revenue.

It is relatively rare for employers to provide paid parental leave that goes beyond disability insurance, paid sick days, or accrued vacation time. Based on my 1997 survey of 389 U.S. worksites with 50 or more employees, I estimate that only 9% of medium and large establishments provide paid maternity leave (beyond disability, sick, or vacation pay) and only 5% of these establishments provide paid paternity leave (again, beyond paid sick days or paid vacation; Kelly, 2004).

Finally, there is evidence of significant noncompliance with the FMLA. My 1997 survey, which included both private and public sector workplaces that were covered by the FMLA, found that about 31% of these establishments violated the FMLA's basic requirements (Kelly, 2004).[2] The survey gathered information on maternity and paternity leaves policies (and on normal practices, if there were no written policies), including the length of leave allowed. Noncompliant organizations tend to be smaller, to be located in the private sector, to lack a separate human resources department, and to have top management that is perceived to be less supportive of work-family issues (Kelly, 2004). Because the organizations that responded to this survey were disproportionately public sector employers and large employers and because sector and size are associated with noncompliance, these figures probably understate the actual extent of employers' noncompliance with the FMLA. Furthermore, the survey does not capture all types of noncompliance. Employers may violate the FMLA by refusing to allow 12 weeks of leave to care for a seriously ill relative or to deal with one's own illness; these questions were not included in my study. Employers may also violate the law's requirements to notify employees of their rights under the FMLA, to continue health insurance during leave time, and to refrain from penalizing leave-takers. Studying noncompliance using reports from workers, rather than data from employers, makes it clear that employees sometimes find it difficult to assert their right to FMLA time, given the power balance between employer and employee, and that noncompliance causes serious stress for many employees (Albiston, 2005).

Family Leave Policies in Other Countries

Other Western, industrialized countries provide much more generous family leaves, with more parents covered and much higher levels of wage replacement during leaves. Gornick and Meyers, in their excellent and thorough review of work-family policies in various countries, described the U.S. leave provisions as "exceptionally meager" and "truly exceptional" (Gornick & Meyers, 2003, p. 123). Paid leaves are provided—and the vast majority of employees are covered by these policies—in all the European comparison countries. Furthermore, paid leaves are generally funded with payroll taxes on a per capita basis. This system discourages employers from discriminating against young women workers, because their costs do not depend on the number of leave-takers in the firm—only on the total number of workers.[3]

Yet there are important differences in the length of time allowed, the pay rate during leave, and the ways leaves are divided between mothers and fathers in the different countries, as Table 5.1 illustrates. The first column in Table 5.1 describes the number of total number of weeks of paid parental leave in which workers receive at least part of their normal wages. Pay provisions during parental leaves are varied across the countries and often complicated, with earnings caps in most countries and a "sliding scale" in which lower-income workers receive a higher proportion of their normal wages (Gornick & Meyers, 2003, Table 5.1). The second column of Table 5.1 summarizes the pay provisions that apply to the majority (or modal group)

TABLE 5.1
Paid Family Leaves for New Parents

	Leave w/ Wage Replacement (weeks)	Basic Pay Provisions (% wages)	Available to Mothers Only (weeks)	Fathers Available to Only (weeks)	Additional Unpaid or Low Benefit Leave (weeks)	Incentives for Fathers' Use: Weeks Lost if Father Doesn't Use
Nordic Countries						
Norway	52	80%	9	4	—	4
Sweden	52	80%	0	2	13	4
Denmark	30	100%	18	2	52	26
Finland	44	66%	18	3	108	—
Continental Countries						
France	18	100%	16	2	156	—
Luxembourg	16	100%	16	2 days	52	26
Netherlands	16	100%	16	2 days	26	13
Germany	14	100%	14	0	156	—
Belgium	15	75%	15	3–4 days	26	13
Austria	16	100%	16		104	—
Italy	26	80%	26	0	24	—
English-Speaking Countries						
Canada	50	55%	15	0	—	—
U.K.	26	90%	26	0	26	13
U.S.*	0	—	0	0	24	12

Sources: Gornick & Meyers (2003); Kamerman & Gatenio (2002); Waldfogel (2001).

*There is no national policy for paid leave in the United States. California provides 6 weeks of paid parental leave and five states provide partially paid maternity leaves of 6–8 weeks through temporary disability insurance.

of workers in each country. The third and fourth columns list the number of weeks that are designated as maternity and paternity leaves per se. The fifth column describes less generous parental leaves that are unpaid or come with a lower, flat-rate benefit (Gornick & Meyers, 2003; Morgan & Zippel, 2003). By adding the first and fifth columns together, readers can see the maximum available parental leave available to married or cohabiting parents in these countries.

To promote fathers' caregiving and gender equity, some countries have "use it or lose it" incentives for fathers' leave time. Individual, nontransferable leave benefits—in which each parent is granted a given number of weeks of leave and fathers are not allowed to pass their weeks to their wives or partners—are one way to set up this incentive. For example, in Denmark, new mothers receive 18 weeks of paid maternity leave, fathers receive 2 weeks of paid paternity leave, and the parents may share 10 weeks of paid parental leave as they wish (for a total of 30 possible weeks with wage replacement). After that, each parent is individually entitled to 26 weeks of leave paid at a lower level. If both parents use this time, they have up to 52 weeks of additional leave; but if the father does not use his leave, it is lost to the family. The situation is similar in the United States because the FMLA creates individual, nontransferable leave rights. However, the economic disincentive of losing men's wages seems to outweigh the loss of men's unused leave time in the United States and elsewhere. In other words, unpaid and minimally paid leaves create disincentives to men's use that are not completely counterbalanced by "use it or lose it" incentives. High wage replacement rates, coupled with public education campaigns about men's family leave rights, may be necessary in order to achieve higher take-up by men (Gornick & Meyers, 2003). These strategies have been used in Sweden and, by the mid-1990s, over 40% of eligible Swedish fathers took some parental leave in their child's first year (Gornick & Meyers, 2003, p. 138).

Although all of the European countries provide more generous family leaves than the United States, the policies of these countries cluster into distinct groups. The Nordic countries provide quite generous family leaves and make them available to both mothers and fathers. These policies reflect the commitment to gender equality and to social citizenship that characterizes these countries. The Continental countries provide generous maternity leaves for a relatively short period of time and then supplement that with gender-neutral, low-paid leaves of a longer duration. However, because the monetary benefit is quite low during these leaves, and because men tend to earn more than women, there are economic disincentives to fathers' use of leave time that are reminiscent of the economic logic at work in the United States. As a result of these economic realities as well as gender norms, these longer parental leaves are also used primarily by mothers (Morgan & Zippel, 2003). This type of policy is appealing to "constituencies that favor maternal care of young children" and seems to "reinforce traditional gender roles in the home" (Morgan & Zippel, 2003, p. 51; see also Gottschall & Bird, 2003). The English-speaking countries are less generous, although there is huge variation among these countries' policies (O'Connor et al., 1999). Canada provides a relatively long period of leave, a maximum of 50 weeks, and much of it is available to either mothers or fathers. However, the wage replacement rate is comparatively low, at 55% of previous wages. The United Kingdom provides a higher wage replacement rate during maternity leave, but for a shorter period of time and to a smaller proportion of mothers. In fact, the 90% wage replacement is available only to mothers who qualify for "Statutory Maternity Pay" (which is determined primarily by the length of service to the employer) and it only covers the first 6 weeks of leave; after that, these mothers receive a flat rate benefit of £100 per week for 20 additional weeks (Department of Trade and Industry, United Kingdom, 2004). Mothers who have not met the eligibility requirements for Statutory Maternity Pay receive a "Maternity Allowance" of £100 per week for 26 weeks (Department of Trade & Industry, United Kingdom, 2004). Australia, an English-speaking country that is not included in Table 5.1, provides paid leave to public sector employees but has no national policy requiring paid family leave in the private sector (Human Rights & Equal Opportunity Commission, Australia, 2002; Pettit & Hook, 2002). Australian workers are guaranteed 1 year of unpaid parental leave. To summarize, the other English-speaking countries offer less generous leaves than the Continental European or Nordic states, but these countries are still more generous than the U.S. policy promising only 12 weeks of unpaid leave to some workers.

Asian countries have recently revised and expanded their family leave policies in an attempt to increase the continuity of women's labor force participation and, in Japan and South Korea, in conjunction with improvements in their sex discrimination laws. These countries now provide more generous family leaves than the United States. Japanese mothers who work in the private sector receive 14 weeks of maternity leave paid at 60% of normal wages, while mothers in the public sector receive 80–100% of their wages during this period (Ministry of Health, Labour, & Welfare, Japan, 2004). Japanese fathers are granted 8 weeks of unpaid paternity leave and either parent can take up to a year of additional parental leave, paid at 30% of wages, with job protection (Ministry of Health, Labour, & Welfare, Japan, 2004). South Korea's family leave policies provide 90 days of maternity leave but pay depends on the insurance plan provided by the woman's employer (Ministry of Health & Welfare, South Korea, 2004). Following that leave, either parent can take up to a year of parental leave with a small monthly benefit (Ministry of Health & Welfare, South Korea, 2004). Singapore provides shorter leaves of 8 weeks for mothers, but mothers receive 100% of their normal wages (paid by employers) while on leave (Ministry of Manpower, Singapore, 2004).

Publicly Supported Child Care in the U.S.

Employed parents must find substitute care for their children. Many families in the United States rely on other members of their families, such as grandparents or older children, and many spouses work different hours—"split shifts"—so that a parent is usually with the children (Casper et al., 1994; Presser, 1988). Still, parents have increasingly turned to nonfamilial care in recent decades (Casper & Bianchi, 2002, p. 185). In the United States—unlike many other countries—nonfamilial care is rarely provided by or subsidized directly by the government.

The United States has a piecemeal child-care policy, with different types of government support for families at different income levels (Kamerman & Kahn, 1987, 1997; Michel, 1999). The federal government provides publicly supported child care for the neediest families, although the demand far exceeds the supply. Other families turn to for-profit or nonprofit centers, "family day care" in the child-care provider's home, or nannies. These private-sector services are indirectly subsidized though federal tax breaks. In addition, a smaller number of families use employer-sponsored child-care programs, which also benefit from federal (and sometimes state and local) tax breaks for the companies that sponsor them. I describe these three parts of the piecemeal system of government supports for child care in turn.

The U.S. federal government does not directly fund child care for the general public. Instead, the federal government subsidizes the child care used by some low-income families, while subsidizing many more families through tax breaks. During national emergencies such as the Great Depression and World War II, the federal government subsidized child-care centers that were intended to employ unemployed teachers, nurses, and social workers, in the first case, and to encourage women's employment in defense industries, in the latter case (Auerbach, 1988; Michel, 1999).

The federal government's most sustained involvement with child-care services has been the Head Start program, which developed as part of the War on Poverty (Zylan, 2000). Head Start was designed to prepare low-income children for school, to "even the playing field" by providing high-quality and comprehensive child care to disadvantaged children. A new initiative for younger children, Early Head Start, was added in 1995 (Smolensky & Gootman, 2001). But, many children who are eligible for Head Start are not served by the program; only 50% of eligible 3- and 4-year-olds and even fewer children under 3 are able to participate (Smolensky & Gootman, 2001, p. 243). Furthermore, Head Start is only minimally helpful to working parents because it is normally a part-day, part-year program (Smolensky & Gootman, 2001; Gornick & Meyers, 2003).

In recent years, the federal government has increased its subsidies for low-income families, particularly for parents who are receiving public assistance and parents who have just left assistance programs. The 1996 "welfare reform," which created the Temporary Assistance to Needy Families (TANF) program, removed the federal guarantee for child-care subsidies for parents trying to move off of public assistance but also infused new funds into the system. The federal government provides block grants to states and then states administer programs as they see fit (Smolensky & Gootman, 2001; Gornick & Meyers, 2003). However, "no state serves all its low-income children" and the percentage of eligible families who receive benefits is sometimes as low as 10 to 15 percent (Smolensky & Gootman, 2001, p. 249). Furthermore, in tough economic times, states may decide to cut the TANF funds for child-care subsidies and the federal government may cut its spending through the TANF reauthorization process. In short, federal support of low-income families has increased in recent years, as part of the effort to move more parents from welfare to paid work, but spending cuts are a very real possibility.

Tax breaks represent the broadest child-care policy in the United States and tax "expenditures" were the most expensive child-care policy for much of the 1980s and 1990s (Kelly, 2003). In other words, until the recent increase in subsidies for low-income families, the federal government lost more money through tax breaks related to child care than it spent funding public child-care programs or subsidizing community programs. By 1997, the revenue lost through child-care tax credits was approximately $7.3 billion dollars (U.S. House Committee on Ways & Means, 1996, Table 14-2).

Tax deductions for child care come in two forms. The first is the Child and Dependent Care Tax Credit (CDCTC) available to all qualified parents who file tax returns.[4] Lower- and middle-income families are able to deduct part of their child-care expenses from their taxable earnings (Gornick & Meyers, 2003). The second tax break is the Dependent Care Expense Account (DCEA)[5] available only to parents whose employers have established these accounts as part of their benefits plans. These expense accounts allow workers to set aside up to $5,000 of their income each year in a special account to pay for qualified child-care expenses. The funds set aside are not considered taxable income, which means parents pay less income tax and employers save on their Social Security and FICA contributions (Beam & McFadden, 1996).

Tax breaks provide greater benefits to higher-income families than to lower-income families for several reasons. First, the tax credit is not refundable, so it is of no use to families that do not earn enough to pay federal taxes. Second, dependent care expense accounts, like other income shelters, are most helpful to middle- and upper-income workers (Buehler, 1998; Samansky, 1998). For example, "a person taxed at the maximum 40% rate would save $2000 [on a $5,000 salary reduction]. A person at the lowest tax rate of 15% would only save $750 in taxes" (Buehler, 1998, p. 200). Third, low-income parents are more likely to rely on unlicensed child care and/or child-care providers who are not reporting their income to the Internal Revenue Service; this means they are less likely to be able to use either tax break.

Tax breaks are a characteristically American form of social policy (Kelly, 2003). They represent a "hidden welfare state" in which the government uses tax policy to subsidize citizens' use of market services rather than developing and providing public services (Howard, 1997). Supporters of tax breaks argue that they represent a "less intrusive, less bureaucratic alternative to government regulations or direct expenditures" and that they "work with the market rather than against it" (Howard, 1997, p. 8). These expenditures are generally uncontroversial, perhaps because they are not characterized as "welfare" or "big government" or perhaps because they are passed as part of large, technical tax bills (Howard, 1997). Tax expenditures can also continue indefinitely because they are not subject to periodic budget battles. These tax breaks also have large and diverse constituencies who would complain loudly if the rules were changed. In contrast, child-care subsidies for low-income families are associated with unpopular "welfare" programs. These programs must be reauthorized by Congress regularly, and the constituents who benefit from them are often unorganized or easily ignored by legislators.

Tax law also affected the development of employer-sponsored child care—a seemingly "private" and "market-based" response to work-family issues (Kelly, 2003). Based on my survey of 389 U.S. work establishments, I estimate that 30% of U.S. workplaces with 50 or more employees offered dependent care expense accounts (described above) and about 5% had an on-site or near-site child-care center. Higher-status and higher-income workers are more likely to report having access to these benefits, largely because they tend to work at larger organizations with more generous benefits. Why did some employers begin providing these benefits? Beginning around 1980, the U.S. federal government tried to encourage employers' investment in child care (Kamerman & Kahn, 1987; Kelly, 2003). In 1981, Congress created a new tax break that advocates hoped would lead to more employer-sponsored child-care centers. Instead, the tax law was reinterpreted (by the Internal Revenue Service, at the request of benefits consulting companies) to allow the creation of dependent care expense accounts described above. Companies jumped on this cheap way to appear "family-friendly" and these accounts quickly became popular, but few companies were willing to take on the extra expense and logistical challenges of on-site or near-site child-care centers (Kelly, 2003).

The federal government is again trying to encourage employer-based child-care services. The Economic Growth and Tax Relief Act of 2001 gives employers a tax credit for the expenses incurred in providing child-care services or referrals. Employers may now claim a credit of 25% of their expenses for establishing and maintaining a child-care center (with a maximum credit of $150,000 per year) and 10% of their expenses for providing child-care referrals to employees. It remains to be seen whether this tax break will help boost employer-supported child care, but the limited publicity the tax break has received and the drive to cut benefits costs (primarily health insurance costs, but also other benefits) make an expansion of child-care benefits unlikely at this time.

The United States subsidizes the private child-care market through direct subsidies and tax breaks for consumers, but the federal government does not regulate the child-care services that parents purchase. Instead, each of the 50 states has its own child-care regulations and they vary widely. The state regulations create a low standard—in terms of child–staff ratio and the educational requirements for staff—and they are rarely proactively enforced (Zigler & Hall, 2000, p. 134). Furthermore, family day care is exempt from regulation in many states (Gornick & Meyers, 2003). The end result is wide variation in the quality of child care, both across states and within states. High-quality child care is costly and, in the private market for child care that exists in the United States, higher-income families are more likely to be purchase high-quality care (Smolensky & Gootman, 2001).

Publicly Supported Child Care in Other Countries

European countries have a fundamentally different system for publicly supported child care. In most of these countries, child care for children ages 3 and up is available as a public service. Child care is regulated by the government and providers are either public employees or licensed by the government. This system ensures that teachers have more training and better wages, which in turn affects staff turnover and children's well-being (Gornick & Meyers, 2003; Zigler & Hall, 2000). In most of these countries, the vast majority of preschool children participate in these public programs, as Table 5.2 illustrates. Fewer young children are enrolled, largely because parents (mothers) are often able to be home due to the generous leave policies described above.

Child care is more affordable and of more consistent quality in these public systems, as compared to the highly variable private system in the United States. Yet consistency does not necessarily mean that all children are in the same type of "institutional" setting, with little parental choice, as Americans often assume. Instead, these countries support a variety of types of child care. For example, in Denmark, there are networks of family day-care providers (both public employees and private providers) for whom the state arranges training, the use of community centers, and help arranging substitute teachers (Gornick & Meyers, 2003, p. 219). Many countries also provide subsidies to parents who choose to hire private care rather than enrolling in the public system (Gornick & Meyers, 2003, Table 7.3).

There are, of course, important differences in the histories, current policies, and trajectories of child-care arrangements across these countries (Michel & Mahon, 2002). The Nordic countries provide the most extensive care during the early years. In these countries, child care is designed to support working parents but also to foster children's integration into the society and preparation for school and later life. Because of these dual goals, child care is usually available even to children whose parents are not in the labor force (Gornick & Meyers, 2003,

TABLE 5.2
Proportions of Children in Publicly Supported Child Care

	1–2 year olds	3–5 year olds
Nordic Countries		
Norway	37	78
Sweden	48+	82
Denmark	74	90
Finland	22	66
Continental Countries		
France	20	99
Luxembourg	3	67
Netherlands	17	71
Germany	5	77
Belgium	42	99
Austria*	3	80
Italy*	6	91
English-Speaking Countries		
Canada	5	53
U.K.	2	77
U.S.	6	53

Sources: Gornick & Meyers (2003); Waldfogel (2001).

+ The figure for Sweden's 1–2 year olds does not include those using family day care, which may be publicly subsidized and supervised (Gornick & Meyers, 2003, Table 7.2).

*The figures for Austria and Italy refer to ages 0–2 and 3–6, respectively (Waldfogel, 2001, Table 5.2).

p. 198). In the Continental countries, the enrollment of very young children is less common, partly because of mothers' use of long child-care leaves (Kamerman & Kahn, 1991; Morgan & Zippel, 2003). Among the Continental countries, France and Belgium stand out for their universal preschool system, which is jointly funded by state revenues, parents' fees, and employer contributions (Gornick & Meyers, 2003; Morgan, 2003). The English-speaking countries—particularly the United States and Canada—enroll fewer children in publicly supported child care than other nations (Kamerman & Kahn, 1997). In the United States, the very low use of publicly supported child care by the youngest children does not reflect parental care while on leave (as it does in many Continental countries); instead, this figure reveals the high use of private child-care services. Also, it is important to note that the 53% figure for American 3–5-year-olds (in Table 5.2) is driven by the almost universal enrollment of 5-year-olds in public kindergartens (Gornick & Meyers, 2003).

Like Europe, and unlike the United States, some Asian countries have well-developed systems of public child-care services. Japan currently has a "dual-care system" that includes both publicly supported "day care" available to children from infancy to age 6 and publicly supported "kindergarten" available to children aged 3–6 (Peng, 2002; Council for Regulatory Reform in the Cabinet Agency Office, Japan, 2003). These two programs have historically focused on caring for children from low-income families and educational preparation, respectively, but the government has discussed unifying the two parts of the system (Council for Regulatory Reform in the Cabinet Agency Office, Japan, 2003). Adding together the two programs, approximately 20% of 1- and 2-year-olds, 65% of 3-year-olds, and 90% of 4- and 5-year-olds participate in publicly supported and regulated child care in Japan (Ministry of Health, Labour, and Welfare,

Japan, 2004; Ministry of Education, Sciences, and Technology, Japan, 2003). Singapore has a variety of public and private child-care facilities, and children under age 7 can receive a subsidy for attending any licensed child-care center. Subsidies for employed parents cover about 25% of the average costs of full-time care, while subsidies for unemployed parents cover about 13% of those costs (Family Services Department, Ministry of Community Development and Sports, Singapore, 2004a, 2004b).

Regulation of Work Time and Work Arrangements in the U.S.

Among work-family policies, the regulation of working time may have the broadest benefits for workers. Family leaves provide crucial time for parents who are adjusting to the arrival of a child (and, in the United States, for those caring for seriously ill relatives). Publicly supported child care facilitates employment and reduces parents' worries about the quality of their children' care. But working-time regulations can help allay work-life conflicts that occur across the life course, among parents whose children are young and older, among those caring for ill or disabled relatives, and even among those workers who do not have many family demands. These regulations can help all workers protect more time for "the rest of life."

In the United States, the laws regulating working time do not provide much leverage for workers who want to control their work hours. The central law on this subject is the Fair Labor Standards Act (FLSA) of 1938, and various state laws supplement this federal law. The FLSA does not create a cap on working hours. It does promise covered workers a higher wage rate (1.5 times the normal wages) for overtime hours, but many employees are classified as "exempt" from the FLSA because they are counted as managers, professionals, or executives and paid on a salaried basis. With the growth of the service sector, an increase in the number of workers who are identified as supervisors and managers, and no inflation adjustments on the income threshold for exemption until 2004, "the share of the labor market that is exempt has grown sharply in recent years, increasing by nine million workers during the 1980s and 1990s alone" (Gornick & Meyers, 2003, p. 152). Some advocates in the U.S. argue that it is time to remove the exemption on professionals and lower-level managers (Jacobs & Gerson, 2004), but new regulations effective August 2004 may actually increase the number of workers who do not receive overtime payments.[6]

Current U.S. regulations do not protect workers against mandatory overtime (except for some state laws that prohibit it for health care workers; Gornick & Meyers, 2003). Furthermore, employers are increasingly demanding overtime from workers in order to avoid hiring additional workers and paying their benefits costs (Golden & Jorgenson, 2002). Mandatory overtime can create huge problems for workers with family responsibilities, particularly when workers do not have much advance notice (Gerstel & Clawson, 2001).

Over the last three decades, American families have experienced a dramatic increase in the number of hours spent on the job and a related feeling of being overworked and rushed (Jacobs & Gerson, 2004). These changes reflect the increase in dual-earner households and a growing number of workers (disproportionately managers and professionals) who work very long hours, rather than an upward trend in the weekly hours of most employees (Jacobs & Gerson, 2004; cf. Schor, 1991). The "bifurcation of working time" is built upon the (lack of) working time regulations in the United States. As Jacobs and Gerson (2004, p. 37) noted,

> By hiring part-time workers with no benefits and simultaneously pressuring some full-time employees—especially salaried workers—to work longer hours, work organizations can lower their total compensation costs. The unintended consequences of these cost-limiting strategies is a division of the work force into those putting in very long workweeks and those putting in relatively short ones.

This bifurcation of work hours reinforces gender inequalities in the workforce, given the existing inequalities in men's and women's family commitments. Faced with the expectation that a "committed" worker will put in very long hours, many workers with extensive family responsibilities, particularly mothers, decide to leave the labor force or move into marginal part-time positions. These long-hour norms fuel the gendered work-family pattern that various scholars have called the "ideal-worker/marginalized caregiver pattern" (Williams, 2000), the "neo-traditional" arrangement (Moen, 2003), or the system of "partial specialization" (Gornick & Meyers, 2003). Of course, many caregivers in working-class and middle-class families are not able to afford working part-time or leaving the labor force. Also, this strategy has significant effects on the lifetime earnings of those who follow it (Noonan, 2002; Williams, 2000; Crittenden, 2001).

Part-time jobs are fairly common in the United States and they are often populated by mothers. Unfortunately, part-time work usually means low-status positions that provide relatively low pay and no benefits. It is harder to find "good" part-time jobs, although some professionals and technical workers have been able to negotiate reduced hours in the same job or to work as consultants on a part-time basis (Barley & Kunda, 2004; Tilly, 1996). U.S. policy permits employers to treat part-time workers differently than full-time workers (Gornick & Meyers, 2003; Williams, 2000), in contrast to European countries. Tax law allows employers to exclude part-time workers from health insurance and other employee benefits. The Employee Retirement Income Security Act (ERISA) precludes part-time workers from participating in employer pension plans. Many U.S. states also treat part-time workers differently by excluding part-time workers from unemployment insurance benefits.

Employed caregivers also seek out flexible work arrangements such as flextime (i.e., setting your own starting and stopping time), telecommuting (i.e., working from home or another remote location), or compressed work weeks (i.e., working four 10-hour days per week) in order to reconcile their work and family responsibilities. In the United States, there are no public policies that require employers to allow workers access to these arrangements and, indeed, some state laws on overtime pay can make it costly to allow workers to have a compressed work week (Kelly & Kalev, 2004). Flexible work arrangements are negotiated on a case-by-case basis by workers and supervisors. This is true even in organizations that have adopted a formal personnel policy covering these arrangements because employers have written these policies to leave these decisions up to supervising managers (Kelly & Kalev, 2004; Lewis, 2003). In other words, company policies on flexible work arrangements promise, at most, the "right to ask" for a flexible work arrangement; managers have discretion on whether to allow any individual worker to use an arrangement or not. The irony is that workers who are already perceived to be more valuable and productive are more likely to get approval for these arrangements, while "average" workers who need a flexible work arrangement in order to manage their dual responsibilities and become "high performers" are less likely to win the manager's approval (Kelly & Kalev, 2004). This dynamic, in which privileged or valued workers can benefit from employers' work-family policies while less privileged and less valued workers cannot, is characteristic of paid leaves, on-site child-care centers, and flexible work arrangements in the United States. The private system of employer-based family benefits therefore helps replicate existing inequalities across occupational groups and among individuals.

Regulation of Work Time and Work Arrangements in Other Countries

Other Western, industrialized countries have more extensive regulations on working time, the treatment of part-time workers, and access to flexible work arrangements. In addition to national labor laws, European employers are affected by collective bargaining agreements (which cover a larger share of the workforce than in the United States) and by European Union (EU) directives on working time and work arrangements (Gornick & Meyers, 2003).

In 1993, the European Union passed a Directive on Working Time that establishes a cap of 48 hours per week, including overtime (Gornick & Meyers, 2003, pp. 309–310). France and Belgium have set normal hours at 35 and 39 hours, respectively. In countries with a legal standard of 40 hours per week (e.g., Norway, Sweden, Finland), collective bargaining agreements usually set a lower limit of 37–39 hours (Gornick & Meyers, 2003, Table 6.1). The EU Directive on Working Time also requires at least 4 weeks of paid vacation each year; in contrast, the United States has no legal requirements about paid vacation time and American workers use, on average, about 11 days of vacation each year (Jacobs & Gerson, 2004, p. 22).

The European Union also has a Directive on Part-Time Work that attempts to "eliminate discrimination against part-time workers and to improve the quality of part-time work" as well as "to facilitate the development of part-time work on a voluntary basis" (quoted in Gornick & Meyers, 2003, p. 312). The Directive affects wages (e.g., requiring the same hourly wage rate for part-time and full-time workers in the same position), benefits, and employment conditions and it encourages employers to accommodate workers' requests to move from full-time to part-time and vice versa.

Other public policies also facilitate part-time work, particularly for parents. Swedish and French parents have a right to part-time work when their children are young (although employers can refuse to allow this under certain, fairly restrictive business conditions; Gornick & Meyers, 2003, pp. 164–165). Other European countries have provisions that push employers to allow workers to have part-time schedules and some of these are available to a wide array of workers, not only to parents. These policies allow employers to turn down requests for part-time work in some cases and they do not necessarily promise a return to full-time work (Gornick & Meyers, 2003, Table 6.2), but even a relatively employer-friendly policy provides more leverage for workers who would like to reduce their hours than we see in the United States. Part-time work is also a less costly choice for European workers than American workers, for several reasons (Gornick & Meyers, 2003). First, the EU directive requires equal pay rates for equal work. Second, in many countries including Norway, France, and Germany, parental leave benefits can be used when a parent is working part-time. These "leave" benefits provide a financial cushion for parents working part-time by replacing some of the wages lost with the reduction in hours. In the United States, parents may be able to negotiate "intermittent leave" (e.g., go to 50% time for 50% pay) but, unlike in other countries, a period of part-time work is not guaranteed.[7]

In the past few years, several countries have also begun promoting flexible work arrangements (such as flextime, telecommuting, and also reduced-hours schedules) through employment law. These laws have not created outright entitlements to flexible work arrangements but instead create a limited employee right—namely the right to request consideration of a flexible work arrangement—*and* the requirement that employers allow flexible work arrangements in most circumstances. For example, in the United Kingdom, the Employment Act of 2002 attempts to "facilitate flexible working" by granting mothers and fathers of children under 6 (or parents of disabled children under 18 years of age) the "right to request a flexible working arrangement." Employers "have a statutory duty to consider such requests seriously and according to a set procedure" and they may only "refuse requests where they have a clear business reason" (Department of Trade & Industry, 2003a; see also Department of Trade & Industry, 2003b; Hegewisch et al., 2005). Similarly, in the Netherlands, the Working Hours (Adjustment) Act 2000 provides a right for employees to decrease their work hours (i.e., move to part-time work), increase their work hours (i.e., return to full-time work), or change their schedules (International Labour Organisation, 2002; Hegewisch et al., 2005). Employers must grant a worker's request "unless it conflicts with weighty company interests" like meeting safety requirements (International Labour Organisation, 2002). Australian states now prohibit discrimination on the basis of employees' family responsibilities or "carer status" (Bourke, 2003). As part of its antidiscrimination statute, New South Wales requires employers to make "reasonable accommodation" for caregiving unless the employee is "unable to carry out the inherent (or essential) requirements of the job" or unless such changes would constitute "unjustifiable hardship" for the employer (Bourke, 2003). Tribunals and courts have generally held that allowing FWA such as telecommuting and flextime are reasonable accommodations, even when employers claimed they were unjustifiable hardships (Bourke, 2003).

Other Policies

In addition to leave policies, child-care supports, and working time regulations, other policies affect caregivers' decisions about whether to remain in the labor force during periods of intensive family responsibilities. For example, in the United States, tax law may discourage the employment of people who are married to high earners because each dollar of the lower-income spouse has her (or his, but more commonly her) wages taxed at the spouse's higher rates (McCaffrey, 1997). Many other nations use individual taxation of each worker, so that the marginal tax rate for additional earnings depends only on the individual's earnings. Caregivers are also affected by the rules of their national pension systems. Describing the U.S. system, Crittenden (2001, p. 262) noted that "Currently, the Social Security system penalizes anyone who spends time working as an unpaid caregiver, and anyone who earns significantly less than their spouse—that is, the great majority of married mothers." Many other industrialized nations have developed "caregiving credits" that either treat time out of the workforce when caring for children as years that count toward a national pension or exclude years out of the workforce from calculations of average wages when determining pension benefits (Orloff, 2002, pp. 23–26). To summarize, tax and pension policies are not generally recognized as work-family policies, but their rules can have important consequences for how caregivers decide to meet work and family responsibilities and how caregivers who stay home for a while fare financially.

EXPLAINING THE CAUSES OF WORK-FAMILY POLICIES

Welfare State Regimes and Work-Family Policies

Why have different countries adopted these different policies? Scholars who study cross-national variation in social and economic policies recognize that there are clusters or "regimes" of countries that have similar policies or whose policies are believed to have similar effects for workers and citizens (Misra, 1998). Esping-Andersen (1990) proposed a typology, which has been widely used—and also critiqued—by welfare state scholars, of social democratic, corporatist/conservative, and liberal welfare states. (The terms conservative and liberal in the welfare state literature do not match the everyday usage of these terms in American political discourse, as I explain below.) These three types basically describe the Nordic, Continental, and English-speaking countries, respectively.

Esping-Andersen (1990) classified countries into these three groups based on (a) whether their policies are available universally to all citizens or are targeted at specific groups of citizens, (b) the generosity and quality of benefits provided, and (c) the extent of "de-commodification," or the degree to which "a person can maintain a livelihood without reliance on the [labor] market" (Esping-Andersen, 1990, pp. 21–22). The idea of de-commodification assumes that industrialized nations require that workers would sell their labor, but that more developed welfare states have expanded social citizenship rights so that citizens have basic housing, income security, health care, et cetera, regardless of their employment status. In other words, Esping-Andersen's original analysis associated social citizenship with the ability to avoid paid labor. Feminist scholars soon pointed out that, because women have historically had their employment restricted or denied, state policies that guarantee access to paid labor, that open up traditionally male occupations, and that facilitate combining work and family are central to achieving social citizenship for women (e.g., Lewis, 1997; Orloff, 1993; Sainsbury, 1994; see also Brush, 2002 and Pateman, 1988).

Feminist theorizing led Esping-Andersen (1999) to add the dimension of "de-familization"—the provision of caregiving services by states or markets, rather than individual family members—to his analysis. The growth of nonfamilial child care (provided by the state in social democratic countries and organized by the market in liberal countries) is one example of de-familization (Michel & Mahon, 2002). De-familization is not welcomed by all. Some feminists argue that a "full-commodification model" (Williams, 2000) in which women join men in prioritizing employment over family responsibilities is not ideal and that states should enable familial caregiving while protecting the financial security of caregivers (see also Fraser, 1994; Gornick & Meyers, 2003).

How do the three types of welfare states differ and how do work-family policies vary across these types? Social democratic states deliberately use social policy to promote equality across different classes and, in some cases, between women and men. Social policies grant rights and benefits to all citizens, rather than targeting only those "in need" (Esping-Andersen, 1990). These states have higher tax rates that support large public sectors (e.g., nationalized health care, public child care) as well as benefits paid directly to citizens (e.g., pensions, paid parental leave). Although familial caregiving is supported through parental leaves, social democratic states presume that most adults will be worker-citizens for most of their lives. Work-family policies encourage women's employment, both by making it easier to meet dual responsibilities and by requiring that workers be employed a certain length of time to be eligible for generous paid leaves (Gornick & Meyers, 2003).

Conservative states also provide fairly generous benefits, but the benefits differ by occupational status more than in the social democratic states. These occupational distinctions occur partly because benefits and work conditions are often determined by collective bargaining rather than national policies. The Continental countries that make up this group have been influenced by the Catholic Church and they generally favor familial caregiving over either public sector or private sector care (Michel & Mahon, 2002; Misra, 2003; Morgan & Zippel, 2003). As Esping-Andersen noted (1990, p. 27), "Day care and similar family services are conspicuously underdeveloped; the principle of 'subsidiarity' serves to emphasize that the state will only interfere when the family's capacity to serve its members is exhausted." As noted above, conservative states tend to have longer child-care leaves, which are used primarily by mothers, and fewer young children enrolled in publicly supported child care (cf. Morgan, 2003 on France).

Liberal welfare states, including the United States and the United Kingdom, provide means-tested and modest benefits to some citizens while attempting to support and stimulate market solutions for most people. The receipt of public benefits is usually stigmatized, rather than being accepted as a normal part of citizenship. Liberal countries exhibit a kind of class "dualism" that limits the development of social policies. As Esping-Andersen (1990, p. 31) described it, in liberal states,

> The welfare state caters essentially to the working class and the poor. Private insurance and occupational fringe benefits cater to the middle classes. Given the electoral importance of the latter, it is quite logical that further extensions of welfare-state activities are resisted.

Many in the United States assume that public policies only help the disadvantaged (hence our narrow use of the term "welfare"). There is little recognition that the occupational "fringe benefits"—including family policies as well as health insurance—that the middle class enjoys are also promoted by public policy. The end result is a failure to see how government policies benefit the middle class or corporations and a consequent disapproval of government policies by many of the more privileged citizens.

Comparative Causal Analyses

The typology of welfare states has proven useful to many scholars, but it raises the question: Why do countries adopt the policies they do? Answering this question in a general way is difficult because historical case studies suggest that there are different motives for the same policy in different countries and even at different times in the same country (Stryker et al., 2004). Nonetheless, comparative welfare state scholars have attempted to identify common conditions for the development of welfare states and of work-family policies specifically. Esping-Andersen (1990, pp. 29–30) argued that welfare states develop in the ways they do because of the (a) mobilization of the working class and its coalitions with other groups and (b) "path dependency," or the ways that the historical legacy of previous coalitions and earlier policies constrain the possibilities for dramatic change.

Huber and Stephens (2000, 2001) described four approaches to these questions and noted that all four have received some empirical support. The *logic of industrialism approach* explains development of welfare states by demographic trends that create new demands and economic conditions that make it harder or easier to meet those demands. The *state-centric perspective* considers how state policymakers (bureaucrats as much as elected representatives) promote different policies according to their own interests, how the administrative capacity of the state affects what policies are adopted and implemented, and how past policies influence new initiatives. *Power resource theory* identifies the relative strength of left-wing parties as the key determinant of welfare state policies. The fourth approach arose from *feminist examinations* of social policies that are directly related to gender, work, and family (e.g., Koven & Michel, 1993; Misra, 1998; O'Connor et al., 1999; Ruggie, 1984; Skocpol, 1992). This perspective argues that women's mobilization and the strength of women's movement allies within the state help explain the development of specific social policies. Additionally, Gauthier (1996) argued that concerns about fertility declines and changes in family structure pushed family policies onto the political agenda in some countries.

Welfare states scholars have recently turned to new methodologies that look for conjunctions of conditions, rather than analyzing the effects of single predictors, and that try to identify which conditions are necessary and sufficient for the adoption of specific policies. These approaches move research beyond a simple "If X, then Y" logic. For example, Misra (2003) utilized Qualitative Comparative Analysis (QCA) to identify distinct "pathways" to the adoption of family allowance policies. She found that countries that adopted family allowances either had strong working-class movements and large Catholic populations that supported family policies of various types *or* strong working-class movements and active women's movements within the Left party (Misra, 2003). Stryker et al. (2004) applied and extended fuzzy-set methods to distinguish political conditions that are causally necessary and causally sufficient for various family policies, as well as the relationships between family policies and labor market outcomes. The distinction between causal necessity and sufficiency has important policy implications, as they noted, because

> finding causal sufficiency in the absence of necessity tells us that there are alternative routes to achieving the desired policy outcome. Finding causal necessity in the absence of sufficiency, however, tells us that, although a particular welfare state or family policy is essential for achieving a particular labor market outcome, its presence alone will not ensure that outcome. (Stryker et al., 2004, p. 16)

Stryker et al. found that long periods of Left government are causally necessary for high levels of public child-care services and that long periods of Left government are causally sufficient for high levels of public sector employment.

EXPLORING THE CONSEQUENCES OF WORK-FAMILY POLICIES

Work-family policies are generally assumed to affect caregivers' (primarily mothers') work decisions and family lives—that is the stated aim of many of these policies—but new research examines these effects in detail. It has been difficult to isolate the effects of specific policies (or clusters of policies). Researchers must be aware of the possibility of endogeneity and spurious associations, and of the difficulties in determining causal order. For example, it is quite plausible that generous work-family policies facilitate women's employment, but it is also possible that high levels of women's labor force participation prompt the development of these work-family policies. There are similar questions about the interplay of fertility decisions, women's work decisions, and family policies. Additionally, there are complex interactions between culture, economic development, and national policies. Comparative researchers realize that these factors come together differently in different contexts. Policies that seem to encourage women's economic advancement in one country may end up further marginalizing female caregivers in another country, depending on the cultural norms and economic opportunities in each setting.

The best research is attuned to these challenges, using sophisticated methodologies as appropriate but also acknowledging the limitations of their methods. Here, I briefly summarize key findings from this vibrant literature, with particular attention to how work-family policies affect mothers' careers (because there is very little research on fathers' or other caregivers' careers) and children's well-being.

Women's Employment

Do work-family policies increase women's employment? Or, by legitimating family caregiving as a valuable social endeavor, do these policies instead encourage full-time caregiving? Alternatively, by making it more expensive or difficult to employ women of childbearing age, do work-family policies unintentionally discourage employers from hiring these women (even if such discrimination is illegal)?

There is no simple relationship between the generosity of work-family policies and patterns of mothers' employment, as Stier et al.'s (2001) findings illustrate. Mothers are most likely to work full-time when their children are young in the United States and Canada (two liberal welfare states with fairly minimal work-family policies) and in Italy, Austria, and Israel (all classified as conservative welfare states with more extensive benefits; Stier et al., 2001, p. 1747). Sweden, the prototypical social democratic state, has the lowest rate of mothers who are out of the labor force for many years while the Netherlands, also classified as a social democratic state, has the highest levels of nonparticipation among mothers (Stier et al., 2001, p. 1747). Mothers' part-time employment is quite common in countries that represent all three welfare regimes: Sweden, Norway, Israel, the United Kingdom, and New Zealand (Stier et al., 2001, p. 1747).

Some scholars assert that the various work-family policies may have distinctive effects on employment, and therefore it is unwise to use an index of policies in analyses of the consequences of these policies (Pettit & Hook, 2002; Stryker et al., 2004). Maternity leave is hypothesized to increase women's labor force participation by minimizing the time women are away from work around a birth. High-quality, affordable child care is also hypothesized to increase women's employment and perhaps encourage longer work hours (i.e., full-time rather than part-time work). In contrast, working time regulations and policies that promote "part-time equity" may increase women's employment, but pull even more women into part-time positions.

Research confirms that family leaves generally increase women's labor force participation, but the effects vary depending on the length of leave (Gornick & Meyers, 2003; OECD, 2001; Ruhm, 1998). The United States provides exceptionally short leaves and studies show that these leaves have had limited effects on women's aggregate employment rates (Waldfogel, 1998b).[8] However, in studies of individual women in the United States, access to maternity leave is associated with continuous labor force attachment (Estes & Glass, 1996; Liebowitz & Klerman, 1995), a higher likelihood of keeping the same job after a birth (Glass & Riley, 1998), and a quicker return to full-time work after a birth (Hofferth, 1996). These findings suggest that short maternity leaves affect the details of women's work decisions in the year after having a child, without dramatically affecting women's basic decisions about whether or not to be employed when their children are young.

Paid leaves of a moderate length (less than a year) seem to have positive effects on women's employment rates. Countries with paid leaves have higher rates of women's labor force participation, as compared to other countries and to the country's employment rates before the leave policy (Ruhm, 1998). Leaves of more than a year may actually discourage women's employment (Gornick & Meyers, 2003; cf. OECD, 2001), although these effects may be spurious because countries that have historically had very low participation rates for mothers have been more likely to create long leaves (Pettit & Hook, 2002). Morgan and Zippel (2003) claimed that the recent establishment of long child care leaves (of 2 or more years) has decreased the labor force participation of mothers of children under age 3 in France and Germany. Yet, in Germany, where mothers often dropped out of the labor force for many years, the longer leaves seem to have made employment more attractive to mothers of *older* children (Morgan & Zippel, 2003, p. 69).

There is also strong evidence that child care costs affect women's employment decisions, with higher child-care costs reducing women's employment rates (Gornick & Meyers, 2003, p. 250). Because public child-care services are subsidized, and because the high-quality care generally provided in these settings is attractive to parents, these policies should increase women's labor force participation. Cross-national research confirms that high levels of public child care for young children do increase women's (especially mothers') labor force participation (Pettit & Hook, 2002; Stryker et al., 2004).

Finally, some research suggests that there are multiple pathways to high levels of women's employment. Stryker et al. (2004) reported that growth in the public sector (which pulls women into employment in that sector), a high level of public child care for young children, and generous maternity leave policies are all *individually* causally sufficient for high levels of women's employment. The implication of this finding is that either de-familization—extensive child care for young children—or support for familial caregiving through family leaves can work to support women's employment.

Women's Wages

Do work-family policies help women's economic achievement or create a "mommy track" of marginalized caregivers? This is a difficult question to answer—and the answer depends on the groups being compared. Recent studies have identified a "motherhood penalty" in wages; mothers earn less than similar women who do not have children, even net of differences in experience, hours worked, type of job, reported effort, and so forth (e.g., Budig and England, 2001; Waldfogel, 1997, 1998a; see also Drago and Golden, chap. 13, this volume). While mothers fare worse than nonmothers in general, research also suggests that mothers who use work-family policies fare better than mothers who quit their jobs when their children are young.

To the extent that work-family policies encourage mothers to remain in the labor force, these policies have positive effects on women's wages. A break from employment reduces women's wages in the near term, but also over the long term. In the United States, the wage penalties associated with a break in employment continue for many years, creating significant cumulative consequences for lifetime earnings (Jacobsen & Levin, 1995; Noonan, 2002). Conversely, longitudinal studies show that American women who take only short breaks after a birth and then return to the same employer earn more than other mothers (Waldfogel, 1998a).[9]

A new line of research examines how the wage penalties associated with time out of the workforce and part-time work differ across countries with different work-family policies and different welfare states. Ruhm (1998) found that longer leaves are associated with bigger wage gaps between men and women, with a jump once the leaves hit 20 weeks or more. In their study of the effects of several family policies (as opposed to family leave on its own), Stier et al. (2001, p. 1754) reported that "high support for women's employment [i.e., more generous work-family policies] minimizes the costs of employment interruptions and the transition to part-time." In other words, women pay smaller penalties for adjusting their work around their family responsibilities in countries that have more generous work-family policies. At the same time, Stier et al. (2001) found no evidence of wage penalties for labor force interruptions in liberal welfare states with low levels of work-family support (such as the United States) once occupation and status in the organization are included in the models of wages. This counterintuitive finding suggests that "acting like a mother" (by dropping out of the workforce for a time or moving to part-time work) pushes women into lower-level jobs or positions that then have a negative effect on their wages (Stier et al., 2001, p. 1756; see also Williams, 2000).

Shifting to part-time work allows caregivers to maintain employment while caring for family members, and hopefully to avoid the wage penalties associated with intermittent work histories. What are the consequences of this strategy? Again, it depends on the policy context. In the United States, where part-time is negotiated by individual workers in the absence of public policies promoting or mandating that part-time work, part-time workers are paid less per hour than full-time workers; part-time workers are less likely to receive employee benefits; and part-time experience is rewarded less than full-time experience (Ferber & Waldfogel, 1998; Budig & England, 2001; Glass, 2004).[10] In a comparative analysis of the differences between the wages of women working full-time and part-time, Gornick and Meyers (2003, p. 63) found that part-timers earner 21% less per hour than full-timers in the United States but only 12% less in Canada, 10% less in the United Kingdom, 9% less in Germany, and part-timers actually earn 3% more per hour than full-timers in Sweden. The high penalties for part-time work in the United States are at least partly due to the occupational segregation of part-time work, that is, part-time jobs are not available in all organizations or positions but instead are concentrated in marginal organizations or lower-level positions (Gornick & Meyers, 2003). One implication of these comparative studies is that work-family policies will not adequately address mothers' lower wages in liberal welfare states like the United States unless those policies help women attain—and remain in—desirable jobs.

Children's Well-Being

Do work-family policies affect children as well as their mothers and fathers? Work-family policies can and do have a positive impact on children, for a number of reasons (Gornick & Meyers, 2003). First, work-family policies have indirect, but important, effects on children by increasing family income because they support mothers' employment (Kamerman et al., 2003). Time spent in poverty is clearly and strongly associated with a host of negative outcomes for children, including poor health, slower cognitive development, lower school achievement, and increased risks of unemployment in young adulthood (Duncan & Brooks-Gunn, 1997).

Second, adequate family leaves facilitate breastfeeding, which has notable benefits for infant health as well as maternal health and bonding (Galtry, 1997), and longer maternity leaves are also associated with other measures of child health in comparative studies (Ruhm, 2000). Third, new research suggests that children who spend more time with their mothers in the first year of life have better scores on cognitive tests than those whose mothers worked full-time when they were infants (Gornick & Meyers, 2003, p. 244). Family leaves that allow mothers to be home with their children, or to work part-time, in that first year will therefore be beneficial to children's cognitive development and school achievement. However, unpaid or poorly paid leaves could create additional challenges for children if these leaves cause families to fall into poverty. Fourth, for older children (ages 3–6), there is clear evidence that participation in high-quality child care has a "positive impacts on children with regard to cognitive, social, and emotional development, school readiness, and school performance" (Kamerman et al., 2003, p. 37). The positive effects of high-quality child care have been found in many studies in many different countries. The difference across countries is whether those high-quality programs are common or rare, and whether they are widely available as part of public policy or limited to those who can afford them in the private sector.

CONCLUSION

This chapter has reviewed public work-family policies and employer-based work-family policies in tandem. Although the literatures on public work-family policies and employers' work-family policies have been quite distinct, we can better understand the American system by linking them. Work-family policies in the United States typify the liberal welfare state's reliance on the market and its relatively meager policies for those who do not fare well in the market system. Those who have done well in the labor market are much more likely to have paid leaves, employer-sponsored child care, and access to flexible work arrangements (Deitch & Huffman, 2001; Kelly, 2003; Weeden, 2004), while many other American workers are trying to "juggle" work and family with much less support than workers in other countries.

In addition to the inequalities in access to work-family policies, this analysis of the United States identifies several other public policy concerns. First, even when employees have access to work-family policies through their employers, they are often afraid to use them for fear that their careers will be curtailed (Blair-Loy & Wharton, 2002; Hochschild, 1997). There is a need for more research comparing the career consequences of work-family policies across different organizations within the same country, but one recent study following a cohort of new mothers in the United States suggests that mothers who used work-family arrangements had a slower rate of wage growth than mothers who did not (Glass, 2004). These findings confirm workers' sense that there is often an economic penalty for taking advantage of family policies and suggest that employer-based policies may not be enough to improve caregivers' careers, at least in a liberal welfare state with few public work-family policies. Second, the U.S. system does not provide security for working families. Important work-family benefits are tied to employment (much like health insurance), and those benefits can be lost if a worker loses a job or if an employer cuts back on benefits for any reason.

The comparative perspective on U.S. work-family policies also raises questions for managers, employees, and their representatives. Employers in the United States are more intimately involved in work-family policies than employers in almost any other country. Providing work-family benefits that go beyond what the law requires can create competitive advantages for organizations. Advocates have long argued—and research increasingly examines the claim—that family-friendly firms do better at recruiting and retaining workers, productivity, and profitability (Kossek & Friede, chap. 29, this volume). Yet this system of employer-based policies requires considerable investments, in both money and management time, and these investments may be increasingly hard to justify in today's competitive global economy. Therefore, it may be wise for concerned managers, employees, and their representatives to concentrate instead on building new public policies to support working families in the United States. However, the current system may make it particularly difficult to develop more generous public policies (Esping-Andersen, 1990; Michel, 1997, 1999). Because the current system serves some workers well, it splits the potential constituency for public work-family policies. More privileged workers (and potentially more powerful citizens) are less likely to demand changes in public policy while their employers are meeting some of their needs and less privileged workers may not have the time, money, or clout to win the public policies that would meet their needs. This dynamic means the current system in the United States will likely be with us for some years to come.

NOTES

[1] Based on my 1997 survey of employers with 50+ workers, I estimate that 60–70% of these establishments provide temporary disability insurance. In some firms, however, this is an optional employee benefit and employees decide whether or not to enroll. Women who expect to become pregnant are likely to enroll in this program but those who become pregnant unexpectedly or who do not learn of the program before their pregnancy would not be covered.

[2] The U.S. Department of Labor's survey of employers, conducted in 2000, finds 84% of covered establishments reporting that they provide at least 12 weeks of leave for all FMLA reasons (Cantor et al., 2001, Table 5.1). The higher level of compliance in this study may reflect improvements in compliance between 1997 and 2000 or, more likely, differences due to the phrasing of the survey questions in the two studies. The government survey asked respondents whether they provide "up to 12 weeks" of leave for each FMLA situation. My survey, in contrast, asked respondents if they provided leave and, if so, how many weeks were allowed. The cue about the 12-week requirement, plus the fact that the survey was sponsored by the federal government, may have led some respondents to report adequate leaves when, in fact, they normally provide illegally short leaves.

[3] Employers with many leave-takers may face additional costs associated with hiring replacement workers, training those workers, and administering leaves. However, as discussed in the section on the consequences of family policies, leaves of up to a year seem to promote women's employment rather than limit it. See Ruhm (1998) for a discussion of the economic debates about the effects of mandated benefits.

[4] To qualify for the Dependent Care Tax Credit, the taxpayer must incur child-care expenses in order to find or keep a job. Married couples may not claim this credit if a parent is available—i.e., is not employed or in school—to care for the child or children.

[5] Dependent care expense accounts are also known as dependent care assistance plans (DCAP), flexible spending accounts, tax-free spending accounts, pre-tax spending accounts, salary reduction programs, and Section 125 plans.

[6] The likely effect of the changes in FLSA regulations is currently the subject of much debate, with the Bush administration claiming the changes will expand eligibility and labor unions claiming the changes define managerial tasks so broadly that many low-level workers will lose their rights to overtime pay.

[7] The FMLA requires employers to allow intermittent leave if it is needed for the worker's own medical care but otherwise employers may choose whether approve these arrangements or not.

[8] Another plausible reason that the FMLA had minimal effects is that existing antidiscrimination law had led many employers to provide maternity leave before the FMLA's passage (Kelly & Dobbin, 1999).

[9] Some of the differences in the wage rates between leave-taking mothers and other mothers reflect selection bias, because more privileged women have access to family leaves in the first place, and this was particularly true before the passage of the FMLA (England, 1997).

[10] However, there are positive returns to part-time work, suggesting that part-time work yields better wages for women, in the long run, than time out of the labor force (Ferber & Waldfogel, 1998). The returns to part-time work are about half the returns to full-time work.

REFERENCES

Albiston, C. (2005). Bargaining in the shadow of social institutions: Competing discourses and social change in workplace mobilization of civil rights. *Law & Society Review, 39*(1), 11–50.

Auerbach, J. D. (1988). *In the business of childcare: Employers' initiatives and working women.* New York: Praeger.

Barley, S. R., & Kunda, G. (2004). *Gurus, hired guns, and warm bodies: Itinerant experts in a knowledge economy.* Princeton, NJ: Princeton University Press.

Beam, B. T., Jr., & McFadden, J. J. (1996). *Employee benefits* (4th ed.). Dearborn, MI: Dearborn Financial Publishing.

Becker, G. S. (1991). *A treatise on the family.* Cambridge, MA: Harvard University Press.

Blair-Loy, M., & Wharton, A. S. (2002). Employees' use of work-family policies and the workplace social context. *Social Forces, 80*(3), 813–845.

Bourke, J. (2003). Using the law to support work/life issues: The Australian experience. *American University Journal of Gender, Social Policy and the Law, 12,* 19–68.

Brush, L. D. (2002). Changing the subject: Gender and welfare regime studies. *Social Politics, 9*(2), 161–186.

Budig, M. J., & England, P. (2001). The wage penalty for motherhood. *American Sociological Review, 66,* 204–225.

Buehler, S. J. (1998). "Child care tax credits the child tax credit, and the Taxpayer Relief Act of 1997." Hastings Women's Law Journal, *9,* 189–210.

Cantor, D., Waldfogel, J., Kerwin, J., Wright, M. M., Levin, K., Rauch, J., Hagerty, T., & Kudela, M. S. (2001). *Balancing the needs of families and employers: The family and medical leave surveys, 2000 update.* Washington, DC: U.S. Department of Labor.

Casper, L. M., & Bianchi, S. M. (2002). *Continuity and change in the American family.* Thousand Oaks, CA: Sage.

Casper, L. M., Hawkins, M., & O'Connell, M. (1994). *Who's minding the kids? Child care arrangements: Fall 1991* (Current Population Reports, Series P-70 No. 36). Washington, DC: Government Printing Office.

Council for Regulatory Reform in the Cabinet Agency Office, Japan. (2003, July). Unification of kindergartens and daycares. *Responses for interim report on the 12 prioritized regulatory reform plans: Toward consumer/user centered society.* Retrieved on May 6, 2004, from http://www8.cao.go.jp/kisei/siryo/030711/1.pdf.

Crittenden, A. (2001). *The price of motherhood: Why the most important job in the world is still the least valued.* New York: Metropolitan Books.

Deitch, C. H., & Huffman, M. L. (2001). Family responsive benefits and the two-tiered labor market. In R. Hertz & N. Marshall (Eds.), *Work and family: Today's vision, tomorrow's realities* (pp. 103–130). Berkeley: University of California Press.

Den Dulk, L., Doorne-Huiskes, A. V., & Schippers, J. (Eds.). (1999). *Work-family arrangements in Europe.* Amsterdam: Netherlands School for Social and Economic Policy Research.

Department of Equal Employment and School Children and Families, Ministry of Health, Labour, and Welfare, Japan. (2001). Figure 2-23: Rates of daycare use by age group. *Year 2001: White papers on women and employment.* Retrieved on May 6, 2004, from http://www.mhlw.go.jp/wp/hakusyo/josei/01/zu8.html#2-23.

Department of Trade and Industry, United Kingdom. (2003a). Employment act 2002: Flexibility and fairness. *Employment relations.* Retrieved on May 10, 2004, from http://www.dti.gov.uk/er/employ/index.htm#Flexibility.

Department of Trade and Industry, United Kingdom. (2003b). Flexible working: The right to request and the duty to consider. *A guide for employers and employees* (PL 520). Crown copyright.

Department of Trade and Industry, United Kingdom. (2004). Employment legislation: Maternity leaves—changes. *Employment relations.* Retrieved on May 10, 2004, from http://www.dti.gov.uk/er/matleafr.htm.

Duncan, G., & Brooks-Gunn, J. (Ed.). (1997). *The consequences of growing up poor.* New York: Russell Sage Foundation.

Elving, R. D. (1995). *Conflict and compromise: How congress makes the law.* New York: Simon & Schuster.

Employment Development Department, State of California. (2005). Paid family leave insurance. Retrieved on June 9, 2005, from http://www.edd.ca.gov/fleclaimpfl.htm.

England, P. (1997). Commentary. In F. D. Blau & E. G. Ehrenberg (Eds.), *Gender and family issues in the workplace* (p. 130). New York: Russell Sage Foundation.

Esping-Andersen, G. (1990). *The three worlds of welfare capitalism.* Princeton, NJ: Princeton University Press.

Esping-Andersen, G. (1999). *Social foundations of postindustrial economies.* Oxford; New York: Oxford University Press.

Estes, S. B., & Glass, J. L. (1996). Job changes following childbirth: Are women trading compensation for family-responsive work conditions? *Work and Occupations, 23*(4), 405–436.

Family Services Department, Ministry of Community Development and Sports, Singapore. (2004a). Government child care subsidy. *Child care link.* Retrieved on May 6, 2004, from http://www.contactsingapore.org.sg/overseas/moving_childneeds_childcare.shtml.

Family Services Department, Ministry of Community Development and Sports, Singapore. (2004b). Statistics on childcare services. *Child care link.* Retrieved on May 6, 2004, from http://www.childcarelink.gov.sg/ccls/uploads/Statistics_on_child_care(STENT).pdf.

Ferber, M., & Waldfogel, J. (1998). The long-term consequences of nontraditional employment. *Monthly Labor Review, 121*(5), 3–13.

Fraser, N. (1994). After the family wage: Gender equity and the welfare state. *Political Theory, 22*, 591–618.

Galtry, J. (1997). Suckling in silence in the USA: The costs and benefits of breastfeeding. *Feminist Economics, 3*(3), 1–24.

Gauthier, A. H. (1996). *The State and the family: A comparative analysis of family policies in industrialized countries.* Oxford, England: Clarendon.

Gauthier, A. H. (2004). Family Policy Project (Database and Selected Links). Retrieved on August 31, 2004, from http://www.soci.ucalgary.ca/fypp/Family_policy.htm.

Gerstel, N., & Clawson, D. (2001). Unions' responses to family concerns. *Social Problems, 48*(2), 277–298.

Gerstel, N., & McGunagle, K. (1999). Job leaves and the limits of the Family and Medical Leave Act: The effects of gender, race, and family. *Work and Occupations, 26*(4): 508–533.

Glass, J. (2004). Blessing or curse? Work-family policies and mother's wage growth. *Work and Occupations, 31*(3), 367–394.

Glass, J., & Riley, L. (1998). Family responsive policies and employee retention following childbirth. *Social Forces, 76*(4), 1401–1435.

Golden, L., & Jorgensen, H. (2002). Time after time: Mandatory overtime in the U.S. economy. *Economic Policy Institute Briefing Paper, January 2002.* Retrieved on May 10, 2004, from http://www.epinet.org/content.cfm/briefingpapers_bp120.

Goodstein, J. (1994). Institutional pressures and strategic responsiveness: Employer involvement in work-family issues. *Academy of Management Journal, 37*(2), 350–382.

Gornick, J. C., & Meyers, M. K. (2003). *Families that work: Policies for reconciling parenthood and employment.* New York: Russell Sage Foundation.

Gottschall, K., & Bird, K. (2003). Family leave policies and labor market segregation in Germany. *Review of Policy Research, 20*(1), 115–134.

Guthrie, D., & Roth, L. M. (1999). The state, courts, and maternity policies in U.S. organizations: Specifying institutional mechanisms. *American Sociological Review, 64*(1), 41–63.

Hegewisch, A., Williams, J. C., Burri, S., Vogelheim, E., Still, M., Bispinck, R., Barnett, D., Heron, A., Fagnani, J., Seifert, H., Morris, J., Lochmann, W., & Reissert, B. (2005). *Working time for working families: Europe and the United States.* Washington, DC: Friedrich-Ebert-Stiftung.

Hochschild, A. R. (1997). *The time bind: When work becomes home and home becomes work.* New York: Metropolitan Books.

Hofferth, S. L. (1996). Effects of public and private policies on working after birth. *Work and Occupations, 23*(4), 378–404.

Howard, C. (1997). *The hidden welfare state: Tax expenditures and social policy in the United States.* Princeton: Princeton University Press.

Huber, E., & Stephens, J. D. (2000). Partisan governance, women's employment, and the social democratic service state. *American Sociological Review, 65*(3), 323–342.

Huber, E., & Stephens, J. D. (2001). *Development and crisis of the welfare state: Parties and policies in global markets.* Chicago: University of Chicago Press.

Human Rights and Equal Opportunity Commission, Australia. (2002). Valuing parenthood: Options for paid maternity leave. *Sex discrimination.* Retrieved on May 6, 2004, from http://www.hreoc.gov.au/sex_discrimination/pml/index.html.

Hyde, J. S., Klein, M. H., Essex, M. J., & Clark, R. (1995). Maternity leave and women's mental health. *Psychology of Women Quarterly, 19*(2), 257–285.

Ingram, P., & Simmons, T. (1995). Institutional and resource dependence determinants of responsiveness to work-family issues. *Academy of Management Journal, 38*(5), 350–382.

International Labour Organization. (2002). Working Hours (Adjustment) Act. Retrieved on October 31, 2003, from www.ilo.org/public/english/employment/gems/ego/law/nether.

Jacobs, J. A., & Gerson, K. (2004). *The time divide: Work, family, and gender inequality.* Cambridge, MA; London: Harvard University Press.

Jacobsen, J. P., & Levin, L. M. (1995). Effects of intermittent labor force attachment on women's earnings. *Monthly Labor Review, September,* 14–19.

Kamerman, S., & Gatenio, S. (2002, Spring). Mother's day: More than candy and flowers, working parents need paid time-off. *The clearinghouse on international developments in child, youth & family policies: Issue brief.* Columbia University (http://www.childpolicyintl.org/). Retrieved on April 10, 2004, from table http://www.childpolicyintl.org/issuebrief/issuebrief5table1.pdf.

Kamerman, S. B., & Kahn, A. J. (1987). *The responsive workplace: Employers and a changing labor force.* New York: Columbia University Press.

Kamerman, S. B., & Kahn, A. J. (Eds.). (1991). *Child care, parental leave, and the under 3s: Policy innovation in Europe.* New York: Auburn House.

Kamerman, S. B., & Kahn, A. J. (1997). *Family change and family policies in Great Britain, Canada, New Zealand, and the United States*. Oxford, England: Clarendon.

Kamerman, S. B., Neuman, M., Waldfogel, J., & Brooks-Gunn, J. (2003). Social policies, family types, and child outcomes in selected OECD countries. *OECD Social, Employment, and Migration Working Paper Series, No. 6*. Retrieved on August 31, 2004, from http://www.oecd.org/dataoecd/26/46/2955844.pdf.

Kelly, E. (2003). The strange history of employer-sponsored child care: Interested actors, uncertainty and the transformation of law in organizational fields. *American Journal of Sociology, 109*(3), 606–649.

Kelly, E. (2004, May). Explaining non-compliance: Family leave and "the law." Paper presented at the Law and Society Association Annual Meeting, Chicago, IL.

Kelly, E., & Dobbin, F. (1999). Civil rights law at work: Sex discrimination and the rise of maternity leave policies. *American Journal of Sociology, 105*(2), 455–492.

Kelly, E., Dobbin, F., Kalev, A., & Ammons, S. (2002). *The Princeton–Minnesota study of employers' family policies: A report to respondents*. Available at www.soc.umn.edu/~elkelly.

Kelly, E., & Kalev, A. (2004). Flexible formalization and limited legalization: Managing flexible work arrangements in the new economy. Manuscript under review.

Knoke, D. (1996). Cui bono? Employee benefit packages. In A. L. Kalleberg, D. Knoke, P. V. Marsden, & J. L. Spaeth (Eds.), *Organizations in America: Analyzing their structures and human resource practices* (pp. 232–253). Thousand Oaks, CA: Sage.

Koven, S., & Michel, S. (1993). *Mothers of the new world: Maternal politics and the origins of the welfare state*. New York: Routledge.

Lewis, J. (1997). Gender and welfare regimes: Further thoughts. *Social Politics, 4*(2), 160–177.

Lewis, S. (2003). Flexible working arrangements: Implementation, outcomes, and management. *International Review of Industrial and Organizational Psychology, 18*, 1–28.

Liebowitz, A., & Klerman, J. A. (1995). Explaining changes in married mothers' employment over time. *Demography, 32*, 365–378.

McCaffery, E. J. (1997). *Taxing women*. Chicago: University of Chicago Press.

McGovern, P., Gross, C., Gjerdingen, D., Dowd, B., Rockwood, T., Kenney, S., Ukestad, L., O'Connor, H., & Lundberg, U. (2003, June). *Changes in health and employment after childbirth: A pilot study*. Paper presented at the Institute for Women's Policy Research Conference, Washington, DC.

Michel, S. (1997). Tale of two states: Race, gender, and public/private welfare provision in postwar America. *Yale Journal of Law and Feminism, 9*, 123.

Michel, S. (1999). *Children's interests/mothers' rights: The shaping of America's childcare policy*. New Haven, CT: Yale University Press.

Michel, S., & Mahon, R. (2002). *Child care policy at the crossroads: Gender and welfare state restructuring*. New York: Routledge.

Milkman, R., & Appelbaum, E. (2004). Paid family leave in California: New research findings. *UCLA Institute of Industrial Relations Research Brief*. Retrieved on September 2, 2004, from http://www.familyleave.ucla.edu/briefingpapers/papers/newresearch.pdf.

Ministry of Education, Sciences, and Technology, Japan. (2003). Figure 2-4-1: Enrollment rates in kindergartens. *Year 2003: White papers on the youth*. Retrieved on April 10, 2004, from http://www8.cao.go.jp/youth/whitepaper/h15zenbun/html/figure/fg020401.htm.

Ministry of Health and Welfare, Republic of Korea. (2004). *Homepage of health and welfare*. Retrieved on May 7, 2004, from http://www.mohw.go.kr/index.jsp.

Ministry of Health, Labour, and Welfare, Japan. (2004). *Ministry of health, labour, and welfare official website*. Retrieved on May 7, 2004, from http://www.mhlw.go.jp/.

Ministry of Manpower, Singapore. (2004). *Lifelong employability great workplaces: FAQs, maternity protection and benefits*. Retrieved on April 10, 2004, from http://www.mom.gov.sg/.

Misra, J. (1998). Mothers or workers? The value of women's labor: Women and the emergence of family allowance policy. *Gender & Society, 12*(4), 376–399.

Misra, J. (2003). Women as agents in welfare state development: A cross-national analysis of family allowance adoption. *Socio-Economic Review, 1*(2), 185–214.

Moen, P. (Ed.). (2003). *It's about time: Couples and careers*. Ithaca, NY: ILR Press.

Moen, P., & Roehling, P. (2005). *The career Mystique: Cracks in the American Dream*. New York: Rowmand & Littlefield.

Morgan, K. J. (2003). The politics of mothers' employment: France in comparative perspective. *World Politics, 55*(2), 259–289.

Morgan, K. J., & Zippel, K. (2003). Paid to care: The origins and effects of care leave policies in Western Europe. *Social Politics, 10*(1), 49–85.

National Child Care Information Center. (2002). Reauthorization of TANF and child care. Retrieved on May 4, 2004, from http://nccic.org/faqs/reauthtanf.html.

Noonan, M. C. (2002). *How much does the long-term cost of a work interruption influence women's employment behavior surrounding first birth?* Unpublished manuscript, Department of Sociology, University of Iowa.

O'Connor, J. S., Orloff, A. S., & Shaver, S. (1999). *States, markets, families: Gender, liberalism and social policy in Australia, Canada, Great Britain and the United States.* New York: Cambridge University Press.

Organisation for Economic Co-operation and Development. (2001). *Economic outlook.* Paris: OECD.

Organisation for Economic Co-operation and Development. (2003). *Babies and bosses: Reconciling work and family life.* Paris: OECD.

Orloff, A. S. (1993). Gender and the social rights of citizenship: The comparative analysis of gender relations and welfare states. *American Sociological Review, 58*(3), 303–328.

Orloff, A. S. (2002). Women's employment and welfare regimes: Globalization, export orientation and social policy in Europe and North America (Social Policy and Development, Programme Paper Number 12). Geneva: United Nations Research Institute for Social Development.

Osterman, P. (1995). Work/family programs and the employment relationship. *Administrative Science Quarterly, 40*(4), 681–700.

Pateman, C. (Ed.). (1988). *Democracy and the state.* Princeton, NJ: Princeton University Press.

Peng, I. (2002). Gender and generation: Japanese child care and the demographic crisis. In S. Michel & R. Mahon (Eds.), *Child care policy at the crossroads: Gender and welfare state restructuring* (pp. 31–56). New York: Routledge.

Pettit, E., & Hook, J. (2002). The structure of women's employment in comparative perspective. Paper presented at the Population Association of America's Annual Meeting, Atlanta, GA, May 8–10, 2002.

Presser, H. B. (1988). Shift work and child care among young dual-earner American parents. *Journal of Marriage and the Family, 50*(1), 133–148.

Ruggie, M. (1984). *The state and working women.* Princeton, NJ: Princeton University Press.

Ruhm, C. (1998). The economic consequences of parental leave mandates: Lessons from Europe. *Quarterly Journal of Economics, 113*(1), 285–317.

Ruhm, C. (2000). Parental leave and child health. *Journal of Health Economics, 19*(6), 931–960.

Sainsbury, D. (Ed.). (1994). *Gendering welfare states.* London; Thousand Oaks, CA: Sage.

Samansky, A. J. (1998). Childcare expenses and the income tax. *Florida Law Review, 50,* 245–294.

Schor, J. (1991). *The overworked American.* New York: Basic Books.

Skocpol, T. (1992). *Protecting soldiers and mothers: The political origins of social policy in the United States.* Cambridge: Harvard University Press.

Smolensky, E., & Gootman, J. A. (Eds.). (2001). *Working families and growing kids: Caring for children and adolescents.* Washington, DC: National Academies Press.

Stier, H., Lewis-Epstein, N., & Braun, M. (2001). Welfare regimes, family supportive policies, and women's employment along the life course. *American Journal of Sociology, 106*(6), 1731–1760.

Stryker, R., Eliagon, S., & Tranby, E. (2004). The welfare state, family policies, and women's labor force participation: A fuzzy-set analysis. Paper presented at the RC-19 Annual Meeting, September 3–7, 2004, Paris.

Tilly, C. (1996). *Half a job: Bad and good part-time jobs in a changing labor market.* Philadelphia: Temple University Press.

U.S. House Committee on Ways and Means. (1996). 104st Congress, 2d sess. *Background material and data on major programs within the jurisdiction of the Committee on Way and Means.* Washington, D.C.: Government Publication Office.

Waldfogel, J. (1997). The effect of children on women's wages. *American Sociological Review, 62,* 209–217.

Waldfogel, J. (1998a). Understanding the "family gap" in pay for women with children. *Journal of Economic Perspectives, 12,* 137–156.

Waldfogel, J. (1998b). The family gap for young women in the United States and Britain: Can maternity leave make a difference? *Journal of Labor Economics, 16,* 505–546.

Waldfogel, J. (2001). International policies toward parental leave and child care. *The Future of Children, 11*(1), 99–111.

Weeden, K. (2004). Is there a flexiglass ceiling? Flexible work arrangements and wages in the United States. *Social Science Research, 34*(2), 454–482.

Williams, J. (2000). *Unbending gender: Why family and work conflict and what to do about it.* Oxford; New York: Oxford University Press.

Winkler, A. E. (1998). Earnings of husbands and wives in dual-earning families. *Monthly Labor Review, April,* 42–48.

Zigler, E. F., & Hall, N. W. (2000). *Child development and social policy.* Boston: McGraw-Hill.

Zylan, Y. (2000). Maternalism redefined: Gender, the state, and the politics of day care, 1945–1962. *Gender and Society, 14*(5), 608–629.

6

Demographic Implications for Work-Family Research

Martha Farnsworth Riche
Cornell University

As the science of the study of populations, demography is essentially a cross-disciplinary field and thus has much to offer work-family researchers. In its most basic form, demography starts with two related informational efforts: It counts people and it places them, either where they live or where they work.[1] Thus, demography brings geographic as well as social and economic dimensions to the study of work and family. This allows other disciplines to analyze the relationship between such important factors as transportation and/or housing and work issues, or early childhood education and maternal employment.

Demography is also a data-intensive discipline, and this offers both advantages and disadvantages to work and family research. The advantages are obvious: identifying, quantifying, and geographically locating populations with concerns and issues that call for policy and program attention as well as research interest. The disadvantages are subtle and arise largely from the long lag between perceiving a need for information and acquiring it. As a rule of thumb, it takes about 20 years to make a major change in data collection. And, it takes much longer if the change is politically controversial.[2]

For instance, demographers find that not all families with work conflicts are reflected in the data currently available for research, as political forces resist broadening the notion of family, say to include unmarried or same-sex parents, even for statistical purposes. The notion of "work" is also undergoing change, but because "family" has religious and social meanings that go beyond a research construct, the barriers to revising family measures are much higher.

In short, demography is largely a descriptive discipline, testing theories and assumptions developed within other disciplines, especially sociology and economics, using the large databases developed by the federal government for measuring the population and changes in it that are important for public policies and programs. In so doing, it uncovers new developments for other disciplines to examine, and thus propose or design new public policies. Work-family conflict is a current example of the ongoing interaction between research and policy. Thus, this chapter focuses on issues in measuring both work and family, as well as on trends that current data suggest for work-family conflict.

125

DATA AND TRENDS: FAMILY

What Is a Family?

Defining the "family" may seem obvious, but the history of family measures in the United States shows that the definition is not fixed. The Latin word *familia* came originally from an Indo-European word meaning "house," and thus included everyone living together, whether they were related or not (Gies & Gies, 1987). In our early, primarily agricultural history, U.S. family measures included everyone living together: blood relatives, people related by marriage, farm employees, servants, and slaves (the latter counting as three/fifths of a person). In modern times, this inclusive residential definition is now labeled a "household." Households of people who are not related by blood or marriage are "nonfamily households," and currently account for nearly a third of all households (U.S. Census Bureau, 2003a). More than twice as many households consist of people related by blood or marriage: "family households."[3].

Though official household and family data assume that families are co-resident, in reality the "family" often encompasses an individual's living relations (by marriage and/or by blood) who live somewhere else. For work-family issues, this broader definition could be particularly relevant. Currently, nearly 7 in 10 children live in the "traditional family" as measured by official data, that is, the nuclear family of a married couple and their minor children living together (U.S. Census Bureau, 2003a). (In a minority of such families, one member of the couple is a stepparent, rather than a biological parent.) That leaves more than 3 in 10 children in some other living arrangement, most often a single-parent household. So for work-family issues, it can be important to know whether nonresident family members such as a divorced parent are involved, whether in terms of care or money. Or, whether others resident in the household might actually be a parent, not married to but cohabiting with the householder.[4]

For example, residence rules designed to prevent double counting oblige official measures to place children who routinely live in more than one family household (as happens in joint custody arrangements) in one household only for counting purposes, thus distorting the work/family portrait. Other, smaller public data sets provide some information about help by nonresident family members, notably the Census Bureau's Survey of Income and Program Participation that produces data every few years on who is minding the nation's children. The most recent data, for 1999, show that 45% of preschool children whose mothers are employed are being minded by a grandparent, sibling, or other relative, while nearly 30% are being cared for by the other parent, wherever they live (U.S. Census Bureau, 2003b).

Most public data sets observe the Census Bureau's residentially based definition of a family: "a group of two persons or more . . . related by birth, marriage, or adoption and residing together."[5] Some data sets created by research institutions (and funded by the federal government) allow for alternative definitions of the family, such as parents who live together but are not married, while others do not. This chapter uses standard demographic data sets, that is, sets that can be disaggregated by such demographic characteristics as age and race, and thus observes the official definition. It would be helpful to have a complete demographic picture of families in relation to work issues, one that would include nonresident family members, but this is not possible with cross-sectional public demographic data sets as they are currently constructed.[6]

Family Trends

The population exposed to work/family conflicts consists largely of families with dependent children under age 15 that have no full-time stay-at-home parent. (This cut-off assumes that children under age 15 need supervision during nonschool time.) Some are two-worker married couples, while others are single parents.[7] Adult family members may also need care from working relatives, whether they are resident or nonresident, but the duration of the need for care tends to be short relative to children's needs, and there tend to be more family members available for caregiving. Thus, this chapter will thus focus primarily on the population that is simultaneously working and raising children.

Work/family issues contribute to determining the population of working parents because these issues influence people's choices about whether to have children, how many to have, and the timing between births (which, in turn, can influence the number of children people eventually have). Most notably, fertility has been decreasing around the world in recent decades while women have entered the workforce in increasing numbers. This trend is resulting in a corollary to the principal theory that demography has developed as a discipline, called the "demographic transition."

The demographic transition, which is still going on in many developing countries, involves decreases from very high fertility levels. This transition begins when public health improves so much that children routinely survive into adulthood. Thus, the child survival rate is a fundamental demographic measure in that it predicts future levels of fertility: People have many more children when they expect that some will die in childhood. It takes at least two decades for prospective parents to begin to perceive that this expectation is no longer valid, and to reduce their fertility accordingly—the second stage in the transition. Demographic theory holds that once the transition is complete, the average family will consist of two children, setting fertility at "the replacement rate," that is, the two children will "replace" the two parents. In 2004, the transition had taken place in more than one third of all countries—containing 43% of the world's people—and was well underway in most other countries (PRB, 2004).

The new development, taking place largely in industrialized countries but also in countries where economic development is proceeding, involves decreases in fertility to below the re-placement rate, that is, to families with one child instead of two, or two instead of three, as well as childless families. Demographers are calling this "the second demographic transition." Researchers have identified many interrelated reasons for this unprecedented decline, and their relative importance varies from country to country, depending on the policies and programs in place as well as cultural differences in family structure and behavior. However, they sum up to the impact of "modernization" and a related increase in the costs of raising children, as conceptualized by economic theory.

On the one hand, parents' rising expectations for their children cause them to incur greater direct expenses, such as the cost of college tuition. On the other hand, women's growing value in the workplace increases the indirect opportunity costs of a reduced or foregone work effort to care for children. As a result, fertility rates have plunged in many countries to record lows, and one-child families have become common in such countries as Germany, Spain, and Japan, where current fertility rates are 1.3 children per woman between the ages of 15 and 44—well below the two-child average that demographic theory posits.

For work-family policy development, it is important to understand why and how the United States has been marked less by this trend than other industrialized countries. In 2002, American women were estimated to be having an average of two children (2.01) over their lifetime, slightly below the rate necessary for replacing the population (Martin et al., 2003). Hispanics were the only population subgroup with a total fertility rate (TFR) above replacement level in 2001—2.7 children over a lifetime, though non-Hispanic Blacks had a rate (2.05) very close to replacement level.[8] Both Asian and Pacific Islander and non-Hispanic White women had a TFR of 1.8, while American Indian women had the lowest TFR of 1.7.

There are many possible explanations for the relatively high U.S. fertility rate—one is the varied racial and ethnic makeup of the population compared to more homogeneous populations elsewhere. However, the fertility rate of the majority non-Hispanic White population is also relatively high, and on a par with rates among Northern European populations that, like the United States, have displayed some flexibility vis-à-vis the growth of work/family conflicts, whether extending shopping hours to accommodate working people, intensifying men's parenting contribution, or making employment practices more flexible.

Nevertheless, work/family issues are clearly part of the explanation for lower fertility rates in the United States as well as elsewhere. According to Census Bureau estimates, American women 40 to 44 years old in 2002 will probably end their childbearing years with an average of 1.9 children, more than one child fewer than the 3.1 average for women in this same age group in 1976 (U.S. Census Bureau, 2003c). Perhaps more revealing, the share of American women who are ending their fertile years childless has nearly doubled over the past quarter century. Among women 40 to 44 years old in 2002, 18% were childless, compared to 10% among women who were the same age in 1976 (U.S. Census Bureau, 2003c). Because birth expectations surveys indicated that most of these women wanted children, and more than one child, when they began their adult lives, a change has clearly taken place.

Tellingly, during the 1990s, the long-standing correlation between maternal employment and fertility reversed in the United States, largely for higher income women (Rindfuss, Guzzo, & Morgan, 2003). McLanahan (2004) argued that women who gain higher education also gain greater resources for parenting in multiple, mutually reinforcing ways. They delay marriage and parenting, thus increasing both their income-earning capacity and their attraction as marital partners for more educated, higher earning men. These are also the men who generally display more egalitarian gender attitudes, and these later formed unions are generally more stable (McLanahan, 2004). Thus, these mothers have more maternal security across a range of dimensions: more individual maturity, more stable unions, the availability of a second income, a partner who is more willing to share domestic work, and a father who is more engaged (in terms of presence, time spent, etc.) with the children.

However, work-family conflicts are still extreme for women who are responsible for providing much or all of their security, and their children's. Low incomes require mothers to work, whether or not a husband or partner is present. Meanwhile, low-income men tend to have more traditional gender role attitudes and thus bear less of the domestic work as well as spend less time with their children, assuming they are present at all (McLanahan, 2004). Thus, for the majority of American women, that is, those who are in low-income households and/or those who are single parents, children and work are still relatively incompatible. This is also true for the relatively small numbers of low-income men who are single parents. Indeed, the difficulty of combining work and family responsibilities may well contribute to the relative low share of single parents who are men.

Given these trends, it is surprising that U.S. fertility is so high compared to other industrial countries. Demographers generally attribute this difference to greater societal flexibility in the United States. The term "societal flexibility" refers to the willingness of communities and individuals to modify established practices and behaviors in response to socioeconomic changes. Perhaps the most important reason for the difference in fertility between industrialized countries is the relative degree of acceptance of nonmarital childbearing. Americans (and most Northern European countries) tolerate nonmarital childbearing, even though they might not favor it, while very low-fertility countries like Italy and Japan do not. In other words, in the former, relatively high-fertility countries, children are more important to society than marriage while very low-fertility countries prioritize marriage. Another important difference relates to society's willingness to make changes to accommodate working parents, particularly mothers. For instance, relatively high-fertility countries like the United States and Northern European countries have adopted important changes such as shopping hours outside the standard workday, while very low-fertility countries like Germany have not been willing to make such changes.

Reflecting these relatively high fertility rates, in 2003 nearly a third of U.S. households contained one or more children under age 18 (U.S. Census Bureau, 2003a).

Total households	111,298,027
Without children	75,814,194
With children	35,483,833

Many childless households consist of people living alone, or with nonrelatives, so for the purposes of this chapter, family households are more relevant. Family households include both married couples and householders with no spouse (present), with and without children. In 2003 the Census Bureau found this picture:

Number of children	none	one	two	three+
Married couples	5,185,012	32,196,168	10,177,105	10,842,188
Male, no spouse present	144,596	2,569,978	1,178,682	532,223
Female, no spouse present	985,893	5,585,248	4,041,290	2,396,843

(U.S. Census Bureau, 2003a)

Note: This tabulation excludes children living in the households of other relatives, most often grand parents.

These data suggest several things to work and family researchers. First, the proportion of families currently raising children continues to decline relative to the numbers of families, and households, as a whole. In part this is due to the small size of families, allied to the increase in Americans' life expectancy. With only two children, on average, and longer lives, Americans have an increasing number of years without children in the home. By one recent estimate, the average American, male or female, spends just over a third of the ages between 20 and 70 raising children (King, 1999).[9]

Second, with fewer children in the home, there is less competition among them for parents' time. One researcher has found that thanks to this shift, today's children get, on average, a few minutes more time a week with mothers than they did when a much smaller proportion of mothers were in the workforce (Bianchi, 2000). And, they get a lot more time from working fathers, at least within married couples, while stay-at-home mothers spend the bulk of their additional nonwork time in housework.

Third, work/family conflict is almost guaranteed for women and men who are raising children on their own. In particular, female-headed families are more likely to contain children than other family types—and much less likely to contain another earner or caretaker, especially one who is engaged with the children.

Finally, avoiding a work/family challenge is most likely for married couples that are able and willing to forego one partner's income. Among women aged 25 to 34 in 2000, one third of married mothers were not in the labor force, compared to one fifth of mothers (never-married, separated, formerly married) who maintained their own household. Mothers who were living with a parent or other relative were also less likely to be in the workforce (Costello, Wight, & Stone, 2002). Nevertheless, compared with 1975, fewer women were stay-at-home mothers regardless of household or family type.

Looking ahead, the population is expected to increase largely among households without children, as increasing life expectancy continues to grow the number of Americans over age 45. In 2015, only 27% of U.S. households are expected to contain dependent children, and their numbers will be little changed from 2003 (Farnsworth Riche Associates, 2003).

Of course, it is always possible that Americans might decide to create another "baby boom," and have three or more children per woman instead of the current average of two. However, the circumstances that produced the "baby boom," were unusual, beginning with the pent-up demand for children following World War II and extended by the effects of the postwar GI Bill, which increased the educational level of young American men relative to their wives. Indeed, it might be fair to say that the relative absence of work/family conflicts in the post-World War II period contributed to the "baby boom." With so many returned veterans using their educational benefits to move from blue-collar jobs into salaried employment, it was cost-effective for their less-educated wives to stay home to take care of the children, rather than trying to hold a (most likely low-paid) job simultaneously. Now that women account for a slight majority of college students, the opportunity costs to them of staying out of the workplace, particularly to raise more than two children, are much higher.

Thus, these projections assume that American women will continue to have an average of around two children. That makes the decline in the share of families with children, in the face of modest growth in numbers, entirely due to the aging of the population as a result of continued improvements in mortality. Put simply, an increasing share of the population, including the working-age population, has raised its children. Whether as employers, managers, or taxpayers, this "empty-nest" population will have a great say in how the United States addresses work/family issues.

Meanwhile, we can expect the aging of the population to enhance concerns over caretaking for elderly relatives. To demographers, the aging of the population does not mean so much that some individuals are living to ever-older ages, but rather that most individuals are now surviving into old age, as seen in Fig. 6.1. At the same time that life expectancy is increasing, so is "health life expectancy," which refers to the number of years before older individuals need help with activities of daily living. At the same time, the number of years that elderly individuals need such help is not increasing—just occurring at older ages. So for a given working individual, the potential burden of such care is not increasing, while more individuals will face such burdens.

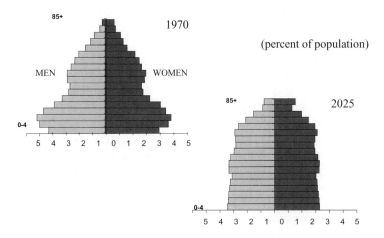

FIG. 6.1.   The changing age structure of the American population.
Source. U.S. Census Bureau.

From a demographic perspective, this increase will be somewhat mitigated for the "baby boomers"—the large generation born between 1946 and 1964, because its members have more siblings than previous or subsequent generations to share caretaking with. However, the "baby boom" generation is the first to include large numbers of women in the paid labor force. In contrast, public programs currently in place were developed in an environment in which policymakers could assume that women would be available for the care of elderly relatives.

The Changing Population Context

Like all issues with a demographic component, work/family issues need to be seen within a new "mental model" of the population as a whole. Thanks to a longer, healthier life expectancy, allied with Americans' continuing preference for the two-child family, the United States population is being transformed.

Throughout world history, the age picture of any population has been a pyramid,

- with a wide base representing a large share of babies born,
- a narrowing midsection in which many died in early childhood and less rapidly with age,
- rising to a pinnacle depicting the few who survived to old age.

In this world, half the population consisted of children, many dying before they had children of their own. The few elderly, along with the children, could be cared for by the people in the middle.

The population pyramid, a basic tool of demographers, is a visual representation of a population according to its composition by age and sex. In 1970, the U.S. population as seen in Fig. 6.1 still resembled the traditional population pyramid (though cinched at the middle by the Depression babies, then widened by the "baby boom"). In contrast, the picture for 2025 is more of a population "pillar," because each age group is roughly the same size except the oldest ones. While the bars at the bottom continue to widen slightly, the bars toward the top are becoming almost as wide as considerably fewer people die before reaching old age.

As a result, the size of each 10-year age cohort is expected to become roughly similar by 2025. As Table 6.1 shows, the seven youngest cohorts, aged 0–70, ranged in size from 20.4

TABLE 6.1
Projections of the U.S. Population by Age: 2025 (in millions)

Age Group	2000	2025
Under age 10	39.7	46.7
10 to 19	40.9	45.4
20 to 29	38.5	43.6
30 to 39	43.2	46.1
40 to 49	42.8	43.0
50 to 59	31.4	40.3
60 to 69	20.4	40.8
70 to 79	16.3	28.3
80 and older	9.3	15.6

Source: U.S. Census Bureau, 2003a.

million people to 43.2 million in 2000. This disparity will be nearly erased by 2025, assuming a continuation of current birth, death, and migration patterns. Thus, each generation from birth until retirement will be roughly equal in size.

In contrast, aside from the distorting effects of the "baby boom" (and subsequent "baby bust"), 10-year age groups were roughly the same size until age 40 until a few decades ago; after age 40, they were much smaller. So the increase in the working-age population is largely among people in later middle age, most of whose children have reached adulthood. Meanwhile, the rise in healthy life expectancy means that most elderly family members need care later in life, and thus later in their adult children's lives, even after those children have retired from the workforce.

Thus, the demographic context implies that the working population in the ages "at risk" of work/family conflicts is growing slowly, relative to the population outside those ages. Other things equal, this trend would tend to reduce the potential costs to employers and to the nation of ameliorating work/family conflicts.

DATA AND TRENDS: WORK

What Is Work?

Just as families are changing, so is work, and current measurements do not reflect all relevant changes. However, in this case the cause of the lag is less political sensitivity than limited financial resources. Overall, government spending on statistics has not kept up with the increasing complexity of economic activities, let alone with simple growth in the economy.

Two kinds of underreported employment are relevant for work/family issues. One is "unpaid" work. Official statistics include people who work in family businesses for no pay—that is, it is not the work that is nonstandard, but the pay status. However, feminists have been arguing with increasing force that housework, particularly the work of raising children, should be included in economic measurements.[10] This work is paid if someone outside the family undertakes it, so not including it skews quantitative analyses of work/family issues.

Paid or unpaid, work done in this "reproductive" economy produces and supports an essential factor of production: the quality as well as the quantity of the future labor force. In recognition of this vital economic role, the internationally harmonized System of National Accounts has designed a satellite account to make the standard national income accounts fully inclusive of key work/family tradeoffs. The United States has not adopted this option, but the Department of Labor has begun a survey, the American Time Use Survey, to collect the data that would be needed to do it. The first estimates from this survey became available in 2004.

An important finding is that employed women aged 18 and older spent about an hour more per day than employed men that age doing household activities and caring for household members. Men and especially women who are not employed spend considerably more time on average on household activities, but women who are not employed spend very little more time than employed women on caring for others, whether in their household or outside it. (Men who are not employed spend considerably less time caring for others, presumably because this group includes large numbers of retirees; U.S. Bureau of Labor Statistics, 2004). This new data source will be a rich resource for researchers of work-family patterns.

Meanwhile, work at home on nonhome jobs seems to be growing. The first official measure also comes from the American Time Use Survey. It found that on the days that they worked, about a fifth of all employed persons did some of their work at home in 2003 (U.S. Bureau of Labor Statistics, 2004).

Technological change has made work more portable, creating new opportunities to blend work and family. Broad surveys of the work-at-home phenomenon have been largely proprietary; however, some researchers have combed large national data sets for clues as to the dimensions of the phenomenon. Using a subset of the 1990 census data, one set of researchers found that home-based workers are more likely than onsite workers to be self-employed, to live in rural areas, to work nonstandard hours, to be women, to be White, and to work in service industries and occupations (Edwards & Field-Hendrey, 1996). Again, the new American Time Use Survey will be a rich resource for such research, as it can be tabulated by age, sex, family composition, and work schedule.

Work Trends

Thanks in particular to the "baby boom," the American labor force has grown rapidly in recent decades. Beginning in 1966, the maturing of this unusually large generation combined with the propensity of its women to stay in the workforce during their childrearing years to raise the nation's labor force participation rate substantially. This rate reached a record high almost every year until 2001, when the first baby boomers reached age 55. In 1966, 59.2% of the population aged 16 and older was in the workforce; by 2000, this share had risen to 67.2%.

Beginning in the 1980s these two demographic changes—an unusually large generation in the working ages and an unprecedented number of wives and mothers in the labor force—made work-family conflict into an increasingly pressing policy concern. The country's basic policy and program assumption—that dependent people had a family member whose primary job was caring for them in the home—no longer held. Of course, many families in the past had not enjoyed that lack of conflict, as both parents needed jobs in families with very low income, single parents were not unknown, and elderly family members relied on children, usually a daughter (who often did not marry), for care. But the new refusal of large numbers of middle-class (i.e., voting) families to withdraw from the work world for family caretaking needs changed the politics around this issue set.

Before describing work-family conflicts from a demographic perspective, it is important to understand how demographers measure such conflicts. In general, demographers tend to estimate the population at risk of such conflict, that is, people who are in the workforce and have dependents in the home. (Dependents are generally described by age and thus usually refer to children, although disability measures can also used to identify dependent adults.) As described earlier, the large databases that demographers use are household based and thus measure dependency in terms of co-residence. However, specialized databases allow demographers to measure the prevalence of family members outside the household who may need care, whether children or disabled adults. For research purposes, such need would be signaled by temporal measures, such as the frequency of care needs and the duration of caregiving, whether by individual episode or over time. In other words, demographers tend to measure caregiving in terms of demonstrated behavior, rather than expressed needs. This approach avoids confronting the politically fraught distinction between care that represents a preference (say spending time with children) and care that represents true need (say leaving young children unsupervised).

Adjusting for the impact of the "baby boom" on the age structure (to remove the impact of its large numbers on particular ages), the labor force participation rate for women rose from 38% in 1960 to 53% in 1980 (Szafran, 2002). The rate has continued to rise, to 62% in 2000, but now work-family conflicts are diminishing for these pioneering parents as they swell the ranks of middle-aged and older workers. In the sense that work-family conflicts have their longest duration, and most consuming demands, for children, work-family issues engage a smaller proportion of the workforce, now and in the future, given the population aging described earlier. In this sense, just as the "baby boom" made work-family issues salient, the aging of this large generation makes it easier to address them.

TABLE 6.2
Labor Force Status by Family Type, 2000

	Number	Percent
Total families	72,261,780	100.0
Married couple families	55,458,451	100.0
Husband in labor force	41,686,722	75.2
Wife in labor force	28,442,464	51.3
Wife in labor force, husband not	3,742,571	6.7
Other families	16,803,329	100.0
Male head, no wife	4,302,568	25.6
In labor force	3,249,123	19.3
Female head, no husband	12,500,761	74.4
In labor force	82,883,81	49.3

Note: This table shows all families at all householder ages and thus includes retired people as well as working-age people.
Source: Riche & Gaquin, 2003.

The demographic onset of work-family conflicts shows up most clearly in comparisons of young women aged 25 to 34 over the past quarter century. In 1975 over one third of American women in this age group reported that they had not been working, almost all of them because they were caring for home and family. By 2000, only 20% reported that they had not been working, only 14% because they were caring for home and family. Meanwhile, the proportion not working because they were in school had doubled (Riche, 2003).

Over this period, women in this age group increasingly delayed marriage and children. Still, the most notable shift toward the work world was among women who followed the traditional path of early marriage and children. In 1975, more than three fourths of women aged 25 to 34 had children and the majority of these mothers were not in the labor force. In 2000, three fifths of women in this age group had children, and all but 30% of these mothers were in the labor force (Riche, 2003).

Table 6.2 shows that in the 2000 census, over half of the nation's married couple families reported that both partners were in the workforce. Many of these couples had responsibility for dependent family members, whether children or adults. However, for most researchers and policymakers, work-family conflicts that involve children are of most concern, due to their long duration as well as their greater prevalence. Table 6.3 shows the 2000 census measure of working parents from a child's point of view (Riche & Gaquin, 2003). As the table shows, the census found 43% of the nation's children living in families where both parents were in the workforce—double the share of children living in "traditional" families, where the father works and the mother does not. Another 21% of the nation's children were living in single-parent families where the parent, most often a mother, was in the workforce. Thus, work-family conflicts are a reality for the nearly two out of three American children who lack a full-time stay-at-home parent.

Looking at the same universe from the perspective of adults, in 2002 over 36 percent of the nation's workforce had (own) children under age 18 (U.S. Bureau of Labor Statistics, 2003). Most analyses focus on mothers, who continue to bear the primary responsibility for caring for children, as demonstrated most recently by the first results of the new American Time Use Survey (U.S. Bureau of Labor Statistics, 2004).[11] In 2002, nearly 40% of women in the labor force had children under age 18. Of these working mothers, nearly 40% had children under age

TABLE 6.3
Labor Force Status of Parents by Age of Child, 2000

	Number	*Percent*
Total own children under 18	6,788,2626	100.0
in families and subfamilies		
Living with two parents	4,877,1265	71.8
both parents in labor force	2,932,8931	43.2
father only in labor force	1,489,1677	21.9
mother only in labor force	20,496,91	3.0
neither parent in labor force	25,009,66	3.7
Living with one parent	1,911,1361	28.2
Living with father	41,443,76	6.1
father in labor force	34,175,17	5.0
Living with mother	1,496,6985	22.0
mother in labor force	1,109,8579	16.3

Source: Riche & Gaquin, 2003.

6—for these more than 10 million mothers, child care was probably a pressing issue. The other 61% of working mothers had school-age children, and faced a different but not necessarily lighter set of work/family conflicts (U.S. Bureau of Labor Statistics, 2003).

Since by far the largest share of the nation's children lives in two-worker married couple families, it is worth taking a closer look at how work-family conflicts play out for these families. In 2002, over half of American wives with children under age 18 *and* with husbands working full-time also worked full-time year-round. Another 23% of worked part-time year-round, while only 27% did not work at all during the year (including the small share of mothers whose husbands did not work either; (U.S. Bureau of Labor Statistics, 2003). In 1970, only 16% of married mothers worked year-round full-time, and as recently as 1992, only 37% did (Hayghe & Bianchi, 1994).

Thus, the work patterns of married mothers are primarily behind the rise of work/family conflicts. When the "baby boom" generation was young, leaving the workforce when they married was the prevailing social pattern for women. This social prescription (made explicit by many employers) had been driven largely by a concern to make room in the workforce for returning veterans after World War II. In 1950 women had a very low labor force participation rate. Indeed, the highest participation rate at that time, 44%, was for women aged 16 to 24, the group that has the lowest rate under age 65 now (Fullerton, 1999). So when "baby boom" women started to join the workforce in the 1960s, society still expected women to withdraw when they had children.

But, "baby boom" women went to college in record numbers, married later, and had their children later. They also had fewer children, on average, than their predecessors. All these circumstances combined to strengthen these women's ties to the labor market, making them less likely to withdraw, or to work part- instead of full-time, when they had children. Moreover, when activists improved women's access to better-paying jobs, the cost to many couples of foregoing the wife's earnings rose significantly (Hayghe & Bianchi, 1994). Thus, Hayghe and Bianchi (1994) found that married mothers who worked full-time year-round have been the primary source of women's increased labor force participation, and the increase in work experience has been as pronounced for wives with very young children as for wives whose children were in school.

Current work patterns of married couples with preschool-age children demonstrate the overwhelming presence of work-family conflicts during an important stage in contemporary lives. Only a third of married mothers who had both preschool-age children and working husbands did not work at all during 2002—that is, followed the traditional path for this life stage. Another third of wives with preschool-age children *and* working husbands worked year-round full-time, while a further 10% worked year-round part-time. Having young children certainly affects mothers' work patterns: by comparison, fully 80% of wives whose children were school-age worked some time during 2002, and nearly half of these mothers worked year-round full-time (U.S. Bureau of Labor Statistics, 2003).

The changing racial and ethnic makeup of the nation's population may be muting this trend somewhat, as Hispanic mothers are less likely to work for pay (especially if they are married), and Hispanics are the nation's fastest growing population group. In 2002, fully 38% of Hispanic wives with children under age 18 *and* working husbands did not work at all, compared to 24 % of White or Black married mothers with working husbands. It is hard to say to what extent this difference reflects different cultural traditions. However, the unemployment rate for women in the prime childrearing ages, 25 to 44, suggests that such differences play a part: It is lower for Hispanic women than for Black women, who are least likely to be married and thus more likely to be seeking work if they are not already employed (U.S. Bureau of Labor Statistics, 2003).

Meanwhile, the proportion of married mothers who work full-time year-round has risen for both White and Black women, while widening the gap between them. In 2002, fully 70% of married Black mothers worked year-round full-time, compared to 49% of married White mothers (and 47% of married Hispanic mothers; U.S. Bureau of Labor Statistics, 2003). In contrast, about 15% of White mothers worked year-round full-time in 1970, compared to 27% of Black mothers (Hayghe and Bianchi, 1994).

Obviously, work/family conflicts are particularly severe for women with very young children who work full-time and/or who are not married. In 2002, three fifths of the nearly 10 million American women who had children under age 3 were in the workforce, and 38% of them worked full-time. Three out of four mothers with very young children lived with a husband and were slightly less likely to work full-time—36%—compared to 41% of mothers with some other marital status (such as spouse not present, divorced/separated, or never married; U.S. Bureau of Labor Statistics, 2003).

Resolving work/family conflict is often framed in terms of developing family-friendly work practices. However, the work experience of mothers of very young children suggests that family-friendly hiring may also be an important concern. It is probably safe to assume that most mothers of children under age 3 without a spouse present have a greater need for work income. Yet in 2002, 16% were working part-time, and another 16% were looking for work and not finding it. In contrast, only 5% of mothers of very young children who were living with husbands reported that they could not find work. Fully 18% were working part-time, which, with a husband's income, would be a less costly response to family/work conflicts than for mothers lacking such a second income (U.S. Bureau of Labor Statistics, 2003).[12]

The Changing Labor Force Context

Recent record high labor force participation rates reflect not only the "baby boom" and the continuing presence in the workforce of mothers, but also the relatively low numbers of people in the cohort that preceded the "baby boom," that is, the cohort currently moving into retirement, and of the cohort that followed it, often referred to as the "baby bust". When these and other effects of the nation's changing age composition are removed, the age-adjusted labor force participation rate rises to 68.2% (Szafran, 2002).

Shifts in the age composition of the population also affect the demographic dimensions of work/family conflicts. At present, they are producing more people of working age who are beyond the ages when children demand a great deal of care (while before the ages when elderly parents may need intensive care). The median age of the workforce has been rising, from 35 in 1982 to 36 in 1993 and 40 in 2002, and is projected to reach 41.4 years in 2012. Between 2002 and 2012, the number of workers aged 55 and older is projected to increase by half, compared to a 10% increase in the numbers aged 25 to 34, the prime ages for having children, and an actual decrease in the numbers aged 35 to 44 (Toosi, 2004).

As a result, the share of the workforce that is simultaneously raising children is becoming smaller. In 2002, fewer than 40% of women in the labor force had children under age 18, as did only 27% of women who worked full-time (two thirds of whom were married; U.S. Bureau of Labor Statistics, 2003). Just 15% of all women in the workforce had a child under age 6, and 30% of them worked part-time. Given that 72% of all women with children under age 18 were in the labor force in 2002, and 64% of women with children under age 6, it is clear that work-family conflicts currently involve a minority of workers. It may well be easier to advance their needs as the costs of doing so, whether to employers or taxpayers, diminish proportionately.

Probably the most intense work-family conflicts were experienced in 2002 by the 3.6 million women with children under age 3 who worked full-time. These workers accounted for only 2.5% of the female labor force, and 7% of all mothers in the labor force. Their small share suggests that policies and programs to ease work-family conflicts should not be overly burdensome for employers or society to undertake.

Moreover, the relative share of the population in need of help with work-family conflicts should continue to decline. In 2002, women ages 25 to 44 accounted for 22% of the labor force, down from 25% 10 years earlier. By 2012, women this age are expected to account for only 20% of the labor force, as the labor force ages (Toosi, 2004). It remains to be seen whether this decline makes employers or taxpayers more willing to address work-family issues, say by providing child care, or simply reduces the pressure on them to do so.

Others will assess the relative costs to economic efficiency (or to the size and quality of the future workforce) of making it difficult for parents to combine work and childrearing. However, the costs to the individual parent, particularly the mother, are substantial, as shown by differences in men's and women's earnings.

Over the years, economists have used increasingly sophisticated methods to explain the persistent gap between men and women's earnings. In the early decades of this work, studies were unable to find any explanation other than sex discrimination for the bulk of the gap. However, attempts to eliminate such discrimination brought an increasing array of data in their wake. Adding data on such important variables as work schedules and work-life interruptions to the standard array of data on education and other individual demographic differences, the U.S. (Government Accountability Office (GAO) formerly the General Accounting Office) has essentially determined that women earn less than men over a lifetime because work-family conflicts are more pronounced for them (U.S. General Accounting Office, 2003).

The GAO found that women earned about 20% less than men in 2000 after accounting for all variables except gender—a decline of about 0.3% a year since 1983, the first year of their analysis. This gap is the unexplained "residual," which could represent discrimination or simply different occupational or workstyle preferences. However, before taking into account women's different work patterns, the male/female earnings gap stands at 44%. In other words, women's choices to manage work-family conflicts by working part-time, part-year, or taking time out of the workforce costs them more in terms of earnings than their preferences for lower-paying jobs or any remaining employer discrimination.

CONCLUSION

The compression of most work-family conflicts into the first half of the prime working years interacts with contemporary demographic patterns in two ways. First, population aging is increasing the share of the workforce that has completed the bulk of its childrearing, thus minimizing the future cost to employers or taxpayers of efforts to ameliorate these conflicts. Indeed, the shift away from a youthful population to one that is evenly divided between young, midlife, and old could foster an increasing societal awareness of the social benefits of broad investment in the young, and a willingness to make it easier for people who wish to have larger families to act on that wish.

Second, trends in education, marriage, and work have produced two different trajectories for work/family conflicts in the United States. On the one hand, higher educated women and men tend to delay marriage and childbearing. As a result, they have more stable marriages and careers when they have children, and thus more individual resources, such as a higher salary and/or a second earner, to deal with the eventual work-related conflicts (McLanahan, 2004). McLanahan (2004) also reported that college-educated fathers tend to spend more time with their children and to score higher on other measures of father involvement, such as reading to the children.

On the other hand, young women who complete their education early tend to have children early, and large numbers have them on their own or cohabit instead of marrying. The decline in jobs for low-skilled men has made them less "marriageable," and the history of income testing for welfare benefits has discouraged both work and marriage for low-skilled single mothers (McLanahan, 2004). Indeed, lacking economic or spousal support, poorly educated young mothers also lack the ability to get well-paying jobs, let alone deal with the conflicts that working would produce. Thus, single mothers are a special concern on both work and family grounds.

With the lower fertility rates described earlier, the U.S. population is growing slowly—even with a steady inflow of immigrants.[13] In the long run, American employers may decide that it would be worthwhile to make a two-handed investment to grow the workforce: address the work-family issues that have kept some women out of the labor market and discouraged others from having as many children as they might have liked. Finding suitable work-life solutions for working householders, such as on-site child care, flexible work schedules, or simply helping working parents make the most of their scarce time is doable, if the will to do it is there.

NOTES

[1] The Census Bureau has begun a research project to link demographic and employment data at small areas of geography, so that researchers can see Americans simultaneously as workers and family members. The Longitudinal Employment and Household Dynamics (LEHD) database is currently available only for projects that reimburse the government for its costs, and its requests for core public funding have not yet been met.

[2] The annual measure of the poverty population is a good example. The current threshold for measuring this population was developed in some haste by the U.S. Department of Health, Education, and Welfare based on household budget data from the U.S. Bureau of Labor Statistics in the late 1960s with the expectation that it would receive the critical evaluation that would enable it to be refined appropriately. This has not happened, although efforts to make it happen have supported a small industry of academics and researchers.

[3] U.S. Census Bureau: "A family household has at least two members related by blood, marriage, or adoption, one of whom is the householder" (www.census.gov).

[4] Of course, an unmarried partner might be the father of some other child, in some other household, but such probing questions are so sensitive that they are limited to surveys conducted by research organizations, such as the Survey of Families and Households conducted occasionally by the University of Wisconsin, on contract to the National Institute of Child Health and Development.

[5] See Zill and Daly (1993) for an inventory of data sets on U.S. families.

[6] A Canadian researcher (Leroy Stone, Statistics Canada and the University of Manitoba) has modeled an interesting approach that could be accomplished by adding a few questions to the basic demographic survey that uses a true probability sample of the population. (In the United States, this is the Current Population Survey.) This would involve asking people how often they see particular family members, who they turn to in need, and who they receive care from or provide care to on a regular basis. Small surveys that are not necessarily generalizable to the population as a whole indicate that nonresident siblings, as well as close friends, are often an important family resource.

[7] As indicated above, U.S. family data place couples who report that they are living together but not married *and* who have children in the household in the single-parent category. This exclusion underestimates the number of two-worker-with-children families. However, there is some evidence, from the Survey of Families and Households, that unmarried partners are relatively uninvolved in care for children who are not their own. In the bulk of such households, the children are the woman's from a previous relationship.

[8] The total fertility rate (TFR) is an estimate of a woman's lifetime childbearing. Specifically, it is the average number of children women will have if, between ages 15 and 44, they bear children at the same rate as women did "this" year, in this case in 2001.

[9] Despite differences due to divorce and custody arrangements, the number of years for men is virtually the same as for women because men are often raising children from a wife's earlier marriage (King, 1999).

[10] The author represented the U.S. Commerce Department at the 1996 Social Summit, one of a series of path-breaking global conferences held by the United Nations during the decade. At that meeting, the U.S. delegation resisted adopting this recommendation because it was framed in a way that did not match U.S. institutional realities. After further work, the U.S. delegation supported provisions in favor of such measures at the Beijing global conference on women held later that year.

[11] In the 1980s, University of Maryland demographer Harriet Presser initiated a line of research into how two-worker families use different work shifts to make sure one spouse or partner is available to care for children or other family members (Presser, 1989). Her recent book, *Working in a 24/7 Economy* (Russell Sage, 2003), addresses the challenges raised for families by growth of nonstandard work schedules. These schedules, particularly in service industries, are to a large extent a response to the demands of people facing work-family conflicts.

[12] Of course, an abundant literature has documented the educational and other employment barriers that confront many young unmarried mothers.

[13] The United States is the only industrialized population that is expected to grow; most others are expected to stabilize or even decline by 2050 (U.S. Census Bureau, 2004).

REFERENCES

Bianchi, S. M. (2000). Maternal employment and time with children: Dramatic change or surprising continuity? *Demography, 37*, 401–414.

Costello, C. B., Wight, V. R., & Stone, A. S. (2002). *The American woman 2003–2004: Daughters of a revolution— young women today.* New York: Palgrave McMillan.

Edwards, L. N., & Field-Hendrey, E. (1996). Home-based workers: Data from the 1990 Census of Population. *Monthly Labor Review, 119,* 26–34.

Farnsworth Riche Associates. (2003). Unpublished household projections.

Fullerton, H. N., Jr. (1999). Labor force participation: 75 years of change, 1950–98 and 1998–2025. *Monthly Labor Review, 121,* 3–12.

Gies, F., & Gies, J. (1987). *Marriage and family in the Middle Ages.* New York: Harper & Row.

Hayghe, H. V., & Bianchi, S. M. (1994). Married mothers' work patterns: The job-family compromise. *Monthly Labor Review, 116,* 24–30.

King, R. B. (1999). Time spent in parenthood status among adults in the United States. *Demography 36,* 377–385.

Martin, J. A., Hamilton, B. E., Sutton, P. D., Ventura, S. J., Menacker, F., & Munson, M. L. (2003). Births: Final data for 2002. *National Vital Statistics Reports, 52.* National Center for Health Statistics, Hyattsville, Maryland.

McLanahan, S. (2004). Diverging destinies: How children fare under the second demographic transition. Presidential address, the 2004 annual meeting of the Population Association of America, Boston, Massachusetts.

Population Reference Bureau. (2004). http://www.prb.org/Template.cfm?Section=PRB&template=/Content/ ContentGroups/04_Articles/The_Double_Divide_Implosionists_and_Explosionists_Endanger_Progress_Since_ Cairo.htm.

Presser, H. B. (1989). Can we make time for children?: The economy, work schedules, and child care. *Demography, 26,* 523–543.

Riche, M. F. (2003). Young women: Where they stand. In C. B. Costello, V. R. Wight, & A. J. Stone (Eds.), *The American woman 2003–2004* (pp. 43–68). New York: Palgrave MacMillan.

Riche, M. F., & Gaquin, D. A. (2003). *The who, what, and where of America: Understanding the census results.* Lanham, MD: Bernan Press.

Rindfuss, R. R., Guzzo, K. B., & Morgan, S. P. (2003). The changing institutional context of low fertility. *Population Research and Policy Review, 22,* 411–438.

Szafran, R. F. (2002). Age-adjusted labor force participation rates: 1960–2045. *Monthly Labor Review, 125,* 37–57.

Toosi, Mitra. (2004). Labor force projections to 2012: The graying of the U.S. workforce *Monthly Labor Review, 127,* 37–51.

U.S. Bureau of Labor Statistics. (2003). http://www.bls.gov/CPS, retrieved July 9, 2003.

U.S. Bureau of Labor Statistics. (2004). Time-use survey—first results announced by BLS. U.S. Department of Labor, news release 04-1797.

U.S. Census Bureau. (2003a). Current population survey, annual demographic file. Unpublished tabulation.

U.S. Census Bureau. (2003b). Who's minding the kids: Child care arrangements, Spring 1999. Detailed Tables (PPL-168). http://www.census.gov/population/www/socdemo/child/ppl-168.html.

U.S. Census Bureau. (2003c). Fertility of American women: June 2002. *Current Population Reports, P-20.*

U.S. Census Bureau. (2004). Global population profile: 2002. *International Population Reports* WP/02.

U.S. General Accounting Office. (2003). Women's earnings: Work patterns partially explain difference between men's and women's earnings. GAO-04-35.

Zill, N., and Daly, M. (Eds.). (1993). *Researching the family: A guide to survey and statistical data on U.S. families.* Washington, DC: Child Trends.

7

Family Studies: Situating Everyday Family Life at Work, in Time, and Across Contexts

Anisa M. Zvonkovic
Texas Tech University

Megan L. Notter
Cheryl L. Peters
Oregon State University

In this chapter, we rely primarily on scholarship from researchers who study family relationships. This work occurs in a variety of academic disciplines, including Sociology, Developmental Psychology, Anthropology, and interdisciplinary departments and programs, including human development and Family Studies (HDFS) departments. Three academic branches have come to shape the interdisciplinary area of research known as Family Studies today: (a) the legacy of "traditional Home Economics" with its interest in every day lives of women; (b) lifespan developmental psychology, with its focus on both the ways development changes over time and the natural ecological contrasts within which individuals and families live out their lives; and (c) family sociology, which has provided a sharp focus on the economic and social contexts of life, incorporating anthropological analysis of comparative cultures. These three areas, with their own theories and preferred methodologies, have combined to form *the family studies perspective, which can be summarized as analyzing development and relationships over the life course, in social and other contexts.*

Because Family Studies draws from such broad content areas, in this chapter we use the concept of time as unifying construct to explore research on work and family that has come from a family studies perspective. The selection of time as a rubric is also responsive to the "social problems" thrust of research in Family Studies. As a field, Family Studies retains strong ties to the application of research results. In this light, family studies has been concerned with the perception among families in North America that time is a problem for them. Researchers first examined stress and perception of time among individuals who reported themselves to be the most stressed and time-deprived. Working parents, especially those aged 35 to 44, overwhelmingly feel a time crunch (Robinson and Godbey, 1997), reporting the lack of family time as a major stressor in their daily lives (Galinsky, 1999). It seems, however, that most everyone feels rushed. When adults were asked how often they "always feel rushed," Robinson and Godbey (1997) reported the following increase: In 1971, 24% of adults reported always feeling rushed; in 1982, 28% of adults reported the same, and in 1992, 38% of adults reported they always felt rushed.

After the groundwork of how family members spend their time has been laid in this chapter, we focus on what families do in terms of their daily activities and how they understand their work and family lives. We bring in prominent theoretical perspectives in Family Studies and exemplar research programs as well as new and innovative perspectives. We attend to how diverse family members experience their everyday lives in work and in interaction with each other, considering differences across family structure, social class, the life course (as children are added to families and as children grow), and time (in terms of cycles and calendars).

Researchers' concerns over family life have coalesced on remarkably consistent themes, regardless of the decade. In reviewing the literature on household time allocation from 1887–1987, Nickols (1986) identified the *enrichment of family life* as the ultimate objective of researchers involved in studying family time. Obstacles to the enjoyment of leisure and family relationships have been continuously identified. These remarkably similar quotes about time, written 16 years apart, are prime examples:

> Time has become more and more scarce in our world . . . . Many conflicting alternatives have claims on our limited time: paid or unpaid work, recreational or social commitments, interaction with our families and friends, and community involvements . . . . We have more choices as to how we can use our time, and scarcity of time becomes a major constraint on our choices. (Walker, 1980, p. 119)

Just as earlier scholars were interested in enriching family life, today's researchers study social problems like the increasing pace of our society, in order to understand everyday family life.

> Whether it be the duties of parenthood, the tasks of household cleanliness, or the incessant demands of a consumer-based culture, there is often little sense of engaged involvement with one another in the experience of family time. The ideal, however, persists: People want to spend more time with their families. . . . Our ideology of what family time is leaves us with an unhappy present. (Daly, 1996a, pp. 204–205)

THE ACADEMIC LEGACY OF FAMILY STUDIES: STUDYING EVERYDAY LIFE

There has been a remarkable persistence of interest in the field regarding family members' daily lives as they spend time in work and in interaction with each other. Though early studies focused on women's time use in the work of homemaking, more modern studies have extended their analyses to paid work, household work, and leisure (Nickols, 1986). Early studies were primarily descriptive, taking the radical position (for their time) that household labor was work. An unintended byproduct of this position was that it prevented information from being aggregated and compared across gender or incorporated with literature on paid work. This work, even through the modern era (the 1970s), tends not to be read or cited by scholars outside of those scholars who trace their academic legacy to the Home Economics branch of the family studies perspective.

Maud Wilson, whose monograph was published in 1929, gathered data on time use of rural families in Oregon from 1926–1927. Her research is "the most comprehensive of numerous time use studies sponsored by the Bureau of Home Economics of the United States Department of Agriculture in the 1920s and 1930s" (Walker, 1980). Based on the traditional agricultural university's mission to serve farmers and their families, she sought to compare how women accomplished family care tasks, depending on whether or not the family farmed. She included information about women, men, and children's time use in household and leisure activities.

Some key findings from Wilson (1929) include an estimate of weekly hours in household work of 51.5 hours for women who did not farm and who lived in nonrural settings. Time devoted to household work and other work revealed in Wilson's study can be compared to time use from research in the modern period. Though methods varied, the average weekly work hours of men and of women who were not employed remained remarkably stable from the classic to the modern era. Wilson reported that homemaking wives put in 7.3 hours of housework per day, quite similar to the 7.6 hours reported by Robinson (1977) and the 6.83 hours reported by Pleck (1985). When work hours were long, women spent less time in sleep, leisure, and personal care. Modern studies of time use have yielded similar findings, with Berk and Berk (1979) reporting that women who were employed tended to rise earlier and to include household tasks in their evening leisure hours, although men who were employed tended to decrease their household contribution in the evening. Wilson also reported on women's time use in leisure activities, finding that the largest chunks of leisure time women reported were devoted to a weekly average of 7.1 hours spent in informal social life and 6.7 hours spent reading. Most other historical and modern studies of household time use have not reported hours spent in leisure activities, so comparisons are difficult to make until the contemporary era.

Because Wilson's (1929) focus was on homemaking as work, she did not provide extensive data about women who might have also been participating in paid work, though she noted that women who provided labor for their family's farm put in an additional 11.8 weekly hours to this task. The total work hours, unpaid in addition to income-producing work, has also remained quite similar across time. Wilson reported a daily workload of farming wives of 8.6 hours, compared to total daily workload of employed women in Robinson's (1977) analysis of 9.3 hours, Walker and Woods' (1976) report of 8.6 hours, and Pleck's (1985) report of 8.96 hours. Wilson did report the hours of assistance women received in homemaking tasks. Ninety percent of the women in her study reported receiving some help, although 49% of this assistance comprised less than 5 weekly hours. Children provided most of the help, averaging 4.6 hours per week, with husbands contributing an average of 2 hours per week, regardless of whether or not the family farmed.

Scholars anticipated that fewer hours in household labor would be necessary due to "modern" technology of the time, but only Wilson (1929) found a difference in hours devoted to household labor, based solely on access to one type of modern convenience: running water. "Time-saving technologies" have been accompanied by elevated standards of housework, resulting in women's household labor hours remaining stable over time (Nickols, 1986). Wilson herself, in a prescient statement, wrote:

> The nature and content of the homemaker's job is rapidly changing. The number of processes carried on in the household is decreasing with the growth of commercial services and community utilities. The number of persons in the household has decreased.... School or work calls children from home sooner.... The effect of recent extension of knowledge regarding child care and training, nutrition, and the link, has been to add to the responsibilities and to increase time demands.... The increase in living standards enjoyed by members of other occupations has had the effect of increasing the desired standard. (Wilson, 1929, pp. 9–10)

Modern scholars of time use, studying women's and men's involvement in household labor and paid work 50 years after Maud Wilson, echo many of the same themes. We see similarities from the quote above to issues studied today, including how scholars in the contemporary period regard child development, standards of living driving workforce participation, and the commercialization of household and family work. Though these historical and modern studies emerged from departments that addressed marital and family well-being, it was not until the late 1980s that the study of time use went beyond description toward connecting family members' time use to family members' satisfaction, interaction with one another, and well-being.

INFLUENTIAL THEORIES AND EXEMPLAR RESEARCH PROGRAMS REGARDING EVERYDAY LIFE IN WORK AND FAMILY

In this section, we review the dominant theories that have been utilized by Family Studies scholars in analyzing work and family activities, and exemplar programs of research that address everyday family life in terms of paid work and family relationships. We believe the dominant theories used by Family Studies scholars, generally developed by scholars in the disciplines from which Family Studies draws, include: (a) the ecological perspective as articulated by Urie Bronfenbrenner (1979, 1986); (b) the family life course perspective (Bengtson & Allen, 1993); (c) social constructionism stemming from the sociological perspective of Symbolic Interactionism (LaRossa & Reitzes, 1993); (d) feminist perspectives (DeReus, Few, & Blume, 2005; Osmond & Thorne, 1993); and (e) General Systems Theory, especially utilized by scholars who focus on stress in families and by interventionists (Broderick & Smith, 1979; Whitchurch & Constantine, 1993). It is outside the scope of this chapter to provide a comprehensive examination of the theories used in family studies; however, the brief descriptions that follow can orient the reader to how dominant theories in the field are connected to research on families and work (see Bengston, Allen, Acock, Dilworth-Anderson, & Klein, 2005; MacDermid, Roy, & Zvonkovic, 2005, for an extended discussion).

The ecological perspective has been central to the training of Family Studies scholars who are developmental psychologists as well as those who trace their roots to the Home Economics perspective. An ecological perspective insists that the actual settings in which humans develop, as well as connections between different settings, are influential in shaping everyday life. Importantly, Bronfenbrenner identified settings which a focal person never enters, but which influence development nonetheless, as a key part of the model (termed "exosystems"). For example, the parents' workplace is an exosystem to the child. Scholars using the ecological perspective have been keenly interested in both variability and in the connections between microsystems, exosystems, and the larger culture, systematically revealing the world outside the developing individual and outside the immediate family.

Ecological perspectives are often combined with life course perspectives. The family life course perspective extends the vision of developing individuals and families through time in several ways. Life course scholars conduct analyses of historical cohorts, and they examine the time and timing of life events. Examples of such work include Elder's (1974) *Children of the Great Depression* and Hareven's analysis of early industrialization (1982), both of which demonstrated how growing up in a particular historical era, in a particular social class, had implications for individual and family life and economic well-being, even extending into future generations. Similarly, Bengtson's study of multiple generations including the baby boom generation (the USC3G study) follows families over time and generation (Bengtson, 1989; Bengtson & Achenbaum, 1994). Family life course scholars examine the trajectory of lives and careers (Moen, 2003) including the individual, marital pair, and family units, so that diverse trajectories, depending on the opportunities available to individuals, can be traced. This perspective offers promise for examining future generations and trajectories of work and family life at the family level.

Family Studies scholars have also capitalized on symbolic interactionism, a theoretical perspective emanating from sociology. As discussed by LaRossa and Reitzes (1993), this theoretical tradition has two schools: In terms of work and family scholarship, one school has been interested in multiple roles and role strain by regarding roles as relatively rigid demands imposed on family members from relatively stable societal demands. Social constructionism, the other school, has been more influential in recent family scholarship, in our view. This perspective regards humans as having *agency*, seen as the ability to construct their work and family roles, at least to some degree, as well as to change and reconstruct how they will enact their family and work lives (Daly, 1996a, 2001a). Scholars who take this perspective tend to gather rich qualitative data from family members in order to discover how they view their work and family lives keying in on the meaning they construct for their everyday lives as well as conflict and contradictory experiences.

Feminist perspectives, generally articulated in critical humanist fields and in sociology, take the examination of women's lives as their central focus. Given the feminist tenet that "the personal is political," feminist perspectives are well suited for examining the connection between family life and political opportunity structures (for example, women's economic oppression; Osmond & Thorne, 1993). Feminist theorists have examined the issue of household labor, articulating how household tasks are indeed work, and providing a lens for viewing women's lives holistically. Feminists have also urged social scientists to be more inclusive of diverse women's lives and to make efforts to conduct emancipatory research that takes action to improve women's lives. Also, feminists were among the first to reject the "separate spheres" dichotomy between work and family, urging scholars to look for connections between home and work, both of which can be sites for conflicting expectations.

Finally, Family Studies as a field has been strongly influenced by General Systems Theory, which focuses is on systems *within* the family, to the near exclusion of regarding anything outside of the family system (Broderick & Smith, 1979; Whitchurch & Constantine, 1993). This perspective has been widely used by applied professionals, in particular, marital and family therapists. Its use in work and family research stems from an interest in family homeostasis (or stability). Potential stressors such as work may enter the family system, disrupt balanced patterns of interaction, and force family members to adjust. The perspective has been used to support homeostatic gendered roles inside families, which feminists view as problematic.

In a review of studies in the broad field of work and family, we identified several "research camps" in Family Studies, each of which uses different methods and addresses time and family activities and relationships in different ways. The University of Michigan (via data gathered in 1965 and 1975) and the University of Maryland (1985 to present) are sites for decades of research on the time use of individuals in society via the *Americans' Use of Time Project*. Books from these research camps connected quality of everyday life with American's use of time in paid and unpaid work and leisure activities (Juster & Stafford, 1985; Robinson, 1977; Robinson & Godbey, 1997). These researchers collected time diaries that covered the complete 24-hour day from a cross-sectional sample of the American public aged 18 and older. Though this research program seems to be a sequel to the Home Economics time use studies, two unique features of these diaries include: (a) incorporating activities in the respondents' own words as opposed to checklists; and (b) collecting information on multiple activities performed at the same time (e.g., multi-tasking).

Other identifiable research camps devoted to understanding how American families spend time in work and in family interaction include the work of researchers at Cornell University and the Pennsylvania State University. Researchers utilized a variety of vantage points, advancing the field by making visible the perceptions and actual time use of couples, children, and their parents (Moen, 2003; Crouter, Perry-Jenkins, Huston, & Crawford, 1989; Crouter & Crowley, 1990). Larson and Richards' (1994) exemplar study of families with adolescents (using experience sampling methodology) illustrates how the use of technology (e.g., pagers) can provide temporally valid estimates of individuals' moods and behaviors, and show the daily transmission of these emotional states to other family members, in addition to documenting time use with family members and alone. These scholars have been deeply influenced by ecological perspectives, articulating the settings in which adults and children spent their lives, with particular focus on the time they spend together in the home and family microsystem with an understanding on how demands from other systems can shape family life.

Other scholars have made use of nationally representative data sets to understand work and family life. *The National Survey of Families and Households* (Coltrane & Adams, 2001), the *Current Population Survey* (Jacobs & Gerson, 2001, 2004; Presser, 1995, 2003), the Child Development supplement to the *Panel of Income Dynamics* (Hofferth & Sandberg, 2001), and the *National Study of the Changing Workforce* (Bond, Galinsky, & Swanberg, 1998) are just a few examples of rich data sets tapped to examine time use trends among subsets of our national population, such as working parents and dual-earner couples.

Finally, an example of merging time diary with behavioral self-report methods and nationally representative data sets is the *National Study of Daily Experiences (NSDE)*. This study's purpose was to examine the daily stressors created by work and family life for individuals who participated in a larger study, the *National Survey of Midlife in the United States (MIDUS)*. The *NSDE* connected daily stress events with aspects of individual development such as personality and health outcomes (Almeida, 2004; Almeida & McDonald, in press; Almeida, Wethington, & Kessler, 2002; Grzywacz, Almeida, & McDonald, 2002). Several research articles stemming from this data set have utilized general systems theory, with a focus on interference from work coming into family systems, but also the potential for work to provide facilitation as an input to the family system.

This list of theoretical perspectives and major research projects is not exhaustive, but is included to illustrate examples of influential perspectives and programs of research. One sound conclusion that can be made is that theoretical underpinning and the methods of measuring time and family activities, as well as the specific tasks that are included, result in the generation of different time use estimates for individuals and families. In this way, this body of research has yielded different conclusions about how individual and family life has unfolded. In the following sections, we systematically consider time spent in paid labor, household labor, and leisure activities.

ACTIVITIES IN EVERYDAY LIFE

Paid Labor

A recent controversy about paid labor hours has enlivened the literature. On one side, Schor, in a series of reports entitled "The overworked American" (1991) and "The even more overworked American" (2003), concluded that U.S. workers spend more time at work than their parents or grandparents did. On the other side, from time use diary data, Robinson and Godbey (1997) compared American time use in 1965, 1975, and 1985 and concluded that Americans have more free time today than they did in 1965. How do we resolve this apparent contradiction?

In an analysis of the *CPS (Current Population Survey)*, Jacobs and Gerson (2001, 2004) attempted to resolve this discrepancy by stating that among highly educated, professionally employed couples, there is less free time than in previous eras. Furthermore, this select group of couples is more prevalent now than in earlier periods, due to increases in women's employment (Clarkberg & Moen, 2001; Jacobs & Gerson, 2001, 2004). The percentage of married women with children in the paid labor force has also increased over time, so that by the end of the 1990s, almost 64% of women with children under the age of 6 were employed and nearly 79% of women with children ages 6 to 17 were employed (Perry-Jenkins, Repetti, & Crouter, 2000). The available free time of these women is thus limited. However, Jacobs and Gerson (2001) also called attention to another contradiction concerning American's paid work hours: A larger sector of American society would like to work more hours but cannot find sufficient paid work, a group that is likely ever growing in the current economic climate. This group of discouraged and underemployed workers may have more available free time than fully employed individuals.

Focusing on family units, rather than total work hours of individuals, reveals how family and work trends have changed, since total work hours mask other trends that are important to consider. For example, the increase in shift work, the prevalence of parents of young children working rotating schedules, and the bifurcation of people working less or more than the traditional 40-hour work week (Clarkberg & Moen, 2001; Presser, 2003) have distinct consequences for family life. One example of a contribution by Family Studies scholars to understanding paid work hours is the Cornell Couples Career's study, which took working couples as their unit of analysis. By focusing on the couple, Clarkberg and Moen (2001) developed a typology of couples' preferences for their work patterns (traditional: wife not in paid work, husband breadwinner; neo-traditional: wife part-time paid work, husband breadwinner; or dual-earner: wives and husbands working full-time). They then examined the match between individuals' preferences and couples' actual work, finding less than half (about 45%) of working couples were working their preferred schedule (Clarkberg & Moen, 2001).

Family structure (marital and parental status) continues to be a key factor in researchers' and the public's consideration of paid work. Given the focus on family, Family Studies scholars are uniquely positioned to capture the richness in American family life as well as to identify our hopes and aspirations for paid work and family life.

Household Labor

From a Family Studies perspective, considering only paid labor when discussing work and family ignores the very real needs of family members for the performance of unpaid labor. Trends in household labor, unlike the increase in maternal employment, seem to reflect less change over time. Scholars have labeled this lack of dramatic change in a variety of ways. For example, changes over time in men's household task participation can be regarded as huge (e.g., men have doubled their weekly hours devoted to household work; Robinson & Godbey, 1997) or as minor (e.g., women still perform three times more routine household tasks as men; Coltrane, 2000; Thompson & Walker, 1989).

Women, employed or not, perform more household labor than men. Studies of time use in the contemporary era demonstrate that women who participate in the paid labor force also put in hours of household labor that result in a total workload exceeding that of men as well as women who do not work for pay (Coltrane, 2000). When regular, daily, inflexibly scheduled labor (e.g., dinner, dishes) is considered, women perform three times more of this sort of work than do men (Coltrane, 2000). Most women (2/3), however, do not describe this imbalance as unfair (Walker, 1999). How extensive the burden of household laboring addition to paid labor appears to depend on whether researchers focus on the number of activities or time spent, as well as supervision of children (an activity in which men are increasingly active) and managing household labor, such as making lists and keeping track of work needed to be done, which is a component of household labor that is more gendered than household work performance (Mederer, 1993). The pattern of activities that women do in the household may create a picture of responsibility and inequity that actual hours spent in household labor do not capture.

Recent researchers have provided some insights into the circumstances under which women's extra household burden is lessened. One finding is that the less husbands' and wives' schedules overlap, the more husbands are involved in family work, especially child care (Brayfield, 1995). Egalitarian attitudes and a good fit between men's and women's gender attitudes also predicted sharing housework (Walker, 1999). As well, women who work longer hours, make more money, and have more education do less housework, and their male partners do proportionately more, though this proportion could be a result of the reduction in women's hours rather than a substantial increase in men's hours (Bianchi et al., 2000; Coltrane, 2000; Walker, 1999). Analyses of national data sets have found that cohabiting men perform more household work than married men, but Ciabattari (2004) found that commitment to the relationship made a difference in cohabiting men's household task performance. In an interesting study of married couples without children in which one or both partners were graduate students, Pittman and his colleagues (2001) found that couples shared housework much more than in studies of broader occupational samples; in fact, women only did one fifth more household labor than men. It seems that the schedule of work or graduate school, ideology, and enhanced education combine to produce a pattern in which household labor is shared.

Leisure Time and Activities

In terms of how and with whom Americans spend their leisure time, recent work suggests that Americans may have as much or more leisure time than in earlier eras, although they do not perceive this as the case (Robinson & Godbey, 1997). This apparent misperception, and the resulting feeling of stress and lack of relaxation, seems to stem from several reasons: (a) Americans' leisure may occur in small chunks of time, around other highly regimented schedules. This chunking of time does not lend itself to deeply engaging or relaxing pursuits; (b) Americans experience such high amounts of stress at work and in other daily commitments that their leisure is seen as "decompression" time, rather than producing positive feelings through actual leisure; and (c) some people, such as parents of young children who work for pay, and individuals who work more than one paid job, actually do have less leisure time than Americans in earlier eras when such patterns were not as prevalent.

From a variety of research programs, across the country, we find support for these explanations. For example, Robinson and Godbey (1997), in their landmark study of time, reported, disappointingly, that 40% of adults' free time is spent watching TV! TV viewing, however, is not ranked by adults as an enjoyable activity. Rather, it is associated with little positive or negative emotions—suggesting an emotionally void activity—perhaps used for decompression (Larson & Richards, 1994). The activities that are ranked most enjoyable, over 30 years of diary data research, include socializing with family and friends, communicating, and playing with children (Robinson & Godbey, 1997). But such activities tend to be difficult to schedule and are not amenable to the 20- or 40- minute chunks of free time individuals might experience in a given evening. The strongest predictor of how adults spend their time is their employment status rather than demographic variables such as age and gender. Not surprising, retired individuals have the most leisure time available, but also spend more time sleeping and in personal care (i.e., eating, bathing). People working long hours, especially those who work more than one job and those who have caregiving responsibilities as well, are found to have less free time. We see a mismatch in what people actually do and what gives people pleasure.

In the Cornell Couples Study, Moen and her colleagues (2003) reported on time couples spend in leisure, again with the couple as the unit of analysis. They characterized leisure as a "jointly consumed (or foregone) commodity," and provided intriguing findings concerning women's work hours and couple leisure. When women worked long hours, they also engaged in more leisure, and their husbands did more housework and child care. In addition, Clarkberg and Merola (2003) claimed that leisure is a lifestyle choice, rather than conceiving of leisure as "residual leftover after other time use accounted for" (p. 45). Similar evidence comes from the leisure studies field (for example, see Shaw's [1991] review article analyzing several surveys conducted in Canada).

At its most negative, evidence concerning work and leisure seems to indicate that most couples do not engage in intentional leisure, but rather dribble out their leisure time in front of the television. At its most positive, for couples who do engage in active leisure, the lifestyle choice of including leisure can allow for more active family time and participation. It is possible, though, that individuals who work hard feel obligated to include leisure in their daily lives, so they are compelled to engage in frantic leisure, rushing into free-time activities as "weekend warriors." Compared to Maud Wilson's time, in which leisure was largely experienced in reading and socializing informally, we see huge changes in how families engage in leisure.

BEYOND TIME USE: DAILY EMOTIONAL SPILLOVER IN WORK AND FAMILY ROLES

Scholars in Family Studies have pursued a deeper analysis than just tracking how family members engage in paid work and leisure by delving into how people *perceive* their time, their emotions, and stress around work and family life. Most of this research has been on samples of workers highly stressed by their family stage (i.e., parents of young children) or by their occupations. Spillover between work and family has been heavily studied as a general phenomenon; in other words, workers who report stressful work life also report that they carry this stress home. The studies reviewed here are exemplary because they measure stress in precise, daily ways, and they connect daily experiences of stress in one sphere (i.e., work or family) to the other sphere. These studies also incorporate methodological sophistication and precision in the conceptualization and measurement of family relationships. In analyses of daily diary data gathered from midlife adults (*NSDE*), Almeida and his colleagues (2002) found that the most prevalent correlate of daily stress came from the occurrence of arguments and tension in interpersonal relationships. The second source of daily stress was work (Almeida, Wethington, & Kessler, 2002). Interestingly, men reported more tension due to work than women, whereas women's primary tension stemmed from household labor. Utilizing the same data set, Grzywacz and colleagues (2002) assessed the extent to which respondent's reports of negative spillover from work to family and from family to work were associated with daily stress. Via multivariate analyses comparing different daily reports of stress, they calculated the odds of reporting a stressful event at work and at home on the same day, which was related to increasing negative spillover from work to family. Less robust, but still significant, were the connections between negative spillover from family to work and the odds of contemporaneous work and family stresses. A strength of the daily diary method was that these researchers could also trace the odds of reporting a stressful event at work one day, followed by a stressful event at home the following day, and vice versa.

These sophisticated analyses of respondent's daily variation in stress provide important evidence that work and family spheres are critical to an understanding of the stress Americans experience. Larson and Richards (1994), in their family study of parents and adolescents' moods, found that men experienced heightened arousal from work to family, affecting what activities men did at home and limiting their interaction with their family. Women, regardless of their stress level at work, engaged in their typical patterns of evening activities, with time use spent in household labor. As earlier researchers identified (Pleck, 1977), there is evidence in the Larson and Richards (1994) study of bi-directional spillover, in that men's work stress affects their family life, whereas women's family stress affects their workdays. This last study begins to assess more of a family and gender context to work and family stress. Data sets that are more limited in terms of their population shed more light on the experience of stress and its specific antecedents and family spillovers. Repetti's (1989, 1994) research program, using a repeated measures methodology in which highly stressful workdays were compared to lower stress workdays within the same individuals, has focused on the work and family lives of men who work as air traffic controllers and their wives. When men experienced stressful workdays (assessed by their self-reports as well as objective indicators such as weather), they tended to withdraw from interaction with their wives, especially under conditions in which their wives were supportive. In their interactions with their children, however, days in which men experienced social stress at the workplace were followed by evenings in which men displayed more anger at their children (Repetti, 1994), which is interesting because their marital relationships on such days were characterized by less interaction and lower displays of anger (Repetti, 1989).

A companion study of an ethnically diverse sample of low-income mothers of preschoolers utilized similar methodology in which mothers' work stress was assessed on a daily basis, followed by reports of family interaction (Repetti & Wood, 1997). Repetti and Wood found that on the days that women experienced high workload or social stress at work, mothers tended to withdraw from interaction with their young children. This study included observations of maternal behavior upon reunion with their children at the end of the workday, for a subsample of the mothers, for whom the findings about maternal withdrawal were robust and quite vivid. From this exemplar research program, we learn some of the mechanisms through which stress at work affects interaction with family members as well as how gender and the nature of the family relationship (e.g., marital partner or parent) shapes the opportunities for being able to withdraw from interaction. Over time, the reader can imagine that such withdrawal would result in less family time and in less interaction with family members, which is precisely how families define "quality time."

A study conducted by Crouter and her colleagues (Crouter, Perry-Jenkins, Huston, & Crawford, 1989) utilized a similar method of obtaining data at multiple time points. In a pilot study of relatively newlywed, first-marriage couples, they requested that men (whose work schedules were standard day shifts) complete questionnaires about their mood at the end of the workday; these questionnaires were linked to measures of their involvement in household labor, leisure, and interaction with their wives later that evening. Days of high stress were days in which men engaged in less household labor and leisure activities. On such days, their wives reported that the husbands interacted with them more negatively. On days of high fatigue at the end of the workday, there was a trend toward less household task participation; and on days of high arousal, a trend for more active leisure (Crouter et al., 1989). These findings show that stress in particular had a clear association to a variety of family behaviors in the evening.

WORKING PARENTS: FAMILY TIME AND ACTIVITIES

As is the case with much research in Family Studies, the work and family research has been spurred by concerns about social problems. In this case, a major concern has been that parents are not spending enough time taking care of their children due to the increase in maternal employment. The research, however, does not support this claim.

Mothers' Time and Activities With Children

Comparing the amount of time mothers spend with children over time, Bryant and Zick (1996) conducted a trend analysis from the mid-1920s to 1981 examining maternal employment and time spent with children. Rather than supporting the claim that contemporary mothers are spending less time with their children, the amount of time mothers spent with their children doing primary care activities (such as feeding, bathing, dressing, putting to bed) actually increased modestly, both for mothers who were employed and mothers who were not employed. However, working mothers in two-parent families spent about 40% less time in primary care for their children than did mothers who were not employed. When time spent per child was considered in the analysis, Bryant and Zick found that each child's time with the mother had increased substantially over time, although this may be attributed to decreasing family size. Similarly, Sandberg and Hofferth (2001) found that in 1997 children actually spent more time with their mothers compared to children in 1981. In fact, when family structure was considered, two-parent families increased time spent with children while single-parent time held constant. The above findings demonstrate that although maternal employment has increased greatly, mothers are still finding ways to maintain time with their children. Maternal employment has not come at the expense of time spent with children, but instead comes at the expense of the time mothers have for their own personal care and leisure activities (Bryant & Zick, 1996) as well as household work, volunteer activities, sleep, and free time (Bianchi, 2000), echoing the way women in the 1920s and 1970s managed heavy workloads. These holistic analyses of women's time use in all spheres of their lives reveal their strategies for managing their time. Many mothers structured their work hours so that they do not conflict with times when their child is home from school, altering work schedules based on the time of day and the time of year (Zvonkovic, Greaves, Schmiege, & Hall, 1996).

In addition to sacrificing their own time, changes have occurred in what constitutes "good mothering" (Arendell, 2001). For example, both employed and nonemployed mothers enroll children in preschool because of the need for children to acquire social and learning skills before kindergarten. Due in part to increased knowledge about the importance of brain development and cognitive development in young children, more direct interaction, more stimulation, and more exposure to special classes and activities have become expectations for young children's lives, and mothers have increasingly become responsible for arranging these complex schedules. Sociologists, anthropologists, and historians have noted that mothers tend to be blamed for a variety of child, adolescent, and adult difficulties (Hays, 1998; Garey & Arendell, 2001), but what is new is that mothers can now be blamed for failure to conform to the emergent "intensive mothering" norm, which has developed at the same time that women's paid work demands have made this norm very difficult to fulfill.

Fathers' Time and Activities With Children

Fathers' time use with children has changed more than their time in household labor, especially when mothers are employed. Family scholars debate the extent to which fathers spending time with their children is a critical aspect of "fatherwork," the work fathers do in families to support their children (Hawkins & Dollahite, 1997). Even researchers who choose to deemphasize fathers' breadwinning as being fatherwork still disagree on the relative importance of fathers' spending time in direct interaction with their children, fathers' being accessible to their children, and fathers' taking responsibility for the care of their children (Coltrane & Adams, 2001; Lamb, Pleck, Charnov, & Levine, 1987). Findings indicate that children spend no less time with their fathers than did children in previous decades (Bianchi, 2000; Sandberg & Hofferth, 2001). In fact, fathers in married families have actually increased their time spent with children significantly (Bianchi, 2000). A major thrust of research on father's time with children has focused on whether fathers who live with employed marital partners provide more parenting time than fathers whose marital partners are not employed. The conclusion, in studies from the contemporary era, is that fathers in dual-earner families do put in more time in direct care of their children than fathers who are single wage earners in their households. In a research program involving fathers who provided daily reports on their household and family care activities, fathers in dual-earner families reported doing more than twice the amount of child care by themselves than do fathers in single-wage earner families (Crouter et al., 1987). In this same study, single-earner fathers spent more time with their sons, but dual-earner fathers did not differ in the amount of time they spent with their children based on gender (Crouter

& Crowley, 1990). In addition, fathers' responsibility for child care when the mother worked increased from 1981 to 1997 (Sandberg and Hofferth, 2001). Children spent about 6 hours more per week with their fathers when their mothers worked, so the authors suggest that this may be because fathers are providing more child care.

In a secondary analysis of the *NSFH* (National Survey of Families and Households), Coltrane and Adams (2001) analyzed 10 different activities parents might do with their children. Though mothers did 9 out of the 10 activities (e.g., helping with homework, having private talks) more often than fathers, attending or coaching youth sports was an activity in which men's contributions exceeded women's. This activity accounted for 2.22 hours per week, just over half the time fathers spent in public pursuits with their children. The specific activities that focused on the child and on nurturing were the most gender segregated and also accounted for the most parenting hours. Coltrane and Adams termed the activities fathers tended to engage in with their children as "adult-centered." Crouter and Crowley (1990) found that little time was spent in father–child dyadic activities and the time fathers did spend with children was characterized by passive activities (e.g., television or homework). Dyadic involvement between fathers and children did increase, however, when work schedules allowed for increased availability. Increased work hours decreased the amount of activities fathers participated in with their children for both single-earner and dual-earner families (Crouter et al, 1987).

Going a step further, Daly (1996b) examined the *meaning* of family time for fathers through in-depth interviews with 32 fathers from married families. In response to interview questions about what it means to be a good father and how important fatherhood is as an identity, Daly reported that fathers felt that spending time with their children was central to being a good father. At the same time, fathers were very aware of their responsibility to provide for their family. One father noted, "I guess being a manager puts bread on the table and being a father doesn't pay the bills, so there's a balance that's required" (Daly, 1996b, p. 471). Men were fatalistic about their time and that work responsibilities are the primary factor in structuring their lives. Unfortunately, this means that family time is a residual commitment. There appears, therefore, to be a disjuncture between the desires fathers expressed to spend time with their children and their ability to do so as a result of work demands (Daly, 1996b). As cultural expectations of fathers continue to call for increased paternal involvement, the contradiction between ideology and reality widens.

Children's Time and Activities

Only in the contemporary time period have researchers extended their interest in household time use to understanding how children use time. Driven by the social problems motivation, scholars have been concerned about what children of working parents might be doing in their time that is not supervised by parents. In addition, the social pressures on contemporary children and the well-documented problems of adolescents (e.g., substance abuse, sexual contact) in many ways spurred this research focus. Rather than identifying problems with how children are spending their time, in general, the research findings about children's time use mirror those of parents' choices in free time and pace of life. Articulating concerns over parents' time with children and with the nature of children's activities changing over time, Bianchi and Robinson (1997) examined the amount of time children spent reading or being read to, watching TV, studying, and doing chores, via a time diary study with respondents aged 3–11. Of the children in the study, 40% took part in housework and 22% spent time studying, during a given day. Consistent with how adults use time, the researchers reported that nearly 90% of children watched TV on a daily basis, while only 25% read or were read to on any given day. College-educated parents were more likely to encourage reading and to limit TV watching. Children's time spent in activities did not vary based on the number of parents in the household, maternal employment, or family size. It did, however, vary according to gender, with teenage girls doing more routine inside chores and boys doing more outside chores, resulting in a pattern in which teenage girls spend twice as much time in household labor as boys (Coltrane, 2000).

Other researchers have also used time methods to document children's time. In a time diary study of 2,818 children aged 12 years and younger, Hofferth and Sandberg (2001) analyzed time use for one weekday and one weekend. Results show that children and adolescents share their parents' pace of life and are often subject to their own calendars and busy schedules of school activities and community programs. Per week, children spend 55% of their time eating, sleeping, and in personal care; 15% of their time at school or day care; and 30% of their time in discretionary activities: 15 hours in free play, 12 hours watching TV, 9 hours in structured activities, 2 hours studying, and 1 hour reading (Hofferth & Sandberg, 2001). Only 45 minutes per week were spent sitting and talking to others. In a similar study, McHale, Crouter, and Tucker (2001) reported that the activities with which children (averaging 10 years old) spend their time are associated with differential social exposure, for example, time spent reading tends to be time alone, whereas time spent in organized sports tended to include parents and nonrelated adults, and time spent watching television tended to be time with parents or alone. Recognizing the social context of activities of children's everyday lives and the links between activities and children's adjustment is important. How children use their free time, leaving little time for socialization and experiencing unstructured "simple delight in life," is a disturbing trend.

Extending information on how children use time to child outcomes, activities such as reading, sports, and family activities have been of paramount concern because they have been associated with some positive child outcomes, such as achievement (Hofferth & Sandberg, 2001), though they have also been associated with depression (McHale et al., 2001). Also, structured activities such as hobbies, sports, and visiting were associated with cognitive and socioemotional well-being (Hofferth & Sandberg, 2001; McHale et al., 2001). Time spent in family activities, increased eating hours, and increased sleeping hours were related to fewer problem behaviors in children (Hofferth & Sandberg, 2001). Doing activities with parents and in the company of adults, as opposed to nonsupervised peers, during middle childhood was associated with less depression, higher achievement, and fewer conduct disorders in early adolescence (McHale et al., 2001).

Asmussen and Larson (1991) used experience sampling methods, which involved students carrying pagers for a week and completing a self-report form when they were beeped at random within every 2-hour period. Students and parents also completed a questionnaire packet at the end of each week to examine adolescents and the quality of family time (students 5th–9th grades). Adolescents in single-parent families spent less time with their parents simultaneously, but did not spend significantly less time with family than adolescents in two-parent families when time with kin was included. Adolescents in single-parent families did not spend more time in maintenance activities (household tasks and chores) than adolescents in two-parent families. Findings indicate, however, that they did spend less time in leisure activities. Adolescents in single-parent families spent more time with their mothers doing instrumental tasks (homework) and more time with their fathers in leisure activities (entertainment).

Recently, scholars have begun to examine trends in teen employment, spurred by an increase in teen paid work and a concern about teenagers' ability to manage their schoolwork along with paid work (Bene & Southers, 1993; Brown, 2001; Johnson & Lino, 2000; Redd, Brooks, & Mc-Garvey, 2002). Across the 1990s, teens from low-income families were less likely to be working than teens from higher-income families (Brown, 2001; Johnson & Lino, 2000). These data are open to interpretation: Is it because higher-class teens are more materialistic and are more connected to the consumer culture (Bene & Southers, 1993), or is it because low-income teens face limited employment opportunities (Brown, 2001)? Teens' ability to manage multiple roles and a detailed examination of how they spend their time and what they are learning about the world of work is an avenue open for future investigation.

In a related vein, Ellen Galinsky (1999) took the bold step of talking to children themselves to uncover their perspectives of their parents' work and family obligations. One conclusion reached in the Galinsky study is that parental work hours, including hours of mothers' paid work, are much less influential in children's ratings than is the children's perception that the parent is stressed by work. In the words of one 12-year-old girl, "We appreciate you. We love you. We understand when you're stressed, tired, and upset about work." The amount of time is less important than the way time at home is experienced.

NEWEST FRONTIERS: VARIATION IN WORK AND FAMILY

As contemporary scholarship has conceptualized families in their daily activities, researchers have been increasingly sensitized to variation in work and family. Such variation includes how family time is viewed as well as variation across family structure, social class, and ages.

What Is Family Time?

Recent research drawing from social constructionism involved listening to family members describe the meaning of family time for them as well as how they experience and construct time. This research has revealed intriguing contradictions between what families perceive, yearn for, and what they do. Daly's 1996 book, *Families and Time,* opened up the field of Family Studies to a reconceptualization of how families experience their lives together, beyond examining their time use to interrogating how families regard their time. Daly (2001a) has examined families' expectations of how family time should be spent. He found that parents were clear that family time was crucial as a mean of carrying on traditions and creating memories for their children. They believed that family time should be positive, involve togetherness, and be unscheduled. Daly found that the time families did spend together was characterized by obligation, demand, and conflict. The historian John Gillis wrote that everyone has two families, "one that they live with, and another that they live by" (1996, p. xv). Parents feel the elusiveness of family time and are plagued with guilt over time not spent with their families, as well as spending time as a couple or in solitude, because that time can be viewed as taken away from the family. Parents try to manage the guilt rather than making changes, demonstrating a systemic contradiction between what time is and how it should be spent.

Expanding Beyond the "Benchmark Nuclear Family"

Innovative researchers have broadened their considerations of work and family to include families of diverse structures and socioeconomic classes, cultures, and ethnicities in their analyses of work and family issues, thereby challenging themselves to expand their definitions of family and to incorporate research methods including qualitative studies, ethnographies, and other approaches. Central to Family Studies is the recognition of diversity in family structures and relationships (Demo, Allen, & Fine, 2000). An influential theoretical book even questioned the use of the term "family" and advocated encompassing a broader understanding of relationship ties (Scanzoni, Polonko, Teachman, & Thompson, 1989). Drawing from the ecological perspective, it is clear that families of different structures will interface with different systems and have different ecological niches.

Two recent examples comparing single-parent mothers and two-parent households are illustrative. In a qualitative investigation of the social time and experiences of time for single-parent mothers of preschool children, women noted how fragile their control was over their work and household time, and felt unrelentingly responsible for their children and households (Hodgson, Dienhart, & Daly, 2001). At the same time, Hodgson and her colleagues reported that mothers valued precious moments of family time and interaction with their children and often strived to make the most of commuting time or other time that they spent in each other's company, while noting the sharp differences between how they experienced time when their children were with their fathers as compared to in their homes. An ecological interpretation would emphasize how the settings their children live in (including mothers' homes and fathers' homes) influence the children's lives, but also that the fathers' home as an exosystem to the mothers has a strong influence on how she experiences her life.

In an interesting study of single-parent mothers of adolescents, utilizing experience sampling methods, Larson (2001) reported that single-parent mothers experienced their time at home as more pleasant than did mothers in dual-earner situations who had teenagers. How positive their experience of household time was, even time spent in household labor, is an intriguing finding. Coupled with data from *NSFH*, it may indicate a reduction of household responsibilities for single-mother households compared to two-parent households (Acock & Demo, 1994). We find it interesting that these two research programs yield such different portrayals of the experience of single-parent mothers' time. Methodological differences between the studies may account for the different findings, as well as the children's ages and different demands of parenting preschoolers as compared to adolescents. A Family Studies perspective that recognizes diversity in family structure as well as family life course differences adds richness to the research findings about the subjective work and family experience.

Variation in Work and Family Experience Across Social Class

Demonstrating how an ecological perspective can acknowledge differences in the context of a parents' workplace, Crouter et al. (1992) investigated the extent to which the occupational status of men's jobs was connected to their ability to reduce their work hours during the summer months and to their feelings of role overload and concern with family time. Fathers with lower-status jobs generally did not reduce their work hours during the summer; these fathers experienced greater strain and overload. Men with higher-status jobs may have more autonomy to reduce the hours they work during the summer, while men in lower-status jobs may actually increase their work hours during the summer because of job demands in occupations such as construction or farming (Crouter et al., 1992). Increased status was associated with decreased strain and overload.

Annette Lareau's recent book, *Unequal Childhoods* (2004), analyzed how parenting practices were strongly connected to parents' social classes, with middle-class parents preparing their children for active roles in interacting with adults in a variety of settings, through intensive parenting practices. By contrast, working-class parents viewed childhood as a process that unfolds naturally, rather than one to be engineered, so that their less intensive parenting practices reflected different views of childhood as well as the limits on their time and availability to their children.

The literature on work and family, even from Family Studies scholars, has tended to examine families in the middle class without serious attention to the difficulties of managing work and family obligations when work provides few resources (MacDermid, Roy, & Zvonkovic, 2005). In a rich analysis of daily life for urban working poor mothers, Roy and his colleagues (2004) investigated rhythms of work, family life, and community interaction. How women interfaced with the "public timetable" in a context in which they had few resources for scheduling or adapting to change was vividly illustrated in their work. While previous studies uncovered weekly and seasonal rhythms, Roy and his colleagues' ethnographic study showed how mothers in urban poor settings must constantly improvise with daily changes, challenging transportation issues, bureaucratic regulations and appointments, work schedules that do not mesh with child care, and school clocks and calendars. The reader is left with appreciation for the density of these women's schedules and the rapid pace in which their days unfold.

Variation in Work and Family Experience Across Family Members' Ages

Conceptualizing across the life course is a new area of work-family research in Family Studies, since the work and family literature regarding social problems has been built on the child-care dilemmas of workers who have children under the age of 6. Dual-earner couples and single-parent families especially feel constraints in making adequate time for raising children (Galinsky, 1999). Working long hours keeps adults busy and family or significant others of the worker feel the crunch of time firsthand, if not in lacking the objective time they spend together, in the strain of a rushed pace of time. Let us remember that these same busy middle-aged adults are also lacking time to spend with their aging parents (Peters, Hooker, & Zvonkovic, under review). Older parents report that they understand why their children are too busy to visit them or converse with them more frequently; however, aging parents also feel ambivalent about this loss of time with their children. It is possible that busy middle-aged adults are missing the last remaining years of their parents' independent lifestyles. Adult children do spend more time with aging parents when parents become ill or develop needs for care-assistance (Ingersoll-Dayton, Neal, & Hammer, 2001). It is unfortunate that time spent with healthy parents is not readily available because of our time-poor lives dominated by paid work. Older parents, when interviewed, remind us that we may come to regret our busy and hurried lives when we are older and reflect back upon what we experienced (Peters, 2003).

Cyclical and Calendar-Linked Variation in Work and Family Experience

As well, variation in work and family time, including the notion that time is not uniform across a year, a season, or even a week, has been pursued by several scholars. This way of looking at the patterning, synchronization, and pace of family time is increasingly adopted for scholars who take a Family Studies perspective, with the emphasis on development in context, as such scholars attend to everyday life, with structural variation in ecological context (Daly, 2001a, 2000b; MacDermid, Lee, & Smith, 2001). The rules that one family schedules by are not necessarily used in different families, the ways families synchronize their lives are not commonly experienced, nor are families' patterns consistent on a daily basis (Daly, 1996a; 2001b).

Anyone with children or any observer of modern life among families has noticed that weekday family life (in families in which adults participate in paid work during the week and in which children attend school) operates at a different pace and with different demands than weekend life. McHale, Crouter, and Bartko (1992) analyzed parents' interaction with their children as reported via daily telephone diaries of behavior, comparing weekends with weekdays. Weekends were the time when more involved fathers (whose children spent at least 43.5% of their time with a parent with their fathers) differed from less involved fathers by spending more time with their kids. Weekends were when the structural constraints of paid labor force work and school were not present, allowing for more time spent together. Whether men were highly involved with their children or not did not relate to mothers' employment status.

This analysis of weekends, a time without school for children, leads into an investigation of the ecology of family life during the summers, when not having public school commitments for children presents work/family scheduling problems. What families do during summertime was not systematically investigated until Crouter and her colleagues studied the phenomenon in the 1990s, as part of a larger study of work and family among parents of school-aged children. Crouter and McHale (1993) developed a typology of parents' year-long work commitments: One group was termed consistently dual-earner families throughout the year; another was consistently single-earner families; and the last group consisted of families in which both parents participated in paid work during the year except for the summer months, when one parent temporarily stopped working for pay, so that the family became single-earner over the summer. Work patterns throughout the year were connected to time in household labor and in child care. Dual-earner families maintained a more egalitarian division of labor over the summer months. All three groups increased their involvement with their children over the summer months (when children were not in school), but this was most evident for single-earner and single-earner over the summer families. The amount of time mothers devoted to their jobs decreased in the summer and the majority of mothers made special arrangements to be available for their children during the summer (Crouter, Hawkins, & Hostetler, 1992). In addition, fathers' involvement changed as a function of change in wives' work hours and parental roles became more traditional during the summer (Crouter & McHale, 1993).

Work Travel and Family Relationships

Our research has been heavily influenced by the idea that time in families and at work is variable. We tried to find a group of workers in which the variability of work and family time would be evident, and obvious enough to the families themselves that they could discuss it. In a series of studies we have conducted on the specific job demand of travel, we have investigated the extent to which travel on the part of one family member affects family involvement. As part of a larger project on commercial fishing, we conducted focus groups, qualitative interviews, and behavioral self-reports among families in which husbands were commercial fishermen, gone from home for extended periods of time (ranging from 5-day cycles to 4-month cycles; Zvonkovic, McGraw, & Manoogian-O'Dell, 2000). We also engaged in a parallel study of long-haul truckers and their wives. Our findings revealed that the travel schedule of the men promoted women's independence in household activities and decisions (Zvonkovic, Manoogian, & McGraw, 2001). As Helen Mederer and Christopher Barker (2001) have described with a similar population of commercial fishermen, men become "periodic guests" in the home rather than fully participating family members. Though women in our studies were aware of this tendency, they alternately fought it by working to promote fathers' authority to discipline, and promoted it by making financial decisions such as purchasing a home without their husbands' knowledge or input.

We also analyzed how travel schedules related to patterns of marital and family life (Zvonkovic et al., 2001), inspired by Repetti's program of research that also focused on specific occupations and daily connection with family members. We uncovered a pattern that the work schedule of traveling husbands invoked on family life, evidence of the problems with synchronizing family schedules discussed by Daly (1996a, 2001a). The first phase, departure, concerns the stressful time when families are preparing the men to leave. Family members work to get the husband ready for the trip and to prepare themselves emotionally for the upcoming absence. Wives and husbands described this phase as emotional, with wives expressing anger, on some level, at being left behind, and husbands sometimes expressing guilt about leaving their wives with so many responsibilities. Separation, the second phase, concerns being away. Husbands and wives experienced this phase very differently, with fishing husbands experiencing their time according to the rhythm and atmosphere at sea, fraught with danger and vigilance, and trucking husbands also operating outside of traditional clock time. During separation', wives tackled all home and family responsibilities. Without fail, wives commented on enjoying their independence and being proud of what they accomplished in their husbands' absence. Most wives in the study thrived under these conditions, relishing their independence.

The third phase, homecoming, starts once the trip is half over and continues as he returned. We viewed this phase as distinct because the husbands reported that at this point, their thoughts and emotions turned more to home. Mostly, the dominant emotion for husbands during home-coming was excitement. Wives' perspectives on the emotions associated with homecoming are related to husbands', but different. Wives' perspectives confirmed the activities of home-coming, but wives did not use language connoting vacation or party to describe his return. The wives generally talked about trying not to overwhelm their husbands with news of what had occurred in their absence, and about trying to create a restful and quiet home environment so that husbands could adjust more quickly.

In many ways, wives were more focused on the final phase, reunion, which was quite different from the homecoming, because families at this point do the work of reintegrating the man into the family. Both wives and husbands identified this phase as distinct from the anticipation and romance of homecoming. Families switch gears from a one-parent system to a two-parent system and negotiate how much intimacy to experience. Men and women voiced many different experiences in the reunion stage. Some couples understood and struggled with the complexities of making room for husbands. There was also some sense that wives might move into the reunion phase before husbands were ready. It could also be that some husbands might be content with homecoming excitement up until the next departure. For the most part, husbands focused on their transition back into the household as disciplinarian (Zvonkovic et al., 2001). Wives also expressed concern about reintegrating husbands back into households, forcing a relinquishment on the wife's part of control over family activities and family time. Articulating the phases family members who experience frequent work-related separation go through illuminates the variable experience of time together and apart in families.

Because the patterns we uncovered are heavily gendered and seemed strongly connected to men as breadwinners, we were very curious to see what the family dynamics would be when the work travelers were women. Our present project involves the study of women in a variety of family structures who are employed in three specific occupations, which differ in travel schedule and other factors: flight attendants, high-tech computer consultants, and nonprofit aid and adoption workers. In general, our preliminary analyses demonstrate that women's travel did not promote men's household independence. Instead, women performed a great deal of household labor preparing their families for their upcoming trip, in contrast to the case of fishermen and truckers in which the family prepared the traveler. Women performed a great deal of household management, compiling plans, posting lists, for example, of their children's after-school activities and special arrangements for them to be transported (Zvonkovic & Peters, 2002). Virtually every woman with a child also described one "totem" household task she focused on before the trip, whether it was ensuring that all the laundry was clean, cooking food for the family to eat during the trip, or cleaning the bathrooms. However, for women who traveled for work and did not have children at home, we saw no evidence that household labor was performed in anticipation of the trip. When children were present, men's involvement in the home and especially with their children was assumed, and men's support for women's breadwinning and career was evident (Zvonkovic & Peters, 2003). This pattern actually minimized women's conflicts between work and family, because they were able to experience work during their trips as their primary demand.

Studying this specialized population demonstrates the importance of synchronization on the part of other families who might have more room for negotiation of their responsibilities (Zvonkovic, Richards, Humble, & Manoogian, 2005). The families we studied had to synchro-nize their calendars, but then, when apart (regardless of whether it was the man or the woman who traveled), the one at home was in charge. This pattern minimized gendered parenting and the tendency for the mother to take over. Yet, women who traveled still felt the pull of home in poignant ways that men did not discuss. In contrast, men were very aware of the pull of the ocean and the road, and breadwinning, in ways women did not discuss. By examining the perceptions of time in family life on the part of men who travel for work, women who travel for work, and their families, we see revealed sharp differences, demonstrating both the cyclical variability of time within these families and the way gender relates to the experience of work and family time.

QUESTIONING BELIEFS AND NORMS ABOUT PAID WORK, FAMILY WORK, AND LEISURE

Recent critical theorizing and research has called into question the traditional conceptualizations of work and family life. One early voice was that of Stephen Marks (1977), who rejected the concept that human time, energy, and commitment were necessarily limited, as had been assumed by those in the role based camp of symbolic interaction. He proposed instead a model of expansion, and articulated how commitments to a person's systems of involvements would lead to time in those involvements being experienced as draining or rewarding. Daly's (1996a) book presented an analysis of time as socially constructed, rejecting the idea that time is necessarily linear. Henderson and Allen (1991) interrogated the concepts of leisure and vacation, revealing that such time often involves an increase in, not a release from, work for women, when unpaid labor is considered. Innovative research has also broadened the consideration of family labor to include a variety of work including emotion work (DeVault, 1991; Hochschild, 1985; Erickson, 1993; Seery & Crowley, 2000). Feminist researchers, particularly those who study household labor, have problematized gender in families in terms of involvement in work and family spheres. As we incorporate these themes, we question the way we experience our leisure, especially the ways in which we "time-deepen" (doing more in less time) and multi-task (doing many actions at once). These activities heighten the pace of our lives, contributing to so many Americans *feeling* time-deprived and stressed.

Given that the objective amount of free time experienced by Americans seems relatively stable over time (Galinksy, 1999; Robinson & Godbey, 1997), we then must ask the question: Why do we feel so busy? Also, what drives us to time-deepen and to multi-task? To answer this question requires a cultural analysis. Anthropologists and sociologists advise us to examine the cultural norms of our technological society. To advance in a career, people feel compelled to put in more hours to show job commitment (termed "face time"). Our desire for material goods (consumerism) drives our intense participation in professional careers, where more income has replaced the priority of more leisure (Clarkberg & Moen, 2001; Hochschild, 1985; Robinson & Godbey, 1997; Schor, 1991). Cultural critiques note our acquisition of expensive leisure time equipment, without our taking the time to actually do the leisure activity!

If norms about working and consumerism were not enough, we currently are experiencing heightened expectations for parenting, with the advent of the intensive mothering norm and the fatherwork movement (Arendell, 2001; Hawkins & Dollahite, 1997; Hays, 1998). Growing expectations that fathers spend time with their children co-occur with continued gendered expectations for them to be breadwinners. Mothers are expected to be home with their children, though most participate in paid work, at the same time ensuring that their children are provided for and able to participate in numerous childhood activities that are increasingly expensive. These parenting norms drive people in paid work to professionalize parenting and household management, which then leads to elevated standards for all parents and households. Even those with little access to professionalizing their parenting and household are not immune to these cultural forces. Earlier life course patterns may set us on trajectories of time use in our families, a concern for adults and for children. Children's pace in contemporary studies reflects the pace set by their parents. We have to wonder whether they will transmit their pace and stress in future generations. Are there pioneers who have found pathways of more intentional use of their time in work and in family, following the challenges described by Daly (1996a) and Robinson and Godbey (1997)? The social issues concerns in Family Studies will compel researchers in the future to tackle these contradictions and problems.

CONCLUSION

A hallmark of research in Family Studies is taking variation and context into account: Families differ by age, work status, socioeconomic status, and the tempo or rhythm of their lives. Undertaking research that includes this diversity provides a deeper inquiry into the nature of family life that might be affected by work. Many studies use families as the unit of analysis (Moen, 2003; Larson & Richards, 1994; Crouter et al., 1992, 1999; Crouter & McHale, 1993). Others delve more deeply into work activities to specify what it is about work that could be carried over into personal life (Repetti, 1989, 1994; Repetti & Wood, 1997; Zvonkovic et al., 2000, 2001; Zvonkovic & Peters, 2003). Starting from Wilson's study of farm and household labor among mothers, the focus on the nature of the job, the setting in which families live, the age and presence of children, and the household focus has been retained. In the postmodern era, we have uncovered many shades of meaning about how we experience work and family life, different concepts that are important to understand, and different populations whose work and family lives need to be taken into account. Future studies will need to continue exploring alternative meanings of work and family life for more diverse populations. Researchers will continue to be challenged by the complexity of the phenomena of paid work, household labor, and leisure time, in ever-more complex families. Clearly, the burgeoning methods used to study families and work and the confluence of different theoretical perspectives and disciplines is an asset to the Family Studies field.

We view individuals in families as active constructors of their time, though we recognize and study their ecological niches including the constraints that some families experience, because of the ages of their children, their economic situations, their urban or rural settings, and their family structures as well as how these factors relate. Nevertheless, collectively, we have the power to change the pace of our lives and to develop new norms that would guide behavior and standards we might actually be able to attain. Only through doing so can we achieve the goal of enriching family life. The applied approach of Family Studies is well suited to studying work and family life, because researchers working in this interdisciplinary field share a mission to conduct research that improves lives. Family Studies professionals can be found advocating and educating on behalf of families, establishing the connection between research to describe needs, offer alternatives, and spur action for families. Uniting these practices pushes us to encourage family members to be mindful about their lives and their connections to each other, including their paid work commitments, their household work, their leisure, and their parenting as well as the pace of their everyday lives.

REFERENCES

Acock, A., & Demo, D. (1994). *Family diversity and well-being*. Thousand Oaks, CA: Sage.
Almeida, D. M. (2004). Using daily diaries to assess temporal friction between work and family. In A. C. Crouter & A. Booth (Eds.), *Work-family challenges for low income parents and their children*. Hillsdale, NJ: Lawrence Erlbaum Associates.

Almeida, D. M., & McDonald, D. (in press). The time Americans spend working for pay, caring for families, and contributing to communities. In J. Heymann (Ed.), *Work, family, and democracy*. New York: Basic Books.

Almeida, D. M., Wethington, E. K., & Kessler, C. C. (2002). The Daily Inventory of Stressful Events: An interview-based approach for measuring daily stressors. *Assessment, 9(1)*, 41–55.

Arendell, T. (2001). The new care work of middle class mothers: Managing childrearing, employment, and time. In K. Daly (Ed.), *Minding the time in family experience: Emerging perspectives and issues* (pp. 163–204). Oxford: JAI.

Asmussen, L., & Larson, R. (1991). The quality of family time among young adolescents in single-parent and married-parent families. *Journal of Marriage and the Family, 53*, 1021–1030.

Bene, P. J., & Southers, C. L. (1993). A resource issue: Employment and the enhancement of adolescent well-being. *Journal of Home Economics, 85*, 23–29.

Bengtson, V. L. (1989). The problems of generations: Age group contrasts, continuities, and social change. In V. L. Bengtson & K. W. Schaie (Eds.), *The course of later life: Research and reflections* (pp. 25–54). New York: Springer.

Bengston, V., & Allen, K. (1993). The life course perspective applied to families over time. In P. Boss, W. Doherty, R. LaRossa, P. Schumm, & S. Steinmetz (Eds.), *Sourcebook of family theories and methods: A contextual approach* (pp. 469–499). New York: Plenum.

Bengtson, V. L., & Achenbaum, W. A. (Eds.). (1994). *The changing contract between generations*. Hawthorn, NY: DeGruyter.

Bengtson, V. L., Allen, K., Acock, A., Dilworth-Anderson, P., & Klein, D. (Eds.) (2005). *Sourcebook of family theories and methods*. Thousand Oaks, CA: Sage.

Berk, R. A., & Berk, S. F. (1979). *Labor and leisure at home: Content and organization of the household day*. Beverly Hills, CA: Sage.

Bianchi, S. M. (2000). Maternal employment and time with children: Dramatic change or surprising continuity? *Demography, 37*, 401–414.

Bianchi, S. M., Milkie, M. A., Sayer, L. C., & Robinson, J. P. (2000). Is anyone doing the housework? Trends in the gender division of household labor. *Social Forces, 79*, 191–228.

Bianchi, S. M., & Robinson, J. (1997). What did you do today? Children's use of time, family composition, and the acquisition of social capital. *Journal of Marriage and the Family, 59*, 332–344.

Bond, J. T., Galinsky, E., & Swanberg, J. E. (1998). *The 1997 National Study of the Changing Workforce*. New York: Families and Work Institute.

Brayfield, A. (1995). Juggling jobs and kids: The impact of employment schedules on fathers' caring for children. *Journal of Marriage and the Family, 57*, 321–332.

Broderick, C., & Smith, R. (1979). The general systems approach to the family. In W. R. Burr, R. Hill, F. I. Nye, & I. L. Reiss (Eds.), *Contemporary theories about the family*, vol. 2 (pp. 112–129). New York: Free Press.

Bronfenbrenner, U. (1979). *The ecology of human development*. Cambridge, MA: Harvard University Press.

Bronfenbrenner, U. (1986). Ecology of the family as a context for human development. *Developmental Psychology, 22*, 723–742.

Brown, B. (2001). Teens, jobs, and welfare: Implications for social policy. *Child Trends Research Brief*. Washington, DC, 1–6.

Bryant, W. K., & Zick, C. D. (1996). Are we investing less in the next generation? Historical trends in time spent caring for children. *Journal of Family and Economic Issues, 17*, 365–392.

Ciabattari, T. (2004). Cohabitation and housework: The effects of marital intentions. *Journal of Marriage and Family, 66*, 118–125.

Clarkberg, M., & Merola, S. S. (2003). Competing clocks: Work and leisure. In P. Moen (Ed.), *It's about time: Couples and careers* (pp. 35–48). Ithaca, NY: Cornell University Press.

Clarkberg, M., & Moen, P. (2001). Understanding the time-squeeze: Married couples' preferred and actual work-hour strategies. *American Behavioral Scientist, 44*, 1115–1136.

Coltrane, S. (2000). Research on household labor: Modeling and measuring the social embeddedness of routine family work. *Journal of Marriage and Family, 62*, 427–452.

Coltrane, S., & Adams, M. (2001). Men's family work: Child-centered fathering and the sharing of domestic labor. In R. Hertz & N. L. Marshall (Eds.), *Working families: The transformation of the American home* (pp. 72–99). Berkeley: University of California Press.

Crouter, A. C., & Crowley, M. S. (1990). School-age children's time alone with fathers in single- and dual-earner families: Implications for the father–child relationship. *Journal of Early Adolescence, 10*(3), 296–312.

Crouter, A. C., Hawkins, A. J., & Hostetler, M. (1992). Seasonal stability and change in dual-earner husbands' psychological responses to work and family roles. *International Journal of Behavioral Development, 15*, 509–525.

Crouter, A. C., Helms-Erikson, H., Updegraff, K., & McHale, S. M. (1999). Conditions underlying parents' knowledge about children's daily lives in middle childhood: Between- and within-family comparisons. *Child Development, 70*, 246–259.

Crouter, A. C., & McHale, S. M. (1993). Temporal rhythms in family life: Seasonal variation in the relation between parental work and family processes. *Developmental Psychology, 29*(2), 198–205.

Crouter, A. C., Perry-Jenkins, M., Huston, T. L., & Crawford, D. W. (1989). The influence of work-induced psychological states on behavior at home. *Basic & Applied Social Psychology, 10*(3), 273–292.

Crouter, A. C., Perry-Jenkins, M., Huston, T. L., & McHale, S. M. (1987). Processes underlying father involvement in dual-earner and single-earner families. *Developmental Psychology, 23*, 431–440.

Daly, K. J. (1996a). *Families and time: Keeping pace in a hurried culture.* Thousand Oaks, CA: Sage.

Daly, K. J. (1996b). Spending time with the kids: Meanings of family time for fathers. *Family Relations, 45*, 466–476.

Daly, K. J. (2001a). Deconstructing family time: From ideology to lived experience. *Journal of Marriage and Family, 63*, 283–294.

Daly, K. J. (Ed.). (2001b). *Minding the time in family experience: Emerging perspectives and issues.* New York: Elsevier Science.

Demo, D., Allen, K. R., & Fine, M. A. (2000). *The handbook of family diversity.* New York: Oxford University Press.

DeReus, L., Few, A., & Blume, L. B. (2005). Theorizing identities and intersectionalities: Third-wave feminism, critical race theory, and families. In V. Bengtson, K. Allen, A. Acock, P. Dilworth-Anderson, & D. Klein (Eds.), *Sourcebook of family theories and methods.*

DeVault, M. (1991). *Feeding the family: The social organization of caring and gendered work.* Chicago: University of Chicago Press.

Elder, G. H. (1974). *Children of the Great Depression.* Cambridge, MA: Harvard University Press.

Erickson, R. J. (1993). Reconceptualizing family work: The effect of emotion work on perceptions of marital quality. *Journal of Marriage and the Family, 55*, 888–900.

Galinsky, E. (1999). *Ask the children: What America's children really think about working parents.* New York: Morrow.

Galinsky, E., Bond, J. T., & Friedman, D. E. (1993). *The changing workforce: Highlights from the national study.* Families and Work Institute.

Garey, A. I. (1999). *Weaving work and motherhood.* Philadelphia: Temple University Press.

Garey, A. I., & Arendell, T. (2001). Children, work, and family: Some thoughts on "mother-blame." In R. H. Hertz & N. L. Marshall (Eds.), *Working families: The transformation of the American Home* (pp. 293–303). Berkeley: University of California Press.

Gillis, J. (1996). *A work of their own making: Myth, ritual, and the quest for family values.* New York: Basic Books.

Grzywacz, J. G., Almeida, D. M., & McDonald, D. A. (2002). Work-family spillover and daily reports of work and family stress in the adult labor force. *Family Relations: Journal of Applied Family & Child Studies, 51*(1), 28–36.

Hareven, T. (1982). *Family time and industrial time.* Cambridge, MA: Cambridge University Press.

Hawkins, A. J., & Dollahite, D. C. (1997). Beyond the role-inadequacy perspective of fathering. In A. J. Hawkins & D. C. Dollahite (Eds.), *In generative fathering: Beyond deficit perspectives.* Thousand Oaks, CA: Sage.

Hays, S. (1998). *The cultural contradictions of motherhood.* New Haven, CT: Yale University Press.

Henderson, K. A., & Allen, K. R. (1991). The ethic of care: Leisure possibilities and constraints for women. *Society and Leisure, 14*, 97–113.

Hochschild, A. R. (1985). *The managed heart.* Berkeley: University of California Press.

Hochschild, A. R. (1997). *The time bind: When work becomes home and home becomes work.* New York: Holt.

Hodgson, J., Dienhart, A., & Daly, K. (2001). Time juggling: Single mothers' experience of time press following divorce. *Journal of Divorce and Remarriage, 35*, 1–28.

Hofferth, S. L., & Sandberg, J. F. (2001). How American children spend their time. *Journal of Marriage and Family, 63*, 295–308.

Humble, A. M., & Zvonkovic, A. M. (2002). Job-related travel: Work conditions and work/family spillover. Paper presented at the Persons, Processes, and Places: Research on Families, Workplaces, and Communities Conference, San Francisco, February 2002.

Ingersoll-Dayton, B., Neal, M. B., & Hammer, L. B. (2001). Aging parents helping adult children: The experience of the sandwiched generation. *Family Relations: Interdisciplinary Journal of Applied Studies, 50*, 262–271.

Jacobs, J., & Gerson, K. (1998). Who are the overworked Americans? *Review of Social Economy, 4*, 442–459.

Jacobs, J., & Gerson, K. (2001). Overworked individuals or overworked families? Explaining trends in work, leisure, and family time. *Work and Occupation, 28*(1), 40–63.

Jacobs, J., & Gerson, K. (2004). *The time divide: Work, family, and gender inequality.* Cambridge, MA: Harvard University Press.

Johnson, D. S., & Lino, M. (2000). Teenagers: Employment and contributions to family spending. *Monthly Labor Review, 123*(9), 15–25.

Juster, F. T., & Stafford, F. P. (1985). *Time, goods, and well-being.* University of Michigan, Ann Arbor: Institute for Social Research.

Lamb, M. E., Pleck, J. H., Charnov, E. L., & Levine, J. A. (1987). A biosocial perspective on paternal behavior and involvement. In J. B. Lancaster, J. Altmann, A. S. Rossi, & L. R. Sherrod (Eds.), *Parenting across the lifespan: Biological dimensions.* New York: DeGruyter.

Lareau, A. (2004). *Unequal childhoods: Class, race, and family life.* Berkely: University of Calfornia Press.

LaRossa, R., & Reitzes, D. (1993). Symbolic interactionism and family studies. In P. Boss, W. Doherty, R. LaRossa, P. Schumm, & S. Steinmetz (Eds.), *Sourcebook of family theories and methods: A contextual approach* (pp. 135–162). New York: Plenum.

Larson, R. (2001). Mother's time in two-parent and one-parent families: The daily organization of work, time for oneself, and parenting of adolescents. In K. J. Daly (Ed.), *Minding the time in family experience: Emerging perspectives and issues* (pp. 85–109). New York: Elsevier Science.

Larson, R., & Richards, M. H. (1994). *Divergent realities: The emotional lives of mothers, fathers, and adolescents.* New York: Basic Books.

MacDermid, S., Lee, M. D., & Smith, S. (2001). Forward into yesterday: Families and work in the 21st century. In K. J. Daly (Ed.), *Minding the time in family experience: Emerging perspectives and issues* (pp. 59– 84). New York: Elsevier Science.

MacDermid, S., Roy, K., & Zvonkovic, A. (2005). Don't stop at the borders: Theorizing beyond "work and family." In V. Bengtson, K. Allen, A. Acock, P. Dilworth-Anderson, & D. Klein (Eds.), *Sourcebook of family theories and methods* (pp. 493–516).

Marks, S. R. (1977). Multiple roles and role strain. *American Sociological Review, 42,* 921–936.

Marks, S. R. (1994). Patterns of commitment. *Journal of Marriage and the Family, 56,* 112–115.

Marks, S. R., & MacDermid, S. M. (1996). Multiple roles and the self: A theory of role balance. *Journal of Marriage and the Family, 58,* 417–433.

McHale, S. M., Crouter, A. C., & Bartko, W. T. (1992). In D. L. Featherman, R. M. Lerner, & M. Perlmutter (Eds.), *Life-span development and behavior* (vol. 11). Hillsdale, NJ: Lawrence Earlbaum Associates.

McHale, S. M., Crouter, A. C., & Tucker, C. J. (2001). Free-time activities in middle childhood: Links with adjustment in early adolescence. *Child Development, 72,* 1764–1778.

Mederer, H. J. (1993). Division of labor in two-earner homes: Task accomplishment versus household maintenance as critical variables in perceptions about family work. *Journal of Marriage and the Family, 55,* 133–145.

Mederer, H. J., & Barker, C. (2001). Reconstructing identities, families, communities, and futures in the wake of fisheries regulation. In S. Hanna & M. Hall-Arbor (Eds.), *Resilience in fishing communities, businesses, and families* (pp. 69–82). Corvallis, OR: OSU Press.

Moen, P. (Ed.). (2003). *It's about time: Couples and careers.* Ithaca, NY: Cornell University Press.

Nickols, S. Y. (1986). Human resources and household time allocation: A long-term view. In R. E. Deacon & W. E. Huffman (Eds.), *Human resources research, 1887–1987 proceedings.* Ames, Iowa: Iowa State University Publications.

Osmond, M. W., & Thorne, B. (1993). Feminist theories: The social construction of gender in families and society. In P. Boss, W. Doherty, R. LaRossa, P. Schumm, & S. Steinmetz (Eds.), *Sourcebook of family theories and methods: A contextual approach* (pp. 591–622). New York: Plenum.

Perry-Jenkins, M., Repetti, R. L., & Crouter, A. C. (2000). Work and family in the 1900s. *Journal of Marriage and Family, 62,* 200–217.

Peters, C. L. (2003). *Mixed emotions in later life: Older parents' experiences of intergenerational ambivalence.* Oregon State University: Unpublished master's thesis.

Peters, C. L., Hooker, K., & Zvonkovic, A. M. (under review). Older parents' experiences of intergenerational ambivalence: Time away from and with their children.

Pittman, J. F., & Kerpelman, J. L. (2001). Stress and performance standards: A dynamic approach to time spent in housework. *Journal of Marriage and Family, 63,* 1111–1121.

Pleck, J. H. (1977). The work-family role system. *Social Problems, 24*(4), 417–427.

Pleck, J. H. (1985). *Working wives/working husbands.* Newbury Park, CA: Sage.

Plionis, E. M. (1990). Parenting, discipline, and the concept of quality time. *Child and Adolescent Social Work, 7*(6), 513–523.

Presser, H. B. (1995). Job, family, and gender—determinants of nonstandard work schedules among employed Americans in 1991. *Demography, 32,* 577–598.

Presser, H. B. (2003). *Working in a 24/7 Economy.* Cambridge, MA: Harvard University Press.

Presser, H. B., & Hermsen, J. M. (1996). Gender differences in the determinants of work-related overnight travel among employed Americans. *Work & Occupations, 23,* 87–108.

Redd, Z., Brooks, J., & McGarvey, A. M. (2002). Educating America's youth: What makes a difference? *Child Trends Research Brief.* Washington, DC, 1–8.

Repetti, R. L. (1989). Effects of daily workload on subsequent behavior during marital interaction: The roles of social withdrawal and spouse support. *Journal of Personality & Social Psychology, 57*(4), 651–659.

Repetti, R. L. (1994). Short-term and long-term processes linking job stressors to father–child interaction. *Social Development, 3*(1), 1–15.

Repetti, R. L., & Wood, J. (1997). Effects of daily stress at work on mothers' interactions with preschoolers. *Journal of Family Psychology, 11*(1), 90–108.

Robinson, J. (1977). *How Americans use time: A social-psychological analysis of everyday behavior.* New York: Praeger.

Robinson, J. P., & Godbey, G. (1997). *Time for life: The surprising ways Americans use their time.* University Park: Pennsylvania State University Press.

Roy, K. M., Tubbs, C., & Burton, L. M. (2004). Don't have no time: Daily rhythms and the organization of time for low-income families. *Family Relations, 53,* 168–178.

Sandberg, J. F., & Hofferth, S. L. (2001). Changes in children's time with parent: United States, 1981–1997. *Demography, 38,* 423–436.

Scanzoni, J., Polonko, K., Teachman, J., & Thompson, L. (1989). *The sexual bond: Rethinking families and close relationships.* Newbury Park, CA: Sage.

Schor, J. (1991). *The overworked American.* New York: Basic Books.

Schor, J. (2003). The even more overworked American. In J. De Graaf, (Ed.), *Take back your time: Fighting overwork and time poverty in American* (pp. 6–11). San Francisco: Berrett-Koehler.

Seery, B., & Crowley, M. S. (2000). Women's emotion work in the family relationship management and the process of building father–child relationships. *Journal of Family Issues, 21,* 100–127.

Shaw, S. (1991). Research note: Women's leisure time—using time budget data to examine current trends and future predictions. *Leisure Studies, 10,* 171–181.

Thompson, L., & Walker, A. J. (1989). Gender in families: Women and men in marriage, work, and parenthood. *Journal of Marriage and Family, 51*(4), 845–871.

Twiggs, J. E., McQuillan, J. A., & Ferree, M. M. (1999). Meaning and measurement: Reconceptualizing measures of the division of household labor. *Journal of Marriage and the Family, 61,* 712–724.

Walker, A. J. (1999). Gender and family relationships. In M. Sussman, S. K. Steinmetz, & G. W. Peterson (Eds.), *Handbook of marriage and the family* (2nd ed., pp. 439–474). New York: Plenum.

Walker, K. E. (1980). Time measurement and the value of nonmarket household production. In C. Hefferan (Ed.), *The household as producer: A look beyond the market* (pp. 119–138). St. Charles, MO: Lindenwood College.

Walker, K. E., & Woods, M. E. (1976). *Time use: A measure of household production of family goods and services.* Washington, DC: The Center for the Family American Home Economics Association.

Whitchurch, G., & Constantine, L. (1993). Family systems theory. In P. Boss, W. Doherty, R. LaRossa, P. Schumm, & S. Steinmetz (Eds.), *Sourcebook of family theories and methods: A contextual approach* (pp. 1325–1352). New York: Plenum.

Wilson, M. (1929). *Use of time by Oregon farm homemakers.* Corvallis: Agricultural Experiment Station, Oregon State Agriculture College.

Zvonkovic, A. M., Greaves, K. M., Schmiege, C. J., & Hall, L. D. (1996). The marital construction of gender through work and family decisions: A qualitative analysis. *Journal of Marriage and the Family, 58,* 91–100.

Zvonkovic, Anisa M., Manoogian, Margaret, M., & McGraw, Lori A. (2001). The ebb and flow of family life: How families experience being together and apart. In K. Daly (Ed.), *Minding the time in family experience: Emerging perspectives and issues* (pp. 135–160). Amsterdam: JAI Press.

Zvonkovic, A. M., McGraw, L. A., & Manoogian-O'Dell, M. (2000). A multi-method research project on commercial fishing families: Multiple windows on resilient women and families. In S. Hanna & M. Hall-Arbor (Eds.), *Resilience in fishing communities, businesses, and families* (pp. 83–96). Corvallis, OR: OSU Press.

Zvonkovic, A. M., & Peters, C. L. (2002). Gender, control, and work-related travel: Women's work and personal lives through the prism of control. Paper presented as part of a symposium on Gender, Control, and Work at the National Council on Family Relations annual conference, Houston, TX.

Zvonkovic, A. M., & Peters, C. L. (2003). Facilitating worker identity and involvement: A qualitative study of women who travel for work. Paper presented at the annual meeting of the National Council on Family Relations, Vancouver, BC.

Zvonkovic, A., Richards Solomon, C., Humble, A., & Manoogian, M. (2005). Family work and relationships: Lessons from families of men whose jobs require travel. *Family Relations, 54,* 411–422.

8

The Anthropology of the Workplace and the Family

Pete Richardson
University of Michigan

When speaking of a "workplace," we are already on the terrain of modern institutions. Prior to the modern reorganization of relations in and of production, most everyone's place of work was household or field; about the closest thing we find to a distinct workplace are the forges and workbenches of craft and artisan labor, or perhaps the intensive organization and division of labor found on the fishing vessel. This is also true of the separation of work and family: at least for those not laboring under bondage, work was usually with family, lineage, and community until the advent of the modern workplace and impersonal markets in labor.

Urbanization, wage labor, specialization within the division of labor, and delayed entrance into labor for youth (tied to education) are among the forces leading to the separation of work and family in space (the workplace from the home) and in time (the working day from leisure time spent with family and/or friends), particularly among global middle classes. Yet we sometimes find, even in the modern workplace, multiple members of the same family being employed by the same firm and family idioms—claims that familylike structures are part of the workplace. For example, groups like unions invoke kindred-ness by using family, brotherhood and sisterhood, as idioms of solidarity. On the whole, family is invoked in the workplace as a way to motivate subjects toward certain ends.

Over the past decade or so, there has appeared in anthropology what has been called "the new kinship," stressing *relatedness*: nongenealogical, yet substantial and binding motives of reciprocity (Carsten, 2000; Franklin & McKinnon, 2001). Rather than accepting the nuclear family as normative, relatedness looks to the ways people forge ties of familiarity with each other through everyday exchanges, through identification, through shared practices. Relatedness rests in a "processual view of kinship and personhood" (Carsten, 1995, p. 223). Kinship arises when it is made, for example, through nurturance, through exchange, and through being sworn—avowed. The new kinship's focus on how the family is made, rather than being simply natural, makes it perfect for exploring what is familylike in the modern workplace and worklike in the family. Relatedness stresses that, rather than being a natural entity, making families takes work.

The major theme of this chapter is how family, or relatedness, is found in the workplace and invoked as an idiom within moral discourses concerning right action in working and how those moral discourses motivate. To achieve this, attention must also be paid to how work enters and structures the family. This is the chapter's minor theme: the recursivity of work and family such that the workplace enters into and structures the home.

The question is not how do we adapt the workplace to the family, but how do we understand the multitude of heterogeneous ways in which the family and the workplace are already bound together and interpenetrating? Once the separation of work and family is recognized to be more of a historically conditioned and strategically placed opposition than a reality, then the question becomes: why this particular constellation of interpenetrations of work and family rather than another? What are the relevant factors at the level of family strategies and institutional opportunities and constraints leading this set of relations to emerge rather than another?

For most people in the United States, work is the path to all other ends. Work is who we are: if Americans have a core principle of identity, it is economic. As Calvin Coolidge said, "The business of America is business." Occupational identity is at the core of American subjectivity, as are economic models of thought, to the point George Marcus can argue that there is a "'doppelganger' quality of economic processes in relation to cultural processes" in the United States (Marcus, 1990, p. 339). At the very least, work, via wages and salary, is how we acquire the means to achieve other goals. As such, work is critical to any understanding of personhood and meaning in the United States.

Occupational identity has been a critical factor shaping the vicissitudes of relatedness, such that we might even speak of "occupational relatedness" existing: That is, who you are proximate with or close to, and whom distance is kept from, in the workplace and outside the workplace is motivated by personhood viewed through occupational lenses. Lawyers and factory workers rarely drink, eat, or otherwise socialize together (unless they are otherwise related—i.e., mother and son, brother and sister); does this mean they have distinct cultures?[1]

Following a short history and review of ethnographic methods and the study of work, culture and other core issues in the anthropology of work are discussed. The next two sections cover the family in the workplace (with a focus on blue-collar workers) and the workplace in the family (focused on professional and/or middle-class work and families). The last section before the conclusion considers some psychological and philosophical anthropological questions about human subjects at work (with a focus on the concept of knowledge work).

WHAT ANTHROPOLOGY OFFERS TO THE STUDY OF WORK AND FAMILY

Work and family have always been among anthropology's core interests. When looking at the foundations of anthropology, it is difficult to find a study that is not marked by a concern with work (e.g., Malinowski's debate with Radcliffe-Brown over the relation of ritual to deep-sea fishing [Malinowski, 1954; Radcliffe-Brown, 1939]), family (Lewis Henry Morgan's or Claude Levi-Strauss' study of kinship [Morgan, 1997; Levi-Strauss, 1969]), or both (Evan-Pritchard's study of the Nuer's segmentary lineages in relation to the "bovine idioms" of cattle herding [Evans-Pritchard, 1982]). Today, there is a resurgent interest among anthropologists in studying the family (e.g., Carsten, 2000, 2004; Franklin & McKinnon, 2001; Strathern, 1992).

Likewise, the past few decades have seen a burgeoning interest in the study of labor processes and the modern workplace. Keeping to Americanist examples, the anthropology and ethnography of the modern workplace can be broken down into five broad categories: (a) agrarian (Goldschmidt, 1947; Gatewood, 1985; Wells, 1996); (b) craft (Harper, 1987); (c) industrial (Gouldner, 1954; Burawoy, 1979b; Nash, 1989; Darrah, 1996); (d) white-collar workers, managers, professionals, and technical experts (Latour & Woolgar, 1986; Orr, 1996; Baba, 2001; Schwartzman, 1987); and (e) personal services (both union and nonunion) and low-wage labor (Durrenberger & Erem, 1999; Luz Ibarra, 2002). There are, of course, borderline cases (Gamst, 1980—a study of railroad engineers, and Applebaum, 1981—a study of construction workers) but the greater point is the anthropology of work has found purchase in a full range of workplaces.

Sociocultural anthropology's methods, distinct from other social scientific approaches, are (a) *holistic* (aimed at investigating the totality of relevant relationships affecting a domain, even if this means crossing boundaries), allowing the (b) pursuit of *patterns* lived by and through (the recognizing and making explicit of patterns, including organizations, known and/or acted through by participants in the studied situation), and (c) the importance of *meaning* (i.e., the centrality of symbols, rituals, etc.) within social life. Given such a methodology, anthropology is well placed to question the degree to which work and family can truly be said to be distinct domains. The work of family and family at work would seem to be natural subjects for anthropological research.

Sociocultural anthropology's core method is ethnography, the attempt to understand what it is like to be part of a social world: what a person's social milieu means to him or her and how they act in that social world, usually accomplished through participant observation. The anthropology of work attempts to understand the modern workplace through comparison with work under different circumstances, in other times and places, with differing principles and ends of organization. Ethnography is the first step in this process. Participant observation aims at the everyday, both what is taken to be significant and to be insignificant. There are differences between what we say and what we do, in good part because we often leave unstated (or hold back from unfamiliar persons) our deepest beliefs and motivations. What people report in interview statements is often what they take to be the normative answer—what they think a person is supposed to say (still, a kind of information). Ethnography often reveals actions and statements that go unspoken in formal interviews (for example, in my own participant observation-based ethnography of a timber mill, after a few months people started to show me where they hid from bosses).

Before returning in the next section to the overlapping of work and family, an elucidation of what is at stake when we try to study the workplace is in order. Theories of motivation in the modern workplace cleave between two ostensive explanations for "Why work?": (a) the pursuit of interests and (b) the desire for recognition as a social being (Taylor, 1998; Mayo, 1933, 1945; Kerr & Fisher, 1964; Burawoy, 1979b). Frederick Winslow Taylor is often credited with making the satistfaction of interests a central principle of scientific management and the motivation of the workforce.

Not usually included in genealogies of the anthropology of work, Taylor has some claim to having been a participant observer: Though the scion of an elite family, Taylor chose to drop out of Harvard and work as shopfloor labor—"[H]e was perhaps the only factory worker in America who was a member of the Philadelphia Cricket Club!" (Kakar, 1970, pp. 10–11). Taylor constantly justified his "scientific methods" through reference to what he had observed while working on the shopfloor: his piecework system, and its appeal to individual interests, was an explicit attempt to tame and channel "systematic soldiering"—labor attempting to collectively control the pace and content of the labor process—which he defined basically as a culture that managers could thwart and redirect by individuating the interests of workers. Taylor brought a moral vision (how a person should properly work) to bear on the question of how best to manage the workplace (so as to *make* such subjects appear). Taylor popularized the idea that the workplace as a social space, and the worker as an individual, could be manipulated by experts toward greater efficiency and harmony.

It was Elton Mayo's interpretation of the Hawthorne studies (the first long-term ethnographic study of a workplace) which led him to first propose that Taylor's assertion that appealing to a worker's interests was the best way to motivate effort was mistaken, or only partially to the point.

Mayo claimed that workers also desired and were motivated toward effort *qua* productivity in the workplace by *belonging*. Mayo believed that the firm should be a functional whole, an integrated social system, with conflict then a symptom of pathology the ethnographer was there to diagnose. If for Taylor the scientific manager's task was to manipulate the culture of workers (e.g., squelch systematic soldiering), for Mayo the firm itself was to become a culture.

By validating workers' contributions to production, even if only by paying attention to what they are doing (the so-called Hawthorne effect, where productivity increases exactly because interest is shown by researchers in productivity), Mayo claimed that conflict on the shopfloor could be ameliorated and functional harmony achieved. Mayo's managers were somewhere between the mental faculties of the firm and good parents willing to listen to the children/workers they then guided toward right action: belonging rubs up against family-ness, but only the vertical, hierarchical, and paternalist dimension of the relation between knowing parents and unruly children.

Mayo began the opposition, unresolved to this day, between interests and familiarity when attempting to explain both how a workplace does and *should* function. This last point is important: when discussing the organization of the workplace, simple references to efficiency are always already normative claims about moral order. How a *person* (someone we expect to act in a certain way) is made in and through relations with other persons (Fortes, 1987; Mauss, 1979; Karp, 1997) and how that person is integrated into a moral cosmos (Beidelman, 1986) are central concerns of anthropology. Even supposedly straightforward claims about one's own interests assume that to be motivated by interests is a moral form of personhood. Both interests and belonging are features of persons, and persons coexist through sameness and familiarity on the one hand and strangeness and antagonism on the other.

Over the past two decades, one way the anthropology of work has been cleaving is along the divide between (a) the use of anthropological methods to refine, focus, and simply understand the emerging importance of knowledge and information work (e.g., Baba, 1999, 2001, 2003; Hakken & Andrews, 1993; Hakken, 1999; Orr, 1996), and (b) the study of the creation and maintenance of what can be loosely called "laboring subjectivities" around the globe (e.g., Burawoy, 1979b; Ong, 1987; Kondo, 1990; Dudley, 1994; Durrenberger and Erem, 1999; Durrenberger, 2002; Freeman, 2000). The former often involves the utilization of the culture concept and anthropological understandings to reform the workplace; the latter's focus is how those employed in such workplaces experience work and its vicissitudes. To attempt to understand a subject's positionality, for example in the workplace, is always also an ethics: an attempt to understand the practice of social relations and interactions as a pursuit of "goods"— goods not reduced simply to interests, but also in terms of what is proper for a person to do (MacIntyre, 1984).

Marietta Baba discussed an aspect of this concern with ethics in her treatment of trust in the workplace: the analysis of expectations is a foundation of modern economic theory (e.g., investment decisions, portfolio theory) and, as Baba pointed out, trust too depends on expectations (Baba, 1999, p. 333). By studying the implementing of new information technology in a variety of workplaces, Baba highlighted how trust is critical to the flow of information and the risks actors perceive in the sharing of information (p. 343). Cooperation in the workplace takes more than designing efficient organizations; it requires the presence of ethics—particularly the presence of standards of character by which we can judge (as Baba also noted) the reliability and competence of others (p. 333).

Helen Schwartzman has documented the importance of *gatherings* (in Erving Goffman's sense) to the construction of organizations (Goffman, 1964). She focused on that ubiquitous aspect of the white-collar workplace, meetings, to demonstrate their importance as a "sense making form" by which a workplace sustains itself as an organization with coherence and common purpose:

It is suggested that decisions, policies, problem solving, and so on, are *not* what meetings are *about*. Instead, we need to reverse this view and examine the possibility that decisions, policies, problems, and crises occur *because* they produce meetings . . . in certain social systems meetings produce "organization." (Schwartzman, 1987, p. 288)

Moreover, rather than power being something an individual with a certain office wields, power is often something negotiated in the workplace through display and interaction at meetings. Meetings produce regularities in the social spacing and timing of organizations; rather than meetings being about producing reasoned decisions and rational action, Schwartzman suggested they are about producing the illusions thereof. But, even if this point is true, even if meetings reveal that power is negotiated between persons rather than being the possession of individuals, the illusion that power is vested in and possessed by individuals is exactly what meetings create. As Arens and Karp (1989) noted: "the key question is not how power is centralized; it isn't . . . [but] how the illusion of power organizes a social formation composed of a center and a periphery emerges and acts in society" (p. xvi).

This brings us to an important rejoinder to Schwartzman (perhaps better described as more of a blind spot): Blue-collar, pink-collar, and most low-wage service workers do not with any regularity participate in meetings. In a sawmill where I worked, and in the auto parts plant where I am doing research, there are sometimes very short meetings where a manager tells the workers what to do, but meetings where conversation takes place are a once a month for an hour affair—a different work world altogether from the three quarters of each day Schwartzman said managers often spend in meetings. If, as Schwartzman claimed, at the mental health center where she did her research "Individuals who did not participate in meetings . . . were essentially 'non-individuals,'" in other words denied personhood, what might we conjecture about the interrelation of white-collar workers to those on the shopfloor, behind the service counter, or taking calls who are not part of these negotiations? I will be returning below to how the experience of occupations in the workplace may have a forming effect on what modes of relatedness, of social models, feel natural. If illusions of power are generated in the "ritual" settings of meetings (and I will be suggesting other ritual aspects of information work) in the modern workplace, what room does that leave for empowering those occupations where meetings may well be occasionally helpful, but hardly a critical part of the labor process?

The anthropology of work, as a subdiscipline within anthropology, has focused primarily on work within the capitalist labor process—that is, market societies and wage labor. In other words, the anthropology of work focuses most on work as a separable and distinct form of action in space and time: as such, the subdiscipline replicates the very divide between work and life, between work and family or relatedness, that is a defining feature of the modern labor process. But, this is not necessarily a fault; the anthropology of work is therefore relatively free of the kinds of romanticizing and search for humanity "degree zero" that sometimes mires anthropology. As such, the anthropology of work is a subfield concerned with what anthropology can offer in way of understanding present conditions globally and therefore help us construct viable paths toward viable futures.

The anthropology of work is loosely affiliated with the sociology of work; much of the most interesting ethnographic work immediately after World War II was done by persons not strictly anthropologists; for example, Alvin Gouldner and Donald Roy, both sociologists, conducted two of the most important ethnographic studies of industrial work (Gouldner, 1954; Roy, 1952a, b). Many sociologists today are again taking up qualitative and ethnographic methods to understand the world of work (e.g., Graham, 1995; Grenier, 1988; Fantasia, 1988). In part, this may be due to the overwhelming influence and allure of the interpretivist and linguistic turns in anthropology which require attention to the details of everyday life that cannot be captured easily, if at all, through quantitative and survey methods associated with sociology.

CULTURE AND WORK

Culture is the central concept of ethnographic anthropology. Recently arguments have arisen that the idea of culture based in co-present persons may be past its heyday as new vernacular modernities unite the globe through media and consumption (see Marcus, 1995; Knauft, 2002; Ortner, 1999). Yet the idea of culture as a unity of meaning and action (or in Clifford Geertz' famous definition, the recursivity of models of and for reality such that our concepts conform to reality while our actions shape reality in conformity with our conceptions) has hardly lost its hold on the ethnographic imagination (Geertz, 1973). Claims that the world of modern economic action is purely rational and objectively oriented may seem to leave anthropological interests in matters such as meaning or ritual with no purchase. Yet the allure of ethnographic methods and the desire to know what members of the workplace *really think* and are up to behind the boss' back (the assumption that workers, like "traditional" anthropological subjects, possess a mysterious culture) have led to a curious mix of claims that ethnography can both increase the efficiency of organization (e.g., Baba's concern with information exchange noted above) and name the means by which coherence and social solidarity (often said to rest in otherwise irrational emotional ties) may be cultivated or at least understood (loosely, Schwartzman's concern).

Christopher Herbert has made a thorough critique of the culture concept, noting that culture, while one of the most pervasive tools for explaining and interpreting social activity today, can be made to mean just about anything. When we critique something as culturally constructed, culture means inauthenticity; yet culture is also invoked as a seat of authenticity—something that a people has a right to defend against intrusion. A final definition is "the supposedly value-neutral one of social science, in which culture refers to a mode of correlation among social phenomena" (Herbert, 1991, p. 2).

Pace Herbert, polyvalence such as that found with the culture concept can be a sign as much of richness of meaning as conceptual confusion. While I do not go as far as Herbert (I will be using the culture concept throughout this chapter), his is an important reminder that the pervasiveness of the culture concept in part comes from the power those wielding it are granted. Culture gives the drive to interpret a certain authenticity, allowing social scientists to claim they are simply providing a *model of* something out there in the world when often what is in fact being done is the positing of a *model for* social activity—that is, normative claims about how persons should behave. Nowhere is this clearer than in how culture is invoked in the business and management literature, where it justifies providing models for desired workplace cultures attuned to the need for efficiency, flexibility, innovation, and so forth. At my current fieldwork site, (an auto parts plant) managers have expressed a repeated interest in curing what they take to be a "bad culture" promoting work habits they would like to purge from the workplace. Culture becomes a catchword for the ability of managers to encourage desired subjective motivations among workers by creating cultures *ex nihilo,* a view Hamada noted may well be a "value supposition [of] the American management subculture itself" (Hamada & Sibley, 1994, p. 24).

The 1980s saw anthropology's core concept, culture, take hold in management circles. Culture promised the possibility of understanding motivating symbols. Stimulated in good part by management gurus like Tom Peters to understand the culture of the workplaces they managed, the social structures of work started to attract more and more interest, leading to a resurgence of applied anthropological studies of firms, commissioned by managers and performed by anthropologist consultants (Peters & Waterman, 1982; Gregory, 1983). The culture concept amounted to a return by management to an interest in social situations at work as distinct from formal institutional structures. Whereas scientific managers in the Taylorist vein assumed informal organization was by definition a force against management, others began to see culture as something savvy managers could utilize within the firm to increase organizational productivity (a position arguably descended from Mayo). Culture became a new name for an old desire to have control over workers' motivations in the workplace (as we shall see below, a model of the sources of motivation in many ways in conflict with relatedness and other family models).

In contrast with official versions of an organization, ethnography reveals facets of social life that are unspoken (at least to strangers), informal, and illicit (at least as gauged by power structures). Gaining insight into these has been a major impetus behind the growth of ethnographic studies of the modern, managed workplace. Formal rules and licit institutions are only part of any fully understood economic structure.

Some hold ethnography becomes more difficult, if not impossible, when attempting to study culture close to home: we are too deeply involved in the structures and sentiments of everyday life to perceive their nuances. The distinction between *etic* studies of experience-distant cultures and the *emic* position of being a full participant or member of a cultural milieu is at best ironic: for the very justification for etic methods rests on their supposed ability to better understand what it is to be in an emic position as a member of a group! Whether the etic/emic distinction is a valid methodological issue, or an ex post facto justification for anthropology's romantic heritage and preference for the so-called primitive and savage over the mundane existence of one's neighbors in the cities of Europe and America toiling in factory or field . . . well, I'll leave that aside here. Schwartzman (1993) noted that the move over the past two decades to question the subjectivity of the ethnographer and the objectivity of the observer means the time for increased attention to the emic may well be at hand.

THE FAMILY IN THE WORKPLACE

Meyer Fortes, a central figure in British social anthropology, argued that we model the world through the nominal structures of the family:

> Here—and not in the structure of the human brain—lies the actor's model for the structure of social groups and relationships at all levels, and it is the experience of the elementary social relationships of filiation and siblingship in this context that is the basis of a person's conception of his social identity. (Fortes, 1987, p. 123)

Fortes suggested the family is a core model of our social relationships. We find in the workplace confirmation of Fortes' point: paternalism, or filiation (by managers) and brotherhood, or siblingship (by unions) are two very common ways to describe how persons in the workplace relate to each other. We must attend to the interrelation between subjective motivation and systems of organization if we are going to understand at all how humans interact in spaces like the workplace (Miller et al., 2001; Bion, 1961). As Fortes suggested, standing between subjects and social systems are "familiar" models: paternalist, sibling, and even (in some cases) that other form of relatedness—marriage. All impinge on the supposedly instrumentally motivated relations of production found in the workplace.

If social models are at once economic, moral, and jural (Fortes, 1987, p. 115), and the lived familiarity of "filiation and siblingship" are always implicated in our social identities, how might we apply this to the modern workplace? What are the moral and jural dimensions of family models in spaces of economic action? Beidelman has stressed the constitutive role of the moral imagination. Rather than sameness always being an oppressive veil over what is unique, imagination has a moral dimension, as Beidelman noted, when it takes social relationships and finds how to make them work; imagination "spans a range of otherwise unbridgeable realms"

(Beidelman, 1986, p. 3). The moral imagination is not checked at the door of the workplace: the bringing of family models into the workplace is a constitutive dimension of the moral imagination in action, the making of relatedness in and through everyday association.

British social anthropology by the mid 20th century had fixed on kinship as a way of explaining "the basis for the orderly functioning of small-scale societies in the absence of government institutions and states" (Carsten, 2004, p. 10). Kinship was a way of explaining what motivated people through both conflict and consensus, to diverge and to cooperate in interests and identity. Kinship served at once to coordinate economic as well as moral integration; Fortes went further by positing that the basic relationships by which we signify, come to understand the world, and have a basic familiarity with the world are familial. This is also a Freudian position, and one which makes family another contender for the role ascribed to culture—a source of models of and for our lifeworlds.

Donald Kalb (1997) has recently produced a historical anthropological study of a European example of paternalism: the Philips Corporation's use of *familism* in the southern Netherlands as a way to discipline its labor force around the beginning of the 20th century. The idea of corporate familism is often associated with the Japanese organization of relations of production (see Hamada & Sibley, 1994). But, as we shall see, family has a much wider and common use as a metaphor (and family is always a metaphor according to the relatedness hypothesis) invoked to motivate and shape relations of and in production. Familism—the mixing of family and work— is ubiquitous: recognizing this, the question becomes more why is it so common to see work and family as parsed from each other? What does imagining work to be opposed to life accomplish?

Beginning in the early 20th century, Philips attempted to replicate a labor force identical to one which had proved efficient (but was not replicating itself) by recruiting whole families to migrate to housing complexes surrounding the company's manufactures. A labor force based on the employment of fathers and daughters (albeit in tasks widely divergent in degrees of power and supervision): in other words, a paternalism where the selfsame parent exerted control in the home and in the workplace.

Family functions (the raising of children, care for the elderly, and the ability to marry), and strategies to achieve these tasks, were all shaped through a relation to work, to gendered and aged spaces or places where work was available. By employing multiple members of the same family, Philips saved costs on what was required for a "living wage" and kept a ready and flexible supply of labor on hand to be expanded and contracted around demand. In the leanest of times, only the father and perhaps one daughter would be employed; when the economy was rolling, multiple daughters would be brought in. The ability of fathers to discipline daughters and invoke familial and household responsibilities (before marriage separated daughters into differing households) became a cornerstone of Philips' labor policy (sons were granted more autonomy in the labor market and also expected to strike out on their own). Kalb termed these relations of production (with an eye on the notion of Fordism) "Philipsism." The problem with Philipsism was it only worked for one generation: families moved up and out of the position of replicating the family strategy on which Philips was depending, so Philips recruited new families to repeat the process. Central to the process was the building of extensive housing complexes and the sociological monitoring of families to make sure they were morally as well as physically replicating themselves.

Like Philipsism, in America (during the progressive era) welfare capitalism sought to tame unionism and preempt state intervention in industrial relations by incorporating "notions of order, community, and paternal responsibility [associated with] the pre-industrial household economy"; creating "in effect, industrial manors" (Jacoby, 1997, p. 4).[2] This managerialist paternalism was a kind of "scientific paternalism" where child care and summer camps for adolescent children of workers sought, as one industrialist put it, to create "a family atmosphere" while also, seeking to keep the sentiments binding this familism "rational" and to maintain the barriers and boundaries separating home from work (Jacoby, 1997, p. 3).

Fordism in its origins is the most important American example of paternalism within industry, and a clear example of paternalism's importance not just as a structure of symbols and sentiments, but also as implicated in how labor is performed in the workplace. Henry Ford's offer of high wages to his workers (the famous "five-dollar day" deal) was meant all at once to (a) compensate for accepting accelerated and more repetitive work on moving assembly lines (and their more finely grained division of labor); (b) allow Ford's workers to be in a position to purchase one of his cars, creating the all-important identification of the worker as also consumer; and (c) allow Ford to pick and choose his workforce, indeed to shape their familial and home life with his infamous "sociology department."

Kalb wants to distinguish between Fordism and Philipsism. Fordism, like Philipsism, was innovative in creating new ways of integrating firms and workers and finding new means of motivating labor. But, whereas Philips rested on the power of fathers over daughters and housing policy, Ford's workforce (at least for the first few decades) was uniformly male and led by the carrot of the five-dollar day into the auto plants. Ford also had a far more extensive "sociology department" entering the homes of workers, managing home and family life: work and family were mixed differently at Philips and Ford, but both relied on a labor force where family and work had blurred boundaries.

In the United States, paternalism as moral ordering within relations of production faded with the Depression's shock to industrial relations and the shifting of responsibility for social welfare programs (or at least the regulation of such programs) to the state (Lichtenstein, 2002). The Wagner Act (1935) marked the advent of decisive federal intervention in regulating labor relations; certainly by the late 1940s (in the wake of the Taft-Hartley Act) explicit paternalism was muted in the United States, replaced by notions that the divide between managers and managed was logical and functional, representing the matching of economic and interest-minded individuals to prestations within the apparatus of production (even as this was the heyday of union brother and sisterhood in America).

Paternalism, owners and managers as parents over laborers, carries with it an imagining of a mutual obligation between senior and junior, between those with power to control and shape the workplace and those within an organization. This is why a simple dismissal or critique of paternalism goes too far: as EP Thompson and James Scott note, we cannot forget that laborers often find in paternalism a moral tone to economic relationships worthy of defense when the other option is the cold hand of the market (Thompson, 1991; Scott, 1985).

Yet we cannot forget that invoking the family in the workplace does not in itself make economic activity equitable: the presence, explicitly or implicitly, of family models in the workplace in no way signals the presence of better or worse relations of production. Corporate paternalism is almost always a way of invoking family as a way of keeping politics out of the workplace: "We're a family here" is almost always accompanied by "no union" (Amazon.com, Wal-Mart, and Whole Foods are current examples).[3]

The rhetoric and activities of Wal-Mart are the best example. Wal-Mart invokes family idioms and images regularly in advertising. Elder employees talk about Wal-Mart as a familylike or homelike space in ads including testimonials from consumers about the need to find low prices to shore up their family's domestic economy. Wal-Mart training videos claim that the family nature of Wal-Mart is incommensurate with the presence of unions (Ehrenreich, 2001), and they are hardly alone in claiming that theirs is a familylike workplace unions would destroy. The implication is family is opposed to the workplace politics a union brings: the workplace is pushed inside family, meaning only the antagonism of politics remains outside the family's purview. In a sense, paternalism like Wal-Mart's is a one-sided relationship where the obligations all fall on one side—workers as children to parents who bear no real responsibility for them—and is therefore distinct from a paternalism stressing the order brought by the interdependence of junior and senior positions within an organization.

In contrast to paternalism's vertical axis, brother and sisterhood foreground lateral relationships. In the workplace, brotherhood and sisterhood are most closely associated with unions (or, in a broader historical frame, guilds). The two blue-collar unionized plants I have studied, a sawmill in Idaho and an auto parts plant in the Detroit area—where I am still conducting research, are noteworthy for having workforces thick with both genealogical kin and unionism (recent anthropological and ethnographic studies concerned with unionism include Burawoy, 1979b; Halle, 1984; Fantasia, 1988; Pred & Watts, 1992; Dudley, 1994; Kalb, 1997; Durrenberger & Erem, 1999; Durrenberger, 2002).

I attended the orientation for new hires at the auto plant, which lasted a week, and both union and managerial persons speaking before the class made repeated references to how the plant was like a family: on closer inspection, this is more literally true than many would think. Out of the group of new hires present at that orientation, 11 out of 12 had significant numbers of family members already working in the plant. It is extremely difficult to get hired without utilizing networks of family connections (the 12th person had leaned on friendships). The hiring practices, in which both union and company cooperate, makes the shopfloor a place where family is ubiquitous. I will stand in the cafeteria with the union's plant chairman and as he introduces a person, he quotes their genealogical relations to others I have met. A joke around the plant is it does not pay to talk behind a person's back—the likelihood is you are talking to someone related to the person you are complaining about! What Philipsism tried to create—an intergenerational workforce—has appeared in many unionized industrial facilities.

My research in an Idaho sawmill involved working as shopfloor union labor until the mill closed its doors after almost a century in operation. The placement of the mill in a small, isolated town, and the fact that the jobs were far better-paying than most options in the area had led to a multi-generational workforce where grandmothers and fathers also preceded sons, daughters, and grandchildren onto the shopfloor. I met a few people in the mill who were cousins on both sides—there were two pairs of identical twins working there and innumerable siblings. Family and intergenerational friendships between families—in other words, relatedness—saturated the workplace: solidarity at the mill was as much an articulation of these ties as anything else.

When genealogical kin saturate a workplace, the bar may well be raised for reciprocity and exchanges: what you do for a union sister and friend will blur with what you do with a genealogical brother or friend. But, this also means the grounds of ambivalence and the stakes in conflict are more intense: the inarguable point is that relationships become "thicker"—the webs of significant relationships deepening and ramifying. I knew two men in the mill who acted entirely personably around each other, but who each told me in asides that they had been at loggerheads for over a decade. Yet they knew each other well enough not to step on each other's toes and worked together in the same work group quite well. Even people who dislike each other but have known each other for years usually have a more flexible relationship than brand-new friends: to quote William Blake, long-standing "opposition is true friendship" (on flexibility as a product of long-term conviviality, see Basso, 1979).

The presence of genealogical kin in the workplace can further a firm's goals of procuring a dependable labor force as well as ground a relatedness that aids and abets solidarity as part of workplace consciousness. All that is assured is that kindred-ness *is motivating* (for better or worse) but not in predictable, and perhaps manageable, ways. Kindred-ness can contribute to illicit goldbricking or be a motivation to give one's full effort—the difference comes down to other facets of how relations of production are organized. For example, in Philips' case, the availability of better work disrupted replication of the workforce between generations; in the auto plant and mill, the high wages of union labor and decreasing prospects for other kinds of work led to many children of workers, even those possessing college degrees, to pursue their parents' occupation.

My current fieldwork in the Detroit area, in many ways the "Mecca" of unionism, has led me to the hypothesis that the relatedness of brotherhood and sisterhood, stretching in and out of the workplace, may extend and broaden shopfloor relationships. For example, I have been encountering sermons and Bible study classes making constant use of moral examples from work on the shopfloor—a preacher in the church I attend with a past union president is the current union local president.

The church's congregation is half African American, half White. One of the deacons was a civil rights activist and organizer who tangled with the Klan and is now a skilled trades worker in the auto industry; another is an engineer in the auto industry. Most members of the church are migrants from the South, where the denomination is nominally segregated. The ability of fraternal and sororal relatedness to overcome differences, race, for example, is an important part of union history (however incompletely realized).

Nelson Lichtenstein noted that referring to each other as brother and sister within unions, regardless of race, began as a CIO practice during the 1930s (Lichtenstein, 2002, p. 76). I am currently exploring whether brotherhood and sisterhood learned on the shopfloor might have had a shaping effect on the desegregated brotherhood and sisterhood of the church. Family, church, and union can become blurred genres where being brother and sister is a meaningful form of personhood cross-cutting and uniting these spaces. One worker at the auto plant told me "my father, my preacher, and my godfather work here"—a fairly complete catalog of the basic forms of relatedness: a shared home, commensality, and support (father); a shared community (church—his preacher is also a union leader—there are quite a few preachers in the auto plant); and shared symbolic, yet nongenealogical, kinship (the godfather).

Freud noted there is a good deal of fantasy and wish fulfillment motivating a desire to do away with paternal relations between generations and create a society marked only by lateral, leveled relationships (Freud, 1922). Yet unions manage to both be brother and sisterhoods while retaining the senior/junior distinction and respect for age through seniority clauses, keeping the locus of paternal relationships among union members rather than between workers and management. Fantasy, as Ethel Person noted, is not always obfuscation; it is also part of Beidelman's aforementioned "moral imagination" whereby differences are overcome (Person, 1995; Beidelman, 1986).

The integration of senior and junior generations through the idioms and practices of work can take place through other mixings of the workplace and the family. I helped a friend of mine (retired from the auto parts plant) and his grandson carry parts for a car the grandson is restoring into the garage the other day. The grandfather, who calls cars a "form of art," passes on both knowledge of how to work and a love for that work on to another generation. He shows his grandson how to scrub a carburetor and the grandson pays close attention—respect for wisdom and knowledge evident in his pose. As Frederik Barth has noted, often "the *same* acts and aspects of acts are *simultaneously* instrumental and communicative, and their form cannot be explained by the analysis of only one of these contexts" (Barth, 1981, p. 81). Work as ethical practice, as a source of relatedness, and as the efficacious transformation of matter into the useful meet here.

What does purifying work and politics from family and the household do—what does it accomplish? For one, it stymies the moral imagination's bridging of family and work—the overcoming of differences across the realms. Primarily, it separates economic interaction from intimacy: those with whom we share familiarity and reciprocity from those who are strangers. Max Weber defined a key aspect of modernity as the replacement of economic particularism—the dividing of the world between insiders (those with whom we share and engage in moral exchanges) and outsiders (those we may exploit or trick in exchanges) with the universal and neutral law of contracts (see Swedberg, 1998). The presence or absence of relatedness would be a measure of this insider versus outsider distinction: for example, one could be opposed or even ostensively enemies with another member of an in-group, but still follow different moral principles when engaging in exchanges with that person than you would with a person with whom you completely lack relatedness of any kind.

The universalism of economic objectivity, where rules and laws rationalizing economic exchanges take precedence, presses intimacy into the private space of the home. As bureaucracy "develops the more perfectly the more the bureaucracy is dehumanized, the more completely it succeeds in eliminating from official business love, hatred, and all purely personal, irrational, and emotional elements which escape calculation" (Weber in Gabriel, 1998, p. 291). While, as Gabriel noted, the study of organizations belies Weber's claim that organizations are purged of affect, this does not in any way undermine Weber's sublime insight into the fantasy behind bureaucracy whereby the human, human frailty, and human relatedness would be banished from institutions in favor of mathematical and technical rationality (Gabriel, 1998, pp. 291–293).

Even if it is not true (as many commentators have noted) that modern institutions and bureaucratic organizations are singularly rational, the fact remains that such de facto rationality remains the justification put forth for such institutions' continued existence—just as it is the justification for Schwartzman's meetings where power is conjured. And, once we remember that those justifications are produced by persons inhabiting such institutions, we are confronted with just how many persons (whose occupational position and identity are within such institutions) believe in those institutions' rationality. It is exactly this rationality that is supposed to serve as, in turn, justification for the exclusion of relatedness and family models from bureaucracy on the grounds that the emotional ties brought with the family impede rational action and efficiency.

THE WORKPLACE IN THE FAMILY

Again, how separate in fact is the home from the workplace? How clearly differentiated are the sentiments found in the home and the workplace? Why would they be different? Let us now consider the question from the opposite angle: how the modern workplace finds its way into the home. The modern workplace we can define as one where the labor process is shaped by the division of labor that comes with industrial production methods: this would span field labor on an industrial farm, sales "associates" at Wal-Mart, through work as a human resources manager in a high-tech firm. A second prototypical feature of the modern workplace is remunerative labor. The notion of class is a third feature: Class is a concept directly related to the emergence of the modern labor process—a reaction to that labor process (Thompson, 1966).

While the death of the working class as a historical force has been widely heralded, this does not mean the end of class. Over the course of the 20th century, the middle class came more and more to be presented as the only putative class, particularly after the onslaught against working-class politics beginning around 1980 in Britain and the United States exemplified by Thatcherism and Reaganism's attack on unions on the one hand and the dismissal of working-class politics as relevant by many left-leaning social critics on the other (Davis, 1986). To become middle class, to aspire to middle class-ness became a desire held by most Americans (Dudley, 1999). Interestingly, this is true both of those positioned in terms of income and education on the lower thresholds of middle-ness and those positioned clearly quite above the middle (it is not hard to find millionaires espousing their middle class-ness). Middle class-ness becomes a core cultural motivation; and middle class-ness first and foremost is articulated through the structure of occupations and that structure's influence on—indeed, penetration of—households.

If, in the early 19th century, the critical class divide was between those who sold and those who bought labor (i.e., between the working classes on one side, and the bourgeoisie or old middle classes on the other), by the 20th century the divide was transformed into a three-way relationship among owners, the new middle classes of managers and experts, and the working class (see Vidich, 1995).[4] Class' primary axis—either as self-identification or as positionality within the productive process—shifted during the 20th century from ownership of the means of production to relations of production in the workplace and (ascribed) differences in organizational knowledge: in other words, the relation of managers to managed, and conceptual engineering to physical labors, became central.

For a few generations during the post-World War II era, there was an unprecedented mixing of middle class-ness and blue-collar workers: it was possible from the late 1950s to be both a manual laborer and middle-class. That mixing has been progressively undone since the 1980s through a mixture of social censure of blue-collar workers, attacks on unionism, and claims that the new knowledge economy effectively devalues all but information work (Davis, 1986; Zweig, 2000; Florida, 2002).

The "professional middle (or managerial) class" (PMC)—the current prototype of middle class-ness—has proved uneasy, particularly since the late 1970s, with any blurring of the boundaries between middle-class and working-class households: "camouflaged by a culture in which it both stars and writes the scripts, [the PMC] plays an overweening role in defining 'America'" (Ehrenreich, 1989, p. 6). Remaining differentiated from working-class persons is a persistent concern of PMC persons, and the workplace (at the very least via the wage) is the central space for marking the rungs on the hierarchical ladder. The attack on the working class *as a culture* gaining momentum during the 1960s and 1970s was uncannily timed to increases in the share of the social product claimed by the PMC, their increased control over the labor process, and the bifurcation of society into high and low—the wallowing out of the middle associated with the emerging hourglass shape of social stratification (Davis, 1986).

I have detailed the presence of the family in the workplace in the blue-collar workplaces I have studied above; to approach work in the family, the PMC is a more appropriate object of study. Gerald Mars argued that it is part of the culture of managers (and, I would argue by extension, professional and technical workers as well) to accept mobility to spaces distant from birthplace and family, and the affective neutrality of workplace relationships: "If we look at managers and their ideology we can see that they are prepared to change homes frequently as the demands of their careers determine, [and] are prepared to accept travel and separation from family as a requirement of their jobs" (Mars, 1981, p. 5). People with occupations making them part of the PMC are more likely to move to where their specialized educations demand, separating them from extended family networks—except on ritual holidays. While celebrating the nuclear family as sacrosanct, PMC workers are also likely to accept mobility in pursuit of the ideal workplace and employment leaving only the nuclear family (and given divorce, not even that) as the only possible semi-enduring social unit over time.

Arlie Hochschild saw emerging a "Taylorized family" based in "deskilling parents at home" as the "cult of efficiency" unleashed on America by middle-class progressive reformers a century ago colonizes the last corners of family time and home space (1997, pp. 209–214). The home becomes a second temple of efficiency, devoted to producing subjects with the proper character and beliefs to succeed in the workplace. Moreover, the division of labor in the home is supplemented by the outsourcing of tasks previously done in the firm: McDonalds replaces home-cooked food and television actors socialize for us in the evening as parents unwind from work, "the main 'skill' still required of family members . . . the ability to forge, deepen, and repair family relationships" becomes more and more difficult to acquire (Hochschild, 1997, p. 210).

The bringing of models of proper action into the home from the workplace would seem inevitable given the American emphasis on one's employment as a visible incarnation of one's character. Recently, I was in a supermarket and witnessed a father in a suit tell his two children—both under 5—that they had to "work as a team" picking out what box of doughnuts to buy . . . the kids were obviously not pleased with his managerial advice. Here we have a parent viewing the world, even his relationship with his children and responsibility to provide them with models of proper social action, through currently fashionable management lingo.[5]

Middle-class families practice their own version of familism: by encouraging an early choice of career paths and supporting children through expensive private educations, the middle class replicates its own occupational aspirations and motivations, hoping one day to be able to say to others in the office "My daughter the doctor . . . ." By supporting their offspring well into adulthood as their children pursue artistic goals or careers requiring prolonged education, such as academia and PhDs, middle-class families mix their destinies in with the mix of work and occupations:

> The new PMC . . . while it still has some of the old emphasis on parenting for ambition and brains, it has also appropriated the institutional mechanisms that the old upper classes relied on, especially trust funds and college legacies. The new PMC is thus increasingly turning itself into a caste like formation analogous to the old upper class. (Ortner, 2003, pp. 272–273)[6]

We maintain the cultural narrative of absolute freedom of choice (at least for middle-class youth) between possible future employments, while in truth family strategies corresponding to specific family constellations are apparent. Children following parents into a plant or sawmill is a fairly open bringing of family to bear on work; white-collar professional workers are more likely to usher their children not into the same space of work, but the same occupational caste. The most likely occupation for sons and daughters remains that of their parents, and the chances are far greater a child of college-educated parents will complete college than the offspring of those without college educations (Zweig, 2000). A child of professional parents not performing in the upper percentiles is likely to be hurried off to tutors, to therapists, and even, if too spirited, to be medicated. A relation between work and family that was truly and completely unmotivated, completely separate, might be the provenance only of unfortunate orphans.

KNOWLEDGE, RELATEDNESS, AND THE EMERGING WORKPLACE

The past few decades have seen prediction after prediction that we have entered a new stage of economic development within the workplace, entailing new hierarchies and priorities, new occupational relationships and relations between persons and their occupations. The postindustrial, information, or simply new economy is said to have supplanted the industrial economy just as the industrial economy replaced agriculture as cynosure and engine of growth.

The last decades of the 20th century saw claims that a new age of information, information exchanged as a business, had supplanted industry at the core of the economy. Heralds of the postindustrial economy can be found as early as the years immediately after World War II, for example among, those involved with the Tavistock Institute (Miller, & Rice, 1967). But, such notions did not come fully into their own until the 1970s alongside crises in industrial capitalism.

We can today find sites in more information and technical orientated fields of work where familism of sorts can be found. For example, Julian Orr's copy machine repairmen/technical workers engage in regular lateral exchanges of information that mark theirs as a community with fraternalism (Orr, 1990, 1996). Orr described copier technicians as a "community of knowledge" with little incentive to hide knowledge from each other, in good part motivated by the "the inability to learn to do [the task] from a theoretical understanding of the task" (Orr, 1990, pp. 170, 174).

Likewise, Gabriella Coleman claimed that open-source programmers have created "guild-like" conditions for their work where they share standards of good work, engage in collective activity, and find expressive identity in what they do. The open-source software movement has "managed to escape the charge of commodification and still produce objects that circulate in the economic sphere also problematizes some characteristics of so-called 'late capitalism' . . . it is productive freedom, to engage in work of a certain style, that largely dictates the moral economy of free software" (Coleman, 2001, p. 31).

But, how new, in fact, is the knowledge economy? The managers of the first decades of the 20th century were knowledge workers, paid for the manipulation of information and logistics in the pursuit of value; the systems theorists of the 1950s were shaping worldwide webs of production with more and more complicated models of information (Vidich, 1995; Mirowski, 2002). Arguably, the knowledge economy is about a century old; at the least, that is when we start to see an explosion of those persons—be they clerks or experts—whose occupation is the manipulation of information (Mills, 1951). Ikujiro Nonaka (and Hirotaka Takeuchi) exemplify proponents of the information economy and theories of knowledge management (Nonaka, 1994; Nonaka & Takeuchi, 1995, 2004; Baba, 1998). Nonaka relies extensively on epistemology and cognitive anthropology, particularly the work of Michael Polanyi and his notion of tacit knowledge (Polanyi, 1967).

Nonaka's notion is that subjects in the workplace can be mined so as to make their implicit, or tacit, knowledge explicit. It is, in a sense, a focus on laboring subjectivity; by "tapping the tacit and often highly subjective insights, intuitions, and hunches of individual employees and making those insights available for testing and use by the company as a whole," Nonaka promises the path to knowledge management and creation (Nonaka, 1994). Yet, as Tsoukas (2003) noted, Nonaka erases the subtlety of tacit knowledge (how it is inseparable from doing and believing) by treating tacit knowledge as potentially translatable into explicit rules, and therefore capable of being operationalized by organizations.[7]

Polanyi analyzed the same terrain as tacit knowledge when considering the question of cybernetics. He asked "whether the operations of a formalized deductive system might conceivably be considered equivalent to the operations of the mind"; he answers: "I believe that such a question involves a logical fallacy" (Polanyi, 1953, p. 312). In other words, there are aspects of the mind that are not capable of being made part of explicit, formal systems. Saying, as Nonaka does, that you can translate those nonformal aspects through poesis into metaphors, and then into explicit and formal knowledge in no way overcomes the difference insisted upon by Polanyi between tacit and explicit knowledge. Nonaka's celebrating of the power of technicians and middle managers to unlock the tacit knowledge in the minds of other persons is explicitly denied by Polanyi: an observing mind cannot in any way completely grasp some aspects of another, observed mind—Polanyi gives the example of convictions (Polanyi, 1953, pp. 314–315).

Tacit knowledge nevertheless serves a critical function in arguments over the value to be mined by knowledge work and creation: it posits a substratum of already existing "factoids" that preexist the search for them; in essence, reifying information into mental models (public models of information become models for subjective mental states). Nonaka claims that "new knowledge always begins with the individual": knowledge then is of a homogeneous kind, capable of being made explicit and communicated as information, yet remains an individual possession (Nonaka, 1994). When Nonaka says knowledge is tacit, he reifies creativity as a metaphysical, almost a priori strata of our minds (despite his claims to be against the Cartesian tradition)—something already known, already organized, waiting to be discovered. Rather than something done in the world, creativity is something done in the head with information.

Professionals and managers, at least in self-conception if not folk understanding, are said to gain and earn capital through individually held knowledge. Managers and professionals are valuable in the workplace because of the individuated contents of their head, whether those are social scientific skills (including manipulation of personality) or facts about the world. Nonaka's notion of tacit knowledge replicates this model of knowledge. Yet, many types of knowledge exist only as part of social groups, as part of a community of practice (Darrah, 1996; Lave & Wenon, 1991) where action happens as a result of "distributed cognition" (Salomon, 1993) not reducible (arguably) to explicit or systemic rules. Knowledge means something to us, in most cases, because it unfolds before us over time through a group of people, a community of practice from whom we wish or need to learn.

While Nonaka cites embodiment as a factor in tacit knowledge, I can find no examples where embodiment is truly a factor. The example he provides of designers of a bread machine watching a master baker work, and realizing his motion when kneading the bread involved a twisting of the dough, may well represent a case where an embodied action is translated into machine action (Nonaka & Takeuchi, 1995, chap. 4; 2004, chaps. 1–3). But, to say there was tacit knowledge involved . . . I doubt that anywhere in the baker's patterns of thought there was a bread machine with a paddle with the "special ribs" the research team used to replicate the effects of the baker's embodied motions (and, frankly, have you tasted bread from a bread machine?).

Gisli Palsson has provided recently an anthropological treatment of Icelandic fishing that notes the "textual" nature of much theory about work, which is also part of the "Cartesian tradition of separating ideas and the real world, learning and doing, experts and laypersons, knowledge and practice" (Palsson, 1994, p. 904). The idea that tacit knowledge can be made explicit requires such knowledge be able to inhere in propositional form (if not already subtend an individual's thought processes as code) such that it can exist independent of embodiment and social groups. It just so happens this is also a tenet of Taylorist scientific management: "The basic premise of scientific management is that one can reduce the best way to do a given job to a set of instructions, and give those instructions to someone who does not know how to do it independently but who will then be able to do the job by following the instructions" (Orr, 1996, p. 107).[8] To claim some type of labor is "cognitive" does not strip it of the contextual, embodied, or shared sources of thought. *Pace* Baba on "globally distributed teams," the information economy does not strip work of the need for co-presence such that "collaboration may take place asynchronously and virtually (i.e., in cyberspace rather than physical space)" (Baba, 2001, p. 20). Claims that the future belongs to work that is contextless and disembodied uncannily reifies information into form abstracted from practice.

Much working knowledge involves embodied and distributed cognition that is also, not surprisingly, just what the idea of relatedness sees as the key communications by which intersubjective social being is cultivated. Factors such as embodiment, group thought processes, and cognition (as part of activities rather than a separable process) are also exactly those factors upon which ethnography has special purchase and cannot easily be discovered through, for example, interview-based methodologies. While I am sure important exceptions can be found, I feel it is fair to say that relatedness requires co-presence at some level (if not in the present, in the past, or at least expected in the future).

CONCLUSIONS AND SUGGESTIONS FOR FURTHER RESEARCH

What is at "work" in the seeming need for some familiarity in the workplace over and against the formal logic and institutions of production? To answer this, I recently have begun to invoke the notion of *avowal*, which I define as the process whereby structures of relatedness (such as the union brotherhood and sisterhood I study) are instantiated in everyday practices, bringing opportunities for commitment and solidarity over time through reciprocal exchanges and enactments of sameness (and, as importantly, antagonism). Avowal is a way to understand everyday practices whereby relatedness is cultivated. Avowal spans petit rituals like joking and horseplay, the exchanging of substances like food and labor, through performative and meta-communicative acts and statements whereby fidelity over time is demonstrated and vowed and relatedness (re)made and tested: rituals, actions, and exchanges that all rest upon the co-presence of persons in space and time—indeed, can only happen there and then.[9]

Co-presence is a richer field of intersubjectivity than that mediated by telephony. When what is being exchanged between persons is pure code (e.g., numbers or computer programs), then there is minimal loss of what co-presence brings; but if there is any need to respond to or understand, say, emotional or affective responses, then the mediation of communication technologies deadens our ability to relate to each other and therefore to accomplish common tasks. It is quite possible that the very communicative channels by which people acquire tacit knowledge from (or with) each other involve mediums depending on co-presence. To think that nothing is lost when we give up co-presence is, for example, to completely neglect the role of the body in our intersubjective dealings, indeed, in our very ability to relate to our lifeworld as sentient beings.

Avowal has the paradoxical nature of being both part of highly integrated and flexible organizations and exactly what is outside the purview of modern management: avowal cannot be designed into systems, nor can it be harnessed simply to other ends. This is because avowal is of a kind with *belief*: I can no more order you to have relatedness with another person than I can order you to believe. Avowal is only possible within intersubjective relationships where there is room for play, a looseness between people.[10] Avowal is best cultivated, I am arguing, slightly askew from the labor process proper: avowal in good part is what happens in the interstices of laboring.

Rather than tacit knowledge being something that managers can mine from workers and transform into operationalized or organizational knowledge, tacit knowledge is often a case of distributed cognition, or socially shared knowledge, that disappears exactly when translation into code is attempted. Moreover, the "connectivity" that allows the flow of such knowledge between subjects is synonymous with what I am calling avowal: the everyday activities by which persons test and retest what kinds of people those around them, and they themselves, are. To the degree such connectivity is foreclosed (for example, by too much stress on formal rule structures), avowal is precluded from occurring. Mark Auslander argued that such activities are most integrative of time and space if "workers 'seize control' of ritual genres" (Auslander, 2002, p. 20). Ironically, these are exactly the sorts of things managers who would like to take control of workplace culture are most likely to want to squelch.

Relatedness other than biological kinship is a field of performative and meta-communicative gestures by which we show our constancy to one another, our ability to stand by our vows. In our promises there is information that cannot be quantified or inserted as a variable into systemic organizational theories, information that allows tacit knowledge to flourish. It is here that allowing the family as sibling structure into the workplace as a model proves its value.

Trust only arises with familiarity, and as the critique of tacit knowledge as used by Nonaka above makes clear, trust often is cultivated by channels of communication that can only take place between co-present persons engaged in mutual succor, or at the very least a mutuality of opposition within the same idioms. The fact that trust cannot be rendered into quantities has made the grounds of trust not just invisible to management, but quite literally unmanageable. If I trust you, I have to stop counting everything you do. Where there is trust, we can expect familiarity, and tolerate weak (or even absent) management.

As further avenues for research, I would suggest more attention be paid to how relationships inside and outside of the workplace shape each other. I hope I have shown treating workplace organization as a "closed system" set off from other activities is a loaded assumption, one that has little to do with the actual intersections of work and home and much to do with how the workplace is structured as social space. We should also pay attention to how persons' notions of what constitutes good or ethical work are consonant or dissonant with their actual world of workday practice: how does work as a moral space integrate with family as a moral space?

I would also like to see more on how children are socialized into their understandings of what work is by their parents, studies that ideally would incorporate ethnographic attention to children's classrooms, their home life and communication with parents, and understandings shared with peers. A study, ideally, that would cover a long enough span of time to see, for example, how such understandings change between pre-adolescence and the entering of the job market or college education.

Peoples' work lives (thought through in comparison with distinct yet overlapping institutions like church and voluntary organizations) deserve attention for how the presentation of social interaction in these various spaces conflicts or is similar. For example, the parliamentary procedure of union meetings is nothing like how most work, even that of meetings, is organized: ethnographic attention could reveal much here.

And, finally, greater attention should be paid to the expression of emotions in the workplace, particularly as part of interactions filling the interstices of work. No one focuses all their effort on work while at work. The closest I can imagine is the lone computer programmer, or perhaps author, slouched over his or her media device. The processual unfolding of relatedness in workspaces through multiple channels of interaction (including embodiment even in white-collar spaces) requires we think through how people are working together, forming a moral order, and emotionally reacting to those interactions, is an important part of the workplace. We should abandon the hope of designing workplace cultures to spec, but this does not mean we should in any way abandon the necessity of understanding the social world of work.

NOTES

[1] An exception here is church and temple. But, even then the correlation of class, occupation, and denomination plays a role in fields of association between persons.

[2] Nelson Lichtenstein wrote that such firms are "not unlike the feudal baronies of old, offering security and identity on return for deference and fealty" (2002, p. 242). While paternalism, or at the very least paternalist models, were defining features of feudalism, paternalism in modern relations of production can be traced back at least to the textile manufactures during the second half of the 18th century in England, where some owners of manufactures sought to turn their company towns into utopian communities (be the good father), while others exerted despotic control over those working in their mills (bad fathers) up to and including the flogging of employees. Patriarchal power was often reinforced in these early manufactures with wage-laboring fathers functioning as mini-foremen or subcontractors, responsible for their wives and children's "subcontracted" labor (Burawoy, 1985, pp. 92–93). Family and family models were explicit parts of the organization of production in these workplaces.

[3] Familism enters the present-tense workplace in a variety of ways. For example, claims beginning a couple decades ago (timed, interestingly, to the discovery of culture in the workplace) that a post-Fordist stage of production had been entered were soon followed by the discovery of "Toyotism": Japanese firms' possession of a familiarity between management and workers that ensured quality. The attempt to cultivate in American firms such patterns of workplace integration began to appear in the early 1980s, largely under the aegis of Total Quality (TQ) programs and the idea that productivity gains could be had through "teamwork." Perhaps the most thoroughgoing attempt to apply the Japanese relations in production model came with Saturn. Both TQ and Saturn rely on a degree of relatedness in the workplace; a sharing of sentiments, goals, and substantial labor between team members. Laurie Graham, based on a stint as a shopfloor labor participant–observer, claimed the case of Toyotism she witnessed at a Midwest auto plant was a failure because, rather than encouraging trust and lateral communication, management used the idea of teamwork to ratchet down rather than loosen control (Graham, 1993). Arguably, the integration necessary for Total Quality or Saturn-style

management to work cannot be engineered into existence: the imperative "Be a team!" cannot be enforced. It will be interesting to see if the quality dividend Toyotism supposedly brings will survive the present wave of structural adjustments happening in Japan (e.g., the end of lifelong employment guarantees).

[4]But, it was only in the late 19th century that what we now think of as middle-class labors appeared (cf. Mills, 1951; Bledstein, 1976). The old middle classes were owners of capital, primarily machinery and land, which they managed as well. But, as the scale of production grew into larger and larger conglomerations, a new middle class of engineers, experts, and managers started to emerge for whom the pursuit of the old middle class' goals of the efficient use of time and materials became itself an occupation. Rather than owning capital, the new middle classes sold their knowledge of the organization of society and nature on the labor market, continuing the mission of making the workplace efficient.

[5]While consumption and lifestyle are important aspects of middle- and working-class identity, Zweig defined class as "in large part based on the power and authority people have at work." He defined the working class as those who "have relatively little control over the pace or content of their work, and aren't anybody's boss"—he figured this amounts to over 60% of the workforce. The middle class he defined as those with "middling authority" and claimed they compose about 30% of the labor force. He put little weight on income and lifestyle (Zweig, 2000, p. 3). While the virtues of aspiring to become middle class are overwhelmingly present in the day-to-day messages promulgated by media sources, another, less-studied, way middle-class persons might have effects on the consciousness of working people is through the "power to shape the realities of workplace life and the daily lives of workers, realities that become encoded as patterns of thought" (Durrenberger, 2002, p. 93). Rather than simply providing ideas that savvy workers mirror, the PMC shapes half of most adults' daily experience through the workplace.

In other words, one way that middle class-ness is spread as an ethos is through the experience of space and time in the workplace. Parents bring these models home to their children, models reinforced by the regimentation of space, time, and knowledge in schools (on the normative middle class-ness of educational institutions and an excellent ethnography of British working-class youth, see Willis, 1977). While cultural models and images in themselves (for example, those found in the media) obviously have an effect on persons, that effect would certainly be less if it did not have the backing of experience.

[6]Zweig asserted that in the end, rather than the myth of the deserving being rewarded, good jobs are distributed by luck and "the most important piece of luck, good or bad, is the family you happen to be born into. Those born into the capitalist class were born on third base (though many may think they personally have hit a triple)" (Zweig, 2000, p. 46). And, for the really wealthy, work and family strategies are bound together by inheritance. It is not going too far to say that the family strategies of the dynastic wealthy, concerned more with status competition than with securing a livelihood (Marcus, 1983) and by placing investment capital in one locus rather than another, affect innumerable other families' strategies as well. Indeed, the workplace itself is made and unmade by the migrations of the finance capital wielded by wealthy families and financiers.

[7]"Our learning is based on believing" (Wittgenstein, et al., 1969, p. 170). When Polanyi claimed "we know more than we say," he explicitly and quite clearly meant the distinction between tacit and explicit knowledge to be in essence unbridgeable: If a type of knowledge were able to be translated into explicit propositions, then it was not tacit to begin with. Tacit knowledge is of a different order than explicit knowledge. Polanyi invented the very concept to account for knowledge that could not be ultimately submitted to objective scrutiny, for example, Popperian notions of falsifiable knowledge (Mirowski, 1997).

[8]Polanyi described tacit knowing as a structure "show[ing] that all thought contains components of which we are subsidiarily aware in the focal content of our thinking, and that all thought dwells in its subsidiaries, as if they were parts of our body. Hence thinking is not only intentional, as Brentano has taught: it is also necessarily fraught with the roots that it embodies. It has a from–*to* structure" (Polanyi, 1967, p. x). Polanyi is grounding thought in neuronal structures, a move that may not be necessary to keep the thrust of his insight that much knowledge is embodied rather than rule-directed.

[9]Meta-communication happens when "the subject of discourse is the relationship between the speakers" (Bateson, 1972, p. 178). The "meta-messages" sent by meta-communicative expressions both frame themselves off from the everyday (e.g., "this is play") and within that space provide room for commentary on everyday social relations. A key feature of meta-communication, and one of the reasons it is invisible or aberrant to formal analysis, is that it (like ritual) makes generous use of reversals: For example, horseplay, a form of meta-communication, overwhelmingly involves what phenomenologically appears as aggression but is, in fact, an expression of familiarity. But, this does not make meta-communication stimulus and response: what makes it a powerful social glue is that it is risky. It can go wrong: the frame "this is play" can be refused by a participant, who then also is refusing familiarity. Meta-communication is close to, but not identical with, performance. For example, performance does not usually involve reversal; instead, performance is closer to an act or statement that creates through expression. Avowal can be made both through performances of competence or skill (Bauman & Babcock, 1984) and through (speech) acts (Austin, 1979). While "akin" to performance, avowal bridges the linguistic and dramaturgical senses of performance: avowal can both be stated and enacted. Avowal is diffused through time; avowal occurs in a multitude of activities, no one of which alone

can be said to be avowal. Just as avowal exists not through a specific act at a specific time (even though such acts can be the simples out of which the composite of avowal arises), it is subject to constant instauration or erasure from time through afterwards-ness and anticipation.

Avowal I link explicitly to the temporality of relationships: how, when, and where a relation unfolds in time and through what mediums it is expressed. The temporality of work involved not only the synchronization of activities around working, but also the ordering of both past events and future expectations between co-present subjects sharing a social milieu. I am particularly interested in how past, present, and future interact in the coordination and synchronization of the labor process.

[10]Horseplay and joking are ludic activities that sublimate aggression into shared-ness: they are forms of play that can only flourish if there is trust that things will not go too far—i.e., spill over into real aggression or into hurtful statements. But, as Henri Bergson noted of joking and humor (Bergson in Meredith & Sypher, 1980), the difference between hurtful and funny often rests on the "flexibility" of the person "subjected" to humor: that is, if a person refuses to be made fun of, this in itself opens further opportunities for humor (both Chaplin and the Marx Brothers made their livings off mockery of the "straight" man or woman). Horseplay and joking are games that can build trust, an understanding of games in the workplace at odds with Burawoy's game theoretical focus on play as about scorekeeping (Burawoy, 1979b).

REFERENCES

Applebaum, H. A. (1981). *Royal blue, the culture of construction workers*. New York: Holt, Rinehart & Winston.

Arens, W., & Karp, I. (1989). Creativity of power: Cosmology and action in African societies. Washington, DC: Smithsonian Institution Press.

Auslander, M. (2002). *Rituals of the workplace*. Retrieved 5 January, 2004, from http://www.bc.edu/bc_org/avp/wfnetwork/rft/wfpedia/wfpROWent.html.

Austin, J. L. (1979). *Philosophical papers*. Oxford, England: Oxford University Press.

Baba, M. (1998). The anthropology of work in the Fortune 1000: A critical retrospective. *The Anthropology of Work Review, 18*(4).

Baba, M. (1999). Dangerous liaisons: Trust, distrust, and information technology in American work organizations. *Human Organization, 58*(3), 331–346.

Baba, M. (2001). The globally distributed team: Learning to work in a new way, for corporations and anthropologists alike. *Practicing Anthropology, 23*(4), 2–8.

Baba, M. (2003). Working knowledge goes global: Knowledge sharing in a globally distributed team. *The Anthropology of Work Review, 24*(1–2), 19–29.

Baldamus, W. (1961). *Efficiency and effort*. London: Tavistock.

Baran, P. A., & Sweezy, P. M. (1968). *Monopoly capital; an essay on the American economic and social order*. Harmondsworth, England: Penguin.

Barley, S. R., & Orr, J. E. (1997). Between craft and science: Technical work in U.S. settings. Ithaca, NY: IRL Press.

Barth, F. (1981). "Models" reconsidered. In (Ed.), *Process and form in social life* (pp. –). London: Routledge & Kegan Paul.

Basso, K. H. (1979). *Portraits of "The Whiteman" : Linguistic play and cultural symbols among the western Apache*. Cambridge, England; New York: Cambridge University Press.

Bateson, G. (1972). *Steps to an ecology of mind*. New York: Ballentine.

Bauman, R., & Babcock, B. A. (1984). *Verbal art as performance*. Prospect Heights, IL: Waveland Press.

Beidelman, T. O. (1986). *Moral imagination in Kaguru modes of thought*. Bloomington: Indiana University Press.

Bion, W. R. (1961). *Experiences in groups*. London: Tavistock.

Bledstein, B. J. (1976). *The culture of professionalism*. New York: Norton.

Bourdieu, P. (1977). *Outline of a theory of practice* (vol. 16). Cambridge, England; New York: Cambridge University Press.

Braverman, H. (1974). *Labor and monopoly capital; the degradation of work in the twentieth century*. New York: Monthly Review Press.

Burawoy, M. (1979a). The anthropology of industrial work. *Annual Review of Anthropology, 8*, 231–266.

Burawoy, M. (1979b). *Manufacturing consent: Changes in the labor process under monopoly capitalism*. Chicago: University of Chicago Press.

Burawoy, M. (1985). *The politics of production: Factory regimes under capitalism and socialism*. London: Verso.

Carsten, J. (1995). The substance of kinship and the heat of the hearth: Feeding, personhood, and relatedness among Malays in Pulau Langkawi. *American Ethnologist, 22*(2), 223–241.

Carsten, J. (2000). *Cultures of relatedness: New approaches to the study of kinship*. Cambridge, England; New York: Cambridge University Press.

Carsten, J. (2004). *After kinship*. Cambridge, England; New York: Cambridge University Press.

Coleman, E. G. (2001). High-tech guilds in the ear of global capital. *The Anthropology of Work Review, 22*(1), 28–32.

Collins, R. (1986). *Weberian sociological theory*. Cambridge, England; New York: Cambridge University Press.

Darrah, C. N. (1996). *Learning and work: An exploration in industrial ethnography*. New York: Garland.

Davis, M. (1986). *Prisoners of the American dream: Politics and economy in the history of the U.S. working class*. London: Verso.

Deal, T. E., & Kennedy, A. A. (1982). *Corporate culture: The rites and rituals of corporate life*. Reading, MA: Addison-Wesley.

Deming, W. E. (1993). *The new economics for industry, government, education*. Cambridge, MA: Massachusetts Institute of Technology Center for Advanced Engineering Study.

Dudley, K. M. (1994). *The end of the line: Lost jobs, new lives in postindustrial America*. Chicago: University of Chicago Press.

Dudley, K. M. (1999). (Dis) locating the middle class. *Anthropology Newsletter, 4*.

Durrenberger, P. (2002). Structure, thought, and action: Stewards in Chicago union locals. *American Anthropologist, 104*(1), 93–105.

Durrenberger, P., & Erem, S. (1999). The weak suffer what they must: A natural experiment in thought and structure. *American Anthropologist, 101*(4), 783–793.

Ehrenreich, B. (1989). *Fear of falling: The inner life of the middle class*. New York: Pantheon.

Ehrenreich, B. (2001). *Nickel and dimed: On (not) getting by in America* (1st ed.). New York: Metropolitan Books.

Evans-Pritchard, E. E. (1982). *The Nuer: A description of the modes of livelihood and political institutions of a Nilotic people*. New York and Oxford, England: Oxford University Press.

Fantasia, R. (1988). *Cultures of solidarity: Consciousness, action, and contemporary American workers*. Berkeley: University of California Press.

Fernández-Kelly, M. P. (1983). *For we are sold, I and my people: Women and industry in Mexico's frontier*. Albany: State University of New York Press.

Fingleton, E. (2003). *Unsustainable: How economic dogma is destroying American prosperity*. New York: Thunder's Mouth Press.

Florida, R. L. (2002). *The rise of the creative class: And how it's transforming work, leisure, community and everyday life*. New York: Basic Books.

Foley, D. H. (1989). Does the working class have a culture in the anthropological sense? *Cultural anthropology, 4*(May), 136–159.

Fortes, M. (1987). *Religion, morality, and the person: Essays on Tallensi religion*. Cambridge, England; New York: Cambridge University Press.

Frankenberg, R. (1982). *Custom and conflict in British society*. Manchester Atlantic Highlands, NJ: Manchester University Press. Distributed in the USA by Humanities Press.

Franklin, S., & McKinnon, S. (2001). *Relative values: Reconfiguring kinship studies*. Durham, NC: Duke University Press.

Freeman, C. (2000). *High tech and high heels in the global economy: Women, work, and pink-collar identities in the Caribbean*. Durham, NC: Duke University Press.

Freud, S. (1975 [1922]).*Group psychology and the analysis of the ego*. New York: Norton.

Gabriel, Y. (1998). Psychoanalytic contributions to the study of the emotional life of organizations. *Administration and Society, 30*(3), 291–315.

Gamst, F. C. (1980). *The hoghead: An industrial ethnology of the locomotive engineer*. New York: Holt, Rinehart & Winston.

Gatewood, J. B. (1985). Actions speak louder than words. In J. W. D. Dougherty (Ed.), *Directions in cognitive anthropology*. University of Illinois Press (pp. –)

Geertz, C. (1973). *The interpretation of cultures: Selected essays*. New York: Basic Books.

Goffman, E. (1964). The neglected situation. *American Anthropologist, 66*(6), 133–136.

Goldschmidt, W. (1947). *As you sow*. New York: Harcourt Brace.

Gouldner, A. W. (1954). *Patterns of industrial bureaucracy*. Glencoe, IL: Free Press.

Gouldner, A. W. (1965). *Wildcat strike: A study in worker–management relationships*. New York: Harper & Row.

Graham, L. (1993). Inside a Japanese transplant: A critical perspective. *Work and Occupations, 20,* 147–173.

Graham, L. (1995). *On the line at Subaru-Isuzu: The Japanese model and the American worker*. Ithaca, NY: ILR Press.

Gregory, K. L. (1983). Native view paradigms: Multiple cultures and culture conflicts in organizations. *Administrative Science Quarterly, 28*(3), 359–376.

Grenier, G. J. (1988). *Inhuman relations: Quality circles and anti-unionism in American industry*. Philadelphia: Temple University Press.

Hakken, D. (1999). *Cyborgs @ cyberspace?: An ethnographer looks to the future*. New York: Routledge.

Hakken, D., & Andrews, B. (1993). *Computing myths, class realities: An ethnography of technology and working people in Sheffield, England*. Boulder, CD: Westview.

Halle, D. (1984). *America's working man: Work, home, and politics among blue-collar property owners*. Chicago: University of Chicago Press.

Hamada, T., & Sibley, W. E. (1994). *Anthropological perspectives on organizational culture*. Lanham, Maryland: University Press of America.

Handelman, D. (1976). Re-thinking "banana time": Symbolic integration in a work setting. *Urban Life, 4*(4), 433–447.

Harper, D. A. (1987). *Working knowledge: Skill and community in a small shop*. Chicago: University of Chicago Press.

Herbert, C. (1991). *Culture and anomie: Ethnographic imagination in the nineteenth century*. Chicago: University of Chicago Press.

Hochschild, A. R. (1997). *The time bind: When work becomes home and home becomes work* (1st ed.). New York: Metropolitan Books.

Jacoby, S. M. (1997). *Modern manors: Welfare capitalism since the New Deal*. Princeton, NJ: Princeton University Press.

Kakar, S. (1970). *Frederick Taylor: A study in personality and innovation*. Cambridge, MA: MIT Press.

Kalb, D. (1997). *Expanding class: Power and everyday politics in industrial communities, the Netherlands, 1850–1950*. Durham, NC: Duke University Press.

Karp, I. (1997). Notions of the person. In J. Middleton (Ed.), *Encyclopedia of Africa* (pp. 100–110). New York: Scribner's.

Kerr, C. (1960). *Industrialism and industrial man; the problems of labor and management in economic growth*. Cambridge, MA: Harvard University Press.

Kerr, C., & Fisher, L. (1964). Plant sociology: The elite and the aborigines. In C. Kerr (Ed.), *Labor and management in industrial society* (pp. 43–82). New York: Doubleday.

Knauft, B. M. (2002). *Critically modern: Alternatives, alterities, anthropologies*. Bloomington: Indiana University Press.

Kondo, D. K. (1990). *Crafting selves: Power, gender, and discourses of identity in a Japanese workplace*. Chicago: University of Chicago Press.

Lamont, M. (2000). *The dignity of working men: Morality and the boundaries of race, class, and immigration*. New York: Cambridge, MA: Russell Sage Foundation; Harvard University Press.

Latour, B., & Woolgar, S. (1986). *Laboratory life: The construction of scientific facts*. Princeton, NJ: Princeton University Press.

Lave, J. & Wenon, E. (1991). *Situated learning: Legitimat*. Peripheral participation. New York: Cambridge.

Lévi-Strauss, C. (1969). *The elementary structures of kinship* (Rev. ed.). Boston: Beacon Press.

Lichtenstein, N. (2002). *State of the union: A century of American labor*. Princeton, NJ: Princeton University Press.

Luz Ibarra, M. d. l. (2002). Transnational identity formation and Mexican immigrant women's ethics of elder care. *The Anthropology of Work Review, 23*(3–4), 16–20.

MacIntyre, A. C. (1984). *After virtue: A study in moral theory* (2nd ed.). Notre Dame, N: University of Notre Dame Press.

Malinowski, B. (1954). *Magic, science and religion, and other essays*. Garden City, NY: Doubleday.

Marcus, G. E. (1983). *Elites, ethnographic issues* (1st ed.). Albuquerque: University of New Mexico Press.

Marcus, G. E. (1990). Once more into the breach between economic and cultural analysis. In (Eds.), *Beyond the marketplace* (pp. 331–352). Friedland & Robertson (Eds.). New York: DeGruyter.

Marcus, G. E. (1995). Ethnography in/of the world system: The emergence of multi-sited ethnography. *Annual Review of Anthropology, 24*, 95–117.

Mars, G. (1981). The anthropology of managers. *RAIN, 42*(Feburary), 4–6.

Mauss, M. (1979). *Sociology and psychology: Essays*. London; Boston: Routledge & Kegan Paul.

Mayo, E. (1933). *The human problems of an industrial civilization*. New York: Macmillan.

Mayo, E., & Harvard University. Graduate School of Business Administration. Division of Research. (1945). *The social problems of an industrial civilization*. Boston: Author.

Meredith, G., Bergson, H., & Sypher, W. (1980). *Comedy: An essay on comedy*. Baltimore: Johns Hopkins University Press.

Miller, E. J., & Rice, A. K. (1967). *Systems of organization*. London: Tauistock publications.

Miller, E. J., Gould, L. J., Stapley, L., & Stein, M. (2001). *The systems psychodynamics of organizations: Integrating the group relations approach, psychoanalytic, and open systems perspectives: Contributions in honor of Eric J. Miller*. New York: Karnac Press.

Mills, C. W. (1951). *White collar; the American middle classes*. New York: Oxford University Press.

Mirowski, P. (1997). On playing the economics trump card in the philosophy of science: Why it did not work for Michael Polanyi. Proceedings of the 1996 Biennial Meetings of the Philosophy of Science Association, 64.

Mirowski, P. (2002). *Machine dreams: Economics becomes a cyborg science*. Cambridge, England; New York: Cambridge University Press.

Morgan, L. H. (1997). *Systems of consanguinity and affinity of the human family*. Lincoln: University of Nebraska Press.

Nash, J. C. (1989). *From tank town to high tech: The clash of community and industrial cycles*. New York: State University of New York Press.

Noble, D. F. (1977). *America by design: Science, technology, and the rise of corporate capitalism* (1st ed.). New York: Knopf.

Nonaka, I. (1994). A dynamic theory of organizational knowledge creation. *Organization Science, 5*(1), 14–33.

Nonaka, I., & Takeuchi, H. (1995). The knowledge-creating company: How Japanese companies create the dynamics of innovation. New York: Oxford University Press.

Nonaka, I. & Takeuchi, H. (2004). *Hitotsubashi on knowledge management*. Singapore: Wiley (Asia).

Ong, A. (1987). *Spirits of resistance and capitalist discipline: Factory women in Malaysia*. Albany: State University of New York Press.

Orr, J. E. (1990). Community memory in a service culture. In Middleton & D. Edwards (Ed.), *Collective remembering*. London: Sage.

Orr, J. E. (1996). *Talking about machines: An ethnography of a modern job*. Ithaca, NY: ILR Press.

Ortner, S. B. (1999). *The fate of "culture": Geertz and beyond*. Berkeley: University of California Press.

Ortner, S. B. (2003). *New Jersey dreaming: Capital, culture, and the class of '58*. Durham, NC: Duke University Press.

Palsson, G. (1994). Enskillment at sea. *Man, 29*(4), 901–927.

Person, E. S. (1995). *By force of fantasy: How we make our lives*. New York: Basic Books.

Peters, T. J., & Waterman, R. H. (1982). *In search of excellence: Lessons from America's best-run companies* (1st ed.). New York: Harper & Row.

Polanyi, M. (1953). The hypothesis of cybernetics. *The British Journal for the Philosophy of Science, 2*(8), 312–315.

Polanyi, M. (1967). *The tacit dimension*. Garden City, NY: Anchor.

Postone, M. (1993). *Time, labor, and social domination: A reinterpretation of Marx's critical theory*. Cambridge, England; New York: Cambridge University Press.

Pred, A. R., & Watts, M. (1992). *Reworking modernity: Capitalisms and symbolic discontent*. New Brunswick, NJ: Rutgers University Press.

Radcliffe-Brown, A. R. (1939). *Taboo*. Cambridge, England: The Cambridge University press.

Reich, R. B. (1983). *The next American frontier*. New York: Times Books.

Roy, D. (1952a). *Restriction of output in a piecework machine shop*. Chicago: University of Chicago Press.

Roy, D. (1952b). Quota restriction and goldbricking in a machine shop. *American Journal of Sociology, 57*, 427–442.

Roy, D. (1954). Efficiency and the fix: Informal intergroup relations in a piecework machine shop. *American Journal of Sociology, 60*, 255–266.

Roy, D. (1959). "Banana time": Job satisfaction and informal interaction. *Human Organization, 18*, 158–168.

Roy, W. G. (1997). *Socializing capital: The rise of the large industrial corporation in America*. Princeton, NJ: Princeton University Press.

Salomon, G. (1993). *Distributed cognitions: Psychological and educational considerations*. Cambridge, England; New York: Cambridge University Press.

Schwartzman, H. B. (1987). The significance of meetings in an American mental health center. *American Ethnologist, 14*(2), 271–294.

Schwartzman, H. B. (1993). *Ethnography in organizations*. Newbury Park, CA: Sage.

Scott, J. C. (1985). *Weapons of the weak: Everyday forms of peasant resistance*. New Haven, CT; London: Yale University Press.

Sennett, R. (1998). *The corrosion of character: The personal consequences of work in the new capitalism* (1st ed.). New York: Norton.

Simmel, G. (1963). The sociology of conflict. In H. M. Ruitenbeek (Ed.), *Varieties of classic social theory* (pp. 259–320). New York: Dutton.

Sklar, M. J. (1988). The corporate reconstruction of American capitalism, 1890–1916: The market, the law, and politics. Cambridge, England; New York: Cambridge University Press.

Strathern, M. (1992). *After nature: English kinship in the late twentieth century*. Cambridge England; New York: Cambridge University Press.

Swedberg, R. (1998). *Max Weber and the idea of economic sociology*. Princeton, NJ: Princeton University Press.

Talamo, P. B., Borgogno, F., & Merciai, S. A. (1998). *Bion's legacy to groups*: Selected contributions from the International Centennial Conference on the Work of W. R. Bion: Turin, July 1997. London: Karnac.

Taylor, F. W. (1998). *The principles of scientific managment*. New York: Dover.

Thompson, E. P. (1966). *The making of the English working class*. New York: Vintage.

Thompson, E. P. (1991). *Customs in common*. New York: The New Press.

Tilly, C. (1988). Solidary logics: Conclusions. *Theory and Society, 17*(3), 451–458.

Tsoukas, H. (2003). Do we really understand tacit knowledge? In M. A. Lyles (Ed.), *The Blackwell handbook of organizational learning and knowledge management* (pp. 410–427). Malden, MA: Blackwell.

Vidich, A. J. (1995). *The new middle classes: Life-styles, status claims and political orientations*. Washington Square, NY: New York University Press.

Wardell, M. L., Steiger, T. L., & Meiksins, P. (1999). *Rethinking the labor process*. Albany: State University of New York Press.

Warner, W. L. (1963). *Yankee city*. New Haven, CT: Yale University Press.

Weber, M. (1958). *The Protestant ethic and the spirit of capitalism*. New York: Scribner's.

Weber, M., Mills, C. W., & Gerth, H. H. (1958). *From Max Weber: Essays in sociology*. New York: Oxford University Press.

Wells, M. J. (1996). *Strawberry fields: Politics, class, and work in California agriculture*. Ithaca, NY: Cornell University Press.

Willis, P. E. (1977). *Learning to labour: How working class kids get working class jobs*. Farnborough, England: Saxon House.

Wittgenstein, L., Anscombe, G. E. M., & Wright, G. H. V. (1969). *On certainty*. Oxford, England: Blackwell.

Wright, S. (1994). *Anthropology of organizations*. London; New York: Routledge.

Zweig, M. (2000). *The working class majority: America's best kept secret*. Ithaca, NY: ILR Press.

9

Advancing a Career Focus on Work and Family: Insights From the Life Course Perspective

Stephen Sweet
Ithaca College

Phyllis Moen
University of Minnesota

In this chapter, we introduce the life course perspective as it applies to the study of work and family. Our goal is to illustrate core insights of this perspective: the need to locate human development within the historically and socially situated roles and contexts that shape self-assessment and preferences, interpersonal linkages, cultural templates, and structural opportunities. As points of contrast, consider some of the ways the life course perspective draws upon, but also broadens, many of the other perspectives and methods outlined in this handbook:

1. In contrast to perspectives that focus on worker experiences at a particular point in time, the life course perspective focuses on biographical processes and how experiences and strategies develop over time.
2. In contrast to perspectives that focus on individuals as isolated entities, the life course perspective pays particular attention to the conjoint influence of significant social relations, such as with spouses, children, parents, friends.
3. Instead of attempting to "control" for "contaminating" factors, the life course perspective focuses on how human development occurs within historical, cultural, structural contexts. As such, locational markers (such as gender, life stage, social class, ethnicity, birth cohort) are of central concern, as are the resources, values, and norms present in a society at a given time.
4. Instead of being either a macro or micro in orientation, the life course perspective examines the reciprocating relations between personal experiences, institutions, and social change.

The life course perspective offers much to benefit the efforts of work and family stakeholders, including human resource personnel, policymakers, teachers, and researchers. Because the life course perspective locates work and family in time and in context, it brings to life the dynamics of "work" and "family" throughout adulthood, along with constraints that shape decisions of managing these affairs along the way. Thus, a life course approach encourages a focus on careers or paths—work careers, family careers, and their complex interlocks throughout adulthood. Doing so orients thinking and research to the *mechanisms* that shape careers, along with the cultural and structural arrangements that impede or promote effectiveness (at work, at home, and in achieving personal goals) for men and women at all life stages. The life course perspective offers a fresh way of framing research and policy questions, especially about the ways that multiple layers of (often conflicting) roles play out over time, the impacts of existing (often outdated) institutional arrangements, and how individuals and families strategically adapt to the challenges embedded in particular role constellations (Elder, 1985; Moen, 2003a; Moen & Wethington, 1992).

Life course scholars always prefer longitudinal data (following workers or families over a period of months or years), but even with cross-sectional data they seek to locate lives in context and in biographical as well as historical time. Consider, for example, the vastly different experiences of two couples whose jobs, ages, and circumstances are virtually identical except that one couple has just had their first child, while the other remains child-free. Clearly, these two couples are operating in different worlds in terms of their needs, resources, and constraints. While cross-sectional comparisons can reveal differences in stress and well-being at one point in time, longitudinal data would permit a focus on the actual transition in becoming parents. By focusing on transitions, the life course perspective helps to focus on the most prevalent life paths followed in a society at a given historical period, the factors (such as gender, race, family situation, etc.) that predispose individuals to follow one path versus another, and the consequences of deviating from culturally and structurally scripted routes.

In this chapter we illustrate the life course perspective by drawing primarily on illustrations from our research on the Ecology of Careers Study, a key initiative of the Cornell Careers Institute: A Sloan Center for the Study of Working Families. This survey was longitudinal, involving two interviews of 1,500 middle-class couples conducted 2 years apart. It permits the analysis of life stage circumstances, work and family lives, career pathways, and expectations for the future.[1] [For further detail on the study methods, see Moen (2003a).] Although in this study we focus on a unique demographic group—dual-earner middle-class couples—the perspective can be (and should be) applied to other subgroups as well, such as single parents, single earners, the unemployed, retirees, and so on.

Our primary interest in this chapter is to introduce core life course concepts. As case examples, we focus on three life course events (transitions) common among working families—the wife's return to school, the entry of children into the family, and retirement. Our goal is not so much to provide comprehensive analysis of these events or of other major transitions that occur over the life course, but, rather, to suggest the types of questions that emerge when one considers lives over time as well as how decisions and experiences are shaped by prevailing cultural and structural forces. We conclude this chapter by assessing the utility of the life course perspective for both research and policy.

In considering these transitions and their work-family implications, we focus on four key interrelated concepts: career pathways, relational contexts, historically situated social structures, and strategic adaptations. Throughout, our overarching emphasis is on the concept of *career* (Barley, 1989; H. Becker, 1966). This concept provides a window into dynamic links between individuals, families, employers, and other institutions. The career concept locates work and family transitions and trajectories as shaped by the weight of existing institutional and cultural arrangements that frame work and the family life (Moen & Sweet, 2004). Although the concept of "career" has been used to discuss the patterns of men's occupational mobility in the workplace, we highlight below its usefulness in depicting the biographical paths followed by women and men as they construct lives with others, broadening the concept to incorporate work careers, family careers, and educational careers.

CAREER PATHWAYS: BIOGRAPHICAL EXPERIENCES AND EDUCATIONAL CAREERS AS ILLUSTRATIONS

One way to apply the life course perspective to work and family is to identify common career patterns as well as their impacts on individual workers, working families, workplaces, and the broader society. Life course researchers move from work-family snapshots to consider *career pathways*, the dominant patterns of development and adjustment (as well as those that are less common) most commonly followed by working families. Within this career focus, a keen attention is placed on the factors contributing to one path versus another and the impacts these paths have on life qualify and life chances.

Using our own biographies as an illustration, Fig. 9.1 models Steve's work, educational, and family careers. We use the thickness of bars to represent the relative time allotted to various dimensions of his life, gaps to represent the absence of major commitments, and the onsets marked by his age. A few things stand out. First, notice the extent to which the paths Steve adopted generally reflects the traditional career path common to men, which is to (1) complete education, (2) establish a work career, and (3) establish a family. If we were to chart Phyllis' career using a similar approach, we would see a very different patterning of educational, family, and work transitions. In Phyllis' case, a return to school followed the formation of her family and the early death of her first husband, an event that profoundly transformed her career goals and parenting responsibilities (Moen, 2004). But, this event notwithstanding, a "disorderly" career sequencing and timing is much more typical of women's lives than men's (Moen, 1992, 2001b; Pavalko & Smith, 1999). This observation is readily apparent in our own lives as well as in the lives of the men and women in our studies.

Second, we can observe points in the life course where Steve's time resources were more plentiful and points at which demands escalated and threatened to outstrip his resources. But, associated with the escalation of time spent in some activities, we see decreases in time spent on other activities, such as the dropping off of hobbies (when he is working as a research associate) and the near elimination of those activities when children are born. This suggests two processes operating in tandem, *external demands* placed on individuals in their various roles, but also *strategic selections* (Moen & Spencer, 2005), as individuals adjust and reconfigure their lives

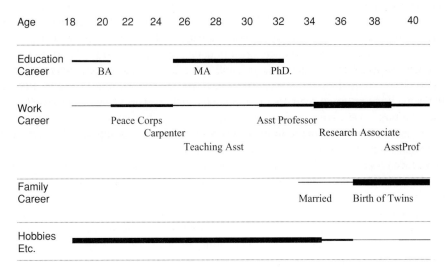

FIG. 9.1. Timing and time demands of an individual's career.
Note: Thicker bars represent heavier time commitments.

to accommodate (as best they can) existing exigencies as well as any new circumstances that confront them. As we will later demonstrate, individuals are not only reactive to the work-family strains in their lives, they are also proactive, planning and adjusting their lives in anticipation of the consequences of making job changes or having additional children.

Documenting career paths requires analyses of timing, durations, and sequences of transitions (Settersten, 1999). *Timing* refers to the point at which events occur in a person's life. These events can be at the societal level (such as the 9-11 terrorist attacks, economic depressions, or the passage of the Family and Medical Leave Act) or at a personal level (such as marriage, divorce, a job shift, a geographical move). *Duration* means the length of individual spells in a particular role or behavior and the frequency of changes between roles. Pavalko and Smith (1999) demonstrated this concern by showing the ways interrupted occupational careers, those marked by periods of nonemployment (a career pattern common for women), are predictive of poorer health in later life. *Sequencing* refers to the ordering of various status changes. For example, Hogan (1980) found that the sequencing of beginning one's work career, having the first child, and completion of education are strongly predictive of, among other things, men's subsequent economic prospects.

Some life course researchers study *"turning points"* (Clausen, 1995, 1998), events or decisions that redirect lives or experiences that orient individuals to pursue very different goals. Turning points can be thought of as objective (such that an outside observer would note marked changes in patterns) or subjective (individuals or families define these), reflecting major shifts in their values, motivations, or relationships (Wethington, Pixley, & Kavey, 2003). Our research points to the birth of the first child as a common turning point in the lives of dual-earner couples, but much more consequential for the lives of wives than husbands, especially in terms of career prospects (Moen & Sweet, 2003). Other consequential turning points include unemployment, marriage, divorce, illness, and retirement. Elder (1995) noted that to understand transitions requires knowledge of the trajectories leading to them. Gauging the effects of major events (including transitions and turning points) depends on prior circumstances and subjective assessments. For example, divorce or early forced retirement do not necessarily constitute "negative" turning points if people were unhappy in their marriages or their jobs (Wheaton, 1990).

To further illustrate the importance of studying transitions and patterns, consider the increasingly common career pathway of returning to school later in life. *The Chronicle of Higher Education* (2004) reported that fully 38% of students enrolled in college are age 25 or older. This high proportion of adult students is one indicator, among others, of the increasing heterogeneity in the timing and sequencing of life course transitions (Moen, 2001a; O'Rand & Henretta, 1996) as well as the increased instability of jobs and occupational careers (Attewell, 1999; Jacobs & Stoner-Eby, 1998; Kets de Vries & Balazs, 1997; Smith & Rubin, 1997).

Women tend to return to school more frequently than men. Why is this the case? The answer lies partially in an earlier decision in the life course, such as couples' decisions to resolve child-care needs by having the wife interrupt or scale back her occupational or educational goals (Moen & Roehling, 2005). Once their children enter school or leave the household, many women return to school to relaunch their occupational careers or to complete an educational program deferred by family obligations (Bradburn, Moen, & Dempster-McClain, 1995; Settersten & Lovegreen, 1998).

Note how one career pathway (education) can be influenced by other pathways (family and work). The choice of returning to school reflects new sets of circumstances. The process of strategic selection, in turn, forces additional shifts. For example, returning women students report high levels of role overload and strain; nearly one in four nontraditional women students report "feeling overwhelmed and conflicted about all my role responsibilities" (Hybertson, Hulme, Smith, & Holton, 1992). We find that women who return to school and who have school-age children report lower marital satisfaction than women at similar life stages who are not in school (Sweet & Moen, under review). Our qualitative interviews with these women indicate that their return to school commonly marks a turning point in their lives, wherein many expect a reordering of domestic obligations and a renewed interest in their career concerns. Their husbands generally do not share this perspective, expecting existing divisions of household chores and child-care responsibilities to continue (Suitor, 1987; Sweet & Moen, under review). As a result, marital satisfaction tends to decline for both partners. The combination of conflicts resulting from work, family, and education explains some of the difficulties older students have in completing their degrees in a timely manner (Jacobs & King, 2002).

In sum, career-related concepts of timing, duration, sequencing, and turning points enable scholars and practitioners to consider how decisions (and roles) unfold, how earlier and recent decisions lead to new sets of constraints and options, and the ways new quandaries are created over time. Not only does this perspective open a window on social norms about being "on" or "off" time, in terms of social roles or personal expectations, but also on the role of *agency* in lives—that strategic decisions (like returning to school, moving, changing jobs, remarrying, or remaining in a job, neighborhood, marriage) can be real forks in the road. One thing is clear: the *lock-step sequencing of careers*—the rigid ordering of educational, work, and family paths throughout the life course—is being rewritten. But, existing lock-step rules remain. For example, jobs and career paths are designed for workers without domestic responsibilities, but both men and women workers now typically have family obligations and goals and are working without the backup of a full-time homemaker (Moen & Sweet, 2003; Moen & Roehling, 2005). Recognizing this mismatch is crucial to understanding the links between work and family, from young adulthood through retirement and beyond.

RELATIONAL CONTEXTS: DUAL-EARNER WORK COMMITMENTS AS ILLUSTRATION

Another life course insight is how *relational contexts*—ties with spouses, children, extended families, friends, and coworkers—impact the lives of members of working families. Surprisingly, most "work-family" research is on *individuals*, not on families, not even on couples. Highlighting the ways in which lives are linked refocuses analysis to consider how problems (and some solutions) to work-family conflict stem from the ways in which multiple roles and multiple career paths intersect throughout the life course. Clearly, the interdependent careers of dual-earner couples affects decisions concerning what jobs to seek, where to live, and how to care for others (e.g., Bielby & Bielby, 1992; Hertz, 2001; Heymann, 2000; Moen, 2003a). Our research leads us to conclude that understanding the challenges confronting working families necessarily involves considering ties to spouses and children as well as ties to broader networks of friends, relatives, and coworkers.

In his pathbreaking book, *The Ecology of Human Development* (1979), Urie Bronfenbrenner criticized the discipline of psychology for its overreliance on laboratory experiments that ostensibly "controlled" (meaning eliminated) the influence of various factors that may "corrupt" analyses. In its stead, he advocated for studies of lives in *context*, and to structure analyses to consider the many ecologies, existing at many levels, that influence the life experiences and decisions (Moen, Elder, & Luscher, 1995). While work-family research purports to assess connections between what happens inside and outside of the workplace, the life course perspective broadens the focus to incorporate the dynamic connections between people as they move through their various roles, what Elder (1998a, b) termed *linked lives*.

We demonstrate below that the decisions of dual-earner couples (now the most common work-family form) are seldom individual ones, and that these couples adopt *couple level*

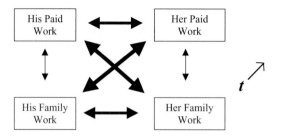

FIG. 9.2.   Conceptual analysis of potential work-family concerns. Bolded arrows represent concerns of linked lives.

strategies to accommodate work and family needs. Our studies indicate that husbands and wives make choices in light of available options, cultural norms, and the impact it will have on those central to their lives (especially their spouses, children, and aging parents; Moen & Sweet, 2004a). At the same time, the people in their lives can restrict—and at times expand—their range of options. For example, even single-parents can be affected by the geographical location and work hours of the other parent, especially when both share custody.

Figure 9.2 points to the relational components that invariably shape dual-earner couples' work and family strategies. Most work-family research takes into account the connections between individual employees' work and family roles (the thinner arrows). One "value added" of the life course perspective is its emphasis on the relationship between the husbands' and wives' work and family roles (bolded arrows) and how these connections play out over their life course or time (t).

The reality of contemporary arrangements is that most jobs and career paths are structured for one breadwinner and one homemaker per household (Moen & Roehling, 2005). As Eileen Boris and Carol Herbst Lewis detail in their chapter in this handbook, for the middle-class households who could afford it in the 1950s, the breadwinner–homemaker division "solved" the problem of competing demands, even as it accentuated gender divisions and inequalities. But, spouses in dual-earner relationships, now the most common work-family arrangement, face the challenge of both members occupying and attempting to satisfy the competing demands of the workplace and the family. As a result, strains are compounded and the need to develop complementary arrangements has become paramount.

Consider how dual-earner couples construct work schedules (modeled in Fig. 9.3) and how these strategies vary across the life course (Clarkberg & Merola, 2003; Clarkberg & Moen, 2001; Presser, 1994). Note that our designation of work-hour arrangements is of *couple* arrangements, not simply men's and women's hours. Note also that the interesting findings do not just concern gender, but also *life stage* (as constructed by people's age and the age of the youngest child).

Given the way jobs and career paths are structured for the unencumbered worker (Moen, 2003a; Williams, 2000), there are considerable incentives for putting in long hours on the job and significant penalties for working shorter hours. As one would expect, husbands and wives at earlier stages in their family careers, those having no children and fewer family obligations, commonly work long hours. But, this arrangement changes in remarkable ways as family demands escalate. New parents are often surprised by the extent of the challenges of maintaining two careers and raising children. When ultimately faced with strained relations and an inability to do all that they expected, many fall back into a variant of conventional gender arrangements (Becker & Moen, 1999). Foremost among these options is to "scale back," having one spouse reduce commitment to work in order to satisfy family needs. Note in Fig. 9.3 that couples with preschool-age and school-age children are most likely to adopt

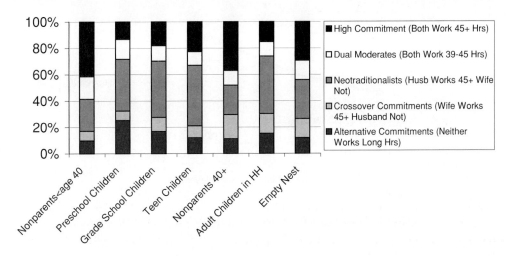

FIG. 9.3.   Work-hour arrangements among middle-class dual-earner couples.

neotraditional work-hour arrangements, with the husband putting in longer hours and the wife working reduced hours. Fewer are able to follow an alternative strategy where both spouses have limited work time (one partner working at most full-time, the other working reduced hours). Both our quantitative data and in-depth interviews with working couples indicate that many more couples would prefer a shorter schedule for both partners but feel they have no choice, as their jobs increasingly require a commitment of long hours (Moen & Sweet, 2003). Faced with a mismatch between the way their jobs are structured and what they feel their families need, the most common strategy for couples is to fall into existing gender scripts once they have children, with wives giving priority to family and husbands emphasizing breadwinning. Not until children are grown and gone do we observe a marked shift away from the neotraditional work-hour arrangement.

"Scaling back" is but one strategy dual-earner couples use to manage the time squeeze. Other common strategies include: having each spouse work alternate schedules (Cox & Presser, 2000; Presser, 2000; Presser & Bamberger, 1993), having the wife working at home or in jobs that offer increased flexibility (Wharton, 1994), reducing expectations for leisure time (working vacations and weekends; Clarkberg & Merola, 2003), redefining household work (such as shopping) into leisure (P. E. Becker & Moen, 1999), or simply going with less sleep (Hochschild & Machung, 1989). Many of these responses to the incompatibility of job demands and family demands fail to work, as well as exacerbate gender inequalities. As Harriet Presser (2000) found, younger couples with young children who have one partner working night shifts are three to six times more likely to divorce than those working day shifts. Having wives work fewer hours at often low-paying, insecure jobs (the kind that permits part-time hours) widens the earnings, status, power, and efficacy divides between husbands and wives within the household, between men and women on the job, and in society at large (Barnett & Gareis, 2000; Moen & Roehling, 2005). Additionally, employees who scale back on work commonly experience a loss of the intrinsic rewards from work, as their job is reduced to nondiscretionary tasks (Barnett & Gareis, 2000).

As Fig. 9.4 shows, while most couples start from a position of fairly equal prioritization of careers, over time, the wife's work career tends to be placed secondary to that of her husband. As husbands remain strongly involved with their paid jobs and wives parent and caregive, career advantages emerge for men and an accumulation of career disadvantages accrue for women.

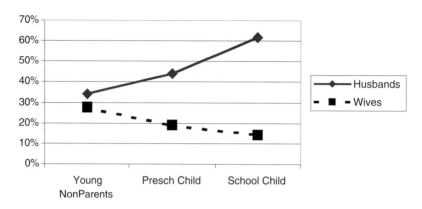

FIG. 9.4.   Husbands and wives reporting that their career was favored.

Men typically experience greater opportunity for upward mobility in their careers as the life course progresses (Padavic & Reskin, 2002). This bifurcation of family and work opportunities poses real challenges to creating dual career success, situations in which both partners feel successful in work, family, and "balancing" both. It is rare to find dual-earner couples to have both partners reporting high success on all three dimensions (Moen, Waismel-Manor, & Sweet, 2003).

In sum, by focusing on social relations as they shape choices and well-being over time, the life course perspective highlights the complex interlocks that link parents and young children (e.g., Gerson, 2001; Lee, Schneider, & Waite, 2003), (adult) children and aging parents (e.g., Gerstel, 2000), and husbands and wives. There are other relational concerns as well, such as the extent to which working parents or retirees are able to participate in civic and community activities (e.g., Michelson, 1985; Putnam, 2000; Sweet, Swisher, & Moen, forthcoming; Swisher, Sweet, & Moen, 2004). The lesson for the field of work-family research is not simply to compare and contrast dichotomies (for example, "employed" workers with "homemakers" or dual-earner families with single-parent families), but to locate lives in the complex web of social ties, and to understand the ways cultural and structural templates about paid work, unpaid care work, children, and gender play out in social relationships as they unfold over time.

HISTORICALLY SITUATED SOCIAL STRUCTURES: RETIREMENT AS ILLUSTRATION

The realities of life at home and at work and the connections between the two have changed in remarkable ways over the last half of the century, as the nation moved from a breadwinner–homemaker norm to the dual-earner family as the modal family form. This is more than simply a matter of women entering the workplace. Most workers today are married to someone who is also in the workforce, and fewer workers have a full-time homemaker to take care of the domestic details of daily life (Moen, 2003a). However, American society has largely failed to adjust to the concerns facing contemporary working families. The result is a mismatch between occupational expectations/reward systems (based on the male breadwinner template) and the realities of families in which most adults are in the workforce. There are other mismatches as well that point to a need to frame work-family research to locate the people and issues we study in their historical and generational contexts.

Three of the most important historical changes transforming the work-family nexus have been (a) revisions in the employer-employee contract, (b) the growth of women's participation in the paid labor force, and (c) advances in technology and the social organization of work. Each succeeding generation has experienced these changes in remarkably different ways: being socialized in very different contexts, experiencing new horizons of opportunity, and watching old structures disintegrate or lag behind. This observation calls attention to the *life course principle*—that the timing of historical events in individual lives, and in particular age-cohorts, shapes subsequent life paths (Elder, 1999; Elder, 1995; Giele & Elder, 1998; Moen, 2001b, 2003a, b).

Existing institutional arrangements tend to change at a glacial pace. As a result, employees and their families confront outmoded employer and governmental practices. These *structural lags* (Riley & Riley, 1994) and *cultural lags* (Ogburn, 1964) reflect the failure to adjust to changing technologies or other emergent social transformations. For contemporary families the prevailing cultural and structural arrangements, designed for husband-breadwinner/wife-homemaker households, present one such lag. By calling attention to the mismatches between existing arrangements and emerging models, the life course perspective encourages scholars to consider the ways in which different cohorts have different opportunities, and the challenges posed by built in, taken-for-granted expectations about work, family, age, and gender. Prevailing (and often outmoded) *institutional arrangements* (legal, economic, organizational, and cultural policies and practices) tend to limit options available to working families.

Consider, as a case in point, retirement. In the early 20th century, retirement was available only to those who could afford to leave their jobs. Most farmers and artisans worked until they died. In the decades following, retirement changed in fundamental ways. With the passage of the Social Security Act of 1935 (and as a means to open up jobs to young [male] heads of households), retirement at age 65 became institutionalized along with government-secured benefits. It also created a new normative age-graded template for later life transitions, offering incentives for a lock-step, one-way, one-time, "quick" exit from the labor force. Coupled with a thriving economy (Levy, 1986) and a paternalistic arrangement that rewarded employee loyalty with job security and employer-sponsored pension programs (Piore & Sabel, 1984), many of the World War II generation had success in making this transition with little personal planning.

For workers in the contemporary economy, the existing structures of Social Security are now being revisited in light of increasing health and longevity as well as the aging of the large baby boom cohort. Social Security, Medicare, health care, and private pensions represent a variety of cultural and structural lags. Rather than intending to retire at age 65, or at the later age now imposed by revisions to the Social Security Act, the average worker in our studies of middle-class, dual-earner couples plans to retire by age 62 (Moen, Sweet, & Swisher, 2005). They also want to have a "second act" in less demanding, more flexible careers/jobs (Moen, Plassmann, & Sweet, 2001). Many would like to continue working on a contractual or part-time basis with their current employer (Hutchens & Dentinger, 2003), but prospects for these types of "bridge" jobs or contingent work following retirement are limited by laws, such as the Fair Labor Standards Act of 1938, that tie health care and other benefits to full-time employment (Moen & Sweet, 2004a).

The regime of career rules and regulations privileges those who work continuously through-out adulthood in (at least) full-time jobs. It disadvantages older women, who often move in and out of part-time and full-time jobs, as well as in and out of the labor force, in tandem with changing family obligations. The edifice of Social Security presumes that women are full-time homemaking wives, "covered" by the spousal benefits. Single, divorced, and wid-owed women's highest 5 years of earnings (on which their Social Security benefits are based) often produce low benefit levels, and women are less apt to be eligible for private pensions or even early buy-outs. Newly widowed women covered by their husbands' earnings are often surprised to find it cut severely with their husbands' deaths, and sometimes husbands' private pension or health care insurance ends as well.

This generation of retirees is the first in which many families are experiencing two retirements: his and hers (Moen et al., 2005). This brings the "work-family" issues to a whole new level, as couples strategize as to when/whether each spouse should retire and when/whether they should work after retirement (Kim & Moen, 1999, 2000, 2001a, b, 2002). Evidence suggests that when couples' retirements are not synchronized there is greater potential for marital discord (Moen, Kim, & Hofmeister, 2000). The age-graded transition into retirement is increasingly fuzzy, and the desires and characteristics of people retiring now evidence greater heterogeneity than was the case for those retiring in the 1960s (O'Rand & Henretta, 1996). At the same time, contemporary men and women can expect to live longer and healthier lives following retirement. Clearly, there is a mismatch between the structure of our aging population and the opportunities present for the baby boom generation as it moves toward and through later adulthood transitions into retirement.

Working families seldom make many "lifestyle" plans for life after retirement, even though they can expect to live much longer and healthier than their parents or grandparents (Farnesworth-Riche, 2000; Moen et al., 2005). But, "planning" is as difficult, given the uncertainties and insecurities. Now even workers in "good" jobs often do not participate in private pension programs. Still, for the more advantaged part of the middle class, financial planning with 401(k)s and other retirement savings plans puts them in greater control of their retirement portfolios, a new structural condition. Our studies indicate that the younger cohorts, those at the trailing edge of the baby boom, are planning more, and beginning their planning earlier than those of the leading-edge baby boom or the World War II generation (Moen et al., 2005).

We believe that one of the challenges confronting new generations of working families is how to transition into retirement and how to manage life after retirement. We believe that what is emerging is a new life stage, one that we call "midcourse," that is, literally *midcourse* between the career and- family building years and the frailties we associate with old age (Moen, 2003b). The fact is that retirement is no longer the passage to old age. Midcourse, as a life stage, has yet to be culturally or structurally defined.

To summarize, the life course perspective offers first a means of moving the work-family interface beyond simply the plight of families with young children. Work-family concerns crop up at every career stage, every family stage, even around the retirement transition. Second, a life course approach points to the importance of locating research and theory in particular historical and policy contexts. Those retiring in the 1950s, for example, came to retirement in a very different way than those retiring in the 2000s or those anticipating retirement in the 2030s.

Third, early life course experiences play out in often unanticipated ways. As a case in point, women who take time out of the workforce when their children are young or else scale back to part-time (Becker & Moen, 1999; Clarkberg & Moen, 2001) pay a price later on in terms of Social Security, health insurance, and other benefits. Earlier experiences, in terms of the timing of events, may also have long-term impacts. Men and women who start their families in their 40s often find they have to postpone retirement to pay their children's college bills (Moen et al., 2005).

Finally, a life course focus underscores the need to recognize and address structural and cultural lags. Again drawing on the retirement example, current policies and practices developed around retirement as an "all or nothing" individual status passage. But, most of the people we interviewed want some form of gradual phasing out or "second act." And, for growing numbers retirement is a *linked* transition, happening over a number of years as both husbands and wives manage two retirements in the face of an uncertain and emerging new life stage (Moen, 2002).

STRATEGIC SELECTION AND ADAPTATION: HOW FAMILIES ADAPT TO ROLE CONFLICTS AS ILLUSTRATION

Our last example explicitly addresses the concept of agency as individuals and families engage in processes of *strategic selection* (into or out of various roles) and *adaptation.* Thus far we have illustrated the way historical contexts, relationships, and career paths shape work and family concerns, while also noting that members of working families make "decisions" as they encounter work and family stresses, overloads, and contradictions. The issue of *agency* is especially challenging for sociologists (like ourselves), since our discipline tends to most heavily emphasize the constraints of structure and culture, social forces existing outside— but not independent—of individuals (Giddens, 1984). To focus exclusively on the structural "weight" and cultural forces, however, would ignore the creativity of individuals and families, suggesting they are simply "role bozos," actors of scripts set forth by existing social conventions (Garfinkel, 1967). Still, any appraisal of decision making *always* occurs in the context of social conventions, powerful forces that guide socialization and behavior, often nonreflectively acted upon in accordance to what one does in a "world-taken-for-granted" (Schutz, [1967] 1932).

As we point out throughout this chapter, some of the most powerful norms shaping current work and family decisions are those imposed by the *gender regime*, an organized and entrenched set of institutional and cultural practices that reinforce an outdated vision of men's and women's responsibilities in the home and paid workforce (Gerson, 2001; Hochschild & Machung, 1989; Moen, 2001b, 2003a; Moen & Roehling, 2005). We observe this dynamic at play in couples planning for retirement (she tends to be concerned about his retirement, but he is less concerned with hers), work commitment following childbirth, and decisions to return to school. Not only does gender have a script, but also so does age, with culturally entrenched notions of when it is appropriate to finish an education, get married, start a family, change jobs, and exit the workforce (Hagestad & Neugarten, 1985; Moen, 2003b). But, existing scripts are out-of-date, producing the structural mismatches and strains that are the common experiences of working families as they respond to job loss, parenthood, divorce, remarriage, death, health problems, and a variety of other concerns that jar their lives from the set image of the autonomous family embraced by American culture (Christensen & Gomory, 1999; Moen, 1994; Riley, Kahn, & Foner, 1994).

Additionally, men and women operate within conventional expectations of what it means to be a "good parent" or a "good employee." These *parent scripts* and *employee scripts* shape the decisions of how to devote oneself to the workplace and the home. As Arlie Hochschild (1997) pointed out, within the culture of the modern workplace, "players" are recognized by a devotion of long hours to the workplace (see also Clarkberg & Moen, 2001; Moen & Roehling, 2005). When asked why they work such long hours, in our research, the most common response was "my job demands it" (Moen & Sweet, 2003). When faced with the contradictions between these two roles, it becomes understandable why couples rely on outmoded gendered strategies of resolving work-family conflicts by prioritizing one career, typically the husband's (Bielby & Bielby, 1992).

Individuals can be, and sometimes are, creative when faced with work-family conflict. But, in our studies of 1,500 working couples, we have been struck by how their strategic selections of roles and behaviors typically accept "as a given" the existing paid work arrangements. Within this framework, they mold their lives to accommodate existing structures, but less often to challenge the structures. As a result, working families are doing their best to modify their *family* circumstances by marrying later, having fewer or no children, having children later in life, sleeping less, and having one spouse move off a more secure career track (Altucher &

Williams, 2003; Becker & Moen, 1999; Clarkberg & Merola, 2003; Moen & Sweet, 2003). But, institutions *are* changing, albeit slowly, in response to the mismatches and family strategies. We offer a few illustrations here.

Consider, for example, the time squeeze dual-earner couples and single parents face as they are pulled between work and home. One way couples respond to the time squeeze is to redefine their realities, for example, the weekly shopping trip becomes the family fun event (Becker & Moen, 1999). Local supermarkets are responding to the needs of working families by including within them child play centers, coffee shops, and restaurants. Thus, we see some organizations outside of the workplace changing in light of the needs of working families.

As individuals tailor their lives to fit into the existing molds, resulting stresses occur. Over two in five (43%) of the men and women who participated in our Ecology of Careers Study reported they do not get enough sleep. Most do not feel highly successful at "balancing" work and family. Although we cannot establish a direct causal relationship with our data, we note the rising popularity of numerous psychotropic drugs and the growth in the pharmaceutical industries. Certainly the difficulty working men and women have in achieving success, or even a night's sleep, plays some role in creating this market.

Couples are also delaying (and sometimes deciding against) having children as a means of compromise between "making a career" and "making a family." The *Statistical Abstracts of the United States* (2002) reports the age at which women have their first child is nearly 4 years later than it was half a century ago. Among professional couples, the age at which women experience their first childbirth has increased even more. Couples now intend to have fewer children and to time them to occur (often with attempts at exacting precision) later in life (Altucher & Williams, 2003). In 2003, nearly one in five (19%) of women between ages 40–44 were childless, compared with only in 1 in 14 women (7%) in 1980. Again, this change represents a personal, not a political, response to incompatibilities of existing institutions. The growth in the number of men and women seeking fertility treatment, and the corresponding increase in the number of multiple births (twins, triplets, etc.), indicates that work-family strains are having a profound effect not only on the lives of individuals but also on the structure of our population. Another social impact relates to the growing demand for nannies and maids, replacing the traditional homemaker with often poor immigrant women who may well have children of their own (Ehrenreich, 2001; Sassen, 1988).

Finally, we find that most members of dual-earner couples espouse egalitarian gender values but still find themselves accepting and relying on prevailing gender schema that places primary responsibility for family matters with the wife, and job/breadwinning responsibilities with the husband. We observe this in couple work-hour arrangements (Moen & Sweet, 2003), the timing of when to retire (Moen et al., 2004), where to move (Moen, Sweet, & Townsend, 2001), and whose career to follow (Bielby & Bielby, 1992; Pixley & Moen, 2003). But, when couples are given structural opportunities to carve more equal priorities between the husband's and wife's career, such as when they both are able to find rewarding work with the same employer, they tend to fair better in both their work and family roles (Moen & Sweet, 2004b; Sweet & Moen, 2004). Optimistically, we observe some employers taking into account dual-career concerns, as many of their professional applicants have "trailing" spouses in need of employment.

On the whole, we are left to conclude that working couples tend to perceive and act on career quandaries as *personal* troubles. Most manage, more or less, by making strategic selections around things they can control—delaying childbearing, following just one person's career, having one member of the couple work part-time. What is needed, as C. Wright Mills (1959) asserted, is the redirection of action and awareness, such that working families recognize these personal problems—experienced in different ways at different points in the life course— as *public* issues. Integrating the work and family careers of men, women, and couples will necessitate changing institutionalized practices—at work, in school, in communities, and in labor market policies.

PRACTICING LIFE COURSE PERSPECTIVE

Application of the life course perspective can create dramatic shifts in the ways workers and supervisors, along with corporate, union, and government leaders, envision response to the needs of working families. But, paths are made by walking them, and the only way to deal with structural and cultural lags is for researchers and policymakers to recast the work-family topic to consider lives lived *across time*, in changing *historical contexts*, and in *enduring relationships* whose impacts cannot be ignored. Specifically, we advocate that the scholarly community expand its initiatives to link family and work to: (a) historically situated social structures and their mismatch with the reality that dual-earner and single-parent households are a fact of 21st-century life; (b) relational connections between partners, children, parents, aging parents, and adult children as well as the broader network of friends, kin, neighbors, and communities; (c) the pathways, turning points, and trajectories that shape men's and women's work, family, and educational careers; and (d) the agentic role of working families as they strategize to manage the multiple dimensions of their lives in the face of the outdated templates and practices. The challenge for stakeholders is to recast "work" and "family" to underscore the need for greater flexibility and variations in both needs and resources over workers' life courses. Here, we offer a few challenges to our colleagues and future work-family activists.

Challenge 1: Consider Individuals and Families in Context

As we discussed above, the life course perspective requires understanding human development, experience, and behavior as it is linked to the locational and temporal contexts that shape opportunities and aspirations. As important as the characteristics of individuals are (i.e., male/female, Black/White, young/old, affluent/poor), future research must go beyond summarizing differences according to single traits, and so long as we conceive of these traits as disconnected "variables," to be "controlled for," much will be missed. This poses real methodological challenges and requires reflection on the synergistic impact that status and environmental combinations may bring to bear on the lives of workers and working families.

One temporal context of central concern is *life stage* and the constellations of resources and demands as they change through a life course. While there is no universal definition of life stage categories, one of the most useful ways of considering this concept is to link it to care-taking responsibilities (Moen & Yu, 1999). We have found that the experiences and needs of working men and women vary significantly depending on the extent to which they are caring for young children, older children, or aging parents. Such observations are critical. While work-family strategies (and needs) shift over the life course, most studies examine the experiences of workers of all ages, often ignoring any age or life stage differences. Moreover, what works for some women and some men at one point in their lives often creates costs at later junctures. Such is the case for women's careers, commonly dislodged by family concerns of raising young children, producing costs in terms of advancement, income, and pension eligibility.

Introducing the "life stage context" is key for future research initiatives. For example, traditional studies of the links between flexible work arrangements and work-family balance would incorporate a "flex arrangement" variable along with a number of "control" variables such as gender, income, age, and so on. A life course perspective would frame the question in a different manner, for example, assessing the extent to which a home office (for instance) or flex time facilitates the bridging of work and family for those caring for young children as compared to those without childrearing responsibilities. The more one considers the idea of context, the more one realizes that many key insights will be revealed by the interactions between variables, rather than as main effects.

The importance of moderators (contexts) is repeatedly underscored in our own studies. For example, in the case of retirement plans (Moen et al., 2004), we found that *organizational contexts* make a difference in the amount of retirement planning individuals engaged in, with employees in some companies planning more than employees of other companies. But, we also found other interesting contextual relationships; for example, younger employees engage in markedly more planning when they work in companies with a greater proportion of older employees. This led us to conclude that working with older employees puts the issue of retirement "in the air," and that having older coworkers likely serves as a reminder to younger employees to plan for their eventual retirement. Such an observation could not have been made without locating the characteristics of individual employees in the context of their relations with coworkers. We also find enduring cohort (or *generation*) effects with the baby boom generation planning more for retirement than the generations that preceded them. Throughout our studies, we observe that the context of *gender* shaped employees lives, on and off the job. But, research on work and family must go beyond its prevailing emphasis on gender to locate it within age, cohort, and life stage contexts (as well as others) and how these contexts intersect with each other.

People's lives play out in a variety of overlapping and interdependent cultural and structural environments, shaped by gender, life stage, organizations, and communities. For example, when we tried to predict which working men and women perceived their communities as being "family friendly" (Swisher et al., 2004), we found few direct relationships between core variables such as gender or even life stage. However, when we constructed models that located the life stages of working couples within the demographic characteristics of their neighborhoods, we found marked differences in the ratings of working families. Dual-earner couples who care for young children and who live in neighborhoods with few other families with young children tend to rate their communities low on family friendliness. By contrast, couples caring for young children with many neighbors at a similar life stage report their communities as being very family friendly. This led us to conclude that perceptions of community family friendliness are linked to a life-stage neighborhood "fit," and that certain types of neighbors can play a key role in buffering work and family strains. Note that in these examples, considering contextual concerns (variables are coupled) reflects the way they operate in the real world. These relationships would be missed in models that just test for main effects.

Space prevents discussion of specific methodologies here, but we will suggest a few strategies. First, even though most everyone recognizes that men and women follow remarkably different career pathways (Moen, 2001b), many continue to use statistical models including gender as a "control" variable. We believe that men's and women's lives should be contrasted in analyses that test the extent variables operate similarly for women and men. Using this strategy, for example, one would look at what types of men use flexible workplace policies and the implications for their (and their spouses' and children's) lives. This analysis can then be contrasted with women's access and use of flexible workplace policies. These two analyses can then be compared. Alternately, one model can be created, with gender interactions established for key variables. Additionally, a life course framing points to the need for *multilevel models* that test interactions between (for example) gender, life stage characteristics, and environmental contexts (i.e., organizations, neighborhoods, or communities). This approach is outlined by Raymond Swisher in this volume. No matter what the methodological strategy, a life course approach encourages a focus on people, not variables, and on the multiple contexts (gender, life stage, spousal linkages, organizational structures, and historical circumstances) that shape their lives.

Challenge 2: Consider Lives Lived Across Time

Most social science research is cross-sectional, as are our visions of working families (e.g., the archetypical parents with young children). But, as we have illustrated, the causes of the different trajectories of women's and men's lives are revealed by considering their decisions at key junctures in the life course. Key from a life course approach is to consider respondents, even in cross-sectional studies, as people with biographies in the making. They are not static objects, they have been influenced by past events, their ties with others, and the historically situated social structures that direct their paths toward the future. We argue that two temporal processes—careers and history—are fruitful avenues for further inquiry.

First, consider how multiple *careers* are linked across time. In its current form, much of the work and family scholarship is devoted to understanding the characteristics of jobs or families and linking the expectations of work to family needs/resources. This is important, but it misses key considerations concerning job or labor market entries and exits, or decisions to scale back on the job, and the challenges these status changes pose for working families. As we observed, some of the biggest work-family challenges stem from decisions to scale back on work commitments to meet family needs, and then to later attempt reentry into the mainstream. Similar focus can be on relational and family careers: moving into or out of marriage or becoming a parent, for example. It is not just new parents who have disorderly occupational paths, but also those having second or third children, those with health problems, those caring for aging parents, and those facing a variety of other needs. Not only do we need assessment of the immediate consequences of work-family strains, but also the long-term implications of the strategic adaptations working families make to the quandaries that confront them.

Second, there needs to be a greater emphasis on *historical time*. Recall the life course principle, that individual development is shaped by the impact of historical events. As it currently stands, cohort and generational concerns are seldom incorporated in work and family research. As we illustrated with retirement planning, the context in which individuals plan for retirement, and the needs they will face in retirement, shift with changes in the social fabric. As the baby boom cohort progresses into retirement, or for that matter, as the current generation of college students progresses into the labor force, each group will reshape the structure of work, retirement, and the broader society. Charting these processes over time and the effects they have on individual's lives is a key concern for understanding the intersections of work and family.

How do we do this? In part, it requires innovatively using currently available data to reframe research questions. One can, for instance, cut data sets into generational cohorts and make comparisons across groups. Although limited, this type of quasi-experimental design can shed light on generational and cohort differences. But, bolder research initiatives are needed that enable us to study lives over time. At the Cornell Careers Institute, we launched a series of longitudinal studies to interview couples at two or, in some instances, three points in time. One of the most striking findings from these studies was the extent to which couples' lives changed in a 2-year time frame. For instance, in the course of the 2 years between surveys, one in three of the participants in the Ecology of Careers Study changed jobs; 1 in 10 either returned to school or completed their educational program; 1 in 10 had a (first or additional) child. A goal to strive for would be a series of longitudinal studies that follow couples' lives over longer time periods. Such projects could involve selecting a particular demographic (e.g., couples that recently had their first child or those approaching retirement) and tracking their experiences over a long duration. Ideally, such efforts will track individuals over time using panel design methods such as those described by Ann Crouter and Amy Pirretti in this volume.

Challenge 3: Consider the Power of Relational Ties

Lastly, much can be learned by examining the ways in which families (as opposed to individuals) respond to work and family opportunities and conflicts. Much of our focus in the Ecology of Careers Study centers on the ways in which couples manage their three careers: two occupational careers (his and hers), along with their conjoint family career. We find that strategies are negotiated in light of changes in resources, opportunities, constraints, and needs. How do dual-earner families and divorced families negotiate geographical moves, for example? There is a wealth of such issues that can fruitfully be researched, including how partners prioritize careers, how they respond to job displacement, how they manage schedules, and a variety of other concerns. Much work is needed to assess the variety of strategies couples adopt as well as to gauge the impact these strategies have on families, employers, and communities. Another fruitful research arena is the broader networks of supports for working families, including kin networks and friendship networks. Our studies of neighborhoods and communities indicate that these relationships can buffer strains in a variety of ways (e.g., Sweet, Swisher, & Moen forthcoming; Swisher et al., 2004). We have been able to capture these dynamics by gathering data on household memberships, caregiving responsibilities, friendship networks, and social relations within the workplace. But, most importantly, we gathered information from both spouses, offering different perspectives within the same household. Additionally, we focus samples on organizations and communities, enabling us to tie personal experiences to networks inside and outside of the workplace. Beyond those concerns, much more work needs to focus on groups outside of the middle-class, and the primarily White, demographic concentrated on in our studies.

As the baby boom generation transitions into retirement, scholars can document the ways this generation responds to the needs of their adult children as they enter into and progress in their own careers. In what ways will they reshape the roles of grandparents, the mature worker, and community citizen? Scholars can also chronicle the ways in which the new generation of workers, those raised in a cultural ethos that is ostensibly challenging traditional gender roles, redefining work and family, and reshaping gendered lines. To do this, we need longitudinal studies sensitive to social contexts and that focus on family transitions over time.

Incorporating a Life Course Approach in Policy Initiatives

Current workplace and government policies rest on an outdated *career mystique*, of devoting heavy commitments of time and energy to jobs (Moen & Roehling, 2005). These presumptions are patterned on the experiences of men in white-collar or unionized blue-collar jobs of the comparatively secure economy of the mid-20th century. These men also had a wife at home managing the unpaid emotional and domestic care work of society. Few in the American workforce now fit this mold.

Contemporary workers are more likely to be in dual-earner relationships, single, or single parents. They are much more likely to work in insecure jobs. And, as the life course perspective highlights, at some points in their lives they will likely need flexibility on the job and even reduced hours to care for children, help aging parents, and/or deal with their own or spouse's health concerns. But, the current regime of policies and practices (around work hours, advancement, health insurance, unemployment, pensions, Social Security, etc.) presume continuous, full-time (or more) paid work, from the completion of schooling until retirement. The social organization of paid work and career paths is poorly designed to accommodate such "disruptions," which are *to be expected* in the normal life course.

Our research evidence points to the need for workplace policies and governmental supports to offer flexibilities, enabling workers to take temporary exists or reduce their work hours without the fear of job loss, disruption of career prospects, loss of health care, and dramatic reductions in pay. Such innovations require rethinking current ways of arranging health insurance, unemployment insurance, family leave, and job security.

Also needed are reevaluations of career ladders, and especially the ways employees are assessed, promoted, and discharged. Taken-for-granted scripts assume the career mystique of uninterrupted demanding and devoted employment (Moen & Roehling, 2005). Such is the case, for example, of tenure-track assistant professors, whose tenure clock begins the moment they accept an appointment. The fact that such clocks often run concurrently with reproductive clocks is rarely acknowledged or accommodated by most universities. Similarly, being a "player" in the high-pressured world of business means being at the office early and home late. Those who do not or cannot play the game by such rules are quickly relegated to the sidelines. The challenge is to resolve such contradictions between what is expected of workers and their responsibilities, goals, and interests beyond their jobs.

Additionally, current workplace practices often fail to address other life course-associated needs of working families. Matters as simple as providing social space and time for breastfeeding/pumping are usually not available to nursing mothers, despite the numerous health benefits (to both the mother and child) that result from nursing children (Galtry, 2000, 2002). Many workers have no private space to make phone calls to their family physicians, children's teachers, or children themselves. The reality is that some aspects of change are less sweeping and dramatic than overhauling a health care system. In this case, a room with a refrigerator, chair, and telephone would likely suffice. The fact is, such amenities are available to only a limited segment of the workforce.

CONCLUSIONS

Although considerable scholarship on work and family has emerged over the past three decades, there is much still to be learned. We believe that the life course perspective can promote understanding of the choices, constraints, strategies, and stresses of working individuals and families as they play out at different ages, career stages, and family stages. This perspective opens a vista of questions, and policy considerations, concerning how working families accommodate stress by adapting to outmoded arrangements and the long-term consequences of these adaptations. The life course paradigm sensitizes observers to lives as they play out over time, pointing to the normality of (among other things) childbirth, sickness, job change, job displacement, geographic moves, divorce, returns to school, and retirement. These transitions not only complicate the lives of individual workers, but also the lives of those to whom they are intimately tied. This approach moves the focus from (ungendered) "workers," to the gendered web of social relations in which they are embedded along with social structures and cultural arrangements that define their options and constraints. As a mechanism for studying both biographies and institutions in dynamic juxtaposition (Barley, 1989; Moen & Roehling, 2005), "careers and the life course" can move "work and family" to center stage and reframe the understanding of work-family challenges and the pool of possible solutions.

NOTE

[1] For further detail on the study methods, see Moen (2003a).

REFERENCES

Altucher, K., & Williams, L. B. (2003). Family clocks: Timing parenthood. In P. Moen (Ed.), *It's about time: Career Strains, strategies, and successes* (pp. 49–59). Ithaca, NY: Cornell University Press.

Attewell, P. (1999). The impact of family on job displacement and recovery. *The Annals of the American Academy of Political and Social Science, 562*, 66–82.

Barley, S. R. (1989). Careers, identities, and institutions: The legacy of the Chicago school of sociology. In M. B. Arthur, D. T. Hall, & B. S. Lawrence (Eds.), *Handbook of career theory* (pp. 41–65). New York: Cambridge University Press.

Barnett, R. C., & Gareis, K. C. (2000). Reduced-hours employment: The relationship between difficulty of trade-offs and quality of life. *Work and Occupations, 27*(2), 168–187.

Becker, H. (1966). *The outsiders: Studies in the sociology of deviance*. New York: Free Press.

Becker, P. E., & Moen, P. (1999). Scaling back: Dual-earner couples' work-family strategies. *Journal of Marriage and the Family, 61*(4), 995–1007.

Bielby, W. T., & Bielby, D. D. (1992). I will follow him: Family ties, gender-role beliefs, and reluctance to relocate for a better job. *American Journal of Sociology, 97*(5), 1241–1267.

Bradburn, E. M., Moen, P., & Dempster-McClain, D. (1995). Women's return to school following the transition to motherhood. *Social Forces, 73*(4), 1517–1551.

Bronfenbrenner, U. (1979). *The ecology of human development*. Cambridge, MA: Harvard University Press.

Christensen, K. E., & Gomory, R. E. (1999, June 2). Three jobs, two people. *Washington Post,* p. A21.

Chronicle of Higher Education Almanac (2004, August 27, 2004). College enrollment by age of students, Fall 2002. *Chronicle of Higher Education,* 16.

Clarkberg, M., & Merola, S. (2003). Competing clocks: Work and leisure in dual-earner couples. In P. Moen (Ed.), *It's about time: Couples and careers* (pp. 35–48). Ithaca, NY: Cornell University Press.

Clarkberg, M., & Moen, P. (2001). Understanding the time-squeeze: Married couples' preferred and actual work-hour strategies. *American Behavioral Scientist, 44*(7), 1115–1136.

Clausen, J. A. (1995). Gender, contexts, and turning points in adults' lives. In P. Moen, G. H. Elder, Jr., & K. Luscher (Eds.), *Examining lives in context: Perspectives on the ecology of human development* (pp. 365–392). Washington, DC: American Psychological Association.

Clausen, J. A. (1998). Life reviews and life stories. In J. Z. Giele & G. H. Elder (Eds.), *Methods of life course research* (pp. 189–212). Thousand Oaks, CA: Sage.

Cox, A. G., & Presser, H. B. (2000). Nonstandard employment schedules among American mothers: The relevance of marital status. In T. L. Parcel & D. B. Cornfield (Eds.), *Work and family: Research informing policy* (pp. 97–130). Thousand Oaks, CA: Sage.

Ehrenreich, B. (2001). *Nickel and dimed: On (not) getting by in America*. New York: Metropolitan.

Elder, G. (1999). *Children of the great depression; social change in life experience*. Boulder, CO.: Westview.

Elder, G. H. (1985). *Life course dynamics: Trajectories and transitions*. Ithaca, NY: Cornell University Press.

Elder, G. H. (1995). The life course paradigm: Social change and individual development. In P. Moen, G. H. Elder, & K. Luscher (Eds.), *Examining lives in context: Perspectives on the ecology of human development* (pp. 101–140). Washington, DC: American Psychological Association.

Elder, G. H. (1998a). The life course and human development. In R. Lerner (Ed.), *Handbook of child psychology, vol. 1: Theoretical models of human development* (pp. 939–991). New York: Wiley.

Elder, G. H. (1998b). The life course as developmental theory. *Child Development, 69*, 1–12.

Farnesworth-Riche, M. (2000). America's diversity and growth: Signposts for the 21st century. *Population Bulletin, 55*(2), 3–43.

Galtry, J. (2000). Extending the "bright line": Feminism, breastfeeding, and the workplace in the United States. *Gender & Society, 14*(2), 295–317.

Galtry, J. (2002). Child health: An underplayed variable in parental leave policy debates? *Community, Work and Family, 5*(3), 257–278.

Garfinkel, H. (1967). *Studies in ethnomethodology*. Englewood Cliffs, NJ: Prentice-Hall.

Gerson, K. (2001). Children of the gender revolution: Some theoretical questions and findings from the field. In V. W. Marshall, W. R. Heinz, H. Krueger, & A. Verma (Eds.), *Restructuring work and the life course* (pp. 446–461). Toronto: University of Toronto Press.

Gerstel, N. (2000). The third shift: Gender and care work outside the home. *Qualitative Sociology, 23*(4), 467–483.

Giddens, A. (1984). *The constitution of society*. Cambridge, England: Polity Press.

Giele, J. Z., & Elder, G. H. (1998). The life course mode of inquiry. In J. Z. Giele & G. H. Elder (Eds.), *Methods of life course research: Qualitative and quantitative approaches* (pp. 5–27). Thousand Oaks, CA: Sage.

Hagestad, G. O., & Neugarten, B. L. (1985). Age and the life course. In R. H. Binstock & E. Shanas & Associates (Eds.), *Handbook of aging and the social sciences* (pp. 35–61). New York: Van Nostrand Reinhold.

Hertz, R. M. N. (2001). *Working families: The transformation of the American home*. Berkeley: University of California Press.

Heymann, J. (2000). *The widening gap: Why America's working families are in jeopardy and what can be done about it*. New York: Perseus.

Hochschild, A., & Machung, A. (1989). *The second shift: Working parents and the revolution at home*. New York: Viking.

Hochschild, A. R. (1997). *The time bind: When work becomes home and home becomes work*. New York: Metropolitan Books.

Hogan, D. P. (1980). The transition to adulthood as a career contingency. *American Sociological Review, 45*, 261–276.

Hutchens, R. M., & Dentinger, E. (2003). Moving toward retirement. In P. Moen (Ed.), *It's about time: Couples and careers* (pp. 259–274). Ithaca, NY: Cornell University Press.

Hybertson, D., Hulme, E., Smith, A., & Holton, M. A. (1992). Wellness in non-traditional-age students. *Journal of College Student Development, 33*, 50–55.

Jacobs, J. A., & King, R. B. (2002). Age and college completion: A life-history analysis of women aged 15–44. *Sociology of Education, 75*(3), 211–230.

Jacobs, J. A., & Stoner-Eby, S. (1998). Adult enrollment and educational attainment. *The Annals of the American Academy of Political and Social Science, 559*, 91–109.

Kets de Vries, M., & Balazs, K. (1997). The downside of downsizing. *Human Relations, 50*, 11–50.

Kim, J., & Moen, P. (1999). *Work/retirement transitions and psychological well-being in late midlife*. Ithaca, NY: Cornell University Press.

Kim, J., & Moen, P. (2001a). Is retirement good or bad for subjective well-being. *Current Directions in Psychological Science, 10*, 83–86.

Kim, J., & Moen, P. (2001b). Moving into retirement: Preparation and transitions in late midlife. In M. Lachman (Ed.), *Handbook of midlife development* (pp. 487–527). New York: Wiley.

Kim, J., & Moen, P. (2002). Retirement transitions, gender and psychological well-being: A life-course, ecological model. *Journal of Gerontology: Psychological Sciences*, 212–222.

Lee, Y.-S., Schneider, B., & Waite, L. J. (2003). Children and housework: Some unanswered questions. *Sociological Studies of Children and Youth*(9), 105–125.

Levy, F. (1986). *Dollars and dreams*. New York: Russell Sage.

Michelson, W. (1985). *From sun to sun: Daily obligations and community structure in the lives of employed women and their families*. Totowa, NJ: Rowman & Allanheld.

Mills, C. W. (1959). *The sociological imagination*. New York: Oxford University Press.

Moen, P. (1992). *Women's two roles: A contemporary dilemma*. Westport, CT: Greenwood.

Moen, P. (1994). Women, work, and family: A sociological perspective on changing roles. In M. W. Riley, R. L. Kahn, & A. Foner (Eds.), *Age and structural lag: The mismatch between people's lives and opportunities in work, family, and leisure* (pp. 151–170). New York: Wiley.

Moen, P. (2001a). Constructing a life course. *Marriage and Family Review, 30*, 97–109.

Moen, P. (2001b). The gendered life course. In L. George & R. H. Binstock (Eds.), *Handbook of aging and the social sciences* (5th ed., pp. 179–196). San Diego, CA: Academic Press.

Moen, P. (2002). The career quandary. *Population Reference Bureau Reports on America, 2*(1).

Moen, P. (2003a). *It's about time: Couples and careers*. Ithaca, NY: Cornell University Press.

Moen, P. (2003b). Midcourse: Navigating retirement and a new life stage. In J. T. Mortimer & M. J. Shanahan (Eds.), *Handbook of the life course* (pp. 267–291). New York: Plenum.

Moen, P. (2004). Unscripted: Continuity and change in the gendered life course. In H. Gans (Ed.), *Our studies, ourselves: Sociologists' lives and work* (pp. 105–114). Cambridge, England: Oxford University Press.

Moen, P., & Roehling, P. V. (2005). *The career mystique*. Boulder, CO: Rowman & Littlefield.

Moen, P., & Spencer, D. (2005, forthcoming). Converging divergences in age, gender, health, and well-being: Strategic selection in the third age. In R. Binstock & L. George (Eds.), *Handbook of aging and the social sciences*. San Diego, CA: Elsevier.

Moen, P., & Sweet, S. (2003). Time clocks: Couples' work hour strategies. In P. Moen (Ed.), *It's about time: Career strains, strategies, and successes* (pp. 17–34). Ithaca, NY: Cornell University Press.

Moen, P., & Sweet, S. (2004a). From "work-family" to "flexible careers": A life course reframing. *Community, Work and Family, 7*, 209–226.

Moen, P., & Sweet, S. (2004b). Two careers one employer. *Journal of Vocational Behavior, 61*, 466–483.

Moen, P., & Wethington, E. (1992). The concept of family adaptive strategies. *Annual Review of Sociology, 18*, 233–251.

Moen, P., & Yu, Y. (1999). Having it all: Overall work/life success in two-earner families. *Research in the Sociology of Work, 7*, 109–139.

Moen, P., Sweet, S., & Swisher, R. (2005). Embedded career clocks: The case of retirement planning. In Macmillan, R. (ed.), The structure of life course-standardized? individual? differentiated?: *Advances in life course research,* vol. 9 (pp. 239–257). New York: Elsevier.

Moen, P., Elder, G. H., & Luscher, K. (1995). *Examining lives in context.* Washington, DC: American Psychological Association.

Moen, P., Kim, J., & Hofmeister, H. (2000). *Couples' work status transitions and marital quality in late midlife.* Ithaca, NY: Cornell Careers Institute.

Moen, P., Plassmann, V., & Sweet, S. (2001). *Cornell midcareer paths and passages study.* Ithaca, NY: Cornell University Press.

Moen, P., Sweet, S., & Townsend, B. (2001). *How family friendly is upstate New York.* Ithaca, NY: Cornell Careers Institute.

Moen, P., Waismel-Manor, R., & Sweet, S. (2003). Success. In P. Moen (Ed.), *It's about time: Couples and careers* (pp. 133–152). Ithaca, NY: Cornell University Press.

Ogburn, W. F. (Ed.). (1964). *On culture and social change: Selected papers.* Chicago: University of Chicago Press.

O'Rand, A. M., & Henretta, J. (1996). *Age and inequality: Diverse pathways through later life.* Boulder, Co: Westview.

Padavic, I., & Reskin, B. (2002). *Women and men at work* (2nd ed.). Thousand Oaks, CA: Pine Forge Press.

Pavalko, E., & Smith, B. (1999). The rhythm of work: Health effects of women's work dynamics. *Social Forces, 77*(3), 1141–1162.

Piore, M., & Sabel, C. (1984). *The second industrial divide: Possibilities for prosperity.* New York: Basic Books.

Pixley, J. E., & Moen, P. (2003). Prioritizing careers. In P. Moen (Ed.), *It's about time: Couples and careers* (pp. 168–182). Ithaca, NY: Cornell University Press.

Presser, H. B. (1994). Employment schedules among dual-earner spouses and the division of household labor by gender. *American Sociological Review, 59*(3), 348–364.

Presser, H. B. (2000). Nonstandard work schedules and marital instability. *Journal of Marriage and the Family, 62*(1), 93–110.

Presser, H. B., & Bamberger, E. (1993). American women who work at home for pay: Distinctions and determinants. *Social Science Quarterly, 74*(4), 815–837.

Putnam, R. (2000). *Bowling alone: The collapse and revival of American community.* New York: Simon & Schuster.

Riley, M. W., Kahn, R. L., & Foner, A. (1994). *Age and structural lag: The mismatch between people's lives and opportunities in work, family, and leisure.* New York: Wiley.

Riley, M. W., & Riley, J. W. J. (1994). Structural lag: Past and future. In M. W. Riley, R. L. Khan, & A. Foner (Eds.), *Age and structural lag: Society's failure to provide meaningful opportunities in work, family, and leisure* (pp. 15–36). New York: Wiley.

Sassen, S. (1988). *The mobility of labor and capital.* Cambridge, England: Cambridge University Press.

Schutz, A. ([1967] 1932). *The phenomenology of the social world.* Evanston, IL: Northwestern University Press.

Settersten, R. (1999). *Lives in time and place: The problems and promises of developmental science.* Amityville, NY: Baywood.

Settersten, R., & Lovegreen, L. (1998). Educational experiences throughout adult life: New hopes or no hope life-course flexibility? *Research on Aging, 20,* 506–538.

Smith, B. T., & Rubin, B. A. (1997). From displacement to reemployment: Job acquisition in the flexible economy. *Social Science Research, 26*(3), 292–308.

Statistical Abstracts of the United States. (2002). Washington, DC: U.S. Dept of Census.

Suitor, J. J. (1987). Marital happiness of returning women students and their husbands: Effects of part and full-time enrollment. *Research in Higher Education, 27*(4), 311–331.

Sweet, S., & Moen, P. (2004). Intimate academics: Coworking couples in two universities. *Innovative Higher Education, 28,* 255–272.

Sweet, S., & Moen, P. (under review). Women's return to school and family life quality: A life course reformulation.

Sweet, S., Swisher, R., & Moen, P. (forthcoming). Selecting and assessing the family-friendly community: Adaptive strategies of middle-class dual-earner couples. *Family Relations.*

Swisher, R., Sweet, S., & Moen, P. (2004). The family-friendly community and its life course fit for dual-earner couples. *Journal of Marriage and the Family, 66,* 281–292.

Wethington, E., Pixley, J. E., & Kavey, A. (2003). Turning points in work careers. In P. Moen (Ed.), *It's about time: Couples and careers* (pp. 168–182). Ithaca, NY: Cornell University Press.

Wharton, C. S. (1994). Finding time for the "second shift": The impact of flexible work schedules on women's double days. *Gender & Society, 8*(2), 189–205.

Wheaton, B. (1990). Life transitions, role histories, and mental health. *American Sociological Review, 55*(2), 209–223.

Williams, J. (2000). *Unbending gender: Why family and work conflict and what to do about it.* New York: Oxford University Press.

10

Role Theory Perspectives on Work and Family

Rosalind Chait Barnett
Karen C. Gareis
Brandeis University

Is combining work and family inevitably associated with distress and conflict? Much research in the work-family tradition has been based on the assumption that the answer is yes. But, research in another tradition—the study of multiple roles and health and quality-of-life outcomes—suggests that the answer may well be no. Sorting out the different assumptions and findings emanating from these two traditions is no mere academic exercise. Decisions affecting individual, corporate, and national policies and practices depend on a clear understanding of the relationships under consideration. In this chapter, we review the major empirical findings from these two bodies of work, propose some strategies for reconciling the differences, and suggest ways to bridge the theoretical divide in future research.

The work-family conflict approach has its origins in studies of inter-role conflict (e.g., Kanter, 1977; Sarbin, 1954) and has as its guiding assumption that work and family are in basic conflict. Moreover, the focus on incompatible role demands is coupled with the notion that human energy is a fixed and limited quantity. This notion is often referred to as the scarcity hypothesis (Barnett, Marshall, & Singer, 1992; Marks, 1977; Sieber, 1974). Accordingly, the more roles a person—usually a woman—occupies, the greater the pressure on her energy and the more depleted her reserves. As a result, incumbents who occupy roles in multiple spheres experience tension and conflict, which, in turn, exacts a cost. In this tradition, the cost of multiple-role occupancy is most often assessed in terms of such outcomes as psychological distress, decreased marital and job satisfaction, and such organizational outcomes as burnout and intention to leave one's current job. The work-family conflict approach remains the dominant perspective in the work-family literature.

In contrast, the role enhancement perspective, restated most recently as the expansionist theory (Barnett & Hyde, 2001; see also Thoits, 1983), has its origins in studies of psychological well-being and has been most concerned with identifying risk factors for health outcomes—mental, physical, and relationship. It has as its first assumption that multiple roles are not harmful per se and are, in general, beneficial for women and men. Underlying this assumption is the belief that human energy is a potentially expandable resource. By engaging in multiple roles, one has the opportunity to increase one's energy supply. The benefits of multiple-role engagement are reflected in positive mental health, physical health, and relationship health. Because this body of literature is less well-known to work-family researchers, in this chapter, we devote disproportionately more space to this approach.

WORK-FAMILY CONFLICT PERSPECTIVE

The phrase "work-family conflict" emerged in the 1980s, a time when married women's labor force participation experienced a steep increase. This increase represented the culmination of a long, 70-year trend beginning in the 1920s. Indeed, the massive movement of women into the labor force has been described as "one of the most significant social and economic trends in modern U.S. history" (Hayghe, 1997). By the 1970s, the 50-year reign of the Ozzie-and-Harriet family was proclaimed to be definitely over (Coontz, 1997, p. 57). The clear boundaries between what had previously been seen as two distinct arenas of life—work (primarily the domain of men) and family (primarily the domain of women)—were eroding.

The prevailing sex-role attitudes in the 1970s and 1980s were more traditional than they are today. Briefly, there was general consensus that women's primary social role was wife and mother, whereas men's primary role was breadwinner. There was also a pervasive belief that multiple roles were "bad" for women; married women with children who took on the added role of employee were inevitably exhausted, highly vulnerable to stress-related problems, and unable to manage adequately the various demands of their complicated and energy-draining lives. Accordingly, the more roles a woman occupied, the greater the pressure on her energy and the more depleted her reserves. Thus, employed married women with children were assumed to be less resilient than men with the same role set and, therefore, at higher risk for such stress-related illnesses as depression and anxiety. They were also assumed to be shortchanging their husbands and children and putting them at risk for emotional problems as well.

The view of work and family as separate, conflicting spheres was reinforced by the then-dominant corporate culture that explicitly required family matters to be left at the work-place door. To be taken seriously on the job, women would have to conform to the traditional one-dimensional view of men as worker drones. This bifurcated model is still unfortunately a part of the corporate landscape. Similarly, the traditional sex-role assumptions underlying this model still have a hold on our thinking. In addition, the scarcity model of energy is consistent with the then (and still) dominant management fixation on "face time" as a reflection of employee commitment and productivity. Because it is believed that family roles deplete employees' energy reserves, the best way to get the most out of employees is to keep them working long hours so that they will be unavailable for such activities.

Because of the dominant assumption that work and family are separate and in competition for such scarce resources as time and attention (Barnett, 1998), the work-family interface has been characterized as involving constant tension and perpetual conflict, especially for employed married women with children. Each employee is viewed as caught in a zero-sum game in which resources expended in one sphere deplete those available for the other, leading inevitably to diminished role quality in the deprived sphere (Gutek, Searle, & Klepa, 1991). Time is the resource most often dealt with in this literature, and this conceptualization has received some empirical support. For example, excessive work hours have been related to increased marital tension (Hughes & Galinsky, 1994). Although most studies of work-family conflict focus on competing time demands, such other aspects as energy, strain, and behavior (Greenhaus & Beutell, 1985; MacDermid et al., 2000) have also been identified. That is, the enactment of one role may (a) reduce the energy available for performing other roles;

(b) increase strain, interfering with the ability to perform other roles; or (c) encourage behaviors that are incompatible with the performance of other roles.

Several major questions arise: (a) Do employed women experience more work-family conflict than employed men? (b) Are long work hours per se related to negative health and quality-of-life indicators? (c) What is the relationship between long work hours and work-family conflict? (d) Is work-family conflict related to health and quality-of-life outcomes? (e) Does work-family conflict moderate or mediate the relationship between long work hours and health and quality-of-life outcomes?

Gender Differences in Work-Family Conflict

A number of studies indicate that men and women report *similar* levels of work-family conflict, a result that challenges the widely held belief that such conflict is higher among women. In one study of 954 employees, gender had far less impact on work-family conflict than did family structure (Kmec, 1999). In a study of 501 employees in four Finnish organizations, there were no gender differences in work-to-family conflict or in family-to-work conflict (Kinnunen & Mauno, 1998). Men and women in dual-earner couples experienced similar levels of conflict and far less work-family stress than did heads of single-parent families. A study of a random sample of 650 parents conducted by the National Parenting Association found that mothers and fathers, by the same percentage, say that work-family balance is their biggest concern (Charney Research, 2000). The 2002 National Study of the Changing Workforce, using a nationally representative sample of 3,000 full-time employed men and women, actually found that men with families reported more work-family conflict than women in the same situation (Bond, Thompson, Galinsky, & Prottas, 2003).

Long Work Hours as a Predictor of Health and Quality-of-Life Indicators

Several studies challenge the assumed link between long work hours and negative outcomes. Some studies find either no relationship or a positive relationship between number of hours worked and outcomes. To illustrate, the more hours worked by women and men in full-time employed couples, the lower their distress (Barnett & Shen, 1997; Ozer, Barnett, Brennan, & Sperling, 1998). And, number of hours worked was unrelated to sexual satisfaction, frequency, or desire in married women, regardless of whether they were homemakers or employed part- or full-time (Hyde, DeLamater, & Hewitt, 1998). Among employees working excessively long hours, some studies do indicate a relationship between work hours and negative outcomes (Gutek et al., 1991), while others do not (Hyde et al., 1998). Inconsistent findings, along with a growing body of research demonstrating work-family synergy (Bailyn, 1993; Greenhaus & Powell, in press) and, as we discuss below, salutary effects of multiple-role involvement (Barnett & Baruch, 1985; Marks & MacDermid, 1996; Thoits, 1992), also challenge the inevitability of the zero-sum assumption.

In a recent within-couples longitudinal analysis of data collected three times in a 2-year period from 211 dual-earner couples (Barnett, Gareis, & Brennan under review), the preliminary results indicate that the relationship between the average number of hours worked and change over time in work hours and four mental health and quality-of-life outcomes—marital-role quality, parent-role quality, work-family conflict, and psychological distress. Among both husbands and wives, increase in wives's work hours over time was related to increase in psychological distress and, surprisingly, increase in parent-role quality. For marital-role quality, increase in spouse's work hours over time was related to decrease in marital-role quality for wives and increase in marital-role quality for husbands.

Long Work Hours and Work-Family Conflict

There is scant empirical evidence linking long work hours to work-family conflict. Gutek and her colleagues (1991) found only weak relationships; that is, correlations ranging from .12 to .34, between time in a domain and the perception of conflict between that domain and others. These relatively low correlations indicate that the perception of work-family conflict is not simply a direct reflection of the amount of time expended (Gutek et al., 1991, p. 567). However, Voydanoff (1988) reported that, for both men and women, work hours was associated with work-family conflict, and van der Hulst and Geurts (2001) reported that overtime work was associated with work-family conflict.

In the above-mentioned within-couples longitudinal analysis (Barnett, Gareis, & Brennan, under review), the researchers also estimated the relationship between each partner's average number of hours worked over the three waves of data collection and work-family conflict. The results provided some support for the direct-effects relationship between work hours and outcomes. The average number of hours husbands worked was related to their reports of work-family conflict. Among wives, increase in work hours over time was related to their experiences of work-family conflict.

Work-Family Conflict as a Predictor of Health and Quality-of-Life Outcomes

It is important to note that, in acknowledging the bi-directional nature of work-family effects, researchers have distinguished two components of work-family conflict, work-to-family conflict and family-to-work conflict, each assumed to have different antecedents and consequences (Frone, Russell, & Cooper, 1992a; Gutek et al., 1991). The findings from several studies support such a distinction (Adams, King, & King, 1996; Frone, Russell, & Cooper, 1997; Gutek et al., 1991; Kinnunen, Vermulst, Gerris, & Makikangas, 2003; Netemeyer, Boles, & McMurrian, 1996).

In a meta-analysis of studies linking work-family conflict with job and life satisfaction, Kossek and Ozeki (1998) found that measures incorporating elements of both family-to-work conflict and work-to-family conflict performed better than measures assessing each type separately. In attempting to identify the antecedents and correlates of work-to-family conflict and family-to-work conflict, there is a critical asymmetry: More studies have focused on work-to-family conflict than on family-to-work conflict, and most have looked at job-related as compared to health and quality-of-life indicators. With those caveats in mind, there is general agreement that work-to-family conflict appears to be more strongly related than family-to-work conflict to outcomes such as life satisfaction and job satisfaction (Kossek & Ozeki, 1998). Work-to-family conflict also appears to be more prevalent than family-to-work conflict. According to Frone, Russell, and Cooper (1992b), work-to-family conflict is three times more common than is family-to-work conflict, and this is equally true for women and for men; other researchers have found similar results (Frone et al., 1997; Kinnunen & Mauno, 1998).

Although the distinction between work-to-family and family-to-work conflict is conceptually useful, results have not always shown the hypothesized relationships between family-to-work conflict and work-to-family conflict and the predicted cross-domain outcomes. For example, Frone et al. (1992a) reported that family-to-work conflict predicted job distress, but work-to-family conflict did not predict family distress, at least among white-collar workers. In a study by Adams et al. (1996), work-to-family conflict predicted reduced job satisfaction, life satisfaction, and family social support, but family-to-work conflict failed to predict job satisfaction. Kinnunen and Mauno (1998) found in a Finnish sample that family-to-work conflict had negative consequences for family well-being, and work-to-family conflict had negative consequences for occupational well-being. Allen, Herst, Bruck, and Sutton (2000) reported very mixed and inconsistent effects of work-to-family conflict on marital and family outcomes.

Work-Family Conflict as a Mediator

Several studies in the work-family conflict tradition have conceptualized work-family conflict as a mediator of the relationship between stressful job conditions (e.g., long work hours) and stress-related health and quality-of-life outcomes (Frone, Yardley, & Markel, 1997; Geurts, Kompier, Roxburgh, & Houtman, 2003; Geurts, Rutte, & Peeters, 1999; Hughes & Galinsky, 1994; Kossek & Ozeki, 1999; Noor, 2003; Vinokur, Price, & Caplan, 1996). That is, stressors at work are linked to negative stress-related outcomes at home only to the extent that they create work-family conflict. For example, Geurts and her colleagues (2003) found that work-home interference fully mediated the relationship linking workload to physical health complaints and to depressive mood and partially mediated the relationship linking workload to work-related negative affect. However, as discussed above, this model has been challenged by several empirical findings indicating weak links between work hours and work-family conflict (Gutek et al., 1991) and between work-family conflict and family distress (Frone et al., 1992a).

ROLE ENHANCEMENT PERSPECTIVE

The basic premise of this approach, as discussed briefly above, is that energy is an expandable quantity; it is not limited and fixed. Operationally, the prediction is that work commitment and family commitment are uncorrelated or perhaps even positively correlated. This prediction is in strong contrast to the work-family conflict approach, with its assumption of a negative correlation between work and family commitment. Indeed, research shows a modest positive correlation between work commitment and family commitment (Marks & MacDermid, 1996). Moreover, a study of male and female senior managers, in which commitment was operationalized as hours spent in paid work and family work, found a modest positive correlation between these two indicators of role commitment (Gutek et al., 1991). In the Wisconsin Maternity Leave and Health Project, work commitment and spouse commitment were significantly positively correlated for wives, although they were not significantly related for husbands (Hyde, DeLamater, & Durik, 2001). These findings lend support to the role enhancement approach and contradict the assumption that work commitment and family commitment are necessarily in conflict.

In practice, most research relating multiple roles to health outcomes is tantamount to the study of the health effects associated with taking on additional roles that are nontraditional for one's gender. For women, the research focus is on the influence of the paid-employee role among married women with children; for men, the focus is on the roles of partner and parent among employed men. Stated differently, studies of women typically ask whether women who combine the roles of wife, mother, and employee differ from women who occupy only the roles of wife and mother—women's "natural" roles. Studies of men, although far fewer in number, focus on the consequences for men of adding the "unnatural" roles of partner and father to the more "natural" role of worker.

In contrast to the popular belief that more roles is synonymous with added stress, little support has been found for the prediction that women and men who engage more roles (i.e., in "nonnatural" roles—e.g., the employee role for women and the parental role for men) experience heightened distress. Indeed, study after study has demonstrated that women and men who are engaged in multiple roles report *lower* levels of stress-related mental and physical health problems and *higher* levels of subjective well-being than their counterparts who are engaged in fewer roles (Barnett & Marshall, 1993; Crosby & Jaskar, 1993; Simons, 1992; Thoits, 1992; Wethington & Kessler, 1989). It appears that "adding" the worker role is beneficial to women, and "adding" or participating in family roles is beneficial for men. This general assumption is supported by two streams of research: The first focuses on the number of roles occupied *per se*; the other focuses on the quality of the experience in each of the multiple roles.

Number of Roles as a Predictor of Health and Quality-of-Life Outcomes

This approach focuses primarily on the rewards associated with multiple-role occupancy, especially the role of employee among married women with children and the roles of husband and father among men. A number of processes contribute to the beneficial effects of multiple roles, including buffering of the negative effects of stress or failure in one role by successes and satisfactions in another role, increased opportunities for social support, multiple opportunities to experience success, an expanded frame of reference, increased self-complexity, and similarity of experiences between women and men (Barnett & Hyde, 2001).

Another benefit of multiple roles is a subjective sense of success in balancing work and family demands. Milkie and Peltola (1999) found that married, employed American women and men reported similarly high levels of success in this balancing act. Although negative aspects of role occupancy are fully acknowledged, the weight of empirical evidence is that overall, for both men and women, the more roles one occupies, the better is one's mental and physical health and quality of life (Barnett & Baruch, 1985; Barnett & Marshall, 1993; Thoits, 1992).

Research on the beneficial effects of employment on women supports the idea that adding the employee role to women's traditional roles as wives and mothers can have positive consequences for health and quality of life. The benefits of adding the employee role has rewards including earning a salary, doing challenging work, utilizing all of one's talents, having access to health benefits, and receiving social support. Of course, not every job confers all these benefits to its incumbents, yet unless one is employed, there is little possibility of enjoying these rewards.

In a review of the research on the effects of employment on women's mental and physical health, Repetti, Matthews, and Waldron (1989) concluded that employment was associated with improved health for single and married women who held a positive attitude toward employment. In a longitudinal approach, Wethington and Kessler (1989) found that women who increased their workforce participation from homemaker to part-time or to full-time worker showed lower levels of depression over the 3-year period of the study; at the same time, employed women who decreased their hours of paid employment from full-time to low part-time or homemaker reported increased symptoms of depression. Several other studies found employed women to be less depressed than nonemployed women (e.g., Aneshensel, 1986; Kandel, Davies, & Raveis, 1985), and in another review, Crosby (1991) concluded that women who juggle multiple roles are less depressed than other women.

The positive effects of the employee role on women appear to extend to women who already fill the challenging role of parent: Repetti et al. (1989) concluded, reviewing studies that examined interactions between work status and parental status, that the mental-health effects of employment are consistent across different parental statuses. Kessler and McRae (1982) found that, although the presence of preschool children in the home was associated with psychological distress among women, employed women showed less distress than nonemployed women, and the effect remained even when the number of children was controlled. Russo and Zierk (1992), using a large national sample, found that, after childbearing was controlled, women's well-being was positively related to employment, although it was negatively related to the total number of children.

Interestingly, for women in multiple roles, the supposedly stressful and unnatural role of employee has been most closely linked to reports of low distress. For example, in a systematic study of middle-class women who varied in employment, marital, and parental status, the factor that accounted for most of the variance in psychological well-being was employment status (Barnett & Baruch, 1985). That is, employed women, whether they were married or parents, reported greater well-being than any of the nonemployed women. Moreover, married women with children who held high-prestige jobs reported the greatest well-being of all.

Although not every study finds a positive effect of employment for women (e.g., Baruch & Barnett, 1986; Repetti & Crosby, 1984; Warr & Parry, 1982) and some studies find positive effects for some groups of women and no effects for other groups of women (Waldron & Jacobs, 1989), in no studies did employed women have worse mental and physical health and lower quality of life than nonemployed women.

As for men, in very early studies, the assumption was made that the worker role was the only role of consequence for men's health. For example, the influential Western Collaborative Group Study (Rosenman, Brand, Jenkins, Friedman, Straus, & Wurm, 1975), the first major prospective study that identified psychosocial stressors as independent risk factors in cardio-vascular disease, did not even ask the 3,000 male participants whether they were married or had children! So convinced were the investigators that men's primary role was that of worker that they inferred that whatever psychosocial stressors or benefits were operative would be at the workplace.

More recent studies do not make that questionable assumption. Several investigations (Farrell & Rosenberg, 1981; Lein, Durham, Pratt, Schudson, Thomas, & Weiss, 1974) con-cluded that men "seek their primary emotional, personal, and spiritual gratification in their family setting" (Lein et al., 1974, p. 118). Using a nationally representative probability sam-ple, Veroff, Douvan, and Kulka (1981) reported similar findings. Male respondents who held all three roles of spouse, parent, and paid worker rated family roles as more critical to their well-being than occupational roles.

Moreover, several studies find that men who are engaged in the roles of employee, spouse, and father report fewer physiological symptoms of distress than men who occupy fewer roles, typically men who are not fathers (Gore & Mangione, 1983). In addition, studies indicate that men's mental health benefits from their occupancy of multiple roles. Specifically, in one study of dual-earner couples, men's psychological well-being benefited equally from their experiences in their employee, spouse, and father roles (Barnett, Marshall, & Pleck, 1992).

When relationship health is the outcome, again the evidence indicates that multiple roles—and, in particular, employment for women and family involvement for men—are beneficial. For example, although some theories (Becker, 1981; Parsons, 1949) predict that marital instability is more likely when women and men expand their "traditional" roles, the empirical data suggest otherwise. In a review of the literature, Oppenheimer (1997) concluded that within couples, income equality is not synonymous with low gains to marriage and may in fact be associated with high gains. In support of this conclusion, one study of couples' relative earnings found that marital dissolution was highest in couples in which the wife had no earnings (Ono, 1998).

In a within-couples analysis of dual-earner couples, wives whose husbands did propor-tionally more child care reported higher marital-role quality and lower psychological distress (Ozer et al., 1998). Kalmijn (1999) found similar effects of father involvement; that is, fathers who were more involved with their children had stabler marital relationships, due to the fact that their wives were happier when their husbands were more involved with the children.

However, it is likely that under certain conditions, the benefits of multiple-role occupancy might diminish. These conditions include the absolute number of roles and the time demands of each. Beyond certain upper limits, overload and distress may occur. To more fully understand the conditions under which multiple roles are beneficial, we turn to a discussion of role quality.

Number of Roles Versus Role Quality as a Predictor of Health and Quality-of-Life Outcomes

Considerable research suggests that role quality is more important to mental and physical health and quality of life than is the number of roles or time spent in a particular role. Just as multiple roles provide opportunities for success, multiple roles also offer opportunities for failure or frustration, especially in the context of low-wage work, work-place discrimination, and sexual harassment. Accordingly, it would be more meaningful to examine the association between subjective role quality and health and quality-of-life outcomes.

What do we mean by subjective role quality? Every social role has rewarding and problematic aspects. Subjective role quality is therefore a construct having two parts: the rewarding aspects and the problematic or "of concern" aspects. Barnett and her team have developed multi-item psychometrically sound measures of both aspects for three major social roles (i.e., partner, parent, and employee). Role quality is calculated by subtracting the average concern score from the average reward score for any particular role. It is important to note that subjective aspects differ from what might more accurately be labeled "job conditions," which include such job aspects as level of salary and benefits, actual work schedule, and presence of a supportive supervisor. Subjective aspects refers to the degree to which such conditions, if present or absent, are experienced as rewarding or problematic.

The hypothesis that role quality is a stronger predictor of health and quality-of-life outcomes than is the number of roles (or time spent in a role) has been widely supported (see Barnett & Hyde, 2001, for a review). For example, mental health benefits do not accrue from the work role when the job is not satisfying or when the person is the victim of discrimination or harassment on the job. Similarly, people may work long hours but benefit psychologically if the work is satisfying. In a review of the multiple-role literature of the 1990s, Perry-Jenkins, Repetti, and Crouter (2000) reported that researchers are now attending more to role *quality* than to role *occupancy*.

Cross-sectional studies indicate that employed women in dual-earner couples report as high levels of job satisfaction as their husbands, and within couples, job-role quality is as strong a predictor of psychological distress for wives as for husbands (Barnett, Marshall, Raudenbush, & Brennan, 1993). Longitudinal studies indicate that, within dual-earner couples, change over time in job-role quality predicts change over time in psychological distress for women and men (Barnett, Raudenbush, Brennan, Pleck, & Marshall, 1995). If the job becomes increasingly rewarding or problematic, distress decreases or increases accordingly. Interestingly, the magnitude of this relationship does not differ by gender. Moreover, for both the men and women in this study, the same two job conditions—time demands and underutilization of skills—were associated both cross-sectionally and longitudinally with psychological distress.

Indirect Effects of Multiple Roles

In addition to the direct effects of multiple roles (number and quality) on health outcomes, many studies indicate that role quality can also have indirect effects on health and quality-of-life outcomes. Indirect effects include moderation (i.e., factors that affect the magnitude of the relationship between multiple roles and beneficial effects) and mediation (i.e., factors through which multiple roles have an effect).

An example of moderation is the buffering effect. Considerable evidence indicates that the negative effects of stress or failure in one role can be buffered by successes and satisfactions in another role. In one study, moderator regression analyses indicated that the main effect of job experiences on psychological distress was conditioned by men's experiences in their family roles (Barnett, Marshall, & Pleck, 1992). When relationships with their wives and/or children were positive, poor experiences on the job did not have significant effects on men's distress. Thus, the effect of job experiences on men's psychological distress was buffered by the quality of their family roles. For women, rewarding experiences on the job, especially those associated with challenging work, offset the negative effects of child-care burdens on mental heath (Barnett, Marshall, & Sayer, 1992).

Similarly, in an examination of the effects of care for elderly parents on adults' psychological distress, Voydanoff and Donnelly (1999) found that job satisfaction and marital happiness acted as buffers or moderators. In an example of moderation with respect to physical health in terms of cardiovascular risk factors, a longitudinal study of 493 women indicated that marriage "confers health benefits for women, but only when marital satisfaction is high" (Gallo, Troxel, Matthews, & Kuller, 2003).

In an example of a mediation effect, when women add the role of employee, they generate additional family income which benefits them and their children and reduces the distress experienced by sole-breadwinner husbands. In contrast, economic hardship has well-documented effects on psychological distress and on marital conflict and distress (e.g., Conger, Rueter, & Elder, 1999). Women's employment can serve as an antidote to the effects of economic hardship by decreasing the poverty rate of married couples (Blank, 1988). In one study, the higher wives' earnings, the higher the family income, which decreased wives' and husbands' perception of economic hardship, which decreased their levels of depression (Ross & Huber, 1985).

FUTURE DIRECTIONS

Integrating the Work-Family Conflict and Role Enhancement Perspectives

The role enhancement approach yields the insight that instead of conceptualizing work and family as separate, conflicting spheres, a more accurate depiction of the work-family interface may be one in which work and family are seen as overlapping spheres that are often in harmony (see Barnett, 1998 for a fuller discussion). Researchers working in the work-family conflict tradition have recently developed the notion of work-family enhancement, which is quite compatible with the overlapping-spheres model. Positive effects of combining work and family roles have been discussed under the terms work-family enrichment (Greenhaus & Powell, in press), positive spillover (Crouter, 1984; Voydanoff, 2001), work-family enhancement (Ruderman, Ohlott, Panzer, & King, 2002), and work-family facilitation (Frone, 2003).

The work-family conflict and role enhancement traditions make contrasting predictions about whether combining work and family roles should lead to negative or to positive effects. These traditions could be integrated by focusing on process; that is, under what conditions are the effects positive? Under what conditions are they negative? Longitudinal studies are one method of illuminating process.

Taking a Systems Approach to the Work-Family Interface

The literature on work-family conflict has been characterized by a focus on employees as autonomous agents, not as members of dyads in which each partner's job and family experiences affect the other partner's social-role experiences in crossover effects from one partner to the other. However, a number of studies provide convincing evidence that couples constitute dynamic, interactive, and fluid interpersonal systems in which each partner's job and family experiences affect the other partner's quality of life (Barling, 1984; Barnett & Brennan, 1995, 1997; Liem & Liem, 1988; Pittman, 1994; Raudenbush, Brennan, & Barnett, 1995; Rook, Dooley, & Catalano, 1991; Vinokur et al., 1996). It is also likely that when there are children or other dependents in the family system, each partner's perceptions of job and family experiences will affect these dependents, who will in turn influence the worker's quality of life. Thus, to adequately model the work-family interface, one must at a minimum take into account the impact of each employee's job characteristics on the other family members.

An example of a systems approach to an aspect of the work-family interface is the concept of schedule fit, or the degree to which each family member's work schedule works well for all of the members of the family (Barnett, Brennan, & Gareis, 1999). The concept of "fit" was first introduced by Pittman (1994; see also Bowen, 1998; Bowen, Orthner, & Bell, 1997). In a dual-earner couple, the assumption is that the partners formulate adaptive strategies for maximizing both of their abilities to meet workplace and family system needs (Moen & Wethington, 1992). When available workplace options permit workers to realize their strategies, they experience compatibility and low distress; otherwise, they experience conflict and high distress. Fit can range along a continuum from good to poor, thereby moving beyond the notion of conflict.

Thus, a third direction for future research on the work-family interface is the development of models that incorporate family-level effects, with the unit of analysis expanded to include partners, children, and other members of the employee's work-family system. Such a systems approach—along with, as discussed above, an acknowledgment of work-family enhancement as well as conflict and a focus on uncovering underlying processes—should serve to greatly enhance theory and improve our understanding of the work-family interface and its effects on health and quality of life.

REFERENCES

Adams, G. A., King, L. A., & King, D. W. (1996). Relationships of job and family involvement, family social support, and work-family conflict with job and life satisfaction. *Journal of Applied Psychology, 81*(4), 411–420.

Allen, T. D., Herst, D. E. L., Bruck, C. S., & Sutton, M. (2000). Consequences associated with work-to-family conflict: A review and agenda for future research. *Journal of Occupational Health Psychology, 5*(2), 278–308.

Aneshensel, C. S. (1986). Marital and employment role-strain, social support, and depression among adult women. In S. E. Hobfoll (Ed.), *Stress, social support, and women* (pp. 99–114). New York: Hemisphere.

Bailyn, L. (1993). *Breaking the mold: Women, men, and time in the new corporate world.* New York: Free Press.

Barling, J. (1984). Effects of husbands' work experiences on wives' marital satisfaction. *Journal of Social Psychology, 124*, 219–225.

Barnett, R. C. (1998). Toward a review and reconceptualization of the work/family literature. *Genetic, Social and General Psychology Monographs, 124*(2), 125–182.

Barnett, R. C., & Baruch, G. K. (1985). Women's involvement in multiple roles and psychological distress. *Journal of Personality and Social Psychology, 49*(1), 135–145.

Barnett, R. C., & Brennan, R. T. (1995). The relationship between job experiences and psychological distress: A structural equation approach. *Journal of Organizational Behavior, 16*, 259–276.

Barnett, R. C., & Brennan, R. T. (1997). Change in job conditions, change in psychological distress, and gender: A longitudinal study of dual-earner couples. *Journal of Organizational Behavior, 18*, 253–274.

Barnett, R. C., Brennan, R. T., & Gareis, K. C. (1999). A closer look at the measurement of burnout. *Journal of Applied Biobehavioral Research, 4*(2), 65–78.

Barnett, R. C., Gareis, K. C., & Brennan, R. T. (under review). *Time to consider time: A longitudinal within-couple analysis of total family work hours.*

Barnett, R. C., & Hyde, J. S. (2001). Women, men, work, and family: An expansionist theory. *American Psychologist, 56*(10), 781–796.

Barnett, R. C., & Marshall, N. L. (1993). Men, family-role quality, job role-quality, and physical health. *Health Psychology, 12*(1), 48–55.

Barnett, R. C., Marshall, N. L., & Pleck, J. H. (1992). Men's multiple roles and their relationship to men's psychological distress. *Journal of Marriage and the Family, 54*, 358–367.

Barnett, R. C., Marshall, N. L., Raudenbush, S., & Brennan, R. (1993). Gender and the relationship between job experiences and psychological distress: A study of dual-earner couples. *Journal of Personality and Social Psychology, 64*(5), 794–806.

Barnett, R. C., Marshall, N. L., & Sayer, A. (1992). Positive-spillover effects from job to home: A closer look. *Women & Health, 19*(2/3), 13–41.

Barnett, R. C., Marshall, N. L., & Singer, J. D. (1992). Job experiences over time, multiple roles, and women's mental health: A longitudinal study. *Journal of Personality and Social Psychology, 62*(4), 634–644.

Barnett, R. C., Raudenbush, S. W., Brennan, R. T., Pleck, J. H., & Marshall, N. L. (1995). Change in job and marital experiences and change in psychological distress: A longitudinal study of dual-earner couples. *Journal of Personality and Social Psychology, 69*(5), 839–850.

Barnett, R. C., & Shen, Y.-C. (1997). Gender, high- and low-schedule-control housework tasks, and psychological distress. *Journal of Family Issues, 18*(4), 403–428.

Baruch, G. K., & Barnett, R. C. (1986). Role quality, multiple role involvement, and psychological well-being in midlife women. *Journal of Personality and Social Psychology, 51*(3), 578–585.

Becker, G. S. (1981). *A treatise on the family*. Cambridge, MA: Harvard University Press.

Blank, R. M. (1988). Women's paid work, household income, and household well-being. In S. E. Rix (Ed.), *The American woman 1988–1989: A status report* (pp. 123–161). New York: Norton.

Bond, J. T., Thompson, C., Galinsky, E., & Prottas, D. (2003). *Highlights of the 2002 National Study of the Changing Workforce* (No. 3). New York: Families and Work Institute.

Bowen, G. L. (1998). Effects of leader support in the work unit on the relationship between work spillover and family adaptation. *Journal of Family and Economic Issues, 19*(1), 25–52.

Bowen, G. L., Orthner, D. K., & Bell, D. B. (1997). Differences in spouses' perceptions of family adaptation. *Journal of Social Behavior and Personality, 12*(1), 53–72.

Charney Research (2000). *What will parents vote for? Update 2000*. New York: National Parenting Association.

Conger, R. D., Rueter, M. A., & Elder, G. H. (1999). Couple resilience to economic pressure. *Journal of Personality and Social Psychology, 76*(1), 54–71.

Coontz, S. (1997). *The way we really are: Coming to terms with America's changing families*. New York: Basic Books.

Crosby, F. J. (1991). *Juggling: The unexpected advantages of balancing career and home for women and their families*. New York: Free Press.

Crosby, F. J., & Jaskar, K. L. (1993). Women and men at home and at work: Realities and illusions. In S. Oskamp & M. Costanzo (Eds.), *Gender issues in contemporary society* (pp. 143–171). Newbury Park, CA: Sage.

Crouter, A. C. (1984). Spillover from family to work: The neglected side of the work-family conflict interface. *Human Relations, 37*(6), 425–441.

Farrell, M. P., & Rosenberg, S. D. (1981). *Men at midlife*. Dover, MA: Auburn.

Frone, M. R. (2003). Work-family balance. In J. C. Quick & L. E. Tetrick (Eds.), *Handbook of occupational health psychology* (pp. 143–162). Washington, DC: American Psychological Association.

Frone, M. R., Russell, M., & Cooper, M. L. (1992a). Antecedents and outcomes of work-family conflict: Testing a model of the work-family interface. *Journal of Applied Psychology, 77*, 65–78.

Frone, M. R., Russell, M., & Cooper, L. M. (1992b). Prevalence of work-family conflict: Are work and family boundaries asymmetrically permeable? *Journal of Organizational Behavior, 13*, 723–729.

Frone, M. R., Russell, M., & Cooper, L. M. (1997). Relation of work-family conflict to health outcomes: A four-year longitudinal study of employed parents. *Journal of Occupational and Organizational Psychology, 70*, 325–335.

Frone, M. R., Yardley, J. K., & Markel, K. S. (1997). Developing and testing an integrative model of the work-family interface. *Journal of Vocational Behavior, 50*, 145–167.

Gallo, L. C., Troxel, W. M., Matthews, K. A., & Kuller, L. H. (2003). Marital status and quality in middle-aged women associations with levels and trajectories of cardiovascular risk factors. *Health Psychology, 22*(5), 453–463.

Geurts, S. A. E., Kompier, M. A. J., Roxburgh, S., & Houtman, I. L. D. (2003). Does work-home interference mediate the relationship between workload and well-being? *Journal of Vocational Behavior, 63*(3), 532–559.

Geurts, S., Rutte, C., & Peeters, M. (1999). Antecedents and consequences of work-home interference among medical residents. *Social Science & Medicine, 48*(9), 1135–1148.

Gore, S., & Mangione, T. W. (1983). Social roles, sex roles, and psychological distress: Additive and interactive models of sex differences. *Journal of Health and Social Behavior, 24*(4), 300–312.

Greenhaus, J. H., & Beutell, N. J. (1985). Sources of conflict between work and family roles. *Academy of Management Review, 10*(1), 76–88.

Greenhaus, J. H., & Powell, G. N. (in press). When work and family are allies: A theory of work-family enrichment. *Academy of Management Review*.

Gutek, B. A., Searle, S., & Klepa, L. (1991). Rational versus gender role explanations for work-family conflict. *Journal of Applied Psychology, 76*(4), 560–568.

Hayghe, H. V. (1997). Developments in women's labor force participation. *Monthly Labor Review, September*, 41–46.

Hughes, D., & Galinsky, E. (1994). Gender, job and family conditions and psychological symptoms. *Psychology of Women Quarterly, 18*, 251–270.

Hyde, J. S., DeLamater, J. D., & Durik, A. M. (2001). Sexuality and the dual-earner couple, Part II: Beyond the baby years. *Journal of Sex Research, 38*(1), 10–23.

Hyde, J. S., DeLamater, J. D., & Hewitt, E. C. (1998). Sexuality and the dual-earner couple: Multiple roles and sexual functioning. *Journal of Family Psychology, 12*(3), 354–368.

Kalmijn, M. (1999). Father involvement in childrearing and the perceived stability of marriage. *Journal of Marriage and the Family, 61*, 409–421.

Kandel, D. B., Davies, M., & Raveis, V. H. (1985). The stressfulness of daily social roles for women: Marital, occupational and household roles. *Journal of Health and Social Behavior, 26*, 64–78.

Kanter, R. M. (1977). *Work and family in the United States: A critical review and agenda for research and policy.* New York: Russell Sage Foundation, Social Science Frontiers.

Kessler, R. C., & McRae, J. A. (1982). The effect of wives' employment on the mental health of married men and women. *American Sociological Review, 47*, 216–227.

Kinnunen, U., & Mauno, S. (1998). Antecedents and outcomes of work-family conflict among employed men and women in Finland. *Human Relations, 51*(2), 157–177.

Kinnunen, U., Vermulst, A., Gerris, A., & Makikangas, A. (2003). Work-family conflict and its relations to well-being: The role of personality as a moderating factor. *Personality and Individual Differences, 35*(7), 1669–1683.

Kmec, J. A. (1999). Multiple aspects of work-family conflict. *Sociological Focus, 32*(3), 265–285.

Kossek, E. E., & Ozeki, C. (1998). Work-family conflict, policies, and the job–life satisfaction relationship: A review and directions for organizational behavior–human resources research. *Journal of Applied Psychology, 83*(2), 139–149.

Kossek, E. E., & Ozeki, C. (1999). Bridging the work-family policy and productivity gap: A literature review. *Community, Work and Family, 2*(1), 7–32.

Lein, L., Durham, M., Pratt, M., Schudson, M., Thomas, R., & Weiss, H. (1974). *Final report: Work and family life.* Cambridge, MA: Center for the Study of Public Policy.

Liem, R., & Liem, J. H. (1988). Psychological effects of unemployment on workers and their families. *Journal of Social Issues, 44*(4), 87–105.

MacDermid, S. M., Barnett, R., Crosby, F., Greenhaus, J., Koblenz, M., Marks, S., et al. (2000). *The measurement of work/life tension: Recommendations of a virtual think tank.* Boston: Alfred P Sloan Foundation.

Marks, S. R. (1977). Multiple roles and role strain: Some notes on human energy, time and commitment. *American Sociological Review, 42*, 921–936.

Marks, S. R., & MacDermid, S. M. (1996). Multiple roles and the self: A theory of role balance. *Journal of Marriage and the Family, 58*, 417–432.

Milkie, M. A., & Peltola, P. (1999). Playing all the roles: Gender and the work-family balancing act. *Journal of Marriage and the Family, 61*, 476–490.

Moen, P., & Wethington, E. (1992). The concept of family adaptive strategies. *Annual Review of Sociology, 18*, 233–251.

Netemeyer, R. G., Boles, J. S., & McMurrian, R. (1996). Development and validation of work-family conflict and family-work conflict scales. *Journal of Applied Psychology, 81*(4), 400–410.

Noor, N. (2003). Work- and family-related variables, work-family conflict and women's well-being: Some observations. *Community, Work & Family, 6*(3), 297–319.

Ono, H. (1998). Husbands' and wives' resources and marital dissolution. *Journal of Marriage and the Family, 60*, 674–689.

Oppenheimer, V. K. (1997). Women's employment and the gain to marriage: The specialization and trading model. *Annual Review of Sociology, 23*, 431–453.

Ozer, E. M., Barnett, R. C., Brennan, R. T., & Sperling, J. (1998). Does child care involvement increase or decrease distress among dual-earner couples? *Women's Health: Research on Gender, Behavior, and Policy, 4*(4), 285–311.

Parsons, T. (1949). The social structure of the family. In R. Anshen (Ed.), *The family: Its function and destiny* (pp. 173–201). New York: Harper.

Perry-Jenkins, M., Repetti, R. L., & Crouter, A. C. (2000). Work and family in the 1990s. *Journal of Marriage and the Family, 62*, 981–998.

Pittman, J. F. (1994). Work/family fit as a mediator of work factors on marital tension: Evidence from the interface of greedy institutions. *Human Relations, 47*(2), 183–209.

Raudenbush, S. W., Brennan, R. T., & Barnett, R. C. (1995). A multivariate hierarchical model for studying psychological change within married couples. *Journal of Family Psychology, 9*(2), 161–174.

Repetti, R. L., & Crosby, F. (1984). Gender and depression: Exploring the adult-role explanation. *Journal of Social and Clinical Psychology, 2*(1), 57–70.

Repetti, R. L., Matthews, K. A., & Waldron, I. (1989). Employment and women's health: Effects of paid employment on women's mental and physical health. *American Psychologist, 44*(11), 1394–1401.

Rook, K., Dooley, D., & Catalano, R. (1991). Stress transmission: The effects of husbands' job stressors on the emotional health of their wives. *Journal of Marriage and the Family, 53*, 165–177.

Rosenman, R. H., Brand, R. J., Jenkins, C. D., Friedman, M., Straus, R., & Wurm, M. (1975). Coronary heart disease in the Western Collaborative Group Study: Final follow-up experience of 81/2 years. *Journal of the American Medical Association, 233*, 872–877.

Ross, C. E., & Huber, J. (1985). Hardship and depression. *Journal of Health and Social Behavior, 26*(4), 312–327.

Ruderman, M. N., Ohlott, P. J., Panzer, K., & King, S. N. (2002). Benefits of multiple roles for managerial women. *Academy of Management Journal, 45*, 369–386.

Russo, N. F., & Zierk, K. L. (1992). Abortion, childbearing, and women's well-being. *Professional Psychology: Research & Practice, 23*(4), 269–280.

Sarbin, T. R. (1954). Role theory. In G. Lindzey (Ed.), *Handbook of social psychology, Vol. I. Theory and method* (pp. 223–258). Cambridge, MA: Addison-Wesley.

Sieber, S. D. (1974). Toward theory of role accumulation. *American Sociological Review, 39*, 567–578.

Simons, R. (1992). Parental role strains, salience of parental identity and gender differences in psychological distress. *Journal of Health and Social Behavior, 33*, 25–35.

Thoits, P. A. (1983). Multiple identities and psychological well-being: A reformulation and test of the social isolation hypothesis. *American Sociological Review, 48*, 174–187.

Thoits, P. A. (1992). Identity structures and psychological well-being: Gender and marital status comparisons. *Social Psychology Quarterly, 55*(3), 236–256.

van der Hulst, M., & Geurts, S. (2001). Associations between overtime and psychological health in high and low reward jobs. *Work & Stress, 15*(3), 227–240.

Veroff, J., Douvan, E., & Kulka, R. A. (1981). *The inner American.* New York: Basis Books.

Vinokur, A. D., Price, R. H., & Caplan, R. D. (1996). Hard times and hurtful partners: How financial strain affects depression and relationship satisfaction of unemployed persons and their spouses. *Journal of Personality and Social Psychology, 71*(1), 166–179.

Voydanoff, P. (1988). Work role characteristics, family structure demands, and work/family conflict. *Journal of Marriage and the Family, 50*, 749–761.

Voydanoff, P. (2001). Incorporating community into work and family research: A review of basic relationships. *Human Relations, 54*(12), 1609–1637.

Voydanoff, P., & Donnelly, B. W. (1999). Multiple roles and psychological distress: The intersection of the paid worker, spouse, and parent roles with the role of the adult child. *Journal of Marriage and the Family, 61*(August), 725–738.

Waldron, I., & Jacobs, J. A. (1989). Effects of multiple roles on women's health: Evidence from a national longitudinal study. *Women and Health, 15*(1), 3–19.

Warr, P., & Parry, G. (1982). Paid employment and women's psychological well-being. *Psychological Bulletin, 91*(3), 498–516.

Wethington, E., & Kessler, R. C. (1989). Employment, parental responsibility, and psychological distress: A longitudinal study of married women. *Journal of Family Issues, 10*(4), 527–546.

11

Experimental Social Psychology and the Study of Work and Family

Francine M. Deutsch
Mount Holyoke College

Social psychologists focus on the intra- and interpersonal processes that drive decisions, perceptions, and psychological outcomes in social life. The cognitive revolution in psychology has also meant that the way people construe their social worlds has become central to the way social psychologists understand social behavior.

To address the question of how mainstream social psychology can inform research on work and family today, I reviewed all the studies that have been published in our two flagship journals, *Journal of Personality and Social Psychology* and *Personality and Social Psychology Bulletin*, since the beginning of the 21st century. Three questions informed my investigation: What evidence exists of a psychological link between behavior and outcomes at home and in the workplace? What social psychological mechanisms perpetuate gendered work/family roles? How can social psychological theories be used to undermine these gendered roles and promote the possibility of gender equality both in the family and on the job? Four social psychological theories seemed particularly relevant to these work/family issues: attachment theory, self-determination theory, social role theory, and norm focus theory. Attachment theory makes clear that behavior at work is deeply tied psychologically to relationships in the family. The other three theories address the mechanisms through which gendered work/family norms are established and maintained and imply ways in which they might be dismantled. Social psychological research on these theories can inform our understanding of work and family life, whether or not the studies are explicitly addressed to work/family issues.

My investigation also showed that although social psychology was born as an experimental social science, today it embraces a wider array of methods, including the correlational and qualitative methods that are typically employed by work and family researchers in other social sciences. Nevertheless, the experimental methods used by social psychologists offer a unique methodological contribution to the field of work and family.

THE ADVANTAGES AND PITFALLS OF EXPERIMENTAL METHODS

Experimental methods are used first and foremost because they can disentangle causal relationships among variables. In an experimental design, one or more *independent* variable/s are manipulated and its/their effects on *dependent* variable/s are measured. The key to an experimental design is that everything in the situation is held constant, except for the manipulated variable, allowing the researcher to isolate the cause of any effect on the dependent variable.

For example, Allen and Russell (1999) conducted an experimental study of perceptions of the work commitment of men and women who take parental leave and the effects of their parental leave-taking on recommendations for work rewards. In this study, advanced undergraduates taking upper-level business classes (half of whom had had supervisory experience) assumed the role of "manager" and read and evaluated the file of an "employee." The participant rated the employee's commitment to the organization, commitment to work and family, and the extent to which the participant would be likely to recommend the employee for six different work rewards, including a salary increase, assignment to a "challenging, high profile project," and admission to an executive training program. The file they read was manipulated such that the employee was depicted as a male or female (Scott/Susan) whose work history included either a previous parental leave, medical leave, or no leave. The employee's performance level was manipulated to appear either high, medium, or low by alterations in the performance ratings in the file, which included supervisor ratings of the employee's characteristics (e.g., leadership, oral communication) as well as objective criteria such as sales performance and client satisfaction.

Parental leave had a more negative impact on men's careers than on women's. Women were just as likely to be recommended for work-related rewards if they had taken medical or parental leave than if they had not. Women who performed at a high level were more likely than those with medium or low performance to be recommended for job rewards. Performance level mattered for men too, but regardless of performance level, men were less likely to be recommended for job rewards if they had taken parental leave than if they had not. Moreover, both men and women were seen as less committed to work in the parental leave condition than in the control (no leave) condition.

In this example, the use of an experiment allows us to rule out potential extraneous variables that might cloud the interpretation of the results obtained in a more real-life setting. Imagine a correlational field study that examined exactly the same issues as this experiment and obtained similar results. In this imagined study, men and women, matched for performance, who had either taken or not taken parental leaves, would be compared on the job-related rewards they had subsequently received. If leaves were associated with fewer rewards, could we conclude that the leaves had been responsible? No, we could not. First, although we are able to control for some aspects of performance, we could never be sure that everything relevant to performance had been controlled. Perhaps those who took leaves differed from their non-leave-taking counterparts because they simply did not like their jobs as much or had subtly tenser relations with their supervisors. Either might encourage them to take leaves and either might account for their diminished rewards at work. The characteristics of the kinds of people who take leaves or their relations with coworkers might be to blame rather than the leaves per se. It is not possible to know every characteristic that might covary with leave-taking that might influence job outcomes. The beauty of the experimental study is that the only information on which the "supervisors" can make a judgment is identical both for men and women and for those who took leaves and those who did not. Therefore, different recommendations for those who took leaves and those who did not can only be attributable to the leaves.

The biggest potential pitfall of experiments is that they may lack external validity, the generalizability of the results to the real world. The artificial environment of the laboratory or the unrepresentative nature of college student samples may call into question whether the results of an experimental study can be applied to a real-world context. Nonetheless, we should not automatically dismiss experimental findings, even when they are obtained in highly artificial settings with very unrepresentative samples. Often, generalizability is not the point (Mook, 1983). For example, many experiments are designed to test theoretical ideas. Explanations for what is happening in a real-life setting might give rise to theories that make predictions for what should occur in the unnatural setting of a laboratory. Take Stanley Milgram's famous obedience study. Milgram (1963) wanted to examine the power of the norm of obedience to elicit evil. In his study, a majority of experimental subjects were induced to give what they thought were dangerous electric shocks to people who they believed were other subjects. They did so simply because the experimenter, the person in authority, told them to. This demonstration of obedience occurred in a laboratory setting. The experimenter, unlike real-life authorities, possessed no real power over the subject. A knee-jerk response for those who worry too much about external validity would be to fault the unnatural setup. However, the results of the experiment show the power of the norm of obedience better than any real-life situation ever could. It is not surprising that those who fear for their lives or even their jobs obey. But, when ordinary people obey an authority and commit evil acts, despite the authority's lack of material power over them, it reveals the enormous power of obedience to authority per se.

Likewise, unrepresentative samples are not always problematic (Mook, 1983). The logic of the claims made must be examined on a case-by-case basis. For example, consider the parental leave study reported above (Allen & Russell, 1999), which showed the discrimination men might suffer if they take parental leave. To what extent should we worry that the subjects were college students, albeit business students who had some work experience? The answer should be based on a careful evaluation of the ways in which we might expect these students to differ from the target population: real-life work managers. If we believe that the students are less family-friendly in their work attitudes than are employed managers, then the students' discrimination would be strong evidence supporting the claim that taking parental leave hurts men at work. However, if we believe that real-life managers are likely to be more family-friendly than students, then the results are suspect.

The best way to ensure against the potential problems of external validity is to use experimental methods in conjunction with field research. The multi-method approach described in another chapter in this volume, which uses qualitative and quantitative methods in tandem to boost convergent validity, can be extended to include experimental methods (Neal, Hammer, & Morgan, chap. 28, this volume).

SOCIAL PSYCHOLOGICAL THEORIES AND WORK/FAMILY LIFE

Attachment Theory

Attachment theory suggests that the quality of family relationships has a direct impact on individuals' functioning at work. Although originally the purview of developmental psychologists, today attachment theory is the source of much contemporary social psychological theory and research on intimate relationships, including family relationships and the connection between family relationships and functioning at work (see Mikulincer & Shaver, 2003, for a review).

John Bowlby, who originally proposed attachment theory, asserted that, as a means of survival, individuals were born with a capacity and need for attachment, which would lead them to seek proximity with their primary caregivers, especially under conditions of threat. If all went well and the caregiver was sensitive and responsive to the child's needs, a secure attachment would be forged in which the attachment figure would be experienced as a "safe haven" from which the child could derive comfort when threatened and from which s/he could explore the world. However, if the attachment figure was unavailable and unresponsive, or unpredictably and unreliably responsive, the child would not develop self-confidence that proximity-seeking will be an effective strategy for reducing threat and obtaining comfort when anxious. An internal working model of attachment figures would be developed that reflected this insecurity. In response, the child would develop one of two alternate means of insecure coping: an anxious attachment style, characterized by desperate attempts to get the attachment figure to respond, or alternatively, an avoidant attachment style, characterized by distancing from the attachment figure. Developmental psychologists have examined both the parental antecedents and the child outcomes that are associated with each of these styles.

Social psychologists have pursued Bowlby's contention that attachment processes are relevant in intimate relationships throughout life, and have shown that adults can be characterized by attachment styles that vary along two dimensions: high or low anxiety about rejection and high or low comfort with relationship closeness (Hazan & Shaver, 1990; Mikulincer & Shaver, 2003). Secure individuals, who are low in anxiety and high in comfort, tend to establish satisfying close relationships, appropriately seek and provide comfort, and effectively deal with conflict. Anxious insecure individuals, whose attachment systems are hyperactivated, tend to cling to partners, to be overly sensitive to partners' rejection or lack of availability, and to make intense demands for attention. At the other end of the continuum, avoidant insecure individuals, whose attachment systems are deactivated, maintain distance in relationships and are defensively self-reliant.

Attachment theory suggests a fascinating link between work and family (Hazan & Shaver, 1990). Work is conceived of as the analogue to childhood exploration. Just as a secure attachment to a reliable caregiver provides the child with a safe haven from which to explore the world freely, a secure attachment style in adulthood provides the psychological freedom needed to pursue the satisfactions of work. In contrast, an anxious attachment style entails a preoccupation with relationships, which could interfere with functioning at work, while an avoidant attachment style could translate into a compulsive work style used to avoid closeness with family members.

Landmark research on romantic couples confirmed this theoretical link between love and work (Hazan & Shaver, 1990). In a survey conducted with newspaper readers, participants with secure attachment styles seemed to have the most positive experience of work. They felt the most job security and were least likely to put off working or to fear rejection from coworkers. At the same time, they enjoyed vacations and put a higher value on intimate relationships than on work. Those with anxious attachment styles felt insecure about their jobs, felt unappreciated by coworkers, and reported that love interfered with work. Notably, they made less money than the other participants, suggesting that their performance may be impaired by their preoccupation with relationship concerns. Participants with avoidant styles were similar to secure participants in work experiences, except that they had more negative views of coworkers. Moreover, their orientation to work seemed to be compulsive. They felt nervous when not working, did not enjoy vacations, and valued work more than love. Avoidant participants appear to be workaholics who use work to avoid closeness.

Although that study focused on attachment security vis-à-vis "romantic" partners, the major attachment figures for married individuals are their spouses. Under conditions of stress, whether generated at home or at work, a husband or wife is the most important source of potential comfort. The ability to receive comfort at home, which is influenced by attachment style, is associated with positive functioning at work.

In marriage, the transition to parenthood is often a stressful period, especially for wives who may seek support from their husbands. Wives' attachment style can shape marital interactions and outcomes during this period. In a study of changes in marriage during the transition to parenthood, anxious insecure women perceived less support from their husbands prenatally than women with less anxiety about attachment. To the extent that those anxious new mothers felt unsupported prenatally, they showed a relatively high decline in marital satisfaction (Rholes, Simpson, Campbell, & Grich, 2001) and an increase in depression (Simpson, Rholes, Campbell, Tran, & Wilson, 2003). Wives' perception of lack of support prenatally was also associated with husbands' anger and husbands' relatively low marital satisfaction at that time, and mediated declines in husbands' marital satisfaction and his support-giving over the transition to parenting. Thus, it appears that a wife's anxious attachment style sets up a negative spiral of interactions.

A longitudinal study of new parents showed the link between family and work benefits of a secure attachment style during the transition to parenting, especially in comparison to an anxious attachment style (Vasquez, Durik, & Hyde, 2002). At both 1 year and 4.5 years postpartum, attachment security in mothers and fathers was associated with relatively more rewards and less stress in their family relationships and with more rewards at work.

It is important to note, however, that both attachment style itself (Cook, 2000) and the interpersonal dynamics it engenders are not fixed. In the transition to parenthood study (Rholes, Simpson, Campbell, & Grich, 2001), despite an insecure anxious attachment style, women who perceived support by husbands prenatally had comparatively good marital relationships postnatally (and presumably better outcomes at work).

Research based on attachment theory shows definitively that work and family are psychologically related. It also suggests some directions for work/family researchers. For example, the negative spillover effects from work to family and vice versa might be moderated by the attachment styles of marital partners. Whether work stress negatively spills over to family life may depend on whether the stressed person can elicit comfort from his or her spouse, which, in turn, is shaped by their attachment styles. Although attachment theory does illustrate a link between work and family, it does not seem to inform our understanding of the gendered nature of work/family life. Social role theory, group norm theory, and self-determination theory do.

Social Role Theory

Male and female stereotypes (at least among white middle-class Americans, the group most studied) roughly parallel the distinction originally proposed by Bakan (1966) between agency and communion. Stereotypically, men are assumed to possess agenic traits, such as self-confidence, independence, assertiveness, and rationality, which are associated with competence, accomplishment, and self-assertion. Women are assumed to possess communal traits, which are associated with relatedness to other people, such as understanding, sympathy, nurturance, and selflessness. Because agenic traits are also associated with suitability for high-power occupations, and communal traits are associated with suitability for family life, they underwrite gendered work/family roles. Thus, the study of how these stereotypes originate, how they get perpetuated, and how they are used to promote power differences between men and women is critical for the work/family field.

Social role theory (Eagly, Wood, & Diekman, 2000) asserts that gender stereotypes are derived from the work/family roles that men and women play in society. Consistent with this view, Twenge (2001) examined self-reports of an agenic personality trait, assertiveness, among American college students over the course of the 20th century, and found an increase in women describing themselves as assertive from the 1930s until World War II, a decrease after World War II, and an increase starting in the late 1960s. This curvilinear pattern parallels changes in women's status in the United States during that historical period, as reflected in their educational attainments, age of marriage, and in media portrayals. In another set of studies that assessed the perceived relation between roles and stereotypes (Diekman & Eagly, 2000), college students and people recruited at airports estimated the distribution of men and women in sex-typed jobs and in the performance of household tasks in the years 1950, the present, or in 2050. Participants' perceptions of the personality characteristics of the average man and woman during those time periods were mediated by their estimates of the distribution of roles, just as social role theory would predict. Personality characteristics were seen as becoming less stereotypical as roles in society became more egalitarian.

Earning money is a part of a stereotypically masculine role. In an experimental study that examined perceptions of people's agenic and communal traits as a function of their earnings, participants rated the personality characteristics of a fictitious man or woman whose income was represented at one of 10 levels, increasing at $20,000 increments from 10,000 to 190,000 dollars (Johannsen-Schmidt & Eagly, 2002). With increases in income, participants rated the target higher on positive agenic traits and lower on communal traits.

Some research also shows that self-ascription of traits depends on the roles one plays. For example, in a longitudinal study of graduates of a German university, career success (as measured by the attainment of a professional job 18 months after graduation) was associated with self-described agency, controlling for sex, GPA, major, and self-described agency a year and a half earlier (Abele, 2003). A professional job led these young people to perceive themselves as possessing more agenic traits. Having a partner and wanting children, however, did not predict self-ascribed communal traits. Although the researchers try to argue that communal traits might be biologically based, they may have not sufficiently measured the kind of role performance that might develop communal traits. Risman's (1986) study of single fathers, who were sometimes thrust into that role by the death of a spouse, demonstrates that caregiving does foster the development of communal traits.

Taken together, these stereotyping studies show that the perception of traits of both the self and others are derived from the occupancy and performance of roles. To the extent that those roles are distributed differently for men and women, gender stereotypes will emerge. In theory, these stereotypes can then lead to the self-fulfilling prophecies that perpetuate gendered family and work roles. If women are assumed to be lacking in agenic traits, they may be passed up for high-powered jobs. If men are thought lacking in communal traits, their wives may not trust them to care for small children. Moreover, self-attributions of gendered traits may perpetuate choice of and success in adopting gendered roles. In Abele's (2003) study, compared to their peers the German graduates who described themselves as relatively more agenic when first surveyed had achieved more "career success" 18 months later, whereas graduates who perceived themselves as relatively more communal, were subsequently more likely to have a partner and to wish for children.

The theoretical reasoning of social role theory, however, ignores power relations between men and women. Gender stereotyping may not be a disinterested assessment of information about people who play particular roles. Men may be motivated to stereotype women to serve their own interests.

Power relations can affect the use of gender stereotypes in ways that disadvantage women. In one experimental study (Vescio, Snyder, & Butz, 2003), male or female "supervisors" interviewed and supervised a female subordinate in a house design project, which entailed tasks that were described as requiring stereotypically masculine abilities, such as logical, mechanical, strategic, and spatial abilities. The "supervisors" were manipulated to believe that a good supervisor focused on either strengths or weaknesses. Male weakness-focused leaders relied on gender stereotypes. They asked the female less about her valued (masculine) attributes, judged the female subordinate to have fewer of them, gave her fewer important tasks, and estimated that she would be less successful than strength-focused leaders did. Female "supervisors," however, showed no such effects. A second study (Vescio et al., 2003) also cast participants in supervisor–worker roles for a marketing task characterized as requiring highly valued masculine attributes. Male and female participants became leaders of a mixed-sex group that consisted of two other male or female participants. In this case, weakness-focused male leaders asked fewer questions of women than men about strengths and more about weaknesses, but again female leaders were unaffected. The male leaders' stereotyping had pernicious effects on female subordinates, who performed worse and felt worse about themselves in those conditions. In these cases, the power of the male supervisor coupled with his weakness orientation led him to rely on negative and detrimental stereotypes of women, despite having no information about those particular women.[1]

The opposite of gender stereotyping is individuating, which means paying attention to the individual characteristics of a person, regardless of gender. Motives shape behavior here, too. In an experiment that supposedly studied first impressions, students viewed two male and two female photographs randomly matched with nongendered traits and were then given a surprise memory task for those traits (Stewart, Vassar, Sanchez, & David, 2000). Students with progressive attitudes about gender made fewer within-gender mistakes for female than for male targets, whereas those with more traditional views made fewer within-gender errors for male than for female targets. Likewise, at a progressive liberal arts college, participants in a similar experiment, individuated women more than men. The desire to see women get ahead seemed to motivate individuation of women (Stewart et al., 2000).

Clearly, stereotypes can and are used by people who are opposed to equal rights for women either at work or at home. But, is stereotyping the basis for discrimination? Would the elimination of stereotypes eradicate discrimination?

Rudman and Kilianski (2000) documented that negative conscious and unconscious attitudes toward women in authority were not related to attributions of agenic traits. Jackson, Esses, and Burris (2001) argued that respect, rather than the attribution of masculine (agenic) characteristics, underlies gender discrimination in hiring decisions for high-status jobs. In an experimental study (Jackson et al., 2001, Study 2), male and female students evaluated applications for a high- or low-status job (i.e., real estate director/short-order cook), to which randomly assigned male and female photographs were attached. Participants rated their respect for the applicant as well as the applicant's suitability for hiring and their agenic and communal traits. Men received better hiring ratings than women for high-status jobs. Both respect and ratings of masculinity (positive agenic traits) were related to hiring ratings, but a regression analysis showed that only respect uniquely contributed to hiring ratings. In fact, males and females were not rated differently on the stereotypic traits, so the differential attribution of agenic traits could not explain gender discrimination in hiring in this study. In a follow-up experiment (Jackson et al., 2001, Study 3), respect, positive masculine traits, and job status were manipulated directly in letters of recommendation, which were the bases for hiring ratings made by student participants. Although all applicants for the low-status jobs were rated as suitable, only those with high respect ratings were viewed as suitable for the high-status jobs. A bias favoring men for positions of authority or high-status positions exists, which seems to be based on respect for them, which is independent of the stereotype that men possess the characteristics (e.g., leadership, assertiveness, etc.) needed for these kinds of positions.

Parenthetically, this set of studies provides an excellent example of how experimental methods can be used powerfully in conjunction with correlational methods to disentangle causal relations. Initially, the researchers controlled the characteristics of male and female job applicants, which allowed them to isolate gender as a source of discrimination (Jackson et al., 2001). Then, participants' respect for and the attribution of communal traits to male and female "applicants" were examined as correlates of gender discrimination. Although both were correlated with discrimination, only respect mediated hiring discrimination. However, the possibility exists that naturally occurring perceptions of respect might be confounded with other unknown factors. Subsequently, the researchers manipulated respect experimentally. The findings confirmed the causal link between respect and hiring ratings.

Taken together, the literature on social roles shows the bi-directional effects of gendered roles and gender stereotypes. When men and women occupy gendered roles, it fosters stereotypes that promote gender discrimination. They may also come to think of themselves in stereotypical ways, which then serve as a basis for stereotypical choices. Both discrimination by others and these stereotypical choices, in turn, serve to maintain gendered family and work roles. However, alternatively, stereotypes about women, whether based on gendered role performance or not, may simply be used to justify discrimination by men and to undermine the resistance of women, as a means of perpetuating male power. And sometimes gender-stereotypical traits do not even fit the low power roles that women fill.

Group Norm Theory

Norms for gendered roles cannot simply be explained by stereotypes. Consider the disproportionate share of housework and child care that women continue to do despite their increasing participation in the paid labor force. Apologists might invoke stereotypes about women's communal traits to explain the assignment of nurturing tasks in the family to women. However, even if women did possess those traits and those traits were relevant to caring for young children, washing the floor or doing the laundry hardly requires one to be understanding, nurturing, or sympathetic. Gender construction theory is the prevailing theory in the work/family field that is invoked to account for the disproportionate housework and child care done by women (West & Zimmerman, 1987). According to this theory, by doing disproportionately less or more housework and child care, men and women are respectively responding to normative conceptions of their genders to which they are accountable. Women "do gender" by doing housework and child care. Conversely, they also "do gender" by not treating their paid work as breadwinning. Men "do gender" by refraining from housework and treating their paid employment as breadwinning. Gender construction theory describes the power of gender norms to shape behavior, but does not explain the internal psychological mechanisms that lead people to feel accountable to those norms.

Group norm theory, which can speak to these issues, has a long history of theoretical and empirical work in social psychology (Sherif & Sherif, 1953). Although this work may not explicitly address work/family issues or even gender, understanding how norms work in general may be applicable to understanding how gender norms operate at home and at work. For example, a recent study examined how people's expression of prejudice changes as they enter and become part of groups with different norms about the appropriateness of expressing those prejudices (Crandall, Eshleman, & O'Brien, 2002). Based on group norm theory, this study found evidence of a very strong relationship between the perceived social acceptability of expressing prejudices toward particular groups and participants' willingness to admit negative feelings toward those groups, acceptance of discrimination toward them, and tolerance of "offensive" jokes about them. The researchers also found evidence of a process in which entry into a new group is accompanied by a feeling of external pressure to support group norms, followed, over time, by an internal pressure to live up to the norms. Internalization has been achieved when people believe that they are following norms out of choice rather than out of either internal or external pressure.

The shift to a more traditional division of labor when couples become parents may reflect similar processes. How do women come to adopt norms that entail taking time off or cutting back at work and assuming the majority of responsibility at home? Becoming a mother puts women in a group in which they incur disapproval for career-strivings or for impatience with infant care. Disapproval might then lead new mothers to feel pressured by their peers or families to express the right feelings and goals. Over time, the suppression of alternate feelings (e.g., boredom, resentment) may become more internally motivated and eventually be experienced as authentic. Women who insist that decisions to compromise their work lives are based on choice may, in fact, feel that way because they have internalized the norms. Their failure to fault their husbands for an unfair division of labor may result from having suppressed resentment by shifting their focus from a comparison between their husbands and themselves to a comparison between their husbands and other men.

The suppression of feelings that clash with gender norms, as described by group norm theory, is akin to the "emotion work" that Hochschild talked about in *The Second Shift* (1989). Hochschild focused on how men and women grapple to feel what they think they should feel about gendered roles; group norm theory focuses on the social context that engenders those "shoulds."

Norms about motherhood are particularly powerful because they are always in focus and because there is so much pressure surrounding them. Recent experiments that manipulated focus on the anti-littering norm show that the norm only influenced behavior when it was made the focus of attention (Kallgren, Reno, & Cialdini, 2000). Moreover, although it is well-documented that deviance from norms elicits disapproval, the type of deviance affects the social response to it (Abrams, Marques, Brown, & Henson, 2000). Anti-norm deviance, which put the deviants' behavior closer to an out-group, elicited more social disapproval than pro-norm deviance. Analogously, in the case of new mothers, more self-sacrifice for the family than is normative might be treated more leniently than less self-sacrifice.

In other recent social psychological research, which demonstrated the power of norms, the relation between values and behavior was attenuated when the behavior was highly normative (Bardi & Schwartz, 2003). In light of those findings, it is easy to see how egalitarian values might get lost in the transition to parenthood, when a shift to a more traditional division of labor can appear universal.

Self-Determination Theory

Self-determination theory also addresses the internalization of social roles as well as the link between work and family roles (Ryan & Deci, 2000). Much of the research derived from self-determination theory focuses on the degree to which an individual's goals are autonomous as well as the predictors and outcomes of autonomy. Autonomy refers to the sense that one's goals are self-determined and reflect one's true self, rather than being externally imposed. According to the theory, at one end of the autonomy continuum, individuals possess intrinsic goals that are motivating because they are interesting, stimulating, or fun in and of themselves. Identification goals, which are defined as those that are not necessarily interesting or fun but are consistent with individuals' values and priorities, are also considered self-determined, although perhaps not as much as intrinsic goals. In contrast, introjected goals are those pursued to avoid guilt or anxiety and tend not to be experienced or defined as self-determined. External goals, which subjectively feel imposed from the outside, are considered the least autonomous. Ryan and Deci (2000) argued that self-regulation often consists of internalizing societally sanctioned goals so that they feel self-determined rather than externally imposed. One way that people pursue their goals is through the enactment of social roles, including gendered work/family roles. Gendered work and family goals are prime examples of socially sanctioned goals. Experiencing these goals as autonomous is critical to individuals' well-being.

Self-determination theory posits that autonomy is one of three primary universal human needs. Competence and relatedness are the other two. Competence is the sense of mastery and effectiveness in one's pursuits. Relatedness is feeling that one has regular intimate contact with people with whom one shares mutual care (Ryan and Deci, 2000). Sheldon, Elliot, Kim, and Kasser (2001) confirmed that satisfaction of these three needs (in addition to self-esteem) was prominent in people's reports of the most satisfying events in their everyday lives.

In a series of studies, Bettencourt and Sheldon (2001) demonstrated that social roles can provide vehicles for fulfilling or thwarting needs for relatedness and autonomy, and can thereby enhance or diminish subjective well-being. The studies, carried out with college students, included investigations of the experience of roles occupied in naturally occurring campus groups as well as roles that were experimentally manipulated in a class discussion group. In both kinds of groups, students whose conceptions of their authentic selves matched the attributes required for roles they occupied, tended to feel both more autonomous and more connected to complementary social actors when they played those roles.

Self-determination theory has also been used explicitly as a lens to understand work/family roles. Senecal, Vallerand, and Guay (2001) showed that when participants felt valued by their spouses, their motivation for family activities, such as assisting children's learning or participating in family leisure activities, was experienced as relatively more autonomous. As self-determination theory predicts, autonomous motivation was negatively related to family alienation, and less family alienation predicted less work-family conflict. Likewise, having a supportive employer (as reported by the participant) increased autonomous motivation at work, which also led to less family alienation, although the relation was not as strong. Nonetheless, the independent effect of autonomous motivation at work on family alienation demonstrates an important link between work and family experience. Moreover, the relation between spousal or employer support and feelings of autonomy in the relevant domain shows how gendered roles can be internalized and maintained. People feel less alienated (i.e., more authentic) in gendered roles when their spouses and employers approve of and value their behavior.

Ideology can also perpetuate gendered roles. Women pushed by discrimination or social pressure into traditional roles may, nonetheless, be reluctant to identify discrimination as such. An experimental study created a simulated job situation in which a male manager (actually a confederate) assigned the job of clerk to a female participant and the job of comanager to a male participant (also a confederate; Major, Granzow, McCoy, Levin, Schmader, & Sidanius, 2002). The more the female participant believed in an ideology of individual achievement-driven mobility, the less likely she was to attribute the male's behavior to sex discrimination.[2]

Likewise, to internalize societally sanctioned goals one must ignore the social pressures that shape behavior and see one's own choices as autonomous. The belief in an ideology of individual choice can facilitate this process. In my study of equally shared parenting (Deutsch, 1999), when I asked dual-earner couples who did not share why the division of labor was unequal in their families, many of the unequal women explained their disproportionate load as their own choices. They ignored socialization in their traditional families and contemporary social pressures as possible explanations for the division of labor at home. They acted as though their greater role at home was unrelated to their being women. This denial of gender is self-protective, because it allows women to retain a sense of control over their lives.

It may also preserve their marriages. Accurately perceiving an inequitable division of labor in the family can foster marital conflict and discontent. In fact, longitudinal research on the transition to parenthood has demonstrated that prenatal marital dissatisfaction leads to postnatal perceptions of inequity, which, in turn, increases conflict and dissatisfaction (Grote & Clark, 2001). The researchers argued that women who are dissatisfied with their marriages before the birth adopt a tit-for-tat exchange mode of calculating contributions in the postnatal period when they are stressed by the new demands of a baby. Given that men are doing disproportionately less child care, attending to each partner's contributions leads women to feel cheated and their husbands to feel guilty. Their findings suggest quite a quandary: How can women get their husbands to do more at home without recognizing an inequity in the division of labor? Is the choice for women really between illusion and unhappiness? Although illusion may bring happiness, it is a strange kind of happiness if it promotes women's subordination in the family and at the work-place.

CONCLUSION

Contemporary social psychology has spawned numerous studies that show how social realities are managed through psychological adoption. Despite the structural and normative constraints of the social worlds we occupy, people usually do not experience themselves as pawns of social forces, but as agents with free choice. Over time, groups need not threaten sanctions for members who deviate because members regulate themselves voluntarily. Studies on social role theory, group norm theory, and self-determination theory all address the internalization processes by which this shift occurs.

Social role theory depicts a loop in which the gendered distribution of social roles leads their occupants and their potential occupants to develop corresponding personalities, which in turn makes it more likely that they will occupy and experience more satisfaction with roles that fit them (Bettencourt & Sheldon, 2001). Group norm theory (Sherif & Sherif, 1953; Crandall et al., 2002) describes how individuals come to internalize the behavioral norms of the groups of which they are a part. Self-determination theory notes that "identification" goals, which are pursued because they represent a person's values and priorities, are experienced as autonomous. Identification goals are often socially sanctioned goals that people come to adopt as their own (e.g., gendered goals), and by doing so, experience all the positive effects of striving for autonomous as opposed to externally imposed goals (Ryan & Deci, 2000).

The dominant theory and research in social psychology has a lot to say about why a gendered world of work and family persists and how it is maintained. Although social psychology has had much less to say about how an inequitable gendered social world can be resisted and changed, the theory, research, and methods of the field could readily be subverted to address a feminist agenda at home and at work.

I am reminded of the classic social psychological study on conformity. Solomon Asch (1951) had participants indicate which of two out of three lines were equal in length, a simple task that was patently obvious to anyone. However, faced with a unanimous majority (in cahoots with the experimenter) who all gave the wrong answer, a large percentage of the research subjects conformed and answered incorrectly. In every introductory psychology book, this classic study is used to highlight the power of groups to elicit conformity. What I found more compelling, however, was the subsequent research that demonstrated that if even one member of the group gave the correct answer, regardless of the size of the majority, research subjects were drastically less likely to conform (Asch, 1951). Even one person's resistance can be powerful.

Equally sharing parents resist gendered norms (Deutsch, 1999). How do they resist? Using self-determination theory as a framework, we might hypothesize that if women interpret gendered roles as externally imposed, they will be more likely to resist those roles. Several equally sharing mothers told me that although they initially tried to play out the traditional role of mother, they were miserable. Lacking intrinsic motivation, they came to see those roles as externally imposed. Likewise, group norm theory speaks to the power of social groups to foster the internalization of norms. But, dominant social norms are not always adopted. Equally sharing parents resist by finding alternative social groups.

Social role theory also provides a lens to understand resistance. For example, the finding that individuals with more income were viewed as more agentic, was especially true for women. Counter-stereotypical role information is especially powerful (Johannsen-Schmidt &

Eagly, 2002). Self-perception is also powerfully affected by counterstereotypic behavior. Self-schemas, which organize and influence processing of information about the self, are more likely to be developed from behaviors that counter rather than conform to stereotypes (von Hippel, Hawkins, & Schooler, 2001). In studies that support this claim, athleticism was assumed to be stereotypical for Black males, and intelligence stereotypical for White males. Self-schemas were indicated by more extreme self-ratings on those traits and faster reaction times when participants had to indicate as quickly as possible whether a trait described them. Better athletic performance was associated with self-schemas of "athletic" for White but not Black males, and a higher GPA was related to self-schemas of "intelligent" for African Americans and White females, but not for White males. Based on these findings, we would expect that resistance to gendered roles would have even a stronger impact on self-perception than conformity to them. As people commit to identities at odds with gendered norms, those identities shape further efforts to resist. Just as conformity to gendered norms can generate a set of processes that perpetuate those norms, so can resistance. According to social role theory, if egalitarian roles were created, gender stereotypes should wither away. My point is that the same theories that explain the psychological mechanisms that maintain the status quo can be used to theorize about and research resistance to the status quo.

Whether women take action to try to change the division of labor in their families may depend on whether they feel powerful. We know that structural power (i.e., a bigger proportion of family income) can translate into less domestic labor for women (Bianchi, Milkie, Sayer, & Robinson, 2000), but it is also clear that women's dollars do not reduce their burden of domestic labor as much as men's do (Izraeli, 1994; Tichenor, 1999).

Power may be a state of mind. In a fascinating set of experiments, power was either manipulated by assigning participants to relatively powerful or powerless roles or by simply invoking their memories of experiences of having been powerful or powerless (Galinsky, Gruenfeld, & Magee, 2003). The experimenters were interested in the relation between power and action. In an unrelated context, participants were given different kinds of opportunities to act, which included taking a hit in a blackjack game, dealing with an annoying fan, or contributing resources in a public goods dilemma. Regardless of the way power was invoked or the kind of action involved, power led to action. Power seemed to lift inhibitions over normative constraints. With or without structural power in the family, women who feel powerful for other reasons may be more likely to take action to change the division of labor.

Social movements, like the women's movement, may, of course, be one of the most important sources of power. Sociology, political science, and economics inform us about the larger social trends that drive social norms. In concert with those social sciences, modern social psychology, with its focus on the individual within a larger social context and its use of experimental methods, can be a useful voice in the scholarly conversation about work and family.

NOTES

[1] We do need to question the external validity of this study. It is possible that more experienced supervisors would rely less on stereotypes, although that possibility needs to be balanced against the more progressive gender attitudes of younger cohorts.

[2] This is an interesting experiment because beliefs cannot be manipulated but must be included as a correlational variable. If this study were simply correlational, however, it would be very difficult to disentangle whether those differing beliefs simply reflected accurately on different experiences of discrimination. However, the laboratory study compared women with differing ideologies but exactly the same experience. Thus, the causal effects of ideology could be clearly seen.

REFERENCES

Abele, A. E. (2003). The dynamics of masculine-agenic and feminine-communal traits: Findings from a prospective study. *Journal of Personality and Social Psychology, 85*, 768–776.

Abrams, D., Marques, J. M., Brown, N., & Henson, M. (2000). Pro-norm and anti-norm deviance within and between groups. *Journal of Personality and Social Psychology, 78*, 906–912.

Allen, T. D., & Russell, J. E. A. (1999). Parental leave of absence: Some not so family-friendly implications. *Journal of Applied Social Psychology, 29*, 166–191.

Asch, S. E. (1951). Effects of group pressure upon the modification and distortion of judgments. In H. Guetzkow (Ed.), *Groups, leadership, and men* (pp. 177–190). Pittsburgh: Carnegie Press.

Bakan, D. (1966). *The duality of human existence*. Boston: Beacon Press.

Bardi, A., & Schwartz, S. H. (2003). Values and behavior: Strength and structure of relations. *Personality and Social Psychology Bulletin, 29*, 1207–1220.

Bettencourt, A., & Sheldon, K. (2001). Social roles as mechanisms for psychological need satisfaction within social groups. *Journal of Personality and Social Psychology, 81*, 1131–1143.

Bianchi, S. M., Milkie, M. A., Sayer, L. C., & Robinson, J. P. (2000). Is anyone doing the housework? Trends in the gender division of household labor. *Social Forces, 79*, 191–228.

Cook, W. L. (2000). Understanding attachment security in family context. *Journal of Personality and Social Psychology, 78*, 285–294.

Crandall, C. S., Eshleman, A., & O'Brien, L. (2002). Social norms and the expression of prejudice: The struggle for internalization. *Journal of Personality and Social Psychology, 82*, 359–378.

Deutsch, F. M. (1999). *Halving it all: How equally shared parenting works*. Cambridge, MA: Harvard University Press.

Diekman, A. B., & Eagly, A. H. (2000). Stereotypes as dynamic constructs: Women and men of the past, present, and future. *Personality and Social Psychology Bulletin, 26*, 1171–1188.

Eagly, A. H., Wood, W., & Diekman, A. B. (2000). Social role theory of sex differences and similarities: A current appraisal. In T. Eckes & H. M. Trautner (Eds.), *The developmental social psychology of gender* (pp. 123–174). Mahwah, NJ: Lawrence Erlbaum Associates.

Galinsky, A. D., Gruenfeld, D. H., & Magee, J. C. (2003). From power to action. *Journal of Personality and Social Psychology, 85*, 453–466.

Grote, N. K., & Clark, M. S. (2001). Perceiving unfairness in the family: Cause or consequence of marital distress? *Journal of Personality and Social Psychology, 80*, 281–293.

Hazan, C., & Shaver, P. R. (1990). Love and work: An attachment theoretical perspective. *Journal of Personality and Social Psychology, 59*, 270–280.

Hochschild, A. (with A. Machung) (1989). *The second shift*. New York: Avon.

Izraeli, D. N. (1994). Money matters: Spousal incomes and family/work relations among physician couples in Israel. *The Sociological Quarterly, 35*, 69–84.

Jackson, L. M., Esses, V. M., & Burris, C. T. (2001). Contemporary sexism and discrimination: The importance of respect for men and women. *Personality and Social Psychology Bulletin, 27*, 48–61.

Johannsen-Schmidt, M. C., & Eagly, A. H. (2002). Diminishing returns: The effects of income on the content of stereotypes of wage earners. *Personality and Social Psychology Bulletin, 28*, 1538–1545.

Kallgren, C. A., Reno, R. R., & Cialdini, R. B. (2000). A focus theory of normative conduct: When norms do and do not affect behavior. *Personality and Social Psychology Bulletin, 26*, 1002–1012.

Major, B., Granzow, R. H., McCoy, S. K., Levin, S., Schmader, T., & Sidanius, J. (2002). Perceiving personal discrimination: The role of group status and legitimizing ideology. *Journal of Personality and Social Psychology, 82*, 269–282.

Mikulincer, M., & Shaver, P. R. (2003). The attachment behavioral system in adulthood: Activation, psychodynamics, and interpersonal processes. In M. P. Zanna (Ed.), *Advances in experimental social psychology* (vol. 35, pp. 53–152). San Diego, CA: Elsevier Science.

Milgram, S. (1963). Behavioral study of obedience. *Journal of Abnormal and Social Psychology, 67*, 371–378.

Mook, D. G. (1983). In defense of external invalidity. *The American Psychologist, 38*, 379–387.

Rholes, W. S., Simpson, J. A., Campbell, L., & Grich, J. (2001). Adult attachment and the transition to parenthood. *Journal of Personality and Social Psychology, 81*, 421–435.

Risman, B. (1986). Can men "mother"? Life as a single father. *Family Relations, 35*, 95–102.

Rudman, L. A., & Kilianski, S. E. (2000). Implicit and explicit attitudes toward female authority. *Personality and Social Psychology Bulletin, 26*, 1315–1328.

Ryan, R. M., & Deci, E. L. (2000). Self-determination theory and the facilitation of intrinsic motivation, social development, and well-being. *American Psychologist, 55*, 68–78.

Senecal, C., Vallerand, R. J., & Guay, F. (2001). Antecedents and outcomes of work-family conflict: Toward a motivational model. *Personality and Social Psychology Bulletin, 27*, 176–186.

Sheldon, K. M., Elliot, A. J., Kim, Y., & Kasser, T. (2001). What is satisfying about satisfying events? Testing 10 candidate psychological needs. *Journal of Personality and Social Psychology, 80*, 325–339.

Sherif, M., & Sherif, C. (1953). *Groups in harmony and tension*. New York: Harper & Brothers.

Simpson, J. A., Rholes, W. S., Campbell, L., Tran, S., & Wilson, C. (2003). Adult attachment, the transition to parenthood, and depressive symptoms. *Journal of Personality and Social Psychology, 84*, 1172–1187.

Stewart, T., Vassar, P. M., Sanchez, D. T., & David, S. E. (2000). Attitude toward women's societal roles moderates the effect of gender cues on target individuation. *Journal of Personality and Social Psychology, 79*, 143–157.

Tichenor, V. J. (1999). Status and income as gendered resources: The case of marital power. *Journal of Marriage and the Family, 61*, 638–650.

Twenge, J. M. (2001). Changes in women's assertiveness in response to status and roles: A cross-temporal meta-analysis, 1931–1993. *Journal of Personality and Social Psychology, 81*, 133–145.

Vasquez, K., Durik, A. M., & Hyde, J. S. (2002). Family and work: Implications of adult attachment styles. *Personality and Social Psychology Bulletin, 28*, 874–886.

Vescio, T. K., Snyder, M., & Butz, D. A. (2003). Power in stereotypically masculine domains: A social influence strategy X stereotype match model. *Journal of Personality and Social Psychology, 85*, 1062–1078.

von Hippel, W., Hawkins, C., & Schooler, J. W. (2001). Stereotype distinctiveness: How counterstereotic behavior shapes the self-concept. *Journal of Personality and Social Psychology, 81*, 193–205.

West, C., & Zimmerman, H. (1987). Doing gender. *Gender and Society, 1*, 125–151.

12

Sociological Perspectives on Families and Work: The Import of Gender, Class, and Race

Naomi Gerstel
University of Massachusetts Amherst

Natalia Sarkisian
Boston College

Since the late 1970s, sociological analyses of work and family have emphasized gender. For its time, this emphasis was a key innovation. But, it is not enough. Although we can occasionally speak of women or of men as a group, we often must attend to variation within each gender group to understand the relationship of families and work. This chapter reviews contemporary sociological research and theories on families and work, describing and explaining differences and similarities across gender, class, and race. More specifically, it concentrates on the work that families do, focusing on unpaid family labor and specifying its relationship to paid work. In particular, we argue that we can explain much of the variation in unpaid family work with variation in paid work across gender, race, and class.

To begin, we first discuss definitions of gender, race, and class that sociologists use. Second, we turn to a discussion of two broad theoretical frameworks that seek to explain variation in unpaid family work: first, a "structural" model that stresses the power of paid work, and second, a "cultural" approach that stresses the role of values and ideology. Third, we turn to the empirical research on unpaid family work and its links to paid work and values. Many discussions of paid and unpaid work focus on housework or parenting, often among married couples. Incorporating race and class, we suggest, helps us move beyond this narrow nuclear family model, with its scant attention to resident and nonresident single parents as well as extended kin. Therefore, in this part of the chapter we address three types of unpaid family work: housework, parenting, and kin work. Finally, we conclude by returning to the theories to assess how effectively they frame and explain the variations in these three types of unpaid family work.

DEFINITION AND OPERATIONALIZATION: GENDER, RACE, AND CLASS

Although gender, race, and class are central to sociological analysis, there is a fair amount of disagreement about definitions and operationalizations of these terms. Even the term "gender" has been subject to much debate in recent years. Many still use "gender" to denote the social and psychological characteristics—masculine/feminine—organized around a binary biological model of male/female. Because of the kind of data typically available, this definition is most often employed, at least implicitly and by default, especially in quantitative analyses that treat gender as a variable and examine statistical differences between women and men. But, it is not the only definition: Others claim "gender" goes far beyond such individual differences. A frequent critique suggests that gender is relational—not something that we are, but something that we do or perform in our interactions with others. Suggesting that gender is relational means that women and men act out gender with one another. It also means that the performances of gender by women and men are connected, even when they do not interact face-to-face. Others add that gender is cultural—a symbolic representation both imposed on and internalized by women and men. Studies that draw upon field work—with its observations and intensive open-ended interviews—are particularly likely to use and elaborate such definitions of gender. Still others suggest gender is a key principle of stratification in both paid and unpaid work: It is built into and shapes institutions that subordinate women to men—such as the economy, families, and state. Analyses of changing labor markets and state policies use this view of gender. (For discussions of the uses of the term gender, see Lorber, 1994; Risman, 1998; Nakano Glenn, 2002.) In our discussion of family and work, we include research using all these definitions, but face limits stemming both from commonly used definitions and the ways research typically operationalizes gender. Taken together, however, these definitions suggest that the image and experience of gender vary, not only across historical periods, but also across race and class.

Discussions of how to define race in many ways parallel discussions of gender. Few sociologists believe that genetic variation and the resulting differences in human bodies, like skin color or other physical attributes, are responsible for the complex social patterns we associate with different races. Some even argue race is purely a historically constructed ideology, invented as a tool of domination that has no basis in objective or bodily reality (e.g., Fields, 1990). Others reject the position that race exists only in the realm of ideology but adopt a relational definition of race, which, like the relational definition of gender, holds that racial categories are fluid, linked, and shaped by shifting social, political, and economic forces that determine their content and organize them as cultural representations and social relations of domination (Omi & Winant, 1994; Almaguer, 1994). Numerous historical studies document the social construction of a White racial identity in opposition to others—whether in the entry of Irish-Americans into the "white race" in 19th-century America (Ignatiev, 1995) or the reclassification of the Chinese in Mississippi from Black to White (Loewen, 1971). Most of the work-family literature, however, takes race as a given, albeit one based in social designations. In quantitative work, race categories are typically based on respondents' self-reports of racial identity (often limited to a small number of categories chosen by those who design the survey), whereas ethnographic studies, using observations and self-reports, more often allow for multiple memberships (but rarely report them as such). In our synthesis of the work-family research, we do not have any choice but to rely on the racial designations used by the researchers, even though we emphasize the limitations of these designations.

Social scientists often use the term "race" when discussing Blacks or Asians, and "ethnicity" when discussing Latinos/as. Therefore, many use the term "race/ethnicity" when discussing these groups at the same time. This distinction between race and ethnicity, however, has been repeatedly challenged as rooted in historical relations of inequality and having no other empirical basis (Nakano Glenn, 2002). In light of these arguments as well as for the sake of brevity, we use the terms "race" and "racial" throughout the chapter.

Although most sociological literature identifies White/Euro-American, Black/African American, Latino/Hispanic, and Asian American as the main racial groups, these labels and their definitions have also been the subject of much contention. This contention culminated with the changes in the 2000 census, which allowed individuals to designate themselves as members of more than one race category (as 2.4 % did). Although this revision begins to capture the reality of race as a social and individual construction rather than an immutable biological fact, it also makes assignment of individuals to one category by researchers problematic and thus makes it more difficult to interpret census data on trends over time.

We should also note from the outset that although the literature on race has grown in recent years, we are still quite limited in our ability to discuss the range of racialized experiences of families and work. Most relevant research compares Whites with Blacks; less examines Latinos/as and still less focuses on other racial categories. In addition, research that finds difference among racial categories (often at some specified level of statistical significance) is more likely to be reported and published than research that shows similarity among them. (For a similar critique of research on gender, see Epstein, 1988.) Moreover, existing research on race tends to focus on differences across broad racial categories rather than differences and/or similarities within them. For example, in the work-family literature studying Latinos/as, almost no research compares Mexican Americans with Puerto Ricans or Cubans. Even less research compares Japanese Americans, Chinese Americans, Vietnamese Americans or Cambodian Americans, or even East Asians and South Asians, within the "Asian American" category. This is unfortunate given that some comparative demographic and a small amount of ethnographic research on individual groups insists there are important distinctions among groups originating from different countries (see, for example, Hein, forthcoming).

In terms of class, we face limits stemming both from the commonly used definitions and the ways they are analyzed. In the research on families and work, especially quantitative analyses, a gradational notion of social class—a version of upper-, middle-, and lower-class division— is most common, typically operationalized as some combination of income, education, and occupation. Critics point out that such a procedure places people on a continuum and then, rather arbitrarily, breaks them up into categories, instead of specifying groups of actors with collective interests and relationships, often adversarial to other groups. These critics champion a relational definition of social class, most often identifying three classes: working class, managers/professionals, and employers.[1] As is the case with the relational definitions of gender and race, however, this specification is rarely used in the families and work literature (Wright, 1997). Most family/work scholars look at classes as independent entities with more or less fixed characteristics. Few look at the relationship among classes or how the privileges of one class are contingent on the disadvantages associated with another. In this review, we introduce those few pieces that do examine the relations between classes; by and large, however, we present findings from the research that treats classes as distinct entities. Even within this tradition, our discussion of class is limited by the greater availability of research on the middle class and poor than on the working or upper class.

In addition, whatever the definition of social class, scholars assume that entire families are of the same class. Some years ago, however, feminist theorists (e.g., Acker, 1973) were deeply embroiled in arguments about determining the class position of *families*: Does the family have a unitary class position? If so, is it determined by the husband's class position or is the family's class position some additive combination of the class of spouses? And, how does unpaid work count? This debate emerged when many families, especially among the White middle class, had only one earner. As more and more couples became dual earners, however, the question of a family's class position determination became even more complicated. On the one hand, families tend to be units of consumption, and therefore we could define a family's class affiliation based on its consumer power. On the other hand, not only do employed husbands and employed wives have a different relationship to the means of production and different experiences on the job, but a fair amount of research also suggests family members do not even share their money (Sorensen & McLanahan, 1987) and differ in their class identification strategies (Yamaguchi & Wang, 2002). To resolve these divisions, Wright (1997) suggested considering using two class locations: "direct" (based on one's own job) and "mediated" (based on other family members' jobs). Much contemporary research on class and paid and unpaid work, however, focuses only on direct class locations.

Furthermore, few studies examine the family/work relationships for lesbians and gays (for exceptions, see the review by Marks in this volume as well as Carrington, 1999; Dalton & Bielby, 2000; Hequembourg, 2002; Reimann, 1997; Sullivan, 2000), much less their variation by race and class. Although the examination of gay/lesbian family experiences is sometimes used to disentangle the particular contribution of gender to the division of paid and unpaid labor, for the most part sociological research has yet to develop a body of literature examining these experiences.

Finally, a growing number of scholars argue that we need to attend to the intersection of race, class, and gender when studying families and work. Black feminist scholars who first developed such an intersectional framework pointed out the interlocking nature of race, gender, and class inequalities (Collins, 2000; hooks, 1981). Their primary concern was bringing race/ethnicity to the center of gender studies and studies of class oppression. A significant number of scholars also examine how social class interacts with race, particularly when attempting to explain racial variation with socioeconomic differences. But, there is an asymmetry with regard to gender: Scholars who focus on race, like scholars of class, seem much less responsive to the incorporation of gender into their analyses. We have shown empirically, however, that it is equally important to introduce gender into the studies of race/ethnicity and social class (Sarkisian & Gerstel, 2004b). Unfortunately, few studies in the families and work field conduct such intersectional analyses. In sum, our discussion of paid and unpaid work looks at the intersection of gender, class, and race within the confines of the limitations of available research.

SOCIOLOGICAL THEORIES OF PAID AND UNPAID WORK

Like sociological definitions of gender and race, sociological theories of work and family emerged and were refined in response to essentialist biological and psychological theories. Typically focusing on gender, what are often referred to as "essentialist theories" argue that differences and inequalities in unpaid work are bound up with the biological makeup of women and men and are, by consequence, if not exactly invariant, at least deep and tenacious (Maccoby, 1998; Marini, 1990; Udry, 2000). Sociological theories also supplement and sometimes challenge psychological theories. Often rooting gender differences in early childhood socialization, psychological theories allow far more room for variation among women and among men than do essentialist biological arguments. Much psychological research, however, has been used to explain uniformity among women and among men on grounds of invariance in gender-specific childrearing practices within a given society. Such arguments and theories have been widely criticized by sociologists for ignoring the variation among women and among men (Connell, 1987; Epstein, 1988; Williams, 1993) as well as for their class-biased and ethnocentric assumptions (Collins, 2000; Segura & Pierce, 1993).

In contrast, sociological theories of family and work often seek to explain social distinctions and inequality. Painting them with broad strokes, this chapter highlights two groups of contemporary sociological theories: (a) those that emphasize structural forces and (b) those that focus on cultural influences operating in adult life. We do, however, want to acknowledge the variation within these broad approaches. Within what we term a cultural approach, some may distinguish, for example, Weberian theories that emphasize shared norms, values, and cultural beliefs that create social cohesion from symbolic interactionism that emphasizes symbolic performances—for example, those entailed in "doing gender" (West & Zimmerman, 1987). Within the broad group of structural approaches, some may distinguish conflict theory, and especially Marxist and neo-Marxist versions, that insist on the primacy of group access to material resources and the contingency of class privilege from some version of rational choice theory (sometimes labeled exchange theory) that stresses individual attempts to maximize utility within given opportunities and constraints and emphasizes individual calculation of costs and benefits. Our broad classification is only one rendition of those sociological theoretical frameworks that have shaped discussions, albeit often only implicitly, of families and work. Furthermore, we focus on contemporary sociological theories of family and work and omit those sociological theories rarely used in discussions of families and work today. This omits, for example, the well-known but now often derided functionalist perspective used by Talcott Parsons half a century ago to explain women's and men's differential involvement in families and work (Parsons & Bales, 1955).

Structural Approach

The first broad sociological approach that we emphasize here—what we are calling the structural approach—currently dominates much of the empirical sociological research on families and work (Epstein, 1988; Gerson, 1993; Lorber, 1994; Risman, 1998; Nakano Glenn, 2002; Gerstel et al., 2002). This approach raises the possibility that if one accounts for structural differences in adult life, variation by gender, race, and class in unpaid work will disappear. Though variously defined, structural factors are typically understood as an array of material and objective constraints and opportunities external to individuals (Hays, 1994; Rubinstein, 2001). Most structural theories assert the primacy of employment in determining involvement in unpaid labor. Employment is deemed important because it imposes restrictions, for example on time or money, that constrain workers' ability to do unpaid work for their nuclear and extended families. It also provides resources and opportunities—which can be opportunities to do unpaid family work (e.g., by allowing flexible schedules or giving access to paid family leaves) as well as opportunities not to do such work (e.g., by making it possible to withdraw from the labor force or purchase paid care).

In terms of gender, structural theories postulate both that the growing similarities between women's and men's paid work explain some of the reallocation of unpaid work and that remaining differences in unpaid work can be explained by their remaining dissimilarities in paid work. Because women and men still have differential access to jobs and access to different types of jobs, men's jobs are more likely to pull or push them away from family responsibilities than women's jobs. Over the last few decades, women—including married women and women with very young children—have joined the labor force in unprecedented numbers. Nevertheless, men, especially married men and fathers, are still more likely to be in the labor force than married women and mothers. Over that same time period, the gender gap in income has narrowed (Blau & Kahn, 2000).[2] Women today, however, still make only 75.5 cents for every dollar that men earn. Moreover, in about three quarters of dual-earner couples, the husband still earns more than his wife; although the numbers are growing, in only about one third of couples in which both spouses work full-time does the wife earn more than the husband (Ameristat, 2002). Women's hours of paid work have also steadily risen. Among the employed (which, of course, excludes those looking for a job as well as those who have exited from the labor force), however, men still spend, on average, more hours on paid work that do women: Employed U.S. men work an average of about 43 hours while employed women work an average of 36 hours per week for pay (Jacobs & Gerson, 2004).

Structural theorists would predict that such changes and differences in paid work are key in the allocation of unpaid work. In general, they predict a movement, although a limited one, toward equality in the division of unpaid work. They emphasize that job effects are cumulative over the life course (Elder & Crosnoe, 2002; Moen, 2003). Some structural theorists also emphasize that changes in state policy—whether revisions in labor regulations, in the provision of child care, or welfare policy—shape paid work, which in turn contributes to changes in the allocation of unpaid work.

Structural influences are also often used to account for the racial differences in unpaid work in nuclear and extended families. Structural theorists argue that the concentration of minorities in less lucrative positions, characterized by lack of promotion opportunities, little job stability, and frequently nonstandard work hours, explains racial variation in the breadth and allocation of unpaid labor. Lower incomes and other characteristics of minority jobs such as lack of promotion opportunities affect the formation and stability of marriages, and therefore increase the prevalence of single mothers and nonresident fathers who in turn have distinctive patterns of balancing work and family. At the same time, low incomes as well as the inability to rely on marital ties are regarded as a motivation for extended family integration that can be used to help make ends meet.[3]

Some also note that gender differences vary by race. For example, Black wives provide almost $4 out of every $10 of household income, compared with about $3 out of $10 for both White and Latina working wives. These differences would lead structural theorists to expect more equality in the division of unpaid labor among Black than White or Latinos/as couples. They might also be associated with lower rates of marriage and unwed parenthood, which in turn shape paid and unpaid work.

In explaining class differences in the division of paid and unpaid labor, structural theories of inequality are often viewed as the only possible framework. In fact, individuals' class position is usually defined in terms of their employment characteristics. This makes it impossible to assess separately the role of employment conditions and class differences in discussions of the relationship of paid and unpaid work. Not all scholars, however, agree with such a purely structural view of social class, suggesting instead that social class distinctions also entail or reflect cultural differences: For instance, some document the cultural processes underlying the intergenerational transmission of class by arguing that one's social class is closely linked to childrearing values (Kohn & Schooler, 1983; Lareau, 2003). By and large, however, scholars of families and work equate social class differences with structural differences. Therefore, the notion of social class is usually employed as an explanatory factor rather than a phenomenon in need of explanation.

Cultural Approach

A second set of sociological theories traces differences in unpaid family labor to the *cultural factors* that operate in adult life. Even though cultural theories have again become fashionable in sociology, only a limited number of studies of families and work empirically examine their propositions. Much of the culture literature in the work and families area, and particularly the qualitative studies, focuses on in-depth understanding of the meaning attached to paid and unpaid work and is usually not primarily constructed to make causal arguments. Much of the literature that does consider cultural explanations for the inequalities in unpaid family work uses a rather limited notion of culture. It usually focuses on individuals' own cultural beliefs and ideologies and the extent to which these beliefs shape involvement in unpaid, as well as paid, work. This literature addresses three sets of cultural beliefs: (a) gender ideologies (especially those concerning what men's and women's roles should be in paid and unpaid labor and nurturance), (b) beliefs concerning the importance of employment, and (c) beliefs concerning the importance of extended family.

A fair amount of literature finds some differences across gender, race, and class in all three sets of ideologies. Across race and class, women hold more egalitarian gender ideologies than do men. These ideologies also differ by race and class: Most research suggests that Blacks hold more egalitarian views than Euro-Americans, whereas Latinos/as, especially Latino men (Sarkisian et al., 2004), hold less liberal views. In terms of class, many argue that working-class men have more traditional gender ideologies and middle-class men more egalitarian ones (Perry-Jenkins & Folk, 1994). There is some evidence that class differences in gender ideologies vary by race. Among Whites, above-average-income men and women hold more egalitarian gender attitudes than those with less income; among Blacks, there are no significant differences by class. Among Latinos/as, wealthier men are more traditional and among Asians, wealthier men and women both hold more traditional attitudes about gender (Aranda, 1998).

The second set of values—centrality of employment—is less represented in research, but some gender, racial, and social class differences have been documented. A study conducted a decade ago found that in general women are less job-centered than men, although further specification finds this primarily among middle-class individuals (Mannheim, 1993). Furthermore, comparing the relative priorities of jobs and families that parents set for their children,[4] Hill and Sprague (1999) found that jobs as long-term goals are more a priority for Black than White parents. But, while Black parents order priorities the same way across class, the priorities of Whites vary substantially by class, with jobs the top priority of working-class Whites and family the top priority for upper-middle-class White parents, especially if they have girls.

Finally, for the third set of values—ideologies concerning the importance of extended families—some report that women find extended kin more important than men (Finley, 1989; Rossi & Rossi, 1990). Many also show that minorities place more value on extended families than do Whites (Connell & Gibson, 1997; Lee, Peek, & Coward, 1998; Sarkisian et al., 2004; Sarkisian & Gerstel, 2004b), although some argue that for Latinos/as and Asians these differences attenuate with acculturation (Rogler & Santana Cooney, 1991; Rumbaut, 1997). Overall, albeit limited, research does find some gender, race, and class differences in internalized cultural beliefs. These differences, according to cultural theories, should shape the inequalities in unpaid as well as paid family work.

In the following sections, we discuss the findings of research on paid and unpaid work. As we will suggest, some of it lends support—often only implicitly—to structural and/or cultural theories. Where possible, we highlight differences and similarities across gender, race, and class—as we attempt to assess the extent to which these are, or can be, tied to structural and/or cultural factors.

RESEARCH ON PAID AND UNPAID WORK

Although often masked by an ideology of the family as a private unit held together by the emotional attachment of its members, economic bonds have been a crucial component of family life throughout U.S. history. In the middle class, the marriage bargain that developed in the 19th century and continued for much of the 20th century involved an exchange, at least according to the prescriptions of the day: Husbands provided income from jobs and received wives' unpaid family labor in return (see the Boris chapter in this volume for a discussion of the history of the emergence of this bargain). Research suggests, however, that the character of economic bonds within families has always depended not only on gender but also on class and race, and continues to do so today. In this section, we look at these intersections by examining contemporary allocation of three kinds of family work: (a) housework, (b) parenting, and (c) kin work.

Housework

Unpaid Housework

Housework, across race and class, remains women's work: Wives still cook, clean, shop, and manage domestic routines more than their husbands. Although even single women do more housework than single men, the gap grows when they marry—men start doing even less, and women begin to do even more (Gupta, 1999). This looks like the old marriage bargain—or, rather, a modified version of that bargain: The gender difference in housework does not reflect equality in total workload (combining paid and unpaid labor) of husbands and wives.

To be sure, Bianchi, Robinson, and Milkie (forthcoming) did find that it is "housework that is the big casualty of increased market work" (p. 192). They found that the hours mothers spent on housework sharply declined during the period when their labor force participation accelerated: Over the last three decades, the average amount of time that mothers spent on housework declined from 32 to 19 hours a week. Notably, women—especially employed women and single mothers—seem to be lowering their housework standards (Coltrane, 2000). Such findings seem to confirm structural arguments about the primacy of paid employment in explaining women's unpaid work. Moreover, numerous studies show that the amount and proportion of household income that women earn, the time they spend on the job, and their job prestige are all negatively associated with the time they spend on housework (Bianchi et al., 2000; Hundley, 2000; for a review of earlier research, see Coltrane, 2000). These findings again suggest the explanatory power of the structural model.[5]

The story is more complicated for husbands. Bianchi et al. (forthcoming) found fathers' hours of housework more than doubled from 1965 to 1985, although they have leveled off since then. Nevertheless, husbands still only "help": They do far less housework than their wives and rarely initiate or manage housework. By 2000, men averaged 9.7 hours per week (about half of what women do). Some scholars even argue that married men do less housework than they create (Shelton & John, 1993; Thompson & Walker, 1991).

Studies of the effects of employment on men's housework are inconsistent (see Coltrane, 2000 for a detailed review of the effects of employment characteristics on men's housework). Most studies suggest that the model for men parallels that for women and similarly supports a structural perspective: Men who do fewer hours of paid work and/or earn less do more housework, although employment characteristics explain much less variance in men's housework than in women's. Other research links men's housework to their wives' employment status, hours, and earnings and finds that by and large, husbands whose wives work more and earn more money do more housework.

Some studies, however, suggest that these findings do not hold across the full range of employment hours and incomes. Importantly, these studies argue that husbands whose wives earn more and husbands without jobs do less domestic work (Brines, 1994; Greenstein, 2000; Bittman et al., 2003). Similar results are reported in qualitative studies (Hochschild & Machung, 2003; Tichenor, 1999). These often-cited findings have led to the claim that culture—especially the centrality of paid work to men's identities and the need to perform heightened masculinity when unemployed or earning less than their wives—explains why such men do less housework. Other research has also suggested that culture matters in determining housework involvement. It shows that some women still do not want to fully share housework because they believe it central to their gender identity and a source of power in the family (Coltrane, 2000). And husbands, whose gender identity is traditionally rooted in paid work, do not object to doing less housework than their wives (Lennon & Rosenfield, 1994). Recent studies, however, find an ideological shift: A growing proportion of women want more help from their husbands. So what happens when one or both spouses have more egalitarian gender ideologies?

Most of the studies that examine the relationship of gender ideologies and housework show that the more egalitarian a husband's gender ideology, the more time he spends doing housework (Coltrane, 2000). And, they find that the more egalitarian a wife's gender ideology, the less time she spends and the more time her husband spends doing housework (Brayfield, 1992; Presser, 1994; Harpster & Monk-Turner, 1998; Pittman & Blanchard, 1996). Research is mixed about whether the ideology of the wife or the husband matters more. Some suggest that one's own attitudes affect one's housework more directly than spouse's attitudes (Baxter, 1993). Others argue that what matters the most is the fit between spouses' attitudes (Greenstein, 1996; MacDermid et al., 1990).

This body of research has mixed implications regarding the explanatory power of the cultural framework. On the one hand, this research on gender ideologies would seem to suggest culture plays a role in determining the allocation of housework. On the other hand, in most of the studies, ideology accounts for only a small portion of variation in husbands' and wives' housework. Furthermore, the research that examines the effects of ideologies on housework does not study how the characteristics of spouses' employment affect ideologies themselves.

Whatever the cause for its unequal distribution by gender, housework often further limits women's ability to achieve financial independence. Researchers (e.g., Noonan, 2001; Hersch & Stratton, 1997) have found that doing housework, especially "feminine" chores, has a negative effect on women's wages. It also affects men's wages, but the size of the wage penalty is larger for women, and they do substantially more housework. Thus, a wife's assumption of housework promotes, and sometimes makes possible, her husband's involvement in his job at the expense of her own. This suggests that employment not only shapes unpaid work but also can be influenced by it.

The gendered division of housework is not, however, identical across racial groups. Research has shown that Black husbands perform a somewhat larger share of housework and spend somewhat more time on it than White husbands (Kamo & Cohen, 1998; McLoyd, Cauce, Takeuchi, & Wilson, 2000; Shelton & John, 1993). And, although Latino husbands do not differ from White husbands in their share of housework, Latinos' hours of housework are higher than those of White men. Latinos spend more time on "feminine" tasks, especially if they are employed part-time or not at all, or if their wives are employed (Coltrane & Valdez, 1993).

Some scholars explicitly attribute race differences in housework to material conditions (McAdoo, 1980; Staples, 1988), often claiming that the greater share of housework performed by men of color derives from their lower incomes relative to women. Studies that compare the division of unpaid labor in different social classes indicate that working-class husbands do more hours of housework overall and more "feminine" tasks than middle-class husbands (Coltrane, 1996; Gutmann, 1996). Furthermore, the findings on gender ideology, race, and class confirm the power of the structural perspective, as the class and race differences in ideological positions often operate in the opposite direction from the actual division of housework. Working-class men who are more traditional in their gender ideologies (Perry-Jenkins & Folk, 1994) do more housework than middle-class ones. And, Latinos who appear to hold less egalitarian views than Whites (Aranda, 1998; Hill & Sprague, 1999; Yancey, 2001; Sarkisian et al., 2004) do more hours of housework than Whites. Only for Blacks is the difference in ideology consistent with the difference in behavior: Across class, Black men's more egalitarian views are reflected in performing more housework than White men.

Variation by gender, race, and class exists not only in the unpaid work of women and men but also in the unpaid work of children. Overall, children are a lot like men: They "help." That is, they do not do very much housework. Some suggest this is a part of parents' ideology of childhood. Today's parents maintain an ideology of the "economically costly" but "emotionally priceless" child (Zelizer, 1994). This entails a vision of a child whose development depends on intensive emotional nurturance, something that, in the modern parent's mind, seems to contradict an insistence on work. Therefore, parents feel ambivalent about getting their kids to do more housework (Goldscheider & Waite, 1991). If they ask their children to do chores, parents say it is because they want to teach them a sense of family, not because they need their help (White & Brinkerhoff, 1981). As they grow up, adult children who remain in their parents' household increase their share of housework but nevertheless do only a small fraction of what needs to get done (Spitze & Ward, 1995). Overall, whether minor or adult, children increase rather than reduce the workload of families.

But, importantly, children's contributions vary by gender: Girls do twice as much as boys (Goldschneider & Waite, 1998). And, their chores vary by gender, too: Girls (like their mothers) do dishes, cleaning, and laundry while boys (like their fathers) do outside chores, consisting primarily of yardwork. Some research has demonstrated that this gender gap in children's housework is related to their parents' (especially mothers') employment characteristics (Benin & Edwards, 1990). In two-parent households where mothers are employed full-time, this gender gap is considerably larger than it is in households where mothers are employed either part-time or not all. Children's own employment experiences might matter as well. A significant proportion of teenagers (about 40%) are employed (Johnson & Lino, 2000), although the numbers are declining, especially among young Black men (Offner & Holzer, 2002). And, although there is little difference in the level of employment of teenage boys and girls, boys' wages are higher than girls'. We might expect that these differences in wages could be related to differential involvement in housework, but no literature directly examines this relationship. Nor has any research explored the role of gender ideologies—whether parents' or children's—in shaping the gender differential in housework.

Furthermore, no research examines the extent to which race or class interacts with gender to shape children's housework. The research does find, however, a racial gap in children's housework: Latino/a and Black children perform greater amounts of housework than their White counterparts (Blair, 2000), perhaps suggesting varying ideologies of childhood across race or varying economic conditions. The latter model receives indirect support from the research that shows that the amount of children's housework indeed depends on household needs: Children in poor families (Dodson & Dickert, 2004), dual-earner families (Benin & Edwards, 1990), and single-mother families (White & Brinkerhoff, 1981) help more with housework.

Housework for Pay

Housework is not only allocated within households between women and men, boys and girls; it is allocated across households—as wealthier women hire other women to do housework for pay. Although far too little research looks at how the privileges of one class or race are contingent on the disadvantages associated with another class or race, research on this transfer of housework makes such contingencies eminently clear. When they can afford it, many families hire poorer women (often women of color) to do the work of the home. So, too, newly created food, laundry, and cleaning services employ low-paid labor to provide much of the unpaid work once provided at home.

The acquisition and provision of such services is a source of gender, race, and class inequality within and across households. Within households, the more power wives have, the more their families spend on such services. Across households, those with more money use more domestic services, even though Blacks with resources equivalent to those of Whites still spend less on such services (Cohen, 1998). In turn, career successes of middle-class women are often predicated on their transfer of housework to others, and therefore, ironically, on the devaluation of "women's work." This devaluation, stemming from the view that housework is women's labor of love and therefore does not require much skill or effort, is used by the affluent to justify the low wages given to those who do domestic labor for pay.

For providers of such services—usually poor women of color, often women who have recently immigrated (Rollins, 1985)—this low-paid work is one of the few employment opportunities available. Paid domestic work, therefore, creates a labor market ghetto, reproducing hierarchical relations of gender and race. In major cities like Los Angeles, Washington, DC, Houston, and San Francisco, women, often from Central America, work as nannies and housekeepers who sometimes live with the families who employ them. These workers, especially those who live-in, often feel isolated, earn subminimum wages, and work round the clock (Hodagneu-Sotelo, 2001).

The 1996 welfare reform—the Personal Responsibility and Work Opportunity Reconciliation Act (PRWORA)—forces increasing numbers of poor women, including many nonimmigrant women of color, to enter such low-paid service occupations. The Act eliminated the federal entitlement program, Aid to Families with Dependent Children (AFDC), and created a new program called Temporary Assistance for Needy Families (TANF), which limits assistance to 5 years over a lifetime and stresses employment (as well as marriage) as the way off welfare. A significant number of jobs that poor women moving off welfare find are service jobs to provide care in and out of households—including cleaning services and child care (Loprest, 2002). These jobs provide low wages with minimal chance for mobility (Jencks & Swingle, 2000). Consequently, most who find jobs do not leave poverty (Blalock, Tiller, & Monroe, 2004). Instead, they are forced to shoulder the increased hardships of combining employment with unpaid carework. These economic hardships are also felt unequally across race: TANF's negative effects are felt disproportionately by African American women, Latinas, and immigrant women (Primus, 1996). Thus, welfare reform intensifies inequalities by class and race (Harrington Meyer & Herd, forthcoming): It helps maintain the position of those affluent, White families who can obtain cheap services from those forced off welfare. Here again, we see how changes in social structure—in the form of state policy shaping paid work—reinforce racial, gender, and class inequality in paid and unpaid work.

Paid Work and Parenting

Parenting remains one of the prime sites of a gender gap—whether we look at two-parent families or single-parent families. In this section, we begin with a broad discussion of mothering and then of fathering. Next, we turn to single parents—both those who share a home with their children and those who do not. Because any discussion of parenting—especially one attentive to race and class divides—is incomplete without a discussion of parenting as paid work, we conclude this section on parenting by examining such paid care. We review empirical research on the ways such experiences of parenting vary not just by gender but also by race and class, and the extent to which structural and cultural models can explain this variation.

Mothering

Across race and class and regardless of marital status, childrearing remains a paramount commitment in mothers' lives. It is often a primary arena in which women express creativity and affection, exercise authority, as well as work out unconscious desires rooted in their own experience as children. Just as women in two-parent households continue to do most of the housework, such mothers continue to do most of the parenting. Here, too, the fathers "help."

Paid employment does not explain this gender gap in parenting entirely: Even mothers employed full-time in demanding careers spend far more time with their children than do their husbands. The birth of a child often makes it even more difficult for those unusual couples that share housework to continue to do so. Because the demands of caring for a baby are unremitting, there is less time to share and more need to specialize. Heterosexual couples usually specialize along gender lines: They invest energy in the husband's job. The mother's share of child care, in turn, expands (Morgan & Waite, 1987). Couples also adjust their gender ideas to that specialization: They become more traditional in their ideas about family and work after the birth of a child. Consequently, most parents, however they divide child care, come to believe that the division is fair (Lennon & Rosenfield, 1994).

Yet the parenting women cherish limits time for other areas of life—spouses, friendships, organizational and civic life (Bianchi et al., forthcoming), but especially employment. Parenting makes it far more difficult for mothers to invest in their jobs (Daniels & Weingarten, 1982). On the one hand, nowhere has the increased employment of women been more dramatic than among married mothers of young children. Such mothers are much less likely to drop out of the labor force today than just a decade ago, even though the dropout rates remain somewhat higher among those with less education and lower wages (Smith & Fields, 2004). On the other hand, mothers still tend to curtail hours on the job that conflict with periods when their young children are at home (Bianchi, 2000). Here again, we witness a way in which unpaid work shapes paid employment. But, the reasons it does so are likely both ideological and structural: Because wives tend to make less money than their husbands, because quality child care outside of the home is often unavailable, and because many women—especially married White women—view "intensive" motherhood as central to their sense of womanhood (Hays, 1996), wives are more likely to curtail their hours of paid work to provide care for their children than are husbands.

Surprisingly little is known, however, about how mothers' allocation of time between work hours and child care varies by race and class. We do know that across race and class there is a substantial wage penalty to mothers for giving care, which once again signifies that parenting is not only shaped by but also influences paid employment and its conditions. Avellar and Smock (2003) have shown that this penalty has not diminished over time. In fact, Anderson, Binder, and Krause (2003) showed that the difference in hourly wages between workers who are mothers and those who are not is now larger than the difference in hourly wages between men and women. Researchers disagree about whether this "wage penalty for motherhood" differs by race: Some argue that Black mothers bear a smaller penalty than White mothers, if they bear one at all (Waldfogel, 1997), even though others find no difference by race (Anderson et al., 2003; Budig & England, 2001).

The lower wage penalty for Black mothers, if it exists, may be a result of the greater contribution that minority mothers, on average, make to family economic well-being in dual-earner families. Even when they are married, there is some evidence that African American mothers are substantially less likely than Latina or Asian mothers and somewhat less likely than White mothers to drop out of the labor force to become full-time mothers (Barron & Mykita, 2004). And, while White mothers often associate motherhood primarily with the emotion and unpaid tasks of the home, for poor and minority women, paid work is often a highly valued part of mothering (Collins, 2002; Nakano Glenn, 1994; Segura, 1994). Although for many years White feminists have seen unpaid family work as the primary site of women's oppression, minority women—Blacks, Asians, and Latinas—consider their marriages and families more generally a unit of survival and a source of resistance against racism and classism in larger society, even if they acknowledge that these families are a site of patriarchal power (Collins, 2002; Kibria, 1990; Moon, 2003; Nakano Glenn, 1994). As the mother's role as a provider ensures survival, childrearing has to be shared among men and women, elders, and children, creating a system of community parenting often referred to as "othermothering" (Collins, 1994; Stack & Burton, 1998) but also "otherfathering" (Lempert, 1999).

Fathering

Research suggests that over the last few decades, as more and more mothers have entered the labor force, residential fathers (i.e., fathers who live with their children) have begun to spend more time caring for their kids (Bianchi et al., forthcoming). Men, however, face less of a wage penalty than women for family-related job interruptions (Huang, 2004). Most fathers, moreover, maintain full involvement in their jobs or careers because their wives assume primary responsibility for child care. Although stay-at-home dads have received much press in recent years and their number has been increasing (Barron & Mykita, 2004), only a small minority (0.5%) of fathers stay at home to provide care for their children, compared to 21% of mothers (Smith & Fields, 2004).

A more salient shift is the transition to a "24-hour economy" that increasingly demands that individuals, including those with children, work in paid jobs outside the regular 9-to-5, Monday through Friday schedule (Presser, 2003a). Minority parents are especially likely to work such nonstandard hours: Even controlling for occupation, Blacks have higher rates of nonstandard shifts than Latinos/as or Whites (Presser, 2003b)—an effect of race independent of social class. As a result, working-class and minority spouses increasingly alternate shifts and consequently also share parenting (Presser, 2004; Glass, 1998). Unlike most fathers, alternate shifters change diapers, give baths, and kiss boo-boos. In the process, these working-class fathers become more attached to their children (Deutsch, 1999). Only a small proportion, however, choose alternate shifts *in order* to share parenting (Presser, 2003b). In most cases, they alternate because other employment opportunities are unavailable. This means that despite sharing parenting, such men often cling to conventional gender ideologies (Deutsch, 1999). Their wives often help them in this process: At work at night and at home during the day, mothers "use the cloak of night to render their employment invisible [and] ... to highlight their maternal visibility" (Garey, 1999, p. 138). Here, structural forces operate in contradiction to cultural values, and it is the former that primarily shape what fathers do.

A very different process operates among fathers in another growing sector of the labor force—professional/managerial occupations like those in Silicon Valley's high-tech economy. On the job 50 or more hours a week, these workers often express an ideological commitment to fatherhood and to an equal division of domestic labor with their wives. Few enact it. Their workplaces are dominated by the cultural assumption that professional/managerial workers do not have any outside obligations; this operates as a mechanism of control that excludes family responsibilities for all but a very small number of exhausted superdads (Cooper, 2002).

Finally, while fatherhood experiences undoubtedly vary by race, much of the literature that compares residential fathers on a variety of parenting tasks suggests that Black, Latino, and White residential fathers are quite similar in terms of their paternal involvement (Harris, Furstenberg, & Marmer, 1998; Julian, McKenry, & McKelvey, 1994; Toth & Xu, 1999; Wilcox, 2002). And, whatever differences exist usually can be explained by structural characteristics of fathers' lives (Ahmeduzzaman & Roopnarine, 1992; Bowman, 1993; Bowman & Forman, 1997; Coley, 1998; Fagan, 1998; Hofferth, 2003; Hudspeth, 2003; Landale & Oropesa, 2001). Thus, even though the media often single out Black and Latino fathers as distinct, often "deadbeat" or at least distant and absent from daily family life, even if they live with their children (Baca Zinn, 1992; Gutmann, 1996; Mirandé, 1997; Roberts, 1998), much research indicates that they only differ insofar as the different structural opportunities and constraints they encounter affect their parental practices.

Single Parents and Nonresident Parents

Although over half of children are still raised by two parents in one home, their numbers are diminishing. In 2003, about three quarters (77%) of White families but only about two thirds of Hispanic families (65%) and a minority (36%) of Black families with children under age 18 included a father and a mother married to each other (U. S. Census Bureau, 2004).[6] To be sure, not all unmarried parents immediately become single or nonresident parents: Approximately one half of nonmarried fathers and mothers are living together when the child is born (Sigle-Rushton & McLanahan, 2002). Similarly, many parents who are currently married will experience spells of single motherhood or nonresident parenthood at some point.

Across race, the vast majority of single parent families are headed by mothers: Even though the number of single fathers is increasing at an even faster rate than the number of single mothers, there are still five times as many single mothers as single fathers. To be sure, single mothers are often poor—whether Asian (14.8%), White (24.1%), Latina (36.4%), or Black (37.4%)—in contrast to 5.3% of married couples (U.S. Census Bureau, 2003). When understanding the sources of these high rates of poverty among single mothers, it is important to distinguish single parenthood that results from a divorce from that which results from non-marital childbearing. In contrast to its effects on men, divorce is a key event in the decline in financial status, often the impoverishment, of White, Mexican-American, and Asian women and children (Stroup & Pollock, 1999; Taylor, 1998). Negligible alimony, unreliable small child-support payments, and lack of state provision have led an increasing number of single mothers to rely on their own typically low earnings. Thus, changing work and family patterns have produced the feminization and juvenilization of poverty. In contrast, divorce rarely throws Black and Puerto Rican mothers into poverty—for them, poverty is a cause of divorce and non-marriage. Research suggests that the poor economic position of Black and Puerto Rican men encourages many Black and Puerto Rican women to leave marriage as well as to forego it altogether (Wilson & Neckerman, 1986).

Consistent with this research, the increase in the proportion of never-married mothers that occurred over the past two decades is especially pronounced among Black and Puerto Rican women. This increase is not a result of increasing rates of adolescent pregnancy. In fact, the rate of teenage pregnancy and childbirth has declined sharply since the late 1950s—with the drop particularly sharp in the last decade for Blacks. Rather, what has happened, especially among Black and Puerto Rican women, is a separation of childbearing from marriage.

Some suggest that this separation and the resulting high level of single motherhood is a result of cultural values. These scholars argue that Black culture is especially characterized by the absence of cultural norms promoting marriage, tolerance for nonmarital childbearing, and a preference for so-called matriarchy, typically implying that Black women prefer to head families themselves and push men away (Moynihan, 1965; Patterson, 1998). These theorists have argued that these internalized cultural factors result in "dysfunctional" single-mother families among Blacks. In the past few decades, these perspectives on minority gender ideologies and their effect on families and work have been repeatedly challenged. Critics argue that the matriarchy argument not only champions the patriarchal nuclear family structure as the norm but also misrepresents the societal position of Black women, who, rather than having a preference for being tough lone mothers, are marginalized by a structure of multiple disadvantage (Baca Zinn, 1989; Collins, 2000; Roschelle, 1997). For example, Furstenberg (2004) suggested that those with low incomes are not against marriage; they do not marry because they believe that stable marriages depend on stable employment with decent wages (and social science evidence supports them).

Unmarried moms, often young and uneducated, face particularly high levels of poverty. This disadvantage, some argue, is further reinforced by recent state policy. While claiming to strengthen the family, recent changes in welfare policy push poor single mothers into the low-wage job market that not only leaves them poor but also makes it harder to care for their children. More than a quarter of welfare recipients work mostly at night and over half struggle to coordinate work schedules with child care. Welfare leavers lose not only money, time, and services but also informal support, especially since they are less able to give care and "giving is as constitutive of communal networks [among the poor] as getting" (Oliker, 2000). They are less able to find the "othermothers" (whether grandmothers or fictive kin) for help in giving care. Consequently, a woman's ability to give care seems to become dependent (again) on financial support from a husband. The new welfare reform in effect and perhaps intentionally reinforces inequality between women and men.

Moreover, this new welfare policy forces single mothers to cooperate in identifying their children's biological fathers and collecting money from them. In doing so, the government insists on the economic dependence of mothers on the biological fathers of their children rather than on the state—children must remain a father's economic responsibility instead of a public responsibility. States are still struggling to set up procedures that comply with these new regulations. Many of the fathers cannot be located. Others simply do not have enough money to pay. In addition, some mothers give false or misleading information to their state's Child Support Enforcement in order to protect the identity of their children's fathers. Mothers mislead the welfare system because state agencies—even with their new mandates—rarely help them get the support they need to survive. These mothers also conceal information because reporting of fathers, which may place them in jail, sometimes makes it impossible for these, often poor, men to continue to offer the financial support and in-kind assistance that they do provide, if only sporadically (Hays, 2003).

To be sure, whereas divorce and nonmarital childbearing often turn women into single resident mothers, many men become nonresident fathers. Like single motherhood, nonresident fatherhood varies substantially by class and race in terms of levels of involvement with children and impact on child development. The more money a nonresident father makes, the more money he contributes toward his child and the more often he visits (Graham & Beller, 1996; Smock & Manning, 1997; Seltzer, Schaeffer, & Charng, 1989). Many poor nonresident fathers desperately want to be a part of their children's lives, but their economic situation makes it difficult for them to provide financial and emotional support to their children (Edin, Lein, & Nelson, 2002). Furthermore, race plays a role: Black men are more likely to be nonresident fathers (Eggebeen, 2002; Taylor, Tucker, Chatters, & Jayakody, 1997) and less likely to pay child support (Garfinkel & McLanahan, 1986; Graham & Beller, 1996; Roberts, 1998). Many of these race differences can be attributed to structural factors: As Black men are more likely to be poor and unemployed, they are less likely to marry or remain married, and less likely to have resources to pay child support (Marsiglio, 1995; McLoyd et al., 2000; Taylor et al., 1997; Tucker & Mitchell-Kernan, 1995).

Despite separate residences, nonpayment of child support, poverty, and even incarceration, many Black nonresident fathers are very involved in the day-to-day work of caring for their children (Hamer, 2001; Lempert, 1999; Samuel, 2002; Thompson & Lawson, 1999). In fact, some researchers find that Black nonresident fathers are as involved as White ones (Seltzer & Bianchi, 1988), and others show Black nonresident fathers are more involved (Mott, 1990; Seltzer, 1991; Stewart, 2004; Stier & Tienda, 1993). Moreover, even though the prevalence of single resident fatherhood is quite low for both groups, Black fathers are significantly more likely than White fathers to head single-parent families (Eggebeen, Snyder, & Manning, 1996). Some also stress Black men's role as "other fathers"—men who, as family members or community members, are deeply involved in parenting children other than their "own" (Lempert, 1999; Whitmore, 1999).

Many scholars argue nonresident fatherhood is linked to numerous negative child outcomes, and they call for policies that might decrease divorce and nonmarital childbearing (McLanahan, 2004; McLanahan & Schwartz, 2002). But numerous critics argue that a father who is unemployed, has a poor relationship with the mother, and may be physically violent would not improve a child's well-being by living in the same household (Scott, London, & Myers, 2002).

Consequently, such critics insist that improvements in the lives of single mothers and their children should come through state provision. They emphasize as well that such improvements should come through economic opportunities for *both* poor men and women.

Parenting (Mothering) For Pay

As more women have entered the labor force, increasing numbers of employed parents rely on others to provide care for their children. Along with widely utilized child-care centers, parents rely on family day-care providers, relatives, neighbors, and nannies. The kind of child care parents use varies greatly by the social class and race of parents.

Child-care centers are the most common and fastest growing nonparental child-care setting in the United States. These centers offer more regulated and higher quality care (on standard measures) and are most often utilized by middle-class and White families (Helburn & Bergmann, 2002). As child care is privately funded, its cost is a significant problem for many parents, but it particularly strains the budgets of poor and single parents. Even though working parents struggle to arrange and pay for private care with its often prohibitive costs, public subsidies for child care go primarily to those with very low incomes, and the majority of families eligible for subsidies do not receive them (Clawson & Gerstel, 2002; Danziger, Ananat, & Browning, 2004). Because women are still held primarily responsible for child care—for reasons both ideological and structural, as discussed above—the inability to find affordable quality care sometimes precludes women's employment or has a depressing effect on their employment hours and wages (Henly & Lyons, 2000; Meyers et al., 2001). This intensifies gender disparities in paid and unpaid labor. Furthermore, it creates disparities in the quality of care that children receive. In many of the child-care arrangements that the poor and minorities can afford to utilize (like family day care), everything possible is done to hold down the expenses, which may have detrimental effects on care quality. In contrast, the more expensive child-care centers used by middle-class Whites appear to bring children numerous benefits.

Around a quarter of parents—especially poor, minorities, and single mothers—rely on relatives, especially grandmothers, to care for their children (Presser, 2003b). Latinas and Black women are more likely than Whites to regard the use of relatives as appropriate (Buriel & Hurtado-Ortiz, 2000; Early & Burchinal, 2001; Becerra & Chi, 1992). Even in the middle class, Black children are raised not just by biological parents but also by a host of kin and neighbors who provide both control and sympathy. As Pattillo-McCoy (1999) argued, however, this is not a result of distinctive values; instead, it is primarily a result of the instability of the middle-class position of Blacks who feel they must rely on extended kin to maintain that class position. In addition, some research suggests that Latinas are especially likely to turn to relatives they trust, feeling that center-based care, with its emphasis on academic learning, does not provide the warmth and moral guidance they seek (Aritomi, 2004). This inclination, however, does not depend solely on beliefs different from those of White women; it also depends on the affordability and the availability of relatives. About one third of kin child care is paid for (Helburn & Bergmann, 2002). The parents who pay kin to provide child care often do so not because they prefer it but because they cannot afford other care (the price of relative care is 20% below that of family child care and 44% below that of child-care centers), and it is a way to provide jobs and income to struggling family members (Uttal, 1999). Thus, considerations of what is best for the child, what is economically most advantageous to the parents, and what works given extended kin relationships all shape decisions about child care.

Another kind of care, family day care with nonrelatives away from home, has declined in recent years—today only around 15% of those who use nonparental child care rely on it. Family day-care providers are almost always women, typically unlicensed and with little formal training, but often of a similar racial and class background to children's parents. Despite the often low quality of care, many parents still choose family day care because of its lower price and greater convenience, as well as the racial and class identification with the providers (Helburn & Bergmann, 2002).

Finally, a small number of mothers, those who are wealthy, become "mother-managers" (Rothman, 1989)—they often prefer to avoid center care in favor of nanny care (Flanagan, 2004). Such "nanny care" is often provided by poor, sometimes illegal, immigrants; they are often paid small salaries with no Social Security, given no opportunity for advancement, are socially isolated, and have only insecure employment (Hodagneu-Sotelo, 2001).

Overall, the system of child-care provision—or parenting for pay—is rooted in a system of inequalities that has three main premises. First, it is based on the low value placed in our society on motherhood (Crittenden, 2001). Just like any carework, the work of child-care providers is grossly undervalued in terms of pay, even though many child-care workers, especially Blacks and Latinas, have to support entire families on these low wages (Armenia, 2004; Helburn & Bergmann, 2002).

Second, it is based on the male-oriented structure of employment, which requires that a worker is unencumbered by family responsibilities. In this system, the employment of affluent, and even middle-class, women and their economic privilege, like that of their husbands', is dependent on the help of those women whom they pay so little to provide child care (Flanagan, 2004). As Hertz (1986) wrote about the hired help of the affluent couples she studied: "The issue is not that some women hire other women and thereby exploit them.... Rather the ability of dual career couples to enjoy the privileges of careers is predicated on the availability of lower paid housework and childcare workers; that is on a systematic and unequal distribution of advantages and disadvantages" (p. 203). At the same time, the work of child-care providers is often structured as if they have no family responsibilities of their own.

Third, this system is increasingly based on a deepening and restructuring of global inequality where the global South provides cheap women's labor to the global North. Many of the nannies have migrated to the United States as "transnational mothers" who must leave behind their own children as a means to support them. Oftentimes their children are raised by grandmothers back home.[7] While the mothers themselves and their families believe that the mother's departure is ultimately for the good of the family and its future, the public, both in their countries of origin and in the United States, disapproves of transnational mothers and their employers. Both the transnational mothers and their women employers are villainized for abandoning their children.

This system may have damaging effects on the lives of middle-class and affluent women and men, but it creates a lose–lose situation for the poor and minorities, especially women. They are often unable to spend much time with their children as the requirements of their (low-paid) jobs take them away from their families for extended hours, and sometimes even months or years. Or, they can stay with their children by taking care of other people's children as family-based child-care providers, usually for even lower pay. The dilemmas faced by these poor and minority mothers are different from those of wealthier mothers, even though both can be attributed to the same structures of inequality. A poor woman's choice is not between a career and stay-at-home motherhood, but between a low-paid job away from her children (often taking care of wealthier women's children or doing their housework) and an even lower-paid job with her children.

Paid Work and Kin Work

Newspapers columns and politicians' speeches routinely present images of people balancing family and work, but these are typically images of paid work and nuclear families. Much scholarship on families and work has this same narrow focus on housework and care of the young, often in the context of nuclear families. By ignoring carework to extended kin, such images and literature contain not only gender but also class and race biases. We have discussed some kin work—and its variations by class and race—in our discussion of child care. But, kin provide many other kinds of care to one another. And this care is divided by gender and varies by race and class.

Women rather than men are the keepers of the modern extended family. Women call, write, and invite kin far more often than do men (Di Leonardo, 1987). Women spend significantly more time giving help to those outside of their households than do men (Abel, 1991; Rossi & Rossi, 1990). To put it quite starkly, women add more than an extra work week to their monthly load by caring for those outside their households. For many, this labor is a "third shift" (Gerstel, 2000), because women do so much of it and because women do it in addition to the "first shift" of paid work and the "second shift" of housework and child care (Hochschild & Machung, 2003).

Women give far more to close relatives, to distant relatives, and to fictive kin than do men. Gender differences in the amount of time spent giving care are matched by differences in the kinds and proportions of care given. Studies find that, where help to kin is concerned, women do a large share of what is conventionally thought of as "men's" work, but men do little of "women's" work (Gerstel & Gallagher, 1994). Finally, there is no caregiving task that men do for a significantly larger number of people than women. Yet, there are many and varied tasks which women do for a significantly larger number of people than men. Furthermore, husbands' kin work tends to increase when their wives do more (Gerstel & Gallagher, 2001). Stated bluntly, these findings suggest there is very little *division* of labor in kin work. Some may argue that perhaps it is part of a wider division of labor in the family: Men do paid work; women do unpaid kin work. Indeed, compared to employed women, the "traditional woman" who does not work for pay is especially likely to do such work—providing care for her family by blood and marriage. Also, the types of tasks a housewife does are different from those an employed woman does: Employed women do help kin, but focus on the kinds of help that require economic resources rather than time. They give more money and gifts while housewives do more time-consuming, hands-on chores, like child care for kin outside the household. In this sense, employed women are beginning to look a little like employed men, as the structural model would predict. Women's increased movement into the labor force and their assumption of "men's jobs" begins to sever the kin work that has organized and sustained the modern extended family (Gerstel, 2000).

Others, however, emphasize that even when women work for pay, they differ from men. The "traditional" man—who holds a paying job—continues to do significantly less kin work than his employed female counterpart. Sarkisian and Gerstel (2004a), once again reaffirming the structural model, showed that a large portion of this gender difference is related to differences in men's and women's job conditions, especially their wages. Many studies, however, find that women still do significantly more than men even if their employment conditions are similar (Gerstel & Gallagher, 1994; Laditka & Laditka, 2001; Marks, 1996). Given that some report that women find extended kin more important than men (Finley, 1989; Rossi & Rossi, 1990), and that others more often expect their female than their male kin to provide care (Aldous, Klaus, & Klein, 1985; Aronson, 1992), the remaining gender differences in kin care can perhaps be attributed to culture.

Race differences in kin work are as large as gender differences (Gerstel, 2000). Latinos/as, Blacks, and Asians are more likely than Whites to live with, live near, and to have more contact with extended kin (Goldscheider & Bures, 2003; Kamo & Zhou, 1994; Miner & Uhlenberg, 1997; Phua et al., 2001; Raley, 1995; Sarkisian et al., 2004; Valenzuela & Dornbusch, 1994). Even though Whites are more likely to give money or advice, minorities exchange significantly more practical care (Sarkisian & Gerstel, 2004b; Sarkisian et al., 2004; Hogan et al., 1993; Jayakody, 1998; Lee & Aytac, 1998). These racial differences are deeply tempered by gender.

In our own research, we have found that Black men are astonishingly similar to White men in their kin support involvement. The only difference between them is in the prevalence of financial transfers, and this difference can be explained by their structural position: Because Black men (as well as women) are more likely to be of low socioeconomic standing, they do not have the resources to transfer money across households. Furthermore, when all types of kin support are combined, Black men are as likely to be involved in kin support as Whites. It looks like Black men are just "being men" when it comes to kin support (Sarkisian & Gerstel, 2004b). In contrast, Black women's kin support is quite different from White women's. Whereas the differences between Black and White women's financial transfers resemble those for men (and can be similarly explained by structural position), Black women are more likely than White ones to be involved in exchanges of household help, transportation help, and child care, and less likely to exchange emotional support (Sarkisian & Gerstel, 2004b).

To be sure, as we suggested above, some of these differences in kin work are associated with cultural values: Many show that Blacks, Latinos/as, and Asians place more value on extended families than Whites (Connell & Gibson, 1997; Lee, Peek, & Coward, 1998; Sarkisian et al., 2004; Sarkisian & Gerstel, 2004b). In our own research (Sarkisian, 2004; Sarkisian et al., 2004; Sarkisian & Gerstel, 2004b), we have found that higher extended familism is related to increased kin work but not responsible for the race differences in it: Structural factors, including education, occupation, income, and wealth, can account for most of such differences.

Indeed, many other scholars also suggest that the racial differences in kin work are better understood in terms of the differences in socioeconomic standing. They argue that minorities are more often poor and therefore more in need of extended family support networks than Whites (Cohen & Casper, 2002; Newman, 2001; Stack, 1974). Because disadvantaged men are often unable to provide women with economic security, poor women regularly turn to extended kin and friends for economic support. Poor women, especially Black, turn friends into "fictive kin," which means that these friends can be counted on to exchange money, goods, and services—not simply love (Stack, 1974). Under these conditions, economic bonds are reconstituted along different lines, emphasizing extended and fictive kin ties rather than conjugal ties. In the absence of marital ties and stable economic opportunities, poor women rely on extended kin as well as adapt the language of family, applying it to their friends. Indeed, some researchers have shown that middle- and upper-class Blacks, unlike the poor minorities, are similar to middle- and upper-class Whites, and both groups are at a remove from kin (Lareau, 2003; Wilkinson, 1990). This suggests that kin work varies by class. Indeed, some scholars have argued that in the working class and among the poor, we should find much more kin work. For instance, Lareau (2003) found that extended kin dominate everyday life for working-class and poor children. The lives of middle-class children are, by contrast, filled with activities with parents and siblings and all but empty of other relatives. These differences are likely due to differences in economic resources, even though class culture may play some role insofar as the familistic values differ by class. Unfortunately, no research unpacks the contributions of each.

CONCLUSION

As we have shown, structural theories postulate that when women and men encounter different economic opportunities and constraints, they will do different kinds of unpaid family work. Men's jobs are more likely to pull or push them away from family responsibilities than women's jobs; when women's jobs come to resemble men's, so too does their unpaid family work. We found much support for this perspective across the three domains of unpaid family work we examined: housework, parenting, and kin work. To be sure, some research suggests that the causal relationships work in both directions: Not only do women do more unpaid family work because they tend to do less paid work and earn less than men, but also they do less paid work and get paid less because they carry more than an equal share of housework, parenting, and kin work. Furthermore, some studies suggest that differences in employment conditions cannot fully explain gender differences in unpaid work. There is no doubt, however, that employment structures shape the unpaid work of both women and men to a large extent.

We have also shown that structural factors often account for racial differences in unpaid work in nuclear and extended families. We saw, for example, that minorities' low incomes as well as their reduced ability to rely on marital ties promote extended family integration; this helps explain the higher rates of kin work, especially involving practical help, among Blacks and Latinos/as compared to Whites. Such studies suggest that class position is key for understanding variations by race in the relationship of paid and unpaid work.

Although the research we reviewed leaves little doubt about the power of structure, a growing sociological literature emphasizes the power of culture. We are limited in our ability to assess the power of culture even at the level of individual values. Much quantitative research attempting to substantiate the cultural theories of inequalities in paid and unpaid work uses a "residual model" of culture. That is, whatever is not explained by structural variables researchers often attribute to culture. As a result, it is difficult to assess the extent to which inequalities in paid and unpaid work are really caused by culture and how much they simply represent a failure to adequately specify structural effects. There are some exceptions, of course: Some quantitative researchers have included measures of individual gender ideologies, familism, or job centrality in their studies of unpaid work. As we have shown, they tend to find some—albeit a limited—effect of such measures on some aspects of unpaid work, especially parenting and kin work. Furthermore, qualitative studies that examine culture more directly (often using observations and intensive interviews) help clarify the utility of cultural theories for understanding race, class, and gender inequalities in paid and unpaid work. For example, researchers have shown the power of culture in some mothers' decisions to work the night shift (Garey, 1999) or to abandon their executive jobs (Blair-Loy, 2003).

Another aspect of culture that sometimes appears in qualitative studies, but eludes most quantitative research, concerns the external expectations that shape paid and unpaid work. A fuller specification of cultural theories rests on the demarcation of what individuals expect of themselves *and* what others expect of them. This distinction between the internal and external elements of culture is important not only because they entail different mechanisms of operation, but also because it avoids referring to culture as unlocalized, as a set of ideas or values residing "out there." The few studies that have examined such external cultural forces find that women and men take into account the expectations of others and that these expectations vary by gender, race, and class. For instance, studies suggest that people more often expect women than men to do unpaid work, especially parenting (Schroeder, Blood, & Maluso, 1992) and kin work (Aldous, Klaus, & Klein, 1985; Aronson, 1992). Others suggest that the pressure to do kin work varies by race: Stack and Burton (1998) documented the extensive pressure to do kin work placed on Blacks, both women and men.

Another caveat is in order: For purposes of exposition and because of the limits of existing research, we presented structure and culture as two distinctive, even rival, theoretical frameworks. A number of scholars have argued (and we concur) that such a dichotomy is unsatisfying. It does not recognize, for example, the ways structural constraints are turned into cultural dictates (Gramsci, 1971) or the ways cultural schemas shape structural constraints (Sewell, 1992)—whether at the macro level of the economy and state, at the meso level of firms and families, or at the micro level of individuals' everyday experiences. Instead of developing such a synthetic model, much empirical research relies on a dichotomous approach that seeks to specify the extent to which either culture *or* structure shapes families and work (for critiques of this dichotomous approach, see Roschelle, 1997; Sudarkasa, 1988). Furthermore, both structural and cultural frameworks tend to view the forces shaping families and work in a deterministic way. Individuals, however, are more than the unwitting subjects of external forces—they are actors who make choices within structural and cultural constraints and therefore actively shape their families and their paid and unpaid labor. We saw this agency, for example, among unemployed men who resist housework, among mothers of color who make decisions about employment and child-care arrangements, and among middle-class and affluent wives who either insist their husbands share domestic work or hire domestic help so they can pursue careers.

To conclude, much sociological research offers support to structural theories of gender, race, and class differences in the division of paid and unpaid labor. The structural framework, we have argued, provides a powerful explanation of the inequalities in families and work, even though it frequently leaves some part of the differences unexplained. Cultural models for understanding family/work relationship hold much potential both in terms of understanding gender differences and in terms of explicating racial and social class variation, but these are in need of further development, both theoretical and empirical. More importantly, the findings summarized in this chapter suggest that cultural models should always be used in conjunction with structural frameworks.

NOTES

[1] Some advocate the existence of unique class distinctions within racial groups: For example, some distinguish two classes among Chinese Americans—"ghetto Chinatown" (small business owners, working-class families, poor immigrants) and the "middle class" (professional Chinese residing outside of Chinatown) (Aponte, 1999).

[2] A reverse trend was observed recently, however: Between 2002 and 2003, median annual earnings for full-time year-round women workers shrank by 0.6%, to $30,724, while men's earnings remained unchanged, at $40,668. The 1.4% decrease in the gender wage ratio is the largest backslide in 12 years—since 1991 (Institute for Women's Policy Research, 2004).

[3] Other structural theorists, however, promote a very different view of minority extended family integration and kin work, emphasizing worsening conditions over time: They perceive a decline in such integration and work and attribute this decline to minorities' worsening economic position (Kaplan, 1997; McDonald & Armstrong, 2001; Murray, 1984; Roschelle, 1997; Wilson, 1987). Both approaches have been criticized for their tendency to generalize "underclass" findings to all minorities, neglecting social class diversity among them.

[4] We must note, however, that these priorities set for children may not reflect the priorities assigned to these areas of parents' own life on a daily basis.

[5] Going beyond the heterosexual family, Carrington (1999) showed that among gays and lesbians, the allocation of housework is also clearly based on employment hours and income.

[6] Recent data are unavailable on Asian families, but data from 1990 show that Asian children are as likely to live in two-parent families as are Whites, whereas Latinos/as and Blacks are considerably less likely to do so (Population Reference Bureau, 1990).

[7] Similarly, Stack (1996) described South–North migration of Blacks within the United States, with young Blacks leaving their children at home with grandparents and going North to earn some money, often working as nannies and domestics and sending money home.

REFERENCES

Abel, E. (1991). *Who cares for the elderly? Public policy and the experiences of adult daughters.* Philadelphia: Temple University Press.

Acker, J. R. (1973). Women and social stratification: A case of intellectual sexism. *American Journal of Sociology, 78*, 936–945.

Ahmeduzzaman, M., & Roopnarine, J. (1992). Sociodemographic factors, functioning style, social support, and fathers' involvement with preschoolers in African-American families. *Journal of Marriage and the Family, 54*, 699–707.

Aldous, J., Klaus, E., & Klein, D. M. (1985). The understanding heart: Aging parents and their favorite children. *Child Development, 56*, 303–316.

Almaguer, T. (1994). *Racial fault lines: The historical origins of White supremacy in California.* Berkeley, CA: University of California Press.

Ameristat. (2002). *Analysis of data from 2002 CPS, March supplement.* Washington, DC: Population Reference Bureau.

Anderson, D. J., Binder, M., & Krause, K. (2003). The motherhood wage penalty revisited: Experience, heterogeneity, work effort, and work-schedule flexibility. *Industrial and Labor Relations Review, 56*, 273–284.

Aponte, R. (1999). Ethnic variation in the family: The elusive trend toward convergence. In M. Sussman, S. K. Steinmetz, & G. W. Peterson (Eds.), *Handbook of marriage and the family* (2nd ed., pp. 111–141). New York: Plenum.

Aranda, L. M. (1998). *Attitudes toward gender roles: Race, ethnic, class, and gender variations.* Paper presented at the Annual Meetings of American Sociological Association, Toronto, Canada.

Aritomi, P. T. (2004). *Matching non-parental child care usage and preferences by race/ethnicity: Is it connected to maternal work stability?* Poster presented at the Annual Meetings of the Population Association of America, April 1–3, Boston, MA.

Armenia, A. (2004). *Invisible subsidies: Racial inequalities in family day care work.* Paper presented at the Sociology Graduate Student Colloquium, April 14, Sociology Department, University of Massachusetts, Amherst, MA.

Aronson, J. (1992). Women's sense of responsibility for the care of old people: "But who else is going to do it?" *Gender and Society, 6*, 8–29.

Avellar, S., & Smock, P. J. (2003). Has the price of motherhood declined over time? A cross-cohort comparison of the motherhood wage penalty. *Journal of Marriage and Family, 65*, 597–607.

Baca Zinn, M. (1989). Family, race, and poverty in the eighties. *Signs, 14*, 856–874.

Baca Zinn, M. (1992). Chicano men and masculinity. In M. S. Kimmel & M. A. Messner (Eds.), *Men's lives* (pp. 67–77). New York: Macmillan.

Barron, D. & Mykita, L. (2004). *Who is home with the kids? The demographics of full time parenthood in the U.S.* Paper presented at the Annual Carework Conference, "Bridging Carework Research, Advocacy, and Policy," August 13, San Francisco, CA.

Baxter, J. (1993). *Work at home: The domestic division of labour.* Queensland, Australia: University of Queensland Press.

Becerra, R. M. & Chi, I. (1992). Child care preferences among low-income minority families. *International Social Work, 25*, 35–47.

Benin, M. H., & Edwards, D. A. (1990). Adolescents' chores: The difference between dual- and single-earner families. *Journal of Marriage and the Family, 52*, 361–373.

Bianchi, S., Milkie, M., Sayer, L., & Robinson, J. (2000). Is anyone doing the housework? Trends in the gender division of household labor. *Social Forces, 79*, 191–228.

Bianchi, S. M. (2000). Maternal employment and time with children: Dramatic change or surprising continuity? *Demography, 37*, 401–414.

Bianchi, S. M., Robinson, J. P., & Milkie, M. A. (forthcoming). *Changing rhythms of American family life.* New York: ASA Rose Monograph Series and Russell Sage Foundation.

Bittman, M., England, P., Sayer, L., Folbre, N., & Matheson, G. (2003). When does gender trump money? Bargaining and time in household work. *American Journal of Sociology, 109*, 186–214.

Blair, S. L. (2000). *Parents and family structure: An examination of ethnic-based variations in children's household labor.* Paper presented at the Annual Meetings of American Sociological Association, August 12–16, Washington, DC.

Blair-Loy, M. (2003). *Competing devotions: Career and family among women executives.* Cambridge, MA: Harvard University Press.

Blalock, L. L., Tiller, V. R., & Monroe, P. A. (2004). "They get you out of courage": Persistent deep poverty among former welfare-reliant women. *Family Relations, 53*, 127–137.

Blau, F. D., & Kahn, L. M. (2000). Gender differences in pay. *Journal of Economic Perspectives, 14*(4), 75–100.

Bowman, P. J. (1993). The impact of economic marginality among African American husbands and fathers. In H. P. McAdoo (Ed.), *Family ethnicity: Strength in diversity* (pp. 120–140). Newbury Park, CA: Sage.

Bowman, P. J., & Forman, T. A. (1997). Instrumental and expressive family roles among African American fathers. In R. J. Taylor & J. S. Jackson (Eds.), *Family life in Black America* (pp. 216–247). Thousand Oaks, CA: Sage.

Brayfield, A. A. (1992). Employment resources and housework in Canada. *Journal of Marriage and the Family, 54*, 19–30.

Brines, J. (1994). Economic dependency, gender and the division of labor at home. *American Journal of Sociology, 100*, 652–688.

Budig, M., & England, P. (2001). The wage penalty for motherhood. *American Sociological Review, 66*, 204–225.

Buriel, R., & Hurtado-Ortiz, M. T. (2000). Child care practices and preferences of native- and foreign-born Latina mothers and Euro-American mothers. *Hispanic Journal of Behavioral Sciences, 22*, 314–331.

Carrington, C. (1999). *No place like home: Relationships and family life among lesbians and gay men.* Chicago: University of Chicago Press.

Center on Fathers, Family and Public Policy. (2004). *Bush budget proposal would benefit wealthy at the expense of the poor.* Retrieved April 10, 2004, from http://www.cffpp.org/briefings/brief_0402.html.

Clawson, D., & Gerstel, N. (2002). Caring for young children: What the U.S. can learn from some European examples. *Contexts, 4*, 28–35.

Cohen, P. N. (1998). Replacing housework in the service economy: Gender, class, and race-ethnicity in service spending. *Gender & Society, 12*, 219–231.

Cohen, P. N., & Casper, L. M. (2002). In whose home? Multigenerational families in the United States, 1998–2000. *Sociological Perspectives, 45*, 1–20.

Coley, R. L. (1998). Children's socialization experiences and functioning in single-mother households: The importance of fathers and other men. *Child Development, 69*, 219–230.

Collins, P. H. (1994). Shifting the center: Race, class, and feminist theorizing about motherhood. In E. Nakano, E. Glenn, G. Chang, & L. R. Forcey (Eds.), *Mothering: Ideology, experience and agency* (pp. 45–65). New York: Routledge.

Collins, P. H. (2000). *Black feminist thought: Knowledge, consciousness, and the politics of empowerment* (2nd ed.). New York: Routledge.

Collins, P. H. (2002). Work, family, and Black women's oppression. In B. R. Hare (Ed.), *2001 Race Odyssey: African Americans and Sociology* (pp. 114–139). New York: Syracuse University Press.

Coltrane, S. (1996). *Family man: Fatherhood, housework, and gender equity.* New York: Oxford University Press.

Coltrane, S. (2000). Research on household labor: Modeling and measuring the social embeddedness of routine family work. *Journal of Marriage and the Family, 62*, 1208–1233.

Coltrane, S., & Valdez, E. O. (1993). Reluctant compliance: Work/family role allocation in dual-earner Chicano families. In J. Hood (Ed.), *Men, work, and family* (pp. 151–173). Newbury Park, CA: Sage.

Connell, C., & Gibson, G. (1997). Racial, ethnic and cultural differences in dementia caregiving: Review and analysis. *The Gerontologist, 37*, 355–363.

Connell, R. W. (1987). *Gender and power: Society, the person and sexual politics.* Cambridge, MA: Polity/Blackwell.

Cooney, T. M., & Uhlenberg, P. (1992). Support from parents over the life course: The adult child's perspective. *Social Forces, 71*, 63–84.

Cooper, M. (2002). Being the go-to-guy: Fatherhood, masculinity and the organization of work in the Silicon Valley. In N. Gerstel, D. Clawson, & R. Zussman (Eds.), *Families at work* (pp. 5–31). Nashville, TN: Vanderbilt University Press.

Crittenden, A. (2001). *The price of motherhood: Why the most important job in the world is still the least valued.* New York: Metropolitan Books.

Dalton, S. E., & Bielby, D. D. (2000). "That's our kind of constellation": Lesbian mothers negotiate institutionalized understandings of gender within the family. *Gender & Society, 14*, 36–61.

Daniels, P., & Weingarten, K. (1982). *Sooner or later: The timing of parenthood in adult lives.* New York: Norton.

Danziger, S. K., Ananat, E. O., & Browning, K. G. (2004). Childcare subsidies and the transition from welfare to work. *Family Relations, 53*, 219–228.

Deutsch, F. (1999). *Halving it all: How equally shared parenting works.* Cambridge, MA: Harvard University Press.

Di Leonardo, M. (1987). The female world of cards and holidays: Women, families, and the work of kinship. *Signs, Journal of Women in Culture and Society, 12*, 440–453.

Dodson, L., & Dickert, J. (2004). Girls' family labor in low-income households: A decade of qualitative research. *Journal of Marriage and Family, 66*, 318–332.

Early, D. M., & Burchinal, M. (2001). Early childhood care: Relations with family characteristics and preferred care characteristics. *Early Childhood Research Quarterly, 16*, 497.

Edin, K., Lein, L., & Nelson, T. (2002). Taking care of business: The economic survival strategies of low-income, noncustodial fathers. In F. Munger (Ed.), *Laboring below the line: The new ethnography of poverty and survival in the global economy* (pp. 125–147). New York: Russell Sage.

Eggebeen, D. J. (2002). The changing course of fatherhood: Men's experiences with children in demographic perspective. *Journal of Family Issues, 23*, 486–506.

Eggebeen, D. J., Snyder, A. R., & Manning, W. (1996). Children in single-father families in demographic perspective. *Journal of Family Issues, 17*, 441–465.

Elder, G. H. Jr., & Crosnoe, R. (2002). The influence of early behavior patterns on later life. In L. Pilkkinen & A. Caspi (Eds.), *Paths to successful development: Personality in the life course* (pp. 157–176). New York: Cambridge University Press.

Epstein, C. (1988). *Deceptive distinctions: Sex, gender and the social order.* New Haven, CT: Yale University Press.

Fagan, J. (1998). Correlates of low-income African American and Puerto Rican fathers' involvement with their children. *The Journal of Black Psychology, 24*, 351–367.

Fields, B. (1990). Slavery, race, and ideology in the U.S. *New Left Review, 181*, 95–118.

Finley, N. J. (1989). Theories of family labor as applied to gender differences in caregiving for elderly parents. *Journal of Marriage and the Family, 51*, 79–86.

Flanagan, C. (2004). How serfdom saved the women's movement: Dispatches from the "nanny wars." *The Atlantic Monthly, 293*, 109–128.

Furstenberg, F. (2004). Mixed messages on marriage. Retrieved March 20, 2004, from http://www.contemporary. families.org.

Garey, A. (1999). *Weaving work and motherhood*. Philadelphia: Temple University Press.

Garfinkel, I., & McLanahan, S. (1986). *Single mothers and their children: A new American dilemma*. Washington, DC: Urban Institute Press.

Gerson, K. (1993). *No man's land: Men's changing commitments to family and work*. New York: Basic Books.

Gerstel, N. (2000). The third shift: Gender and care work outside the home. *Qualitative Sociology, 23*, 467–483.

Gerstel, N., Clawson, D., & Zussman, R. (Eds.). (2002). *Families at work*. Nashville, TN: Vanderbilt University Press.

Gerstel, N., & Gallagher, S. (1994). Caring for kith and kin: Gender, employment, and the privatization of care. *Social Problems, 41*, 519–539.

Gerstel, N., & Gallagher, S. K. (2001). Men's caregiving: Gender and the contingent character of care. *Gender & Society, 15*, 197–217.

Glass, J. (1998). Gender liberation, economic squeeze, or fear of strangers: Why fathers provide infant care in dual-earner families. *Journal of Marriage and the Family, 60*, 821–834.

Goldscheider, F. K., & Bures, R. M. (2003). The racial crossover in family complexity in the United States. *Demography, 40*, 569–587.

Goldscheider, F. K., & Waite, L. J. (1991). *New families, no families: The transformation of the American home*. Berkeley and Los Angeles, CA: University of California Press.

Goldscheider, F. K., & Waite, L. J. (1998). Children's share in household tasks. In K. V. Hansen & A. I. Garey (Eds.), *Families in the U.S.: Kinship and domestic politics* (pp. 809–817). Philadelphia: Temple University Press.

Graham, J. W., & Beller, A. H. (1996). Child support in Black and White: Racial differentials in the award and receipt of child support during the 1980s. *Social Science Quarterly, 77*, 528–542.

Gramsci, A. (1971). *Selections from the prison notebooks*. New York: International Publishers.

Greenstein, T. N. (1996). Gender ideology and perceptions of the fairness of the division of household labour: Effects on marital quality. *Social Forces, 74*, 1029–1042.

Greenstein, T. N. (2000). Economic dependence, gender and the division of labor in the home: A replication and extension. *Journal of Marriage and Family, 62*, 322–335.

Gupta, S. (1999). The effects of transitions in marital status on men's performance of housework. *Journal of Marriage and the Family, 61*, 700–711.

Gutmann, M. C. (1996). *The meanings of macho: Being a man in Mexico City*. Berkeley and Los Angeles: University of California Press.

Hamer, J. (2001). *What it means to be daddy: Fatherhood for Black men living away from their children*. New York: Columbia University Press.

Harpster, P., & Monk-Turner, E. (1998). Why men do housework: A test of gender production and the relative resources model. *Sociological Focus, 31*, 45–57.

Harrington Meyer, M., & Herd, P. (forthcoming). *Retrenching welfare, entrenching inequality*. New York: American Sociological Association and Russell Sage Foundation.

Harris, K. M., Furstenberg, F. F., & Marmer, J. K. (1998). Paternal involvement with adolescents in intact families: The influence of fathers over the life course. *Demography, 35*, 201–216.

Hays, S. (1994). Structure and agency and the sticky problem of culture. *Sociological Theory, 12*, 57–72.

Hays, S. (1996). *The cultural contradictions of motherhood*. New Haven, CT: Yale University Press.

Hays, S. (2003). Off the rolls: The ground level results of welfare reform. *Dissent, 50*, 48–53.

Hein, J. (forthcoming). *Homeland diversity and the adaptation of immigrants: Responses to race, ethnicity, and discrimination among refugees in small and large American cities.* New York: Russell Sage Foundation.

Helburn, S. W., & Bergmann, B. R. (2002). *America's childcare problem: The way out*. New York: Palgrave/St. Martin's Press.

Henly, J. R., & Lyons, S. (2000). The negotiation of child care and employment demands among low-income parents. *Journal of Social Issues, 56*, 683–706.

Hequembourg, A. L. (2002). *Territories of lesbian motherhood: Meanings in flux*. PhD Dissertation, State University of New York, Buffalo, NY.

Hersch, J., & Stratton, L. S. (1997). Housework, fixed effects and wages of married workers. *The Journal of Human Resources, 32*, 285–307.

Hertz, R. (1986). *More equal than others*. London and Berkeley: University of California Press.

Hill, S. A., & Sprague, J. (1999). Parenting in Black and White families: The interaction of gender with race and class. *Gender & Society, 13*, 480–502.

Hochschild, A., & Machung, A. (2003). *The second shift: Inside a two-job marriage.* New York: Penguin.

Hodagneu-Sotelo, P. (2001). *Doméstica: Immigrant workers cleaning and caring in the shadows of affluence.* Berkeley, CA: University of California Press.

Hofferth, S. (2003). Race/ethnic differences in father involvement in two-parent families: Culture, context, or economy. *Journal of Family Issues, 24*, 185–216.

Hogan, D. P., Eggebeen, D. J., & Clogg, C. C. (1993). The structure of intergenerational exchanges in American families. *American Journal of Sociology, 98*, 1428–1458.

Hooks, B. (1981). *Ain't I a woman: Black women and feminism.* Boston: South End.

Huang, P. (2004). *Father as breadwinner: Gendered wage penalties for job interruptions.* Paper presented at the Annual Meetings of the Population Association of America, April, Boston, MA.

Hudspeth, C. D. (2003). *Does class matter in father–child interaction?* PhD Dissertation, Mississippi State University.

Hundley, G. (2000). Male/female earnings differences in self-employment: The effects of marriage, children, and the household division of labor. *Industrial and Labor Relations Review, 54*, 95–114.

Ignatiev, N. (1995). *How the Irish became White.* New York: Routledge.

Institute for Women's Policy Research. (2004). Women's earnings fall; U.S. Census Bureau finds rising gender wage gap. Washington, DC: Institute for Women's Policy Research. Retrieved September 25, 2004, from http://www.iwpr.org/pdf/WageRatioPress_release8-27-04.pdf.

Jacobs, J. A., & Gerson, K. (2004). *The time divide: Balancing work and family in contemporary society.* Cambridge, MA: Harvard University Press.

Jayakody, R. (1998). Race differences in intergenerational financial assistance: The needs of children and the resources of parents. *Journal of Family Issues, 19*, 508–533.

Jencks, C., & Swingle, J. (2000). Without a net. *The American Prospect, January*, 37–41.

Johnson, D., & Lino, M. (2000). Trends in teenage employment and contributions to family spending. *Monthly Labor Review, 123*(9), 15–25.

Julian, T. W., McKenry, P. C., & McKelvey, M. W. (1994). Cultural variations in parenting: Perceptions of Caucasian, African-American, Hispanic, and Asian-American parents. *Family Relations, 43*, 30–37.

Kamo, Y., & Cohen, E. L. (1998). Division of household work between partners: A comparison of Black and White couples. *Journal of Comparative Family Studies, 29*, 131–145.

Kamo, Y., & Zhou, M. (1994). Living arrangements of elderly Chinese and Japanese in the United States. *Journal of Marriage and the Family, 56*, 544–558.

Kibria, N. (1990). Power, patriarchy, and gender conflict in the Vietnamese immigrant community. *Gender & Society, 4*, 9–24.

Kohn, M. L., & Schooler, C. (1983). *Work and personality: An inquiry into the impact of social stratification.* Norwood, NJ: Ablex.

Laditka, J. N., & Laditka, S. B. (2001). Adult children helping older parents: Variations in the likelihood and hours by gender, race, and family role. *Research on Aging, 23*, 429–456.

Landale, N. S., & Oropesa, R. S. (2001). Father involvement in the lives of mainland Puerto Rican children: Contributions of nonresident, cohabiting, and married fathers. *Social Forces, 79*, 945–968.

Lareau, A. (2003). *Unequal childhoods: Class, race and family life.* Berkeley, CA: University of California Press.

Lee, G. R., Peek, C. W., & Coward, R. T. (1998). Race differences in filial responsibility expectations among older parents. *Journal of Marriage and the Family, 60*, 404–412.

Lee, Y. J., & Aytac, I. A. (1998). Intergenerational financial support among Whites, Blacks, and Latinos. *Journal of Marriage and the Family, 60*, 426–441.

Lempert, L. B. (1999). Other fathers: An alternative perspective on Black community caring. In R. Staples (Ed.), *The Black family: Essays and studies* (pp. 189–201). Belmont, CA: Wadsworth.

Lennon, M. C., & Rosenfield, S. (1994). Relative fairness and the division of household labor: The importance of options. *American Journal of Sociology, 100*, 506–531.

Loewen, J. W. (1971). *The Mississippi Chinese: Between Black and White.* Cambridge, MA: Harvard University Press.

Loprest, P. (2002). Making the transition from welfare to work. In A. Weil & K. Feingold (Eds.), *Welfare reform: The next act* (pp. 17–31). Washington, DC: Urban Institute Press.

Lorber, J. (1994). *Paradoxes of gender.* New Haven, CT: Yale University Press.

Maccoby, E. (1998). *The two sexes.* Cambridge, MA: Belknap.

MacDermid, S. M., Huston, T. L., & McHale, S. M. (1990). Changes in marriage associated with the transition to parenthood: Individual differences as a function of sex-role attitudes and changes in division of household labor. *Journal of Marriage and the Family, 52*, 475–486.

Mannheim, B. (1993). Gender and the effects of demographics, status, and work values on work centrality. *Work and Occupations, 20*, 3–22.

Manning, W. D., & Smock, P. J. (1997). Children's living arrangements in unmarried-mother families. *Journal of Family Issues, 18*, 526–544.

Marini, M. M. (1990). Sex and gender: What do we know? *Sociological Forum, 5*, 95–120.

Marks, N. F. (1996). Caregiving across the lifespan: National prevalence and predictors. *Family Relations, 45*, 27–36.

Marsiglio, W. (1995). Young nonresident biological fathers. *Marriage and Family Review, 20*, 325–348.

McAdoo, H. P. (1980). Black mothers and the extended family support network. In L. F. Rodgers-Rose (Ed.), *The Black woman* (pp. 125–144). Beverly Hills, CA: Sage.

McLanahan, S. (2004). *Diverging destinies: How children fare under the second demographic transition.* Presidential address given at the Annual Meetings of the Population Association of America, April 1–3, Boston, MA.

McLanahan, S., & Schwartz, D. (2002). Life without father: What happens to the children? *Contexts, 1*, 35–44.

McLoyd, V. C., Cauce, A. M., Takeuchi, D., & Wilson, L. (2000). Marital processes and parental socialization in families of color: A decade review of research. *Journal of Marriage and the Family, 62*, 1070–1093.

Meyers, M., Han, W., Waldfogel, J., Garfinkel, I., & Villeneuve, P. (2001). Child care and single mother families in the wake of welfare reform: Evidence from New York. *Social Service Review, 75*, 29–59.

Miner, S., & Uhlenberg, P. (1997). Intragenerational proximity and the social role of sibling neighbors after midlife. *Family Relations, 46*, 145–153.

Mirandé, A. (1997). *Hombres y machos: Masculinity and Latino culture.* Boulder, CO: Westview.

Moen, P. (2003). Linked lives: Dual careers, gender, and the contingent life course. In W. Heinz & V. Marshall (Eds.), *Social dynamics of the life course: Transitions, institutions, and interrelations* (pp. 237–258). Hawthorne, NY: DeGruyter.

Moon, S. (2003). Immigration and mothering: Case studies from two generations of Korean immigrant women. *Gender & Society, 17*, 840–860.

Morgan, P., & Waite, L. (1987). Parenthood and attitudes of young adults. *American Sociological Review, 42*, 541–547.

Mott, F. L. (1990). When is a father really gone? Paternal-child conduct in father-absent homes. *Demography, 27*, 499–517.

Moynihan, D. P. (1965). *The Negro family: A case for national action.* Washington, DC: Government Printing Office.

Nakano Glenn, E. (1994). Social constructions of mothering: A thematic overview. In E. Nakano Glenn, G. Chang, & L. R. Forcey (Eds.), *Mothering: Ideology, experience, and agency (perspectives on gender)* (pp. 1–29). New York: Routledge.

Nakano Glenn, E. (2002). *Unequal freedom: How race and gender shaped American citizenship and labor.* Cambridge, MA: Harvard University Press.

Newman, K. (2001). Local caring: Social capital and social responsibility in New York's minority neighborhoods. In A. S. Rossi (Ed.), *Caring and doing for others: Social responsibility in the domains of family, work, and community* (pp. 157–177). Chicago: University of Chicago Press.

Noonan, M. C. (2001). The impact of domestic work on men's and women's wages. *Journal of Marriage and Family, 63*, 1134–1145.

Offner, P., & Holzer, H. (2002). *Left behind in the labor market: Recent employment trends among young Black men.* Washington, DC: Brookings Institution, Center on Urban and Metropolitan Policy. Retrieved September 20, 2004, from http://www.brookings.edu/dybdocroot/es/urban/publications/offnerholzer.pdf.

Oliker, S. J. (2000). Examining care at welfare's end. In M. Harrington Meyer (Ed.), *Care work: Gender, labor, and welfare state* (pp. 167–185). London: Routledge.

Omi, M., & Winant H. (1994). *Racial formation in the United States: From the 1960s to the 1990s.* New York: Routledge.

Parsons, T., & Bales, R. (1955). *Family socialization and interaction process.* Glencoe, IL: Free Press.

Pattillo-McCoy, M. (1999). *Black picket fences: Privilege and peril among the Black middle class.* Chicago: University of Chicago Press.

Patterson, O. (1998). *Rituals of blood: Consequences of slavery in two American centuries.* Washington, DC: Civitas/Counterpoint.

Perry-Jenkins, M., & Folk, K. (1994). Class, couples, and conflict: Effects of the division of labor on assessments of marriage in dual-earner families. *Journal of Marriage and the Family, 56*, 165–180.

Phua, V. C., Kaufman, G., & Park, K. S. (2001). Strategic adjustments of elderly Asian Americans: Living arrangements and headship. *Journal of Comparative Family Studies, 32*, 263–281.

Pittman, J. F., & Blanchard, D. (1996). Effects of work history and timing of marriage on the division of household labor: A life-course perspective. *Journal of Marriage and the Family, 58*, 78–90.

Population Reference Bureau. (1990). *The challenge of change: What the 1990 Census tells us about children, Table 14.* Washington, DC: Center for the Study of Social Policy.

Presser, H. B. (1994). Employment schedules among dual-earner spouses and the division of household labor by gender. *American Sociological Review, 59*, 348–364.

Presser, H. B. (2003a). *Working in a 24/7 economy.* New York: Russell Sage Foundation.

Presser, H. B. (2003b). Race-ethnic and gender differences in nonstandard work shifts. *Work and Occupations, 30*, 412–439.

Presser, H. B. (2004). Employment in a 24/7 economy: Challenges for the family. In C. F. Epstein & A. Kalleberg (Eds.), *Fighting for time* (pp. 46–76). New York: Russell Sage Foundation.

Primus, W. (1996). Immigration provisions in the new welfare law. *Focus, 18*, 14–18.

Raley, R. K. (1995). Black–White differences in kin contact and exchange among never-married adults. *Journal of Family Issues, 16*, 77–103.

Reimann, R. (1997). Does biology matter?: Lesbian couples' transition to parenthood and their division of labor. *Qualitative Sociology, 20*, 153–185.

Risman, B. (1998). *Gender vertigo: American families in transition.* New Haven, CT: Yale University Press.

Roberts, D. (1998). The absent Black father. In C. R. Daniels (Ed.), *Lost fathers: The politics of fatherlessness in America* (pp. 145–161). New York: St. Martin's Press.

Rogler, L. H., & Santana Cooney, R. (1991). Puerto Rican families in New York City: Intergenerational processes. *Marriage and Family Review, 16*, 331–349.

Rollins, J. (1985). *Between women: Domestics and their employers.* Philadelphia: Temple University Press.

Roschelle, A. R. (1997). *No more kin: Exploring race, class, and gender in family networks.* Thousand Oaks, CA: Sage.

Rossi, A. S., & Rossi, P. H. (1990). *Of human bonding: Parent–child relations across the life course.* New York: DeGruyter.

Rothman, B. K. (1989). Women as fathers: Motherhood and child care under a modified patriarchy. *Gender & Society, 3*, 89–104.

Rubinstein, D. (2001). *Culture, structure, and agency: Toward a truly multidimensional sociology.* Thousand Oaks, CA: Sage.

Rumbaut, R. G. (1997). Paradoxes (and orthodoxies) of assimilation. *Sociological Perspectives, 40*, 483–511.

Samuel, J. V. (2002). Breaking the cycle of absent fathers: Highly involved African-American nonresidential fathers describe their roles and responsibilities beyond biological paternity. PhD Dissertation, University of Tennessee.

Sarkisian, N. (2004). *Assessing the myth of familial AWOL: Kin support among Euro and African American men.* Paper presented at the Annual Meetings of the Population Association of America, April 1–3, Boston, MA.

Sarkisian, N., & Gerstel, N. (2004a). Explaining the gender gap in help to parents: The importance of employment. *Journal of Marriage and the Family, 66*, 431–451.

Sarkisian, N., & Gerstel, N. (2004b). Kin support among Blacks and Whites: Race and family organization. *American Sociological Review, 69*, 812–837.

Sarkisian, N., Muñoz, R., & Gerstel, N. (2004b). The myths of ethnic fatherhood: Mexican American and Euro American residential father–child involvement. Unpublished manuscript.

Sarkisian, N., Gerena, M., & Gerstel, N. (2004). Detecting distinctions: Extended family integration among Latinos/as and Euro Americans. Unpublished manuscript.

Schroeder, K. A., Blood, L. L., & Maluso, D. (1992). An intergenerational analysis of expectations for women's career and family roles. *Sex Roles, 26*, 273–291.

Scott, E. K., London, A., & Myers, N. A. (2002). Living with violence: Women's reliance on abusive men in their transitions from welfare to work. In N. Gerstel, D. Clawson, & R. Zussman (Eds.), *Families at work: Expanding the bounds* (pp. 302–316). Nashville, TN: Vanderbilt University Press.

Segura, D. (1994). Working at motherhood: Chicana and Mexican immigrant mothers and employment. In E. Nakano Glenn, G. Chang, & L. Forcey Rennie (Eds.), *Mothering: Ideology, experience, agency* (pp. 211–236). New York: Routledge.

Segura, D. A., & Pierce, J. L. (1993). Chicana/o family structure and gender personality: Chodorow, familism, and psychoanalytic sociology revisited. In K. Hansen & A. I. Garey (Eds.), *Families in the U.S.: Kinship and domestic politics* (pp. 295–314). Philadelphia: Temple University Press.

Seltzer, J. A. (1991). Relationships between fathers and children who live apart: The father's role after separation. *Journal of Marriage and the Family, 53*, 79–101.

Seltzer, J. A., & Bianchi, S. M. (1988). Children's contact with absent parents. *Journal of Marriage and the Family, 50*, 663–677.

Seltzer, J. A., Schaeffer, N. C., & Charng, H. W. (1989). Family ties after divorce: The relationship between visiting and paying child support. *Journal of Marriage and the Family, 51*, 1013–1031.

Sewell, W. H. (1992). A theory of structure: Duality, agency, and transformation. *American Journal of Sociology, 98*, 1–29.

Shelton, B. A., & John, D. (1993). Does marital status make a difference? *Journal of Family Issues, 14*, 401–420.

Sigle-Rushton, W., & McLanahan, S. (2002). The living arrangements of new unmarried mothers. *Demography, 39*, 415–433.

Smith, K., & Fields, J. (2004). *Transition dynamics for stay-at-home parenthood.* Paper presented at the Annual Meetings of the Population Association of America, April 1–3, Boston, MA.

Smock, P. J., & Manning, W. D. (1997). Nonresident parents' characteristics and child support. *Journal of Marriage and the Family, 59*, 798–808.

Sorensen, A., & McLanahan, S. (1987). Married women's economic dependency: 1940–1980. *American Sociological Review, 93*, 659–687.

Spitze, G., & Ward, R. (1995). Household labor in intergenerational households. *Journal of Marriage and the Family, 57*, 355–361.

Stack, C. (1974). *All my kin: Strategies for survival in a Black community.* New York: Harper & Row.

Stack, C. (1996). *Call to home: African Americans reclaim the rural South.* New York: Basic Books.

Stack, C., & Burton, L. M. (1998). Kinscripts. In K. Hansen & A. I. Garey (Eds.), *Families in the U.S.: Kinship and domestic politics* (pp. 405–417). Philadelphia: Temple University Press.

Staples, R. (1988). The Black American family. In C. H. Mindel, R. Beberstein, & R. J. Wright (Eds.), *Ethnic families in America: Patterns and variations* (3rd ed., pp. 303–323). New York: Elsevier.

Stewart, S. D. (2004). *The sociology of African American nonresident fatherhood.* Paper presented at the Annual Meetings of the Population Association of America, April 1–3, Boston, MA.

Stier, H., & Tienda, M. (1993). Are men marginal to their families? In J. C. Hood (Ed.), *Men, work, and family* (pp. 23–44). Newbury Park, CA: Sage.

Stroup, A. L., & Pollock, G. E. (1999). Economic consequences of marital dissolution for Hispanics. *Journal of Divorce and Remarriage, 30*, 149–166.

Sudarkasa, N. (1988). Interpreting the Black heritage in Afro-American family organization. In H. P. McAdoo (Ed.), *Black families* (2nd ed., pp. 27–43). Beverly Hills, CA: Sage.

Sullivan, M. E. (2000). *Conscious kinship: Lesbian coparent families and the undoing of gender.* PhD Dissertation, University of California, Davis.

Taylor, R. J., Tucker, M. B., Chatters, L. M., & Jayakody, R. (1997). Recent demographic trends in African American family structure. In R. J. Taylor & J. S. Jackson (Eds.), *Family life in Black America* (pp. 14–62). Thousand Oaks, CA: Sage.

Taylor, R. L. (1998). Minority families and social change. In R. Taylor (Ed.), *Minority families in the U.S.* (2nd ed., pp. 251–295). Englewood Cliffs, NJ: Prentice-Hall.

Thompson, A., & Lawson, E. J. (1999). African American men and fatherhood: A look from divorced fathers. *Journal of African American Men, 4*, 37–51.

Thompson, L., & Walker, A. J. (1991). Gender in families: Women and men in marriage, work, and parenthood. In A. Booth (Ed.), *Contemporary families: Looking forward, looking back* (pp. 76–102). Minneapolis, MN: National Council on Family Relations.

Tichenor, V. J. (1999). Status and income as gendered resources: The case of marital power. *Journal of Marriage and the Family, 61*, 638–650.

Toth, J. F., & Xu, X. (1999). Ethnic and cultural diversity in fathers' involvement: A racial/ethnic comparison of African American, Hispanic, and White fathers. *Youth and Society, 31*, 76–99.

Tucker, M., & Mitchell-Kernan, C. (1995). Trends in African American family formation: A theoretical overview. In M. Tucker & C. Mitchell-Kernan (Eds.), *The decline of marriage among African-Americans* (pp. 8–26). New York: Russell Sage.

Udry, J. R. (2000). Biological limits of gender construction. *American Sociological Review, 65*, 443–457.

U.S. Census Bureau (2003). Poverty in the United States: 2002, Current Population Reports. Washington, DC.

U.S. Census Bureau (2004). Families and living arrangements: 2004, Current Population Reports. Washington, DC.

Uttal, L. (1999). Using kin for child care: Embedment in the socioeconomic networks of extended families. *Journal of Marriage and the Family, 61*, 845–857.

Valenzuela, A., & Dornbusch, S. M. (1994). Familism and social capital in the academic achievement of Mexican origin and Anglo adolescents. *Social Science Quarterly, 75*, 18–36.

Waldfogel, J. (1997). The effects of children on women's wages. *American Sociological Review, 62*, 209–217.

West, C., & Zimmerman, D. (1987). Doing gender. *Gender & Society, 1*, 125–151.

White, L. K., & Brinkerhoff, D. B. (1981). The sexual division of labor: Evidence from childhood. *Social Forces, 60*, 170–181.

Whitmore, G. (1999). African American father figures and children's achievement. *Journal of African American Men, 4*, 25–35.

Wilcox, W. B. (2002). Religion, convention, and paternal involvement. *Journal of Marriage and the Family, 64*, 780–792.

Wilkinson, D. Y. (1990). Afro-Americans in the corporation: An assessment of the impact on the family. *Marriage and Family Review, 15*, 115–129.

Williams, N. (1993). Elderly Mexican American men: Work and family patterns. In J. C. Hood (Ed.), *Men, work, and family* (pp. 68–85). Newbury Park, CA: Sage.

Wilson, W. J., & Neckerman, K. (1986). Poverty and family structure: The widening gap between evidence and public policy issues. In S. H. Danziger & D. Weinberg (Eds.), *Fighting poverty: What works and what doesn't* (pp. 232–259). Cambridge, England: Cambridge University Press.

Wright, E. O. (1997). *Class counts: Comparative studies in class analysis.* New York: Cambridge University Press.

Yamaguchi, K., & Wang, Y. (2002). Class identification of married employed women and men in America. *American Journal of Sociology, 108*, 440–475.

Yancey, G. A. (2001). *Differences in the gender attitudes of European-Americans, African-Americans, Hispanic-Americans and Asian-Americans.* Paper presented at the Annual Meetings of Southern Sociological Society.

Zelizer, V. A. (1994). *Pricing the priceless child: The changing social value of children* (2nd ed.). Princeton, NJ: Princeton University Press.

13

The Role of Economics
in Work-Family Research[1]

Robert Drago
Lonnie Golden
Pennsylvania State University

Conflicts between work and family occur when three conditions hold. First, a family has dependent care responsibilities. Second, all able-bodied adults in the family are employed during hours of the day or week such that there is a gap in family coverage of dependent care because employers do not provide sufficient time and flexibility for employees to meet family commitments. And, third, governmental supports for dependent care are insufficient to fill the gap. In other words, work-family conflict emerges when there is a care gap to be filled and the caregiver is not fully accommodated by his or her employer or government. Typically, "caregiving" and "family" refer to care for dependent children, but the definition is intended to be broader, extending to time caring for elderly parents, other relatives, and spouses and partners. Although conflicts may also arise between work and nonfamily commitments, such as religious, community, athletic or various avocations, these are ignored in what follows for brevity.

For most of its history, economics had little to say about work-family conflict. In part, the lack of attention was related to a presumption that women were not employed and hence were available and willing to fill the care gap. In addition, economics became more narrowly focused on market activities rather than work per se heading into the 20th century, leaving little space for considerations of care and unpaid work. What came to be known as "mainstream" economics emerged with a focus on self-interested individuals operating in markets for goods and services, labor, and capital (e.g., Marshall, 1920).

These circumstances changed rapidly with the mass movement of women and ultimately mothers into the labor markets of the developed economies in the last half of the 20th century. Labor economists began researching the factors driving women into the labor force and the possibility of labor market discrimination. Ultimately, a large body of research, mainly produced by feminist economists, came to address issues of work-family conflict and prospective solutions.

After reviewing the relevant writings of early economists, this chapter turns to issues of the definition of work and related measures of value in the national accounts, the division of labor in the home, the motherhood wage gap, the supply of work hours, inflexible hours, and overwork. The conclusion provides a brief summary and directions for future research.

EARLY ECONOMISTS AND WORK-FAMILY ISSUES

In what is usually considered the primary starting point of economics, as a discipline, Adam Smith in his 1776 book, *The Wealth of Nations*, introduced two ideas that survive in one form or another to the present. The first is the distinction between those who engage in productive labor and those who do not, with productive labor implicitly defined as involving tangible goods made for market exchange. Smith regarded "reproduction," including tasks such as childrearing, cooking and cleaning, as useful and necessary, but unproductive.[2] The second is the notion that an extensive division of labor helps an economy to increase its production and wealth. Both ideas appear initially on the first page of the work (Smith, 1904, p. 1).

These two ideas are gendered. Men were more often engaged in productive labor, even in the 18th century, hence men were privileged in Smith's analysis. Additionally, the rationale for keeping women out of the labor market was implicitly traced to the efficiency of the bread-winner/homemaker model of the family due to the division of labor involved, although this argument did not become explicit until much later (i.e., Becker, 1965). Within a generation or two after Smith, some political economists began to employ the distinction between the productive and unproductive spheres to make the case for better educating women, so as to integrate them into what were considered productive roles. Thomas Malthus, writing somewhat later, is perhaps most well-known for the "Malthusian" argument that population tends to outstrip growth in the economy and impoverish many as a result (1798). Surprisingly, Malthus did not see women's entry into the labor force as a mechanism for staving off starvation.[3] Instead, he saw periodic misery and impoverishment as the mechanisms necessary to keep populations in check. However, around the same time, J. B. Say, who regarded the gendered division of labor as "natural," proposed that certain professions be reserved for women (remaining excluded from all others), so as to deter women from entering prostitution. This marked a transition of thought from entirely ignoring the role of women to treating them more as rational, economic agents. The occupational confinement of women and restriction of their choices, however, presaged overcrowding theory and the suppression of women's wages by the mid-18th century.[4]

Karl Marx was the first economist to foreshadow work-family issues (1954 [1867]). In an agricultural context, David Ricardo (1911 [1817]) had argued that some corn from the end of one season needs to be held back to produce the same amount of corn the next season; this seed corn is needed to reproduce the economy. Marx expanded the notion of reproduction to include workers, thereby implicitly raising the possibility that paid or unpaid child care is necessary for the economy.[5] Homemaking therefore took on heightened status in Marx's theoretical framework.

More directly, Marx believed that capitalist economies have an inexorable appetite for workers, and hence that women and mothers would eventually be drawn into the labor market. Although he did not pursue this idea at length, he did predict the potential development of child-care and domestic services labor markets as a result.[6]

Marx's framework was eventually discarded by the mainstream of economics. This discarding had probably occurred by the time the eighth edition of Alfred Marshall's *Principles of Economics* was published in 1920. Marshall mentioned the employment of women in this work, but women are more often mentioned in the context of family expenditures and childbearing. Indeed, Marshall claimed explicitly that women should not be employed.[7]

Less directly but of perhaps greater importance was Marshall's focus on the supply and demand for goods and services in *markets*, a focus that necessarily excluded unpaid housework and child care. As McNulty (1980) has argued, many labor economists in the first half of the 20th century ignored the mainstream and maintained an interdisciplinary approach with an emphasis on institutions, or laws, customs and practices that are sufficiently regular and consistent to warrant study, and which affect behavior in the workplace (e.g., tax laws, norms around work effort, or health and safety practices in the workplace). Recognition of work-family issues might have occurred among the institutionalists, but did not. For example, among the most prominent institutionalists, both Thorstein Veblen (1899) and Sydney and Beatrice Webb (1965 [1897]) wrote fairly extensively on women, yet never discussed issues of child or family care. The lesser-known Charlotte Perkins Gilman (1966 [1898]) addressed work-family conflict in *Women and Economics*, arguing that women needed to enter the labor market to achieve economic independence, and that even if this meant mothers would spend less time on child rearing, "our babies would be better off if part of their time was passed in other care than their mothers" (p. 212).

Gilman foreshadowed the emergence of a later body of research by feminist economists that challenged mainstream economics on a variety of fronts—including the reasons for and appropriate solutions to work-family conflict. Feminist economists draw on the empirical tools of mainstream economics, the institutionalist emphasis on the importance of specific practices, laws and regulations, and Marx's focus on systematic power relations. These strands are drawn together through the lens of gender inequality or, somewhat differently, through efforts to track and reduce systematic differences in political and economic power according to race, class, and gender categories. Among those mentioned below, we can count as leading feminist economist researchers Randy Albelda, Teresa Amott, Eileen Appelbaum, Barbara Bergmann, Francine Blau, Marianne Ferber, Nancy Folbre, Heidi Hartmann, Jane Humphries, Laura Leete, Julie Matthaei, Margaret Reid, and Juliet Schor.

By the 1950s, however, most labor economists were following Marshall's lead and analyzing markets and market forces alone (McNulty, 1980, p. 5). This narrowing of the field pushed work and family issues further into the background of economics, if that were possible, until the massive entry of women and mothers into the labor market in the latter half of the 20th century.

After the economic mainstream had honed in on market behavior, it became more formal and accepted the notion that individuals are self-interested and make decisions based on the rational pursuit of self-interest. The scope for examining unpaid child care and the motivations to perform such tasks was therefore extremely limited. Additionally, the tools to analyze such behavior were distorted by an increasing if often implicit presumption that all human behavior can be cast in the mold of rational decision making in a market setting (Folbre, 2001).

THE MEANING OF "WORK" AND THE NATIONAL ACCOUNTS

Nancy Folbre (1991) documented the way in which the U.S. Census has historically treated housework and unpaid child care.[8] Should the performance of such tasks be treated as productive and valuable? Were the answer cast in the negative, then if two househusbands hire each other to perform the same tasks in each others' households, they switch from being nonproductive to productive. At a fundamental level, this argument is nonsensical, because the men are still performing exactly the same tasks and should therefore be classified as productive regardless of whether pay is involved. After a series of battles, the U.S. Census settled on classifying anyone performing housework and child care full-time without pay as "unoccupied," and eventually as "dependents," a term that survives today in both the census and the U.S. tax code. Unsurprisingly, it was not househusbands whose efforts were typically devalued and ultimately ignored in this process; it was housewives.

A better definition of work was and is available. As Margaret Reid wrote in 1934, work can be viewed as any "*activity ... that ... might be delegated to a paid [employee]*" (p. 11).[9] Thus, we might distinguish paid from unpaid work, but the fact that virtually identical tasks may be undertaken for high, low, or no pay implies that relevant activities should all fall under the category of work.

The relevance of unpaid work was heightened when the developed nations began constructing national accounting systems in the 1930s and 1940s.[10] These systems set criteria for gauging whether an economy is improving or deteriorating, originally relying mainly on the concept of Gross National Product (GNP) and later focusing on the construct of Gross Domestic Product (GDP). Both measures place zero value on unpaid work. Therefore, returning to our earlier example, and using either the GNP or GDP yardstick, when the two househusbands hired each other, the economy grew. If they returned to their own households, the economy apparently shrank. By extension, the entry of women and mothers into the labor market, even if their entire paychecks went toward covering homemaker replacement services, would appear to generate economic growth.

The logical deficiency of ignoring unpaid work led a steady stream of mainstream economists, starting in the 1940s, to support an extension of the national income accounting system to include unpaid work; the group included the likes of Simon Kuznets, William Nordhaus, James Tobin, and John Kendrick (Eisner, 1989). Such extended accounts now exist, but are far from replacing GDP as the primary yardstick for measuring economic well-being and devising economic policies.

The use of GDP to gauge the health of the economy promotes, for example, a tendency to permit environmental degradation; to push women, men, and children into paid work; and to reduce fertility rates. Anything that is unpaid, whether it is work in the home, childbearing, or maintaining clean air, is necessarily excluded and devalued.

The debate over measuring GDP may strike some readers as esoteric and of little practical importance. Such is not the case.

Take electoral behavior. It is now a mantra among pundits that GDP growth is a major factor for incumbent presidents seeking reelection (e.g., Aversa, 2003). As a result, presidents have an incentive to force individuals to switch from unpaid to paid work in the runup to elections. If unpaid work were included in GDP, this incentive would not exist.

Or, consider current divorce law. Williams noted that present divorce law weighs heavily on the side of breadwinner men because of a presumption that "he-who-earns-it-owns-it" (1999, p. 5). As a result, millions of American women and children are left in poverty following divorce. If unpaid work counted in GDP, the grounds for courts to rely on this presumption would be considerably weakened, and it would be less likely that poverty would represent a legally sanctioned fruit for performing unpaid labor as a housewife.

By similar logic, the 1996 Personal Responsibility and Work Opportunity Reconciliation Act (PRWORA) sought to force millions of poor mothers off of the welfare roles, in large part by replacing unpaid with paid work. If unpaid work around childrearing were valued, it is at least possible that the PRWORA would not have passed, at least with heavy "work" requirements.

Finally, the devaluing of unpaid work has shaped recent debates concerning overwork. The book that set off this debate, Juliet Schor's *The Overworked American* (1991), actually included housework and child care in calculations related to overwork. Nonetheless, responses to the book uniformly dropped unpaid work from working time calculations,[11] presumably because the only possible source of overwork is paid employment.

In general, the exclusion of unpaid work in studies of working time tends to privilege men. As Hochschild and Machung (1989) argued, if unpaid work is excluded from working time figures, it typically appears that men work more than women while, if it is included, women appear to "work" more than men. In a time diary study of elementary school teachers, evidence supported the claim that "overwork" is better understood in the latter case—parents performing less paid work but far more unpaid work in the home also slept less, had less leisure time, and exercised less, all consistent with the possibility that they are often overworked.[12]

The overarching implication of devaluing unpaid work is that both the government and researchers end up weighing in on work-family conflicts in a lopsided fashion: in favor of the paid work side. As Folbre (2001) and Schor (1991) argued, family supports and time with families, whether facilitated by corporate or government policies, are antithetical to GDP growth. They both concluded that it is the improper measurement of GDP that should be changed to facilitate family life and child development.

THE DIVISION OF LABOR IN THE HOME AND WOMEN'S LABOR FORCE PARTICIPATION

In addition to unpaid work, many women were performing paid work during the corpus of the 19th and 20th centuries (Bergmann, 1986). This was particularly true for women of color (Amott & Matthaei, 1996). Over the course of the first half of the 20th century, however, women's labor force participation declined, men's wages improved, and the breadwinner father/homemaker mother model of the family became viable for more people. That decline halted and reversed beginning in the 1950s (Appelbaum, 1981). The percentage of adult women in the labor force rose from 33.9% in 1950 to 59.8% in 1998, with the largest increase occurring during the decade of the 1970s, when the figure rose by 8.1% (Fullerton, 1999). Of greater relevance to the question of work and family conflict, labor force participation rates for mothers of young children continued to rise, and are now in fact *higher* than for other adult women at 61.5% as of 1998, with a particularly large recent increase in rates for single mothers, consistent with passage of the PRWORA in 1996 (Martin & Kats, 2003).

The single most important mainstream economist who has weighed in on work and family issues is undoubtedly Nobel prize-winner Gary S. Becker. Becker's work was mainstream in that he believed in the importance of market forces and self-interested, rational individuals. His work is important because he carried relevant analytical tools into areas where markets did not exist. For example, it is reasonably safe to assert that prior to Becker's (1966) analyses of education as productive of "human capital," most individuals and policymakers (and students) viewed higher education as a luxury more associated with middle- or upper-class status than with the ability to earn a higher income. Becker also studied marriage, religion, parenting, discrimination, and the division of labor in the home (1976).

Becker's work has been criticized by a variety of economists. When phenomena such as marriage, education, or religion come under the purview of economics, the results make little intuitive sense. Individuals rarely pay each other a "price" to marry, cannot purchase education and simply inject it into their minds, and rarely wake up and check the latest price configuration to help determine whether to attend a mosque, church, or synagogue. Instead, motivations and social structures around love, power, and cultural norms are probably of greater relevance for understanding these phenomena (Albelda, Drago, & Shulman, 2001). Nonetheless, Becker's research has been highly influential and insightful.

In his 1965 article, "A Theory of the Allocation of Time," Becker predicted that women would continue to enter the labor market in increasing numbers. As he put it, "an increase in the value of a mother's time may induce her to enter the labor force and spend less time cooking by using pre-cooked foods and less time on child-care by using nurseries, camps or baby-sitters" (1965, p. 110). Becker noted the dramatic increases in women's participation in higher education, a trend that continues to this day (National Coalition for Women and Girls in Education, 2002), along with the development of labor-saving devices in the home, such as laundry and dishwashing machines, electric and gas stoves, refrigerators, vacuum cleaners, and precooked meals, and believed that these changes would reduce the value of a woman's time in the home and increase her value in the labor market, driving women to seek employment. He also foresaw the development of the child-care labor market.

Becker did not, however, understand the care gap that emerged with the rise of dual-earner couples in a context where neither employers nor the government provided relevant supports for caregiving. This omission was not accidental: Becker did not believe dual-earner couples were efficient, so believed they would not become the modal family form (as in fact occurred). A paper published in 1985 on the sexual division of labor marked a dramatic breakthrough in Becker's research—for the first time, he clearly labeled unpaid child care and housework as "work." Up to this point, most economic research on discriminatory wage differentials traced them to differences in the treatment of men and women per se, rather than to the gender division of labor in the home (e.g., Bergmann, 1986). Once the idea of unpaid work was admitted, along with the fact that it mainly falls on women, Becker concluded that differences in wages between men and women are partly attributable to discrimination and differences in hours of work and human capital investments, but also due to the fact that women devote substantially more time and effort to children and the household. In short, raising children is work, and jobs are structured to advantage those who perform no child care because, as Adam Smith's work implied, a strong division of labor and attendant specialization in either unpaid or paid labor is efficient.

Once unpaid work was considered, Becker believed the efficiency of the division of labor favored breadwinner/homemaker over dual-earner families. Indeed, the 1985 paper concluded that the way forward to gender equality lay not in the equal sharing of employment and child care across men and women, but instead in a situation where "husbands would be more specialized to housework and wives to market activities in about half the marriages, and the reverse would occur in the other half" (p. S56). The conclusion that breadwinner/homemaker families are efficient is, for most couples, probably incorrect. Indeed, Becker's earlier (1965) research explained the emergence of dual-earner couples due to women's increasing levels of education, in tandem with the development of labor-saving devices in the home and child-care labor markets. These developments had, if anything, continued through the 1980s and to the present.

Nonetheless, the central insight of the 1985 paper regarding unpaid work is crucial, and was largely ignored for at least a decade. On one side, feminist economists were hesitant to admit that a subset of women—those with child-care responsibilities—were less productive in the workplace than men.[13] Such an admission would feed the backlash against women's entry into the labor force (Faludi, 1991). On the other side, mainstream labor economists continued to focus on markets and market forces, relegating unpaid work to the sidelines.[14]

This issue reappeared with the development of research on the motherhood wage gap, discussed below. But, it should be mentioned in closing that some feminist economists took a very different approach to women's entry into the labor market and the division of labor in the home. Heidi Hartmann started with Marx's argument that capitalism "threatened to bring all women and children into the labor force and hence to destroy the family..." (1979, p. 207). In Hartmann's view, the puzzle was not why women entered the labor force in the last half-century, but rather why it took so long for women to enter. Her answer lay in the patriarchal power of men over women, particularly in the household. Men had a direct stake in preventing the employment of women to maintain women's dependence on men. Men engaged in various tactics, ranging from the passage of so-called protective legislation to restrict the hours of women, to the exclusion of women from trade unions, and the prevention of skills acquisition by women. Men ultimately lost this battle, but in the process were able to shape the labor market such that most women would be locked into low-wage, dead-end jobs and hence still be reliant on marriage and men to achieve economic security and success.

Ultimately, Hartmann's predictions seem to have been realized with the development of what Phyllis Moen (2000) has labeled the "neotraditional family." In these families, there is greater gender overlap in terms of paid and unpaid work, but women continue to perform a higher proportion of unpaid work in the family, and men continue to earn most of the income, thereby maintaining inequality.

THE MOTHERHOOD WAGE GAP

Becker's later research suggested that there might be a wage penalty associated with parenting. Because most parenting work was and continues to be performed by mothers, the research further implied that there might be a wage gap specifically associated with motherhood: Among women, mothers may systematically earn less than nonmothers.

As discussed earlier, the gender wage gap literature largely ignored any potential role for motherhood per se. Becker's 1985 work implied that the phenomenon warranted study. Other economists were reaching the same conclusion by around the mid-1980s. As Victor Fuchs wrote in 1988, mothers suffered lower wages than nonmothers because their careers are interrupted: "even when mothers stay in the labor force, responsibility for children frequently constrains their choice of job ... [and] women who devote a great deal of time and energy to childcare ... are often less able to devote maximum effort to market work" (1988, p. 60). Similar arguments appeared in Barbara Bergmann's (1986) work.

These works suggested the existence of a motherhood wage gap. But, in retrospect, the gap was still emerging at that time. Only later was the new pattern clearly identified and documented, a task performed by Jane Waldfogel in 1998. Waldfogel compared wage figures from 1980 and 1990 for respondents at age 30, and found the gender wage gap had shrunk substantially over the period.[15] The overall wage gap between women and men, corrected for differences in education and the like, was $4.73 per hour in 1980, a figure that fell to $1.86 per hour by 1990. In both years, men experienced higher wages. This decline in the gender gap reflected dramatic gains for women in the labor market.

However, Waldfogel found a new wage gap emerging, a gap affecting women who are employed and responsible for dependent children. Among women in the sample, the motherhood gap, as Waldfogel called it, rose from $.42 in 1980 to $2.07 in 1990. The difference in hourly wages between women who are and are not mothers became larger than the overall difference between men and women.

More recently, Michelle Budig and Paula England (2001) decomposed the motherhood wage gap into various factors. They found that a portion of the gap (around two sevenths) was related to mothers having less job experience than nonmother women, and that the jobs mothers took, particularly part-time jobs, also played a role in their lesser wages. The main causes of the motherhood wage gap were, however, located either in mothers being less productive or employers discriminating against mothers. Budig and England were unable to disentangle these two effects because precise gauges of individual productivity were not available.

The main question this research raises is whether, in fact, the work of caring for children leaves employees with less energy, time, and commitment for their jobs, or if instead employers simply view mothers as less productive regardless of actual job performance—engaging in discrimination against mothers. Research by Hersch and Stratton (2000) on the marriage wage premium for men is consistent with the discrimination argument in that they found employers favoring married over unmarried men, regardless of how many hours the married men spent on household tasks; the flip side of this argument is that employers may discriminate against mothers as opposed to nonparenting women. Lundberg and Rose (2000) similarly found that it is not the tasks of parenting per se, but instead signals mothers send to employers regarding parenting responsibilities—such as extended time off for childbearing and reduced hours of employment—that generate the motherhood wage gap.

To establish directly that discrimination is involved here, it might be worthwhile to employ testing procedures used to identify racial discrimination (Darity & Mason, 1998). In such tests, individuals are differentiated only by racial characteristics and apply for jobs to ascertain whether people of color experience lower rates of second interviews, are less frequently offered a job, are offered lower wages when offered jobs, and are placed at lower levels on the employer's job ladders (all of these typically occur for Black as opposed to White testers). Tests involving job applications by pregnant and nonpregnant women could be performed, as could tests involving only pregnant women who are distinquished only in plans for time off the job following childbirth. These tests would not establish that discrimination is the only factor involved, but could confirm that discrimination against mothers operates in the labor market. If discrimination against mothers exists, either existing civil rights legislation or new antidiscrimination laws may be warranted (Williams, 1999).

UPDATING ECONOMIC MODELS OF LABOR SUPPLY

In addition to employer behavior, empirical efforts to isolate the sources of the motherhood wage gap suggest that household behavior is also involved, and particularly the division of labor between husbands and wives and decisions regarding the supply of labor to the market.

The individual's labor supply curve appears as the starting point in virtually all labor economics textbooks, including those focused on work and family.[16] The foundation for the decision to enter or exit the labor force and to prefer to supply a certain number of hours of market work is the notion of worker welfare or "utility." The conventional economic approach to labor supply then rests on three-legged stool of utility maximization behavior, equilibrating markets, and stable preferences (see Humphries, 1998). That is, individuals seek the amount of paid work activity that will attain the highest possible level of well-being for themselves (or family). The wage they earn is assumed to reflect their "marginal productivity"—the monetary value they create for their employer. Their market wage rate also reflects their "marginal rate of substitution"—the value they ascribe to the last hour of unpaid ("leisure") time they sacrifice by working. Finally, individuals are assumed to possess their own unique, inherent taste or distaste for work (which may change over the life cycle, but not randomly). It is assumed that "more is better" when it comes to both income and leisure time, but each additional unit of income or leisure yields individuals smaller and smaller gains to their well-being.

Each one of these three assumptions of the basic model is either too simplistic or fundamentally flawed. First, worker welfare increasingly depends on more than just the standard determinants of income (Y) and leisure (L), even when the model is expanded to Becker's third component of time allocation, unpaid household production. Second, market forces in the labor market may never actually reach equilibrium. Even when they do, the result may be suboptimal for workers and families, in part because of negative spillover effects, to others in the household or community in general. Third, preferences for income and leisure are determined not only by individuals or even the family context, but instead may be increasingly influenced and ultimately altered by perceived gender roles, the surrounding workplace, and general culture (Jacobs & Gerson, 2004; Hakim, 2002; George, 2001; Jalilvand, 2000).

MODELING DIMENSIONS OF TIME: FROM INDIVIDUAL TO FAMILY TO SOCIAL CONTEXT

As more and more household time, and particularly women's time, is spent in the workforce—longer weekly hours and more weeks worked per year—the nature of both work and leisure hours gains in importance. The standard utility function:

$$U = f(Y; L),$$

where utility (U) is a function (f) of income (Y) and hours of leisure (L), needs to be expanded to capture this development. Becker's insight was to introduce unpaid household production as a distinct, third argument in the utility function, P, which has elements of both work and leisure—as is true for housework, caregiving, childrearing, and so on:

$$U = f(Y; L; P).$$

The introduction of household production provided a rationale for the division of labor and specialization along traditional gender lines: To maximize total consumption of all goods and services, men should be fully employed and women should engage exclusively in household production. Surprisingly little attention has been paid in economics-based research to the specific uses and distinct types of nonmarket "leisure" time, which may have economic consequences in the longer run. For example, "productive" leisure may build one's own human capital to supply labor more efficiently in the future. "Nonproductive" leisure may promote the recuperation necessary for supplying future labor to peak efficiency, while any counterproductive types of leisure activities produce the reverse, future inefficiency. Consumptive leisure time (e.g., shopping) transforms income into the goods and services that contribute to utility. Social reproduction leisure (P) fosters human capital development of the future workforce.[17] Finally, "pure" leisure time is an end in itself that increases utility.

However, the increasing prominence of the dual-earner household has elevated the importance of *combining* market work and unpaid work activities, on a daily basis, throughout most of workers' life cycles. Thus, a separate and distinct contributor to individuals' well-being, even for those without direct care responsibilities, is the timing or scheduling of work activities (S). For a given duration of work time and leisure time, a worker's well-being may be maximized if the schedule is as preferred by the worker, and diminished if the scheduling does not fit (see Barnett, Gareis, & Brennan, 1999):

$$U = f(Y; L; P; S).$$

The importance of S appears to be increasing, as not only working parents but also younger and older workers are placing a higher value on their ability to synchronize or stagger work schedules, such as occurs with flextime and compressed workweek initiatives in the workplace. For dual-earner parents, the value lies in an improved capacity to coordinate caregiving activities and by reducing the frequency, size, or risk of time gaps around child care. Such coordination may involve more tag-team parenting and nontraditional shift working (e.g., Presser, 2003). Indeed, many workers that have more flexible daily starting and ending times are either working excessively long hours or are employed part-time to achieve coordination, sacrificing either leisure time or average hourly compensation (Golden, 2005).

Moreover, as the complexity of household reproduction activities grows with more time spent in the paid workforce, the ability to adjust both the number and the scheduling of work hours in response to either unanticipated or anticipated changes in preferences, gains in importance. Hence, even if the number and scheduling of work hours are as desired at any one point in time, workers benefit from an ability to transition between income-earning, caregiving and leisure activities over the course of the day and over the life course, suggesting the need to include flexibility (F) in the model, or

$$U = f(Y; L; P; S; F).$$

Lacking the ability to make seamless transitions, workers become more prone to multi-tasking. Overlapping activities are quite common, and not only cut into leisure time but also cause stress (Floro & Miles, 2003).

Another dimension of people's working time is the extent to which some hours are worked involuntarily. The conventional model assumes that workers and firms sort themselves in ways that match desired and required hours of paid work, at least in the long run. But, in the interim, and maybe indefinitely, there may be disequilibrium in the market for labor. Individuals' actual hours worked can exceed their desired hours if, for example, there is unwelcome but mandatory overtime, no opportunity to cut back hours to part-time, or inadequate vacation time in a job. Workers thus can experience "overemployment," being employed beyond their desired number of hours of work, being willing but unable to trade income for reduced hours. A worker might rationally settle for a longer than optimal workweek. This may occur because switching to a shorter-hours job is too costly, either in terms of a transition to a new career or because wage and benefits losses associated with part-time status are too severe. Thus, while individuals might not alter their employment or hours—technically experiencing an equilibrium—the outcome is suboptimal. Moreover, because parents with young children are more prone to experience "overemployment," the reduced time spent with family may create a negative externality to the extent there are adverse effects on children, marriage quality, and the creation of social capital.

By focusing on work hours preferences almost exclusively as a reflection of changes in wages that generate opposing income and substitution effects, the conventional model of labor supply has paid insufficient attention to the importance of labor-supply preference formation.[18] The factors that shift the entire labor supply curve are typically relegated to the status of exogenous changes in innate preferences or constraints. This lacunae is not only unfortunate, because these shifts are important for understanding recent trends, but may also be mistaken because some of these factors may be "endogenous." This endogeneity violates the standard model's assumption that preferences are stable and external. For example, an individual experiencing a bout with overemployment creates time scarcity in the household. This scarcity might in turn lead a household to eventually change their preference from self-produced to more market-produced goods and services. The household may now want to shift from time-*using* toward more time-*saving* goods and services. This shift requires more income. In addition, households are likely to shift preferences from time-intensive to income-intensive leisure activities. Together, these effects ratchet upward individuals' targeted consumption levels and gradually dissipate the initial desire for shorter work hours (Rothschild, 1982).[19] On the other end, socioeconomic class, religion, and cultural attitudes may influence how much time women prefer to spend (or limit themselves) in the paid labor force (Jalilvand, 2000). Moreover, the individual in the household who provides the superior income may hold sway in household decision making. A cultural bias is that such leverage is not symmetrically derived from bringing home more "leisure" time. Thus, increasing hours of labor force activity may boost the relative weight one's preferences receive in decisions such as consumption purchases, leisure time use, and allocations among sons versus daughters. This effect may also impede any initial desire to reduce hours of paid work. Furthermore, there is some evidence that the generally heightened inequality of earnings among individuals, households, and particularly within occupations has led individuals, especially among those losing ground, to supply more labor to the market in order to sustain the household's relative income and consumption levels.[20] Finally, high-performance workplaces, even with their greater formal employee supports and involvement, promote additional time commitment that is detrimental to work and family balance.[21]

Long hours of labor, even if voluntary but especially if involuntary, may lead to symptoms of "overwork." Overwork occurs when individuals experience some adverse health conditions attributable to fatigue, stress, or burnout. Overwork occurs with the combination of paid plus unpaid work, not just the former (as Schor's critics failed to recognize, see above). Individuals are thus at risk with either an increase in paid work or unpaid work, but particularly when pursuing both roles simultaneously with intensity. Perhaps this combined effect explains why conflict between work and family demands escalates as individuals make greater commitments of time and attention to either their work or their family role.[22] The upshot of overwork is a higher risk of negative outcomes for relationships with spouse, children, and friends.[23]

ECONOMICS-BASED SOLUTIONS: PERSPECTIVES OF ECONOMICS ON FAMILY-FRIENDLY POLICIES

The gradual crowding out of nonmarket time for families creates a market failure. Even if the time crunch is due to voluntary overwork, many of the resulting social costs will not be internalized or borne by the worker him or herself.[24] If the labor market is failing to provide the optimal amount of time for efficient reproduction in households and for the production of future human capital, there is a basis for policy intervention in favor of promoting family-friendly workplaces.[25] An adverse selection issue exists here such that many companies may balk at introducing family-friendly features for fear not only of its initial cost, but also of attracting employees who would use the policies.[26] In addition, there is a problem of asymmetric information such that workers may consistently underestimate the long-run negative effects of overwork on their own health and on others. Thus, there are at least three reasons why market forces alone cannot be relied on to yield the socially optimal amount of family-friendly workplace benefits and flexibility.

Economics thus can be applied as a basis for public policy efforts to encourage a greater provision and wider dissemination of workplace supports through some combination of mandates, taxes, and subsidies. Over the two and a quarter centuries since Adam Smith's era, work and family time has been transformed from separate spheres of life to ones that are increasingly in direct conflict with each other, both within the daily life of households and for individuals themselves. As a result, analysts have evolved from work-family conflict and imbalance to work-life integration.[27] Integrating rather than separating these once separate realms requires a multipronged effort to modify workplaces to accommodate rather than penalize employees seeking to fulfill multiple commitments. Ensuring more options for the flexible supply of labor time is crucial to achieving this ends.[28] Needed improvements also involve eliminating the documented compensation penalty facing employees who attempt to reduce their hours in the workforce via either part-time or nonstandard and contingent jobs.[29]

INSIDE THE BLACK BOX

An additional challenge for economists interested in understanding conflicts between work and family is posed by ethnographic research. Ethnographers gather samples of rich, detailed qualitative data from a handful of research subjects and strive to let the resulting interpretation of reality come from the subjects themselves. Excellent examples of this approach in the work-family field can be found in the work of Hochschild (1997), Risman (1998), Deutsch (1999), or Garey (1999). These works rely on the inductive rather than deductive method common to economic theorizing, and what generalizations are found are based on samples that are sufficiently small that they would never see the light of day in the pages of a reputable economics journal.

Economists could continue to ignore ethnographers. But, we believe that would be a mistake. What instead should be pursued is to take hypotheses generated by ethnographic research and test these in larger data sets, using economic methods to do so.[30] That promising line of research leads us down a very daunting path, however, since an acceptance of the value of ethnographic research among economists would have us generating theoretical predictions drawn from empirical findings rather than just deductive thinking.

Nonetheless, for ascertaining where the crux of work-family conflicts will be found and for identifying viable solutions, an approach combining of traditional economic methods with ethnographic research offers us a great source of hope. Whether others will follow that path remains to be seen.

IMPLICATIONS FOR RESEARCH, TEACHING, AND PUBLIC POLICY

Among all of the disciplines that research issues relevant to work-family, the contribution from the economics field probably holds the most untapped potential. It can most directly make the "business case" and "public goods" argument that work-family issues remain insufficiently resolved. However, work-family conflict and imbalance continue to be framed most often as individual, private concerns only. Economic models have evolved somewhat, mainly to capture the "work" aspect of work-family, by recognizing that unpaid work takes time and energy from paid work and leisure time. It is useful in understanding individual and household decision making regarding whether to be in the paid labor force; the types of jobs sought or taken to combine work and family; the number of hours of preferred each day/days worked each week/weeks worked each year; the price paid by workers who wish to prioritize time and effort for family and caregiving activities; and the illogic and bias inherent in excluding the value of unpaid work in our measures of aggregate "production," and particularly in GDP, while including similar services involved in market transactions.

Thus, future research should employ a more nuanced and realistic, albeit more complex, model to understanding individual and family behavior. Moreover, it needs to further develop analyses of the economic and social consequences of choices, constraints, and institutions that ultimately determine the health and well-being of individuals, families, relationships, communities, and society at large. The costs of work-life conflict have escalated and are likely to continue to rise. The benefits of facilitating work-life integration will remain largely ignored or discounted by economists until the spillover costs and benefits are brought onto their radar screens in next-generation models and empirical testing.

Finally, for the teaching of economics, the major challenges this chapter suggests are those common to any interdisciplinary approach. To give students a solid understanding of the public goods aspects of children, of the importance of including unpaid work in the national accounts, and of the externalities involved in overwork requires a firm grounding in mainstream economic theory. Students often find the mainstream notions of self-interested individuals (or families) interacting only through markets attractive and useful. But, it is also incumbent on teachers to provide understandings brought from ethnographic research, from sociology, and particularly from feminist economics in order for students to garner a reasonably accurate picture of the gender and racial inequalities, power relationships, and institutions involved in creating work-family conflict. Such an understanding among students and the general populace could help move us toward a society where the care gap is bridged, with help from both employers and the government, and with improved levels of gender equity in both the home and the workplace.

NOTES

[1] The authors both thank the Alfred P. Sloan Foundation for financial support and thank Jennifer Fazioli for research assistance.

[2] Dimand et al. (2004). Such labor was considered unproductive because it created neither a commodity nor capital. Note this is well prior to the modern notion of human capital formation, which is clearly fostered by reproduction-type services.

[3] This argument is implicit in the following statement: "When therefore a woman was connected with a man, who had entered into no compact to maintain her children; and aware of the inconveniences that he might bring upon himself, had deserted her, these children must necessarily fall for support upon the society, or starve" (Malthus, 1798, chapter 10, para. 27).

[4] Dimand et al. (2004).

[5] "Hence the sum of the means of subsistence necessary for the production of labour-power must include the means necessary for the labourer's substitutes, i.e., his children, in order that this race of peculiar commodity-owners may perpetuate its appearance in the market" (Marx, 1954, p. 168).

[6] As women are drawn into the labor market, "the diminished expenditure of labor in the house is accompanied by an increased expenditure of money. The cost of keeping the family increases, and balances the great income [from the employment of wives]" (Marx, 1954, p. 373).

[7] "The wages of women are for similar reasons rising fast relatively to those of men. And this is a great gain in so far as it tends to develop their faculties; but an injury in so far as it tempts them to neglect their duty of building up a true home, and of investing their efforts in the personal capital of their children's character and abilities" (Marshall, 1920, chapter 12, para. 40).

[8] For a brief history of what society has considered "work," employment, and "idleness," see Wolfe (1997).

[9] The italics are ours, and the word "employee" has been substituted for the word "worker" in the quotation to preclude the use of the term being defined within the definition.

[10] The following history is recounted by Eisner (1989).

[11] See, e.g., Robinson and Bostrom (1994) or Jacobs and Gerson (1998, 2004).

[12] See Drago et al. (1999).

[13] For example, as late as 1994, Folbre relegated the paper to a footnote (1994, p. 19).

[14] For example, as recently as 1991, Jacob Mincer produced a study of women's labor force participation and, even though he found strong evidence regarding the effects of children, placed the relevant information in appendices. For a summary of mainstream research on wage discrimination by gender, see Albelda, Drago, and Shulman (2000, chapter 5). For a recent example, see Barth, Roed, and Torp (2002).

[15] Waldfogel (1998) used Current Population Survey data and applied a natural log transform to the wage data. The log wage approach typically provides a better fit for wage regressions, such that a higher percentage of the variance in wages is explained following the transformation, as opposed to using simple dollar figures. We undo that transformation to yield the dollar figures reported in this paragraph. However, because the transformation alters the relationships between variables, undoing the transformation only yields an approximation that would not be replicated if absolute dollar values were used consistently in the analysis. The figures provided here are gotten by taking the anti-log of the figures for male and female log wages in 1980 and 1991, and subtracting to obtain the gender gap (see the first four sets of numbers in Waldfogel's Table 7, 1997, p. 147), and performing a similar operation for the nonmothers' and mothers' log wage figures (see the bottom of the table).

[16] Such standard contemporary texts include Blau, Ferber, and Winkler (2001); Hoffman and Averett (2004); and Albelda, Drago, and Shulman's (2001) sections describing the neoclassical approach.

[17] See Altman and Golden (2004).

[18] For the historical development and critique of the "marginalist" school's emphasis on substitution vs. income effects, see Nyland (1989).

[19] There is evidence that while only a minority (estimates range from 6 to 30%) of the workforce would prefer to reduce their work hours currently (with proportional adjustment in earnings), a much greater proportion, almost half, would consider this in the future (see Altman & Golden, 2004). This suggests that workers feel locked in by today's financial commitments, but in due time could make the adjustments in consumption allowing for reduced hours of paid work.

[20] See, e.g., Bell (2000). Generally, rising earnings inequality also has helped to preserve the large gender gap in earnings. Because skill differentials in pay are generally increasing, they are offsetting potential relative gains for women that might have occurred due to women's improvement in education and successful entrance into many once segregated occupations (Blau & Kahn, 2000).

[21] Generally, high-performance practices, because so many of them generate greater work demands, often tend to conflict with work-life balance policies (White et al. 2003). In particular, required overtime work negatively affects workers' ability to balance work and family responsibilities (Berg et al., 2003). The negative effects of work on family concerns appear to be much stronger than the negative effects of family on work (Cappelli et al., 2000).

[22] Cappelli et al. (2000).

[23] Galinsky, Bond, and Kim (2001).

[24] Altman and Golden (2004).

[25] Holzer (2003).

[26] Ruhm (2004).

[27] See, e.g., Kimmel and Hoffman (2002), Leete (2001), and Appelbaum (2000).

[28] See Bailyn, Drago, and Kochan (2001). There are voices that express doubt that the work-life balance campaign can succeed by focusing on employers and the business case only (Shorthose, 2004).

[29] See Ferber and Waldfogel (1998) for part-time and Belman and Golden (2002) for nonstandard jobs.

[30] For example, Drago (2001) took the notion of "time transfer" as developed in Rogers' (2001) ethnographic study, to understand and test in a relatively large survey data set for transfers of work tasks from parents to nonparents in the workplace.

REFERENCES

Albelda, R. (1997). *Economics and feminism: Disturbances in the field.* Woodbridge, CT: Twayne.

Albelda, R., Drago, R., & Shulman, S. (2001). *Unlevel playing fields: Understanding wage inequality and discrimination.* Boston: Dollars and Sense.

Altman, M., & Golden, L. (2004). Alternative approaches of regulating hours: Labor demand, labor supply or institutional innovations? In M. Oppenheimer & N. Mercuro (Eds.), *Alternative approaches in law and economics* (pp. 286–307). Armonk, NY: Sharpe.

Amott, T., & Matthaei, J. (1996). *Race, gender, and work: A multicultural economic history of women in the United States.* Boston: South End Press.

Anderson, D., Binder, M., & Krause, K. (2003). The motherhood wage penalty revisited: Experience, heterogeneity, work effort and work-schedule flexibility. *Industrial and Labor Relations Review, 56*(2), 273–294.

Appelbaum, E. (1981). *Back to work: Determinants of women's successful re-entry.* Westport, CT: Auburn House.

Appelbaum, E. (Ed.). (2000). Balancing acts: Easing the burdens and improving the options for working families. Economic Policy Institute.

Appelbaum, E., Bailey, T., Berg, P., & Kalleberg, A. L. (2000). *Manufacturing advantage: Why high-performance work systems pay off.* Ithaca, NY: Cornell University Press.

Aversa, J. (2003). GDP revised higher; mood brighter. *Associated Press*, November 26.

Bailyn, L., Drago, R., & Kochan, T. (2001). *Integrating work and family life: A holistic approach.* Report for Alfred P. Sloan Foundation Work-Family Policy Network, September.

Barnett, R. C., Gareis, K., & Brennan, R. (1999). Fit as a mediator of the relationship between work hours and burnout. *Journal of Occupational Health Psychology, 4*(4), 307–317.

Barth, E., Roed, M., & Torp, H. (2002). *Towards a closing of the gender pay gap: A comparative study of three occupations in six European countries.* Oslo, Norway: Institute for Social Research.

Becker, G. S. (1965). A theory of the allocation of time. *Economic Journal, 75*(299), 493–517.

Becker, G. S. (1966). *Human capital: A theoretical and empirical analysis, with special reference to education.* New York: Columbia University Press.

Becker, G. S. (1976). *The economic approach to human behavior.* Chicago: University of Chicago Press.

Becker, G. S. (1985). Human capital, effort, and the sexual division of labor. *Journal of Labor Economics, 3*(1), Part 2, S33–S58.

Bell, L. (2000). The Incentive to Work Hard. In *Working Time: International Trends, Theory and Policy perspectives*, (ed.) L. Golden and D. Figart. New York: Routledge, 106–26.

Belman, D., & Golden, L. (2002). Which workers are nonstandard and contingent and does it pay? In I. U. Zeytinoğlu (ed.), *Flexible work arrangements: Conceptualizations and international experiences.* The Hague, The Netherlands: Kluwer Law International, 241–267.

Berg, P., Kalleberg, A., & Appelbaum, E. (2003). Balancing work and family: The role of high-commitment environments. *Industrial Relations*, April *42*(2), 168–188.

Bergmann, B. (1986). *The economic emergence of women.* New York: Basic Books.

Blau, F., Ferber, M., & Winkler, A. (2001). *The economics of women, men and work* (5th ed.). Englewood Cliffs, NJ: Prentice-Hall.

Blau, F., & Kahn, L. (2000). Gender differences in pay. *Journal of Economic Perspectives, 14*(Fall), 75–99.

Brandon, P. D. (1999). Determinants of self-care arrangements among school-aged children. *Children and Youth Services Review, 21*, 497–520.

Braverman, H. (1974). *Labor and monopoly capital: The degradation of work in the twentieth century.* New York: Monthly Review Press.

Budig, M. J., & England, P. (2001). The wage penalty for motherhood. *American Sociological Review, 66*(2), 204–225.

Cappelli, P., Constantine, J., & Chadwick, C. (2000). It pays to value family: Work and family tradeoffs reconsidered. *Industrial Relations, 39*(2), April, 175–198.

Darity, W. A., & Mason, P. L. (1998). Evidence on discrimination in employment: Codes of color, codes of gender. *Journal of Economic Perspectives, 12*(Spring), 63–90.

Deutsch, F. (1999). *Halving it all: How equally shared parenting works.* Cambridge, MA: Harvard University Press.

Dimand, R., Forget, E., & Nyland, C. (2004). Retrospectives: Gender in classical economics. *Journal of Economic Perspectives, 18*(1), Winter, 229–241.

Drago, R. (2000). Trends in working time in the U.S.: A policy perspective. *Labor Law Journal, 51*, 212–218.

Drago, R. (2001). Time on the job and time with their kids: The cultures of teaching and parenthood in the U.S. *Feminist Economics, 7*(3), 1–31.

Drago, R., Caplan, R., Constanza, D., Brubaker, T., Cloud, D., Harris, N., Kashian, R., & Riggs, T. L. (1999). New estimates of working time for elementary school teachers. *Monthly Labor Review, 122*(4), 31–40.

Ehrenberg, R. G., & Smith, R. S. (1991). *Modern labor economics* (4th ed.). New York: HarperCollins.

Eisner, R. (1989). *The total incomes system of accounts.* Chicago: University of Chicago Press.

Faludi, S. (1991). *Backlash: The undeclared war against women.* New York: Crown.

Fenwick, R., & Tausig, M. (2001). Scheduling stress: Family and health outcomes of shift work and schedule control. *American Behavioral Scientist, 44*(7), 1179–1198.

Ferber, M. A., & Waldfogel, J. (1998). The long-term consequences of nontraditional employment. *Monthly Labor Review, 121, 5*, May 3–12.

Floro, M. S., & Miles, M. (2003). Time use, work and overlapping activities: Evidence from Australia. *Cambridge Journal of Economics, 27*, 881–904.

Folbre, N. (1991). The unproductive housewife: Her evolution in nineteenth-century economic thought. *Signs: Journal of Women in Culture and Society, 16*(3), 463–484.

Folbre, N. (1994). *Who pays for the kids? Gender and the structures of constraint.* New York & London: Routledge.

Folbre, N. (2001). *The invisible heart: Economics and family values.* New York: New Press.

Frank, R. H. (1995). *The Winner-take-all society: Why the few at the top get so much more than the rest of us.* New York: Penquin.

Fuchs, V. R. (1988). *Women's quest for economic equality.* Cambridge, MA: Harvard University Press.

Fullerton, H. N., Jr. (1999). Labor force participation: 75 years of change, 1950–1998 and 1998–2025. *Monthly Labor Review*, December, *122*(12), 3–12.

Galinsky, E., Kim, S., & Bond, J. T. (2001). *Feeling overworked: When work becomes too much.* New York: Families and Work Institute.

Garey, A. I. (1999). *Weaving work and motherhood.* philadelphia: Temple University Press.

George, D. (2001). Driven to spend: Longer work hours a by-product of market forces. In L. Golden & D. Figart (Eds.), *Working time: International trends, theory and policy perspectives* (pp. 127–142). New York: Routledge.

Gilman, C. P. (1966 [1898]). *Women and economics: A study of the economic relation between men and women as a factor in social evolution.* New York: Harper & Row.

Golden, L. (2005). The flexibility gap: Access to flexible work schedules in 2001. In I.U. Zeytinoglu (Ed.), *Flexibility in workplaces: Effects on workers, work environment and the unions* (pp. 38–56). Geneva: IIRA/ILO. ISBN Web pdf: 92-2-116130-7; Web html: 92-2-116131-5.

Hakim, C. (2002). Lifestyle preferences as determinants of women's differentiated labor market career. *Work and Occupations, 29*(4), November, 428–461.

Hartmann, H. (1979). Capitalism, Patriarchy, and Job Segregation by Sex. In Z. Eisenstein (Ed.), *Capitalist patriarchy and the case for socialist feminism* (pp. 206–247). New York Monthly Review Press.

Hersch, J., & Stratton, L. S. (2000). Household specialization and the male marriage wage premium. *Industrial and Labor Relations Review, 54*(1), 78–94.

Hochschild, A., & Machung, A. (1989). *The second shift.* New York: Avon.

Hochschild, A. (1997). *The time bind: When work becomes home and home becomes work.* New York: Metropolitan Books.

Hoffman, S., & Averett, S. (2004). *Women and the economy: Family, work and pay.* Reading, MA: Addison-Wesley.

Holzer, H. (2003). Work and family life: The perspective of employers. Conference on Work, Family, Health and Well-Being, June 16–18.

Humphries, J. (1998). Toward a family-friendly economics. *New Political Economy, 3*(2), 223–240.

Jacobs, J. A., & Gerson, K. (1998). Who are the overworked Americans? *Review of Social Economy, 56*(4), 442–459.

Jacobs, J. A. (2004). *The time divide: Work, family, and gender inequality.* Cambridge, MA: Harvard University Press.

Jalilvand, M. (2000). Married women, work and values. *Monthly Labor Review, 123*(8), August, 26–31.

Kimmel, J., & Hoffman, E. (2002). *The economics of work and family.* Kalamazoo, MI: W.E. Upjohn Institute for Employment Research.

Leete, L. (2001). History and housework: Implications for work hours and family policies in market economies. In L. Golden & D. Figart (Eds.), *Working time: international trends, theory and policy perspectives.* New York: Routledge.

Lundberg, S., & Rose, E. (2000). Parenthood and the earnings of married men and women. *Labour Economics, 7*(6), 689–710.

Malthus, T. R. (1798). *An essay on the principle of population.* Library of Economics and Liberty. Retrieved January 29, 2004 from the World Wide Web: http://www.econlib.org/library/Malthus/malPop1.html.

Marshall, A. (1920). *Principles of economics.* Library of Economics and Liberty. Retrieved January 29, 2004 from the World Wide Web: http://www.econlib.org/library/Marshall/marP1.html.

Martin, G., & Kats, V. (2003). Families and work in transition in 12 countries, 1980–2001. *Monthly Labor Review, 126*(9), 3–31.

Marx, K. (1954 [1887]). *Capital, volume I.* Moscow: Progress Publishers.

McNulty, P. J. (1980). *The origins and development of labor economics.* Cambridge, MA: MIT Press.

Mincer, J. (1991). Education and unemployment of women. Working Paper #3837, National Bureau of Economic Research. Cambridge, MA: NBER.

Moen, P. (2000). The career quandary. *Reports on America 2*(1). Washington, DC: Population Reference Bureau.

National Coalition for Women and Girls in Education. (2002). *Title IX at 30: Report card on gender equity.* Washington, DC: American Association of University Women. http://www.aauw.org.

Nyland, C. (1989). *Reduced worktime and the management of production.* Cambridge, UK.

Presser, H. (2003). *Working in a 24/7 economy.* New York: Russell Sage Foundation.

Reid, M. (1934). *Economics of household production.* New York: Wiley.

Ricardo, D. (1911 [1817]). *The principles of political economy and taxation.* New York: Dutton.

Risman, B. (1998). *Gender vertigo: American families in transition.* New Haven, CT: Yale University Press.

Robinson, J., & Bostrom, A. (1994). The overestimated workweek? What time diary measures suggest. *Monthly Labor Review, 117*(8), 11–23.

Rogers, J. K. (2001). There's no substitute: The politics of time transfer in the teaching profession. *Work and Occupations, 28*, 64–90.

Rothschild, K. (1982). A note on some economic and welfare aspects of working time regulations. *Australian Economic Papers, 21*, 214–218.

Ruhm, C. (2004). How well do parents with young children combine work and family life? *NBER Working Paper No. W10247,* January.

Schor, J. B. (1991). *The overworked American: The unexpected decline of leisure.* New York: Basic Books.

Schor, J. B. (1998). *The overspent American: Upscaling, downshifting, and the new consumer.* New York: Basic Books.

Shorthose, J. (2004). Like summer and good sex? The limitations of the work-life balance campaign. *Capital & Class, 82,* Spring, 1–8.

Smith, A. (1904). *An Inquiry into the Nature and Causes of the Wealth of Nations*, London: Methuen and Co., Ltd., ed. Edwin Cannan, Fifth edition.

Veblen, T. (1899). *The theory of the leisure class.* New York: Macmillan.

Waldfogel, J. (1998). Understanding the "family gap" in pay for women with children. *Journal of Economic Perspectives, 12*(1), 137–156.

Webb, S., & Webb, B. (1965 [1897]). *Industrial democracy.* New York: Sentry Press.

White, M., Hill, S., McGovern, P., Mills, C., & Smeaton, D. (2003). "High-performance" management practices, working hours and work-life balance. *British Journal of Industrial Relations, 41*(2), June, 175–196.

Williams, J. (1999). *Unbending gender: Why work and family conflict and what to do about it.* New York: Oxford University Press.

Wolfe, A. (1997). The moral meanings of work. *The American Prospect, 8*(34), September–October, 82–90.

14

Work and Family
From an Industrial/Organizational
Psychology Perspective[1]

Cynthia A. Thompson
Baruch College, CUNY

Laura L. Beauvais
University of Rhode Island

Tammy D. Allen
University of South Florida

Industrial/organizational (I/O) psychologists study human attitudes and behavior in the workplace. Their goals are to understand and measure human behavior to improve employees' satisfaction and job performance, enhance employers' ability to select and promote the best people, and generally make the workplace better for employees (www.siop.org). Although I/O psychologists focus on the interrelatedness of the individual, the group, and the organization, it has only been in the last 20 years or so that they have considered the relationship between work and family. Fortunately, the field has advanced tremendously since then and has added substantially to the work-family literature.

It is a challenge to tease out the unique contributions of I/O psychology to the field of work and family as there is much overlap with the management disciplines of organizational behavior and human resource management. Indeed, academic I/O psychologists can be found in ample numbers within management departments as well as within departments of psychology. Work-family research by I/O psychologists also overlaps with research by sociologists, developmental psychologists, social psychologists, anthropologists, economists, and social workers, as can be seen in the diversity of authors in this handbook. Further confusing the issue is that it is not uncommon for sociologists to publish in psychology journals (e.g., Moen, 1996) and I/O psychologists to publish in sociology and management journals (e.g., Williams & Alliger, 1994). However, each of these fields focuses on different, albeit sometimes overlapping, aspects of the work-family interface. Developmental psychologists, for example, tend to focus on the impact of work on attitudes and behaviors of children of working parents (Major & Cleveland, 2005), economists on labor market issues such as the need of employers to find a dependable and reliable workforce (Holzer, 2003), and sociologists on the domestic division of labor among employed couples with children (Glass, 2003).

I/O psychologists largely focus on the work side of the work-family interface (Major & Cleveland, 2005); on the individual employee rather than the employee's family, workgroup, or community (Allen, Herst, Bruck, & Sutton, 2000; Major & Cleveland, 2005); and on employee attitudes and behavior as they affect organizational functioning and ultimately the bottom line. In addition, they focus on organizational structures and processes that may affect individual and group-level functioning. This chapter reviews research from I/O psychology that sheds light on the role of the individual and the role of the organization in the work-family interface. In addition, in the section "Overcoming Barriers to Family-Supportive Workplaces," we describe research that exemplifies the application of I/O psychology theory to the challenges facing organizations as they attempt to enhance their employees' ability to manage work and family.

THE ROLE OF THE INDIVIDUAL IN WORK AND FAMILY

Work-Family Linkages: Conflict versus Enrichment

To understand how individuals perceive the relationship between work and family, researchers have proposed a number of ways in which the two domains may be linked (Edwards & Rothbard, 2000; Lambert, 1990; Zedeck, 1990), recognizing that more than one may be operating at the same time. Spillover theory suggests that work and family can influence each other positively or negatively through transfer of affect, values, skills, and behavior. For example, a good mood from a successful experience at work may influence the employee's mood at home. According to the accommodation theory, employees may accommodate the demands of one role by reducing involvement in another role (Lambert, 1990). Compensation theory suggests that individuals attempt to compensate for dissatisfaction in one domain by pursuing more satisfying experiences in another (Lambert, 1990; Zedeck, 1990). According to segmentation theory, some employees intentionally segment their work and family roles such that when they are participating in one role they do not allow the other role to impinge on their thoughts, behaviors, or feelings (Greenhaus & Singh, 2004; Lambert, 1990).

By far the most common explanation for the nature of the relationship between work and family is derived from the scarcity theory of role accumulation, which suggests that the sum of human energy is fixed and that adding more roles creates a greater likelihood of overload, conflict, strain, and other negative consequences for well-being (Marks, 1977). Similarly, the role conflict perspective, based on role theory (Kahn, Wolf, Quinn, Snoek, & Rosenthal, 1964; Katz & Kahn, 1978), suggests that multiple roles lead to role conflict and stress. I/O researchers predominantly have used the role conflict perspective as the underlying theoretical foundation for their research; indeed, most work-family researchers, whatever their background, tend to use the conflict perspective to understand the work-family interface (Eby, Casper, Lockwood, Bordeaux, & Brinley, 2005; Greenhaus & Powell, in press).

More recently, researchers have begun to consider possible positive links between work and family (e.g., Barnett & Hyde, 2001; Frone, 2003; Greenhaus & Powell, in press; Grzywacz & Marks, 2000; Rothbard, 2001; Thompson & Prottas, in press). Specifically, there is growing evidence that role accumulation can be beneficial for individuals such that experiences in one role can enhance the experiences in another role (Barnett & Hyde, 2001). In the following two sections, we highlight research representative of the role conflict and role enhancement perspectives. We focus on the role conflict perspective as it has dominated research to date and on the role enhancement perspective as it shows great promise in moving the field forward.

Role Conflict Perspective

Work-family conflict (denoted WFC when referring to overall work-family conflict) is a type of interrole conflict in which the demands of the work role and the demands of the family role are mutually incompatible in some respect (Greenhaus & Beutell, 1985; Parasuraman & Greenhaus, 1997a). When an employee is in a meeting at work, for example, it is physically impossible for her to attend her child's soccer game. It is also possible that an individual is physically present but psychologically elsewhere (Greenhaus & Beutell, 1985). Although originally conceptualized as a unidimensional construct (e.g., Kopelman, Greenhaus, & Connolly, 1983), more recent conceptualizations include two forms of conflict: work interference with family conflict (WIF) and family interference with work conflict (FIW; Frone, Russell, & Cooper, 1992b; Gutek, Searle, & Klepa, 1991; Kelloway, Gottlieb, & Barham, 1999; Thompson, 1989).

Most research on work-family conflict has investigated the extent to which work interferes with family life rather than the extent to which family interferes with work, and in fact, the former appears to be more prevalent among employees (e.g., Eagle, Miles, & Icenogle, 1997; Frone, 2003; Gutek et al., 1991; Williams & Alliger, 1994). Bellavia and Frone (2005) reviewed three large-scale, national surveys of the U.S. population that were conducted between 1990 and 1997 and found that between a quarter and a half of the population experienced some form of WIF. The prevalence of FIW was much lower (approximately 10 to 14%).

According to Greenhaus and Beutell (1985), there are three types of work-family conflict. *Time-based conflict* occurs "when the time demands of one role make it difficult or impossible to participate fully in another role" (Parasuraman & Greenhaus, 1997a, p. 4). For example, early morning breakfast meetings make it difficult for single parents to get their children to day care. *Strain-based conflict* occurs "when symptoms of psychological strain (e.g., anxiety, fatigue, irritability) generated by the demands of the work or family role intrude or 'spill over' into the other role, making it difficult to fulfill the responsibilities of that role" (Parasuraman & Greenhaus, 1997a, p. 4). A production supervisor anxious about his child's illness may not be able to fully concentrate on his job; an accountant working long hours to meet the April 15 tax deadline may be irritable or too exhausted to fully respond to her family's needs. *Behavior-based conflict* occurs "when the behaviors that are expected or appropriate in the family role (e.g., expressiveness, emotional sensitivity) are viewed as inappropriate or dysfunctional when used in the work role" (Parasuraman & Greenhaus, 1997a, p. 4), or when behaviors appropriate for work (e.g., aggressiveness) are dysfunctional at home. For example, a manager in a financial services organization may be expected to be aggressive and hard-driving to be accepted and promoted at work, yet these same behaviors can create conflict and tension at home.

Antecedents of Work-Family Conflict. There are numerous demographic, attitudinal, and workplace characteristics that are associated with both WIF and FIW. Not surprisingly, employees with young children or large families are more likely to experience conflict (Behson, 2000; Carlson, 1999; Frone, Russell, & Cooper, 1992b; Greenhaus & Beutell, 1985; Grzywacz & Marks, 2000), as are employees whose aging parents need care. In one study, for example, employees who were caring for elderly dependents were more likely to experience work-family conflict and to have stress- and health-related problems (Scharlach & Boyd, 1989). Higgins, Duxbury, and Lee (1994) found that gender and life-cycle stage were related to the experience of work-family conflict. For men, work-family conflict decreased as their families went through three stages: Stage 1, families with preschool children; Stage 2, families with grade-school children; and Stage 3, families with adolescents. For women, work-family conflict did not decrease until the third stage, when their children were adolescents.

Other research also suggests that women experience more work-family conflict than men (e.g., Behson, 2002; Gutek et al., 1991; Wallace, 1999), which is not surprising as women are still responsible for the majority of household chores and child-care activities, although men's participation in household chores appears to be increasing (Bond, Thompson, Galinsky, & Prottas, 2003). One recent large-scale, nationally representative study of the nation's labor force found that on workdays, working mothers reported spending nearly an hour more than fathers caring for and doing things with their children (3.5 vs. 2.7 hours) and an hour more a day doing home chores (Bond et al., 2003). Nevertheless, some research suggests that there are no gender differences (Frone, 2003) or that men experience more conflict (Parasuraman & Simmers, 2001). Indeed, a recent meta-analysis (Byron, in press) found that gender was not related to WIF and that gender was weakly related to FIW; however, the confidence interval for FIW included zero. These findings suggest that there is little difference in the degree that men and women report experiencing either form of work-family conflict.

Rather than looking at gender per se, some researchers have considered the attitudes that employees have toward women working. For example, employed mothers who held traditional attitudes about women working (i.e., belief that everyone is better off if the man earns the money and the woman takes care of the home and children) experienced more work-family conflict than women with less traditional attitudes (Bond et al., 1998). In another study, women who were highly involved in their jobs before deciding to stay home full-time with their infants tended to be more depressed and irritable, compared to women who were not so involved in their jobs (Pistrang, 1984). In fact, women were least depressed when their decision to work or not work was consistent with their own and their husbands' preferences, and most depressed when they were stay-at-home mothers but wanted to be working (Spitze, 1988). Thus, the attitudes women have toward mothers working, the degree that they are involved in a job or career, and their own comfort level with working (or not working) while raising children appear to play important roles in predicting their level of conflict and well-being.

Workplace characteristics can also contribute to higher levels of work-family conflict. Researchers have found that the number of hours worked per week, the amount and frequency of overtime required, an inflexible work schedule, unpredictability in work routines, unsupportive supervisors, and an inhospitable organizational culture for balancing work and family all increase the likelihood that employees will experience conflict between their work and family roles (Allen, 2001; Bond et al., 2003; Carlson & Perrewe, 1999; Fox & Dwyer, 1999; Grzywacz & Marks, 2000; Greenhaus & Beutell, 1985; Thompson, Beauvais, & Lyness, 1999). Having an unsympathetic boss or a job that requires heavy amounts of overtime or travel, for example, can make employees feel stressed and conflicted over the effect their job is having on their family. Part of the stress comes from employees feeling they have no control over their work life (Thompson & Prottas, 2004), and in fact, many employees tend to adjust their family or personal lives to accommodate work requirements (Thomas & Ganster, 1995). Some "family-friendly" policies and practices, described in a later section, are designed to give control back to employees. Supportive practices such as flexible scheduling and supportive supervisors have been shown to have a positive effect on employee perceptions of control and, ultimately, can reduce levels of work-family conflict (Galinsky et al., 1996; Thomas & Ganster, 1995).

Finally, certain characteristics of a person's *job* can affect the level of work-family conflict experienced. In two large-scale studies of the U.S. workforce, the Families and Work Institute found that employed parents experienced less conflict between their work life and their family/personal life when they had greater autonomy in their jobs, more schedule flexibility, less demanding or hectic jobs, and more job security (Bond et al., 2003; Galinsky et al., 1996). Other job characteristics predictive of work-family conflict include nonchallenging, routine, or unimportant tasks; role ambiguity; poor person–job fit; role conflict; stressful events at work; and boundary-spanning activities (Batt & Valcour, 2003; Clark, 2002; Frone, Yardley et al., 1997; Greenhaus & Beutell, 1985; Parasuraman & Greenhaus, 2001).

Consequences of Work-Family Conflict.   Although not everyone who attempts to jug-gle multiple work and nonwork roles experiences conflict, a substantial number of employees do. Researchers have found that work-family conflict is related to job and life dissatisfaction, depression, anxiety, anger/hostility, hypertension, greater alcohol consumption and substance abuse, and perceptions of a lower quality of life (e.g., Bond et al., 2003; Bruck, Allen, & Spector, 2002; Duxbury & Higgins, 1991; Frone et al., 1992b; Frone, Russell, & Cooper, 1997; Kelloway et al., 1999; Kossek & Ozeki, 1998; Thomas & Ganster, 1995). There are also unhealthy consequences for the organization such as absenteeism, tardiness, greater turnover intentions among employees, and actual turnover (Greenhaus, Collins, Singh, & Parasuraman, 1997; Greenhaus, Parasuraman, & Collins, 2001; Kossek, 1998). (See Allen et al., 2000, and Eby et al., 2005, for comprehensive reviews of research on the consequences of work-family conflict.) As noted by Allen et al. (2000), psychological research consistently demonstrates a main effect for WFC on such organizational outcomes. What is needed now is to exam-ine possible personal and organizational moderators that may affect the relationship between work-family conflict and its consequences.

Work-Family Enrichment Perspective

Although the findings described above appear to support the scarcity theory of role accumu-lation (Marks, 1977), there is a growing body of research that suggests that individuals with multiple life roles (e.g., spouse, parent, employee) are less depressed, have higher self-esteem, and are more satisfied with their marriages and their jobs compared to women and men who are not married, are unemployed, or are childless (see Crosby, 1991, and Greenhaus & Powell, in press, for a review of this literature). In other words, up to a point, the more roles one participates in, the better one's mental and physical health. Barnett and Hyde (2001) argued that it is the *quality* of roles rather than the *quantity* of roles that matters. That is, there is a positive association between multiple roles and mental health when employees are satisfied with their jobs and satisfied with their home life. The greater the quality of the roles (e.g., a job that is interesting and challenging and uses the employee's skills and talents), the greater an individual's self-esteem and freedom from depression (Barnett & Hyde, 2001; Baruch & Barnett, 1987).

According to the enrichment theory of role accumulation (also referred to as work-family enhancement, positive spillover, and work-family facilitation), multiple roles may increase one's energy by increasing sources of identity, self-esteem, rewards, and resources available to cope with the multiple demands (Barnett & Hyde, 2001; Greenhaus & Powell, in press; Ruderman, Ohlott, Panzer, & King, 2002; Thoits, 1987). For example, participating in multiple roles creates more opportunities for gratification, positive self-experiences, and subsequent enhanced feelings of self-worth (Ruderman et al., 2002). In addition, resources acquired in one role (e.g., connections, leadership skills) may be used to enhance functioning in another role (Sieber, 1974).

Consistent with a broader movement in psychology to examine not just mental illness but also mental health (e.g., Seligman & Csikszentmihalyi, 2000), we need to expand our think-ing about the positive connections between work and family. However, given the competing predictions of the role conflict and role enrichment perspectives, it behooves researchers to develop a comprehensive theoretical framework that can guide our examination of the positive *and* negative effects of combining work and family roles. That is, we need to determine which personal and organizational factors influence whether individuals experience their multiple roles positively or negatively, and we need to determine the process through which positive and negative outcomes occur.

Although Grzywacz (2002) has proposed a preliminary model of work-family facilitation, based on ecological theory, it focuses on positive interdependencies only. Similarly, Greenhaus and Powell (in press) have proposed a model of work-family enrichment, which they define as "the extent to which experiences in one role improve the quality of life in the other role" (p. 6). While both models move the field toward a more complex view of the work-family interface, neither proposes a process for understanding how and when certain role experiences lead to positive outcomes and how and when they lead to negative outcomes. To date, only Rothbard (2001) has proposed a model that describes a process (i.e., psychological engagement in a role) through which work and family roles might influence each other positively or negatively. However, future models need to include possible personal, job, and organizational factors that may influence the extent to which roles are experienced positively or negatively.

Individual Differences in Experiencing Work-Family Linkages

Psychologists have a rich history of examining individual differences, and this has recently carried over into the study of work and family. Specifically, there has been a growing interest in examining the dispositional variables that relate to work and family linkages, particularly WFC. The dispositional variable that has been most frequently associated with WFC is negative affectivity (NA). Research has consistently demonstrated that individuals higher in negative affectivity also report greater WFC (Bruck & Allen, 2003, Carlson, 1999; Frone, Russell, & Cooper, 1993; Stoeva, Chiu, & Greenhaus, 2002). Indeed, several studies examining multiple situational and dispositional predictors suggest that NA may be one of the strongest predictors of WFC (Allen, & Bruck, 2004; Carlson, 1999).

A few studies have examined the relationship between Type A and WFC, but the results have been mixed. Individuals who display Type A behavior are generally described as ambitious, competitive, impatient, and aggressive or hostile (Spence, Helmreich, & Pred, 1987). Burke (1988) found that police officers with more of a Type A personality were more likely to report WFC than were police officers with less of a Type A personality. However, Carlson (1999) did not replicate Burke's finding. Bruck and Allen (2003) used a multidimensional measure of Type A behavior that separated the construct into two components, impatience–irritability and achievement strivings. As expected, a significant correlation between the impatience–irritability aspect of Type A and WFC was observed. However, Type A did not contribute unique variance toward the explanation of WFC after controlling for other demographic and dispositional variables.

The Big Five personality variables have been examined in relation to WFC (Costa & McCrae, 1991). Not surprisingly, neuroticism, which is highly related to negative affectivity, has been associated with both forms of work-family conflict (Grzywacz & Marks, 2000; Wayne, Musisca, & Fleeson, 2004). In addition to neuroticism, there is some evidence linking agreeableness and conscientiousness with WFC. Specifically, after controlling for demographics and other dispositional variables, Bruck and Allen (2003) found that more conscientious individuals were less likely to report FIW, but found no relationship with overall WFC or with WIF. Wayne et al. (2004) found that more conscientious individuals were less likely to report both FIW and WIF. Wayne et el. also found that more agreeable individuals were less likely to report WIF. Neither Bruck and Allen nor Wayne et al. found support for a relationship between extraversion and openness to experience with WFC.

Less research has examined dispositional variables and work-family enrichment or facilitation. In their study that included the Big Five variables, Wayne et al. (2004) found that individuals who were more extraverted, less neurotic, and more open to experience were more likely to report that work facilitated family. More extraverted, agreeable, and conscientious individuals were more likely to report that family facilitated work. Thus, their results demonstrate that the same dispositional variables that relate to WFC do not necessarily relate to work-family enrichment. Grzywacz and Marks (2000) also found that extraversion was related to positive spillover in both directions.

In sum, the research concerning personality seems to indicate that dispositional factors may serve as either risk factors or protective factors against work-family conflict. Individuals with negative affectivity may be most at risk for work-family conflict while conscientiousness and agreeableness may serve as protective factors. Little data are available yet concerning dispositions and work-family enrichment, but the extant research seems to suggest that extraversion enhances the likelihood that individuals will report that work and family are mutually enriching. Moreover, it appears WFC and work-family enrichment have different dispositional antecedents. Thus, it should not be assumed that the dispositional variables that relate to WFC also relate to work-family enrichment.

Individual Role Management Strategies

Researchers have identified several strategies for coping with multiple role demands (Behson, 2002; Greenhaus & Parasuraman, 1986; Hall, 1972). In Hall's (1972) typology of coping, for example, individuals may choose to *modify the stressful situation* through direct action. That is, the employee must figure out the root cause of the stress and attempt to change the situation (e.g., others' expectations) that produces the stress. Another strategy is to *modify the meaning of the situation* by changing their personal concept of role requirements or by changing self-expectations for career and family. This might involve establishing priorities (e.g., family comes first), overlooking less important role expectations (e.g., not worrying about the house being a mess), and keeping things in perspective (e.g., focusing on the positive aspects of one's life). Hall's (1972) third type of coping is *reactive coping*, which involves trying to meet everyone's expectations. Instead of trying to confront the source of the stress or change the meaning of the stressful situation, some individuals try to plan or schedule better, work harder to meet everyone's expectations, or use no conscious strategy at all. Most research suggests that this third style of coping is not very effective (Hall, 1972; Kirchmeyer, 1993).

Some individuals cope by *managing the symptoms* of stress (e.g., by exercising, eating well, getting enough sleep, meditating, listening to music). However, while this strategy may alleviate stress symptoms, it does nothing to resolve the source of the stress (Latack, 1984). More recently, Behson (2002) found that an informal coping strategy of making temporary and informal accommodations to the employee's usual work patterns attenuated the relationship between family-to-work conflict and work stress. In general, active styles of coping tend to be more effective than emotion-focused or passive coping (Behson, 2002; Kirchmeyer, 1993).

Another important resource for coping with the stress of balancing multiple roles is *support from others* (Carlson & Perrewe, 1999; Cohen & Wills, 1985). Support may come from one's spouse, significant other, friends, family, supervisor, coworkers, or others in the form of instrumental, emotional, and informational support (House, 1981). *Instrumental support* refers to tangible assistance, such as providing time, skill, advice, or resources to help solve the problem. *Emotional support* refers to caring behaviors such as providing empathy, trust, love, or simply listening. *Informational support* refers to providing information to help solve the problem. Research has shown that support in the workplace (e.g., from supervisors and coworkers) can affect employees' perceptions of their job, quality of life, and experience of work-family conflict and stress (Allen, 2001; Bond et al., 2003; Goff, Mount, & Jamison, 1990; Parasuraman, Greenhaus, & Granrose, 1992; Thomas & Ganster, 1995). Carlson and Perrewe (1999), for example, found that social support at work and at home was related to fewer perceived stressors. However, once an individual perceived his or her role as stressful, social support did little to reduce subsequent feelings of work-family conflict.

THE ROLE OF THE ORGANIZATION IN WORK AND FAMILY

Programs and Policies

Both I/O psychologists and management scholars investigate the programs and policies that organizations implement to help employees manage work and nonwork responsibilities. There are four general types of work/life programs offered by companies to support employees (Lobel & Kossek, 1996). *Time-based strategies* help employees manage time pressures and include flexible schedules (e.g., flextime, compressed workweeks, permanent part-time work, telecommuting, or job sharing) and various leave programs (e.g., vacation time, sick leave, parental leave, child- or elder care leave, phased return to work, and unpaid or personal leaves of absence). *Information-based strategies* are policies and programs that provide information to employees to help them make decisions regarding balancing work and nonwork responsibilities. They include resource and referral programs, support groups, stress and time management seminars, relocation assistance, dependent care provider fairs, preretirement planning, and employee assistance programs. *Money-based strategies* are programs that provide financial assistance to employees in managing their responsibilities, such as affordable health or long-term care insurance, flexible spending accounts (i.e., deposits of pretax wage dollars into company accounts designated to reimburse child- or elder care expenses), tuition reimbursement, and adoption assistance. Lastly, *direct services* include programs provided directly to employees from the company, such as onsite child or elder care, sick child care, emergency child-care services, holiday and vacation care programs, and before and after school programs.

However, offering programs or services such as those described above does not guarantee that employees perceive a company as "family-friendly" or ensure that their lives are any less stressful. In fact, several studies have found either nonexistent or weak relationships between benefits offered and/or used by employees and work-family conflict (Anderson, Coffey, & Byerly, 2002; Batt & Valcour, 2003; Thompson & Prottas, in press). As will be discussed in a later section, that having supportive bosses and a supportive organizational culture makes it more likely that the programs will have their intended effects in that the programs can be used without fear of negative job or career consequences.

Even supporters of work-family programs are somewhat guarded in their enthusiasm for options that require employees to "accommodate" their lives to work. Underlying the accommodation view is the assumption that traditional business practices (e.g., lengthy work hours and total commitment to the firm) are the norm, and family-friendly practices are paternalistic corporate welfare benefits that may have no or perhaps even negative relationships with the efficiency and profitability of firms. This assumption prevents us from challenging the more fundamental ways in which business strategies are highly *unresponsive* to families (Friedman & Johnson, 1996; Kingston, 1990).

For example, consider typical relocation policies in most companies. Many promotion decisions at mid- to upper-levels of management are contingent on an employee's willingness to relocate, the assumption being that one must have a variety of experiences in different parts of the organization in order to succeed in these positions. The psychological and social costs of such relocations are significant, especially for the dual-earner couple who also must consider the spouse's job-related needs. Many companies "accommodate" these couples' needs by providing job search assistance to the trailing spouse. However, a more fundamental approach to this problem would be to reexamine the need for relocation in the first place. For example, perhaps employees can gain the experience needed by remaining in the same area but taking on different responsibilities (Cooper & Lewis, 1994). Viewing the work-family interface as an accommodation process prevents us from developing more creative solutions to these problems.

The next section explores in more detail the various barriers to creating workplaces that enable employees to have a life outside of work.

Barriers to Promoting a Family-Supportive Workplace

Despite efforts to develop organizations that are more family-friendly, there are a number of barriers that impede the implementation or reduce the effectiveness of work-family programs in organizations. These barriers include: (a) ingrained societal and organizational values and assumptions regarding work and family, (b) structural difficulties in implementing work-life programs, (c) lack of support from managers and supervisors, (d) the perception that family issues are women's issues, (e) maintaining equity among all employees, and (f) lack of evaluation data on work-life programs. This section draws extensively on Thompson and Beauvais (2000) and Allen (2003).

Ingrained Cultural Values and Assumptions Regarding Work and Family. Of all the barriers to implementing work-life programs, this one is probably the most significant because it stems from deeply held beliefs developed over the course of social history in the United States. When the United States was first settled, most people worked on family farms that allowed for the integration of work and family lives. Both men and women engaged in economic, childrearing, and household work. However, as industrialization grew, the domains of work and family began to split into separate spheres of activities. Men went into the factories to work for wages, while most women remained at home, taking care of the household and childrearing activities. Families could be supported wholly on men's wages, and therefore women no longer needed to be engaged in the production of goods, either in the home or the factory. The home became the private domain of families, where intimate relationships, socialization of children, and relaxation took place. Work became the public sphere where (mostly) men carried out economic activity. In essence, work became the masculine domain while home became the feminine domain (Kanter, 1977; Thompson, Thomas, & Maier, 1992).

Today, the separation of the two spheres is still deeply ingrained in how we think about our work and nonwork lives. The reality for most people, however, is that the two domains are intricately linked. Women are in the workforce in greater numbers and, due to technological innovations in work processes, work is now increasingly performed at home. Family and work lives are not segmented as clearly today as they were even 20 years ago. However, most corporate cultures still operate as if men are the primary wage earners who have wives who stay home to take care of the children and housework.

Especially with regard to managerial and professional workers, the majority of organizations demand "single-mindedness" from their employees, requiring them to invest excessive time and psychological energy in work. The "ideal worker" is the one who works full-time and overtime and takes little or no time off from work for childbearing or childrearing (Williams, 2000). A successful managerial career usually requires these investments just when child rearing is at its most intense, curtailing many women's (and increasingly, men's) ability to advance in an organization designed for industrial-age lives. Furthermore, common practices and assumptions regarding *"face time"* abound, where employees feel they need to be at work for long hours each day to show dedication and commitment to their careers.

Another outcome of the view that work and family are separate spheres is that many organizations place no value on the experiences one gains from the family domain. Managers fail to recognize that many valuable work skills and habits (e.g., time management, budgeting, asset management, coaching and training, cooperation and teamwork) are developed and honed in the family sphere (Levine & Pittinsky, 1997). In addition, we often fail to see how employee's home lives may be a source of stability (or instability) for the organization.

Structural Difficulties in Implementing Work-Life Programs.   This barrier refers to the problems that managers have when trying to develop and carry out the procedures associated with work-life programs. Many companies still have rigid, hierarchical systems of organizing work, whereas many work-life programs require flexibility and continuous negotiations among workers and their managers in order to work effectively. Scheduling the appropriate number of employees, managing the increased paperwork, calculating benefits, satisfying client demands, and arranging for special equipment for telecommuters are some of the additional responsibilities managers have in running these programs. Not only do these duties take time and effort away from other activities, but they also may be perceived as diluting the autonomy and control that managers take for granted in managing their subordinates (Parasuraman & Greenhaus, 1997b; Thompson et al., 1992).

Lack of Support from Managers and Supervisors.   This third barrier is often a consequence of the structural problems previously described. Policies such as flexible work arrangements are difficult to successfully implement without support and commitment from management and supervisors. Supervisors may be resistant to enacting flexible work options and make it difficult for employees to utilize the benefit (Allen, 2001; Brewer, 2000; Thompson et al., 1992). This resistance likely stems from several factors. The administrative aspect of family-supportive policies and programs may increase supervisory workloads. As the ranks of middle management and first-level supervisors continue to decrease due to downsizing, these employees are likely to balk at any attempts to add more responsibilities to their jobs. In some cases, managers may find that they are required to administer policies for which they themselves are not eligible, due to their key positions in the organization. Furthermore, managers may find it difficult to choose and prioritize among employees with regard to who is able to take advantage of certain programs. For example, what happens when two employees in a four-person team ask for family leave at the same time? In essence, how does one continue to meet business objectives, treat all employees fairly, and help individuals balance work and life demands (Christensen, 1997)? Lastly, managers and supervisors may resist work-life programs because they hold traditional views of the separation of work and nonwork. To obtain their current positions of authority and responsibility, managers often sacrificed family life for work, and may resent providing the flexibility to aspiring leaders that was not given to them. Indeed, Parker and Allen (2001) found that older employees had less favorable views regarding family-friendly benefits than did younger employees.

As managers and supervisors play a crucial role in ensuring the development and implementation of work-life policies, their resistance is a key barrier to overcome. Not only do supervisors need to support and effectively manage family-supportive policies, but they also need to use the benefits themselves when possible. Kossek, Barber, and Winter (1999) found that managerial use is critical to the implementation of family-friendly benefits such as flexible schedules as managers serve as role models to their employees. If managers take advantage of benefits, they send a signal to employees that benefit use is okay.

The Perception that Family Issues are Women's Issues.   Separate role expectations for men and women are at the heart of how work and family issues are currently framed (Bailyn, 1993). Consistent with the belief of separate private and public lives discussed earlier, successful workers are those who keep a strict separation between work and family, never letting family concerns intrude into the workplace. Additionally, the belief continues to persist that women are more committed to family than to work, and that men are more committed to work than to family (Cook, 1994). Consequently, family supportive policies continue to be seen as policies primarily designed to "help" women (Lewis, 2001).

When managers view work-life programs as primarily benefiting women with children, they may fail to regard them as a legitimate business strategy that will impact corporate profitability and competitiveness. Furthermore, these programs may result in discrimination against women in the long run (Gonyea & Googins, 1996). That is, if women are perceived as less successful than are men in managing the work-family interface, they are less likely to receive the training and promotional opportunities that will advance their careers.

In reality, despite gender role expectations and corporate beliefs, balancing work and family is not just a woman's issue. As noted earlier, recent findings from the National Study of the Changing Workforce supports the notion that men are taking on greater responsibility for domestic labor than in the past (Bond et al., 2003). Specifically between 1977 and 2002, men have increased their participation in activities such as routine child care and cleaning. Other research has shown that working fathers as well as women and men without children are just as likely as working mothers to benefit from flexible schedules in terms of greater job satisfaction and reduced work–nonwork conflict (Marshall & Barnett, 1994).

Interestingly, men make use of family supportive policies to a greater extent than people realize. Working fathers use flexible schedules as well as leaves to spend more time with children. However, men use these options in ways that are not perceived by employers and coworkers as work-family accommodations (e.g., they take "informal" paternity leave by using vacation and sick days; Levine & Pittinksy, 1997). The informal leaves they take are short-term, involve no loss of pay, and require no formal application and approval. Thus, informal leaves allow men to take time off without publicly admitting that they are trying to balance work and family demands. As a result, men avoid possible negative evaluations from employers and coworkers, such as being uncommitted to one's career or even being perceived as unmasculine (Pleck, 1993). However, this strategy perpetuates the perception that family issues are mainly women's issues. Recent research conducted in Sweden, which has strongly advocated men becoming more active in the care of children, found that men were more likely to use paternity leave when performance was evaluated based on results rather than time on task and when the company was perceived as committed to gender equality (Haas, Allard, & Hwang, 2002). Encouraging men to make use of family-supportive benefits and openly participate in childrearing is an important step in overcoming the view that family issues are women's issues.

Maintaining Equity Among all Employees.   As indicated earlier, an important barrier to work-life accommodation in organizations is the fear of treating employees differently. Grandey (2001) suggested that perceptions regarding the fairness of work and family policies may impede their effectiveness. For example, many programs focus on dependent care concerns (i.e., parental leaves and child care). Employees without children may resent that the organization provides such benefits to their coworkers who are parents but not to them. Researchers at the Families and Work Institute in New York found that 40% of workers surveyed were at least somewhat resentful of employers that offered benefits not all workers could use (Bond et al., 1998). It has been argued that childless adults are unfairly paying for benefits and perks that are available primarily to middle-class parents (Burkett, 2000). On the other hand, Parker and Allen (2001) found that individuals generally reported that offering work and family benefits such as child care and flexible scheduling was fair. That is, they found little evidence of a "family-friendly backlash." To deal with issues of perceived fairness, many organizations try to offer "something for everyone" to avoid slighting singles and childless couples, and have changed the name of "work and family programs" to "work-life programs" (Schafer & Salmon, 2001).

Lack of Evaluation Data on Work-Family Programs.   A final barrier to work-life programs has been the lack of "hard" evidence that they actually have positive effects on employee attitudes and behaviors, such as satisfaction, commitment, recruitment, retention, absenteeism, and performance (Aldous, 1990; Kossek, 2005). Most reports on their effectiveness have been anecdotal or impressionistic, not based on rigorous cost-benefit analyses. Lacking company-specific evaluation data, some managers are unconvinced that there is a strategic benefit to implementing these programs, especially if a large proportion of their workforce is contract-based labor or low-skilled workers in great supply (e.g., clerks, cashiers, waitresses). As described below, a few researchers have begun the difficult process of demonstrating a relationship between work-family programs and firm productivity.

Overcoming Barriers to Family-Supportive Workplaces: Application of I/O Psychology

Much has been written about the strategies and practices that organizations might use to overcome barriers to work-family integration. Some of these strategies focus on implementing specific human resource initiatives (e.g., flexible schedules, telecommuting, child care, etc.) to help employees balance the demands of work and family, while others involve examining the organization-level predictors and outcomes associated with implementing work-family policies and practices. At the human resource initiative level, studies have examined how such practices are related to attracting employees, scheduling work and designing jobs, training and development, and retention. At the organization level, most research has focused on how firms adapt in response to institutional pressures and norms to integrate work and family domains (Goodstein, 1994, 1995; Ingram & Simons, 1995; Milliken, Martins, & Morgan, 1998) and less so on the effects of work-family program implementation on organizational performance and profits (Arthur, 2003; Meyer, Mukerjee, & Sestero, 2001; Perry-Smith & Blum, 2000). In addition, recent research on family-supportive cultures and climates has added greatly to our understanding of how organizational family-friendly policies and practices influence work attitudes and performance.

Human Resource Practices and Work-Family Integration.   Modifying human resource practices has been suggested as a method of overcoming the barriers of achieving work and family integration in the workplace. Specifically, modifying practices such as work hours, job design, work schedules, training and career opportunities, supervisor training, attendance and leave policies, and so on is assumed to better attract, manage the performance of, develop, and retain employees who are attempting to balance their work and family domains.

Recruiting.   Many organizations offer family-friendly benefits with the intention that these will attract and retain more qualified employees. Unfortunately, there is very little research on the impact of such practices on actual recruitment and retention rates, due to the costs and difficulties in doing such research. Galinsky and Stein (1990) reported the results of two studies that found child-care programs increased employers' ability to attract employees. A 1994 Families and Work Institute report commissioned by the U.S. Department of Labor concluded that family-friendly policies positively affect recruitment, productivity, and retention, and thus enhance individuals' abilities to participate successfully in the labor force (Schwartz, 1994). Nord, Fox, Phoenix, and Viano (2002) recently examined family-friendly practices (i.e., flextime, reduced hours, telecommuting, and internal job rotation) in two firms and found that participants perceived that these programs helped in recruiting talented employees to the firms. However, the experiences of users were not universally positive due to perceptions of inadequate technical support, policies and procedures, human resource systems, supervisory support, and communications associated with the work-family practices.

With regard to specific research on recruitment practices, Honeycutt and Rosen (1997) explored whether type of role identity salience (family, career, and balance of work and family) predicted a job candidate's attraction to an organization. Results showed that all candidates were attracted to organizations with flexible career paths; however, those individuals who had a "balanced" career and family identity were more attracted to organizations that offered both dual career paths and traditional career paths than candidates who had either salient family or career identities.

Perry-Smith and Blum (2000), in an examination of the effects of "bundles" of human resource practices on firm-level performance, found that organizations that offered a larger package of work-family options were perceived by managers to be more effective in attracting key employees than those firms that offered fewer options. Although attraction of key employees made up only a small part of the organizational performance measure, Perry-Smith and Blum's results indicate that work-family policies and programs might serve as a source of competitive advantage for firms, especially for those in industries where adoption of such practices is limited.

Rau and Hyland (2002) found that the level of role conflict experienced by job seekers determined how attracted they were to organizations offering flexible work arrangements (e.g., flextime and telecommuting). Those individuals with high work-to-family, family-to-work, and work-to-school conflict were more attracted to organizations with flextime options than those with low role conflict in these areas. Conversely, individuals with low role conflict were more attracted to organizations with telecommuting options, while individuals with high role conflict did not express a preference for organizations with or without such options. The authors drew on boundary theory (Ashforth, Kreiner, & Fugate, 2000) to explain these results. Boundary theory describes how employees transition between home and work roles, and is based on the assumption that individuals seek to minimize difficult role transitions and the frequency of role interruptions. Rau and Hyland argued that flexible schedules and telecommuting options differentially affect costs associated with crossing role boundaries and the blurring of roles between work, family, and school domains. As such, boundary theory may be a promising framework for understanding how work and family role conflicts affect the attractiveness of different human resource practices.

Work Scheduling and Job Design.   Much research has been conducted with regard to work-family integration and work hour requirements, job design, and work-scheduling practices. With regard to work hour requirements, the research evidence is clear that requiring employees to work long hours (or "face time") hurts their ability to integrate work and family domains (Carlson & Perrewe, 1999; Greenhaus, Bedeian, & Mossholder, 1987; Grzywacz & Marks, 2000; Major, Klein, & Ehrhart, 2002; Shamir, 1983). Similarly, employees who express greater time commitment to work (Parasuraman & Simmers, 2001) and who perceive heavy organizational time demands (even after controlling for actual hours worked; Thompson et al., 1999) report higher levels of work-family conflict.

With regard to job design, Thompson, Andreassi, and Prottas (2005) suggested that the technology that transforms inputs into goods and services influences the design of jobs in firms and their ability to successfully implement flexible management strategies. Specifically, firm technology determines different forms of task interdependencies among employees; therefore, jobs that are reciprocally interdependent might be difficult to redesign for flexibility as employees in such jobs are vitally dependent on other employees' inputs and outputs. Perlow (1997) discovered that type of coordination among members of software engineering groups affected the number of hours they worked and how much flexibility they had in choices of when and where to work. Another factor to consider is the degree to which a job is comprised of nonanalyzable tasks (Perrow, 1970). Because the performance of employees working in jobs comprised of nonanalyzable tasks (e.g., managerial and professional) is difficult to evaluate, "face time" or visibility at work is often used as a proxy to measure successful performance (Bailyn, 1993; Thompson et al., 2005). This renders many work-family programs unacceptable to employees who rightly perceive they will be penalized for not being physically present at work. Finally, Batt and Valcour (2003) found that work design characteristics explained a significant amount of variance in employees' ability to control demands from work and family (i.e., coordination responsibilities and longer work hours decreased employee control, while decision-making autonomy and technology use increased employee control). These findings suggest that job design characteristics influence the degree to which work-family practices can be implemented and how successful they might be in helping employees manage the demands of both work and family domains.

Work-scheduling practices, such as flexible schedules, telecommuting, shift and weekend work, and unpredictable schedules, may positively or negatively affect work and family integration. As noted earlier, variability in work schedules (Fox & Dwyer, 1999) and working weekends or rotating shifts (Shamir, 1983) are positively related to work-family conflict. Hill, Miller, Weiner, and Colihan (1998) failed to find any evidence that telecommuting helps employees balance work and family domains, although telecommuting does seem to enhance productivity as measured by self-report performance ratings and morale.

Lee, MacDermid, Williams, Buck, and Leiba-O'Sullivan (2002) found that managers and professionals who engaged in a formal human resource program that provided them with reduced workloads were happier and reported greater work-family balance, although they also indicated that they likely missed some career opportunities and worked more hours than they had contracted for in these arrangements. They also found that supportive senior management and organizational culture, along with the human resource department's assistance in implementing and managing these formal arrangements, made these practices more successful.

In summary, it appears that some of the work-scheduling practices intended to help employees balance work and family domains have mixed results on attitudes and performance. It is clear that face time requirements associated with long work hours are detrimental to maintaining work-family balance. On the other hand, work-scheduling flexibility may need careful planning and implementation to serve as an effective mechanism for reducing work-family conflicts and enhancing performance (Kossek, 2005). In the Nord et al. (2002) study cited above, employees reported many negative experiences associated with flexible schedules and telecommuting that affected their levels of productivity and stress. Specifically, employees indicated that the inadequacies of the technological infrastructure; lack of technical support; poorly defined policies and procedures for participating in telecommuting; failure of the organization to adjust selection, appraisal, project management, and motivational systems for consistency with work performed under new scheduling options; and lack of work schedule fit with the needs of clients presented the greatest obstacles for employees. This research highlights the need for executives to conduct a thorough evaluation of current human resource systems when implementing flexible work-scheduling practices. An integrated change implementation process must be undertaken to improve the success rates of work scheduling initiatives. In addition, we need to examine work-scheduling arrangements in conjunction with job design characteristics (e.g., task interdependencies, task analyzability; Thompson et al., 2005) to determine the most appropriate ways to structure flexibility while maintaining appropriate performance levels.

Training and Career Development.   Schwartz (1996) has suggested that traditional practices for developing managers and the structure of career paths must be redesigned so that family-friendly policies and practices will be utilized successfully. The impact of training and career development opportunities on work-family integration can be examined in three ways: (a) Are there particular training and development opportunities that employees might undertake to help them balance their work and family domains better? (b) Does supervisor training in managing work and family programs help employees maintain work and family integration successfully? and (c) Does work-family conflict and participation in work-family programs hurt employees' career advancement?

Surprisingly, there is little research on each of the above questions. With regard to the first issue, there have been few research attempts to examine the effects of particular training and career development programs for employees that might help them integrate work and family. The only research in this area is on the effects of mentoring on reducing employees' work-family conflict. Nielson, Carlson, and Lankau (2001) found that having a mentor, receiving role modeling and mentor support, and having a mentor who is perceived to have similar work-family values were related to less work-to-family conflict.

With regard to the second issue, it has been assumed that supervisors play a key role in whether or not employees participate in family-friendly programs and in reflecting the organizational cultural norms surrounding work and family integration. Research examining the effect of supervisor support on work-family conflict indicates that it is a significant variable in helping employees integrate work and family (Allen, 2001; Anderson, Coffey, & Byerly, 2002; Fox & Dwyer, 1999; Perlow, 1995; Schwartz, 1996; Thomas & Ganster, 1995; Thompson et al., 1999). Given the importance of supervisor support, researchers have suggested that training supervisors to better accommodate family concerns might promote the use of work-family programs in a way that enhances employee work productivity and quality of family life (Galinsky & Hughes, 1987; Lobel & Kossek, 1996). In particular, Lobel and Kossek (1996) argued that training supervisors in such skills as flexibility, promoting cross-training among employees, communication, coordination, and team-building would encourage the use of family-friendly initiatives. Unfortunately, there are few published empirical studies that actually examine the effect of supervisory training on supervisor support of work-family initiatives and employee work-family integration.

Finally, there appears to be a dearth of research on the relationship between use of family-friendly policies and career advancement. Most studies in this area have examined the effects of work and family variables, not the use of family-supportive policies, on career progress. In her examination of gender differences in the determinants of managerial career success, Kirchmeyer (1998) found that, in general, having family responsibilities did not affect objective or subjective career success. However, women with family responsibilities had more career interruptions, which resulted in lower salaries. Kirchmeyer suggested that effective family-friendly policies might help employees cope with demands from multiple domains and ameliorate the effects of potential career interruptions on career success.

In a study of Spanish employees, it was found that employees with high levels of work-family conflict had limited internal occupational mobility in terms of having fewer promotions and lateral transfers within the organization (Carnicer, Perez, & Sanchez, 2003). Knoke and Ishio (1998) examined gender differences in training program participation and found evidence that women's greater involvement in part-time work and marital and child-care obligations decreased their involvement in training opportunities. The authors argued that employers likely believe that women's familial responsibilities result in transient attachment to the labor force and thus are less willing to invest company resources in developing women. Similar to Carnicer et al. (2003), these authors suggested that enlightened corporations should consider how to bundle training and development opportunities as important components of work-family programs.

Researchers have suggested that using family-friendly policies may hurt career progress (Anderson et al., 2002, Thompson et al., 1999). In general, career interruptions have been found to negatively affect subsequent earnings (Jacobsen & Levin, 1995; Schneer & Reitman, 1997). However, most studies in this area have not examined the specific effects on income or career progress due to family-related career interruptions, with the exception of Judiesch and Lyness (1999), who found that managers who took leaves of absence, for illness or for family reasons, subsequently were promoted less often and received smaller salary increases. Furthermore, there appears to be little evaluation of whether companies have actually altered their career management practices upon implementation of family-friendly policies, and if so, whether these new practices are effective in advancing employees' careers.

In summary, there is virtually no research on the effectiveness of various training and career development programs for employees trying to integrate work and family lives. Not only do we need to conduct more research on identifying effective career management and training strategies for employees seeking balance, but future research also needs to focus on examining the effects of supervisor training in helping managers become more knowledgeable about and skillful in implementing supportive work-family programs. In addition, work-family researchers need to conduct empirical studies to determine how participation in work-family programs affects employees' career prospects. We agree with Lobel and Kossek (1996) and Schwartz (1996) that we need to identify and evaluate the effectiveness of training and career development initiatives that accompany the development of a family-friendly organizational culture and help employees advance in their careers as well as effectively manage their family lives.

Retention.   Most studies on the effects of work-family linkages on retention have not examined objective turnover rates, but turnover intentions. In this regard, WIF has been found to be significantly and positively related to turnover intentions (Anderson, Coffey, & Byerly, 2002; Greenhaus, Parasuraman, & Collins, 2001; Kirchmeyer & Cohen, 1999). In addition, family-supportive work cultures are significantly and negatively related to turnover intentions (Allen, 2001; Thompson et al., 1999). In one study that measured actual turnover, Greenhaus et al. (2001) found that accountants who had low psychological involvement in their careers and who perceived greater levels of work-to-family conflict were more likely to leave their profession. Batt and Valcour (2003) suggested that a combination of human resource incentives for increasing attachment to the firm, work-family policies, and work redesign practices might be effective in reducing work-family conflict and turnover intentions. In addition, studies conducted within large organizations by the Families and Work Institute provide some empirical evidence on the effectiveness of work-family programs in promoting retention. Research conducted at Johnson & Johnson (Families & Work Institute, 1993) and at Fel-Pro (Lambert et al., 1993) both show that the most consistent benefit of work-family programs is enhanced retention.

In summary, research on the effects of work-family conflict on retention has focused mainly on measuring turnover intentions rather than actual turnover or retention rates. The few studies that have measured actual retention rates support the contention that work-family practices are positively related to employee retention.

Organizational Adoption and Evaluation of Work-Family Programs

At the organizational level, recent research has focused on examining factors that lead to firm adoption of work-family programs and the effectiveness of such programs on organizational performance. Institutional and resource dependence theories provide useful frameworks by which to examine these issues. Institutional theory describes how firms adopt policies and practices in response to pressures placed on them from forces in the institutional environment (e.g., state regulations, societal and/or professional norms and expectations, etc.), while resource dependence theory describes how organizations minimize their dependencies on other organizations for the supply of scarce resources (such as key human resources) and find ways of influencing the organizational environment to make these scarce resources available (Jones, 2004).

Goodstein (1994, 1995) and Ingram and Simons (1995) have used institutional theory to examine firm variations in dealing with pressures to adopt work-family policies and programs. Goodstein (1994) found that companies were more likely to adopt family-friendly practices (i.e., workplace flexibility practices and child-care benefits) when the practice was broadly diffused in an industry, when the organization was large and employed a large percentage of women, and when the practice was expected to result in significant benefits to the firm in terms of productivity and performance outcomes. In a later study on implementation of eldercare practices, Goodstein (1995) found that issue visibility in the industry, assessment of eldercare needs, scope of other work-family benefits offered, and the perceived importance of eldercare in increasing employee productivity resulted in greater employer adoption of eldercare practices. Similarly, Ingram and Simons (1995), taking an institutional and resource dependence view of work-family benefits adoption, found that factors within the institutional environment and important stakeholder demands for work-family practices (i.e., firm size, percentage of women and women managers employed in the firm, public sector organizations, greater diffusion of the practice in the industry, and firms in industries with low unemployment rates for women) were related to firm responsiveness to work-family issues. More recently, Arthur (2003) found a significant and positive relationship between firm adoption of work-family initiatives and share prices, with these relationships being higher in high-tech industries and in those that employ higher proportions of women.

In addition to institutional and resource dependence effects, Milliken, Martins, and Morgan (1998) examined the role of human resource executives in framing work-family issues for the firm. They found significant differences across industries in adoption of work-family programs (e.g., health care and financial industries offered more than manufacturing); no significant differences across firms based on the percentage of women employed in the organization; and significant differences across firms based on how salient work-family issues were to human resource executives and the degree to which these executives believed that organizational performance would be detrimentally affected if programs were not offered. Therefore, it appears that human resource staffs play a critical role in framing the importance of adopting work-family programs for effective organizational performance.

Osterman (1995) framed the adoption of work-family programs as one element of an organization's employment strategy to implement a high-performance (high-commitment) work system. He found that organizations that adopt such high-performance systems are more likely to adopt work-family programs. Along with Milliken et al.'s findings, the research suggests that work-family programs need to be conceptualized as an important part of a whole human resource strategy that focuses on building high-commitment workplaces.

In an attempt to determine if adoption of work-family programs results in positive organizational performance, several researchers have examined the effects of "bundles" of work-family benefits. Perry-Smith and Blum (2000) examined the effects of work-family bundles as a strategic human resource initiative that could provide competitive advantage to firms. Using data from 527 U.S. firms, these researchers found that firms that offer more extensive work-family policies are perceived to have higher overall performance as measured by quality of products, ability to attract essential employees, relations between managers and employees, market share, profit, and sales growth. These effects may be stronger in older firms and firms that employ more women. In addition to providing strategic advantage, Perry-Smith and Blum suggested that work-family bundles serve as "positive symbols" (p. 1114) that signal to employees that employers care about their well-being and value their contributions, which in turn may increase their commitment and loyalty. Lambert's (2000) research, which found positive relationships between employee perceptions of the usefulness of work-family benefits and organizational citizenship behaviors, lends support to this interpretation. Further support for the view of the symbolic nature of work-family benefits comes from Kopelman, Prottas, Thompson, and Jahn

(2003), who found that at both the individual and work-unit levels, offering more rather than fewer work-family practices had positive effects on perceived organizational family support and affective commitment.

In an investigation of the effects of work-family programs on profits, using data from the 100 best companies for working mothers, Meyer, Mukerjee, and Sestero (2001) found that overall, work-family programs have a positive effect on profitability, but not all programs added equally to the profit equation. Specifically, job sharing and child-care subsidies were more costly than the benefits that they provided, whereas allowing workers to take time off when family members were sick and telecommuting strongly contributed to profitability. This study implies that organizations need to conduct more sophisticated analyses of the organizational benefits of work-family programs and implement and retain those that provide the most cost-effective solutions for working families.

Impact of Work-Family Practices and Supportive Culture on Organizational Outcomes

Recent research has focused on examining the effects of supportive organizational culture and climate on employee work attitudes and performance. For example, Thompson et al. (1999) developed a measure of work-family culture (i.e., the shared assumptions, beliefs, and values regarding the degree to which the organization supports and values work-family integration) and discovered three dimensions of work-family culture: managerial support for work-family balance, career consequences associated with using work-family benefits, and organizational time expectations that may interfere with family responsibilities. They found that employees were more likely to use work-family benefits when the culture was supportive, and that both the availability of work-family benefits and supportive work-family culture were positively related to affective commitment and negatively related to work-to-family conflict and turnover intentions. Furthermore, the effects of work-family culture on employee attitudes remained significant even after controlling for availability of work-family benefits. In addition, the three dimensions of work-family culture had different relationships with the outcomes measured: lower organizational time demands were related to higher affective commitment, greater managerial support and fewer negative career consequences were related to lower intentions to leave, and fewer negative career consequences and lower organizational time demands were associated with less work-to-family conflict.

Allen (2001) examined the role of family-supportive organization perceptions (FSOP) in managing work-family integration. These perceptions were significantly related to the number of work-family benefits offered, their usage, and perceptions of supervisory family support. In addition, Allen found that FSOP accounted for significant variance in work-family conflict, job satisfaction, organizational commitment, and turnover intentions, above and beyond the effects of work-family benefits and supervisor support. Furthermore, FSOP mediated the relationship between work-family benefits and employee attitudes and behavioral intentions, as well as between supervisor support and work-family conflict. Other research by Kossek, Colquitt, and Noe (2001) examining the effects of work-family climate on caregiving decisions, and by Clark (2001) on the reciprocal nature of the relationship between work-family culture and work-family balance, further underscores the promise associated with continuing research on the role of work-family culture in helping employees achieve work-family integration.

SUMMARY

In this chapter, we have examined the contributions that I/O psychology research has made in better understanding the linkages between work and family domains. Current research supports the beneficial effects of work-life policies, programs, and supportive work-family cultures on work and family balance. To advance research and practice in the work and family field, we need to conduct studies that will provide evidence that links work-family policies, practices, family-friendly culture, and work and family perceptions to firm and employee performance outcomes. In addition, we need to learn how these issues become integrated into the strategic planning of the organization. To do this, more research needs to focus on examining the links between work-life initiatives and human resource practices such as employee recruitment, retention, training and development, and performance management.

With regard to managerial practice, resistance to such policies and practices continues to be problematic. One way to break down such resistance to work-life programs is to show that they have effects that are important to business success. For example, research is beginning to document the effects of various work/life programs and supportive practices on recruiting, retention, absenteeism, tardiness, stress, job satisfaction, organizational commitment and loyalty, and performance (Kossek, 1998). The links between individual policies and anticipated organizational effects must be clarified as different policies and practices may have different effects and usefulness for different employees (Meyer et al., 2001; Perry-Smith & Blum, 2000). In addition, this research might show which programs have little return on their investment. Holding work-life programs to the same strict cost-benefit analysis as other business initiatives encourages more open attitudes toward the programs, reduces the stigma of paternalism associated with them, and paves the way for new and creative solutions for managing work-life dilemmas (Thompson & Beauvais, 2000). Kossek (2005) suggested going beyond making the business case by using a stakeholder or criterion-related approach for evaluating the usefulness of work-life programs that would take multiple interests and goals (e.g., those of the employee, families, and communities) into account. Ultimately, unique configurations of work and family "best practices" for each organization will be developed that become the foundation of a new social contract of "mutual flexibility" between employers and employees (Gonyea & Googins, 1996). These new social contracts should be based on "principles of trust, independence, and choice" (Christensen, 1997, p. 36). Joint problem-solving around work-life issues needs to occur so that the trust and commitment needed to compete in the global marketplace can be generated.

In summary, industrial/organizational psychology has contributed a great deal to understanding the individual issues related to the integration of work and family roles. Moreover, this area of research has revealed that certain organizational policies and practices, including a supportive work-family culture, can help employees successfully manage multiple roles and also benefit organizations. It is encouraging to see that new models of work-family linkages are beginning to include potential positive outcomes. Future theoretical work should include possible personal, job, and organizational factors that might influence whether work and family roles are experienced positively or negatively. In addition, we have many unanswered questions regarding how work-family practices and policies can best be integrated into the overall business strategy and human resource practices of organizations. For example, which work-family programs might be part of a package of organizational "best practices"? How should human resource strategy and practices be changed to incorporate and reinforce work-family practices? What are the best ways to orchestrate changes in the work culture so that work-family linkages are more productive and satisfying? What criteria should we use to evaluate the "success" of work-family practices? As I/O psychologists have expertise in integrating individual and organizational perspectives, they are especially suited to answering these questions and contributing to the field of work and family for years to come.

NOTE

[1]This chapter is a substantially revised and updated version of Thompson and Beauvais (2000).

REFERENCES

Aldous, J. (1990). Specification and speculation concerning the politics of workplace family policies. *Journal of Family Issues, 11*, 355–367.

Allen, T. D. (2001). Family-supportive work environments: The role of organizational perceptions. *Journal of Vocational Behavior, 58*, 414–435.

Allen, T. D. (2003). Organizational barriers. In M. Pitt-Catsouphes & E. Kossek (Eds.), *Work-family encyclopedia*. Chestnut Hill, MA: Sloan Work and Family Research Network at Boston College. Online at www.bc.edu/wfnetwork.

Allen, T. D., & Bruck, C. S. (2004, July). A dominance analysis approach to understanding factors associated with work-family conflict. In J. Cleveland (Chair) Work family: Constructing a view using multiple methods, occupations, culture. Symposium presented at the American Psychological Association Convention, Honolulu, Hawaii.

Allen, T. D., Herst, D. E., Bruck, C. S., & Sutton, M. (2000). Consequences associated with work-to-family conflict: A review and agenda for further research. *Journal of Occupational Health Psychology, 5*, 278–308.

Anderson, S., Coffey, B. S., & Byerly, R. T. (2002). Formal organizational initiatives and informal workplace practices: Links to work-family conflict and job-related outcomes. *Journal of Management, 28*, 787–810.

Arthur, M. M. (2003). Share price reactions to work-family initiatives: An institutional perspective. *Academy of Management Journal, 46*, 497–505.

Ashforth, B. E., Kreiner, G. E., & Fugate, M. (2000). All in a day's work: Boundaries and micro role transitions. *Academy of Management Review, 25*, 472–491.

Bailyn, L. (1993). *Breaking the mold: Women, men and time in the new corporate world*. New York: The Free Press.

Baltes, B. B., Briggs, T. E., Huff, J. W., Wright, J. A., and Neuman, G. A. (1999). Flexible and compressed workweek schedules: A meta-analysis of their effects on work-related criteria. *Journal of Applied Psychology, 84*, 496–513.

Barnett, R. C., & Hyde, J. S. (2001). Women, men, work, and family: An expansionist theory. *American Psychologist, 56*, 781–796.

Baruch, G. K., & Barnett, R. C. (1987). Role quality and psychological well-being. In F. J. Crosby (Ed.), *Spouse, parent, worker: On gender and multiple roles* (pp. 63–73). New Haven, CT: Yale University Press.

Batt, R., & Valcour, P. M. (2003). Human resource practices as predictors of work-family outcomes and employee turnover. *Industrial Relations, 42*, 189–220.

Behson, S. J. (2000). Which dominates? The relative importance of work-family organizational support and general organizational context on employee outcomes. *Journal of Vocational Behavior, 61*, 53–72.

Behson, S. J. (2002). Coping with family-to-work conflict: The role of informal work accommodations to family. *Journal of Occupational Health Psychology, 7*, 324–341.

Bellavia, G. M., & Frone, M. R. (2005). Work-family conflict. In J. Barling, E. K. Kelloway, & M. R. Frone (Eds.), *Handbook of work stress* (pp. 113–148). Thousand Oaks, CA: Sage.

Bond, J. T., Galinsky, E., & Swanberg, J. E. (1998). *The 1997 National Study of the Changing Workforce*. New York: Families and Work Institute.

Bond, T. J., Thompson, C. A., Galinsky, E., & Prottas, D. (2003). *Highlights of the 2002 National Study of the Changing Workforce*. New York: Families and Work Institute.

Brewer, A. M. (2000). Work design for flexible work scheduling: Barriers and gender implications. *Gender, Work and Organization, 7*, 33–44.

Bruck, C. S, & Allen, T. D. (2003). The relationship between big five personality traits, negative affectivity, Type A behavior, and work-family conflict. *Journal of Vocational Behavior, 63*, 457–472.

Bruck, C. S., Allen, T. D., & Spector, P. E. (2002). The relation between work-family conflict and job satisfaction: A finer-grained analysis. *Journal of Vocational Behavior, 60*, 336–353.

Byron, K. (in press). A meta-analytic review of work-family conflict and its antecedents. *Journal of Vocational Behavior*.

Burke, R. J. (1988). Some antecedents and consequences of work-family conflict. *Journal of Social Behavior and Personality, 3*, 287–302.

Burkett, E. (2000). *The baby boon: How family-friendly America cheats the childless*. New York: Free Press.

Carlson, D. S. (1999). Personality and role variables as predictors of three forms of work-family conflict. *Journal of Vocational Behavior, 55*, 236–253.

Carlson, D. S., & Perrewe, P. L. (1999). The role of social support in the stressor–strain relationship: An examination of work-family conflict. *Journal of Management, 25*, 513–540.

Carnicer, M. P. D., Perez, M. P., & Sanchez, A. M. (2003). Human resources mobility management: A study of job related and non-related factors. *International Journal of Human Resources Development and Management, 3*, 308–328.

Christensen, P. M. (1997). Toward a comprehensive work-life strategy. In S. Parasuraman & J. H. Greenhaus (Eds.), *Integrating work and family: Challenges and choices for a changing world* (pp. 25–37). Westport, CT: Quorum Books.

Clark, S. C. (2001). Work cultures and work/family balance. *Journal of Vocational Behavior, 58*, 348–365.

Clark, S. C. (2002). Employees' sense of community, sense of control, and work/family conflict in Native American organizations. *Journal of Vocational Behavior, 61*, 92–108.

Cohen, S., & Wills, T. A. (1985). Stress, social support, and the buffering hypothesis. *Psychological Bulletin, 98*, 310–357.

Cook, E. P. (1994). Role salience and multiple roles: A gender perspective. *Career Development Quarterly, 43*, 85–95.

Cooper, C. L., & Lewis, S. (1994). *Managing the new work force: The challenge of dual-income families*. San Diego, CA: Pfeiffer.

Costa, P. T., & McCrae, R. R. (1991). *Revised NEO personality inventory (NEO PI-R) and NEO five-factor inventory (NEO-FFI): Professional manual*. Odessa, FL: Psychological Assessment Resources.

Crosby, F. J. (1991). *Juggling: The unexpected advantages of balancing career and home for women and their families*. New York: The Free Press.

Duxbury, L. E., & Higgins, C. A. (1991). Gender differences in work-family conflict. *Journal of Applied Psychology, 76*(1), 60–74.

Duxbury, L. E., Higgins, C. A., & Thomas, D. R. (1996). Work and family environments and the adoption of computer-supported supplemental work-at-home. *Journal of Vocational Behavior, 49*, 1–23.

Eagle, B. W., Miles, E. W., & Icenogle, M. L. (1997). Interrole conflicts and the permeability of work and family domains: Are there gender differences? *Journal of Vocational Behavior, 50*, 168–184.

Eby, L. T., Casper, W. J., Lockwood, A., Bordeaux, C., & Brinley, A. (2005). Work and family research in IO/OB: Content analysis and review of the literature (1980–2002). *Journal of Vocational Behavior, 66*, 124–197.

Edwards, J. R., & Rothbard, N. P. (2000). Mechanisms linking work and family: Clarifying the relationship between work and family constructs. *Academy of Management Review, 25*, 178–199.

Families & Work Institute. (1993). *An evaluation of Johnson & Johnson's work-family initiative*. New York: Families and Work Institute.

Fox, M. L., & Dwyer, D. J. (1999). An investigation of the effects of time and involvement in the relationship between stressors and work-family conflict. *Journal of Occupational Health Psychology, 4*, 164–174.

Friedman, D. E., & Johnson, A. A. (1996). *Moving from programs to culture change: The next stage for the corporate work-family agenda*. New York: Families and Work Institute.

Frone, M. R. (2003). Work-family balance. In J. C. Quick & L. E. Tetrick (Eds.), *Handbook of occupational health psychology* (pp. 143–162). Washington, DC: American Psychological Association.

Frone, M. R., Russell, M., & Cooper, M. L. (1992a). Prevalence of work-family conflict: Are work and family boundaries asymmetrically permeable? *Journal of Organizational Behavior, 13*, 723–729.

Frone, M. R., Russell, M., & Cooper, M. L. (1992b). Antecedents and outcomes of work-family conflict: Testing a model of the work-family interface. *Journal of Applied Psychology, 77*, 65–78.

Frone, M. R., Russell, M., & Cooper, M. L. (1993). Relationship of work-family conflict, gender, and alcohol expectancies to alcohol use/abuse. *Journal of Organizational Behavior, 14*, 545–558.

Frone, M. R., Russell, M., & Cooper, M. L. (1997). Relation of work-family conflict to health outcomes: A four-year longitudinal study of employed parents. *Journal of Occupational and Organizational Psychology, 70*, 325–335.

Frone, M. R., Yardley, J. K., & Markel, K. S. (1997). Developing and testing an integrative model of the work-family interface. *Journal of Vocational Behavior, 50*, 145–167.

Galinsky, E., Bond, J. T., & Friedman, D. E. (1996). The role of employers in addressing the needs of employed parents. *Journal of Social Issues, 52*, 111–136.

Galinsky, E., & Hughes, D. (1987). *The Fortune Magazine Child Care Study*. Paper presented at the American Psychological Association, New York.

Galinsky, E., & Stein, P. J. (1990). The impact of human resource policies on employees. *Journal of Family Issues, 11*, 368–377.

Glass, J. (2003). Sociological perspectives on work and family. Paper presented at the NICHD/Sloan Foundation conference, "Workforce/workplace mismatch? Work, Family, Health, and Well-being," Washington, D.C., June.

Goff, S. J., Mount, M. K., & Jamison, R. L. (1990). Employer supported child care, work-family, and absenteeism: A field study. *Personnel Psychology, 43*, 793–809.

Gonyea, J. G., & Googins, B. K. (1996). The restructuring of work and family in the United States: A new challenge for American corporations. In S. Lewis & J. Lewis (Eds.), *The work-family challenge: Rethinking employment* (pp. 63–78). London: Sage.

Goodstein, J. D. (1994). Institutional pressures and strategic responsiveness: Employer involvement in work-family issues. *Academy of Management Journal, 37*, 350–382.

Goodstein, J. D. (1995). Employer involvement in eldercare: An organizational adaptation perspective. *Academy of Management Journal, 38*, 1657–1671.

Grandey, A. (2001). Family friendly policies: Organizational justice perceptions of need-based allocations. In R. Cropanzano (Ed.), *Justice in the workplace: From theory to practice* (Vol. 2). Series in applied psychology (pp. 145–173). Mahwah, NJ: Lawrence Erlbaum Associates.

Greenhaus, J. H., Bedeian, A. G., & Mossholder, K. W. (1987). Work experiences, job performance, and feelings of personal and family well-being. *Journal of Vocational Behavior, 31*, 200–215.

Greenhaus, J. H., & Beutell, N. J. (1985). Sources of conflict between work and family roles. *Academy of Management Review, 10*, 76–88.

Greenhaus, J. H., Collins, K. M., Singh, R., & Parasuraman, S. (1997). Work and family influences on departure from public accounting. *Journal of Vocational Behavior, 50*, 249–270.

Greenhaus, J. H., & Parasuraman, S. (1986). A work–nonwork interactive perspective of stress and its consequences. *Journal of Organizational Behavior Management, 8*, 37–60.

Greenhaus, J. H., Parasuraman, S., & Collins, K. M. (2001). Career involvement and family involvement as moderators of relationships between work-family conflict and withdrawal from a profession. *Journal of Occupational Health Psychology, 6*, 91–100.

Greenhaus, J. H., & Powell, G. N. (in press). When work and family are allies: A theory of work-family enrichment. *Academy of Management Review*.

Greenhaus, J. H., & Singh, R. (2004). Work-family linkages. *A Sloan work and family encyclopedia* entry, www.bc.edu/wfnetwork/encyclopedia.

Grzywacz, J. G. (2002). Toward a theory of work-family facilitation. Paper presented at the 2002 Persons, Processes, and Places: Research on Families, Workplaces and Communities Conference. San Francisco, CA.

Grzywacz, J. G., & Marks, N. F. (2000). Reconceptualizing the work-family interface: An ecological perspective on the correlates of positive and negative spillover between work and family. *Journal of Occupational Health Psychology, 5*, 111–126.

Gutek, B. A., Searle, S., & Klepa, L. (1991). Rational versus gender role explanations for work-family conflict. *Journal of Applied Psychology, 76*, 560–568.

Haas, L., Allard, K., & Hwang, P. (2002). The impact of organizational culture on men's use of parental leave in Sweden. *Community, Work, & Family, 5*, 319–342.

Hall, D. T. (1972). A model of coping with role conflict: The role behaviors of college educated women. *Administrative Science Quarterly, 1*, 471–486.

Higgins, C., Duxbury, L., & Lee, C. (1994). Impact of life-cycle stage and gender on the ability to balance work and family responsibilities. *Family Relations, 43*, 144–150.

Hill, E. J., Miller, B. C., Weiner, S. P., & Colihan, J. (1998). Influences of the virtual office on aspects of work and work/life balances. *Personnel Psychology, 51*, 667–683.

Holzer, H. (2003). Work and family life: The perspective of employers. Paper presented at the NICHD/Sloan Foundation conference, "Workforce/workplace mismatch? Work, Family, Health, and Well-being," Washington, DC., June.

Honeycutt, T. L., & Rosen, B. (1997). Family friendly human resource policies, salary levels, and salient identity as predictors of organizational attraction. *Journal of Vocational Behavior, 50*, 271–290.

House, J. S. (1981). Work stress and social support. Reading, MA: Addition-Wesley.

Ingram, P., & Simons, T. (1995). Institutional and resource dependence determinants of responsiveness to work-family issues. *Academy of Management Journal, 38*, 1466–1482.

Jacobsen, J. P., & Levin, L. M. (1995). Effects of intermittent labor force attachment on women's earnings. *Monthly Labor Review, 118*, 14–19.

Jones, G. R. (2004). *Organizational theory, design, and change.* (4th ed.). Upper Saddle River, NJ: Pearson Prentice-Hall.

Judiesch, M., & Lyness, K. (1999). Left behind? The impact of leaves of absence on managers' career success. *Academy of Management Journal, 42*, 641–651.

Kahn, R. L., Wolfz, D. M., Quinn, R. P., Snoek, J. D., & Rosenthal, R. A. (1964). Organizational Stress: Studies in role conflict and ambiguity. New York: Wiley.

Kanter, R. (1977). *Work and family in the United States.* New York: Russell Sage.

Katz, D., & Kahn, R. L. (1978). The social psychology of organizations (2nd edition). New York: Wiley.

Kelloway, E. K., Gottlieb, B. H., & Barham, L. (1999). The source, nature, and direction of work and family conflict: A longitudinal investigation. *Journal of Occupational Health Psychology, 4*, 337–346.

Kingston, P. W. (1990). Illusions and ignorance about the family-responsive workplace. *Journal of Family Issues, 11*, 438–454.

Kirchmeyer, C. (1993). Non-work to work spillover: A more balanced view of the experience and coping of professional women and men. *Sex Roles, 28*, 531–552.

Kirchmeyer, C. (1998). Determinants of managerial career success: Evidence and explanation of male/female differences. *Journal of Management, 24*, 673–692.

Kirchmeyer, C., & Cohen, A. (1999). Different strategies for managing the work/non-work interface: A test for unique pathways to work outcomes. *Work & Stress, 13*, 59–73.

Knoke, D., & Ishio, Y. (1998). The gender gap in company training. *Work and Occupations, 25*, 141–167.

Kopelman, R. E., Greenhaus, J. H., & Connolly, T. F. (1983). A model of work, family, and interrole conflict: A construct validation study. *Organizational Behavior & Human Decision Processes, 32*, 198–215.

Kopelman, R. E., Prottas, D. J., Thompson, C. A., & Jahn, E. W. (2003). *A multilevel examination of work-life practices: Is more always better?* Paper presented at the 63rd Annual Meeting of the Academy of Management. Seattle, WA: August.

Kossek, E. E. (1998). Organizational payback from work/life policies. In S. D. Friedman, J. DeGroot, & P. M. Christensen (Eds.), *Integrating work and life: The Wharton resource guide* (pp. 265–277). San Francisco: Jossey-Bass/Pfeiffer.

Kossek, E. E. (2005). Workplace policies and practices to support work and families: Gaps in implementation and linkages to individual and organizational effectiveness. In S. M. Bianchi, L. M. Casper, K. E. Christensen, & R. Berkowitz King (Eds.), *Workforce/workplace mismatch? Work, family, health and well-being*. Mahwah, NJ: Lawrence Erlbaum Associates.

Kossek, E. E., Barber, A. E., & Winters, D. (1999). Using flexible schedules in the managerial world: The power of peers. *Human Resource Management, 38*, 33–46.

Kossek, E. E., Colquitt, J. A., & Noe, R. A. (2001). Caregiving decisions, well-being, and performance: The effects of place and provider as a function of dependent type and work-family climates. *Academy of Management Journal, 44*, 29–44.

Kossek, E. E., & Ozeki, C. (1998). Work-family conflict, policies, and the job–life satisfaction relationship: A review and directions for the organizational behavior–human resources research. *Journal of Applied Psychology, 83*, 139–149.

Lambert, S. J. (1990). Processes linking work and family: A critical review and research agenda. *Human Relations, 43*, 239–257.

Lambert, S. J. (2000). Added benefits: The link between work-life benefits and organizational citizenship behavior. *Academy of Management Journal, 43*, 801–815.

Lambert, S. J., Hopkins, K., Easton, G., Walker, J., McWilliams, H., & Chung, M. S. (1993). *Added benefits: The link between family responsive policies and job performance. University of Chicago study of Fel-Pro Incorporated.* Chicago, IL.

Latack, J. (1984). Career transitions within organizations: An exploratory study of work, nonwork, and coping strategies. *Organizational Behavior and Human Performance, 34*, 296–322.

Lee, M. D., MacDermid, S. M., Williams, M. L., Buck, M. L., & Leiba-O'Sullivan, S. (2002). Contextual factors in the success of reduced-load work arrangements among managers and professionals. *Human Resource Management, 41*, 209–223.

Levine, J. A., & Pittinsky, T. L. (1997). *Working fathers: New strategies for balancing work and family.* Reading, MA: Addison-Wesley.

Lewis, S. (2001). Restructuring workplace cultures: The ultimate work-family challenge? *Women in Management Review, 16*, 21–29.

Lobel, S. A., & Kossek, E. E. (1996). Human resource strategies to support diversity in work and personal lifestyles: Beyond the "family-friendly" organization. In E. E. Kossek & S. A. Lobel (Eds.), *Managing diversity: Human resource strategies for transforming the workplace* (pp. 221–244). Oxford, UK: Blackwell.

Major, D. A., & Cleveland, J. N. (2005). Psychological perspectives on the work-family interface. In S. M. Bianchi, L. M. Casper, R. Berkowitz King (Eds.), *Workforce/workplace mismatch? Work, Family, Health and Well-being* (pp. 169–186). Mahwah, NJ: Lawrence Erlbaum Associates.

Major, V. S., Klein, K. J., & Ehrhart, M. G. (2002). Work time, work interference with family, and psychological stress. *Journal of Applied Psychology, 87*, 427–436.

Marks, S. R. (1977). Multiple roles and role strain: Some notes on human energy, time and commitment. *American Sociological Review, 42*, 921–936.

Marshall, N. L., & Barnett, R. C. (1994). Family-friendly workplaces, work-family interface, and worker health. In G. P. Keita & J. J. Hurrell (Eds.), *Job stress in a changing workforce* (pp. 253–264). Washington, DC: American Psychological Association.

Meyer, C. S., Mukerjee, S., & Sestero, A. (2001). Work-family benefits: Which ones maximize profits? *Journal of Managerial Issues, 13*, 28–44.

Milliken, F. J., Martins, L. L., & Morgan, H. (1998). Explaining organizational responsiveness to work-family issues: The role of human resource executives as issue interpreters. *Academy of Management Journal, 41*, 580–592.

Moen, P. (1996). A life course perspective on retirement, gender, and well-being. *Journal of Occupational Health Psychology, 1*, 131–144.

Nielson, T. R., Carlson, D. S., & Lankau, M. J. (2001). The supportive mentor as a means of reducing work-family conflict. *Journal of Vocational Behavior, 59*, 364–381.

Nord, W. R., Fox, S., Phoenix, A., & Viano, K. (2002). Real-world reactions to work-life balance programs: Lessons for effective implementation. *Organizational Dynamics, 30*, 223–238.

Osterman, P. (1995). Work/family programs and the employment relationship. *Administration Science Quarterly, 40*, 681–700.

Parasuraman, S., & Greenhaus, J. H. (1997a). The changing world of work and family. In S. Parasuraman & J. H. Greenhaus (Eds.), *Integrating work and family: Challenges and choices for a changing world* (pp. 3–14). Westport, CT: Quorum Books.

Parasuraman, S., & Greenhaus, J. H. (1997b). *Integrating work and family: Challenges and choices for a changing world.* Westport, CT: Quorum Books.

Parasuraman, S., Greenhaus, J. H., & Granrose, C. S. (1992). Role stressors, social support, and well-being among two-career couples. *Journal of Organizational Behavior, 13*, 339–356.

Parasuraman, S., & Simmers, C. A. (2001). Type of employment, work-family conflict and well-being: A comparative study. *Journal of Organizational Behavior, 22*, 551–568.

Parker, L., & Allen, T. D. (2001). Work/family benefits: Variables related to employees' fairness perceptions. *Journal of Vocational Behavior, 58*, 453–468.

Perlow, L. A. (1995). Putting the work back into work/family. *Group and Organization Management, 20*, 227–239.

Perlow, L. A. (1997). *Finding time: How corporations, individuals, and families can benefit from new work practices.* Ithaca, NY: Cornell University Press.

Perrow, C. (1970). *Organizational analysis: A sociological view.* Belmont, CA: Wadsworth.

Perry-Smith, J. E., & Blum, T. C. (2000). Work-family human resource bundles and perceived organizational performance. *Academy of Management Journal, 43*, 1107–1117.

Pistrang, N. (1984). Women's work involvement and experience of new motherhood. *Journal of Marriage and the Family, 46*, 433–447.

Pleck, J. H. (1993). Are "family-supportive" employer policies relevant to men? In J. C. Hood (Ed.), *Men, work, and family* (pp. 217–237). Newbury Park, CA: Sage.

Rau, B. L., & Hyland, M. M. (2002). Role conflict and flexible work arrangements: The effects on applicant attraction. *Personnel Psychology, 55*, 111–136.

Rothbard, N. P. (2001). Enriching or deleting? The dynamics of engagement in work and family roles. *Administrative Science Quarterly, 46*, 655–684.

Ruderman, M. N., Ohlott, P. J., Panzer, K., & King, S. N. (2002). Benefits of multiple roles for managerial women. *Academy of Management Journal, 45*, 369–386.

Schafer, S., & Salmon, J. L. (2001). Childless employees want equal flextime and more. *Washington Post*, April 21, A01.

Scharlach, A. E., & Boyd, S. L. (1989). Caregiving and employment: Results of an employee survey. *The Gerontologist, 29*, 382–387.

Schneer, J. A., & Reitman, F. (1997). The interrupted managerial career path: A longitudinal study of MBA's. *Journal of Vocational Behavior, 51*, 411–434.

Schwartz, D. B. (1994). *An examination of the impact of family-friendly policies on the glass ceiling.* Families and Work Institute, New York, NY.

Schwartz, D. B. (1996). The impact of work-family policies on women's career development: Boon or bust? *Women in Management Review, 11*, 5–19.

Schwartz, F. N. (1992). *Breaking with tradition: Women and work, the new facts of life.* New York: Warner Books.

Seligman, M. E. P., & Csikszentmihalyi, M. (2000). Positive psychology: An introduction. *American Psychologist, 55*, 5–14.

Shamir, B. (1983). Some antecedents of work–nonwork conflict. *Journal of Vocational Behavior, 23*, 98–111.

Sieber, S. D. (1974). Toward a theory of role accumulation. *American Sociological Review, 39*, 567–578.

Spence, J. T., Helmreich, R. L., & Pred, R. S. (1987). Impatience versus achievement strivings in the Type A pattern: Differential effects on students' health and academic achievement. *Journal of Applied Psychology, 72*, 522–528.

Spitze, G. (1988). Women's employment and family relations: A review. *Journal of Marriage and the Family, 50*, 595–618.

Stoeva, A. Z., Chiu, R., & Greenhaus, J. H. (2002). Negative affectivity, role stress, and work-family conflict. *Journal of Vocational Behavior, 60*, 1–16.

Thoits, P. A. (1987). Negotiating roles. In F. J. Crosby (Ed.), *Spouse, parent, worker* (pp. 11–22). New Haven, CT: Yale University Press.

Thomas, L. T., & Ganster, D. C. (1995). Impact of family-supportive work variables on work-family conflict and strain: A control perspective. *Journal of Applied Psychology, 80*, 6–15.

Thompson, C. A. (1989). Effects of work-family conflict: The mediating role of stress. Presented at the Fourth Annual Conference of the Society of Industrial and Organizational Psychology, Boston.

Thompson, C. A., Andreassi, J., & Prottas, D. (2005). Work-family culture: Key to reducing workforce–workplace mismatch? In S. M. Bianchi, L. M. Casper, & R. Berkowitz King (Eds.), *Workforce/workplace mismatch? Work, family, health and well-being* (pp. 117–132). Mahwah, NJ: Lawrence Erlbaum Associates.

Thompson, C. A., & Beauvais, L. L. (2000). Balancing work/life. In D. M. Smith (Ed.), *Women at work: Leadership for the next century* (pp. 162–189). Upper Saddle River, NJ: Prentice-Hall.

Thompson, C. A., Beauvais, L. L., & Lyness, K. S. (1999). When work-family benefits are not enough: The influence of work-family culture on benefit utilization, organizational attachment, and work-family conflict. *Journal of Vocational Behavior, 54*, 392–415.

Thompson, C. A., & Prottas, D. J. (in press). Relationships among organizational family support, job autonomy, perceived control, and employee well-being. *Journal of Occupational Health Psychology.*

Thompson, C. A., Thomas, C. C., & Maier, M. (1992). Work-family conflict and the bottom line: Reassessing corporate policies and initiatives. In U. Sekaran & F. T. Leong (Eds.), *Womanpower: Managing in times of demographic turbulence* (pp. 59–84). Newbury Park, CA: Sage.

Wallace, J. E. (1999). Work-to-nonwork conflict among married male and female lawyers. *Journal of Organizational Behavior, 20*, 797–816.

Wayne, J. H., Musisca, N., & Fleeson, W. (2004). Considering the role of personality in the work-family experience: Relationships of the big five to work-family conflict and facilitation. *Journal of Vocational Behavior, 64*, 108–130.

Williams, J. (2000). *Unbending gender.* New York: Oxford University Press.

Williams, K. J., & Alliger, G. M. (1994). Role stressors, mood spillover, and perceptions of work-family conflict in employed parents. *Academy of Management Journal, 37*, 837–868.

Zedeck, S. (1990). Work in the family and employing organization. *American Psychologist, 45*, 240–251.

15

A Legal Perspective on Family Issues at Work

Mary C. Still
American University

Joan C. Williams
University of California
Hastings College of the Law

What does the law have to do with work/life scholarship and activism? This chapter examines existing laws related to work and family conflict, discusses the legal issues that have arisen in the courts as a result of workers suing their employers, and details the underlying process of stereotyping that can turn employer actions against workers with family or caregiver conflicts into litigable (and increasingly, winnable) court cases. We conclude with a discussion of how new and existing labor laws hurt or help ease work/family conflicts, and how litigation and public policy-making can be used in conjunction with the business case to make American workplaces more family-friendly.

Only recently have scholars begun to shift their attention from the corporate arena of voluntary policies to the broader arenas of public policy and law. Of the six dimensions of work/family public policy—leaves, child care, working time, tax and benefits, labor market incentives, and discrimination—the greatest attention has been paid to leaves and child-care subsidies.[1] Although both paid leave and subsidized child care are important tools for reducing work/family conflict, an emphasis on these solutions has meant other potential solutions are only now coming into the public conversation. We focus on two potential solutions, both related to law: discrimination litigation and working time public policy.

THE DISCRIMINATION APPROACH: LITIGATION AS SOCIAL CHANGE AGENT

A substantial literature documents the legal environment as one of the most important institutions guiding workplace organizations and influencing change. Organizations must pay particularly close attention to law and its implications for managing their workforce, because law is a significant source of their legitimacy (DiMaggio & Powell, 1983; Meyer & Rowan, 1977). To new institutional sociologists such as DiMaggio, Powell, Meyer, and Rowan, legitimacy is a key concept in understanding why organizations behave as they do. Organizations need legitimacy—the broad acceptance by the public that their actions are desirable, proper, or appropriate (Suchman, 1995, p. 576). Legitimacy is necessary to be accepted, to be admired, and even to function, and much of organizational action is geared toward gaining this legitimacy. Thus, when an organization adopts a family-friendly practice such as paid parental leave, it is not behaving "rationally" as traditional economists would define it, since it is not required to pay employees to take care of their newborns or family members and doing so can be expensive, and since retention and recruitment linkages are often indirect and difficult for companies to measure. The organization is instead behaving in a way that increases its legitimacy in the eyes of its constituents: Paying employees for parental leave is what socially responsible, "good" companies do. Such seemingly irrational action is difficult to explain by a simple behavioral view of the world, in which organizations are composed of individual decision makers making choices that aggregate to a single, strategic collective behavior (Powell & DiMaggio, 1991). Instead, in the institutionalist view, individual preferences are shaped by the norms, values, and beliefs in the larger culture rather than the other way around. In such a world, organizations that "do the right thing" or act in seemingly irrational ways are not just anomalies, but the norm.

As the codified formalization of a society's values and beliefs, law—and proposed changes to it—can be ambiguous, creating a great deal of uncertainty for organizations (Sutton & Dobbin, 1996; Sutton, Dobbin, Meyer, & Scott, 1994; Edelman, 1990, 1992). Organizations dislike uncertainty, and their attempts to overcome it as well as their drive toward legitimacy cause them to pay close attention to legal issues that may impact them. For example, Kelly and Dobbin (1999) studied organizational adoption of family leave policies and found that companies voluntarily adopted policies giving employees paid or partially paid time off after *media coverage of lawsuits* brought against employers by pregnant women. The power of law was constituted, in significant part, by the public "conversation" around, rather than the mere passage of, the Pregnancy Discrimination Act. Edelman (1992) found that companies paid close attention to equal employment opportunity and affirmative action law, proactively forming their responses to avoid being proclaimed to be violating the law. Both Edelman's and Kelly and Dobbin's (1999) studies confirm earlier assertions by new institutionalists that the social process of litigation is a closely watched and influential force on the actions of organizations.

The new institutionalists' observation of the complex interactions between litigation, social norms, and the press parallels discussions among legal historians who advocate legal history that includes not only discussion of statutes and cases, but also of "rights talk" and more generally of legal consciousness (Hartog, Marcus, & Scheiber, 1987). These historians inspired one co-author (Williams) to reframe work/life issues through the lens of discrimination law as a way to shift social norms. "Rights talk" helps to reframe work/family conflict as a problem with American institutions and the way work is structured, rather than in terms of individual workers' personal problems. If employers define the ideal worker as an individual who works 40 years straight without time off for childbearing, rearing, or any kind of caregiving, then the workplace is designed for individuals with particular bodies and social roles—men (Williams, 2000). Designing the workplace around the bodies and traditional life patterns of men discriminates against women. Thus, it should not be the responsibility of the individual experiencing work/family conflict to make a hard "choice"—to quit work, find part-time work, find a job with fewer demands. Instead, it is the responsibility of larger societal institutions, notably laws and workplace policies, to find new ways to work that do not perpetuate gender bias.

The discrimination approach has its roots in "rights talk," which frames discrimination as a violation of fundamental human rights and has been successfully used to galvanize social change for African Americans, women, individuals with disabilities, and homosexuals. Rights talk is a powerful rhetorical and legal tool that shows promise for influencing social norms in liberal societies. Especially during times of social change, conversations about "who owes what to whom" are an important part of people's ideas about both what is legal and what is ethical. Court cases are one important forum, but private conversations and consciousness-raising also play an important role. The history of sexual harassment serves as an important example of how litigation can reshape behavioral norms. Women—and men, too—won the right to a workplace environment free of sexual advances, innuendo, and lewdness. Only 20 years before, such a "right" might well have seemed ridiculous to the average worker.

EXISTING LAWS RELATED TO WORK/LIFE CONFLICT

Some laws already exist to resolve cases in which workers are penalized because of their family caregiving responsibilities. No federal statute explicitly protects workers from adverse actions by their employer because of family obligations; however, in a systematic review of cases involving work/family claims, we have identified more than 200 cases where legal theories have been successfully used in court to gain settlements or verdicts for family caregivers (WorkLife Law, 2005). Below, we describe the laws most frequently used in cases involving discrimination against caregivers.

Title VII

Title VII is the most commonly used statute in legal cases claiming unfair treatment of family caregivers in the workplace. Title VII is the basic federal statute prohibiting discrimination in employment. Claims under Title VII have been brought under a number of distinct theories, including disparate treatment, disparate impact, hostile work environment, constructive discharge, and retaliation. *Title VII disparate treatment* claims can be brought if an employer treats male and female applicants or workers differently. In the early Title VII case *Phillips v. Martin Marietta Corp.* (1971), the Supreme Court established that employers cannot treat employees differently based on their sex "plus" a facially neutral characteristic such as having young children. This "sex-plus" theory meant that Martin Marietta was liable for refusing to allow mothers of school-aged children to apply for jobs that were open to men with young children. More modern disparate treatment cases sometimes rely on sex-plus; sometimes they are litigated as straightforward gender discrimination cases (WorkLife Law, 2005).

Title VII disparate impact is used in cases where practices or policies that appear to be gender neutral actually have a negative impact on workers of one sex. In *EEOC v. Warshawsky & Co.* (1991), for example, a mother challenged a policy of terminating any first-year employee who required long-term sick leave. She proved that the policy had a disparate impact on women by showing that women were 11 times more likely to be fired for absences than men, and that, of the 53 employees fired under this policy, 50 were women and 20 were pregnant in a 4-year period.

Title VII hostile work environment theory is used when an employee has been subjected to severe and pervasive intimidation, ridicule, or insults based on her sex. In *Walsh v. National Computer Systems, Inc.* (2002), a top salesperson with outstanding performance evaluations experienced a hostile environment after she had a child, including intensive scrutiny of her hours when no other employee's hours were scrutinized; requiring the mother to stay at work while allowing her coworkers to go to a crafts fair to "pay them back" for covering for her while she was on maternity leave; refusal to allow her to pick up her sick child from day care; referring to the plaintiff's child, who was subject to ear infections, as "the sickling"; declaring "You better not be pregnant again" when the plaintiff fainted due to the stress of workplace hostility; and throwing a phone book on her desk with an order to find a new pediatrician who was open after business hours. The plaintiff was awarded $625,525.

A *Title VII constructive discharge* claim is made when an employer makes working conditions so intolerable they would compel a reasonable employee to quit. *Walsh v. National*

Computer (2002) involved a constructive discharge claim as well as a hostile environment claim.

Title VII retaliation occurs when the employee has been punished for being involved in an activity protected by Title VII, such as filing a charge against the company. In *Flores-Suarez v. Turabo* (2001), the plaintiff had sued once under Title VII and won, but was retaliated against upon her return. The jury awarded the plaintiff $570,000, which the judge increased to $940,000.

Equal Pay Act

Designed to rectify the disparity between men's and women's wages, the Equal Pay Act is a federal statute that prohibits employers from paying men a higher wage than women based on sex. It has interesting applications to work/family issues. For example, in *Corning Glass Works v. Brennan* (1974), women workers who worked during the day were being paid less than male nightshift workers doing the same job. The court ruled in favor of the women. Similarly, in *Lovell v. BBNT Solutions* (2004), the court upheld an award of $403,125 against an employer that had paid a part-timer a lower wage than its full-time workers who had similar job titles, similar educational backgrounds, worked under the same supervisor, and had virtually identical duties and responsibilities.

Constitutional Equality Mandates

Employees who work for the state or local governments can be sued under the U.S. Constitution, using Section 1983 (Civil Rights Act, 1994). Examples include *Back v. Hastings* (2004) and *Knussman v. Maryland* (2001; discussed below).

Family and Medical Leave Act (FMLA)

This 1993 statute requires employers with more than 50 employees to give workers up to 12 weeks of unpaid leave per year if they or their spouse, children, or parents have a serious health condition or for the birth or adoption of a child (Family and Medical Leave Act of 1993). The leading FMLA caregiver case, *Schultz v. Advocate Health* (2002), involved a hospital maintenance worker who was fired in retaliation for taking intermittent family leave to care for his ailing parents. His FMLA claim was accompanied by a state claim for intentional infliction of emotional distress, yielding a verdict for the plaintiff of over $11.65 million (Family Leave Suit, 2002).

Americans With Disabilities Act (ADA)

The ADA prohibits not only discrimination against workers with disabilities, but also discrimination against workers who have a "relationship or association" with an individual with a disability (Americans with Disabilities Act of 1990, 1994). An example is *McGrenaghan v. St. Denis Schools* (1997), where a court held that it was an adverse employment action when a teacher was demoted from full-time teacher to part-time teacher/part-time aide, with a decrease in salary, after her son was born with a disability.

ERISA

ERISA governs pension plans and certain benefits plans. For example, a mother denied employment because the employer feared her son's medical bills would be too costly successfully sued under ERISA (*Fleming v. Ayers and Associates*, 1991).

State Statutes

Many states have antidiscrimination laws that are at least as protective if not more so than federal laws. In addition, several states and localities have passed laws expressly prohibiting discrimination against parents. One example is the District of Columbia's Human Rights Act that protects workers against discrimination because they are also family caregivers (1981). In *Simpson v. D.C. Office of Human Rights* (1991), a worker was fired for refusing a change in her work schedule that would have kept her from caring for her sick father. Her case was settled under the D.C. Human Rights Statute.

State Causes of Action

Caregivers have also successfully sued their employers for discrimination using claims of intentional infliction of emotional distress, tortious interference with contract, breach of contract, and breach of the covenant of good faith and fair dealing. A common practice is to add state tort claims to suits filed under state or federal statutes, largely because this allows plaintiffs access to potentially much larger damage awards.

THE MECHANISMS OF DISCRIMINATION

In 2003, the U.S. Supreme Court case of *Nevada Department of Human Resources v. Hibbs* upheld the right of state employees to sue states for violations of the Family and Medical Leave Act (1993), noting that, "The fault line between work and family [is] precisely where sex-based generalization has been and remains strongest." The majority opinion, written by conservative Supreme Court Chief Justice Rehnquist, continued: "Stereotypes about women's domestic responsibilities are reinforced by parallel stereotypes presuming a lack of domestic responsibilities for men. These mutually reinforcing stereotypes created a self-fulfilling cycle of discrimination" (*Hibbs*, 2003, p. 1983). Lower federal and state courts have reiterated that stereotypes that mothers are neither competent nor committed can play an important role in "maternal wall" discrimination, which refers to the unequal treatment of women in the workplace leading to their being passed over for promotions, paid lower wages, or even being fired (e.g., see *Back v. Hastings on the Hudson Union Free School District*, 2004; *Sivieri v. Commonwealth of Massachusetts Department of Transitional Assistance*, 2003).

Social psychologists have identified a number of specific stereotypes that affect mothers. Negative competence assumptions are a major source of maternal wall bias. A series of studies by Susan Fiske, Peter Glick, Jun Xu, and Amy Cuddy documents that, while businesswomen are considered highly competent, similar to businessmen and millionaires, housewives are considered very low in competence, alongside the elderly, blind, "retarded," and disabled (1999, p. 476). A more recent study by Amy Cuddy, Susan Fiske and Peter Glick documents that working mothers are rated as more similar in competence to low-competence housewives than to high-competence businesswomen (2004).

These studies help explain the problems faced by mothers on their return from maternity leave. "When I returned from maternity leave," said one Boston lawyer, "I was given the work of a paralegal; I wanted to say, 'Look, I had a baby, not a lobotomy '" (Williams & Segal, 2003, p. 77). Stereotypes also can be triggered when a woman gets pregnant, as in the case of *Sigmon v. Parker* (1995). In *Sigmon*, a law firm associate sued because, after she got pregnant, a rumor spread that she planned to work short hours and weeks while being compensated for full-time work; her department excluded her from high-profile firm activities, notably ending her participation in recruitment; her department head said in her presence, upon seeing another pregnant associate, "With all these pregnant women around, I guess we should stop hiring women" (p. 4).

Such comments help explain the findings of a study showing that the job evaluations of pregnant women managers "plummeted" (Halpert, Wilson, & Hickman, 1993, p. 651). Another study by Sara Corse found that some coworkers worried that pregnant women were overly emotional and irrational, while others expected pregnant colleagues to conform rigorously to the mandates of traditional femininity—to be understanding, empathetic, nonauthoritarian, easy to negotiate with, gentle, nice, and neither intimidating nor aggressive (1990, pp. 40, 49; Williams, 2003). This study suggests that pregnant managers and professionals may face a catch-22: They can meet colleagues' expectations of a pregnant woman and behave too demurely to qualify as an effective "hard-driving" professional, or they can meet workplace expectations of a hard-driving manager in which case they risk being considered irrational or disliked as inappropriately "aggressive" due to unspoken expectations that pregnant women should be "nice" (Corse, 1990; Williams, 2004).

Pregnancy and parental leave are two common triggers for maternal wall stereotyping; similar stereotypes may be triggered when a woman goes part-time or on a flexible work arrangement (FWA). Sociological studies document that women who go on FWAs suffer career detriments (Hochschild, 1997; Glass, 2004). Though stereotyping studies are inconsistent, one concluded that women who work part-time were viewed as less warm and nurturing than homemakers, but as having the same lack of go-getter qualities—they seemed to get the worst of both worlds (Eagly & Steffen, 1986; see also Etaugh & Moss, 2001).

Evidence from human resources suggests that fathers who request FWAs or go part-time may actually experience greater workplace hostility than mothers do (Eagly & Steffen, 1986; Williams & Segal, 2003). Anthropologists and other writers document that fathers who fail to perform as ideal workers face assumptions that they are neither manly men (Gould, 1974) nor good fathers(!) (Townsend, 2002).

A shocking number of legal cases involve "loose lips"—*hostile prescriptive stereotyping* in which employers express open hostility to working mothers and prescribe traditional gender roles (Glick & Fiske, 1997). A clear example is a Virginia wrongful discharge case, *Bailey v. Scott-Gallaher* (1997), in which a mother called her employer to find out when she should return from maternity leave, only to be fired with the statement (among others) that a mother's place was home with her child. Hostile prescriptive stereotyping of fathers played a major role in *Knussman v. Maryland* (1999); Mr. Knussman's boss fired him for wanting to care for his newborn, stating that "God made women to have babies" and his wife had to be "in a coma or dead" in order for him to be the primary caregiver (p. 630). In *Moore v. Alabama State University* (1997), a company vice president told a female employee he would not promote her because she was married, pregnant and a mother, and he believed she should stay at home to take care of her family. Pointing to her belly—she was 8 months pregnant—he said, "I was going to put you in charge of the office, but look at you now" (p. 431). In *Santiago-Ramos v. Centennial P. R. Wireless Corp.* (2000), the only woman executive in a company was fired after her employer, which had used a job profile excluding women with children because they did not "give 150%," learned of her plans to have a second child; she was also asked whether her husband minded that she was not home to cook dinner for him (pp. 22, 33). In *Sheehan v. Donlen Corp.* (1999), a supervisor blurted out, "Oh my God, she's pregnant again," and told the plaintiff "you're not coming back after this baby" (p. 1042).

These cases are not subtle. Indeed, they suggest that, whereas most employers know not to say "We don't want women here," many do not understand that it is also illegal to say, "We don't want mothers." The ideology that mothers "naturally" belong at home, or that good mothers "choose" to stay home, are felt by many to be legitimate, as indicated by the greater than two thirds of Americans who agreed with the statement that everyone in the family benefits when women take care of the children and home and men provide financially for the family (General Social Survey, 1996).

Other cases draw on the prescriptive stereotype of the "good mother." Studies show that a "good mother," unlike the "good father," is expected to be always available to her children (Kobrynowicz & Biernat, 1997). This 24/7 ideal, of course, clashes with the norm of the ever-available ideal worker (Williams, 2000). The result is *role incongruity*, in which mothers' workforce potential is challenged on the grounds that their parental role precludes their ability to be good workers (Eagly & Karau, 2002). Thus, in *Trezza v. The Hartford, Inc.* (1998), a mother's boss opined that women could not be both good workers and good mothers, stating, "I don't see how you can do either job well" (p. 2). In another case, the president of a mother's company told her, "You have to decide: do you want babies, or a career here?" (Belser, 2003).

In addition to prescriptive stereotyping, mothers often face cognitive bias, also called *descriptive stereotyping* (Burgess & Borgida, 1999). In cases involving cognitive bias, employers do not *prescribe* traditional roles; instead, they simply *describe* mothers as adhering to traditional roles, whether or not they actually do so. In *Back v. Hastings on Hudson* (2004), a court held that an employer's description of a mother was guided by stereotype rather than her actual behavior. Workers on flexible or part-time arrangements report that they are common targets of descriptive stereotyping. One part-time worker noted that, so long as she was working full-time, when she has to give a slower-than-desired turn-around, she was given the benefit of the doubt: "They assumed I was giving them as fast a turn-around as was humanly possible" (Williams & Segal, 2003, p. 97). This ended after she went part-time, and people attributed a slower-than-desired turn-around to her part-time schedule. She also found, after she went part-time, that coworkers assumed that if she was not at her desk she was home with her children—even if she was at a business meeting. Both problems track documented patterns of stereotyping. The first is called the "leniency bias," in which in-groups (here, full-time workers)—but not out-groups (here, part-timer workers)—are given the benefit of the doubt (Brewer, 1996, pp. 64–67). The second is "attribution bias": Her colleagues attributed her absence to work-related reasons when she was a "serious, committed" worker, but to family-related reasons after she went part-time (Deaux, 1976; Krieger, 1995).

The third major type of maternal wall bias is *benevolent stereotyping*, in which employers with good intentions police couples into traditional gender roles in a kinder, gentler tone of voice (Burgess & Borgida, 1999). A classic example is that of a couple who both worked for the same long-hours employer and had a baby, only to find that the mother was sent home promptly at 5:30 P.M.—she had a baby to take care of—whereas the man was kept working later than ever—he had a family to support (Williams & Segal, 2003). Another example is *McGrenaghan v. St. Denis School* (1997), the case mentioned earlier in which a school district shifted a mother from a full-time teaching position to a half-time teacher/half-time resource aide after the birth of her disabled child, presumably to "help" her care for her son. Note that the employer did not ask the plaintiff whether she wanted the transfer, and refused to return her to her (higher-paid) teaching position even after she filed suit. In *Trezza* (1997), the plaintiff was not considered for a promotion because the job required extensive travel and the supervisor assumed she did not want to travel because she had children. In fact, the plaintiff did not mind travel.

In short, gender bias often is triggered when working women get pregnant, take maternity leave, or switch to part-time or a flexible work arrangement. Evidence also suggests that mothers and other carers are increasingly likely to sue, and to gain relief in the courts, when they feel they have been treated unfairly due to family caregiving responsibilities. WorkLife Law has now documented over 200 cases in which mothers and other carers have sued successfully (WorkLife Law, 2005). In only the first 4 years of the new decade, there have already been nearly as many cases won as in the entire 1990s (WorkLife Law, 2005). This trend is particularly striking because plaintiffs lose most discrimination cases that are filed (Clermont & Schwab, 2004); federal courts are becoming increasingly conservative (The Federal Judiciary, 2005);

and most aggrieved individuals do not file suit because of the steep economic and emotional costs of a lawsuit (Lind, Greenberg, Scott, & Welchans, 2000).

LIMITS OF LITIGATION

Legal scholars have expressed doubts that litigation can bring about the kind of social change needed for mothers and caregivers to be treated fairly (e.g., Becker, 2001; Kessler, 2001; Dowd, 1989). This stems from a concern that cases brought by mothers do not "fit" existing law. Thus, the argument goes, the rights-based cases mothers bring will not be powerful enough to persuade courts to mandate sweeping workplace redesign. Critics are looking for the "Lancelot" model—in which a flawless case instigates a broad court order—since it is the more memorable but less common type of legal case leading to social change. Instead, as sociologists and social historians have observed, the interactive, gradually unfolding dialogue among *numerous* actors embedded in important social institutions (including law) is how most change occurs. The power of law is not only in the high-profile case that results in Lancelot-like crusaders winning a test case spurring rapid social progress. The more common process is for modest cases to be heard initially. The first sexual harassment case, for example, seemed to be about the claims of a particular woman against a particular boss (*Meritor Savings Bank, FSB v. Vinson*, 1981).

Litigation is an important part of this incremental process of social change, since lawsuits often prompt "rights talk" in larger circles. As theorists have long observed, law serves an expressive function in society and is constitutive of who we are (Sunstein, 1996; Gordon, 1984). Rights talk raises questions about the distinction between normative and legal claims. If people experience court rulings as misaligned with their lay understandings of law, they may demand changes so that law becomes aligned with the rights they believe they have. The social dynamic that occurs around these conversations, many of which are spurred or guided by case law, can have transformative effects on the workplaces that monitor them.

A second criticism of a litigation approach is that legal challenges entail an unconvincing demand for "accommodation" of mothers' special needs. In fact, virtually no successful cases are framed in this way; WorkLife Law has long argued this framing is flawed (Williams & Segal, 2003, pp. 82–89). Requesting "accommodation" leaves intact the discriminatory ideal-worker norm, which is what makes mothers and other family caregivers appear defective and in need of "accommodation" or "special treatment" (Williams & Segal, 2003, p. 86).

Another common assumption is that maternal wall cases will lose because the federal judiciary is increasingly conservative. This may be inaccurate. Much to the astonishment of many commentators, (conservative) Chief Justice Rehnquist wrote the majority opinion in *Nevada Department of Human Resources v. Hibbs* (2003), which upheld the constitutionality of certain provisions of the Family and Medical Leave Act. The *Hibbs* opinion was filled with strong language decrying the stereotyping often experienced by mothers—not the sort of language often associated with Justice Rehnquist (in fact, significant sections of the majority opinion come straight out of the briefs for Mr. Hibbs (Respondent's Brief, 2003). Furthermore, *Hibbs* astonished constitutional commentators because its holding—that states can be sued for violations of the FMLA—placed sharp limits on the constitutional doctrine that limits congressional power to enforce antidiscrimination statutes against state governments, a doctrine commonly considered one of Justice Rehnquist's chief legacies as Chief Justice (Killenbeck, 2004).

Rehnquist's language in *Hibbs* was quickly picked up by Judge Calibresi of the Second Circuit Federal Court of Appeals, one of the most important courts in the country, in the landmark case of *Back v. Hastings-on-Hudson* (2004). *Back* involved a school psychologist who generally received outstanding job evaluations during her 3-year pre-tenure period, along with repeated assurances she would get tenure. She did not. As the tenure decision approached, the officials in charge of her case began to make comments, including "Please do not get pregnant until I retire" (p. 115) and "It is not possible for you to be a good mother and have this job" (p. 115), expressing the opinion that her job performance was "just an act" and that once she was granted tenure she would not show the same level of commitment because she had "little ones at home" (p. 115).

The Second Circuit found for Ms. Back at summary judgment. Citing WorkLife Law's law review article on the maternal wall stereotyping and maternal wall case law as well as *Hibbs'* memorable statement about the persistent "fault line between work and family" (Williams & Segal, 2003, p. 113), the Second Circuit held that Ms. Back had been the subject of stereotyping and that her case could go forward to trial. *Back* surprised many because it accepted (without the need for expert testimony) that mothers suffer from negative competence assumptions, and—even more important—because it did not require Ms. Back to produce a similarly situated man who had been treated better than she had (a "comparator"). The former is important because it allows courts to find maternal wall stereotyping without requiring plaintiffs to hire expensive expert witnesses; the latter because it opens up to potential maternal wall lawsuits the roughly three quarters of American women who work in sex-segregated environments where no male comparator typically can be found (Williams, 2000). Many employment law practitioners immediately recognized *Back* as a landmark case (Williams, 2004).

Increasingly, the potential exists for significant liability. One company has now been sued three times, by three different mothers (*Trezza*, 1998; *Goldstick*, 2000; *Capruso*, 2001). A hospital maintenance worker was awarded $11.65 million when he was penalized for caring for his ailing parents (*Schultz*, 2002); phone company workers were awarded roughly $10 million in back pay when their company denied service credit to their pension accounts (*EEOC v. Bell Atlantic*, 2002; Williams, 2003b); an engineer won a $3 million jury verdict (later overturned) when her employer told her she needed to choose between having babies and having a job (Belser, 1999; Williams & Segal, 2003); a director of finance was awarded $730,000 when her employer "stripped her of her managerial role" after she returned from maternity leave (*Zimmerman*, 2001, p. 73); 22 female corrections officers were awarded $2.2 million after their employer demanded that they have abortions if they wanted to continue working (*Alversa*, 1991); a medical technician who was fired after she needed bed rest while she was pregnant received $940,001 (*Flores-Suarez*, 2001); Walsh was awarded $625,000, as noted above (*Walsh*, 2002); an assistant dance professor won a tentative settlement of $495,000 in a tenure case that involved a memo stating that her child-care responsibilities were inconsistent with her tenure-track status (Schneider, 2000).

Once a social phenomenon is interpreted as being a potential legal liability, as in the above cases, many institutional actors will converge around the resulting uncertainty and urge employers to be proactive. Such action can lead to organizations going beyond what is eventually required by law, as was the case in adoption of parental leave policies (Kelly & Dobbin, 1999). Thus, in a well-respected human resources publication, a management-side law firm responded to the initial publication of WorkLife Law's 20-page press report, *The New Glass Ceiling: Mothers—and Fathers—Sue for Discrimination* (Williams & Segal, 2002), by advising employers to not only avoid stereotyping of employees by ceasing to ask questions about applicants' and employees' family situations and avoiding assumptions about employees' ability to meet job requirements based on their family situation, but also to consider setting up leave banks, pro-rating at least some benefits for part-time employees, and offering flexible schedules and/or telecommuting if they do not impede productivity (Krukowski, 2002).[2]

PUBLIC POLICY: USING EXISTING LAWS TO INCREASE
THE LIKELIHOOD OF PASSING NEW ONES

Given the inevitable limitations of litigation, it may seem more prudent simply to pass new laws. This question looms particularly large given the central role of U.S. public policy in *creating* acute work/life conflict. This section first discusses how present policies contribute to tensions between work and family and then details laws in other countries that may serve as models for the United States. The European experience, our particular focus here, suggests that developing a robust litigation strategy may help build the political will for legislation that places limits on how much employees work and gives them rights to certain alternative schedules—what we call "working time policies."

The Role of Public Policy in Creating Work/Family Conflict

At medium and large companies in the United States, workers average about 10 days' vacation a year in their first year with a company and about 14 days in the next 5 years (U.S. Department of Labor, http://www.bls.gov/news.release/ebs3.nws.htm, data retrieved April 20, 2004). In comparison, the European Union mandates 4 weeks of paid vacation a year and many European countries go beyond that, with some allowing as much as 25 to 30 days off, or 5 to 6 work-weeks (Gornick & Meyers, 2003; European Union Online, http://europa.eu.int/scadplus/citizens/en/fr). The United States is also lacking in its parental and sick leaves in comparison with other countries. Mothers in many other countries are paid by either the government or their employers during 14 or more weeks of maternity leave (Gornick & Meyers, 2003; Clearinghouse, 2002). In Germany, mothers are given 14 weeks' leave at full pay and after that either parent can take leave and may receive a monthly sum from social security (up to the child's 3rd birthday); in Canada, maternity benefits are paid for 15 weeks and parental benefits up to an additional 35 weeks; in Finland, mothers can take 106 paid days and then either parent may take 158 paid days after that (European Union Online, 2003; Human Resources Development Canada, 2003; Clearinghouse, 2002; Stebbins, 2001).

Similarly, the United States lags behind most of the industrialized world in affording leaves to care for sick family members. The FMLA allows for unpaid leave to care for "serious health conditions" of the employee or his or her family members. However, more than 40% of U.S. employees are not covered by the FMLA because they either do have not enough tenure or work for smaller employers, and most companies do not allow workers to care for such relatives as in-laws or grandparents or to take such leave for routine medical needs (Gornick & Meyers, 2003). In particular, the lowest income workers are left especially vulnerable. Nearly three of every four parents living at or below the federal poverty line have no paid sick leave; 57% have no vacation leave; and 54% lack both sick and vacation leave (Heymann et al., 2002). Other policies and norms enable workers in Europe to manage work and family more easily, including subsidized child care and shorter work weeks. In much of Northern Europe, child care is seen as an investment in the resources critical to the future economy (Bergmann, 1996). In the United States, nonfamilial care tends to be seen as consigning one's child to "strangers." These fundamental viewpoints have concrete consequences: The United States leaves parents to negotiate and pay for care privately, whereas many European countries offer government-sponsored child care and preschool. In addition, long work hours logged by Americans means their children have to be in daycare for long hours—an unappealing prospect for many parents. Americans work longer than citizens in any other industrialized nation (Gornick & Meyers, 2003).

Much of Americans' work/family conflict stems from this long-hours culture, a problem that no amount of short-term leaves and subsidized child care can remedy. Working hours legislation is needed; luckily, some international models already exist. As described below, a Europe Union directive requires proportional pay and benefits for part-time work ("part-time equity"); another European Union directive sets overall limits on working time and three individual countries—Germany, the Netherlands, and the United Kingdom—also allow workers to request shorter hours or flexible schedules *in their existing job*.

A first step in introducing working hours legislation into the public policy debate in the United States must begin with an analysis of why the leaves-and-child-care model has exercised such a hold. Three important constituencies are supportive of paid leaves and subsidized child care but are wary of working hours legislation. First, some women's groups fear that working hours legislation may in the end simply reinforce traditional gender roles, by creating a mommy track that only women will use. American feminists have tended to focus on "equal opportunity" for ideal-worker women rather than on solutions more protective of caregiver women (Crittenden, 2001; Fineman, 1992).

Unions are a second important stakeholder wary of working hours legislation but highly supportive of a leaves-and-child-care approach. Though some unions are receptive (notably the Service Employees International Union, or SEIU) to part-time equity, others view their key constituency as members who want to work full-time and overtime. They tend to be deeply skeptical of initiatives to limit work hours or protect part-timers (Kessler-Harris, 2001). These unions have traditionally fought flexibility on the ground that it gives employers unfettered discretion over workers' lives (Gerstel & Clawson, 2001). They are equally anxious about part-time work; their traditional goal has been to eliminate "bad" part-time jobs that, in their view, threaten to erode high-quality jobs for the breadwinners who have been their traditional constituency.

Antipoverty advocates are a third important stakeholder. They often argue that scarce political capital should be spent on subsidized child care and paid leaves targeted at the neediest Americans, rather than on gaining minimum protections for Americans better able to protect themselves. Arguments that decades of social programs tightly targeted to the poorest Americans have eroded political support for social subsidies pale, for these advocates, beside the urgent and immediate needs of the poor (Skocpol, 2000).

These three influential stakeholders—women's organizations, unions, and antipoverty advocates—have reinforced the tendency in the United States for work/life public policy to follow the leaves-and-child-care model. As a result, victories at the federal level have been few and far between. Of 25 bills proposed that relate to work and family in the past 3 years (106th–108th Congress), none has resulted in a public law. With the present budget shortfall, job losses, and a stagnant economy, new subsidies for leaves and child care have become an elusive goal. Child care and paid leaves cost money, and it is hard to see the political will emerging to support new social programs in the near future.

Americans are far more unified in their support of flexible work arrangements: In a 1996 random-sample survey, fully 90% said employers should allow workers more flexible hours (GSS, 1996). Clearly, flexibility is something nearly all Americans favor, yet only 23% of surveyed employees reported being able to change their start and quit times daily (Bond et al., 2002, p. 31), and fewer than half reported being able to change those times periodically ("traditional" flextime).

These data may suggest the potential for working hours legislation in the United States Certainly, European models exist. The European Union, for example, has adopted a twin approach to addressing the quality of part-time jobs. This twin approach makes it illegal to give someone less favorable terms and conditions (pro rata) merely because they work less hours as well as encourages part-time jobs in higher-paid occupations and sectors so that part-time work is no longer synonymous with low-paid, low-quality work. In 1997, the European Union adopted a directive giving part-time workers the right to treatment equal to full-time workers regarding all terms of their contracts. The directive, which began in 2000 and is in force in all 25 European Union member states, applies the same principles as the Equal Pay Act, only that here it is not an individual man or woman comparing themselves to someone of the opposite sex, but a part-time worker taking a full-time worker as the comparator.[3]

At the same time, several individual European countries have adopted legislation giving employees individual rights to change their working hours. The furthest-reaching of these is the Dutch 2000 Law on Working Time Adjustment.[4] The law gives employees with a minimum of 1 year's service in companies with at least 10 employees the right to demand a reduction in working hours;[5] the request for what in effect amounts to a permanent change in contract has to include the desired weekly hours, their distribution between different days, and the effective starting date. The employer must grant the request unless there are demonstrated serious business reasons (see Burri et al., 2003 for a detailed discussion). An employee also has a right to ask for extended hours, although here there are fewer restraints on employers. The German Part-time Law,[6] which took effect in 2001, is similar to the Dutch law, although employers only have to demonstrate "business and organizational reasons" (not *serious* business reasons as in the Dutch case) to refuse a request (Burri et al., 2003). One important difference, however, exists between the two laws: The German law provides equal protection for decisions regarding the distribution of hours as it does regarding the overall length of the working week; the Dutch law (and case law as well) views the scheduling of working time as a prerogative of the employer— clearly an approach not necessarily helpful to people with caring responsibilities (Burri, 2004). The UK law provides much weaker rights but combines these with a broader approach to work/life balance: The law[7] is limited to parents who have children under the age of 6 or a disabled child under 18 requiring changes in work organization specifically to care for a child. Moreover, employees only have a right to "request" a change; as long as the employer follows a given timetable and format in preparing a response, employees cannot externally challenge the decision. On the other hand, the UK approach is broader than the Dutch and German laws in that it encourages employees to consider a broad menu of when, where, and for how long work is done when putting together their request. Interestingly, in spite of its weak employer-friendly approach, the UK law has been surprisingly effective; 1 year after the introductions of both the German and the UK laws, usage was 10 times as high as in Germany, with successful requests going significantly beyond the designated group of parents of young children (Hegewisch, 2004).

Americans would benefit from legislation that drew upon these models: While the 3-month leave offered by the FMLA remains an extraordinarily important step in the right direction, raising a child in the United States takes not 3 months but nearly 20 years! New working time laws are vital; the question is how to build the political will to pass them, given that experts currently estimate that a decade or more will be required (Feldblum, 2004). What is the relationship of litigation in this public policy context? Litigation is important, first, as a stopgap, to give carers some minimal rights in the absence of working time legislation. Second, litigation can help build the case that working time laws are needed, given that legal cases by their nature often involve dramatic facts in which working parents have been discriminated against and badly treated. Cases such as those discussed in this chapter help move the public's perception of work/family conflict out of the "mothers' choice" logic into the "something ought to be done" logic.

In this and other ways, litigation can help pave the way for public policy solutions. At a recent conference held by WorkLife Law,[8] European work/family experts described the 20 years of litigation in which depressed wages and lack of pension benefits for part-timers were struck down as illegal gender discrimination because of their disproportionate impact on women (parallel to disparate impact theory in the United States; Heron, 2004). A number of experts present were of the opinion that the pathbreaking European Union Part-Time Directive had been passed only because the case law had evolved to the extent that the directive did not give part-timers that much more than the courts already had given them under existing legislation. The strategies of using existing laws seems an integral part of the effort to pass new working time legislation in the United States, rather than an alternative.

THE FUTURE: INCORPORATING LITIGATION AND THE BUSINESS CASE TO GALVANIZE CHANGE

Practitioners, attorneys, policymakers, activists, and scholars should not abandon the traditional business case, which uses evidence from the workplace to show that work/family policies and practices can be good for the bottom line, but can strengthen the case with evidence from discrimination litigation.

Why the Business Case Is Important in Litigation

The business case plays a formal doctrinal role in some lawsuits. In disparate impact suits, after a plaintiff has proven the existence of an employer policy that has a disparate impact on women, the employer can still win the suit if it can show that it had a business necessity to use the policy in question despite its disproportionate impact on women (Civil Rights Act of 1991, 2000). Thus, the literature on the business case, which details the cost benefits of attracting and retaining women and caregivers in the workplace, plays an important role in meeting the plaintiff's burden of proof that the employer has no business necessity to run a family-hostile workplace, given that family-friendly policies can help an employer's bottom line by decreasing attrition and absenteeism and possibly enhance recruitment and productivity.

Even plaintiffs who sue under statutes that do not formally require them to prove that it is economically feasible to change the workplace in the ways plaintiffs propose would be well advised, in many situations, to offer evidence that the proposed flexible schedules or other workplace changes are economically feasible. Simply put, if a judge is convinced that what the plaintiff is requesting is infeasible from an economic standpoint, one can expect that the judge will find some doctrinal reason why the plaintiff should lose.

Why the Business Case Is Important in Public Policy

The same logic holds true for politicians. If faced with a bill that benefits caregivers but imposes additional costs on employers, politicians will have real difficulties overcoming arguments about "keeping America competitive." Rigorous data are needed to document that many public policies have long-term benefits. Savvy politicians know this. Senator Ted Kennedy, for example, recently introduced the Healthy Families Act (2004), which proposes mandatory sick leave for American employees. Rather than relying solely on language about basic human rights or social responsibility, the bill's press release cited a study by Cornell University exacting the cost employers incur—$180 million—when people who have no sick leave come to work ill and are physically present but unproductive (a phenomenon known as "presenteeism"; press release distributed at Kennedy-DeLauro press conference, Dirksen Senate Office Building, June 15, 2004).

Litigation costs are another expense that should be tallied in making the business case. Without careful attention to the potential costs of litigation, employers' interest in family-responsive policies will fluctuate and their implementation will continue to vary widely. Employers stand to lose hundreds of thousands in discrimination suits, à la *Walsh v. National Computer Systems*

(2002). Incorporating the potential costs of litigation with the potential savings of family-responsive policies is what we refer to as "the business case linked with the discrimination model."

CONCLUSION AND SUGGESTIONS FOR FUTURE RESEARCH

The interplay of law and social norms is a particularly complex dynamic that has been shown increasingly to be the engine of much social change. We have argued that both existing and new laws are a critical component of the social process that will bring about genuine change in work organizations. Litigation has an important role to play in the public discourse surrounding work/family conflict, as has been observed in the United States in regard to such social issues as civil rights and women's rights, and in Europe in regard to working time flexibility. Incorporating discrimination with traditional business case arguments will make organizations more motivated to move beyond merely symbolic adoption of work/life programs.

We detailed present laws related to work/family conflict and provided examples of cases in which those laws were brought to bear on specific workplace incidents. In addition, we described the underlying social psychological mechanisms that lead to such conflicts, summarizing *hostile prescriptive stereotyping, prescriptive stereotyping, cognitive bias,* and *benevolent stereotyping,* all forms of stereotyping that can lead to discrimination against mothers and others with caregiving responsibilities.

We argued that current public policy plays a role in contributing to the conflict American workers feel between work and family, and provided a glimpse into European models for relieving that conflict. We propose that the momentum growing in the courts through an increasing number of caregiving discrimination cases in which large monetary awards are awarded should be tapped into to reenergize the field of work/life, which has relied mostly on traditional business case arguments to motivate social change, with limited success.

We will conclude by suggesting a few suggestions for future research, practice, and teaching. For legal practitioners, the important message is that a new wave of gender discrimination litigation appears to be picking up steam: Our ongoing inventory currently shows that more successful maternal wall cases have emerged since 2000 than did in the entire decade of the 1990s (WorkLife Law, 2005). The legal dimension of work/family issues has begun to be explored, but much more needs to be done, not only by legal scholars but also by scholars in fields as diverse as sociology, business administration, industrial relations, economics, and women's studies. This topic will be of particular interest to sociologists who write in the tradition of the new institutionalism, who can compare the complex interplay between litigation, intermediary actors, and social norms to the interplay in different social areas.

This also offers a new arena for analysis by political scientists who are developing an overlapping literature in "cause lawyering" (Sarat & Scheingold, 1997) and for legal historians who study the interplay between cases, statutes, and legal consciousness (Hartog, Marcus, & Scheiber, 1987). For law professors, the message is that casebooks in employment law and feminist jurisprudence should consider including a discussion of maternal wall litigation; indeed, one feminist jurisprudence course already has been designed around work/family issues (Tami, 2000). Business school professors should consider including a case study that informs their students of the potential for legal liability if work/life issues are mishandled. Sociologists and others who teach work/family courses may want to consider adding a legal case or two to their course materials.

Ultimately, the message of this chapter—both its authorship and its analytical approach—shows the promise for interdisciplinary research. To this arena, law professors can bring their knowledge of how to manipulate legal doctrine, their background knowledge about what kinds of lawsuits are feasible, and their experience with judging legal trends; sociologists can bring their rigorous training in the work/family literature, their quantitative training, and their commitment to social "science." This combination of skills holds the promise to deepen the study of the complex interactions between social norms and social and legal change.

NOTES

[1] Areas identified and named by sociologist Janet Gornick. Personal communication to Joan Williams, February 10, 2004, on file with authors.

[2] The hardest cases, no doubt, involve plaintiffs who seek to require their employers to create a part-time track where none currently exists. Yet a major employer consulted the first author about implementing a part-time policy directly in response to a lawsuit. In cases where plaintiffs want to create a part-time track, lawyers need to find out whether the employer has granted part-time schedules to anyone else.

[3] Council Directive 97/81/EC of December 15, 1997 concerning the Framework Agreement on part-time work concluded by UNICE, CEEP, and the ETUC, *OJ* 1998, L 14/9; see Burri (2004).

[4] *Wet aanpassing arbeidsduur*, *Stb.* 2000, 114, in force since July 1, 2000.

[5] Employees in organizations with less than 10 workers have weaker rights; see Burri (2004).

[6] The Act on Part-time work and Fixed Term Contracts (*Teilzeit und Befristungsgesetz*), January 1, 2001: BGBl 2000 I, 1966.

[7] Department of Trade and Industry: "Flexible working: the right to request and the duty to consider," http://www.dti.gov.uk/er/individual/flexwork-pl520.pdf.

[8] Symposium on "Working time for working families: Europe and the USA," American University Washington College of Law: Washington, DC; June 7–8 2004.

REFERENCES

Alversa v. City of New York, 8 NY Jury Verdict Rptr. Issue 50, at 16 (S.D.N.Y. 1991).

Americans with Disabilities Act of 1990, 42 U.S.C. § 12111 (1994).

Back v. Hastings on Hudson Free School District, 365 F.3d 107 (2004).

Bailey v. Scott-Gallaher, 480 S.E.2d 502, 503 (Va. 1997).

Becker, M. (2001). Caring for children and caretakers. *Chicago-Kent Law Review, 76*, 1441–1493.

Belser, A. (1999). *Mommy track wins*. Retrieved May 21, 2003, from Pittsburgh Post Gazette Online: http://www.postgazette.com/regionstate/19990430lawsuit2.asp.

Bergmann, B. R. (1996). *Saving our children from poverty: What the United States can learn from France*. New York: Russell Sage Foundation.

Bond, J., Thompson, C., Galinsky, E., & Prottas, D. (2002). Highlights of the National Study of the Changing Workforce. Families and Work Institute, No. 3.

Brewer, M. B. (1996). In-group favoritism: The subtle side of intergroup discrimination. In D. M. Messick & E. Tenbrunsel (Eds.), *Codes of conduct: Behavioral research into business ethics* (pp. 58–68). New York: Russel Sage Foundation.

Burgess, D., & Borgida, E. (1999). Who women are, who women should be: Descriptive and prescriptive gender stereotyping in sex discrimination. *Psychology, Public Policy, & the Law, 5*, 665–687.

Burri, S. (2004, June 7). *Working time adjustment policies in the Netherlands*. Paper presented at Symposium on Working Time for Working Families: Europe and the USA, Washington, DC.

Burri, S., Opitz, H., & Veldman, A. (2003). Work family policies on working time put into practice. A comparison of Dutch and German case law on working time adjustment. *The International Journal of Comparative Labour Law and Industrial Relations, 19*, 321–346.

Capruso v. The Hartford, Inc., No. 01 Civ. 4250 (complaint filed and removed to S.D.N.Y. May 18, 2001).

Civil Rights Act of 1964, 42 U.S.C. §§ 2000e-2000e-16 (1994).

Civil Rights Act of 1964, 42 U.S.C. § 1983 (1994).

Civil Rights Act of 1991, Pub. L. No. 105, 105 Stat. 1071 (codified as amended at 42 U.S.C. § 2000e-2(k) (2000).

Clearinghouse on International Developments in Child, Youth and Families Policies at Columbia University. (2002). *Mother's Day: More than candy and flowers, working parents need paid time-off*. Retrieved October 26, 2003, from http://www.childpolicyintl.org/issuebrief/issuebrief5.pdf.

Clermont, K. M., & Schwab, S. J. (2004). How employment discrimination plaintiffs fare in federal court. *Journal of Empirical Legal Studies, 1*(2), 429–458.

Cockey, R. R. (2003). The family medical leave act: What you see and what you get. *American University Journal of Gender, Social Policy and the Law, 12*(1), 1–18.

Corning Glass Works v. Brennan, 417 U.S. 188 (1974).

Corse, S. J. (1990). Pregnant managers and their subordinates: The effects of gender expectations on hierarchical relationships. *Journal of Applied Behavioral Science, 26*, 25–47.

Crittenden, A. (2001). *The price of motherhood: Why the most important job in the world is still the least valued.* New York: Metropolitan Books.

Cuddy, A. J., Fiske, S. T. & Peter Glick. (2004). When professional become mothers warmth doesn't cut the ice. *The Journal of Social Issues, 60*(4), 701–719.

D.C. Human Rights Act, D.C. CODE ANN. § 1-2512 (1981).

Deaux, K. (1976). Sex: A perspective on the attribution process. In J. H. Harvey, W. J. Ickes, & R. F. Kidd (Eds.), *New directions in attribution research* (pp. 335–352). Hillsdale: Lawrence Erlbaum Associates.

Department of Trade and Industry. (1993). Flexible working: The right to request and the duty to consider. Retrieved September 29, 2004, from http://www.dti.gov.uk/er/individual/flexwork-pl520.pdf.

DiMaggio, P. J., & Powell, W. W. (1983). The iron cage revisited: Institutional isomorphism and collective rationality in organizational fields. *American Sociological Review, 48*(2), 147–160.

Dowd, N. (1989). Work and family: The gender paradox and the limitations of discrimination analysis in restructuring the workplace. *Harvard Civil Rights–Civil Liberties Law Review, 24*, 79–172.

Eagly, A. H., & Karau, S. J. (2002). Role congruity theory of prejudice toward female leaders. *Psychological Review, 109*(3), 573–598.

Eagly, A. H., & Steffen, V. J. (1986). Gender stereotypes, occupational roles, and beliefs about part-time employees. *Psychology of Women Quarterly, 10*, 252–262.

Edelman, L. B. (1990). Legal environment and organizational governance: The expansion of due process in the American workplace. *American Journal of Sociology, 95*(6), 1401–1441.

Edelman, L. B. (1992). Legal ambiguity and symbolic structures: Organizational mediation of civil rights law. *American Journal of Sociology, 97*(6), 1531–1576.

E.E.O.C. v. Bell Atlantic, 2002 U.S. Dist. Lexis 19156 (S.D.N.Y. 2002).

E.E.O.C. v. Warshawsky & Co., 768 F.Supp. 647 (N.D. Ill. 1991).

Etaugh, C., & Moss, C. (2001). Attitudes of employed women toward parents who choose full-time or part-time employment following their child's birth. *Sex Roles, 44*, 611–619.

European Union Online. (n.d.b.). *Parental leave.* Retrieved April 30, 2003, from http://www.europa.eu.int/scadplus/citizens/en/fr/01018.htm.

Family and Medical Leave Act of 1993, 29 U.S.C. §§ 2601–2654 (1994).

Family Leave Suit Draws Record $11.65M Award. (2002). *National Law Journal*, November 11. at A4.

The Federal Judiciary and Key Issues. (2004). Retrieved October 1, 2004, from the Independent Judiciary: http://www.independentjudiciary.com/issues/.

Feldblum, C. (2004). Plenary Panel "Building Political Will, Changing Public Policy: Is Flexible Work in our Future?" Alfred P. Sloan Foundation Conference on Workplaces and Working Families, "Changing Structures, Changing Lives: Resolving the Workplace/Workforce Mismatch," Cambridge, MA, May 19–21.

Fineman, M. A. (1992). Feminist theory in law: The difference it makes. *Columbia Journal of Gender & Law, 2*, 1–23.

Fiske, S. T., Glick, P., Xu, J., & Cuddy, A. J. C. (1999). (Dis)respecting versus (dis)liking; status and interdependence predict ambivalent stereotypes of competence and warmth. *Social Issues, 55*, 473–489.

Fleming v. Ayers and Associates, 948 F.2d 993 (6th Cir. 1991).

Flores-Suarez v. Turabo Medical Center Partnership, 165 F. Supp. 2d 79 (D.P.R. 2001).

General Social Survey. (1996). Retrieved April 17 from http://sda.berkeley.edu:7502.

Gerstel, N., & Clawson, D. (2001). Unions' responses to family concerns. *Social Problems, 48*(2), 277–297.

Glass, J. L. (2004). Blessing or curse? Family responsive policies and mothers' wage growth. *Work and Occupations, 31*(3), 367–394.

Glick, P., & Fiske, S. T. (1997). Hostile and benevolent sexism: Measuring ambivalent sexist attitudes toward women. *Psychology of Women Quarterly, 21*(1), 119–135.

Goldstick v. The Hartford, Inc., No. 00 Civ. 8577, 2002 U.S. Dist. LEXIS 15247 (S.D.N.Y. November 9, 2000).

Gordon, R. W. (1984). Critical legal histories. *Stanford Law Review, 36*, 57–124.

Gornick, J. (2004). Personal correspondence to Joan Williams, February 10, 2004, on file with authors.

Gornick, J. C., & Meyers, M. (2003). *Families that work: Policies for reconciling parenthood and employment.* New York: Russell Sage Foundation.

Gould, R. (1974). Measuring masculinity by the size of a paycheck. In J. Pleck & J. Sawyer (Eds.) *Men and masculinity* (pp. 96–100). Englewood Cliffs, NJ: Prentice-Hall.

Halpert, J., Wilson, M., & Hickman, J. (1993). Pregnancy as a source of bias in performance appraisals. *Journal of Organizational Behavior, 14*, 649–663.

Hartog, H., Marcus, M., & Scheiber, H. N. (1987). The constitution and American life. Part II: Rights consciousness in American history. *Journal of American History, 74*(3), 795–1034.

Healthy Families Act, S.2520, introduced by Senator Edward Kennedy June 15, 2004.

Hegewisch, A. (2004). *Individual workplace flexibility in Europe.* Paper presented at American University Symposium, Working Time for Working Families: Europe and the USA. June 7, Washington, DC.

Heron, A. (2004, June 7). *Promoting and protecting reduced hours work: European Union law and part-time work.* Paper presented at American University Symposium, Working Time for Working Families: Europe and the USA. June 7, Washington, DC.

Heymann, J., Boynton-Jarrett, R., Carter, P., Bond, J. T., & Galinsky, E. (2002). *Work-family issues and low-income families.* Retrieved October 26, 2003, from http://www.economythatworks.org/PDFs/ford_analysisfinal.pdf.

Hochschild, A. R. (1997). *The time bind: When work becomes home and home becomes work* (1st ed.). New York: Metropolitan Books.

Human Resources Development Canada (n.d.). Digest of benefit entitlement principles. Retrieved October 26, 2003, from http://www.hrsdc.gc.cq/en/ei/digest/12_1_0.shtml 12_1_4.

Kelly, E., & Dobbin, F. (1999). Civil rights law at work: Sex discrimination and the rise of maternity leave policies. *American Journal of Sociology, 105*(2), 455–492.

Kelly, E. L. (1999). Theorizing corporate family policies: How advocates built "the business case" for "family-friendly" programs. *Research in the Sociology of Work, 7*, 169–202.

Kessler, L. (2001). The attachment gap: Employment discrimination law. *University of Michigan Journal of Legal Reform, 34*, 371–468.

Kessler-Harris, A. (2001). *In pursuit of equity: Women, men, and the quest for economic citizenship in 20th-century America.* New York: Oxford University Press.

Killenbeck, M. R. (2004). Affirmative action and diversity: The beginning of the end? Or the end of the beginning/ Policy Information Perspective. Educational Testing Service.

Knussman v. Maryland, 65 F. Supp. 2d 353 (D. Md. 1999), 272 F.3d 625 (4th Cir. 2001).

Kobrynowicz, D., & Biernat, M. (1997). Decoding subjective evaluations: How stereotypes provide shifting standards. *Experimental Social Psychology, 33*, 579.

Krieger, L. H. (1995). The content of our categories: A cognitive bias approach to discrimination and equal employment opportunity. *Stanford Law Review, 47*, 1161–1248.

Krukowski, C. (2002). A glass ceiling for parents. *D.C. Employment Law Letter, 3*(6), 1.

Lind, E. A., Greenberg, J., Scott, K. S., & Welchans, T. D. (2000). The winding road: From employee to complaints: Situational and psychological determinants of wrongful-termination claims. *Administrative Science Quarterly, 45*(3), 557.

Lovell v. BBNT Solutions, Inc., 295 F. Supp. 2d 611 (E.D. Va. 2003).

McGrenaghan v. St. Denis Schools, 979 F Supp. 323 (E.D. Pa. 1997).

Meritor Savings Bank, FSB v. Vinson, 106 S. Ct. 2399 (1981).

Meyer, J. W., & Rowan, B. (1977). Institutionalized organizations: Formal structure as myth and ceremony. *American Journal of Sociology, 83*(2), 340–363.

Moore v. Alaska State University, 980 F. Supp. 426, 431 (M.D. Ala. 1997).

Nevada Department of Human Resources v. Hibbs, 123 S. Ct. 1972 (2003).

Phillips v. Martin Marietta Corp., 400 U.S. 542 (1971) (per curium).

Powell, W. W., & DiMaggio, P. (1991). *The new institutionalism in organizational analysis.* Chicago: University of Chicago Press.

Respondent's Brief, Nevada Department of Human Resources v. Hibbs, 528 U.S. 721 (2003) (No. 01–1368).

Rones, P. L., Ilg, R. E., & Gardner, J. M. (1997). *Trends in the hours of work since the mid-1970s.* Washington, DC: Department of Labor, Bureau of Labor Statistics.

Santiago-Ramos v. Centennial P.R. Wireless Corp., 217 F.3d 46, 57 (1st Cir. 2000).

Sarat, A., & Scheingold, S. (1997). *Cause lawyering: Political commitments and professional responsibilities.* New York: Oxford University Press.

Schneider, A. (2000). U. of Oregon settles tenure lawsuit over maternity leave. *Chronicle of Higher Education.* Retrieved May 21, 2003, from http://www.chronicle.com/free/v46/i46/46a01202.htm.

Schultz v. Advocate Health and Hopps. Corp., et al., No. 01C-0702, 2002 U.S. Dist. LEXIS 9517 (N.D. Ill. June 5, 2002).

Sheehan v. Donlen Corp., 173 F.3d 1039, 1044 (7th Cir. 1999).

Sigmon v. Parker, 901 F. Supp. 667 (1995).

Simpson v. D.C. Office of Human Rights, 597 A.2d 392 (D.C. App. 1991).

Sivieri v. Commonwealth of Massachusetts. Department of Transitional Assistance, 2003 Mass. Super. LEXIS 201 (June 25, 2003).

Skocpol, T. (2000). *The missing middle: Working families and the future of American social policy*. New York: Norton.

Stebbins, L. (2001). *Work and family in America: A reference handbook*. Santa Barbara, CA: ABC-CLIO.

Suchman, M. C. (1995). Managing legitimacy: Strategic and institutional approaches. *Academy of Management. The Academy of Management Review, 20*(3), 571–610.

Sunstein, C. R. (1996). Against tradition. *Social Philosophy & Policy 1996, 13*(1), 207–228.

Sutton, J. R., Dobbin, F., Meyer, J. W., & Scott, W. R. (1994). The legalization of the work-place. *American Journal of Sociology, 99*(4), 944–971.

Sutton, J. R., & Dobbin, F. (1996). The two faces of governance: Responses to legal uncertainty in U.S. firms, 1955 to 1985. *American Sociological Review, 61*(5), 794–811.

Tami, Molly. (2001). The work-family axis. Course syllabus. University of Cincinnati Law School. On file with authors.

Townsend, N. W. (2002). *The package deal: Marriage, work, and fatherhood in men's lives*. Philadelphia: Temple University Press.

Trezza v. The Hartford, Inc., No. 98 Civ. 2205, 1998 U.S. Dist. LEXIS 20206 (S.D.N.Y. 1998).

United States Department of Labor. (1999). *Employee benefits in medium and large private establishments, 1997*. Retrieved April 20, 2004, from http://www.bls.gov/news.release/ebs3.nws.htm.

Walsh v. National Computer Systems, Inc., No. 00-CV-82, slip op (D. Minn. August 27, 2002).

Williams, J. (2000). *Unbending gender: Why family and work conflict and what to do about it*. New York: Oxford University Press.

Williams, J. C. (2003a). Beyond the glass ceiling: The maternal wall as a barrier to gender equality. *Thomas Jefferson Law Review, 26*(1), 1–14.

Williams, J. C. (Ed.) (2003b). Litigating the glass ceiling and the maternal wall: Using stereotyping and cognitive bias evidence to prove gender discrimination. *Employee Rights and Employment Policy Journal, 7*(2), 101–154.

Williams, J. C. (2003c). The social psychology of stereotyping: Using social science to litigate gender discrimination cases and defang the cluelessness defense. *Employee Rights and Employment Policy Journal, 7*(2), 401–458.

Williams, J. (2004). *Hibbs* as a federalism case; *Hibbs* as a maternal wall case. *Cincinnati Law Review, 73*(2), 365–398.

Williams, J. & Calvert, C. (2001). *Balanced hours: Effective part-time policies for Washington law firms*. Washington, DC: American University Washington College of Law, Project for Attorney Retention.

Williams, J., & Segal, N. (2002). *The new glass ceiling: Mothers—and fathers—sue for discrimination*. Washington, DC: American University Washington College of Law, Program on WorkLife Law.

Williams, J., & Segal, N. (2003). Beyond the maternal wall: Relief for family caregivers who are discriminated against on the job. *Harvard Women's Law Journal, 26*, 77–162.

WorkLife Law. (2005). Technical guidance: Using employment and civil rights laws to protect working families. Alfred P. Sloan Foundation and the Washington College of Law, American University.

Zimmerman v. Direct Federal Credit Union, 262 F.3d 70 (8th Cir. 2001).

16

Connecting Social Work Perspectives to Work-Family Research and Practice

Marcie Pitt-Catsouphes
Boston College

Jennifer E. Swanberg
University of Kentucky

During the 1970s and 1980s, social workers were among the trailblazers of the emerging area of work-family studies. Since then, they have continued to add their voices to those of other academics who have noted the importance of focusing research, policy, and practice attention on the needs of working families. Sheila Kamerman, for example, has made significant and noteworthy contributions to the work-family discourse for more than three decades (e.g., Kamerman & Hayes, 1982; Kamerman & Kahn, 1978, 1981, 1987, 1991, 1997).

The field of social work offers unique insights about work and family situations and experiences. The "value added" by social work to the work-family area of study reflects the orientation of the social work profession itself. Social work rests on a set of values that are anchored in an explicit commitment to social justice and social equity. The field of social work focuses its research, policy analysis, and practice on the well-being of individuals, families, groups and communities, with an emphasis on populations who are marginalized, vulnerable, and/or have limited access to resources and opportunities. As described in the 1999 Code of Ethics adopted by the National Association of Social Workers (NASW):

> The primary mission of the social work profession is to enhance human well-being and help meet the basic human needs of all people, with particular attention to the needs and empowerment of people who are vulnerable, oppressed, and living in poverty.... The mission of the social work profession is rooted in a set of core values. [which] ... are the foundation of social work's unique purpose and perspective.

Social work values not only guide the research agendas of social workers but also create strong linkages between their studies and social work practice. Indeed, social workers emphasize the connections between research, policy, and practice. Furthermore, social workers believe that one of the fundamental purposes of their investigations is to provide the "evidence base" for practice and social change interventions.

In this chapter, we discuss how work-family issues have been examined in academic journals that contain much of the scholarly social work discourse. We explain how the person-in-environment conceptual framework, which is salient in much of the social work literature, helps social workers to consider the experiences of working families in different social settings. After commenting on our analysis of 100 work-family articles in social work literature, we discuss selected themes and topics. Finally, we conclude the chapter with observations of the implications that social work perspectives have for direct practice and social change initiatives.

METHODS

It is difficult to define the boundaries of the social work body of knowledge. This challenge results in part because social work attempts to think about social issues holistically and draws insights from different social science disciplines, including theories and empirical studies conducted by social workers themselves. Social Work Abstracts, the premier indexing source for social work journals in the United States, helps to organize the social work body of knowledge (Williams, 2001). Social Work Abstracts is a database that identifies and catalogs journal articles considered to be relevant to the social work profession. This database was originally established by the National Association of Social Workers in 1965 and, starting in 1977, began to include the citations and annotations of social work research literature. According to the managing editor of the Social Work Abstracts, the following criteria are used for selecting articles to be included in the database: all articles in journals associated with/published by social work professional associations, such as *Social Work* and *Social Work Education* (journals of the National Association of Social Work and the Council on Social Work Education, respectively); articles in journals that have the words "social work" in the journal title; and articles in journals affiliated with disciplines/professions that contribute to the social work knowledge base (e.g., psychology) and that have relevance to social work research, education, and/or practice. Currently, articles from over 450 journals are referenced in the Social Work Abstracts database (Personal conversation with Fredda Payne, managing editor of Social Work Abstracts, March 2004 and information obtained online at http://www.columbia.edu/cu/libraries/indexes/social-work-abs.html).

We used the search engine of Social Work Abstracts to identify work-family articles relevant to social work. In our effort to generate a sample of articles, three search terms were used: "work and family," "work/life," and "mother and work." We recognized that this preliminary search would not surface every article in the Social Work Abstracts pertinent to the lives of working families; however, we felt that these terms would result in a sufficient number of articles that could be analyzed for the purposes of this chapter.

A total of 1,742 articles were initially identified using the term "work and family," 805 articles using the term "mother and work," and 34 articles using the term "work/life." The abstracts for each of the 2,581 articles were reviewed to determine if they discussed issues pertaining to the intersection of work and family life (rather than either just "work" or "family"). A total of 2,330 abstracts were eliminated, leaving 251 abstracts for further scrutiny. Both authors of this chapter read the 251 abstracts to assess whether the abstracts were directly relevant to work-family issues, making independent decisions about the inclusion or exclusion of each abstract. When differences in opinions resulted, we discussed our respective interpretations of the abstracts and then mutually decided to include or exclude the article. Doctoral dissertations, letters to editors, and essays were excluded from the final literature review.

Our examination of the abstracts resulted in the identification of 128 articles, of which all were selected for full review. During the final review phase, an additional 28 articles were eliminated from the final analysis because 11 articles were duplicates, 16 articles did not directly address work-family experiences, and one article did not arrive in time from interlibrary loan. In the end, 100 work-family articles retrieved from journals contained in Social Work Abstracts were included in the analysis of the literature.

As mentioned above, the database of Social Work Abstracts includes articles published in social work journals as well as in journals affiliated with disciplines and fields aligned with social work. It should be noted, therefore, that many of the articles referenced in this database were authored by scholars from disciplines/fields other than social work (e.g., sociology). Approximately half ($n = 49$) of the articles reviewed for this chapter were published by authors affiliated with schools of social work; that is, the author(s) either received a degree from an accredited social work program or they were employed by an accredited social work program when the article was originally published. The remaining articles were published by authors from other disciplines including anthropology, economics, family studies, public health, psychology, psychiatry, and sociology. We have included these articles in our review because they are considered to be part of the social work body of knowledge.

There are some limitations of the methodology adopted for this analysis. First, books and reports on work-family topics were not identified because they are not included in the database of the Social Work Abstracts. Unfortunately, it was not feasible for us to use other databases to identify and review work-family books because there is no structure, such as Social Work Abstracts, which could define whether or not the books are considered to be part of the social work body of knowledge. As a result, many important work-family books authored by social workers are not examined in this chapter.[1] Second, the search may have missed pertinent articles because the terms we used—"work-family," "work/life," and "mother and work"—were not included in the titles or the abstracts.[2] Finally, articles published by journals not included in Social Work Abstracts were, obviously, not included in the search results. Therefore, some relevant work-family articles published by social workers or scholars affiliated with schools of social work were not identified.[3] Due to these restrictions and because we felt it was important to elucidate some of our discussions by referencing literature not identified through our search, we have used footnotes in this chapter (rather than in-text citations) when we cite publications that were not included in the results of our search of Social Work Abstracts.

Each of the articles included in our analysis was summarized. We noted whether the article focused primarily on theories/conceptual frameworks, research, policy, and/or practice. We analyzed the content of each article, paying particular attention to important topics discussed by the authors. Study variables were recorded for research articles, and key findings and recommendations were recorded. Table 16.1 includes abbreviated versions of these summaries.

Two primary themes emerged from our content analysis of the 100 social work articles. Each of them either discussed particular "population groups" (and also commented on their "environments") or they discussed "social–political–economic environments" (and also commented on the impacts of these environments on different "population groups"). Consequently, we used the person-in-environment perspective to analyze each of the articles.

THE PERSON-IN-ENVIRONMENT PERSPECTIVE

Numerous epistemological traditions and theoretical perspectives have contributed to the social work literature in general and to social work publications about work-family issues in particular. The "person-in-environment" perspective, which was articulated in the earliest social work literature at the beginning of the 20th century, frames a number of basic social work assumptions and constructs.[4] As explained by the National Association of Social Work, "A historic and defining feature of social work is the profession's focus on individual well-being in a social context and the well-being of society. Fundamental to social work is attention to the environmental forces that create, contribute to, and address problems in living" (NASW Code of Ethics, 1999).

TABLE 16.1
Combined Charts—100 Articles

Author/Citation	Comments
Akabas, S. (September–October 1984). Workers are parents, too. *Child Welfare, 63*(5), 387–399.	Type of Article: Theoretical Highlights: Author presents theoretical and empirical arguments for importance of changes in "welfare policies" (e.g., employer policies, public policies, and policies of voluntary organizations) needed to support working families across the life cycle. Suggestions for services, such as counseling at the workplace and in the community.
Anastas, J., Gibeau, J., & Larson, P. (1990). Working families and eldercare: A national perspective in an aging America. *Social Work, 35*(5), 405–411.	Type of Article: Research Highlights: National Survey of Caregivers. Survey of employees (40 + years) working for employers with 1,000+ employees (*n* = 436). 36% identified self as caregivers, evenly divided males/females. Women reported more conflict than men. Suggestions for workplace-based supports, such as information about eldercare services.
Applewhite, L., & Mays, R. (1996). Parent–child separation: A comparison of maternally and paternally separate children in military families. *Child and Adolescent Social Work Journal, 13*(1), 23–39.	Type of Article: Research Highlights: Comparison of psychosocial functioning of children (*n* = 288) who experienced extended maternal separation (*n* = 139) with children who experienced extended paternal separation (*n* = 149). No significant differences found in the quality of child psychosocial functioning between the two groups. Practice implications discussed.
Avioli, P. (1985). The labor-force participation of married mothers of infants. *Journal of Marriage and Family, 47*(3), 739–745.	Type of Article: Research Highlights: Data from the Panel Study of Income Dynamics were used to examine the factors affecting the decisions of married women whether to enter the labor force during the first 3 years of a child's life. Multivariate analysis found prior work experience and attitudes toward future employment were the most predictive factors.
Axinn, J., & Stern, M. (July–August 1987). Women and the postindustrial welfare state. *Social Work, 32*(4), 282–286.	Type of Article: Research/Policy Highlights: Analysis of 1973 and 1983 Census data to consider impact of women's labor force participation on poverty rates. Modeling analyses suggest that dramatic increases in poverty among women would have occurred without their increased labor force participation. Policies for temporary and long-term unemployed; policies for retirement.
Bowen, G. (1987). Single fathers in the air force. *Social Casework: The Journal of Contemporary Social Work, 68*(6), 339–344.	Type of Article: Research Highlights: Study examines the work, personal, and family demands and adjustments of single fathers (*n* = 87) in the Air Force. Semi-structured interviews found that, overall, single fathers in Air Force adjust successfully to the demands of Air Force life. Discussion of possible supports to military families.

Broman, C. (2001). Work stress in the family life of African Americans. *Journal of Black Studies, 31*(6), 835–846.

Type of Article: Research
Highlights: Using data from 2 panels of the American's Changing Lives Survey (ACL) [first wave ($n = 3,617$) second wave ($n = 2,867$)], study examines the link between job-related stressors and family life among African American workers. Regression analysis found job characteristics play a critical role in family life. Implications for job redesign and stress management explored.

Brownwell. J. (1998). Striking a balance: The future of work and family issues in the hospitality industry. *Marriage & Family Review, 28*(1/2), 109–123.

Type of Article: Practice
Highlights: Discussion of employer responsiveness in hotel industry. Work conditions including work hours, earnings, and employer-supported initiatives addressed. Suggestions for employers and for educators offered.

Burud, S., Collins, R., & Divine-Hawkins, P. (May–June 1983). Employer supported child care: Everybody benefits. *Children Today, 12*(3), 2–7.

Type of Article: Practice
Highlights: Discussion of factors that promote workplace responsiveness to work-family needs of working parents.

Cancian, M. (2001). Rhetoric or reality: Work-based welfare reform. *Social Work, 46*(4), 309–314.

Type of Article: Policy
Highlights: Reviewing the social welfare policy literature, author found former welfare recipients earn low wages in unstable employment and require broad supports to move toward self-sufficiency. Implications for social work advocacy presented. Author argues for social policy reforms.

Cannon, D. (1998). Better understanding of the impact of work interferences on organizational commitment. *Marriage & Family Review, 28*(1/2), 153–166.

Type of Article: Research
Highlights: Survey of employees at all levels of hotel ($n = 300$). Regression analyses found child-care needs and medical problems predict variance in organizational commitment. Child care, personal activities, and medical problems related to job satisfaction. Age and education predictors of interferences with work.

Casey, J., & Pitt-Catsouphes, M. (1994). Employed single mothers: Balancing job and homelife. *Employee Assistance Quarterly, 9*(3/4), 37–53.

Type of Article: Research
Highlights: Article describes experiences of employed single mothers. Data from three studies presented: focus group data; a substudy of a larger work and family survey that compared employed single mothers to dual-earner mothers; results from a survey of single mothers ($n = 71$). Working single mothers have limited financial and economic sources to meet work and family demands. Implications for EAP programs considered.

Chilman, C. (1993). Parental employment and child care trends: Some critical issues and suggested policies. *Social Work, 38*(4), 451–460.

Type of Article: Policy
Highlights: Article summarizes research about the effects of parental employment and substitute child care on young children and their parents. Federal legislation provisions (e.g., child care, job training, and income supports) for young low-income parents discussed.

Chung, B. (1998). Accounting for changing times: Aligning human resource practices to employees' nonwork lives. *Marriage & Family Review, 28*(1/2), 143–152.

Type of Article: Practice
Highlights: Review of rationale for increased employer involvement including: employer need for workers, changing social values, changing demographics, possibilities of increased productivity, and desire for improved customer service and decreased costs.

(Continued)

TABLE 16.1
(Continued)

Author/Citation	Comments
Clayton, H., Odera, V., Emenheiser, D., & Reynolds, J. S. (1998). The relationship of job satisfaction and family life: Female managers in health care food service. *Marriage & Family Review, 28*(1/2), 167–185.	Type of Article: Research Highlights: Survey of female managers in health care food service ($n = 122$). Correlation analyses found relationships between the number of hours worked and limited opportunities for advancement related to dissatisfaction. 55% respondents reported positive impact of job on family life. 40% of respondents reported perceptions of discrimination. Recognition of need for organizational change strategies.
Collins, S. (1984). A comparison of top and middle level women administrators in social work, nursing & education: Career supports and barriers. *Administration in Social Work, 8*(2), 25–34.	Type of Article: Research Highlights: A nationally stratified sample of female administrators ($n = 259$) within three fields (SW, nursing, education) to determine factors that influence their career development. Top administrators in SW and education receive moderate to high career support from their husbands. Workplace factors including presence of role models, organizational support, and discrimination noted. Suggestions for addressing issues in social work curriculum offered.
Crouter, A. (November 1984). Spillover from family to work: The neglected side of the work-family interface. *Human Relations, 37*(6), 425–442.	Type of Article: Research Highlights: Interviews conducted with parents of young children ($n = 55$). Work demands/work structures associated with negative spillover from family to work. Spillover related to family roles and responsibilities (which tend to be assumed in a gendered manner). Implications for workplace supports considered.
Crouter, A. (July–August 1982). The children of working parents. *Children Today, 11*(4), 25–28.	Type of Article: Policy [workplace policy] Highlights: Reviews historical literature pertaining to the effects of parental employment on children. Argues that child care and workplaces are two systems that can enhance or impede a child's development. Discussion of adjustments that could be made by workplaces and child-care centers.
Danes, S., & Keskinen, S. (Summer 1990). The extent of off-farm employment and its impact on farm women. *Human Services in the Rural Environment, 14*(1), 10–14.	Type of Article: Research Highlights: Survey of farm women ($n = 216$). 46% reported employment off the farm. Less than half received any benefits (e.g., vacation time, sick leave, health insurance, unemployment compensation, etc.) from employers. 17% reported that employment greatly reduced time with spouse. Employed farm women reported greatest dissatisfaction with work-family balance and leisure. Importance of human service workers understanding the work and family demands on farm women who are also employed off farm discussed.
DeBord, K., Canu, R. F., & Kerpelman, J. (July 2000). Understanding a work-family fit for single parents moving from welfare to work. *Social Work, 45*(4), 313–324.	Type of Article: Research/Theoretical Highlights: Interviews conducted with TANF recipients ($n = 30$) to identify characteristics of the work environment as well as personal characteristics associated with success at the workplace. Success at the workplace reflects work-family "fit" when needs of families and demands at the workplace met. Strategies for social service agencies highlighted.

Dinerman, M. (1992). Is everything women's work? *Affilia, (7)*2, 77–93.

Type of Article: Policy

Highlights: Discussion of the ramifications of women entering into the labor force. Advocates for changes at the home, maternity leave policies, and modifying workplace practices. Spells out an "action agenda" including: maternity policy, domestic changes, increase in dependent care, and equity in the workplace.

Eggebeen, D., & Hawkins, A. (1990). Economic needs and wives' employment. *Journal of Family Issues, 11*(1), 48–66.

Type of Article: Theoretical

Highlights: Author finds that White, married mothers whose partners earn adequate income were more likely to move into the labor force than those whose husbands do not. Personal choice, rather than economic need, was identified as the primary motive for entering the labor force.

Etaugh, C., & Folger, D. (1998). Perceptions of parents whose work and parenting behaviors deviate from role expectations. *Sex Roles, 39*(3/4), 215–223.

Type of Article: Research

Highlights: Study examines the perceptions of college students (*n* = 200) with parents whose work and parenting behaviors deviate from role expectations. FT employment enhanced perception of professional competence of fathers but not of mothers, and lowered evaluations of nurturance for both parents, especially mothers. Discusses effects of gender stereotypes on full-time/part-time working mothers and fathers.

Finn-Stevensen, M., & Trzcinski, E. (October 1991). Mandated leave: Analysis of federal and state legislation. *American Journal of Orthopsychiatry, 6*(4), 567–575.

Type of Article: Policy

Highlights: Importance of leave for dependent care, particularly following birth/adoption of child. History and provisions of Family and Medical Leave Act.

Fischel-Wolovick, L., Cotter, C., Masser, I., Kelman-Bravo, E., Jaffe, R., Rosenberg, G., & Wittenberg, B. (1988). Alternative work scheduling for professional social workers. *Administration in Social Work, 12*(4), 93–102.

Type of Article: Research

Highlights: Case study of a Department of Social Services at a medical center that employed alternative work scheduling (AWS) as a strategy to reduce employees' work-family stress. Flex schedules associated with increase in # of cases opened and # of direct services.

Fox Folk, K., & Beller, A. (1993). Part-time work and child care choices for mothers of preschool children. *Journal of Marriage and the Family, 55*(1), 146–157.

Type of Article: Research

Highlights: Study examines level of employment and child-care arrangements using a sample of mothers of preschool children (*n* = 976) from the National Survey of Families and Households. 40% of mothers of preschool children combine employment and caregiving by working part-time. A combination of factors affects the choice of combining part-time employment with parent or relative child care. Implications for child-care policy discussed.

Freedman, R., Litchfield, L., & Warfield, M. (October 1995). Balancing work and family: Perspectives of children with developmental disabilities. *Families in Society: The Journal of Contemporary Human Services, 76*(8),507–514.

Type of Article: Research

Highlights: Four focus groups (*n* = 26) used to explore work and family responsibilities of working parents of children with developmental disabilities. Study found work plays a vital role in the lives of families with developmental disabilities. Implications for workplace-based supports considered.

Garrett, P., & Wenk, D. (1990). Working around childbirth: Comparative and empirical perspectives on parental-leave policy. *Child Welfare, 69*(5), 401–413.

Type of Article: Policy

Highlights: Discusses international legislation and national trends. Examines mothers' reentry into the work force during child's first year, and the age of infants when child care is first needed. Offers policy recommendations for job protection and wage replacement.

(Continued)

TABLE 16.1
(Continued)

Author/Citation	Comments
Gelles, R. J., & Hargreaves, E. F. (1981). Maternal employment and violence toward children. *Journal of Family Issues, 2*(4), 509–530.	Type of Article: Research Highlights: Study examines the relationship between maternal employment and violence toward children using interviews with a nationally representative sample (*n* = 1, 146). Considers relationship to paternal unemployment. Working mothers are not more likely to be violent.
Gonyea, J. (1993). Family responsibilities and family-oriented policies: Assessing their impacts on the work place. *Employee Assistance Quarterly, 9*(1), 1–29.	Type of Article: Policy Highlights: Reviews the research focusing on the effects of child care, elder care, and family-oriented personnel policies on employees. Six dimensions of employees' work experience are explored: stress, morale and job satisfaction, absenteeism and tardiness, job performance, job search and acceptance, and career development and turnover. Implications given for organizational policy.
Googins, B., & Burden, D. (July–August 1987). Vulnerability of working parents balancing work and home roles. *Social Work, 32*(4), 295–300.	Type of Article: Research Highlights: Exploratory study assessed job–family role strain among employees (*n* = 711). Study identified employee groups vulnerable to reduced levels of physical and emotional well-being. Implications for workplace policy and family practitioners.
Grahame, K. M. (2003). For the family: Asian immigrant women's triple day. *Journal of Sociology and Social Welfare, 30*(1), 65–90.	Type of Article: Research/Policy Highlights: Qualitative examination of Asian immigrant women's (*n* = 7) management of the demands of family, job training, and paid work in their new country. Implications for social policy highlighted.
Gray, E., Lovejoy, M., Piotrkowski, C., & Bond, J. T. (June 1990). Husband supportiveness and the well-being of employed mothers of infants. *Families in Society: The Journal of Contemporary Human Services, 71*(6), 332–341.	Type of Article: Research Highlights: Analysis of data from Mothers in the Workplace Study Survey of pregnant employees (*n* = 490 married mothers of infants working full-time). Negative relationships noted between supportiveness of husband and mothers' stress and marital strain.
Greenberger, E., & Goldberg, W. (1989). Work, parenting, and the socialization of children. *Developmental Psychology, 25*(1), 22–35.	Type of Article: Research/Practice Highlights: Employed mothers (*n* = 194) and fathers (*n* = 104) in dual-earner families with 3–4-year-old were surveyed about work, parenting, child's socialization practices, and perceptions of their child's behavior. Parental investment was a stronger predictor of fathers' and mothers' demands for mature child behavior than was work investment. Women with high commitments to work and parenting were more likely than others to engage in authoritative parenting. Parenting styles were related to mothers' ratings of child's behavior.

Grimm-Thomas, K., & Perry-Jenkins, M. (1994). All in a day's work: Job experiences, self-esteem, and fathering in working-class families. *Family Relations, 43*(2), 174–181.

Type of Article: Research
Highlights: Examined how working-class fathers' job experiences affected their self-esteem and parenting styles (*n* = 59). In-person interviews with working class fathers in dual-earner families with children between 8–12 years. Positive relationships between fathers' work experiences and self-esteem, which predicted a more accepting parenting style. Implications for work redesign considered.

Gringeri, C. E. (1995). Flexibility, the family ethic, and rural home-based work. *Affilia, 10*(1), 70–86.

Type of Article: Research
Highlights: Interviews with home-based workers (*n* = 80) in two rural communities to explore how flexible work arrangements influence home responsibilities. Work can become flexible only when tasks are no longer rigidly defined. Workplace and public policy options suggested.

Grosswald, B. (2002). I raised my kids on the bus: Transit shift workers' coping strategies for parenting. *Journal of Sociology and Social Welfare, 29*(3), 29–49.

Type of Article: Research
Highlights: Study investigates coping strategies for parenting of transit shift workers. Interviews were conducted with parents (*n* = 30) of school-age children. The principal impact of job on relationships with children was the lack of time they had together. Public policy implications of hours and wages considered.

Haddock, S. A., Zimmerman, T. S., Current, L. R., & Harvey, A. (2003). The parenting practices of dual-earner couples who successfully balance family and work. *Journal of Feminist Family Therapy, 14*(3/4), 37–56.

Type of Article: Research
Highlights: Using qualitative interviews, this study investigates the parenting practices of middle-class, dual-earner couples (*n* = 27) who perceive themselves as successful in balancing family and work. Four primary strategies were identified. Options for intervention suggested.

Hattery, A. (2001). Tag-team parenting: Costs and benefits of utilizing non-overlapping shift work in families w/ young children. *Families in Society: The Journal of Contemporary Human Services, 82*(4), 419–427.

Type of Article: Research
Highlights: Face-to-face interviews conducted with women working full-time (*n* = 10), part-time (*n* = 10), and staying at home (*n* = 10). Despite difficulties negotiating schedules, overlapping shifts allows families to provide their own child care. Implications for practitioners and policy advocates considered.

Herring, C., & Wilson-Sadberry, K. (May 1993). Preference or necessity? Changing work roles of Black and White women, 1973–1990. *Journal of Marriage and the Family, 55*(2), 314–325.

Type of Article: Research
Highlights: Data from 11 General Social Surveys used to investigate changes in the degree to which Black and White women have participated in the labor market out of economic necessity versus preference. Sample consisted of Black and White female respondents (*n* = 6,483) between the ages of 18 and 65. Most working women from both racial groups reported that they participated in the labor force for reasons other than economic necessity alone.

Hofferth, S. (1999). Child care, maternal employment and public policy. *Annals of the American Academy of Political and Social Science, 563*, 20–38.

Type of Article: Policy
Highlights: Article focuses on relationship between child care and self-sufficiency among low-income mothers. Factors affecting the demand and availability and cost and quality considered. The role of public subsidies in increasing access to quality child care mentioned. Author notes mismatch between job schedules and child-care center hours.

(Continued)

TABLE 16.1
(Continued)

Author/Citation	Comments
Hofferth, S., & Deich, S. G. (September 1994). Recent U.S. child care and family legislation in comparative perspective. *Journal of Family Issues, 15*(3), 424–448.	Type of Article: Policy Highlights: Cross-national comparisons of US and four European countries according to 5 dimensions of policies for working families: supply of child care, support for maternal employment, easing burdens of childrearing, permitting parental choice, and program quality. Authors conclude that, with exception of reducing burdens of childrearing (in tax credits), the US has not adopted broad national policies that support any of these social goals.
Home, A. (1997). Learning the hard way: Role strain, stress, role demands, and support in multiple-role women students. *Journal of Social Work Education, 33*(2), 335–347.	Type of Article: Research/Education/Policy Highlights: Study examines the relationships between stress, income, role strain, perceived role demands, and perceived social support in women ($n = 443$) with family and job responsibilities while studying in Canadian social work, nursing, or education programs. Students with multiple roles had most difficulty. Income was the stronger predictor of life situation and types of support provided by family.
Jackson, A. (1993). Black, single working mothers in poverty: Preferences for employment, well being and perceptions of preschool age children. *Social Work. 38(1)* 26–34.	Type of Article: Research Highlights: Investigation of role strain and emotional well-being among 111 single, Black, low-income employed mothers with 3–4-year-old. Mothers who prefer employment reveal less stress and perceive their preschool-age children more positively than mothers who prefer to stay home. Parenting boys may be especially stressful for these working mothers. Implications for family and social support policy outlined.
Jackson, A. (1994). The effects of role strain on single, working Black mothers' perceptions of their young children. *Social Work Research, 18*(1), 36–41.	Type of Article: Research Highlights: Investigation of role strain and emotional well-being among 111 single, Black, low-income employed mothers with 3–4-year-old. Regression found mothers with some education beyond high school have more positive views of their children regardless of child's sex. Implications for economic support policy and for practice explored.
Jackson, A. (September 1992). Well-being among single, Black, employed mothers. *Social Service Review, 66*(3), 399–408.	Type of Article: Research Highlights: Investigation of emotional well-being among 111 single, Black, low-income employed mothers with 3–4-year-old. Sample was at risk for depression. Those with no education beyond high school and a preschool-age boy predicted the least favorable well-being outcomes. Implications for economic support policy and for practice considered.
Jackson, A. P., & Huang, C. C. (1998). Concerns about children's development: Implications for single, employed Black mothers' well-being. *Social Work Research, 22*(4), 233–240.	Type of Article: Research Highlights: Analysis of data from ongoing investigation of single Black mothers employed in low-wage jobs in NYC ($n = 93$) found relationships between role strain with preference to stay home; appraisals of greater child problem behaviors and lower pay with depression symptoms. Implications for policies and programs related to child care and wages discussed.

Jayaratne, S., Chess, W., & Kunkel, D. (January–February 1986). Burnout: Its impact on child welfare workers and their spouses. *Social Work, 31*(1), 53–59.

Type of Article: Research
Highlights: Impact of burnout of welfare workers on marital/family relationships ($n = 75$ female child welfare workers and their spouses). Data from spouses compared to responses of welfare workers themselves. Study found negative relationships between burnout and mental health of welfare workers.

Johnson, B. (July–August 1987). The changing role of women and social security reform. *Social Work, 32*(4), 341–344.

Type of Article: Policy
Highlights: Changing roles of women and social security reform explored. Disadvantages of women's less continuous employment for retirement. Reforms suggested to remove gender-based penalties from social security.

Johnson, P. (1983). Divorced mothers' management of responsibilities: Conflicts between employment and child care. *Journal of Family Issues, 4*(1), 83–103.

Type of Article: Research
Highlights: Using the theory of asymmetrically permeable boundaries between employment and family, study examines how divorced mothers manage potentially conflicting situations between employment and child care. Sample consisted of women employed full-time in clerical and sales positions ($n = 381$). Mothers allowed child care to take precedence over employment demands.

Jordan, C., Cobb, N., & McCully, R. (January 1989). Clinical issues of the dual-career couple. *Social Work, 34*(1), 29–32.

Type of Article: Practice
Highlights: Discussion of clinical interventions—such as values clarification, communication training, stress management, training in negotiating, and time/stress management—to help the dual-career couple. Clinical interventions for dual-career couple suggested.

Kahne, H. (September 1994). Part-time work: A reassessment for changing economy. *Social Service Review, 68*(3), 418–436.

Type of Article: Policy
Highlights: Article reviews reasons for the increase in part-time work. Part-time work can increase job flexibility, reduce pressures on dual-earner families, and increase productivity. Suggests that public welfare and private sector training programs providing part-time work with pro-rated wages and benefits and subsidized part-time training can be beneficial.

Kaye, L., Alexander, L., & Kauffman, S. (1999). Factors contributing to job quality and satisfaction among ethnically diverse, lower income elderly part-timers. *Journal of Gerontological Social Work, 31*(1/2), 143–166.

Type of Article: Research
Highlights: Study determines factors that contribute to job satisfaction among ethnically diverse, low-income older (55+) workers employed part-time ($n = 164$). Job satisfaction levels were high for all employees; no difference for age, gender, or type of senior citizen program. Implications for practice and workplace policy summarized.

Kingston, P., & Nock, S. (August 1985). Consequences of the family work day. *Journal of Marriage and the Family, 47*(3), 619–629.

Type of Article: Research
Highlights: Analysis of 1977 Quality of Employment Survey using responses of married individuals with working spouses ($n = 668$) to consider relationship between well-being and stress with parents' combined work hours. Parents' longer hours associated with less time with children. Every additional 2 hours at work, time with children reduced 14–21 minutes. No significant impact on marital adjustment or life satisfaction. Authors note there is little evidence to suggest that the quality of family life is altered in major ways by hours worked or the scheduling of those hours."

(Continued)

TABLE 16.1
(Continued)

Author/Citation	Comments
Kissman, K., & Solar Silva, M. (1994). Women in Chile: Wage labor and child care in families headed by mothers. *International Social Work, 37*(1), 37–46.	Type of Article: Policy/Education Highlights: Article summarizes the social and demographic changes among working women and families in Chile. Policy recommendations suggested for ways to promote maternal and child welfare, and gives suggestions for how to integrate this material into the social work curriculum.
Kolodinsky, J., & Shirey, L. (2000). The impact of living with an elderly parent on adult daughters' labor supply and hours of work. *Journal of Family and Economic Issues, 21*(2), 149–175.	Type of Article: Research/Policy Highlights: Using a sample from the Panel Study of Income Dynamics ($n = 1,451$), study examines impact of individuals and household characteristics on labor supply probabilities and work hours of adult employed and unemployed daughters living in: (1) households where daughter co-resides with elder parents; (2) households in which adult daughters have living parents but they do not reside with parents. Co-residence with an elder suppresses labor market participation. Implications for labor and family policy considered.
Krauskopf, M., & Akabas, S. (1998). Children with disabilities: A family/workplace partnership in problem resolution. *Social Work Papers, 21,* 28–35.	Type of Article: Research Highlights: Descriptive study examines types of work-family problems experienced by employed parents of children with disabilities ($n = 160$). Sample drawn from a list of union members who had used maternity benefits or hospitalization benefits for a young child.
Lechner, V. (July 1993). Support systems and stress reduction among working workers caring for dependent parents. *Social Work, 38*(4), 462–469.	Type of Article: Research Highlights: Study of employees at 3 hospitals providing care to frail elders ($n = 133$). Three types of support examined: social support from family and friend, workplace support, and community services on stress and health outcomes. Formal and informal supports reduced stress. Supportive work environments reduced negative health outcomes. Author advocates for increasing workplace responsiveness as mediator of negative health outcomes.
Lechner, V., & Sasaki, M. (1995). Japan and the US struggle with who will care for our aging parents when caregivers are employed. *Journal of Gerontological Social Work, 12*(1/2), 97–114.	Type of Article: Policy Highlights: Summarizes work-family problems and government, workplace, and community responses in Japan and US. Discussion of US and Japan's ideology pertaining to caregiving responsibilities. Implications for social policy, advocacy for elders, elder care policy.
Leiter, M., & Durup, M. (March 1996). Work, home and in-between: A longitudinal study of spillover. *Journal of Applied Behavioral Science, 32*(1), 29–47.	Type of Article: Research Highlights: Longitudinal study of demands (stressor) and resources of the workplace and home among health care professionals ($n = 151$). Models indicate more work to family impact than family to work. Authors note "active personal conflict, not simply an absence of support, is required before family concerns noticeably disrupt the work of health care providers." Suggestions for workplace-based supports, such as EAPs.

Linbloom, J. (1995). Addressing the needs of working mothers: The changing context of occupational social work education. *Journal of Teaching in Social Work, 12*(1/2), 85–103.

Type of Article: Education/Policy/Practice
Highlights: Overview of changing work and family social systems and their relationship to needs of employed mothers. Author argues that occupational social work curricula should include issues salient to working mothers and the systemic factors that lead to poor coping.

Lowry, C., Paul, S., Morrill, W., & Oviatt, B. (1987). Examining person and environment variables related to work performance, work satisfaction, and psychological adjustment: Preparation for preventive interventions. *Social Work Papers, 24*(3), 55–66.

Type of Article: Research/Theory/Practice/Education
Highlights: Study of work and family experiences of university staff ($n = 274$). Together, personal competencies, work environment, and family environment accounted for 23.9% of variance in psychological adjustment. Together, work environment, family environment, and personal competencies predicted work satisfaction. Authors explore opportunities to reduce stressors at the workplace and for involving family system in interventions.

Lundgren-Gaveras, L. (1996). The work-family needs of single parents: A comparison of American and Swedish policy trends. *Journal of Sociology & Social Welfare, 32*(2), 131–147.

Type of Article: Policy
Highlights: Comparison of US and Swedish policies. In US, public policies focus on welfare (paid to mother) vs. Swedish policies where emphasis is on integration of mothers into workforce. However, in US as well as Sweden, private (employer) policies also promote integration. Author concludes that single mothers more disadvantaged in US due to their weak labor market position. Additional US public policy suggested.

MacDermid, S., & Williams, M. (1997). A within-industry comparison of employed mothers' experiences in small and large workplace. *Journal of Family Issues, 18*(5), 545–567.

Type of Article: Research
Highlights: Research focuses on the relationships between mothers' ($n = 110$) perceptions of their parenting practices, their parenting values, their children's behavior, and work conditions at small and large workplaces. Analyses revealed significant direct and indirect relationships between work conditions and parenting, and significant differences between small and large workplaces, even when backgrounds were controlled.

Marlow, C. (Spring 1993). Coping with multiple roles: Family configuration and the need for workplace services. *Affilia, 8*(1), 40–55.

Type of Article: Research Practice
Highlights: Survey of female clerical workers ($n = 226$). Cross-tabulations found married women with children reported more difficulty coping than single moms.

Marlow, C. (1991). Women, children and employment: Responses by the United States and Great Britain. *International Social Work, 34*(3), 287–297.

Type of Article: Policy
Highlights: Comparison of policies, programs, and services viewed as supportive of employed mothers in the United States and Great Britain. Author advocates for employer responsiveness such as: counseling, flexible work schedules, control over work hours, assistance accessing child care. Implications for role of social workers at the workplace noted.

McNeeley, R. L. (1988). Managing work and family demands: Strengths, weaknesses and barriers to implementing twenty innovative programs. *Social Work Papers, 21*, 1–15.

Type of Article: Practice
Highlights: Discussion of the potential benefits and costs of workplace policies and programs established to help employees manage work and family responsibilities.

Moen, P., & Yu, Y. (2000). Effective work/life strategies: Working couples, work conditions, gender, and life quality. *Social Problems, 47*(3), 291–326.

Type of Article: Research
Highlights: Analysis of 1992 National Study of the Changing Workforce ($n = 824$ men and 844 women) to examine relationships of structural mismatch/fit between needs of workers/families and demands of workplace. In general, life quality for couples appears highest when both husband and wife work "regular" (but not excessive) hours. Study found strategies and life quality are gendered.

(Continued)

TABLE 16.1
(Continued)

Author/Citation	Comments
Mor Barak, M., Nissly, J., & Levin, A. (December 2001). Antecedents to retention and turnover among child welfare, social work and other human service employees: What can we learn from the past research: A review and metanalysis. *Social Service Review, 75*(4), 625–661.	Type of Article: Research Highlights: Metanalysis of articles (*n* = 25) concerning the relationships between demographic variables, personal perceptions, organizational conditions, and turnover/intent to leave among social service workers. Job burnout, job dissatisfaction, availability of employment alternatives, low organizational and professional commitment, stress, and lack of social support are strongest predictors of turnover/intention to leave. Implications for workplace policy and for child welfare policy examined.
Mukhopadhyay, S. (1996). Working status and health of middle-class Calcutta women. *The Indian Journal of Social Work, 57*(2), 327–336.	Type of Article: Research Highlights: Study examines effects of working status on selected physical and mental health traits of working (*n* = 95) and nonworking mothers (*n* = 95). There were no differences in physical or mental health status between two groups.
Noor, M. (1996). Women, work and family: Emerging issues and their implications on social work education. *Asia Pacific Journal of Social Work, 6*(2), 87–104.	Type of Article: Policy Highlights: Summarizes changes in women's roles in Malaysia. Argues that public policy should stop rewarding and supporting traditional role distribution and work policies should take into account dual-earner lifestyle. Implications for social work education and practice examined.
Olsen, F. (1992). Does enough work make women free? Part-time and full-time work strategies for women in the US and Germany. *The Indian Journal of Social Work, 53*(4), 599–610.	Type of Article: Policy Highlights: Examines the effects of work outside the home on the status of women living in the US and West Germany. Compares the work and care giving of women in US with women in West Germany. Public policies options presented.
Osterman, P. (1995). Work/family programs and the employment relationship. *Administrative Science Quarterly, 40*(4), 681–700.	Type of Article: Research Highlights: Survey of American establishments (*n* = 875) with 50+ employees to document workplace responsiveness. Regression analyses found relationships between employers supporting high-commitment work systems and those offering work-family programs. Author identifies factors related to employer responsiveness.
Paulson, S. (1996). Maternal employment and adolescent achievement revised: An ecological perspective. *Family Relations, 45*(2), 201–208.	Type of Article: Research/Practice Highlights: Study examines relationship between maternal employment and attitudes toward employment to achievement in adolescents (*n* = 240). Adolescents whose parents' attitudes toward maternal employment were not consistent with mothers' employment had lower grades than other adolescents. Implications for family practitioners and educators considered.

Pleck, J., Staines, G., & Lang, L. (March 1980). Research summaries: Conflicts between work and family life. *Monthly Labor Review, 103*(3), 29–32.

Type of Article: Research
Highlights: Analyses of DOL Quality of Employment Survey. Study found both men and women reported work-family conflict, with parents having more work-family conflict than others. Relationships between work-family conflicts and excessive work time, schedules, irritability/fatigue. Consideration of outcomes of scheduling demands on employees with caregiving responsibilities.

Prasad, B. D. (July 2001). Maternal employment and child abuse. *Indian Journal of Social Work, 62*(3), 328–346.

Type of Article: Research
Highlights: Study of dual-earner ($n = 133$) and single-earner ($n = 136$) couple families. Women who were not in the labor force were more likely to report more violent behaviors with their children, particularly younger children. Among dual earner couples, stress from work and low income status were correlated with child abuse. Suggestions for family life education.

Presser, H. B., & Baldwin, W. (1980). Child care as a constraint on employment: Prevalence, correlates, and bearing on the work and fertility nexus. *The American Journal of Sociology, 85,* 1202–1213.

Type of Article: Research
Highlights: Explores social and demographic correlates of child care, labor-force participation of women with children under 5 years, and fertility. Analysis is based on data from June 1977 Current Population Survey for the U.S., which was based on a sample of 53,500 households. A substantial minority of women feel constrained in their labor force participation due to lack of child-care options.

Price, R. (1985). Work and community. *American Journal of Community Psychology, 13*(1), 1–12.

Type of Article: Theoretical
Highlights: Connection between work (through family) to community. Impact on psychological well-being of individuals.

Riger, S., Ahrens, C., & Blickenstaff, A. (2000). Measuring interference with employment and education reported by women with abusive partners: Preliminary data. *Violence and Victims, 15*(2), 161–172.

Type of Article: Research
Highlights: Examines reliability and convergent validity of the work/school abuse scale, a measure of the ways that abusive men interfere with women's participation in education and employment. Sample consists of domestic violence victims residing in a Chicago shelter ($n = 35$). Implications for federal welfare policy, specifically the Family Violence Option.

Romito, P., Cubizolles, M., & Cuttini, M. (1994). Mothers' health after birth of the first child. *Women & Health, 21*(2/3), 1–24.

Type of Article: Research
Highlights: Examines the health and work outcomes of first-time mothers employed during pregnancy and residing in Italy ($n = 141$). Within 15 months, 84% of women had returned to paid jobs. Nonemployed women opted to stay home due to personal preference or because they lost their jobs.

Root, K. (September 1984). The human response to plant closings. *Annals of the AAPS, 475.* 52–65.

Type of Article: Research
Highlights: Comparison of longitudinal qualitative data from workers employed in a Midwest meat-packaging closed in early 1970s ($n = 35$) with displaced manufacturing and farm workers ($n = 27$) during the early 1980s. Qualitative interviews. Family coping strategies discussed.

(Continued)

TABLE 16.1
(Continued)

Author/Citation	Comments
Rosenzweig, J. M., Brennan, E. M., & Ogilvie, M. (2002). Work-family fit: Voices of parents of children w/ emotional and behavioral disorders. *Social Work, 47*(4), 415–424.	Type of Article: Research Highlights: Describes the strategies used by employed parents of children with disabilities and their perceptions about "fit" between caregiving and employment responsibilities. Five focus groups of employed parents ($n = 41$) whose children had emotional or behavioral disorders. Parents lack needed community-based services and resources. Implications for social work policy/practice (e.g., employment, child care, schools, and mental health care domains).
Rossi, A. (April 1993). The future in the making: Recent trends in the work-family interface. *Journal of Orthopsychiatry, 63*(2), 166–176.	Type of Article: Theoretical Highlights: Sociological/demographic/economic trends in family life and work discussed. Feminist perspective of changes in women's labor force participation, lack of pay equity, and gendered division of labor at home. Author notes importance of addressing concerns such as employer responsiveness, employment flexibility, portability of benefits, and pensions.
Rotman, A. (1989). Female social workers: Career or family. *Affilia, 4*(4), 81–90.	Type of Article: Research Highlights: Study of social workers ($n = 54$), interviewed about their commitment to work and family responsibilities during their working years. No difference in the commitment to work based on the degree of family responsibility.
Sancier, B., & Mapp, P. (Summer 1992). Who helps working women care for the young and the old? *Affilia, 7*(2), 61–76.	Type of Article: Research/Policy Highlights: Examination of policy supports for employed caregivers in Wisconsin. Responses to surveys of employers in Wisconsin Manufacturers and Commerce in 1985 ($n = 276$) and 1989 ($n = 418$) compared. Increases noted in "time-off" options. Suggestion for political platform to address needs of working women. Need noted for occupational social workers to respond.
Scharlach, A.. & Boyd, S. (1989). Caregiving and employment: Results of an employee survey. *The Gerontological Society of America, 29*(3), 382–387.	Type of Article: Research Highlights: Examines prevalence of elder care responsibilities among an employed population ($n = 3,658$). Multivariate analyses indicate that employed care providers, when compared to other employees, are more likely to experience interference between their jobs and family responsibilities and more likely to miss work. Implications for Employee Assistance Programs.
Secret, M., Sprang, G., & Bradford, J. (November 1998). Parenting in the workplace: Examining a unique infant care option. *Journal of Family Issues, 19*(6), 795–815.	Type of Article: Research Highlights: Option for infant care at the workplace at small, nonprofit workplace. Survey of all employees ($n = 26$). Bi-variate analyses found parenting at workplace had little/no negative impact on other employees, who in general expressed positive attitudes. Importance of considering impact of work-family supports on coworkers as well as on the employees who use them.

Secret, M., Sprang, G., Rompf, E., & Anderson, D. (2000). Community-based study of family-friendly workplaces. *Journal of Community Practice, 8*(1), 1–20.

Type of Article: Research
Highlights: Survey of business/nonprofit and public sector workplaces (*n* = 88) of all sizes in single community. Flexibility reported by the highest number of employers as work-family response (78% indicating availability). Larger organizations tend to report greater availability of work-family supports. Possibilities for partnerships between schools of social work and municipal governments interested in promoting more family-friendly employers in community.

Seyler, D., Monroe, P., & Garand, J. (March 1995). Balancing work and family: The role of employer-supported child care benefits. *Journal of Family Issues, 16*(2), 170–193.

Type of Article: Research
Highlights: Survey of workplaces in Louisiana with 50+ employees (*n* = 178). Correlation analyses found that businesses in the medical industry more likely to offer financial assistance to their employees. Regression analyses found workplace responsiveness related to % women in workforce and size of firm. Need to provide employers with evidence about organizational responsiveness in business' self-interest.

Solomon, B. (2001). The ins and outs of welfare to work: Women as they enter and exit a nursing assistant employment and training program. *Journal of Sociology and Social Welfare, 28*(3), 157–186.

Type of Article: Research/Policy
Highlights: Using participant observation and follow-up interviews, study explores the multiple work accountabilities that women receiving public assistance (*n* = 28) must manage as they enter and exit a welfare-to-work nursing assistant and training program. Concludes that the shift from welfare to work is incomplete. Implications for federal welfare policy, employment policy.

Sprang, G., Secret, M., & Bradford, J. (Spring 1999). Blending work and family: A case study. *Affilia, 14*(1), 98–116.

Type of Article: Research
Highlights: Option for infant care at the workplace at small, nonprofit workplace. Survey of all employees (*n* = 26). Bi-variate analyses found parenting at workplace had little/no negative impact on other employees, who in general expressed positive attitudes. Importance of considering impact of work-family supports on coworkers as well as on the employees who use them.

Swick, K., & Rotter, M. (Winter 1981). The workplace as a family system support. *Day Care and Early Childhood Education, 9*(2), 7–11.

Type of Article: Practice
Highlights: Workplace as an important support system for working families. Discussion about specific policies and programs that could promote quality of family life. Need for family-centered practice at the workplace. Suggests "family advisory councils" for businesses.

Van Breda, A. (November 1999). Developing resilience to routine separations: An occupational social work intervention. *Families in Society: The Journal of Contemporary Human Services, 80*(6), 597–605.

Type of Article: Practice Research
Highlights: Evaluation of pilot training intervention (Separation Resilience Seminar) (*n* = 24) designed to increase families' resilience to separations resulting from work commitments. Suggestions for social workers as supports to employees/their families and advocates for organizational change discussed.

Voydanoff, P. (June 1984). Economic distress and families. Policy Issues. *Journal of Family Issues, 5*(2), 273–288.

Type of Article: Policy
Highlights: 5 dimensions of economic changes outlined including increases in unemployment, shifts in jobs in different sectors, shift in geographic location of jobs, polarization of high and low earnings jobs, and decline of unionized jobs. Discussion of policies and programs designed to prevent/reduce families' economic distress through policies such as job creation, expansion of unemployment insurance, and supports for securing new employment.

(Continued)

TABLE 16.1
(Continued)

Author/Citation	Comments
Voydanoff, P., & Kelly, R. (November 1984). Determinants of work-related family problems among employed parents. *Journal of Marriage and the Family, 22*(1), 881–892.	Type of Article: Research/Theoretical Model at Individual/Family/Work Levels. Highlights: Interventions at macro, meso, and micro levels considered. Options examined with regard to criteria including anticipated effectiveness, equity, cost, stigma and work disincentive, preference satisfaction, and feasibility.
Voydanoff, P., & Kelly, R. (November 1984). Determinants of work-related family problems among employed parents. *Journal of Marriage and the Family, 22*(1), 881–892.	Type of Article: Research; Theoretical Model at individual/family/work levels. Highlights: Survey data collected from working parents (*n* = 468) in single firm examined to consider relationships between stressors and resources with work-related family problems. Sex predicted most of variance related to time shortage. Families with higher incomes report less time shortage.
Wardlaw, L. (June 1994). Sustaining informal caregivers for persons with AIDS. *The Journal of Contemporary Human Service, 75*(6), 373–384.	Type of Article: Research Highlights: Descriptive study designed to identify the type of care provided by informal caregivers (*n* = 642) to person with AIDS. Costs of caring for loved one, the resources available to assist caregivers, and benefits associated with providing care are considered. Author views the experiences of caregivers of people with AIDs as being idiosyncratic.
Winett, R., Neale, M., & Williams, K. (1982). The effects of flexible work schedules on urban families with young children. Quasi-experimental, ecological studies. *American Journal of Community Psychology, 10*(1), 49–64.	Type of Article: Research Highlights: Quasi experiment with introduction of limited flextime for parents (either single-earner, dual-earner, or single-parent families) at 2 federal agencies (*n* = 97 experimental groups; *n* = 37 in control group). Even limited flextime related to more time in evening with families. In one agency, less commuting time. Importance of organizational change for family well-being.
Zimmerman, I. L., & Bernstein, M. (1983). Parental work patterns in alternative families: Influence on child development. *American Journal of Orthopsychiatry, 53*, 418–425.	Type of Article: Research Highlights: Documents the increasing return to work by mothers of young children among samples of mothers in families representing traditional marriages, single-mother units, social-contract relationships, and communal living groups. Data from Family Styles Project (*n* = 200) analyzed. No evidence was found of negative effects on children's social, emotional, and cognitive development due to maternal absence secondary to employment.
Zvonkovic, A., Schmiege, C., & Hall, L. (1994). Influence strategies used when couples make work-family decisions and their importance for marital satisfaction. *Family Relations, 43*(2), 182–188.	Type of Article: Research/Practice Highlights: Survey of 61 couples (*n* = 122) examining types of decisions made by couples and strategies used by husbands and wives to influence decisions. 31% of decisions related to husband's employment, 59% related to wives' employment, and 13% to both. No gender differences in types of strategies used. The use of emotional influence was associated with lower marital satisfaction. Suggests that programs be developed to help couples enhance their decision-making skills.

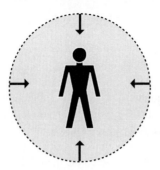

FIG. 16.1.   Person in Environment: Demands/Resources and Responses/Adaptations.

The person-in-environment lens (sometimes referred to as PIE or P-E) emerged from the human ecology or "ecosystems" tradition.[5] Several disciplines, such as psychology and organizational studies, have also adopted and modified the person-in-environment perspective to guide examinations of phenomena that are contextualized in different types of social settings. The common thread among different P-E variants is the recognition that individuals and groups have dynamic relationships with their social, physical, and natural environments.

A simplified depiction of the person-in-environment construct is illustrated by Fig. 16.1, where the solid arrow represents the impact of the characteristics of a specific environment (i.e., demands, resources, opportunities, constraints) on a person and the dotted arrow represents the person's response to the outcomes of the interaction between the person and that social setting.

Some studies using the P-E framework focus more on the effect that environments have on individuals, whereas others focus on the agency of the individuals who act upon (and, therefore, affect) their environments.[6] Interactions between individuals and their environments are sometimes seen as process mediators between various independent variables, such as employment status, and dependent variables, such as measures of well-being.

The P-E perspective has spawned a number of theories. Theories of "fit" and "mismatch," for instance, suggest that stress is (at least in part) an outcome of the extent of fit/misalignment between individuals' needs and preferences with environments' expectations and resources (for example, see Leiter & Durup, 1996; Price, 1985).[7] As explained by DeBord, Canu, and Kerpelman (2000, p. 314), "The work-family fit approach views work and family as interconnected systems, where connections between these two systems are conceived as the 'fit' between the demands of work and the individual's abilities to meet those demands and the fit between the family's needs and the resources available from work to meet those needs. Both work and family are seen as active contributors to this exchange process, and bidirectional influences are assumed to exist between the two dimensions of fit." The person–environment fit theory is a particularly powerful one for social workers because it urges these scholars to simultaneously focus on people as well as their social contexts (for example, see Paulson, 1996).

FOCUS ON PEOPLE IN VULNERABLE CIRCUMSTANCES

As explained by the NASW Code of Ethics (1999), social workers have a commitment to identify and respond to the needs of vulnerable populations: "Social workers should act to expand choice and opportunity for all people, with special regard for vulnerable, disadvantaged, oppressed, and exploited people and groups." It is widely recognized that population groups may become vulnerable, and often marginalized in society, as a result of factors such as demographic characteristics (e.g., race/ethnicity) or having less access to institutional resources and supports (e.g., education, employment, financial assistance).[8]

Fit theories suggest that working families in two types of circumstances could be considered vulnerable: those who confront extraordinary demands or stressors (such as families with children with profound disabilities or families where the adults routinely work for an excessive number of hours) or individuals with limited resources (such as low-income employees who have limited access to financial resources or single parents who typically have fewer adults living in the household who can assume responsibilities for income earning/home management/family caregiving tasks). Individuals in both of these situations could be considered "at-risk" because there is a mismatch between the demands on them and their ability to access resources that could help them respond to those demands.

Critical insights about the work-family experiences of diverse populations across the range of socioeconomic groups are embedded in social work literature. As a result of our analysis, we identified numerous articles that discussed salient work-family issues experienced by populations at-risk, including: women receiving public assistance (for example, see Cancian, 2001; Jackson, 1992, 1993, 1994; Solomon, 2001), families of color (for example, see Broman, 2001; Herring & Wilson-Sadberry, 1993; Jackson & Huang, 1998; Kaye et al., 1999), immigrant families (for example, see Grahame, 2003), working-class families (for example, see Grimm-Thomas & Perry-Jenkins, 1994; Grosswald, 2002; Hattery, 2001; Root, 1984), rural families (for example, see Danes & Keskinen, 1990; Gringeri, 1995), divorced mothers (for example, see Johnson, 1983), and working women who are victims of domestic violence (for example, see Riger et al., 2000). These investigations were designed to gain an understanding of the circumstances unique to the specific study population. Many of these studies found that the groups are often able to fulfill their work and family responsibilities, despite the challenges they confront.

A majority ($n = 57$) of the articles explored the experiences of working parents, often focusing on the role demands experienced by working mothers (for example, see Avioli, 1985; Chilman, 1993; Collins, 1984; Crouter, 1982, 1984; Eggebeen & Hawkins, 1990; Etaugh & Folger, 1998; Fox Folk & Beller, 1993; Greenberger & Goldberg, 1989; Romito et al., 1994; Zimmerman & Bernstein, 1983). For instance, Avioli (1985) conducted a study to investigate why some married mothers of infants opt to return to paid employment, while others make the decision to stay out of the labor force during the first 3 years of their children's lives. Using data from the Panel Study of Income Dynamic, the results of multivariate analyses suggest that working mothers' prior work experiences and attitudes toward future employment were predictive of whether women returned to their paid job after the birth of their child. Several of the articles included in our content analysis discuss the findings of studies about the experiences of single-parent families (for example, see Cancian, 2001; Casey & Pitt-Catsouphes, 1994; Dinnerman, 1992; Marlow, 1993; Olsen, 1992). Finally, the authors of two of the articles identified in Social Work Abstracts focus on parents in the military (Applewhite & Mays, 1996; Bowen, 1987). Bowen (1987) examined the work, family, and personal demands of single fathers ($n = 87$) employed by the U.S. Air Force. Overall, these single fathers adjusted successfully to meeting the demands of single fatherhood and the demands of Air Force life. However, Bowen's findings suggested that periods of transition are stressful for single fathers and recommended family counseling and parenting skills programs.

Articles included in the body of social work literature have made important contributions to our understanding of the diverse nature of caregiving assumed by working families. Several of the articles that we analyzed focused on employees who provide care to aging relatives (for example, see Anastas et al., 1990; Kolodinsky & Shirey, 2000; Lechner & Sasaki, 1995; Lechner, 1993; Sancier & Mapp, 1992; Scharlach & Boyd, 1989). For instance, Scharlach and Boyd's (1989) national survey of working people found that employees with elder caregiving responsibilities were more likely to miss work than employees without such responsibilities.

Three of the articles discussed the experiences of working parents who have children with disabilities and behavioral disorders (for example, see Freedman et al., 1995; Krauskopf & Akabas, 1998; Rosenzweig et al., 2002). Freedman et al. (1995) found that the extent of access to work-family benefits and polices (including flexible work schedules, health insurance, and part-time employment) significantly influenced working parents' decisions about caretaking responsibilities. Finally, one of the articles (Wardlaw, 1994) examined the experiences of employees who provide care to loved ones with AIDS.

Most of the work-family articles reviewed for this chapter contextualized the experiences of these working families in the broader socioeconomic–political environments, drawing attention to the different social settings that frame their daily life experiences.

FOCUS ON SOCIAL CONTEXTS

The P-E focus on social settings encourages researchers and practitioners alike to consider the demands, resources, opportunities, and systemic constraints that affect the work-family situations of vulnerable families. The P-E perspective also focuses the analysis of the work-family experiences on three different types of ecosystems: the micro, meso, and macro social settings or levels.[9]

The ecosystems model, which serves as the foundation for the P-E perspective, conceptualizes the micro system as those situations or "settings" in which a person has direct interactions with other people of significance. This level would, therefore, include intrafamilial relationships (i.e., in the "home" "setting") and friendship networks (i.e., in the informal neighborhood setting). The meso system is the level where two or more micro systems connect. Social organizations, such as religious organizations, schools, and workplaces, are often viewed as being part of the meso sytem level. Macro systems are considered to include social institutions that frame larger societies and would include normative values and social values.[10]

The dynamic relationships between a person and different social settings are suggested by Fig. 16.2. It is important to understand that this diagram significantly oversimplifies the experiences of individuals, who typically have experiences in multiple meso and macro social settings each day. Furthermore, each person in a working family presumably has experiences in social settings that differ from some of the settings experienced by other family members. For example, each spouse in a dual-earner family would have experiences in the same "home social setting" at the micro level, but the wife and husband might go to work at different workplaces, and each spouse could be involved in different community organizations (in the meso level).

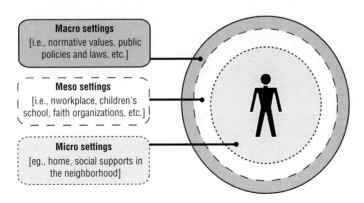

FIG. 16.2.   Person in Environment: Experiences in Micro, Meso, and Macro Social Settings.

Some studies have begun to consider how the meso settings of one family member might have an indirect impact on the experiences of other family members.

Investigations included in the social work literature often consider work-family experiences at two or even all three of these levels (for example, see Gray et al., 1990; Gringeri, 1995; Voydanoff, 1984; Voydanoff, & Kelly, 1984), for instance, discussed a range of macro factors such as the fluctuations in the accessibility of employment opportunities in different regions of the country and also made recommendations about interventions that could help individuals find employment.

Micro Social Settings

Our analysis of the social work work-family articles suggests that studies which focus on the experiences of working families at the micro level typically address either the relationships among family members with regard to their work-family responsibilities and/or the personal/family outcomes of work-family circumstances. Nearly two thirds ($n = -62$) of the articles reviewed for this chapter focused specifically on issues at the micro system level.

The attitudes and behaviors of family members can have a profound affect on the work-family experiences of other family members. Gray et al. (1990) conducted a study of the stresses associated with caring for a newborn child and with returning to work as experienced by working mothers. They found that the wives' perceptions of their husbands' supportiveness and their assessments of perceived economic need to return to work contributed to mothers' stress. (In addition, workplace factors, such as employer-supported leave, contributed to the stress levels. Workplace factors, which are considered to be in the meso level, are discussed below.) The consequences of unequal distribution of labor at home—particularly for working women—have long been studied by work-family scholars (for example, see Dinnerman, 1992; Googins & Burden, 1987; Kahne, 1994; Marlow, 1993; Zvonkovic et al., 1994). Googins and Burden (1987) reported that employed mothers spent more hours on home chores and child-care activities than fathers. Moreover, they found that mothers had lower levels of health and energy and were absent more from work compared to fathers. Another study comparing married mothers to single mothers found that married mothers reported more difficulties coping than single mothers, suggesting that the additional role of spouse may cause additional strain (Marlow, 1993). Riger et al. (2000) developed the Work/School Abuse Scale, a measurement tool to assess the ways that abusive men interfere with women's education and labor force participation. The authors reported that intimate partner violence can be a critical barrier to employment for welfare recipients and other working women.

Many of the articles identified through our preliminary search of Social Work Abstracts highlight factors that contribute to the stress/well-being among members of certain groups of working families (see, for example, Mukhopadhayay, 1996). Jackson (1992) found that among working-poor Black mothers, low educational status (high school completion or less) and having a male preschool child were predictive of increased role strain and depressive symptoms. Two studies examined family violence in working families (Gelles & Hargreaves, 1981; Prasad, 2001). Prasad (2001) examined the relationship between stress and child abuse among working and nonworking mothers in dual- and single-earning families. She found that nonworking mothers were more likely to abuse infants than working mothers. However, fathers in dual-earner households were more likely to abuse children if the wife was working.

A number of work-family articles consider the interface between work and family, and often examine how experiences in one setting, such as the workplace, affect the experiences of working families in the home (a key micro system). For instance, Crouter (1984) interviewed parents of young children ($n = 55$) to determine which workplace factors contributed to negative spillover from work to home. She found that work demands and specific types of work structures had a negative affect on family roles and responsibilities, in particular roles and responsibilities of working women. In another study, Lowry, Paul, Morril, and Oviatt (1987) examined the personal competencies and work environment variables that influenced the family experiences of university workers ($n = 274$). The study found that work environment factors in combination with family environment factors plus personal competencies predicted 55% of the variance in psychological adjustment of women and 43% of the adjustment of men. Studies such as these establish links between micro social systems and meso social systems.

Meso Social Settings

Researchers who examine work-family phenomena at the meso level document the experiences of individuals as they interact with groups and organizations in different community settings. We located 39 articles indexed in Social Work Abstracts that focus on work-family experiences in meso social systems.

Although some work-family scholars have begun to consider how work-family experiences are relevant to different types of organizations and social settings in the meso systems level, work-family investigations at this level typically focus on the workplace. Social work literature that examines the experiences of people at the workplace is often located in the "occupational social work" field.[11] Occupational social work publications typically consider different facets of social issues/social problems, such as discrimination/valuing diversity and inclusion, as they are observed at the workplace (see Clayton et al., 1998).[12] Work-family experiences are also sometimes considered from the perspective of occupational social work.[13] A recent study conducted by Mor Barak, Nissly, and Levin (2001) found that the turnover among social workers was affected by several factors; however, work-family conflict was not a predictor of turnover among these workers.

As a result of our analysis of the work-family studies contained in the social work literature, we discovered that approximately one fifth of them focus on employee groups which hold less privileged positions at the workplace or on those employed in industries that tend to hire more vulnerable employees. For example, Marlow (1993) analyzed information gathered from clerical workers ($n = 226$) and found that the "most sought-after service was for flexible work hours for themselves and for their husbands in the case of married women" (p. 50). Other authors have focused on specific industry sectors, such as the service or hospitality sectors, which tend to employ hourly workers (for example, see Brownell, 1998; Cannon, 1998; Chung, 1998; Danes & Keskinen, 1990). Brownell (1998) discussed the work conditions, such as the unpredictability of tasks, sexualized jobs, low wages, and pressures for relocation, commonly found in the hospitality industry. MacDermid and Williams (1997) investigated the experiences of employees who work at small businesses (which often hired hourly wage workers) and compared their work-family experiences with those working at other workplaces. Finally, several of the articles examined the work-family experiences of human service/health care employees (see, for example, Collins, 1984; Fischel-Wolovick et al., 1988; Home, 1997; Jayaratne et al., 1986; Leiter & Durup, 1996; Mor Barak et al. 2001).

As a result of our analysis of the work-family articles, a dominant theme emerged: the consequences of workplace practices on employees. Specifically, studies investigated the consequences associated with long work hours (Brownell, 1998; Grosswald, 2002; Kingston & Nock, 1985), poor working conditions (Brownell, 1998; Grosswald, 2002; Kaye et al., 1999; Pleck et al.,1980), schedule incompatibility (Hattery, 2001; Grosswald, 2002), and involuntary plant closings (Root, 1984). Other studies have demonstrated that poor working conditions, such as limited job autonomy and scarcity of benefits, negatively impacted employee satisfaction and well-being (for example, see Gonyea, 1993; Home, 1997; Pleck et al., 1980; Seyler et al., 1995). Kingston & Nock (1985) analyzed the 1977 Quality of Employment Survey

($n = 668$) to determine the relationships between the number of hours worked and quality of life indicators. They found that variables related to work schedules affect the wives' quality of life experiences more than the husbands'. One of the interesting contributions of this study was the researchers' use of the measure of "family work day" (i.e., the combined hours worked by husbands and wives). This innovation facilitated analysis of work time at the family level, rather than only at the individual level.

Three of the articles identified as a part of our search studied families' experiences with job-induced separation, where one family member had moved to a location away from the rest of the family members due to job demands (Applewhite & Mays, 1996; Bowen, 1987; Van Breda, 1999). Van Breda (1999) identified several sets of factors that contributed families' resilience in these situations: emotional continuity, positive perspectives on separations, support systems, financial preparation, "partner-aware family structure," resilient children, and flexible marriage.

Some of the work-family articles included in the social work body of knowledge considered the resources needed by specific groups of employees at the workplace, and several of the articles focused on experiences of individuals transitioning from public assistance to paid employment (Cancian, 2001; DeBord et al., 2000; Solomon, 2001). DeBord et al., (2000) found that the presence of a job coach and employers' flexibility affect the extent of "fit" between the employees' family responsibilities and work expectations.

Our analysis of the social work articles found that many of them provided information about the adaptive strategies used by individuals and families as they either responded to the demands/expectations/constraints of the workplace or as they used different types of resources available in the meso settings (for example, see DeBord et al., 2000; Gringeri, 1995; Grosswald, 2002; Haddock et al, 2003;Hattery; 2001; Hofferth, 1999; Moen & Yu, 2000; Voydanoff, 1984; Voydanoff & Kelly, 1984; Wardlaw, 1994). For example, Wardlaw (1994) found that caregivers of people with AIDS used multiple strategies to adequately care for their loved ones and to minimize role strain, including changing jobs to those that offered work hours more aligned with caregiving demands, reducing work hours, or resigning from work. Grosswald (2002) examined the coping strategies for parenting adopted by public transportation shift workers, most of whom were from an ethnic minority population. She concluded that these workers could not rely exclusively on formal child care because the operating hours of most child-care centers could not accommodate their job schedules. As a consequence, the working parents found creative ways to care for their children, including allowing children to ride the bus, working shifts that accommodated their partners' job shifts, and using siblings to assist with child care. In other articles, authors discuss the outcomes associated with the work-family tactics and strategies adopted by working families. Hattery (2001) considered the costs and benefits to parents who work on shifts and who used tag-team parenting. This study found that families preferred this child-care strategy because it saved money and allowed for parents to be the sole caregivers. Finally, Gringeri (1995) identified the advantages and disadvantages of home-based piecework for working rural families. Although such arrangements were found to be extremely flexible and allowed parents to schedule the completion of their paid job responsibilities around their caregiving responsibilities, the author noted that piecework pays poorly, provides limited job benefits, and suffers from uneven work cycles.

Two of the articles reviewed for this chapter provide some insight about the impact that employer-supported work-family policies can have on the coworkers of employees who use those policies. Secret, Sprang, and Bradford (1998) gathered information about the outcomes of an informal policy adopted at one worksite, which allowed parent employees to bring their infants to the workplace and care for them while they worked (see also Sprang et al., 1999). This study found the coworkers reported that the "at-work infant care" policy had little or no negative impact on coworkers, who generally stated that they had positive attitudes toward the infant care option.

Although most work-family studies that document variables in meso social settings focus on workplaces as they are connected to the lives of working families, Secret et al. (2000) gathered information about the work-family responsiveness of workplace organizations that were all located in a single geographic community. The design of this study enabled the researchers to consider how communities might be able to facilitate the responsiveness of workplaces. Price (1985) also considered workplace–community relationships.

Our review found that many of the articles which analyzed work-family situations at the micro and/or meso levels commented on the impact that demographic trends and public policies have on the experiences of working families and on the responsiveness of employers. Consequently, macro social settings were perceived to be important contexts that frame the experiences of working families.

Macro Social Settings

The analysis of work-family experiences at the macro level considers the impact of society-at-large on organizations (such as the workplace) in the meso level as well as on families and on individuals in the micro level. Macro studies may analyze demographic trends (see, for example, Presser & Baldwin 1980), characteristics of the economy, social shifts, or public policies.

With few exceptions, the articles identified by our search of Social Work Abstracts acknowledged that work-family experiences are important social issues because macro economic circumstances and social policies have a profound impact on the experiences of working families. Many authors commented on macro issues in the introduction of their articles; 22 of the articles reviewed were specifically concerned about macro setting issues.

For some time, publications included in the social work literature have contended that work-family issues should be framed as "societal issues" relevant to public policy. The authors of these publications argue that work-family issues are not only "private issues" relevant to working women and men as well as their families, nor are they only "business issues" with implications for the workplace. Rather, work-family issues are social issues that are affected by public policy.[14]

The analysis of U.S. work-family policy is complicated because governmental bodies (at the local, state and/or national levels), employers, and nonprofit organizations *all* have some roles and responsibilities for the well-being of working families. Nearly three decades ago, Akabas (1984) authored an article that discussed these three components of the U.S. welfare system. She noted that boundaries of the roles assumed by the public sector, the business sector, and the nonprofit sector often seem "blurry," in part because the public sector has increasingly contracted with nonprofit organizations to provide services and has also established incentives/mandates for employers to respond to specific social issues, including the well-being of working families.[15] Akabas explained that society has responsibility for promoting the well-being of working families, particularly those families who have limited employment security, because families fulfill important societal functions, such as producing and nurturing future workers.

Many of the work-family articles discussed the inequities that have resulted from the transformation of labor market which occurred during the 1980s and 1990s (see, for example, Axinn & Stern, 1987; Johnson, 1987; Kahne, 1994). For example, social security policies have been problematic for many women who have worked part-time, have been employed as temporary workers, or have accepted lower-paying jobs with limited benefits so that they could better manage their work and family responsibilities (see discussion in Johnson, 1987).[16]

The body of social work literature includes analyses of current public policies as well as recommendations for policy change (see, for example, Finn-Stevensen & Trzcinski, 1991;

Hofferth & Deich, 1994). Finn-Stevensen and Trzcinski (1991) provided a comprehensive review of efforts to pass legislation for parental leave at the state and national levels. Other authors have compared U.S. policy to the policies promulgated in other countries (see, for example, Garrett & Wenk, 1990; Kissman & Solar Silva, 1994; Lundgren-Gaveras, 1996; Marlow, 1991). Lundgren-Gaveras (1996) considered the impact of public policies as well as employer-sponsored policies in the United State and in Sweden on working single parents. She concluded that single-parent families in the United State are more vulnerable due their disadvantaged positioning in the workforce.

SEEKING SOCIAL JUSTICE: CONNECTING RESEARCH TO PRACTICE AT THE MICRO, MESO, AND MACRO LEVELS

Social work's long-standing interest in the well-being of vulnerable populations reflects the profession's commitment to social justice. Since the early decades of the 20th century, a time when large numbers of immigrants arrived in urban communities in the United States, the field of social work has worked to end discrimination, oppression, poverty, and other forms of injustice. Constructs of social justice are often linked to assumptions about human rights.[17] Although there is variation in the operationalization of social justice, the definition often refers to two types of "person-in-environment" equities/inequities. Distributive justice refers to the differences in the access that specific individuals/populations have to the resources/forms of capital (including nonmonetary capital, such as social capital and political capital) that are distributed within society. Relational or procedural justice refers to the differences in the extent to which specific individuals/ populations are involved in the decision-making processes that directly or indirectly affect their well-being.[18] The social justice value that underpins all of the activities of the social work profession—research, education, and practice—encourages social workers to ask two fundamental questions with regard to work-family phenomena: Which families may become at-risk as a result of the demands placed on them or as a result of the limited resources available to them? What could be done to prevent or minimize unjust consequences?

The inequities embedded in the structure of the interactions that individuals and groups have with their environments help to frame the social justice agenda for social work scholars. Many of the work-family articles reviewed for this chapter consider social justice dimensions of work-family situations (for example, see Axinn & Stern, 1987; Clayton et al., 1998; Rossi, 1993). Axinn & Stern (1987), for example, identified changes in the social and economic environment (such as the growth of the service sector—which tends to pay low wages—and changes in social policies) as factors that have exacerbated the inequities faced by working women with dependent care responsibilities. Rossi (1993) used a feminist perspective to examine the lack of pay equity and the gendered division of labor at home.

The social work vision of social justice urges social workers to consider the possibilities of practice interventions and social change—at the micro, meso, and/or macro levels—that could improve the well-being of vulnerable populations. Studies that focus on the micro level may discuss options for intervention and support (see, for example, Jordan, Cobb & McCully, 1989). Some authors suggest that training or clinical interventions designed to enhance in-trafamilial relationships and/or to reduce stress/promote specific aspects of well–being should be considered. Van Breda (1999), for instance, pilot-tested seminars to enhance the resilience of the members of working families.

Social work publications that focus on the possibility of social change at the meso level often consider how the introduction of organizational changes could benefit working families, particularly those who are most vulnerable.[19] Social workers view organizational change as an opportunity to maximize person–environment fit, with the potential of creating healthy organizations that support healthy individuals at work (for example, see Burud et al., 1983; Chung, 1998; Faul, 2002; Fischel-Wolovick et al., 1988; Seyler et al., 1995; Swick & Rotter, 1981; Winett et al., 1982). Fischel-Wolovick et al. (1988) pilot-tested an intervention within a social work department at a major medical center to reduce employees' stress related to their work-family situations. The intervention consisted of the introduction of three types of flexible schedule arrangements. Overall, the results of the pilot project were positive, as measured by indicators such as an increase in the number of direct service hours and in the number of new cases opened by the social workers. In another article, Broman (2001) suggested that practitioners educate employees about stress management techniques as one way to help them manage job stress. Several of the articles reviewed recommended that employers consider expanding the resources of their Employee Assistance Programs (EAPs) to help employees meet the demands of work and caring for dependent family members (Casey & Pitt-Catsouphes, 1994; Scharlach & Boyd, 1989). Casey and Pitt-Catsouphes (1994) suggested that EAPs could provide support to working single mothers as they attempt to manage some of their work-family responsibilities. Other authors suggested options for improving work environments for employees, including those with caregiving responsibilities (for example, see Dinerman, 1992; Googins & Burden, 1987; Kahne, 1994; McNeeley, 1988; Osterman, 1995; Rossi, 1993). Dinerman (1992) outlined an action agenda, including the establishment of better maternity leave policies, child care, and greater equity in the workplace. In her review of social welfare and labor policies, Kahne (1994), a feminist economist, argued that the creation of quality part-time work with prorated wage and benefits could help to reduce burdened working parents by allowing more flexibility.

At the macro level, social work interventions might focus on options for increasing the equitable access that working families have to needed resources and supports. In a very forward-thinking article, Axinn and Stern (1987) suggested several public policy changes that could improve the well-being of working families, such as extending unemployment benefits, providing job training, offering earned income tax, and modifying the penalties associated with "quasi-retirees" who would like to work part-time but still remain eligible for social security and Medicare. These examples illustrate the connections made between policy analysis and social change in the social work literature.

CONCLUSION

The contributions made by many different disciplines and fields have enriched the state of work-family knowledge. The social work literature has added both depth and breadth to our understanding of the experiences of working families in several ways. First, the commitment of the social work profession to social justice offers a "human rights" framing of important work-family experiences. In addition, social work's focus on vulnerable populations facilitates the pursuit of research questions related to the full engagement of diverse individuals at the workplace and also fosters inquiries about the experiences of diverse families at home. The person-in-environment perspective contextualizes the experiences of working families in different social environments. Finally, the emphasis on "evidence-based practice" helps to connect social work studies to training and education (for example, see Linbom, 1995; Noor, 1996) and to the work-family experiences of practitioners who are employed by social service organizations that offer support to working families (for example, see Leiter & Durup, 1996; Mor Barak et al., 2001; Rotman, 1989).

Clearly, other disciplines have also conducted studies about social justice/equity, the experiences of marginalized populations, and opportunities for social change. However, these issues constitute the heart and soul, as well as the intellectual framework, for the social work approach to understanding the experiences of working families.

NOTES

[1] For example, Andrew Scharlach has written extensively on a range of work-family topics and recently co-edited an important volume with another social work scholar (Fredriksen-Goldsen & Scharlach, 2000).

[2] For instance, Susan Lambert's (1993) article, "Workplace Policies as Social Policy," was not identified during the search.

[3] As examples, articles authored by Lambert (1999, 2000) and Pitt-Catsouphes (MacDermid, Litchfield, & Pitt-Catsouphes, 1999) were published in social science journals but not in journals referenced in the Social Work Abstracts.

[4] Johnson, 1999; Meyer & Mattaini, 1998.

[5] Meyer & Mattaini, 1998. See also Bronfenbrenner, 1986.

[6] See discussion in Kondrat, 2002.

[7] For further discussion, see Kemp et al., 1997, pp. 41–43.

[8] Social exclusion theory also helps to define groups that may be considered to be at-risk. The International Labor Organization (2001) defined social exclusion as, "a state of poverty in which individuals cannot access the living conditions which would enable them to both satisfy their essential needs (food, education, health, etc.) and participate in the development of the society in which they live. The analysis of social exclusion is concerned with the causes of poverty, the specific nature of the essential *needs in different societies, access to the services and opportunities which would make it possible to meet these needs and the civil and political rights of individuals.*" (http://portal.unesco.org/shs/en/ev.php-URL_ID=3016&URL_DO=DO_TOPIC&URL_SECTION=201.html (italics added by authors). We have used the ILO's working definition of social exclusion because it links social exclusion to vulnerable populations, offers a functional operationalization, and reflects an international interpretation. As well, the definition identifies both individual and system factors associated with social exclusion.

[9] The ecosystems theory also recognizes a fourth system: the exosystem. This system is used to designate settings that can have an indirect impact on an individual. For example, a parent's workplace would be an exosystem for a child. The designation of exosystems varies depending on the focus of the analysis; therefore, we have omitted this system from our discussion.

[10] For further discussion, see Kemp et al., 1997, pp. 70–73.

[11] As noted by Mor Barak & Bargal (2000), occupational social work attempts to: "Improve the fit between the needs of individuals and their families, work organizations, and communities; help people in need of employment transition into jobs and become gainfully employed; introduce to the workplace social work values and principles, such as valuing diversity and balancing family needs with work demands; and generate knowledge in the area of social work and the world of work that will inform practice and policy" (p. 4).

[12] See also Faul, 2002; Mor Barak, 2000a. Poverny (2000) noted that employers' definitions of "family" determine the experiences of inclusion/exclusion at the workplace with regard to access to benefits (adoptive parents, foster parents, gay/lesbian parents).

[13] See also the impact of layoffs and health and wellness issues (Bargal, 2000).

[14] See Googins, 1991; Lambert, 1993; and Pitt-Catsouphes & Googins, 2005.

[15] In an article that has become one of the "seminal" publications on work-family, Lambert (1993) concluded that it is important for the public sector to assume different roles for the well-being of working families, in part because some employer-sponsored work/life policies and programs (such as weekend child care) are initiated in response to business needs but may, in fact, exacerbate the tension and stress experienced by some working families.

[16] As noted by Iversen (1998), "economic restructuring and radical changes in welfare policy are producing increasing social dislocation and disadvantage among both employed and unemployed people in the United States. Such disadvantage is experienced strongly by women, members of racial and ethnic minority groups, and youths" (p. 551).

[17] See Lowery (1998).

[18] See discussion in Longres & Scanlon, 2001.

[19] Johnson (1999) referred to social workers' efforts to facilitate the successful interface between individuals and their environments as "indirect" social work. Indirect practice is usually considered in contrast to "direct practice," which often takes the form of services (such as counseling) provided to individuals/groups who are in need of assistance.

REFERENCES

Akabas, S. H. (1984). Workers are parents too. *Child Welfare, 63*(5), 387–399.

Akabas, S., & Gates, L. (2000). A social work role: Promoting employment equity for people with serious and persistent mental illness. *Administration in Social Work, 23*(3/4), 163–184.

Anastas, J. W., Gibeau, J. L., & Larson, P. J. (1990). Working families and eldercare: A national perspective in an aging America. *Social Work, 35*(5), 405–411.

Applewhite, L. W., & Mays, R. A. (February 1996). Parent child separation: A comparison of maternally and paternally separated children in military families. *Child and Adolescent Social Work Journal, 13*(1), 23–39.

Avioli, P. (1985). The labor-force participation of married mothers of infants. *Journal of Marriage and the Family, 47*(3), 739–745.

Axinn, J., & Stern, M. J. (1987). Women and the postindustrial welfare state. *Social Work, 32*(4), 282–286.

Bargal, D. (2000). The future development of occupational social work. *Administration in Social Work, 23*(3/4), 139–156.

Bowen, G. L. (June 1987). Single fathers in the air force. *Social Casework, 68*(6), 339–344.

Broman, C. L. (July 2001). Work stress in the family life of African Americans. *Journal of Black Studies, 31*(6), 835–846.

Bronfenbrenner, U. (1986). Ecology of the family as a context for human development: Research perspectives. *Developmental Psychology, 22*(6), 723–742.

Brownell, J. (1998). Striking a balance: The future of work and family issues in the hospitality industry. *Marriage and Family Review, 28*(1/2), 109–123.

Burud, S. L., Collins, R. C., & Divine, H. P. (1983). Employer supported day care. *Children Today, 12*(3), 2–11.

Cancian, M. (October 2001). Rhetoric and reality of work based welfare reform. *Social Work, 46*(4), 309–314.

Cannon, D. F. (1998). Better understanding the impact of work interferences on organizational commitment. *Marriage and Family Review, 28*(1/2), 153–166.

Casey, J. C., & Pitt-Catsouphes, M. (1994). Employed single mothers: Balancing job and homelife. *Employee Assistance Quarterly, 9*(3/4), 37–53.

Chilman, C. (1993). Parental employment and child care trends: Some critical issues and suggested policies. *Social Work, 38*(4), 451–460.

Chung, B. G. (1998). Accounting for changing times: Aligning human resources practices to employees nonwork lives. *Marriage and Family Review, 28*(1/2), 143–152.

Clayton, H. R., Odera, V., Emenheiser, D. A., & Reynolds, J. S. (1998). The relationship of job satisfaction and family life: Female managers in health care food service. *Marriage and Family Review, 28*(1/2), 167–185.

Collins, S. K. (1984). A comparison of top and middle level women administrators in social work, nursing, and education: Career supports and barriers. *Administration in Social Work, 8*(2), 25–34.

Crouter, A. C. (1982). The children of working parents. *Children Today, 11*(4), 25–28.

Crouter, A. C. (1984). Spillover from family to work: The neglected side of the work family interface. *Human Relations, 37*(6), 425–441.

Danes, S., & Keskinen, S. (Summer 1990). The extent of off-farm employment and its impact on farm women. *Human Services in the Rural Environment, 14*(1), 10–14.

DeBord, K., Canu, R. F., & Kerpelman, J. (2000). Understanding a work family fit for single parents moving from welfare to work. *Social Work, 45*(4), 313–324.

Dinerman, M. (Summer 1992). Is everything women's work? *Affilia: Journal of Women and Social Work, 7*(2), 77–93.

Eggebeen, D., & Hawkins, A. (1990). Economic needs and wives' employment. *Journal of Family Issues, 11*(1), 48–66.

Etaugh, C., & Folger, D. (1998). Perceptions of parents whose work and parenting behaviors deviate from role expectations. *Sex Roles, 39*(3/4), 215–223.

Faul, A. (2002). Comprehensive assessment in occupational social work: The development and validation of the corporate behavioral wellness inventory. *Research on Social Work Practice, 12*(1), 47–70.

Finn-Stevenson, M., & Trzcinski, E. (October 1991). Mandated leave: An analysis of federal and state legislation. *American Journal of Orthopsychiatry, 61*(4), 567–575.

Fischel-Wolovick, L., Cotter, C., Masser, I., Kelman-Bravo, E., Jaffe, R. S., Rosenberg, G., & Wittenberg, B. (1988). Alternative work scheduling for professional social workers. *Administration in Social Work, 12*(4), 93–100.

Fox Folk, K., & Beller, A. (1993). Part-time work and child care choices for mothers of preschool children. *Journal of Marriage and the Family, 55*(1), 146–157.

Fredriksen-Goldsen, K., & Scharlach, A. (Eds.). (2000). *Families and work. New directions in the twenty-first century.* New York: Oxford University Press.

Freedman, R. I., Litchfield, L. C., & Warfield, M. E. (October 1995). Balancing work and family: Perspectives of parents of children with developmental disabilities. *Families in Society, 76*(8), 507–514.

Garrett, P., & Wenk, D. (1990). Working around childbirth: Comparative and empirical perspectives on parental-leave policy. *Child Welfare, 69*(5), 401–413.

Gelles, R. J., & Hargreaves, E. F. (1981). Maternal employment and violence toward children. *Journal of Family Issues, 2*(4), 509–530.

Gonyea, J. G. (1993). Family responsibilities and family oriented policies: Assessing their impacts on the work place. *Employee Assistance Quarterly, 9*(1), 1–29.

Googins, B. (1991). *Work/family conflicts: Private lives—public responses.* New York: Auburn House.

Googins, B., & Burden, D. (1987). Vulnerability of working parents: Balancing work and home roles. *Social Work, 32*(4), 295–299.

Grahame, K. M. (March 2003). "For the family": Asian immigrant women's triple day. *Journal of Sociology and Social Welfare, 30*(1), 65–90.

Gray, E. B., Lovejoy, M. C., Piotrkowski, C. S., & Bond, J. T. (June 1990). Husband supportiveness and the well being of employed mothers of infants. *Families in Society, 71*(6), 332–341.

Greenberger, E., & Goldberg, W. (1989). Work, parenting, and the socialization of children. *Developmental Psychology, 25*(1), 22–35.

Grimm-Thomas, K., & Perry-Jenkins, M. (April 1994). All in a day's work: Job experiences, self esteem, and fathering in working-class families. *Family Relations, 43*(2), 174–181.

Gringeri, C. E. (Spring 1995). Flexibility, the family ethic, and rural home-based work. *Affilia: Journal of Women and Social Work, 10*(1), 70–86.

Grosswald, B. (September 2002). "I raised my kids on the bus": Transit shift workers' coping strategies for parenting. *Journal of Sociology and Social Welfare, 29*(3), 29–49.

Haddock, S. A., Zimmerman, T. S., Current, L. R., & Harvey, A. (2003). The parenting practices of dual-earner couples who successfully balance family and work. *Journal of Feminist Family Therapy, 14*(3/4), 37–56.

Hattery, A. J. (July–August 2001). Tag-team parenting: Costs and benefits of utilizing nonoverlapping shift work in families with young children. *Families in Society, 82*(4), 419–427.

Herring, C., & Wilson-Sadberry, K. (1993). Preference or necessity? Changing work roles of Black and White women, 1973–1990. *Journal of Marriage and the Family, 55*(2), 314–325.

Hofferth, S. (1999). Child care, maternal employment and public policy. *Annals of the American Academy of Political and Social Science, 563,* 20–38.

Hofferth, S. L., & Deich, S. G. (September 1994). Recent U. S. childcare and family legislation in comparative perspective. *Journal of Family Issues, 15*(3), 424–448.

Home, A. M. (Spring/Summer 1997). Learning the hard way: Role strain, stress, role demands, and support in multiple-role women students. *Journal of Social Work Education, 33*(2), 335–346.

Iversen, R. (November 1998). Occupational social work for the 21st century. *Social Work, 43*(6), 551–578.

Jackson, A. P. (September 1992). Well being among single, Black, employed mothers. *Social Service Review, 66*(3), 399–409.

Jackson, A. P. (January 1993). Black, single, working mothers in poverty: Preferences for employment, well-being, and perceptions of preschool-age children. *Social Work, 38*(1), 26–34.

Jackson, A. P. (March 1994). The effects of role strain on single, working, Black mother's perceptions of their young children. *Social Work Research, 18*(1), 36–40.

Jackson, A. P., & Huang, C. C. (1998). Concerns about children's development: Implications for single, employed Black mothers' well-being. *Social Work Research, 22*(4), 233–240.

Jayaratne, S., Chess, W., & Kunkel, D. (January–February 1986). Burnout: Its impact on child welfare workers and their spouses. *Social Work, 31*(1), 53–59.

Johnson, B. B. (1987). The changing role of women and social security reform. *Social Work, 32*(4), 341–345.

Johnson, P. J. (1983). Divorced mother's management of responsibilities: conflicts between employment and childcare. *Journal of Family Issues, 4*(1), 83–103.

Johnson, Y. (July 1999). Indirect work: Social work's uncelebrated strength. *Social Work, 44*(4), 323–345.

Jordan, C., Cobb, N., & McCully, R. (January 1989). Clinical issues of the dual-career couple. *Social Work, 34*(1), 29–32.

Kahne, H. (September 1994). Part-time work: A reassessment for a changing economy. *Social Service Review, 68*(3), 417–436.

Kamerman, S., & Hayes, C. (Eds.). (1982). *Families that work: Children in a changing world.* Washington, DC: National Academy Press.

Kamerman, S., & Kahn, A. (1978). *Family policy: Government and families in fourteen countries.* New York: Columbia University Press.

Kamerman, S., & Kahn, A. (1981). *Child care, family benefits, and working parents: A study in comparative policy.* New York: Columbia University Press.

Kamerman, S., & Kahn, A. (1987). *The responsive workplace: Employers and a changing labor force.* New York: Columbia University Press.

Kamerman, S., & Kahn, A. (1991). *Child care, parental leave, and the under 3s: Policy innovations in Europe.* New York: Auburn House.

Kamerman, S., & Kahn, A. (1997). *Family change and family policies in Great Britain, Canada, New Zealand, and the United States.* Oxford, UK: Clarendon Press.

Kaye, L. W., Alexander, L. B., & Kauffman, S. (1999). Factors contributing to job quality and satisfaction among ethnically diverse, lower income, elderly part-timers. *Journal of Gerontological Social Work, 31*(1/2) 143–166.

Kemp, S., Whittaker, J., & Tracy, E. (1997). *Person-environment practice. The social ecology of interpersonal helping.* New York: DeGruyter.

Kingston, P. W., & Nock, S. L. (1985). Consequences of the family workday. *Journal of Marriage and the Family, 47*(3), 619–629.

Kissman, K., & Solar Silva, M. (1994). Women in Chile: Wage labor and child care in families headed by mothers. *International Social Work, 37*(1), 37–46.

Kolodinsky, J., & Shirey, L. (April 2000). The impact of living with an elder parent on adult daughters' labor supply and hours of work. *Journal of Family and Economic Issues, 21*(2), 149–175.

Kondrat, M. (October 2002). Actor-centered social work: Re-vision "person-in-environment": Through a critical lens. *Social Work, 47*(4), 435–449.

Krauskopf, M. S., & Akabas, S. H. (1988). Children with disabilities: A family/workplace partnership in problem resolution. *Social Work Papers, 21*, 28–35.

Lambert, S. (1993). Workplace policies as social policy. *Social Service Review, 67*(2), 237–278.

Lambert, S. (1999). Lower-wage workers and the new realities of work and family. *The Evolving World of Work and Family: New Stakeholders, New Voices. The ANNALS of the American Academy of Political and Social Science, 562,*174–190.

Lambert, S. (2000). Added benefits: The link between work-life benefits and organizational citizenship behavior. *Academy of Management Journal, 43*(5), 801–815.

Lechner, V. M. (July 1993). Support systems and stress reduction among workers caring for dependent parents. *Social Work, 38*(4), 461–469.

Lechner, V. M., & Sasaki, M. (1995). Japan and the United States struggle with who will care for aging parents when caregivers are employed. *Journal of Gerontological Social Work, 24*(1/2), 97–114.

Leiter, M. P., & Durup, M. J. (March 1996). Work, home, and in-between: A longitudinal study of spillover. *Journal of Applied Behavioral Science, 32*(1), 29–47.

Lindbom, J. (1995). Addressing the needs of working mothers: The changing context for occupational social work education. *Journal of Teaching in Social Work, 12*(1/2), 85–103.

Longres, F., & Scanlon, E. (Fall 2001). Social justice and the research curriculum. *Journal of Social Work Education, 37*(3), 447–467.

Lowery, C. T. (1998). Social justice and international human rights. In M. Mattaini, C. T. Lowery, & C. H. Meyer (Eds.). *The foundations of social work practice: A graduate text* (p. 20–42). Washington, DC: NASW Press.

Lundgren-Gaveras, L. (March 1996). The work-family needs of single parents: A comparison of American and Swedish policy trends. *Journal of Sociology and Social Welfare, 23*(2), 131–147.

MacDermid, S., Litchfield, L., & Pitt-Catsouphes, M. (1999). Organizational size and work-family issues. *The Evolving World of Work and Family: New Stakeholders, New Voices. The ANNALS of the American Academy of Political and Social Science, 562,* 111–126.

MacDermid, S., & Williams, M. (1997). A within-industry comparison of employed mothers' experiences in small and large workplace. *Journal of Family Issues, 18*(5), 545–566.

Marlow, C. (1991). Women, children and employment: Responses by the United States and Great Britain. *International Social Work, 34*(3), 287–297.

Marlow., C. (Spring 1993). Coping with the multiple roles: Family configuration and the need for workplace services. *AFFILIA: Journal of Women and Social Work, 8*(1), 40–55.

McNeeley, R. L. (1988). Managing work and family demands: Strengths, weaknesses and barriers to implementing twenty innovative programs. *Social Work Papers, 21*, 1–15.

Meyer, C., & Mattaini, M. (1998). The ecosystems perspective: Implications for practice. In M. Mattaini, C. T. Lowery, & C. H. Meyer (Eds.), *The foundations of social work practice: A graduate text* (p. 3–19). Washington, DC: NASW Press.

Moen, P., & Yu, Y. (August 2000). Effective work/life strategies: Working couples, work conditions, gender and life quality. *Social Problems, 47*(3), 291–326.

Mor Barak, M. E. M. (2000a). Beyond affirmative action: Toward a model of diversity and organizational inclusion. *Administration in Social Work, 23*(3/4), 47–68.

Mor Barak, M. E. M. (2000b). Repositioning occupational social work in the new millenium. *Administration in Social Work, 23*(3/4), 201–210.

Mor Barak, M. E. M., & Bargal, D. (2000). Human services in the context of work: Evolving and innovative roles for occupational social work. *Administration in Social Work, 23*(3/4), 1–11.

Mor Barak, M. E., Nissly, J. A., & Levin, A. (December 2001). Antecedents to retention and turnover among child welfare, social work, and other human service employees: What can we learn from past research? A review and metanalysis. *Social Service Review, 75*(4), 625–661.

Mukhopadhayay, S. (1996). Working status and health: A study of middle-class Calcutta women. *The Indian Journal of Social Work, 57*(2), 327–336.

National Association of Social Workers. (1999). Code of Ethics. Alexandria, VA: NASW Press. Avasilable online at: http://www.socialworkers.org/pubs/code/code.asp.

National Association of Social Workers. (2000). Social work speaks. In *National Association of Social Workers Policy Statements* (p. 229–233). 2000–2003. Alexandria, VA: NASW Press.

Noor, N. M. (September 1996). Women, work and family: Emerging social issues and their implications on social work education. *Asia Pacific Journal of Social Work, 6*(2), 87–104.

Olsen, F. (October 1992). Does enough work make women free? Part-time and full-time work strategies for women in the United States and Germany. *Indian Journal of Social Work, 53*(4), 599–610.

Osterman, P. (December 1995). Work/family programs and the employment relationship. *Administrative Science Quarterly, 40*(4), 681–700.

Paulson, S. (1996). Maternal employment and adolescent achievement revised: An ecological perspective. *Family Relations, 45*(2), 201–208.

Pitt-Catsouphes, M., & Googins, B. (2005). The paradox of corporate solutions: Accomplishments, limitations, and new opportunities. In J. Heymann & C. Beam (Eds.), *Unfinished business: Building equality and democracy in an era of working families* (pp. 224–250). New York: The New Press.

Pleck, J. H., Staines, G. L., & Lang, L. (1980). Conflicts between work and family life. *Monthly Labor Review, 103*(3), 29–32.

Poverny, L. (2000). Employee assistance practice with sexual minorities. *Administration in Social Work, 23*(3/4), 69–91.

Prasad, B. D. (July 2001). Maternal employment and child abuse. *Indian Journal of Social Work, 62*(3), 328–346.

Presser, H. B., & Baldwin, W. (1980). Child care as a constraint on employment: Prevalence, correlates, and bearing on the work and fertility nexus. *The American Journal of Sociology, 85*(5), 1202–1213.

Price, R. H. (1985). Work and community. *American Journal of Community Psychology, 13*(1), 1–12.

Riger, S., Ahrens, C., & Blickenstaff, A. (Summer 2000). Measuring interference with employment and education reported by women with abusive partners: Preliminary data. *Violence and Victims, 15*(2), 161–172.

Romito, P., Saurel Cubizolles, M. J., & Cuttini, M. (1994). Mothers' health after the birth of the first child: The case of employed women in an Italian city. *Women and Health, 21*(2/3), 1–22.

Root, K. (September 1984). The human response to plant closures. *Annals of the American Academy of Political and Social Science, 475*, 52–65.

Root, L. (2000). Education and training in the workplace: Social work interventions in the private sector. *Administration in Social Work, 23*(3/4), 13–28.

Rosenzweig, J. M., Brennan, E. M., & Ogilvie, M. (October 2002). Work family fit: Voices of parents of children with emotional and behavioral disorders. *Social Work, 47*(4), 415–424.

Rossi, A. S. (1993). The future in the making: Recent trends in the work family interface. *American Journal of Orthopsychiatry, 63*(2), 166–176.

Rotman, A. (Winter 1989). Female social workers: Career or family? *Affilia: Journal of Women and Social Work, 4*(4), 81–90.

Sancier, B., & Mapp, P. (Summer 1992). Who helps working women care for the young and the old? *Affilia, 7*(2), 61–76.

Scharlach, A. E., & Boyd, S. L. (1989). Caregiving and employment: Results of an employee survey. *The Gerontologist, 29*(3), 382–387.

Secret, M., Sprang, G., & Bradford, J. (November 1998). Parenting in workplace: Examining a unique infant care option. *Journal of Family Issues, 19*(6), 795–815.

Secret, M., Sprang, G., Rompf, E. L., & Anderson, D. G. (2000). A community based study of family friendly workplaces. *Journal of Community Practice, 8*(1), 1–20.

Seyler, D. L., Monroe, P. A., & Garand, J. C. (March 1995). Balancing work and family: The role of employer-supported childcare benefits. *Journal of Family Issues, 16*(2), 170–193.

Solomon, B. (September 2001). The ins and outs of welfare to work: Women as they enter and exit a nursing assistant employment and training program. *Journal of Sociology and Social Welfare, 28*(3), 157–186.

Sprang, G., Secret, M., & Bradford, J. (Spring 1999). Blending work and family: A case study. *AFFILIA—Journal of Women and Social Work, 14*(1), 98–116.

Swick, K., & Rotter, M. (Winter 1981). The workplace as a family system support. *Day Care and Early Childhood Education, 9*(2), 7–11.

Van Breda, A. D. (1999). Developing resilience to routine separations: An occupational social work intervention. *Families in Society, 80*(6), 597–605.

Voydanoff, P. (1984). Economic distress and families: Policy issues. *Journal of Family Issues, 5*(2), 273–288.

Voydanoff, P., & Kelly, R. F. (1984). Determinants of work related family problems among employed parents. *Journal of Marriage and the Family, 46*(4), 881–892.

Wardlaw, L. A. (June 1994). Sustaining informal caregivers for persons with AIDS. *Families in Society, 75*(6), 373–384.

Williams, J. (2001). Journals of the century in social work. *The Serials Librarian, 39*(3), 69–77.

Winett, R. A., Neale, M. S., & Williams, K. R. (1982). The effects of flexible work schedules on urban families with young children: Quasi-experimental, ecological studies. *American Journal of Community Psychology, 10*(1), 49–64.

Zimmerman, I. L., & Bernstein, M. (1983). Parental work patterns in alternative families: Influence on child development. *American Journal of Orthopsychiatry, 53*(3), 418–425.

Zvonkovic, A. M., Schmiege, C. J., & Hall, L. D. (April 1994). Influence strategies used when couples make work-family decisions and their importance for marital satisfaction. *Family Relations, 43*(3), 182–188.

PART III: Methodological Approaches

Introduction: How Diverse Methodologies Inform Understandings of Work and Family Relations

Stephen Sweet
Ithaca College

Marcie Pitt-Catsouphes
Boston College

Ellen Ernst Kossek
Michigan State University

Disciplinary traditions vary not only in their perspectives on the connections between work and family, as amply demonstrated in Section II of this volume, but also in the approaches or methods used to understand phenomena. The chapters that follow in Section III have been selected to enable readers to gain an appreciation of the diversity of methodologies being applied to the study workplace and family relationships. In order for epistemologies to be shared, not only do basic assumptions and fundamental views need to be bridged, but also approaches to and ways of knowing. When we looked at the existing books on work and family, we saw a critical gap—there is a lack of discussion of the breadth of methods, the varieties of technologies, and the range of sampling strategies being used by the different discipilines. Bridging these divides opens a horizon of new opportunities in the work and family field.

It was clear to us that the disciplinary perspectives of the scholars influenced their selection of the preferred unit of study. These can range from individuals, couples, work groups, organizations, communities, legal structures, and other structural and cultural arrangements. We also saw conventional differences in what was measured and not measured. Sometimes the center of attention was on psychological dispositions, and at other times the focus for work and family researchers was on organizational-level decision making in response to strategic change, productivity outcomes, family relationship qualities, or time resources. To collect this information, a variety of strategies were used, including direct observation, participant–observer surveys, interviews, organizational records, and legal archives. In essence, because work and family is a multi-disciplinary endeavor, it is also necessarily a multi-methodological endeavor that requires adoption of a variety of approaches for the empirical study of workplace and family connections.

In developing this section, we asked authors to provide an overview of their customary methodologies and the types of knowledge they can reveal about working families, jobs, and employers. We asked them to bring us into their world of research and to highlight some of the challenges they faced, as well as the strategies they used to overcome these concerns. We also asked them to reflect on the limitations of their methodologies as well as share advice for shaping future research agenda.

Social science is not particularly conducive to the application of rigorous scientific methods, in part due to the ethical considerations of studying people and the logistical challenges of cataloguing human experience, development, and organization. For work-family researchers the problems of finding and effectively applying the right methodology are particularly vexing, owing to the need of infiltrating and connecting the unique institutional arrangements of the workplace and family. As Lewis Coser (1974) argued, the family and the workplace share much in common as "greedy institutions." These institutions can require intense loyalty and demand much on the part of their members, not the least of which are heavy time and emotional commitments. Most importantly from a methodologist's perspective, as cultural institutions, the workplace and the family tend toward privacy rather than disclosure. Work-family researchers must convince families and organizational gatekeepers to permit members to take time from their busy schedules and open their lives and experiences for study.

Consider, for instance, the insights Charles Darrah offers in his overview of ethnographic methodology (chapter 17), the methodological approach favored by cultural anthropologists. Darrah demonstrates the challenges and rewards of creating rich, thick, in-depth descriptions of the contexts of work and family lives. For Darrah, ethnography is as much a goal as it is a methodology, because it is uniquely designed to provide measures of the subjective experiences and understandings of the worlds that engage working families. For work and family researchers, this involves time-intensive activities, such as shadowing working men and women in the home and workplace, and their travels between. By bringing us inside the life-worlds of 14 working families in Silicon Valley, Darrah demonstrates the limited ability of the commonly accepted metaphors of "balance" and "juggling" to accurately capture the objective and subjective realities of work and family life. Better, argues Darrah, is the notion of "busyness," a concept that highlights the fragmented demands and selves created by contemporary arrangements.

While Darrah's ethnographic approach emphasizes the use of shadowing techniques and the analysis of field notes, Elinor Ochs, Anthony Graesch, Angela Mittmann, Thomas Bradbury, and Rena Repetti approach ethnographic research with the use of video cameras and systematic tracking of family members within household space (chapter 18). Ochs and her team stress the importance of understanding the interpersonal dynamics within situational encounters that form social rituals that charge family cohesion, such as the moments when working men and women return home, as well as the interaction of families with the material objects that surround their lives. By tracking families within the home, videotaping their encounters, and studying their conversations, her team documents the extent to which family members contact one another as well as the terms and qualities of these interactions. In their studies, they find low occurrence of all family members congregating or participating in similar activities within the first few hours of returning home from work. Additionally, the sequencing of the mother's and father's returns from work influence the nature of encounters with children, with fathers on the whole arriving later and experiencing greater difficulty integrating themselves into family interactions established in their absence. This research highlights the challenges families face in forging cohesive bonds, which tend to be hampered by the scheduling demands associated with dual-earner lives.

As Darrah and Ochs and her colleagues note, the quantity and quality of observations can be remarkably impressive with the use of methods developed by anthropologists. However, an inherent limitation in ethnographic research, as applied to work and the family, is the small number of families that can be observed by any research team, which in turn influences the prospects of generalizing findings to more diverse populations, or to make comparisons between distinct groups. In contrast, the capacity to generalize and make statistically significant comparisons is one of the strengths of survey research. In chapter 19, James Bond and Ellen Galinsky provide an overview of the substantial work that has been conducted by the Families and Work Institute using survey methods. By illustrating the types of surveys they (and others) have conducted and identifying some key findings emerging from those studies, Bond and Galinsky show how carefully worded questions, fielded to large samples of participants across major corporations, offer the opportunity to detail how work and family experiences, needs, and opinions vary. In a useful overview of the central concerns of survey methods, the authors offer a helpful guide through considerations of sampling strategies, designing, and successfully implementing survey instruments.

Generally, telephone surveys, such as those developed by Bond and Galinsky, are conducted as directed dialogues between the interviewers and individual participants. Alternate strategies of interviewing are equally valuable, such as in-depth face-to-face interviews. In chapter 20, Janet Smithson outlines yet another methodology, the use of focus groups and group interviews. The focus group usually comprises a homogenous assembly of 6 to 12 people who maintain shared interests, and is guided by a moderator. "Running" the conversation is actually a group activity, as the pursuit of related issues emerge as a result of collective discussion. There are considerable advantages to using discussion groups as the unit of analysis because it affords researchers the opportunity to examine how group members "co-construct" their knowledge and perspectives. For example, Smithson shows how a discussion of family leave policy quickly became redefined as "unfair" to people who do not have children. By posing issues and recording the emergent dialogue, the focus group method especially lends itself to understanding how people form their perspectives on work and family concerns and policy.

In the previous section on disciplinary perspectives, many authors advocated for studies conducted over time—through the course of the day, through the course of a life, or even across historical eras. Ann Crouter and Amy Pirretti (chapter 21) offer an overview of longitudinal research methodologies and demonstrate how they can be applied to work and family issues over the life course. By performing repeated measurements on the same individuals or groups over time, longitudinal research is one of the most productive means of testing hypotheses of cause and effect relationships. These repeated measurements (i.e., data of the same indicators assessed multiple times on the same subject) can occur in a variety of temporal patterns, such as changes that occur after a long interval of time has elapsed or changes that occur annually, weekly, daily, or in accordance with life stage (such as transitions into parenthood or retirement). Crouter and Pirretti accomplish two important tasks in their chapter. First, they show that longitudinal research, in accordance with a variety of temporal conditions, has been applied to the study of work and family. Second, they show how longitudinal findings substantiate causal effects that remain merely "associational" in cross-sectional data. Although many challenges are inherent to longitudinal methods (including concerns of participant attrition, monetary expense, and time demands), these authors offer a compelling argument for the expansion of longitudinal research efforts, as they are crucial to the advancement of life course, life span, and evaluation research.

In chapter 22 Barbara Schneider extends the concern of integrating a temporal dimension to work and family research, illustrating the unique and robust contributions of the experience sampling method (ESM). First developed in the 1970s, ESM studies time use with the assistance of beepers, personal digital assistants (PDAs), or programmable wristwatches that signal participants to record their primary and secondary activities, as well as their affect, at random or specified moments in the day and week. By charting these observations across time, Schneider documents the devotion of family members to different activities throughout the day, how they feel about those activities, stress issues that emerge, and the times in the day and week at which family members' subjective experiences enhance or deteriorate. The potential of ESM to enhance understanding of family time use, applied through projects at the University of Chicago's Sloan Center's Study of Youth and Social Development, is now reaching fruition. One notable observation, for instance, is the trajectories the subjective experiences of husbands and wives take during transitions from work to home in the late afternoon and evening. This methodology complements, and in some respects improves on, the reliability concerns that are present in retrospective accounts of the use of time (such as those obtained in time diaries or surveys).

Most of the methods we have discussed thus far tend to focus on the personal aspects of work and family research. Other methods are uniquely designed to focus on characteristics and operations of the organizations in which working families are employed. In chapter 23, Suzan Lewis, Maria Das Dores Guerreiro, and Julia Brannen make a case for the case study method. They argue that an intensive analysis of a single company, workplace, or group of workers can reveal the workplace structures, practices, and cultures that limit (or potentially expand) opportunities to harmonize work and family responsibilities. Their descriptions of existing case studies reveal that these methods are best suited to describing *how* particular policies or cultures impact workers' lives, as well as generating understandings of *why* people behave in the manner that they do. In some respects, the case study (like ethnography) is better characterized as an "approach" than a specific methodology, as the types of data collected vary depending on both the research questions and the extent to which opportunities are afforded research teams. The authors highlight successful strategies of gaining access to organizations, selecting and interviewing key informants, and gauging formal and informal organizational hierarchies.

Susan Lambert extends this concern in chapter 24, discussing methods of obtaining and analyzing organizational documentation. Lambert makes a compelling argument that the types of data customarily collected by companies (such as absenteeism, promotion, employee turnover, performance reviews, family leave usage, sales figures, profit statements, etc.) are both under-utilized and central to making the "business case" for work-family policy. She notes, however, that these data can be prone to concerns of limited validity, which is the degree to which researchers can be sure that they accurately measure what they purport to measure. They also can have uncertain reliability or contain systematic variation that results from inconsistent record-keeping practices. Despite these potential limitations, Lambert argues that they are generally more accurate than self-reports, which are the most commonly relied on indicators of employee productivity and work commitment.

Some of the challenges of using organizational documents involve gaining the trust of organizational gatekeepers (such as managers or owners), learning the types of data that are available, gauging the strengths and limitations of the information recorded, adjusting analytic strategies to accommodate those concerns, and harmonizing research questions with data availability. In a demonstration of its application, Lambert shows that existing data in a mid-sized manufacturing plant revealed that workers tend to reciprocate their appreciation for family-friendly policies with increased productivity. She also shows that organizational records can sometimes be used to distinguish employer *policy* (what is formally stated) from employer *practice* (what is actually implemented). Such is the case when a program or policy is on the books, but records show it seldom used or has little impact on the lives of employees.

As Lambert discusses, one of the challenges of using organizational records is in gaining access to these files. Anticipating this concern, some readers will be especially interested in chapter 25, wherein MaryAnne Hyland and Susan Jackson consider the types of outcomes that are of interest to owners and investors, customers, top management, employees, spouses and children, and communities. They argue that the availability of data and the unique interest of academic research should not be the sole driving force in determining research methodology. Instead, they argue for crafting research projects to correspond with the interests of other stakeholders, which in turn will open doors with greater ease. A significant contribution of their chapter is a careful consideration of the varieties of data of interest to groups that have a vested concern in work-family issues. By summarizing key findings and approaches to gathering those data, they bring us closer to matching research activities and design to suit the interests of receptive audiences.

Among the most significant recent developments in social science research are advances in statistical techniques. As Raymond Swisher demonstrates in chapter 26, the application of hierarchical models holds great potential in connecting the experiences of individuals and couples to the companies and communities in which their lives are embedded. These multi-level models offer innovative ways of assessing person and environmental fits and mismatches. Although only of recent invention, multi-level applications are already present in many statistical programs and have been used by many of the authors in this handbook. We believe Swisher's assertion is correct – that the future of work-family research will necessarily involve greater attention to the dynamic interplay of the characteristics of individuals, families, and their environmental contexts. Although grasping hierarchical methodology can be challenging even for those with advanced statistical capabilities, Swisher offers one of the most accessible illustrations available, as well as applies it to work and family research.

Work and family research involves making connections between institutional arrangements, and therefore also requires the consideration of causal relationships. In chapter 27, Shelley MacDermid and Ashley Harvey consider the concept of work and family conflict and challenge the work and family community to consider the causal connections that are implied in its study. On the one hand, work and family conflict can be an outcome—the result of institutionalized practices that put work roles and family roles at odds with one another. Alternately, it can be viewed as a predictor of a variety of experiences (such as stress) or shape decisions (such as when to have a child). MacDermid and Harvey suggest that one important direction to pursue is to not only understand the predictions and outcomes, but also why some individuals fare better or worse in similar circumstances. They suggest that this may require pursuing the study of work and family conflict in the manner outlined by other methodologies outlined in this section, such as the need for longitudinal study and hierarchical analyses that link individuals with their environmental contexts.

The final chapter in this section, by Margaret Neal, Leslie Hammer, and David Morgan, ties together many of the methodologies discussed by other authors. Rather than focusing on a single methodology, these authors outline the strategies of applying multiple methodologies to the study of work and family. They suggest that some research projects will benefit immensely by combining quantitative (statistical) and qualitative (discursive) methods. One advantage of these methods, when applied to individuals and organizations, is that they can facilitate the creation of hierarchical analyses, such as those described by Swisher. These authors argue that mixed methodologies also offer the advantage of complementing and overcoming the inherent limitations of single method studies. For example, the integration of qualitative methods (such as the focus group method described by Smithson) offers the advantage of creating inductive insights, and these insights can then later be used in the development of quantitatively oriented instruments such as surveys (such as those described by Bond and Galinsky). The successful application of mixed methods can lead to the creation of convergent findings that bolster confidence in the conclusions generated by a single methodology, as well as create connections between discrete findings. Additionally, the careful consideration of multiple methods can enable researchers to close the holes of questions left unanswered by a single methodology. Neal, Hammer, and Morgan provide a significant contribution by identifying the logistical challenges in implementing mixed methodologies (including staffing, time, expense, and coordinating activities), as well as highlighting the empirically driven concerns of methodology selection, sequencing of activities, and weighting study components in a multi-methodological design.

We hope readers find these chapters of value to their research activities. We believe that no single methodology or combination of methodologies is inherently superior. Our hope is that this presentation of the current diversity of methodologies being applied to the study of work and family will further stimulate the integration and cross-fertilization of approaches developed by the different disciplines. By bridging methodological divides and integrating findings, not only can we triangulate the state of the knowledge of working families and their employers (from their successes to failures, their needs to their resources), but also better fine-tune our instruments, approaches, and analytic techniques to answer the emerging questions in the challenging field that attempts to connect the workplace to the family.

REFERENCE

Coser, L. (1974). *Greedy institutions: Patterns of undivided commitment*. New York: Free Press.

17

Ethnography and Working Families

Charles N. Darrah
San Jose State University

Ethnography, once largely associated with anthropologists studying apparently "exotic" cultures, has become an increasingly accepted research approach in the social sciences and beyond. Of course, the association of ethnography itself with anthropology has always been imperfect. Likewise, anthropology is a broad discipline and its research methods are not exhausted by ethnography. Nonetheless, ethnography has been central to cultural anthropology, and it is there that it has arguably been most developed and refined as a research approach. This chapter argues that ethnography, as it is conceptualized and practiced by anthropologists, can provide a productive source of research strategies for family and work researchers.

Already a somewhat eclectic approach to social research, its very definition has become murky as ethnography has become popularized. It is frequently defined as a set of research methods (or techniques) for learning about social phenomena, with specific ways of interviewing and observing cited as its hallmarks. Claims to be conducting ethnographic interviews, for example, assume that an interview has characteristics, such as a structure of open-ended questions, that make it essentially ethnographic. Yet while the ways that ethnographers conduct interviews are perhaps distinctive, they are far from unique. What makes interviewing (or observing) ethnographic has to do both with how it is conducted and with its place in a larger research process.

In order to understand how ethnography can be useful to work-family researchers, the interplay between discrete methods (and techniques) and this larger process must be explicated. Doing so is the goal of this chapter. It seeks to provide an overview to a set of methods that are associated with ethnography, but that may be used independently by work-family scholars who may not identify themselves as ethnographers. It also describes a larger ethnographic research process in which various methods and techniques are incorporated. While the goal of the chapter is not one of conversion to anthropology, the ethnographic research process makes sense within a broader set of assumptions and values about people and societies. Ethnography as a research process is thus as much about thinking about social life as it is about collecting data.

Ethnographic studies of working families are especially important today. The family takes variable form and performs different functions in different societies (Harrell, 1997), and it is being remade yet again due to societal changes. These include the widespread availability of new technologies; economic restructuring that is affecting jobs, skills, and careers; intensified globalization (however defined); and redefinitions of the role of the state. The family, which in its modern form has been increasingly organized around providing support and companionship to its individual members, has suddenly been thrust into the role of buffer against the risk of uncertainties that are themselves dynamic. Under such conditions, ethnographic studies that allow us to trace the effects of macro-level change on everyday lives and social institutions are critical.

This chapter attempts to provide an overview to an ethnography that is relevant to such conditions. It begins by presenting a narrow view of ethnography as a set of methods and techniques. Next, it situates ethnographic methods in the discipline of anthropology with its four-field approach, characteristic concepts and theories, and use of the comparative method. An ethnographic case study of work and family is then presented, one that hopefully provides a sense of the rhythms of ethnography as well as its advantages and limitations. Finally, the chapter closes by describing the larger cycles of research in which the case study is embedded in order to answer the question, Why "do" ethnography?

ETHNOGRAPHY AS METHOD

Despite its increased use, definitions of ethnography vary. Its popularity likely reflects acknowledgment of the limitations of quantitative, positivist methodologies, but it is not synonymous with qualitative research (Bernard, 2002). While it is true that many ethnographies are long on text and short on numerical data, ethnography often begins with a census, and surveys may provide data used in ethnographic accounts. Participant observation is, for some researchers, synonymous with ethnography (Hammersley & Atkinson, 1983, p. 2), while for others it is but a first step in a larger methodology (Agar, 1996). Ethnography is sometimes portrayed as a fundamentally descriptive endeavor, but ethnographers acknowledge the role of theory in shaping their initial observations. If, as Hammersley and Atkinson (1983) claimed, ethnography is the most basic form of social research, resting as it does on how people ordinarily investigate and understand unfamiliar social settings, then the variety of definitions is unsurprising. After all, we use a variety of strategies to comprehend social life, and so ethnography should reflect that epistemological and methodological diversity.

Definition by enumeration provides another way to define ethnography. LeCompte and Schensul (1999) argued that it is carried out in the natural (or "cultural") settings where people live their lives, rather than in a researcher's office, laboratory, or other contrived setting. Even when interviews are undertaken, they are usually carried out on the interviewee's "turf," or where an activity typically occurs. Despite a recent fascination with online communities, ethnography has historically entailed intimate face-to-face contact between the researcher and the members of the group, community, or category of people being studied. Such intimacy is a function of the prolonged personal engagement of the ethnographer in a community, allowing ethnographers and community members to encounter each other in a variety of settings. Indeed, it is the very absence of control that permits the depth and breadth of insights that can emerge through ethnographic fieldwork.

In order to capture the behaviors and perspectives of the participants in an activity or community, the ethnographer adopts the role of a learner who is attempting to figure out the appropriate questions to ask, rather than that of the expert who knows the questions and is only trying to get them answered. Although ethnographers necessarily become conversant with relevant literatures about people, issues or ideas, it is equally true that most are motivated by the sense that there is something important but hidden that can only be learned through extended participation in local settings. Ethnography is inductive and recursive, using multiple forms of quantitative and qualitative data in order to explicate and model local knowledge. Ethnographers are keenly sensitive to the meanings of action to people and the larger contexts within which they exist. Situating beliefs and actions within cultural contexts is at the heart of the ethnographic enterprise, and so bold generalizations are often eschewed in favor of more modest specifications of the conditions under which actions occur and make sense. Ethnographers are thus students of conditions and contexts as much as they are of actions and beliefs.

Ethnography, like any research methodology, is useful under particular conditions, and knowing them is essential (LeCompte & Schensul, 1999; Bernard, 2002). The methodology is especially useful when phenomena are just emerging or are poorly understood. It can clarify both the characteristics of a phenomenon and its relationships to specific conditions, and is especially useful in explicating hidden processes or systems of things, people, and meanings. Ethnographers are able to capture espoused assumptions and values as well as those inferred from practices and the unintended consequences of activities. Although it is largely inductive and based on an abiding respect for fine-grained data (and not sweeping generalizations), it also explicates assumptions, problematizes basic categories of thinking, and thereby allows us to imagine the consequences of alternative social arrangements.

Because of its flexibility, ethnography also articulates with other methodologies. Its focus on emergent or poorly understood phenomena, and the often taken for granted categories by which we think about social life, allow it to play an important role in pilot projects for quantitative approaches. Ethnography can support developing clearer conceptualizations of a phenomenon from the perspectives of different stakeholders, and to thereby develop more sensitive indicators and measures. It is also used to explore the implications of quantitative findings in the lives of actual people, thereby bringing such findings to life and further exploring their consequences (Bernard, 2002).

Although both work and family are familiar cultural domains, each the subject of extensive scholarly literatures, both are being transformed today and we cannot take for granted their meanings. Furthermore, many questions cannot be answered by looking deeply into each domain, but rather they require us to explore the interstices between them. Questions about the latter merge with questions about the communities in which people live, and the global flows of ideas, capital, and people that shape them. Accordingly, work-family research provides the very conditions under which ethnographic fieldwork is appropriate.

If ethnography is often defined by its methods, those methods are heterogeneous. Precisely which methods make a research project ethnographic are unclear, as is what a researcher means when claiming to be "doing ethnography." Alternatively, the *sine qua non* of ethnography may not be its individual methods, but the way they are incorporated into a larger process. From this perspective, we may use one or more of the methods of ethnography without "doing ethnography," if we reserve the latter for a larger process that is grounded in the assumptions and values of anthropology. This larger process has at least three characteristics. First, it unfolds over months or years so that even a seeming snapshot of a social setting or system incorporates its history. Second, it captures the meaning of activities to different participants who often hold inconsistent views. And, third, it has a direction that begins with open inquiry and that gradually (and using multiple methods) converges on topics whose importance emerges through fieldwork. It is how the methods of ethnography fit into this process that makes a project ethnographic.

Specific ethnographic methods are well described in numerous books,[1] and they will only be introduced here. The starting point is typically participant observation, which is less a specific method than a strategy for collecting data, especially during the initial stages of fieldwork. It can, however, constitute the primary strategy for data collection in specific projects. Participant observation involves living with the people being studied, observing social settings and the activities that occur in them, and participating as appropriate in people's lives. Ethnographers undoubtedly differ in their relative preferences for active participation and reflective observation, and the conditions of fieldwork can limit the opportunities for either. Regardless, participant observation dispels the notion that the ethnographer is a neutral scientist standing apart from the action. Ideally, he or she is in the thick of things, and it is by studying there that the ethnographer develops the relationships necessary for fieldwork, experiences that provide the basis for subsequent interviews and systematic observations, and an intuitive sense of cultural rules. By demonstrating the commitment to learning, the ethnographer develops the trust that encourages the people being studied to deem him or her worthy of their time, attention, and confidences.

Interviews, too, comprise an essential set of methods that allow the ethnographer to capture what people say they are doing and what they say they should be doing. Cycles of ethnographic interviewing typically begin with loosely structured, open-ended interviews that sound almost conversational as they proceed. In fact, they do not follow the normal rules of conversational turn taking, and are carefully structured to elicit basic cultural domains, often building on the hunches gleaned from participant observation. Schensul, Schensul, and LeCompte (1999, pp. 137–138) suggested structuring such interviews around asking for lists (e.g., "What are the activities you do together as a family?" or "In what ways do you think your job affects your children?") and narratives of experience (e.g. "Tell me about what you did the last time you were ill.").

Semistructured interviews assume the relevance of particular domains (usually established through participant observation and unstructured interviewing) and allow the ethnographer to flexibly explore them. Although the line between them and unstructured interviews is fuzzy, they are used to further elaborate specific cultural domains that are relevant to the goals of the project and to develop more sensitive variables and instruments for further data collection. They thus lie at the intersection of exploratory and explanatory phases of research. Such interviews are carefully structured, but at the heart of both unstructured and semistructured interviews is the ability to spontaneously probe an interviewee in order to elicit more detailed information and to follow up on emerging themes. Probing is important because it places the ethnographer in the role of attentive student or learner, and because it helps generate information that is salient to the interviewee.

Structured interviewing converts exploratory data into instruments that conceptualize and measure the relationships between cultural domains. Such instruments take the form of questionnaires and cultural domain analyses, both of which underlie the creation of formal models of culture. Ethnographic surveys may appear similar to others used in the social sciences, but they are only the final step in an often lengthy process of discovery of the categories that are salient to people in a setting. Cultural domain analysis consists of a variety of techniques used to rigorously study how people "think about lists of things that somehow go together" (Bernard, 2002, p. 280), as well as their characteristics and the principles of classification. Both ethnographic surveys and cultural domain analyses represent the culmination of the ethnographer's role as learner in those settings.

Systematic observation complements interviewing as a basis of ethnography, and indeed the commitment to getting at what people actually do is a distinct contribution of ethnography. Observation should not be undertaken lightly, for it is time-consuming and so drives up the costs of fieldwork. An interview conducted with just the right person can effectively compress weeks or even years of potential observation into minutes or hours, thereby enhancing the efficiency of data collection. Yet as useful as interviews are, they provide a thin and potentially distorted understanding of social life, especially if they focus on the question of what people do or did. Not only can people lie, but also memory is selective and not all behavior can be verbalized. Interview-based accounts of behavior can present the latter as more rational and predictable than it really is, and through observation we capture the contingencies and improvisations that characterize everyday life. It is not that observation is paramount, but rather it is by exploring how verbalized descriptions articulate with observable actions that ethnography's potential to deliver insights is realized.

Bernard (2002, pp. 390–426) distinguished between direct and indirect strategies for observing. In direct observation, the ethnographer observes behavior as it occurs, using such techniques as continuous monitoring, spot sampling, and time allocation studies. In indirect observation, the ethnographer observes only the traces of previous behavior. Examples include observations of buildings and built landscapes, as well as features such as graffiti or outputs like garbage. Archival research, too, constitutes a form of indirect observation since it results from previous behaviors that are not directly observed. Strategies for observing have been most dramatically transformed by new information technologies, and the use of videotaping, digital photography, and pagers is widespread in contemporary ethnography, although use of such devices in natural settings does not mark a project as ethnographic.

Two facets of ethnography that are salient to work-family researchers can thus be distinguished. It can be viewed as a set of methods and techniques that can be independently adopted. From this perspective, knowing about ethnography is useful because it provides research tools that can be used even if a project is not fully ethnographic. Alternatively, work-family researchers can focus on ethnography as a larger methodology, quite apart from its specific methods. It provides a systematic way to address research questions while retaining a methodological flexibility that is responsive to local conditions. Here its value is less in its methods per se than in the way it structures our thinking about how to investigate a phenomenon. The danger lies in separating the methods from the larger methodology that gives them meaning and power.

ETHNOGRPAHY AS ANTHROPOLOGY

Ethnography is also situated within the discipline of anthropology, which provides an intellectual context that gives the methods their meaning. The discipline is not silent on issues of families and work, and the American Anthropological Association has published a research agenda on middle-class working families (Overbey & Dudley, 2000). Research to date has focused on work and families, the importance of material culture, and the uses of technology to mediate work and family. Future research into the life course, public life, and personhood are suggested.

Apart from a research agenda, the discipline of anthropology has several characteristics that are germane to ethnographers of families. These include a four-field approach to studying humans, a distinctive conceptual and theoretical basis, and a comparative perspective.

The discipline's constituent fields of archaeology, linguistic anthropology, physical anthropology, and cultural anthropology are distinct in the social sciences. Cultural anthropologists are especially concerned with practices that link social organization, including families, with cultural models and their material embodiments. They are sensitive to inconsistencies or contradictions between structural constraints, lived experience, and familiar cultural assumptions, values, and norms. Distinctive characteristics of cultural anthropology include a holistic analysis of social systems, attention to the often-divergent understandings of people, and concern with the meaning of action to participants.

Linguistic anthropology focuses both on the primary means by which children are socialized into social practices and the categories into which fundamental cultural models are organized.

The paradigm of language socialization, for example, assumes that "language is a form of social action, as well as a critical means of social reproduction and transformation across generations" (Paugh, 2002, p. 2). By adopting the paradigm, anthropologists examine the activities and interactions of everyday life in which children both participate and observe. It is thus useful for understanding how children gain practical knowledge of adult spheres of life, such as family and community obligations, work practices, and notions of the good life. Research within the paradigm explicates how a family is created and maintained through talk, such as through recounting personal narratives, issuing and listening to directions or instructions, and choosing topics of conversation (Paugh, 2002, pp. 5–13).

Physical anthropology draws our attention to the interplay of cultural practices and meanings with human biology. For example, the work of Carol Worthman and her colleagues at the Emory University Center for Myth and Ritual in American Life (MARIAL) seeks to create a biocultural model that systematically links social structure, culture and meaning, and the well-being of people. Their working model combines the methods and concepts of cultural consensus modeling, status incongruity, and the analysis of cultural models with psychobiological models of stress, affective regulation, and reactivity (Worthman, DeCaro, & Brown, 2002).

Archaeology provides tools for handling and drawing inferences from material artifacts and configurations. It can be used to analyze the material worlds of families who, after all, are profoundly shaped by the constraints of space and time. The methods of archaeology can be used to analyze the architecture of houses, the organization and use of spaces within them, and their provisioning with artifacts (Arnold & Graesch, 2002), as well as homes and yards (Arnold & Lang, 2003).

Just as anthropology's four-field approach provides one context for ethnography, the discipline's master concepts provide another. While a summary of the theoretical bases of the discipline is far beyond the scope of this chapter, Perry (2003) provided a useful starting point for further exploration. Perry argued that the discipline has developed around five "key concepts" which anthropologists simultaneously embrace and debate. Positions vis-à-vis these concepts are reflected in the formulation of questions or problems that ethnographers investigate, how they collect data, and the way they typically frame analyses and interpretations.

The concept of evolution sensitizes anthropologists to time and the relativity of observations, as well as to the importance of adaptation to constraints and the transformation of social systems. It also underlies their concern with humans as biological organisms. The anthropological concept of culture as being learned, shared, and symbolic provides the discipline's enduring contribution to the social sciences. Simultaneously central and diversely defined, culture underlies the ethnographer's concern with symbolism and the meaning of actions to people. In contemporary anthropology, it links a concern with the larger systems in which actions are taken and rendered meaningful, with the knowledge that individual actors possess in order to demonstrate competence. The related concept of relativism is also variously defined, but minimally can be expressed as a methodological principle that analysts cannot explain action without understanding the social and cultural systems in which it is produced. The concept of structure suggests that the parts of society, however conceived, are less important than their relationships and how they form emergent phenomena, such as a family emerging from a collection of individuals. Furthermore, it suggests that such structures conform to rules about which humans may be unaware, such as rules of reciprocity. Finally, the concept of function suggests that practices and institutions may have effects in society quite apart from those that human participants may acknowledge.

In addition to these broad organizing concepts, anthropology, like any discipline, provides specific theories that can be used as models to explain different phenomena. For example, theories of optimal foraging strategies (Cashdan, 1989; Halperin, 1994), originally developed to apply a microeconomic approach to how hunters and gatherers allocate their time to procure specific resources, can in principle stimulate theorizing about the allocation of time in middle-class working families. Likewise, an emerging synthesis of human ecological and political–economy perspectives to explain the effects of childhood poverty in Andean families can potentially generate insights into the effects of work-family juggling on the children of dual-career couples (Thomas, 1998). Such models are not simply transferred to a different phenomenon, but rather they stimulate new questions and propositions about it.

Anthropology also is predicated upon the value of cross-cultural comparisons. While such comparison is not systematically incorporated into every ethnographic monograph, anthropologists are sensitive to the possibilities of cultural variation and they eschew bold, broad generalizations based on just one culture. Even when a specific project is narrowly focused, anthropology's adherence to the comparative method can debunk crude notions of causality or necessity and expand thinking about the range of possible family arrangements.

From one perspective, nearly the entire corpus of ethnographic studies can be viewed as a source of cross-cultural information about families, as well as the myriad other topics ethnographers typically include when describing a social system. Such ethnographies may seem archaic or exotic to the contemporary work-family researcher, but they document the creative capacity of humans to adapt to different circumstances. Other publications address topics that may be of more direct use and interest to prospective work-family ethnographers. Anthropologists have long conducted cross-cultural studies of families (e.g., Harrell, 1997), kinship (e.g., Schweizer & White, 1998), and household economies (e.g., Small & Tannenbaum, 1999), each of which can enrich ethnographies of working families. Comparative studies of childhood (e.g., Olwig & Gullov, 2003), parenting (e.g., Harkness & Super, 1996), and aging (e.g., Sokolovsky, 1997) can help ethnographers of working families frame new questions around the human life-course. Specific studies, too, may incorporate an explicitly cross-cultural perspective, such as Tsuya and Bumpass's (2003) comparative study of marriage, work, and family in Japan, South Korea, and the United States.

Several resources directly or indirectly support the comparative perspective of anthropology. The Human Relations Area File (HRAF) is an archive of ethnographic materials from about 360 societies that can be used in formulating cross-cultural hypotheses. The literature of anthropology can be explored using databases such as Anthropological Index Online, Anthropological Literature, and Abstracts in Anthropology.

Understanding "doing ethnography" thus involves more than our earlier distinction between methods and methodology, for it also establishes our relationship to intellectual traditions and corpuses of data. Researchers as reflective practitioners must think through the consequences of how their use of ethnography articulates with the tenets of their own discipline, and how it can potentially be enriched by using anthropological resources. Ethnography is central to anthropology precisely because it reflects the basic assumptions and values of the discipline. Its power inheres not just in its methods or methodology, but in the larger intellectual tradition in which its practitioners are socialized. The implication is that it is possible to master the methods and methodology of ethnography without producing the kind of analyses and insights that they do when anthropologists use them.

HEADING FOR THE FIELD: THE ETHNOGRPAHY
OF DUAL-CAREER FAMILIES

Methods, methodology, and discipline connote a tidiness that often vanishes during fieldwork. The very power of ethnography lies in the commitment to study social life for extended periods in natural settings, and so it ultimately translates into a distinctive engagement with people on their own terrain. Ethnographers do not simply implement a research plan. Rather, the latter provides a base from which to launch an effort to learn what is important about a social setting, and the lessons may not be the ones we expected to learn. Fieldwork can thus seem messy and profoundly frustrating, but its very difficulties and dilemmas also provide the opportunities for serendipitous insights. Recognizing these opportunities, and using even the pitfalls of fieldwork as means to collect data and refine analyses, is central to the promise of ethnography.

Here we explore ethnography in practice by delving into a project undertaken by the author, J. A. English-Lueck, and J. M. Freeman in the Silicon Valley region of northern California. The purpose of the 2 year project was to understand how 14 dual-career families addressed the often-competing obligations of jobs, careers, and family.[2]

Because our sample was small, selection of families was critical.[3] Random sampling was both impossible and inappropriate, and instead a major objective was to maximize the variability within the sample along several dimensions. First, income provided a relatively poor criterion for middle-class status in a region where the median house price hovered at about $500,000. Still, the team sought several families whose members expressed middle-class values about lifestyle and education, but who were struggling financially to realize their aspirations. In addition, the team sought at least one family whose income and lifestyle placed it beyond the middle class, at least from the perspective of professors at a public university.

In addition, we sought to include families that varied in ethnicity or country of origin. The intention here was not to seek a representative sample, since to do so was meaningless with such a small sample size. Instead, we assumed that a culturally diverse sample of families would increase the variety of strategies used to balance work and family that we could observe during fieldwork, thereby making our analysis more robust. We also recruited families that included a sample of workers from the public and private sectors as well as from different industries. In addition, we tried to select some families with parents who held similar jobs (e.g., two attorneys) and others whose jobs are dissimilar (e.g., a firefighter and a high-tech marketer).

Recruitment was time-consuming and difficult due to the intrusive nature of the fieldwork and the duration of the study. We used several strategies to publicize the project and to invite participation. First, we drafted advertisements to run repeatedly in newspapers directed at parents in the region and several families were recruited through such means. Second, we prepared advertisements to be run in several newspapers targeted at specific ethnic or religious communities. Developing this publicity was a time-consuming and iterative process. For example, finding Vietnamese-American families that would participate required effort by Freeman over 4 months, culminating in a successful advertisement that appeared in a Vietnamese-language newspaper. Third, the team aggressively sought opportunities to speak about its research, using such events as opportunities to recruit potential families. Ultimately, several speeches facilitated the distribution of flyers that found their way into the hands of people interested in the project. Fourth, we produced and mailed a newsletter that updated the participants from a previous project and tried to enlist them in finding families for the new project. This strategy was strikingly unproductive, and so most of the participating families turned out to be complete strangers to all members of the team prior to their agreement to participate.

Inquiries about the project arrived by e-mail, telephone, and through face-to-face meetings. They ranged from a few casual remarks to well-prepared cases advocating for a family. Because inquiries were heterogeneous (and frequently ambiguous), it is difficult to enumerate them, but we estimate that we responded to over 200 inquiries. In some cases, people simply wanted to vent frustration at their own pace of life and they acknowledged they did not even meet the criteria for participation (e.g., they had no children or a spouse was not employed).

A member of the team handled each inquiry so that (ideally) the person responding to the initial inquiry would be the one who would ultimately be responsible for the fieldwork. The team member described the project and determined if the family in question included a dual-career middle-class couple. Then, he or she described the nature of the fieldwork in order to eliminate those families and individuals that believed that participation consisted merely of answering a survey, an all too common misunderstanding. If the family met the criteria to participate, fit into the sampling strategy, and remained interested, a meeting was scheduled with either the person who initiated contact or with the entire family. No family was allowed to participate without a meeting between the fieldworker and all family members.

Recruitment to participation was accordingly far from simple, easy, and direct; after all, only a small minority of inquiries resulted in participating families. Many families were initially interested, but they subsequently decided that they were too busy or under too much stress to allow our intrusion into already hectic schedules. Sometimes one person strongly advocated participation, but others were indifferent or even opposed. And, in still others, it was impossible to obtain all the necessary human subjects permissions in order to proceed. Participation thus necessitated a sequence of decisions by family members followed by agreements from schools, child-care providers, and employers, as well as favorable assessments by the project team.

Family members reportedly participated for one or more reasons. Many people were familiar with various traditions of empirical research through their education or job. They valued such an approach to social issues and contrasted it with the often-unsupported pronouncements they encountered in the media. Some were especially fascinated by the idea of ethnography and wanted to experience it firsthand. In addition, many people were sympathetic to the goal of better understanding how middle-class families try to balance or juggle the demands of work and family. They believed that the topic was important yet overlooked, and they viewed participation as a way to contribute to their community. Most families, too, had at least one person who viewed participation as a way of reflecting on the family's practices. They were proud of their family and sought ways to improve its capacity to cope with complex responsibilities. Although the ethnographers made it clear that therapy was not forthcoming, some families sought to use their participation as such. Finally, some individuals recognized the importance of the project and wanted to make sure that families of their ethnicity or ancestry were included.

From the start, we faced fundamental logistical choices concerning where to conduct fieldwork and who to conduct it with, since we expected family members to be mobile and separated during much of the day. A first decision was that only one ethnographer would study each participating family in order to maximize logistical continuity. Indeed, each member of the team never met the members of families they did not personally study. A drawback of this approach might be the absence of alternative field perspectives and practices, but we believe the gains in trust and intimacy (not to mention convenience for the participants) were essential to meeting the project goals.

Fieldwork was divided into three rough phases that were adapted to the circumstances of each family. First, the ethnographer accompanied the individual family members during their days, often remaining with them for 10–12 hours at a time. For adults, this meant arriving at the family home before that day's family member departed on his or her commute, "shadowing" the person while they worked, and then returning home with them at the end of the day, often stopping to collect children or dinner on the way. For children, the ethnographer typically arrived at home to accompany the child to school (or day care prior to school), spent the day sitting in classes, and accompanied the child to his or her after school activities. Child and fieldworker returned home together, usually after being picked up by a parent. The fieldworker usually terminated the day's fieldwork upon returning home, since the "shadowee" was usually ready to escape the company of the ethnographer. Likewise, the intensity of note taking often left the fieldworker exhausted, so ending fieldwork at this juncture was mutually agreeable.

This first and most intense phase of fieldwork typically lasted 2 to 4 months, depending on the number of families under study and the schedules of the members. A fieldworker usually spent 4 complete days with each family member, resulting in between 140–170 hours of initial contact time per family. This first phase of fieldwork focused on the lives of individual family members (although they were sometimes physically or virtually co-present). The second phase focused on more collective "family activities." The ethnographer often began this phase by arriving at the family home when one or more family members had arrived after school, work, or errands. He or she joined the family for dinner and after dinner activities, such as completing homework, attending meetings (e.g., Cub Scouts), watching television, or playing video games. The ethnographer also scheduled time with the family on weekends in order to observe activities ranging from running errands or performing chores, to hosting baptisms or family reunions. In addition, the individuals were asked to think about activities or events that expressed something important or distinctive about their family, and to notify the fieldworker when an appropriate opportunity to participate–observe arose. This phase concluded after about 2 months, although some significant activities or events were often not observed until much later (or sometimes, earlier).

Finally, we remained in touch with family members for another 4 to 8 months, asking about changes in the family and the work routines of its members, and visiting to capture important activities or events. Phone calls and e-mails were used to keep up with the family, sometimes augmented by monthly lunches or coffees. Indeed, the fieldworkers remain in touch with most families, some of whom have been assimilated into their own network of friends. Although not a formal part of the research design, this continued contact has contributed to our understanding of family rhythms and changes.

The basic output of fieldwork was field "jottings" made in several ways. Ideally, we made jottings with a laptop computer or mobile field device (e.g., Hewlett Packard Jornada), but we often switched to a steno book under some conditions. For example, the electronic devices were difficult to use while riding in automobiles or walking around, and they made people uncomfortable in some settings (e.g., performance reviews with supervisors, religious services, etc.). Whatever the form, field jottings had to be converted into fleshed-out, word-processed field notes, a chore that could take as many hours as the original observations (especially when working from handwritten notes).

Fieldwork thus took the form of classic ethnographic participant observation. Sometimes participation dominated, as a fieldworker joined a family at a party, Easter egg hunt, or holiday dinner. At other times, especially while a family member was at work or school, observation dominated. The interplay of participation and observation was extremely fine-grained. For example, laws and occupational, professional, or organizational policies and practices sometimes constrained fieldwork, as when English-Lueck shadowed a pair of attorneys or I, a fireman. In the former, English-Lueck could not be present during client meetings, nor could she have access to client materials. In the latter, I was always instructed where to stand and what to say to observers who might not understand my role. In neither case were we invited to participate respectively in the work of litigation or fire fighting. Yet the balance could shift abruptly to participation. For example, I shadowed someone at a corporate board meeting and was asked to sign a nondisclosure agreement and admonished to remain silent throughout the meeting, which, I was informed, could prove to be tense or even hostile. Yet within 30 minutes, board members solicited my opinions about the organization of the company. Thus, participant observation often had a roller-coaster quality of oscillations between involvement and detachment, coolness and intimacy, and informality and formality.

Ethnographic fieldwork, like all research, involves ethical issues, and research with families can be especially sensitive. Ethnographers share with other researchers the obligation to prevent harm to the people involved in their projects. That participants must consent to participate in the research is a basic obligation, but one which can nonetheless be difficult to achieve. Consider requests to complete a survey or questionnaire in which the person completing it can explicitly do so. Ethnography presents different conditions, for people who have not given their consent, and who may not even be aware of the project, are often encountered in the course of fieldwork. Such occurrences were common in our project, as we shadowed members of our focal families at work, school, and in myriad settings that we could not anticipate.

Consent must not only be freely given, but it must also be informed. It is rare that participants in a research project will or can have the same understandings of its purpose as do the researchers. This translation problem is exacerbated in ethnography by its exploratory nature, for we often cannot specify with precision what we hope to discover and how we plan to do so. Even what counts as data can be problematical. In the ethnography of dual-career families, we were often asked if we would be jumping out of bushes or peering in bedroom windows, all in the name of ethnography. We carefully explained that the ethnographer and family members would discuss and jointly decide the schedule of participant observation: There would be no surprise visits. Yet soon into fieldwork we discovered that the telephone calls we made to schedule visits were fertile sources of data. People had become sensitized to what we were interested in and used the calls to provide updates on their family, and even to think through impending family decisions. From our perspective, these conversations functioned as informal, de facto interviews in which the salience of the family member's remarks could be assumed. Weeks later, we realized that while *we* viewed these conversations as rich sources of data, *they* might not since they occurred outside the boundaries of a scheduled visit. The solution was to continue scribbling notes during the calls, but to confirm the comments during fieldwork.

Provisions for privacy, confidentiality, and anonymity must also accompany informed consent. Informed consent was always secured through signed forms, approved by the university's Institutional Review Board, that explained participants' rights of privacy, confidentiality, and anonymity. Separate forms were completed for each family member, by the principals of children's schools, and by employers. Such permissions sometimes took lengthy negotiations, and on several occasions the unwillingness of even one party to sign prevented an otherwise willing family from participating.

Despite the general precautions taken, ethical issues abound in fieldwork and ethnographers can feel caught between contradictory admonitions. When we encountered a family member's acquaintances in a new setting, we could neither assume they knew about the project nor could we inform them that the person we were with was a participant, for doing so would violate their privacy. Usually, the participant would introduce the ethnographer as such and briefly explain the project, as when the author's presence at a large birthday party was explained by the announcement, "Some families have psychologists, but ours has an anthropologist." Although greeted by good-natured laughter, this points to the much broader issue of how to collect data in settings with people whose consent is tacit at best. It also reflects how the families are represented, especially when those representations depend on interactions with a wider network of kin, friends, classmates, and coworkers.

Another peculiarity of ethnography is the extended duration and unpredictability of fieldwork. Ethnographers witness things that could be embarrassing, harmful to reputations, or even illegal, and fieldwork results in deep intrusions that expose mutual vulnerabilities. For example, we sometimes knew of children left alone before parents returned home from their jobs, and had to ask if what we were witnessing constituted child endangerment. While we were comforted that we never confronted anything that required us to report activities to legal authorities, we were well aware that conditions could change instantaneously.

The intrusiveness of fieldwork is manifested not only in what we see, but also in the relationships that develop between ethnographers and those they study. Those relationships do not (and need not) always result in close friendships, but it is difficult to maintain the stance of dispassionate scientist for a year. Initially, families were uncertain about the limits of the relationship, and more than once we were asked if they had to pretend we were not present while they were eating dinner, all in the interest of science. Even if that had been ethnographically desirable, it clearly violated rules of hospitality, and we routinely dined with the families. Doing so yielded important data and avoided an awkward situation, but it also meant we broke bread with the people we were studying. Clearly, friendships formed, but they were friendships of a special kind and had to be treated as such by both participants and researcher.

The complications of friendship can be categorized as advice, intervention, and advocacy. The participants in the study were living lives not unlike our own, and it could be tempting to offer advice. For example, a parent might be struggling to find a supervised activity for a child at a particular time and, because we lived in the same region, we might know of a likely possibility. If we offered it we were helping someone who was clearly helping us, but we would also be shaping the very strategies we were there to observe; thus, we remained silent. More typical were requests from a family member for advice. Parents might ask us about how to improve a child's school performance because, after all, we typically knew more about what went on in class than they did: We had spent days sitting in the classroom, chatting with the teacher, and watching kids play during after school programs. One of us was asked for advice about how to respond to negative performance reviews at work, and another to suggest ways the couple, a very generous pair, could avoid being taken advantage of in the future. Advice could shade into intervention, as when we were asked to participate in family decisions about what college would be appropriate for a child or to help interview a potential day-care provider.

Requests for advocacy, too, were based on the closeness of the researcher–family relationship, the knowledge the researcher had about the family, and his or her professional qualifications. When one couple that had an adversarial relationship with their children's school was traveling for business, they suggested that I attend the annual meeting of parents and school officials to advocate on their behalf. The request was accompanied by humorous asides, but I have no doubts that my agreement to do so would have been welcomed. Likewise, attempts were made to sweep another member of the team into a highly contentious local political issue, one that had potential legal ramifications for all involved. He was compelled to formally reject the offer to become involved in order to protect both himself and the integrity of the project.

Underlying the complexity of friendships in the field is the notion of reciprocity. Although each family was given a $1,500 honorarium for participating, this was intended as a token of appreciation and not as direct payment for access to information. From the team's perspective, that information was beyond monetary remuneration. Besides, once fieldwork began the logic of reciprocity became evident. While we eschewed the role of family advisor, families often asked us about our own families, and we often answered those questions. Not to do so would have exposed the asymmetry in information about respective lives and it could have severely constrained fieldwork in some families. At the same time, we were careful to avoid normative judgments and always explained that our way of handling a situation was just one of many alternatives, as was theirs.

Reciprocity thus swept us into the lives of the families. Often the requests were blatant and humorous in their self-interest. On several occasions, people scheduled days to be shadowed based on their need for another person—the ethnographer—to get them into a carpool lane during a particularly horrific commute. "You might as well be good for something," they would joke. I agreed to meet with a colleague of Eleanor, one parent, to share information about Silicon Valley and to serve on an advisory board for an organization she was founding. Eleanor was ecstatic (and explicit) about how being able to "deliver" me would help build her professional network, and she explained that this was the way she had built a successful career.

At other times, reciprocity was far from a joking matter. Following the "play date" with my young children that one family had requested, I was taken aside by the father and asked why my children had largely obeyed my instructions, while he said his own children always ignored his. He speculated on the reasons, including his fear that the number of hours he and his wife worked made them reluctant to lose scarce time with their children by meting out punishment. He did not wish to chat abstractly about children, but rather he wanted specific advice and was not put off by my explanation that my children had been warned to behave themselves while in this new house. His request was clearly grounded in the relationship we had formed over the months and by the fact that he and his wife had exposed their own family life to my scrutiny.

What these and many other incidents reveal is that just as we as ethnographers are using other people for our purposes, and so have an obligation to protect them from harm, so too can others use us. This is certainly unsurprising in a study of dual-career families, many of whom juggle work and family by adopting an instrumental attitude to social relationships. To do extended fieldwork is both to use others and to agree to be used by them, often for purposes we can only dimly see. We can become unwittingly entangled in the agendas of those we study and the consequences can indeed be serious. How we protect them from risk must be accompanied by sensitivity to the uses to which we as individuals or professionals can be put.

Each family member understood us and our purposes in their own way, for we effectively but tacitly educated them as to our interests and goals. They, of course, brought their own perspectives to bear. One child, for example, explained to her friends that I was writing her life history for a book, while a middle school boy from a troubled background explained to friends that I was his bodyguard, and a teenager joked that I was his stalker. When I explained that he would select the occasions when I shadowed him so as not to embarrass him, he responded, "There is nothing you can do that won't embarrass me."

The families made decisions about who we were and what to reveal to us, and the latter were always selective. One man proclaimed that his family was utterly alone in the region, and only later did we discover that his brother's family lived only a few blocks away; he was embarrassed by the latter's success. A child in another family had a criminal record that was not revealed until well into fieldwork. Family members thus sought to control how at least some facets of their lives were represented, and their understandings of what is ethnographically interesting seldom corresponded exactly to how we saw their family. They, for example, had simply never systematically compared themselves to other families in the way that we could do and so they did not know how they were doing; indeed, finding out was a common motivation to participate.

Our individual characteristics also entered the fieldwork equation, often in ways we could only see in retrospect. Freeman, for example, conducted his original doctoral research in a temple town in India and for many years taught a university course on anthropology and religion. Whether coincidentally or not, his four families revealed much about their religious beliefs. I had long studied the use of technology at work and home, and my fieldnotes are replete with meticulous descriptions of Palm Pilots, usage of cellular phones, and the minutiae of jobs. At the time of fieldwork, Freeman was the 60-year-old father of an adult child, and families placed him in the role of fictive grandfather. English-Lueck and I, although middle-aged, were parents of younger children and we were understood as fellow jugglers of work and family obligations. How we were understood, as well as our potential uses, was thus only partially under our control, for the families drew their own conclusions.

The ethical issues and interpersonal dynamics of ethnography with families can seem over-whelming, but they are also benefits of the methodology, for the unfolding dilemmas allow us to learn deeper lessons. Arguably, they are why we are there in the first place, participating in the messiness and ambiguity of daily life instead of the sanitized comfort of "controlled conditions." While lies can complicate fieldwork, they also open the door to deeper conver-sations about why a lie was told and why it took the form it did. While it can be tiresome guarding against offering advice or being used in others' agendas, the very fact that people try to involve us in their lives on their terms, too, gives us the chance to discuss those lives with greater sensitivity.

The very difficulties and even limitations of fieldwork are thus viewed by the ethnographer as additional sources of data. Reciprocity need not be provided by offering answers to life's imponderables, but rather by providing an opportunity for a particular form of dialogue that is otherwise largely missing from the lives of busy families. Indeed, many families asked at the onset of fieldwork if they would receive a metaphorical "report card" at the end, but none actually asked for it when the time arrived. Through the reflections and conversations about their practices that they had engaged in over the months, there was no need.

A RESEARCH TRAJECTORY

If this chapter is doing its job, then the reader is aware of both the usefulness and complexity of the ethnographic endeavor as well as the magnitude of its obligations and commitments. Ethnography is often viewed as a source of interesting anecdotes that bring to life survey results or secondary research analyses, yet this is not sufficient grounds to undertake projects such as the one just described; the costs in time and money are too great. Rather, ethnography can be placed in a larger trajectory of research so that its use becomes a logical or necessary next step to address a set of compelling problems, issues, or questions. And, so this chapter closes with neither a grand summing up nor a clarion call to the reader to embrace ethnography. Instead, it revisits the fundamental questions, Why "do ethnography" in the first place, and when we do it, what difference can it make?

We begin by exploring the genesis of the project just described, at least from my perspective; English-Lueck and Freeman would undoubtedly tell slightly different tales. Tracing the linkages between projects and their integration into a larger process demonstrates the recursive nature of ethnography, its capacity to generate new and often unanticipated lines of inquiry, and its role as a source of data that can be mined—and remined—for new ideas. From this perspective, the division of the research process into discrete projects is somewhat arbitrary for it distorts a continuous process of inquiry that was punctuated by new findings, opportunities for fieldwork, insights, and sources of funding.

My own interests in the issues explored in the ethnography of dual-career families began in the late 1980s when, as a doctoral student at Stanford University, I undertook ethnographic fieldwork on the shopfloors of Kramden Computers, an assembler of computer workstations, and Calhoun Wire and Cable, a manufacturer of specialized high-tech products (both pseudonyms). The fieldwork focused on the emerging skill requirements of jobs that were changing under the impact of new technology (e.g., workplace computers) and organizational roles (e.g., teamwork). One finding was that workers did not simply learn a set of required or basic skills, but rather they gradually became incorporated into a community of practice that was at least as important to their subsequent success (Darrah, 1996). Yet while I studied the community that emerged around work practices, I learned little about the wider community and families of which workers were a part. In fact, I consciously dampened my curiosity since exploring home life seemed an unwarranted intrusion into the lives of workers who had only agreed, after all, to discuss with me their jobs. Still, questions of communities and families persisted, as did the relationship of each to work.

In 1991 the opportunity arose to explore life beyond the workplace. Now in a tenure track position at San Jose State University, colleague J. A. English-Lueck and I launched a project designed to understand the high-tech Silicon Valley of northern California as a distinctive culture region. Through a series of interview-based projects, we learned that work, and its articulation with family, community and education, was the issue that connected the narratives of seemingly diverse lives. Along with J. M. Freeman, in 1994 we began the multi-year Work, Identity, and Community in Silicon Valley project.[4] The project was based on a series of three semistructured interviews conducted with theoretically drawn samples of 175 people working in high-tech industries and other economic sectors. Ideally, each person was interviewed in a public place (e.g., cafeteria, park), their workplace, and in their home. Interviews included "grand tours" of workplaces in which the interviewee was asked to explain the contents of their desks, piles of papers, and the presence of artifacts such as business cards, cartoons, photographs, and ubiquitous Post-its. The project resulted in over 10,000 pages of transcribed and coded interviews that provide a glimpse into the lives of ordinary people in a high-tech region.

Although these interviews captured in limited ways the perspectives of different people, and even allowed us to explore them in some depth, they raised two important questions. First, they were necessarily about what people said they did, wanted to do, or should do, but they did not reveal what people actually did. Occasionally, we caught glimpses of a reality that was more complex than what we were being told. For example, many interviewees repeatedly told us they kept work and home strictly separate, even as they blithely packed a briefcase to lug materials and laptop home for the night.

Second, we wondered what other people in an interviewee's life would say about his or her coping strategies. When, for instance, someone claimed to work 50–60 hours a week without disrupting his or her family life, we wanted to know what their significant other and children would have to say, and how such a work week was affecting families in ways no one could verbalize.

We were thus excited when contacted by the Alfred P. Sloan Foundation to undertake fieldwork that would answer some of our nagging questions. Fieldwork began with a set of assumptions and questions about dual-career middle-class families that were based on both reviews of the literature and our own previous research in the Silicon Valley region. We assumed that although work can be characterized by some significant general trends, specific characteristics of work, jobs, and careers affect individual families. Accordingly, these specific characteristics must be part of an analysis of the work-family intersection. In the earlier project, we found consensus that work was affecting family, but the specific pathways were heterogeneous. For example, some interviewees focused on the practical, logistical constraints of work (e.g., hours, travel, locations, interruptions), while for others it was their inability to "shut off" work as an internal dialogue.

The specifics of family life also mattered. We expected the specific needs, interests and schedules of children, other family members, and friends to profoundly affect work and careers. For example, we hoped to explore how spouses regulated the work habits of their partners and whether their own jobs and careers affected their willingness to do so.

We also wanted to explore how work affected home life, a daunting task. Number of hours worked is useful only as proxy for those effects. For example, our interviews indicated that people bring models and metaphors from the workplace into family life. Talk about efficiency and productivity, various techniques to manage interpersonal relationships, and management tools such as total quality management can thus penetrate family settings. Yet these transfers from work settings to home and family are simply overlooked by an exclusive focus on hours worked. Furthermore, much from family and community life is imported into the workplace. Assumptions and values about proper relations between the genders, the relationship between family and work, and the responsibilities of superiors and subordinates may be modeled on family life. These may vary by cultural background, and we expected they would be striking in multi-cultural workplaces marked by work processes requiring close interactions among people in order to accomplish collective goals.

The effects on children of family-work management strategies are often unexamined or they are reduced to gross indicators such as providing "quality time." The more subtle effects of allowing the household to be penetrated by demands for "accessibility" or the incorporation into childhood of work-based rhythms, metaphors, and models were seldom noted by our interviewees, but they could be inferred from their stories about work and family.

To summarize, we presupposed that work and family constituted clear and distinct cultural domains that were separable from each other as well as other domains. We assumed that work, jobs, and careers were characterized by objective characteristics that could be used to describe them and their effects on families. Regarding families, we assumed that "family" was a clear cultural domain and specific families had clear boundaries around them so that determining what or who constituted a family was a simple descriptive chore. Artifacts, people and ideas, we expected, were imported and exported between the domains of work and family, and their movements would be fairly easy to follow. Tracing these flows was at the heart of the relationship between a specific family and the work of its members. It followed then that what drove the characteristics of specific families was largely external to them. The family reacted to the flows of artifacts, people, and ideas from other domains, including work, and so a basic challenge for the family was to manage obligations imposed by external "others." Finally, this initial framing of the research problem tacitly assumed that demands of jobs and careers created problems for families. Furthermore, these problems were the primary impact of work on family, and the idea that work might also provide resources or solutions was not articulated. At an even deeper level, this framing implied that family was basically good, albeit buffeted by the (negative) exigencies of work.

This initial framing of the intersection of work and family provided a useful heuristic for initiating fieldwork. However, ethnographic fieldwork typically involves much more than simply finding confirming or disconfirming evidence for a set of hypotheses. Instead, a goal is to develop a deeper understanding of the research questions by a process of engagement with people in the field. In the present project, this process took the form of exploring how family members defined and used the familiar categories of work and family in their own lives. What each fieldworker encountered was a rich and complex reality that, not surprisingly, challenged the initial assumptions and compelled us to refine our assumptions and questions. We were struck by the blurring of these common spheres of life, making it difficult to distinguish what was work and what was family. Pamela and her husband, for example, had traded convenience for space in Silicon Valley's overheated housing market by living in cramped quarters but having short commutes to and from work. There was simply no space for a home office in which she could work. That space had become their toddler son's bedroom, and his prolonged and exacting bedtime ritual meant that the space could not be shared. Pamela's workplace thus became the only site where she could attend to some personal and family chores. She sometimes went on virtual shopping excursions and completed assignments for her graduate degree in her cubicle. One afternoon she headed for the company fitness room to simultaneously exercise her surgically repaired knee, while using her cellular phone to participate in a conference call with her East Coast business "start-up" partners.

When asked why she was performing an activity, Pamela offered specific reasons, often articulating obligations to employer and family that made her way of acting commonsensical and moral. Each family member juggled their own obligations in distinctive ways, so the mutual interpenetration of work and family blurred the boundary between them. Work, in the sense of clear and unambiguous tasks, was not merely moved around, but what constituted work was ambiguous and conditional. The workplace, too, became a site for exploring family issues, and while it was often a source of strain, it was also where the very resources used to cope with those strains could be found. Each family's daily life was hectic and ordinary, but through it they engaged a larger moral universe that often failed to provide clear guideposts. Their daily lives compelled them to ask who they were and what should they become.

Just as familiar cultural domains became problematic, new ones emerged in importance. We were struck by how many tasks were chosen or voluntarily assumed. Parents who were already burdened by long work hours, job stress, and the logistics of transporting children made additional commitments, such as to serve as a room parent. These chosen burdens suggested that there was more going in the families' lives than simply coping with inexorable, externally imposed burdens. Consumption of products and services, too, emerged as a significant activity within most families, although they seldom spoke of its significance. In fact, sometimes a family would comment that fieldwork on a particular Saturday would be boring to us because they were "only running errands" that day. Such "running around" appeared trite and unworthy of serious consideration as a family activity, although it could provide the most opportunities for face-to-face interaction among members that week. Even time spent investigating possible purchases on the Internet, learning to use new devices, and then troubleshooting or arranging for service when something went wrong could be significant and the basis for collective action.

The blurrings and emergent phenomena ultimately compelled us to revise how we conceptualized work and family, and thus, the analysis of our fieldnotes. There is, of course, no statistical test that told us that a threshold had been crossed and a new conceptualization was warranted, much less what the latter would be. Instead, we proceeded as ethnographers usually proceed, by repeatedly reviewing our fieldnotes and discussing them with each other and other colleagues, and by writing conference papers.

Reconceptualizing both data and problem then proceeded through a two-step process. First, the inadequacies of the initial conceptualization were articulated in several papers and presentations that critiqued the metaphor of work-family "balancing" or "juggling" (Darrah, English-Lueck, & Freeman, 2001; Darrah & English-Lueck, 2001; English-Lueck & Darrah, 2001). Second, an alternative conceptualization around the idea of busyness was introduced and developed (Darrah 2002a, 2002b; Darrah, English-Lueck, & Freeman, 2003; Darrah, 2003a, 2003b). Busyness is both broader than the narrow focus on work and family, and yet it is also more precise in that it points to a distinctive phenomenon, the emergence of a tacit work of managing the fragmented and shifting activities that comprise quotidian existence and that are affecting the longer trajectories of our lives.

The concept of busyness does not imply that people are simply working harder than ever; indeed, there is evidence to the contrary. Rather, it sensitizes us to a panoply of ways that lives have been reconfigured around the demands of busy schedules, regardless of their ultimate causes. It provides a conceptual framework that allows us to connect and make sense of previously disparate activities, assumptions and values, and then situate the latter in a changed society and global system. Managing busyness permeated our fieldnotes, and it was through compiling them that we recognized the phenomenon. It was reflected in the extensive planning and rehearsals for improvisations that we witnessed in so many families, as well as their anticipation of possible surprises and formulation of contingency plans. Busyness was reflected in how families used technological devices to be in touch with people throughout the day and to keep track of essential information. It also permeated social relationships, such as the networks of helpers they created out of potentially any and all encounters, the division of labor within the family, and their use of employers to provide resources that could ameliorate the effects of busyness.

By refocusing our analysis using the concept of busyness, we are also able to ground the minutiae of everyday life that was captured through ethnography in larger contexts, such the penetration of metaphors of productivity and efficiency, and an instrumental logic, into potentially any sphere of life or activity. Busyness also provides a perspective on the activity settings in which children find themselves, and which prepare them for their own lives as busy adults. Indeed, documenting the lives of children, their reflections on those lives, and their own theorizing about a larger social world was an unintended benefit of the fieldwork. The result is that we are able to theorize not only busy days and busy lives, but also a society that is itself organized around the proliferation of activities and ways to manage them. And, doing so only occurred because of ethnography and the close up, flexible view of families it afforded us. Surveys asking people how much time they spend on work or family would reveal neither the phenomenon of busyness nor its complexity and pervasiveness.

What ethnography of working families offers then is an opportunity to participate in the messiness of their everyday lives and the ways they think about and organize them. It offers the possibilities of genuine insight (we hope) and reformulating problems in ways that suggest new ways to address them. Yet it is also an exercise in humility as "the family" yields to "families," each a self-referencing social universe that can challenge and debunk our most precious assumptions. We thus lose some certainty and a sort of false clarity, but we gain a refined sense of what really matters to families—and why.

The implications of ethnographies of working families are thus significant. They can allow us to better understand what is happening to families at a time when communities, governments, and the economy are being dramatically altered. Exploring these changes and their impact on families is important, for lives are indeed being transformed, and not always for the better. Yet by focusing on what is being lost or threatened, we also risk reifying families as essential, timeless forms. Ethnography thus has the equally important task of understanding families as sites of creative adaptation to new realities. The outcomes may be families with renewed importance in society, albeit in ways that we are only beginning to anticipate.

NOTES

[1] The following discussion is largely based on Agar (1996), Bernard (2002), Hammersley and Atkinson (1983), and LeCompte and Schensul (1999). James Spradley's books on ethnographic interviewing (1979) and participant observation (1980) remain useful guides to those methods. Fetterman (1997) provided a useful introduction to the ethnographic process, and Bryman's (2001) four-volume series (*The Nature of Ethnography, Ethnographic Fieldwork Practice, Issues in Ethnography,* and *Analysis and Writing in Ethnography*) is a valuable reference for the reader seeking a deeper exploration of the methodology.

[2] The Ethnography of Dual-Career Middle-Class Families project was generously supported by the Alfred P. Sloan Foundation, which also supported the author during a sabbatical year. I thank Kathleen Christensen for her insistence on involving anthropologists in a research agenda to better understand working families. The fieldwork and subsequent writing were also facilitated by sabbatical support by the College of Social Sciences, San Jose State University. Of course, the project would not have been completed without the collaboration of Jan English-Lueck and Jim Freeman.

[3] This section is partially based on Darrah, English-Lueck, and Freeman (2001).

[4] The Work, Identity, and Community in Silicon Valley project was partially supported by a grant from the National Science Foundation.

REFERENCES

Agar, M. (1996). *The professional stranger* (2nd ed.). New York: Academic Press.

Arnold, J., & Graesch, A. (2002). Space, time and activities in the everyday lives of working families: An ethnoarchaeological approach (Working Paper No. 2). Los Angeles: UCLA Center on Everyday Lives of Families.

Arnold, J., & Lang, U. (2003). The changing landscape of home: Reflecting and reshaping middle-class family lives (Working Paper No. 20). Los Angeles: UCLA Center on Everyday Lives of Families.

Bernard, H. R. (2002). *Research methods in anthropology: Qualitative and quantitative approaches* (3rd ed.). Walnut Creek, CA: AltaMira Press.

Bryman, A. (2001). *The nature of ethnography*. Thousand Oaks, CA: Sage.

Bryman, A. (2001). *Ethnographic fieldwork practice*. Thousand Oaks, CA: Sage.

Bryman, A. (2001). *Issues in ethnography*. Thousand Oaks, CA: Sage.

Bryman, A. (2001). *Analysis and writing in ethnography*. Thousand Oaks, CA: Sage.

Cashdan, E. (1989). Hunters and gatherers: Economic behavior in bands. In S. Plattner (Ed.), *Economic anthropology* (pp. 21–48). Stanford, CA: Stanford University Press.

Darrah, C. N. (1996). *Learning and work: An exploration in industrial ethnography*. New York: Garland.

Darrah, C. N. (2002a). *Blurring the edges of work and family: Tales from Silicon Valley*. Emory Center for Myth and Ritual in American Life. Emory University, Atlanta.

Darrah, C. N. (2002b). We're this kind of family: Creating the good family in busy times. Families That Work: Cross-Currents in Sloan-Sponsored Research on Working Families, Alfred P. Sloan Foundation annual conference of Centers for the Study of Working Families. Emory University, Atlanta.

Darrah, C. N. (2003a). *Anthropology, ethnography and the thesis of a workplace/workforce mismatch*. Work, Family, Health and Well-Being Conference. National Institute of Child Health and Human Development of the National Institutes of Health, the Alfred P. Sloan Foundation, the Office of Behavioral and Social Science Research of the National Institutes of Health, the National Institute for Occupation Safety and Health of the Centers for Disease Control and Prevention, and the Child Care Bureau of the Administration for Children and Families. Washington, DC.

Darrah, C. N. (2003b). *Busy bodies: The anthropology of busy lives*. Winter Symposia Series, Center for Science, Technology and Society, Santa Clara University.

Darrah, C. N., & English-Lueck, J. A. (2001). *Ethnography and thinking about dutiful occasions*. Alfred P. Sloan Foundation annual conference of Centers for the Study of Working Families. University of Michigan, Ann Arbor.

Darrah, C. N., English-Lueck, J. A., & Freeman, J. M. (2001). *Ethnography of dual career middle class families: Final report to the Alfred P. Sloan Foundation*.

Darrah, C. N., English-Lueck, J. A., & Freeman, J. M. (2003). Shock-absorbing and sense-making: American families and a public anthropology. *Anthropology News, 44*(2), 12.

English-Lueck, J. A., & Darrah, C. N. (2001). *The dutiful dance: Scenes from the ethnography of Silicon Valley families*. Alfred P. Sloan Foundation annual conference of Centers for the Study of Working Families. University of Michigan, Ann Arbor.

Fetterman, D. M. (1997). *Ethnography: Step-by-step*. Thousand Oaks, CA: Sage.

Halperin, R. H. (1994). *Cultural economies: Past and present*. Austin: University of Texas Press.

Hammersley, M., & Atkinson, P. (1983). *Ethnography: Principles in practice*. New York: Tavistock.

Harkness, S., & Super, C. M. (Eds.). (1996). *Parents' cultural belief systems: Their origins, expressions, and consequences*. New York: Guilford.

Harrell, S. (1997). *Human families*. Boulder, CO: Westview.

LeCompte, M., & Schensul, J. J. (1999). *Designing and conducting ethnographic research*. Walnut Creek, CA: AltaMira.

Olwig, K. F., & Gullov, E. (Eds.). (2003). *Children's places: Cross-cultural perspectives*. New York: Routledge.

Overbey, M. M., & Dudley, K. M. (2000). *Anthropology and middle class working families: A research agenda*. Arlington, VA: American Anthropological Association.

Paugh, A. (2002). *Child language socialization in working families* (Working Paper No. 6). Los Angeles: UCLA Center on Everyday Lives of Families.

Perry, R. J. (2003). *Five key concepts in anthropological thinking*. Upper Saddle River, NJ: Prentice-Hall/Pearson.

Schensul, S. L., Schensul, J. J., & LeCompte, M. (1999). *Essential ethnographic methods: Observations, interviews, and questionnaires*. Walnut Creek, CA: AltaMira.

Schweitzer, T., & White, D. R. (1998). *Kinship, networks, and exchange*. Cambridge, New York: Cambridge University Press.

Small, D. B., & Tannenbaum, N. (Eds.). (1999). *At the interface: The household and beyond*. Lanham, MI: University Press of America.

Sokolovsky, J. (Ed.). (1997). *The cultural context of aging: Worldwide perspectives* (2nd. ed.). Westport, CT: Begin & Garvey.

Spradley, J. P. (1979). *The ethnographic interview*. San Francisco: Holt, Rinehart & Winston.

Spradley, J. P. (1980). *Participant observation*. San Francisco: Holt, Rinehart & Winston.

Thomas, B. (1998). The evolution of human adaptability paradigms: Toward a biology of poverty. In A. Goodman & T. L. Leatherman (Eds.), *Building a new biocultural synthesis: Political–economic perspectives on human biology* (pp. 43–73). Ann Arbor: University of Michigan Press.

Tsuya, N. O., & Bumpass, L. L. (2003). *Marriage, work and family life in comparative perspective: Japan, South Korea, and the United States*. Honolulu: University of Hawaii Press.

Worthman, C., DeCaro, J., & Brown, R. (2002). *Cultural consensus approaches to the study of American family life* (Working Paper No. 13). Atlanta, GA: The Emory Center for Myth and Ritual in American Life.

18

Video Ethnography
and Ethnoarchaeological Tracking

Elinor Ochs
Anthony P. Graesch
Angela Mittmann
Thomas Bradbury
Rena Repetti
University of California, Los Angeles

This chapter delineates how video ethnography and ethnoarchaeological tracking can illuminate working family life. These methodologies were integrated into the UCLA Sloan Center on Everyday Lives of Families (CELF) project to document how working parents manage to raise a family and maintain a home. Our discussion begins with a general introduction to the use of video ethnography and ethnoarchaeological tracking methods in anthropology and other disciplines. The chapter next considers how these methodologies have been incorporated, elaborated, and integrated in the CELF project. To demonstrate the analytic potential of video ethnography and tracking, the authors turn to a specific study that relies on these methodologies. The study examines the social cohesiveness of working families by documenting how and how much family members come together when parents and children return home after work and school. The video ethnography provides documentation on how working parents are welcomed home by their spouse and children (interactional cohesion). The ethnoarchaeological tracking provides timed observations of the proximity of family members (spatial cohesion) from the time parents return home until the time the children go to bed at the end of the evening.

VIDEO ETHNOGRAPHY

Ever since sociologist Erving Goffman (1964) appealed to social scientists to turn their attention to the internal complexities of the "social situation" and linguistic anthropologists John Gumperz and Dell Hymes (1964) established the discipline called "ethnography of communication," scholars of social interaction have relied on electronic recordings, film, and photography to closely document social life as it transpires moment-by-moment. Whereas earlier scholarship relied on note-taking to capture the behaviors of social interactants (Leopold, 1939–1949; Sapir, 1949; Kroeber, 1916), audio and eventually video recording allowed more accurate renditions and more detailed analysis of the dynamics of human social encounters in situ.

Electronic recordings provided the methodological grounding for a wide range of research endeavors. Within the field of psychology, for example, child language research burgeoned in the late 1960s and the 1970s, when portable audio recording machines allowed scholars to reliably capture the exact spontaneous utterances of children and analyze developmental changes in utterance length; grammatical, lexical, and discursive complexity; intonation; and voice quality, among other linguistic and communicative forms (Bloom, 1973; Brown et al., 1968; Keenan & Schieffelin, 1976; Kernan, 1969). Researchers could also record caregivers and others interacting with children and assess children's developing competence in relation to the input to which children were exposed (Snow & Ferguson, 1977). At first film and video were costly, but some child language researchers used this technology to examine nonverbal dimensions of social interactions involving children, especially the role of eye gaze and gesture in children's emergent communicative competence (Bates et al., 1979; Greenfield, 1979).

In addition to child language studies, audio and video technology was essential to the flourishing of sociological studies of human interaction, including ethnomethodology (Lynch, 1985), cognitive sociology (Cicourel, 1987), and conversation analysis (Drew & Heritage, 1992; Sacks et al., 1974; Sacks, 1992; Schegloff, 1987), among others. Varying in the scope of their focus, these pursuits emphasized the importance of close analysis of the recorded data and detailed transcription as a sine qua non of analytic rigor. For these fields, recording equipment serves as an essential tool, a microscope that allows the researchers' eyes and ears to apprehend the emergent structuring of utterances, gestures, facial expressions, gaze direction, silences, conversational turns, transitions between speakers, turn sequences, and more extended units of social activity. These structurings in turn are seen as interactional building blocks of social life.

Within the field of anthropology, linguistic anthropologists have championed a form of ethnography sometimes referred to as micro-ethnography. Rather than providing a general account of a society (what members do, how they think and feel, their material worlds, etc.), micro-ethnography focuses on a small facet of a society, such as a particular social group (e.g., an occupation, adolescent peers), setting (e.g., a workplace, schoolyard), activity (e.g., political, religious, or educational practice), performance (e.g., storytelling), or process (e.g., language socialization).

Micro-ethnography abides by the general methodological orientations of ethnography (see Darrah, chap. 17, this volume), in that it relies on participant observation in an attempt to document "the social organization, social activities, symbolic and material resources, and interpretive practices characteristic of a particular group of people" (Duranti, 1997a, p. 85). Participant observation entails prolonged involvement with a social group, using all of the researcher's senses to get a feel for what is happening from the group members' perspective, to the best of the observer's ability, given limitations of outsider status and the impossibility of true intersubjectivity (Clifford & Marcus, 1986). A number of linguistic anthropologists augment participant observation by electronically recording social life as it unfolds in day-to-day human encounters. With the availability of lightweight portable video equipment, contemporary linguistic anthropologists have exercised the opportunity to follow members of a social group with a camera in hand.

In many ways, linguistic anthropologists are like visual anthropologists, but rather than filming events to produce an edited film narrative, the linguistic anthropologist tends to video-record events to collect a corpus of data that can be broken down and analyzed as situations, activities, interactions, or behaviors of the same type. An ethnographic sensibility informs the linguistic anthropologist's use of video data, such that recordings are mined for what they reveal concerning a group's social practices; institutions; social relationships; systems of knowledge, understanding, and feeling; and repertoires of symbols and meanings. Micro-video ethnography involves documenting the moment-by-moment actualization of social order and cultural orientations in a range of locally relevant contexts. Researchers analyze who says and does what, when, how and to what end, in an attempt to examine how historically grounded sociocultural categories (such as "family" and "home") are realized and possibly transformed in ordinary social encounters.

The use of video ethnography in no way assures observer objectivity. Video ethnography depends on the quality of data captured through the camera lens. Video ethnographers need to be trained in how to minimize observer bias and how to be discreet when filming. In addition, they need to be sensitive to what is encompassed in the frame of the picture, specifically to open up the lens as much as possible to include all participants in a social situation and the physical environment in which social activity transpires. Optimally, the video ethnographer should use a wide-angle lens as primary camera equipment. In certain cases, there is a need to use the zoom capacity of the video camera, however. For example, it is sometimes important to document more precisely what participants are viewing, reading, writing, drawing, or otherwise producing. At these times, the video ethnographer should briefly zoom in to capture the detailed information and then return to the wide-angle format.

In addition, video ethnographers are trained to be sensitive to camera angle. Video ethnographers sometimes feel that they have to decide which participants' faces and which participants' backs will be photographed. Expert video ethnographers, however, try to situate the camera in such a way that most faces are captured. Rather than shooting from behind one or another set of participants, the video camera is placed at some point to one side between the participants. Thus, in recording family dinnertimes, the camera might be positioned at an angle between those seated around a table, avoiding the back of any one family member.

In doing video ethnography, the camera does not usually remain static. Rather, participants move fluidly in their environments. Video ethnographers are trained to follow the participants, using smooth tracking shots by bending their knees as they pursue the paths taken by the participants. In this manner, the video recording is not a series of jerky frames that induce sea-sickness!

Equally important as visual skills is the sound component of video ethnography. The video recording is only as good as the quality of its sound. Because participants in spontaneous social life are constantly moving, the microphone on the camera cannot always capture what people are saying. For this reason and others, it is important to use a wireless microphone. The wireless microphone can be pinned on a central participant, to capture sounds no matter which way the participant turns. It will also capture sounds from a relatively distant point from where the camera is positioned. As such, the wireless microphone allows the video ethnographer to be less intrusive, which is important for capturing so-called naturalistic data. Ideally, it is optimal to be able to use both the wireless microphone and the video camera's external microphone at once. The wireless will provide high-quality sound of focal participants; the external microphone will provide ambient sound. To use both microphones, a mixer can be attached to the bottom of the video camera. The mixer inputs sound from the wireless and the external camera microphones into the recording.

Because electronic recordings are relatively durable, they have a distinct advantage over seeing and listening through our primary senses, which rely on memory and intermittent or delayed annotation of events. Video recordings can be reviewed repeatedly and slowed down, allowing researchers to analyze features that are easily missed with only one opportunity to observe. Researchers are able to document facial expressions, tone of voice, gestures, bodily stances, and the emergent construction of utterances and actions that shape social activities and propel social encounters (C. Goodwin, 1981, 1994; M. Goodwin, 1990).

Video ethnography relies on not only recorded data but also transcriptions of the recordings. Transcriptions reflect the focal interests of the researchers and thus are selective representations of what is recorded (Ochs, 1979). Linguistic anthropologists, for example, generally privilege transcription of utterances over nonvocal behavior. Over the past decade, however, the representation of nonvocal behavior has been improved through the incorporation of still images from the video recordings at relevant points in the transcript (Goodwin, 1996). Yet another alternative is to view the transcript and video recording simultaneously, either side by side or in the form of subtitles. This possibility allows the recordings and transcriptions to inform each other. The transcription clarifies what people are saying; the video recording provides invaluable situational dynamics. This possibility, however, remains at present largely restricted to the laboratory setting, oral presentations, and Web dissemination rather than print publication.

The assembling of a corpus of recordings and adequate transcriptions is tremendously time-consuming. Moreover, the more one views the recorded data and transcription, the more one is drawn into the systematic complexities of the briefest of social situations. As such, while video ethnography provides documentation of on-the-ground, coordinated enactments of social order and cultural orientations, it cannot stand on its own in capturing the life worlds of either an entire society or a particular social group. Video ethnography needs to be combined with other ethnographic methodologies that tap into broader social time frames and different dimensions of the human experience. To this end, we now turn to ethnoarchaeological tracking as a complement to video ethnography.

ETHNOARCHAEOLOGICAL TRACKING

Situated at the crossroads of anthropological, archaeological, and ethnographic method, eth-noarchaeology is a line of anthropological inquiry addressing the relationship of material culture to everyday behavior and to culture as a whole (David & Kramer, 2001).[1] Ethnoarchae-ologists are often also archaeologists who seek to gain insights into fragmentary archaeological pasts by constructing cultural analogies with ethnographic data from the present. It follows that ethnoarchaeology may be regarded as a form of ethnographic research performed for the pur-pose of informing archaeological concepts and interpretation (David & Kramer, 2001; Gould, 1978; Kramer, 1996; Longacre, 1991). To this end, a great deal of ethnoarchaeological research has focused on aspects of the production, use, exchange, and consumption of craft goods and tools in small-scale societies. With regard to household- and family-level research, studies by Horne (1994), Janes (1983), Kent (1984), and Kramer (1982) among others exemplify the high utility of intensive ethnoarchaeological research programs that address the relationships between built habitats, household organization, economic status, and the production and use of domestic space. Similar lines of inquiry, including questions regarding family identity and the role of domestic architecture in the construction of everyday activities, are pursued in CELF's ethnoarchaeological research on modern-day Los Angeles families (Arnold & Graesch, 2002; Arnold & Lang, 2003; Graesch, 2004).

A hallmark of ethnoarchaeological research is diversity of primary data-collection tech-niques. Participant-observation (documented with written field notes), interviewing, mapping, photography, video and audio recording, and questionnaires are among the most common data-collection procedures, although not all are incorporated in any given project. Each method of collecting data has its advantages, limitations, and biases. However, the application of a combi-nation of procedures yields a dataset with potentially greater explanatory power and an overall fuller picture of everyday life. Here, we discuss a specific method employed in CELF ethnoar-chaeological research—ethnoarchaeological tracking—and consider its broader application to the study of family cohesion.

Tracking is a term we apply to a procedure in which family members are systematically observed in and around their homes at timed intervals. The term originated in CELF group discussions on how ethnographers could most effectively *track* the movement and activities of individual family members through their homes. In the broader community of behavioral science scholars, this method of observation is better known as a variant of *scan sampling*,[2] a technique originating in early 20th-century behavioral psychology and used to obtain behavioral data from a group of organisms by observing individuals in turn and recording the behavioral state at the instant of observation (Altmann, 1974; Dunbar, 1976).

In performing ethnoarchaeological tracking, CELF field researchers sequentially observed and recorded individuals at 10-minute intervals during the course of all four filmed visits in the home. Recorded observations reflect the location, the focal activities, and the objects incorporated in the activities for each family member at the instant of assessment (Arnold & Graesch, 2002; Graesch, 2004). The sequential observation and coding of these primary variables for each family member constitutes an *observation round*. Because family homes in our sample rarely exceed 3,000 square feet, observation rounds typically consumed no more than 2 or 3 minutes. Scanning the behavior of all group members in a short period of time can provide a near simultaneous sample of individual behavior (Altman, 1974, p. 258). In other words, tracking data reflect the location and activities of all family members at nearly the same moment in time. This rapid scanning and recording of individual behavior helps reduce sample biases, such as overrepresentation of group activities, that can emerge when individuals are widely dispersed (e.g., in different areas of a village) and observation rounds take longer periods of time to complete (Borgerhoff Mulder & Caro, 1985; Cromley, 1999; Hawkes et al., 1987).

Various methods of standardized observation, including spot observation and focal person follows, have been applied to studies of human activity and everyday behavior by numerous anthropologists (e.g., Draper, 1975, Erasmus, 1955, Hawkes et al., 1987; Johnson, 1975; Konner, 1976; Munroe & Munroe, 1971; Nerlove et al., 1974; O'Connell et al., 1991). Many of these studies share a common goal of documenting the total time humans allocate to a range of everyday activities (see review in Gross, 1984), while others emphasize standardized observation of behavior for the purpose of understanding the distribution of activities across space (e.g., O'Connell et al., 1991). Scan sampling, or tracking, can be distinguished from other quantitative data collection procedures, such as spot observation or point sampling, in that behavior is repeatedly recorded at predetermined points in time (Hinde, 1985). Because observation periods, the frequency of observation, and behavioral coding are all rigorously structured by the sampling procedure, tracking is well-suited to research in which intra- and intergroup comparisons of activities, uses of objects, and uses of space are an analytic goal.

Tracking, however, emphasizes controlled observation at the expense of participation in family home life. In this respect, tracking is not appropriate for examining *emic* perspectives on family activities, interactions, and uses of home spaces. Insights into such matters are perhaps better acquired with informal interviews, questionnaires, and creative exercises, such as those in which family members draw maps of their homes (e.g., Kent, 1984) or film and narrate "home tours" with a video camera (e.g., Arnold and Graesch, 2002; Graesch, 2004). Tracking is a method better suited to questions regarding the *frequency* and *spatial distribution* of activities in the home and within the community (e.g., O'Connell et al., 1991).

Furthermore, tracking data can be used to generate quantitative assessments of activity budgets, but are not always analytically comparable to data generated with other standardized observation methods, such as focal person follows (e.g., Hawkes et al., 1991). While two or more sequential tracking records may be identical and thus imply temporal continuity in individual (or group) behavior, there is no guarantee that individual family members remained in the same location or engaged in the same activity in the 10 minutes that transpired between observation rounds. Whereas focal person follows can report discreet allocations of time to particular activities, tracking data only reflect the frequency at which certain behaviors were recorded during observation rounds over the course of a home visit.

VIDEO RECORDING AND TRACKING OF WORKING FAMILY LIFE

In this section, we consider how video ethnography and ethnoarchaeological tracking method-ologies are integrated into the larger project conducted by the UCLA Sloan Center on Everyday Lives of Families (CELF). Below we present the general outline of the CELF study and the role of video recording and tracking in the study.

Overview of Participants and Procedures

The CELF study examines the everyday experiences of 30 middle-class dual-earner families. Each family comprises two parents who work 30 hours or more per week, has two or three children, with one child 8–10 years old, owns a home, and pays a mortgage. The families reside in different neighborhoods in the Los Angeles area, are ethnically diverse, and include same-sex as well as heterosexual parents.

In research endeavors involving human populations, analysts weigh the advantages and disadvantages of diverse methods. A large sample size, for example, has the advantage of potentially capturing a representative swath of the population under study. Large samples, however, preclude or inhibit collecting in-depth information on each participant in the sample. Alternatively, small sample sizes allow researchers the opportunity to capture a range of de-tails relevant to a particular research question or dilemma. The limited number of participants, however, makes it more difficult for researchers to generalize findings and perform certain statistical analyses. In other words, there is a tension between the costs and benefits of large-scale and fine-grained studies. In the CELF project, we believe that there is much to be learned from intensively video-recording, photographing, tracking, interviewing, and collecting bio-logical data from 30 working families. The 30-family corpus is sufficiently large to allow for certain quantitative analyses and at the same time is manageable for qualitative inquiry into the complex dynamics of everyday family life.

An integrated set of data collection methods from the social and life sciences document each family over a 1-month period. Prior to data collection, informed consent was obtained from all family members and visitors to the home. The next five steps undertaken to gather information on each family, shown in Table 18.1, involve a wide range of procedures, including standardized questionnaires; interviews; digital photography; videotaped home tours guided and narrated by participants; and a repeated salivary sampling of cortisol, which can be an indicator of a stress response. All maps, photographs, video and audio recordings, tracking observations, transcripts, questionnaire responses, biological data, and subjective reports of moods and stressors are digitized, stored, and integrated on a server. To ensure anonymity, pseudonyms were used to identify study participants in transcripts. The server, which is only accessible to CELF researchers, facilitates the use of multiple databases and the blending of different disciplinary methodologies to explore the dynamics of working family life.

As shown in Part III of Table 18.1, the heart of the CELF study is documentation of a *week in the life of working families* across the workweek and the weekend. On 4 days, family activities and interactions are documented by three ethnographers, two of whom make video recordings of the family and one of whom records family members' locations and activities. The procedures followed by these ethnographers are detailed below.

Video Ethnography of Working Families

In documenting a week in the life of working families, video ethnography plays a central role. We used two semiprofessional digital video cameras with wide-angle lenses to capture the rou-tine activities that occupy parents and children across the week, including weekends. The deci-sion to employ two cameras was based on the need to dedicate a camera to each working parent,

TABLE 18.1
Organization of Data Collection Procedures

Telephone Screening Interview

Part I: Home Visit to Introduce Project
            Describe study to family
            Review informed consent procedures
            Identify other possible visitors to the home
            Leave consent forms and first set of questionnaires for family

Part Ia: Collect signed consent forms
            Collect completed questionnaires

Part II: Home Visit for first set of interviews
            Conduct interviews on daily routines, social networks, and educational practices
            Measure and map home
            Photograph home interior, exterior, and artifacts
            Provide instruction on self-guided home tour filming and camera use

Part IIa: Introduce procedures for collecting salivary cortisol
            Introduce procedures for collecting daily mood reports

Part III: Documenting a Week in the Lives of Working Families
            Collection of Salivary Cortisol and Mood Ratings
            Assessments occur four times per day on 3 weekdays (upon awaking, before lunch, before leaving
                work or school, and before going to bed). On two of these days, videotaping and tracking are also
                taking place.
            Videotaping
                Two ethnographers with digital videocameras film family activities in and away from home
                    during 2 weekdays (in the morning before school and work, in the afternoon and in the
                    evening), Saturday morning, and Sunday morning and evening.
            Tracking
                During filming days, an ethnoarchaeologist records on a hand-held computer in 10-minute
                    intervals family members' activities in the home, members they interact with, location of
                    activities, and objects they are using.

Part IV: Home Visits for second set of interviews
            Conduct parents' interview on health and well-being
            Conduct guided, videotaped tour of refrigerator and medicine cabinet
            Conduct children's interview on school, extra-curricular activities, friends, work
            Administer a children's psychological measure
            Leave second set of parents' questionnaires

Part V: Collect questionnaires and home tour camera and tapes
            Pay family and provide children with gift certificate

---

to obtain comparative data on their day-to-day experiences. When a parent was not present, the second camera focused on other family members, such as children playing with their friends, siblings, or members of their extended family. The video ethnographers recorded each working family not only in the home but also in the car and in a variety of community settings.

Field researchers filmed family members' interactions during 2 weekdays and 2 weekend days. The weekday recordings included early mornings from the time family members woke up until they left for work and school and afternoons and evenings when parents and children returned home until the children went to bed. Weekend recordings documented family life on Saturday and Sunday mornings and Sunday evenings. The video corpus for each family includes approximately 50 hours of recordings.

Graduate students and postdoctoral fellows from diverse disciplines were trained to carry out video ethnography in the CELF study. The overarching goal of training was for field researchers to achieve a high comfort level with the video camera and the sound equipment. When researchers are familiar with the recording equipment, they emit a greater sense of ease to those being recorded, which is crucial in entering the intimate space of family and home and doubly crucial when two cameras are on the scene. When video ethnographers know where to position themselves to be out of the way of those being recorded, can move fluidly in and out of occupied spaces, change tapes easily, and locate by touch the important controls on the camera, then family members come to see the camera as part of the researcher's persona.

Before traveling to each family to record, each researcher assembled and readied equipment and supplies. In addition to the digital video camera, the following items were essential: camera batteries; sound mixer; high-quality external microphone; wireless microphone set; batteries; fanny pack (to hold wireless microphone transmitter on person being recorded); earphones; tripod, monopod, or body brace to secure camera; and prelabeled digital video tapes. Additional batteries and tapes were placed in the pockets of a photographer's vest worn for the duration of the video-recording session. This arrangement allowed the video ethnographer to easily change tapes and batteries in the course of recording.

The researchers arrived in front of the family home (or other location) before the appointed time. This period was used to connect the external and wireless microphones and the earphones to the camera and the camera to either a body brace or monopod and check the functioning of the microphones. When the family indicated that that they were available, the researchers turned the cameras on as they approached the family.

During the recording itself, the video ethnographers strove to be as discreet as possible, remaining at a close enough distance to allow accurate recording but far enough to preserve a degree of insularity for the family members. We found that wearing earphones is also a good way of distancing the researcher from the ongoing social interaction. In the CELF project, researchers had the additional challenge of the video ethnographers staying out of the way of each other. During recording, the researchers usually relied on the body brace or monopod as family members moved around the house and yard and in community spaces. Recording in the car was usually done with a handheld camera, sometimes aimed toward the back seat and sometimes toward the driver.

The completed digital video tapes for each working family are copied, digitized, and up-loaded to the CELF server. Once accessible in the server, the tapes undergo the following postproduction procedures:

1. Transcribers produce an Activity Log of the family and home activities that occur during each recording. A set of Key Terms (e.g., homework, TV, exercise) is used to identify activities of particular import to the CELF study. The Activity Log and Key Terms offer an efficient overview of tape contents, so that researchers can locate analytically relevant events in the lives of working families, such as the returning home of family members at the end of the day.

2. Transcribers produce a transcript of selected tapes. Because researchers at CELF are centrally interested in the systematic ways in which families interact when they are together, it is essential not only to log video recordings but also to carefully represent what family members are saying and doing. Transcribers write down family members' words, voice quality, emphatic stress, pauses, and overlapping conversational turns as well as gestures, facial expressions, and actions. The transcribers utilize the software program vPrism to synchronize the transcribed behavior with corresponding moments in the video recordings. Using vPrism, the co-authors of this chapter were able to simultaneously view video footage and detailed transcripts of family togetherness when parents return home from work during the week. Looking at both video and transcript, we were able to see much more than each of these media on its own can provide, including subtleties of family communication and affect.

Ethnoarchaeological Tracking of Working Families

In addition to capturing family interactions through video recordings and transcripts, CELF researchers used ethnoarchaeological tracking to document how family members spatially situate themselves when they are at home. Tracking procedures were integrally tied to a broader set of ethnoarchaeological data-collection techniques used to study contemporary Los Angeles families and their material worlds (Arnold & Graesch, 2002). Prior to tracking families' activities and interaction in their home spaces, archaeologists on our team first documented the *physical attributes of the family home* (see Table 18.1, Part II). Interior and exterior home dimensions, architectural features, and major furnishings were systematically mapped using a combination of digital and conventional measuring tools. Floor plans for each family home were initially drawn in the field and later digitized using architectural design software embedded in Microsoft Visio. Upon digitizing the home map, interior and exterior home spaces were assigned numerical labels that later organized observations of family activities (Fig. 18.1). As discussed below, the floor plan of each home is central to tracking and analyzing how family members move through and utilize the spaces in their home.

Next, the material *contents* of each family home were documented with comprehensive digital photography in each home space. This included digital images of all objects in these settings as well as 360-degree panoramic photographs capturing the location and association of architectural features and artifact assemblages. All digital images were then uploaded to a central database where each was evaluated and assigned keywords to facilitate archival searches. Panoramic photographs were cleaned and stitched together using a combination of Adobe Photoshop and Quicktime VR software.

Prior to embarking on family home visits (see Table 18.1, Part III), a tracking database was customized for each family using FileMaker Pro desktop software and uploaded to a Visor handheld computer using FileMaker Mobile. The handheld database features preprogrammed drop-down lists from which relevant time, location, and activity data can be inputted for each family member (Fig. 18.2). All home spaces were numerically coded (see Fig. 18.1) but also included a common name (e.g., kitchen, living room, bedroom) for ease of data entry and onsite navigation. Similarly, each family member was coded with a letter (A = mother, B = father, C = 8–10-year-old child, D–G = remaining children [oldest to youngest], additional family members, and visitors), but were also listed by name. The letter codes helped trackers verify that all family members were sequentially documented at the conclusion of each observation round, including those that did not return home during our visit.

Observation rounds began shortly after arriving at the family's home and concluded when children were put to bed at night. Trackers moved through the home every 10 minutes, recording not only the space number in which family members occurred, but also their relative location, posture, and activities. Data inserted into these fields could be selected from drop-down lists of commonly observed behavior (e.g., sitting on west chair, eating dinner) or inputted manually using an onscreen keyboard.

Trackers were trained to remain on the periphery of family activities and interactions as well as to minimize their presence in front of the video cameras. To this end, trackers preplanned alternate routes through the family home for walking observation rounds and constantly strove to anticipate changes in activities that led to the movement of family members *and* video ethnographers when collecting data. Smaller houses often posed greater constraints on movement through home spaces, and trackers sometimes had to exit the house through one door and reenter through another in order complete an observation round without disrupting the social setting. An effort was made by all field researchers to avoid obstructing regularly traveled passageways so as to not affect patterns of family interaction and movement through home spaces. Prior to home visits, trackers consulted with video ethnographers and used the digitized

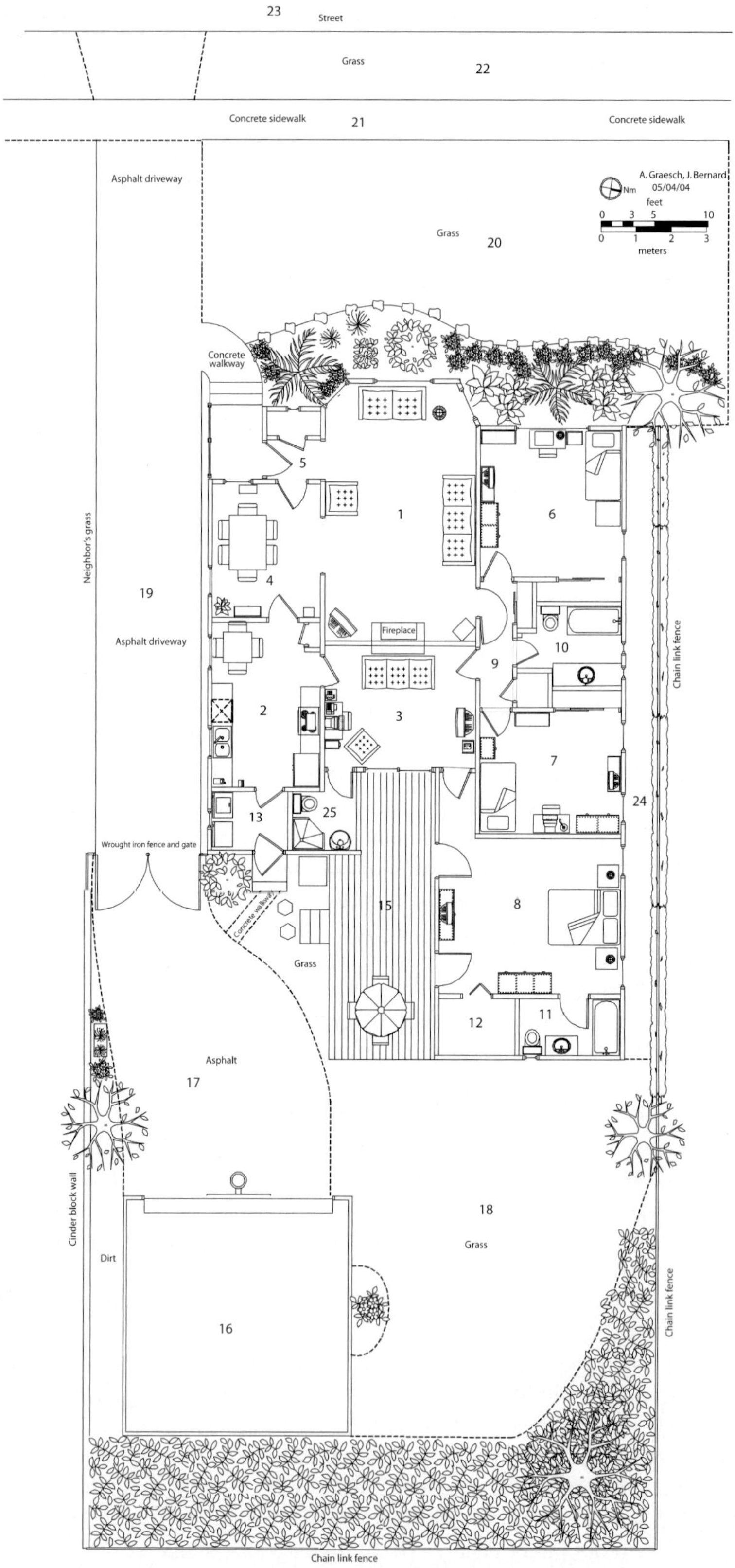

FIG. 18.1. Example of family home floor plan.

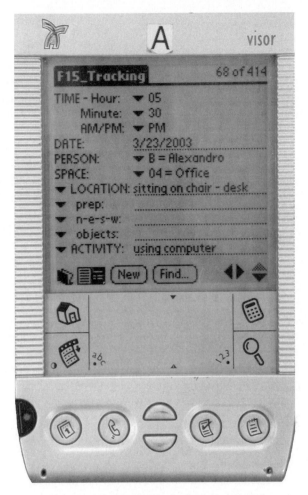

FIG. 18.2.   Tracking screen on hand held computer.

map to strategize potential filming locations and ways to physically minimize intrusiveness in the house.

Between observation rounds, trackers often attended to small data-collection tasks that were noted when archiving Part II ethnoarchaeology data (see above). Specifically, the 6 to 7 minutes between each round were used to correct mapping errors and omissions as well as to address any gaps in the photographic record. Trackers also used this time to opportunistically document conversation, activities, and uses of space not captured on camera or during observation rounds. Descriptive field notes were recorded on small paper tablets or with the handheld computer and a portable keyboard.

Ethnoarchaeology data-collection equipment, including the handheld computer, a digital camera, digital and conventional measuring equipment, a small notepad, batteries, and a flash-light, were stored and carried in the many pockets of a photographer's vest when conducting field research. Trackers were also encouraged to pack snacks and water to help counteract the effects of fatigue and hunger when collecting data in family homes for 6 or more hours per visit.

VIDEO AND TRACKING METHODS IN ACTION:
STUDYING FAMILY COHESION

In this section, we apply video and tracking methods to illuminate the state of contemporary working families as cohesive social units and the practices and processes that may facilitate or hinder family members' interconnectivity. Using video and tracking data, we probe the dynamics of family cohesion through two questions: (a) To what extent do family members greet one another when parents return home from work? and (b) To what extent are family members together in the same room when parents return home from work? The first question considers family cohesion in interactional terms, that is, family members as co-participants who coordinate in the activity of greeting a parent who is returning home from work. The second question considers family cohesion in spatial terms, that is, the togetherness of family members in a single home location.

The concept of cohesion enjoys widespread use in psychological analyses of the family. Defined commonly as the "emotional bonding that family members have toward one another" (e.g., Olson et al., 1983, p. 70), family cohesion has been approached typically as a global, traitlike characteristic of family functioning or the outcome of family interaction processes. Assessment of cohesion has been undertaken almost exclusively with self-report procedures, and the questions used to capture family members' perceptions of cohesion reflect the broad terms in which it is defined. For example, with the Family Adaptability and Cohesion Scales (version III; Olson et al., 1985), cohesion is reflected by such items as "Family togetherness is very important" and "Family members like to spend free time with each other."

Although information gathered in this way has proven useful for understanding the perception of bonding experiences in the families, in the present analysis we adopt a rather different perspective on the concept of cohesion. Specifically, we view cohesion as a quality of the transactions between family members that can be inferred by outside observers based, for example, on the physical proximity of family members to one another, particularly in different locations in the home, and on the coordinated reunions that occur between family members after they have been separated. Because cohesion is viewed as a characteristic of an ongoing, enacted process between family members, the methods used here are designed specifically to capture the flow of contact between family members, across different physical spaces, across time, and across different groupings of parents and children. Defining and assessing cohesion in this way is advantageous because it permits analysis of how emotional connections are achieved and maintained within families and, more specifically, how family members' experiences outside the home—for example, at work, in school—come to affect events within the home. In short, rather than view cohesion as a relatively global perception of interaction provided by family members, we approach cohesion as an aspect of family interaction that outside observers can infer based on the quality and topography of behaviors displayed by family members. Details of the methods used to assess cohesion in the present analysis are considered next.

Below we report on two analyses of family cohesion we conducted using the CELF database. First, we consider the interactional cohesion of the working families at the moment family members reunite after parents return home from work. Second, we analyze the spatial cohesion of working families after parents return home from work, drawing on ethnoarchaeological tracking observations. The interactional analysis primarily relies on the video recordings and transcripts of working family life. Both analyses focus on 2 weekdays for 20 families in our study. These 20 families were families for whom data collection had been completed at the time of analysis. All families were headed by both a mother and a father, and had both parents working outside the home on both videotaped weekdays. Left out of the analyses were one family for whom data collection had not yet been completed (F21), one family that included a mother who worked from home (F2), and two same-sex parent families (F10, F11).

Video Ethnography of Family Cohesion

We have examined the social togetherness of family members as co-participants in family interactions. We ask, "How do members of working families engage one another in social encounters?" Our focus is on family interactional cohesion when family members return home at the end of the day after parents are at work and children at school. We focus specifically on how parents returning from work are received by family members in the home. Returning parents' own behavior was not part of the current analysis. While our analysis of spatial dimensions of family cohesion (discussed below) will capture the entire period from the time the first family member returned home to the time that the children were in bed, the interactional analysis of family cohesion considers the moment when a parent returns home from work and reunites with the rest of the family. In some cases, a reunion takes place in the driveway; in others, it occurs in the entryway to the home; and in still others, it transpires in interior rooms. Reunion encounters did not always occur immediately upon the parent entering the home, depending on family members' location in the home. A reunion was defined as the returning parent's first encounter with a family member who was home at the time of the parent's arrival. Each parent could be involved in as many as three to four reunions per night as families in our study range in size from four to five members; however, not every family member was necessarily home at the time of a parent's arrival. In the 20 families under analysis, a total of 98 reunions were videotaped when parents returned home after work, that is 4.9 reunions per family, or 2.5 reunions per day. The length of these initial interactions ranged from very brief (1–2 seconds) to drawn-out (5 minutes or more).

In our study, we used the video images and transcribed text to analyze two important components of families reuniting after parents return home from work. First, we analyzed the *ecology of family reunions* during the workweek. That is, we examined the video record for which parent returned home first and which parent picked up the children after work. Second, we analyzed the *character of family reunions* for each working parent returning home. To examine the character of family reunions, the co-authors examined transcripts and video recordings for family members' use of greetings, kinship terms, requests for assistance, reports of the day, displays of affect, and attention directed toward the returning parent.

Ecology of Working Family Reunions.   Because parents in our study are all dual-income earners, we were able to investigate the family reunions that occur when working fathers and working mothers return home at the end of their workdays. Our initial analysis of the data shows there are fundamental differences between the returns home of mothers and fathers. Regarding which working parent arrives to the home first after work, across the 39 weekdays under analysis mothers returned home first on 28 of the days (72%).[3] On 11 of the days (28%), fathers returned home first. Regarding which parent picks up the children from school or after school programs, across 38 weekdays in the analysis mothers picked up children on 29 of the days (76.3%).[4] On 6 of the days (15.8%), fathers picked up children. On 3 of the days (7.9%), another family member or a babysitter picked up the children. These results indicate a gender asymmetry between parents, with mothers primarily arriving home before their spouse and taking on the task of picking up the children. Conversely, fathers in our sample tend to work later and arrive home later, reducing their opportunities to bring their children home.

In addition to investigating gender roles, we also examined whether relative income influences which parent arrives home first and/or picks up the children. There is evidence that income may influence both these activities. Using data from the 19 families who reported on their income, we found that the spouse who earns the higher income is less likely to arrive home first and less likely to pick up the children. Considering the 12 families in which fathers reported the higher income, there were only 2 out of 24 days (6%) when the father arrived home first, and on both these days the father arrived home only 15 minutes before the mother. Among the seven families in which mothers reported the higher (or in one case equivalent) income, the fathers arrived home first with greater frequency (9 out of 14 days, 64%). As such, in these seven higher-earner mother families we see an attenuation of the earlier-reported gender asymmetry in who returns home first. When his spouse makes a higher income, it appears to increase the likelihood that the father will be the first to arrive home.

Such a pattern is again evident when looking at which spouse is responsible for picking up the children from school or after school activities. Among the 12 families in which fathers reported the higher income, the fathers never picked up their children at the end of the school day (0%). However, among the seven families in which mothers reported the higher (or in one case equivalent) income, their husbands picked up the children 50% of the time. Again, in these seven families we see an attenuation of the earlier-reported gender asymmetry in who is responsible for bringing children home after school. When his spouse makes a higher income, it appears to increase the likelihood that a father will be the one to pick up the children. The role of income becomes especially important when one considers that out of the 4 fathers in our sample of 20 families who picked up their children, all had a spouse who was making the higher income.

One important note of qualification: While income does appear to attenuate the gender asymmetry, this effect is not absolute. Even among those families in which mothers were the higher-earners, they still arrived home before their spouse on 36% of the days, and assumed the task of picking up children 50% of the time. Compare these figures to the very low number of higher-earner fathers who arrived home first (6%) and performed child pick-ups (0%), and we see that the gender asymmetry still remains even when income is taken into account.

The implication of these results is that the typical context surrounding reunions differs for working mothers and fathers. For example, as mothers tend to pick up the children, children's reunions with mother are likely to occur immediately after the ending of the mother's workday, and often occur in a car outside the child's school/activity. In contrast, before reuniting with their fathers, children have usually already seen their mothers and have been home for some period of time. These differences are important to consider when interpreting the data we present next regarding the qualitative nature of working mothers' and fathers' reunions.

Character of Working Family Reunions.   Turning to the character of family reunions, we examine how working parents are welcomed home by the rest of the family. How do wives welcome husbands and husbands welcome their wives when they return from work? How do children welcome home their fathers and mothers? Reunion moments were recorded in the field as one of many types of naturally occurring family activities that occurred at the end of the weekday (along with such events as, e.g., dinner preparation, phone calls, children's bedtime, etc.). After these recordings were digitized and stored on the server, each parent's first hour home was transcribed in detail, allowing us to conduct the current analysis. The authors used not only video recording of reunion moments, but also the transcription of talk that took place, no matter how brief. Use of the recordings in the absence of the transcript or vice versa would have resulted in less clarity in our qualitative understanding of each reunion, since video recordings capture verbal and nonverbal behavior, and careful transcription ensures that brief but important utterances get noted.

Reunions after parents return from work are opportunities for the family to reconstitute itself as a social and emotional unit and for returning parents to recognize their transition from public to private life worlds. Across the world's societies, people tend to acknowledge one another when they encounter one another after being apart (Goffman, 1963, 1967, 1971; Duranti, 1997b). Such acknowledgments ratify the status and emotional value of the person encountered. In the initial moments of a social encounter, a display of deference, that is, appreciation of another, indicates that one upholds the social face that another wishes to assume and have ratified (Goffman, ibid.). In our study of family reunions, we are interested in the extent to which deference is displayed to returning parents.

To understand reunion behavior in the 20 families in our analysis, each of the 98 reunions that occurred between a returning parent and a family member was carefully observed for four types of behaviors:

1. Positive Attention was coded for displays of appreciation toward the returning parent such as: salutations ("hello," "how are you?," "Daddy!"); affection (excited intonation, hugs and kisses); assistance (e.g., taking father's coat or offering mother a soda); or scaffolding a child's greeting (a parent directs child's greeting of returning parent such as, "Go give Daddy a hug").
2. Negative Affect was coded for anger, criticism, or whining that occurred during the reunion, either directed at the returning parent ("I asked you to come home early, and you're home so late!") or due to another situation (family members arguing when parent enters).
3. Logistical Talk was coded for: requests or directives for help from the returning parent ("Go pick Bobby up from soccer"; "Can you help me with this game?"); questions and statements having to do with the activities of the household ("Did you pick Bobby up from soccer?"); or household business ("That bill came in the mail").
4. Distraction was coded when a family member did not show recognition of the parent's return and either completely ignored the parent or treated the parent in a distracted manner, a "side involvement" (Goffman, 1971), often due to primary involvement in another ongoing activity.

Reunions were categorized based on the one predominant code that best defined the tone or activities of the reunion, that is, identified the most frequent or dominant behavior. Results are shown in Table 18.2. A reunion was coded as "Positive Attention" when the welcoming family member displayed appreciation and was generally attentive to the positive social face of the returning parent. One of the latter three codes was applied when the parent was received with generally nonattentive, nonappreciative behaviors. A reunion that contained a combination of positive attention, negative affect, logistical talk, and distraction was categorized based on

TABLE 18.2

Interactional Cohesion of Family: Predominant Character of Reunions after Work

	Positive Attention	Negative Affect	Logistical Talk	Distraction
When Fathers are Greeted By:				
Spouse ($n = 22$)	36%	27%	18%	18%
Child ($n = 46$)	32%	6%	11%	50%
When Mothers are Greeted By:				
Spouse ($n = 11$)	55%	9%	18%	18%
Child ($n = 19$)	63%	0%	0%	37%
Total ($n = 98$)	42% ($n = 41$)	10% ($n = 10$)	11% ($n = 11$)	37% ($n = 36$)

Data presented as percentages of all coded reunions.

which code was most evident or seemed to be most dominant in the reunion. Coding was completed by two coders who each coded every reunion. Agreement between the two coders was above 80%. Any disagreements in the coding of a reunion were resolved through discussion between the coders.

The following excerpt of a father returning home to his wife and toddler illustrates two "positive attention" reunions.

Mother:	Hello:!
	((pause))
	((to Joshua)) Who's here?
Joshua:	*((waves to father))* (Daddy.)
Father:	Hi, sweetie.
Mother:	Hello.
Joshua:	*((runs to father and hugs him))*

It was surprising to us that, considering family members' welcoming behavior across all 98 reunions in the 20 families, positive attention to the returning parent was not the predominant behavior (see Table 18.2). Instead, when parents arrived home at the end of the day, family members were about as likely to be distracted and treat the reunion as a side event as they were to fully engage in receiving the returning parent. This is indicated by the similar frequencies of Positive Attention reunions (42%), and Distracted reunions (37%).

A lack of positive attention was most predominant in the receptions toward fathers. Positive attention toward fathers was displayed in only 34% of family members' reunions and, most striking, was equally absent in the welcomings by spouses and by children (36.3% of spouse reunions and 32.5% of child reunions). This finding indicates that fathers' returns home tended to be marked by a general absence of attentive reunions across family members. In contrast to fathers, when mothers returned home from work positive attention was displayed in 60% of the 30 reunions, both by spouse and by children (63% spouse Positive Attention, and 55% child Positive Attention).

The following excerpt of transcript from a family occurred directly after the father (Vee) arrives home with a pizza for dinner and is met by his wife and two sons (Virat and Harun). The transcript gives a sense of the general high level of activity in the home and lack of positive attention to the returning father. The interaction also contains a display of negative affect by the son, Virat, as well as logistical talk from the spouse.

Virat:	*((whining))* PAPA! What did you buy for ME:::?
Father:	What do you want?
Mother:	VEE!
Harun:	Sure, you bought him a Quizzno.
Mother:	*((from other room))* VEE, PICK UP THE PHONE!
Virat:	You didn't buy anything for me::!

Children were more likely to be distracted when welcoming fathers than they were when welcoming mothers (50% and 37%, respectively). In fact, when welcoming fathers, children were more likely to be distracted than they were to greet him with positive attention (50% and 32.5%, respectively); whereas when welcoming mothers, children were more likely to display positive attention than they were to be distracted (63% and 37%, respectively). Mothers and fathers displayed equal levels of distractedness in their welcoming home of their returning spouse (18% for both husbands and wives). In the excerpt below, the father arrives home and goes to the computer room to greet his sons (Jeremy and Alan). The father makes numerous bids for connection with his sons, who are distracted and either do not respond or respond only minimally while playing a computer game with a friend.

> *((As Dad enters room, Alan is playing video game, while Jeremy and a friend are watching))*
>
> Father: Hey, dudes!
>   *((1.8 second pause))*
>   What are you playing?
> Alan?:   *((unclear utterance))*
> Jeremy: What the *heck*?
> Father: *((rubs and pulls Alan's head up towards Father))*
>   *((looking down at Alan))* Hey, dudes!
> Alan: *((softly))* Hi.
>   *((looks briefly at Father then back to video))*
> Friend: *((Reacts to video game))* Hey! We didn't do that one.
> Father: How was school? *((Gives high five to Jeremy))*
> Jeremy: *((looking at video))* Good.
> Father: Hey there, dude!
>   *((taps Jeremy on his head))*
> Jeremy: *((continues looking at video))*
> Father: *((extends open palm to Jeremy))*
> Jeremy: *((continues looking at video))*
> Alan: Dad, this is not working good . . .
> Friend: No, it is.
>   Alan—do it—
>   Pass it.
> Father: *((pokes Jeremy's shoulder))*
> Alan: *((looks at Father, gives a high fiver, then looks back to video))*
> Father: *((rubs Alan's head))*
> Alan: *((continues looking at video))*

Despite these and further attempts by the returning father to communicate with the children, they remain glued to the video game they are playing. After repeated bids for attention, Father walks out of the room, muttering to the video ethnographer, "God forbid they should know anything else besides play, huh?"

In addition to being more distracted, children engaged in more logistics-related talk when receiving fathers than when receiving mothers (11% and 0%, respectively). This percentage actually underrepresents the logistical character of children's reunions with fathers, as distracted children often eventually asked father for assistance with an activity ("Dad, this is not working good").

While displays of negative affect were low across all the 98 reunions, returning fathers were also more likely than mothers to encounter negativity. Of the 10 displays that occurred in our sample of 98 reunions, 9 of these displays occurred during a father's reunion, and 6 of these instances of negative affect actually concerned some purported wrongdoing by the father. Negative affect assumed the greatest salience when fathers were welcomed home by their wives (27.3% of these reunions). The following negative welcome transpires just after Mother and Father talk by cell phone as Father drives home from work and they discover that

Father forgot to refrigerate the chicken that he had prepared for dinner. Mother finds the plate of chicken sitting on the kitchen counter:

Father:	*((enters kitchen area))*
Mother:	So does that mean that's all spoiled?
Father:	I think so.
Mother:	What did you do *that* for?
Father:	Well, I'll have to look at it and see.
Mother:	*((walks away from father as she speaks))*
	But you need to answer my *question*.
Father:	*((does not reply to mother))*

In sum, by using video ethnography we have revealed a number of patterns running across working families in our study. At the end of the day, mothers tend to be the parent who arrives home first from work and picks up the children from their school or after school activities. When either parent returns to the family after work, he or she is likely to be received by family members in a distracted, task-oriented, and even negative manner rather than be greeted attentively and with appreciation. This finding of a lack of positive attention is especially prevalent in the receptions of returning fathers. Frequent distractedness, especially in children, seems to be the primarily reason behind the low rate of positive receptions.

Although the small sample size precludes definitive conclusions, these observations on how families reconstitute at the end of the day serve as useful indicators of family cohesion. Results have important implications for active, dual-earner families as they indicate one way in which the level of interactional cohesiveness in families can suffer if activities, tasks, and individual pursuits are overprioritized. These results can be better understood by turning now to our ethnoarchaeological analysis of family cohesion in which we present results on the proximity of family members when at home at the end of the weekday.

Tracking Family Cohesion

In addition to analyzing family cohesion from the point of view of interaction, we use ethnoarchaeological tracking data to examine the *spatial* cohesion of family members when they came home after work and school. Our analysis of tracking data collected from 20 families suggests that family members rarely come together within several hours of returning home. This may be explained in part by the irregularity in the timing of family home reunions on weekday afternoons and evenings. Parents frequently coordinate hectic work schedules and commutes in order to transport children to and from after-school activities at various points in the afternoon. For many families, no two afternoon schedules may be identical, and there is seemingly always some degree of unpredictability in the schedules of parents and children alike such that simultaneous convergence on the home is impeded. Our tracking rounds, for instance, typically began when one of the parents (usually the mother; see discussion of video data above) returned home with one or more of the children.

The number of rounds during which both parents were observed in the home is typically much lower than the total rounds recorded for each family, indicating considerable variability in the times at which family members return home on weekday afternoons and evenings (Table 18.3). Moreover, the frequency at which we observed all family members in the home is highly correlated with the frequency at which we observed both parents in the home ($R = 0.9$).[5] These data suggest that opportunity for family togetherness is largely influenced by parents' afternoon schedules.

TABLE 18.3
Family Togetherness: Tracking Data

Family	Total Observation Rounds[1]	All Home[2]		Parents Home[3]		All Together[4]		Parents Alone[5]		Parents Together[6]	
		n	%	n	%	n	%	n	%	n	%
1	22	13	59.1%	13	59.1%	0	0.0%	0	0.0%	0	0.0%
3	43	5	11.6%	5	11.6%	0	0.0%	0	0.0%	0	0.0%
4	50	24	48.0%	27	54.0%	0	0.0%	4	16.7%	0	0.0%
5	34	12	35.3%	12	35.3%	1	8.0%	1	8.3%	3	25.0%
6	73	18	24.7%	32	43.8%	0	0.0%	2	11.1%	3	9.4%
7	42	24	57.1%	24	57.1%	6	25.0%	4	16.7%	4	16.7%
8	48	26	54.2%	30	62.5%	6	23.0%	1	4.3%	1	3.3%
9	53	29	54.7%	29	54.7%	5	17.0%	8	27.6%	2	6.9%
12	26	24	92.3%	26	100.0%	2	8.0%	2	8.3%	4	15.4%
13	69	36	52.2%	37	53.6%	10	28.0%	3	8.6%	5	13.5%
14	22	17	77.3%	17	77.3%	1	6.0%	5	29.4%	0	0.0%
15	52	22	42.3%	22	42.3%	8	36.0%	4	18.2%	1	4.5%
16	21	17	81.0%	17	81.0%	5	29.0%	2	11.8%	1	5.9%
17	41	26	63.4%	26	63.4%	4	15.0%	1	4.0%	1	3.8%
18	50	17	34.0%	17	34.0%	0	0.0%	4	23.5%	1	5.9%
19	29	13	44.8%	15	51.7%	3	23.0%	1	7.7%	0	0.0%
20	57	15	26.3%	15	26.3%	3	20.0%	3	20.0%	1	6.7%
22	34	23	67.6%	23	67.6%	4	17.0%	1	4.3%	2	8.7%
23	51	22	43.1%	23	45.1%	2	9.0%	6	27.0%	3	13.0%
24	58	35	60.3%	35	60.3%	7	20.0%	3	8.6%	6	17.1%

[1] Total number of tracking rounds (at 10-minute intervals) on 2 weekday afternoons/evenings beginning when at least one family member was home and ending when children were put to bed.

[2] Tracking rounds during which all family members were observed in/at the home.

[3] Tracking rounds during which *both* parents were observed in/at the home.

[4] Tracking rounds during which all family members were observed in/at home *and* all family members were together in the same home space.

[5] Tracking rounds during which all family members were at home and neither parent shared space with another family member.

[6] Tracking rounds during which both parents were observed in/at the home *and* alone together in the same home space.

When all of the family members finally do congregate under one roof, they rarely situate themselves in the same home spaces or participate in activities in which more than one or two people are engaged. The daily return from work and school to home is seemingly a phased transition during which family members physically and psychologically reorient themselves to the relationships and tasks central to home life. Family members who have been home for longer periods of time are often at a different phase of this transition than that experienced by family members who have only recently walked through the door. As our analysis of video data suggests, these phases may be discernible by varying displays of attention and varying levels of commitment on the part of children to reestablishing group togetherness at the end of the day. Furthermore, parents and children often attend to a wide range of tasks and activities that physically situate family members in different areas of the house on weekday afternoons. Recurring activities observed during tracking rounds include meal preparation, schoolwork, play, laundry, work-related phone calls, and watching television. While many of these activities involved two or more people, we rarely observed all family members coming together in the first several hours home.

However, the frequency of group congregation is just as low throughout the remainder of afternoon and evening observations. Among the 20 families analyzed, the frequency of observations in which all family members are at home *and* recorded in the same home space ranges between 0% and 36% (Table 18.3; median = 16%). Ten of our families came together in less than 16% of total observations in which all members were in the home, and 10 families came together in greater than 16% of these observations. However, only 6 of our 20 families congregated in the same house space more than 20% of these tracking rounds, and members of five of the families *never* collectively shared space during our weekday visits to their homes. These data indicate a surprisingly low occurrence of *group-level* interaction following the family's return to home on weekday afternoons and evenings.

It is important to note that variability in the frequency of family congregation among these 20 families is *not* strongly correlated with variability in the total time we spent studying each ($R = 0.2$). In other words, we did not observe family members coming together more frequently among families for which we have a greater number of total observation rounds (e.g., Family 6; see Table 18.3).

However, parents are rarely found alone in home spaces. The frequency of observations in which a parent was found individually occupying a house space ranged between 0% and 29% (median = 10%; see Table 18.3). These data indicate that while families rarely congregate as a group, parents are sharing space with at least one other family member between 71% and 100% of tracking rounds performed when all family members had returned home. Furthermore, parents are typically recorded as sharing space with one or more children rather than with each other. Tracking data indicate that parents in only 6 of the 20 families shared exclusive space (i.e., in the absence of their children) in greater than 10% of the total observation rounds (range = 13–25%; median = 16%). In contrast, parents of nine of the sampled families came together between only 3% and 9% (median = 6%) of the tracking rounds in which both parents were in the house, and parents of five families *never* shared exclusive space during our visits to their homes. These data indicate that parents are carving out very little time for private conversation and interaction prior to putting children to bed on weeknights.

The analytical limitations of tracking data as a measure of family togetherness lie chiefly in the rate at which observations of family members are recorded. That is, people can and do interact more frequently than that documented at 10-minute intervals. The completion of children's homework, for instance, is an activity often attended by either or both parents, although sustained physical proximity of activity participants is not the norm. Our between-round observations (see above) indicate that parents frequently move in and out of home spaces in which homework and school-related projects are situated while simultaneously attending to other late afternoon and early evening tasks (e.g., dinner preparation, finances, job-related phone calls). Thus, interaction among family members is often intermittent yet frequent, although we rarely observed instances in which *all* family members came together in the 10-minute span of time between tracking rounds.

Our measure of daily family togetherness may also be underestimated by data derived from only 2 weekdays of family observation. We recognize that some families, in the midst of juggling chaotic weekday schedules, may strive to schedule more time with each other on days other than those we observed (e.g., a family game night). We expect, however, that families who have volunteered (self-selected) for our study would want to highlight and perhaps even exaggerate the frequency of these occurrences, thereby augmenting the number of observations in which all family members congregate in certain home spaces. Furthermore, our comprehensive data on daily routines collected during interviews conducted *prior* to tracking days do not reflect these types of scheduled interactions.

Family Cohesion Summary

We have suggested that family togetherness can be profitably analyzed along two dimensions: (a) interactional cohesion, determined by the participatory involvement of family members in social encounters with one another; and (b) spatial cohesion, determined by spatial proximity of family members to one another. Our analysis of the interactional cohesiveness of working families focused on family encounters when parents returned home from work. Our spatial analysis rested on ethnoarchaeological tracking observations of family members' movements and activities when they were at home. Our interactional analysis relied on video recordings and transcripts of the verbal and non verbal behavior of family members as they engaged one another and otherwise carried out their daily life activities.

Our study of how working families reunite after work indicates that working mothers tended to return home earlier and pick up the children more often than did working fathers. This was the case even when the mothers were the higher-income earners in their families. Therefore, compared to husbands, working mothers had fewer opportunities to be welcomed home by their spouses and children who were often not home when mothers arrived. At the same time, while spouses and children tended to be home when fathers arrived, reunion interactions were often not positively attentive. Working fathers were less likely to be welcomed with deference by their spouses and children than were working mothers who returned home after their husbands. One possible reason for this finding is that fathers tended to arrive home later in the evening. Since our tracking data show that family members become very involved in a variety of tasks and activities over the course of an evening, it may have been the case that by the time fathers arrived home, family members were so involved in their activities that they were distracted and limited in their availability to fully welcome the returning father. The spatial cohesion results also show that members of working families in this study rarely even congregated all together in a single location in the home during the week. Even more rarely were spouses in the same location, just the two of them together as a couple. Rather, family cohesiveness in the home took the form of one parent together with one or more children, usually engaged in one or more tasks.

CONCLUDING COMMENTS

Understanding fully the everyday lives of families requires methods that capture family members' activities and coordinated behavioral exchanges, as they unfold in real time and across different situations in and around the home. This chapter provides an introduction to two procedures—video ethnography and ethnoarchaeological tracking—that are designed to enhance the information that can be gathered on exchanges within families and the contexts in which they occur. As demonstrated in this chapter, application of these methods to questions about the interactional and spatial cohesion of families illustrates how they yield data not readily available from questionnaires and interviews.

Although these methods are likely to prove informative in addressing a wide range of questions, they are not without important limitations. For example, intensive data collection of this sort can impose a significant burden on participants (or discourage other families from participating), limit the amount of information that can be collected from a given family, and force the investigator to make numerous decisions about who, when, and where to record, and with what frequency. The procedures themselves might alter the very processes we seek to clarify, they result in a large and sometimes unwieldy corpus of data, and they entail a high degree of logistical planning and organization. Finally, because administering these procedures with large samples is likely to be prohibitively expensive, caution must be exercised in generalizing observations from a small sample to working families more generally.

Notwithstanding these qualifications, video ethnography and ethnoarchaeological tracking are powerful tools that build on established traditions in anthropology, archaeology, psychology, and sociology, and they promise to expand the repertoire of social scientists seeking to gain insight into the dynamic properties of working family life.

NOTES

[1] See David and Kramer (2001) for a comprehensive discussion of the history, scope, and application of ethnoarchaeology over the last 50 years.

[2] *Scan sampling, instantaneous sampling,* and *instantaneous scan sampling* are terms applied to similar data-collection techniques (Altmann, 1974; Hawkes et al., 1987).

[3] For one family, parents' return home from work on 1 weekday was not recorded.

[4] On 2 days, after-school pick-ups were not captured on film.

[5] Spearman's Rank Order Correlation was used to measure the association between tracking data.

REFERENCES

Altmann, J. (1974). Observational study of behavior: Sampling methods. *Behaviour, 49,* 227–267.

Arnold, J. E., & Graesch, A. P. (2002). Space, time, and activities in the everyday lives of working families: An ethnoarchaeological approach. Working Paper No. 2. Los Angeles: UCLA Center on Everyday Lives of Families.

Arnold, J. E., & Lang, U. A. (2003). The changing landscape of home: Reflecting and shaping middle-class family lives. Working Paper No. 20. Los Angeles: UCLA Center on Everyday Lives of Families.

Bates, E., Camaioni, L., & Volterra, V. (1979). The acquisition of performatives prior to speech. In E. Ochs & B. B. Schieffelin (Eds.), *Developmental pragmatics* (pp. 111–131). New York: Academic Press.

Bloom, L. (1973). *One word at a time.* The Hague: Mouton.

Borgerhoff Mulder, M., & Caro, T. M. (1985). The use of quantitative observational techniques in anthropology. *Current Anthropology, 26,* 322–335.

Brown, R., Cazden, C., & Bellugi, U. (1968). The child's grammar from I to III. In C. Cofer & B. Musgrave (Eds.), *Verbal behavior and learning: Problems and processes* (pp. 158–197). New York: McGraw-Hill.

Cicourel, A. (1987). The interpenetration of communicative contexts: Examples from medical encounters. *Social Psychology Quarterly, 50,* 217–226.

Clifford, J., & Marcus, G. E. (1986). *Writing culture: The poetics and politics of ethnography.* Berkeley: University of California Press.

Cromley, E. K. (1999). Mapping spatial data. In J. J. Schensul, M. D. LeCompte, R. T. Trotter II, E. K. Cromley, and M. Singer (Eds.), *Mapping social networks, spatial data, and hidden populations* (pp. 51–124). Walnut Creek, CA: AltaMira.

David, N., & Kramer, C. (2001). *Ethnoarchaeology in action.* Cambridge, UK: Cambridge University Press.

Draper, P. (1975). Cultural pressure on sex difference. *American Ethnologist, 4,* 600–616.

Drew, P., & Heritage, J. (Eds.). (1992). *Talk at work.* Cambridge, UK: Cambridge University Press.

Dunbar, R. I. M. (1976). Some aspects of research design and their implications in the observational study of behavior. *Behaviour, 58,* 78–98.

Duranti, A. (1997a). *Linguistic anthropology.* Cambridge, UK: Cambridge University Press.

Duranti, A. (1997b). Universal and culture-specific properties of greetings. *Journal of Linguistic Anthropology, 7,* 63–97.

Erasmus, C. J. (1955). Work patterns in a Mayo village. *American Anthropologist, 57*(2), 322–333.

Goffman, E. (1963). *Behavior in public places: Notes on the social organization of gathering.* New York: Free Press.

Goffman, E. (1964). The neglected situation. In J. Gumperz & D. Hymes (Eds.), *The ethnography of communication. Special issue of the American Anthropologist* (pp. 133–136). Washington, DC: American Anthropological Association.

Goffman, E. (1967). *Interaction ritual: Essays in face to face behavior.* Garden City, NY: Doubleday.

Goffman, E. (1971). *Relations in public: Microstudies of the public order.* New York: Harper & Row.

Goodwin, C. (1981). *Conversational organization: Interaction between speakers and hearers.* New York: Academic Press.

Goodwin, C. (1994). Professional vision. *American Anthropologist, 96,* 606–633.

Goodwin, C. (1996). Transparent vision. In E. Ochs, E. Schegloff, & S. Thompson (Eds.), *Interaction and grammar* (pp. 370–404). Cambridge, UK: Cambridge University Press.

Goodwin, M. H. (1990). *He-said-she-said: Talk as social organization among Black children.* Bloomington: Indiana University Press.

Gould, R. A. (Ed.). (1978). *Explorations in ethnoarchaeology.* Albuquerque: University of New Mexico Press.

Graesch, A. P. (2004). Notions of family embedded in the house. *Anthropology News, 45*(5), 20.

Greenfield, P. (1979). Informativenes, presupposition, and semantic choice. In E. Ochs & B. Schieffelin (Eds.), *Developmental pragmatics* (pp. 159–166). New York: Academic Press.

Gross, D. R. (1984). Time allocation: A tool for the study of cultural behavior. *Annual Review in Anthropology, 13,* 519–558.

Gumperz, J., & Hymes, D. (1964). *The ethnography of communication. Special issue of the American Anthropologist.* Washington, DC: American Anthropological Association.

Hawkes, K., Hill, K., Kaplan, H., & Hurtado, A. M. (1987). A problem of bias in the ethnographic use of scan sampling. *Journal of Anthropological Research, 43*(3), 239–245.

Hawkes, K., O'Connell, J. F., & Blurton Jones, N. G. (1991). Hunting income patterns among the Hadza: Big game, common goods, foraging goals and the evolution of the human diet. *Philosophical Transactions of the Royal Society, Series B, 334,* 243–251.

Hinde, R. A. (1985). Comment to M. Borgerhoff Mulder and T. M. Caro's "The use of quantitative observational techniques in anthropology." *Current Anthropology, 26,* 331.

Horne, L. (1994). *Village spaces: Settlement and society in northern Iran.* Washington, DC: Smithsonian Institution Press.

Janes, R. R. (1983). *Archaeological ethnography among Mackenzie Basin Dene, Canada. Technical Paper 28.* Calgary: Arctic Institute of North America.

Johnson, A. (1975). Time allocation in a Machiguenga community. *Ethnology, 14,* 301–310.

Keenan, E., Ochs, E., & Schieffelin, B. (1976). Topic as a discourse notion: A study of topic in the conversations of children and adults. In C. N. Li (Ed.), *Subject and topic* (pp. 335–384). New York: Academic Press.

Kent, S. (1984). *Analyzing activity areas.* Albuquerque: University of New Mexico Press.

Kernan, K. (1969). *The acquisition of language by Samoan children.* Berkeley: University of California Press.

Konner, M. J. (1976). Maternal care, infant behavior and development among the !Kung. In R. B. Lee & I. De Vore (Eds.), *Kalahari hunter–gatherers: Studies of the !Kung San and their neighbors* (pp. 218–245). Cambridge, MA: Harvard University Press.

Kramer, C. (1982). *Village ethnoarchaeology: Rural Iran in archaeological perspective.* New York: Academic Press.

Kramer, C. (1996). Ethnoarchaeology. In D. Levinson & M. Ember (Eds.), *Encyclopedia of cultural anthropology* (pp. 396–399). New York: Holt.

Kroeber, A. L. (1916). The speech of a Zuni child. *American Anthropologist, 18,* 529–534.

Leopold, W. F. (1939–1949). *Speech development of a bilingual child: A linguist's record.* Evanston, IL: Northwestern University Press.

Longacre, W. A. (Ed.). (1991). *Ceramic ethnoarchaeology.* Tucson: University of Arizona Press.

Lynch, B. (1985). *Art and artifact in laboratory science.* London: Routledge & Kegan Paul.

Munroe, R. H., & Munroe, R. L. (1971). Household density and infant care in an East African society. *Journal of Social Psychology, 83,* 3–13.

Nerlove, S. B., Roberts, J. M., Klein, R. E., Yarbrough, C., & Habicht, J. P. (1974). Natural indicators of cognitive development: An observational study of rural Guatemalan children. *Ethos, 2,* 265–295.

Ochs, E. (1979). Transcription as theory. In E. Ochs & B. Schieffelin (Eds.), *Developmental pragmatics* (pp. 43–72). New York: Academic Press.

O'Connell, J. F., Hawkes, K., & Blurton Jones, N. G. (1991). Distribution of refuse producing activities at Hadza residence base camps: Implications for analyses of archaeological site structure. In E. M. Kroll & T. D. Price (Eds.), *The interpretation of archaeological spatial patterning* (pp. 61–76). New York: Plenum.

Olson, D. H., Portner, J., & Lavee, Y. (1985). *FACES III.* St. Paul: University of Minnesota, Family Social Science.

Olson, D. H., Russell, C. S., & Sprenkle, D. H. (1983). Circumplex model of marital and family systems: 6. Theoretical update. *Family Process, 22,* 69–83.

Sacks, H. (1992). *Lectures on conversation: Volumes I and II.* Cambridge, MA: Blackwell.

Sacks, H., Schegloff, E., & Jefferson, G. (1974). A simplest systematics for the organization of turn-taking for conversation. *Language, 50,* 696–735.

Sapir, E. (Ed.). (1949). *Selected writings of Edward Sapir in language, culture, and personality.* Berkeley and Los Angeles: University of California Press.

Sapolsky, R. M. (1998). *Why zebras don't get ulcers.* New York: Freeman.

Schegloff, E. (1987). The routine as achievement. *Human Studies, 9,* 111–151.

Smith, P. K., & Connolly, K. (1972). Patterns of play and social interaction in pre-school children. In N. Blurton Jones (Ed.), *Ethological studies of child behaviour* (pp. 65–94). Cambridge, UK: Cambridge University Press.

Snow, C., & Ferguson, C. (1977). *Talking to children.* Cambridge, UK: Cambridge University Press.

19

Using Survey Research
to Address Work-Life Issues

James T. Bond
Ellen Galinsky
Families and Work Institute

Survey research is generally viewed as distinct from experimental—or quasi-experimental—research in which the researcher is interested in estimating the impact of a specific intervention or treatment on persons subjected to the intervention/treatment.[1] In practice, however, it is difficult to draw such clear distinctions, as when random samples of a population are surveyed (questioned) before and after implementation of a particular public policy to estimate the impact of that policy. Survey research is also most often associated with the questioning of *cross-sectional samples* of the population as in political polling or market research. However, the decennial *census* that attempts to question *all* U.S. citizens, not a sample, is generally considered to be a survey as is the Current Population Survey that incorporates a *longitudinal sample* using a panel design with continuous refreshment of new people. Surveys of voter behavior also are frequently longitudinal, involving data collection on the same sample before and after an election. Though some methodologies for data collection—specifically in-person interviews and self-administered paper questionnaires—are most often associated with survey research, increasingly questionnaires administered over the Internet are also used and even individual *tests* and direct *observations* are sometimes utilized. Epidemiological surveys frequently employ longitudinal designs as well as individual medical tests and observations of rather large samples. Despite these differences, the most distinguishing common feature of what we will call *scientific* survey research is its concern with being able to generalize research findings to a specific *population* or *group*.

Survey research also has other characteristics that are distinguishing in most, but not all, instances. It generally relies on standardized measurement and quantification of variables, infrequently employing such qualitative methodologies as participant observation, unstructured interviews, or focus groups. Surveys typically include large numbers of individuals—either whole populations or samples large enough to provide statistically reliable estimates of population attributes. Because surveys generally collect data from large samples, the measurements taken are often not as comprehensive or "high fidelity" as the measurements made in more intensive small-scale studies due to budgetary constraints and the challenge of gaining cooperation from large numbers of individuals for the time needed to ask more complex questions.

The truth be told, large-scale survey research is generally not as fertile a source of new insights and hypotheses about human behavior as more intimate and intense small-scale studies. In work and family research, it is often these smaller studies, frequently incorporating survey methodology, that have generated the hypotheses that inform larger-scale research. For example, Rena Repetti from UCLA explored the notion of work-family spillover by looking at the working conditions of a small, non-randomly selected group of fathers who were Air Traffic Controllers (ATC) during the day and how they then behaved toward their children at night. On 3 consecutive days, each ATC filled out a questionnaire that assessed his perceptions of the workload, interactions with coworkers, and then interactions with his children when he returned home. She found that on days when fathers perceived that their work was more demanding, they tended to withdraw from their children (Repetti, 1994). In another project, she and Wood conducted a study of the mothers of 30 preschool children for 5 consecutive workdays. The mothers filled out a questionnaire assessing their day at the end of the workday. Then, 13 mother-child pairs were videotaped for 10 minutes at pick-up time. They found that mothers were more withdrawn on days when they felt their workload was higher and the stress among coworkers more pronounced (Repetti & Wood, 1997). These in-depth, smaller-scale studies have shaped the development of more finely tuned measures of how work spills over into family life. Other studies illustrating the creative methodologies that various researchers have used to examine work-life issues include Repetti (1994), Lee and Waite (2005), Moen (2003), and Moen, Sweet, and Swisher (2004). We strongly encourage readers to review these and other seminal work-life studies to broaden their perspectives on the range of possible research designs and methodologies.

As valuable as small scale surveys of nonrepresentative samples are, in this chapter we highlight the important contributions made by large-scale surveys of representative samples. Many such surveys have been conducted by the Families and Work Institute (FWI), a nonprofit research organization founded in 1989 and located in New York City. FWI's mission is to provide unbiased information that supports public- and private-sector decision making related to the changing workforce, workplace, family, and community. While FWI has conducted many surveys of quite different kinds since its founding in 1989, it has certainly not exhausted all survey research possibilities. We hope, however, that by sharing our experiences in greater depth we can clarify important issues of design and methodology and encourage new research that contributes to better understanding of work-life issues.

MAJOR DECISIONS IN DESIGNING SURVEY RESEARCH PROJECTS

This chapter is not intended to replace survey research methodology texts. Aspiring sampling statisticians would be well-advised to take the demanding graduate-level courses appropriate to this career. Here, we attempt only to provide a conceptual framework that individuals might use to think through the basic issues involved in conducting a valid survey that addresses specific questions of interest, illustrating these issues and various survey research approaches using examples from our own experience. There are numerous general texts on survey research methods that provide greater detail than can be provided here and should be consulted before actually undertaking a survey for the first time (e.g., Fowler, 2002; Rea, 1997).

DEFINING THE RESEARCH QUESTIONS AND THE POPULATION

Step 1 in survey research—and any research project, experimental or otherwise—is to decide what questions are being addressed or what hypotheses are being tested. In practice, however, decisions about research questions and populations of interest are made jointly. For example:

- Do employees (men and women) experience less work-family interference when employers offer more flexible work arrangements?
- Do new mothers return to work sooner and are they more likely to be retained when they are allowed to work part-time schedules upon return?
- Do adolescent boys have more positive views of maternal employment when their own mothers are not only employed but also enjoy their jobs and provide good parental support?

It is worth considerable up-front effort to articulate research questions in fully operational terms and in the language of one's primary audience—"natural English" in the case of public and private decision makers. It is surprising how often this is not done, leaving intended audiences scratching their heads about the meaning and significance of research findings. Involving intended audiences—academic, business, government—in the initial process of formulating research questions and population definitions can make enormous contributions to the study, ensuring that the ultimate questions asked are of significant interest and that findings will be used.

Related to the research question is the population of interest. Who will be the subjects of research and to whom do we hope our findings will apply? Are we interested in characterizing the attitudes and behaviors of students in this semester's sociology class, college students in general, adults in the U.S. population, all employed persons, all employers...who? Once the population or universe of interest has been selected, there are two options for survey research—either attempt to collect data from all individuals or institutions in the population (e.g., U.S. population, all employees of a company, all members of an organization, all students in a school, all state governments, all police departments)—a *census*—or to collect data from smaller representative *samples*. Seldom do resources permit surveying every member of a population, and therefore survey researchers generally use various sampling strategies to select appropriate representatives of the population.

MAJOR SAMPLING STRATEGIES

Samples of Convenience

Samples of "convenience"—friends, people who are readily available or who volunteer—are often useful sources of information and feedback during the process of developing a survey questionnaire. For example, college students interested in conducting scientific surveys of undergraduates at their universities could interview undergraduate friends about the topics of interest, such as their views of how they plan to manage their work and family lives in the future, to get a better idea of how to ask questions and to identify related issues of interest. This information might be collected through individual interviews or discussions with several students in the cafeteria or a dorm room. However, such samples of convenience do not provide a basis for reaching general conclusions about undergraduates, much less a basis for estimating sampling error. Such research is more along the lines of "journalistic research" that attempts to characterize a population based on highly selective interviews. It may be very informative, provocative, and lead to hypotheses that can be tested, but is seldom sufficient to guide decision making in and of itself.

Scientific sampling differs from the preceding example by starting with a sampling frame that defines the population of interest (generally in the form of a list of population units—households, people, institutions, etc.) and applying a sampling procedure that maximizes the representativeness of the final sample within the constraints of available information and financial resources.

Research using samples of convenience can, of course, meet scientific standards if the *population of interest* is in fact the sample of convenience. For example, many corporations regularly survey their own employees—a "sample of convenience"— regarding work-life issues. Generally, all employees are invited to participate in the survey (a census of the population). Assuming that managers only want to generalize to their own employees, the only threat to such generalizations is potential response bias. Another example might be an association of human resource professionals that surveys its entire membership. If the purpose of the survey is to describe characteristics and attitudes only of the membership and characteristics of the places where they work, there is no problem. Problems arise, however, when either the association or others attribute characteristics of association members and their companies to all human resource professionals and/or the organizations in which they work—assuming that not all human resource professionals belong to the association.

Systematic Samples

Systematic samples are drawn by count from a comprehensive list of units in the population (people, institutions). The researcher begins by determining the number of units in the list, then divides that number by the desired sample size to obtain the sampling interval. For example, if the population of interest is 1,000 people and the desired sample size is 100, the sampling interval would be 10—that is, every 10th person would be selected from the list. Selection should begin at a randomly selected start point in the list to ensure selection by chance. Unless there is a recurrent pattern or periodicity in the list that correlates with the selection interval and with specific characteristics of the units that are related to variables of interest in the study, a systematic sample will be as representative of the population as a true random sample. Seldom is bias introduced by systematic sampling, but one should be alert to the possibility. Generally the same estimates of sampling error, sample weights, and other statistics are applied to systematic samples as to simple random samples.

Simple Probability Samples

Simple random sampling requires a comprehensive list of the population of interest, with each member (ideally) listed only once. This may be a list of telephone numbers, a list of members or employees of an organization, a list of schools in a school district, or whatever. Members of the population are selected randomly, one at a time, independently of one another, each with an equal probability of selection. With the advent of computers, random selection of any given sample size from a population has become a fairly simple matter.

Stratified Probability Samples

If anything is known about characteristics of members of the population prior to sample selection, stratified random sampling can be used to reduce sampling variation and produce a sample that is more representative of the population than a simple probability/random sample. For example, region of residence is almost always used in national surveys as a stratification variable to ensure that the sample drawn is distributed in the same way as the total population across regions. Stratification increases the reliability of estimates of variables correlated with the stratification variables and the representativeness of the sample.

Sometimes researchers oversample particular subgroups in a population, selecting a higher proportion of people in particular subgroups than their proportions in the population distribution. Typically this is done to achieve large enough numbers in particular subgroups of interest—for example, ethnic minorities, very large companies—to permit more reliable generalizations to the same subgroups in the population. For example, a national survey of 1,000 employers that is intended to provide reliable information on large employers must oversample larger employers given their smaller number in the universe of employers nationwide. Sampling employers in proportion to number of employees addresses this issue, when followed by weighting the sample back to the number of employers of different sizes in the universe. Whenever oversampling is used, the sample must be weighted accordingly before generalizing to the population as a whole.

Cluster Probability Samples

Cluster sampling designs are typically used to increase efficiency and reduce costs. For example, if the researcher is interested in surveying school-age children, collecting data from students in representative schools, which have clusters of students, is likely to be the most efficient way to proceed. Cluster sampling draws samples from natural clusters where members of the population of interest are co-located—neighborhoods, census tracts, workplaces, schools, and so on. The U.S. Bureau of the Census uses this approach in its Current Population Survey conducted for the U.S. Bureau of Labor Statistics. Methods are available for computing sample statistics (sampling error and design effects) for cluster samples; however, this is best discussed with sampling statisticians.

"Snowball" Samples

When members of a population are difficult to locate or no comprehensive list exists, researchers commonly rely on "snowball samples," wherein initial survey participants play an instrumental role in locating other participants. Snowball samples originate with "seeds," an individual or small group of individuals who fit the characteristics of the group one is interested in studying. The researcher then asks these participants for referrals to other members of the same group for inclusion in the study. For example, a researcher or journalist may be interested in new mothers who have left their jobs to raise children and use referrals from one or several new mothers in this situation to identify others for interviewing. In some cases, snowball sampling may be the only practical way of proceeding. For example, if the researcher is interested in the connection between domestic violence and work-life issues, personal referrals among women who know one another and have experienced similar domestic violence could be an effective way to identify and engage potential study participants who may be embarrassed and distrustful of strangers.

Though snowball samples may provide very important insights into human behavior, typically they do not provide a strong basis for generalizing to all individuals sharing the sample's characteristics. Unfortunately, the least robust snowball samples are those focused on the *rarest* populations in which there may be major differences between persons who are widely known by others and those who are not. That said, some snowball samples are quite robust, such that it may even be possible to estimate sampling error by applying procedures generally used for cluster samples (e.g., Sudman, 1976).

How Large a Sample Is Large Enough?

This is probably the most frequent question asked by researchers new to survey research and one of the most difficult to answer. There is a common misconception that the proportion of the population surveyed is the determinant or primary determinant of adequate sample size. To the contrary, it is the size of the sample and not its proportion of the population that primarily determines its adequacy.

Often, the sole consideration is obtaining a sample large enough to provide acceptable *sampling errors* when generalizing to the population of interest—as sample size increases, sampling error decreases, other things being equal. In survey research intended to provide very precise population estimates for purposes of policymaking—for example, the U.S. Bureau of the Census Current Population Survey (CPS), which provides unemployment data for the U.S. Bureau of Labor Statistics—sample sizes are very large (about 60,000 households in the case of the CPS with maximum sampling errors of about $\pm 0.004\%$). On the other hand, political polls of voter intentions frequently rely on samples of 800–1,000 adult voters and report maximum sampling errors of about $\pm 2\%$ (the sampling error of estimates—sometimes referred to as the "margin of error"—at the 95% confidence interval) for whole sample statistics. A first step in choosing a sample size is to decide what level of precision of estimates is acceptable given the purposes of the research project. When conducting a census of a population, of whatever size, the main issue is not "sampling error" (which would be 0 if a 100% response rate were achieved) but "response rate" and "selection bias" among those who respond and do not respond.

If the researcher does not obtain a 100% response rate for a population or sample, it is not possible to determine with absolute precision the reliability of population estimates. This situation describes almost all survey research. However, *estimating approximate sampling error* is a fairly simple matter for proportions in simple and stratified random samples that do not involve sample weighting.[2] It is also important to note that sampling error decreases slowly after sample sizes reach 200. Thus, depending on the purposes of the research project and plans for subsample analyses, it may not be necessary to obtain very large samples to achieve study goals.

In most research projects, the size of subsamples should also be considered. If the researcher wants to make generalizations to subgroups in the population being sampled, the corresponding subsamples in the survey must be large enough to support these generalizations at the desired level of precision. If, for example, along with other generalizations one wants to make reliable general statements about employed women with children under 3 years old in the population, the number of such women in the survey sample should be large enough to achieve the desired level of precision in population estimates. If the proportion of such women in the population is known, the researcher can draw a large enough general sample of the population to ensure that there are enough employed women with children under 3 in the final survey sample. Alternatively, the researcher can oversample such women to achieve the desired numbers in the subsample, then weight the total sample to account for oversampling of this subgroup when generalizing to the population as a whole. As the preceding discussion suggests, plans for data analysis should guide sampling decisions. Similarly, knowledge about the likely distribution of various characteristics of the sample should be considered to the extent that these can be projected.

Issues of sample size also arise when one is concerned about *statistical power* in estimating correlations and/or comparing subsamples. Statistical power is the odds or probability that one will be able to detect a real, not chance, difference or relationship if it occurs in an experiment or a survey sample. There are numerous statistical texts and articles that discuss the calculation of statistical power in great detail (e.g., Cohen, 1990). However, when the survey sample and subsamples of interest will be relatively large (several hundred or more) and the correlations or differences of interest are expected to be of at least moderate magnitude, power analysis is not essential.

DATA COLLECTION METHODOLOGY

Deciding on the method for collecting data is fundamental. There are three basic methods of data collection, each having its own strengths, weaknesses, and costs:

1. **Self-Administered Questionnaires:**
   - Paper-based questionnaires are the simplest tools for collecting information in a survey. They can be prepared in different languages, but all presume that respondents are sufficiently literate to respond. The literacy assumption may exclude important segments of the population of interest. Another important limitation of paper-based questionnaires is the difficulty of incorporating complicated skip patterns that allow one to tailor questions to respondents with different characteristics. Many respondents have great difficulty following complicated skip instructions in paper-based questionnaires—for example, "If you answered 'No' to question 35, please skip to question 40." Thus, it is not easy to ask long series of questions *only* of employed women, *only* of parents, *only* of single parents, *only* of persons living in dual-earner couples, and so on in paper-based questionnaires administered to diverse samples.

     Paper-based questionnaires can be mailed to a sample of selected respondents or delivered by other means. Broad-scale mailings typically result in very low response rates, while targeted mailings (to new mothers, for example) can elicit acceptable levels of response. Distribution to a "captive audience" such as employees of a particular company—with leverage provided by urging from the CEO—can generate higher response rates. In our studies of children where we distribute questionnaires in individual classrooms under teacher supervision, the response rate is virtually 100% of students present. Various examples are presented below.
   - Internet surveys—using print-based questionnaires—are beginning to take hold. In many companies, for example, all employees—or all employees of interest in a particular study—may have Internet access and e-mail addresses, making it relatively simple to draw a random sample or even a stratified random sample (using demographic data available from the organization) to survey. A number of survey research companies have developed sophisticated software for conducting Internet surveys, providing for complicated skip patterns and stop/restart options that fit employees' time availability. A side benefit of this methodology is that responses are automatically coded into electronic data files suitable for analysis.

     At least one survey research company has developed large state and national samples that appear to be fairly representative of the U.S. population.[3] With proper adjustments for bias in the universe of Internet users when compared with the total population, this company has demonstrated that it is possible to conduct political polls by Internet that are just as predictive of election outcomes as telephone polls. Given the growing difficulty of conducting telephone surveys, a number of survey research experts think this is the wave of the future (Tuckel, 2001). Whether the future has yet arrived, however, is a matter of some debate.
   - Intranet surveys: Some companies conduct surveys on their own intranets. However, it can be difficult or virtually impossible to guarantee respondent anonymity given existing software used to monitor intranet communications. If the questions being asked are completely innocuous, intranet surveys present no problem. Otherwise, large companies with which we are familiar tend to conduct *Internet* surveys relying on outside vendors to manage the survey and guarantee confidentiality.

2. Telephone Interviews:

We have relied on random-digit-dial (RDD) and computer-assisted telephone interviews (CATI) for many of our surveys. However, it has become increasingly difficult to keep response rates high. Repeated follow-up calls definitely help, as do financial incentives to participate. Personalized invitation letters sent to members of the calling sample whose addresses can be identified from their telephone numbers may also help, though this is difficult to determine unless experimental studies are conducted.

In 1995–1996, approximately 50% of households had answering machines, 25% had caller ID, and 6% had voice mail—additionally it was estimated that 25% of households had more than one telephone line, frequently used for Internet access (Piekarski, Kaplan, & Prestegaard, 1999). The situation has grown worse. In 2000, 67% of households had call-answering devices of one sort or another and 45% had caller ID (Tuckel, 2001). Call screening is rampant. No answers and busy signals have become the norm.

According to the Council for Marketing and Opinion Research, the current average response rate for industry surveys (a sample of 473 surveys) is 24% and the comparable figure for RDD surveys of the population is only 12% (a sample of 227 surveys)— not high enough to ensure representative samples (Council for Marketing and Opinion Research, 1999). In order to maintain relatively acceptable response rates, many more calls are required than was the case a decade ago.

Wireless telephony presents additional problems. By law, survey researchers are not allowed to use automated dialing equipment to deliberately call cell phone numbers. Thus, known wireless prefixes and blocks of numbers used for wireless phones must be removed from RDD samples. A small, but growing number of households rely exclusively on cellular phones. This is particularly true for young adults. Although the implications of this situation for the validity of telephone-based survey research are unclear at the moment, if the trend away from landlines and toward wireless continues, it will become a problem in the near future.

Bottom line: Telephone surveys of the general population that achieve scientific rigor are becoming increasingly difficult at *any* cost.

3. In-Person Data Collection:

- As a first step in developing a questionnaire, focus groups, unstructured interviews, and participant observation can play extraordinarily important roles in identifying the issues of importance and the appropriate language for asking standardized questions in survey research. Families and Work Institute frequently employs qualitative research as the first step in focusing its survey research, just as it always pretests surveys with the target population to determine whether questions are clear and properly understood.

- As a method of large-scale survey data collection, in-person research tends to be quite expensive, particularly when the research sample is located in many places across the country. For example, using in-person interviews, rather than telephone interviews, to conduct our surveys of the U.S. workforce would increase the (already considerable) cost by a factor of 2–3. On the other hand, in-person data collection can be relatively cost-efficient if one's research is focused on a well-defined, co-located, and small "population" as might be the case if, for example, one were examining work-family issues for nurses in a single hospital. If the audience were the hospital administration and if one collected in-person data from all or a representative sample of nurses, such a survey could provide a very solid basis for policy changes.

  Taking the previous example, the survey researcher wants to be able to make generalizations—sometimes conditional and qualified—about nurses in a particular hospital . . . not simply statements about "the nurse I talked to." A hospital administrator may be interested in the opinions of one nurse, but will not be prepared to assume that the opinions of just one nurse reflect the views of others. She does care, however, about the views of the nursing staff as a whole.

Obviously, researchers must always be sensitive to the language they use in questioning respondents. It is important not to use jargon or slang, unless it is the jargon or slang of the population being surveyed, in which case it may be the most effective way of eliciting information. In general, stick with *plain* English. Avoid language that might be offensive to particular segments of the population being surveyed and get advice as to what that might be. Adjust vocabulary and grammar difficulty to the anticipated educational levels and English mastery levels of respondents, whether the questionnaire is administered orally or in writing. Non-English versions of the questionnaire must be created if one wants to include respondents who are not English speakers or whose English language skills are very poor. It is important that the people creating these surveys are knowledgeable about the nuances of the languages being used so that the exact meaning of a question is captured. This does not necessarily happen with a literal word-for-word translation. For telephone and in-person interviews, it may also be necessary to use bilingual interviewers. As the U.S. population becomes more ethnically diverse, sensitivity to language differences becomes ever more important for researchers wanting to make generalizations about the U.S. population or ethnically diverse subsegments thereof. Always pretest the survey instrument with a sample (random or not) of respondents representing important dimensions of diversity in the population of interest.

FWI SURVEY RESEARCH EXAMPLES

Families and Work Institute (FWI) is a nonprofit research organization founded in 1989 and located in New York City. FWI's mission is to provide unbiased information that supports public- and private-sector decision making related to the changing workforce, workplace, family, and community. We ask ourselves three questions before we begin any study: First, is the topic of the study one where the findings will make a difference? Next, how can we design the study so that its findings will be unbiased and convincing? Finally, how will we communicate the findings to the right groups in the most effective way?

Given our questions, sample selection is critical. Although data collection on *samples of convenience* that are not necessarily representative of particular groups or populations can reveal important issues and relationships among variables, particularly when the samples are diverse, information collected from demonstrably representative samples or entire populations of interest generally provides a much more convincing basis for decision making by government, business, other institutions, and individuals. For that reason, FWI has given high priority to conducting research on representative samples or entire populations of individuals—eschewing research on groups that may not be representative of populations about which private or public policy decisions might be made.

In the examples below, we describe how each of several studies addresses these three questions: Is this a study that can make a difference? How can we design the study so that its findings are unbiased and convincing? How can we communicate the findings?

SURVEYS OF EMPLOYEES IN STATES

Is This a Study That Can Make a Difference?

In 1989, Families and Work Institute (FWI) undertook one of its first studies—*Beyond the Parental Leave Debate* (Bond, Galinsky, Lord, Staines, & Brown, 1991)—in four states:

Minnesota, Oregon, Rhode Island, and Wisconsin. We decided to pursue this topic because national and state parental leave policies were being vigorously debated and the states that had already implemented such laws provided a natural laboratory for evaluating the impact of this kind of legislation on families and on businesses. Furthermore, there were no other studies that had stepped into this breach to provide data on such a hot policy topic.

These states were selected because they already had parental leave laws that differed with respect to the policy dimensions being debated on the federal and state levels—some had shorter while others had longer leaves, some exempted companies with fewer than 21 employees whereas others set the exemption level at 50 employees, and one state required employers to provide temporary disability insurance plans providing wage replacement for women taking leave for maternity. The study was intended to affect policy debates and action related to parental leave at both the state and national levels by providing information heretofore unavailable to policymakers.

How Can the Study be Designed so That Its Findings Are Unbiased and Convincing? How Can the Results Best Be Communicated?

In order to address our second criterion for research—designing a study that is unbiased and convincing—we invited the Governor or Lieutenant Governor in each state to be the study's state sponsor. This person then convened an Advisory Panel that brought together key individuals on all sides of the debate—elected officials, unions, women's groups, and business leaders. The Advisory Panel of opponents and proponents of the law in their state met together to suggest questions for the study to address. Subsequently, they reviewed the questions, methodology, design, and findings. If one is interested in influencing key decision makers, we believe it helps to involve them in the study from its very beginning. In addition, by including noted individuals representing organizations on all sides of the debate, no one could accuse the study of being an advocacy study. To have an impact on public and private policy, researchers need to know what decision makers want and need to know in order to make decisions. And, it is vital that decision makers view the findings of research as valid for the findings to have maximum impact.

Finally, by assembling this diverse group of opponents and proponents of family leave legislation, we addressed our third criterion. The people selected as advisors were prestigious. They were listened to in the "court" of public opinion. They could (and did) become spokespersons for the results.

Defining and Drawing the Sample

Representative cross-sectional parent samples were obtained in each state of approximately 1,000 biological mothers whose children were born 3 to 9 months before enactment of the state parental leave law and 1,000 biological mothers whose children were born 6 to 12 months after enactment of these laws. Samples of 1,000–1,500 employers were also drawn in each state, using establishment data from unemployment insurance agencies. Employers were surveyed approximately 2–3 years after enactment of state parental leave statutes.

In some instances employees and employers were randomly selected from existing lists; in other instances, they were systematically selected by starting at a random point and then taking, for example, every fourth person/company to obtain a sample of 1,000 from a list of roughly 4,000 entries. *Systematically drawn samples* are generally as representative as *random samples* if there is no bias associated with *periodicity* (in this example, being every fourth person or company in the list). All data were collected using mailed questionnaires, followed by reminder postcards a week after the initial mailing, and the additional mailing of another copy of the questionnaire 3 weeks later, if necessary.

Assessing Response Rates

Response rates for mothers ranged from 47 to 68% for the prestatute samples and 45 to 79% for poststatute samples. Samples were drawn from official birth records in two states and from lists of new mothers maintained by direct mail firms in the other two. Employer response rates ranged from 30–40%. Since the response rate for employers was somewhat low, an analysis was conducted to determine whether employers that responded differed from those that did not with respect to location, industry, or size. No significant differences were found, and no sample weighting seemed to be necessary.

Evaluating Evidence

Findings from the study played an important role in debates of the Family and Medical Leave Act in various states as well as the U.S. House of Representatives and U.S. Senate. Testimony was provided before state and federal legislative committees, and extensive consulting on research findings was provided to legislative staff—all at their request. A brief summary of findings follows:

> Statutes like the unpaid parental leave laws in the four states included in this study have the effect of institutionalizing employers' leave practices by specifying a certain number of weeks of leave and providing job guarantees. This study shows that the most immediate effect of the passage of parental leave laws seems to be a small reduction in the proportion of women who take fewer than 6 weeks off after childbirth (less than the medically recommended length) and a small increase in the proportion of fathers who take leaves. The study finds that very few employers report difficulty in complying with the new laws. Given this lack of difficulty in compliance and the lack of significant costs for the majority of employers, the passage of federal parental leave laws would present few operational problems for the vast majority of employers. Nor would it lead to significantly increased costs for employers.

> Of utmost importance to parents is the eventual provision of paid leave so that families of at all economic levels can afford to take time off to care for their children. The study found that lower-income mothers in Rhode Island, which mandates temporary disability insurance for virtually all employees, took more time off work following childbirth than those in the other states without wage replacement.

SURVEYS OF NATIONAL SAMPLES OF THE U.S. WORKFORCE

The National Study of the Changing Workforce (NSCW) has surveyed random samples of the U.S. workforce in 1992, 1997, and 2002 by telephone (Bond, Galinsky, & Friedman, 1993; Bond, Galinsky, & Swanberg, 1998; Bond with Thompson, Galinsky, & Prottas, 2003). The NSCW has included numerous questions from the U.S. Department of Labor's 1977 Quality of Employment Study (QES) to make deeper historical comparisons possible (Quinn & Staines, 1979).

Is This a Study That Can Make a Difference?

When the Quality of Employment Survey ended in 1977, a void was left in the field. There were no nationally representative studies being conducted on a regular basis that examined employees' lives on and off the job. Our decision to field the NSCW was to fill that void, in order to detect historical trends in the workforce and to add new questions to investigate emerging issues. Although the NSCW has sought to test some specific hypotheses, it has been largely descriptive—providing a broad base of information for use by public and private decision makers. An additional purpose has been to provide data on a nationally representative sample to work-life researchers.

How Can the Study Be Designed so That It Is Rigorous and Unbiased? How Can the Results Best Be Communicated?

In all three of its iterations, the development of NSCW questionnaires has been guided by the "burning" questions of business leaders, public policymakers, and academics, which we have spent months eliciting through telephone calls, focus groups, mailings, and meetings. It is our intent that this study belongs to the field and investigates many of its most important questions. By designing the study with input from its intended recipients, they become both the audience for and the communicators of the results.

Methodology and Response Rates

To this point in time, the NSCW has employed random-digit-dial telephone interviews and faced increasing difficulty in achieving acceptable response rates. Interview lengths have ranged from an average of 40 to 45 minutes, which certainly seems daunting. However, once interviewers have established the *eligibility* of someone from the household called, completion (or "cooperation") rates have exceeded 80% (98% in 2002) employing the most conservative calculation proposed by the American Association of Public Opinion Research (AAPOR: COOP1). We highly recommend AAPOR publications for guidance in calculating response rates (American Association for Public Opinion Research, 2004). The major problem the NSCW has faced has been *contacting* someone in the household and *screening* for eligibility.

Establishing telephone contact with a individual and screening them into the sample has become much more difficult over the past 10 years (1992–2002). In 1992, interviewers from Mathematica Policy Research made up to 10 calls to make contact and screen potential respondents; in 1997, interviewers from Louis Harris and Associates made up to 20 calls to contact and screen potential respondents; and in 2002, interviewers from Harris Interactive (formerly Louis Harris and Associates) made 30 or more calls to contact and screen potential respondents. It is important to note that we were not screening for members of a "rare" or particularly difficult to interview population: All persons 18 or older who worked any number of hours for pay or operated a business, and spoke English or Spanish were eligible to be interviewed.

Response rates for the 1992, 1997, and 2002 NSCW surveys have been quite similar despite increasing levels of effort over this period. Using conservative response rate calculations recommended by the Council of American Survey Research Organizations (CASRO) and the American Association for Opinion Research (AAPOR, 2004), the response rates for these three iterations of the NSCW range from 51 to 53%. In 2002, we made an effort to adjust for the growing number of residential and nonresidential telephone lines that are not used for voice communications. In this case, telephone numbers that were called 30 times with no response or a busy signal were considered ineligible numbers. If our adjustments are correct, the actual response rate for the 2002 NSCW may actually be 60% or slightly higher—still lower than we would like, but much better than most telephone surveys. (See discussion of data collection methodology—telephone interviews, above.)

Weighting the Sample and Design Effects

Sample weighting is widely used in survey research to adjust for potential sampling bias. The most common adjustment is for *differential probability of selection*. In telephone surveys that interview whoever picks up the phone or the first eligible contacted, there is really no way to adjust for selection bias. That is why scientific surveys of households typically interview a randomly selected eligible member of each household, if there is more than one eligible. To adjust for differential probability of selection in the latter case, one simply weights by the reciprocal of the probability of selection. Respondents in households with one eligible adult are weighted by 1; those in households with two eligible adults, by 2; those in households with three eligible adults, by 3; and so on. The net effect of this adjustment is to multiply the number of times respondents appear in the sample by their weights. Contemporary statistical analysis packages apply sample weights as instructed. Because respondents with weights greater than 1 appear more than once in a weighted sample, it is necessary to adjust weights to produce the actual sample size in order not to *artificially* reduce estimated sampling errors or inflate the power of statistical tests. If the actual sample size were 2,000 and the (preliminarily) weighted sample size were 2,500, the weighted sample size would be adjusted to the actual size by multiplying weights by (2,000/2,500 = 0.8).

In preparing NSCW data for analysis, we also perform additional sample weighting in each survey year. The full 2002 NSCW sampling scheme is briefly described here. Weighting was iterative, with each additional weighting step operating on weights from the preceding step. Weighting factors were selected because of their known correlations with variables of interest in the NSCW survey and because sample distributions were found to differ appreciably from population distributions as measured by March 2002 Current Population Survey (CPS) conducted by the U.S. Bureau of the Census for the U.S. Bureau of Labor Statistics.

After weighting for selection probability (above), we then weighted the sample to the proportions of households in the U.S. population with different numbers of eligibles as defined by our screening characteristics. Weights from the previous step were adjusted to reflect the proportions of households in the CPS with 1, 2, 3, 4, and 5 or more eligibles. If the preceding weight was 1, it was multiplied times the proportion of CPS households with 1 eligible divided by the proportion of sample households with 1 eligible. . . . and so on through households with 5 or more eligibles.

We also identified several other demographic variables on which our sample differed appreciably from the CPS after applying the weights generated to this point. Differences in the gender distributions seemed most problematic given the purposes of the study. We included gender as a weighting factor in previous surveys and did so again in 2002. Women have consistently been somewhat more likely to respond to NSCW surveys than men. The preceding weights were adjusted separately for men and women by multiply these weights times the proportion of eligible men/women in the CPS divided by the proportion of men/women in the sample to produce the same sex ratio in the sample as in the eligible population.

After weighting for gender, in addition to the preceding factors, the sample and population distributions became more similar. However, we still found disconcerting differences in the distributions of respondents and population eligibles by level of education completed. Since education is correlated with many of the variables of interest in the NSCW survey, it seemed imperative to make further adjustments. Following the same basic procedures used above, we then adjusted the weights generated to this point by education. This was the last weighting factor included for the 2002 NSCW. When the final weights were applied, sample and population distributions on various demographic variables were quite similar.

Whenever population demographics are available, sample weighting is possible; however, weighting does not guarantee that bias will be eliminated. This is particularly so when response rates are low, samples are not randomly drawn, and sample-population discrepancies are large. Moreover, when samples are not random, it is not possible to estimate the effects of weighting on sampling error.

Various sampling designs and sample weighting are associated with what are called *design effects*. When the design effect (DEF) is greater than 1 (no effect), the DEF increases sampling error by reducing the *effective sample size*. When DEFs are on the order of 1.1 or 1.2, many social scientists will simply ignore them because of their small effects on sampling error. However, those concerned with making the most accurate estimates of population statistics possible (not always the purpose of survey research) based on their sample data should adjust their estimates of sampling error for any design effects. It should also be noted that different design effects may be associated with different subsamples and with different variables in the same sample. When reporting on total samples, however, estimated average design effects across variables are generally used unless a very high degree of precision is called for.

Another situation in which DEFs are important is in comparisons of independent samples of the same population, perhaps obtained at different points in time—for example, the 1977 QES versus the 2002 NSCW. These two studies have different design effects, both greater than 1. Unless the DEFs are taken into account in statistical comparisons of the two samples, the power of tests will be artificially inflated by virtue of the fact that the *effective* sample sizes for each survey are smaller than the *actual* sample sizes. Fortunately, there is a simple fix. If sample weights are divided by sample DEFs producing DEF-adjusted weights, one need only apply these DEF-adjusted weights when comparing the two independent samples.

Calculating DEFs can be quite complicated depending on the sampling design, weighting scheme, and analysis plan, which may rely heavily on comparisons of and generalizations from subsamples. Although approximate *overall* sample DEFs can be rather easily calculated for simple probability samples, readers should consult advanced statistical texts or statisticians before attempting such calculations.[4]

Evaluating Relevance

Data and findings from National Study of the Changing Workforce surveys have broad relevance to business, government, public policymakers, researchers, advocates, and the media. Findings from these surveys have had significant influence on workplace policy and practice. Public-use data files are available for use by other researchers, and literally hundreds have used these data in their own research.[5] Because of the great expense of conducting national surveys, the NSCW has become a—if not *the*—primary source of work-life data on large, representative national samples. Findings from the NSCW have helped to refocus work-life initiatives from their early emphasis on specific *programs* to an emphasis on *policies*, *practices*, and the *workplace culture* that address the needs of employees as whole persons at different points in the life cycle and appear to have a much greater impact on organizational bottom lines and employee/family well-being. They have also been the source of two collected academic volumes (MacDermid, Galinsky, & Bond, 2001; MacDermid, Galinsky, & Bond, 2005), as well as the source for Issue Briefs on specific topics, such as *Generation and Gender in the Workplace* (FWI, 2004), and reports, such as *When Work Works* (Bond, Galinsky, & Hill, 2004) written by FWI.

SURVEYS OF NATIONAL SAMPLES OF U.S. EMPLOYERS

In 1998, Families and Work Institute conducted the Business Work-Life Study (BWLS) surveying *employers* with more than 100 employees nationwide by telephone (Galinsky & Bond, 1998). Another cross-sectional survey, the National Study of Employers (NSE, renamed from BWLS), was conducted in 2004. Questions were developed in collaboration with business leaders and work-life researchers.

Is This a Study That Can Make a Difference?

Many BWLS questions were specifically designed to parallel those in our 1997 NSCW survey of *employees*, enabling us to selectively compare employer with employee perspectives. In addition, other questions were designed to parallel those used in the *Working Mother* magazine's 100 Best Companies for Working Mothers, which we had revised for them in 1997. Because most surveys of employers on work-life issues are conducted of members or clients of specific organizations, or other self-selected groups, there is little nationally representative data on employers. The BWLS was created to fill that gap and to provide *benchmarks* for employers interested in knowing how their fringe benefits and policies measure up. Our hope was to assess change over time. In addition, since the initial study was conducted at the request of then Secretary of the Treasury, Robert Rubin, following a 1997 White House Conference on Child Care, and was used as the basis of a Treasury Department report, the intent by the government was to stimulate improvements in work-life practices, programs, and policies demonstrated (in the NSCW and elsewhere) to be associated with benefits to both employers and employees (U.S. Department of the Treasury, 1998).

In 2004, the NSE was designed to serve as the research basis for a new award—the Sloan Awards for Business Excellence in Workplace Flexibility. With funding from the Alfred P. Sloan Foundation and in collaboration with the Center for Workforce Preparation (an affiliate of the U.S. Chamber of Commerce) and the Center for Emerging Futures, we are developing a new locally based award. Legislation to be introduced in Congress in 2005 will establish a national Sloan Award. Questions from the NSE are used in surveys of employers and employees for purposes of award application. It is our intent that by having nationally representative data on employer practices, the awards will be given to employers that exceed the national norms, thus continuing to raise the bar for and improving employer practice.

How Can the Study Be Designed so That It Is Rigorous and Unbiased? How Can the Results Best Be Communicated?

The BWLS and the NSE have been designed by leaders in the work-life field to provide the kind of data they need for business and policy decision making. For example, a group of national leaders from the Alliance for Work Life Progress, the Boston Center for Work & Family, Corporate Voices for Working Families, The Conference Board Work-Life Leadership Council with the Center for Workforce Preparation, the Center for Emerging Futures, and academics from the Sloan network all met to discuss the study design and reviewed the survey. These processes help ensure that what is found will be used by the field. In addition, using the NSE as the basis for local and national awards increases its utility.

Methodology and Response Rates

Because the 2004 NSE is still in process, we describe the 1998 BWLS in discussing this program of research. The sample of companies surveyed for the BWLS was randomly drawn from lists maintained by Dun and Bradstreet (D&B), which maintains a database of approximately 14 million U.S. companies. The call list was randomly selected by D&B and purchased by Families and Work Institute. Although D&B lists are not exhaustive, particularly with respect to very small companies, they represent the most comprehensive database commercially available.

The BWLS surveyed a stratified random sample of private for-profit and nonprofit companies with 100 or more employees in the United States. Selection was proportional to the number of people employed by each company. This resulted in oversampling larger companies, which are underrepresented in the total universe of companies, to ensure that the sample would support generalizations to companies of all sizes greater than 100 employees.

The final sample included 1,057 companies—84% private for-profit and 16% nonprofit. Interviews were conducted by senior interviewers from Louis Harris and Associates (now Harris Interactive). Human resource directors or others directly responsible for personnel policies were interviewed. The response rate was 45%, based on the percentage of all companies on the call list that completed interviews. Although a higher response rate would have been desirable, it is quite difficult and growing more difficult to gain the cooperation of company managers to participate in outside research when cold-calling.

Because larger companies were oversampled, it was necessary to weight the sample so that it would be representative of companies in general. The sample weights were created by dividing the proportion of companies with more than 100 employees in the full D&B database of a particular size by the proportion of companies in the BWLS sample of the same size. Weighting by company size was particularly important because our own and others' research has often demonstrated strong relationships between company size and particular fringe benefits and policies.

Evaluating Relevance

Findings from the 1998 Business Work-Life Study were used by Secretary of the Treasury Robert Rubin as the basis for formulating policy recommendations. In addition, these findings have and continue to be used by many companies to benchmark their own benefits, policies and practices, resulting in changes motivated by desires to keep up with one's competitors in order to be employers of choice. Moreover, business leaders have encouraged us to repeat the study to bring national benchmarks up to date, which we are doing with the 2004 National Study of Employers.

SURVEY OF EMPLOYEES IN A SINGLE ORGANIZATION

Much can be learned by surveying employees in a single organization, even though it is not possible to generalize without qualification to other organizations not studied. In 1990, Johnson & Johnson (J&J) and Families and Work Institute partnered to survey J&J employees in four divisions before and after their implementation of a major work-life initiative—the *Balancing Work and Family Program* (BWFP; FWI, 1993).

Is This a Study That Can Make a Difference? How Can the Study Be Designed so That It Is Rigorous and Unbiased? How Can the Results Best Be Communicated?

We undertook this study because we knew that companies that had not ventured into the work-life arena wanted hard data on the impact of this kind of initiative. Although Johnson & Johnson was less interested in knowing about the specific impact of their own Balancing Work and Family Program (because, in their words, they knew "it is the right thing to do"), they agreed to partner with us in this endeavor for the "public good" as well as to have us share the findings publicly, which is unlike so many corporate research projects in which research findings are considered proprietary. Because this was one of the first studies to rigorously assess the impact of work and family policies and programs, its results were widely anticipated and used by companies to put their own initiatives into place.

Methodology and Response Rates

This study is an example of using longitudinal and cross-sectional survey methodology for program evaluation in a pre-post quasi-experimental design. The longitudinal sample comprised employees who responded at both points in time; the cross-sectional samples, those who responded at each point in time. Although such designs are not as robust as true experimental designs when evaluating program effects, often they are the only alternative (Campbell & Stanley, 1963). The survey (*census*) was conducted using self-administered questionnaires mailed to *all* employees in the four divisions of J&J targeted for the BWFP initiative. Questions were developed in close collaboration with J&J staff to provide relevant pre-intervention benchmarks and measure changes after a year of BWFP implementation.

All employees did not, of course, respond. Of the 5,679 questionnaires mailed in 1990, 2,402 were returned in usable form, for a response rate of 42.3%. Of 5,285 questionnaires mailed in 1992, 2,417 were returned in usable form for a response rate of 45.7%. It is likely that the response rate was depressed because individual employees were identified by their employee numbers written on the questionnaires for purposes of linking pre- and post-responses in the longitudinal design. Even though employees were told that the survey was being conducted by an independent research organization that guaranteed their anonymity (i.e., not to share individual information with the company), it is very likely that some employees were skeptical. Moreover, there was no penalty for not responding. Approximately 50% of the sample responded to *both* the 1990 and 1992 questionnaires. Again, issues of confidentiality may have played some role in the rate of response across time. However, the research burden—"How many times are they going to ask me about this?"—must also be considered, as well as attrition of respondents from the J&J workforce. Our impression from our own and others' research is that these response rates are not unusually low even for surveys that have company support.

Weighting the Sample

This study was conducted early in the life of Families and Work Institute when there were no research staff on board sensitive to or knowledgeable about weighting to reduce potential sample bias. And, thus, no sample weighting was performed. When 1990 and 1992 respondents were compared with the full workforce of employees, a number of statistically significant differences were found—occupational status, gender, race/ethnicity, marital status, and tenure at the company—and presented in the report. Differences were smaller in 1992 and modest in both years. Readers were simply cautioned "not to generalize these findings to the entire workforce, without qualification." Today, we would certainly explore sample weighting options to improve the generalizability of findings.

Evaluating Relevance

The findings, even with qualifications, were extremely relevant to J&J management and reinforced their commitment to the BWFP and broader work-life initiatives. Other employers that perceive the findings to be generalizable have also looked to this study to guide their own development of work-life initiatives. Some analyses were longitudinal, comparing the responses of the same employees in 1990 and 1992. Other analyses were cross-sectional, using data from the 1992 sample to assess change over the past 2 years as reported retrospectively by employees. A sample of those findings are presented here to indicate how provocative longitudinal and even cross-sectional findings can be:

- *Employees report that from 1990 to 1992 their immediate supervisors became significantly more responsive to their family and personal needs.* (longitudinal finding)

- *According to employees, their immediate supervisors' attitudes toward flexible work arrangements grew significantly more positive from 1990 to 1992.* (longitudinal finding)
- *Employees who used flexible time and leave policies were significantly less likely to think they paid a price for doing so in 1992 than in 1990.* (longitudinal finding)
- *More than half of employees surveyed in 1992 felt that their work environment had improved over the last 2 years because of Johnson & Johnson's work-family initiative. Women, employees with dependent care responsibilities, and married employees with employed spouses were significantly more likely to report improvements than men, employees without dependents, and employees with nonemployed spouses.* (cross-sectional finding)

If a *prospective* longitudinal design is not feasible, one might rely on a *retrospective* design only, asking employees how things have changed since the intervention occurred. However, a longitudinal (or mixed longitudinal–cross-sectional design) is more robust.

SURVEY OF EMPLOYEES IN A NONREPRESENTATIVE SAMPLE OF ORGANIZATIONS

Beginning in 2000, Families and Work Institute, Catalyst, and the Boston College Center for Work & Family supported a group of 12 multinational corporations in their efforts to examine the experiences of women business leaders in the global economy.

Is This a Study That Can Make a Difference?

All of the participating companies depend heavily on women in executive roles, want to increase their numbers, and want to improve retention. Although most of the participating companies had conducted their own surveys on issues of women's leadership, they turned to the three nonprofits as partners in hope of deepening their understanding and of obtaining comparative data from the other companies. The participating nonprofits saw this study as an opportunity to better understand issues of women's advancement and to promote the findings with the many other companies in their orbits.

How Can the Study Be Designed so That It Is Rigorous and Unbiased? How Can the Results Best Be Communicated?

This study, *Leaders in a Global Economy*, had several stages. In the first stage, researchers conducted unstructured interviews with four or five very senior women in each of the participating companies to ascertain what helped them and what stood in the way of their own success at work and home, in connecting to their communities, and in caring for themselves. Based on that information, 90 senior women from nine of the participating companies participated in a 3-day seminar in Prague to go over the findings, to learn from each other, to shape the next stage of the study—a survey of the top leadership—and to make action plans in their own companies to promote women's advancement.

One of the recommendations of the Prague seminar was to include men in the survey to provide a point of comparison. In addition, the women leaders were invited to frame questions that they would like to see the survey address and to e-mail them to the researchers. The study genuinely reflects the questions posed by women leaders in the companies as well as the researchers. For this reason, its findings have generated widespread interest and use by companies, women leaders, and the media.

Defining and Drawing the Sample

In 2002, 10 of these companies participated in a global survey of high-level executive women and men (Galinsky et al., 2003): Baxter International, Inc.; Citigroup; J.P. Morgan Chase & Co.; Deloitte Touche Tohmatsu; Dow Chemical Company; Eli Lilly and Company; Goldman Sachs; IBM Corporation; Marriott International; and the Procter & Gamble Company. The sample of executives was selected from comprehensive company lists of their international employee universes, which is a great advantage in sampling. The top 100–125 male and top 100–125 female executives were selected from each company. Executive level was defined as the reporting distance away from the CEO—reporting directly to the CEO (Level 1), reporting to someone who reported directly to the CEO (Level 2), reporting to someone 1 level away from the CEO (Level 3), and reporting to someone 2 levels away from the CEO (Level 4). In all companies we included all employees at Levels 1 and 2. When additional employees at Level 3, combined with those at Levels 1 and 2, exceeded 125, we randomly sampled employees at Level 3 to complete the company sample. When there were not enough employees at Levels 1, 2, and 3 to complete the company sample—due to the way in which the company was organized internally and on an international basis—we randomly sampled employees (generally a small number) from Level 4 to complete the company sample.

Internet-Based Methodology and Response Rates

The survey was conducted via the Internet. As previously noted, the questionnaire was developed over the period of a year with input from work-life and diversity experts and company representatives, and multiple reviews by each participating company, including their legal departments in some instances. All employees in the sample had ready access to the Internet, were Internet-savvy, and had personal Internet addresses.

Executives selected for the sample were first contacted by their CEOs or other top-level officers via e-mail to advise them of the survey and encourage their participation. Subsequent emails provided the Web site address for the survey and a personal ID for entering the site. A survey consultant developed the Web site to present the questionnaire with skip patterns to ensure that respondents were not asked irrelevant questions. Respondents could exit the questionnaire at any point and reenter where they left off. Company staff were available to provide assistance if problems arose, and reminders were emailed as appropriate.

Families and Work Institute maintained all files that could be used to link individual employees to their survey responses. This required having considerable trust in our relationships with companies, built up over a decade of institutional history. For some companies, releasing such information to outside organizations of any type went against standard corporate policy and required special waivers. All files containing identifying information were destroyed once the survey was completed. Of 2,157 executives selected into the original sample, 1,100 provided completed questionnaires for an overall response rate of 51%. Given the hectic lives of these executives and the experiences of other researchers who have studied executive-level employees, this response rate is quite good.

Evaluating Relevance

The findings of the survey have been extremely useful to the executives and human resource staff of participating companies in their diversity initiatives, and in provoking important rethinking of strategies for supporting and retaining women executives. A sampling of findings follows:

- Although the majority of high-level executives (61%) are work-centric, a substantial minority (32%, men and women alike) are dual-centric, placing an equivalent emphasis on work and on their personal or family lives. Interestingly, women who are dual-centric have advanced to higher reporting levels than other women.

- Women executives face many more obstacles to advancement than men—specifically, being excluded from important networks, having a limited number of role models, having limited opportunities for experiences in line or general management positions, and being in dual-career families.
- While it is true that support and mentoring by higher-level executives—both male and female—are essential to developing leaders, we find that women mentoring women is of special importance.

Companies took these and other findings from the survey back to their diversity councils and women's networks to stimulate discussion and guide forward planning for more effective advancement of women into executive ranks and more effective retention. Another survey is currently being planned by the participating companies and other corporations to focus on leadership in Europe.

SURVEYS OF CHILDREN

In 1998 Ellen Galinsky, President of Families and Work Institute, conducted a survey of parents and children examining work and family life issues. This study became the first in an ongoing series of surveys of children called *Ask the Children*® (Galinsky, 1999). Our position is that young people have a great deal of importance to say about the issues they face growing up that adults need to hear. Surveys in this series provide children with a powerful voice.

Is This a Study the Can Make a Difference?

Here we describe the *Youth and Employment* survey that was designed to document young people's experiences in the workforce, their motivations for working, their educational and employment aspirations, their thoughts about work and family life, their expectations of employment as adults, and so forth (Galinsky, Kim, Bond, & Salmond, 2000). Our hope was to glean insights into tomorrow's workforce that would be useful to educators, parents, and employers.

How Can the Study Be Designed so That It Is Rigorous and Unbiased?
How Can the Results Best Be Communicated?

The questionnaire was developed after reviewing the literature in collaboration with business leaders, educators, youth employment experts, and others. In addition, and very importantly, focus groups with young people were used to shape the final questionnaire so that it reflected their experiences and voices.

Defining and Drawing the Sample

A nationally representative sample of high schools and 10th-, 11th-, and 12th-grade students was drawn by Harris Interactive. The sample of schools and students was based on a highly stratified two-stage sampling design with clustering. This design employs features similar to designs used in various national surveys of students and schools that are conducted by the National Center for Education Statistics (NCES) within the U.S. Department of Education.

The sampling frame for schools was provided by the NCES. In the first stage, a sample of schools was selected from a list of all schools in the United States. The primary stratification variables were school type (public, parochial, private), grade coverage, urbanicity, and region. Within the basic strata defined by these dimensions, further stratification was carried out by state, grade enrollment, and zipcode. Within each substratum, the required number of schools was selected with probabilities proportional to the number of students. When particular schools were unable to participate because of district policies or refused to participate, replacement schools were selected by finding the closest match by zipcode for selected schools in the same stratum and group size.

Data Collection Method and Response Rates

Data were collected using self-administered questionnaires. Questionnaires were distributed by English teachers during English classes that all students attend. Teachers received written instructions regarding administration of the survey. Students received sealable envelopes into which they placed their completed questionnaires for return to the survey research firm. Questionnaires contained no identifying information, and students' anonymity was guaranteed and maintained. Overall, 1,028 students completed useable questionnaires. The response rate of students attending their English classes on the day of data collection was virtually 100%. The sample was weighted according to information in the NCES database for all schools in the United States—the distribution of students by grade, region, size of place, gender, and race/ethnicity.

Evaluating Relevance

The findings from the study have been widely cited and used to inform action. Select findings follow:

- 78% of 10th-, 11th-, and 12th-grade students have a job during the current school year or had one during the previous summer.
- 59% of students work to save for college or other long-term goals and 16% work because their families need the money they earn.
- As adults, most students want to find jobs that are personally meaningful (84%) and to find jobs where they can be creative and use their special skills (69%). Fewer will look for jobs where they can make a lot of money (58%) or be able to succeed very quickly (49%).
- 79% of students want adult jobs that will allow time for personal and family activities—a strong message to many organizations that currently place very high demands on employee time.

Findings from the original *Ask the Children* survey and the *Youth and Employment* survey were used in the development of activities for the Ms. Foundation for Women's 2003 and 2004 *Take Our Daughters and Sons to Work Day*. About 11% of employed Americans—14.4 million people—participated in the program, bringing some 15.8 million children to their workplaces.

Although surveys of nationally representative samples of students or teachers are quite complicated and expensive, more modest surveys of representative samples of students or teachers within a single school district can provide extremely valuable information for local decision making.

CONCLUSION

Survey research can serve many purposes as suggested here. Although we focus on surveys of fairly large and representative samples in this chapter, small-scale surveys of nonrepresentative samples can provide very provocative data for hypothesis generation and the tweaking of prevailing theory. More often than not, student-initiated survey research projects may fit into this category. A major advantage of small-scale surveys is that they can examine issues in much greater detail than large-scale survey research. There are, however, numerous representative data bases available for secondary analyses, and we urge student researchers to take these resources into account[6]—either relying solely on these sources to test important hypotheses or using statistics from representative samples as points of reference in evaluating findings from their own research.

NOTES

[1] Although qualitative, experimental, and survey research methods can be applied to animals (cattle), things (water pollution levels), and events (automobile accidents) as well as human beings, here we consider only human behavioral research.

[2] Estimating sampling error:

se = standard error
p = proportion
n = sample size
$se(p)$ = square root of $(p\,(1 - p))\,/\,(n - 1)$
Sampling Error (95% confidence interval) = $1.96 * se(p)$

Applying the preceding formula, the sampling error for a sample of 300 in which the characteristic of interest has a 50/50 percent distribution would be the square root of $(.5\,(1-.5)\,/\,299) * 1.96$ or $\pm 6\%$—the maximum sampling error for generalizations from the total sample of 300 to the population from which it was drawn. Most textbooks on survey research (e.g., Fowler, 2002; Rea, 1997) provide this formula and formulas for estimating the sampling errors for means as well as tables for samples of different sizes and different proportional distributions. It is important to note that sampling error is greatest (maximum error) when 50% of the sample exhibits the characteristic and 50% does not, while sampling errors decrease as distributions become more imbalanced.

[3] www.HarrisInteractive.com (panels).

[4] In-depth discussions of variance estimation and design effects (intermediate/advanced statistics) can be found in *Practical Methods for Design and Analysis of Complex Surveys* (Lehtonen & Pahkinen, 2004) and in *Introduction to Variance Estimation* (Wolter, 1985). An example of design effects associated with the complex Panel Study of Income Dynamics (PSID) can be found in *Panel Study of Income Dynamics: A User's Guide* (Hill, 1991). This book is also an excellent general guide to the PSID dataset that is available to faculty and students for analysis (http://psidonline.isr.umich.edu).

[5] NSCW public-use files and reports are available from www.familiesandwork.org.

[6] Large representative national samples addressing work-life questions that are readily available to academic researchers include not only FWI's National Study of the Changing Workforce, but also the longitudinal Panel Study of Income Dynamics (http://psidonline.isr.umich.edu) and the U.S. Department of Labor's National Longitudinal Surveys (www.bls.gov). An interesting study of life transitions using data from the NLS can be found in Klerman (1993).

REFERENCES

American Association for Public Opinion Research (AAPOR). (2004). *Standard definitions: Final dispositions of case codes and outcome rates for surveys* (3rd ed.). Lenexa, KS: AAPOR.

Bond, J. T., Galinsky, E., & Friedman, D. E. (1993). *The changing workforce: Highlights of the national study.* New York: Families and Work Institute.

Bond, J. T., Galinsky, E., & Hill, E. J. (2004). *When work works—flexibility: A critical ingredient in creating an effective workplace.* New York: Families and Work Institute.

Bond, J. T., Galinsky, E., Lord, M., Staines, G. L., & Brown, K. (1991). *Beyond the parental leave debate: The impact of laws in four states.* New York: Families and Work Institute.

Bond., J. T., Galinsky, E., & Swanberg, J. E. (1998). *The 1997 national study of the changing workforce.* New York: Families and Work Institute.

Bond, J. T. with Thompson, C., Galinsky, E., & Prottas, D. (2003). *Highlights of the 2002 national study of the changing workforce.* New York: Families and Work Institute.

Campbell, D., & Stanley, J. (1963). *Experimental and quasi-experimental designs for research.* Chicago: Rand-McNally.

Cohen, J. (1988). *Statistical power analysis for the behavioral sciences* (2nd ed.). Mahwah: Lawrence Erlbaum Associates.

Council for Marketing and Opinion Research (CMOR). (1999). *Respondent cooperation and industry survey image.* December.

Families and Work Institute. (1993). *An evaluation of Johnson & Johnson's work-family initiative.* New York: Families and Work Institute.

Families and Work Institute. (2004). *Generation and gender in the workplace.* New York: Families and Work Institute.

Fowler, F. J. (2002). *Survey research methods* (3rd ed.). Beverly Hills, CA: Sage.

Galinsky, E. (1999). *Ask the children: What America's children really think about working parents.* New York: Morrow.

Galinsky, E., & Bond, J. T. (1998). *The 1998 business Work-Life study: A sourcebook.* New York: Families and Work Institute.

Galinsky, E., Kim, S. S., Bond, J. T., & Salmond, K. (2000). *Youth and employment: Today's students; tomorrow's workforce* [Summary and Discussion Guide]. New York: Families and Work Institute.

Galinsky, E., Salmond, K., Bond, J. T., Kropf, M. B., Moore, M., & Harrington, B. (2003). *Leaders in a global economy: A study of executive women and men* [Executive Summary]. New York: Families and Work Institute.

Hill, M. S. (1991). *Panel study of income dynamics: A user's guide.* Beverly Hills, CA: Sage.

Jacobs, J. A., & Gerson, K. (2004). *The time divide: Work, family, and gender inequality.* Cambridge, MA: Harvard University Press.

Kerlinger, F. N. (1964). *Foundations of behavioral research: Educational and psychological inquiry.* New York: Holt, Rinehart & Winston.

Klerman, J. (1993). *Characterizing leave for maternity: Modeling the NLSY data.* Retrieved October, 2004, from http://www.bls.gov/ore/abstract/nl/nl930010.htm.

Lee, Y. S., & Waite, L. (forthcoming 2005). How much time husbands spend on housework depends on who you ask, how you ask and what you ask.*Journal of Marriage and Family.*

Lehtonen, R., & Pahkinen, E. (2004). *Practical methods for design and analysis of complex surveys* (2nd ed.). New York: Wiley.

MacDermid, S., Galinsky, E., & Bond, J. T. (Guest Eds.). (2001). *Journal of Family and Economic Issues, 22.*

MacDermid, S., Galinsky, E., & Bond, J. T. (Guest Eds.). (forthcoming 2005). *Journal of Family Issues.*

Moen, P. (2003). *It's about time: Couples and careers.* Ithaca, NY: Cornell University Press.

Moen, P., & Sweet, S. (2004). From "work-family" to "flexible careers": A life course reframing. *Community, Work and Family, 7*(2), 209–226.

Moen, P. (2001). *Customizing the career clock: Retirement planning and expectations.* Ithaca, NY: Cornell Employment and Family Careers Institute.

Piekarski, L., Kaplan, G., & Prestegaard, J. (1999). *Telephony and telephone sampling: The dynamics of change.* Presentation to the AAPOR Annual Conference, May, 1999.

Quinn, R. P., & Staines, G. L. (1979). *The 1977 quality of employment survey.* Ann Arbor: Institute for Social Research, University of Michigan.

Rea, L. M. (1997). *Designing and conducting survey research* (2nd ed.). New York: Jossey-Bass.

Repetti, R. L. (1987). Linkages between family and work roles. *Applied social psychology annual, vol. 7.* Beverly Hills, CA: Sage.

Repetti, R. L. (1994). Short-term and long-term processes linking job stressors to father–child interaction. *Social Development, 3,* 1–15.

Repetti, R. L., & Wood, J. (1997). The effects of daily stress at work on mothers' interactions with preschoolers. *Journal of Family Psychology, 11,* 90–108.

Sudman, S. (1976). *Applied sampling.* New York: Academic Press.

Sweet, S., & Moen, P. (2004). Intimate academics: Coworking couples in two universities. *Innovative Higher Education, 24*(4), 255–272.

Tuckel, P. (2001). *The vanishing respondent in telephone surveys.* Presentation to the AAPOR Annual Conference, May, 2001.

U.S. Department of the Treasury. (1998). *Investing in child care: Challenges facing working parents and the private sector response* (USDT Report-3110).Washington, DC: U.S. Government Printing Office.

Wolter, K. (1985). *Introduction to variance estimation.* New York: Springer-Verlag.

20

Using Focus Groups to Study Work and Family

Janet Smithson
Manchester Metropolitan University

Focus groups are increasingly being used as a research tool in work-family and work-life research, and are popular as a source of information on a wide range of work-family issues, experiences, and dilemmas. Focus groups are usually defined either as group interviews (Hughes & DuMont, 1993) or group discussions (Kreuger, 1998). In most cases, a focus group is understood to be a group of 6–12 participants, with an interviewer, or moderator, asking questions about a particular topic. The emphasis is on the way the group discusses the issues, with interactions between participants in the group being the distinctive characteristic of focus group methodology. This interaction within groups generates a particular type of data (Kitzinger, 1995), something in between a natural discussion of a relevant topic and a constrained group interview with set questions.

This chapter sets out some of the main advantages and limitations of using focus groups in work-family research projects together with suggestions on how to use and analyze the groups most effectively. First, some of the reasons for using focus groups in work-family research are considered, with reference to some key studies that have used focus groups. In section 2, design and procedure are considered, including sampling and selecting participants, the logistics of recording and managing the data, and ethical considerations. Third, the role of the moderator, including strategies for moderating focus groups, is discussed. In section 4, some of the specific issues that arise in analysis of focus groups are considerd. Finally, section 5 looks at the use of focus groups in specific contexts: within organizational research, in cross-cultural and cross-national work-family studies, and the growing use of online focus groups. Extracts from focus groups used in recent work-family research projects in the UK[1] are used to illustrate the points made.

WHY USE FOCUS GROUPS IN WORK-FAMILY RESEARCH?

The nature of the research question should drive the methodology used. In this section, some of the unique features and opportunities offered by focus groups are described.

Framing in Words of Participants

A central feature of focus groups is that they provide researchers with direct access to the language and concepts participants use to structure their experiences and to think and talk about a designated topic. Using standard focus group methodology, focus groups are composed of fairly homogenous groups, for example, all men, or new parents, or managers working in a particular organization. This "within-group homogeneity" is intended to encourage focus group participants to talk about issues in their own words, elaborating stories and themes that help researchers understand how participants structure and organize their social world (Hughes & DuMont, 1993). A particular strength of the methodology is the possibility for research participants to develop ideas collectively, bringing forward their own priorities and perspectives, "to create theory grounded in the actual experience and language of [the participants]" (Du Bois, 1983).

Development of New Constructs

Focus groups are often used at an early stage of research to develop new constructs or to develop themes and ideas for larger research projects. The method is particularly strong in exploring issues in a general way, and the group dynamics frequently result in new concerns and perspectives being aired and discussed, often in ways unexpected by the initial research agenda. For example, in a study of young European adults' expectations of future work and family, the theme of job insecurity and its perceived impact on starting a family emerged in participants' discussions regularly, despite not having been part of the original research agenda. Because of this, job insecurity became a major theme for the second stage of the research (Brannen, Lewis, Nilsen, & Smithson, 2002).

Studying Cultural Variations and Minority Groups

One of the claims made in favor of focus groups as a methodology is that they can be a powerful method for minority groups or groups who are often ignored in other research methods to express their views and experiences (Wilkinson, 1998). The formulation of issues and concerns in participants' own words, and the emphasis on the issues that participants view as important to the topic, can be particularly useful for highlighting issues for disadvantaged or minority groups by validating and publicizing their views. Examples for work-family research include studying the work-family orientations of ethnic minority populations or of diverse family forms.

Studying the "Dynamics" of Attitudes and Opinions

Focus group researchers are often particularly interested in the way that group dynamics can provide researchers with an understanding of how opinions are formed, changed, and expressed in a social situation (Morgan, 1988). Typically, focus group data are not just a response to the researcher's preconceived questions (as may happen in more structured interviews) but include discussion and elaboration by the group, with participants developing links between individual and collective experiences (Smithson, 2000; Pini, 2002). Some of the ways in which group members build on each other's accounts can be seen in the following extract, where two women complete each other's utterances and so jointly build a description of their experiences on maternity leave—what Jacoby and Ochs (1995) termed "co-construction" of accounts:

Extract 1: Expectant mothers, organizational focus group [2]

Rachel: I'm going to every single coffee morning that they say you know [pause]
Wendy: ... and especially if you're on maternity you sort of lose contact with your work mates, don't you?
Rachel: You forget how to have a conversation [pause]
Wendy: ... and then you're not, unless you can go to things like that [pause]
Rachel: Yes
Wendy: ... Otherwise you're totally on your own.

In this extract, Rachel and Wendy together build a picture of their experiences of maternity leave. This type of collaborative construction of accounts is common in focus group situations, demonstrating how people are encouraged and also influenced by feedback from other group members to elaborate on their experiences (Smithson & Diaz, 1996).

An Enjoyable and Empowering Experience for Participants

One further feature of focus groups is that they can also be a creative and enjoyable experience for participants. Many participants enjoy the groups and the opportunity to discuss their opinions with others in a fairly relaxed research environment. This can lead to instances of shared humor and storytelling by group members. People also often use the groups to gain new information. For example, in an organizational study of new parents in the workplace, an expectant mother learned from the new mothers in the group about her rights and entitlements from the company policies. Focus groups with children have been shown to be a very effective approach for collecting data in a setting in which children feel comfortable (Ronen et al., 2001).

Key Work-Family Studies That Have Used Focus Groups

Work-family researchers are increasingly using focus groups in their research. Ingersoll-Dayton, Neal, and Hammer (2001) used focus groups to inform the first stage of a study on Dual Earner Couples in the Sandwiched Generation. They conducted 17 focus groups with 63 participants to investigate the ways in which couples who balance multiple responsibilities have devised unique ways of handling these various demands. Findings from the focus groups, including the help that elders could provide to the sandwich generation (financial, child care, and emotional), were used to inform the next stage of the research—a survey questionnaire. Barnett used focus groups in a study of the effects on children's well-being of mothers working shift work. In the first phase of the study, focus groups were conducted to explore the reasons why mothers chose to work the shifts they worked and to learn what shift-related concerns they had about their children's well-being. Instruments assessing these dimensions of shift work were then developed. Gallinsky, Kim, and Bond (2001) used focus groups to study feelings of being overworked, using the findings to inform the design of a telephone survey. A European study of young adults in five countries used focus groups to look at orientations to work and family (Brannen, Lewis, Nilsen, & Smithson, 2002). The study found that job insecurity was a major issue across Europe, hindering expectations of family formation or career progression.

DESIGN AND PROCEDURE

The practicalities of organizing focus groups are covered in various guides, for example, Vaughn et al., 1996, Morgan and Kreuger, 1998, and Bloor et al., 2001. Some of the main issues are summarized in this section.

Sampling Design and Size of Groups

The number and composition of groups will be driven by the research question. For example, the research may entail the need for groups of men and women at particular life stages or working in a particular organization. It may be desirable to compare the opinions of people before and after having children, or to compare the experiences of people in different jobs but at the same life stage. While researchers are encouraged (e.g., Ritchie & Lewis, 2003) to aim for within-group homogeneity—that is, single sex, all parents, at same life stage or career level—this is not always feasible. There are many other variables that may need to be taken into consideration, such as nationality, sexuality, and ethnic background. For work-family topics, having people at similar life stages—for example, all parents or all expectant parents—can be particularly relevant. In our research we found that when parents of young children are in focus groups with nonparents, the parents take on the role of "experts" in work-family issues, to the extent that nonparents have trouble joining in. However, heterogenous groups can produce very interesting discussions, for example, in mixed-sex groups participants can challenge the typical male and female discourses on these topics. The size and the composition of the focus group should be driven by the research question itself. So, for instance, if the author is examining issues salient to work/family conflict among men and women, and she is especially interested in the gender differences in the perception of conflict, it may be important for the focus groups to be segregated by gender. Furthermore, organizational research cautions against putting supervisors and supervisees in the same focus group, as the latter group may not speak up.

While the literature often (e.g., Vaughn et al., 1996) recommends focus groups of up to 12 participants, there are practical and methodological reasons why many focus groups are smaller. In larger groups, there is a likelihood that some participants will remain silent or speak very little, while smaller groups (say 4–8 participants) often provide an environment where all participants can play an active part in the discussion. In work-family studies, smaller groups have often yielded interesting and relevant data, giving more space for all participants to talk and to explore the various themes in detail (Brannen et al., 2002). Richie and Lewis (2003) suggested that if groups are smaller than four they can lose some of the qualities of being a group, while they see triads and dyads as an effective hybrid of in-depth interviews. Practically, it can be difficult to get an exact number of participants to turn up for a focus group, especially if trying to get a specific subgroup, for example, new parents working in specific jobs or expectant mothers of a particular age. For these reasons, groups may be based on availability rather than representativeness of sample, with implications for analysis. Possible ways of reaching hard-to-get participants include offering incentives (money, refreshments) and providing child care. Sometimes focus groups may be practically unfeasible, for example, interviewing people who are geographically distant, who have very little time, or who will be being interviewed in a second language. Telephone and online focus group methods are being developed (Chappell, 2003) and will be discussed later in this chapter.

Procedure

The focus group procedure is typically to follow a relatively unstructured interview guide, which generates a list of topics for discussion. The aim is to cover the topics set by the research agenda but with some flexibility to allow related topics to emerge in this context. The focus group moderator (who may or may not be the researcher) guides the discussion, making sure that all topics are covered and that all group members are given the chance to speak. Groups will ideally last from 1–2 hours. Just as with other forms of semistructured interview, testing the guide on a pilot group is highly recommended to ensure that the length of the schedule is realistic in the time available, that the questions are understood by the participants, and that the moderator is familiar with the questions.

Logistics

Focus group methodology has specific data-management issues. It is not possible to moderate a group and take detailed notes simultaneously, so groups will either need to be recorded or a dedicated note-taker will be required. Most research focus groups are recorded on audio- or video-tape, and it is often suggested that an observer also be present to make notes. A common problem for focus group recording is the quality of sound recording for a large group. Standard audiocassette recorders are often not capable of recording the talk of many people in a large room, although recent mini-disc technology makes this easier. Especially in larger groups, it is often impossible to tell from an audio recording alone which group member is speaking. Having a dedicated note-taker who makes a record of who is speaking and the first words of their utterance can be useful for attributing authorship to each comment. Suggestions for managing the data include taking great care with recording, using high-quality instruments, and also back-up instruments. Another useful tactic is for the moderator (and observer) to write detailed notes immediately after focus group if possible. When using focus group data, it is standard practice to change names and other identifying details of participants to ensure group members' anonymity.

Ethical Considerations

A particular concern with using focus group methodology is the ethical issues involved of having more than one research participant at a time. The researcher cannot guarantee that all discussion in this context will remain totally confidential—though they can guarantee it on their part, the other group members may not be discreet. A useful strategy is to start the focus group with a list of "dos and don'ts," including asking participants to respect each other's confidences and not repeat what was said in the group; however, this cannot be enforced. The moderator can guarantee that he or she will keep the data anonymous and confidential, especially in an organizational setting. The moderator can also try and move the discussion on if group members appear uncomfortable with sensitive issues.

Suitability of Topics for Focus Groups

Certain topics are commonly understood to be unsuitable for the focus group context. In particular, topics that participants may view as personal or sensitive are often better left for other methods, such as individual interviews. These may include people's personal experiences or life histories, their sexuality, and topics such as infertility or financial status. Overall, a focus group is likely to elicit "public" accounts (Smithson, 2000; Sim, 2002) in contrast to the private accounts that may emerge in individual interviews or in everyday interactions. However, Kitzinger and Farquhar (1999) contended that focus groups sometimes provide an opportunity for "sensitive" topics to be raised, as there is the space for discussion and reflection and time to explore issues in a more in-depth way than might be the case in more routine dialogue. They argued that focus groups can be used to unpack the social construction of sensitive issues, uncover different layers of discourse, and illuminate group taboos and the routine silencing of certain views and experiences. The age of participants, gender, occupational status, and ethnic background will affect what participants feel comfortable discussing, as will be seen in the examples presented in this chapter. However, as will be seen in section 3, much depends on how the topic is introduced by the moderator and how it is taken up by the group: Groups may be happy to discuss sensitive topics such as sexual orientation and parenting in a general way but not to give personal details about their own lives. There are implications for analysis, too: Through attention to sensitive moments, researchers can identify unspoken assumptions and question the nature of everyday talk, as will be seen later in this chapter. Telephone and online focus groups, which are discussed in section 5, are a possible means of conducting group discussions on more sensitive topics.

MODERATING FOCUS GROUPS

In market research, moderators tend to be specifically trained and employed to perform this task, while in the social sciences researchers often moderate the group themselves. There are some advantages to the researcher being the moderator—it is easier to ensure that the relevant topics are covered, and interpretation and analysis of the data are easier when the researcher was present at the group. The role of the moderator is complex and can make a big difference to the group dynamics (Pini, 2002). In this section, some specific issues for focus group moderation are considered.

How to Start the Group

In many focus groups, participants will be strangers to each other and often unsure about what is required of them in a focus group. It is useful for the moderator to recount the purpose of the study and the main topics to be discussed. At this point it is often useful to remind participants about confidentiality and to explain how the data might be used, and also to ask people in the group, including the moderator, to introduce themselves. Possible strategies for starting the focus group discussion and "warming up" the participants include starting the group with a couple of simple, easy-to-answer general questions. For example, in a study of young adults' expectations of the future, participants were first asked what was important to them in a job at the moment. Another option is to start with a warm-up exercise, for example, in a recent study of new parents in Europe, participants were asked, "What are the first words that come into your head to describe being a parent?"

How Closely to Keep to the Schedule?

A particular issue for focus group moderation is how far to encourage lively in-depth discussion of some topics, at the risk of not leaving enough time to cover other topics on the schedule. The moderator is expected to strike a balance between generating interest in and discussion about a particular topic, while not pushing his or her own research agenda ending in confirming existing expectations (Vaughn et al., 1996; Sim, 2002). For analysis reasons, covering all the major topics in the focus group schedule is important, but groups will vary in how much or enthusiastically they talk about each topic.

Moderating Sensitive Issues

While sensitive topics are often left to more private research methods, it is unlikely that focus groups on work-family issues will never touch on potentially sensitive issues. Moreover, sensitive topics can be discussed in a general way in a focus group context, but with the emphasis on general discussion rather than individual experience, unless this is volunteered by a group member. In the following example, taken from a study of young adults' expectations of future work and family, the research team was interested in diversity of family forms and in young adults' attitudes to parenting, including lone parents, young parents, and same-sex parenting. In this context, homosexuality was brought up in a general way by the moderator, by asking the group for views on lesbian or gay parenting.

Extract 2: 18-year-old women, secretarial course

Mod: What do you think about lesbian couples, homosexual couples having children, do any of you know any people in that position?
Sally: I don't, I don't think it's right really, two lesbians to bring up a child.
Vicky: I don't know
Sally: because they're [pause]
Tina: It depends if they're happy
Rachel: if that's what they want

Some young people expressed their views on this subject, but the issue was always positioned from a heterosexual point of view. Here, Tina and Rachel, in common with many of the participants, expressed a tolerance of homosexuality while clearly positioning themselves as heterosexual (e.g., "It depends if *they're* happy"). These normative influences are not limited to focus groups (Bradburn & Sudman, 1979; Bryman, 1988) but are affected in focus group research by fear of peer group disapproval. From a perspective of hoping to influence policy-makers and employers toward a wider acceptance of "family needs," this was frustrating for the research team and demonstrates a limitation of the focus group methodology. However, the research did illuminate the current norms of the under-30 generation. One possible solution for this would be to include in the research design specific focus groups with young lesbians and gay men in order to understand their orientations to family life (Smithson, 2000; Stokoe & Smithson, 2002).

Moderator Influences on the Discussion

While focus group literature may sometimes give the impression that the ideal moderator is a neutral person with the ability to encourage the discussion and pick up on participants' responses and narratives, in practice the moderator can never be a neutral bystander and sometimes inevitably influences the discourse. In the study of young adults' orientations to family and work from which Extract 2 was taken, the moderator aimed to avoid what might be seen as heterosexist language, for example, by using the word "partner" instead of boyfriend/girlfriend. It is possible that the moderator's positioning of homosexual couples as "other" in this way encouraged this distancing of participants from the topic. However, in the UK, teenage girls such as those in Extract 2 are unlikely to use the gender-neutral term "partner" but will typically talk about "boyfriends." A moderator has the option to use the terms the group commonly uses, as she did in the example shown, despite the assumption of heterosexuality in the term, or to use inclusive terms that risk alienating the group. Her choice either way may influence the discussion. A good moderator will aim for reflexivity and awareness of the way his or her characteristics and behavior may be influencing the group, rather than assuming it is possible to be totally uninfluential (Wilkinson & Kitzinger, 1996; Stokoe & Smithson, 2002).

Dealing with Silences and Omissions in the Focus Groups

Silences and pauses are issues both for focus group moderation and for analysis. Silence is an "enduring feature of human interaction," present in research communicative contexts as elsewhere (Poland & Pederson, 1998, p. 308). Silences after a specific question can be an indicator to the moderator that the group is not comfortable with talking about a particular issue (Myers, 1998). For example, in a recent study of new parents people were asked what they felt about mothers with young children working outside the home (often a heated topic in the UK context), and gave very bland responses with minimal discussion. This type of general question often elicits stock, socially acceptable responses when it is likely that the individuals in the group hold stronger views than this.

Extract 3: New parents in organizational study

Mod: Do you think people still feel it's important for mothers to be at home with their children, among the people you know? Is there that sort of expectation still?

Tom: Oh I think there's, there's uhm, people we know, there's a wide spectrum of those working, went back full-time, went back full-time only stayed longer, went back full-time, went part-time, stayed at home. There's a, there's a wide range [pause]. There's a diversity of approaches.
        [pause]

Mod: Did anyone here take time off when their children were born?

Here, the moderator's general, nonpersonal approach to the topic—"Do you think people feel . . . ?" "among the people you know . . . ?"—elicited a vague response by Tom, which is typical of responses to this question in the other focus groups in this study. This general question strategy was a tactic discussed in advance by the research team, as a way of introducing a potentially sensitive topic. This sort of question may be useful as an ice-breaker topic, but as Sim suggested, does not adequately demonstrate the range of views people hold on such topics (Sim, 2002). Here, the moderator continued by probing for more specific personal experiences of whether anyone did stay at home with their children, which led to people sharing their opinions more freely. While focus groups are primarily concerned with the public discourses on topics, people's personal experiences can be a useful way to talk about these issues. Sometimes the group is silent because the question is not clear; here, too, probes for more specific examples and personal experiences can be useful.

Moderating Quiet People

Inevitably, some participants speak freely in focus groups and others remain silent or need encouragement to speak. Individuals can be silent in focus groups for a variety of reasons: They may feel awkward in group situations or in this particular group. They may feel uncomfortable with the topic or with the tone of the discussion. In focus group literature, moderators are often exhorted to try and draw out the quieter group members to express their views (Kreuger, 1994; Vaughn et al., 1996). Kreuger (1994) suggested moderators use eye contact to involve quieter group members. Vaughn et al. (1996) suggested using a "polling technique" to elicit each participant's feelings. However, it is natural for some people to be quieter in groups than others, and inevitably some people will not contribute as much to the discussion, particularly in a larger group context.

ISSUES IN ANALYSING FOCUS GROUP DATA

Many of the moderator issues, such as dealing with sensitive issues, silences, and disagreements, are also concerns for the focus group analyst. An important characteristic of focus group data is that groups, rather than individuals within groups, are the unit of analysis (Kreuger,

1988; Morgan, 1988). This makes systematic analysis tricky. Sample populations in the focus groups are small and nonrepresentative. Topics are not all discussed in equal depth in all groups. Some information is volunteered in some groups and not others, some individuals are more forthcoming than others, and the group interactions will determine the discussion. Literature on analyzing focus groups stresses the key issue that the analytic focus is not on what individuals say in a group context but on the discourses that are constructed within this group context (e.g., Wilkinson, 1998; Smithson, 2000; Sim, 2002). For this reason, analytical approaches that explicitly consider interactive effects and group dynamics are particularly appropriate (Jacoby & Ochs, 1995; Myers, 1998; Puchta & Potter, 1999, 2002; Stokoe & Smithson, 2002). These approaches all focus on how discourses, or themes, are constructed jointly by participants in a group context. In this section, some particular issues that regularly arise in analysis of focus groups are considered and strategies for analysis suggested.

Analyzing Consensus and Disagreement

The emergence of dissonant views and opinions between participants—what Kitzinger (1994) called "argumentative interactions"—is a distinctive feature of the focus group method and often makes an important contribution to the richness of the data obtained (Sim, 2002). Disagreements, challenges, and resistances are seen as important parts of the construction of collective opinions. However, there are limitations to how disagreements are expressed in this peer group context. It can be that focus groups replicate a dominant social discourse on a topic. People with unpopular views or less confident group members may be reluctant to air their views in a group context. As seen in Extracts 2 and 3, people are often reluctant to disagree openly with a stated view, especially in groups of strangers. It is important, therefore, not to assume consensus just because no one has disagreed openly (Sim, 2002). If a divergence of views emerges, it is safe to assume that participants do hold different views; however, if no divergence appears, this does not indicate consensus.

When people do disagree in a focus group, it is often in an indirect, polite way. Here, the moderator is asking a different group the question about mothers of young children working outside the home, asked in Extract 3. As in Extract 3, the moderator asks the question generally: "Do you think people think ... ?," but when this gets no response she probes with asking a direct question about personal experience to one of the group:

Extract 4: New parents in organizational study

Mod: Do you think people think it's important for a mother to be at home with young children still?
[pause]
I mean you were saying you wanted your wife to be at home but [pause] do you think it matters if it's the woman or ... ?

Ben: I prefer the woman to be at home.

Ruth: As a mother I'd, I'd say, it's [pause] I think some involvement of parents, it doesn't matter male or female at home with the children [pause] is, is important [pause] but I not, I don't think it has to be necessarily full-time, I think nursery, I think a mix of both [pause] I think has got to be the most ideal.

Mod: In an ideal world

Ruth: Yeah

Pam: Yeah, I again the mix, I er think that er, grandparents as well, you know a mix of parents, grandparents and nursery, then I think that works fairly well.

Here, Ben does give a definite opinion (the mother should be at home), followed by Ruth giving a different opinion (a mixture of parental and nursery care is better), but there is not explicit debate or argument on the topic. Ruth starts her account by positioning her different opinion "as a mother," demonstrating one strategy by which focus group participants may express opposing views while avoiding direct conflict. She refers directly to her personal experience as a mother as the reason for her view, rather than engaging directly with Ben's statement. She then moderates the tone of her disagreement with pauses and modifiers such as "I think" and "I don't think," which serve to make her disagreement less direct (Smithson & Diaz, 1996; Stokoe & Smithson, 2002).

While focus group dynamics do often lead to modified or indirect disagreement rather than direct confrontation, a detailed study of group data suggests the opposite can also happen and they can be a forum for contrasting opinions to emerge and develop (Smithson, 2000; Pini, 2002). There are various powerful counterexamples to the expected "rule" that focus groups replicate the dominant discourse. Sometimes participants make gentle or overt challenges to the status quo, and there are particular strengths in the challenging of views by other participants rather than by the moderator. Kitzinger (1994) showed how difference can be examined in the focus group context and how the method can be used as a way of studying how differences are negotiated and understood. When analyzing the focus group data, it is important to note the lone voices (such as Ben's in this extract) and also when a statement is met with silence or swift topic change, which may signify disagreement by group members.

Analyzing Cultural Variations and Sensitive Topics

Sometimes focus groups will yield seemingly contradictory accounts, particularly when discussing sensitive topics. To illustrate this, it is interesting to compare two discussion from UK focus groups in which people are asked about expectations of current and future relationships and marriage. The first is with a group of British Asian women undergraduate students, with a White British woman moderator.

Extract 5: Asian women students

Mod:	How about the idea of living with someone before you got married? I mean, in this country it's getting more and more common, but from what you've all been saying it would be not very acceptable.
Sabiya:	But we still do it
Tara:	When you're away from home, you
Asiya:	While you're at Uni you do
Mod:	So people [pause]
Asiya:	Wouldn't openly do it, I wouldn't like move next door to my mum and bring my boyfriend and, but
Mod:	But it does happen a lot?
Several:	Yeah
Asiya:	I think when people go away, especially Asian girls, they tend to do so much in the 3 years that probably no one does in a lifetime, I think they fulfill every dream possible. One of my mates, I mean she's engaged as well, back in Pakistan, but she's come here and she's like, she's doing all sorts, and like you just wonder to yourself.
Vera:	Can you define that?
Asiya:	Well um, she's like practically living with her boyfriend as well.

It is interesting to compare this discussion with the discussion following a similar question in a group of male Asian undergraduate students at the same UK institution, with a British Asian woman moderator:

Extract 6: Asian men students

Mod:	Would you settle down with somebody without being married?
All:	No
Mod:	Would you live with somebody?
All:	No
Asim:	We don't believe in that.
Mod:	Is that because of your religion?
All:	Yeah, yeah.
Asim:	Yeah, religion.
Mod:	What about yourselves, what do you think about it?
Abdul:	Yeah, I think
Asim:	No, I agree with my culture, my religion
Abdul:	Religion.
Sid:	Whatever your religion says, that's what you follow so, if that says that, that says that's wrong, then we see that.

Officially, the extracts are from two comparable groups—male and female university students of Asian origin, of similar ages (18–22) from the same institution, recruited by contacts among the Asian students. Gender was therefore the only planned different variable between the groups. This might lead to the conclusion that the different discourses obtained on the same topic are due to the women are being more open about their relationships, while the men are possibly repeating the official line. However, there are several other interpretations of the discrepancy between the two discourses. First, these groups of students, though comparable on paper, may be from different religious/social/cultural backgrounds. In fact, the women were mostly from a Sikh or Hindu background and the men from Muslim backgrounds. However, the women were including Muslim friends in their discussion (for example, the woman from Pakistan, a country which is 99% Muslim). Another possibility is that by chance, the group of women was mainly composed of women with liberal, Westernized perspectives on relationships, while the men happened to be more traditional. It is also likely that young Asian women students in the UK do experience more conflict between traditional expected roles for women and the reality of their behavior, especially while living away from home at university (Rana et al., 1998).

Study of the discourses in the male and female groups demonstrates that everyday talk can include many contradictions, norms, and both official and unofficial perspectives on a sensitive topic—in this case, premarital sex in a context where this is taboo. These two extracts from "comparable" groups also demonstrate some of the limitations of generalizing from focus group data, especially about "ethnic minority views," and especially demonstrates the dangers of having a "token" ethnic minority group in a study. These extracts are also interesting as in this context it is the young men who appear more conservative about sexual behavior than the young women, which might not have been expected.

Development of New Constructs

As described in section 1, while researchers construct the focus group schedules around their research topics, members of focus groups take up these discourses or themes in ways unanticipated by the researchers and often also introduce new themes unanticipated in the research design. Focus groups can be particularly useful at an early stage of research as a means of eliciting general viewpoints, which can be used to inform the development of new constructs and the design of larger studies (Vaughn et al., 1996). For example, in the following extract the moderator was interested in new parents' attitudes to recent changes in UK parental leave regulations, whereby all parents of a child under 5 now have the right to up to 4 weeks' unpaid leave per year.

Extract 7: New parents in organizational study

Mod: Do you think people would be more likely to take parental leave, if it was more flexible how you could . . .
Alex: Hmm, possibly yeah . . .
Mod: What about if it was paid, do you think you'd be more likely to take it?
Ray: If it was paid, yeah—laughter—
Mod: It's paid in most other countries but . . .
Ray: I just go back to the point I made earlier, if you start introducing things like that, it's very unfair on singles, and I just don't think it's right.
Jane: Yeah, seems like an extra holiday almost.
Ray: Well the thing is, you've chosen to have children, so that's your choice.
Sally: Why should others suffer?
Ray: . . . and other people chose to be single, so why, I . . . it might seem strange coming from a father of three young girls but, you know, I . . . there's got to be a balance.
Mod: So you've got to provide things for other people without children?
Ray: Yes, absolutely.

The discussion of the unfairness of a right to leave that nonparents do not have was unexpected. This was particularly interesting in the context of a cross-European study of new parents and different national contexts, as new parents in many of the other countries have the right to far more leave, often fully or partially paid, but did not view this as unfair to nonparents. Similar discussions took place in the other UK focus groups but not in the other countries taking part in the study, reflecting a national debate in the UK about fairness of work-life policies. The concerns raised in the focus groups about "backlash" to policies designed to help parents balance work and family therefore became a major topic of inquiry for the next stage of this study.

SPECIFIC USES OF FOCUS GROUPS
IN WORK-FAMILY RESEARCH

Using Focus Groups in an Organizational Context

Conducting focus groups in an organizational context has particular implications, some of which are discussed in the chapter on organizational case studies (see Lewis, Das Dores Guerreiro, & Brannen, chap. 23, this volume). While it can be an advantage having people from the same departments and work teams, who have shared experiences and are often comfortable talking together, there can be problems with how freely people feel they can express themselves in a workplace situation. Shared workplace experiences such as restructuring, management experiences, and enthusiasm or resistance to work-life initiatives can encourage feelings of solidarity among team members. Groups can share common knowledge about relevant issues in the company even when the people were strangers. For example, in a recent study of new parents in organizations, participants used the focus group to enhance and share their own knowledge of the organization—a useful outcome for the participants of this methodology.

Possible drawbacks of using focus groups in organizational settings include people feeling unable to speak out in front of superiors or people from different parts of the organization. It is generally advisable not to put managers and employees in the same group. This will vary with the nature of the organization. In this study, the UK participants did not find it difficult to voice criticisms of the organization or of unnamed managers and colleagues, but this will vary in different organizations and was not found in other European countries in the study. Overt criticism was directed mainly at company policies, unnamed managers and colleagues, and management decisions. Issues that generated the most emotion included bad treatment by the company, managers, or colleagues and apparent lack of understanding by managers or colleagues of difficult job or family situations.

The main issues for organizational focus groups concern privacy and confidentiality. The general guidelines on ethics and anonymity suggested in section 2 need to be applied with especial rigor. Participants and managers need to know in advance exactly how the data will be used, and extra precautions need to be taken to ensure that participants' comments are not identifiable.

Using Focus Groups in Cross-Cultural Work-Family Research

Focus groups are being increasingly suggested as a good method for understanding cultural variations and differences. The involvement of minority community groups through focus groups has been shown to be a powerful tool in developing culturally appropriate methods (Hughes & DuMont, 1993; Pollack, 2003; Willgerodt, 2003) and in including culturally diverse perspectives in research. There are issues in the running of focus groups in different cultural contexts—in some cultures dissent is not expressed in public, some cultures have more subjects that are not discussed in public, and in some cultures variables such as gender will be a bigger concern.

Which topics work well in the focus group context vary greatly in different contexts and cultures. For example, as shown above, in the UK participants in an organizational study did not have a problem with openly criticising the organization, while in other European countries people were unlikely to publicly criticize their organization in a group context. Thus, in a recent study of new parents in different European countries, the UK focus group moderators reported lively discussions with a good deal of criticism expressed toward management but marked by a relaxed, jokey atmosphere. Other countries did not report the same level of humor and criticism in their organizational contexts. The Swedish team suggested that discussions were "consensual" and turn taking was easily managed, while in Bulgaria, unlike in the UK groups, there was little cross-talking or butting in.

Online and Telephone Focus Groups

While "virtual" or online focus groups are becoming popular in market research, they have until recently been little used in academic research (Murray, 1997; Kendall, 1999; Bloor et al., 2001). There are two main ways of conducting online focus groups: in real time, with users all connected and posting their comments simultaneously, *or*, as Murray (1997) described, when recounting his use of online focus groups to study health professionals, using an asynchronous discussion form or mailing list and keeping the discussion going over days or weeks, which encouraged active discussion to develop between group members. The type of interaction here is very different from face-to-face focus groups, and specific discussion characteristics emerged, such as "threading"—the simultaneous conduct of multiple topics of conversation, which is also found in naturally occurring online discussions (chatrooms and discussion forums). Participants have hours or days to reflect on the discussion and post considered comments, which can lead to a depth of discussion not always seen in standard focus groups. The issues of anonymity and confidentiality are also different for online groups. The possibilities for total anonymity by group members can lead to more open discussions and may therefore make online groups especially suitable for sensitive topics. However, the possibilities for group participants to be "creating" a character, including experimenting with gender identities, are also high (Bloor et al., 2001). Online groups may be a suitable method for geographically distant participants, for example, when researching a topic where people are not able to join in standard groups for a variety of reasons (physical disability, geographical remoteness, child-care commitments).

Another focus group variation with possible uses for work-family research is telephone focus groups. While telephone focus groups occur in "real time," the invisibility and relative anonymity of participants have been shown to be useful for permitting anonymity and more open responses (Smith, 1995; White & Thompson, 1995). As with online groups, this may be useful for investigating difficult-to-recruit groups or for discussing sensitive topics.

CONCLUSIONS: STRENGTHS AND LIMITATIONS OF FOCUS GROUPS FOR WORK-FAMILY RESEARCH

There are conceptual, methodological, and ethical issues in focus group research. As with other qualitative research methods, there are opportunities for consciously or unconsciously manipulating the participants' responses. Focus groups also have specific dilemmas that we need to be aware of, such as normative effects, dominant "voices," and respect for individuals' privacy. It is also vital to remember that, while focus groups produce seemingly "natural" discussions, these discussions are occurring in a formal research setting and are influenced by that. Hughes and DuMont (1993) argued that the researcher compromises ecological validity of observations in favor of control over the research topics. This works well for certain research questions, particularly at an exploratory stage of the research.

For which work-family topics are focus groups unsuitable? Some perspectives that rarely come out in "mainstream" groups, though these vary in different cultural contexts and are affected by age, gender, and background of the participants as well as the setting and context of the focus group. From experience of our work-family studies, perspectives that rarely emerge in focus groups unless specifically designed include gay and lesbian views and other nonstandard family set-ups, and also ethnic minority and religious minority perspectives. Separate focus groups can cover some aspects of these perspectives, but for other aspects, more "private" methods such as individual interviews may be more suitable. However, as shown in the examples in this chapter, the limitations of what is discussed and what is omitted vary and it is possible to get unexpected and extremely interesting discussions about topics that are not always "recommended" in focus group manuals.

As this chapter has demonstrated, the focus group method has particular strengths. It enables research participants to discuss and develop ideas collectively and articulate their ideas in their own terms, bringing forward their own priorities and perspectives. It can be seen from the examples shown in this chapter that in the focus groups not only can a wide variety of opinions be given and considered, but the development of collective opinions can also be studied. Participants engage in a range of argumentative behaviors, which results in a depth of dialogue not often found in individual interviews. Another plus is that they are often enjoyable and creative experiences for the participants (Wilkinson, 1998; Smithson, 2000; Pini, 2002). The effects of group dynamics in the focus groups can therefore be a distinct advantage over other qualitative methods, for exploring issues from the perspective of the participants, in a way that is culturally sensitive to participants' priorities and experiences.

NOTES

[1] Details of research projects here. The reconciliation of future work and family life: Young Europeans talk about work and family is a qualitative cross-national research project funded by the European Commission looking at young European adults' expectations of future work and family in five countries. Transitions: Gender, parenthood and the changing European workplace is a qualitative cross-national research project which examines how young European adults negotiate parenthood and work-family boundaries in the context of labour market and workplace change. It is funded by the Fifth framework programe of the European Commission (2003–2005).

[2] All participants' names have been changed. Mod = focus group moderator.

REFERENCES

Bloor, M., Frankland, J., Thomas, M., & Robson, K. (2001). *Focus groups in social research*. London: Sage.
Bradburn, N. M., & Sudman, S. (1979). *Improving interview method and questionnaire design*. San Francisco: Jossey-Bass.
Brannen, J., Lewis, S., Nilsen, A., & Smithson, J. (Eds.). (2002). *Young Europeans, work and family: Futures in transition*. London: Routledge.
Bryman, A. (1988). *Quantity and quality in social research*. London: Unwin Hyman.
Chappell, D. (2003). *A procedural manual for the online work-family focus group*. Guelph, Canada: Centre for Families, Work and Well-being.
Du Bois, B. (1983). Passionate scholarship: Notes on values, knowing and method in feminist social science. In G. Bowles & R. D. Klein (Eds.), *Theories of women's studies* (pp. 105–116). London: Routledge.
Gallinsky, E., Kim, S., & Bond, J. T. (2001). *Feeling overworked: When work becomes too much*. New York: Families and Work Institute.
Hughes, D., & DuMont, K. (1993). Using focus groups to facilitate culturally anchored research. *American Journal of Community Psychology, 21*(6), 775–803.
Ingersoll-Dayton, B., Neal, M. B., & Hammer, L. B. (2001). Aging parents helping adult children: The experience of the sandwiched generation. *Family Relations, 50*, 262–271.
Jacoby, S., & Ochs, E. (1995). Co-construction: An introduction. *Research on Language and Social Interaction, 28*(3), 171–183.
Kendall, L. (1999). Recontextualising "cyberspace": Methodological considerations for online research. In S. Jones (Ed.), *Doing Internet research*. Newbury Park, CA: Sage.
Kitzinger, J. (1994). The methodology of focus groups: The importance of interaction between research participants. *Sociology of Health and Illness, 16*(1), 103–121.
Kitzinger, J. (1995). Introducing focus groups. *British Medical Journal, 311*, 299–302.
Kitzinger, J., & Farquhar, C. (1999). The analytical potential of "sensitive moments" in focus group discussions. In R. S. Barbour & J. Kitzinger (Eds.), *Developing focus group research: Politics, theory and practice* (pp. 151–172). London: Sage.
Kreuger, R. A. (1994). *Focus groups: A practical guide for applied research* (2nd ed.). Newbury Park, CA: Sage.
Kreuger, R. A. (1998). *Analyzing and reporting focus group results. Focus group kit, volume 6*. Newbury Park, CA: Sage.
Morgan, D. L. (1988). *Focus groups as qualitative research*. Newbury Park, CA: Sage.
Morgan, D. L. (1998). *The focus group guidebook. Focus group kit, volume 1*. Newbury Park, CA: Sage.
Morgan, D. L., & Kreuger, R. A. (1998). *The focus group kit*. Newbury Park, CA: Sage.
Murray, P. (1997). Using virtual focus groups in qualitative research. *Qualitative Health Research, 7*(4), 542–549.
Myers, G. (1998). Displaying opinions: Topics and disagreement in focus groups. *Language in Society, 27*, 85–111.
Pini, B. (2002). Focus groups, feminist research and farm women: Opportunities for empowerment in rural social research. *Journal of Rural Studies, 18*(3), 339–351.
Poland, B., & Pederson, A. (1998). Reading between the lines: Interpreting silences in qualitative research. *Qualitative Inquiry, 4*(2) 293–312.

Pollack, S. (2003). Focus-group methodology in research with incarcerated women: Race, power, and collective experience. *Affilia*, *18*(4), 461–472.

Puchta, C., & Potter, J. (1999). Asking elaborate questions: Focus groups and the management of spontaneity. *Journal of Sociolinguistics*, *3*, 314–335.

Puchta, C., & Potter, J. (2002). Manufacturing individual opinions: Market research focus groups and the discursive psychology of attitudes. *British Journal of Social Psychology, 41*, 345–363.

Rana, B., Kagan, C., Lewis, S., & Rout, U. (1998). British South Asian women managers and professionals: Experiences of work and family. *Women in Management Review*, *13*(6), 221–232.

Ritchie, J., & Lewis, J. (eds). (2003). Qualitative Research Practice: A guide for social science students and researchers. Thousand Oaks, CA: Sage 2003.

Ronen, G. M., Rosenbaum, P., Law, M., & Streiner, D. L. (2001). Health-related quality of life in childhood disorders: A modified focus group technique to involve children. *Quality of Life Research*, *10*(1), 71–79.

Sim, J. (2002). Collecting and analysing qualitative data: Issues raised by the focus group. *Journal of Advanced Nursing*, *28*(2), 345–352.

Smith, H. W. (1995). Ethics in focus groups: A few concerns. *Qualitative Health Research*, *5*(4), 476–486.

Smithson, J. (2000). Using and analysing focus groups: Limitations and possibilities. *International Journal of Methodology: Theory and Practice*, *3*(2), 103–119.

Smithson, J., & Diaz, F. (1996). Arguing for a collective voice: Collaborative strategies in problem-oriented conversation. *Text*, *16*(2), 251–268.

Stokoe, E. H., & Smithson, J. (2002). Gender and sexuality in talk-in-interaction: Considering conversation analytic perspectives. In P. McIlvenny (Ed.), *Talking gender and sexuality* (pp. 79–110). Amsterdam: John Benjamins.

Vaughn, S., Shay Schumm, J., & Sinagub, J. (1996). *Focus group interviews in education and psychology*. Newbury Park, CA: Sage.

White, G. E., & Thompson, A. N. (1995). Anonymised focus groups as a research tool for health professionals. *Qualitative Health Research*, *5*(2), 256–261.

Wilkinson, S. (1998). Focus group methodology: A review. *International Journal of Social Research Methodology, Theory and Practice*, *1*(3), 181–204.

Wilkinson, S., & Kitzinger, C. (1996). *Representing the other*. London: Sage.

Willgerodt, M. A. (2003). Using focus groups to develop culturally relevant instruments. *Western Journal of Nursing Research*, *25*(7), 798–814.

21

Longitudinal Research on Work and Family Issues

Ann C. Crouter
Amy E. Pirretti
Pennsylvania State University

Longitudinal research designs rely on repeated occasions of measurement on the same individuals or groups over time. Such designs take different forms depending on the nature of the research questions being addressed and the sample being studied, but a hallmark of longitudinal research is a dual focus on continuity and change. Longitudinal researchers who are interested in the interconnections between work and family life typically focus on which aspects of work, family, or the individual stay the same, which aspects change, how they change, and whether those changes can be predicted with other data the investigator has available. Although longitudinal investigations in the area of work and family are still somewhat rare, they have the potential to reveal important insights about the work-family interface that cannot be ascertained from cross-sectional snapshots of individuals, families, or workplaces at a single point in time. Longitudinal research designs are an important part of the toolkit for work-family researchers for several reasons.

First, longitudinal designs can help researchers address hypotheses about cause–effect associations. Note that a longitudinal study typically does not provide enough information to definitively establish directional, causal relationships unless it includes an experimental design with random assignment to conditions. Experimental designs with random assignment are the only way to eliminate the possibility that research results are attributable to selection effects, threats to validity that are whimsically referred to by developmental psychologists Scarr and McCartney (1983) as "niche-picking." Experimental designs with random assignment, however, are rare in the work-family literature. After all, it very difficult to randomly assign adults to different work conditions or young children to different child-care arrangements, or to experimentally manipulate who has access to "family-friendly" workplace policies and practices and who does not.

But, with the necessary caveats underscored, longitudinal research often can provide a stronger basis for developing causal explanations than a cross-sectional study can because longitudinal investigations depict the temporal sequencing of phenomena under study. Longitudinal studies can also provide information on when certain effects emerge and how long they are sustained. Take, for example, the National Institute of Child Health and Human De-velopment's Study of Early Child Care (SECC), an ambitious, multisite longitudinal study that enrolled 1,364 infants in 1991 and is following their development into their adolescent years (see, for example, NICHD Early Child Care Network, 1997, 2001, 2002a, 2002b). The original impetus for the SECC was the hotly debated question of whether infants were developmen-tally at risk if they experienced high levels of nonmaternal child care during the 1st year of life (Belsky, 2001; Belsky & Eggebeen, 1991; Belsky & Rovine, 1988). In general, with only a few exceptions (e.g., Brooks-Gunn, Han, & Waldfogel, 2002), the SECC has found very little evidence that maternal employment, or time in nonmaternal care, has negative associations with children's subsequent psychosocial functioning, a question that can only be answered by following children and their parents over a long period of time.

Longitudinal designs can also be used to eliminate some causal explanations. For example, Crouter, Tucker, Head, and McHale (2004) asked whether "family time," defined as time that mothers, fathers, and two adolescent siblings spent together in joint activities, predicted enhanced psychosocial functioning for family members 2 years later. They found that family time predicted decreased depressive symptoms for firstborns, mothers, and fathers in certain family situations. Concerned, however, that these findings might reflect selection processes whereby less adjusted individuals simply opted out of family time and better adjusted family members chose to spend more time with family members, they turned their model around and used individual adjustment to predict subsequent involvement in family time using the same analytic approach. These analyses revealed no support for the selection effect explanation, a finding that strengthened (but did not prove) their argument that family time may be beneficial for some people under certain circumstances.

A second, related advantage that longitudinal research offers work-family researchers is that it can reveal patterns of individual development: systematic intraindividual gains in phys-ical, social, cognitive, and emotional competencies that unfold as individuals learn to adapt to, master, and shape their changing circumstances. A cross-sectional study may reveal an association between, for example, the degree of occupational self-direction employed adults enjoy on the job and their intellectual flexibility, but a longitudinal design can provide addi-tional information about whether working in complex, challenging jobs *precedes* subsequent increases in competence (see, for example, Kohn & Schooler, 1983).

Finally, longitudinal research reveals the dynamic nature and the intricate complexity of work and family life that cannot be conveyed by a onetime assessment of work and family circumstances. Indeed, a researcher may identify a sample in which, at baseline, the partic-ipants look very similar to one another. A longitudinal design, however, reveals the fanning out that often happens over time as individuals make certain choices and experience an ar-ray of life events. Over the years, individuals change jobs and alter their work hours and schedules; health challenges arise that require adaptation; families change neighborhoods; couples marry and divorce; children move in and out of child-care situations, schools, and extracurricular activities; workplaces downsize or even close, or, in good economic times, hire new staff or increase employee overtime hours; and so on. These naturally occurring changes are humbling for longitudinal researchers who must grapple conceptually and analytically with the complex realities that their research participants experience as they move through time.

In this chapter, we review several types of longitudinal designs, providing some examples of work and family research that have used these different strategies and noting strengths and weaknesses of each approach. We conclude with some thoughts about the challenges longitudinal research poses for researchers and some strategies for maximizing the advantages and minimizing the disadvantages that characterize this type of research.

TYPES OF LONGITUDINAL RESEARCH DESIGNS

In developmental science, some of the most sophisticated thinking about longitudinal methodology has come from the fields of life-span development, particularly the field of gerontology, and life course sociology. In gerontology, the emphasis has been on tracking individuals over time to map continuities and discontinuities in different domains of cognitive competence as people age. Life course sociologists have been interested in understanding how social change impacts the life trajectories of individuals (Elder, 1998) and in how individuals' work and family careers take shape (e.g., Moen, 2003; Moen, Kim, & Hofmeister, 2001).

In the mid-1960s, developmental psychologist Warner Schaie (1965) and sociologist Norman Ryder (1965) drew attention to the inherent confounds between three interrelated longitudinal phenomena: age, history, and cohort. To illustrate this point, imagine that a research project identified a group of people who were all age 25 in the year 1985 and then followed that group until the year 2000, a 15-year period. Although such a data set would undoubtedly yield many interesting findings, it would be impossible to disentangle whether the observed findings reflected the effects of developmental processes (i.e., aging) that unfold from age 25 to 40 or the effects of having been born in a specific cohort that was exposed to a unique set of historical circumstances at the same point in their development.

An example of the potential importance of these issues can be found in Elder's research (see Elder, 1998, for summary) on the life course trajectories of two groups who experienced the Great Depression of the 1930s at different points in their development: a sample of children who were of preschool age at the height of the economic downturn and a sample of youth who were adolescents during that period. For the most part, the adult employment and family trajectories of youth who experienced the Depression as adolescents were quite positive, even for those whose families experienced considerable economic deprivation. In contrast, the life course trajectories of those who experienced the brunt of the Depression as young children were much less positive, especially for boys. Elder surmised that teenagers were old enough to be able to make active contributions to their families that not only helped families adapt to changing economic circumstances but were also valued and appreciated by parents and other family members, a set of processes that would be likely to instill self-esteem and self-reliance in youth. In contrast, the children who experienced the Depression's impact in early childhood were too young to understand the turmoil going on around them or to take on paid jobs or pitch in with housework in ways that could make meaningful contributions to their families.

Life-span methodologists have developed sophisticated longitudinal research designs to disentangle age and period effects, such as cohort-sequential designs (Schaie & Baltes, 1975; Schaie & Hertzog, 1983) that involve following more than one cohort of individuals over the same age period. Similarities in results for different cohorts would suggest that age-related findings might be characteristic of the aging process in that particular ecological context rather than limited to a specific group of people that experienced a specific, unique sequence of historical events at the same time in their development. Differences in age-related results for different cohorts, in contrast, would suggest that historical circumstances may have sent cohorts on somewhat different trajectories.

The field of work and family would seem to be a natural place to find research designs that are sensitive to the age–history confound. After all, individuals and couples construct their work and family lives against a historical backdrop of changing social, political, and economic circumstances. A good example of the role that history plays in shaping work and family circumstances is historian Tamara Hareven's (1982) monograph, *Family Time, Industrial Time*, a study that focused on the unfolding work-family interface for workers at the New England textile firm, Amoskeag, across almost 100 years of industrial, economic, technological, and social change. Using company records, church and community archives, and workers' diaries and letters, Hareven depicted the very different levels of control textile workers had over their employment situations in times of economic prosperity, when the Amoskeag mills were operating at full capacity, compared to times of economic contraction, when the surplus of available workers made the employer less responsive to individual and family circumstances. Although Hareven's work provides compelling evidence that work-family researchers should be attentive to the role of history, and although there are some outstanding exceptions (e.g., Elder, 1998), in general, work and family researchers have *not* designed their longitudinal studies in ways that permit them to disentangle age and history effects.

The body of longitudinal research in the area of work and family is quite diverse and can be parsed in a variety of ways. We have grouped the relevant studies under five broad subheadings. The first group of studies is characterized by long intervals of time between occasions of measurement. For example, Kohn and Schooler's (1983) groundbreaking longitudinal research on the implications of occupational self-direction for adults' intellectual flexibility relied on two occasions of measurement, spaced 10 years apart. The second group of studies relies on annual assessments of individuals, dyads, or families. A third approach relies on repeated assessments of individuals multiple times a year. Sometimes these designs are tailored to the developmental status of the sample. In other instances, researchers are interested in seasonal patterns. The fourth group of studies uses repeated assessments, usually across multiple days, to examine intraindividual variability in rapidly changing phenomena such as emotions and positive and negative interactions. These designs are ideal for addressing research questions in which the researcher is interested in the conditions under which individuals deviate from their personal central tendencies, such as how people behave on high- and low-stress days. Finally, a fifth type of longitudinal design follows individuals or dyads across a key work or family transition such as retirement or the transition to parenthood. In these quasi-experimental designs, the individual functions as his or her own "control." Taking advantage of "before" and "after" data, the researcher typically asks whether, and how, individuals change as a function of a key transition.

Longitudinal Designs in Which Assessments Are Far Apart

There are a handful of studies in research areas pertaining to work and family in which investigators had access to data on individuals across long intervals of time. Kohn (1969, 1977), for example, conducted a survey of over 3,000 employed men in the early 1960s, data he published in his enduring monograph, *Class and Conformity* (1969, 1977). Kohn and Schooler (1983) followed the sample up 10 years later, using the new data to examine whether and how early occupational self-direction predicted subsequent intellectual flexibility as well as the proverbial chicken–egg question of whether men systematically selected themselves into or out of jobs with varying levels of self-direction as a function of their intellectual flexibility. Similarly, in 1986, a group of investigators led by Moen and Williams were able to interview a group of women who had first been studied in 1956 (see Moen, Erickson, & Dempster-McClain, 1997). The follow-up study also included interviews with many of the original sample's grown daughters, enabling the research team not only to examine intraindividual continuity and change in the original sample's gender role ideologies but also to investigate the link between the original sample women's attitudes in 1956 and their daughters' work identities 30 years later.

Studies with wide intervals between data collection are ideal for investigating phenomena that slowly develop or unfold over a long period of time. Because these designs cover such a wide slice of the life course, evidence that baseline measures predict functioning 10 or even 30 years later is quite compelling.

There are drawbacks of these designs, however. In research of this kind, the investigators know a lot about individuals' work and family situations at several points in the life course, but the areas in between those widely spaced occasions of measurement are uncharted. This can be frustrating for researchers who are interested not only in predicting behavior or attitudes across time but also in understanding the *mechanisms* through which an experience or phenomenon is linked to something about the individual or family many years later. Researchers can attempt to fill in the gaps by asking participants to provide retrospective accounts of events and decisions that took place during the uncharted interval, but such data are problematic because they are filtered through the research participants' current views of self and current work and family circumstances. Such retrospective data may not coincide with how the participants would have responded had they actually been assessed during the time period in question.

The longer the time interval between occasions of measurement, the more challenging it becomes to retain sample participants. Participant attrition is a potentially serious problem for longitudinal research studies. It can occur for several reasons. Participants may die or become incapacitated and unable to participate. They may change addresses or telephone numbers and become lost to the research team, or they may refuse to continue participating. Attrition poses problems for investigators not only because it reduces sample size, and therefore statistical power, but also because it is often nonrandom. Indeed, sometimes the very people the researcher is most interested in may be those most likely to drop out of a study or to be difficult to track down. Miller and Wright (1995) provided a heuristic example of a longitudinal study on the implications of divorce for mental health. As they explain, if people who are depressed systematically are less likely to participate in the study, the study will underestimate the links between divorce and poor mental health. We will discuss ways to track individuals and families and to minimize attrition and provide a summary of some techniques to deal with missing data in our concluding remarks.

Longitudinal Designs With Annual Assessments

A second type of longitudinal design involves repeated annual assessments of individuals. Because this strategy is somewhat common, we provide two illustrations of longitudinal investigations that have taken this approach. The Penn State Family Relationships Project (FRP; Crouter, Helms-Erikson, Updegraff, & McHale, 1999; McHale, Crouter, & Tucker, 1999) has conducted annual assessments on fathers, mothers, and two target children in 200 dual-earner families since 1995. The study began when the two eldest children in each family were approximately 10 and 8 years of age and is now in its ninth wave of annual data collection. At each year of measurement, family members participate in a 2- to 3-hour-long home interview in which individuals separately complete a variety of questionnaires and open-ended questions. Mothers' and fathers' interviews focus on their work circumstances, their relationships with each of the two target children and with one another, their gender attitudes and orientations, and their psychosocial functioning. Children's interviews focus on their relationships with parents and siblings, their gender development—including their ideas about future work and family roles—and their psychosocial adjustment. After the home interview, families participate in a series of seven evening telephone calls that focus on family members' time use, including the content of their time use (e.g., leisure activities; household tasks; homework) and the social context of their time use (e.g., maternal and paternal involvement with children; time spent with same-sex peers, etc.), and parents' knowledge of their sons' and daughters' daily experiences.

Fortner, Crouter, and McHale (2004) used FRP longitudinal data to examine whether and how the quality of parent–adolescent relationships predicted mothers' and fathers' temporal and emotional involvement in their jobs 2 years later, a rare look at the implications of family life for work, the often neglected direction of influence in the work-family literature (Crouter, 1984). Controlling for year 1 work involvement, Fortner and her colleagues found that less accepting relationships predicted increased emotional involvement in work for mothers of sons and fathers of daughters, as well as increased work hours for fathers of daughters, a pattern of findings that suggests that less positive parent–adolescent relationships may lead parents to invest their time and emotional energies in other roles such as employment. One explanation for why this pattern emerged for parents of opposite-sex offspring but not for parents of same-sex offspring is that fathers of sons and mothers of daughters may feel that they are essential players in their children's lives, and that they therefore cannot afford to de-invest in the relationship, a constraint that may not be perceived by parents with regard to opposite-sex children.

Another work-family study that has employed annual waves of data collection is a longitudinal study of dual-earner couples, funded by the National Institute of Mental Health and led by Rosalind Barnett (Barnett & Brennan, 1997). Barnett and her colleagues identified a random sample of 300 dual-earner couples between the ages of 25 and 40 who were living in two towns in eastern Massachusetts. The sample was stratified initially by parental status with 60% of the sample being parents. Barnett selected her sample from the town census lists of two towns that had high levels of women's labor force participation. Households were screened by telephone. Almost 70% of couples that fit the criteria (i.e., dual earners, parental status, English-speaking, and had performed in role for at least 3-months prior) agreed to take part in the study. The sample was interviewed at three points across 2 years. Across the three waves, the attrition rate was only 8%. The sample was 97% White and highly educated, with 73% of men and 74% of women having at least a bachelor's degree.

Data were collected by trained interviewers who completed the interviews in homes or offices of the respondents. The average interview took 1.5 hours. Couples were also given a packet of questionnaires to fill out prior to each interview. Husbands and wives were encouraged to complete the questionnaires independently and paid $25 for each of the three waves of data collection. Respondents were asked many questions about their job experiences, family roles, and psychological distress (Barnett & Brennan, 1997).

Barnett and her colleagues utilized this dual-earner sample to address work-family questions pertaining to change. Longitudinal data with at least three data points allow researchers to distinguish between linear patterns of change and more complex patterns, such as quadratic patterns (u-shaped or inverted u-shaped curves). Additionally, Barnett and her team utilized multi-level modeling (MLM) techniques to understand individual change as well as couple-level change (Barnett & Brennan, 1997; Brennan, Barnett, & Gareis, 2001; Barnett, Raudenbush, Brennan, Pleck, & Marshall, 1995). Multi-level modeling (MLM) techniques allow researchers to examine two or more levels of analysis in the same model (see Bryk & Raudenbush, 1992; Swisher, chap. 26, this volume). For example, Brennan, Barnett, and Gareis (2001) used their data to investigate change in couples' marital quality relative to changes in salary. Women's change in salary relative to their husbands' had no effect on how they perceived their marital quality over time. For men, however, as their relative earnings in comparison to their spouses increased, so too did men's assessments of marital quality, especially for men reporting high rewards of salary. Barnett and Brennan (1997) used the longitudinal data set to examine the associations between changes in psychological distress and changes in job demands and skills discretion and changes in marital quality. Increases over time in skill discretion on the job predicted decreased psychological distress across time for both husbands and wives. Increases in job demands over the three waves, however, were associated with increased psychological distress for all respondents.

Like other longitudinal designs, designs that rely on one annual occasion of measurement have strengths and limitations. The key limitation is that the annual snapshot of the family or family member may not do justice to the variability in the phenomena of interest across the whole year. Each year the FRP, for example, asks mothers and fathers about their hours of employment, but data are not collected about whether those hours were stable throughout the year. For continuously employed parents this may not be a problem, but the project does not adequately capture seasonal and temporary employment.

Another drawback of the annual approach is that there is no theoretical reason to believe that a year is necessarily the appropriate marker of development or change. It is an arbitrary choice. The annual interval may be very useful for some outcomes and not useful for others. For phenomena that change very slowly, such as adults' gender role ideologies or personality qualities, collecting annual data may be inefficient because the researcher is unlikely to detect meaningful patterns of change over such short periods of time. Other phenomena, however, such as psychological well-being, relationship quality, parenting, or job satisfaction, may respond more sensitively to changing work and family circumstances and therefore may be worth the time, energy, and monetary investment of annual data collection.

The annual approach has certain important strengths, too. Regular contact with participants helps researchers keep track of the individuals they are studying. In the case of the FRP, families are interviewed every spring. The annual face-to-face meeting and series of telephone interviews, coupled with correspondence throughout the year, help to connect families to the project. Some families have even contacted the project on their own when they have changed residences or telephone numbers. When individuals or families feel as though they are an integral part of an ongoing research endeavor, it is easier to keep track of them.

Another positive feature of annual assessments is that a year is probably a long enough time interval to minimize reactivity or practice effects. Reactivity occurs when subjects in a research investigation become sensitized to the content of the study's questions in a way that changes their subsequent behavior or self-reports. A year may be enough time for busy family members to forget the content of the previous year's interviews, especially their own answers to questions, so that they are able to complete the next year's interview with an open mind. One way to assess whether reactivity is a problem in a longitudinal study is to periodically collect parallel data on a control group of individuals or families who are like the participants in as many ways as possible but have not been exposed to prior data collections. Although this step would provide useful information to many longitudinal studies, in practice most longitudinal studies do not implement it because it is costly to do well.

Developmental scholars and family researchers have recently begun to use data analytic tools that lend themselves well to longitudinal data with annual assessments, and especially to longitudinal data on multiple members of a unit such as a couple or a family. Recall that Barnett and her colleagues made use of MLM techniques to study husbands and wives in dual-earner families over time. This approach is ideal for studying couples or families because data on individuals (i.e., husbands and wives) can be nested within the couple or family unit of analysis, and the researcher can use variables at both levels to predict an outcome such as individuals' perceptions of marital quality (see Bryk & Raudenbush, 1992; Klute, Crouter, Sayer, & McHale, 2001; Maguire, 1999; Raudenbush, Brennan, & Barnett, 1995). Similarly, MLM techniques provide an efficient, flexible approach for studying siblings. If a research team has collected data on all children in a sample of dual-earner families, for example, the children's data can be nested within the family level of analysis. A family with only one child would have that child's data nested within the family level of analysis, whereas families with two or more children represented in the data set would have data from multiple children nested within the family level. MLM techniques adjust for the fact that data from family members are not independent.

In longitudinal studies, occasions of measurement can be nested within individuals, giving the researcher using MLM potentially three levels of analysis. For the marriage researcher, those levels would be time, the individual husband or wife, and the couple. For the family researcher interested in studying children in families, the three levels would be time, the individual child or sibling, and the family. MLM approaches can also be used to study individual employees within work groups that in turn are nested in companies, making it a flexible tool for researchers on both ends of the work-family research continuum.

MLM techniques offer longitudinal researchers other advantages, too. For example, these techniques handle missing data very flexibly. If, for instance, a researcher had data on 200 individuals over 5 years but some of the individuals did not participate at some of the waves, MLM approaches would utilize the available data to estimate the relevant coefficients, giving more weight to the individuals who provided more data. In contrast, many other data analytic tools require complete data, with the result that families with missing data are eliminated from those analyses. Another feature of MLM approaches is that they provide estimates of the intercept and the slope in the same analysis. In other words, a longitudinal researcher can, in the same analysis, predict where individuals were at baseline on a given outcome variable and also predict their longitudinal trajectories. Depending on the research question, the researcher can also define the intercept in different ways. For example, depending on the nature of the research questions, researchers using FRP data could choose to use a given calendar year as the intercept or they could center the data at a specific chronological age.

Longitudinal Designs With Assessments at Multiple Times of Year

For some research questions, it makes sense to collect data more frequently than once a year. We will discuss two scenarios of this type. One approach focuses on differences across seasons of the year. Another type of study calibrates the frequency of data collection based on the rapidity of development and change expected.

Almost 70 years ago, sociologists Sorokin and Merton (1937) argued that time is not merely a linear, chronological phenomenon; it is also a social phenomenon. As they explained (p. 623):

> Social time, in contrast to the time of astronomy, is qualitative and not purely quantitative; . . . these qualities derive from the beliefs and customs common to the group . . . and reveal the rhythms, pulsations, and beats of the societies in which they are found.

The field of work and family is replete with examples of social time such as daytime, afternoon and evening work shifts, weekday and weekend work, vacation time, and so on. For families with children, the school year and summer vacation are good examples of contrasting social times that children and parents experience within a year. School-age children have a qualitatively different experience during the academic year compared to during the summer months, and their parents face different supervisory challenges at these two different times of the year as well.

In an early longitudinal research project, Crouter and McHale (1993) gathered three waves of data on school-aged children and mothers and fathers living in single- and dual-earner two-parent families; these occasions of measurement took place during the school year, over the following summer, and during the subsequent school year. As part of this study, Crouter and McHale were interested in continuity and change in mothers' work hours across these three occasions of measurement and the implications of different patterns of continuity or change in maternal work hours for family processes such as parent–child involvement and parental monitoring. They identified three groups of families based on mothers' work hours at each of the three time points: (a) a continuously single-earner group in which mothers were either not employed or employed very few hours at each point in time; (b) a continuously dual-earner group in which both mothers and fathers were employed during all three occasions; and (c) a discontinuous group in which mothers were employed during both school year time points but not in the summer. Analyses revealed that mothers in the discontinuous group increased their involvement with their children significantly during the summer, creating a situation in which the parents' division of child care became temporarily more traditional: That is, the gap between mothers and fathers' levels of involvement in joint activities with their children became more pronounced in the summer, favoring mothers. These patterns of involvement returned to a more egalitarian arrangement in which mothers and fathers were involved at similar levels the following school year once mothers had returned to the workplace. Similarly, husbands of women with discontinuous employment became less knowledgeable about their children's lives over the summer but recovered the following school year, suggesting that fathers in dual-earner families may calibrate their involvement in their children's lives in part on the basis of their wives' availability.

Another goal of studies that build in multiple occasions of measurement within a year is to accurately map the anticipated developmental trajectories of the target participants. In such studies, data collection points are closely spaced during times of rapid change and spaced farther apart during periods when less development or change is expected. This approach is common in studies of child development. An example of such a study is a new program project being conducted by investigators at the University of North Carolina and Penn State University, the Family Life Project (FLP). Led by Lynne Vernon-Feagans and Martha Cox, this study focuses on the development of 1,200 young children growing up in three rural, low-income counties in North Carolina and three rural, low-income counties in Pennsylvania. One component project within the multi-faceted, interdisciplinary program project focuses on work and family. Led by Ann Crouter, this investigation examines the connections over time between mothers' and fathers' employment circumstances, the quality of the home environment and parent–child interaction, and child development. The fact that the sample is disproportionately low-income and rural gives Crouter and collaborators a unique opportunity to examine the connections between mothers' and fathers' jobs and the quality of family life for parents in low-income jobs; low-income work has not received sufficient attention in the mainstream work-family literature (Lambert, 1999). The research team is interested in understanding the risk factors that shape family processes and ultimately child development, including such work-related issues as low wages, meager benefits, job insecurity, long hours (exacerbated by long commutes in rural areas), underemployment, nonstandard shifts, low occupational self-direction, and high levels of work pressure. The project is also interested in protective factors that may help parents maintain responsive, sensitive parenting even under stressful conditions. Potential protective factors include workplace flexibility, supervisor and coworker support, and strong marital relationships. Families in the program project were identified through local hospitals shortly after mothers had given birth. A few screening questions were asked of all mothers in the hospital, and families were subsequently selected at random and invited to participate. Data are being collected when the target children are 2, 6, 15, 24, and 36 months of age via a series of home visits that integrate a variety of methods including parent interviews, child assessments, observations of parents and children, and collection of biomarker data (i.e., mothers' and children's saliva to be assayed for cortisol; child heart-rate data to monitor stress reactivity).

Note that in the early part of the study, occasions of measurement are spaced closely together. This is not only because infants undergo tremendous changes in physical, social, cognitive, emotional, and linguistic development in the early months of life, but also because, during such times of rapid development, mothers and fathers must adapt their parenting in response to the changing competencies and behavioral repertoires of their young children. Annual points of measurement would miss much of the action.

How does one choose how often to study individuals or families in a situation like this one? Researchers have to weigh theoretical and pragmatic considerations; research design decisions often involve trade-offs. Perhaps in the FLP it would have been ideal, theoretically, to study the children and their families even more often, but data collection is expensive, demanding of participants, and labor-intensive for staff. Closely spaced assessments may increase the likelihood of practice or reactivity effects for some measures. Subject burden is not inconsequential. It is not sensible to commit resources to collecting data at such frequent intervals that busy families become overwhelmed and drop out of the study. Closely spaced time intervals place demands on research staffs as well. In the FLP, families were recruited into the study across a full year. This means that, once the study passed the point at which the first babies recruited turn 6 months of age, 2- and 6-month visits happened simultaneously. Later on in the life of the project, 6- and 15-month visits overlap as well, creating organizational challenges for those charged with tracking families and training home visitors, who must be up-to-speed on two sets of data collection protocols.

Strengths and limitations of longitudinal designs that involve multiple time points during the year include many of the same issues we have covered in previous sections. The primary strength is that researchers can try to capture the pattern of development or change that is most relevant to their research questions. Analytic approaches such as MLM are flexible about the length of time between occasions of measurement, making uneven intervals less of a concern than they are with some other statistical techniques.

The primary disadvantages of designs that rely on multiple occasions of measurement across a year are potentially reactivity, subject burden, and expense. When data points are closer together, there is a greater likelihood that participants will be sensitized by the questions asked or the procedures undertaken during the previous occasion of measurement. In addition, closely spaced data collection points require more time and attention from participants. If the burden is perceived as too great, participants may refuse to participate, creating a retention problem. High levels of attrition bias the sample and make it more difficult for researchers to interpret their results. Another factor that the researcher must weigh is expense. Collecting data and tracking participants are expensive enterprises. The research team has to be sure that the closely spaced measurement intervals are theoretically justifiable and likely to produce meaningful variations in patterns of stability and change.

Using Repeated Measures of Individuals to Understand Intraindividual Variability in Emotional Experience

Thus far, our examples of longitudinal research have all pertained to understanding how individuals, couples, or families change over time. There is another body of research, however, that utilizes repeated measures of individuals in another way. For this group of investigations, the emphasis is not on time, or the aging or maturational or experiential processes thought to be captured by time, but on understanding within-person variability in experience, usually emotional experience (see review by Larson & Almeida, 1999). In the literature on work and family, much of this work has focused on implications of daily stressors (e.g., Almeida, 2004; Bolger, DeLongis, Kessler, & Wethington, 1989; Repetti, 1989; Repetti & Wood, 1997; Wells, 1988).

A typical study of work-family stress might correlate a measure of work stress with a measure of individual health or well-being or a measure of family relationship quality. In such a study, each participant is represented by one piece of data on each construct. In contrast, the small body of research that has focused on intraindividual variability collects data from each individual on multiple occasions. These occasions are often spaced very closely together. Typically, researchers gather these data using daily diaries or evening telephone interviews about the specific day's events. Researchers who use the Experience Sampling Method (ESM) ask participants to carry electronic pagers or alarm watches (see Schneider, chap. 22, this volume, for a discussion of experience sampling methods). The pager or watch beeps at random times of the day, prompting participants to complete an immediate, quick report about their current activities, interactions, and emotions. A recent innovation in this genre is the use of preprogrammed handheld computers. These small devices emit a signal when respondents are supposed to enter their data. An advantage of using this technology is that these machines can record in real time exactly when the participant actually responded to the signal, whereas with some of the other methods of collecting daily data, the researcher never knows whether respondents complied with the request to complete their forms immediately or whether they filled them out before or after they were supposed to.

In data analysis, researchers typically treat the day or beep as the unit of analysis and control for the dependency between data points provided by the same participant analytically. Such analyses provide information on, for example, how individuals respond at home on days that have been "high" or "low" on work stress (defining high and low with regard to each individual participant's own central tendencies).

A pioneering investigation in this genre is a study by Bolger et al. (1989) of the connections between daily work and family stressors. This research team had access to 42 consecutive days of daily diary data from a sample of 166 married couples. The diaries, completed separately each night by husbands and wives, consisted of short questionnaires about a variety of stressors that might have occurred that day, including the experience of "overloads" (e.g., having too much to do) and "tensions or arguments" both at work and at home. In the analyses of these data, "day" was treated as the unit of analysis, and controls were entered to hold constant individual differences that were stable across days; thus, the analyses focused on intraindividual variability in the experience of stressors across days. Analyses of work-to-home spillover of stress revealed that, on days when husbands experienced an argument at work with a coworker or supervisor, they came home and engaged in more arguments with their wives. The pattern was similar—though not statistically significant—when wives experienced arguments at work. On days when husbands experienced "overloads" at work, they performed less work at home; interestingly, on those stressful days, their wives stepped in and performed more work at home. The parallel compensatory pattern did not occur, however; when wives experienced overloads at work they too performed less work at home, but their husbands did not step in and perform more. This is a nice example of a study that relies on repeated measures of work and family phenomena across multiple days being able to reveal a family process (i.e., wives compensating for husbands' work stress by doing more housework, and husbands failing to compensate for their wives' work stress) that could probably have not been uncovered in any other way.

Repetti (1989) used a similar strategy in a study of air traffic controllers. She chose air traffic control as an occupation because these jobs are characterized by high levels of stress and because variations in weather, flights delays, and the like create naturally occurring variability in day-to-day stress. In this study, 33 air traffic controllers and 27 of their spouses completed short surveys on three different evenings about their experiences on the job that day as well at home that evening. These self-report data were complemented with objective, daily FAA data on airport conditions. Results revealed that air traffic controllers tended to withdraw from social interaction with their spouses and to express lower rates of anger on days that had been stressful at work, withdrawal processes that were facilitated by spousal support.

Research that focuses on intraindividual variability has a somewhat limited applicability to work and family research in that it is best suited for studying fast-changing phenomena such as emotional states and negative and positive interactions (Larson & Almeida, 1999). Studies in this genre provide great insight into these phenomena, however, because they exploit what can be learned from repeated measures of the same person across hours or days. In controlling for individual differences in temperaments, personalities, worldviews, and coping styles, research studies of this type enable the systematic associations between daily work and family emotions or interactions to shine through.

There are pitfalls to watch for, however. There are no clear norms, for example, about how many occasions of measurement are needed to have an accurate sense of individual participants' emotion and interaction repertoires. The more occasions, the more likely central tendencies will be accurately pinpointed. From this point of view, the 42 consecutive days of daily diary data that Bolger et al. (1989) analyzed would appear satisfactory, assuming that those 6 weeks reflected the participants' usual experiences. The 3 days that Repetti relied on in her air traffic controller study, however, would seem to be a scant basis on which to assess intraindividual patterns of work stress and interaction at home. It is also possible, however, that researchers run an increased risk of encountering practice effects when they ask participants to complete the same questionnaires on many, closely spaced occasions. As research in this area grows, presumably norms about best practice will develop with it.

Larson and Almeida (1999, p. 12) noted that researchers also need to carefully match their research questions with the methods available:

> Experience sampling has the advantage of capturing specific actions and events when they happen, thus increasing the ability to evaluate short-term, rapidly occurring changes in family members' emotions. This approach, however, may not be effective if the researcher is studying events that do not occur frequently during the course of a day (e.g., arguments and disagreements). The rarer the event of interest, the more unlikely that the participant will be signaled at the right time to obtain the information.

For less common events, it may be more appropriate to ask participants to complete daily diaries that cover the entire day's events or to telephone them in the evening and to ask for a summary of their activities and interactions on that particular day.

Longitudinal Designs That Follow Participants Over Key Work and Family Transitions

Certain work and family questions deal with key milestones and transitions during individuals', couples', and families' lives. Sometimes these transitions can be anticipated by the researcher and a study designed accordingly. Such transitions include becoming a parent and retiring from the workforce. Other transitions cannot be easily anticipated, but a longitudinal researcher may discover that a data set happens to provide before and after data on a key transition.

Research on life course transitions captures participants' functioning prior to and following the identified transition. Goldberg and Perry-Jenkins (2004), for example, used data on 97 dual-earner, working-class couples experiencing the transition to parenthood for the first time to understand the effects of this transition on women's mental health and marital outcomes. Couples were recruited via hospital prenatal classes. To be enrolled in the study, both members of the couple had to be working full-time, planning on returning to work full-time after the birth of the baby, married or cohabiting, and meet the working-class criterion. Goldberg and Perry-Jenkins (2004) used the prebirth occasion of measurement to ask questions about prospective parents' expectations about what life would be like after the baby's arrival. They found that mothers who, prior to giving birth, had expected to perform more child care but who, in fact, performed less postnatal child care than anticipated reported higher levels of depression at Time 2. This finding was especially evident for mothers who worked part-time and those who held traditional gender ideologies.

Utilizing the same sample, Perry-Jenkins, Goldberg, Pierce, and Sayer (under review) compared the mental health and marital quality of 46 same-shift couples and 45 alternating-shift couples across the 1st year of parenthood. During the prenatal period, they found no differences in mental health or marital quality as a function of shift. After the transitions to parenthood and back to work, however, wives in alternating-shift couples reported significant declines in both mental health and marital love, compared to wives in same-shift couples. A year after the first child's birth, alternating-shift husbands were also less in love with their wives than were husbands in same-shift couples.

Another important work-family transition is retirement. The Cornell Retirement and Well-Being Study, led by Phyllis Moen, collected data on 762 individuals ages 50 to 72 identified from six employers in upstate New York. Husbands and wives were interviewed every other year for a total of three waves. Moen, Kim, and Hofmeister (2001) reported that following the transition to retirement both women and men reported lower levels of marital quality. Marital conflict increased for individuals across the transition to retirement, especially if their spouse continued to work. However, directly following the transition to retirement men reported heightened levels of morale possibly due a reduction in the number of roles and associated strains (Kim & Moen, 2002).

Studies of transitions are ideal for assessing change associated with a specific event. With before and after data, the individual essentially serves as his or her own "control" during the transition. Thus, changes that occur between these two data points can be fairly safely attributed to the transition itself (e.g., becoming a parent). Certain types of transitions lend themselves well to being studied in this way, such as the transition to parenthood. The pregnancy period provides a window for researchers to identify individuals and couples who are about to experience this transition. Age-graded transitions such as retirement can also be anticipated and studied with a before and after design. Note that researchers using a before and after design often still must grapple with the issue of selection effects, however. To the extent that participants *choose* to make the transition (e.g., planned pregnancies, optional retirements), those who make the transition may differ in important ways from those who do not.

Selection effects are less problematic in transitions that are imposed, as in a company's decision to close a plant. Although it would be ideal to be able to use before and after designs to study organizational changes such as plant closings and their implications for individuals, couples and families, in practice these transitions are hard to study without insider organizational knowledge. Ordinarily, by the time the research community hears about a potential plant closing or a similar large-scale organizational event, employees undoubtedly already know about it, making it difficult to attain true "before" data.

FINAL CONSIDERATIONS: WHEN ARE LONGITUDINAL DESIGNS MOST USEFUL?

Having provided a primer on some of the most common longitudinal designs in the area of work-family research, we conclude with a pragmatic discussion of some of the issues researchers should take into account when considering whether or not to mount a longitudinal study. These issues include (a) theoretical considerations, (b) trade-offs and pragmatic considerations, (c) resources, (d) missing data, and (e) developmental equivalence of measurement.

Theoretical Considerations

It does not make sense to invest in a longitudinal study unless the researcher has some clear, theoretically grounded research questions that involve continuity and change. Over the proposed time span of the study, what do the researchers expect to see unfold in the workplace, family, or developing individual? If the researcher is really interested in associations between variables but not in the conditions underlying continuity and change in those phenomena, a cross-sectional design may make more sense.

Sometimes a longitudinal design is the result of luck rather than planning. Elder (1998), for example, made the discovery that researchers during the 1920s and 1930s had collected data on children and youth and their parents. Years later, he was able to follow up the children and adolescents to see how their adult years had unfolded. The combination of two data sets waiting to be taken full advantage of, coupled with the fact that one of the most dramatic economic events in American history (the Great Depression) had occurred during the period in which the original researchers had collected the data, made following up these cohorts theoretically interesting. Elder could bring to bear theoretical work about economic stress, social change, and intergenerational relations to a data set that was uniquely suited for these research questions.

Trade-Offs and Pragmatic Considerations

Longitudinal research is a waiting game. Researchers invest tremendous time and resources up front and, depending on the design of the study, may have to wait quite a long time for the phenomena of interest to unfold. This strategy may be risky, especially for junior investigators, unless the study yields interesting findings along the way that can be presented and published. There are some shortcuts that can reduce the waiting game, however. For example, for some questions one can design a synthetic cohort. Imagine that a researcher is interested in how gender role attitudes unfold from middle childhood into early adulthood. The researcher identifies a cohort of 10-year-olds in 2005 and plans to follow them at regular intervals until they are 25 years old. This plan will mean waiting for 15 years to have a full picture of development and change in this phenomenon. If our hypothetical researcher is impatient, however, he or she could add two additional 5-year longitudinal samples to this design. This would mean in 2005 the researcher would also identify a sample of 15-year-olds and a sample of 20-year-olds and follow them each for 5 years. Combining the first 5 years of data from the 10-year-olds with the 5 years of data from the samples of 15- and 20-year-olds will give the researcher a synthetic representation of how gender role attitudes may unfold across the years from age 10 to 25. Moreover, creating this synthetic picture would take only 5 years to accomplish.

The researcher would need to make sure that the three samples are drawn from the same populations, that is, that they differ only on age and not on other potential confounds such as social class, race, ethnicity, and so on. The researcher still runs the risk that the samples will differ in certain ways, however, because, as discussed above, they would have been exposed to prevailing social and historical events at different periods in their development. Eventually, however, the investigator would be able to compare the synthetic data with the 15 years of longitudinal data provided by the participants who began participating in the study as 10-year-olds. That comparison would help establish how effective the synthetic cohort approach turned out to be. Ideally, the synthetic cohort strategy gives the researcher an opportunity to preview the phenomena of interest while real time is ticking slowly along in the full longitudinal study.

Resources

Longitudinal research is expensive, and researchers must weigh the trade-off between what can be learned by following people over time versus the costs. In addition to the data collection, data management, and data analysis costs that all research projects face, longitudinal researchers must provide incentives for participants to stay involved and track participants' whereabouts.

Many longitudinal projects provide a monetary payment to participants each time they provide data. Often this amount is not enough to cover the participants' time, but it is an important symbolic gesture, and for some participants it is an incentive to join a study and to remain involved. Researchers handle subject payments in different ways. When the FRP began studying its middle childhood sample in 1995, the project provided a $100 honorarium to families. This annual honorarium was increased to $200 in 2000 partly to account for inflation and also to provide an extra incentive for families to remain in the study. The honorarium is given at the beginning of the home interview to signify that it is a "no strings attached" thank you. Some research projects organize their subject payments so that they increase steadily over time. Others provide modest honoraria at each occasion of measurement and arrange for families or individuals to receive a larger lump sum at the end of the study if they have participated at every wave.

The Family Life Project takes a somewhat different approach. Preliminary focus groups with parents in low-income, rural communities indicated that some families did not have bank accounts and would find cashing a check difficult. Thus, for this project, the subject payments come in the form of $50 gift cards to department or grocery stores. FLP home visitors also bring a small baby gift each time they visit the family. These include bibs and onesies decorated with the project logo, children's books, packets of diapers, and so on. In addition, at the first visit, each family receives a colorful refrigerator magnet with the project's logo on it and all the contact information for the project, including a toll-free telephone number. The hope is that families will hold on to the magnet and refer to it when they need to change appointments with home visitor staff.

Longitudinal researchers must also invest resources in staying in touch with participants. Each year, the FRP stays in touch with families by sending a summer newsletter, a December holiday card and letter, and birthday cards to the two participating siblings. In the summer newsletter, we provide short bios and photos of our staff and summarize some new findings from the study (we focus on benign findings that are not likely to influence how families respond to subsequent interviews). When the children were younger, the newsletter included a "kids' page" with puzzles, riddles, and information about Web sites that children might find fun. Creating these communications takes some work and mailing them takes resources, but such mailings help connect the families to the project as well as provide valuable information to the project about changes in address.

At times it is also necessary to track down missing participants, a time-consuming endeavor. Many projects ask participants as they join the project to provide contact information for several people who are likely to always know who they are, usually extended family members and close friends. Staff charged with tracking missing participants can begin with those contacts, but they may also have to use Web-based white pages, make queries to state departments of motor vehicles, and even knock on doors in participants' old neighborhoods to ask neighbors if they know where the missing family can be found. These efforts can be expensive, but given the havoc that high levels of attrition can wreak on a longitudinal project's ability to provide useful information, they are often worth the time and expense.

Dealing With Missing Data

Even the most organized longitudinal research project will, over time, have some missing data. Participants will skip questions, fail to complete measures, or refuse to participate in one wave but return for the next. Small amounts of missing data are generally not viewed as a serious problem, especially if the missingness is not systematic. Researchers can either conduct their analyses without those few cases or use standard techniques such as substituting mean values to fill in the gaps. As noted earlier, some analytic strategies, such as multi-level modeling, are quite flexible about missing data.

In other situations, however, missing data can be very troublesome. Heckman (1976, 1979) has proposed a two-stage procedure that some family scholars (see, for example, Miller & Wright, 1995) have used to correct for attrition in longitudinal research. More recently, Schafer (1997) has developed a sophisticated multiple imputation software program for researchers to estimate missing data values (see Collins, Schafer, & Kam, 2001, for an example).

Developmental Equivalence of Measures

Work and family researchers who are interested in children and adolescents face the issue of developmental equivalence of measures. Ideally, longitudinal researchers want to use the same measures at each data point in order to track continuity and change. Sometimes, however, a measure that is appropriate at one development period is not appropriate in another. For example, when the FRP began following families in 1995, the two target children were 8 and 10 years of age. The research team chose to measure depressive symptoms with the Children's Depression Inventory (CDI; Kovacs, 1981), a measure that had been established for use with school-age children. As the children became adolescents and neared the end of the age window for this measure, the researchers faced a dilemma: Should they continue using the CDI, even though its wording at this point may strike adolescent participants as decidedly babyish, or should they switch to an adult measure of depressive symptoms? They elected to continue using the CDI but also to add the Center for Epidemiological Studies Depression measure (CES-D; Devins & Orme, 1985). They reasoned that having both measures at one point in time would enable them to assess how intercorrelated these measures were and whether the same results would emerge with the new measure as with the tried-and-true measure.

The issue of developmental equivalence of measurement is even more challenging in infancy, when development unfolds at such a fast rate. For example, separate measures of temperament have been developed for infants (Infant Behavior Questionnaire; Rothbart, 1981) and toddlers (Toddler Behavior Assessment Questionnaire; Goldsmith, 1996). Longitudinal researchers have to be developmentally attuned to the phenomena they are studying and prepare carefully for each occasion of measurement. One way that the NICHD's Study of Early Child Care research team has handled this challenge has been to periodically add new investigators to the team in anticipation of the sample's transitions into new stages of development. Thus, the research team, originally comprised of researchers with expertise in the infant and toddler years, now includes investigators with knowledge about development in middle childhood and adolescence.

Concluding Note

Longitudinal designs offer researchers interested in work and family issues important tools with which to learn about individual, dyadic, and familial continuity and change, and the ecological conditions that give rise to these patterns over time. As we have attempted to show, longitudinal research is appropriate for some research questions and not for others. For certain research questions, however, only a longitudinal design can provide theoretically satisfying answers to the questions posed because they focus on fundamental issues having to do with change.

To mount a successful study, a longitudinal researcher must define a set of interesting research questions, acquire resources to conduct the research, identify an appropriate sample, design a study that follows that sample at time intervals that are consistent with the research question, identify appropriate measures (keeping in mind concerns about practice effects and developmental equivalence), track the sample carefully, implement strategies to minimize attrition, be attentive to missing data and find the best ways to deal with it analytically, and analyze the data appropriately. This is a tall order. Given the many, diverse concerns that longitudinal researchers must address and the fact that no one person's substantive expertise usually covers all these substantive and methodological areas, interdisciplinary teamwork may be an excellent strategy. Longitudinal research has made and will continue to make important contributions to our growing understanding of the interrelationships between work and family. We hope to see many new and exciting contributions in this area in the years to come.

ACKNOWLEDGMENTS

Work on this chapter was supported by two grants from the National Institute for Child Health and Human Development: R01-HD32336 (Ann Crouter & Susan McHale, Co-PIs), which provides support for the Penn State Family Relationships Project, and P01 HD39667-01 (Lynne Vernon-Feagans & Martha Cox, Co-PIs), which provides support for the cross-site Family Life Project.

REFERENCES

Almeida, D. M. (2004). Using daily diaries to assess temporal friction between work and family. In A. C. Crouter & A. Booth (Eds.) *Work-family challenges for low-income parents and their children* (pp. 127–136). Mahwah, NJ: Lawrence Erlbaum Associates.

Barnett, R. C., & Brennan, R. T. (1997). Change in job conditions, change in psychological distress, and gender: A longitudinal study of dual-earner couples. *Journal of Organizational Behavior, 18*, 253–274.

Barnett, R. C., Raudenbush, S. W., Brennan, R. T., Pleck, J. H., & Marshall, N. L. (1995). Change in job and marital experiences and change in psychological distress: A longitudinal study of dual-earner couples. *Journal of Personality and Social Psychology, 69*, 839–850.

Belsky, J. (2001). Developmental risks (still) associated with early child care. *Journal of Child Psychology and Psychiatry, 42*, 845–859.

Belsky, J., & Eggebeen, D. (1991). Early and extensive maternal employment and young children's socioemotional development: Children of the National Longitudinal Survey of Youth. *Journal of Marriage and the Family, 53*, 1083–1098.

Belsky, J., & Rovine, M. J. (1988). Nonmaternal care in the first year of life and the security of infant–parent attachment. *Child Development, 59*, 157–167.

Bolger, N., DeLongis, A., Kessler, R. C., & Wethington, E. (1989). The contagion of stress across multiple roles. *Journal of Marriage and the Family, 51*, 175–183.

Brennan, R. T., Barnett, R. C., & Gareis, K. C. (2001). When she earns more than he does: A longitudinal study of dual-earner couples. *Journal of Marriage and Family, 63*, 168–182.

Brooks-Gunn, J., Han, W. J., & Waldfogel, J. (2002). Maternal employment and child cognitive outcomes in the first three years of life: The NICHD Study of Early Child Care. *Child Development, 73*, 1052–1072.

Bryk, A. S., & Raudenbush, S. W. (1992). *Hierarchical linear models.* Newbury Park, CA: Sage.

Collins, L. M., Schafer, J. L., & Kam, C. M. (2001). A comparison of inclusive and restrictive strategies in modern missing data procedures. *Psychological Methods, 6*, 330–351.

Crouter, A. C. (1984). Spillover from family to work: The neglected side of the work-family interface. *Human Relations, 37*, 425–442.

Crouter, A. C., Helms-Erikson, H., Updegraff, K., & McHale, S. M. (1999). Conditions underlying parents' knowledge about children's daily lives in middle childhood: Between- and within-family comparisons. *Child Development, 70*, 246–259.

Crouter, A. C., & McHale, S. M. (1993). Temporal rhythms in family life: Seasonal variation in the relation between parental work and family processes. *Developmental Psychology, 29*, 198–205.

Crouter, A. C., Tucker, C. J., Head, M. R., & McHale, S. M. (2004). Family time and the psychosocial adjustment of adolescent siblings and their parents. *Journal of Marriage and Family, 66*, 147–162.

Devins, G. M., & Orme, C. M. (1985). Center for Epidemiological Studies Depression Scale. In D. J. Keyser & R. C. Sweetland (Eds.), *Test critiques* (pp. 144–160). Kansas City, MO: Test Corporation of America.

Elder, G. H. (1998). The life course and human development. In R. M. Lerner (general editor, W. Damon), *Handbook of child psychology, volume 1: Theoretical models of human development* (pp. 939–992). New York: Wiley.

Goldberg, A. E., & Perry-Jenkins, M. (2004). Division of labor and working-class women's well-being across the transition to parenthood. *Journal of Family Psychology, 18*, 225–236.

Goldsmith, H. H. (1996). Studying temperament via construction of the toddler behavior assessment questionnaire. *Child Development, 67*, 218–235.

Hareven, T. K. (1982). *Family time and industrial time.* Cambridge, MA: Cambridge University Press.

Fortner, M. R., Crouter, A. C., & McHale, S. M. (2004). Is parents' work involvement responsive to the quality of relationships with adolescent offspring? *Journal of Family Psychology, 18*, 530–538.

Heckman, J. J. (1976). The common structure of statistical models of truncation, sample selection and limited dependent variables and a simple estimator for such variables. *Annals of Economic and Social Measurement, 5*, 475–492.

Heckman, J. J. (1979). Sample selection bias as a specification error. *Econometrica, 47*, 153–161.

Kim, J. E., & Moen, P. (2002). Retirement transitions, gender, and psychological well-being: A life-course, ecological model. *Journal of Gerontology, 57*, 212–222.

Klute, M. M., Crouter, A. C., Sayer, A. G., & McHale, S. M. (2001). Occupational self-direction, values, and egalitarian relationships. *Journal of Marriage and Family, 64*, 139–151.

Kohn, M. L. (1969). *Class and conformity: A study in values*. Homewood, IL: Dorsey.

Kohn, M. L. (1977). *Class and conformity: A study in values* (2nd ed.). Chicago: University of Chicago Press.

Kohn, M. L., & Schooler, C. (1983). *Work and personality: An inquiry into the impact of social stratification*. Norwood, NJ: Ablex.

Kovacs, M. (1981). The children's depression inventory: A self rated depression scale for school-aged youngsters. Unpublished manuscript, University of Pittsburgh School of Medicine.

Lambert, S. J. (1999). Lower-wage workers and the new realities of work and family. *The Annals of the American Academy of Political and Social Science, 562*, 174–190.

Larson, R., & Almeida, D. (1999). Emotional transmission in the daily lives of families: A new paradigm for studying family process. *Journal of Marriage and the Family, 61*, 5–20.

Maguire, M. C. (1999). Treating the dyad as the unit of analysis: A primer on three analytic approaches. *Journal of Marriage and the Family, 61*, 213–223.

McHale, S. M, Crouter, A. C., & Tucker, C. J. (1999). Family context and gender socialization in middle childhood: Comparing girls to boys and sisters to brothers. *Child Development, 70*, 990–1004.

Miller, R. B., & Wright, D. W. (1995). Detecting and correcting attrition bias in longitudinal family research. *Journal of Marriage and Family, 57*, 921–929.

Moen, P. (2003). *It's about time: Couples and careers*. Ithaca, NY: ILR Press.

Moen, P., Erickson, M., & Dempster-McClain, D. (1997). Their mothers' daughters? The intergenerational transmission of gender attitudes in a world of changing roles. *Journal of Marriage and the Family, 59*, 281–293.

Moen, P., Kim, J. E., & Hofmeister, H. (2001). Couples' work/retirement transitions, gender, and marital quality. *Social Psychology Quarterly, 64*, 55–71.

NICHD Early Child Care Research Network. (1997). The effects of infant child care on infant–mother attachment security: Results of the NICHD study of early child care. *Child Development, 68*, 860–879.

NICHD Early Child Care Research Network (2001). Nonmaternal care and family factors in early development: An overview of the NICHD Study of Early Child Care. *Journal of Applied Developmental Psychology, 22*, 457–492.

NICHD Early Child Care Research Network. (2002a). The interaction of child care and family risk in relation to child development at 24 and 36 months. *Applied Developmental Science, 6*, 144–156.

NICHD Early Child Care Research Network. (2002b). Child-care structure > process > outcome: Direct and indirect effects of child-care quality on young children's development. *Psychological- Science, 13*, 199–206.

Perry-Jenkins, M., Goldberg, A., Pierce, C., & Sayer, A. (under review). Shift work, role overload, and the transition to parenthood.

Raudenbush, S. W., Brennan, R. T., & Barnett, R. C. (1995). A multivariate hierarchical model for studying psychological change within married couples. *Journal of Family Psychology, 9*, 161–174.

Repetti, R. L. (1989). Effects of daily workload on subsequent behavior during marital interaction: The roles of social withdrawal and spouse support. *Journal of Personality and Social Psychology, 57*, 651–659.

Repetti, R. L., & Wood, J. (1997). Effects of daily stress at work on mothers' interactions with preschoolers. *Journal of Family Psychology, 11*, 90–108.

Rothbart, M. (1981). Measurement of temperament in infancy. *Child Development, 52*, 569–578.

Ryder, N. B. (1965). The cohort as a concept in the study of social changes. *American Sociological Review, 30*, 843–861.

Scarr, S., & McCartney, K. (1983). How people make their own environments: A theory of genotype → environment effects. *Child Development, 54*, 424–435.

Schafer, J. (1997). *Analysis of incomplete multivariate data*. London: Chapman & Hall.

Schaie, K. W. (1965). A general model for the study of developmental problems. *Psychological Bulletin, 64*, 92–107.

Schaie, K. W., & Baltes, P. B. (1975). On sequential strategies in developmental research: Description or explanation. *Human Development, 18*, 384–390.

Schaie, K. W., & Hertzog, C. (1983). Fourteen-year cohort-sequential analyses of adult intellectual development. *Developmental Psychology, 19*, 531–543.

Sorokin, P. A., & Merton, R. K. (1937). Social time: A methodological and functional analysis. *American Journal of Sociology, 42*, 615–629.

Wells, A. J. (1988). Variations in mothers' self-esteem in daily life. *Journal of Personality and Social Psychology, 55*, 661–668.

22

In the Moment: The Benefits of the Experience Sampling Method

Barbara Schneider
University of Chicago

"Where did the time go?" is a common phrase used by individuals when reflecting on how their time was spent and their memories of recent experiences. In certain types of scientific experiments conducted in laboratories, researchers try to interpret how individuals feel when confronted with different simulated life experiences and their reactions to them. In contrast, the Experience Sampling Method (ESM) is a unique method for estimating how individuals actually spend their time, who they are spending it with, what activities they are engaged in, and how they subjectively interpret the experience. Unlike the laboratory experience, individuals are randomly notified by a beeper during everyday experiences and, when signaled, record what they are doing and how they are feeling. Developed by Mihaly Csikszentmihalyi and colleagues in the 1970s (Csikszentmihalyi, Larson, & Prescott, 1977; Csikszentmihalyi & Csikszentmihalyi, 1988; Csikszentmihalyi & Larson, 1984), the ESM is especially useful for revealing the subjective experiences of persons in their natural environments. The data obtained from the ESM make it possible to investigate how differences in location, time, and physical and social environments affect individuals' quality of experience. Not without methodological problems, particularly with respect to sampling bias, burden, and nonresponse, the ESM continues to be one of the favored methods for studying time use and the emotional states associated with reported activities. This chapter describes the strengths and weaknesses of the ESM, how it compares with other methods for studying time use, and its advantages for understanding the daily experiences of adults and adolescents.

MEASURING TIME USE

One of the key problems in studying how individuals spend their time and how they feel when engaged in specific activities is finding the most efficient and accurate method for recording human behaviors and emotional responses. This can be challenging as people have a tendency to exaggerate time spent on socially desirable activities and underreport time spent on activities viewed as socially undesirable, such as excessive use of alcohol. Whatever method is used for collecting time use information, it is likely subject to inherent sources of bias. Clearly, a preferable method would be direct and unobtrusive observations of human life, such as using some type of hidden surveillance device to record individual behaviors throughout the course of a day. While likely to be the most accurate for measuring time use, this method, even with the respondent's approval, raises ethical issues as well as being logistically problematic and prohibitively expensive. When people know they are being observed, they may change their behaviors, thus producing nontypical estimates of their time use. However, there are some studies that involve extensive videography that have been able to overcome this problem (see Ochs, this volume). When participants become accustomed to the researcher's presence, they are less likely to be defensive and alter their behavior. Over time, the camera is hardly noticeable and becomes an unobtrusive part of the environment.

The most common method for obtaining information on time use is to ask individuals retrospective questions, such as those traditionally used by the U.S. Census Bureau, which ask the respondent how many hours he or she worked in the previous week. Although less intrusive, this method and others that rely on retrospective questions have been shown to produce unreliable time use estimates (Mulligan, Schneider, & Wolfe, 2003). An alternative to retrospective survey questions is the time diary method, which requires individuals to record their activities and the times at which they occurred. There are several types of time diaries. Perhaps the most well known is the full-day diary, used in a series of studies at the Universities of Maryland and Michigan (Juster & Stafford, 1985; Robinson & Godbey, 1997; Bianchi, Milkie, Sayer, & Robinson, 2000). In full-day diary studies, respondents are asked to name the activity or activities they were engaged in during each of ninety-six 15-minute intervals over a 24-hour period. These full-day diaries are collected using a variety of procedures including in-person interviews, telephone interviews, or return mail surveys. Some studies ask individuals to report their previous day's activities, while others introduce respondents to the diary and ask them to begin using it when they wake up the next day. Another form of time diary, used primarily for estimating the number of hours worked, is the travel schedule diary (Jacobs, 1998). Individuals report what time they leave for work, how much time they spend commuting, and what time they return home.

The ESM is another method for studying time use (Csikszentmihalyi & Csikszentmihalyi, 1988; Csikszentmihalyi & Larson, 1984). The term "experience sampling" refers to the collection of data about individuals' self-reported feelings and actions within the context of everyday life. The common procedure used in an ESM study is to notify individuals by a beeper and have them, when signaled, record what they are doing and feeling. Experience sampling designs vary in terms of when events are sampled: at fixed intervals, randomly throughout the day, or in response to some event or set of events over the course of a few days to a month (for excellent reviews, see Bolger, Davis, & Rafaeli, 2003; Reis & Gable, 2000). A critically important aspect of the ESM is that it permits individuals to report on experiences as they occur in a natural setting, thus minimizing the likelihood of retrospective bias.

The Csikszentmihalyi studies typically ask participants to respond to eight signals per day over the course of a week, which has the advantage of sampling over 7 consecutive days rather than on a given day. Researchers have the option of choosing the frequency and duration of the signaling schedule. Obtaining sufficient responses allows investigators to address questions about within- and between-person differences in emotion. In contrast to a single-report item, where respondents tend to give more weight to recent or intense experiences, the ESM captures how they feel at each moment signaled, thus minimizing systematic and random sources of measurement error (Redelmeier & Kahneman, 1996; Stone & Neale, 1980). One of the most valuable aspects of instruments like the ESM, where participants answer questions over several consecutive days, is that it is possible to learn how moods fluctuate from morning to night; are experienced over the weekend versus the weekday; and, if data are collected over a period of months or years, how individuals change over time. The ability to measure temporal effects is one of the major strengths of this type of method.

One major investigation that used the ESM over the course of 5 years is the Alfred P. Sloan Study of Youth and Social Development. In this national initiative designed to learn how young people form ideas about careers, over 1,000 adolescents participated in the ESM through their teenage years into adulthood. This study was able to investigate not only variations across a week in how adolescents experienced their relationships with parents, friends, and teachers, but also replicated this methodology longitudinally over a 5-year period (Csikszentmihalyi & Schneider, 2000; and the special issue of *Applied Developmental Science*, edited by Csikszentmihalyi & Schneider, 2001).[1]

ESM studies have been conducted with diverse populations, including adults and adolescents, and provide estimates on how much time adults watch television (Kubey & Csikszentmihalyi, 1990), do housework, and work at their jobs (Schneider & Waite, 2005) and how much time adolescents spend on homework, socializing with friends, or being home alone (Csikszentmihalyi, Rathunde, & Whalen, 1993; Csikszentmihalyi & Schneider, 2000). One of the major findings of the adolescent study was how much time adolescents actually spend at home alone, a finding that has been validated with data from other survey instruments. Unstructured time, particularly for adolescents, can be an especially negative experience. In the adolescent study, Hispanic high school students spent considerably more time than other groups milling around outside and inside school, and traveling to and from school and work. Milling around time, much like time alone, tends to promote low self-esteem and disengagement (Csikszentmihalyi & Schneider, 2000; Schneider & Stevenson, 1999).

There is considerable variation in ESM research technology, including beepers, watches, and handheld computers, such as Palm Pilots (see Bolger, Davis, & Rafaeli, 2003, for a review of the strengths and limitations of these methods). A new handbook is forthcoming that summarizes ESM procedures and the types of studies and findings that rely on the ESM (Csikszentmihalyi, Hektner, & Schmidt, forthcoming). Because there are so many new and extensive materials on ESM methods, rather than reviewing these sources, this chapter focuses on one major initiative, the 500 Family Study, which examines how working families and their children spend their time at work, at school, and at home and how they interpret these experiences (Schneider & Waite, 2005). To illustrate how the ESM can be used and its methodological strengths and limitations, this chapter reviews selected findings from ESM analyses.

In the 500 Family Study, researchers preprogrammed wristwatches (a Casio brand that emitted unobtrusive beeps) according to a schedule that signaled the parents and their children randomly seven times a day at different intervals from 7:30 A.M. through 10:30 P.M. over the course of a normal week. The beeping schedule was tailored to each family member's sleep and wake patterns, in order to take into account nonstandard work schedules. This procedure, it could be argued, more accurately captures the waking experiences of working parents and their children than methods that do not consider nonstandard work schedules. The predetermined schedule of signals was designed to be unpredictable to the respondent, thus providing a representative sample of each person's moods and activities for that day and week. The respondents were asked to fill out a one-page, two-sided form each time they were signaled. The form takes about 2 to 3 minutes to complete. Figure 22.1 displays the two-sided ESM form used in the 500 Family Study.

As seen in Fig. 22.1, the front page of the form asks the respondent to verify the date, time when signaled, and the time when responding. As might be expected, individuals are occasionally beeped at times when it is difficult to respond, for example, when in the shower, listening to a concert, or in the midst of an argument. Asking two questions, the time when signaled and the time when responding, allows the analyst to determine the time lapse from signal to response. If the duration between the time beeped and time answered is longer than

Date_____ Time you were beeped _____am/pm   Time you responded _____am/pm

As you were beeped...

Where were you? _____
                                    PLEASE BE SPECIFIC
_____

What was the main thing you were **doing**? _____
                                               PLEASE BE SPECIFIC
_____

What **else** were you doing at the same time? _____
                                               PLEASE BE SPECIFIC
_____

What was on your mind? _____
                              PLEASE BE SPECIFIC
_____

Were you alone... Yes___ No___ ... or were you with... (please check all that apply)

Your Spouse___ Your Boss____ Co-Workers ___ Friend(s) ___ Girl/Boyfriend____

Your Mother___ Your Father ___Teacher____ Classmates/Peers ____ Other(s) ____

Your Child(ren) ____ (please indicate who) _____

Your Sibling(s) ____ (please indicate who) _____

Think back on how you got into this activity...
Were you doing this **main activity** because you... (check all that apply)

    (1) Wanted to ___   (2) Had to ___   (3) had nothing else to do ___

Indicate how you felt about the main activity.   (Please circle one number for each question)

	Not at All	A Little	Somewhat	Very Much
Did you **enjoy** what you were doing?	0	1	2	3
Was this activity **interesting**?	0	1	2	3
How well were you **concentrating**?	0	1	2	3
Were you living up to **your expectations**?	0	1	2	3
Did you feel **in control** of the situation?	0	1	2	3
Did the situation allow you to be **involved** or **to act**?	0	1	2	3
Did you have **the abilities** to deal with the situation?	0	1	2	3
Was the activity **important to you**?	0	1	2	3
Were others **expecting** a lot from you?	0	1	2	3

Were you **succeeding** at what you were doing?	0	1	2	3
Did you wish you were **doing something else**?	0	1	2	3
Did you **feel good** about yourself?	0	1	2	3

FIG. 22.1.   The Experience Sampling Method (ESM) form.

How did you feel as you were beeped? (For every pair of opposites, please circle only one mark.)							
Happy	*Sad*	*Weak*	*Strong*	*Passive*	*Active*	*Excited*	*Bored*
O o o o o O		O o o o o O		O o o o o O		O o o o o O	

As you were being beeped, were you feeling…?   (Circle one number for each question)

	Not at all	A little	Some what	Very Much		Not at all	A little	Somew hat	Very Much
Cheerful	0	1	2	3	**Worried**	0	1	2	3
Lonely	0	1	2	3	**Caring**	0	1	2	3
Nervous	0	1	2	3	**Irritated**	0	1	2	3
Cooperative	0	1	2	3	**Relaxed**	0	1	2	3
Angry	0	1	2	3	**Stressed**	0	1	2	3
Responsible	0	1	2	3	**Proud**	0	1	2	3
Frustrated	0	1	2	3	**Friendly**	0	1	2	3
Competitive	0	1	2	3	**Hardworking**	0	1	2	3
Strained	0	1	2	3	**Productive**	0	1	2	3

Did you feel any **physical pain** or **discomfort** as you were beeped? None Slight Bothersome Severe
(Please describe) _____   0   1   2   3

If you were talking with people, please answer the following 3 questions:	Not at All	A Little	Somewhat	Very Much
Were you able to **express** your opinion?	0	1	2	3
Were others really **listening** to what you had to say?	0	1	2	3
Did you **care** about what others were saying?	0	1	2	3

If you felt a **strong emotion** since the last report, what did you feel and why did you feel that way?

I felt _____ because _____
                                                    PLEASE BE SPECIFIC
_____

_____

If anyone else you were with expressed a strong emotion to you since the last report, what did they feel and why?
(who) _____ felt _____ because _____
                                                    PLEASE BE SPECIFIC
_____

_____

COMMENTS, ETC.

FIG. 22.1.   (Continued).

20 minutes, the information is discarded as the responses are no longer regarded as "in the moment," but instead are retrospective analyses of the event. Time signaled is also important as it can be verified with the predetermined random time schedule and used to check the reliability of the participant's response patterns.

The place indicator is particularly valuable as it describes where the participant is. The place codes were constructed similar to a Dewey Decimal system with the first set of numbers as the main identifiers followed by additional numbers that signify more specific categories. Presently there are approximately 200 place codes used in various ESM studies conducted at the

University of Chicago (see Csikszentmihalyi & Schneider, 2000 and Schneider & Waite, 2005, for more detailed descriptions of these place codes). Following place codes are the "doing" or activity codes. Respondents report what activities they are engaged in when signaled, and these activities are coded using a classification system similar to that for the place codes. Because people spend so much time multitasking, participants are asked to report both their primary and secondary activities. Having both primary and secondary activity codes is valuable for estimating time use, especially at work and at home. For example, an individual at work could be beeped when eating lunch and reading e-mails, raising the question whether this activity should be considered as personal care or working. If seen as working, then the issue is whether the secondary activity should be assigned the same weight as the primary activity.

Primary and secondary activity codes are also helpful for more accurately estimating time spent on housework, such as doing laundry while cooking dinner (see Lee, 2005, on this issue). Wives are more likely to multitask, perhaps leading to an underestimate of how much time they spend on housework. The final code in this series is the thinking code, designed to determine congruence between cognitive engagement and activity codes. Returning to the housework example, most estimates of housework exclude the planning of household tasks. Thinking codes allow researchers to include in their estimates of time spent on housework these "invisible" mental tasks. Over 400 activity and thinking codes have been constructed for the 500 Family Study.[2]

To obtain the fraction of total time spent in an activity using ESM responses based on a beeping schedule that extends over a week, the typical calculation is made by dividing the number of beeps for which the respondent reports doing a particular task by the total number of beeps to which he or she responded. Ratios are then transformed into hours by multiplying that number by the number of days beeped and the number of waking hours in a day. For the 500 Family Study, the percentage of time would be this ratio times 112 hours (i.e., 7 days × 16 hours per day). In cases of secondary activities, analysts will sometimes add additional time to the primary activity to obtain more accurate estimates of time use. However, to minimize inflation of estimates, most analysts will add to the primary activity only a proportion of time for the secondary activity.

The next set of categories describes who the respondent is with. The codes for these items are useful for determining time spent with family, friends, and being alone. In the 500 Family Study, these items were particularly useful for determining how much time family members spent together and how they felt during shared activities. An additional item, sometimes referred to as the volition measure, asks respondents whether they were engaged in the activity because they had to, wanted to, had nothing else to do, or some combination of these response options. This item makes it possible to assess the strength of the respondents' motivations for engaging in certain tasks such as housework, schoolwork, and paid work.

Following these items is a series of Likert-type scales that measure how the respondent feels about the activity, including such items as enjoyment, interest, concentration, control, and involvement. Embedded within this list of items are another series of questions that are internal assessments, including living up to one's expectations of oneself and others, having the ability to deal with the situation, how successful and good the individual feels about what he or she is doing, and how motivated he or she feels about the activity. (The actual item asks the extent to which the respondent wishes to be doing something else.) In the 500 Family Study, issues of expectations are important for understanding whether individuals believe their actions are viewed as legitimate and meeting with others' approval. Expectations can be assessed in reference to marriage, work, childbearing, and schoolwork.

The second side of the ESM form continues with more scaled items pertaining to the respondent's emotional states, including measures of positive affect (happy, cheerful, and friendly) and negative affect (irritated, angry, and worried). At the top of the page are a set of items designed as bipolar adjective pairs (e.g., sad–happy) and several monopolar ones. Both bipolar and monopolar items are used to determine relative degrees of stability and consistency across items (see Diener & Larson, 1984, and Diener, Smith, & Fujita, 1995, on this point). Some controversy exists regarding whether one type of scale is more accurate and reliable than the other. In the 500 Family Study, the decision was made to include both types of scales.

Several modifications to the ESM form were made in the 500 Family Study to accommodate the adult sample, including expanded activity, place, and thinking codes. To provide an additional view on physical health, an item was developed to detect instances of pain and their frequency. The third set of items on the second page of the ESM is an attempt to learn about perceptions of "voice." Several researchers have suggested that communication patterns differ markedly between men and women (see, e.g., Tannen, 1990). These items were constructed to obtain personal assessments of opportunities to express oneself and to learn if they vary from work to home. To provide more temporal contextual information for a specific beep, the last set of items before the comments section was designed to provide a self-report of prior emotional experiences.

Much like time diaries, the ESM has been criticized as being too burdensome; that is, the time and cognitive demands made on the respondent are more excessive than the demands typically made by surveys. There may also be an inherent selection bias with these methods if the people who agree to participate differ systematically from those who do not (Zuzanek, 1999). Critics have also suggested that individuals may underreport what they are doing simply because they do not wish to be interrupted. Such underreporting is often thought to occur more frequently outside the home where respondents may be unwilling to answer the beeps. Recent studies suggest that this is not the case and that people are more likely to respond at work and at school (Mulligan, Schneider, & Jeong, 2004).

USING THE ESM IN THE 500 FAMILY STUDY

The purpose of the 500 Family Study, conducted in 1999–2000, was to understand how working families balance work and life experiences. Recognizing that the composition of the family would likely make different demands on the responsibilities of mothers and fathers, the study was designed to include 300 families with adolescents and 200 with kindergarten children. Drawing from a sample of families from eight communities across the United States, multiple methods were used to explore a variety of questions regarding the influence work had on family life, the quality of relationships among working families, and stresses and conflicts parents and their children experience when both parents are working full-time.

The sites for the study were selected to vary in their levels of urbanization, labor force composition, and socioeconomic characteristics. Four of the communities are predominately upper-middle class, where the majority of the parents are college-educated professionals with family incomes above $50,000. The four remaining communities are middle or lower-middle class in which 20 to 30% of the adults have earned college or advanced degrees and are employed in managerial or professional jobs; the median family income in these communities ranges from $40,000 to $44,000 per year (U.S. Department of Commerce, Bureau of the Census, 2002).

Families in the study were recruited through solicitation by phone, mail, and newspaper advertisements. At each of the sites, permission to send out informational packets about the study was obtained from local high schools and elementary schools. Two sites included letters in school newsletters inviting families to participate. Advertisements were also run in local newspapers asking families to contact the university if interested in participating in the study. Additionally, families were referred by parents already participating in the study, and these families were contacted by phone. (For a full description of the design, sample, and procedures for the 500 Family Study, see Hoogstra, 2005.)

Several methods were used to examine the family and work experiences of the parents and children in the study, including surveys, in-depth interviews, and the ESM. By triangulating data obtained through these different methods, a fairly comprehensive picture of work and family life can be constructed. Several items included in the survey correspond to questions in the ESM, thereby allowing analysts to assess reliability of time use estimates for such activities as housework and television viewing. Following procedures outlined by Csikszentmihalyi and Larson (1987), respondents were asked to wear wristwatches preprogrammed to emit several signals each day. The schedule was set so that the watch beeped at random times in 2-hour blocks during respondents' waking hours, with the restriction that no two signals occurred less than 30 minutes apart. To the extent possible, members of the same family were placed on identical signaling schedules so that it would be possible, as during the dinner hour, to analyze individuals' responses to shared activities. Trained coders, using detailed schemes, coded the open-ended responses. Inter-rater reliabilities on the ESM coding, based on person agreement, ranged from .79 to .95.

Respondents provided more than 45,000 ESM responses during the week of experience sampling. Participants were typically signaled eight times each day for 7 consecutive days, for a total of 56 signals per person for an entire week. Signaling schedules were modified slightly in cases where participants were typically awake for substantially fewer or greater than 16 hours each day. Although participants were asked to respond as often as possible, there were times when it was difficult or inconvenient to respond (e.g., while driving, attending religious services, or talking with a client). In such instances, participants were asked to complete the ESM form as soon as possible after being signaled. On average, mothers responded to 44 signals over the course of a week (a 78% response rate), and fathers responded to 41 signals (a 73% response rate). Response rates were slightly lower among adolescents. Teenagers responded to an average of 30 out of 56 beeps over the course of the week, with girls having higher response rates than boys (girls responded to 34 signals on average, while boys responded to 27). Thus, adults in the study only failed to respond to one in seven beeps, on average. In other words, they responded to most signals.

It is important to understand differences in response rates for the ESM in comparison with surveys or other types of instruments. In a typical national survey, the average nonresponse rate across items varies from 5 to as much as 30% (see, e.g., frequency distributions on items in High School Beyond and the National Educational Longitudinal Study of 1988–2000). Nonresponse to items is different than nonresponse by participants (i.e., failing to complete the survey at all). In large national surveys, the number of cases lost because of nonresponse to critical items can be considerable, and sophisticated imputation procedures have been developed for missing items so that the population estimates are not biased by nonresponse. For an individual's ESM records to be considered in an ESM analysis, he or she must have responded to, at a minimum, more than a fourth of the signals.

Nonresponse in ESM studies could be systematic; that is, there may be patterns across individuals, times, or places that influence when individuals respond. In analyzing ESM data, it is important to understand how missing responses are related to other variables in the data set. Jeong (2005) has developed new weighting procedures that take into account both response rates of individuals and the distribution of responses within clusters of activities. For example, adolescent boys tend to answer more beeps when in school than out of school (Mulligan,

Schneider, & Jeong, 2004). Jeong found that ESM response rates vary over the course of the week; the response rate for the first day of participation is greater than 83%, but gradually declines to 67% by the final day. Response rates also vary by day of the week, with higher response rates occurring on weekdays compared to weekends. Jeong cautioned potential ESM analysts to consider varying the days on which participants begin the ESM and to devise special incentives so that individuals will continue to participate throughout the course of the week.

ESM data are typically stored and analyzed at two levels: beep and person. In beep-level analyses, multiple beeps from the same individual are treated as independent records. Person-level analyses are based on percentages, means, and other aggregate scores of a group variable or variables for each respondent, often in conjunction with information from other instruments. In most statistical analyses of ESM data, mean values are calculated for each person's responses to a given item, and these means, rather than specific responses, are used in analysis. Thus, the unit of analysis is the person, not the response. In examining whether fathers or mothers report greater stress, for example, the appropriate comparison is between the mean stress scores of fathers and mothers. However, because ESM data consist of responses nested within individuals, it is possible to analyze the data at two levels—the beep level and person level—using multilevel modeling techniques, such as hierarchical linear modeling (HLM).

With respect to time use, ESM findings show that mothers spend less time than fathers on work-related activities, findings which were verified with survey results. In contrast to fathers, mothers spend more time engaged in social activities with family members and others, and on maintenance activities such as housework. Mothers and fathers in the sample spent comparable amounts of time in leisure activities and "other" activities such as commuting. Regarding measures of emotion obtained from the ESM, both mothers and fathers reported relatively low levels of stress, anger, worry, frustration, and irritation over the week of ESM participation. In contrast, they reported feeling moderately cheerful, cooperative, caring, relaxed, and friendly. While the general patterns of response are similar for mothers and fathers, some significant gender differences emerged. Mothers scored significantly higher than fathers on measures of caring, but reported feeling significantly more worried and significantly less cooperative, friendly, and relaxed.

Figure 22.2 shows the time period of 5 to 9 P.M. for one family, including the mother, father, and adolescent. The lines show individual responses for enjoyment at each beep relative to each family member's own mean. In ESM studies, analysts often use z scores in their analyses. Recognizing that people use scales differently and that some individuals may never feel very sad or happy, z scores allow the analyst to create a standardized score for each affect measure as well as more global mood scores. Comparisons of affect are consequently made in reference to an individual's overall mean. The benefit of the z score is that it is calculated relative to a person's entire schedule of beeps, not to a specific time. In this way it is possible to learn if a person, for example, feels more bored than average when working on the computer. Z scores also provide opportunities to compare and contrast different affective states on a standardized scale; it is thus possible to determine which person is happier and more cooperative at home than at work. Having a standardized score also allows for comparisons between individuals, so it is possible to ascertain whether fathers are happier than mothers at home taking into account both fathers' and mothers' average level of happiness. The formula for calculating the z score is $\frac{X-\mu}{\sigma}$, where X is the score to be standardized, μ is the mean, and σ is the standard deviation, resulting in a mean of zero and a standard deviation of 1.[3]

As shown in Fig. 22.2, the adolescent has the highest and lowest enjoyment score from 4:56 P.M. until 9:23 P.M. The father and mother show similar trends in enjoyment, although father's enjoyment remains higher than mother's until the final beep. Since the ESM also

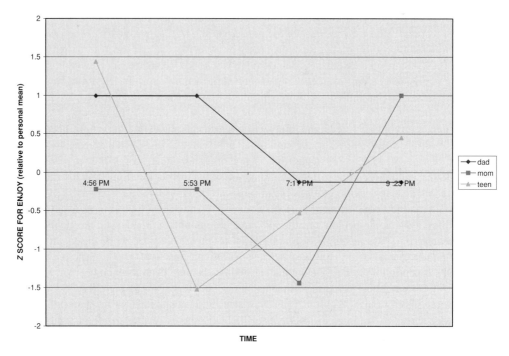

FIG. 22.2.   Experience Sampling Method (ESM) reports of individual enjoyment (scaled as a z score relative to a personal mean) in an evening after work for mother, father, and adolescent.

includes place and activity codes, it is possible to determine what activities the family members were engaged in during each emotional state. Using the place and activity codes, at 4:56 P.M., the teenager was in the family room watching television, the mother was in the home office writing and helping another child in the family, and the father was in the kitchen cooking while talking to the teenager watching television. The mother reports that writing was her primary activity while helping her child was secondary; the father indicated that cooking was his primary activity and talking was secondary. With the "who with" item, we are also able to learn that the father was talking with the teenager, who at the same time was watching television. The teenager, however, did not indicate that he was talking to his father.

At 5:53 P.M. the father continues cooking, but the mother has moved into the family room and is talking with the children. The teenager is engaged in general cleaning, which may account for his sharp decrease in enjoyment. By 7:11 P.M., the father has moved into the home office and is on the Internet engaged in job-related work. This decline in enjoyment while working at home is fairly consistent across mothers and fathers. Overall, when a mother or father is engaged in job-related work at home, he or she does not reap the same positive affective and cognitive benefits found when engaged in tasks at work (Schneider & Waite, 2005). By 7:00 P.M., the mother is now in the kitchen doing the dishes, and her enjoyment has clearly dropped from 5:53 P.M. when she was talking with her children. This is also fairly consistent with other trends in the 500 Family Study; that is, housework is a task disliked by all family members, and mood tends to be positive only when the whole family is involved in the task (Lee, 2005). The teenager is in the bathroom taking care of personal grooming, which may account for an increase in enjoyment. At the time of the last beep, both mother and father are in their bedroom watching a drama on television, and the teenager has returned to the living room and is also watching television.

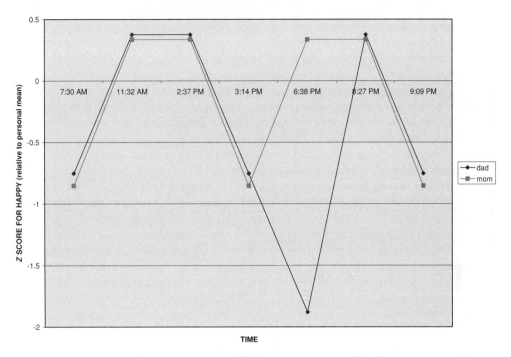

FIG. 22.3.   Experience Sampling Method (ESM) reports of individual happiness (scaled as a *z* score relative to a personal mean) for a couple with similar levels of happiness throughout a regular day.

COMPARING COUPLES USING THE ESM

One advantage of using the ESM in a family is the ability to analyze triads, dyads, and individuals and examine different types of families. In the 500 Family Study, there are approximately 235 couples with children who have ESM measures that can be analyzed as triads or dyads. What is perhaps somewhat surprising is that many family and couple studies fail to extract information from all family members at the same time. A notable exception is the excellent work by Larson and Richards (1994), who have examined the emotional spillovers and crossovers among fathers, mothers, and children in the same family.

Studying couples can provide extraordinarily rich insights into the constancy and dissonance of emotion to similar situations, thus allowing a more penetrating look into issues of gender and the division of household labor. In the next example, Figs. 22.3 and 22.4 show for the same couple over the course of a day two emotional states—one positive (happiness) and one negative (frustration). What is most interesting is how similar their positive and negative emotional patterns are regardless of the activities in which they are engaged. In examining the emotional worlds of couples, Koh (2005) found that they appear to be more similar than when comparisons are made at the individual level, suggesting a selection effect; that is, people who are similar in emotional makeup tend to marry each other. Alternatively, over many years of sharing life together, spouses may become more alike in the emotional experiences.

In this example, when the beeping begins at 7:30 A.M., Dad is engaged in general cleaning and Mom is in the bathroom. At 11:30 A.M., Dad is at work talking over business matters with his coworker and Mom is at home talking in her office. These experiences for both the mother and father are reported as enjoyable and low on frustration. These patterns are also evident at 2:37 P.M., when Dad is in the mailroom faxing a document and Mom is at home preparing for a meeting. Forty-five minutes later, Mom is continuing to prepare for her meeting and Dad is

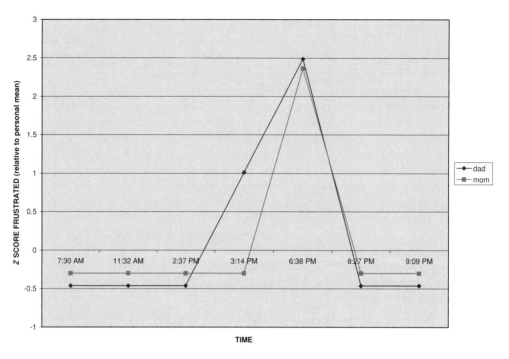

FIG. 22.4.   Experience Sampling Method (ESM) reports of individual frustration (scaled as a *z* score relative to a personal mean) for the same couple on the same day.

having a meeting. At this time, both parents' happiness begins to decline, and both report an increase in frustration that peaks at the next beep. At 6:38 P.M., Dad is at the subway waiting for his train and Mom is at her child's school coaching. While both parents report high levels of frustration, Mom's happiness does not seem to be affected, while Dad reports both frustration and unhappiness. Both parents report high levels of happiness and low levels of frustration at 8:27 P.M., when Dad is eating a meal and Mom is reading the newspaper. Happiness begins to decline, and frustration remains low when at 9:09 P.M. Dad is running errands for the family and Mom is making social plans on the phone.

In this example, mother's and father's experiences throughout the day appear quite similar to one another with the exception of the early evening, when the father is returning home from work and the mother is coaching at school. It has been suggested that workplace demands may carry over into the family and influence the emotions of other family members. The frustration experienced by the father while coming home from work may be transmitted to his spouse or child. Using the 500 Family Study ESM data, Matjasko and Feldman (2005) found evidence for emotional transmission between mothers and adolescents but not between fathers and adolescents. Mothers' happiness and anger are significantly related to adolescent happiness and anger. Fathers' and adolescents' reports of happiness are more in line with each other when fathers report working more than 40 hours a week. It may be that adolescents feel more secure when their fathers are working, or it could be that the time they have together is limited and so they are generally happier when with each other.

The Matjasko and Feldman analyses of ESM data were estimated using two-level Hierarchical Linear Modeling (HLM; Bryk & Raudenbush, 1992), a multivariate modeling procedure that allows for within- and between-person analyses. HLM is particularly advantageous for analyzing ESM data as it nests individual beeps within persons, eliminating the *z*-score computation. (For a more detailed description of HLM, see Swisher in this volume.) In the next example, HLM is used to examine emotional states at work and at home for workers employed in different occupations.

NESTING EMOTIONS WITHIN INDIVIDUALS: MULTILEVEL MODELS

Multilevel modeling allows for the analysis of both real-time data (ESM beeps) and individual-level characteristics that may predict moment-to-moment emotional assessments. A second advantage of multilevel analysis is the ability to incorporate individual-level variables that otherwise would be difficult to include in an analysis at the "beep" level. Multilevel models, in this example, were constructed to examine the effects of both individual- and beep-level characteristics on emotional outcomes.[4] The analysis was designed to examine emotions at work and at home. At work, the analysis focused on the task individuals were performing and how they felt when performing them.

An example of how HLM can be used is found in work by Sexton (2005), in which she examines differences in engagement at work and at home based on individual work orientations. Building on Kohn and Schooler's (1969, 1982, 1983) studies in which they distinguished between two work orientations, self-directed and conforming, all full-time workers ($n = 421$) in the 500 Family Study were categorized along these two dimensions. Workers with self-directed orientations were characterized by having more autonomy and flexibility over work tasks and finding their work cognitively engaging, whereas those identified as conforming were more likely to be closely supervised and be engaged in work tasks seen as routine and less substantively complex. The categories were created from ESM self-reports regarding control, interest, and intellectual complexity (among the sample of those identified as self-directed $n = 209$, and conforming $n = 212$). The emotional state that was examined was cognitive engagement, that is, how productive, concentrated, active, and responsible the individual felt. These variables were combined into a single composite measure. Specifically, the analysis was designed to learn if individuals who were self-directed felt more engaged at work and at home than those described as conforming.

In an HLM analysis using ESM data, all engagement beeps were considered at level 1, and a second variable was created indicating whether the beep occurred at home or work.[5] Essentially, a level-1 analysis considers all the engagement beeps at home and school for a single individual, in this way obviating the need for a standardized score (z score). At level 2, individual person-level variables are entered into the model; they included work orientation (self-directed versus conforming) and other factors likely to influence engagement, such as gender, educational attainment, hours worked, occupation, and salary.

When conducting an HLM, the first consideration is whether there is sufficient variation at both levels. Initial analyses indicated sufficient variation both within and between individuals.[6] This justified the addition of variables at level 2. Because individual-level characteristics are of primary interest, the proportion of between-person variance in the outcome variables was calculated. (This proportion is represented by the intraclass correlation and is calculated using the formula $\rho = \gamma_{00}/(\gamma_{00} + \sigma^2)$.) The coefficients for the final model for each outcome are presented in Table 22.1.

To determine the possible predictors of engagement, an initial random coefficient regression model was run with place entered as a level-1 predictor such that the intercept represented engagement at home. Adding place at level 1 accounts for approximately 19% of the variance within persons ($\sigma^2 = 5.31$, reduced from $6.56 : (6.56 - 5.31)/6.56 = .19$). The coefficients for both the intercept and slope are significant ($t = 83.75$, $p < .001$ and $t = 28.49$, $p < .001$, respectively). The positive t-value for the slope suggests that engagement increases when at

TABLE 22.1
Beep- and Individual-Level Effects on Engagement

	Engagement
Home (level-1 intercept)	
Conforming (level-2 intercept)	5.93***
Self-Directed (level-2 slope)	7.04***
Work (level-1 slope)	
Conforming (level-2 intercept)	7.73***
Self-Directed (level-2 slope)	8.65**
Proportion of variance within Individuals	0.19
Proportion of variance between Individuals	0.16

* p < .05; ** p < .01; *** p < .001.

work versus at home. Therefore, individuals find their work experiences to be more engaging than their experiences at home. Overall, individuals show a 30% increase in engagement when moving from home to work.

The addition of self-directed/conforming on the level-1 intercept explains 16% of the variance in engagement between individuals at home ($\gamma_{00} = 1.65$, reduced from 1.96 in the random coefficient regression model: $(1.96 - 1.65)/1.96 = .16$). The coefficient for self-directed/conforming at the intercept (home) is significant ($t = 7.70$, $p < .001$), suggesting that being self-directed or conforming is highly associated with engagement at home. Individuals who are self-directed in work orientation score 18% higher on engagement at home than those who are conforming (coefficients are reported in Table 22.1).

The addition of the self-directed/conforming variable on the slope (work) explains approximately 10% of the variation in engagement between individuals ($\gamma_{11} = 0.98$, reduced from 1.09 in the random coefficient regression model: $(1.09 - 0.98)/1.09 = .10$). Again, the coefficient for self-directed/conforming on the slope is significant ($t = 2.97$, $p < .01$), suggesting that individuals who are self-directed have significantly higher engagement while at work. Self-directed individuals score 12% higher on engagement when at work compared to those who are conforming. Thus, while engagement is higher overall at work, those who are self-directed find both home and work experiences to be more engaging than individuals who are conforming in work situations. Being at work explains nearly one fifth of the variation that occurs within an individual's moment-to-moment assessments of engagement for beeps occurring at home and work. Similarly, incorporating self-direction at level 2 explains 16% of the variation in engagement that occurs between persons. It appears that self-direction has a strong association with task engagement. These analyses combine to suggest that it is not necessarily the characteristics of the job itself that determine whether someone is self-directed or not, but how engaged the individual is with the task.

Figure 22.5 shows these results in graph form. The difference in the slope for the two groups is significant, suggesting that individuals who are self-directed in work are more engaged at home and at work than those who are conforming. It would appear that work orientations may in fact be more encompassing with respect to a person's total life experiences than just their experiences on the job, at least with respect to engagement. Additional analyses (not shown) suggest that when moving from home to work, those who are self-directed are less likely than those who are conforming to experience negative affect.

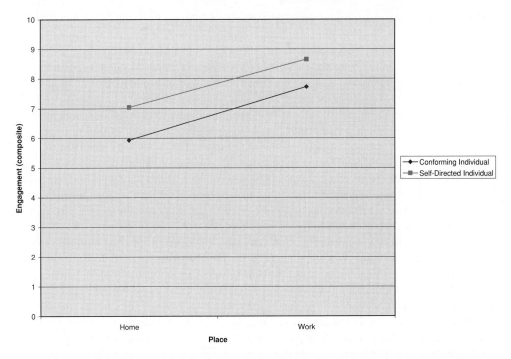

FIG. 22.5. Coefficients for engagement composite variable by beep-level (place) and individual-level (work orientation) effects.

These results, while interesting, represent an evaluation of emotional experiences and job satisfaction over the course of only a week, and drawing conclusions concerning long-term job satisfaction is problematic. However, it is important to stress that this ESM analysis is consistent with results reported by Kohn and Schooler (1969) and expands their focus into additional emotional states that appear to affirm their conclusions (see Sexton, 2005).

PROBLEMS IN MEASURING TIME USE

The ESM presents certain challenges and problems in measuring time use. Some of the measurement problems associated with the ESM also occur with other instruments designed to measure time use and affect. One major concern that researchers often face is whether the question asked results in a response that can be considered a valid measure of affect. The issue pertaining to the validity of self-report affect measures rests on the notion that people may be unable to recognize or admit their own feelings. However, extensive validation research conducted with the ESM has demonstrated that these concerns may be unwarranted since the average level of affect tends to be consistent over time and verifiable by other observers (see Schimmack, 2003; Csikszentmihalyi & Schneider, 2001; Csikszentmihalyi & Larson, 1987). In longitudinal studies, such measures also allow analysts to chart changes in emotion over time.

Moneta, Schneider, and Csikszentmihalyi (2001), for example, used ESM longitudinal data to address the question: How real is the *Sturm und Drang* of adolescence? Items measuring self-esteem and locus of control show a steady linear improvement over several years. In contrast, living up to one's expectations and feeling successful in sixth grade are strong and positive, but begin to decline in eighth grade, fall further in 10th grade, and start moving upward after that time. Feeling good and feeling happy are positive but continue to fall through middle and high school, showing no improvement by Grade 12. There was some variation in these general trends when considering certain adolescent background characteristics such as race and ethnicity and family composition (e.g., adolescents in single-parent homes and those in reconstituted families). However, even when considering these factors, there appears to be a 10th-grade trough, suggesting that the conventional view of a "sophomore slump" may be closer to reality than some have assumed.

Tied to the issue of validity of self-report is the problem of recall bias. Respondents may erroneously estimate the time they spend on a given activity or activities during the period in question. When such retrospective items are compared with answers obtained through other methods, they have been shown to be somewhat unreliable, with individuals tending to overestimate the amount of time spent on certain activities such as paid work or housework (Robinson and Bostrum, 1994; Lee, 2005). Comparisons of ESM data with survey data show that time diary data tend to be more accurate, especially when estimating time use for frequently occurring activities like housework (Juster & Stafford, 1991; Marini & Shelton, 1993). Surveys tend to produce estimates that can be as much as 50% higher than time diary estimates (Press & Townsley, 1998). Adults as well as children are prone to give socially desirable answers regarding a variety of tasks, raising time estimates for activities such as helping with homework and lowering time estimates for watching television. Thus, recall items not only are biased by memory failure and peak experiences, but also by social desirability.

One of the benefits of time diaries is that they account for an entire 24-hour period so that random errors occurring in one time use category are cancelled by random errors occurring in another category. Furthermore, time diaries obtain specific information about the day and time when an activity occurs. This is also the case for the ESM since respondents report their activities at the moment signaled. But, while time diaries can provide very comprehensive information on the daily life of a person, they do not necessarily provide accurate estimates of time use over the course of a week or a month. For example, suppose an individual, using the single-day diary method, reports spending 8 hours at work. Can we infer that person worked 40 hours in the week? Or 56 hours? This point is made by Jacobs (1998) where he argued that synthetic workweeks used in time diary studies are subject to regression to the mean, so that they tend to under- or overestimate time at work. Gershuny et al. (1986) suggested that people tend to organize their lives by weekly schedules. A study of one day may misrepresent a person's weekly schedule. For example, a person may typically work longer on Tuesdays but leave earlier on Fridays (see Gerson & Jacobs, 2004, on this issue).

There are other inference problems using full-day diaries that relate to reporting activities of short duration. Diaries may cause substantial under- or overestimates of activities of short duration, primarily because respondents may feel encouraged to report time use in regular blocks, such as 15- or 20-minute intervals, during which a short duration activity would either be ignored or grossly overstated. For this reason, it is important, regardless of the instrument, to include units of shorter and longer duration. In a recent study, Mulligan, Schneider, and Jeong (2004) compared ESM responses and time diary entries for the same time period and found that about 2% of nonidentical records seem to occur because respondents do not remember the exact time at which they were doing certain activities, especially those that were not work-related. For instance, while ESM records indicate that respondents were eating a meal when signaled, diary entries typically report that they were eating 20 minutes before or after the scheduled signal. The ESM has limitations, however, mainly because participants are asked to specify the activity they are engaged in at a given moment. They are not asked to specify the duration of the activity or prior or later activities. The duration and sequencing of activities are thus more likely to be better estimated using the time diary method.

One strength of the ESM is the inclusion of primary and secondary activities. By having respondents identify the main activity they were involved in and the secondary activity, it is possible to gauge individual time use with respect to multitasking. With the changes in technology, such as e-mail, and the various types of codes in the ESM, it is possible to distinguish between times allocated for personal messaging in contrast to business messaging. However, such calculations in studies like the 500 Family Study are relatively unstable because of the number of times individuals report e-mailing. With larger population samples, it could be possible to assess such time use patterns on a momentary basis although adjustments, either through addition of items or changes in beeping times, would have to be made to incorporate issues of duration and sequencing.

Since the ESM covers an entire week, it enables researchers to examine respondents' activities across the week, thus allowing researchers to study individuals across time, thus minimizing the impact of inquiring about feelings before or after a single event. With the ESM, single events are examined in the context of daily life, allowing the researcher to investigate the subjective experiences of events that are routine or out of the ordinary. Considering that people tend to organize their lives on a weekly schedule (Gershuny et al., 1986), this aspect of the ESM is noteworthy.

Another problem with time diaries relates to respondent burden and its implications regarding sample selection. Assume time diaries could be obtained from an individual over the course of a week. Having to complete a diary every day may in fact be too burdensome, and individuals might over- or underreport activities or simply stop participating. Now assume a group of individuals agreed to participate in such a project. One might suspect that they represent a biased group since it is likely that few respondents would tolerate the burden of reporting for seven consecutive days. The question of selection bias—that is, who would willingly participate in an ESM study and comply with study demands—is a serious consideration in constructing such studies.

The ESM shares many of the problems of time diaries, including respondent burden, but has several advantages over both surveys and time diaries: immediate response to signals, which minimizes recall bias; randomization of beeps, which eliminates stereotypical categorizations of time use; and data collection over several consecutive days rather than on a single day. Several recent studies have been undertaken to evaluate the burden of the ESM and its effects on response bias and compare it with other instruments (see, e.g., Mulligan, Schneider, & Wolfe, 2003). Mulligan et al. compared adolescent time use across three different datasets, one of which uses the ESM. Results suggest that it may not be burden or "busyness" that dissuades people from responding to beeps. Rather, the problem may be one of compliance, and this is where systematic differences across respondents occur. To correct for such compliance factors, which will undoubtedly differ by the populations being surveyed, Mulligan et al. developed a demographic-weighting strategy to adjust for nonresponse.

ESM AND OTHER METHODS OF DATA COLLECTION: SOME CONCLUDING COMMENTS

Social scientists have a wide variety of instruments at their disposal in conducting their work. The ESM, though not without its own set of methodological constraints, fills an important gap in understanding time use and, more importantly, everyday emotional experiences. It is the small, often nuanced reactions of people to other people and particular events that cannot be overlooked when examining psychological states and change. Over 35 years of work has shown that the ESM can provide reliable quantitative measures of variation in individual experiences from the moment they wake up to the time they go to sleep.

Recent studies that use the ESM including the 500 Family Study have shown the potential of this instrument for examining work-family conflict, shared family time, and experiences of marriage, childrearing, and employment. One of the strengths of the ESM in the 500 Family Study is the ability to analyze individual experiences within the context of the family. Thus, the study has revealed how adolescents feel about their parents, how parents feel about themselves, and how both view parents' ability to manage work and family responsibilities. Combined with data from other instruments used in the 500 Family Study, including interviews, surveys, and census information, analyses of ESM data provide a comprehensive and in-depth picture of contemporary life in working families. Though not captured on videotape or simulated in a laboratory, these combined data sources provide a realistic view of "in the moment" experiences of parents and children.

NOTES

[1]This special issue presents five articles that use the ESM to illustrate various applications of the method for studying both adolescents and families.

[2]The Alfred P. Sloan Study of Youth and Social Development constructed codes for place, activity, and thinking, building on earlier categories created by Csikszentmihalyi developed for his study with Reed Larson on adolescents, and a later study on Talented Teens co-authored with Samuel Whelan and Kevin Rathunde. In the 500 Family Study, which included both adults and children, the categories were expanded based on the verbatim responses of the participants.

[3]Some analysts have concerns with using z scores and suggest other transformations (see Rooney, 2003).

[4]For all multilevel analyses, the statistical package HLM (Raudenbush, Bryk, & Congdon, 2000) was used. Model development followed standard protocol by beginning first with the simplest model (unconditional), followed by the continual addition of predictors at both level 1 and level 2 based on statistics from previous models.

[5]The place variable was created as a dummy variable with home equal to 0 and work equal to 1. With this method, the place variable can be entered uncentered and the intercept then represents the value at home.

[6]This was an unconditional model conducted as a one-way ANOVA with random effects.

REFERENCES

Bianchi, S., Milkie, M., Sayer, L., & Robinson, J. (2000). Is anyone doing the housework? Trends in the gender division of household labor. *Social Forces, 79,* 191–228.

Bolger, N., Davis, A., & Rafaeli, A. (2003). Diary methods: Capturing life as it is lived. *Annual Review of Psychology, 54,* 579–616.

Bryk, A., & Raudenbush, S. (1992). *Hierarchical linear models: Applications and data analysis method.* Newbury Park, CA: Sage.

Csikszentmihalyi, M., & Csikszentmihalyi, I. (1988). *Optimal experience: Psychological studies of flow in consciousness.* Cambridge, UK: Cambridge University Press.

Csikszentmihalyi, M., Hektner, J., & Schmidt, J. (Forthcoming). Measuring the quality of everyday life: The ESM handbook.

Csikszentmihalyi, M., Larson, R., & Prescott, S. (1977). The ecology of adolescent activities and experiences. *Journal of Youth and Adolescence, 6,* 281–294.

Csikszentmihalyi, M., & Larson, R. (1984). *Being adolescent: Conflict and growth in the teenage years.* New York: Basic Books.

Csikszentmihalyi, M., & Larson, R. (1987). Validity and reliability of the experience sampling method. *Journal of Nervous and Mental Disease, 175,* 526–536.

Csikszentmihalyi, M., Rathunde, K., & Whalen, S. (1993). *Talented teenagers: The roots of success and failure.* New York: Cambridge University Press.

Csikszentmihalyi, M., & Schneider, B. (2000). *Becoming adult: How teenagers prepare for the world of work.* New York: Basic Books.

Csikszentmihalyi, M., & Schneider, B. (2001). Conditions for optimal development in adolescence: An experiential approach. *Applied Developmental Science, 5,* 122–125.

Diener, E., & Larson, R. (1984). Temporal stability and cross-situational consistency as affective, behavioral and cognitive processes. *Journal of Personality and Social Psychology, 47,* 580–592.

Diener E., Smith, H., & Fujita, F. (1995). The personality structure of affect. *Journal of Personality and Social Psychology, 69,* 130–141.

Gershuny, J., Miles, I., Jones, S., Mullings, C., Thomas, G., & Wyatt, S. (1986). Time budgets: Preliminary analyses of a national survey. *Quarterly Journal of Social Affairs, 2,* 13–39.

Gerson, K., & Jacobs, J. (2004). *The time divide: work, family, and gender inequality.* Cambridge, MA: Harvard University Press.

Hoogstra, L. (2005). The design of the 500 Family Study. In B. Schneider & L. Waite (Eds.), *Being together, working apart: Dual-career families and the work-life balance* (pp. 25–52). Cambridge, UK: Cambridge University Press.

Jacobs, J. (1998). Measuring time at work: Are self-reports accurate? *Monthly Labor Review, 121,* 42–51.

Jeong, J. (2005). Obtaining accurate measures of time use from the ESM. In B. Schneider & L. Waite (Eds.), *Being together, working apart: Dual-career families and the work-life balance* (pp. 643–672). Cambridge, MA: Cambridge University Press.

Juster, T., & Stafford, F. (Eds.). (1985). *Time, goods, and well-being.* Ann Arbor: The University of Michigan Survey Research Center, Institute for Social Research.

Juster, T., & Stafford, F. (1991). The allocation of time: Empirical findings, behavioral models, and problems of measurement. *Journal of Economic Literature, 29,* 471–522.

Koh, C. (2005). The everyday emotional experiences of husbands and wives. In B. Schneider & L. Waite (Eds.), *Being together, working apart: Dual-career families and the work-life balance* (pp. 234–265). Cambridge, UK: Cambridge University Press.

Kohn, M., & Schooler, C. (1969). Class, occupation and orientation. *American Sociological Review, 34,* 659–678.

Kohn, M., & Schooler, C. (1982). Job conditions and personality: A longitudinal assessment of their reciprocal effects. *American Journal of Sociology, 8,* 1257–1286.

Kohn, M., & Schooler, C. (1983). *Work and personality: An inquiry into the impact of social structure.* Norwood, NJ: Ablex.

Kubey, R., & Csikszentmihalyi, M. (1990). *Television and the quality of life: How viewing shapes everyday experience.* Hillsdale, NJ: Lawrence Erlbaum Associates.

Larson, R., & Richards, M. (1994). *Divergent realities: The emotional lives of mothers, fathers, and adolescents.* New York: Basic Books.

Lee, Y. (2005). Measuring the gender gap in household labor: Accurately estimating wives' and husbands' contributions. In B. Schneider & L. Waite (Eds.), *Being together, working apart: Dual-career families and the work-life balance* (pp. 318–347). Cambridge, UK: Cambridge University Press.

Marini, M., & Shelton, B. (1993). Measuring household work: Recent experience in the United States. *Social Science Research, 22,* 361–382.

Matjasko, J., & Feldman, A. (2005). Emotional transmission between parents and adolescents: The importance of work characteristics and relationship quality. In B. Schneider & L. Waite (Eds.), *Being together, working apart: Dual-career families and the work-life balance* (pp. 195–225). Cambridge, UK: Cambridge University Press.

Moneta, B., Schneider, B., & Csikszentmihalyi, M. (2001). A longitudinal study of the self-concept and experiential components of self-worth and affect across adolescent. *Applied Developmental Science, 5,* 125–142.

Mulligan, C., Schneider, B., & Jeong, J. (2004). Working Paper: University of Chicago, Alfred P. Sloan Center on Parents, Children, and Work.

Mulligan, C., Schneider, B., & Wolfe, R. (2003). Non-response and population representation in studies of time use. Working Paper: University of Chicago, Alfred P. Sloan Center on Parents, Children, and Work.

Press, J., & Townsley, E. (1998). Wives' and husbands' housework reporting: Gender, class, and social desirability. *Gender and Society, 12,* 188–218.

Rauderbush, S., Bryk, A. & Congdon, R. (2000). HLM5 Hierarchical linear and nonlinear modeling. Scientific Software International.

Redelmeier, D., & Kahneman, D. (1996). Patients' memories of painful medical treatments: Real-time and retrospective evaluations of two minimally invasive procedures. *Pain, 66,* 3–8.

Reis, H., & Gable, S. (2000). Event sampling and other methods of studying everyday experience. In H. Reis and C. Judd (Eds.), *Handbook of research methods in personality and social psychology* (pp. 199–222). Cambridge, UK: Cambridge University Press.

Robinson, J., & Bostrum, A. (1994). The overestimated workweek? What time diaries measures suggest. *Monthly Labor Review, 117,* 11–23.

Robinson, J., & Godbey, G. (1997). *Time for life: The surprising ways Americans use their time.* University Park: The Pennsylvania State University Press.

Schimmack, U. (2003). Affect measurement in experience sampling research. *Journal of Happiness Studies, 4,* 79–106.

Schneider, B., & Stevenson, D. (1999). *The ambitious generation: America's teenagers motivated but directionless.* New Haven, CT: Yale University Press.

Schneider, B., & Waite, L. (Eds.). (2005). *Being together, working apart: Dual-career families and the work-life balance.* Cambridge, UK: Cambridge University Press.

Sexton, H. R. (2005). Spending time at work and at home: What workers do, how they feel about it, and how these emotions affect family life. In B. Schneider & L. Waite (Eds.), *Being together, working apart: Dual-career families and the work-life balance* (pp. 64–96). Cambridge, UK: Cambridge University Press.

Stone, A. A., & Neale, J. M. (1982). Development of a methodology for assessing daily experience. In A. Baum and J. E. Singer (Eds.), *Advances in environmental psychology: Environment and health* (Vol. 4: 49–83). Hillsdale, NJ: Lawrence Erlbaum.

Tannen, D. (1990). *You just don't understand: Women and men in conversation*. New York: Morrow.

U.S. Department of Commerce, Bureau of the Census. (2002). *Table DP-3: Profile of selected economic characteristics 2000 (by town or city). Census 2000 Summary File 3 (SF-3)—Sample Data*. http:factfinder.census/gov.

Zuzanek, J. (1999). Experience sampling method: Current and potential research applications. Paper presented for the Time-Use Measurements and Research Workshops of the Committee on National Statistics, organized by the National Research Council. May 27–29, 1999.

23

Case Studies in Work-Family Research

Suzan Lewis
Manchester Metropolitan University

Maria das Dores Guerreiro
ISCTE

Julia Brannen
University of London

Although the field of work-family research is characterized by bringing together research on workplaces, families, communities, and other institutions and recognizing the interdependence of these domains, a focus on understanding organizations and organizational processes provides one important perspective contributing to this bigger picture. The in-depth study of organizations helps us to understand and explain workplace structures, working practices, and cultures that can make it difficult for employees to integrate paid work and personal life. It also helps to identify and evaluate change initiatives and to understand resistance and barriers to changes to support people in combining work and nonwork roles. In this chapter, we first discuss the case study approach in general and then provide some examples of the ways in which organizational case studies have been used in the study of organizational responses to work-personal life issues. We then consider some practical issues in carrying out case study research, drawing primarily on an ongoing international study involving case studies in private and public sector organizations in seven European countries.

THE CASE STUDY APPROACH TO RESEARCH

Although often stereotyped as a weak research strategy, case studies have been used in a wide range of research contexts and the strengths of this strategy are increasingly recognized (Yin, 2003a, b). In particular, this is a very useful way of gathering in-depth, contextualized data on organizational processes informed by theory and systematic inquiry. Indeed, case studies can be more rigorous than other research strategies because of the systematic and theoretically informed use of different forms of data gathered from multiple stakeholders, providing a holistic and in-depth understanding of social or organizational phenomena and processes in real-life contexts. Some also argue that they provide explanations and causal processes analogous to statistical analysis (see Hammersley et al., 2000 for a discussion).

The use of case studies is not a method but a research strategy or mode of empirical inquiry that covers design, methods of data collection, and data analysis and which epistemologically organizes the research procedures to shed light on understanding a "case." Single or multiple cases can be used to address specific research questions in different social fields, and they seem particularly appropriate for studying organizations (Crozier, 2000) and their contexts (Sainsaulieu, 1997), either individually or on a comparative basis. They may be studied either iteratively or in parallel. The evidence from multiple case studies can sometimes be considered as being more valid though single case studies can also be useful (Yin, 2003a). Moreover, case studies involve different levels so that care must be taken in extrapolating the conclusions to the level of "the case," that is, to the organization in organizational case studies rather than the individual employee (see Yin, 2003a for a discussion)

Like other research approaches or strategies, case studies can be used for exploratory, descriptive, or explanatory purposes. Case studies are particularly appropriate for answering *"how"* and *"why"* questions—for example, how does flexible working impact on workers and the organization and why is it effective or of limited effectiveness? They help to explain processes and examine links over time in relation to specific interventions and contexts.

Case studies are useful for *understanding complex phenomena and processes within specific contexts*. For example, a study of the impact of the introduction of flexible working arrangements may use a survey or interviews with employees from a wide range of organizations. However, changes in one part of an organizational system inevitably affects other parts. A case study of one organization or multiple case studies would reveal much more than a survey or series of interviews about the processes by which flexible working practices may impact on individual employees, their colleagues and managers, and other stakeholders such as customers or service recipients, and the dynamics of these effects in a given organization. So case studies provide a holistic approach recognizing the complexities of organizations. As Yin (2003a) put it, the case study approach "allows investigators to retain the holistic and meaningful characteristics of real-life events" (p. 20) and has been described as a direct and satisfying way of adding to experience and improving understanding (Stake, 2002).

A case study approach is particularly appropriate to investigate a *contemporary phenomenon in a real-life context*, where boundaries between the phenomenon and context are not clearly evident (Yin, 2003a). In such contexts, where there is limited historical or past evidence, or where there is rapid social and organizational change, the investigator sets out to focus on contextual conditions because it is believed that they may be highly pertinent to the topic or process in question.

Case studies incorporate *multiple methods and multiple perspectives*. Methods used within case studies include documentary analysis, qualitative and quantitative methods, participant observation, and action research. A preference for particular methods may be framed by underlying philosophical positions (Lincoln & Guba, 1989), although in the practice of creating research designs more practical issues take priority. Case study research typically combines methods drawn from both sides of the qualitative and quantitative divide. However, in the analysis phase, the use of different data drawn from different methods is or should be governed by the theoretical ways in which the research questions are framed (Bryman, 2001; Brannen, 2004).

The methods used in case studies are informed (though not dictated) by the development of theoretical propositions and by the research questions that guide design, data collection, and analysis. Multiple (and sometimes conflicting) perspectives are generated by collecting and triangulating data from diverse participants at various levels in an organization and often from stakeholders beyond the organization, such as family members (Hochschild, 1997).

Case studies are often criticized for lack of *generalizability,* but this criticism is typically underpinned by the assumption that statistical generalization is the only basis for generalizability (Hammersley et al., 2000). Indeed, a weakness of many other approaches in work-life research—for example, surveys of work-life policies and practices—is the failure to take account of the specificity and diversity of organizational contexts. As Yin explained, "Case studies, like experiments, are generalizable to theoretical propositions and not to populations" (2003a, p. 10), or, as Mitchel said, "The validity of the extrapolation depends not on the typicality or representativeness of the case but upon the cogency of the theoretical reasoning" (2002, p. 183).

A case study approach is often used in *evaluation research*, for example, evaluating the outcomes of specific initiatives or programs. Case studies can be used to describe an initiative—such as a flexible working program, or illustrate a particular effect (descriptive), explain presumed causal links in real-life contexts (explanatory), or to explore processes, barriers, and facilitators in situations with no single set of outcomes (exploratory).

The use of theory is important for case study research; Yin (2003b) argued that theory is important for:

- Selecting the case or cases to be studied
- Specifying what is being explored in exploratory case studies
- Defining a complete and appropriate description in descriptive case studies
- Stipulating rival theories in explanatory case studies and
- Generalizing results to other cases and contexts.

EXAMPLES OF CASE STUDIES IN WORK-LIFE/FLEXIBLE WORKING RESEARCH

One area of organizational studies to have received much recent research attention is that of flexible or alternative working arrangements. This is often linked with debates about work-life "balance" or integration although some research also approaches flexible forms of work as an issue for organizational efficiency and productivity (Lewis, 2003). As flexible, innovative, and atypical working practices are highly topical in the context of an increasingly diverse workforce, advances in information and communication technology, and the need for organizations to adapt to constant change, this is a *contemporary issue* that benefits from a case study approach. Research questions include: which policies are associated with positive outcomes for employees and employers in different contexts; why do certain policies or flexible practices have positive outcomes or why do they not have the predicted outcomes; how do they work, how can they be more effective, what are the processes undermining effectiveness, and how does their impact differ across different contexts?

Case studies have been used to address a range of questions concerning flexible or "family-friendly" policies. First, they have been used to address the question of which flexible or family-friendly policies work in what contexts and for whom. Often, this is done through case studies of what is considered to be "good practice" and role models for other organizations. For example, the UK Government Department of Trade and Industry provides examples of "good practice" organizations (www.dti.gov.uk). While this can fulfill a useful role, it is often a descriptive PR exercise rather than based on empirical research, particularly if the case study is not theory-driven or analytic in terms of process. Often, the policies alone are presented rather than the processes of development, implementation, and learning that take place leading to new organizational practices.

Cases studies are used more critically in studies evaluating policy and practices (e.g., Lewis, 1997, 2001; Guerreiro et al., 2003). Often based on theories of organizational change processes, organizational culture, and work-family conflict, evaluation studies examine possible links between specific policies and individual and organizational outcomes. While these links can be examined by other approaches such as multi-organizational surveys (Kossek & Ozeki, 1999), a case study approach enables the researchers to supplement survey findings and examine how policies and practices are implemented in specific contexts and with what outcomes. This, in turn, can lead to further theory development. For example, case studies evaluating the use of family-friendly policies in accountancy firms and public sector organizations (Lewis, 1997, 2000) involved the analysis of written policies (document analysis) and interviews with multiple stakeholders (employers, line managers, human resource managers, trade union representatives, etc.). These studies pointed to the impact of specific aspects of organizational culture (defined in terms of shared values and assumptions), especially the ways in which time is articulated and valued within specific organizations. Gender differences in subjective feelings of entitlement to take up flexible working policies also emerged from these studies, pointing to the significance of concepts such as perceived entitlement and equity, central concepts in social justice theory (Lewis & Smithson, 2001). By gathering data from various sources, it is possible to explore how policies were developed in a specific case organization, how they have been implemented, who has been instrumental in this process, what has helped the process, and what barriers have emerged. Building on this work, subsequent case studies have explored in greater detail the role of organizational culture and time discourses and practices (e.g., Lewis, 2001; Lewis & Cooper, 2005). For example, a case study may explore the introduction of flexibility using different theoretical perspectives and by interviewing employees at home as well as at work. As a study that sought to develop a methodology for the TRANSITIONS project described below (Brannen et al., 2001) reveals, employees' experience of increased autonomy arising from flexible work practices may be at odds with their experience of time, in particular the feeling they are never off the treadmill of work and care as work intensifies and the boundaries between work and home become blurred (Brannen, 2005).

Most research shows that policies alone are of limited value since they are often not well implemented in practice and tend to be undermined by workplace cultures. Other case studies have been used to addresses the question of how to move beyond policy to practice. For example, a case study of the Xerox Corporation in the United States (Fletcher & Rapoport, 1996; Rapoport, Bailyn, Fletcher, & Pruitt, 2001) was one of several case studies using action research to bring about organizational change to meet a dual agenda of enhanced workplace effectiveness and enhanced work-personal life integration and gender equity. These studies were based on, and also contributed to the further development of, gender theory, particularly theories of the gendered nature of organizations and the myth of separate and gendered spheres which also leads to the valuing of different types of behavior, and also theories of organizational change processes. These researchers demonstrated the importance of a specific action research approach, which they termed collaborative interactive action research (CIAR). CIAR involves looking at working practices through a work-family/work-life/gender equity lens, listening, reflecting, collaborating in problem solving, and experimenting to find win-win solutions. Case studies of other organizations using this method have not always been so successful but also contribute to the understanding of processes and inform theory and practice. For example, a case study of organizational change in an accountancy firm using this method illustrated how deep-seated assumptions can undermine flexible working policies (as demonstrated in the Xerox study) and also showed the importance of support from the top for such changes, which was absent in this case. The prior identification of a problem is also crucial. In this case issues such as long, intensive working hours and the underutilization of women had not yet been widely identified as problems, though some employees and managers had made these connections (Lewis & Cooper, 2005). Portuguese teams involved with companies to promote family-friendly practices and gender equal opportunities reached similar conclusions (CITE, 2003).

Case studies are also useful for understanding the links between what happens in organizations, social policy, and the wider context. This can be illustrated by an ongoing European study: Gender, Parenthood and the Changing European Workplace: young adults negotiating the work-family boundary (TRANSITIONS; see http://www.workliferesearch.org/transitions.html). A major objective of this study is to develop an understanding of the impact of workplace environment and organizational change on younger adults who become parents, in the context of diverse social and economic policies and situations, in seven European countries. It is based on theories relating to welfare states and the links between social policy and sense of entitlement to work in nonstandard ways, theories of organizational change and well-being, and theories relating to the negotiation of work-family boundaries. Multiple case studies were selected as one of the main approaches. As the aim is to study the impact of both organizational change and national social policy, the research design was to select two types of workplace (one private and one public sector) across a range of countries with very different social policies on, for example, parental leave. The methods adopted in the case studies included document analysis (on workplace policies as well as other organizational documents), focus groups with parents of young children drawn from all parts of the organization (see also Smithson, chap. 20, this volume), interviews with HR and line managers, and questionnaires (on well-being). Each of the research instruments was clearly underpinned by the aims of the study and the concepts to be employed in the national and cross-national analysis.

PRACTICAL ISSUES IN CASE STUDIES (ILLUSTRATED BY THE ONGOING TRANSITIONS STUDY)

Below we discuss some practical issues in carrying out case studies, with reference to the TRANSITIONS study. Processes and issues include:

- Background research
- Gaining access
- Getting interviews with key informants for background and to identify appropriate documents and participants for case studies
- Understanding the organizational structures—organizational charts
- What is an organization: core and periphery workers
- Getting theoretical samples
- Developing and piloting research instruments
- Analytic strategies and issues
- Reporting: maintaining anonymity and other ethical issues

General Background Research

Preliminary research is necessary whatever research strategy is used. As case studies, like other research, build on current research and trends, the first stage of the TRANSITIONS research was a literature review carried out in each country covering relevant issues. But national trends and context are also very important for the research questions, so a context mapping exercise examining relevant policies, debates, and statistical trends was also carried out. This enabled the case study instruments (interview schedules, questionnaires) to build not only on theory and past research, but also on the cross-national picture: factors such as differences in statutory policies, demographic trends, and current national discourses and debates. As an example of the latter, the mapping exercise shows how discussions about family and employment issues tend in the UK to focus on the business case and workplace change, in France on fertility arguments, and in Sweden on gender equity. Thus, it can be hypothesized that these debates impact differently on parents' experiences of work and family in different countries.

Gaining Access

Getting access to the organization is a key issue in the case study research process. This is the case for all organizational research, of course, but case studies can be very demanding for the organizations under scrutiny. We have to remember that "almost always data gathering is done on somebody's 'home grounds,' involving a certain invasion of someone's privacy" (Stake, 1995, p. 57). In some situations access is taken for granted, for example, when the studies are promoted internally to understand and solve organizational problems or to introduce changes. But organizations may be resistant to case study research by outsiders. According to an old Portuguese saying, "secrecy is the business soul" and many companies fear possible intruders: From their perspective, confidential information could either be captured and transferred to their competitors or used to harm their credibility in the market. Moreover, data gathering for case studies can make more demands on participants' time than other approaches using single methods such as surveys. Time use is rationalized in most organizations and if managers do not see a clear benefit from their cooperation in a piece of research, they tend to be reluctant to permit access to research teams.

The case study procedures, therefore, need to include strategies for overcoming these difficulties and getting access to the field. Initial contact may be made through senior management, HR, or others (the more senior, the better). A common strategy is to gain access via the research team's existing contacts with key personnel. Focusing on the reputation of the research team, the credibility of the research institution, and the profile of the funders of the study can also help. However, all workplace contacts will need to be convinced by the researchers that the organization will benefit in some way. First of all, it is important to decide which topic or perspective on the project is to be emphasized to gain organizational interest, and this may depend either on the specificities of the organization or on its context. For example, some organizations may be interested in work-family policies, others in stress management.

It is always important for the researcher to produce strong evidence of the likely organizational benefits of being a case study subject. This is easiest when one goal of the research is publicizing company "good practices" in the domain of work and family integration, or of including it in a quality ranking among other organizations (Guerreiro & Lourenço, 2000). Other incentives can include the possibility of obtaining a credible and cost-free diagnosis of organizational life, for example, feedback on how certain policies and practices are experienced by different sections of the workforce. The research team might mention the opportunity for good PR that comes from a willingness to be involved in research and identified as a progressive leading-edge organization, especially if the study is cross-national. However, participating organizations will usually be offered anonymity, unless they particularly want to be identified when they have seen the findings. Therefore, the PR argument is generally more risky.

A number of strategies were used in the TRANSITIONS project to gain access to organizations in different national contexts. In some cases, the agreement was granted on the basis of knowledge and contacts already made by the team from previous research. In other countries, the status of the research team's university, of which some employees had studied, facilitated access to a key manager. Some organizations were attracted to the idea of being the only organization in their sector to take part in an international project, funded by the

European Union, with the promise of feedback on their own organization as well as similar organizations across Europe.

The practicalities of gaining access involved informal and formal contacts by phone calls, e-mails, and letters. Managers were identified and were sent letters from the research director and/or from the national team together with a leaflet presenting briefly the main goals of the study, the countries, research teams and universities involved, the funding institution, and some predicted outcome. Permission for access came usually at senior management levels but involved in most cases extensive negotiation at other management levels, depending on the sector (public sector organizations had many more levels) and the country. Whatever the levers used to engage organizational interest, persistence was always necessary: first in getting access to key contact persons; second, ensuring that these persons (usually from HR in the private sector) followed through with requests for interviewees and arranged the focus groups; and, third, gaining individual agreement from employees to take part in the study.

Two factors were particularly significant in relation to gaining access to the case studies in the TRANSITIONS project (see Brannen, 2004a). The first was the complexity and hierarchical nature of the organization, both in terms of personnel and geographical location. Complexity was particularly difficult in public sector, highly bureaucratic organizations where lengthy and complex negotiations were necessary with "gatekeepers" before access could be granted. Flatter organizations were usually much easier to access. Geographical dispersion of an organization could also make access difficult. The second issue was the degree of threat the proposed case study presented to management, some of whom in one East European country were in acute fear of losing their jobs, and was most problematic in the private (finance) sector organizations. This was particularly the case in Bulgaria, where the organization had only recently been privatized. It was less of a problem in organizations where family-friendly work practices fitted with the expressed goals of the organization.

In gaining the agreement of the workforce to be interviewed, it is important to recognize the motives for participation, which could differ from those of the organization's senior management. This implies, for instance, the need to emphasize one aspect of the research's relevance while retaining the coherence of its overall objectives. Within the TRANSITIONS project, the international research team made use of different strategies according to the country or the organization's profile, and even the researcher's identity. Most of the research teams underlined the work-family life issues and/or the transition to parenthood, but some also focused on the management of change, organizational well-being, and recruitment and retention issues (where skilled workers were in high demand).

Getting Interviews With Key Informants: For Background and to Identify Appropriate Documents and Research Participants

Knowledge about the background of the case study organization is crucial to understanding the case (the organization) and for the analysis. Web-based material was an important source of information in some case studies (for example, the UK public sector). Persons must be identified to provide information, help in the collection of documents, and identify potential interviewees. Sometimes the person who permits access is already a key informant. Formally or informally, key informants can provide: overviews of the organization and its current position in the business environment; perceptions of the workplace culture; and identification of strategic actors, critical problems in the organization, and their location. These are issues to take into account in later stages of the case study process.

Other key informants may appear when the researchers are already inside the organization, particularly the contact person who is designated to host them and help to engage participants (usually someone more junior than the person granting access).

The design of the TRANSITIONS project included interviews with the HR managers as key informants. Although some background had been gleaned informally during the processes of gaining access to the organization, the HR managers were asked to provide information regarding the organizational background and also to identify participants for the interviews. HR was less often the more important route in the public sector, where negotiation of access could include national, regional, and local level managers as well as local politicians.

Topics of the HR interview schedule focused not only on workplace policies and organizational change, but also on the perceptions of how managers manage and on their own parenthood and work-family boundaries experience. At the same time, written documentation was sought about the organization and its workforce profile. Indicators like levels of pay, rotation and absenteeism rates, training programs, and so forth were also collected. However, documentation was not readily forthcoming in most of the case studies, as much of the organizational information was considered confidential in the private sector, whereas in the public sector it was not always collected or in accessible format.

The process of identifying the interviewees took different forms. Some of the organizations did not have a database that identified parents (not all could identify mothers who had recently taken maternity leave and only the organizations in Portugal routinely kept information on men's and women's parental status). Because of this, strategies had to be developed, one method being to send a screening questionnaire to those in the relevant age group attached to monthly pay slips (not particularly successful), another to access parents via a Christmas present list for the children of employees (a successful strategy although this later presented difficulties of confidentiality!).

Having identified potential interviewees and focus group participants, the next stage was to gain their permission. Sometimes this was achieved through a convoluted process in which permission had to be first gained before an approach could be made to a parent, in other cases through more informal contact with managers. Of course, some potential participants might decline and this has implications for the nature of the sample that must be taken into account at the analysis stage.

Understanding Organizational Structures

Interviews with key informants and document analysis can be used to acquire an organizational chart (or, to develop one if none is available). This can be useful for locating participants in the structure of their organizations and contribute to an understanding of their discourses. The size and the activity of the organization, the type of work done there, and the hierarchical position and degree of autonomy, for instance, may all be relevant for defining the position of the employees regarding the organization and their working lives and identities (Sainsaulieu, 1977, 1997; Costa, Guerreiro, Ferreira, & Freitas, 1984; Mintzberg, 1982). For example, Crozier (see Crozier & Fieldberg, 1977; Crozier, 2000) used organizational charts to analyze formal and informal rules of interaction inside organizations and identify what he called "uncertainty zones."

Within the TRANSITIONS project, organizational charts helped us to understand the organizational structures, to compare them across the countries, and at the same time to locate the positions of the interviewees.

Getting Theoretical Samples

A theoretical sample represents data gathering driven by concepts derived from the theory evolving over the course of case study (Strauss & Corbin, 1998). In a case study, fieldwork information is collected in order to get answers to research questions developed from theory, which are further developed during the study. Unlike statistical samples, which require statistical procedures to extract from a parent population a representative number of survey participants, theoretical samples are selected for theoretical reasons.

The TRANSITIONS project defined its theoretical sample according to the theoretical framework and its concern regarding the ways in which a new generation of parents in different countries, experiencing different forms of welfare state and changing forms of employment, experience parenthood, combine work and family life, and express their feelings of well-being.

First, in designing the project, we selected countries with different welfare regimes (Esping-Anderson, 2000)—social-democratic, continental, liberal—southern and eastern countries, and different traditions and patterns of female employment. This led to the selection of two Nordic countries—Sweden and Norway—as examples of the first model; France as belonging to the continental model; the Netherlands and the UK as representing the liberal model; and Portugal as a southern country where the welfare system is not highly developed; and Slovenia and Bulgaria, former Eastern block countries, which have a different history of welfare states to that understood in the West.

Second, the research aimed to analyze the changing forms of organizations and employment across the countries, to look at the differences and similarities and their impact on parents regarding work-family balance and well-being/life quality. The option for studying the same kind of organizations (finance sector and social services) in all countries provided a basis for making comparisons.

In each case study organization, mothers and fathers were selected to participate in focus groups according to criteria that again related to the project's theoretical goals, being organized by gender, age, parental status, and occupational level. Individual interviews were then carried out with their line managers to generate managerial perspectives, in particular on flexible working practices.

What Is an Organization? Core and Peripheral Workers

A major issue that arose in the TRANSITIONS project was that in almost every organization and country, low-skilled workers such as cleaners and catering staff were outsourced to agencies and were not therefore officially part of the organization. Since they were not managed in the organization, we were not able to access them via the means described above. This raises the issue: What is an organization (and what is the case)? Which workers are included? If both core and peripheral workers are to be included in an organizational case study, different methods of gaining access may be required, including accessing some participants via the agencies or other organizations for whom they work.

Developing and Piloting Research Instruments

As in any field research, instruments have to be developed and piloted. In single case studies, these can be designed with a very specific organizational focus, informed by the background information gained at the key informant stage. Where multiple case studies are used, a balance may need to be struck both between methods that are specific to the organization and those aimed to achieve comparable data.

In the TRANSITIONS research, it was important that the research instruments reflected the reality of the different contexts involved. That is, the researchers needed to take account of the fact that the research was being done by different national teams with different research traditions as well the fact of their working in different national contexts. This was not always easy and a number of theoretical/conceptual and interpretation problems arose. For example, a well-being questionnaire was used, including questions on individual satisfaction, enjoyment and happiness, but the distinction between these latter concepts was not always clear in different languages or cultures. For this reason, it was vital that all members of the transnational team were involved in piloting and commenting on the research instruments.

While these issues may have less relevance to research that is not cross-national, there are nevertheless wider lessons to be learned. Methodological and theoretical language varies across social science disciplines and its translation via particular methods will vary across organizations and social contexts. It is therefore advisable to test out the languages used through consultation with representatives of organizations while being attentive to using a differently nuanced language in different organizations.

Analyzing the Data

Data analysis first involves data from different sources: interviews with people of different status or differently placed within the organizational structures, questionnaires, group interviews, participant observation, and document analysis. Although each method may have its own analytical logic, in case study research the different methods have to be brought together to provide a holistic understanding of the organization and to build theoretical explanations. With multiple case studies, the cases have to be compared in order to search for patterns of similarity, while attempts may also be made to test out explanations for differences between cases (Ragin, 1987; Ragin & Becker, 1992).

Yin (2003a) stressed the need for an analytic strategy, which should ideally follow the strategy adopted in the choice of research question and design. He described three general strategies:

1. *Working from theoretical propositions.*
   Yin argued that this is the preferred strategy. It involves following the theoretical propositions that led to the choice of case in the first place. Thus, in the TRANSITIONS study, data analysis is guided by research questions—for example, understanding parents' experiences of managing work and family in relation to organizational change and social policy context.
2. *Thinking about rival explanations.*
   If the case study has been set up to test rival theories, this would guide the analysis. Although this was not explicitly the case, overall, for TRANSITIONS, it is the case that the teams cover a number of disciplines and are likely to apply different and possibly rival theories. Moreover, one aspect of the project, examining how managers make decisions in relation to staff requests for flexibility, involved asking questions that could be used to test two rival theories of management decision making: disruption theory (managers will grant flexibility to staff when it causes least disruption) versus dependency theory (managers are more inclined to support the flexibility of staff on whom they depend most); see Lewis, 2003). The case studies allow these theories to be tested in the different organizational contexts.
3. *Developing a case description.*
   The cases in the TRANSITIONS projects may be regarded as both the organizations and the employee groups. Generating a case description involves developing a framework for organizing the case study analysis. This may be an end in itself or one step toward a theoretical analysis. Because of the complexity of doing cross-national research as well as carrying out multiple case studies, in the TRANSITIONS project a common descriptive analytic framework, in terms of organizing the data analysis under clearly specified analytic themes and fieldwork questions, was developed to facilitate comparison across the organizations and individual employees.

Therefore, in TRANSITIONS all three strategies are being used to some extent.

A number of issues and problems may arise at the analytic stage. One such question is how to deal with diverse perspectives among managers and employees. One approach is to triangulate data, in the sense of looking for consistencies, to find the "correct" or "valid" accounts of organizational processes. However, this assumes that there is just one way of accounting for what is going on in organizations. Another view is that there are multiple realities and that it is important to understand all of these rather than searching for a single "truth." For example, in the private sector company in the TRANSITIONS project in the UK (an insurance company), different perspectives on recent changes in work-family policies emerged, as indeed they do in most organizations. One such change involved a new flexitime system, which comprised a shift from a formal flexitime (key-based, clocking in) system to what managers described as an informal, "trust-based" flexitime system. Managers portrayed this as a move toward greater autonomy for employees. As one manager put it:

> We wanted to get to a culture where you know there's trust in the environment . . . . clocking in and clocking out was felt to be quite a factory mentality and we want people [managers] to . . . think about things flexibly rather than be very stringent and dogmatic.

Staff, on the other hand, tended to focus on the reduction in entitlements that the new system entailed. They had lost the right to save up time to take off extra flexi days and felt that the informal system was much less "fair." There was much mistrust around the concept of trust in this context. Many employees felt that the new system increased management control.

So, is the new system based on trust and an attempt to increase worker autonomy or is it a management tool to ensure that staff work harder and give management more control? A case study provides the opportunity to treat both perspectives as valid within their own terms: the managers' perspectives and rationale on the one hand and the employees' experiences on the other hand. Moreover, it is important to view this within the wider context. This includes new legislation in the UK that provides employees with the "right" to request flexible working, which the employer must consider unless there are good business reasons to the contrary. This may influence the perceptions of both managers and staff, legitimizing the discussion of alternative ways of working.

Maintaining Anonymity and Ethical Issues

As in other types of research, the anonymity of organizations and individual participants is crucial in the reporting of case studies. While anonymity may be fairly easy to maintain in research that covers many organizations, the singularity of the case study makes it more problematic to preserve the anonymity of all involved. The need to protect our sources is a fundamental rule for any social researcher and is part of their professional ethical code (see, for example, Portuguese Sociological Association Code of Ethics, British Psychological Society Code of Ethics, British Sociological Association Code of Ethics). As Stake stated "Qualitative researchers are guests in the private spaces of the world [and] the value of the best research is not likely to outweigh injury to a person exposed" (2000, p. 447). The same idea is voiced by many other authors (Steele et al., 1999; Lee, 2000).

Not all case study participants have the same concern regarding anonymity. In some cases, participants like to be mentioned in the study report. This can even be the appeal for their collaboration. For example, in a case study by one of the authors carried out in an old urban neighborhood in Portugal, it was obvious from the beginning that all the interviewees and other informants would like to be recognized in the research report (Costa & Guerreiro, 1984). The research team had the difficult task of paying particular attention to what they included about them in their reporting, even when omitting information was to the disadvantage of the overall report. As Steele et al. said, "No research, be it pure or applied, is worth the cost of harming the individual or individuals being studied (Steele et al., 1999, p. 199).

The same desire for visibility can occur in companies that are seeking a ranking on accredited lists, for example, on family friendliness or equal opportunities policies. Here, the challenge is to avoid colluding with companies' desires to present themselves favorably and to report on them in an unbiased way so as to maintain ethical principles. Other problems can appear, not because the researchers are biased in their analysis, but because the media "misunderstands" the scientific conclusions of the study (Morgan, 1982). In reporting the case studies in the TRANSITIONS project, each organization was given a pseudonym and individual participants were either not named or given a pseudonym or, in some cases, their details were changed to protect anonymity. As the project involves only two organizations in each country, each from a different sector, it would be fairly easy to guess which organizations are being studied. Particular attention was given to guarding against this. The same caution was exercised regarding the workers, especially those in smaller organizational structures where they could easily be identified by colleagues or managers.

Ethical issues must also be considered if faced with evidence that some participants may be acting illegally. What should a researcher do, for instance, if he or she found that a company is breaking equal opportunities law by setting out not to recruit women, or, for example, if a woman is asked to sign a resignation declaration if she becomes pregnant? Steele et al. (1999) recommended, "If you observe or if the respondent tells you that he or she is committing a criminal act, it is your legal responsibility to report it" (p. 200). Similarly, Stake (2000) observed that the case study researcher needs constant feedback from his or her conscience, from stakeholders, and from the research community. In the insurance firm studied by the UK team for TRANSITIONS, it was noted that employees were obliged to take all their paid annual leave before they could request unpaid parental leave. This contravenes the spirit of the law, but the research team decided, after much consideration, that it was not their role to point this out in this instance.

Finally, a word needs to be said about the increasing "participative" approach adopted in social science research, that is, to working collaboratively with research participants. This may be an explicit contract in organizational case study research of the action research variety and hence the process may be open to negotiation when researchers discuss their findings with participants. However, in other studies, feeding back may be more problematic as, for example, when the gatekeepers in the organization challenge the researcher's analysis (see Coffey, 1996). Thus, deciding what to feed back to the organization and when to do it requires careful thought if this is to take place in the course of the case study. Moreover, the nature of the relationship with the organization will affect the power of both parties to shape the published output.

CONCLUSION

We have argued that organizational case studies are useful ways of exploring how organizational structures, cultures, and processes can undermine initiatives designed to support employees in managing work and nonwork responsibilities as well as identifying and evaluating potential initiatives and processes for making effective interventions in organization, for example, by using action research. The case study approach recognizes the complexity of organizations and the diversity of perspectives within them. It allows organizations to be studied in a parallel or iterative way (Verschuren, 2003) and brings into the analysis internal and external contextual factors. In building explanations, case studies may suggest that what happens in one organization may not occur in another and the reasons why an initiative is successful in one organization are likely to vary in different contexts. A particular practice developed in one context may not be generalizable across other organizations. For example, a trust-based, flexible working program may be rejected by employees in one organization but not in another organization where the history and context are different. However, a case study may enable extrapolation at a theoretical level A hypothesis that, for example, an informal system of flexible working, even if it apparently enhances individual employee autonomy, may be resented by employees collectively if it replaces a formal system of entitlements which had formerly been popular with the workforce. This can then be tested in different contexts and will contribute to creating theory about the conditions that generate feelings of autonomy and control among employees.

There is considerable scope for developing workplace case studies in relation to work-family issues. Some case studies also extend the holistic picture beyond a specific workplace or workplaces to include the perspectives of the families of employees (Hochschild, 1997; Lewis & Taylor, 1996; Brannen et al., 2001), and community perspectives could also be incorporated. As we have discussed, the case study approach is not without problems and unresolved issues. Nevertheless, it does offer a research strategy that takes account of organizational systems and processes, and can provide a way of getting beyond "quick fix" solutions that promote uncritical acceptance of "good practice" and moving toward deeper understanding of the conditions under which work may best be integrated with family responsibilities and the rest of life.

REFERENCES

Brannen, J. (2004a). Consolidated report of organizational case studies: Methodological issues. TRANSITIONS.

Brannen, J. (2004b). Working qualitatively and quantitatively. In C. Seale, G. Gobo, J. Gubrium, & D. Silverman (Eds.), *Qualitative research practice*. (pp. 312–327) London: Sage.

Brannen, J. (2005). Time and the negotiation of work-family boundaries: Autonomy or illusion? *Time and Society, 14*(1), 113–131.

Brannen, J., Lewis, S., & Moss, P. (2001). Workplace change and family life, Report on two case studies. London: Report to the Tedworth Trust.

Bryman, A. (2001). *Social research methods*. Oxford, UK: Oxford University Press.

CITE (2003). *Agir para a Igualdade. Equal Report*. Lisboa.

Coffey, A. (1996). The power of accounts: Authority and authorshipin ethnography. *Qualitative Studies in Education, 9*(1), 61–74.

Costa, A. F., Guerreiro, M. D., Ferreira, M., & Freitas, F. (1984). *Artes de Ser e de Fazer no Quotidiano Operário*. Lisboa: CIES.

Costa, A. F., & Guerreiro, M. D. (1984). *O Trágico e o Contraste. O Fado no Bairro de Alfama*. Lisboa: Publicaçes Dom Quixote.

Crozier, M. (2000). *À quoi sert la sociologie des organizations?* Paris: Éditions Seli Arslan.

Crozier, M., & Friedberg, E. (1977). *L'acteur et le système*. Paris: Le Seuil.

Esping-Anderson, G. (2000). *Social foundations of postindustrial economies*. Oxford, UK: Oxford University Press.

Fletcher, J., & Rapoport, R. (1996). Work-family issues as a catalyst for organizational change. In S. Lewis & J. Lewis (Eds.), *The work-family challenge* (pp. 142–158). London: Sage.

Guerreiro, M. D., Abranches, M., & Pereira, I. (2003). *Conciliação entre Vida Profissional e Vida Familiar, Políticas Públicas e Práticas dos Agentes em Contexto Empresarial*. Lisboa: CIES.

Guerreiro, M. D., & Lourenço, V. (2000). *Best practices for reconciling work and family life*. Lisboa: CITE.

Hammersley, M., Gomm, R., & Foster, P. (2000). Case study and theory. In R. Gomm, M. Hammersley, & P. Foster (Eds.), *Case study method: Key issues, key texts*. (pp. 234–258) London: Sage.

Hochschild, A. (1997). *The time bind*. New York: Henry Holt.

Kossek, E. E., & Ozeki, C. (1999). Bridging the work-family policy and productivity gap: A literature review. *Community, Work and Family, 2*(1), 7.

Lee, M. R. (2000). *Unobtrusive methods in social research*. Buckingham, UK: Open University Press.

Lewis, S. (1997). Family friendly organizational policies: A route to organizational change or playing about at the margins. *Gender, Work and Organization, 4*, 13–23.

Lewis, S. (2000). Organizational change and gender equity. Case studies from the UK. In L. Haas, P. Hwang, & G. Russell (Eds.), *Organizational change and gender equity*, (pp. 181–196) London: Sage.

Lewis, S. (2001). Restructuring workplace cultures: The ultimate work-family challenge? *Women in Management Review, 16*(1), 21–29.

Lewis, S. (2003). Flexible working arrangements; implementation, outcomes and management. In I. Roberson & C. Cooper (Eds.), *Annual review of industrial and organizational psychology* (vol. 18). London: Wiley.

Lewis, S., & Cooper, C. L. (2005). *The integration of work and personal life: Case studies of organizational change.* London: Wiley.

Lewis, S., & Smithson, J. (2001). Sense of entitlement to support for the reconciliation of employment and family life. *Human Relations, 55*(11), 1455–1481.

Lewis, S., & Taylor, K. (1996). Evaluating the impact of employer family friendly policies. A case study. In S. Lewis & J. Lewis (Eds.), *The work family challenge.* London: Sage.

Lincoln, Y. S., & Guba, E. G. (1989). *Naturalistic inquiry.* London: Sage.

Mintzberg, H. (1982). *Structure et Dynamique des Organizations.* Paris: Editions d'organization.

Mitchel, J. C. (2002). Case and situation analysis. In R. Gomm, M. Hammersley, & P. Foster (Eds), *Case study method* (pp. 165–186). London: Sage.

Morgan, D. H. J. (1982). The British association scandal: The effect of publicity on a sociological investigation. In Robert G. Burgess (Ed.), *Field research: A sourcebook and field manual* (pp. 254–263). London: George Allen & Unwin.

Ragin, C. (1987). *The comparative method.* Berkeley and Los Angeles: University of California Press.

Ragin, C., & H. S. Becker. (1992). *What is a case?* Cambridge, UK: Cambridge University Press.

Rapoport, R., Bailyn, L., Fletcher, J., & Pruitt, B. (2001). *Beyond work-family balance: Advancing gender equity and work performance.* Jossey-Bass.

Sainsaulieu, R. (1977). *L'identité au travail. Les effets culturels de l'organization.* Paris: Presses de la Fondation Nationale des Sciences Politiques.

Sainsaulieu, R. (1997). *Sociologie de l'entreprise.* Paris: Presses de la Fondation Nationale des Sciences Politiques.

Stake, R. E. (1995). *The art of case study research.* London: Sage.

Stake, R. E. (2000). Case studies. In N. K. Denzin & Y. S. Lincoln (Eds.), *Handbook of qualitative research*, (pp. 435–454). London: Sage.

Stake, R. E. (2002). The case study method in social inquiry. In R. Gomm, M. Hammersley, & P. Foster (Eds.), *Case study method* (pp. 19–26). London: Sage.

Steele, S. F., Scarisbrick-Hauser, A., & Hauser, W. (Eds.). (1999). *Solution centered sociology. Addressing problems through applied sociology.* Thousand Oaks, CA: Sage.

Strauss, A., & Corbin, J. (1998). *Basics of qualitative research. Techniques and procedures for developing grounded theory.* Thousand Oaks, CA: Sage.

Verschuren, P. (2003). Case study as a research strategy: Some ambiguities and opportunities. *International Journal of Social Research Methodology: Theory and Practice, 6*(2), 121–141.

Yin, R. K. (2003a). *Case study research. Design andl methods* (3rd ed.). London: Sage.

Yin, R. K. (2003b). *Applications of case study research* (2nd ed.). London: Sage.

24

Both Art and Science: Employing Organizational Documentation in Workplace-Based Research[1]

Susan J. Lambert
University of Chicago

Organizations can be a veritable treasure trove of information on work processes and practices and worker performance and behavior. In the work-life field, organizational documentation can provide useful information on the conditions of work that matter in the lives of employees and to the bottom lines of employers. Information from employers, however, can be difficult to obtain and less than complete and trustworthy, being collected for purposes far different than producing reliable, valid indicators of theoretical concepts. Fortunately, with a little cleverness and a great deal of persistence, researchers can often secure organizational documentation and transform it into high-quality measures that tap the realities of everyday organizational life.

My focus in this chapter is on organizational documentation reviewed directly by the researcher or by organizational informants who draw on it during in-person interviews with the researcher. Not included is survey research in which respondents may (or may not!) consult organizational documentation when responding to particular questions posed via a telephone interview or a written questionnaire. Organizational documentation as defined here includes published written reports used to inform the public, shareholders, or other external constituencies on organizational operations and outcomes (e.g., annual reports, profit statements) or the organization's unpublished, proprietary records used to inform internal decision makers about workers and workplace practices (e.g., personnel files, attendance records, sales numbers, scrap rates). The particular uses of organizational documentation discussed in this chapter have been primarily employed in case study research designed to investigate in-depth a single organization or a selected set of them (Yin, 2003).

Including organizational documentation in workplace-based research is often a quest to improve measurement validity, which is how well a measure captures what it is supposed to capture. If, for example, we want to understand the role *organizational* policies, *employer* practices, and *job* structures play in the lives of workers, then data at the organizational and job levels are likely to be more valid than data at the individual level. Understandably, scholars are reluctant to sacrifice reliability (consistency) for validity (accuracy). Organizational documentation—especially private employer records—can be full of inconsistencies. Researchers may choose survey methods that gather data on working conditions directly from workers in order to maintain control over data collection, thus helping ensure relia-bility.

Surveys may not, however, produce particularly valid (accurate) measures of organizational practices and policies. Just as individuals' views of their family are shaped by their unique roles in them, so too are workers' self-reports of working conditions biased by their personal experiences at work. By developing a sound strategy for using organizational documentation in work-life research, scholars may be able to improve the validity of their measures of or-ganizational and job conditions while acknowledging and potentially limiting problems with reliability.

Including organizational documentation in workplace-based research may be also driven by an interest in reducing common-method variance. Because each type of data source (e.g., in-person interviews, questionnaires, administrative records) has its own set of biases and errors, measures developed from the same source are likely to vary together—regardless. Common-method variance is problematic because at least part of the estimated association between an independent and dependent variable is likely to be due to the fact that both measures are derived from the same source (e.g., the worker), using the same method of data collection (e.g., questionnaires). Adding measures developed from organizational documentation to those obtained from other data sources, such as questionnaires, reduces the probability that estimated associations will be artificially inflated.

In this chapter, I first summarize the key uses organizational documentation can be put to in work-life research, providing examples from the broader organizational literature as well as the work-life literature. I then discuss some of the practical issues researchers are likely to encounter in conducting workplace-based research that employs existing organizational documentation in the process of measurement. I conclude by presenting examples from my own research that employs organizational documentation in workplace-based research on work-life issues, highlighting the important role theory has played in guiding my use of company records.

KEY USES OF ORGANIZATIONAL DOCUMENTATION IN WORK-LIFE RESEARCH

In this section, I briefly summarize the uses organizational documentation can be put to in work-life research. As Lambert and Kossek (2005) have lamented, work-life researchers still rely primarily on self-report data to measure individual performance, job conditions, and most aspects of both work and life. Nonetheless, creative uses of organizational documentation can be found in the work-life literature, some of which are reported here. Although not an exhaustive review, I also include examples from the broader organizational literature that use organizational documentation to capture aspects of the workplace of particular relevance to work-life scholars. Table 24.1 summarizes alphabetically the studies I refer to as I discuss uses of organizational documentation in work-life research.

Employee Performance

One purpose that immediately comes to mind when thinking of the uses organizational docu-mentation can be put to in work-life research is to measure employee performance. Different aspects of employee performance may require information from different data sources, from personnel records to computer output recording scrap levels and re-makes.

Absenteeism.   One aspect of performance is showing up at work. Researchers interested in absenteeism as a marker of employee performance would be wise to think through what

TABLE 24.1

Examples of Studies Using Organizational Documentation in Workplace-Based Research

Citation	Title of Article	Summary of Study	Use of Organizational Documentation
Allen, David, Lynn Shore, & Rodger Griffeth (2003)	Role of Perceived Organizational Support and Supportive Human Resource Practices in the Turnover Process	Investigated the antecedents of perceived organizational support (POS) and the role it plays in predicting voluntary turnover using data from two samples of employees. Perceptions of supportive human resources practices contributed to POS and POS was negatively related to turnover.	Organizational records used to assess turnover of individual employees 1 year after surveys assessing POS were administered.
Benkhoff, Birgit (1997)	Ignoring Commitment Is Costly: New Approaches Establish the Missing Link Between Commitment and Performance	Investigated the link between employee commitment and organizational performance in terms of sales targets met and change in profits. Setting was a bank with multiple branches. Employee commitment was significantly related to the financial success of bank branches.	The planning department of the bank provided information on sales targets for each branch and each branch's contribution to the bank's profit.
Blair-Loy, Mary & Amy Wharton (2002)	Employees' Use of Work-Family Policies and the Workplace Social Context	Estimated a multilevel model to identify the extent to which individual-level and work-group level factors were associated with professionals' use of work-family policies available in a financial services company. The more powerful their supervisor and colleagues, the more likely employees were to use policies.	Used personnel records to examine sample selection bias introduced by nonresponse to a survey. Also drew on organizational documents to identify what policies were available at the company.
Dalton, Dan R. & Debra J. Mesch (1990)	The Impact of Flexible Scheduling on Employee Attendance and Turnover	A natural occurring experiment of the implementation of a flexible scheduling program at a Western utility company. Examined the relationship between flexible scheduling and absenteeism and turnover. A 6-year assessment of effects revealed lower absenteeism among those in the experimental group, as compared to those in the control group. When the program was terminated, absenteeism rose to base-rate levels in the experimental group. Employee turnover was unaffected by the flexibility program.	Used monthly records of the number of unexcused absences and the number of employees who left voluntarily. Absenteeism and turnover rates were calculated for the 3 years prior to the intervention, the year of the intervention, and the 2 years following discontinuation.

(Continued)

TABLE 24.1
(Continued)

Citation	Title of Article	Summary of Study	Use of Organizational Documentation
Duarte, Neville, Jane R. Goodson, & Nancy R. Klich (1993)	How Do I Like Thee? Let Me Appraise the Ways	Examined the relationship between leader–member exchange (LMX) and employee performance (measured with records) and the supervisor's rating of that performance. The site for the study was a telephone company; data were collected from and on hourly workers. Among low LMX employees, objective measures of performance were associated with supervisor's ratings of performance; among high LMX employees, supervisor ratings were high regardless of objective performance.	Measures of daily employee performance were derived from department records. The performance of call operators was measured in terms of time taken to complete a call, cable splicers and joiners according to established standards for speed and accuracy, and dispatch clerks in terms of the time taken to record complaints.
Fernandez, Roberto, Emilio Castilla, & Paul Moore (2000)	Social Capital at Work: Networks and Employment at a Phone Center	Examined how hiring new workers via employee referrals can foster "social capital" that benefits the organization through three processes: the "richer pool," the "better match," and the "social enrichment." The site was a large, globally diversified financial services institution; the job studied is phone customer service representative, a full-time hourly position. The study finds that the firm's investment in the social capital of its employees pays off in several ways for the company itself.	Example of a particularly creative method that employed information from a company's database used to track the application and hiring process. Information from employment records was used to see how referrers' qualities were related to subsequent hiring decisions and the retention of those referred.
George, Jennifer (1991)	State or Trait: Effects of Positive Mood on Prosocial Behaviors at Work	Examined the relationship between positive mood at work and performance of both extra-role and role-prescribed prosocial organizational behaviors. Positive mood was related to prosocial behavior and when this behavior was directed at customers, it was linked to sales performance.	Sales data were collected for the month in which a survey was fielded, standardized within departments.
Griffin, Ricky W. (1981)	A Longitudinal Investigation of Task Characteristics Relationships	Investigated the stability of individuals' perceptions of their work and their reactions to these perceptions across a 3-month period. Perceptions were then related to individuals' productivity. Individuals' perceptions of task characteristics were relatively stable over the 3 months but workers' reactions to these perceptions and to productivity were less stable.	A key dependent variable was an index measuring individual productivity that the organization calculated for most employees on a daily basis. The index was based on an employee's total output for the day, controlling for problems in the production process such as down-time and set-up time.

Reference	Title	Description	Data/Method
Knez, Marc & Duncan Simester (2001)	Firm-Wide Incentives and Mutual Monitoring at Continental Airlines	Investigated the effectiveness of an incentive scheme implemented at Continental Airlines in 1995 that included monthly bonuses to all hourly employees if the company met its firm-wide performance goals. The results provide little evidence for "free-riding," and instead show how the scheme led to mutual monitoring among work group members.	Airplane departure time (on-time or not) was secured from industry records. The dependent variable was improvement in on-time departures based on monthly data that recorded the proportion of flights departing on time (within 15 minutes of scheduled departure time).
Kossek, Ellen Ernst, Alison Barber, & Deborah Winters (1999)	Using Flexible Schedules in the Managerial World: The Power of Peers	Examined managers' use of flexible scheduling options and their concerns about productivity. Survey data were collected from 1,000 managers at a telecommunications firm. Managers were more likely to use a flexibility option if they were female or had peers who also did so.	Used archival records to group respondents into work groups (all reported to the same manager). Work group variables included the percentage of women in the work group, average age of work group members, and average level of dependent care responsibility.
Kossek, Ellen Ernst, M. Huber, & J. Lerner (2003)	Sustaining Economic and Psychological Well-being of Mothers on Public Assistance: Individual Deficit and Social Structural Accounts	Examined the well-being and labor market experiences of mothers mandated to participate in work activities in order to receive public assistance in Michigan.	Used zip codes from administrative records of public aid recipients' addresses to code community characteristics using 1990 census data. Variables captured the average years of education completed by community residents and the average percentage of gross income community members spent on rent.
Kossek, Ellen, Brenda Lautsch, & Susan Eaton (2005)	Flexibility Enactment Theory: Relationships Between Type, Boundaries, Control and Work-Family Effectiveness	Examined the experiences of approximately 300 workers who varied in their access and use of flexibility in the location and timing of their work. Initial findings suggest that the amount and type of flexibility mattered in terms of work performance and work-family conflict. Flexible scheduling did not always translate into reduced conflict and users of formal flexibility had lower supervisor performance ratings, on average.	Measured access to flexibility using company records indicating whether the worker had formal permission to telework and was wired offsite.
Krackhardt, David, John McKenn, Lyman Porte, & Richard Steers (1981)	Supervisory Behavior and Employee Turnover	An experimental study that introduced changes in supervisor behavior in a subset of branches of a commercial bank. Turnover among bank tellers was significantly lower in the experimental branches than in the matched control branches.	Dependent variable was the voluntary turnover rate for each branch of the bank.

(Continued)

TABLE 24.1
(Continued)

Citation	Title of Article	Summary of Study	Use of Organizational Documentation
Lambert, Susan & Karen Hopkins (1995)	Occupational Conditions and Workers' Sense of Community: Variations by Gender and Race	Examined the extent to which workers' sense of community could be explained by their personal characteristics (race, gender, age, parental status) and their occupational conditions (job characteristics, hours, supervisor relationship). African American men and women experienced a lower sense of community than Caucasian and Hispanic workers, even after taking job conditions into account.	Used personnel records to gather data on both respondents and nonrespondents to a survey. Estimated a selection model to adjust regression equations for sample selection bias introduced by the varying response rates of workers of different race and gender.
Lambert, Susan & Elaine Waxman (2005)	Organizational Stratification: Distributing Opportunities for Balancing Work and Personal Life	Examined how opportunities for work-life balance are structured in policy, implemented in practice, and experienced by workers in lower-level jobs, lodged in 22 workplaces in the Chicago area. Firms varied more in terms of policy than in terms of actual workplace practices.	Used organizational documentation as a source of information on formal policies (wages benefits, flexibility, training, etc.) and actual workplace practices (percentage of workers who have received training, turnover rates, up-take of health insurance).
Lyness, Karen & Michael Judiesch (2001)	Are Female Managers Quitters? The Relationships of Gender, Promotions, and Family Leaves of Absence to Voluntary Turnover	Investigated the relationships among leaves of absence, timing of promotions, and voluntary turnover among managers working at a multinational financial services company during a 3-year period. After controlling for human capital, female managers were less likely to turnover than their male counterparts. Men and women taking family leaves had higher turnover rates than other managers.	All the data were obtained from databases created and maintained by the company.
Mesch, Debra & Dan Dalton (1992)	Unexpected Consequences of Improving Workplace Justice: A Six Year Time Series Assessment	A naturally occurring field experiment at a public utility company in which an intervention to improve a grievance process was introduced and then removed. Upon removal, there was an increase in the number of compromise resolutions and in the number of grievances filed.	Organizational records of all grievances filed over a 6-year study period were used to create four measures of the grievance process: grievance rate, grievance resolution (outcome from grievant's view), rate of compromises, and grievance resolution level (level of company where grievance was resolved).

Author (Year)	Title	Description	Measures
Milkovich, George & Luis Gomez (1976)	Day Care and Selected Employee Work Behaviors	Investigated the link between use of a particular day-care center and employees' job performance. The performance of 30 mothers with children enrolled in the day-care facilities was compared to the performance of a matched sample of mothers with young children not enrolled in the center and a sample of 30 other employees who either were not parents or had older children. All worked at the same company assembling electronic components. Day-care participants' average monthly rates of turnover and absenteeism were significantly lower than those of comparison employees.	Personnel records were used to measure absenteeism and turnover. Performance appraisal ratings submitted by supervisors were also secured from company records.
Pierce, Jon & John Newstrom (1983)	The Design of Flexible Work Schedules and Employee Responses: Relationships and Process	Examined the relationship between six dimensions of flexible work schedules and satisfaction and performance-related employee attitudes and behaviors. Results reveal a positive association between work schedule flexibility and employee performance and absenteeism, but no significant relationship with job satisfaction.	Used employee records to measure absenteeism and performance (score given by supervisor). The study also employed company HR policies/records to measure work schedule flexibility on five dimensions—core minutes, change approval, schedule variability, job bank, and schedule flexibility.
Tharenou, Phyllis (1993)	The Test of Reciprocal Causality for Absenteeism	Assessed reciprocal causality between absence and job satisfaction, performance, training achievement, and supervisory style. The study collected data at multiple time points, 2 years apart. The site for the study was an electricity authority and the workers were apprentices. Causal tests indicated that unexcused absences led to lower job satisfaction, training achievement, and supervisor-rated performance and attendance—rather than the reverse.	Three measures of absenteeism were drawn from company records: time lost (total uncertified hours absent), frequency (number of uncertified times absent), and certified absence (total hours for formally sanctioned absence). Supervisor performance ratings were also used.

type of absenteeism is likely to show the effects of their independent variables, specifically, whether it makes sense to gather information on all days missed or just on unscheduled time taken. As summarized in Table 24.1, Dalton and Mesch (1990) used monthly records of unexcused absences to examine changes in absenteeism before and after the implementation of a flexible scheduling program. Similarly, Tharenou (1993) distinguished between absenteeism in terms of certified (formally sanctioned) and uncertified hours of absence when investigating reciprocal causality between absence and job satisfaction, performance, training, and supervisory style; she found that, rather than vice versa, uncertified absences *led* to lower job satisfaction, training achievement, and supervisor-rated performance. Similarly, in a study of the relationship between use of day care and absenteeism, Milkovich and Gomez (1976) effectively focused on unplanned absences by calculating a ratio of the number of hours worked over the number of hours scheduled; workers using formal day care had significantly lower rates of unplanned absenteeism than other groups of workers.

In relying on company records to capture absenteeism, the researcher should know *a priori* whether or not different types of absenteeism can be distinguished. If not, the researcher should use care when interpreting associations or, better yet, should consider securing data on absenteeism through other means.

Turnover.   Another aspect of performance that is often documented by organizations is turnover. Again, it is important that researchers specify the type of turnover of interest in their study. Who leaves is often as important a question as how many leave; turnover of underperforming employees may be desirable. Researchers investigating turnover usually distinguish between employees terminated for performance problems from those who leave voluntarily. For example, Krackhardt, McKenn, Porter, and Steers (1981) employed organizational records of voluntary turnover to investigate the effects, via a quasi-experimental design, of changes in supervisor behavior on the turnover of bank tellers in a commercial bank, comparing voluntary turnover rates across experimental and comparison branches; branches implementing changes in supervisor interactions with tellers had lower rates of turnover than comparison branches. Allen, Shore, and Griffeth (2003) also used organizational records to identify voluntary turnover, in this case of individual employees in two organizations 1 year after they had filled out questionnaires assessing their *perceived organizational support* (POS); POS was negatively related to this measure of actual turnover as well as to a self-report measure of intentions to leave.

Appraised Performance.   Most companies regularly evaluate the performance of individual employees and record it on some kind of form, stored physically or, increasingly, electronically. The extent to which evaluations accurately capture performance varies with the evaluation process; formal evaluations can reflect office politics and wage policies as much as actual employee performance. Whether or not the recorded evaluation captures performance accurately, supervisor ratings can be an important source of information on the extent to which workers' contributions are valued by their supervisor. For example, in a study that examined the relationship between leader–member exchange (indicating a good relationship with one's supervisor) and supervisors' ratings of performance, Duarte, Goodson, and Klich (1993) found that the performance of workers who reported strong leader–member exchange was rated highly by their supervisor regardless of their objective performance as documented in department productivity records.

Daily Performance.   Several studies that employ organizational records to capture daily work performance can be found in the broader organizational literature. For example, in the study by Duarte et al. (1993) discussed above, measures of objective performance were derived from department records and vary depending on the workers' job; performance of call operators was measured in terms of the average time taken to complete calls whereas the performance of cable splicers was measured according to established standards for completion of daily work assignments. Griffin (1981) related workers' perceptions of and reactions to their job characteristics to their performance—calculated using an index created by the company to capture employees' daily productivity.

Because retailers often track sales at the store and worker level, sales records are often available in these settings. For example, George (1991) used questionnaires to examine how positive mood at work promoted extra-role prosocial behaviors and then linked these prosocial behaviors to sales performance, measured in terms of workers' average sales per hour in the month following the questionnaire. Benkhoff (1997) compared sales targets with actual sales records in an examination of the relationship between employee commitment and the performance of branches of a commercial bank.

A key point is that organizations often track the type of performance that is most meaningful in their industry. In retail, it is sales. In production settings, it may be time-to-delivery, scrap rates, re-makes. By finding out what is key in the industry, and to the company or companies under study, researchers are likely to find company records that may produce particularly meaningful—and thus valid—measures of performance. For example, Knez and Simester (2001) investigated the effectiveness of an incentive system implemented at Continental Airlines by examining records of airplane departure times, a key indicator of performance in the airline industry.

Employer Policies

Organizational documentation can be a key source of information on formal employer policies that may extend or limit what workers in particular jobs are entitled to as a part of their employment. Fortunately, most mid-sized and large corporations document pretty much everything. A good place to start learning about flexibility options, for example, is to read the company's guidelines for implementation. For example, Blair-Loy and Wharton (2002) drew on employee handbooks and official brochures, in addition to interviews with human resources staff, to identify the major work-family policies offered by a large financial services company; they then asked employees, via a survey, whether they had used each of the policies available "on-the-books."

Documentation is often available on compensation policies such as pay-bands for different classifications of jobs, on benefit plans for exempt versus nonexempt and full-time versus part-time workers, and on the rules for accumulating and actually using sick and personal days, securing holiday pay, and scheduling paid vacation time. Employers are also likely to have codified procedures for grievances from workers and dismissals by supervisors and may have formal rules guiding movement into a different job or onto another shift.

Without written documentation, researchers must, and often do, rely on informants' reports of employer policies—often to good effect. For example, Goodstein (1994) examined the factors that help explain which organizations adopt work-life policies by drawing on data from a survey conducted by the Washington State Employment Security Department that asked organizational informants to report on their company's provision of particular work-life supports (e.g., child-care benefits, flexible work arrangements) as well as characteristics of their institutional environment (e.g., percentage of working parents and female employees). Kelly and Dobbins (1999) examined factors that help explain why some companies adopted maternal leave policies before the United States enacted the Family and Medical Leave Act, using a survey mailed to an industry-stratified sample of organizations with 50 or more employees located in three states. They found that rather than a response to the increase of women in the workforce, maternal leave policies were more a response to changes in the legal environment, specifically EEOC guidelines that threatened to extend discrimination protections to pregnancy.

Although employer representatives can provide valuable information on and insight into the workplace, researchers should remember that informants are not immune to misunderstanding or misrepresenting company policies. Written guidelines can provide those specifics on eligibility and details of benefit plans that some individuals have a hard time recounting. In sum, written documentation on policies can be used itself to develop measures of organizational policies, for example, to categorize a company's formal flexibility options (Blair-Loy & Wharton, 2002). At the least, written employer policies can help researchers when interpreting variations in workers' self-reported experiences, such as with work-life supports, differentiating those circumstances when workers' lack of use may be more a matter of employer policy than employee choice.

Employer Practices

Many researchers have observed that often there is a disconnect between supports offered on paper and those available to workers in practice (Blair-Loy & Wharton, 2002; Eaton, 2003; Kossek, Barber, & Winters, 1999; Lambert, 1998). Organizational documentation can be a crucial source of information on employer practice, which includes how formal policies are implemented in daily organizational life as well as informal routines not covered by formal policy. For example, turnover rates broken down by job classification can provide valuable insight on how job security is practiced across and within organizational levels. Benefit participation rates can help reveal the extent to which benefits available as a matter of employer policy are delivered to workers as a matter of practice. Lambert and Waxman (2005), for example, drew on documentation of benefit take-up rates to look at the extent to which health insurance is distributed to lower-level workers; only a small fraction of workers in many of the lower-level jobs they have studied are covered by insurance available in policy.

Administrative records also can be used to reveal how employer practices "show up" at the individual-worker level by coding, for example, each study participant's use of sick time, vacation days sacrificed, use of parental leave, and so forth. This is one of the most common purposes of organizational data in work-life research. For example, Lyness and Judiesch (2001) combined data from multiple databases of a multinational financial services corporation to trace the relationships among family leaves of absence, voluntary turnover, and timing of promotions. They found that, on average, managers taking family leave had a higher rate of turnover than other managers, but that those with graduate degrees were no more likely to quit than comparable colleagues. Moreover, contrary to hypotheses, women's voluntary turnover rates were slightly lower than those of men, once human capital variables were controlled.

Mesch and Dalton (1992) examined records of grievances filed over a 6-year period to investigate how grievance practices in a public utility company changed when an intervention to improve the grievance process was introduced and then canceled. Pierce and Newstrom (1983) coded organizational documents to create six measures that capture different dimensions of the flexible work arrangements used by office staff in five insurance companies. They then examined the relationship between these dimensions of flexibility and workers' absenteeism and supervisor performance ratings, also collected from organizational records.

Another example of how organizational documentation can be used to reveal employer practice is Fernandez, Castilla, and Moore's (2000) study of hiring practices at a large financial services institution. They used the company's database designed to track its application and hiring process to investigate how hiring new workers via employee referrals can foster "social capital" that benefits the organization itself. The researchers were able to link information on referrers with information on referrals to see how preferences for employee referrals played themselves out in the hiring process and, ultimately, in employee retention.

Although employee reports of their experiences with formal policies and informal organizational routines are invaluable in helping inform understandings of everyday organizational life, relying solely on employees to capture employer practice is problematic. Response rates to surveys rarely approach 100%, making it hard to discern whether respondents' experiences of the organization represent the exception or the rule. And, workers may be motivated to over- or underreport their use of benefits and other workplace experiences. For example, Kossek, Lautsch, and Eaton (2005) created a variable from organizational records of formal approvals for flexible scheduling and found that it is negatively related to supervisor performance ratings, which runs counter to other studies that rest on workers' self-reports of teleworking. Kossek et al. posited that the difference in results might be due to employees overreporting their use of flexible work arrangements in surveys; employees may be reluctant to provide information that could jeopardize their opportunity to elect a flexible schedule at a later date.

In sum, organizational documentation of participation rates in various employer-sponsored programs can be used to provide a context for interpreting self-report data and can itself be used to create indicators of employer practice at the organizational and job levels.

Strengthening Analyses

Another use of organizational documentation in work-life research is to strengthen the rigor of research designs by introducing additional independent or control variables into analyses and by taking nonresponse bias into account. For example, Kossek, Barber, and Winters (1999) used personnel records to identify respondents' work groups, which allowed them to construct variables of work group composition (percent women, percent with children) themselves rather than relying on either employee or employer accounts. Personnel records, often computerized even in small firms, can be used to document a variety of worker characteristics, for example, workers' job tenure, internal mobility, and wage/salary history. Home addresses can be placed in census tracks for developing variables on workers' neighborhoods, availability of public transportation, and other community-level variables. For example, in a study of women receiving public aid in Michigan, Kossek, Huber, and Lerner (2003) matched census data with zip codes to create a variable indicating the affordability of rental housing in the women's communities. Women in communities where rents were high relative to wages received the greatest amount of cash assistance during the 3-year study period.

Although basic demographic information may be directly gathered from workers, using organizational documentation in lieu reduces the burden on respondents and leaves more room on the survey for other items. It also allows for the possibility that some research questions can be addressed without the need for costly interviews or questionnaires.

Organizational documentation can also be employed to take nonresponse bias into consideration when conducting a survey of workers. Nonresponse bias is one source of sample selection bias; respondents and nonrespondents are likely to vary in ways related to the issue under study, thus biasing estimates of population parameters such as betas in regression analyses (cf. Heckman, 1979). Information from personnel records on all workers sent a survey (both those who responded and those who did not) can prove useful in estimating a statistical model that differentiates respondents and nonrespondents, calculating what is called a selection term.

Basically, this selection term becomes an additional independent variable in one's substantive model, effectively controlling for nonresponse bias—to the extent the model estimated distinguishes respondents and nonrespondents well. For example, Lambert and Hopkins (1995) estimated selection with the goal of controlling for the low questionnaire response rate of African American men in a study that investigated the relationship between workers' occupational characteristics and workers' sense of community; introducing the selection term into multivariate regressions reduced the once significant difference between African American men and women's sense of community. Blair-Loy and Wharton (2002) also used employee records to compare survey respondents and nonrespondents at the individual and work-group levels. The selection variable they created was not statistically significant in their models examining employees' use of work-family policies and, thus, they did not include it in their final analyses. In sum, although securing a high response rate is clearly superior to statistically correcting for nonresponse bias, the availability of organizational documentation on both respondents and nonrespondents presents the opportunity for work-life researchers to assess rather than simply lament how nonresponse may influence study results.

TIPS OF THE TRADE

Given the abundance of documentation in organizations and its potential uses in work-life research, it may seem puzzling that organizational documentation remains underutilized in work-life research. It is more understandable when one recognizes the difficulties of using it. Some of the challenges include the time and effort it takes to gain access to existing documentation, wariness of potential problems with reliability, and unfamiliarity with the task of moving from documentation to measurement. In this section, I discuss some of the pragmatics of accessing, appraising, and employing organizational documentation in work-life research; I also highlight the rationale for doing so. My focus is on workplace-based research aimed at developing knowledge of the work side of work-life issues.

Tip 1. Know which level(s) of the organization you want to understand and try to secure data at that level.

Organizations, being systems, can be conceptualized and studied at different levels: individual worker level, work group level, job level, macro structure level (division or department), the organizational level, and the organizational network level. Organizational scholars often contribute to knowledge by peeling back these layers to examine how they are related to one another—or not. Doing so requires data relevant to different levels of analysis. Studying workers is not the same as studying work groups, in the same way that studying individuals' experiences of their family is not the same as studying families.

Although variables can be created by combining workers' responses together, perhaps averaging them to make a variable of organizational culture or supportiveness, data from individuals provide the best insight into individual-level phenomenon. They tell us about workers' experiences in particular jobs, but not about how that job is embedded within the larger organizational context. For example, suppose we want to assess the extent to which a job is designed for retention. We could survey workers about their intentions to leave. This information would give some sense of workers' commitment to the organization, but it would not tell us much about the structured probability that workers in that job are likely to stay in it. In some universities, the majority of junior faculty may intend to stay and may want to stay, but few may actually get tenure. Their probability of job security is low, no matter what their intentions or commitment.

Note that the turnover rate for the overall organization will not tell us whether a particular job is structured for retention either. Turnover rates can vary enormously among jobs within the same company, as do turnover rates among faculty and administrative staff in university departments. The information we would need is the actual turnover rate for the particular job. In sum, workers' intentions to leave, job retention rates, and organizational turnover are all related to one another, but each tells us something different about the workplace.

In the studies summarized in Table 24.1, some measures of performance were at the individual worker level and others at the department or organizational level. The level of measurement should, of course, depend on the relationship being assessed. For example, Allen et al. (2003) measured turnover at the worker level, which makes sense because they were investigating its link to workers' perceptions of organizational support. Dalton and Mesch (1990), on the other hand, measured turnover at the level of bank branch, comparing the average turnover and absenteeism of branches before and after a flexible scheduling program was implemented and then withdrawn in these branches. Knez and Simester's (2001) use of online departure as an indicator of performance is at the organizational level, which fits well with their focus on the outcomes of a firmwide incentive program.

Gathering data at particular levels of the organization—differentiating worker-level data from job-level data, for example—is not only a matter of ensuring a good fit between theory and data. Gathering data that capture different organizational levels is also important if we are to consider multiple avenues for change because interventions are often targeted to whatever level(s) under study. As demographer Barbara Reskin (2003) concluded, "individual-level explanations are the *only* explanations possible with individual-level data" (p. 6). If we hope to identify aspects of workplaces that can be improved to foster work-life balance, then our data need to include variables at the job and organizational levels. One cannot just study *workers* when seeking to improve *workplaces*.

Incorporating measures at different levels of analysis creates challenges for statistical analysis. Many multivariate statistical techniques are based on the assumption of independence of errors. This assumption is violated when respondents' scores on variables do not vary independently, for example, when more than one respondent comes from the same department and variables include the gender and race of the supervisor. Fortunately, new statistical techniques are available that take into account correlated error terms, allowing researchers to appropriately estimate multi-level models, such as, workers within departments, departments within organizations. For example, Haley-Lock (2003) employed hierarchical linear modeling (HLM; Raudenbush & Bryk, 2002) to differentiate the contributions of individual worker characteristics, such as human capital and network ties, versus workplace policies and practices in explaining the extent to which social service workers in different agencies realized opportunities for advancement, skill development, and full-time work. Blair-Loy and Wharton (2002) also used HLM to estimate a multi-level model distinguishing the contributions of individual level and work-group level variables in explaining professionals' use of available work-life policies; they found that "social context," defined in terms of the power of one's supervisor and coworkers, helped explain professionals' use of policies beyond their family caregiving responsibilities.

Tip 2. Try to earn the trust of organizational representatives at all levels.

Gaining the trust of company representatives who have the decision-making authority to grant or restrict access to organizational documentation, especially proprietary company records, is obviously essential to being able to incorporate documentation in one's data collection efforts. Without the trust of organizational representatives, access to the organization overall is likely to be circumscribed, perhaps restricted to collecting anonymous surveys. A researcher should not underestimate the amount of trust required to gain access to even a company's most basic information. Information the researcher may view as fairly straightforward, such as on the demographic characteristics of workers, may be deemed sensitive by the employer, or perhaps by employees. Key organizational representatives can be found at all levels of an organization. Senior managers may grant access on paper but if lower-level managers and workers are not invested in the study, they may impede timely access to documents and may withhold their own opinions and insights on possible data sources.

Establishing trust with company representatives—at all levels—takes more than simply explaining the study's procedures and protections. Trust is developed through multiple actions and interactions, through honesty and candor. It takes time to establish. One likely reason researchers addressing work-life issues continue to rely on self-report data is that they do not have, or are reluctant to take, the time needed to identify and gain access to sources of information that come from the workplace. Although there are no shortcuts to mutual trust, there are several steps researchers can take to help them earn the trust of organizational representatives while they locate and appraise organizational documentation of potential use:

1. Set the stage for adding organizational documentation to a survey study. Employers are often comfortable with survey techniques; most major employers conduct their own surveys to keep tabs on worker morale and employees' emerging needs. Thus, initial entrée to an organization often centers around the fielding of a survey to be distributed to workers. As trust develops between the researcher and company representatives, it may be possible—with appropriate human subjects' approval—to expand the scope of the study to include measures developed from performance appraisals, production records, or personnel files.

Regardless of whether access to organizational documentation is granted prior to entrée or following it, if information from organizational documentation is to be linked to survey data, surveys from employees cannot be anonymous. Winning company approval to field a survey that ensures the confidentiality of respondents but not their anonymity can be as difficult as gaining access to company records. Managers have to know that ethical and legal protections are in place, employees have to be assured that their identity will remain confidential, and the researchers have to be confident that they will not be pressured to provide analyses that could reveal worker identities. If enough trust cannot be developed to field surveys with assurances of confidentiality rather than anonymity, then organizational data may be of little value and may not warrant the time or cost of their collection. Researchers can help set the stage for the incorporation of organizational documentation in their research by readying other elements of their study for its eventual inclusion.

2. Get to know what data are collected by the organization. One of the key steps that can facilitate company representatives granting access to documentation is to be able to specify exactly what information would be useful and from what source it could come. The more people at the company researchers talk with about how and what information is collected and disseminated, the better. Many companies collect so much information that relying on a limited array of informants may hinder the identification of promising sources of data. Moreover, researchers may think they are making a simple request, but the way the data are collected and stored may render the request anything but simple. In sum, the more researchers know about a company's data collection processes and reporting conventions, the better able they will be to make reasonable, specific requests for documents of particular value to their study.

3. Don't ask for everything. A key piece of advice is to limit requests for documentation to those pieces most essential to addressing the research questions posed. Just as survey researchers are tempted to pack questionnaires with items they think would be "interesting," so too is it tempting to ask for documentation that seems readily available or that might prove "useful." Organizational representatives can be easily overwhelmed by data requests; they have a business to run after all.

What kind of documentation is likely to be of most use depends on the research questions posed, but there are some general factors that should be considered. One is to consider where common-method variance is most likely to limit the strength of the conclusions drawn. If, for example, one is interested in linking worker attitudes to worker performance, then using self-report data to measure both is unlikely to be satisfying. Moreover, as argued earlier, organizational documentation is likely to be more convincing than self-report data when the goal is to capture phenomena at the organizational or job level. Finally, documentation that yields measures of interest to the company as well as to the theory merits special consideration because, as discussed more fully below, it is likely to be more consistent (reliable) and meaningful (valid).

In sum, specifying what information would be most useful, the documents from which it can be gathered, and how it will be incorporated into ongoing data collection efforts can help overcome reluctance on the part of company representatives to share proprietary information. The more sensitive the information from the point of the company, the more trust needed to gain access. There are no substitutes for spending the time needed to get to know both the company and its representatives and for being responsive and honest in interactions with staff at all levels.

Tip 3. Develop a strategy for dealing with errors in documentation.

Appraising the quality of organizational documentation can be discouraging, at least initially. Errors often can be found in the coding of even basic personnel information. Consider, for example, that companies may not even have accurate addresses for all their employees, as evidenced by surveys returned because they were undeliverable by the postal service. Moreover, records may not be up-to-date; the last date for a performance evaluation may be 3 years ago, which makes it difficult to use supervisory ratings as a dependent variable for a study you are beginning to field.

Perhaps the most important tip for using organizational documentation in research is to examine it carefully for errors. Often, you can see errors just by looking at the data, such as running a distribution on "date of review." In any case, it is useful to assess likely errors by discussing with company representatives the uses of the data and the kinds of decisions that they inform. Information that is used for important purposes, such as the calculation of bonuses or even a free lunch in the company cafeteria, is likely to have a lot of eyes on it and a number of people invested in its accuracy. To the extent insurance providers, for example, base their rates partly on employee utilization of health care (which many do), utilization of health services is likely to be tracked carefully. Other types of information that hold little relevance for employer expenditures or employee recognition are likely to be more prone to error and neglect.

Assessing as carefully as possible the accuracy of particular organizational documentation allows the researcher to consider several possible avenues of action. First, the researcher may decide that the errors are so great, the documentation is of little value. In this case, the researcher may want to consider developing alternative ways of gathering the information. For example, in reviewing formal performance evaluations within a hospital, Kossek and Nichol (1992) found that they would be unable to combine data for workers in different job categories because performance evaluation forms varied; they decided instead to design their own rating form for supervisors. Obviously, it is better to find problems of comparability, and any other limitations, before one gets to the analysis stage.

Another strategy is to make inconsistencies part of the study itself. Incorporating measures of the same construct (e.g., performance) from multiple sources (e.g. worker, supervisor, department records) allows the researcher to investigate possible reasons for inconsistencies—and consistencies. Incorporating in the study variables that may help explain contradictions (e.g., attribution bias) among data sources can only occur, however, if the researcher attends to such possibilities prior to data collection.

Another possible strategy for the researcher is to consider how the type of error in the data limits interpretation. For example, employers may not have exact information on turnover rates for each job of interest. But, documentation on recruitment and hiring as well as interviews with staff may make it possible to rank particular jobs in terms of turnover or to rate jobs as having high, medium, or low turnover. Although the researcher may have little confidence in putting an exact number on turnover for some jobs, there may be ample evidence to differentiate high-turnover from low-turnover jobs, and, depending on the purposes of the study, this distinction may be sufficient.

Another direction the researcher can take is to develop ways to improve the reliability and validity of existing organizational documentation. For example, the researcher may work with the employer to update employees' addresses, to ensure that performance reviews are current, and to develop procedures for recording turnover by job type. Again, such actions can only be taken if time is spent up-front assessing the adequacy of possible data sources rather than waiting until analysis to discover that, for example, information on income or family structure is missing for half of the sample. Just as pretesting a survey is an important step in survey research and conducting a pilot is useful in field experiments, so too is pretesting the use of organizational documentation when conducting workplace-based research.

In sum, by assessing, rather than ignoring or assuming, errors in existing organizational documentation, researchers can develop an informed strategy for employing organizational documentation given the particular focus of their study. Doing so makes it possible to employ organizational documentation that may have its problems without overstepping its limits or dismissing its value.

EXAMPLES EMPLOYING ORGANIZATIONAL DOCUMENTATION IN WORK-LIFE RESEARCH

The examples provided below highlight both the challenges and rewards of employing organizational documentation to develop knowledge on work-life issues and underscore the usefulness of theory in guiding its selection and use. Both examples come from my own research in which organizational documentation was used as part of a multi-method data collection strategy. In the first example, information from company records was combined with questionnaire data from workers; in the second example, a variety of organizational documentation, both published and proprietary, was combined with in-depth interview data from human resource professionals and managers and with onsite observation.

Using Organizational Documentation to Measure Organizational Citizenship Behavior (OCB)

In the early 1990s, I conducted a study at Fel-Pro, Incorporated, a mid-size manufacturing firm in Skokie, Illinois. The company, then family-owned, was renowned for its supports for workers and their families, providing, for example, onsite child care, legal and mental health counseling, a fitness center, and a summer camp for workers' children. The purpose of the study was to examine workers' use and appreciation of the menu of work-life benefits offered at Fel-Pro and their relationship to worker performance. The study's main findings and details of the methodology are reported in articles authored by myself and former doctoral-student colleagues (cf. Hopkins, 2001, 2002; Lambert, 1998, 2000; Lambert & Hopkins, 1995). A key finding is that the more workers appreciated the work-life benefits available to them, the more likely they were to submit suggestions for quality improvement and to participate in meetings on quality methods. Here, I focus on some of the strategies we developed for dealing with potential errors in organizational documentation and the use of theory in directing us toward particular data sources.

The key issue in investigating the link between workers' appreciation of work-life supports and worker performance was how to capture performance. As explained in Lambert (2000), social exchange theory provided a basis for hypothesizing reciprocity between employees and their employer; the more workers appreciated available work-life benefits, the more likely they would be to repay their employer through their work performance. But, what kind of performance would "show" workers' efforts to repay their employer? There are a lot of reasons workers show up for work on time every day and do their basic job well, reasons that may have little to do with how well they are treated by their employer. Theories of social exchange and what is termed extra-role performance suggested that workers would be likely to repay their employer for "extra" benefits with "extra" performance.

One type of extra-role performance is organizational citizenship behavior (OCB), defined for that study as behavior that (a) goes beyond the basic requirements of the job, (b) is to a large extent discretionary, and (c) is of benefit to the organization. I decided that we should try to develop "hard" measures of OCB, to complement workers' self-reports of their OCB collected via a mailed questionnaire. In reviewing the performance evaluations used in the company, we found that information on "extra" performance was rarely mentioned as a source for a rating in supervisors' narratives. The focus, especially in lower-level jobs, was on absenteeism and workers' performance of basic job tasks. In talking with supervisors, it was clear that when workers were rated as "exceeds expectations," the basis for the evaluation was still on how well workers performed their basic job. Thus, supervisory ratings and narrative evaluations did not seem very good sources of information on OCB per se.

In the many months I was at the company developing and then fielding the questionnaire, it became clear that one of the greatest challenges facing managers was how to more fully engage lower-level workers in quality-improvement initiatives. The company had invested a great deal of time and money in training all workers in a quality-improvement methodology and had implemented several forums that required workers' active participation to be deemed successful, including meetings on quality methods, a suggestion program for process and product improvement, department-level Quality Circles, and work-unit tracking of scrap levels and time-to-delivery. This was an area of performance important to the organization and for which workers obviously had some discretion, since participation at meetings and in the suggestion program was lower than managers desired and work units varied in their recording of scrap and delivery times.

In order to identify which aspects of participation would be useful indicators of citizenship behavior, I recruited George Easton, then a faculty member in the University of Chicago's Graduate School of Business and an examiner for the National Baldrige Quality Award, to assess Fel-Pro's quality-improvement program. From Dr. Easton's assessment, the suggestion program and quality meetings seemed the most promising indicators. Gathering data on scrap levels and time-to-delivery had been my original focus, but Easton's analysis revealed that these were more the result of work group and department processes than individual effort. On the other hand, workers' participation in quality meetings and their submission of suggestions varied within job categories and within and across departments and, hence, seemed a better indicator of individual discretion and effort. Thus, conceptual understandings of OCB guided our search for and subsequent selection of the indicators I employed to capture workers' organizational citizenship behavior.

Once I selected submission of suggestions and participation in quality meetings as possible indicators of OCB, I began looking closely at sources of information on these behaviors. I found that information on who submitted suggestions was carefully recorded. Workers earned free lunches in the cafeteria for every three suggestions submitted and were eligible for cash awards when suggestions were adopted. Moreover, a committee was responsible for responding to each and every suggestion. Workers were known to complain when their submission was not recorded or responded to, but this was rare. Thus, our assessment of likely errors revealed that organizational documentation of suggestions by workers was likely to be reliable. We then set to the task of coding the number of suggestions each worker at Fel-Pro made. First, we tallied suggestions for 2 years: the year prior to fielding the survey and the year the survey was fielded. Later, we coded the submission of suggestions for the 2 years following the survey, adding a longitudinal component to the study. We also coded whether or not each suggestion was implemented; we did not employ this count in our measure of OCB because, conceptually, adoption seems to reflect the discretion of the employer rather than the goodwill of the employee.

My initial assessment of meetings on quality issues, on the other hand, suggested that records of attendance were spotty. A sign-up sheet was passed around during the meeting and, from my observation, some attendees signed and some did not. I worked with quality improvement (QI) staff to improve the reliability of attendance sheets. For example, one QI staff person was positioned at the door with a clipboard on which workers were to sign in as they entered the room. Fortunately, QI staff were open to this because they wanted to make sure every name was recorded so that they could document the popularity of their presentations. Probably most importantly, only when workers signed in did they get a ticket for the raffle that was (and had been always) conducted at the end of the meeting. My research team's subsequent observations of these meetings revealed a dramatic improvement in the accuracy of the attendance sheets.

The use of organizational documentation allowed me to develop a longitudinal design that captured workers' citizenship behavior at two points in time. As reported in Lambert (2000), controlling for the number of suggestions submitted prior to the survey helped rule out the possibility of reverse causation when estimating the relationship between workers' appreciation of available supports and their OCB 2 years later, thus strengthening the research design. The coding of suggestions also allowed us to estimate differences in the OCB of respondents versus nonrespondents to the questionnaire; differences were not statistically significant.

Of course, our measure of workers' organizational citizenship behavior was limited by the documentation that was available in this particular company. We could not find a source of documentation, for example, that captured the extent to which individual workers helped one another and, instead, relied solely on workers' self-reports of this aspect of OCB.

In sum, social exchange theory and conceptualizations of extra-role behavior provided useful guides for identifying documentation on a particular type of worker performance, organizational citizenship behavior. By examining the accuracy of organizational documentation, we were able to work with the company's managers and staff to secure and, importantly, to improve the reliability of documentation pertaining to aspects of performance important to the company and to assessing a theoretical model. Moreover, because records of suggestions were maintained over time, employing this documentation made it possible to add a longitudinal dimension to what would have been a cross-sectional survey design.

Using Organizational Documentation to Disentangle Employer Policy From Employer Practice

For the past several years, I have been working with a team of doctoral students to conduct a study of lower-level jobs in major Chicago-area corporations.[2] The goal of the study is to understand how, and the mechanisms by which, employers distribute opportunities for work-life balance, defined quite broadly, to jobs lodged at lower organizational levels. At this point, we have data on 84 specific lower-skilled jobs, housed in over 22 workplaces throughout Chicago, in four key industries: retail (stores, distribution centers), hospitality (hotels, airline catering), transportation (airlines, package delivery), and financial services (banks).

Because what is a matter of employer policy is not always a matter of employer practice, my colleagues and I have developed a three-step approach to assessing the distribution of work-life opportunities that draws on the theories and analytic methods of firm-level labor markets (Henly & Lambert, 2005; Lambert & Haley-Lock, 2004; Lambert & Waxman, 2005). Here, I focus on how we are employing organizational documentation in our assessment.

Step 1: Opportunity in Policy.   In the first step, we follow traditional firm-level labor market approaches by collecting detailed information on organizationwide policies and practices. Because our definition of work-life opportunities is quite expansive, we gather data not only on job ladders and legal protections, but also on training provided and funded, tuition reimbursement, turnover rates, scheduling guidelines, flextime programs, and policies related to the use of temporary, part-time, and other nonstandard jobs. In this step, our basic goal is to capture the many opportunities that are available in today's workplaces and to discern how employers structure access to these opportunities through their formal policies.

One key source of information on employer policies are just that: employer policies. We collect from our informants as much written text as we can on, for example, compensation policies (such as pay bands and wage ranges), rules guiding the accumulation and use of sick days and vacation time, formal guidelines around flexibility, benefit plans for different levels/types of workers, written procedures for dismissals and grievances, training offerings and requirements, tuition reimbursement policies, and so forth. We use this information to help assess whether, according to employer policy, specific opportunities are to be extended to workers in lower-level jobs and, if so, which ones. This documentation is used to complement information we gain through in-depth interviews with company representatives; we follow up by phone or e-mail when the information included in the documentation conflicts with what our informants have told us.

Step 2: Opportunity in Practice.   In the second step, we collect information on the extent to which opportunities available in policy are extended in practice to workers in four particular lower-level jobs: (a) a lower-skilled, entry-level job selected because of its importance, in the view of the employer, for the organization's success (a core job); (b) a lower-skilled, entry-level job selected because of its relative unimportance to the organization's success (a noncore job); (c) a lower-skilled job found in all the organizations studied (i.e., an entry-level clerical job); and (d) a job filled by a public aid recipient (which we know *a priori*).

It can take several phone calls and in-person interviews to identify those corporate representatives who have data on particular organizational practices. We seek out those who know, or can help us calculate, the proportion of workers in each of our target jobs who has realized the different types of work-life opportunities available at least in policy. For example, we try to specify the proportion of workers in each job who have received the different kinds of training for which they are technically eligible, the proportion currently eligible for "universal" health insurance and actually covered right now, and the proportion of workers in each job who make it past any probation period and who move into a different job with the company. We also seek detailed information on the employment status, scheduling practices, and turnover rates for each job.

Before our interview, we send our interviewees a letter listing the specific information we will be requesting. Most interviewees are well prepared and have documentation on their desk. Sometimes they need to consult with other staff or to pull up data files on their computer; other times they ask to send us the information later or refer us to colleagues in other units. In some cases, it becomes obvious that the detailed information we would like to secure cannot be gathered and that it is not just a matter of finding the right person to ask. In these cases, we switch to questions that employ a different response categorization. That is, if respondents cannot give us proportions (ratio-level data), we ask them if they are knowledgeable enough to provide ordinal-level data, that is, whether they can rate turnover, for example, as "high, moderate, or low" or whether "most, few, or none" of the workers in a target job are currently covered by their company's health insurance. If so, we then discuss with them the basis for their judgment and look for other sources of information that might shed additional light on the accuracy of their assessment.

The downside of these data collection techniques is that they produce data with varying levels of specificity. The upside is that we have greater confidence in the data we are able to secure than we would have if we collected them via a mailed or telephone questionnaire. Organizational representatives often want to appear knowledgeable and to comply with information requests; some are more than happy to provide estimates that may or may not be based on sound information. Moreover, many surveys conducted by mail or phone employ ordinal scales because researchers recognize that not all respondents will have specific data on organizational structures and processes. This results in an information loss because some respondents are likely to possess detailed, "harder" data on important workplace conditions.

In addition, unless you talk with the respondent or write out very detailed instructions, respondents may be reporting apples when you are interested in oranges. For example, companies vary in how they calculate turnover rates. Some calculate it for the fiscal year rather than the calendar year, which may not be all that different. Consider, however, that some companies only calculate turnover among workers who have passed a probation period, which, if you are conducting a study of lower-level jobs, is quite problematic if left uncorrected.

Step 3: Opportunity as Experienced.   My colleagues Julia Henly and Elaine Waxman have extended the investigation of opportunity to the worker level by interviewing women employed in jobs in the retail settings we have investigated in prior steps.[3] By linking data on opportunity in policy and practice to interview data, they are able to place a woman's experience in a larger context, differentiating when her experiences seem to represent the rule or the exception. We trace how workplace practices designed to allow flexibility in labor costs translate into unpredictable schedules for sales associates, leading mothers in these jobs to either set up child care "just-in-case" or to scramble for it at the last minute (Henly & Lambert, 2005).

In sum, organizational documentation can help distinguish employer policy from employer practice, in this study, advancing understanding of stratification in the workplace (Lambert & Haley-Lock, 2004; Lambert & Waxman, 2005) and of new forms of instability in workers' lives (Lambert, Waxman, & Haley-Lock, 2002). By talking with employer representatives about the sources of their information and how it is recorded, it is possible to understand both the limits and strengths of the data being recorded and thus to report results with both more care and more confidence.

CONCLUSION

Understanding the work side of work-life issues, that is, how organizational structures, employer practices, and job conditions shape workers' personal lives, requires studying workplaces as well as workers. Although organizational documentation may be viewed as a supplemental source of information when studying workers, it is an essential source of information when investigating workplaces. The additional time it takes to gain access to relevant documentation, to appraise its accuracy, and to develop a strategy for its use can be overwhelming. The very process of developing a strategy for employing organizational documentation can, fortunately, reduce the burden on both the research team and the employer and can help ensure that resources are put to good use.

In most studies, not all components of one's theoretical model require organizational documentation to be measured well. Certainly workers' own experiences with and views of their job and employer are best reported by them via survey methods. Concepts relating to organizational and job level conditions, as well as employees' behaviors at work, on the other hand, may be best captured with information that comes from the workplace rather than the worker. Thus, targeting the use of documentation to measuring particular organizational, job, and work-related variables can help minimize resources expended while maximizing contributions to knowledge.

Not all kinds of work-life research are good candidates for including organizational documentation as a source of measurement, even when concepts are at the organizational and job levels. It may be impractical, for example, to use organizational documentation as a primary source of information in studies that seek to represent a population of organizations; the time needed to identify let alone develop, accurate and reliable sources of information would be prohibitive when gathering data on a large number of organizations. Moreover, efforts to incorporate organizational documentation may be a waste of resources in studies of small workplaces; the best path to knowledge development there may require a focus on informal relationships rather than formal organizational policies or practices.

To the extent there is interest in understanding the work side of work-life issues, there should be interest in increasing the use of organizational documentation as a source of measurement in work-life research. Developing (some) measures from organizational documentation affords the opportunity to reduce problems with common-method variance, to more accurately capture job and organizational-level concepts, and to incorporate aspects of performance that are particularly meaningful to employers. As in any field, by being attuned to promising sources of data and probable sources of bias, work-life researchers can improve methods as they advance theory and practice.

NOTES

[1] My gratitude to the editors and reviewers who provided exceptionally useful feedback on an earlier version of this chapter. Also, thank you to Timothy Hilton for his help in identifying some of the examples provided in this chapter of studies incorporating organizational documentation in workplace-based research.

[2] Our study of workplaces is part of The Project on the Public Economy of Work at the University of Chicago, a multi-year study of the key institutions involved in implementing changes in welfare legislation: public welfare offices, labor market intermediaries, and private employers. The Project is supported by grants from the Ford Foundation, the National Science Foundation, and the Soros' Open Society Institute. Co-Directors: Evelyn Brodkin and Susan Lambert.

[3] The Study on Work–Child Care Fit is supported by a research grant from U.S. Health and Human Services in collaboration with the Joint Center for Poverty Research, and by additional funds from the McCormick-Tribune Center for Early Childhood Research and the Louise R. Bowler Faculty Research Award, School of Social Service Administration.

REFERENCES

Allen, D., Shore, L., & Griffeth, R. (2003). The role of perceived organizational support and supportive human resource practices in the turnover process. *Journal of Management, 29*, 99–118.

Benkhoff, B. (1997). Ignoring commitment is costly: New approaches establish the missing link between commitment and performance. *Human Relations, 30*, 701–726.

Blair-Loy, M., & Wharton, A. (2002). Employee's use of work-family policies and workplace social context. *Social Forces, 80*, 813–845.

Blalock, H. (1982). *Conceptualization and measurement in the social sciences.* Beverly Hills, CA: Sage.

Dalton, D., & Mesch, D. (1990). The impact of flexible scheduling on employee attendance and turnover. *Administrative Science Quarterly, 35*, 370–387.

Duarte, N., Goodson, J., & Klich, N. (1993). How do I like thee? Let me appraise the ways. *Journal of Organizational Behavior, 14*, 239–249.

Eaton, S. (2003). If you can use them: Flexibility policies, organizational commitment, and perceived performance. *Industrial Relations, 45*, 145–167.

Fernandez, R., Castilla, E., & Moore, P. (2000). Social capital at work: Networks and employment at a phone center. *American Journal of Sociology, 5*, 1288–1356.

George, J. (1991). State or trait: Effects of positive mood on prosocial behaviors at work. *Journal of Applied Psychology, 76*, 299–307.

Goodstein, J. (1994). Institutional pressures and strategic responsiveness: Employer involvement in work-family issues. *Academy of Management Journal, 37*, 350–382.

Griffin, R. (1981). A longitudinal investigation of task characteristics relationships. *Academy of Management Journal, 24*, 99–113.

Haley-Lock, A. (2003). *Advancing in one's calling: The roles of internal labor markets and social capital in human services career plateauing.* Unpublished doctoral dissertation, School of Social Service Administration, University of Chicago.

Heckman, J. (1979). Sample selection bias as a specification error. *Econometrica, 47*, 153–161.

Henly, J. R., & Lambert, S. J. (2005). Nonstandard work and child care needs of low-income parents. In S. Bianchi, L. Casper, & R. King (Eds.), *Work, family, health, and well-being.* Mahwah, NJ: Lawrence Erlbaum Associates.

Hopkins, K. (2001). Manager intervention with troubled supervisors: Help and support start at the top. *Management Communication Quarterly, 15*, 83–99.

Hopkins, K. (2002). Interactions of gender and race in workers' help seeking and personal/family problems: Perceptions of supervisor support and intervention. *Journal of Applied Behavioral Science, 38*, 156–176.

Kelly, E., & Dobbin. F. (1999). Civil rights law at work: Sex discrimination and the rise of maternity leave policies. *American Journal of Sociology, 105*, 455–492.

Knez, M., & Simester, D. (2001). Firm-wide incentives and mutual monitoring at Continental Airlines. *Journal of Labor Economics, 29*, 743–772.

Kossek, E. E., Barber, A. E., & Winters, D. (1999). Using flexible schedules in the managerial world: The power of peers. *Human Resource Management Journal, 38*, 36–46.

Kossek, E. E., Huber, M., & Lerner, J. (2003). Sustaining economic and psychological well-being of mothers on public assistance: Individual deficit and social structural accounts. *Journal of Vocational Behavior, 62*, 155–175.

Kossek, E. E., Lautsch, B., & Eaton, S. (2005). Flexibility enactment theory: Implications of flexibility types, control, and boundary management for work-family effectiveness. In E. Kossek & S. Lambert (Eds.), *Work and life integration: Organizational, cultural and Individual perspectives* (pp. 243–261). Mahwah, NJ: Lawrence Erlbaum Associates.

Kossek, E. E., & Nichol, V. (1992). The effects of employer-sponsored child care on employee attitudes and performance. *Personnel Psychology, 45*, 485–509.

Krackhardt, D., McKenn, J., Porter, L., & Steers, R. (1981). Supervisory behavior and employee turnover: A field experiment. *Academy of Management Journal, 24*, 249–259.

Lambert, S. (1998). Workers' use of supportive workplace policies: Variations by race and class-related characteristics. In A. Daly (Ed.), *Workforce diversity: Issues and perspectives* (pp. 297–313). Washington, DC: NASW Press.

Lambert, S. (2000). Added benefits: The link between work-life benefits and organizational citizenship behavior. *Academy of Management Journal, 43*, 801–815.

Lambert, S., & Haley-Lock, A. (2004). The organizational stratification of opportunities for work-life balance: Addressing issues of equality and social justice in the workplace. *Community, Work & Family, 7*, 181–197.

Lambert, S., & Hopkins, K. (1995). Occupational conditions and workers' sense of community: Variations by gender and race. *American Journal of Community Psychology, 23*,151–179.

Lambert, S., & Kossek, E. E. (2005). Future frontiers: Enduring challenges and established assumptions in the work-life field. In E. Kossek & S. Lambert (Eds.), *Work and life integration: Organizational, cultural and Individual perspectives* (pp. 513–532). Mahwah, NJ: Lawrence Erlbaum Associates.

Lambert, S., & Waxman, E. (2005). Organizational stratification: Distributing opportunities for balancing work and personal life. In E. Kossek & S. Lambert (Eds.), *Work and life integration: Organizational, cultural, and individual perspectives* (pp. 103–126). Mahwah, NJ: Lawrence Erlbaum Associates.

Lambert, S., Waxman, E., & Haley-Lock, A. (2002). Against the odds: A study of sources of instability in lower-skilled jobs. Working Paper of *The Project on the Public Economy of Work*, School of Social Service Administration, University of Chicago.

Lyness, K., & Judiesch, M. (2001). Are female managers quitters? The relationship of gender, promotions, and family leaves of absence to voluntary turnover. *Journal of Applied Psychology, 86*, 1167–1178.

Mesch, D., & Dalton, D. (1992). Unexpected consequences of improving workplace justice: A six-year time series assessment. *Academy of Management Journal, 35*, 1099–1114.

Milkovich, G., & Gomez, L. (1976). Day care and selected employee work behaviors. *Academy of Management Journal, 19*, 111–115.

Pierce, J., & Newstrom, J. (1983). The design of flexible work schedules and employee responses: Relationships and process. *Journal of Organizational Behavior, 4*, 247–262.

Raudenbush, S., & Bryk, A. (2002). *Hierarchical linear models: Applications and data analysis methods* (2nd ed.). Thousand Oaks, CA: Sage.

Reskin, B. (2003). Including mechanisms in our models of ascriptive inequality. *American Sociological Review, 68*, 1–121.

Tharenou, P. (1993). A test of reciprocal causality for absenteeism. *Journal of Organizational Behavior, 14*, 269–290.

Yin, R. (2003). *Case study research: Design and methods*. Thousand Oaks, CA: Sage.

25

A Multiple Stakeholder Perspective: Implications for Measuring Work-Family Outcomes

MaryAnne Hyland
Adelphi University

Susan E. Jackson
Rutgers University

This chapter addresses various outcomes related to work/family research. Our objectives are to describe several general categories of outcomes, identify specific outcomes that have been or should be measured in work/family research, and encourage work/family researchers to adopt a framework that recognizes the need to consider outcomes of interest to multiple stakeholders and multiple disciplines. Unlike other chapters in this section, this chapter does not focus on a specific research method, such as experimental interventions or case studies. Instead, we describe several measures that can be used in a variety of research designs.

We begin by considering the perspectives of several groups of organizational stakeholders. Stakeholders are individuals or groups that have legitimate rights and interests in the organization. Their concerns provide a backdrop for our subsequent summary of organization research relevant to evaluating work/family initiatives. After describing the concerns of multiple stakeholders, we present a simple framework that we used to organize this review. Our framework reflects the fact that the concerns of a few stakeholders tend to dominate the organizational literature—not all stakeholders' concerns have been considered.

Next, we tackle the task of summarizing research that illustrates the variety of criteria that organizational researchers have used to assess the effectiveness of work/family initiatives. Throughout this discussion, we address the nature of the various measures, the appropriate level(s) of analysis, and the challenges associated with various measurement approaches. We also provide examples of measures used in past studies.

Finally, we conclude with a discussion of possible future directions for organizational research that evaluates the effectiveness of work/family initiatives. This section addresses some additional methodological issues and describes three specific suggestions for future research: paying more attention to the multiple stakeholder approach, studying work/family practices in the context of an organization's total system for managing human resources, and adopting a multi-disciplinary perspective.

UNDERSTANDING THE PERSPECTIVES
OF MULTIPLE STAKEHOLDERS

A complete assessment of the effectiveness of an organization's human resource management policies and practices—including work/family policies and practices—should consider their impact on all of an organization's primary stakeholders (see Jackson & Schuler, 2006, for a detailed discussion). Typically, the primary stakeholders of an organization include the "owners" (e.g., founders, investors), customers, top-level executives and managers, the organization's employees, and society in general. Here, we describe briefly the concerns of these various stakeholders. Our goal is to illustrate the many possible perspectives that *could* (and, we believe, *should*) be adopted when evaluating the effectiveness of work/family initiatives (see also Mirvis, 1999).

Owners and Investors

Owners and investors are among the most important stakeholders because without their capital, the business could not continue. Regardless of whether an organization operates on a for-profit or not-for-profit basis, the concerns of owners must be satisfied in order for the organization to be assured of long-term survival. When owners evaluate the effectiveness of management practices, they consider whether the practices contribute to the organization's ability to achieve its goals. Thus, for example, workforce management practices are considered effective to the degree that they support the achievement of objectives such as improving productivity, improving profitability, and ensuring the organization's long-term survival. Studies that adopt the perspective of owners often use cost–benefit ratios, financial accounting measures, and stock prices to assess the effectiveness of management practices (Becker & Gerhart, 1996; Becker & Huselid, 1998; Gerhart, 1999).

Customers

The effectiveness of workforce management practices also can be assessed against their effects on customers. Ultimately, customers are satisfied when an organization's management practices serve to improve the quality and variety of products available to customers, the price at which those products can be purchased, the service received, and so on. As the U.S. economy has evolved toward services, the voices of customers have begun to influence numerous management practices. For example, their input is sought to design the jobs of employees, their preferences shape the criteria used to select new employees, and their evaluations may be used to assess employee performance (Schneider & White, 2004). We found no published research that evaluated the effectiveness of work/family practices against criteria that reflected the customer perspective. However, it is reasonable to assume that managers would not be eager to support work/family initiatives that they believe are likely to adversely affect customers. Thus, when Ernst & Young introduced work/family initiatives designed to improve employee retention, they made an effort to ensure that the firm's clients understood why Ernst & Young was changing aspects of how employees worked with clients and how clients were likely to benefit from the firm's new practices (Friedman, Thompson, Carpenter, & Marcel, 2000).

Top Management

Top-level managers and executives are another distinct group of stakeholders whose concerns must be satisfied. The concerns of top-level executives and managers are (ideally) aligned and somewhat redundant with those of owners and customers. In addition, their evaluations of management practices typically include assessments of how much they contribute to achieving strategic goals. Managing the workforce strategically involves developing a comprehensive understanding of the organization's goals and objectives, and then finding ways to help the organization achieve those goals and objectives through the effective management of human resources (Jackson & Schuler, 2003). Generally, workforce management practices are recognized as having strategic value when they help differentiate the organization as an employer of choice, create changes in employee behaviors that add increased value to the organization, and/or reduce labor-related expenses. Long-term HR practices that accomplish these three objectives can be assumed to contribute to improved organizational performance.

Employees and Their Families

Employees and their families also are legitimate stakeholders whose concerns must be addressed. Increasingly, employers recognize that organizational strategies that depend on total quality management, innovation, and/or customer service cannot be met unless employees are dedicated to achieving the goals of the organization. Thus, "soft" indicators of employees' feelings about the organization (e.g., how attractive it is to job applicants, how committed employees feel) are recognized as relevant indicators of effectiveness that are worthy of top management's attention (Schneider & Bowen, 1995). Family considerations, in turn, are often assumed to partially determine these employee attitudes.

Society

Finally, the effects of an organization's management practices on the local community and the broader society should be considered when assessing their effectiveness. The work-family agenda should be considered from a corporate social responsibility view (Pitt-Catsouphes & Googins, 2005). Unfortunately, few for-profit organizations in the United States give much weight to the societal perspective when evaluating management practices, except to the extent that these concerns are embodied in laws and regulations. Nevertheless, proponents of employer initiatives that support work-family balance have argued that such initiatives are consistent with the social responsibilities of employers.

Some types of work/family practices can provide clear benefits to a community. When employers build and manage day-care centers, for example, they provide a service that may decrease the incidence of child neglect and perhaps improve early childhood social and cognitive development. To the extent that such services make it possible for some members of the community to maintain their employment, welfare costs should be lower and tax revenues should be higher.

Ideally, a complete evaluation of work/family initiatives would include assessments of their consequences for all of an organization's primary stakeholders. Our review of the existing organizational literature reveals an incomplete picture, however. To date, most researchers have evaluated work/family practices using criteria that reflect the perspectives of top management and employees and their families. This does not mean that the concerns of all other stakeholders have been completely ignored. Undoubtedly, cost considerations and the potential impact on an organization's customers are routinely taken into account when organizations decide whether or not to adopt a particular work/family initiative. Human resource practitioners and top-level managers often refer to the presumed benefits to society when they describe their organizations' more progressive work/family practices. Nevertheless, we found very little research that documented the many presumed effects of work/family initiatives on outcomes that reflect the concerns of owners, customers, or society in general.

Criteria Used in Organizational Research Relevant to Evaluating Work-Family Initiatives

Outcomes Studied	Degree of Concern for Stakeholder Group (High, Med, Low)				
	Owners	Top Mgt	Customer	Employees and Families	Society
Work Outcomes					
Attracting and Retaining Employees	M	H	M	H	M
Work Performance	H	H	H	M	L
Work Behaviors	L	M	H	M	L
Cost-Related Measures	H	H	M	L	L
Family Outcomes					
Psychological Outcomes	L	L	M	H	M
Family Performance	L	L	L	H	H
Career Outcomes					
Advancement	L	M	L	H	L
Satisfaction	M	M	M	H	M
Income	L	L	M	H	H

Note: The ratings in this table reflect the opinions of the authors. They were not derived empirically. A high rating indicates that members of the stakeholder group are likely to recognize that outcome is directly related to their primary interests. A medium rating indicates our judgment that the outcome has a clear but indirect influence on outcomes that are of primary interest to this stakeholder group. A low rating indicates that we believe members of this stakeholder group would consider this outcome to be, at best, weakly related to their primary concerns.

FRAMEWORK USED TO ORGANIZE OUR REVIEW OF RELEVANT RESEARCH

Table 25.1 provides a summary of the criteria that have been used by organizational researchers interested in work and family issues. The criteria are listed in the order they are discussed in this chapter: work outcomes, family outcomes, and career outcomes. For each category of criterion, we also indicate our assessment of the stakeholder perspectives that are most closely related to use of the criterion.

Work Outcomes

We begin by describing studies that focus on work outcomes. Studies of work outcomes best reflect the concerns of top management and owners. By extension, the concerns of customers also are reflected in these studies. However, the views of customers are seldom directly solicited.

Family Outcomes

Next, we consider studies of family outcomes. Studies of family outcomes usually include the perspectives of employees and they sometimes also directly assess the attitudes and experiences of family members. What distinguishes studies in this category is that the criteria of interest reflect consequences that are realized at home rather than at work.

Career Outcomes

Finally, we consider several outcomes that span the categories of work and family and do not fit neatly into either of these categories. The notion of a career spans the boundaries of work and family since employers are concerned with their employees' careers and the employees themselves also have a personal interest in their career success.

In presenting this review, our primary objective is to summarize the relevant research that has been conducted and published to date. We do not provide a full critique of this work.

WORK-FAMILY INITIATIVES AND WORK OUTCOMES

We have organized work outcomes into four categories: employee attraction and retention, work performance, work behavior, and cost-related measures. Within each of these categories, we have provided what we believe are the primary constructs of interest. However, we recognize that there are other constructs that may be of interest; our list is not exhaustive.

Employee Attraction and Retention

Organizations offering family-friendly policies have been recognized by publications such as *Fortune* and *Working Mother*. These organizations have publicized their placement on popular magazine lists as a recruiting tool. As the composition of the workforce has changed to include more dual-career couples and single parents, attracting such individuals to an organization has become increasingly important. Person–organization fit (Chatman, 1991) may result in applicants choosing organizations that offer family-friendly policies. Subsequently, satisfaction with work/family balance may influence employees' decisions about whether to remain with the organization.

Attracting Employees. We are aware of only two studies that have examined attraction of potential employees as an outcome related to offering family-friendly policies. This is surprising because it implies that many organizations are offering family-friendly policies without having evidence that suggests that such polices do indeed improve the organization's reputation as an employer and thereby increase applicant attraction. Honeycutt and Rosen (1997) found that individuals were attracted to an organization with flexible career paths and policies, but that differences in attraction existed with regard to individuals' salient identities (career primary or family primary). Rau and Hyland (2002) found that attraction to organizations offering flexible work arrangements varied according to level of role conflict and the type of work arrangement offered.

Both Honeycutt and Rosen (1997) and Rau and Hyland (2002) created their own measures of attraction to the organization. Other measures exist in the more general recruitment literature (e.g., Cable & Judge, 1994; Schwoerer & Rosen, 1989). Measures of organizational reputation may be of particular value for understanding how work/family practices influence the perceptions and employment choices of actual and potential job applicants (for a discussion of these and other measures that can be used to assess recruitment activities, see Harris & Lasson, 2003). As applicant attraction is an individual level construct, existing measures use self-reported, individual level data. Clearly, measures of applicant attraction assess the effects of recruitment efforts early in the recruitment and selection process. However, applicant attraction is important to understanding early recruitment efforts (Barber, 1998) and it has been found to be related to applicant beliefs later in the hiring process as well as performance and turnover (Barber, 1998; Cable, Aiman-Smith, Mulvey, & Edwards, 2000).

Retaining Employees. Many employers offer or have considered offering family-friendly policies as a retention strategy (Batt & Valcour, 2003). However, relatively few studies have specifically examined employee retention (or its opposite—turnover) as an outcome of work-family conflict (Boyar, Maertz, Pearson, & Keough, 2003). Recent research on turnover in relation to work/family polices also is quite limited. Batt and Valcour (2003) found that access to flexible scheduling predicted lower turnover intentions; yet, as predicted, dependent care benefits were not related to turnover intentions. Early research on flexible work arrangements found mixed results (e.g., Golembiewski & Proehl, 1978; Nollen & Martin, 1978; Ramsower, 1985), while early research on dependent care benefits generally found that turnover was reduced when such benefits were available or used (Milkovich & Gomez, 1976; Youngblood & Chambers-Cook, 1984).

Although a vast and long-standing literature on turnover exists outside of the work-family arena, there still is no consensus on how to best measure turnover. First, there is the difficulty of measuring actual turnover because individuals who have already quit will not be available to complete interviews or questionnaires. Second, there are challenges related to measuring turnover intentions, because even though most research finds a positive relationship between turnover intentions and actual turnover (e.g., Prestholdt, Lane, & Matthews, 1987; Steel & Ovalle, 1984), the two are not perfectly correlated. Third, despite the fact that turnover models have been developed and tested for over 20 years, a recent reconceptualization of the turnover decision process suggests that past models have not accurately captured the decision of an individual to leave an organization (Steel, 2002).

Turnover is an individual-level construct. Although actual turnover data are most readily garnered from organizational records, managerial reports and individual self-report data can be used to measure turnover. At the most basic level, turnover is measured as a dichotomous variable. However, richer measures may include whether the turnover was voluntary or involuntary as well as more detailed reasons for the separation (e.g., found another job, spouse's job relocated, poor performance, position eliminated).

Lyness and Judiesch (2001) used archival organizational data to measure turnover as voluntary or involuntary, with family-related reasons considered to be voluntary. Two recent studies from the work/family literature measured turnover intentions rather than actual turnover. Batt and Valcour (2003) used an additive scale that consisted of five items. Each item received a score of 0 to 4, with lower scores indicating a serious intention to quit. Boyar, Maertz, Pearson, and Keough (2003) used four items to create a turnover intentions scale. The co-efficient alpha was .90. Other studies have used previously existing measures (e.g., Mobley, Homer, & Hollingsworth, 1978).

Although all turnover and turnover intentions measures must begin at the individual level, departmental or organizational turnover rates can be calculated by aggregating individual-level turnover data. These rates are generally computed as the percentage of employees who leave within a 1-year period; however, other time frames could be used.

Work Performance

Traditionally, researchers interested in measuring the performance of employees assessed how well they accomplished the core tasks that comprised an employee's "job." As the nature of work has changed, managers and researchers alike have gradually adopted a broader view of effective work performance (Arvey & Murphy, 1998; Ilgen & Pulakos, 1999; Murphy & Jackson, 1999). In addition to performing core tasks, the best employees are able to adapt to continuously changing organizational conditions and are willing to accept a broad array of responsibilities associated with being good organizational citizens. In other words, total work performance includes task performance, adaptive performance, and contextual performance (also referred to as organizational citizenship).

Task Performance.   Task performance focuses on core tasks, rather than organizational citizenship that may fall beyond basic performance of one's job duties. Although understanding the distinction between task performance and organizational citizenship is important for all disciplines that study performance, it is especially important for work/family research. Employees participating in certain work/family programs, such as flexible work arrangements, may have difficulty engaging in citizenship behavior due to time restrictions related to their work arrangement, yet they still are able to excel in their task performance. Therefore, using a measure that combines task performance with citizenship behavior may underestimate benefits or overestimate problems associated with a work/family program. For example, if one studied the effect of flextime on overall performance, results may suggest that the effect on overall performance is small. However, if performance is dissected into task performance and organizational citizenship, it may be discovered that flextime has a positive effect on task performance but a negative effect on organizational citizenship, which results in a small effect on overall performance.

Task performance can also be distinguished from productivity, which is the ratio of production divided by the time required for that production (Calvasina & Boxx, 1975), yet not all studies have made this distinction (e.g., Kim & Campagna, 1981). Some organizations have taken the more straightforward approach of measuring sales per employee as a measure of performance (O'Connell, 1996). For many organizations, behavioral measures such as absenteeism and lateness are relevant. Absence and lateness can be highly disruptive for organizations when jobs are designed around teams of employees who are highly interdependent. For employees in jobs that involve providing customer service, absence and lateness interfere with rapid and reliable customer response times. Task performance can be studied at the individual or group level. Employees would be the target of individual-level analysis and work groups would be the target of group level-analysis. We were unable to identify any studies that examined the effects of work-family practices on group-level performance. However, research on individual performance is plentiful. (Although researchers have not always stated that they measured task performance as such, readers can often determine whether the performance measure focused on the task and/or encompassed citizenship behavior.)

Work/family research that studied task performance as an outcome variable has found mixed results. A meta-analysis by Baltes, Briggs, Huff, Wright, and Neuman (1999) found differing effects of various flexible work arrangements on performance or productivity. For example, flextime was found to have positive effects, whereas compressed work weeks had a negative effect on productivity. Supporting earlier work by Milkovich and Gomez (1976), Kossek and Nichol (1992) found no direct effect for using onsite child care on performance.

To measure task performance, many organizations rely on the subjective performance ratings of supervisors and peers. One of the greatest methodological challenges of measuring task performance is obtaining ratings that are reliable, unbiased, and valid. The challenges associated with measuring performance are not solely methodological, however—defining the appropriate domain to be measured can also be a challenge (Arvey & Murphy, 1998). Indeed, entire books have been written about the difficulties associated with measuring employee performance (e.g., Coens & Jenkins, 2000; Ilgen & Pulakos, 1999; Murphy & Cleveland, 1991; Smither, 1998). Because no approach to measuring task performance (or any type of performance) is problem-free, researchers may find it useful to use multiple approaches. For example, an estimated 5% use the employees' own self-ratings of performance (for a full discussion, see Atwater, 1998). However, such self-ratings often differ from ratings by others (e.g., Atkins & Wood, 2002). In addition to subjective ratings, organizational researchers have also measured performance using behavioral measures such as absenteeism and lateness as well as objective indicators of productivity (see Baltes et al., 1999). Adopting this approach, Kossek and Nichol (1992) measured performance using both supervisor-rated performance and absenteeism. Ultimately, the choice of measures should depend on the research objective. At times, theoretical considerations may dictate the decision of how to measure performance. When the objective includes influencing how an organization manages its employees, however, researchers may find it most effective to use the performance measures that the organization has adopted for use in its own internal decision making.

Contextual Performance.   Several terms have been used to describe the notion of good organizational citizenship, including extra-role performance, pro-social behavior, and contextual performance. Regardless of which term is used, the focus is the beneficial things that people do at work that are beyond the scope of their required work. Social exchange theory (Blau, 1964) and the norm of reciprocity (Gouldner, 1960) suggest that individuals feel obligated to reciprocate when they receive something from another individual or entity. If workers feel the need to reciprocate for the organization offering them work-family benefits, discretionary contextual performance may be the preferred form of reciprocal payment (Lambert, 2000; see also Lambert, 1999).

Contextual performance has traditionally been measured at the individual level (e.g., Podsakoff, MacKenzie, Moorman, & Fetter, 1990). Although some studies have tried to measure the contextual performance of work groups (e.g., Bachrach, Bendoly, & Podskaoff, 2001; Bommer, Miles, & Grover, 2003), we are unaware of any work-family studies that have considered contextual performance at any level other than the individual level. Even research on individual-level contextual performance is rare in the work-family arena. Lambert (2000) found that workers' perceptions of the usefulness of work-family benefits were positively related to organizational citizenship behaviors. Her study used three measures: a four-item index of helping behaviors, a dichotomous variable indicating whether or not an individual had submitted any suggestions as part of a company suggestion system during a 2-year period, and attendance at lunch hour quality meetings. Again, the dearth of work-family research in this area may be due to the fact that many individuals believe that work-family benefits and contextual performance should not have a positive relationship; yet according to Lambert's (2000) study, this is not the case.

Adaptive Performance.   Unlike task performance and contextual performance, both of which have been studied a great deal, adaptive performance has only recently been proposed as an important dimension of work performance (Campbell, 1999; Hesketh & Neal, 1999; Pulakos, Arad, Donovan, & Plamondon, 2000). Adaptive performance can be loosely defined as the ability to manage new experiences by adapting or being flexible. However, recent research suggests that this construct is more complex than implied by this simple definition. Pulakos et al. (2000) developed a taxonomy of adaptive performance that takes into account multiple dimensions, such as handling emergencies or crisis situations and handling work stress. These researchers also developed a psychometrically sound measure of this outcome, called the Job Adaptability Inventory (JAI).

Although to our knowledge no work-family studies have examined adaptive performance, we think it is an important outcome to consider, given that work-family benefits often result from workplaces experiencing changes in the composition of the workforce (e.g., an increased percentage of women) and that work-family benefits may be related to a worker's ability to adapt to a changing environment if such benefits improve the employee's flexibility.

Work Behaviors

Although many consider performance to be the ultimate work outcome, work behaviors also are important to measure, either because they are known to be antecedents to performance or because they are considered valued outcomes in and of themselves. Absenteeism and tardiness are two work behaviors often discussed in the work-family literature. Presumably, work-family benefits have the potential to alleviate otherwise incompatible role pressures that may result in high rates of absenteeism or lateness (see Katz & Kahn, 1978, for a detailed discussion of role theory.) Some work-family benefits, such as flexible work arrangements, may even alter the relevance of absenteeism and lateness as they are traditionally measured if such arrangements do not require employees to be working at specified times or on specified days. Cooperativeness is another potentially important work behavior; employees may be more cooperative at work if stress in their home life is reduced by work-family benefits.

Absenteeism.   On a typical day in the United States, 2 to 3% of employees fail to show up for work, costing employers millions of dollars in lost productivity. A long tradition of research has shown that having children is positively related to absenteeism, and more recent research has shown that having elder care responsibilities also is positively related to absenteeism (Boise & Neal, 1996).

Although measuring absenteeism may seem straightforward, there are different approaches to doing so. One decision that researchers must make is whether they want to measure all absenteeism or only absenteeism related to family matters. For example, Anderson, Coffey, and Byerly (2002) used the measure designed for the National Study of the Changing Workforce (Bond, Galinsky, & Swanberg, 1998), which asked respondents about the frequency of their absenteeism due to (a) the need to care for a sick child, (b) because their usual child care was not available, or (c) for other family reasons. Hammer, Bauer, and Grandey (2003) used a one-item measure that asked respondents how many days they have missed work due to family/personal-related issues. Both of these examples point out another important component of an absenteeism measure: One must determine the relevant period of time to be included. For the previous examples, Bond et al. (1998) asked respondents to base their response on their experience in the previous 3 months, and Hammer et al. (2003) asked respondents to consider the previous 4 months. Another possibility for measuring absenteeism is to use organizational records. This approach has the advantage of being more objective than the self-reported measures. However, unless the organization collects data on the reason for an employee's absence, such organizational data cannot serve as a measure of family-related absenteeism, but rather must serve as an overall measure of absenteeism. Interestingly, in a meta-analysis on personality and absenteeism (not specific to the work-family literature), only non-self-report measures of absenteeism were included (Ones, Viswesvaran, & Schmidt, 2003). Most were from organizational records and a few were from supervisory records. Although supervisory reports could yield richer data than organizational records, this would require that the supervisors know whether or not an employee's absence was due to family reasons. Kossek and Nichol (1992) used such a measure by having supervisors report their perception of the degree to which child care affected employee attendance, including partial absences such as lateness. The authors stated that they chose this measure because organizational records did not permit the distinction between absence related to child care and other causes.

As one of the goals of this review is to address levels of analysis, we would be remiss to only acknowledge absenteeism at the individual level. Like other individual behaviors, absence behaviors can be aggregated to study group-level phenomena. It is possible that the true effects on absence of work-family initiatives would be more accurately captured by studying absence rates for work units. As many organizations have learned, programs that reward and recognize employees with outstanding attendance records are one effective approach to minimizing absenteeism. When work-family initiatives make it possible for more employees to maintain better attendance records, organizations may find that they can raise the criteria used in such programs (e.g., require longer records of perfect attendance or lower the number of allowed absences in order to receive recognition or a reward). If the criteria for excellence are raised for the work unit, it is likely that absenteeism for the unit will decline.

Lateness.   Like absenteeism, lateness is a type of work withdrawal behavior (Hammer, Bauer, & Grandey, 2003). Some researchers have identified lateness as a form of partial absence (e.g., Hepburn & Barling, 1996). Other aspects of partial absence include leaving work early and nonwork telephone conversations. Studies have found that work–eldercare conflict is related to partial absenteeism (Barling, MacEwen, Kelloway, & Higginbottom, 1994; Hepburn & Barling, 1996). In a study of dual-earner couples, Hammer and colleagues (2003) found that work-family conflict is related to wife lateness but not husband lateness. Blau (1995) pointed out that in the management literature, lateness has experienced "empirical neglect" compared to other withdrawal behaviors, such as absenteeism and turnover (p. 1483).

Lateness can be measured from self-report data, managerial report data or organizational records, although for upper-level employees, the organization may not track lateness. One early study on lateness (Adler & Golan, 1981) used time clock records to obtain an objective measure of lateness. Lateness was defined by organizational policy (which was being more than 7 minutes late in the sample organization). As with absenteeism, the authors needed to determine the relevant time frame over which to examine lateness. They chose a 1-year period. Another study (Blau, 1995) used a 9-month period. Both Adler and Golan (1981) and Blau (1995) used frequency (the number of times an individual was late) and duration (the total number of minutes the individual was late) measures for lateness. However, Adler and Golan (1981) measured duration as the number of minutes late per incident, whereas Blau (1995) measured the total number of minutes late for the 9-month period. Following his earlier work (Blau, 1994), Blau calculated an overall lateness score by multiplying frequency by duration. As with absenteeism, there does not seem to be a readily apparent way to calculate group-level lateness.

Cooperativeness.   Although we were unable to find any work-family studies that considered cooperativeness as an outcome of interest, we feel that this construct is worthy of a brief discussion as a work behavior. Both the academic and practitioner literatures address many employers' desire to be recognized as a "great place to work." Such places are characterized by positive relationships between employees and their managers and coworkers (Great Place to Work Institute, 2004). Establishing a culture in which people cooperate is beneficial for employers, who can invest less in managing conflict and the problems that arise when employees fail to work as an integrated team or work unit. We feel that this construct could be informative for work-family research because cooperativeness is possible even when employees have flexible work arrangements or dependent care arrangements that result in rigid schedules. Including measures of cooperativeness in future research would be relatively easy, as several measures of this construct have already been developed and used in psychological research (e.g., Ross, Rausch, & Canada, 2003).

Cost-Related Measures

During the past decade, human resource managers have experienced increasing pressure to document the effects of HR practices on "the bottom line." Among researchers who study HR practices, the most well-developed approaches to estimating the cost-effectiveness of specific HR practices are utility analysis (e.g., Schmidt, Hunter, MacKenzie, & Muldrow, 1979; Boudreau, 1991; Boudreau, 2003; Boudreau & Ramstad, 2003) and cost accounting (see Cascio, 2000; Flamholtz, 1999). The goal of both approaches is to determine whether the dollar value of the benefits associated with introducing a new practice (e.g., a work-life initiative) is greater than the total dollar value of all costs associated with the new practices. Essential to both utility analysis and cost accounting is the ability to accurately determine the true costs and all benefits of both current practices and the new initiatives being considered.

Regardless of the technical merits of utility analysis and cost accounting and their potential usefulness, these methods for assessing the effectiveness of HR practices—including work-family initiatives—have not been widely adopted by organizations. Instead, most firms continue to rely on subjective estimates and intuition when assessing the effectiveness of their HR practices (Becker, Huselid, & Ulrich, 2001). Undoubtedly, there are many explanations for the slow adoption rate of utility analysis and cost accounting methods, including the fact that these measures may not reflect fundamental strategic objectives or the concerns of a broader set of important stakeholders (Donaldson & Preston, 1995; Jayne & Rauschenberger, 2000).

Recently, however, there has been renewed interest in developing cost-related metrics for evaluating workforce management practices. HR consultants now offer a broader variety of more sophisticated measures intended to assess HR effectiveness, including measures that estimate the economic value added or return-on-investment for a variety of activities (e.g., see Becker et al., 2001; Fitz-Enz, 2002). Much of this work adopts the perspective of human capital theory. The crux of this theory is that people are of value to the organization to the extent they make it productive (Becker, 1964; Becker & Huselid, 1998; Lepak & Snell, 1999). Thus, organizations make decisions about investing in people just as they make decisions about investing in machinery, viewing them as a form of capital. Costs related to attracting, training, retraining, motivating, and monitoring the organization's workforce are viewed as investments in the human capital of the firm, just as maintenance of machinery would constitute an investment in the capital of the firm (Flamholtz, 1999; Wright et al., 1994; Wright, Dunford, & Snell, 2001). This reasoning suggests that the value of human resource management practices can be estimated using macro-level financial indicators of firm performance, such as stock price or the ratio of the market-to-book valuation.

A recent study illustrates the type of research associated with this more macro-level approach to evaluating HR practices (see Arthur, 2003). The investigator focused on firms that appeared in the annual list of Fortune 500 companies for the years 1971 through 1996. For these firms, the investigator used public announcements of work-family initiatives as predictors of the firm's performance in the stock market. The results showed that shareholder returns increased significantly on the day a work-family initiative was announced. Furthermore, this effect remained over the subsequent 3-day trading period. The effect was somewhat stronger for high-tech firms and those that employed more women. Presumably, these stronger effects were found because attracting and retaining talent was more challenging for these firms and being successful was more likely to lead to improved firm performance over time. A similar methodology was used by Cascio (2004) in a study that found that the *Working Mother* Best 100 companies had superior stock performance to the S&P 500 companies. Hannon and Milkovich (1996) also studied firms identified as one of "the best" companies for working mothers and found that being on this list resulted in stock price gains of .69%.

Research strategies such as those just described are quite new and interpreting the results of such studies is fraught with many challenges. Nevertheless, such findings may help to shift researchers away from a narrow focus on estimating the costs and benefits associated with work/family initiatives and toward understanding the more interesting question of why investors are willing to pay a premium to own stock in family-friendly firms.

WORK-FAMILY INITIATIVES AND FAMILY OUTCOMES

We turn next to research that provides insights into how the family lives of employees can be affected by employers' work-family policies and practices. To organize the research relevant to the family domain, we have grouped studies into two major categories: employees' psychological reactions and outcomes that more directly reflect an employee's family role performance.

Psychological Outcomes

Employees' psychological reactions to issues that arise from involvement in work and family roles are too numerous to list. However, those that have drawn the most attention from researchers can be easily categorized into three types: the experience of conflict, strain, and relationship/marital satisfaction.

Role Conflict.   Although early research on work/family conflict did not distinguish between conflict that emanates from work and affects family and conflict that originates at home and affects work, the bi-directional nature of such role conflict is now widely accepted. Thus, work/family research includes measures of work-to-family conflict and family-to-work conflict, even though the subject of the research may only specify work/family conflict. For purposes of this discussion, we refer to work/family role conflict as the general construct related to conflict flowing either into or out of work and we refer to work-to-family and family-to work conflict as the directional measures related to the construct.

A great deal of the existing literature on work/family conflict has examined such conflict as a predictor of various outcomes. A meta-analytic review of 34 sample groups examined the relationship of work-to-family and family-to-work conflict on the outcomes of job satisfaction and life satisfaction (Kossek & Ozeki, 1998). Other recent studies have also considered work/family conflict as a predictor (e.g., Boles, Howard, & Donofrio, 2001, O'Driscoll et al., 2003). However, work/family conflict also is an important outcome itself. A recent study examined the effects of telecommuting on work/family conflict (Madsen, 2003). Another study examined the effects of a supportive work-family culture on work-family conflict (Thompson, Beauvais, & Lyness, 1999).

Work/family conflict is an individual level construct that is generally measured using self-reported data. Many reliable, valid scales have been developed and used by organizational researchers. For example, Netemeyer, Boles, and McMurrian (1996) developed and validated work-to-family and family-to-work measures. In addition to addressing the bi-directional nature of work/family conflict, Carlson, Kacmar, and Williams (2000) took a multi-dimensional approach to the development of a work/family conflict measure by identifying three forms of work-family conflict: time, strain, and behavior-based. The lack of consistency among measures of work-family conflict may be responsible for differences in research results (Kossek & Ozeki, 1998). Avoiding measurement variation was the purpose of Carlson et al.'s (2000) development of a comprehensive measure that followed Kossek and Ozeki's (1998) suggestion to distinguish between attitudinal and activity-based measures of work-family conflict.

Strain.   Psychological strain and self-reported symptoms of related health problems have been studied as work/family outcomes for many years. For example, Cooke and Rousseau (1984) examined the effects of holding work and family roles on role strain, psychological distress, and somatic complaints. Today, research on the effects of work/family conflict on psychological strain and stress continues, but with various mediating and moderating factors taken into account. For example, like earlier researchers, O'Driscoll et al. (2003) found an overall correlation between work/family conflict and psychological strain, but they did not find that family-supportive organizational policies mediated this relationship.

Psychological strain is measured at the individual level. Most researchers have used preexisting scales to measure such strain. For example, O'Driscoll et al. (2003) used a 13-item measure developed by Caplan, Cobb, French, Harrison, and Pinneau (1980). In the marketing literature, Boles, Johnston, and Hair (1997) used an adaptation of the Maslach Burnout Inventory (Maslach & Jackson, 1981) to measure emotional exhaustion in relation to work/family conflict. A study by Hammer, Saksvik, Nytro, Torvatn, and Bayazit (2004) measured job stress by using Cooper's Job Stress Scale (Cooper, 1981). This study also included subjective health symptoms, which were measured using a scale from the European Foundation (1997). Frone, Russell, and Cooper (1997) also studied physical manifestations of stress, including overall health and hypertension.

Relationship/Marital Satisfaction.   This psychological outcome has traditionally been thought of as marital satisfaction; however, as organizations increasingly recognize domestic partnerships, more inclusive measures of relationship satisfaction may become commonplace. Unlike most work/family measures, marital satisfaction is most useful when considered in studies of couples. Those studies in which marital satisfaction is not a focal construct are most likely to measure only one partner's level of marital satisfaction (e.g., Chiu, Man, & Thayer, 1998). Studies that focus on marital satisfaction more often include data from both partners. For example, Schulz, Cowan, Cowan, and Brennan (2004) used the validated Marital Adjustment Test (MAT; Locke & Wallace, 1959) to measure husbands' and wives' marital satisfaction in their study of the impact of workday experiences on couples' interactions. Although Roehling and Bultman (2002) also focused on couples, their measure of marital satisfaction was much simpler. They used a single item that asked respondents to rate on a scale from 0 (not satisfied at all) to 100 (absolutely satisfied) how satisfied they were with their current relationship. Such single-item measures generally are not recommended because it is impossible to separate the different sources of variability in the indicator (Pedhazur & Schmelkin, 1991).

Family Performance

Although family performance includes the ability of individuals to fulfill all of their family roles, the work and family literature focuses primarily on outcomes related to children. This is largely due to debates on the effects of parental employment, specifically maternal employment, on children. Friedman and Greenhaus (2000) developed a model to explain how work affects the ability of parents to care for their children. The outcomes in this model are parental performance, parental satisfaction with child care, children's health, and children's school performance. We focus our discussion on child-related outcomes and collapse other outcomes into a category labeled "accountability to family."

Child General Health.   The physical and mental health of children can be affected by parental employment. General health may be improved as a result of the income produced from a parent's employment due to improved access to medical care (Friedman & Greenhaus, 2000). However, most research on child health focuses on mental health and development.

Child Adjustment.   Behavioral functioning of children also has been shown to be related to parental employment. Much of the research on such child adjustment comes from the psychology literature. Studies often rely on national samples, such as the National Longitudinal Survey of Youth (NLSY), and the measures that such studies include. For example, past research using the NLSY for samples have included measures of short-term memory and attentiveness, compliance, behavior problems, and self-esteem (Harvey, 1999; Vandell & Ramanan, 1992). These measures are individual level self-report scales, scales that are completed by the child's mother, or child assessment scores. The child's mother completes the Behavior Problems Index (BPI; Peterson & Zill, 1986). It assesses peer conflicts, hyperactivity, and anxiety, along with other behavior problems (Vandell & Ramanan, 1992). Self-esteem is measured with the Self-Perception Profile for Children (Harter, 1985), which is a self-report questionnaire for children ages 8 and older. Compliance is reported by the mother using a temperament scale developed specifically for the NLSY (United States Bureau of Labor Statistics). The NLSY also includes many other measures of child adjustment.

Child Cognitive Development.   Studies on early maternal employment have found negative effects of maternal employment on child cognitive development, although these effects generally are not universal and are sometimes offset by positive effects of later maternal employment (e.g., Blau & Grossberg, 1992; Harvey, 1999; Waldfogel, Han, & Brooks-Gunn, 2002). Most of the research on the effects of parental employment rely on achievement test scores to measure cognitive development or intellectual ability. The Peabody Picture Vocabulary Test (PPVT) and Peabody Individual Achievement Tests (PIAT) for math and reading are commonly reported in the literature. These and other assessments of cognitive development are included in the NLSY child surveys.

Accountability to Family.   In addition to child health, adjustment, and development, work/family balance can affect other outcomes in the family domain. The availability for various household chores is one potential outcome. Creating a supportive home environment is another. The NLSY has included the Home Observation Measurement of the Environment (HOME) for one cohort that it tracks. This inventory assesses the quality of a child's home environment, as measured by such factors as the ways in which parents spend time with their children, emotional support, and access to educational materials (Earle, 2001). Other studies have used questionnaires to measure outcomes such as paternal contribution to child care, housework, and percentage of overall family income (Almeida, Maggs, & Galambos, 1993; Deutsch, Lussier, & Servis, 1993). For example, husband's contribution to housework was measured with a seven-item scale and husband's contribution to child care was measured by a five-item scale, both of which were completed by both husbands and wives in a study that focused on paternal participation in child care and housework as the outcomes of interest (Deutsch, Lussier, & Servis, 1993).

WORK-FAMILY INITIATIVES AND CAREER OUTCOMES

As mentioned previously, the career outcomes of employees are of concern to employers and employees alike. Many employees consider advancement to be an important reward for doing well, and employers understand that frustration over lack of advancement is one of the primary reasons for turnover among top performers. Thus, both have a common interest in work practices that facilitate the ability of employees to advance at an acceptable rate over time. Similarly, maintaining high levels of employee satisfaction serves both employees, who benefit directly, and employers, who benefit from the improved work performance and reduced costs associated with work behaviors that are associated with dissatisfaction.

Advancement

Advancement is a well-known issue in the work-family literature, largely because of "glass ceiling" and "mommy track" research. Unfortunately, there has been little effort among researchers to develop valid and reliable measures of career advancement. One reason for the lack of development of such measures may be the fact that advancement can be measured objectively with organization data. If an organization tracks job titles or uses a tier system that classifies jobs by level, researchers can easily compute a measure of advancement by looking at changes in individuals' jobs (see Dreher & Bretz, 1991, or Lyness & Judiesch, 2001, for examples). Tharenou (1999) used a three-item measure that was the average of managerial level, salary and managerial promotions, with each of the three measured on a six-point scale. However, some researchers try to measure advancement using surveys. Such research often asks respondents for information regarding their advancement intentions (e.g., Cutler & Jackson, 2002). The Power and Fast Track Job (PFTJ) scale was developed to address job advancement potential and was found to be valid and reliable by its authors (Kelly & Marin, 1998). Although such measures of behavioral intentions are important, research also should examine the relationship between advancement intentions and actual advancement.

Satisfaction

There are several forms of satisfaction that are relevant to work/family research. Job satisfaction is most closely related to work, whereas career satisfaction and life satisfaction are outcomes associated with the personal domain.

Job Satisfaction. Although job satisfaction can be classified as a work-related outcome, we have categorized it as a career outcome because of the potential impact of such satisfaction on an individual's career. It is an individual-level construct that has generally been measured by self-report surveys. Kossek and Ozeki's (1998) meta-analysis found that the studies included in the analysis used preexisting measures of job satisfaction, but unlike life satisfaction, there was no consistency in the measures of job satisfaction that were used.

Career Satisfaction. Work/family conflict has been suggested to have important effects on individuals' career satisfaction (Powell & Mainiero, 1992). As an individual-level attitude, such satisfaction has been measured using self-reported survey instruments. Martins, Eddleston, and Veiga (2002) used a three-item measure that drew from earlier measures of career satisfaction. Burke (2002) also relied on a previously developed measure.

Life Satisfaction. One of the advantages of studying life satisfaction as an outcome is it comprehensiveness, as it relates to all life domains. It is an individual-level construct and has traditionally been measured by self-report surveys. In Kossek and Ozeki's (1998) meta-analysis on job and life satisfaction in relation to work-family conflict, almost all of the included studies used Quinn and Staines' (1978) measure of life satisfaction. Other studies have examined quality of work life, which includes an assessment of life satisfaction (e.g., Greenhaus, Bedeian, & Mossholder, 1987).

Income

Another outcome with both work and family implications is income. Surprisingly, work/family research often excludes this construct, despite debates in the literature about whether it is possible to "have it all" in terms of work or family, or whether sacrifices must be made in one realm or the other. Two notable exceptions to the dearth in the literature are studies by Schneer and Reitman (1990, 1993), which tracked the income of MBA couples and examined differences in the couples' working patterns. Income can be measured at the individual level or the family level. Self-reports or organizational records are straightforward approaches to collecting income data.

DIRECTIONS FOR FUTURE RESEARCH

Methodological Challenges

As is true for any body of work, the studies that we have referred to throughout this chapter vary greatly in terms of methodological rigor and statistical sophistication. Generally, however, organizational research on work/family initiatives is conducted using cross-sectional designs that prevent researchers from ruling out reverse causality. Many studies are conducted using only self-report data, which often is biased, and may not yield conclusions that are as valid as studies that gather data from multiple sources. In addition, most studies examine outcomes in either the work or the family domain, but not both. Due to the difficulty of conducting true field experiments, even the conclusions that flow from the most rigorous research available should be accepted with caution. The problem of reverse causality is created by the fact that observed relationships between work/family initiatives and so-called outcomes may be due to cause-and-effect relationships other than the one of interest to researchers. For example, if a study shows that organizations that invest more heavily in work/family initiatives are more profitable, what can one conclude? One possibility is that investments in work/family initiatives lead to greater profitability. Alternatively, perhaps profitable organizations are more likely to invest in work/family initiatives. Rigorous study designs can be used to greatly reduce this problem, but such designs are seldom used because the time and expense required makes them less feasible.

Spillover theory (Crouter, 1984) proposes that what happens at work "spills over" into the home realm and what happens at home "spills over" into the work realm. That is, according to spillover theory, "work" outcomes such as attendance and productivity are likely to also have consequences for family life. Some of these outcomes may be positive (e.g., more pay) while others may be negative (e.g., more fatigue). Conversely, "family" outcomes may spill into work. It follows that research on the effects of work/family initiatives can most accurately assess the full range of outcomes when it includes assessments of outcomes in both domains. Unfortunately, very few studies achieve this goal. Instead, most studies assess only work-related outcomes *or* family-related outcomes. Thus, most research does not permit conclusions to be drawn about the total effectiveness of work/family initiatives.

As is true for the field of management in general, there is a great need for more research that employs rigorous methods to evaluate the effectiveness of various approaches to managing work/family issues. Excellent scholarly resources are available to guide anyone interested in conducting such research (e.g., see Edwards, Scott, & Raju, 2003). What is less certain is whether organizations are willing to devote the time and effort that is needed to adequately assess the full range of outcomes that could be influenced by their work/family initiatives.

Multiple Stakeholders Approach

We began this chapter by briefly describing the concerns of several primary stakeholder groups that must be satisfied in order for an organization to be assured of long-term prosperity. These stakeholders include investors/owners, top management, customers, employees and their families, and society. To date, research relevant to establishing the effectiveness of work/family practices has typically adopted the perspective of only one group of stakeholders. For example, a study might consider outcomes of interest primarily to employees and their families while ignoring consequences of more direct concern to top management (e.g., job performance). Of course, studies that do the opposite also are prevalent.

Going forward, research that adopts the perspective of multiple stakeholders would be valuable. The principle that effective management requires attending to all relevant stakeholders is as true for work/family initiatives as it is of other management practices. Work-family practices cannot be designed solely to meet the needs of employees and their families. Nor can they be designed by considering only their consequences for customer service or the bottom line. To the extent that researchers can establish that progressive work/family practices can improve the satisfaction of multiple stakeholders simultaneously, such practices are more likely to be adopted by employers and retained even in the face of difficult economic conditions. We acknowledge that in many cases, individual studies will focus on one or a few stakeholders. This is often necessary due to the constructs that are being studied or the samples that are available. However, the work/family literature as a whole must adapt a multiple stakeholder approach that uses a variety of measures for examining work/family practices and issues.

Work/Family Initiatives and Integrated Human Resources Systems

Recent theoretical developments in the management literature provide compelling reasons to include the views of multiple stakeholders in future research on work/family initiatives. Recently, research in the general field of human resource management has been significantly influenced by the resource-based view of organizations. The resource-based view emphasizes the need for resources as being primary in the determination of policies and procedures (Wernerfelt, 1984). Organizations are viewed as being able to succeed by gaining and retaining control over scarce, valuable, and inimitable resources (Barney, 1990; Porter, 1980).

In larger organizations, the HR department can be viewed as controlling scarce resources to the extent that it controls access to the skills necessary for the achievement of strategic goals (Lepak & Snell, 2003). Thus, for example, an appealing approach to work/family balance should be valuable to firms that face stiff competition in their efforts to lure and retain top talent. Furthermore, the resource-based view emphasizes the importance of ensuring that a firm's work/family practices are integrated elements of a coherent HR *system*. Whereas it may be relatively easy for competitors to copy or imitate any single HR practice, it is more difficult to copy an entire system of practices that are aligned with each other and that serve the specific needs of the organization (Wright et al., 1994; Lado & Wilson, 1994).

The resource-based view highlights the importance of understanding how all the elements of an HR system work in concert with each other. For example, it suggests that specific work/family initiatives are more likely to be effective when they are aligned with all of the other elements of the organization's HR system. This idea is consistent with some of the assumptions that seem to be prevalent in organizations. For example, it is widely believed that work/family initiatives are ineffective in retaining top talent when employees believe that the criteria used to make promotion decisions penalize employees who make use of those initiatives. Another common belief is that progressive work/family practices can be used to counterbalance the otherwise negative effects of offering pay that is somewhat below the market average.

Research that attempts to shed light on the issue of how the elements of an HR system work in concert to influence the reactions of employees and the performance of organizations is in its infancy, emerging only during the last decade. Much of this research has sought to identify the so-called best practices and high-performance work systems (e.g., Becker & Huselid, 1998; Cappelli & Neumark, 2001). The logic underlying this research is that properly aligned HR practices are mutually reinforcing, which bolster their overall effectiveness; when mismatched, HR practices may work against each other and their effectiveness is diminished (Delery, 1998; Lawler, 1992; Lawler, Mohrman, & Ledford, 1992).

Several empirical studies have shown that firms that have an entire set of so-called high-performance HR practices outperform firms with none or only a few of these practices. However, as critics have pointed out, there has been some inconsistency in the specific practices that various authors consider to be among the preferred practices, making it difficult to draw general conclusions about which practices qualify as "best practices" (e.g., see Becker & Gerhart, 1996). Perhaps most disturbing for those interested in work/family initiatives, researchers in this area almost never include work/family initiatives in their measures of "best practices." Thus, there is clearly an opportunity for new research that adopts the perspective of the emerging field of strategic HRM and also incorporates measures of work/family practices as components of a total HR system.

Multi-Discipline Research

We have attempted to draw from several disciplines when compiling this chapter. Human resource management, psychology, and sociology are heavily drawn on in this review. However, more accounting, economics, and marketing information would help to inform the business case for work/family initiatives. Likewise, education and health care information would improve the understanding of the family outcomes of work/family initiatives. Given the dual outcome realms of work and home associated with this line of research, more multi-discipline research could change the pattern of business scholars focusing more on business outcomes and family specialists focusing more on family outcomes. Teams of researchers from different disciplines working together could provide broader perspectives that improve the quality of work/family research.

CONCLUSION

This chapter has attempted to clarify how measures from work/family research can be classified as well as to provide an overview of specific measures and the advantages and disadvantages of several possible measures. We hope that the information provided here is useful for individuals who are trying to choose a measurement approach for their work. We also hope that our discussion in this chapter may spark ideas about how to better measure outcomes in work/family research. With improved research attention on measures related to work/family practices, we hope that the quality and cohesiveness of this body of research will result in significant advances in our shared understanding of the phenomena related to the worlds of work and family.

Due to space constraints, we were not able to describe specific steps for measuring all of the constructs we discussed. For more details about measures, we encourage readers to study the original sources cited throughout this chapter. In addition, readers may wish to consult the Center for Work and Family's *Metrics Manual* (1999), which includes specific items that can be used to assess many of the constructs we have referred to as potential measures for assessing how work/family initiatives influence various outcomes.

ACKNOWLEDGMENTS

We wish to thank Tanille Edwards for her assistance with this chapter.

REFERENCES

Adler, S., & Golan, J. (1981). Lateness as a withdrawal behavior. *Journal of Applied Psychology, 66,* 544–554.
Almeida, D. M., Maggs, J. L., & Galambos, N. L. (1993). Wives' employment hours and spousal participation in family work. *Journal of Family Psychology, 7,* 233–244.

Anderson, S. E., Coffey, B. S., & Byerly, R. T. (2002). Formal organizational initiatives and informal workplace practices: Links to work-family conflict and job-related outcomes. *Journal of Management, 28*, 787–810.

Arthur, M. M. (2003). Share price reactions to work-family initiatives: An institutional perspective. *Academy of Management Journal, 46*, 497–505.

Arvey, R. D., & Murphy, K. R. (1998). Performance evaluation in work settings. In J. Spence (Ed.), *Annual review of psychology* (pp. 141–168). Stanford, CA: Annual Reviews.

Atkins, P. W. B., & Wood, R. E. (2002). Self- versus others' ratings as predictors of assessment center ratings: Validation evidence for 360-degree feedback programs. *Personnel Psychology, 55*, 871–904.

Atwater, L. E. (1998). The advantages and pitfalls of self-assessment in organizations. In J. W. Smither (Ed.), *Performance appraisal: State of the art in practice* (pp. 331–369). San Francisco: Jossey-Bass.

Bachrach, D. G., Bendoly, E., & Podsakoff, P. M. (2001). Attributions of the causes of group performance as an alternative explanation of the relationship between organizational citizenship behavior and organizational performance. *Journal of Applied Psychology, 86*, 1285–1293.

Baltes, B. B., Briggs, T. E., Huff, J. W., Wright, J. A., & Neuman, G. A. (1999). Flexible and compressed workweek schedules: A meta-analysis of their effects on work-related criteria. *Journal of Applied Psychology, 84*, 496–513.

Barber, A. E. (1998). *Recruiting employees: Individual and organizational perspectives*. Thousand Oaks, CA: Sage.

Barling, J., MacEwen, K. E., Kelloway, E. K., & Higginbottom, S. F. (1994). Predictors and outcomes of elder-care based interrole conflict. *Psychology and Aging, 9*, 391–397.

Barney, J. B. (1990). Firm resources and sustained competitive advantage. *Journal of Management, 17*, 99–120.

Batt, R., & Valcour, P. M. (2003). Human resources practices as predictors of work-family outcomes and employee turnover. *Industrial Relations, 42*, 189–220.

Becker, B., & Gerhart, B. (1996). The impact of human resource management on organizational performance: Progress and prospects. *Academy of Management Journal, 39*, 779–801.

Becker, B. E., & Huselid, M. A. (1998). High performance work systems and firm performance: A synthesis of research and managerial implications. In G. Ferris (Ed.), *Research in personnel and human resources management* (pp. 53–101). Greenwich, CT: JAI Press.

Becker, B. E., Huselid, M. A., & Ulrich, D. (2001). *The HR scorecard: Linking people, strategy, and performance*. Boston: Harvard Business School Press.

Becker, G. S. (1964). *Human capital*. New York: National Bureau of Economic Research.

Blau, F. D., & Grossberg, A. J. (1992). Maternal labor supply and children's cognitive development. *The Review of Economics and Statistics, 74*, 474–481.

Blau, G. (1994). Developing and testing a taxonomy of lateness behavior. *Journal of Applied Psychology, 70*, 442–450.

Blau, G. (1995). Influence of group lateness on individual lateness: A cross-level examination. *Academy of Management Journal, 5*, 1483–1496.

Blau, P. M. (1964). *Exchange and power in social life*. New York: Wiley.

Boise, L., & Neal, M. B. (1996). Family responsibilities and absenteeism: Employees caring for parents versus employees caring for children. *Journal of Managerial Issues, 7*, 218–238.

Boles, J. S., Howard, W. G., & Donofrio, H. H. (2001). An investigation into the inter-relationships of work-family conflict, family-work conflict and work satisfaction. *Journal of Managerial Issues, 13*, 376–390.

Boles, J. S., Johnston, M. W., & Hair Jr., J. F. (1997). Role stress, work-family conflict and emotional exhaustion: Inter-relationships and effects on some work-related consequences. *The Journal of Personal Selling & Sales Management, 17*, 17–28.

Bommer, W. H., Miles, E. W., & Grover, S. L. (2003). Does one good turn deserve another? Coworker influences on employee citizenship behavior. *Journal of Organizational Behavior, 24*, 181–196.

Bond, J. T., Galinsky, E., & Swanberg, J. E. (1997). *The 1997 national study of the changing workforce*. New York: Families and Work Institute.

Boudreau, J. W. (1991). Utility analysis for decisions in human resource management. In M. D. Dunnette & L. M. Hough (Eds.), *Handbook of industrial and organizational psychology* (2nd ed., Vol. 2., pp. 621–745). Palo Alto, CA: Consulting Psychologists Press.

Boudreau, J. W. (2003). Strategic knowledge measurement and management. In S. E. Jackson, M. A. Hitt, & A. S. DeNisi (Eds.), *Managing knowledge for sustained competitive advantage* (pp. 360–396). San Francisco: Jossey-Bass.

Boudreau, J. W., & Ramstad, P. R. (2003). Strategic I/O psychology and the role of utility analysis models. In W. Borman, R. Klimoski, & D. Ilgen (Eds.), *Handbook of industrial and organizational psychology* (pp. 53–101). New York: Wiley.

Boyar, S. L., Maertz, C. P., Pearson, A., & Keough, S. M. (2003). Work family conflict: A model of linkages between work and family domain variables and turnover intentions. *Journal of Managerial Issues, 15*, 175–190.

Burke, R. J. (2002). Organizational values, job experiences and satisfactions among managerial and professional women and men: Advantage men? *Women in Management Review, 17*, 228–236.

Cable, D. M., Aiman-Smith, L., Mulvey, P., & Edwards, J. R. (2000). The sources and accuracy of job applicants' beliefs about organizational culture. *Academy of Management Journal, 43,* 1076–1085.

Cable, D. M., & Judge, T. A. (1994). Pay preferences and job search decision: A person–organization fit perspective. *Personnel Psychology, 47,* 317–348.

Calvasina, E. J., & Boxx, W. R. (1975). Efficiency of workers on the four-day workweek. *Academy of Management Journal, 18,* 604–610.

Campbell, J. P. (1999). The definition and measurement of performance in the new age. In D. R. Ilgen & E. D. Pulakos (Eds.), *The changing nature of performance: Implications for staffing, motivation, and development* (pp. 399–430). San Francisco: Jossey-Bass.

Caplan, R. D., Cobb, S., French, J. R. P., Jr., Harrison, R. V., & Pinneau, S. R. (1980). *Job demands and worker death: Main effects and occupational difference.* Ann Arbor: University of Michigan Institute for Social Research.

Cappelli, P., & Neumark, D. (2001). Do "high-performance" work practices improve establishment-level outcomes? *Industrial and Labor Relations Review, 54,* 737–775.

Carlson, D. S., Kacmar, K. M., & Williams, L. J. (2000). Construction and initial validation of a multidimensional measure of work-family conflict. *Journal of Vocational Behavior, 56,* 249–276.

Cascio, W. F. (2000). *Costing human resources.* Mason, OH: South-Western College.

Cascio, W. F. (2004). Work-family balance: Does the market reward firms that respect it? In D. F. Halpern & S. G. Murphy (Eds.), *Changing the metaphor: From work-family balance to work-family interaction.* Mahwah, NJ: Lawrence Erlbaum Associates.

Center for Work and Family. (1999). *Metrics manual: Ten approaches to measuring work/life initiatives.* Boston: The Center for Work & Family.

Chatman, J. A. (1991). Matching people and organizations: Selection and socialization in public accounting firms. *Administrative Science Quarterly, 36,* 459–484.

Chiu, R. K., Man, J. S., & Thayer, J. (1998). Effects of role conflicts and role satisfactions on stress of three professions in Hong Kong: A path analysis approach. *Journal of Managerial Psychology, 13,* 318–333.

Coens, T., & Jenkins, M. (2000). *Abolishing performance appraisals.* San Francisco: Berrett-Koehler.

Cooke, R. A., & Rousseau, D. M. (1984). Stress and strain from family roles and work role expectations. *Journal of Applied Psychology, 69,* 252–260.

Cooper, C. L. (1981). *The stress check.* New York: Prentice-Hall.

Crouter, A. (1984). Spillover from family to work: The neglected side of the work-family interface. *Human Relations, 37,* 425–442.

Cutler, M. M., & Jackson, A. L. (2002). A "glass ceiling" or work/family conflicts? *Journal of Business & Economics, 8,* 73–82.

Delery, J. E. (1998). Issues of fit in strategic human resource management: Implications for research. *Human Resource Management Review, 8,* 289–309.

Deutsch, F. M., Lussier, J. B., & Servis, L. J. (1993). Husbands at home: Predictors of paternal participation in childcare and housework. *Journal of Personality & Social Psychology, 65,* 1154–1166.

Donaldson, T., & Preston, L. E. (1995). The stakeholder theory of the corporation: Concepts, evidence, and implications. *Academy of Management Review, 20,* 65–91.

Dreher, G. F., & Bretz, R. D. Jr. (1991). Cognitive ability and career attainment: Moderating effects of early career success. *Journal of Applied Psychology, 76,* 392–397.

Earle, A. (2001). The impact of parental working conditions on school-age children: The case of evening work. *Community, Work, & Family, 4,* 305–325.

Edwards, J. E., Scott, J. C., & Raju, N. S. (Eds.). (2003). *The human resources program-evaluation handbook.* Thousand Oaks, CA: Sage.

European Foundation. (1997). *Working conditions in the European Union: Second European survey on working conditions.* Dublin, Ireland: EURF.

Fitz-Enz, J. (2002). *How to measure human resource management.* New York: McGraw-Hill.

Flamholtz, E. G. (1999). *Human resource accounting* (3rd ed.). New York: Kluwer.

Friedman, S. D., & Greenhaus, J. H. (2000). *Work and family: Allies or enemies? What happens when business professionals confront life choices.* New York: Oxford University Press.

Friedman, S. D., Thompson, C., Carpenter, M., & Marcel, D. (2000). *Proving Leo Durocher Wrong: Driving work/life change at Ernst & Young (A case study on the role of senior business leaders in driving work/life change).* Philadelphia: The Wharton Work/Life Integration Project.

Frone, M. R., Russell, M., & Cooper, M. L. (1997). Relation of work-family conflict to health outcomes: A four-year longitudinal study of employed parents. *Journal of Occupational Health Psychology, 70,* 325–335.

Gerhart, B. (1999). Human resource management and firm performance. *Research in Personnel and Human Resource Management, Supplement 4,* 31–51.

Golembiewski, R. T., & Proehl, C. W. (1978). A survey of the empirical literature on flexible work hours: Characters and consequences of a major innovation. *Academy of Management Review, 3,* 837–853.

Gouldner, A. W. (1960). The norm of reciprocity: A preliminary statement. *American Sociological Review, 25,* 161–177.

Great Place to Work Institute (2004). What makes a great place to work? Retrieved September 7, 2004, from www.100best.org/great/index.php.

Greenhaus, J. H., Bedeian, A. G., & Mossholder, K. W. (1987). Work experiences, job performances, and feelings of personal and family well being. *Journal of Vocational Behavior, 31,* 200–215.

Hammer, L. B., Bauer, T. N., & Grandey, A. A. (2003). Work-family conflict and work-related withdrawal behavniors. *Journal of Business & Psychology, 17,* 419–436.

Hammer, T. H., Saksvik, P. O., Nytro, K., Torvatn, H., & Bayazit, M. (2004). Expanding the psychosocial work environment: Workplace norms and work-family conflict as correlates of stress and health. *Journal of Occupational Health Psychology, 9*(1), 83–97.

Hannon, J. M., & Milkovich, G. T. (1996). The effect of human resource reputational signals on share prices: An event study. *Academy of Management Journal, 35,* 405–424.

Harris, M. M., & Lasson, E. D. (2003). Recruitment. In J. E. Edwards, J. C. Scott, & N. S. Raju (Eds.), *The human resources program-evaluation handbook* (pp. 71–88). Thousand Oaks, CA: Sage.

Harter, S. (1985). *Manual for the self-perception profile for children.* Unpublished manuscript, University of Denver.

Harvey, E. (1999). Short-term and long-term effects of early parental employment on children of the National Longitudinal Survey of Youth. *Developmental Psychology, 35,* 445–459.

Hepburn, C. G., & Barling, J. (1996). Eldercare responsibilities, interrole conflict, and employee absence: A daily study. *Journal of Occupational Health Psychology, 1,* 311–318.

Hesketh, B., & Neal, A. (1999). Technology and performance. In D. R. Ilgen & E. D. Pulakos (Eds.), *The changing nature of performance: Implications for staffing, motivation, and development* (pp. 21–55). San Francisco: Jossey-Bass.

Honeycutt, T. L., & Rosen, B. (1997). Family friendly human resource policies, salary levels, and salient identity as predictors of organization attraction. *Journal of Vocational Behavior, 50,* 271–290.

Ilgen, D. R., & Pulakos, E. D. (Eds.). (1999). *The changing nature of performance* (pp. 325–365). San Francisco: Jossey-Bass.

Jackson, S. E., & Schuler, R. S. (2006). *Managing human resources through strategic partnerships,* 9th Edition. Mason, OH: Thomson.

Jayne, M. E. A., & Rauschenberger, J. M. (2000). Demonstrating the value of selection in organizations. In J. F. Kehoe (Ed.), *Managing selection in changing organizations* (pp. 73–122). San Francisco: Jossey-Bass.

Katz, D., & Kahn, R. (1978). *The social psychology of organizations* (2nd ed.). New York: Wiley.

Kelly, R. M., & Marin, A. D. (1998). Position power and women's career advancement. *Women in Management Review, 13,* 53–66.

Kim, J. S., & Campagna, A. F. (1981). Effects of flexitime on employee attendance and performance: A field experiment. *Academy of Management Journal, 24,* 729–741.

Kossek, E. E., & Nichol, V. (1992). The effects of on-site child care on employee attitudes and performance. *Personnel Psychology, 45,* 485–509.

Kossek, E. E., & Ozeki, C. (1998). Work-family conflict, policies, and the job-life satisfaction relationship: A review and directions for organizational behavior-human resources research. *Journal of Applied Psychology, 83,* 139–149.

Lado, A. A., & Wilson, M. C. (1994). Human resource systems and sustained competitive advantage: A competency-based perspective. *Academy of Management Review, 19,* 699–727.

Lambert, S. J. (1999). The value-added approach: Establishing the link with business strategies. In *Metrics manual: Ten approaches to measuring work/life initiatives* (pp. 117–142). Boston: The Center for Work & Family.

Lambert, S. J. (2000). Added benefits: The link between work-life benefits and organizational citizenship behavior. *Academy of Management Journal, 43,* 801–815.

Lawler, E. E. III (1992). *The ultimate advantage: Creating the high involvement organization.* San Francisco: Jossey-Bass.

Lawler, E. E. III, Mohrman, S. A., & Ledford, G. E. (1992). *Employee involvement in America: An assessment of practices and results.* San Francisco: Jossey-Bass.

Lepak, D., & Snell, S. (1999). The human resource architecture: Toward a theory of human capital allocation and development. *Academy of Management Review, 24,* 31–48.

Lepak, D. P., & Snell, S. A. (2003). Managing the human resource architecture for knowledge-based competition. In S. E. Jackson, M. A. Hitt, & A. S. DeNisi (Eds.), *Managing knowledge for sustained competitive advantage* (pp. 127–154). San Francisco: Jossey-Bass.

Locke, H. J., & Wallace, K. M. (1959, August). Short marital adjustment and predictions test: Their reliability and validity. *Marriage and Family Living, 2,* 251–255.

Lyness, K. S., & Judiesch, M. K. (2001). Are female managers quitters? The relationships of gender, promotions, and family leaves of absence on voluntary turnover. *Journal of Applied Psychology, 86,* 1167–1178.

Madsen, S. R. (2003). The effects of home-based teleworking on work-family conflict. *Human Resource Development Quarterly, 14,* 35–58.

Martins, L. L., Eddleston, K. A., & Veiga, J. F. (2002). Moderators of the relationship between work-family conflict and career satisfaction. *Academy of Management Journal, 45,* 399–409.

Maslach, C., & Jackson, S. E. (1981). *The Maslach burnout inventory.* Palo Alto, CA: Consulting Psychologists Press.

Milkovich, G. T., & Gomez, L. (1976). Day care and selected employee work behaviors. *Academy of Management Journal, 19,* 111–115.

Mirvis, P. (1999). Measuring impact on external stakeholder relationships. In *Metrics manual: Ten approaches to measuring work/life initiatives* (pp. 227–250). Boston: The Center for Work & Family.

Mobley, W. H., Homer, S. O., & Hollingsworth, A. T. (1978). An evaluation of the precursors of hospital employee turnover. *Journal of Applied Psychology, 63,* 408–414.

Murphy, K. R., & Cleveland, J. N. (1991). *Performance appraisal: An organizational perspective.* Needham Heights, MA: Allyn & Bacon.

Murphy, P. R., & Jackson, S. E. (1999). Changing work role performance: Challenges for twenty-first-century organizations and their employees. In D. R. Ilgen & E. D. Pulakos (Eds.), *The changing nature of performance* (pp. 325–365). San Francisco: Jossey-Bass.

Netemeyer, R. G., Boles, J. S., & McMurrian, R. (1996). Development and validation of work-family conflict and family-work conflict scales. *Journal of Applied Psychology, 81,* 400–410.

Nollen, S. D., & Martin, V. H. (1978). *Alternative work schedules.* New York: Amacom.

O'Connell, S. E. (1996). The virtual workplace moves at warp speed. *HR Magazine, 41,* 50–54.

O'Driscoll, M. P., Poelmans, S., Spector, P. E., Kalliath, T., Allen, T. D., Cooper, C. L., & Sanchez, J. I. (2003). Family-responsive interventions, perceived organizational and supervisor support, work-family conflict, and psychological strain. *International Journal of Stress Management, 10,* 326–344.

Ones, D. S., Viswesvaran, C., & Schmidt, F. L. (2003). Personality and absenteeism: A meta-analysis of integrity tests. *European Journal of Personality, 17,* S19–S38.

Pedhazur, E. J., & Schmelkin, L. P. (1991). *Measurement, design, and analysis: An integrated approach.* Hillsdale, NJ: Lawrence Erlbaum Associates.

Peterson, J. L., & Zill, N. (1986). Marital disruption, parent-child relationships, and behavior problems in children. *Journal of Marriage and the Family, 48,* 295–307.

Pitt-Catsouphes, M., & Googins, B. (2005). Recasting the work-family agenda as a corporate social responsibility. In E. Kossek. & S. Lambert, S. (Eds.), *Work and life integration: Organizational, cultural and psychological perspectives* (pp. 469–490). Mahwah, NJ: Lawrence Erlbaum Associates.

Podsakoff, P. M., MacKenzie, S. B., Moorman, R. H., & Fetter, R. (1990). Transformational leader behaviors and their effects on followers' trust in leader, satisfaction, and organizational citizenship behaviors. *Leadership Quarterly, 1,* 107–142.

Porter, M. E. (1980). *Competitive strategy: Techniques for analyzing industries and competitors.* New York: Free Press.

Powell, G., & Mainiero, L. (1992). Cross-currents in the river of time: Conceptualizing the complexities of women's careers. *Journal of Management, 18,* 215–237.

Prestholdt, P. H., Lane, I. M., & Matthews, R. C. (1987). Nurse turnover as reasoned action: Development of a process model. *Journal of Applied Psychology, 72,* 221–227.

Pulakos, E. D., Arad, S., Donovan, M. A., & Plamondon, K. E. (2000). Adaptability in the workplace: Development of a taxonomy of adaptive performance. *Journal of Applied Psychology, 85,* 612–624.

Quinn, R. P., & Staines, G. L. (1978). *The 1977 quality of employment survey.* Ann Arbor, MI: Institute for Social Research.

Ramsower, R. M. (1985). *Telecommuting: The organizational and behavioral effects of working at home.* Ann Arbor: UMI Research Press.

Rau, B. L., & Hyland, M. M. (2002). Role conflict and flexible work arrangements. The effects on applicant attraction. *Personnel Psychology, 55,* 111–136.

Roehling, P. V., & Bultman, M. (2002). Does absence make the heart grow fonder? Work-related travel and marital satisfaction. *Sex Roles, 46,* 279–293.

Ross, S. R., Rausch, M. K., & Canada, K. E. (2003). Competition and cooperation in the five-factor model: Individual differences in achievement orientation. *The Journal of Psychology, 137,* 323–337.

Schmidt, F. L., Hunter, J. E., MacKenzie, R., & Muldrow, T. (1979). The impact of valid selection procedures on workforce productivity. *Journal of Applied Psychology, 64,* 627–670.

Schneer, J. A., & Reitman, F. (1990). Effects of employment gaps on the careers of M.B.A.'s: More damaging for men than for women? Alternate family structures on managerial career paths. *Academy of Management Journal, 33,* 391–406.

Schneer, J. A., & Reitman, F. (1993). Effects of alternate family structures on managerial career paths. *Academy of Management Journal, 36,* 830–843.

Schneider, B., & Bowen, D. E. (1995). *Winning the service game.* Boston: Harvard Business School Press.

Schneider, B., & White, S. S. (2004). *Service quality: Research perspectives.* Thousand Oaks, CA: Sage.

Schulz, M. S., Cowan, P. A., Cowan, C. P., & Brennan, R. T. (2004). Coming home upset: Gender, marital satisfaction, and the daily spillover of workday experience into couple interactions. *Journal of Family Psychology, 18,* 250–263.

Schwoerer, C., & Rosen, B. (1989). Effects of employment-at-will policies and compensation policies on corporate image and job pursuit intentions. *Journal of Applied Psychology, 74,* 653–656.

Smither, J. W. (1998). *Performance appraisal: State of the art in practice.* San Francisco: Jossey-Bass.

Steel, R. P. (2002). Turnover theory at the empirical interface: Problems of fit and function. *Academy of Management Review, 27,* 346–360.

Steel, R. P., & Ovalle, N. K. (1984). A review and meta-analysis of research on the relationship between behavioral intentions and employee turnover. *Journal of Applied Psychology, 69,* 673–686.

Tharenou, P. (1999). Is there a link between family structures and women's and men's managerial career advancement? *Journal of Organizational Behavior, 20,* 837–863.

Thompson, C. A., Beauvais, L. L., & Lyness, K. S. (1999). When work-family benefits are not enough: The influence of work-family culture on benefit utilization, organizational attachment, and work-family conflict. *Journal of Vocational Behavior, 54,* 392–415.

United States Bureau of Labor Statistics. (n.d.). *NLSY79 Child and Young Adult User's Guide 2000.* Retrieved September 7, 2004, from http://stats.bls.gov/nls/y79cyaguide/nlsy79cusg.htm.

Vandell, D. L., & Ramanan, J. (1992). Effects of early and recent maternal employment on children from low-income families. *Child Development, 63,* 938–949.

Waldfogel, J., Han, W. J., & Brooks-Gunn, J. (2002). The effects of early maternal employment on child cognitive development. *Demography, 39,* 369–392.

Wernerfelt, B. (1984). A resource-based view of the firm. *Strategic Management Journal, 5,* 171–180.

Wright, P. M., Dunford, B. B., & Snell, S. A. (2001). Human resources and the resource-based view of the firm. *Journal of Management, 27,* 701–721.

Wright, P. M., McMahan, G. C., & McWilliams, A. (1994). Human resources and sustained competitive advantage: A resource-based perspective. *International Journal of Human Resource Management, 5,* 301–326.

Youngblood, S. A., & Chambers-Cook, K. (1984). Child care assistance can improve employee attitudes and behavior. *The Personnel Administrator, 29,* 45–50.

26

Hierarchical Models for Work-Family and Life Course Research[1]

Raymond Swisher
Cornell University

Work and family researchers are increasingly recognizing the importance of the social, temporal, and geographic contexts within which individual workers and their families are embedded. One critical context is the workplace and the family-friendliness of policies in place to enable workers to negotiate the competing demands of work, family, and community (Glass & Estes, 1997). Other relevant contexts include the couple and family, the temporal trajectory of a worker's career, cohorts and historical periods, and the neighborhoods and communities in which workers live, to name but a few. Illustrative research questions might include:

- Do family-friendly workplace policies influence the ability of dual-earner families to manage work-family conflicts?
- Do the age compositions of workplaces influence employees' use of family-friendly policies? And if so, for which types of employees?
- Do the demographic characteristics of neighborhoods influence residents' perceptions of neighborhood family-friendliness?
- Do characteristics of couples shape responses of individuals to workplace or family stressors, and does this vary by gender?

Examining properly the role of these contexts requires adjustments to existing research methods, including sampling strategies in which both contexts and the individuals within them are randomly sampled, as well as statistical techniques that account for the clustering of individuals within contexts. One such statistical technique is known as hierarchical (or multilevel) modeling (Bryk & Raudenbush, 1992; Goldstein, 1995; Hox & Kreft, 1994; Muthen, 1997; Snijders & Bosker, 1999). Hierarchical refers to the multiple levels at which data are collected or clustered. Most typical are two-level models with, for example, individuals (level 1) clustered within workplaces (level 2) or families clustered within neighborhoods.

The purpose of this chapter is to provide work and family researchers with an overview of hierarchical modeling, some of the statistical issues involved, possible applications, and options for software implementation. It will do so with illustration from two empirical applications: (a) the retirement planning of workers within organizations and (b) how perceptions that the community is family-friendly are shaped by the fit between a couple's life stage and the life course characteristics of neighbors. Though statistical formulas will necessarily be introduced, more emphasis will be placed on their theoretical and applied utility than on issues of model derivation, estimation, and other technical details (see Bryk & Raudenbush, 1992 for such details). It is hoped that researchers will gain a greater appreciation of the reasons why hierarchical models might be appropriate for their research questions and data, as well as directions for where to look for additional information. See also the potentials of using hierarchical models to analyze the nesting of emotional experiences at work and at home within persons of varying work orientations, as described by Schneider in this volume.

THE THEORETICAL UTILITY OF HIERARCHICAL MODELS

There are a number of statistical reasons for using hierarchical models, such as accounting for the clustering of individuals within contexts (i.e., correlated error terms), which will be described in the next section. Perhaps of most importance, however, is their suitability to theoretical questions within work-family and life course research.

Examining Lives in Context

A foundational principle of the life course perspective is that lives are shaped by the social, historical, and geographical contexts in which they are embedded (Elder, 1999; Elder, 1998; Moen, Elder, & Luscher, 1995). In the work-family literature, the context most often examined is the workplace (Glass & Estes, 1997). Family leave, flextime and other policies, and even supportive managers may significantly contribute to the ability of dual-earner couples to balance the demands emanating from work, family, community, and other roles.

If we have samples in which significant numbers of respondents work for the same organizations, we can examine both workplace and individual-level predictors of work-family outcomes. For example, MacDermid and colleagues used multilevel models to show that smaller organizations were associated with higher perceptions of job quality and better work-family relationships, while controlling for individual-level variables (MacDermid, Hertzog, Kensinger, & Zipp, 2001). Less often considered by work-family researchers are characteristics of the communities and neighborhoods within which dual-earner couples reside (Swisher, Sweet, & Moen, 2004). Labor markets, regions, and states, which may vary in work, social welfare, and family policies, are also likely to be of importance.

Another important context is the couple itself. If we have data from both members of a couple, as is increasingly common within work-family research, we can treat this as a multilevel situation, with individuals nested within couples. In other words, we can analyze the experiences of individuals and relate these to both individual characteristics (e.g., gender, age) and characteristics of the couple itself (e.g., combined household income, joint marital quality). From a statistical standpoint, analyzing such data with multilevel models also represents a considerable improvement over other approaches to dealing with the nonindependent nature of paired data (Kenny, 1996), such as running the models separately or using couples as the unit of analysis and ignoring individual variation within the couple. Rosalind Barnett and colleagues, for example, have used hierarchical models to study psychological stress and its relationship to job and couple-level characteristics among dual-earner couples (Barnett et al., 1993; Maguire, 1999; Newsom, 2003; Raudenbush, 1995). Other research on couples has used multilevel models to study individual and couple predictors of marital satisfaction (Wendorf, 2003) and the adjustment of wives' work and family-related preferences to those of their husbands during the transition to parenthood (Johnson & Huston, 1998). (For more information about techniques for analyzing dyadic data, see Maguire, 1999; Newsom, 2003; Raudenbush et al., 1995).

The life course perspective also directs attention to the importance of conceptualizing lives as composed of multiple trajectories or careers (Moen, 2003). In addition to what we traditionally think of as a work career, life course researchers conceive of other roles or life domains (family careers, educational careers) as possessing long-term and career-like characteristics. Han and Moen (1999) identified five common career trajectories (e.g., high-geared, orderly, intermittent) and linked these to gender differences in retirement transitions. Hierarchical modeling, also known in this case as growth curve modeling, is well suited to studies of such careers or trajectories (Bryk & Raudenbush, 1992). In this case, multiple observations over time (level 1) are nested within an individual respondent (level 2). Hierarchical models assess between- and within-person variation in the levels, directions, and rates of change of these trajectories. One limitation of growth curves, however, is that they generally assume only one general trajectory exists in the population and that all individuals must vary randomly around the overall pattern.[2]

Ecological Models: Interactions Between Persons and Contexts

A limitation of much of the contextual literature is a tendency to pose contextual effects against individual-level influences. We tend to allow the possibility of a contextual effect only after every possible individual-level variable has been controlled. There are sound methodological reasons for doing so, of course, including wanting to rule out competing composition or selection effects. For example, when attempting to show that neighborhood poverty has an effect on a given outcome, researchers want to control for the socioeconomic characteristics of the individuals who live there (i.e., compose the neighborhood). Alternatively, they want to control for the fact that socioeconomic status is associated with differences in the ability of individuals or families to select or choose the neighborhoods in which they live. In the work-family literature, we might imagine that workers in small firms have greater job satisfaction than those in larger, more bureaucratic organizations. On the other hand, it may simply be that highly entrepreneurial individuals who tend to enjoy their jobs are drawn to or even start up these small firms, so that the causal effect is individual and not organizational. Given these concerns, the common practice is to include every possible individual-level variable in the model. Yet many of the variables controlled are themselves influenced by neighborhoods. As a result, we miss much of the life course influence of contexts and are left with only their most immediate or short-term influences.

These methodological concerns also tend to limit people's thinking about contextual effects. By posing individual and contextual effects against one another, they also assume that contextual effects will be the same for all individuals (i.e., at all levels of the control variables). An ecological or life course approach, on the other hand, conceives of development as inherently interactive (Elder, 1998). For example, Lewin's (1951) famous dictum that behavior is a function of a person and the environment clearly treats the relationship between individuals and contexts as interactive. Working within the same framework, Bronfenbrenner (1979) asserted that "in ecological research, the principal main effects are likely to be interactions" (p. 38).

Work-family researchers should be similarly cognizant of the fact that the effect of a given contextual variable (e.g., a flexible workplace policy) likely depends on a variety of individual factors. Whether someone takes advantage of such a policy, for example, likely depends on whether or not the boss is supportive, status within the organization, gender, and spouse's or partner's employment characteristics, to imagine just a few possibilities.

The strategies by which individuals and families adapt to their environments also moderate the influence of contexts in their lives (Becker & Moen, 1999; Moen & Wethington, 1992). A classic example from the neighborhood literature is the use of authoritarian-style parenting in dangerous environments. In an average or more advantaged environment, use of authoritative parenting, characterized as demanding and responsive, is associated with a wide range of positive outcomes. The highly demanding yet unresponsive style of authoritarian parents, in contrast, is thought to limit youth autonomy and is associated with poorer outcomes (Steinberg, Mounts, Lamborn, & Dornbusch, 1991). Research considering parenting style within ecological contexts, however, suggests that authoritarian parenting might represent a good fit for the demands and challenges posed in poor or minority neighborhoods (Furstenberg, Cook, Eccles, Elder, Glen & Sameroff, 1998; Lamborn, Dornbusch, & Steinberg, 1996).

Building on the concept of person–environment fit and the life course's life stage principle, Swisher, Sweet, and Moen (2004) coined the phrase "life stage–neighborhood fit" to capture the interactive effects of neighborhood demographic structure and life stage on perceptions that the community is family-friendly. In particular, they found that a strong presence of married couples with children in the neighborhood was associated with more positive perceptions of community family-friendliness, but only among couples with children of their own.

The point of this discussion, of course, is that hierarchical models are well-equipped to handle each of these important contextual and life course theoretical questions. They can examine the conventional direct effects of contexts, controlling for composition, selection and other individual-level explanations. In the statistical discussion to follow, these direct effects are called "random intercept" models, in that contextual characteristics will be associated with differences in the mean levels (i.e., the intercepts) of a given outcome across contexts. The more interactive theoretical questions, such as how worker and workplace characteristics interact, will be assessed by "random slope" models.

STATISTICAL MOTIVATIONS FOR HIERARCHICAL MODELS

Even if one were not interested in the theoretical issues just raised, there are a number of important statistical reasons for using hierarchical models. If we are using any type of clustered dataset, and this includes many of the school- or organization-based samples common today, we may be violating assumptions of ordinary least squares (OLS) regression models.

A well-known assumption of OLS models is that the error terms associated with individual observations are independent (i.e., no auto-correlation). This is part of what we mean when we say we have drawn a random sample. Many multi-stage and other complex sample designs, which involve random sampling of some larger geographic or social unit (e.g., schools or census tracts) and random samples taken within each of these units, may violate the assumption of independent samples. In a truly random sample, the full amount of variation in the population will be represented. In a multi-stage or clustered sampling design, in contrast, we are artificially constraining the amount of variation observed. This is not a problem if the larger units are completely unrelated to the outcomes or independent variables we are studying. But, if the clustering is at all related to the dependent variable, as is frequently the case, we will have limited the total amount of variation observed in the resulting sample.

Artificially constrained variation is problematic because it influences the standard errors of coefficient estimates in our models, and hence our tests of statistical significance and model fit. In other words, constrained variation means smaller standard errors and an increased risk of concluding that relationships are statistically significant, when in fact they are not (i.e., Type 1 errors). There are techniques, of course, for adjusting standard errors for "design effects" (Lee, Forthofer, & Lorimer, 1989) in software packages such as SUDANN or STATA. What is unique to hierarchical modeling, however, is that rather than treating this clustering as error that needs to be corrected, it treats the cluster as something of substantive and theoretical importance that should be considered, measured, and modeled in its own right.

Another assumption of OLS models is that the error terms are uncorrelated with the explanatory variables. This assumption is likely to be violated if the characteristics of workplaces, schools, or neighborhoods are of substantive importance. For example, if presence of other families with children in a neighborhood influences the ability of dual-earner couples with children to manage work-family stressors, and this is unaccounted for in our models, we end up with the classic problem of omitted variable bias. The effect of the unmeasured neighborhood characteristic is captured in the error term of our model, and since this variable is also likely to be correlated with independent variables in the model (e.g., number of children in the home), the resulting coefficients will be biased. One might try within OLS models to include measures of the contextual characteristics, but the problem of correlated errors and deflated standard errors would remain.

HIERARCHICAL MODELING GRAPHS AND EQUATIONS

The structure of hierarchical models is illustrated below using two examples from the Cornell Ecology of Careers Study. In presenting these models, I am following the general conventions of Bryk and Raudenbush (1992). Please consult this source for additional details about model assumptions, estimation, and diagnostics, which are beyond the scope of this chapter.

The first example is of the retirement planning of dual-earner households, using a subsample in which at least one spouse works for one of the 10 participating organizations ($N = 1,063$ individuals) in the utilities, health care, and higher education industries. Sampling within organizations is random, yet the selection of organizations is not. The analysis is limited to the focal respondent and does not include their spouses or partners. The outcome is an index of lifestyle planning for retirement, combining the degree to which respondents have developed hobbies and interests for retirement, have thought of a second or third career after retirement, or have thought about volunteer work after retirement (alpha $= .60$). It is hypothesized that the intensity of an individual's lifestyle planning for retirement will be a function of their age, other control variables, and, at the organizational level, the average age of coworkers. Average age is constructed by averaging the ages of individual respondents who work within the same organizations. Several limitations of the sample are discussed in the analysis sections to follow.

The second example is based on the Cornell Community Study (1999–2000), an extension of the Couples and Careers project. The Community Study randomly sampled within census block groups with high representations of Couples and Careers Study respondents. Fifty-seven block groups are included, with an average of 26.9 respondents per block group. The analysis is limited to the half of respondents randomly given a module of questions about the "family-friendliness" of their communities ($N = 727$). The outcome variable is the respondent's assessment of the overall family-friendliness of their communities, on a scale of 0 (*extremely family-unfriendly*) to 100 (*extremely family-friendly*). While fairly representative of dual-earner couples in upstate New York, both samples are composed primarily of White, middle-class respondents.

Hierarchical models avoid violating the assumptions of OLS by explicitly modeling variation, and allowing for unique error terms, at each level of the data. If we are studying individuals nested within organizations, for example, we would have two models: an individual-level and organization-level model. Extensions to designs with three or more level models are also possible (Bryk & Raudenbush, 1992).

Before presenting the equations, it is useful to grasp the models more intuitively, using the example of retirement planning within organizational context. In essence, what hierarchical models do is estimate a separate regression model in every one of the 10 organizations. Figure 26.1 depicts such organization-specific regressions of the amount of lifestyle planning

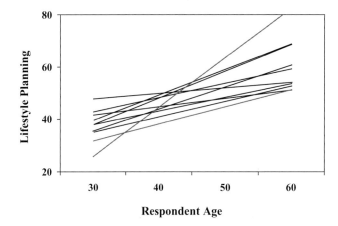

FIG. 26.1.   Regressions of retirement planning on age in 10 organizations.
Source: Cornell Ecology of Careers Study.

on respondent's age. As the graphs illustrate, there appears to be considerable variation in the average levels of lifestyle planning across organizations (i.e., the intercepts), but less so in the relationship between age and planning (i.e., the slopes). The lines are all upward sloping, indicating that age is positively associated with lifestyle planning, and they tend to be parallel to one another, with the exception of the single organization with a very steep slope.

Why not simply use the OLS results from Fig. 26.1? The problem with these equations is twofold. First is that each suffers from the limits of relatively small sample sizes, which affects the variability of the estimates and thus tests of statistical significance. Second, we have no way to systematically combine the results to assess an overall effect of age, nor a way to account for the variation in the intercepts and slopes we observe. Hierarchical modeling avoids the small samples problem by borrowing degrees of freedom from all of the organizations in the sample. It also produces a combined or overall model, by averaging together the intercepts and slopes from each individual organization's model, while giving more weight to those with a larger number of workers. The resulting intercept and slope coefficients from the weighted-average model are known as the "fixed effects," in that they are assumed to be the same (or fixed) across all organizations. In other words, this is the part of the model for which context does not matter. Older workers are likely to plan more intensively for retirement regardless of the characteristics of their coworkers.

Intra-class Correlations

Our visual inspection of Fig. 26.1 suggested considerable variation between the organizations in their intercepts or average levels of lifestyle planning. Hierarchical models allow us to test whether this between-organization variation is statistically significant. A common first step in hierarchical modeling is to see whether the outcome of interest (i.e., lifestyle planning) actually varies significantly across contexts. This is a simple analysis of variance procedure (i.e., a one-way ANOVA) that partitions total variation in lifestyle planning into two sources: within-organization variation (i.e., that associated with individual characteristics) and between-organization variation. We can then also assess the percentage of variation due to both sources. The percentage of total variation between contexts is known as the intra-class correlation.

The model at the individual level (i.e., level 1) is:

$$Lifestyle_{ij} = \beta_{0j} + r_{ij} \tag{26.1}$$

TABLE 26.1
One-Way ANOVA of Lifestyle Planning

Random Effects	Variance	SE	z	p-value
Organizational mean, uoj	21.29	12.84	1.66	0.0487
Residual, rij	516.39	22.52	22.93	< 0.0001

Notes: Cornell Couples and Careers Study.
N is 1,063 respondents in 10 organizations.

with the lifestyle planning of respondent i working in organization j ($Lifestyle_{ij}$) modeled as a function of a level-1 intercept (β_{0j}) and an error term (r_{ij}) capturing the unique error associated with individual i working in organization j. At the second level, the regression coefficients from the level-1 model are allowed to randomly vary (i.e., the previously fixed intercept becomes random) and are treated as the outcomes to be modeled. In this case, we only have a random intercept. The model at level-2 is:

$$\beta_{0j} = \gamma_{00} + \mu_{0j} \tag{26.2}$$

in which each organization's mean level of lifestyle planning (β_{0j}) is a function of a grand mean across all organizations (γ_{00}), and a unique residual associated with that organization. By allowing both individual-level (r_{ij}) and organizational-level (μ_{ij}) error terms, we avoid the problem of correlated errors that might be present in an OLS model.

The analysis of variance results are presented in Table 26.1. The interclass correlation is calculated by dividing the variance component associated with the organizational intercepts (21.29) by the total variance (21.29 + 516.39), which yields 0.0396. Thus, 3.96% of the total variation in lifestyle planning is observed between organizations.

Models With Individual-level Covariates

To test the hypothesis that lifestyle planning is associated with a worker's age, we add age and other control variables to the level-1 model. The model then becomes:

$$Lifestyle_{ij} = \beta_{0j} + \beta_{1j}Age_{ij} + \ldots + \beta_{kj}X_{kij} + r_{ij} \tag{26.3}$$

in which within-organizational variation in the amount of lifestyle planning ($Lifestyle_{ij}$) is modeled as a function of an intercept and individual-level independent variables (Age_{ij} and X_{kij}) such as age, gender, family income, and so forth and the error term. The model is unchanged at level-2 (see model 26.2 above).

For ease of interpretation of the intercepts and stable statistical estimation, it is advised that researchers "center" individual- and contextual-level variables around some standard (Bryk & Raudenbush, 1992). Looking back at Equation 26.3, the intercept represents the expected value of a person in organization j, who has values of 0 across all the independent variables. In many cases, such as in our focal variable of age, a value of 0 makes little sense, rendering the intercept uninterpretable. If we center the independent variables, for example, around their respective means, the intercept then represents the expected value of someone with average values on the independent variables. (See Bryk & Raudenbush, 1992 for an extended discussion of centering.) In analyses reported here, all individual- and organizational-level variables are grand mean centered.

TABLE 26.2
Hierarchical Linear Models of Lifestyle Planning

	(1)	(2)	(3)
Intercept	47.25***	47.49***	47.65***
	(1.69)	(1.32)	(0.69)
Individual-level variables			
Age		0.63***	0.59***
		(0.09)	(0.09)
Female		0.14	−0.42
		(1.48)	(1.42)
Years of Education Completed		−0.01	−0.09
		(0.27)	(0.27)
Household Income		0.09*	0.1*
		(0.04)	(0.04)
Organization-level variables			
Mean Age			1.33**
			(0.33)
Variance Components			
Organizational mean, uoj	21.29	10.88	0.00
Residual, rij	516.39	494.34	495.21
Total	537.68	505.22	495.21
Percent of Variation Explained			
Individual-level	—	4.3	4.2
Organization-level	—	48.8	100.0
Total	—	6.0	7.9

Notes: *** $p < 0.001$,** $p < 0.01$,* $p < 0.05$, +$p < 0.10$.
Cornell Couples and Careers Study. N is 1,063 respondents in 10 organizations.

Results are presented in column 2 of Table 26.2, with the first column reporting variance components from the previous one-way ANOVA model. The intercept is 47.49, representing the expected level of financial planning for an individual with average values across the independent variables. As expected, age is associated with a greater intensity of lifestyle planning. One additional year of age is associated with 0.63 additional units of lifestyle planning (on the 0 to 100 scale). Of other independent variables, only family income is significantly associated with lifestyle planning, perhaps suggesting that serious consideration of volunteering, hobbies, and other activities requires financial security, even among a predominantly middle-class dual-earner sample.

By comparing the original variance components in column 1 to those produced by our new model, we can calculate the percentage of variation at each level explained by the independent variables. Inclusion of the individual-level predictors explains 4.3% of within-organization variation and 6.0% of total variation in lifestyle planning (e.g., [[537.68 − 505.22] / 537.68]] = 0.06). Note that almost half (48.8%) of the between-organization variation in lifestyle planning is also explained, suggesting that much of the difference in lifestyle planning is associated with age, income, and other compositional differences across organizations.

Random Intercept Models With Contextual Variables

Now we turn to modeling the remaining between-organization variation in lifestyle planning. The question now becomes which characteristics of organizations are associated with this variation? It is hypothesized that the average age of coworkers within an organization would be associated with greater discussions of retirement issues, including lifestyle planning for retirement (see Moen, Sweet, & Swisher, 2005). To assess this, organizational-level variables are added to the "random-intercept" model (26.2) above. It thus becomes:

$$\beta_{0j} = \gamma_{00} + \gamma_{01} MeanAge_j + \gamma_{02} W_{2j} + \ldots + \gamma_{0S} W_{Sj} + u_{0j} \qquad (26.4)$$

with mean lifestyle planning in organization $j(\beta_{0j})$ a function of a level-2 intercept (γ_{00}), level-2 independent variables (W_S), such as the mean age of workers within that organization, and the organization-level residual (μ_{0j}).

Results are displayed in column 3. As expected, organizations with a higher mean age of coworkers have higher average levels of lifestyle planning. The slope coefficient indicates that a 1-year increase in the average age of coworkers is associated with 1.33 units of additional lifestyle planning. Examination of the variance components suggests that average age of coworkers and the other independent variables explain 100% of the variation between organizations and 7.9% of the total variation in lifestyle planning.

Caution must be registered against overinterpretation of the effects of the organizational variable. One problem is the small number of organizations involved. The sampling design of the Ecology of Careers Study is really not ideal for multilevel modeling. Having only 10 organizations limits both the power to detect significant effects and the number of organizational variables that can be considered simultaneously. Moreover, it precludes estimation of random-slope models (to be discussed in the next section) that require greater degrees of freedom.

In addition to the problem of having only 10 organizations, Fig. 26.1 suggests that most of the variation between organizations was in the intercepts, not the slopes. A way to formally test whether variation in slopes across organizations is statistically significant is to run a model allowing the slopes to vary randomly and examine the significance of the associated variance component. The results of such a model (not shown) suggest that variation in the slopes of worker's age is not statistically significant for lifestyle planning.

Another limitation is that the organization-level variables considered (see Moen et al., 2004 for more comprehensive analyses) are simply constructed as the average of individual respondent characteristics. Very few of the organizations were able or willing to provide more objective measures of workers' ages or a variety of other variables that might be related to retirement planning. More extensive discussion of issues of sampling design and contextual measurement will be covered in a subsequent section about practical implementation issues.

Despite these limitations, hierarchical models enabled a consideration of how organizational characteristics influence the life course planning of individual employees, a fundamental issue within the work and family literature. Perhaps most interestingly, they illustrate how the same variable, measured at two levels (in this case, an individual's age and his or her workplace's age structure), may have independent and significant influences. At the individual level, older workers were found to engage in more retirement lifestyle planning. Moreover, the hierarchical random intercept models enable the additional insight that the age structure of coworkers may facilitate, or discourage, retirement planning. One might plausibly expect that an organization's age and life course structure would be associated with other outcomes of interest, such as presence of family-friendly policies and the encouragement of employees to use them.

Random Slope Models

An important theoretical motivation for multilevel modeling is the ability to examine the interactive relationship between individuals and the contexts within which they are embedded. In particular, we can examine how the effects of individual-level variables (i.e., the slopes) vary as a function of contextual characteristics. These are referred to as "random slope" models. To

TABLE 26.3

Multilevel Models of Perceived Community Family-Friendliness

	(1)	(2)
Individual Level Variables		
Intercept	78.63***	78.43***
	(0.62)	(0.62)
Women with Young Children	7.62***	6.88***
	(1.82)	(1.84)
Women with Older Children	1.71	0.26
	(2.37)	(2.45)
Women with No Children	1.56	1.52
	(2.04)	(2.05)
Men with Young Children	8.10***	7.56***
	(1.92)	(1.95)
Men with Older Children	2.00	2.21
	(2.48)	(2.72)
Household Income	0.00	0.00
	(0.00)	(0.00)
Educational Attainment	0.58*	0.63**
	(0.23)	(0.23)
Life Course Fit Interactions		
Families with Children		−0.11
		(0.07)
Neighborhood Families * Women with Young Children		0.47**
		(0.16)
Neighborhood Families * Women with Older Children		0.66**
		(0.21)
Neighborhood Families * Women with No Children		0.24
		(0.18)
Neighborhood Families * Men with Young Children		0.42*
		(0.16)
Neighborhood Families * Men with Older Children		0.26
		(0.23)
−2 Log Likelihood	6,193.4	6,188.2
Percent of Total Variation Explained	3.8	5.0

Notes: N is 727 individuals in 57 census block groups.
$+p < 0.10,$ $^* p < 0.05.,$ $^{**} p < 0.01.,$ $^{***} p < 0.001.$

illustrate them, we turn to the second example of the community perceptions of dual-earner couples in upstate New York.

In this case, the two levels are respondents nested within 57 census block groups. Perceptions that the community is family-friendly are modeled as a function of individual-level character-istics (e.g., life stage), features of the block group (i.e., percent of married with children house-holds), and the interaction of life stage and percent of married with children households (for more complete models and analyses, see Moen, Sweet, & Swisher, 2005). The focal hypothesis is that perceptions of community family-friendliness will depend on the fit between a couple's life stage and the life course demographic structure of the neighborhood in which they are living.

At level-1:

$$FF_{ij} = \beta_{0j} + \beta_{1j} FemaleYoungKid_{ij} + \ldots + \beta_{kj} X_{kij} + r_{ij} \qquad (26.5)$$

within-context variation in perceptions of community family-friendliness (FF_{ij}) are modeled as a function of indicator variables representing the gender and life stage of respondents (*Female*

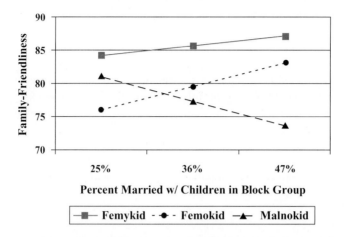

FIG. 26.2.   Perceived family-friendliness of community by life-stage neighborhood fit.

Young Kid$_{ij}$), and control variables (X_{kij}) such as family income and educational attainment. Six gender (male and female) by life stage (young children at home, older children at home, and no children at home) categories are examined, with men with no children being the excluded category. The interactive hypothesis is then tested by allowing the slope coefficients for the life-stage groups to vary at level-2:

$$\beta_{1j} = \gamma_{10} + \gamma_{11} TwoParentsWithChildren_j + u_{1j} \qquad (26.6)$$

and modeled as a function of the percentage of households in the block group made up of two parents with children families (*TwoParentsW/kids*$_j$).

The results from simplified versions of these models are presented in Table 26.3. The first column presents the random intercept model with individual-level covariates, including the gender by life stage indicators. Compared to the excluded category of men with no children, having young children at home is associated with considerably higher perceptions of community family-friendliness. Model 2 presents the random slope results (also sometimes called cross-level interactions). Although the percentage of families with children in a block group is found to have no direct effect on perceptions of family-friendliness, it is associated with higher family-friendliness among women and men with children at home (again compared to men with no children).

Interpreting interaction effects such as these just by looking at the coefficients themselves is difficult, as the predicted value for a given individual is the joint product of several coefficients. Thus, Fig. 26.2 presents a graphic simulation of these interactions for three subgroups: women with young children, women with older children, and men with no children (the excluded category). It shows predicted ratings of family-friendliness for the three groups, in block groups with varying percentages of married with children households. A visually interesting contrast is between women with older children at home and men with no children. In neighborhoods with a relatively low percentage of married with children households (i.e., 25%, corresponding to 1 standard deviation below the mean), men without children actually rate their communities as more family-friendly than do women with older children. As the percentage of married couples with children increases in the block group, however, their relative ratings reverse. In block groups with a high presence of married couples with children, women with older children rate their communities almost 10 points higher than do men without children.

Although the results just presented suggest support for the notion of life stage–neighborhood fit, lack of information at the neighborhood level (i.e., beyond census data) about social processes within neighborhoods limits our ability to know precisely what it is about the match between life stage and neighborhood characteristics that matters.

Nonetheless, hierarchical models enabled consideration of the interactive relationship between family and neighborhood environments. This insight would have been missed, moreover, had one simply applied the intra-class correlation litmus test, as mean levels of perceived family-friendliness did not vary significantly across block groups. A similar pattern of results might be expected in other areas of work-family research. For example, the diversity of workers within organizations might lead a researcher to find no variation in mean levels of work satisfaction across organizations and thus conclude that workplace policies are inconsequential. In reality, however, it is quite likely that workplace policies matter to employees, but that they matter in different ways to different employees depending on life stage, gender, socioeconomic status, and a host of other individual characteristics.

EXTENSIONS, COMPLICATIONS, AND APPLICATIONS

Multiple and/or Overlapping Contexts

Though the examples we have considered have been limited to two levels, hierarchical models can be extended to three or more levels. For example, if reports of community family-friendliness had been provided by both members of the couple, we could estimate three-level models with individuals nested within couples, and couples nested within block groups. Similarly, if both members of couples in the retirement example were working for the same organization (they were not), we could estimate individuals within couples within organizations models. There are also ways to estimate what are called cross-classified models, in which individuals are nested imperfectly within multiple or overlapping contexts (Goldstein, 1994), such as individuals nested within couples but working for different organizations.

Categorical Outcomes

Both examples considered here involved continuous outcomes and thus hierarchical *linear* models. Linear models are inappropriate, however, for use with dichotomous, ordinal, or multiple category outcomes. Fortunately, generalized hierarchical models are also available (Guo, 2000; Raudenbush, Bryk, Cheong, & Congdon, 2000) for these categorical outcomes.

Sample Designs and Appropriate Contexts

In an ideal world, researchers would incorporate the multilevel nature of their research questions at the outset of the research and sample design process. The importance of random sampling in non-multilevel research is well understood. Yet the same issues of representativeness and bias apply to multilevel research as well. Unfortunately, most applications of multilevel modeling utilize random samples of individuals, with contexts considered after the fact or limited to particular contexts due to issues of cost and availability. In even some of the very best neighborhood research today, for example that done by Sampson and colleagues (Sampson, Morenoff, & Earls, 1999), findings are limited by the fact that neighborhoods are drawn from only one or a small set of cities. An ideal approach would be a multi-stage design, with random sampling at both the contextual and individual levels.

This raises the related issue of identifying the appropriate context(s) to consider. For many work and family outcomes, some combination of workplaces, neighborhoods, and couples might be most appropriate. Yet even within the context of the workplace, one might argue for finer contextualizations, such as workers nested within work teams, or divisions, or exempt versus nonexempt statuses. Similarly, the community or neighborhood might be treated as an entire metropolitan area, a zip code, a census tract, a block group, or some smaller, more socially defined boundaries.

Sample Sizes and Measurement of Contextual Variables

Once the appropriate contexts have been identified, a next critical issue is sample size. For reasons of both statistical power (i.e., ability to detect significant relationships) and reliability, multilevel designs are improved by a larger number of units at each level of the hierarchy. Though no exact rules exist, some have argued for a minimum of 30 contextual units, with even more preferable if one is interested in cross-level random slopes models (Hox, 1998; Kreft, 1996). The example of retirement planning within organizations clearly falls short of these rules of thumb. Multilevel models are also generally improved by a larger number of individuals within each context. Rules of thumb again vary, with a suggested average of 10 to 30 per context (Hox, 1998; Kreft, 1996). In the case of modeling trajectories over time, growth curves can be estimated with as few as three measurements per respondent and can also handle missing data and varying measurement times. Note that these rules are averages so that some contexts may have considerably fewer respondents, including as few as one.

Measurement issues are also critical within multilevel research, though the statistical properties of contextual measures (sometimes called "ecometrics") are not as well understood as the psychometric properties of individual-level measures (Raudenbush & Sampson, 1999). One common technique for measuring contextual characteristics is to construct aggregated averages of individual-level variables, such as in the use of the average age of coworkers as a contextual variable in the retirement example. In general, the reliability of such contextual measures depends on a variety of factors, including the variability of the concept across contexts, inter-rater reliability (i.e., the agreement of persons within the same context), and the number of respondents per context (Raudenbush & Sampson, 1999).

Just as is true when measuring multiple concepts at the individual level, having independent measures of contextual- and individual-level measures is preferred. One frequent approach is to rely on administrative data, such as measures from the decennial censuses. This works relatively well for the more objective demographic and socioeconomic characteristics of census geographies, such as the percentage of single-parent households or the percent of families below poverty.

Administrative records, however, tend not to capture well the more proximal social processes through which contexts are likely to have their greatest influence. One technique used in neighborhood research is known as systematic social observation. In short, researchers drive through neighborhoods with video cameras, taping randomly selected "face-blocks" (i.e., sides of the street). The videos are then systematically rated to assess social processes within the neighborhood such as informal social control or social disorder (Raudenbush & Sampson, 1999; Sampson & Raudenbush, 1999). Precisely how one might apply this technique within contexts such as private organizations is not clear. Yet the idea of independent assessments of organizational characteristics still seems feasible.

Software Implementation

There are an increasing number of options for implementing hierarchical models within widely available software packages. Perhaps best-known is the HLM software (Raudenbush et al., 2000), now in its sixth edition, which supports a wide range of linear and nonlinear models. The accompanying manuals and Websites are user-friendly and provide many examples and answers to frequently asked questions. Other specialized hierarchical packages include MLWIN and MPLUS.

Hierarchical linear and generalized models may also be estimated within SAS statistical software using PROC MIXED and the GLIMMIX macro. One limitation of PROC MIXED is that it tends not to be as user-friendly as HLM and other software designed specifically for multilevel modeling. Fortunately, a number of researchers have developed detailed applications of hierarchical models within SAS, including step-by-step instructions (Guo, 2000; Singer, 1998). Given the increasing use of hierarchical models in the social sciences and applied professions, procedures for estimating such models with other large packages such as SPSS and STATA have recently been developed. See the Web sites of these programs for details.

CONCLUSION

If readers are not already familiar with hierarchical linear models, it is hoped that this review has sparked interest in the strong fit between the types of life course questions that work and family researchers frequently ask and the modeling possibilities of hierarchical models. They allow us to take seriously the life course tenet that lives are made up of trajectories embedded within social times and places. Moreover, they allow us to move beyond artificial individual versus contextual dichotomies to a more ecological approach that conceives of development as involving an inherently interactive relationship between characteristics of persons, couples, families, and the contexts within which they are embedded. Though not intended as a complete how-to guide, it is also hoped that this review has raised some of the theoretical, conceptual, and methodological issues that need to be considered as well as directions to look for more information about this rapidly growing technique.

NOTES

[1] Data used in this chapter are from the Cornell Ecology of Careers Study, designed by Principal Investigator Phyllis Moen, and supported by the Alfred P. Sloan Foundation (#96-6-9; 99-6-23; 2002-6-8) and National Institute on Aging (NIA#2p50-AG11711-86).

[2] This assumption can be relaxed by the related techniques of sequence analysis (Abbott & Tsay, 2000) and semi-parametric trajectory modeling (Nagin, 1999), which allow multiple trajectories and complex sequence of events.

REFERENCES

Abbott, A., & Tsay, A. (2000). Sequence analysis and optimal matching methods in sociology: Review and prospect. *Sociological Methods and Research, 48*(6), 3–33.

Barnett, R. C., Marshall, Nancy L., Raudenbush, Stephen W., & Brennan, Robert T. (1993). Gender and the relationship between job experiences and psychological distress: A study of dual-earner couples. *Journal of Personality and Social Psychology, 64*(5), 794–806.

Becker, P. E., & Moen, P. (1999). Scaling back: Dual-earner couples' work-family strategies. *Journal of Marriage and the Family, 61*(4), 995–1007.

Bronfenbrenner, U. (1979). *The ecology of human development.* Cambridge, MA: Harvard University Press.

Bryk, A. S., & Raudenbush, S. W. (1992). *Hierarchical linear models.* Newbury Park, CA: Sage.

Elder, G. (1999). *Children of the Great Depression; social change in life experience.* Boulder, CO: Westview.

Elder, G. H. (1998). The life course and human development. In R. Lerner (Ed.), *Handbook of child psychology, vol. 1: Theoretical models of human development* (pp. 939–991). New York: Wiley.

Furstenberg, F. F., Cook, T. D., Eccles, J., Elder, Glen H. Jr., & Sameroff, A. D. (1998). *Managing to make it: Urban families and adolescent success.* Chicago: University of Chicago Press.

Glass, J. L., & Estes, S. B. (1997). The family responsive workplace. *Annual Review of Sociology, 23*, 289–313.

Goldstein, H. (1994). Multilevel cross-classified models. *Sociological Methods and Research, 42*(3), 364–375.

Goldstein, H. (1995). *Multilevel statistical models.* London: Arnold.

Guo, G. (2000). Multilevel modeling for binary data. *Annual Review of Sociology, 26*, 441–462.

Han, S. K., & Moen, P. (1999). Clocking out: Temporal patterning of retirement. *American Journal of Sociology, 105*(1), 191–236.

Hox, J. J. (1998). Multilevel modeling: When and why. In I. Balderjahn, R. Mathar, & M. Schader (Eds.), *Classification, data analysis, and data highways* (pp. 147–154). Berlin: Springer-Verlag.

Hox, J. J., & Kreft, I. G. G. (1994). Multilevel analysis methods. *Sociological Methods and Research, 42*(3), 283–299.

Johnson, E. M., & Huston, T. L. (1998). The perils of love, or why wives adapt to husbands during the transition to parenthood. *Journal of Marriage and the Family, 51*(5), 195–204.

Kenny, D. A. (1996). Models of nonindependence in dyadic research. *Journal of Social and Personal Relationships, 13*, 279–294.

Kreft, I. G. G. (1996). *Are multilevel techniques necessary? An overview, including simulation studies.* Los Angeles: California State University.

Lamborn, S. D., Dornbusch, S. M., & Steinberg, L. (1996). Ethnicity and community context as moderators of the relations between family decison making and adolescent adjustment. *Child Development, 45*(1), 283–301.

Lee, E. S., Forthofer, R. N., & Lorimer, R. J. (1989). *Analyzing complex survey data.* Newbury Park, CA: Sage.

Lewin, K. (1951). *Field theory in social science, selected theoretical papers.* New York: Harper.

MacDermid, S. M., Hertzog, J. L., Kensinger, K. B., & Zipp, J. F. (2001). The role of organizational size and industry in job quality and work-family relationships. *Journal of Family and Economic Issues, 50*(1), 191–216.

Maguire, M. C. (1999). Treating the dyad as the unit of analysis: A primer on three analytic approaches. *Journal of Marriage and the Family, 61*, 213–223.

Moen, P. (Ed.). (2003). *It's about time.* Ithaca, NY: Cornell University Press.

Moen, P., Elder, G. H., & Luscher, K. (1995). *Examining lives in context.* Washington, DC: American Psychological Association.

Moen, P., Sweet, Stephen, & Swisher, Raymond R. (2005). Customizing the career clock: Retirement planning and expectations. In R. Macmillan (Ed.), *Advances in life course research: The structure of the life course: Standardized? individualized? differentiated?* Stamford, CT: JAI Press.

Moen, P., & Wethington, E. (1992). The concept of family adaptive strategies. *Annual Review of Sociology, 18*, 233–251.

Muthen, B. (1997). Latent variable modeling of longitudinal and multilevel data. *Sociological Methodology, 45*(6), 453–480.

Nagin, D. (1999). Analyzing developmental trajectories: A semiparametric, group-based approach. *Psychological Methods, 4*(2), 139–157.

Newsom, J. T. (2003). A multilevel structural equation model for dyadic data. *Structural Equation Modeling, 51*(6), 431–447.

Raudenbush, S. W., Brennan, Robert T., & Barnett, Rosalind C. (1995). A multivariate hierarchical model for studying psychological change within married couples. *Journal of Family Psychology, 9*(2), 161–174.

Raudenbush, S. W., Bryk, A. S., Cheong, Y. F., & Congdon, R. (2000). *HLM5: Hierarchial linear and nonlinear modeling.* Lincolnwood, IL: Scientific Software International.

Raudenbush, S. W., & Sampson, R. J. (1999). Ecometric: Toward a science of assessing ecological settings, with application to the systematic social observation of neighborhoods. *Sociolgical Methodology, 29*, 1–41.

Sampson, R. J., Morenoff, J. D., & Earls, F. (1999). Beyond social capital: Spatial dynamics of collective efficacy for children. *American Sociological Review, 64*(5), 633–660.

Sampson, R. J., & Raudenbush, S. W. (1999). Systematic social observation of public spaces: A new look at disorder in urban neighborhoods. *American Journal of Sociology, 48*(3), 603–651.

Singer, J. D. (1998). Using SAS PROC MIXED to fit multilevel models, hierarchical models, and individual growth models. *Journal of Educational and Behavioral Statistics, 24*(4), 323–355.

Snijders, T. A. B., & Bosker, R. J. (1999). *Multilevel analysis. An introduction to basic and advanced multilevel modelling.* London: Sage.

Steinberg, L., Mounts, N. S., Lamborn, S. D., & Dornbusch, S. M. (1991). Authoritative parenting and adolescent adjustment across varied ecological niches. *Journal of Research on Adolescence, 39*(5), 19–36.

Swisher, R., Sweet, S. A., & Moen, P. (2004). The family-friendly community and its life course fit for dual-earner couples. *Journal of Marriage and the Family, 66*(May), 281–292.

Wendorf, C. A. (2003). Comparisons of structural equation modeling and hierarchical linear modeling approaches to couples' data. *Structural Equation Modeling, 51*(6), 126–140.

27

The Work-Family Conflict Construct: Methodological Implications

Shelley M. MacDermid
Ashley Harvey
Purdue University

Work and family activities clearly dominate the lives of many adults. Consider that:

- The average adult is awake for 6,192 of the 8,766 hours in a year (National Sleep Foundation, 2002).
- Employed adults who are parents devote about 70% of their waking time to paid work, housework, and child care (Bianchi, 2000; Mishel, Bernstein, & Schmitt, 1999).

Thus, even without considering leisure time, the management of work and family responsibilities commands significant attention by working adults. Given the compelling nature of the work-family phenomenon, it is not surprising that researchers have devoted increasing attention to work-family research over the past 20 years.

The construct of work-family conflict has been a predominant theme in the study of the relationship between family and work (MacDermid, 2005). Given the salience of this topic in the work-family literature, we use this chapter to trace the evolution of the construct in the scholarly research and theoretic literature. Given the centrality of the work-family construct, this analysis is important because it provides a unique lens through which it is possible to also consider the development of the work-family area of study over time.

We describe our thoughts about work-family conflict from three vantage points: as a predictor, as an outcome, and as a process (with thanks to our colleague Michael Frone [2003], who inspired our format). This framework enables us to focus attention on different dimensions of the work-family construct, different research questions associated with the construct, and different implications for measurement and analysis. It is important to note that, in our discussion, we limit our consideration to paid work and to work-family conflict as it is experienced within (as opposed to across) individuals. As is suggested in the concluding section of this chapter, there continue to be many challenges associated with the precision of our operationalization of work-family conflict; however, due to the pivotal position that the work-family conflict construct holds in the work-family literature, it is essential that scholars continue to engage in these discussions.

RESEARCH ABOUT THE CONSEQUENCES
OF WORK-FAMILY CONFLICT

Work-family conflict has been studied as a precursor to and predictor of many outcomes (see reviews by Burke, 1988; Greenhaus & Beutell, 1985; Kossek & Ozeki, 1998; and Pleck, Staines, & Lang, 1980). In the most recent and comprehensive review of existing evidence, Allen, Herst, Bruck & Sutton (2000) conducted a meta-analysis of 67 quantitative studies of work-to-family conflict (we use this term to make clear that Allen et al.'s analysis focused only on conflict originating at work) published between 1980 and 1999. The studies fell into three groups according to whether the outcomes were related to work, nonwork, or stress. Job satisfaction was the most widely studied work outcome and in most studies was negatively related to work-to-family conflict, with a weighted correlation of $r = -.24$ across studies. The strongest relationship to work outcomes was found between work-to-family conflict and turnover intent ($r = .29$). A weak negative relationship to self-reported work performance was observed ($r = -.12$). In terms of nonwork outcomes, findings across the studies indicated that work-to-family conflict was negatively related to satisfaction with life ($r = -.28$), marriage ($r = -.23$), and family ($r = -.17$). Relationships between work-to-family conflict and stress were the strongest observed and were consistently positive: Across studies, reports of greater work-to-family conflict were associated with elevated general psychological strain ($r = .29$), physical symptoms or somatic complaints ($r = .29$), depression ($r = .32$), job burnout ($r = .42$), work-related distress ($r = .41$), family-related distress ($r = .31$), and alcohol use ($r = .13$).

Allen et al.'s analyses show that work-to-family conflict is significantly related to many important aspects of well-being and positive functioning. Why have so many researchers hypothesized such relationships? According to Near, Rice, and Hunt (1980), the theoretical origins of these hypotheses go back to Durkheim, Marx, Weber, and others who were concerned about the impact on individuals of the large social institutions that emerged early in the last century. Regardless of whether the predicted result was normlessness, alienation, or integration, these scholars shared a conviction that powerful influences linked organizations and individuals. For research on work-family conflict conducted during the past 20 years, the foundational theory is organizational stress theory as proposed by Kahn, Wolfe, Quinn, Snoek, and Rosenthal (1964), who defined role conflict as the result of incompatible role pressures. Kahn proposed that role conflict would have three consequences for individuals: (a) distress, in the form of anxiety, tension, frustration, a sense of futility, worry, or reduced general satisfaction that might in turn depress productivity and elevate absenteeism and turnover; (b) reduced trust, respect, and liking for role senders (the individuals imposing the conflicting expectations); and (c) psychological and social withdrawal in the form of reduced communication with role senders.

Allen et al.'s (2000) review summarizes considerable evidence supporting distress, the first consequence of conflict between roles that Kahn et al. (1964) predicted. So far, there is considerably more evidence of connections to psychological well-being than to productivity, absenteeism, or turnover. We are not aware of a research literature linking role conflict to attitudes toward role senders. Social withdrawal has been observed in a small number of studies, in response to stressful days or events at work (e.g., Repetti, 1994).

Despite an extensive research literature, our understanding of the consequences of work-family conflict remains incomplete (MacDermid, 2005). In most existing studies, conflict and outcomes are measured with the same self-report methods, which may inflate the relationships observed between them (Allen et al., 2000; Carlson, 1999). Grant-Vallone and Donaldson (2001) exposed such inflation when they used ratings by both workers and coworkers to assess links between work and family role conflict and psychological well-being. Although statistically significant relationships were evident regardless of the ratings used, the relationships using coworkers' ratings were only about half the strength of those obtained using workers' ratings. Greater precision will be obtained in future studies if researchers can find ways to reduce or control for variance attributed to shared methods, such as through the use of multiple raters (Grant-Vallone & Donaldson, 2001) and objective assessments (e.g., hypertension; Frone, Russell, & Barnes, 1996).

Since almost all existing studies are cross-sectional, the degree to which work-family conflict is a cause or a consequence (or both) of psychological well-being is not yet clear (see also MacDermid [2005] for a discussion of concerns regarding discriminant validity). Although Allen et al. (2000) tried to select studies that focused on "plausible outcomes," existing longitudinal studies raise questions about how relationships unfold over time. For example, Leiter and Durup (1996) found a reciprocal relationship in a study of health care workers: Work-to-family conflict and emotional exhaustion each significantly predicted the other 3 months later. In a study of 426 employed Finnish men and women with spouses or children, Kinnunen, Guerts, and Mauno (2004) found that work-family conflict was quite stable over a 1-year period and that it and well-being were about equally predictive of one another over time. Kelloway, Gottlieb, and Barham (1999) found that work interference with family was not a predictor but a result of general distress measured 6 months earlier.

Finally, Allen et al. (2000) found many inconsistencies in findings across studies. These could be due to differences across studies in samples, measures, or methods (Kossek & Ozeki, 1998). They also could be due to inaccuracies in theoretical models. We are especially concerned about the omission of relevant predictor variables because it can compromise the precision of research findings in two ways. First, omitting relevant variables reduces the ability of the researcher's model to explain the phenomenon under study. For example, had Greenhaus, Parasuraman, and Collins (2001) not included career involvement as a moderating variable in their study of work-to-family conflict and turnover among accountants, they would have failed to discover that work-to-family conflict was linked to withdrawal only for accountants who were uninvolved in their careers; those who were very involved were relatively unbothered. Second, omitting relevant predictors can lead researchers to overestimate the importance of work-family conflict because it is not forced to "compete" with other explanations of the outcomes. For example, if we know that one of the best-known predictors of intent to turnover is job satisfaction (Weiss, Beal, Barros, & MacDermid, 2003) and we do not include job satisfaction along with work-family conflict in an examination of turnover, we risk assigning more importance to work-family conflict than it deserves.

In summary, work-family conflict is significantly correlated with many indicators of well-being, in particular to indicators of psychological distress. It is not clear whether conflict predicts distress or the reverse; the few longitudinal studies that have been completed yield mixed results. There is less evidence of relationships to behavior, although at least one longitudinal study has found links to objective measures of alcohol use. We now turn our attention from the consequences of work-family conflict to its antecedents or causes.

RESEARCH ABOUT THE CAUSES OF WORK-FAMILY CONFLICT

When one considers work-to-family conflict as an outcome, the research questions that spring to mind include, "Who experiences conflict?" and "How much conflict is experienced?" Many studies have focused on the prevalence and severity of work-family conflict, often via group comparisons. For example, researchers have compared conflict among men and women, finding mixed results (e.g., Gutek, Searle, & Klepa, 1991; Pleck, Staines, & Lang, 1980) and overall more similarities than differences (Frone, 2003). Another popular strategy has been to base comparisons on family arrangements, such as earner status or children's ages. For example, Higgins, Duxbury, and Lee (1994) found in a large study of private and public employees in

Canada that gender and life cycle stage were both important. For men, work-family conflict was lower at each successive stage of the family life cycle (based on cross-sectional comparisons); for women, levels of conflict were similar in two early stages and lower in later stages.

Unlike gender and age, minority status is a social category that has received relatively little attention from work-family researchers. Underrepresented groups may be defined by ethnicity, but also by religion, gender, sexual orientation, social class, disability, family structure, or other factors (Voydanoff, 2002; Marks & Leslie, 1999), and minority status may increase the likelihood of stressful experiences in several ways. First, members of minority groups may be more likely to perceive—accurately or inaccurately—the occurrence of demands as a partial function of their underrepresentation, such as perceiving certain work pressures as being imposed on them because they have smaller numbers with which to resist. Due to their underrepresentation, the views of members of minority groups may differ from those of the majority population, which can create potentially stressful demands to conform or adjust. Finally, members of minority groups may feel that they constantly must manage their presentation of self to others so that they do not provoke negative reactions or reveal information that could be used to disadvantage them—over time, this can be draining and stressful.

On its own, membership in social categories such as gender, earner, or minority status has not proven very fruitful in revealing the causes of work-family conflict. The specific pressures that individuals face, in combination with the features of their niche in society, are more likely to account for their experiences of conflict (Frone, 2003). Research and theory on these specific pressures or demands is the next focus of our discussion.

Most measures of work-family conflict spring from a framework proposed by Greenhaus and Beutell (1985). Based on Kahn et al.'s aforementioned theory, they defined work-family conflict as "a form of interrole conflict in which the role pressures from the work and family domains are mutually incompatible in some respect" (p. 77). According to Greenhaus and Beutell, conflict may be time-based, where time pressure such as long or inflexible work hours in one role interfere with performance in the other; strain-based, where stress in role affects performance in the other; and behavior-based, when behavior in one role makes it difficult to fulfill expectations in another.

Greenhaus and Beutell (1985) also endorsed Kahn et al.'s proposal that role conflict would be more severe when the roles generating pressure or demands were central to the individual's sense of self. Subsequent research suggests that this hypothesis may need to be fine-tuned. Using cross-sectional data from a randomly selected community sample of 795 employed adults, Frone, Russell, and Cooper (1995) found limited support for the stress-exacerbating influence of role salience. High levels of salience exacerbated 3 of 10 relationships tested: between role ambiguity and physical health, role ambiguity and heavy alcohol use, and work pressure and heavy alcohol use. The researchers concluded that salience of the work role may not exacerbate the effect of all job stressors, only those that impede successful role performance. In the study mentioned earlier by Greenhaus, Parasuraman, and Collins (2001), however, salience of the work role among accountants had a moderating effect *opposite* the one found by Frone et al. (1995): Work-family conflict mattered most for turnover among accountants who were *least* involved in their careers. Perhaps role salience has different effects on work and family outcomes, or perhaps there is a level of salience beyond which job stressors no longer matter.

The Kahn and Greenhaus perspectives are "bottom-up" perspectives in that they focus very much on the relationships between specific roles. In contrast, Goode's (1960) "role strain" perspective focuses on the role system as a whole (Marks & MacDermid, 1996). Defining strain as "felt difficulty in fulfilling role obligations" (Goode, 1960, p. 483), Goode argued that the role obligations of most individuals would at times exceed their capacity to respond. For Goode, total role overload was more important for psychological well-being than conflict or ambiguity within a role or between any pair of roles. Hecht (2001) put these ideas to the test in a comparison of overload and conflict in a cross-sectional study of 279 employed Canadian mothers. She accurately predicted that respondents would perceive conflict as more difficult to manage than overload, explaining that conflict is the result of simultaneous incompatible demands. She also correctly predicted that time spent in roles would be more strongly related to overload than conflict. Resources such as income, flexibility, child care, and emergency child care were significantly and negatively related to conflict but not to overload. Hecht's hypotheses and findings illustrate the importance of precise hypotheses driven by theory. Her results have strong practical implications because they suggest that resources and policies and programs might reduce conflict, but leave overload untouched until work hours are reduced.

As MacDermid (2005) and others have noted, several refinements to early formulations of work-family conflict gained popularity in the 1990s. Considerable evidence has now accumulated that it is productive to consider separately conflict that originates in the home and in the workplace (Frone, 2003; Gutek, Searle, & Klepa, 1991). In their meta-analysis of relationships between conflict and satisfaction with work and with life, Kossek and Ozeki (1998) observed stronger findings for measures that clearly specified the direction of conflict than measures that did not do so. Findings generated by the use of directional measures suggest that work-to-family conflict and family-to-work facilitation are more common than family-to-work conflict and work-to-family facilitation (Frone, 2003; Kossek & Ozeki, 1998; Leiter & Durup, 1996). Although work-to-family and family-to-work conflict are correlated, they both appear to have implications for health or well-being (Frone, Russell, & Cooper, 1997).

Based on the available (mostly correlational) evidence, Frone (2003) concluded in a recent review that family-to-work conflict and work-to-family conflict are both positively related to time spent, psychological involvement, dissatisfaction or distress, conflict, ambiguity, and demands in the source domain (i.e., family is the source domain of family-to-work conflict). In turn, each type of conflict is associated with elevated dissatisfaction or distress and poor (self-reports of) performance in the outcome domain as well as general distress, poor physical health, and alcohol use. Higher levels of social support at work and higher levels of personal resilience, such as hardiness, extraversion, and self-esteem, are related to lower levels of conflict. One work outcome—turnover—may violate this symmetrical pattern by being more strongly related to conflict emanating from work than from family.

A second refinement that has gained in popularity is to attend not only to conflicting but also enhancing or facilitating elements of the interaction between work and family, which Wayne, Musisca, and Fleeson (2004) defined as performance or functioning in one role being enhanced by virtue of participation in another (p. 110). A 30-year literature proposes that roles generate resources (Sieber, 1974), energy (Barnett & Hyde, 2001; Marks, 1977), skills (Crouter, 1984), or positive mood (Stephens, Franks, & Atienza, 1997) for one another (Kirchmeyer, 1992). In a recent study, Grzywacz & Marks (2000) found that decision latitude and work and family support at home were associated with less conflicting and more enhancing relationships between the domains. In contrast, pressure at work and disagreements at home were associated with more conflict and less enhancement.

Third, several recent studies have improved their precision by taking personality characteristics into account. Kahn et al. (1964) predicted that the vulnerability of workers to role conflict would be in part a function of their personality traits, and the accumulating evidence supports this prediction. For example, individuals with certain traits may be less likely to perceive demands as stressful. Wayne, Musisca, and Fleeson (2004) studied the role of the "big five" personality traits in the consequences of conflict and facilitation emanating from work and from family. They used a random-digit dialing procedure and two-stage sampling to assemble a sample of 2,130 employed individuals; the response rate was 70%. Personality characteristics accounted for about 15% of the variance in work-family conflict and 8% of the variance in work-family facilitation. Individuals who scored higher on neuroticism and lower on conscientiousness and agreeableness were more likely to report conflict between work and family. Individuals who scored higher on extraversion, conscientiousness, agreeableness, and openness to experience were more likely to report facilitation between work and family.

In addition to main effect relationships, some researchers propose that certain personality traits may blunt the effects of conflict, playing a moderating or buffering role. Kinnunen, Vermulst, Gerris, and Mäkikangas (2003) studied 296 fathers in the Netherlands. In cross-sectional data, more emotionally stable fathers (i.e., those with low neuroticism and negative affectivity) reported weaker relationships between work-to-family conflict and job exhaustion or depression. Fathers who scored higher on agreeableness displayed weaker relationships between family-to-work conflict and marital satisfaction. The authors concluded that emotional stability and agreeableness may protect fathers from negative consequences of work-family conflict.

Another improvement in the study of relationships between work and family life has been increasingly sophisticated attention to the characteristics of workplaces. Workers' experiences are clearly related to the size and structure of their organizations (Kalleberg, Knoke, Marsden, & Spaeth, 1996). Workers in small workplaces generally report less work-family conflict, for example, than workers in larger workplaces (MacDermid, Hertzog, Kensinger, & Zipp, 2001). Other important environmental features include workers' access to supportive programs, policies, or supervision (Anderson, Coffey, & Byerly, 2002; Kossek & Ozeki, 1998; Lambert, 1990). For example, McManus, Korabik, Rosin, and Kelloway (2002) studied the degree to which single and married mothers at different occupational levels were offered support by their organizations and their supervisors and the degree to which they made use of formal policies intended to reduce work-family conflict. They found that regardless of marital status and family demands, mothers in lower-level occupations reported less work-to-family conflict when they perceived higher organizational and supervisor support and made greater use of formal policies.

Workplaces are also social environments where workers share experiences, interactions and perceptions, and work-family researchers have paid considerable attention to the supportiveness of supervisors and workplace cultures. Until recently, it has been very difficult to incorporate collective perceptions and experiences of workers into statistical models. Now, multi-level analyses offer the important capability of incorporating both individual and shared experiences of demands and support without the statistical distortions that previously could not be avoided (e.g., Bliese & Castro, 2000; Blair-Loy & Wharton, 2002).

As with consequences, the map of the causes of work-family conflict and facilitation contains several uncharted regions. For example, Kahn et al. (1964) and Greenhaus and Beutell (1985) agreed that conflict between work and family is generated by *simultaneous* pressure from the two domains, and that work-family conflict would be strongest in the presence of negative sanctions for noncompliance with role demands. Researchers have rarely tested these propositions, although Greenhaus and Powell (2003) are an exception. They presented 207 MBA students with vignettes asking them to choose between an overtime work session and a surprise birthday party for a family member. The vignettes were constructed so that students were presented with varying combinations of pressure and support from work and from home. Findings showed that students responded to the *combined* role pressures from work and from home when making their choices, and that they were especially responsive to pressure from salient roles.

The work-family literature has emphasized conflict between only these two roles as opposed to conflict involving other roles, but Barnett and colleagues have done considerable work to show that all roles are not created equal when it comes to compensating for or adding to the overall demands individuals face (Baruch & Barnett, 1986; Barnett, Marshall, & Pleck, 1992;

Barnett, Marshall, & Sayer, 1992). More recently, Blanchard-Fields, Chen, and Hebert (1997) studied the roles of self, spouse, parent, and professional among 244 married adults recruited through community organizations and newspaper ads. They found that role combinations differed in the ways they appeared to generate conflict, in part as a function of employment status and gender. For example, employed mothers experienced more conflict than unemployed mothers—not with their professional role—but between the roles of spouse and parent.

In summary, research on the causes of work-family conflict has sometimes focused on membership in social categories, but this approach has yielded less consistent results than approaches that also consider the specific pressures faced by individuals. Conflicting—or facilitating—influences may originate in either the work or family role as a function of pressure, distress or dissatisfaction, time spent, and psychological involvement. Enhancing or facilitating influences appear to occur less frequently than conflict (according to current measures), and certain personality characteristics may elevate or reduce vulnerability to conflict. Conflict may be more troublesome when it involves highly salient roles, although findings from one study suggest the opposite pattern. Other research suggests that all roles are not equal when it comes to generating conflict or enhancement. Role conflict may be more strongly related than role overload to psychological well-being, and also may be more responsive than overload to supportive policies and programs within workplaces.

THE PROCESSES OF WORK-FAMILY CONFLICT AND FACILITATION

Perhaps the most compelling questions of all about work-family conflict and facilitation are "How?" and "Why?" How do work and family influence one another, and why are these effects stronger for some workers than for others—these questions are at the cutting edge of our knowledge. In order to address them, researchers will need to emphasize "process" approaches. Research in the social sciences has tended to concentrate more on w*hether* than *how* phenonena are related. According to Mohr (1982), "variance" perspectives focus on relationships among variables and predicting an outcome from them. In contrast, process approaches focus more on how outcomes develop over time (Markus & Robey, 1988).

What does it mean to study processes? Monge, Farace, Eisenberg, Miller, and White (1984) referred to processes as "patterns . . . seen in reference to time" (p. 22). Thus, one key requirement when studying process is to address the time structure or the sequence in which processes unfold. Usually, longitudinal data are required to accomplish this goal, but through careful selection of variables some researchers have also been able to reveal time structures (e.g., Moen and colleagues have made very effective use of life history variables [Moen & Yu, 2000]). A second requirement of studying processes is that researchers must pay careful attention to factors that condition the way that processes unfold. For example, relationships between some variables are moderated by factors that reduce negative impacts or enhance positive ones; mediating factors intervene between other variables. Third, researchers must acknowledge the role of individuals in actively shaping their own experience by selecting roles in which to participate, monitoring and adjusting their performance within roles, and working toward goals over time (MacDermid, Franz, & De Reus, 1998). Fourth, answering questions of "how" and "why" requires attention to causal mechanisms. This means not only that the time structure and the contingencies that shape processes must be established, but also that alternative explanations must be ruled out in order to identify the most accurate and efficient explanation.

There have been repeated discussions among work-family researchers during the past 25 years about causal processes (Lambert, 1990; Staines, 1980; Zedeck, 1992; Zedeck &

Mosier, 1990). Recently, Edwards and Rothbard (2000) undertook a major rearticulation of six well-known processes: spillover, compensation, segmentation, resource drain, congruence, and work-family conflict. We applaud their contribution but wonder whether the need for (a)symmetry that these models impose is helpful in advancing knowledge. For example, constructs are suitable for inclusion in models of spillover or compensation if they display the required pattern of similarities or differences between work and family, but (a)symmetry does not seem to tell us much about causal mechanisms (e.g., knowing that stress in one domain is positively related to stress in the other reveals little about how or why this occurs). As an alternative approach, we take a closer look at the literature on occupational stress to generate ideas for future research.

Widely studied by researchers from many disciplines, work-related stress is a key construct in the connections between life on and off the job (Perry-Jenkins, Repetti, & Crouter, 2000). Existing evidence shows that stress is implicated in a variety of physical, psychological, behavioral, and social aspects of human behavior. For example, negative stress at work can impair psychological well-being; interfere with job performance by decreasing concentration (Wilson & Gottman, 1996), increasing substance use or counter productive behavior (Spielberger, Vagg, & Wasala, 2003); and elevate health complaints and the occurrence of disease, such as cardiovascular, musculoskeletal, immunological, and gastrointestinal disorders (Fitzgerald, Haythornthwaite, Suchday, & Ewart, 2003; Grebner, Elfering, Semmer, Kaiser-Probst, & Schlapbach, 2004). Work-induced stress also can interfere with social relationships by causing workers to withdraw from social interaction with their spouse and children (Repetti & Wood, 1997).

Although there are many theories about why stress processes unfold the way they do, there does appear to be a consensus that they include at least four elements: occurrence of an event or demand, followed by primary and secondary appraisal, an affective or emotional reaction, and a response in the form of coping. Most measures of work-family conflict make it difficult to determine whether these processes are operating because they conflate the precipitating event and perceptions of stress (Perry-Jenkins et al., 2000). For example, work-family conflict scores are usually analyzed as indicators of stress or strain, implying that an *emotional* reaction has been provoked. Yet the items on such measures typically use the approach in this sample item— "My work schedule makes it difficult for me to do things with my family," which sounds like a *cognitive* assessment or a primary appraisal of a mismatch between a demand (work schedule) and a desired goal (time with family), with no indication of the degree to which the worker is worried or upset by the mismatch. And, according to Edwards and Rothbard's (2000, p. 192) definition, work-family conflict sounds like a response to a demand or a form of coping *behavior*: "Work-family conflict is a form of resource drain, in which time or attention transferred from a domain hinders role performance in that domain but facilitates role performance in the receiving domain." The processes through which work, family, and perhaps other roles hinder and facilitate one another have cognitive, emotional, and behavioral elements that have not yet been fully explored.

Several major theories of organizational stress offer hints about why some demands and resources may be more important than others in the production of conflict between roles. Person–environment fit theory proposes that stress is lower when the characteristics of individuals and their work environment are well-matched, and some researchers have applied this theory to fit between work and family (e.g., Barnett, Gareis, & Brennan, 1999; Pittman, 1994; Voydanoff, 2002). Karasek's (1979) demand–control theory posits that autonomy and control are key variables, suggesting that stress results when workers experience high job demands and low decision-making power (Thomas & Ganster, 1995). Siegrist (1996) proposed that occupational stress occurs when individuals think they will not be rewarded in proportion to their effort. Lazarus' (1991b) transactional theory says that demands are perceived as stress-producing when they exceed the resources individuals can muster to cope with them. Hobfoll's (1989) conservation of resources perspective is the result of individual efforts to minimize the loss and maximize the gain of resources (Espino, Sundstrom, Frick, Jacobs, & Peters, 2002, p. 310; Grandey & Cropanzano, 1999). And, the effort–recovery model focuses on the need for recovery from workload effects during nonworking hours. If opportunities for recovery are insufficient and workers must "gear up" when they have not yet recovered, the negative effects will multiply during subsequent periods of work (Geurts, Kompier, Roxburh, & Houtman, 2003).

Voydanoff (2002) included elements from several of these theories in a recent conceptual framework. In her view, work and family characteristics generate conflict, balance or enhancement, depending on the moderating effects of social categories and coping resources. Strain or ease are affective or emotional reactions to conflict, balance, or enhancement, and they lead to perceptions of work-family fit (subject to mediation or moderation by coping strategies) and then to well-being outcomes.

To date, studies of work-related stress and its connections to life off the job have produced "weak and inconsistent" results (Perry-Jenkins et al., 2000). Findings from small homogenous samples have not tended to generalize to heterogeneous samples, probably because the individual differences that loom large in heterogeneous samples are not sufficiently taken into account in existing models and measures. Paying closer attention to the conditions that produce different outcomes in different individuals should allow us to account for more variability, omit fewer important predictors unnecessarily, and generate more realistic assessments of the role of work conditions in nonwork life. If conflict between work and family is essentially a special case of stress, it is especially important to study cognitive appraisals of demands posed by multiple roles, the emotions generated by such appraisals, and the coping efforts with which individuals respond—these are the foci of the following discussion.

WORK-FAMILY CONFLICT AND COGNITIVE APPRAISAL

Appraisal is the assessment of demands and the capacity to respond to them. Various theories define demands as heavy workloads, unpredictable schedules, financial strain, or heavy caregiving responsibilities. Resources might include financial, social and instrumental supports, and personal traits that help individuals to cope with stressors; these might include problem-solving skills, adequate income, emotional support from family and friends, and family-friendly programs and policies in the community or the workplace (Fredriksen & Scharlach, 1999; Haveman, Van Berkum, Reijnders, & Heller, 1997; Scharlach, Sobel, & Roberts, 1991). As demands rise, individuals' capacities to meet them may shrink unless new resources are found (Campbell & Moen, 1992; Eckenrode & Gore, 2000; Neal, Chapman, Ingersoll-Dayton, & Emlen, 1993; Parcel & Menaghan, 1994). For example, two workers who face the same demands on the job are likely to experience them very differently if one worker has very good support from family, friends, or community and the other is socially isolated.

Appraisals have two components. In primary appraisal, individuals assess the degree to which the demand or potential stressor is relevant to them, the degree to which it is threatening, and the degree to which it is challenging (Peacock & Wong, 1990, as cited in Dewe, 1991). Secondary appraisal occurs when the individual determines whether or not he or she can mobilize sufficient resources to meet the demand. Psychological stress occurs when the individual concludes that the magnitude of the demand is too great for the available resources (Ortony, Clore, & Collins, 1988). Few studies have been conducted on the processes of primary or secondary appraisal in the production of work-family conflict and facilitation.

Because events, appraisals and emotions happen quickly, perhaps many times over the course of a day, they must be observed using research methods designed for capturing life "in the moment." Experience sampling or momentary assessment methods, whereby respondents are prompted via a signal or paging device several times a day to answer a small set of questions, have proven very useful in this effort (Larson & Almeida, 1999). Williams, Suls, Alliger, Learner, and Wan (1991) studied 20 working mothers over a period of 8 days. At each signal, the mothers were asked whether their current activity had been interrupted in the 30 minutes prior to the signal, causing them to juggle two or more tasks at once. If their response was affirmative, they were asked to indicate what role or roles were juggled—responsibilities within the work role, the family role, or from both roles at once. Respondents also were asked to indicate their emotional state at the time of the signal. With this strategy, Williams et al. were able to measure separately the occurrence of an event with the potential to produce stress (i.e., juggling role responsibilities) from its consequences. Results showed that different types of juggling had different implications for distress. Juggling tasks from different roles was more difficult than juggling tasks within the same role. Juggling overall was perceived as more troublesome than work-family juggling per se. And, respondents appeared to habituate to juggling over time, becoming less likely to evaluate it as difficult or stressful. Thus, all events were clearly not appraised as equal.

How might stress theories explain why some work-family events are more likely than others to be appraised as stressful? Demand–control theory suggests that one of the most important moderators of the stress process is the degree to which persons believe that they can control the circumstances they experience and respond successfully (Karasek, 1979). Persons who perceive high levels of control may be less likely to appraise a demand as relevant to their well-being, reducing the likelihood that anxiety or depression will be experienced. Even when they consider a demand to be stressful, such persons also may by more likely than others to believe that they can respond successfully, thus moderating the relationship between primary and secondary appraisal. Specifically regarding processes of work-family conflict, Williams et al. speculated that workers might be better able to control competing responsibilities when they come from one domain as opposed to multiple domains. For example, workers might find it easier to rearrange competing work tasks than to deal with a family issue that erupts during business hours.

WORK-FAMILY CONFLICT AND EMOTIONS

Anxiety and depressed mood are the two most commonly measured manifestations of psychological distress (Grimshaw, 1999, p. 219) and have both been studied as consequences of work-family conflict. Although they both can become chronic disorders, we are more interested in their statelike manifestations. As emotions, anxiety and depressed mood are "valenced reactions to events, agents, or objects" (Ortony et al., 1988, p. 13); we use the inclusive term "demand" as shorthand for events, agents, or objects. Emotion word synonyms for anxiety might be "tense," "worried," or "anxious"; synonyms for depressed mood might be "miserable," "depressed," and "gloomy" (Holman & Wall, 2002). Emotions fall into groups based in part on their valence (positive, negative) and intensity (low, high). As a negative high-arousal emotion, anxiety falls into a group of emotions associated with fear, while depressed mood is a negative low-arousal emotion and falls into a group defined by sadness (Holman & Wall, 2002).

The valence of an emotion is based on whether the demand is viewed positively or negatively (Lazarus, 1993). Intensity is determined by the *degree* of positive or negative reaction to the demand. To the degree that demands seem real or likely and are sudden, immediate, or unexpected, intensity will be greater (Boss, 2002; Ortony et al., 1988). Work-family researchers have so far not devoted much attention to these dimensions of demands. Lazarus (1993) argued that emotions are joint functions of the stressor or demand and the goals of the individual. Without considering goals, there is no way to determine the relevance or importance of the demand. To the extent that the salience or importance of a role to the individual could be considered an indicator of his or her goals, most studies of role salience and work-family conflict have found salience to be important to responses to role pressure.

The antecedents of anxiety appear to be distinct from those of depressed mood (Lazarus, 1991a). For example, both anxiety and depressed mood result from evaluations of demands as undesirable, but anxiety is about future events while depressed mood is about events in the past. Anxiety is negative because the prospective demand is undesirable, and the intensity of the anxiety is a function of just how undesirable it is (Ortony et al., 1988). Depressed mood is associated with a negative demand that has already occurred and a consequent sense of loss (Lazarus, 1993). The consequences of anxiety and depressed mood also may differ. Emotions affect judgments and lead to particular behaviors (Brief & Weiss, 2002; MacDermid, Weiss, & Seery, 2002), and different emotions lead to different behaviors. For example, since depressed mood is a low-arousal emotion, it may be more likely than anxiety to stimulate a passive coping response.

Conservation of resources theory (Grandey & Cropanzano, 1999) may be particularly relevant to understanding anxiety as it relates to work-family conflict, because this theory deals with worry about the possible loss of resources in the future. Potential or actual losses of resources lead to a negative "state of being," which may include dissatisfaction, depression, anxiety, or physiological tension. Some type of behavior is needed to replace or protect the threatened resources. If efforts are not made to replace or protect the threatened resources, they may be so depleted that burnout ensues.

Work-family conflict has been linked to a variety of indicators of psychological distress but only a narrow range of emotions. Other emotional states deserve consideration, such as anger, guilt, excitement, and contentment. Better understanding of occasions when a potential stressor is appraised as nonthreatening and fails to generate an emotional response would do much to explain individual differences.

WORK-FAMILY CONFLICT AND COPING

Emotions lead to coping, "constantly changing cognitive and behavioral efforts to manage . . . demands that are appraised as taxing or exceeding the resources of the person" (Lazarus & Folkman, 1984, p. 141). In other words, coping is what individuals and families do to mobilize resources in response to emotions generated by demands that have been appraised as stressful.

Many different coping strategies have been documented, and individuals vary considerably in the number and diversity of strategies they favor. Historically, strategies have been classified as "problem-focused," where energy is directed to eliminating the provoking problem, or "emotion-focused," where the primary goal is to control emotional responses. A more fine-grained classification focuses on the degree to which the strategy aims at avoiding the stressor, taking action to remove it, seeking support, or changing the way one thinks or feels about it (Folkman & Moskowitz, 2004, p. 752). Multiple strategies may be implemented at once, as individuals try to cope simultaneously with negative emotions as well as the logistical or other demands of stressful circumstances. As coping strategies are tried and have varying results, individuals reappraise their situations, experiencing new emotional reactions as the ratio between demands and resources shifts.

As described earlier, anxiety is an emotion generated in relation to the possibility of a future threat. Because of ambiguity about whether, when, and how the threat might occur, it is difficult for the individual to know how to respond. As a result, anxiety may be associated with coping strategies that aim to avoid or escape the potential threat. In contrast, depression grows from sadness and resignation associated with past events and is often accompanied by a sense of helplessness that inhibits action (Lazarus, 1991a).

With a few exceptions (e.g., McCubbin, Thompson, & McCubbin, 1996; Moen & Yu, 2000), coping responses to have received relatively little attention in research on work and family. Behson (2002) tackled the difficult task of operationalizing informal work accommodations as a strategy for coping with work-family conflict (e.g., increasing boundary permeability to benefit the family), finding that such accommodations reduced subsequent distress.

Left for future examinations are whether or when efforts to cope with work-family conflict are appropriately chosen, their degree of success, and the degree to which they are the result of a first or later attempt to deal with a stressor. It is also important to consider the personal or contextual circumstances that might condition the suitability or the success of coping efforts. Perhaps the primary example of such a condition is the amount of control available to the individual to be sure that he or she can implement the strategies choosen. Here, we see another key difference between anxiety and depression, for example. Whereas anxiety carries uncertainty about the degree to which circumstances may be controlled, depression is more likely to be associated with resignation at a loss of control (Lazarus, 1993).

Control also is implicated in the selection of coping strategies. To the extent that it is not possible to control the stressor, emotion-focused coping might be appropriate and adaptive; to the extent that the stressor can be controlled, it might be best to try to do so using problem-focused strategies (Lazarus, 1993). Empirical research provides considerable support for this proposition. For example, Holman and Wall (2002) found that job control reduced strain and also increased learning. Price, Choi, and Vinokur (2002) concluded that loss of personal control was a pathway through which economic adversity was transformed into chronic problems of poor health and impaired role and emotional functioning. Grebner et al. (2004, p. 42) observed that high control seemed to make it easier for individuals to calm themselves in stress-producing situations.

Our goal in the preceding sections has been to suggest a conceptual approach to a key process linking work and family. In order to accomplish the goal, our approach needed to account for the unfolding of the process over time, systematic patterns of change, and individual variations in outcomes. It also needed to specify antecedents, outcomes, and linking mechanisms. Attending to specific features of stress processes as they might relate to work-family conflict may enrich the models on which the work-family literature has relied for the past quarter century. Stress theories offer ways to account for individuals' idiosyncratic appraisals of demands, their emotional reactions, and the likely results. They suggest a temporal structure of demand–appraisal–emotion–response. They lead us to learn about individuals' assessments of the relevance of events, how well-prepared they feel to respond, and how successful their responses turn out to be. Addressing these issues will help us to determine more precisely how and why work-family conflict occurs, and how important it is in the configuration of causes of psychological well-being and role performance.

EXPANDING LEVELS OF ANALYSIS

This chapter has focused exclusively on work-family conflict as it occurs within individuals. Stressful demands may have implications far beyond the individual worker, however. Ultimately, demands also may affect marital or parental dyads, groups of family members or coworkers, workplace environments, and possibly even communities.

Studying processes that unfold across levels of analysis is challenging because it is easy to make errors in logic, where there is a mismatch between the levels at which data are gathered and inferences are made. Neuman (1997) described two particularly common errors in causal explanation. Ecological fallacy occurs when a researcher draws a conclusion about individuals based on data gathered at a higher or aggregate level (see also Bliese & Jex, 2002), such as when researchers draw conclusions about individual workers based on assessing some characteristic of an organization. This was a controversial element of several studies conducted by Menaghan and Parcel in the 1980s and 1990s, where some occupational characteristics were coded based on the dictionary of occupational titles as opposed to the perceptions of the workers being studied (Parcel & Menaghan, 1994).

In contrast, reductionism occurs when researchers explain macro-level events based only on evidence from specific individuals. This used to occur frequently when researchers used the perceptions of only one partner to characterize a marriage overall (Thomson & Williams, 1982). Today, it is likely to occur when employer characteristics are assessed, usually through one of the following approaches: a representative of the human resources area of an employing organization is invited to complete a survey or interview that focuses on corporate policies and programs, or to designate someone else within the company to do so; or one or more workers in an organization are asked to describe the availability and their use of programs and policies, as well as their impressions of other characteristics of organizations. Strangely, while data from small groups of workers are not generally considered to provide a "true" picture of organizational characteristics, the practice of asking an HR representative to characterize the organization is both well-established and well-accepted. In the future, better use could probably be made of organizations' internal administrative data. Multi-level methods of data collection and analysis also offer hope for achieving greater precision in understanding the relationships between organizational- and individual-level phenomena.

Studying higher-level or cross-level phenomena also requires great clarity on the part of researchers with regard to measurement, analysis, and inference. Level of measurement is determined by who actually reports the data to be considered. When individuals describe their subjective experiences, measurement is clearly at the level of the individual. When characteristics of organizations are indicated by aggregate figures such as sales or profitability, measurement is clearly at the level of the organization. In a gray area are instances where data are gathered from individuals who are asked to characterize organizations. In this case, measurement is at the level of the individual, but the content of the measures is at the level of organizations. Nonetheless, the data should be treated as data from individuals in statistical analyses. Data analyses also must carefully distinguish between individual and higher levels. For example, when groups of workers are asked to assess the supportiveness of their supervisor, their observations are not independent and should not be treated as such in analyses. A variety of multi-level analytic techniques are available to meet this challenge. Finally, researchers must be careful to limit their inferences to the levels for which they have appropriate data, avoiding the problems of reductionism and ecological fallacy described above.

It is a worthy but difficult challenge to conclusively demonstrate the operation of cross-level processes. Bronfenbrenner, Moen, and Garbarino (1984) offered useful insights in their description of the necessary conditions for documenting the influences of communities on individuals. The same prescriptions apply to demonstrating the effects of organizations. Thus, the researcher must not only show that organizations vary in structure and that there are systematic differences across organizations in individuals' psychological experiences of them; it is also necessary to show that the effects occur at the level of the organization and are not simply an aggregation of processes at the individual level, to distinguish organization-level processes from the effects of indivduals' self-selection into them, and to identify the sources and mechanisms of organization effects.

It is also important to give explicit attention to different rhythms of time. The vast majority of existing studies of work-family conflict use survey methods that focus on periods of a few weeks or months. A few studies have used experience sampling methods to capture hour-to-hour and day-to-day variations. And, a few studies have used longitudinal methods to capture longer-term implications of work-family conflict extending several years into the future. But, large gaps remain in researchers' consideration of the time structure of work-family conflict. For example, theories of work-family conflict say little about how it is likely to be manifest in the short, medium, and long term. Most measurement strategies rely on individuals' perceptions of whether work and family conflict, but perhaps there are types of conflict that are visible only through objective observations of large-scale populations (e.g., inequitable distributions of opportunities in the labor force that interfere with family life), very long periods of time (e.g., truncated life expectancies as a function of chronic mismatches between work and family), or very precise physiological markers (e.g., stress hormones).

Recent theory and research have begun to pursue these possibilities. Several scholars have turned their focus to workers' daily navigation of responsibilities within and between roles. For example, Kossek, Lautsch, and Eaton (2005) are considering how individuals "enact flexibility." Ashforth, Kreiner, and Fugate (2000) asked how individuals engage in daily role transitions as part of their organizational life, creating, maintaining, and managing role boundaries over the course of a day. Clark (2002) has studied the content of cross-boundary communication, finding that certain topics of communication are more important for conflict than others. At the other end of the time spectrum, scholars are considering workers' efforts to cope with structural conflicts between work and family over the life course. For example, Carr (2002) examined the differing consequences of trade-offs between work and family for three cohorts of men and women. Becker and Moen (1999) documented how gender and life course factors shape work family strategies, showing that dual-earner husbands and wives (mostly wives) use "scaling back" as a strategy for reducing negative impacts of paid work on family life.

IMPLICATIONS FOR FUTURE RESEARCH

Many other important aspects of work-family conflict deserve further study. For example, important outcomes for individuals and families include physical health, effective social functioning (Moore & Keyes, 2003), and quality of relationships with family members and friends. In workplaces, the dynamics of relationships with supervisors and coworkers are not yet well-understood and much also remains to be learned about organizational programs and policies as they shape workers' experiences and important organizational outcomes such as profitability, performance, and morale (Arthur, 2003; Grover & Crooker, 1995; Kossek & Ozeki, 1999; Perry-Smith & Blum, 2000).

The study of emotional experiences in relationships between work and family is still in its early stages, and many emotions remain only lightly examined. One example is anger. Like anxiety, anger is a negative high-arousal emotion that can interfere with job performance and may lead to cardiovascular disease. For example, Fitzgerald, Haythornthwaite, Suchday, and Ewart (2003) found that dissatisfied workers with less job control and social support not only were more angry, but also more likely to feel threatened by and evoke hostility from customers, coworkers, or supervisors. Given established connections between violence at home and at work (Macmillan & Gartner, 1999; Melzer, 2002), anger and hostility deserve much greater attention.

There are also processes to be examined in greater depth. Creative scholars such as Nippert-Eng (1996) and Rothbard (2001) are developing new ideas about ways in which work and family may influence each other. Better understanding of the processes through which individuals select and manage participation in roles and restrict the flow of negative influences between roles would be very helpful, especially when it comes to considering the implications of work-family conflict for children or work performance.

Researchers who want clearly articulate the mechanisms that connect work and family may find the following principles helpful for future studies:

- Attend to the time structure of the process under consideration. Of course, this is best accomplished by gathering longitudinal data, but even then variables must be operationalized to match the rhythm or frequency of the phenomenon under study.
- Push beyond descriptive questions. Make specific directional predictions and test competing explanations.
- Make sure predictions are grounded in theories that clearly specify the mechanism that links the work and family (or other) domains.
- Consider the role of mediating and/or moderating effects, but do so with an eye on parsimony—the most comprehensive explanations are not necessarily the most efficient.
- Reduce variance due to shared methods by using multiple informants, objective measures (e.g., observers, physiological), or questions about objective events.
- Provide evidence of the discriminant validity of all measures, not just convergent validity or internal consistency.

Some existing studies illustrate these strategies. For example, Matthews, Conger, and Wickrama's (1996) study of marital outcomes used longitudinal data to trace the causal sequence from work-family conflict through psychological distress of workers and partners to marital functioning. Crouter, Bumpus, Head, and McHale (2001) demonstrated that workers' long hours were corrosive for relationships with children and spouses only when combined with perceptions of overload and strain. Several short-term longitudinal studies provide excellent insight into work-family conflict as it unfolds over the course of a day (Larson & Almeida, 1999; Repetti, 1989; Schulz, Cowan, Pape Cowan, & Brennan, 2004).

Much of the research about relationships between employment and family life is motivated by researchers' convictions that these domains influence one another. Studies conducting the rigorous tests required to support such convictions are just beginning to appear. We are eager to see what the studies yet to come will teach us!

ACKNOWLEDGMENTS

We wish to express our appreciation to the editors for the invitation to submit this manuscript. Thanks also to Howard Weiss for his helpful suggestions. Preparation of this manuscript was supported in part by Cooperative Agreement # DASW01-00-2-0005, awarded to S. MacDermid and H. Weiss by the U.S. Department of Defense, and by a grant from the Alfred P. Sloan Foundation to S. MacDermid and M. Pitt-Catsouphes.

REFERENCES

Allen, T. D., Herst, D. E. L., Bruck, C. S., & Sutton, M. (2000). Consequences associated with work-to-family conflict: A review and agenda for future research. *Journal of Occupational Health Psychology, 5*, 278–308.
Anderson, S. E., Coffey, B. S., & Byerly, R. T. (2002). Formal organizational initiatives and informal workplace practices: Links to work-family conflict and job-related outcomes. *Journal of Management, 28*, 787–810.
Arthur, M. (2003). Share price reactions to work-family initiatives: An institutional perspective. *Academy of Management Journal, 46*, 497–506.

Ashforth, B. E., Kreiner, G. E., & Fugate, M. (2000). All in a day's work: Boundaries and micro role transitions. *Academy of Management Review, 25*, 472–491.

Barnett, R. C., Gareis, K. C., & Brennan, R. T. (1999). Fit as a mediator of the relationships between work hours and burnout. *Journal of Occupational Health Psychology, 4*, 307–317.

Barnett, R. C., Marshall, N. L., & Pleck, J. H. (1992). Men's multiple roles and their relationship to men's psychological distress. *Journal of Marriage and the Family, 54*, 358–367.

Barnett, R. C., Marshall, N. L., & Sayer, A. (1992). Positive spillover effects from job to home: A closer look. *Women and Health, 19*, 13–41.

Baruch, G. K., & Barnett, R. C. (1986). Role quality, multiple role involvement, and psychological well-being in midlife women. *Journal of Personality and Social Psychology, 51*, 578–585.

Becker, P. E., & Moen, P. (1999). Scaling back: Dual-career couples' work-family strategies. *Journal of Marriage and the Family, 61*, 995–1007.

Behson, S. J. (2002). Coping with family-to-work conflict: The role of informal work accommodations to family. *Journal of Occupational Health Psychology, 7*, 324–341.

Bianchi, S. M. (2000). Maternal employment and time with children: Dramatic change or surprising continuity? Presidential address to the Population Association of America.

Blair-Loy, M., & Wharton, A. S. (2002). Employees' use of work-family policies and the workplace social context. *Social Forces, 80*, 813–845.

Blanchard-Fields, F., Chen, Y., & Hebert, C. E. (1997). Interrole conflict as a function of life stage, gender, and gender-related personality attributes. *Sex Roles, 37*, 155–174.

Bliese, P. D., & Castro, C. A. (2000). Role clarity, work overload and organizational support: Multilevel evidence of the importance of support. *Work and Stress, 14*, 65–73.

Bliese, P. D., & Jex, S. M. (2002). Incorporating a multilevel perspective into occupational stress research: Theoretical, methodological, and practical implications. *Journal of Occupational Health Psychology, 7*, 265–276.

Boss, P. (2002). *Family stress management: A contextual approach (2nd ed.).* Thousand Oaks, CA: Sage.

Brief, A. P., & Weiss, H. M. (2002). Organizational behavior: Affect in the workplace. *Annual Review of Psychology, 53*, 279–307.

Bronfenbrenner, U., Moen, P., & Garbarino, J. (1984). Family, community, and children. In R. Parke (Ed.) Review of child development research (Vol. 7, pp. 283–328). Chicago, IL: University of Chicago Press.

Bumpus, M. F., Crouter, A. C., & McHale, S. M. (1999). Work demands of dual-earner couples: Implications for parents' knowledge about children's daily lives in middle childhood. *Journal of Marriage and the Family, 61*, 465–475.

Burke, R. J. (1988). Some antecedents and consequences of work-family conflict. *Journal of Social Behavior and Personality, 3*, 287–302.

Campbell, M. L., & Moen, P. (1992). Job–family role strain among employed single mothers of preschoolers. *Family Relations, 41*, 205–211.

Carlson, D. S. (1999). Personality and role variables as predictors of three forms of work-family conflict. *Journal of Vocational Behavior, 55*, 236–253.

Carr, D. (2002). The psychological consequences of work-family trade-offs for three cohorts of men and women. *Social Psychology Quarterly, 65*, 103–124.

Clark, S. (2002). Communicating across the work/home border. *Community, Work & Family, 5*, 23–48.

Crouter, A. C. (1984). Participative work as an influence on human development. *Journal of Applied Developmental Psychology, 5*, 71–90.

Crouter, A. C., Bumpas, M. F., Head, M. R., & McHale, S. M. (2001). Implications of overwork and overload for the quality of men's family relationships. *Journal of Marriage & the Family, 63*, 404–416.

Dewe, P. (1991). Primary appraisal, secondary appraisal and coping: Their role in stressful work encounters. *Journal of Occupational Psychology, 64*, 331–351.

Eckenrode, J., & Gore, S. (1990). Stress and coping at the boundary of work and family. In J. Eckenrode & S. Gore (Eds.), Stress between work and family (pp. 1–16). New York: Plenum.

Edwards, J. R., & Rothbard, N. P. (2000). Mechanisms linking work and family: Clarifying the relationship between work and family constructs. *Academy of Management Review, 25*, 178–199.

Espino, C. M., Sundstrom, S. M., Frick, H. L., Jacobs, M., & Peters, M. (2002). International business travel: Impact on families and travelers. *Occupational Environmental Medicine, 59*, 309–322.

Fitzgerald, S. T., Haythornthwaite, J. A., Suchday, S., & Ewart, C. K. (2003). Anger in young Black and White workers: Effects of job control, dissatisfaction and support. *Journal of Behavioral Medicine, 26*, 283–296.

Folkman, S., & Moskowitz, J. T. (2004). Coping: Pitfalls and promise. *Annual Review of Psychology, 55*, 745–754.

Fredriksen, K. I., & Scharlach, A. E. (1999). Employee family care responsibilities. *Family Relations, 48*, 189–196.

Frone, Michael R. (2003). Work-family balance. In J. C. Quick & L. E. Tetrick (Eds.), *Handbook of occupational health psychology* (pp. 143–162). Washington, DC: American Psychological Association.

Frone, M. R., Russell, M., & Barnes, G. M. (1996). Work-family conflict, gender, and health-related outcomes: A study of employed parents in two community samples. *Journal of Occupational Health Psychology, 1*, 57–69.

Frone, M. R., Russell, M., & Cooper, M. L. (1995). Job stressors, job involvement and employee health: A test of identity theory. *Journal of Occupational and Organizational Psychology, 68*, 1–11.

Frone, M. R., Russell, M., & Cooper, M. L. (1997). Relation of work-family conflict to health outcomes: A four-year longitudinal study of employed parents. *Journal of Occupational and Organizational Psychology, 70*, 325–335.

Goode, William J. (1960). A theory of role strain. *American Sociological Review, 25*, 483–496.

Grandey, A. A., & Cropanzano, R. (1999). The conservation of resources model applied to work-family conflict and strain. *Journal of Vocational Behavior, 54*, 350–370.

Grant-Vallone, Elisa J., & Donaldson, Stewart I. (2001). Consequences of work-family conflict on employee well-being over time. *Work and Stress, 15*, 214–226.

Grebner, S., Elfering, A., Semmer, N. K., Kaiser-Probst, C., & Schlapbach, M. (2004). Stressful situations at work and in private life among young workers: An event sampling approach. *Social Indicators Research, 67*, 11–49.

Greenhaus, J. H., & Beutell, N. J. (1985). Sources of conflict between work and family roles. *Academy of Management Review, 10*, 76–88.

Greenhaus, J. H., Parasuraman, S., & Collins, K. M. (2001). Career involvement and family involvement as moderators of relationships between work-family conflict and withdrawal from a profession. *Journal of Occupational Health Psychology, 6*, 91–100.

Greenhaus, J. H., & Powell, G. N. (2003). When work and family collide: Deciding between competing role demands. *Organizational Behavior and Human Decision Processes, 90*, 291–303.

Grimshaw, J. (1999). *Employment and health: Psychosocial stress in the workplace.* London: The British Library.

Grover, S. L., & Crooker, K. J. (1995). Who appreciates family-responsive human resource policies: The impact of family-friendly policies. *Personnel Psychology, 48*, 271–299.

Grzywacz, J. G., & Marks, N. F. (2000). Reconceptualizing the work-family interface: An ecological perspective on the correlates of positive and negative spillover between work and family. *Journal of Occupational Health Psychology, 5*, 111–126.

Geurts, S. A. E., Kompier, M. A. J., Roxburgh, S., & Houtman, I. L. D. (2003). Does work–home interference mediate the relationship between workload and well-being? *Journal of Vocational Behavior, 63*, 532–559.

Gutek, B. A., Searle, S., & Klepa, L. (1991). Rational versus gender role explanations for work-family conflict. *Journal of Applied Psychology, 76*, 560–568.

Hecht, L. M. (2001). Role conflict and role overload: Different concepts, different consequences. *Sociological Inquiry, 71*, 111–121.

Higgins, C., Duxbury, L., & Lee, C. (1994). Impact of life-cycle stage and gender on the ability to balance work and family responsibilities. *Family Relations, 43*, 144–150.

Hobfoll, S. E. (1989). Conservation of resources: A new attempt at conceptualizing stress. *American Psychologist, 44*, 513–524.

Holman, D. J., & Wall, T. D. (2002). Work characteristics, learning-related outcomes, and strain: A test of competing direct effects, mediated, and moderated models. *Journal of Occupational Health Psychology, 7*, 283–301.

Kahn, R. L., Wolfe, D. M., Quinn, R. P., Snoek, J. D., & Rosenthal, R. A. (1964). *Organizational stress: Studies in role conflict and ambiguity.* New York: Wiley.

Kalleberg, A. L., Knoke, D., Marsden, P. V., & Spaeth, J. L. (1996). *Organizations in America: Analyzing their structures and human resource practices.* Thousand Oaks, CA: Sage.

Karasek, R. A. (1979). Job demands, job decision latitude, and mental strain: Implications for job redesign. *Administrative Science Quarterly, 24*, 285–309.

Kelloway, E. K., Gottlieb, B. H., & Barham, L. (1999). The source, nature, and direction of work and family conflict: A longitudinal investigation. *Journal of Occupational Health Psychology, 4*, 337–346.

Kinnunen, U., Geurts, S., & Mauno, S. (2004). Work-to-family conflict and its relationship with satisfaction and well-being: A one-year longitudinal study on gender differences. *Work & Stress, 18*, 1–22.

Kinnunen, U., Vermulst, A., Gerris, J., & Mäkikangas, A. (2003). Work-family conflict and its relations to well-being: The role of personality as a moderating factor. *Personality and Individual Differences, 35*, 1669–1683.

Kirchmeyer, C. (1992). Perceptions of nonwork-to-work spillover: Challenging the common view of conflict-ridden domain relationships. *Basic and Applied Social Psychology, 13*, 231–249.

Kossek, E. E., Lautsch, B. A., & Eaton, S. C. (2005). Flexiblity enactment theory: Relationships between type, boundaries, control and work-family effectiveness. In E. Kossek & S. Lambert (Eds.), *Work and life integration: Organizational, cultural, and psychological perspectives.* Mahwah, NJ: Lawrence Erlbaum Associates.

Kossek, E. E., & Ozeki, C. (1998). Work-family conflict, policies, and the job–life satisfaction relationship: A review and directions for organizational behavior–human resources research. *Journal of Applied Psychology, 83*, 139–149.

Lambert, S. (1990). Processes linking work and family: A critical review and research agenda. *Human Relations, 43*, 239–257.

Larson, R. W., & Almeida, D. M. (1999). Emotional transmission in the daily lives of families: A new paradigm for studying family process. *Journal of Marriage & the Family, 61,* 5–20.

Lazarus, R. S. (1991a). *Emotion and adaptation.* New York: Oxford University Press.

Lazarus, R. S. (1991b). Psychological stress in the workplace. In P. L. Perrewe (Ed.), *Handbook on job stress* (pp. 1–13). Corte Madera, CA: Select Press.

Lazarus, R. S. (1993). From psychological stress to the emotions: A history of changing outlooks. *Annual Review of Psychology, 44,* 1–21.

Lazarus, R. S., & Folkman, S. (1984). *Stress, appraisal, and coping.* New York: Springer.

Leiter, M. P., & Durup, M. J. (1996). Work, home, and in-between: A longitudinal study of spillover. *Journal of Applied Behavioral Science, 32,* 29–47.

MacDermid, S. M. (2005). (Re)considering conflict between work and family. In E. E. Kossek & S. Lambert (Eds.), *Work and life integration in organizations: New directions for theory and practice* (pp. 19–40). Mahwah, NJ: Lawrence Erlbaum Associates.

MacDermid, S. M., Franz, C. E., & De Reus, L. (1998). Generativity: At the crossroads of social roles and personality. In D. P. McAdams & E. de St. Aubin (Eds.), *Generativity and adult development: How and why we care for the next generation* (pp. 181–226). Washington, DC: American Psychological Association.

MacDermid, S. M., Hertzog, J. L, Kensinger, K. B., & Zipp, J. F. (2001). The role of organizational size and industry in job quality and work-family relationships. *Journal of Family & Economic Issues, 22,* 191–216.

MacDermid, S. M., Weiss, H. M., & Seery, B. L. (2002). An emotional examination of the work-family interface. In R. Lord, R. Klimoski, & R. Kanfer (Eds.), *Emotions in the workplace: Understanding the structure and role of emotions in organizational behavior* (pp. 402–427). San Francisco: Jossey-Bass.

Macmillan, R., & Gartner, R. (1999). When she brings home the bacon: Labor-force participation and the risk of spousal violence against women. *Journal of Marriage and the Family, 61,* 947–958.

Marks, S. R. (1977). Multiple roles and role strain: Some notes on human energy, time, and commitment. *American Sociological Review, 42,* 921–936.

Marks, S. R., & Leslie, L. A. (1999). Family diversity and intersecting categories: Toward a richer approach to multiple roles. In D. Demo, K. Allen, & M. Fine (Eds.), *Handbook of family diversity* (pp. 402–423). Cambridge, England: Oxford University Press.

Marks, S. R., & MacDermid, S. M. (1996). Multiple roles, role balance and role ease. *Journal of Marriage and the Family, 58,* 417–432.

Markus, M. L., & Robey, D. (1988). Information technology and organizational change: Causal structure in theory and research. *Management Science, 34,* 583–598.

Matthews, L. S., Conger, R. D., & Wickrama, K. A. S. (1996). Work-family conflict and marital quality: Mediating processes. *Social Psychology Quarterly, 59,* 62–79.

McCubbin, H. I., Thompson, A. I., & McCubbin, M. A. (1996). *Family assessment: Resiliency, coping, and adaptation.* Madison: University of Wisconsin Press.

McManus, K., Korabik, K., Rosin, H. M., & Kelloway, E. K. (2002). Employed mothers and the work-family interface: Does family structure matter? *Human Relations, 55,* 1295–1324.

Melzer, S. A. (2002). Gender, work, and intimate violence: Men's occupational violence spillover and compensatory violence. *Journal of Marriage and Family, 64,* 820–832.

Mishel, L., Bernstein, J., & Schmitt, J. (1999). *The state of working America 1998–1999.* Ithaca, NY: Economic Policy Institute, Cornell University Press.

Moen, P., & Yu, Y. (2000). Effective work/life strategies: Working couples, work conditions, gender and life quality. *Social Problems, 47,* 91–326.

Monge, P. R., Farace, R. V., Eisenberg, E. M., Miller, K. I., & White, L. L. (1984). The process of studying process in organizational communication. *Journal of Communication, 34,* 22–43.

Moore, K. A, & Keyes, C. L. M. (2003). A brief history of well-being in children and adults. In M. Bornstein, L. Davidson, C. Keyes, & K. Moore (Eds), *Well-being: Positive development across the life course. Crosscurrents in contemporary psychology* (pp. 1–11). Mahwah, NJ: Lawrence Erlbaum Associates.

National Sleep Foundation. (2002). Sleep in America Poll. Washington, DC: National Sleep Foundation.

Neal, M. B., Chapman, N. J., Ingersoll-Dayton, B., & Emlen, A. C. (1993). *Balancing work and caregiving for children, adults, and elders.* Thousand Oaks, CA: Sage.

Near, J. P., Rice, R. W., & Hunt, R. G. (1980). The relationship between work and nonwork domains: A review of empirical research. *The Academy of Management Review, 5,* 415–429.

Neuman, W. L. (1997). *Social research methods: Qualitative and quantitative approaches* (3rd ed.). Boston: Allyn & Bacon.

Nippert-Eng, C. (1996). Calendars and keys: The classification of "home" and "work." *Sociological Forum, 11,* 563–582.

Ortony, A., Clore, G. L., & Collins, A. (1988). *The cognitive structure of emotions.* Cambridge, UK: Cambridge University Press.

Parcel, T. L., & Menaghan, E. G. (1994). *Parents' jobs and children's lives.* New York: DeGruyter.

Peacock, E. J., & Wong, P. T. P. (1990). The Stress Appraisal Measure (SAM): A multidimensional approach to cognitive appraisal. *Stress Medicine, 6*, 227–236.

Perry-Jenkins, M., Repetti, R. L., & Crouter, A. C. (2000). Work and family in the 1990s. *Journal of Marriage and the Family, 62*, 981–998.

Perry-Smith, J. E., & Blum, T. C. (2000). Work-family human resource bundles and perceived organizational performance. *Academy of Management Journal, 43*(6), 1107–1117.

Pittman, J. (1994). Work/family fit as a mediator of work factors on marital tension: Evidence from the interface of greedy institutions. *Human Relations, 47*, 183–209.

Pleck, J. H., Staines, G. L., & Lang, L. (1980). Conflicts between work and family life. *Monthly Labor Review, 103*, 29–32.

Price, R. H., Choi, J. N., & Vinokur, A. D. (2002). Links in the chain of adversity following job loss: How financial strain and loss of personal control lead to depression, impaired functioning, and poor health. *Journal of Occupational Health Psychology, 7*, 302–312.

Repetti, R. L. (1989). Effects of daily workload on subsequent behavior during marital interaction: The roles of social withdrawal and spouse support. *Journal of Personality & Social Psychology, 57*, 651–659.

Repetti, R. L. (1994). Short-term and long-term processes linking job stressors to father–child interaction. *Social Development, 3*, 1–15.

Repetti, R. L., & Wood, J. (1997). Effects of daily stress at work on mothers' interactions with preschoolers. *Journal of Family Psychology, 11*, 90–108.

Rothbard, N. P. (2001). Enriching or depleting? The dynamics of engagement in work and family roles. *Administrative Science Quarterly, 46*, 655–684.

Ruderman, M. N., Ohlott, P. J., Panzer, K., & King, S. N. (2002). Benefits of multiple roles for managerial women. *Academy of Management Journal, 45*, 369–386.

Schulz, M. S., Cowan, P. A., Pape Cowan, C., & Brennan, R. T. (2004). Coming home upset: Gender, marital satisfaction, and the daily spillover of workday experience into couple interactions. *Journal of Family Psychology, 18*, 250–263.

Sieber, S. D. (1974). Toward a theory of role accumulation. *American Sociological Review, 39*, 467–478.

Siegrist, J. (1996). Adverse health effects of high-effort/low-reward conditions. *Occupational Health Psychology, 1*, 27–41.

Spielberger, C. D., Vagg, P. R., & Wasala, C. F. (2003). Occupational stress: Job pressures and lack of support. In J. Quick & L. Tetrick (Eds.), *Handbook of occupational health psychology* (pp. 185–200). Washington, DC: American Psychological Association.

Staines, G. L. (1980). Spillover versus compensation: A review of the literature on the relationship between work and nonwork. *Human Relations, 33*, 111–129.

Stephens, M. P., Franks, M. M., & Atienza, A. A. (1997). Where two roles intersect: Spillover between parent care and employment. *Psychology & Aging, 12*, 30–37.

Thomas, L. T., & Ganster, D. C. (1995). Impact of family-supportive work variables on work-family conflict and strain: A control perspective. *Journal of Applied Psychology, 80*, 6–15.

Thomson, E., & Williams, R. (1982). Beyond wives' family sociology: A method for analyzing couple data. *Journal of Marriage & the Family, 44*, 999–1008.

Van der Doef, M., & Maes, S. (1999). The job demand-control(-support) model and psychological well-being: A review of 20 years of empirical research. *Work & Stress, 13*, 87–114.

Voydanoff, P. (2002). Linkages between the work-family interface and work, family, and individual outcomes: An integrative model. *Journal of Family Issues, 23*, 138–164.

Voydanoff, P. (2004). The effects of work demands and resources on work-to-family conflict and facilitation. *Journal of Marriage and Family, 66*, 398–412.

Wayne, J. H., Musisca, N., & Fleeson, W. (2004). Considering the role of personality in the work-family experience: Relationships of the big five to work-family conflict and facilitation. *Journal of Vocational Behavior, 64*, 108–130.

Weiss, H. M., Beal, D. J., Barros, E., & MacDermid, S. M. (2003). *Conceptualizing performance processes: A model to guide research linking quality of life and performance.* West Lafayette, IN: Military Family Research Institute, Purdue University.

Weiss, H. M., MacDermid, S. M., Strauss, R., Kurek, K. E., Le, B., & Robbins, D. (2002). *Retention in the armed forces: Past approaches and new research directions.* West Lafayette, IN: Military Family Research Institute, Purdue University.

Westman, M. (2002). Gender asymmetry in crossover research. In D. Nelson & R. Burke (Eds.), *Gender, work stress, and health* (pp. 129–149). Washington, DC: American Psychological Association.

Williams, K. J., & Alliger, G. M. (1994). Role stressors, mood spillover, and perceptions of work-family conflict in employed parents. *Academy of Management Journal, 37,* 837–868.

Williams, K., Suls, J., Alliger, G. M., Learner, S. M., & Wan, C. K. (1991). Multiple role juggling and daily mood states in working mothers: An experience sampling study. *Journal of Applied Psychology, 76,* 664–674.

Wilson, B. J., & Gottman, J. M. (1996). Attention—the shuttle between emotion and cognition: Risk, resiliency and physiological bases. In E. Hetherington & E. Blechman (Eds.), *Stress, coping and resiliency in children and families* (pp. 189–228). Mahwah, NJ: Lawrence Erlbaum Associates.

Zedeck, S. (1992). Introduction: Exploring the domain of work and family concerns. In S. Zedeck (Ed.), *Work, families and organizations* (pp. 1–32). San Francisco: Jossey-Bass.

Zedeck, S., & Mosier, K. L. (1990). Work in the family and employing organization. *American Psychologist, 45,* 240–251.

28

Using Mixed Methods in Research Related to Work and Family

Margaret B. Neal
Leslie B. Hammer
David L. Morgan
Portland State University

The study of work and family is an inherently interdisciplinary field that draws on a wide variety of theories and methods. Given the complexity of the topics addressed, it is hardly surprising that researchers have pursued it with both qualitative (e.g., focus groups) and quantitative (e.g., large-scale survey) methods. Qualitative designs can provide more contextual information on the nature and dynamics of work and family relationships that are not easily captured using solely traditional quantitative methods. Nonetheless, a content analysis of work and family research in the industrial/organizational and organizational behavior literature revealed that between 1980 and 2002, only 20 out of 190 studies (or 10.5%) included qualitative data (Eby, Casper, Lockwood, Bordeaux, & Brinley, 2005).

Recently, there has been growing interest in research designs that *combine* qualitative and quantitative methods, or "mixed methods" research (Tashakorri & Teddlie, 2003a). Such designs have intrinsic appeal in fields such as the intersection of work and family, given the breadth of types of research questions asked and potential sources of data. We believe that the field of work and family can benefit by expanding its research designs to integrate more qualitative methods with existing quantitative methods. As one example of a broad research program that has integrated both quantitative and qualitative methods, Heymann (2000) has provided a detailed analysis of the difficulties faced by working-class families, using a combination of in-depth interviews, daily diary methods, and existing national-level quantitative data. Other examples will be discussed throughout the chapter. Thus, in this chapter, we describe the use of mixed methods to address research questions related to the intersection of work and family. First, we provide an overview of mixed-methods approaches, including an answer to the question of "what" mixed methods are. Second, we discuss the questions of "why" and "when" one might wish to use mixed methods, addressing various reasons for using mixed methods and the advantages and potential disadvantages of such designs. Third, we provide examples from our own work and that of others in the work-family literature to illustrate the "how" of using mixed methods. Finally, we offer some practical guidelines for using mixed methods in research related to work and family.

OVERVIEW AND DEFINITION: WHAT ARE MIXED METHODS?

A rather confusing array of terms has been employed to describe research in which a combination of methods is used, including "multiple methods" (e.g., Johnson & Turner, 2003), "mixed methods" (e.g., Tashakkori & Teddlie, 2003a), and "multimethod" research (e.g., Hunter & Brewer, 2003). One simple definition is offered by Hunter and Brewer (2003), in which they state that such research "calls for the use of multiple methods with complementary strengths and different weaknesses in relation to a given set of research problems" (p. 580). Creswell, Plano Clark, Gutmann, and Hanson (2003) provide another definition:

> A *mixed methods study* involves the collection or analysis of both quantitative and/or qualitative data in a single study in which the data are collected concurrently or sequentially, are given a priority, and involve the integration of the data at one or more stages in the process of research. (p. 212)

In addition to differences in definition, other disagreements and inconsistencies exist as well. Most notably, and not surprisingly, numerous typologies of mixed methods designs have been developed (e.g., Greene, Caracelli, & Graham, 1989; Morgan, 1998; Tashakkori & Teddlie, 1998; see Creswell et al., 2003, for an overview). Moreover, there is a lack of agreement regarding the criteria that should be used to select the best design for one's research project (Tashakkori & Teddlie, 2003a).

In sum, then, the field of mixed methods inquiry is an emerging one, with an abundance of interesting ideas but a lack of consensus. In particular, the inconsistent terminology and a range of typologies indicate a lack of agreement about what the basic research design options are as well as a corresponding disagreement about when any given option would be most appropriate. Nonetheless, Tashakkori and Teddlie (2003a) have declared the field of mixed methods to be the "third methodological movement," a movement that has evolved "as a pragmatic way of using the strengths of both [quantitative and qualitative] approaches" (p. ix). We believe this pragmatic approach to research is highly consistent with the types of research questions posed in the arena of work-family integration and, as such, has much to offer the field. Thus, the position we take here is pragmatic: We argue that the researcher should select the method or methods that can best illuminate the phenomenon of interest.

In this chapter we focus specifically on research designs involving combinations of qualitative and quantitative methods, and we use the term "mixed methods" or simply "combining qualitative and quantitative data." We adopt this focus because different combinations only of qualitative methods (e.g., focus groups and structured personal interviews) or only of quantitative methods (e.g., survey and archival organizational data) can usually be handled by standard procedures, whereas special consideration must be given when qualitative and quantitative approaches are used together (Morgan, 1998; forthcoming). Although we concentrate on examples in which approaches are combined within a given study, we also provide examples of when they are used across a program of research.

In addition, we present a typology of designs that we feel most simply and clearly represents the major options for ways of combining qualitative and quantitative methods. We then illustrate these designs with examples from our own research and from other studies in the work-family literature. We conclude with some issues to consider with respect to the implementation of mixed methods research. First, however, let us look at several reasons to adopt, or not adopt, mixed methods design strategies.

WHY (OR WHY NOT) USE MIXED METHODS?

The central rationale for using mixed methods in research is that different methods have different purposes and different strengths, as outlined in earlier chapters of this handbook. Thus, a study that employs mixed methods can benefit from the advantages associated with each of the methods used (Morgan, 1998). This makes it possible to address research questions that cannot be answered by any one method, providing both stronger inferences and the opportunity for presenting divergent views (Tashakkori & Teddlie, 2003a).

Because different methods have different purposes and different strengths, the decision as to which method(s) to use depends on the goals for the research and the available designs that might meet those goals (Caracelli & Greene, 1997; Greene, Caracelli, & Graham, 1989). As Morgan (forthcoming) notes, *qualitative research* is inductive, subjective, and contextual. That is, it emphasizes using observations to generate theory, relying on the researcher's own interpretations of events, behaviors, or responses, and collecting detailed data concerning the situation or context. *Quantitative research*, in contrast, is deductive, objective, and generalized. It typically emphasizes using observations to test theories, relying on procedures that minimize the researcher's impact on the results, and collecting data that can be generalized to a wide variety of settings and circumstances (Morgan, forthcoming). When elements of each of these approaches are desirable, mixing qualitative and quantitative methods may be advisable.

At the same time, although the purposes and procedures associated with qualitative and quantitative research are well known, both the justification for, and the conduct of, mixed methods research are less established. Moreover, it is generally agreed that it can be difficult to combine qualitative and quantitative approaches, for both technical and epistemological reasons (Morgan, 1998). Technical challenges arise because using two methods more than doubles the complexity of a study: Not only must each method itself be used effectively, but the two methods also must be combined effectively (Morgan, forthcoming), thus requiring additional skill, time, and resources. We discuss these technical issues later in greater detail.

The second explanation for the difficulty of combining qualitative and quantitative methods is rooted in the different paradigms represented by quantitative and qualitative research and is related to the "paradigm wars" (Gage, 1989; Tashakkori & Teddlie, 2003a) that resulted from the differences in worldview between these two major approaches to research. These differences in worldview, or paradigm, concern the basic beliefs or assumptions that guide a researcher and frame his or her beliefs about research methods, including the researcher's ontological beliefs (beliefs about the nature of reality), epistemological beliefs (beliefs about what it is possible to know), and axiological beliefs (beliefs about what is ethical and the role of values in research) (Creswell, 1994; Greene & Caracelli, 1997; Rocco, Bliss, Gallagher, & Pérez-Prado, 2003a). Several chapters in Tashakkori and Teddlie's (2003) *Handbook of Mixed Methods in Social & Behavioral Research* address the controversies around combining approaches to research that rely on different philosophical assumptions (e.g., Creswell et al., 2003; Greene & Caracelli, 2003; Maxcy, 2003; Maxwell & Loomis, 2003; Moghaddam, Walker, & Harré, 2003; Rallis & Rossman, 2003; Rocco et al., 2003b; Tashakkori & Teddlie, 2003a, 2003b).

Although the issue of combining the different paradigmatic assumptions of qualitative and quantitative *research* or methodologies remains problematic, there is considerably less controversy about combining qualitative and quantitative *methods*. Thus, although there are continuing disagreements about the feasibility of combining different *views* about the nature of reality and knowledge (i.e., ontologies and epistemologies), there is far more agreement about the possibility and value of combining different kinds of *data*—especially given the number of mixed methods studies that have been conducted successfully (Brannen, 1992; Brewer & Hunter, 1989; Bryman, 1984, 1988; Cook & Reichardt, 1979; Morgan, 1998; Tashakkori &

Teddlie, 2003a). Hence, our aim here is to provide a guide for resolving the *technical* difficulties in combining qualitative and quantitative methods by highlighting a set of practical research designs.

SPECIFIC MOTIVATIONS FOR USING MIXED METHODS

As noted earlier, the primary reason for using mixed methods in research is to be able to take advantage of the different strengths associated with each of the types of methods. Johnson and Turner (2003) referred to this as "the fundamental principle of mixed methods research" and noted that "methods should be mixed in a way that has complementary strengths and nonoverlapping weaknesses" (p. 299). Morgan (forthcoming) outlined three main purposes, or motivations, for using mixed methods: *Convergent Findings*, *Comprehensive Coverage*, and *Connected Contributions*. Figure 28.1 depicts these three purposes.[1]

Notation for Describing Mixed Methods Designs

Before we describe the three motivations in detail, let us first offer some convenient shorthand notation that can be used to graphically depict all of the various types of mixed methods designs, as illustrated in Fig. 28.1. This notation was originally developed by Janice Morse (1991, 2003) and is "the standard currently used in the mixed methods research area" (Tashakkori & Teddlie, 2003a, p. 27). As detailed in the next section, when mixed methods are used, often one of the two methods is considered as core, or primary, and the other as complementary. Using Morse's (1991, 2003) notation, this decision is depicted by showing the core method, abbreviated, in uppercase letters (i.e., either "QUANT" or "QUAL") and the complementary method, abbreviated, in lowercase letters (i.e., "qual" or "quant"). Morse's notation also can be modified to indicate study designs in which both methods receive equal attention by simply writing "Quant" and "Qual" (i.e., capitalizing the first letter of each method), as shown in Fig. 28.1.

Morse (1991, 2003) used an arrow ("→") to depict the order of data collection for the two methods; others, including us, however, use it to indicate order of *use* of the data (Creswell

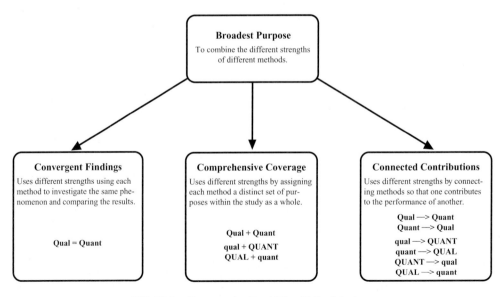

FIG. 28.1.   Purposes for Combining Methodologies.

et al., 2003; Morgan, 1998, forthcoming). A "+" is used to indicate designs in which both methods are used simultaneously and one adds something to the other (e.g., Quant + Qual). Finally, we have extended Morse's notation to include as well the use of an equal sign ("=") to depict projects that pursue Convergent Findings, which we explain below (e.g., Quant = Qual). We will use the above notation throughout the remainder of our discussion.

The Convergent Findings Motivation

The Convergent Findings motivation, also called "cross-validation," "convergence," and "triangulation,"[2] uses both quantitative and qualitative methods to investigate the same research question. Ideally, both methods produce similar results (hence, the "=" sign), thereby providing a form of quality control to guard against threats to validity that result from artifacts or limitations in either of the separate methods (Morgan, 1998). The work of Donald Campbell and his colleagues, who were particularly interested in the question of how to confirm, or cross-validate, results, originally provided the impetus for combining mixed methods to make use of the methods' different strengths (Campbell & Fiske, 1959; Morgan, 1998; Tashakkori & Teddlie, 2003a; Webb, Campbell, Schwartz, & Sechrest, 1966). In Convergent Findings designs, the data from the two methods are used simultaneously, for example, when one indicator is compared with another.

This motivation for combining qualitative and quantitative methods, however, has been somewhat rare in recent research, due to: (a) the logistical problems presented (i.e., how to support two very different field efforts at the same time); (b) the relatively large amount of time and expense required for realizing the limited (or even, as Morse, 2003, suggested, potentially wasteful) goal of producing convergent findings, that is, the goal of "finding the same thing twice" (Morgan, 1998, p. 365); and, perhaps most importantly, (c) problems of coordination that emerge when results fail to converge (Morgan, 1998).

An example of a study in the work-family literature with a convergent findings motivation is one by Grzywacz, Almeida, and McDonald (2002). This well-designed, thorough study involved using both diary and questionnaire archival data to explore the distribution of work-family spillover across working adults in the United States and to examine the relation between different types of spillover between work and family. As we describe later, however, the findings yielded by the two types of data were inconsistent, and no obvious explanation for the inconsistency could be found.

The Comprehensive Coverage Motivation

The Comprehensive Coverage motivation calls for using both quantitative and qualitative methods to make their own unique contribution to the project as a whole. The strengths of each type of method are matched to a specific set of purposes, with each method used to study a different part of the overall project (Morgan, forthcoming). Both methods may have equal priority, or one may be more important than the other, as shown in Fig. 28.1.

This approach, too, is not without its problems. Practical problems may arise because two full data sets are generated, and coherent analysis of this combination of data can be difficult (Morse, 1991). Moreover, paradigm problems may arise again because there is the potential that knowledge gained from the two methods may be difficult to compare or even contradictory (Morgan, 1998).

To briefly illustrate the Comprehensive Coverage motivation in the work-family literature, we will use a study by Winston et al. (1999). This large-scale project combined three different methods to understand how the federal "welfare to work" legislation of 1996 affected the lives of low-income families. The first component was a longitudinal survey that followed more than

2,000 families for several years, concentrating on both the development of children within low-income families and the work experiences of their parents. This survey was paired with an intensive developmental study of 700 children from families in the survey sample, including video-taping of mother–child interaction. The final portion of the project used ethnographic methods to study 200 additional families who lived in the same neighborhoods as the original survey respondents, observing not only their home life but also their experiences with work and welfare.

The Connected Contributions Motivation

The Connected Contributions motivation (Morgan, forthcoming) is similar to the Comprehensive Coverage motivation, with each method chosen according to its strengths for accomplishing a particular task. It differs from Comprehensive Coverage, however, in that it explicitly *links* the methods so the results of one can enhance the effectiveness of the other. Typically, one method is designated as the primary tool for gathering the data and the other serves as either a preliminary input or a follow-up extension. As Fig. 28.1 shows, this results in a set of sequential connections between different methods.

This third motivation, Connected Contributions, is a particularly promising and potentially useful application of a mixed methods approach, in contrast to either Convergent Findings, where both the benefits and limitations of this approach are well known, or Comprehensive Coverage, where the appropriate procedures remain poorly understood due to ongoing controversy about the extent to which it is possible to compare the results derived from qualitative and quantitative methods (Morgan, forthcoming). Our own work, as described in the next section, provides several examples of Connected Contributions.

THE "HOW" OF MIXED METHODS: EXAMPLES FROM OUR STUDY OF DUAL-EARNER COUPLES IN THE SANDWICHED GENERATION

To further illustrate some of the Connected Contributions mixed methods designs, we will use a study that we recently completed with funding from the Alfred P. Sloan Foundation (Neal & Hammer, in press). This research had several mixed methods design components, or embedded studies, involving the gathering and analysis of both qualitative and quantitative data. Specifically, included were examples of the following designs: qual → QUANT, quant → QUAL, and QUANT → qual.

The study as a whole employed three modes of data collection: focus groups (qualitative) conducted locally at both the beginning and end of the study, mailed surveys (quantitative), and follow-up telephone interviews (qualitative). In the core, quantitative study, Wave 1 survey data were collected by mail from a total of 309 dual-earner couples in the sandwiched generation identified through telephone screening from across the United States; Wave 2 data were collected from 234 (74.4%) of the original 309 couples. Prior to the survey, 17 focus groups were held with a total of 63 participants, and the procedures recommended by Morgan (1997) for conducting and transcribing data from focus groups were followed. Following the survey, additional qualitative follow-up interviews were conducted by telephone with 48 respondents to the original survey. Four follow-up focus groups with some of the original focus group participants were held as well. These interviews and focus groups, too, were taped and transcribed.

In our study, the criteria for sample selection for both the local focus groups and the national mailed survey were identical: (a) the couple had been married or living together for at least 1 year; (b) one person in the couple worked at least 35 hours per week and the other worked at least 20 hours per week; (c) there were one or more children 18 years of age or younger living in the home at least 3 days a week; and (d) one or the other or both members of the couple together spent a minimum of 3 hours per week caring for a frail or disabled parent, step-parent, or parent-in-law. The type of assistance provided to parents could encompass a wide array of activities, including transportation, shopping, hands-on care, assistance with finances, home maintenance, emotional support, and so forth. Because of the interest of the study's primary funding source, the Alfred P. Sloan Foundation, in middle- and upper-income families, the final study criterion was that the couple had a household income of $40,000 or greater.

The survey was both national in scope and longitudinal, with two waves of data. Another feature of the study, not discussed here, is that a family systems approach was taken in which both members of couples, rather than just one member, were included as participants. This enabled examination not only of individual differences, but also between- and within-couple differences. In addition to the items on coping strategies that are described below, the survey instrument for the quantitative study included questions concerning the nature and quality of participants' roles, workplace supports available and used, and various work and well-being outcomes. (See Neal and Hammer [in press] for additional study details and findings, as our purpose here is illustrative only, to detail various mixed methods design options.)

Preliminary Studies to Aid in Developing the Sampling Strategy for the Quantitative Study (qual → QUANT design)

We designed three preliminary studies, each using a different recruitment strategy for the initial focus groups, to aid in the development of a prototype sampling strategy for the core quantitative study (the national mailed survey). Thus, this portion of the project represented a qual → QUANT design (see Fig. 28.1). In essence, these were three preliminary case studies that provided a systematic assessment of the pluses and minuses associated with different sampling strategies. Ultimately, this allowed us to pick a sampling strategy for the national survey that was both effective and cost-efficient.

In Study 1, the sample was identified and recruited via computer-assisted telephone interviews (CATI) conducted with a sample generated using random-digit dialing (RDD) techniques (25% of the focus group sample). In Study 2, another 25% of the focus group sample was obtained through advertising in local newspapers. In Study 3, the remaining 50% of the sample was recruited via computer-assisted telephone interviewing (CATI) using a purchased, targeted list of telephone numbers of households believed to have at least one adult between the ages of 30 and 60. This last strategy proved to be the most time- and cost-effective in identifying couples who met the study criteria.

Preliminary Qualitative Study to Aid in Instrument Development for a Quantitative Study (qual → QUANT design)

The second, but primary, purpose for conducting the local focus groups was to ascertain the types of coping strategies used by dual-earner couples caring for children and aging parents so that we could then design a quantitative measure for inclusion in the mailed survey instrument. Again, this illustrates a qual → QUANT design. In this case, we wanted to develop items measuring coping that would identify the full range of types of strategies that couples used to manage their work and family responsibilities, and to hear the words and phrases couples used to describe those strategies.

Analysis of the qualitative data proceeded in four basic stages: (a) "open coding" (Strauss & Corbin, 1990) to identify the full range of focus group participants' responses concerning how they coped with the demands of work and family; (b) sorting the data (statements) by both the various theoretical categories suggested by existing conceptual models and the key themes mentioned by participants as they emerged in the data; (c) synthesizing the two sorting efforts into a single conceptual system; and(d) using the focus group participants' statements to aid in developing items for use in the mailed survey instrument, to measure the extent to which those surveyed used the various coping strategies.[3]

Preliminary Quantitative Study to Identify Participants for a Qualitative Study (quant → QUAL design)

Following completion of both waves of the quantitative mailed surveys, the next component of our project design called for conducting qualitative telephone interviews with study participants who had experienced changes in well-being between the two waves of the survey. We were particularly interested in exploring the reasons for these changes. Thus, we used the quantitative data in a preliminary fashion to determine which individuals had experienced the greatest amount of change in well-being between the two waves of the survey and to select equal numbers of women and men to be interviewed by telephone. This design can serve as an example of a quant → QUAL design (see Fig. 28.1), as the quantitative data were used to select those individuals whom we wished to study more in depth. Telephone interviews were conducted with 48 individuals who exhibited the most change in well-being, half for the better and half for the worse.

This example also illustrates how the designation of a study's "priority" is a matter of how that study is *used*, rather than the absolute size of the study. Thus, within the project as a whole, the survey not only required the most resources but also received the most analytic attention. For the purposes of this particular qualitative study, however, the survey played the purely supplementary role of locating a theoretically driven sample for the open-ended interviews.

Preliminary Qualitative Study That Informed Instrument Development, Then Aided in Explaining Nonintuitive Findings (qual → QUANT → qual design)

A final mixed methods design example can be gleaned from our larger study. In the preliminary focus groups that we held, some unexpected topics emerged as important, including sibling relationships among adult children caring for aging parents (Ingersoll-Dayton, Neal, Ha, & Hammer, 2003a, 2003b) and the provision of help *by* aging parents *to* their adult child caregivers (Ingersoll-Dayton, Neal, & Hammer, 2001). With respect to this latter topic, we content-analyzed the data from focus group transcripts, identifying and coding, by type of help, each of the instances in which participants talked about receiving help from the parent or parent-in-law for whom they were caring. As we did with respect to the coping strategies used by couples (see above), we used those findings to inform the development of items asking how often each type of help was received from the parent/in-law and included these items in the mailed survey.

As a second step, we then analyzed the quantitative data to identify the extent of help received from the aging parents, whether the quantity and nature of help differed by the adult child's gender, what the effects of receiving help from aging parents were on the adult child's relationship with the parent, caregiver performance, and work performance. Finally, because some of the survey findings were perplexing (e.g., receipt of forms of support other than emotional support was not consistently beneficial), we conducted further analyses of focus group data to help in explaining these nonintuitive survey results (Ingersoll-Dayton et al., 2001). In sum, we used the same set of qualitative data both to inform the development of the quantitative study and to explain some unexpected results. This design would be depicted as follows: qual → QUANT → qual. These examples demonstrate the practical application of research designs that use the Connected Contributions approach to combining qualitative and quantitative methods.

In the next section, we turn to other studies in the work-family literature for further illustrations of not only the Connected Contributions but also the Convergent Findings and Comprehensive Coverage motivations for mixed methods study designs.

THE "HOW" OF MIXED METHODS: ADDITIONAL EXAMPLES FROM THE WORK-FAMILY LITERATURE

Above we gave some detailed examples of Connected Contributions mixed methods designs from our own work. In this next section, we provide examples of others' designs, including designs with Convergent Findings and Comprehensive Motivations, as they have appeared in the work-family literature. These studies were located through a systematic search (using electronic bibliographies and databases) for studies in the work-family literature that used mixed methods. From that larger set of studies, we have selected the ones that provided the most explicit information about their research designs for combining qualitative and quantitative data.

Convergent Findings Motivation Design

As mentioned above, the substantive purpose of the Grzywacz et al. (2002) study was to explore the distribution of work-family spillover across working adults in the United States and to examine the relation between different types of spillover between work and family. To do this, the researchers merged data gathered from working adults who participated in the National Survey of Midlife Development in the United States (MIDUS) (data from a telephone interview and two mailed questionnaires) ($n = 2,130$) and data gathered from a subsample ($n = 741$) of those same adults (participants in the National Study of Daily Experiences [NSDE], an 8-day daily diary study which assessed daily work and family stresses through a semistructured daily telephone interview). As Grzywacz et al. (2002) noted, "This is the first study to use different types of data to comprehensively explore the distribution of multiple types of work-family spillover across a wide range of sociodemographic characteristics" (p. 35).

The findings, however, were paradoxical, in that there was a relatively low correlation between the two types of data (i.e., the investigator-created measures from the 8-day diary data and the self-reported measures) and a dissimilar pattern of results in the multivariate models between the self-report and daily diary outcomes.

This study represents a Quant = Qual design, although the qualitative data were "quantitized" (Miles & Huberman, 1994; Tashakkori & Teddlie, 2003a). Moreover, it illustrates the challenges that can be encountered when the findings using each type of data are inconsistent, thus (depending on one's viewpoint) either thwarting the effort to triangulate or contributing to the diversity of viewpoints.

Comprehensive Coverage Motivation Design

A Qual + Quant Design.   Dorfman (2002) gathered data via personal interviews using a semistructured interview schedule consisting of tape-recorded open-ended questions and a written questionnaire using a sample of college professors over age 70 who chose to stay in their jobs ($N = 17$) versus those who chose to retire ($N = 54$). Both the interview and questionnaire responses from the professors were of equal priority and were used simultaneously.

The interviews were "designed to provide a qualitative assessment of professors' reasons for continuing to work or to retire, their attitudes toward professional and nonprofessional activities, and their preparation for and plans regarding retirement" (Dorfman, 2002, p. 20). The written questionnaire, "consisting mainly of forced-choice and scale items, was designed to provide a more quantitative assessment of attitudinal and behavioral responses" (p. 20). Personal characteristics of age, self-perceived health, income, and marital and family status also were assessed. Content analyses were conducted based on the responses to the interviews, and major themes were identified related to reasons for continuing to work versus reasons for retiring. Statistical comparisons were made between the retired and employed group on personal characteristics and satisfaction levels. The data were analyzed and interpreted separately, characterizing the Qual + Quant design.

A Quant + Qual Design.   Agazio, Ephraim, Flaherty, and Gurney (2002) examined both quantitative and qualitative data to understand factors related to health promotion behaviors and work-family experiences of mothers. More specifically, survey data from 140 active-duty mothers were used to test relationships between various factors (i.e., demographic characteristics, self-efficacy, and interpersonal factors) and health promotion behaviors. A subset of 28 women was then interviewed concerning their work and family experiences as well as barriers to health promotion. The authors stated that they used mixed methods for "methodological triangulation," or validating and expansion purposes. Because the two types of data provided unique contributions to the study as a whole and were used simultaneously, however, we would classify the study as representing a Comprehensive Coverage design.

Connected Contributions Motivation

A QUANT → qual Design.   Hawkins, Roberts, Christiansen, and Marshall (1994) conducted a study with a Connected Contributions motivation, using qualitative data to shed light on the quantitatively driven evaluation of the effectiveness of a family life education program. The program was designed to help dual-earner couples with children devise mutually satisfactory arrangements for sharing domestic labor. Data collection consisted of: (a) an intake interview, primarily quantitative in nature, in each couple's home with wives and husbands interviewed separately; (b) administration of the same questionnaires at the conclusion of the program, along with a tape-recorded open-ended interview asking participants to share their reactions to, and evaluations of, the program and how it affected them; (c) in-home interviews 6 months after the post-assessment to determine change or stability in respondents' situations and including open-ended questions, along with a letter written by the couple as a unit at the end of the program describing their feelings during the program and their plans for sharing domestic labor.

Both types of data suggested the program produced desired and persistent (for 6 months) effects, and the quantitative results were presented along with "qualitative data that enriched . . . understanding of the program outcomes and helped . . . interpret the statistical results" (p. 216). In particular, the qualitative data were used to aid in understanding some of the puzzling quantitative results.

A QUAL → quant Design.   In another example of a study based on a Connected Contributions motivation, but with the opposite priority (i.e., a QUAL → quant design), Zimmerman, Haddock, Current, and Ziemba (2003) conducted a qualitative study with a very small complementary quantitative component to examine how a convenience sample of 47 dual-earner couples with children practice marital partnership to support work-family balance. To be eligible, couples had to perceive themselves as successful in balancing family and work, as indicated by their agreement with five statements that defined "success" in balancing work and family. Data were collected through a self-report questionnaire and a 90-minute conjoint interview that included open-ended questions regarding successful work-family balance strategies. The qualitative data were analyzed prior to the quantitative data "to avoid bias during the coding process" (p. 112). A grounded theory approach was used, as was a qualitative data analysis program to code the information fragments in the interviews.

The authors stated that they used quantitative methods because "multiple methods allows for triangulation of results" (p. 112) and because quantitative measures provide more "fine-tuned . . . analysis of participants' perceptions of behaviors, which complement and add depth to the more . . . broad-stroked qualitative findings" (p. 112). The description of the findings was organized around each of the six themes identified through the qualitative data, and both qualitative and quantitative findings (where available) were presented. Based on the authors' description of the reasons for using quantitative methods, their presentation of findings around the six themes identified in the qualitative analysis, and the use of the data sequentially, although they were gathered simultaneously, this study illustrates a QUAL → quant design.

A quant → QUAL Design.   An example of the relatively uncommon design involving a quantitative study conducted to inform a core qualitative study is afforded by Chusid and Cochran (1989), who investigated the question of whether career change reflects earlier "dramas" from one's family of origin. Specifically, theirs was a case study approach but also involved quantitative data from Q-sorts. Q-sorts are a process whereby a subject rank-orders items in piles along a continuum, evaluating items relative to each other (McKeown & Thomas, 1988). In this case, the Q-sorts were used to inform a primary, qualitative study involving interviews. The authors explicitly described their rationale for using both quantitative and qualitative data: "Because persons are the sole arbiters of what is meaningful to them, independent sources of data are not possible. Rather, one can elicit different kinds of evidence and evaluate convergence in this manner" (p. 35); and "Although the [Q-sort] analysis revealed a pattern, interviews were required to elaborate the meaning of this pattern" (p. 36). Thus, based on both types of data, narrative portrayals of meaning for each of 10 subjects were developed and analyzed. As the authors stated, "The quantitative results of the Q-sorts were secondary and supportive, whereas the qualitative results in the form of portraits were primary, for they allowed us to understand the meaning of enactments" (p. 36).

A Qual → Quant Design.   In an examination of the benefits of multiple roles among managerial women, Ruderman, Ohlott, Panser, and King (2002) used both qualitative and quantitative data to assess the enrichment associated with multiple role occupation. Two separate, stand-alone studies were conducted and are characteristic of the Qual → Quant design, in which both studies have equal priority. The qualitative study aimed at identification of the resources and skills in managerial women's nonwork roles that contribute to their work roles. The quantitative study allowed for examination of the relationship between such nonwork roles and work and well-being. In particular, Ruderman et al. suggested that the quantitative study "allowed us to generalize the links between personal roles and managerial skills suggested by the first study to a more generic relationship between nonwork and managerial effectiveness" (p. 371).

Sixty-one managerial women participated in the qualitative study, which consisted of 1-hour telephone interviews addressing questions related to aspects of their nonwork lives that enhance their work lives. Data were content-analyzed, and six broad themes were identified, representing areas in which personal roles enhance professional roles. To further examine these themes, a mailed questionnaire, administered to 276 women, gathered data on investment in five life roles, psychological well-being, and managerial skills. Results indicated that commitment to life roles was related to well-being and managerial skills. The authors argued that, together, the findings of these two studies help to support the contention that work and family roles can enrich one another.

A Quant → Qual Design. Krüger and Baldus (1999) examined the impact of family and labor market forces on male and female life course patterns using both quantitative and qualitative data that were gathered between 1988 and 1994 from German women and men. Quantitative data were gathered via mailed survey ($N = 220$). A subset of women ($n = 52$) was then chosen to represent the range of life course structures identified in the 220 cases, using the principles of theoretical sampling outlined by Glaser and Strauss (1967), and "problem-centered interviews" were conducted. The authors analyzed the two types of data separately, reached contradictory conclusions, and noted the pitfalls associated with each when examined alone. Although the data were gathered sequentially, however, analysis and reporting were done working back and forth between the two types of data to integrate them, and no priority was given to either method. Thus, although the authors of the study consider it as having a Convergent Findings motivation, it is probably best characterized as an equal priority Connected Contributions design (Quant → Qual).

The following examples represent designs that constitute *programs* of research in the work-family literature in which qualitative and quantitative methods have been combined with a Connected Contributions motivation.

A Program of Research: qual → [QUANT + qual] Design. Shaffer and Harrison (2001), through a sequence of qualitative and quantitative investigations, developed and tested a model of spouse adjustment to international assignments. First, to identify potentially important sources of adjustment, in-depth interviews were conducted with expatriate spouses ($n = 5$ women with clearly positive experiences, and $n = 5$ women with clearly negative experiences; all were members of or referrals from a spouse support group). Next, the constructs identified were integrated with others from identity theory and earlier research on expatriates to develop a conceptual model of spouse adjustment. The model and hypotheses generated then were tested by analyzing quantitative data collected via a mailed survey of 221 international assignee couples working in 37 countries. The survey instrument consisted mostly of quantitative measures but included open-ended questions as well. The qualitative data were used for illustrative purposes in reporting the findings. Thus, this study had a qual → [QUANT + qual] design.

A Program of Research: qual → qual → qual → quant → QUANT Design. Using a series of quantitative and qualitative studies, Curbow, McDonnell, Spratt, Griffin, and Agnew (2003) conducted a program of research (spiral design) that led to development of the Work-Family Interface Scale (W-FIS). They then assessed the scale psychometrically and explored the conceptual linkages among work-family interface, the theoretical components of job stress (job demands, job control, and job resources), and depression using multivariate analyses of data collected from a sample of child-care providers.

Of particular interest here is the program of research leading to the development of the W-FIS. The first study involved intensive face-to-face interviews with 100 randomly selected family child-care providers in Baltimore County and Baltimore City. The second study involved the conduct of 17 focus groups with family child-care center workers randomly selected from throughout the state of Maryland. The third study included conducting interviews with and collecting physiological data from family and center child-care providers in Baltimore City and County, along with interviews with mothers linked to the family child-care providers. The fourth study consisted of a statewide mailed survey of family and center child-care providers.

A program of Research: quant + [quant → QUANT → qual] Design. A final example in the work-family literature is a series of component studies involving the combining of quantitative and qualitative data by Phyllis Moen and colleagues (2003). As explained in the book edited by Moen (2003), *It's About Time,* the primary goal was "to understand the complex interface between work and family among middle-class dual-earner couples" (p. 350), using a "multitmethodological approach to study middle-class dual-earner workers and their spouses" (p. 352).

In the book, the authors highlighted a number of studies that emerged from their larger *Cornell Couples and Career Study*, funded by the Alfred P. Sloan Foundation. They examined not only the couples themselves, but also the organizations in which the couples worked and the associated policies that helped the couples manage their multiple role responsibilities. They began with quantitative surveys and in-depth qualitative interviews with the human resource personnel to identify family-friendly policies and practices of the organization. Then, within each organization, a sample of employees and their spouses was identified and sent a survey asking them to participate in the broader study. All who responded affirmatively were then interviewed by telephone ($N = 1,236$ workers; $N = 979$ couples with both members participating). Random samples were selected to participate in focus groups ($n = 112$) and one-on-one interviews ($n = 150$). In their book, Moen et al. (2003) focused on time use among these couples and drew on the multitude of quantitative and qualitative data to describe the ways in which these couples are managing their work and family lives, fully integrating the data.

TECHNICAL ISSUES IN IMPLEMENTING MIXED METHODS RESEARCH

In this chapter, we have provided readers with an overview of mixed methods research, presented a typology of mixed methods research designs based on the basic purposes for combining qualitative and quantitative methods, and provided examples of designs from our own work and that of other work-family researchers. Once the design decisions have been made, however, appropriate sampling strategies must be crafted, the data gathered (concurrently or sequentially), analyses conducted, findings integrated, and results reported. A detailed discussion of each of these phases is beyond the scope of this chapter. For excellent discussions of these and other issues, we refer readers to Tashakkori and Teddlie's (2003) edited *Handbook of Mixed Methods in Social & Behavioral Research*.[4] We would, however, like to highlight what we see as some of the particularly salient issues in implementing mixed methods studies, regardless of the substantive field of inquiry. These include the challenges of additional time and expense required and the knowledge and expertise necessary for collecting, analyzing, integrating, and reporting findings.

The Issues of Time and Expense

Central among the technical issues in implementing mixed methods research are the additional time and resources required in mixed methods studies. Costs are incurred because of the multiple data collection and analysis efforts as well as the effort required to integrate the results. In particular, studies conducted and analyzed independently, such as those with a Convergent Findings motivation, require more time and are more costly. Moreover, they pose a significant risk for researchers to assume, should the results derived from the two methods be contradictory, as even more time and resources will be required to resolve the conflict through additional analysis or data collection (Jick, 1979; Morgan, 1998).

The Issues of Knowledge and Expertise

As Morse (2003) noted, "research strategies and methods are only tools—tools that are only as good as the researcher's knowledge and skill" (p. 207). Professionals need broader skills and understanding to conduct effective mixed methods research (Morgan, 1998; Morse, 2003; Newman, Ridenour, Newman, & DeMarco, 2003; Tashakorri & Teddlie, 2003a, 2003b). In practice, however, few university courses are devoted specifically to mixed methods research (Tashakkori and Teddlie, 2003a). Moreover, there remain many professors in graduate programs in various disciplines in the United States who consider themselves and their students purely as quantitative researchers or as qualitative researchers. There is a growing need to train students to be "trilingual," as increasingly, organizations and funding agencies require employees to be able to use an array of research methods (Tashakorri & Teddlie, 2003b, p. 696).

Aside from addressing the current organizational pedagogical limitations, how can individual researchers obtain the expertise required to implement effective mixed methods projects? There are two basic ways. First, a researcher can develop expertise in both qualitative and quantitative research methods (Morgan, 1998). The advantages are that the researcher is aware of not only the contributions but also the requirements of each method (e.g., timeline, field logistics, resource issues) and is able to be self-reliant in data collection, analysis, and integration. The limitation, of course, is the difficulty of developing complete mastery of both quantitative and qualitative research methods. Particularly in research designs where one method is secondary to the other, however, the researcher may have or be able to acquire the requisite skills, as complete mastery of the complementary method may not be necessary (Morgan, 1998). In addition to being able to conduct their own mixed methods research, such "boundary crossers" will be especially valuable members of a research team (Lazarsfeld, 1944; Morgan, 1998).

Thus, a second way in which the necessary expertise can be obtained is by creating a team of researchers who together have the requisite knowledge and skills to implement the project successfully. Mixed methods research is particularly well served by collaboration, or the team approach (Shulha & Wilson, 2003), as high levels of expertise in each research method can be secured. If the team members also represent different substantive disciplines, an added advantage is the multidisciplinary perspective that will guide the research.

For maximum team effectiveness, all researchers on a project ideally would have a minimum level of competency in both qualitative and quantitative methods (Tashakorri & Teddlie, 2003a). However, there are very real challenges associated with working together as a team. Teamwork is often demanding even when all members share the same research tradition, qualitative or quantitative, and the same discipline (e.g., psychology or sociology or anthropology); collaborations among researchers who are trained in different disciplines and/or who use different methods can be even more arduous. As Petter and Gallivan (2004) noted: "When multiple researchers, each one well-versed in a different methodological tradition, analyze and report findings from a [mixed methods] study, difficulty and frustration can surface as conflicting values, assumptions, and terms cause confusion during the research process . . . " (p. 9). Also, especially in mixed methods designs in which one method is dominant, team-related problems can become further exacerbated, since one set of professionals is asked to play a subordinate role (Morgan, 1998). Finally, another difficulty can arise when levels of commitment to the project or other demands (e.g., teaching loads, other research projects, family responsibilities) vary among team members. Such circumstances can further compound the problems associated with teamwork.

SOME PRACTICAL SUGGESTIONS FOR IMPLEMENTING MIXED METHODS STUDIES

The following are our suggestions related to conducting research using mixed methods. We include some recommendations of a more general nature as well, related to pedagogy, promotion and tenure, publications, and teamwork.

Articulate the study's purpose and how the two types of data will be linked. Before a mixed methods study is embarked upon, the central purpose of using both qualitative and quantitative methods in the project should be articulated. Moreover, how the methods, especially the data generated, will be linked should be determined. Simply deciding to gather both qualitative and quantitative data is not adequate; "more is better" is not reason enough to conduct a mixed methods study, considering the added time and expense that will be required.

Decide which method is dominant and the order of use of the data. The priority and sequence decisions must be made. Which method will have priority, or be the dominant or core method, and which will be supplemental or complementary (Morgan, 1998; Morse, 2003)? In some cases, the methods will have equal priority, but not usually. Then, a decision must be made regarding the order in which the data will be used: Can the effectiveness of the principal method be maximized by having the complementary method serve as preliminary input or by having it serve as follow-up?

Make explicit the rationale for using mixed methods. Once the study has been completed and it is time to write up the results, careful attention should be paid to making explicit the rationale for using mixed methods and to describing the specific design and methods employed. When we reviewed the work-family literature for studies to include as examples in this chapter, we often found that we were required to guess at the researcher(s)' motivations for using mixed methods and the procedures they used to implement their studies.

Integrate the results. When reporting on a mixed methods study, the results from both methods should be integrated, particularly if the motivation for the study is Connected Contributions, and in some cases, Comprehensive Coverage. We found several examples of studies in which mixed methods were used but the results were presented separately, with little if any attempt to integrate the information yielded. This may be simply a matter of poor presentation. For example, Maxwell and Loomis (2003) found that some studies actually involved more integration of qualitative and quantitative methods than was apparent from the descriptions of their methods. Without explicit details about the integration process, however, the reader cannot be sure.

Obtain the necessary methodological expertise. To successfully implement mixed methods research, certain skills are necessary. Academic departments must begin training students with broader skills and understanding; separate courses in both quantitative and qualitative methodologies should be required as well as courses in mixed methods research (Currall & Towler, 2003; Newman, Ridenour, Newman, & DeMarco, 2003; Tashakkori & Teddlie, 2003a, 2003b). As Newman and colleagues (2003) asserted, "We need to train a new generation of researchers who are comfortable in looking beyond a single technique" (pp. 187–188). For students, our advice is to actively seek courses in a wide range of methodologies and courses that integrate those methodologies. Gaining practical experience by working with a research team can also be helpful.

For currently practicing work-family researchers who may be interested in conducting mixed methods studies, we suggest that they, too, develop at least a minimum competency in both quantitative and qualitative research methods. We concur with Morse (2003), who noted that "Building one's toolbox, both qualitatively and quantitatively, aids the quality of one's research, as does thoughtful deliberate action coupled with foresight and skill" (p. 207). Some hints for how one might go about this are provided by Franklin (1996), who chronicled her experiences as a quantitative researcher who became a teacher of qualitative research. For example, she developed relationships with qualitative researchers who served as mentors, did a literature search on qualitative research methods in substantive areas related to hers, talked to qualitative researchers about how they collected and analyzed data, gathered syllabi from faculty in other universities, taught a qualitative research course and received feedback, arranged to work with a qualitative researcher on an ethnographic study, and wrote a proposal, ultimately funded, to conduct a qualitative study.

Recognize the value of mixed methods research through policies concerning promotion and tenure and in editorial policies. Currall and Towler (2003) argued that the emphasis by many promotion and tenure committees on number of publications, rather than the impact of research, results in the narrow specialization of researchers in either qualitative or quantitative techniques. We support their recommendation that promotion and tenure policies that reward methodological breadth should be established, such as through the creation of promotion and tenure committees composed of members who are "sufficiently knowledgeable to fairly evaluate the overall contribution and impact of a candidate's research" and who "have the sophistication to understand publications that use or integrate both qualitative and quantitative techniques" (p. 524).

With regard to journal editorial policies, we again concur with Currall and Towler (2003) and urge that consideration be given to deemphasizing purely qualitative or quantitative studies and including broader, more ambitious, integrative studies that use both qualitative and quantitative techniques. In this regard, authors should make explicit the methods they used so that readers can adequately evaluate and replicate those methods (Currall & Towler, 2003).

Learn to be a good collaborator and team member. Work-family research is, by its very nature, an interdisciplinary field. To maximize the quality of the research conducted, we suggest that work-family researchers embrace a team approach. As might be noted from the authorship of this chapter, we have taken our own advice. Together, the three of us have substantive expertise in gerontology, organizational psychology, and sociology and methodological expertise in quantitative methods, qualitative methods, and combining the two general types of methods. Our experience has led us to believe that the team approach to empirical research, despite its challenges, can be highly rewarding, professionally and personally, and superior in terms of the quality of the work produced than that likely to be done individually. As Shulha and Wilson (2003) documented, "collaboration itself can transform the nature of data collection and analysis . . . [creating] the potential for learning that is more than additive" (p. 666).

The following are, from our perspective, key "Rules of Engagement" for a successful mixed methods team of work-family researchers:

1. Each researcher appreciates and respects the research tradition, disciplines, and skills of the others.
2. Each researcher is not only open to, but also interested in, learning from the others.
3. The project team meets together regularly (in person, ideally, but via telephone conferencing or real-time electronic conferencing if necessary).
4. Task deadlines are mutually set and agreed on by all team members.
5. Each researcher makes every effort to meet deadlines.
6. Team members recognize and respect the efforts and work-family situations of their fellow team members, exhibit flexibility, and revise plans accordingly.

CONCLUSION

In addition to being useful for answering complex questions, such as many of those addressed in the field of work and family integration, mixed methods research, in which qualitative and quantitative methods are combined, can aid in the development of hypotheses regarding why results were found as well as the development of more valid data collection instruments, often yielding richer, more thorough, insightful, and trustworthy findings (Currall & Towler, 2003; Johnson & Turner, 2003; Mertens, 2003; Rossman & Wilson, 1985; Tashakkori & Teddlie, 2003a, 2003b). Also, the process of conducting mixed methods research can be personally and professionally enriching for the researchers who are involved (Tashakkori & Teddlie, 2003a).

At the same time, mixed methods research is still viewed by some as a controversial approach to conducting research in the social and behavioral sciences (Onwuegbuzie & Teddlie, 2003), and there is a lack of consensus, even among proponents, with respect to terminology, types of designs, and appropriate uses of mixed methods approaches. This lack of consensus results in confusion and creates challenges for researchers seeking to design mixed methods studies.

Our position has been pragmatic: We argue the researcher should select the method or methods that can best illuminate the phenomenon of interest. Our goal has been to inform work-family researchers and students of the benefits of using mixed methods in research and the basic motivations for designing studies that use both qualitative and quantitative methods. Toward this end, we have provided examples of mixed methods study designs from our own work and that of other work-family researchers. We also have identified several challenges one faces when undertaking this kind of research. It is our hope that readers have gained a greater understanding of what mixed methods research is, how qualitative and quantitative methods can be combined successfully, and the gains to be realized in quality and scope in work-family research.

NOTES

[1] These three purposes are consistent with, but simplify, the five purposes for adopting mixed methods design strategies outlined by Greene, Caracelli, and Graham (1989) (i.e., triangulation, complementarity, development, initiation, and expansion).

[2] Although "triangulation" is another term used to describe the process of conducting two different studies with the hope of reaching the same conclusions to demonstrate that results are not due to invalidity or to an artifact of a particular method, it also has several other meanings as well. Hence, Morgan (1998) argued that "convergence" or "confirmation" are better terms to use to describe this goal of seeking cross-validation between methods.

[3] The original qualitative analysis located coping strategies that involved (a) increasing resources or (b) decreasing demands in one of three ways: (1) behaviorally, (2) emotionally, or (3) cognitively. Subsequent analyses of the quantitative survey data (Neal & Hammer, in press) revealed only three factors that fit the data reasonably well: emotional coping strategies that increase resources, cognitive coping strategies that increase prioritization, and behavioral coping strategies that decrease social involvement. Each factor contained from two to four items.

[4] In particular, for an overview of the various classifications of mixed methods designs that have been proposed and an examination of additional design possibilities, see Creswell, Plano Clark, Gutmann, and Hanson (chap. 8). For an alternative approach to design selection, see Maxwell and Loomis (chap. 9). For a discussion of sampling strategies in mixed methods research, see Kempler, Stringfield, and Teddlie (chap. 10), and for an examination of data collection strategies in mixed methods research, see Johnson and Turner (chap. 11). Sandelowski's chapter (chap. 12) on the challenges of describing the results of mixed methods studies is illuminating, as are those concerning data analytic frameworks (chap. 13, by Onwuegbuzie and Teddlie) and computer programs for analyzing data gathered through mixed methods research (chap. 14, by Bazeley). Miller (chap. 15) and Erzberger and Kelle (chap. 16) tackle the issue of making inferences in mixed methods research.

REFERENCES

Agazio, J. G., Ephraim, P. M., Flaherty, N. B., & Gurney, C. A. (2002). Health promotion in active-duty military women with children. *Women & Health, 35(1),* 65–82.

Brannen, J. (1992). Combining qualitative and quantitative methods: An overview. In J. Brannen (Ed.), *Mixing methods: Qualitative and quantitative research* (pp. 3–38). Brookfield, VT: Avebury.

Brewer, J., & Hunter, A. (1989). *Multimethod research: A synthesis of styles.* Newbury Park, CA: Sage.

Bridges: Mixed Methods Network for Behavioral, Social and Health Sciences. http://www.fiu.edu/~bridges/.

Brink, B., & de la Rey, C. (2001). Work-family interaction strain: Coping strategies used by successful women in the public, corporate and self-employed sectors of the economy. *South African Journal of Psychology, 31,* 55–61.

Bryman, A. (1984). The debate about quantitative and qualitative methods: A question of method or epistemology. *British Journal of Sociology, 35,* 75–92.

Bryman, A. (1988). *Quantity and quality in social research.* Boston: Unwin Hyman.

Campbell, D. T., & Fiske, D. W. (1959). Convergent and discriminant validity in the multitrait–multimethod matrix. *Psychological Bulletin, 56,* 81–105.

Caracelli, V. J., & Greene, J. C. (1997). Crafting mixed-method evaluation designs. In J. C. Greene & V. J. Caracelli (Eds.), *Advances in mixed methods evaluation: The challenges and benefits of integrating diverse paradigms* (pp. 19–32). San Francisco: Jossey-Bass.

Chusid, H., & Cochran, L. (1989). Meaning of career change from the perspective of family roles and dramas. *Journal of Counseling Psychology, 36(1),* 34–41.

Cook, T. D., & Reichardt, C. S. (1979). *Qualitative and quantitative methods in evaluation research.* Beverly Hills, CA: Sage.

Creswell, J. W. (1994). *Research design: Qualitative and quantitative approaches.* Thousand Oaks, CA: Sage.

Creswell, J. W., Plano Clark, V. L., Gutmann, M. L., & Hanson, W. E. (2003). Advanced mixed methods research designs. In A. Tashakkori & C. Teddlie (Eds.), *Handbook of mixed methods in social & behavioral research* (pp. 209–240). Thousand Oaks, CA: Sage.

Curbow, B., McDonnell, K., Spratt, K., Griffin, J., & Agnew, J. (2003). Development of the work-family interface scale. *Early Childhood Research Quarterly, 18,* 310–330.

Currall, S. C., & Towler, A. J. (2003). Research methods in management and organizational research: Toward integration of qualitative and quantitative techniques. In A. Tashakkori & C. Teddlie (Eds.), *Handbook of mixed methods in social & behavioral research* (pp. 513–526). Thousand Oaks, CA: Sage.

Dey, I. (1993). *Qualitative data analysis: A user-friendly guide for social scientists.* London: Routledge.

Dorfman, L. T. (2002). Stayers and leavers: Professors in an era of no mandatory retirement. *Educational Gerontology, 28,* 15–133.

Eby, L. T., Casper, W. J., Lockwood, A., Bordeaux, C., & Brinley, A. (2005). Work and family research in IO/OB: Content analysis and review of the literature (1980–2002). *Journal of Vocational Behavior, 66,* 124–197.

Erzberger, C., & Kelle, U. (2003). Making inferences in mixed methods: The rules of integration. In A. Tashakkori & C. Teddlie (Eds.), *Handbook of mixed methods in social & behavioral research* (pp. 457–490). Thousand Oaks, CA: Sage.

Erzberger, C., & Prein, G. (1997). Triangulation: Validity and empirically based hypothesis construction. *Quality & Quantity, 2,* 141–154.

Franklin, C. (1996). Learning to teach qualitative research: Reflections of a quantitative researcher. In M. B. Sussman & J. F. Gilgun (Eds.), *The methods and methodologies of qualitative family research* (pp. 241–274). New York: Haworth.

Gage, N. (1989). The paradigm wars and their aftermath: A "historical" sketch of research and teaching since 1989. *Educational Researcher, 18(7),* 4–10.

Glaser, B. G., & Strauss, A. L. (1967). *The discovery of grounded theory: Strategies for qualitative research.* New York: DeGruyter.

Greene, J. C., & Caracelli, V. J. (1997). Defining and describing the paradigm issue in mixed method evaluation. In J. C. Greene & V. J. Caracelli (Eds.), *Advances in mixed methods evaluation: The challenges and benefits of integrating diverse paradigms* (pp. 5–18). San Francisco: Jossey-Bass.

Greene, J. C., & Caracelli, V. J. (2003). Making paradigmatic sense of mixed methods practice. In A. Tashakkori & C. Teddlie (Eds.), *Handbook of mixed methods in social and behavioral research* (pp. 91–110). Thousand Oaks, CA: Sage.

Greene, J. C., Caracelli, V. J., & Graham, W. F. (1989). Toward a conceptual framework for mixed-method evaluation designs. *Educational Evaluation and Policy Analysis, 11,* 255–274.

Grzywacz, J. G., Almeida, D. M., & McDonald, D. A. (2002). Work-family spillover and daily reports of work and family stress in the adult labor force. *Family Relations, 51,* 28–36.

Guba, E. G., & Lincoln, Y. W. (1994). Competing paradigms in qualitative methods. In N. Denzin & Y. Lincoln (Eds.), *Handbook of qualitative research* (pp. 105–117). Thousand Oaks, CA: Sage.

Hawkins, A. J., Roberts, T., Christiansen, S. L., & Marshall, C. M. (1994). An evaluation of a program to help dual-earner couples share the second shift. *Family Relations, 43,* 213–220.

Heymann, J. (2000). *The widening gap: Why America's working families are in jeopardy—and what can be done about it.* New York: Basic Books.

Hunter, A., & Brewer, J. (2003). Multimethod research in sociology. In A. Tashakkori & C. Teddlie (Eds.), *Handbook of mixed methods in social & behavioral research* (pp. 577–594). Thousand Oaks, CA: Sage.

Ingersoll-Dayton, B., Neal, M., & Hammer, L. (2001). Aging parents helping adult children: The experience of the sandwiched generation. *Family Relations, 50,* 262–271.

Ingersoll-Dayton, B., Neal, M. B., Ha, J., & Hammer, L. B. (2003a). Redressing inequity in parent care among siblings. *Journal of Marriage and Family, 65,* 201–212.

Ingersoll-Dayton, B., Neal, M. B., Ha, J., & Hammer, L. B. (2003b). Collaboration among siblings providing care for older parents. *Journal of Gerontological Social Work, 40(3),* 51–66.

Jick, T. D. (1979). Mixing qualitative and quantitative methods: Triangulation in action. *Administrative Science Quarterly, 24,* 602–611.

Johnson, B., & Turner, L. A. (2003). Data collection strategies in mixed methods research. In A. Tashakkori & C. Teddlie (Eds.), *Handbook of mixed methods in social & behavioral research* (pp. 297–320). Thousand Oaks, CA: Sage.

Krüger, H., & Baldus, B. (1999). Work, gender and the life course: Social construction and individual experience. *Canadian Journal of Sociology, 24,* 355–379.

Lazarsfeld, P. F. (1944). The controversy over detailed interviews: An offer for negotiation. *Public Opinion Quarterly, 8,* 38–60.

Maxcy, S. J. (2003). Pragmatic threads in mixed methods research in the social sciences: The search for multiple modes of inquiry and the end of the philosophy of formalism. In A. Tashakkori & C. Teddlie (Eds.), *Handbook of mixed methods in social & behavioral research* (pp. 51–90). Thousand Oaks, CA: Sage.

Maxwell, J. A., & Loomis, D. M. (2003). Mixed methods design: An alternative approach. In A. Tashakkori & C. Teddlie (Eds.), *Handbook of mixed methods in social and behavioral research* (pp. 241–272). Thousand Oaks, CA: Sage.

McKeown, B., & Thomas, D. (1988). *Q methodology*. Newbury Park, CA: Sage.

Mertens, D. (2003). Mixed methods and the politics of human research: The transformative–emancipatory perspective. In A. Tashakkori & C. Teddlie (Eds.), *Handbook of mixed methods in social & behavioral research* (pp. 135–166). Thousand Oaks, CA: Sage.

Miles, M. B., & Huberman, A. M. (1994). *Qualitative data analysis: An expanded sourcebook* (2nd ed.). Thousand Oaks, CA: Sage.

Moen, P. (Ed.). (2003). *It's about time: Couples and careers*. Ithaca, NY: Cornell University Press.

Moghaddam, F. M., Walker, B. R., & Harré, R. (2003). Cultural distance, levels of abstraction, and the advantages of mixed methods. In A. Tashakkori & C. Teddlie (Eds.), *Handbook of mixed methods in social & behavioral research* (pp. 111–134). Thousand Oaks, CA: Sage.

Morgan, D. L. (1997). *Focus groups as qualitative research* (2nd ed.). *Qualitative research methods series 16*. Thousand Oaks, CA: Sage.

Morgan, D. L. (1998). Practical strategies for combining qualitative and quantitative methods: Applications to health research. *Qualitative Health Research, 8,* 362–376.

Morgan, D. L. (forthcoming). *Practical strategies for combining qualitative and quantitative methods*. Thousand Oaks, CA: Sage.

Morse, J. M. (1991). Approaches to qualitative–quantitative triangulation. *Nursing Research, 40,* 120–123.

Morse, J. M. (2003). Principles of mixed methods and multimethod research design. In A. Tashakkori & C. Teddlie (Eds.), *Handbook of mixed methods in social & behavioral research* (pp. 189–208). Thousand Oaks, CA: Sage.

Neal, M. B., & Hammer, L. B. (in press). *Working couples caring for children and aging parents: Effects on work and well-being*. Mahwah, NJ: Lawrence Erlbaum Associates.

Newman, I., Ridenour, C. S., Newman, C., & Demarco, G. M. P., Jr. (2003). A typology of research purposes and its relationship to mixed methods. In A. Tashakkori & C. Teddlie (Eds.), *Handbook of mixed methods in social & behavioral research* (pp. 167–188). Thousand Oaks, CA: Sage.

Onwuegbuzie, A. J., & Teddlie, C. (2003). A framework for analyzing data in mixed methods research. In A. Tashakkori & C. Teddlie (Eds.), *Handbook of mixed methods in social & behavioral research* (pp. 351–384). Thousand Oaks, CA: Sage.

Orlikowski, W. J., & Baroudi, J. J. (1991). Studying information technology in organizations: Research approaches and assumptions. *Information Systems Research, 2,* 1–28.

Petter, S. C., & Gallivan, M. J. (2004). Toward a framework for classifying and guiding mixed method research in information systems. Proceedings of the 37th Hawaii International Conference on System Sciences, 2004. Available at: http://csdl.computer.org/comp/proceedings/hicss/2004/2056/08/205680257a.pdf.

Rallis, S. F., & Rossman, G. B. (2003). Mixed methods in evaluation contexts: A pragmatic framework. In A. Tashakkori & C. Teddlie (Eds.), *Handbook of mixed methods in social & behavioral research* (pp. 491–512). Thousand Oaks, CA: Sage.

Rocco, T. S., Bliss, L. A., Gallagher, S., & Pérez-Prado, A. (2003a). Taking the next step: Mixed methods research in organizational systems. *Information Technology, Learning, and Performance Journal, 21,* 19–29.

Rocco, T. S., Bliss, L. A., Gallagher, S., Pérez-Prado, A., Alacaci, C., Dwyer, E. S., Fine, J. C., & Pappamihiel, N. E. (2003b). The pragmatic and dialectical lenses: Two views of mixed methods use in education. In A. Tashakkori & C. Teddlie (Eds.), *Handbook of mixed methods in social & behavioral research* (pp. 595–615). Thousand Oaks, CA: Sage.

Rossman, G. B., & Wilson, B. L. (1985). Numbers and words: Combining quantitative and qualitative methods in a single large scale evaluation. *Evaluation Review, 9,* 627–643.

Ruderman, M. N., Ohlott, P. J., Panser, K., & King, S. N. (2002). Benefits of multiple roles for managerial women. *Academy of Management Journal, 45,* 369–386.

Sandelowski, M. (2003). Tables or tableaux? The challenges of writing and reading mixed methods studies. In A. Tashakkori & C. Teddlie (Eds.), *Handbook of mixed methods in social & behavioral research* (pp. 321–350). Thousand Oaks, CA: Sage.

Shaffer, M. A., & Harrison, D. A. (2001). Forgotten partners of international assignments: Development and test of a model of spouse adjustment. *Journal of Applied Psychology, 86,* 238–254.

Shulha, L. M., & Wilson, R. J. (2003). Collaborative mixed methods research. In A. Tashakkori & C. Teddlie (Eds.), *Handbook of mixed methods in social & behavioral research* (pp. 639–670). Thousand Oaks, CA: Sage.

Sieber, S. D. (1973). The integration of fieldwork and survey methods. *American Journal of Sociology, 78,*1335–1359.

Smith, J. K., & Heshusius, L. (1986). Closing down the conversation: The end of the qualitative–quantitative debate among educational inquirers. *Educational Researcher, 15,*4–12.

Strauss, A. L., & Corbin, J. M. (1990). *Basics of qualitative research: Grounded theory procedures and techniques.* Newbury Park, CA: Sage.

Tashakkori, A., & Teddlie, C. (1998). *Mixed methodology: Combining qualitative and quantitative approaches.* Thousand Oaks, CA: Sage.

Tashakkori, A., & Teddlie, C. (2003a). Preface. In A. Tashakkori & C. Teddlie (Eds.), *Handbook of mixed methods in social & behavioral research* (pp. ix–xv). Thousand Oaks, CA: Sage.

Tashakkori, A., & Teddlie, C. (2003b). The past and future of mixed methods research: From data triangulation to mixed model designs. In A. Tashakkori & C. Teddlie (Eds.), *Handbook of mixed methods in social & behavioral research* (pp. 671–701). Thousand Oaks, CA: Sage.

Webb, E. J., Campbell, D. T., Schwartz, R. D., & Sechrest, L. (1966). *Unobtrusive measures: Nonreactive research in the social sciences.* Chicago: Rand McNally.

Winston, P., Angel, R., Burton, L., Cherlin, A., Moffitt, R., & Wilson, W. J. (1999). Welfare, children, and families: A three city study; overview and design report. Baltimore: Johns Hopkins University Press. Available at www.jhu.edu/~welfare/welfare_publication.html.

Zimmerman, T. S., Haddock, S. A., Current, L. R., & Ziemba, S. (2003). Intimate partnership: Foundation to the successful balance of family and work. *American Journal of Family Therapy, 31,* 107–124.

PART IV: Advancing Policy and Organizational Change

Introduction: Cultivating Organizational Change and Advancing Public Policy

Marcie Pitt-Catsouphes
Boston College

Ellen Ernst Kossek
Michigan State University

Stephen Sweet
Ithaca College

The contours of the work-family area of study have been dynamically shaped by business practitioners and policymakers as well as by academics. Each of these different stakeholder groups has contributed unique perspectives and different types of leadership that have enhanced our understanding of work-family phenomena.

The importance of linking academic research to social change in organizations and to public policymaking is a long-standing tradition in the work and family field. In fact, Rosabeth Moss Kanter's 1977 seminal monograph, *Work and Family in the United States: A Critical Review and Agenda for Research and Policy*, includes chapters that consider "Research and Policy Agenda" and "Social Policy Innovations and Experiments." In these chapters, Kanter makes a range of recommendations, such as expanding the availability of flextime/flexible working hours, community-based supports and services, and different types of short- and long-term paid leaves of absence.

Many of the preceding chapters in this handbook comment on the extent to which the lives of working families are significantly impacted by employer policies as well as by public policies. These authors understand that the findings of work-family research can contribute to informed decision making by leaders at the workplace as well as by government representatives. Section IV of this handbook introduces readers to the work of several scholars who have stepped outside of traditional academic settings in an effort to link academic inquiries to the work of business leaders and policymakers.

In chapter 29, Ellen Kossek and Alyssa Friede consider different business cases for implementing family-responsive practices. Focusing on the concerns of managers, Kossek and Friede provide a nuanced discussion about employers' perspectives of work-family issues and different decision-making rationales for responding to them. The authors identify three basic dimensions of employer support for work and family: formal work and family policies and practices, employment conditions and the way jobs are designed, and occupational and organizational cultures. They then pose one of the most important questions related to social change at the workplace: What are the motivations behind employer adoption of work and family policies? Kossek and Friede indicate that there are multiple business cases or management perspectives that help to explain workplace responsiveness to work-life issues and managers' approaches to them, in addition to the more standard argument that work/life policies can add to a firm's competitive advantage. These business cases include: change management orientations, the dual agenda, work/life bundles, high commitment work systems, social exchange, and diversity and employer-of-choice perspectives. Kossek and Friede provide descriptions of each of these approaches, offer examples of scholarship that reflect these management perspectives, and include analytic observations about the strengths and limitations of each. They close with some important and provocative suggestions and also caution academics and managers against making the misassumption that organizations with work and family policies on the books must be family-friendly.

Although it has long been acknowledged that work-family issues are affected by public policy (and therefore relevant to policymaking), few academics are formally trained to move scholarly discourse about work-family issues into the public policy arena. It can be a challenge to mobilize research to advance the development and analysis of law. In chapter 30, "Legislatures, Agencies, Courts, and Advocates: How Laws Are Made, Interpreted, and Modified," Chai Feldblum and Robin Appleberry illuminate the hurdles as well as some of the strategies of policymaking. Using the passage and implementation of the 1993 Family and Medical Leave Act as a detailed case study, Feldblum and Appleberry connect legal research, legal advocacy, and lawmaking activities. The chapter begins with a reminder of the roles that each of the three branches of government can have in policymaking at both the state and federal levels. The authors then weave together descriptions of the lawmaking process with analytic comments about the opportunities for academics and advocates to participate in the process. A key message embedded in this chapter is that scholars who are interested in contributing to lawmaking need to understand the importance of engaging in persistent conversations with policymakers in all three branches of government. They stress that ongoing dialogue and relationship building is critical when different versions of bills are considered during different congressional sessions, when the bills are discussed during the comment periods for proposed regulations developed by executive branch agencies, and when laws are interpreted by the courts. The authors offer significant insight into the behind-the-scenes politics that influence both the pace and the outcomes of policymaking activities. This chapter concludes with some nuts and bolts assistance offered to scholars not trained in the law about strategies for conducting legal research.

In chapter 31, "Work-Family Interventions & Experiments: Workplaces, Communities, and Society," Lotte Bailyn, Ann Bookman, Mona Harrington, and Tom Kochan present a compelling case for using work redesign as one intervention that can result in meaningful and sustainable change at the workplace. Focusing on projects at the MIT Workplace Center, these authors discuss the strategies they have used to coordinate the goals of traditional research with the priorities of businesses. As a result, their projects advance a dual agenda of creating interventions that simultaneously improve organizational effectiveness *and* the integration of family and personal life. The work of the MIT Workplace Center creatively connects research with action, a synthesis that catalyzes a model for change at three levels: the workplace level, the association level, and the state level. The process that Bailyn, Bookman, Harrington, and Kochan utilize reflects the Collaborative Interactive Action Research (CIAR) model, a method that contextualizes the needs of a specific workforce group in the conditions present at their workplace. One of the key assumptions of the CIAR model is that "the issues faced by working families are social, not individual, problems requiring broad social responsibility and public solutions" This CIAR method involves cultivating collaborative relationships between members of the research team, employers, and employees. In the chapter, the authors discuss the iterative stages of interventions based on the CIAR model. They emphasize that researchers can use virtually every interaction as an opportunity for a micro-intervention with their partners in the experiment (e.g., employees and business leaders at the workplace). Drawing on studies conducted by the MIT Workplace Center in the health care sector as well as in other industries, they demonstrate how their involvement as researchers has helped both the employees and employers recognize the negative impact that some taken-for-granted work practices can have on employees' performance at work and on their lives outside the workplace. It is important to note that the MIT Workplace Center places a premium on disseminating the findings of their studies beyond the organizational boundaries of the workplace to key stakeholders, including professional associations, employee representatives, business groups, and policy leaders. Thus, ideas for positive social change can cascade into different industry sectors and into the public sector.

Brad Harrington and Jacquelyne James continue conversations started in other chapters of the handbook about academic–business leader partnerships in chapter 32, "The Standards of Excellence in Work-Life Integration: From Changing Policies to Changing Organizations." They start with a basic but complicated question posed by the business leaders themselves: What are the most appropriate and effective measures to chart the progress that organizations make toward greater responsiveness to work/life issues? Harrington and James describe the instrument developed by the Boston College Center for Work & Family in partnership with work-life managers, The Standards of Excellence in Work/Life Integration Index. One of the unique aspects of The Standards of Excellence Index is that it rests on a foundation of guiding principles that address organizational effectiveness through a work/life lens. The principles of Excellence are operationalized in seven elements of the Index: leadership, strategy, infrastructure, accountability, relationship building, communications, and measurement. The Harrington and James chapter illustrates how scholarly theory and constructs, such as theory about organizational learning, can be relevant to practitioners' interest in promoting effective organizational change. The development and use of The Standards of Excellence Index is evidence of the potential power of practitioner–academic partnerships, such as that established between the Boston College Center for Work & Family and its corporate members.

Arbitration is another approach used to advance family-responsive workplaces. In chapter 33, "The Arbitration of Work-Family Conflicts," Benjamin Wolkinson and Russell Ormiston focus on a subset of workplaces—unionized workplaces—and explain the processes used to resolve contentious interpretations of employer and employee contractual obligations, rights, and responsibilities. As they point out in the chapter, access to arbitration is virtually limited to employees who are union members (approximately 17 million workers), but arbitration discourse and decisions can resonate beyond the specific organizational confines. The research presented in this chapter offers tremendous insight into the arbitration process and explores how the resolution of arbitration can affect decisions made at the workplace. The authors contend that changing contractual arrangements between workers and employers and examining the extent of conformity to legal mandates will, ultimately, affect how workplaces accommodate family needs. However, Wolkinson and Ormiston reveal that there is considerable ambiguity about the interpretation of specific statutory and regulatory provisions and that different employers may utilize different definitions of legal concepts, such as the interpretation of a legitimate absence from the workplace. In a comprehensive review of recent arbitration decisions concerning parental absences for child-care needs, Wolkinson and Ormiston outline the approach arbitrators use to determine if employers exercise "just cause" in disciplining employees. This process entails examining factors such as contractual agreements, past practice with other employees, existing laws that are external to the contract, the specifics of particular situations, duties of the employee to act responsibility, past attendance histories, extenuating circumstances, and employer operational needs. But, as much as the authors argue for the potential of arbitration as a means of creating reasonable resolutions to discordant opinions, Wolkinson and Ormiston also consider situations where employees and employers were unable to identify common ground.

The last chapter in this handbook, "Leadership in Action: A Work and Family Agenda for the Future," encourages readers to reflect on the origins of the work-family field as well as consider the future directions of work-family research, policy, and practice. Kathleen Christensen, currently the Director of the Workplace, Workforce and Working Families Program at the Alfred P. Sloan Foundation, was one of the early scholars in the work-family area of study and has had firsthand opportunities to observe how the intricate intersections of the academic and the practice roots of the work-family field have created a healthy tension between *what we know*, *what we need to know*, and *what we do*. It is of particular interest to note the linkages that Christensen makes between the results of research conducted in the 1990s and the possibilities for reaching out to employers and policymakers in the 21st century. Since 1994, Christensen has served as the Foundation's in-house leader in the area of work-family. In that capacity, she has played a key role both in articulating a vision for the work-family area of study and in developing and implementing grant-making strategies that have made it possible for numerous academics to contribute to that vision. This chapter provides commentary and analytic insight into the influential roles that scholars can assume outside of university settings, such as at a national foundation. Christensen's chapter describes her analysis of the evolution and purposive development of the work-family area of study from mid-1990s to the present, and then uses these observations to chart some of the areas that will be needed for continued progress as scholars add their voices and contribute their insights to the work of business leaders and public policymakers.

Each of the chapters in Section IV contributes to the articulation of new types of collaborations between researchers from different disciplines, business practitioners, and policymakers. Ultimately, efforts such as those described in this last section of the handbook will not only increase the insightfulness of the findings of research studies but, in the end, will also increase the relevance of work-family investigations to a range of stakeholders. Thus, this concluding section of the handbook extends the tradition of linking work and family scholarship to social change.

REFERENCE

Kanter, R. (1977). *Work and family in the United States: A critical review and agenda for research and policy.* New York: Russell Sage Foundation.

29

The Business Case: Managerial Perspectives on Work and the Family

Ellen Ernst Kossek
Alyssa Friede
Michigan State University

In this chapter, we discuss the different management approaches used by employers for framing, adopting, and managing work and family policies in organizations and by researchers examining work-family issues. The field of management focuses on ensuring that when workers come together in an enterprise, they are organized with the dual goals of achieving effectiveness in accomplishing the organizational mission and efficiency in motivating employees to work toward maximizing productivity (Stroh, Northcraft, & Neale, 2002). Management tends to take a rational and prescriptive perspective and assumes there is an optimal way to organize a firm and its workforce depending on the organization's strategy, culture, power and resources, and external environment. The field of management is closely aligned with organizational behavior, which is multi-disciplinary, drawing from many fields in the social sciences, and seeks to understand behavior in organizations by examining individual, group, organizational, and interorganizational dynamics (Miner, 2002). It is relatively recently that work and family issues have been viewed as a mainstream and core management concern. As managers have become more cognizant of the importance of work and family issues to efficiency and effectiveness, the management field is gradually moving in practice toward recognition that like other business issues, work and family problems must be analyzed in the context of organizational behavior.

Kossek (2005) noted that the traditional research on managerial work family policy can be organized into several streams: an *adoption* stream, a *demographic* stream, and *a policy impact* stream. Research from the *adoption* stream tends to focus on the organizational level of analysis and examines employer characteristics predicting policy adoption or availability and work-life responsiveness, as well as variation in availability by industries and job groups. Research from the *demographic* stream tends to focus on the individual employee level of analysis, with regards to the perceived attractiveness, access, satisfaction, and use of policies by various demographic groups focusing on employee family-relevant demographics (e.g., gender, age, number and ages of dependents). The *policy impact* stream examines how policy use relates to individual and organizational outcomes (Kossek & Ozeki, 1999). Past reviews of management streams such as these are descriptive and reflect where much of the state of the development of the field is to date. The approach, while valuable, does not shed light on the variation in management justification for work-family policy.

A main goal of this chapter is to argue that it is critical to identify and recognize the wide diversity in employer rhetoric used to understand work and family policies in practice, an issue that has not been fully examined in previous research reviews. We believe it is important to not only focus on prevailing norms and existence of formal policies, but also to question the universalization of managerial interests (Alvesson & Deetz, 1996) that predominates the managerial work and family literature. By this we mean that the management literature on work and family has had a tendency to view work-family problems as if the way that employers deem they should be properly managed are serving everyone's interests. Yet critical and postmodern theorists (cf. Alvesson & Deetz, 1996) note that management is ascribed a privileged position in terms of being able to define the interests of corporations in such a way that minimizes the interests and investments made to organizational effectiveness by other stakeholders, such as employees, families, community and society, and maximizes those made by financial investors and owners.

By showing the wide variety in the rhetoric used by employers in their response to work and family issues, we seek to encourage future scholarship and practice that examines and scrutinizes the formal managerial rationale for the adoption of work and family policies. Such an approach will lead to a greater definition of the predictors and consequences of work and family policy, which may ultimately lead to multiple perspectives on the effectiveness of management progressivism in responding to and supporting employees' work and family needs. Before exploring managerial perspectives on work-life policies and practices, we will review the distinct ways in which organizations' support and practices impact employees' work and family well-being.

DOMAIN OF EMPLOYER SUPPORT OF WORK AND FAMILY

The domain of employer support of work and family includes three main areas: formal human resource policies to support work and family, job design and terms and conditions of employment, and informal occupational and organizational culture and norms (Kossek, 2005). The first area involves the development and implementation of *formal human resource policies and practices* that influence the extent to which a workplace has supports available that are designed to reduce conflicts and stresses related to the delivery of work and nonwork roles. Table 29.1 includes some examples of these policies, which include but are not limited to flexibility in working time or place, direct work-life services for child or elder care or self care, and information and social supports. As these policies illustrate, although employers often initially define work-family integration as a parenting and dependent care issue, over time in many firms there is a broadening of policies and practices to support participation in additional life roles such as community, elder care, teen supervision, personal health care, those related to personal values (e.g., political, religious), military service, domestic chores, or exercise (Kossek, 2005). This trend shows growing management recognition of the need to support not only those with visible dependent care needs (e.g., child care), but all employees at many life stages who may experience work-life stresses regardless of family status or who may have important nonwork identities (e.g., National Guard, education, religious) that require flexibility to enable effective participation (Kossek, 2005).

The second area of employer support, job design and terms of employment, refers to *employment conditions* such as pay, work hours, or other human resource policies. Employment conditions may dictate the manner in which work and family roles can be combined, controlled, or performed in ways that create psychological and/or physical distress as well as enrichment.

TABLE 29.1
Description of Types of Work-Life Policies/Programs

Policy/Program Category	*Flexibility of Working Time*
Definition	Policies/practices designed to allow employees to have more control over the amount of hours that they work or when those hours are worked.
Examples	*Reduced-Hours or Part-time work*: Working less than full-time with a commensurate decrease in salary.
	Flextime: Employees vary their beginning and ending times (within a given flex range and established core hours), but generally work full-time.
	Compressed work-week: Employees work extra hours on some days of the week in order to have part of the day or a whole day off at another time.
	Job-sharing: Two employees share one full-time job.
	Compensatory time: Employees working long hours get subsequent time off in order to recoup.
	Leaves of absence: Employees get time off for maternity, paternity, military service, education, elder and child care, and other life pursuits and can return to their jobs or a similar job.

Policy/Program Category	*Flexibility of Working Place*
Definition	Policies/practices that allow employees to choose to work outside of the office or worksite (all or some of the time).
Examples	*Telework*: Employees work part or all of the time at an off-site location and use technology (e.g., e-mail, fax, mobile phone) in order to communicate with others.

Policy/Program Category	*Support with Care Responsibilities*
Definition	Policies/practices that assist employees in providing care for others (child and elder) or for self and household.
Examples	*Child/elder care*: Employees have access to employer-provided care for children or elders either at their worksite or in communities.
	Child/elder care provider referral service: Employees can call/e-mail a service which will assist them in finding regular child/elder care providers.
	Financial support for dependent care: Employees receive financial help in the form of flexible spending accounts that use pretax dollars to help pay for care, direct subsidies, or discounts.
	Emergency/sick child/elder care: Employee has access to child/elder care for unexpected situations.

Policy/Program Category	*Informational and Social Supports*
Definition	Policies/practices that provide emotional support to employees facing nonwork or balance challenges.
Examples	*Support hotlines*: Employees can call a number to receive emotional support for dealing with work-life issues.
	Support groups: Employees can join a support or networking group for informational and psychological support.

*Some of the definitions in this table were adapted from Hyland, 2003; Kossek, 2003; Lee, MacDermid, & Buck, 2000.

For example, a single parent who works the second shift may find her job design makes it virtually impossible for her child to participate in after school activities that require parent involvement or for her family. Yet if the same single parent were able to take a longer dinner break at her home near the plant, she would be able to eat weekday meals with her children and still fulfill her breadwinning role. In one of the few published studies that linked work-family policies to job design and other conditions of employment, Batt and Valcour (2003) examined relationships between access to work-family policies, human resource incentives such as salary or work hours, and job design such as control for a nonrandom sample of over 500 dual earners. They found that human resource incentives had a stronger relationship to work-family conflict and turnover than job design or work family policies. Perhaps one reason for the findings that employment conditions were more important than policies is that the scale used summed access to dependent care and flexibility policies and not use of specific policies, which future research might want to further examine.

The third area refers to *organizational and professional cultures and norms*. These cultures and norms often shape informal work practices and supervisor preferences for managing work and family. The culture of the organization toward work-family issues has been defined as the "shared assumptions, beliefs, and values regarding the extent to which an organization supports and values the integration of employees' work and family lives" (Thompson, Beauvais, & Lyness, 1999, p. 394). A supportive culture includes the extent of organizational time demands for long work hours, perceived career consequences for using family-friendly policies, and managerial support of family needs (Thompson et al., 1999). Thompson et al. (1999) found that a work-family supportive work culture was associated with increased employee use of work-family benefits, increased organizational commitment, and decreased work-family conflict and intention to turnover. Kossek, Colqiutt, and Noe (2001) focused on positive cross-domain climate relationships between work and family and found that the ability to share concerns about work when at home or home when at work, was related to better performance and well-being.

While the categories in Table 29.1 do not reflect every possible policy or practice associated with employer support for work-life integration, they cover a broad range of the human resource policies and practices offered in today's workplaces. Although useful for describing organizational activities, these groupings are limited in their ability to capture management beliefs about these policies or assumptions about *why* or *how* they impact employee, group, and organizational outcomes; nor do they give insight into how these policies are embedded in practice in relation to job design and conditions of employment, organizational culture and norms, or supervision.

MANAGEMENT PERSPECTIVES ON IMPLEMENTING WORK-LIFE POLICIES

We have argued that the preceding review of work-life policies, practices and research, while important for understanding the nature of work-life in organizations today, does not necessarily indicate the motivations behind policy adoption and implementation, nor the degree to which management posits connections between the policies and other organizational factors (e.g., strategy, job design, etc.). After reviewing the strategic human resource management business case, what follows is a review of the main perspectives we see used to explain the employer practice of adopting work and family policies. Table 29.2 provides a brief summary of these perspectives, including their definitions, key terms, and a sample article reference. It should be noted that these approaches are not discrete and may overlap in firms and research studies.

TABLE 29.2
Summary of Managerial Perspectives

Managerial Perspective	Definition	Key Terms	Recent Empirical Reference
Implementation Orientations	The management orientation toward implementing work and family policies and state of organizational development	• Management orientation • Accommodation • Elaboration • Transformation	Lee, MacDermid, & Buck (2000)
Dual Agenda	The degree to which an organization views work-family issues as a trade-off or as mutually beneficial	• Trade-offs • Integrated approach • Leveraged approach	Lautsch, Kossek, & Eaton (2004)
Work-Life Bundles	The degree to which work and family policies are clustered with each other and implemented with other HR policies and how this relates to organizational performance and other key outcomes	• Bundles • Clusters • Adoption • Human Resource Management	Perry-Smith & Blum (2000)
High Commitment Work Systems	The degree to which bundles of human resource practices create a high commitment work environment which, in turn, may affect employee work-family balance	• Empowerment • Human capital • High commitment	Berg, Kalleberg, & Appelbaum (2003)
Social Exchange	The degree to which employees respond to an organization's work-life policies by engaging in voluntary behaviors to help the organization	• Norms of reciprocity • Organizational citizenship behaviors	Lambert (2000)
Employer of Choice	The degree to which an organization offers work-life policies and practices in order to be perceived as a high-quality employer by internal and external stakeholders	• Share price • Employer of choice • *Working Mother* Top 100	Cascio & Young (2005)
Diversity	The degree to which work-life policies/practices are implemented in order to attract and retain a diverse workforce. This perspective may also emphasize culture change toward joint accommodation as opposed to assimilation.	• Recruiting • Retention • Demographics • Multiculturalism	Catalyst (2004)

Strategic Human Resource Management Grounding for the Business Case

Nearly all of the management perspectives we reviewed incorporate some strategic human resource management (SHRM) rhetoric related to the business case for work and family. Here, managers implicitly or explicitly draw on Barney (1991), who held that a quality-motivated, high talent workforce can be a source of competitive advantage. This view suggests that resources such as talent can become a competitive advantage when the resource is not easily imitated. Under this perspective, an organization's work-life policies enhance organizational performance due to their role in adding value to the firm. Research reflecting this perspective includes a variety of research questions: What is the relative economic performance of firms that provide such work-family balance? Do the firms that provide the best work-family balance for their employees do better in the marketplace? Are they more profitable? Are employees of those firms more productive? Potential benefits from work-life policies include increased competitiveness, profits, and stock price, reduced labor costs, and other work-related criteria that may benefit the firm over the long term. The latter might include: turnover and absenteeism; stress; unhealthy behaviors; substance abuse; and attitudes such as job satisfaction and extra-role behaviors (e.g., making suggestions, volunteering to help a coworker), commitment, and loyalty.

Using telework as an example, Hill, Ferris, and Martinson (2003) contended that work-life flexibility policies can help the organization meet strategic business needs by encouraging a reevaluation of what it means to be a productive employee. Due to the fact that employees who work in nontraditional ways (e.g., less than full-time, telework, job-share, etc.) may have reduced "face-time" in the office, performance cannot be judged solely along the lines of who is in the office and seems to be working hard. Instead, performance evaluation must shift to a more "results oriented" culture, in which performance is evaluated based on the results of the individual's work behaviors rather than his or her face-time in the office (Hill et al., 2003). This shifting emphasis on results within a company may be responsible for performance increases at the individual, group, and organizational levels.

SHRM approaches can help researchers and organizations identify the long-term strategic outcomes that may be associated with effectively managing the human resources within an organization. By emphasizing important overarching linkages between performance and new ways of working, work-life practitioners can use a SHRM approach to gain buy-in for work-life policies/practices from organizational leaders who may be reluctant to implement policies/practices for fear that they will have short-term negative business outcomes.

Organizational Implementation Orientation: Management Response to Change

Organizational implementation perspectives generally focus on variation in organizational ways of responding to workforce changes resulting in the adoption of policies and new management practices to support work-life integration. For example, after analyzing over 350 interviews with professionals who were users of company reduced workload arrangements, their bosses, their subordinates, and a family member such as a spouse, Lee, MacDermid, and Buck (2000) proposed three paradigms to describe organizational responses to the strategic change—namely the changing work-life needs of professionals and their requests to work reduced loads for at least some portion of their careers. Traditional management paradigms historically have assumed full-time managers and professionals are able and willing to work as many hours as are needed to get the job done. This resulted in many managers and professionals working long hours, sometimes 50–60-hour work weeks, which did not fit the needs of the changing demographics of the workforce. Increasing numbers of employees have non-work interests that necessitate they set some limits to the hours of work. In the first paradigm, *accommodation*, organizations make limited adjustments on a case-by-case basis in response to individual requests to work less than full-time. Although work-life accommodations were often made in order to retain a top performer, reduced-load options were allowed reluctantly and usually not written into formal organizational policy (Lee et al., 2000). Under this approach, while employers may be willing to *accommodate* individual needs in order to retain better-performing employees, they do so with restrained enthusiasm and a belief that widespread implementation of work-life policies and practices would have negative implications for the firm. Under the second orientation, *elaboration*, employees and managers were beginning to jointly manage arrangements and policies are beginning to be developed to support reduced load. There was, however, some disagreement in management perspectives regarding the individual and organizational implications of individuals choosing to work less (Lee et al., 2000). Under the third paradigm, a *transformation* approach was followed where major culture change to support new ways of working occurred. Here, there was little controversy regarding the importance or use of reduced workload arrangements, and they were seen as benefiting both the individual and the organization. Although Lee et al. (2000) focused on reduced workload management practices, these implementation paradigms can be used to think about the cultural acceptance and implementation of any work-life policy or practice.

A benefit of adopting an implementation orientation is that these orientations exist at the intersection of many work-family issues. In each paradigm, culture, policies, practices, and belief systems combine to create an overall image of an organization's orientation toward work-life. However, one must be careful not to oversimplify the nature of an organization by simply putting it into a single paradigm. Organizations and business units may have conflicting characteristics of accommodating, elaborating, and transformational paradigms. This perspective can be used as a tool by practitioners to then identify which paradigms tend to prevail in their firm and to which paradigm they aspire. Strategies for being a transformational organization, if that were the goal, could be developed with key organizational stakeholders. Diagnosing prevailing orientations could help change agents develop strategies for mobilizing change.

Dual Agenda

When management first handles work and family issues, there is often a *trade-off* approach, in which managers believe that employees are trading off time and energy between work and family, with one or the other domain "winning." In this case, the focus is on minimizing the cost of accommodating workers' personal needs (Lautsch, Kossek, & Eaton, 2004). Often consistent with a transformation perspective toward implementation, the *dual agenda* perspective seeks to avoid this win–lose framing. Instead, managers seeking to better handle work-family issues focus on broad changes to the work process and norms that will respond to personal concerns as well as benefit the organization's performance (Bailyn & Fletcher, 1997). Here, the job and the workplace are redesigned to jointly support work and family. The dual agenda approach is aligned with Friedman, Christensen, and DeGroot's (1998) writings supporting either an *integrated approach* that assumes a win–win solution is possible for resolving work and family conflicts that can jointly improve work and family or a *leveraged approach*, where managers strive to diagnose workers' personal concerns and build on them in order to catalyze broad workplace changes that benefit workers and organizations. Other than these excellent qualitative studies, little referred quantitative work has examined the dual agenda approach.

One exception is a study by Lautsch et al. (2004). Using a matched sample of 90 supervisors and 90 professional employees, regression analysis showed that supervisors who adopted the same monitoring behaviors in terms of job formalization for teleworkers and nonteleworkers, who provided higher levels of social support, and who viewed personal issues as an opportunity to catalyze improvements in the work process for all workers—a leveraged approach—had employees with higher performance.

A dual agenda approach can be useful for helping researchers and practitioners reframe the work-family issue. By focusing on how use of work-family policies can increase their work performance and their personal effectiveness, researchers can identify the mutually beneficial outcomes associated with work-life policies/practices. Managers, if aware of mutually beneficial outcomes, may be more willing to support employee work-life needs, which may result in mutually beneficial outcomes for their firms. One potential pitfall associated with the dual agenda approach can be the assumption that work-life policies/practices will be mutually beneficial on a daily basis, under all circumstances. For example, there may be times when an employee who works a reduced load is unable to make an important meeting or when a family event must be missed for work requirements. Adopting an unrealistic expectation of constant mutual beneficiality may lead to dissatisfaction with work-life policies by all parties. By realistically discussion the pros and cons, managers and employees can make an informed decision about when it is a good decision to use a policy in a given situation.

Work-Life Bundles

The work-life bundles perspective suggests that work and family policies are more effective and have a greater relation to organizational performance if they are clustered with each other and implemented with other HR policies than if adopted piecemeal. This perspective focuses less on the effects of individual initiatives and more on the joint effects of multiple policies that are configured in a consistent way, such as a high performance or high commitment workplace. The emphasis is on examining the bottom-line benefits of having a group of complementary overlapping HR policies that foster a core organizational approach, philosophy, or mindset.

Using a national sample of 527 U.S. firms, Perry-Smith and Blum (2000) developed four profiles of work-family cluster adoption: low offerings of all policies, offering leaves and less traditional dependent care (elder care and money to support child care), offering leaves and traditional dependent care (onsite child care, information and flexible scheduling), and high offerings of all work-family policies. The outcome measures were (a) perceptual, including the ability to attract essential workers, quality of relations between management and employees, and product quality; and (b) objective, that is, the percentage increase in sales and profits (profit sales growth) in the last 12 months. They found that extensive work-family policies were linked to higher perceptual measures of firm-level performance. Their findings did not strongly vary by proportion of women in the company or firm age.

Perry-Smith and Blum suggested that the way in which work-family bundles add value to the firm is socially complex and not always obvious. They surmised that work-life bundles help better connect employees' families to the firm and employees to their families. This represents a fundamental paradigm shift of greater trust and relinquishing of management control and sends a signal to investors and the marketplace about willingness to invest in employees. It should be noted that the mechanism by which the policies actually affect performance was not measured, nor was policy use. Perry-Smith and Blum identified some potential moderators for future research: firm strategy and industry connectedness, availability of community-based work-family support, and top management support.

By examining the effects of combinations of work-life policies and practices rather than the effects of a single policy, researchers may gain a more complete picture of the psychological and organizational outcomes associated with work-life policy availability and use. For managers, considering work-life issues as a whole may lead to a more consistent and clear vision of organizational acceptance of and culture toward employee work-life issues. However, a potential downside to the work-life bundles perspective may be that the implications of a given policy/practice are ignored. There is considerable value in understanding whether a particular policy is perceived unfairly, is not utilized appropriately, or is ineffective. Furthermore, some policies such as elder care or infant care may be used by only a relatively small portion of the workforce at any given time and hence may seem unrelated in the short run to other overarching policies such as selection or performance, yet may have long-term relationships to these and other policy clusters.

High Commitment Work Systems

The high commitment work systems approach (also known as high performance work systems, or HPWS) suggests that when employees are highly empowered and involved, they can provide a source of competitive advantage. Barling, Kelloway, and Iverson (2003) suggested that the assumptions of this management approach are that (a) employees are viewed as resources difficult to imitate, (b) there is significant investment in human capital (skills, information, motivation, latitude), and (c) human resource management practices are mutually reinforcing so that their sum is greater than their individual parts. Osterman (1995) noted that this management approach involves firms moving away from a traditional structure of highly formalized, narrowly defined jobs to a configuration of human resource practices that involve team-based decision making and a focus on quality and higher employee commitment than traditionally designed jobs. He surmised that employee work-life benefits may play an important role in eliciting desired employee behaviors supporting high commitment, especially those that are not under constant supervision or direct control. Osterman's empirical study (1995) found that organizations categorized as having high commitment work systems (measured by the goals espoused by the organization, the degree to which employees have discretion in their jobs, and the use of specific practices within the organization) were more likely to offer work-life benefits.

A recent example of a study on the perspective that holds there is a relationship between work and family policies and high performance work systems is provided by Berg, Kalleberg, and Appelbaum (2003). They argued that high commitment work environments (characterized by high-performance work systems, understanding supervisors, and jobs with intrinsic rewards) are positively related to employee perceptions that the company is helping them balance their work and nonwork lives. Berg and his colleagues suggested that the nature of the work environment such as culture and job design, not just the organization's work-life policies and programs, will influence how employees are able to balance work and nonwork aspects of their lives. Similar to Eaton (2003), they hypothesized that high commitment work environments give people a sense of control and self-efficacy that has a positive spillover into their ability to manage their nonwork life, enabling a better balance between the two roles.

An important benefit of the high commitment perspective is the recognition that employee work-family effectiveness is not simply the result of the work-family policies/practices available. The work environment as a whole, and its impact on the employee, can impact how employees feel about and react to the relationship between their work and nonwork lives. However, a focus on a high commitment work system, if enacted without regard to specific work-life issues, may leave some employees feeling that the organization does not care about their specific work-life needs. Practitioners with an eye to specific work-life issues in a firm and more broad work environment characteristics may be best able to help employees jointly manage work and family roles while at the same time maximizing their effectiveness as a company human resource.

Social Exchange

Mirroring some of the assumptions of the high commitment work systems perspective, the social exchange perspective implicitly underlies management beliefs that workers are willing to engage in more discretionary performance (i.e., behaviors not required by the job such as making suggestions or volunteering to help out a coworker) when the employer is supportive of work and family (Lambert, 2000). Work-family policies are seen as a social exchange mechanism to promote norms of reciprocity from employees. Employees are willing to give back more to the company in terms of organizational citizenship behaviors or higher loyalty, since employers have acted to create greater feelings of obligation by supporting employees' work-life integration needs. An example of a study in this stream is by Lambert (2000). In return for "extra" benefits from the organization (such as work-family supports), Lambert surmised that employees may feel obliged to perform "extra" behaviors for the organization.

Konrad and Mangel (2000) contended that those "extra" efforts on the part of the employee are likely to be in the form of discretionary work behaviors. Since the extra benefits are being offered by the organization as an entity (rather than by a specific supervisor, coworker, or department), Lambert (2000) suggested that reciprocation efforts will likely be those that benefit the firm as a whole. She found that employees who perceived the work-life benefits offered by the organization to be more useful were more likely to exhibit organizational citizenship behaviors (discretionary voluntary performance behaviors) such as submitting suggestions for organizational improvement, attending nonrequired meetings, and assisting others with their job duties. Such research typifies a prevailing management view that if you give employees "an inch of work-family support," they will give you back a mile of productivity.

A beneficial outcome associated with the adoption of a social exchange perspective is that it examines the effects of work-life policies/practices at the psychological level of the individual. While more research is needed to verify this assumption, this perspective suggests that the effects of norms of reciprocity are unlikely to be conscious. In other words, employees are unlikely to decide to put a suggestion into the suggestion box *because* the organization offered them a work-life policy/practice. Instead, psychological tendencies to want to reciprocate goodwill are the mechanism in use in the social exchange perspective. A related pitfall is the expectation that the implementation of work-life policies and practices will be associated with a visible and large increase in organizational citizenship behaviors in the entire workforce. A work-life practitioner who tries to "sell" work-life policies/programs to management in this way may be setting up unrealistic expectations. Nonetheless, practitioners who are able to think about and describe the intra-psychic effects of work-life policies/practices may be better able to *explain* why certain outcomes of policy/practice implementation may be expected.

Employer of Choice

Some organizations may offer work-life policies and practices because of the management perspective that such offerings are likely to increase the ability of the organization to attract and retain employees. This will lead to being perceived by internal (e.g., employees) and external (e.g., applicants) stakeholders as a desirable company for which to work. Konrad and Mangel (2000) offered a stress-reduction hypothesis to support this employer of choice argument. They suggested that if employees are experiencing considerable amounts of stress between their work and family lives, they may be likely to move to positions or organizations that are more supportive of balance between the roles.

Cascio and Young (2005) examined absolute and industry-adjusted productivity (defined as total sales divided by the total number of employees), profitability (operating income before depreciation and taxes divided by total assets), and returns on common stock of the *Working*

Mother 100 Best Firms from 1995–2002 for those firms that are publicly traded. They compared the performance of these firms relative to two equity benchmarks—the Standard & Poors 500 and the Russell 3000. Results showed that the productivity and profitability of the *Working Mother* 100 Best companies did not consistently exceed those of the S&P 500. However, stock performance consistently did exceed that of the two equity benchmarks. Cascio and Young surmised a possible cause of higher stock prices was that for the average investment analyst, 35 % of his or her investment decision is determined by nonfinancial information (Low & Siesfield, 1998). They noted that one of the top five nonfinancial variables considered in rating stock attractiveness is the "ability to attract and retain talented people." Cascio (2000) argued that "best employers to work for" typically receive twice as many job applications per position as firms not deemed as best employers. An important caveat is that the Cascio and Young study is correlational in nature. Therefore, causal relationships between being a "best employer," number of job applicants, and stock prices cannot be drawn. It is possible that other characteristics of these companies (e.g., strong leadership) may impact the relationship of the variables above. However, public recognition of work-life policies/practices may not only affect how attracted individuals are toward working in a particular organization but also the public opinion about the quality of the organization.

The adoption of an "employer of choice" perspective can be beneficial if the implementation of work-life policies/practices makes the organization more attractive to current and future employees while simultaneously improving shareholder opinion of the organization. However, the "employer of choice" perspective may be problematic if organizational actions are viewed by employees as the organization simply trying to "look good" (by making the *Working Mother Magazine's Top 100* list, for example), especially if those actions are not associated with a genuine intent on the part of the organization to help employees balance work and nonwork. Such actions may be viewed as hypocritical. Practitioners who endorse work-life policies/programs as a means to gain external approval should emphasize the need to make sure that policies/programs are also internally supported. Furthermore, there has been considerable competitive gamesmanship about applying for the *Working Mother* and other similar awards. Organizations need to have a person dedicating a significant part of their time to complete the application. One wonders if the employer resources being allocated to the annual application might better serve employees by being focused on how to help the workforce on a day-to-day basis.

Workforce Diversity

This perspective focuses on the development and implementation of formal organizational practices that influence the extent to which a workplace becomes more diverse (Kossek & Lobel, 1996) and then links the greater diversity to organizational performance. The assumption is that employers should adopt employment practices that enable women to have upward mobility into the management and executive ranks so that the human resource policies/practices reflect the needs of the demographics of the organizations. According to Kossek, Markel, and McHugh (2002), one way that organizations may attempt to manage demographic change is through their hiring practices. Work-life policies and practices may be conceptualized as a strategy for recruiting and retaining a more diverse workforce at all levels.

SHRM diversity research (Kossek, Lobel, & Brown, 2005) often measures the associations between the presence of diversity (often gender) and performance outcomes measured at either the individual (turnover) or organizational level (financial performance.) Although they did not formally measure work-life policies, Catalyst (2004) studied linkages between gender diversity of the top management executive team and business performance from 1996–2000 for 353 Fortune 500 companies from a cross-section of industries. Work-life progressiveness might be implicitly captured if one assumes that if top management jobs were not accommodating of family or required long hours and travel, these jobs would be undesirable to talented women who would otherwise seek to opt out of the rat race. After controlling for size and the financial performance of industries, the study showed that firms with higher top management gender diversity had a 35% higher return on equity and a 34% higher total return to shareholders than other firms, an effect that held up for four out of five industries studied. A benefit of the diversity perspective is clearly its ability to meet the needs of a workforce demographic group. However, when work-life policies/practices are only available to certain subgroups within a population (e.g., parents), there is the potential for resentment on the part of other employees. Practitioners should keep in mind the work-life needs of all of the demographic groups represented, including those not seen as traditional work-*family* issues, such as the needs of individuals without children and older employees nearing retirement age. Focusing policies only on visible work-family diversity may give short shift to critical work-family needs related to seemingly "invisible" issues such as depression, stress from workloads, and substance abuse.

IMPLICATIONS FOR RESEARCH AND PRACTICE

While the findings from each perspective raise unique research questions and have distinct implications for how organizations approach work-family issues, some common threads run throughout the perspectives that have important implications for both research and practice.

Expanding the levels perspective. First, both researchers and managers have had the tendency to look at the work-family domain as an individual, rather than a contextual, issue. As Kossek and Lambert (2005) noted with regards to research, much of the traditional management literature has implicitly adopted a largely individual, psychological perspective emanating out of role theory (Katz & Kahn, 1966), which has considerable focus on the individual predictors and consequences of employees having perceived conflicts between work and family roles. This has resulted in considerably less focus on what organizations can do to alleviate work-family conflict, and greater focus on the responsibility of the individual in his or her own experiences of conflict. The relationship of organizational context (e.g., job design, culture, leadership) to individual balance between work and family has received relatively less attention. Which policies, practices, leadership styles, cultures, and other contextual elements are effective in ameliorating work-family conflict remains somewhat unclear. Future research should examine how predictors at all organizational levels (e.g., dyad-level predictors such as the supervisor/subordinate dyad and work-group level predictors such as team supportiveness) are associated with the use of, satisfaction with, and effectiveness of work-life policies and practices for organizations and individuals.

When managers and policymakers in organizations take an individual perspective on work-family balance, their attitudes toward work-life issues may be affected. Organizations that respond to work-family issues as a need to "manage individual employee problems" perpetuate the myth of work and family as separates worlds that Rosabeth Moss Kanter (1977) pointed out almost 30 years ago in her classic treatise: Traditional employing organizations are designed based on the assumption that most employees do have family or personal demands that compete for their primary identities and attention during working time. Policies, practices, and norms that emphasize individual responsibility for managing work and family may be overemphasized (e.g., self-help groups) and structural changes that may help employees find balance may not be deemed necessary (e.g., flextime).

In sum, managers and researchers need to be cognizant of the many influences upon which the business case for work-family issues can be examined. Some assumptions that distinguish this chapter in the handbook are the importance placed on measuring levels of analysis beyond the individual and identifying management perspectives in use. These are crucial to designing interventions that matter. Some of the perspectives we reviewed such as the dual agenda demonstrate a recognition that individual difficulties in managing work and family can be due to organizational and group behavior. Greater cognizance of the fact that individual behavior in organizations is embedded in group and organizational contexts and that these contexts shape the work and family realities of individuals is needed in management research and practice.

Moving beyond policy adoption. Another historical trend of the management literature is a focus on the availability of formal workplace policies and minimal attention to effectiveness and utilization. Managers had a tendency to take policies at face value, often assuming that if a firm adopted a lot of work-family policies "on the books," it must be family-friendly. The evaluations that were done were often largely informal testimonials or involved public relations successes like being listed on magazines' Best Company lists (e.g., *Working Mother*). Kossek et al. (2005) noted that like other diversity interventions, there has been limited rigorous evaluation of policy effectiveness by employers (Comer & Soliman, 1996) as well as linkage to business and human resource strategy (for an exception, see Perry-Smith & Blum, 2000).

Nor have sufficient concerted efforts been made by managers to understand social barriers to use. For example, frequently even if policies were available, career-minded employees did not feel free to use them without fear of penalties (Eaton, 2003). Or, these policies were not uniformly well-publicized or supported by managers throughout the corporation, creating unevenness in how the policies were implemented in practice even in the same firm. "Management discretion" and "needs of the business or work group" are the caveats and language included in a majority of employee-initiated flexibility policies, for example. This creates the situation where an individual can experience the social dissonance of working for a company on the *Working Mother* list, yet not experience life in his or her own work unit as particularly family-friendly. In addition, the business and popular media may have overstated the availability of policies—a problem exacerbated by the fact that research published in management journals involves larger employers that are most likely to allow research access (Kossek, 2005).

Traditionally, given their role in the firm and their position in the hierarchy, managers also tend to take for granted and dictate the prevailing workplace cultural assumptions and norms about the hegemony of work and family. These norms are powerful as they structure the social reality and construction about how "good employees" jointly manage work and family demands. The management field generally has not questioned the roles of existing norms and social systems, management processes, and the managerial determination of workplace structures and jobs in creating and perpetuating conflict (for an exception, see Fletcher & Bailyn, 2005).

Researchers too must expand their focus to consider work-life issues beyond policy availability. While examining the relationship of the number and type of work-life policies available may be useful (e.g., the work-life bundle perspective), the subtext that exists within and beyond policy availability must also be examined. Researchers should examine whether policies are available to all workers or only to a small subset (e.g., professionals) and whether they are available under all circumstances or only in particular instances (e.g., maternity but not adoption leave). Furthermore, as discussed above, there may be cultural and social barriers to policy use, such as disapproval from leadership or being taken off the "fast track." Also, researchers should identify what constitutes effective policy design and implementation. Policies that are ineffective or incompatible with worker needs may do little to alleviate the challenges of balancing work and family.

In sum, both managers and researchers should take into consideration not only the policies available for employees on paper, but also how those policies play out in the day-to-day lives of employees. Only by understanding the nature, availability, effectiveness, and social and cultural implications of policies will the true status of work-life within organizations be revealed.

In closing, a main goal of this chapter was to expose readers to the wide variety of managerial perspectives on work-family issues that are reflected both in organizations and in the research literature. Our purpose was not to help readers decide what the "best" perspective is or which perspective researchers should be adopting. Instead, we propose that both individuals and organizations will benefit from thoughtfully considering the implications of each perspective.

For managers and work-life policymakers, acknowledging multiple management perspectives may encourage a more realistic weighing of the pros and cons of particular work-life focused actions. For example, consider a manager who is focused on the diversity perspective desires to retain high-level working mothers. That manager might be inclined to implement a policy that suits the needs of that particular demographic group, such as onsite child care. However, this manager also might benefit from considering the implications of the social exchange perspective before implementing such a policy. The manager may recognize that those employees who do not have children may feel left out or unimportant to the organization. The principle of norms of reciprocity suggests that if those employees feel like they are being devalued by the organization, they may be less likely to engage in organizational citizenship behaviors. By taking on the multiple managerial perspectives discussed in this chapter, managers may be able to better understand the full ramifications of how organizations approach work-life issues and to be able to make more informed decisions and offer a cafeteria of work-life supports.

Research will also be enhanced through the consideration of multiple managerial perspectives. By trying to understand the relationships between culture, policies, practices, leadership, a multiple perspective angle is more likely to lead to an accurate understanding of the nature of organizational decision making and individual outcomes. For example, consider a researcher who adopts an "employer of choice" perspective and examines how the implementation of work-life policies enhances stakeholder opinion of (and willingness to invest in) the organization. This researcher might neglect to collect data on the degree to which policy use is seen as meeting a dual agenda for the organization. If policy use is considered a trade-off, employees who use work-life policies may be considered less effective contributors to the organization or not eligible for promotions. Consequently, employees may be less likely to use the policies, less able to balance work and family, and more likely to leave the organization. By considering multiple managerial perspectives, researchers may be able to predict and explain the pros and cons associated with different organizational work-life decisions.

CONCLUSIONS

We have shown in the chapter that there is varied rhetoric in the management field for the reasons employers respond to employees' work and family needs and the employer payback from these policies. Drawing on strategic human resource management rhetoric, the predominant perspectives we identified in the literature to understand management practice surrounding work-life policies included the following: organizational implementation orientation, dual agenda, work-life bundles, high performance work systems, social exchange, employer of choice, and diversity.

It is important for researchers and practitioners to recognize these varying rhetorics, because the rationales given by organizations to sell work-life issues have implications for how they are viewed in practice as being effective and how they are understood and promulgated by employees, managers, and researchers. Practitioners and researchers can help individuals and organizations by examining work-life issues from a multi-faceted perspective beyond simple policy adoption, with attention to sometimes simultaneously conflicting managerial framings.

We believe more attention needs to be given in the work-family field to the rhetoric that organizations, managers, and researchers use to discuss the adoption and implementation of work-life policies. Such an approach would recognize that conflict between work and family is largely due to a structural workforce/workplace mismatch, where the formal and informal design of the workplace does not fit changing workforce characteristics, and that many long-term organizational and societal goals can be better served by examining the utility of prevailing management assumptions.

ACKNOWLEDGMENTS

Portions of this chapter were presented in a speech written by the first author on the employer perspective on links between work-life policies and employment for the Workplace Strategies and Interventions for Improving Health and Well-Being Conference. The conference was the second in a series sponsored by the National Institute of Child Development and the National Institute of Health, among other agencies, and was held in Baltimore, Maryland in April 2004.

REFERENCES

Alvesson, M., & Deetz, S. (1996). Critical theory and postmodernism approaches to organizational studies. In S. Clegg, C. Hardy, & W. Nord (Eds.), *Handbook of organizational studies* (pp. 191–217). Thousand Oaks, CA: Sage.

Bailyn, L., & Fletcher, J. K. (1997). Unexpected connections: Considering employees' personal lives can revitalize your business. *Sloan Management Review, 38,* 11–19.

Barling, J., Kelloway, K., & Iverson, R. (2003). High-quality work, job satisfaction, and occupational injuries. *Journal of Applied Psychology, 88,* 276–283.

Barney, J. (1991). Firm resources and sustained competitive advantage. *Journal of Management, 17,* 99–120.

Batt, R., & Valcour, P. (2003). Human resources practices as predictors of work-family outcomes and employee turnover. *Industrial Relations, 42,* 189–220.

Berg, P., Kalleberg, A., & Appelbaum, E. (2003). Balancing work and family: The role of high-commitment environments. *Industrial Relations, 42,* 168–188.

Cascio, W., & Young, C. (2005). Work-family balance: Does the market reward firms that respect it? In D. F. Halpern & S. G. Murphy (Eds.), *Changing the metaphor: From work-family balance to work-family interaction* (pp. 49–63). Mahwah, NJ: Lawrence Erlbaum Associates.

Cascio, W. F. (2000). *Costing human resources: The financial impact of behavior in organizations* (4th ed.). Cincinnati, OH: South-Western College Publishing.

Catalyst. (2004). *The bottom line: Connecting corporate performance and gender diversity.* New York: Catalyst.

Comer, D., & Soliman, C. (1996). Organizational efforts to manage diversity: Do they really work? *Journal of Managerial Issues, 8,* 470–483.

Eaton, S. (2003). If you can use them: Flexibility policies, organizational commitment and perceived performance. *Industrial Relations, 42,* 145–167.

Fletcher, J., & Bailyn, L. (2005). The equity imperative: Redesigning work for work-family integration. In E. Kossek & S. Lambert (Eds.), *Work and life integration: Organizational, cultural and individual perspectives* (pp. 171–189). Mahwah, NJ: Lawrence Erlbaum Associates.

Friedman, S. D., Christensen, P., & DeGroot, J. (1998). Work and life: The end of the zero-sum game. *Harvard Business Review*, November–December, 119–129.

Hill, J., Ferris, M., & Martinson, V. (2003). Does it matter where you work? A comparison of how three work venues (traditional office, virtual office, and home office) influence aspects of work and personal/family life. *Journal of Vocational Behavior, 63,* 220–241.

Hyland, M. (2003). Flextime entry. In M. Pitt-Catsouphes & E. Kossek (Eds.), Sloan Work and Family Research Network Resources for Teaching: Work and Family Encyclopedia (http://www.bc.edu/bc_org/avp/wfnetwork/rft/wfpedia/index.html).

Kanter, R. (1977). *Work and family in the United States: A critical review and agenda for research and policy.* New York: Russell Sage Foundation.

Katz, D., & Kahn, R. (1966). *The social psychology of organizations.* New York: Wiley.

Konrad, A., & Mangel, R. (2000). The impact of work-life programs on firm productivity. *Strategic Management Journal, 21*, 1225–1237.

Kossek, E. E., & Lobel, S. (Eds.). (1996). *Managing diversity: Human resource strategies for transforming the workplace.* Oxford, England: Blackwell.

Kossek, E. (2003). Telecommuting entry. In M. Pitt-Catsouphes & E. Kossek (Eds.), Sloan Work and Family Research Network Resources for Teaching: Work and Family Encyclopedia (http://www.bc.edu/bc_org/avp/wfnetwork/rft/wfpedia/index.html).

Kossek, E. E. (2005). Workplace policies and practices to support work and families: Gaps in implementation and linkages to individual and organizational effectiveness. In S. Bianchi, L. Casper, & R. King (Eds.), *Workforce/workplace mismatch? Work, family, health, and well-being.* Mahwah, NJ: Lawrencce Erlbaum Associates.

Kossek, E. E., Colquitt, J. A., & Noe, R. A. (2001). Caregiving decisions, well-being, and performance: The effects of place and provider as a function of dependent type and work-family climates. *Academy of Management Journal, 44*, 29–44.

Kossek, E. E., & Lambert, S. J. (2005). "Work-family scholarship": Voice and context. In E. E. Kossek & S. J. Lambert (Eds.), *Work and life integration: Organizational, cultural and individual perspectives* (pp. 1–17). Mahwah, NJ: Lawrence Erlbaum Associates.

Kossek, E. E., Markel, K., & McHugh, P. (2003). Increasing diversity as a HR change strategy. *Journal of Organizational Change Management, 16*(2), 328–352.

Kossek, E. E., & Ozeki, (1999). Briding the work-family policy & productivity gap. *International Journal of Community, Work & Family, 2*(1), 7–32.

Kossek, E. E., & Ozeki, C. (1998). Work-family conflict, policies, and the job–life satisfaction relationship: A review and directions for the organizational behavior–human resources research. *Journal of Applied Psychology, 83*, 139–149.

Kossek, E. E., Lobel, S., & Brown, J. (2005). Human resource strategies to manage work force diversity: Examining "the business case." In A. M. Conrad, P. Prasad, & J. K. Pringle (Eds.), *Handbook of workplace diversity.* Thousand Oaks, CA: Sage.

Lautsch, B., Kossek, E., & Eaton, S. (2004). Supervising telecommuting and the work-family dual agenda. Simon Fraser University. Working Paper.

Lambert, S. J. (2000). Added benefits: The link between work-life benefits and organizational citizenship behavior. *Academy of Management Journal, 43*, 801–815.

Lee, M. D., MacDermid, S., & Buck, M. (2000). Organizational paradigms of reduced-load work: Accommodation, elaboration, and transformation. *Academy of Management Journal, 43*, 1211–1226.

Low, J., & Siesfield, T. (1998). *Measures that matter.* Boston: Ernst & Young. Lyness, K., & Judiesch, M. 2001. Are female managers quitters? The relationships of gender, promotion, and family leaves of absence to voluntary turnover. *Journal of Applied Psychology, 86*, 1167–1178.

Miner, J. B. (2002). *Organizational behavior: Foundations, theories, analyses.* New York: Oxford University Press.

Osterman, P. (1995). Work/family programs and the employment relationship. *Administrative Science Quarterly, 40*, 681–700.

Perry-Smith, J. E., & Blum, T. C. (2000). Work-family human resource bundles and perceived organizational performance. *Academy of Management Journal, 43*, 1107–1117.

Stroh, K., Northcraft, G., & Neale, M. (2002). *Organizational behavior: A management challenge.* Mahwah, NJ: Lawrence Erlbaum Associates.

Thompson, C. A., Beauvais, L. L., & Lyness, K. S. (1999). When work-family benefits are not enough . . . The influence of work-family culture on benefit utilization, organizational attachment, and work-family conflict. *Journal of Vocational Behavior, 54*, 392–415.

30

Legislatures, Agencies, Courts, and Advocates: How Laws Are Made, Interpreted, and Modified

Chai Rachel Feldblum
Robin Appleberry
Georgetown University

This chapter explains the nature and practice of lawmaking, legal advocacy, and legal research as they relate to the field of work and family. Through reference to the Family and Medical Leave Act of 1993 as a case study, we explain the dynamic processes by which laws are made, interpreted and modified by legislatures, administrative agencies and courts, with the help of legal advocates. Our goal is not to provide substantive analysis of laws related to work and family, but rather to enable researchers from a range of disciplines to understand and access the legal system, as it currently exists and as it is evolving. In addition, for those inclined to change the current system through legal advocacy, this chapter provides a window into how advocates may use the lawmaking process to promote their preferred work and family policies.

BACKGROUND: THE STRUCTURE OF THE U.S. LEGAL SYSTEM

To make use of legal resources in research or to effect change through the lawmaking process, it is necessary first to understand the framework in which our laws are created and shaped. We begin with the Constitution, which provides both the structure and the boundaries of our government and laws. Since its ratification in 1788, the U.S. Constitution has been the supreme law of our land; no law and no governmental action may run afoul of its precepts.

Many Americans think of the Constitution as establishing and safeguarding their basic individual rights. That is correct. But, the rights that the Constitution provides to individuals are actually somewhat limited. They provide a certain number of rights as against the *government*. Thus, for example, the government is not permitted to restrict our freedom to speak or to travel or to practice our religion absent certain compelling circumstances. But, the Constitution offers us very limited rights against private parties, such as private employers.

Americans do, however, enjoy a number of additional legal rights in the private employment sector. These are rights that have been created by federal or state legislatures. Thus, many rights that Americans might think of as their "constitutional" rights are really their "statutory" rights—that is, rights created by statutes passed by legislatures.

The Constitution, however, remains key in creating the framework in which the three branches of government together create this statutory law. The Constitution establishes a national government with three branches—legislative, executive, and judicial—and enumerates the respective powers of each. The powers of these branches are both fluid and fixed: The Constitution establishes certain limits beyond which each branch must not pass, but allows the specific meaning of those limits to change over time and to be determined through a process of constant negotiation among the three branches.

The Constitution imposes no particular system of government on the individual states; it merely provides that "the United States shall guarantee to every State in this Union a Republican Form of Government." Thus, each state is left to adopt its own constitution and create its own government. Today, there are perceptible and at times important differences among the constitutions of the 50 states, but their systems of government are alike in that their basic contours mirror those established at the national level by the federal Constitution.

While all three branches are bound to enforce and to uphold the Constitution, each fulfills a distinct role within the legal system—the legislature drafts statutes, the executive carries out laws through regulations and enforcement orders, and the judiciary interprets laws through case decisions. Thus, when we speak of "the law" we refer to many types of legal authority, each associated primarily with one branch of the government and resulting from the legal process unique to that branch.

LAWMAKING AND THE FAMILY AND MEDICAL LEAVE ACT

This section uses the example of the Family and Medical Leave Act (FMLA) to describe the three branches of government, their processes, and the type of legal authority that each creates. As we examine each in turn, note that the functions of each branch are essentially the same at both the national and the state levels. While specific practices, inter-branch relationships, and intra-branch structures may vary from state to state, or between a state government and the national government, the basic structures are the same: The Maine legislature works much like Montana's, and both work like the federal Congress.

THE FAMILY AND MEDICAL LEAVE ACT OF 1993

The Family and Medical Leave Act is a federal law that guarantees certain workers the right to take up to 12 weeks of unpaid, job-protected leave per year to care for a sick relative or new child (born, adopted, or fostered) or if they themselves have a serious health condition. The Act contains an exception for small and medium-sized businesses (those with fewer than 50 employees) and limits coverage to those employees who have worked at least 1,250 hours in the 12 months before leave is taken.

With its passage, the FMLA represented the culmination of nearly a decade of work by a diverse coalition of advocates and policymakers. Before it was passed by the House and Senate on February 3rd and 4th and finally signed into law by President Clinton on February 5, 1993, the FMLA had been passed by Congress twice before. Both times the bill had been vetoed by President George H.W. Bush. The story of the bill's final passage into law reflects a number of compromises that were reached along the way and also directly informs the continuing debate about the meaning of the law, as seen in the bill's subsequent application by the executive branch and interpretation by the courts (Elving, 1995).

Given these complexities, the FMLA provides a thorough illustration of the processes of legislative drafting, executive rulemaking, judicial interpretation, and legislative modification.

As is true in most cases of lawmaking and legal advocacy, the FMLA is an unfinished story. The practical impact of this law for workers, for businesses, for families, and for society continues to develop in federal and state legislatures, agencies, and courts. As we will see, lawyers and other work-family advocates are critical in shaping this impact.

THE LEGISLATIVE BRANCH: CONGRESS AND THE FMLA

Background: The United States Congress

The U.S. Congress is established in Article 1 of the Constitution and vested with "all legislative powers," meaning that only that body has the power to "write" federal law. The Congress is bicameral, with a Senate and a House of Representatives. Each state sends two delegates to the Senate and some number of delegates to the House, depending on its population. The House is considered the most direct link between the people and the national government for two reasons: First, proportionality allows representatives to be elected from relatively small districts, while senators speak for an entire state. Second, all representatives are elected every 2 years, while senators are elected every 6 years in staggered elections.

The laws passed by Congress are called **statutes**, and thus the body of law generated by legislators is called **statutory law**. With a few exceptions, laws may be initiated in either congressional house and ultimately must be passed in identical form by a majority of both houses (51 in the Senate and 218 in the House) in order to go to the president for signature and to become law.

Bill Introduction (and Reintroduction and Reintroduction . . .)

The bill that ultimately became the FMLA was introduced in the House on January 5, 1993 and in the Senate on January 26, 1993, a remarkably short time before its passage on February 4th. But, as noted above, this was not the first time that the bill had been introduced—in fact, the bill had been introduced in some form 10 *times* over the preceding 9 years. Why was it introduced so many times?

The reason for such repeated reintroduction stems from the requirement that passage of any bill must occur within a single "Congress." Because the makeup of the Congress (the entire House of Representatives and one third of the Senate) can change every 2 years, each 2-year period is considered a distinct legislative cycle, called a "Congress." Every Congress consists of two 1-year sessions, beginning in January. A bill must pass *within* the Congress in which it has been introduced. Otherwise, the bill expires and must be reintroduced in the next Congress (Oleszick, 2004; Dove, 1997; Johnson, 2003).

For example, the FMLA was first introduced in 1985, which was the first session of the 99th Congress. When the bill was introduced (or "dropped") in the House, and then when a companion bill was later introduced in the Senate, the bill was assigned a number within each chamber based on its chronological place among the bills introduced during that Congress—in this case, H.R. 2020 in the House and S. 2278 in the Senate. Because the bill was not passed by both houses and signed into law before the 99th Congress ended in January of 1987, the bill expired. In order to be considered again, it had to be reintroduced as a separate bill in the 100th Congress. Thus, in the 9 years from its first drafting to its final passage, the FMLA was introduced in five separate Congresses, each time with new bill numbers in each chamber.

Such a prolonged history is not unusual. Indeed, for significant bills that need time to build public and hence legislative support, the entire first stage of a bill's life may consist solely in its consistent reintroduction over a period of Congresses, with each introduction simply displaying the addition of some new cosponsors of the bill. Usually, as in the case of the Family and Medical Leave Act, the content of the bill will stay relatively the same through the early years of this process. The few changes in the bill—in select substantive provisions and/or in the title—usually will reflect "deals" that have been made to bring on specific new sponsors, or will include clarifications or changes that have been made to rebut or respond to arguments against the bill.

The potential for compromises at this stage also will depend on the purpose of the bill. For example, if the sponsors of a bill primarily want a "message bill," they will not try to make significant compromises in the bill prior to introduction. Conversely, if the sponsors want a bill that has significant momentum and broad coalition support upon introduction, important compromises will be made in the bill's substantive provisions before the bill is introduced.

For example, the FMLA was first conceived and drafted in 1984 and 1985, when Ronald Reagan was president and the Senate was under Republican control. Under these circumstances, proponents of the bill knew that passage was impossible. In light of that political reality, advocates did not attempt to negotiate the details of the bill with opponents, but instead used the bill primarily to raise awareness about the need for the law. At the same time, because the House was controlled by Democrats throughout the FMLA's consideration, it was possible to get attention for the bill in the form of House committee hearings. These hearings provided a chance to spark debate on the issue of family and medical leave while advocates built support for the bill within Congress and among interest groups and the public at large.

Referral to Committee

Once a bill is introduced, the House or Senate Parliamentarian "refers" the bill to one or more committees or subcommittees whose areas of concern relate to the substance of the proposed law. These are known as the "committees of jurisdiction." While the name and jurisdiction of committees in each house are largely parallel, they do vary in significant respects. In addition, a bill might be sent to several committees in the House, while it might be sent to only one committee in the Senate. This is primarily because there are far fewer senators to conduct the business of lawmaking than representatives, and hence senators must limit the focus of their work.

For example, when the final version of the FMLA was introduced in the Senate, it was referred solely to the Committee on Labor and Human Resources (now the Committee on Health, Education, Labor and Pensions, or the "HELP" Committee). By contrast, when the bill was introduced in the House, it was referred to the Committee on Education and Labor (the counterpart to the Senate labor committee) *and* to the Post Office and Civil Service Committee and the House Administration Committee.

This difference was not because there were not equivalent civil service and congressional administration committees in the Senate; there were. Instead, it reflected the reality that there was already too much work for too few senators to do. Thus, the Senate civil service and congressional administration committees were ready to let the Senate labor committee deal with the FMLA, while they focused on other pieces of legislation.

The dominant party in each house appoints the chair of each committee and subcommittee; the nondominant party in each house appoints the "ranking minority member" of each committee and each subcommittee. Each committee and subcommittee also includes a majority of members from the dominant party. In this way, the dominant party ensures effective control over the outcome of most full and subcommittee actions. For example, during the first several years of the FMLA's consideration in Congress, both the Senate and the White House were Republican. As we discuss below, this control by Republicans during the early years of the bill effectively kept the FMLA from moving forward. What little progress the bill made had to happen in the House, which was controlled by Democrats throughout the period. Only when the Senate came under Democratic control in 1987 did the bill have a real chance for success. Even then, it was not until 1993 when the White House was again occupied by a Democrat that the bill became law.

Once a bill has been referred to the appropriate committee (or subcommittee), the chair of that committee (or subcommittee) decides whether or not to give the bill any attention. The vast majority of bills never progress past the stage of committee referral. The reason for "committee constipation" is simple. Many more bills are introduced each year than a committee possibly has time to consider. On average, thousands of bills are introduced in each Congress while a scant few hundred make it through the whole process. For instance, in the 107th Congress (2001–2003), 7,439 bills and joint resolutions were introduced. Only 377 of these bills became public law. Furthermore, a great number of the bills that passed were relatively small and inconsequential, serving only to rename a federal building or designate a national day of awareness on some uncontroversial topic.

For these reasons, as a veteran congressional observer has noted: "Time is the most precious commodity on Capitol Hill." This includes the time to engage the attention of a staff person or member of Congress as well as the legislative time needed for a committee and a full house to consider and vote on a bill. Lawmakers on each committee are busy with their own legislative priorities; rarely do they have time to advance the legislative priorities of their colleagues. If a bill actively conflicts with the priorities of a lawmaker on the committee, he and she certainly will not be interested in moving that bill forward.

While the chairs of committees retain the most power to block a bill, a committee chair often will seek to accommodate the wishes of other members of the committee from his or her political party with regard to blocking or moving a bill. Thus, advocates who wish to promote action on their legislative priorities in Congress always try to find congressional champions who have a position (and, if possible, a senior position) on the relevant committee of jurisdiction. Indeed, sometimes lawyers will draft a bill in a certain manner simply to ensure that it is sent to a particular committee of jurisdiction where the advocates have a strong champion. The "dream team" for a bill is sponsorship by a committee chair *and* the ranking minority member of that committee. Achieving that level of sponsorship usually means advocates have succeeded in building a coalition and making compromises prior to introduction of the bill.

Two cosponsors particularly important to passage of the FMLA because of their committee status (as well as their party affiliation and gender) were Senator Chris Dodd (Democrat of Connecticut) and Representative Marge Roukema (Republican of New Jersey). In 1986, Senator Dodd was the ranking minority member of the Senate Subcommittee on Children, Family, Drugs and Alcoholism (now the Subcommittees on Children and Families and Substance Abuse and Mental Health Services), which had jurisdiction over the FMLA. Dodd was a staunch supporter of family leave, and when Democrats gained control of the Senate in 1987, making Dodd Chair of the subcommittee, he used his position to raise public awareness of the issue by holding numerous hearings around the country and devoting significant subcommittee time to the bill. Driven by his personal ideology and dedication to families, Dodd became a committed and tenacious advocate of the bill. Ultimately, his role as chair of the subcommittee was critical to the bill's success (Lenhoff & Bell, 2002).

Throughout consideration of the FMLA, Representative Roukema was the ranking minority member of the House Subcommittee on Labor–Management Relations and a member of the Education and Labor Committee, which had jurisdiction over the main portions of the bill in that chamber. In contrast to Dodd's ideological motivations, Roukema's support was rooted in her experiences as a stay-at-home mother and caregiver for her elderly mother as well as the death of her teenage son from leukemia. These experiences motivated her to consider supporting the bill when it was expanded to cover leave for purposes of caring for an ill parent or child. Because Roukema's support on the committee was so critical to moving the bill forward, proponents of the bill eventually acceded to many of her demands on the bill. Even when it meant a significant compromise in the content of the bill, Roukema's cosponsorship of the bill was seen as worth its price: In becoming a supporter of the bill, Roukema agreed not only to help move it through her subcommittee but also to recruit Republican support for the bill, particularly among women. With Roukema's conversion in the fall of 1987, the bill suddenly had gained three new Republican women cosponsors and had regained its momentum in the House at a critical stage. Thus, even as a minority member of the committee of jurisdiction, Roukema played an important role in ensuring the FMLA's success (Elving, 1995; Lenhoff & Bell, 2002).

Upon introduction and referral to committee, a bill gets its first public showing. Groups who feel they will be adversely or positively affected by the bill, but who were not invited to participate in the crafting of the bill, will now get their first look at the legislative proposal and will decide how much attention to pay it. Again, the controlling mantra of Washington is: "Time is the most precious commodity on Capitol Hill." This includes the time of those who advocate on Capitol Hill. Thus, advocates will decide how much time to spend reacting to a bill based on how directly the bill affects their constituents' interests and based on who has sponsored the bill.

For the first several years of its history, the FMLA suffered the same fate as thousands of other bills that die in committee—as noted above, the Republican Senate refused to devote attention to a bill that was fiercely opposed by business interest groups. While the Democratic House gave some attention to the bill in the form of hearings, representatives of both parties did not feel sufficient pressure, either from advocates or from constituents, to schedule a vote on the bill until 1990, 5 years after its first introduction. Over time, advocates used sophisticated media and grassroots strategies to raise public awareness of the bill and to educate and influence members of Congress. In this way the bill garnered additional cosponsors and broader support among diverse interest groups, all of which increased the pressure on congressional leadership to give the bill attention.

So who does all this work behind the scenes? In most cases, there is a group of two to five organizations that forms the core of a legislative advocacy effort. That core group is not always readily discernible to non-Washington ("outside the Beltway") players. When such core groups exist, they usually are surrounded by a larger coalition that can include anywhere from 10 to 40 or more groups, depending on the magnitude and scope of the effort. The more major the effort, however, the more likely it is that there is a core group of two to five organizations that is the stabilizing and constant force behind sustained legislative activity (Feldblum 2003).

In the case of the FMLA, the coalition was led by the efforts of the Women's Legal Defense Fund (now the National Partnership for Women and Families), whose staff worked persistently over the years to identify and persuade congressional champions and to create the public support for the bill that would convince those members to devote time to the bill. Their strategy also included framing the issue in broad terms that appealed in some way to both political parties, uniting diverse and unlikely allies (such as pro-choice feminist groups and the United States Catholic Conference) behind a common, value-based theme. Likewise, by extending the message and the content of the bill beyond new mothers, advocates brought in the support of key constituency groups like the American Association of Retired Persons and various labor unions. Ultimately, this diverse coalition and creative framing made it hard for lawmakers to oppose the bill, even in the face of powerful opposition by business interests (Lenhoff & Bell, 2002).

While a success story in many respects, this history nonetheless hints at one of the ugliest truths of legislative process, that is, that lawmaking truly is a "sausage factory"—it is messy inside, and for many, the process is one that they would rather never see. But for policy advocates, the inside of this process is absolutely critical. Indeed, this phase of the legislative cycle—before the text of the bill is finalized, before positions are staked out beyond retreat—may offer the *single greatest point of influence on the formulation of policy*. An effective advocate knows that if she sets the terms of the debate, she is much more likely to win. The Women's Legal Defense Fund knew this when it spent countless hours negotiating language and building broad support for the bill, well before it reached the floor of either house for debate and, in some cases, before hearings were held. Even with such negotiation, the FMLA took nearly a decade to pass into law and its proponents had to accept significant compromises along the way. As this demonstrates, it is crucial always to consider the "back story" to a legislative win or loss and to be present in writing that story from the very beginning.

Hearings

If and when a bill does get attention, it will receive its first "public" legislative activity: a hearing on the bill, held by the chair of a subcommittee or committee of jurisdiction. In the case of the FMLA, the first hearings were held on October 17, 1985 as Joint House Oversight Hearings by the Subcommittees on Labor–Management Relations and Labor Standards, of the Committee on Education and Labor, and the Subcommittees on Civil Service and Compensation and Employee Benefits, of the Post Office and Civil Service Committee. Eight years later and in a far different political climate, the bill underwent its final hearings on January 26, 1993. As with any hearings, all of these constitute important pieces of legislative history, but not in the ways one might expect.

Congressional hearings ostensibly are designed to gather information and to engage in fact-finding; members of Congress, at least according to our high school government texts, use hearings to decide whether a bill is necessary, whether it is correctly drafted, and whether they should vote for or against the bill.

In reality, hearings in Washington are highly choreographed theater. The testimony of the majority of witnesses called to the hearing will be remarkably consistent with the current views of the committee chair. The ranking minority member of the committee is usually given a few slots for which he or she can propose additional witnesses. The views of these witnesses will tend to be remarkably consistent with the views of the ranking member of the committee. In this way, hearings serve primarily to justify a bill that is already supported by the chair or another member of the dominant party. Surprises are not the norm in Washington hearings.

This does not mean that members of Congress have not engaged in fact-finding and sophisticated analysis about whether a bill is necessary, how the bill should be drafted, and whether they should support the bill. On the contrary, staff to members (and sometimes the members themselves) often engage in extensive research and consideration. But they tend to do so before, rather than during, a hearing. For instance, as noted above, advocates for the FMLA spent countless hours before any hearings were held—discussing the issues with congressional staff, explaining why federal legislation was necessary, considering what provisions should be included in the bill and even proposing how those provisions should be written, down to the last word. In this process, decades of research and analysis on families, the changing workforce, workplace management, and early child development were relied on, both on and off Capitol Hill. This research is evidenced in the extensive findings and purpose of the law as well as in the committee reports that accompanied the final versions of the bill.

After introduction and hearings, the analysis, fact-finding, and decision making that have occurred behind the scenes up to that point often continue, again outside of public view. Thus, another stage at which negotiations and compromises on a bill may occur is after a hearing on the bill has been held or announced. The hearing will bring to the fore the supporters and opponents of a bill. While it is a rare sight in Washington for witnesses opposing a bill ever to equal or outnumber witnesses supporting a bill, hearings will serve to focus attention on a bill and to highlight what provisions of a bill might need to be modified in order to gain the requisite political support to actually pass the bill.

Of course, in the case of the final bills that became the FMLA, the relevant subcommittees held hearings and the committees of jurisdiction voted to approve the bill within weeks of its introduction. Such quick action is *not* the usual course; as noted earlier, the speed with which Congress acted in 1993 was the direct result of the bill having successfully passed both houses of Congress twice before, only to be vetoed by President Bush. With a Democrat in the White House for the first time in 12 years, Congress knew that the FMLA would not be vetoed and acted quickly to ensure that the FMLA would be the first bill signed into law by President Clinton.

By contrast, in previous years, the content of the FMLA had changed significantly after hearings to reflect compromises that would enable its passage. For instance, in 1988, after multiple Senate hearings had been held on the FMLA bill in the form of S. 249, Senator Dodd introduced an entirely new version of the bill—S. 2488—that provided significantly shorter periods of leave but broader coverage than the earlier bill. This modification by the bill's lead sponsor reflected his conclusion that the bill simply would not move in its current form. Most important, the new bill succeeded in garnering the key cosponsorship of two Republicans on the Senate Labor Committee, whose support would be pivotal (Elving, 1995).

True to Washington form, the hearings held on the FMLA in 1993 were a surprise to absolutely no one. Particularly after the previous passage of the bill on two separate occasions, these hearings represented the reenactment of years of well-rehearsed debate, rather than the formation or exchange of new ideas. Indeed, the witnesses at the 1993 hearings—the president of the Women's Legal Defense Fund, which had led the fight for family leave protections, and the president and CEO of the Society for Human Resource Management, an association of human resources professionals that had raised concerns about the bill—had testified at *nine* previous hearings on similar legislation, making their cases for and against the same proposals.

Committee Markup and Voting

After a hearing, if a bill is simple and noncontroversial, the committee usually proceeds directly to a vote on the bill. The session in which this occurs is called a "markup." For complicated or controversial bills, however, there is often an interim period, following one or more hearings, in which significant legislative activity can occur. (As you might guess, the FMLA saw both versions of this process over the course of its history.) As noted, there are few surprises at a hearing. But, hearings can help to crystallize changes that will be needed to move a bill forward. In addition, once a hearing has been held, members of the committee who were not involved in the drafting of the bill will focus on the legislation and decide if they would like to ask for changes in the bill.

Thus, following a hearing, the sponsor of a bill may engage in additional negotiations and agree to certain changes in the bill. These changes will be designed either to secure necessary votes for the bill's passage or to address an issue and/or a request made by a member already inclined to support the bill. These negotiations will occur outside of public view and with no official record.

For example, in 1988, the House Committee on Education and Labor voted to approve an amendment to the pending version of the FMLA by Representative Roukema, the ranking minority member whose support was key. As we have described, Roukema was committed to the idea of family leave but insisted that the impact of the bill on small businesses be softened. In her own version of the bill, introduced in 1987, Roukema had included an exemption for businesses employing fewer than 50 employees, as opposed to the five-employee threshold set by the original bill. Before markup, the bill's champions struck a deal with Roukema, agreeing to many of her demands. As a result of this deal, the committee approved a Roukema amendment during markup "in the nature of a substitute," meaning that the amendment replaced the original provisions of the bill and substituted new provisions. The changes to the bill were substantial—in addition to raising the small business threshold, the amended bill reduced the period of leave from 18 weeks to 10 weeks for family care and from 26 weeks to 15 weeks for one's own medical condition.

In many markup sessions, each amendment to a bill is offered by the member seeking the change. If a majority of the members on the committee vote to accept the amendment, the original provision of the bill will be modified to reflect that amendment.

In certain situations, however, all of the changes accepted by the sponsor of a bill will be incorporated into a new version of the bill. This version is called the "chairman's mark." The chairman's mark retains the same bill number that the bill received upon introduction and simply strikes all the original language of the bill and substitutes entirely new text.

If a chairman's mark has been prepared, the first vote at the markup is on accepting the chairman's mark. As one can imagine, members of a committee are always happier to have their policy proposals adopted by the chair and rolled into the chairman's mark. Since the dominant party holds a majority of seats on each committee and subcommittee, the chairman's mark almost invariably passes.

If the chair has not prepared a new version of the bill, or after the initial vote on the chairman's mark if she has prepared a new version, members of the committee will move through each section of the bill, offering amendments to various provisions. If the chair has refused to accept a change offered by a member of her own party, this is the opportunity for that member to try to get his or her proposal adopted by winning enough votes through a cross-party vote on the committee. In most cases, however, amendments at markups are offered by members of the nondominant party and fail relatively consistently on party-line votes. For instance, when the final version of the FMLA was marked up by the House Education and Labor Committee, Republicans offered five amendments and suggested nine other modifications, each aimed at softening, delaying, or derailing the bill. All five amendments failed, mostly along party lines. The only amendment passed by the committee was a substitute text offered by the chair of the relevant subcommittee (a Democrat), which contained technical changes and a few specific revisions authored by the proponents of the bill (Elving, 1995).

If a bill has been referred to a subcommittee, the subcommittee members will mark up the bill and then vote on whether to forward it to the full committee. If the subcommittee does so, the chair of the full committee then decides whether to schedule a markup on the bill. (The chair of the full committee also can choose to hold a hearing, but rarely does so if a subcommittee chair has already held one or more hearings on the bill.) Markup in full committee provides yet another opportunity to modify the bill, or to express partisan opposition to the bill, by offering amendments to significantly alter the bill. Again, these amendments usually are defeated in party-line votes. Of course, if a bill is not particularly controversial, hearings usually will reflect the unanimity on the bill and the markup will be similarly courteous and swift.

The final step in a markup session is a vote by the full committee on whether to forward the bill to the full chamber with a recommendation that it be passed. If this vote is successful, the bill is forwarded to the full chamber for consideration.

Committee Reports

When a committee votes to recommend a piece of legislation, it almost always issues an accompanying report. Such reports often include a summary of the bill, explanation of any changes to the text of the bill made during markup, the background and need for legislation, and the views of the committee on its action.

Committee reports often become the basis for judicial interpretation of a law after its passage, since courts may look to these documents as evidence of legislative intent when the language of a statute is not plainly clear or specific. Because of this ability to influence judicial interpretation, the content of these reports is extremely important.

The drafting of a committee report is typically closed to most of the outside world; the committee staff is charged with writing the report. However, as noted above, two to five organizations tend to form the core of any legislative advocacy effort. In most situations, committee staff will share an early version of the committee report with this smaller group of advocates to receive input and suggestions. The report is also an opportunity for those with dissenting views to reiterate their opposition—almost all reports will include a statement of the minority's views. As a result, members of Congress (and advocates working with them) may use the report as a chance to repeat arguments that did not prevail during markup or to state their understanding of the committee's action, where they believe that the meaning may be subject to dispute.

In the case of the FMLA, the final Senate Committee report offers insight into the political and policy reasoning behind the bill's success. In voting to recommend the FMLA, the committee had to walk a fine political line. On the one hand, the law had to seem important, solving a pressing problem; otherwise there was no need for federal legislative action. On the other hand, the solutions offered by the law could not be seen as a radical departure from existing policy or they would be seen as a potentially destabilizing departure from the status quo.

In explaining the necessity of the FMLA, the committee's report stated that changes in the makeup of the workforce, the demographics of the population, and the structure of the family had created a profound need for the protections afforded by the law. Specifically, the committee noted that the increased number of women in the paid labor force meant that more families consisted of two working parents, with no parent available to provide unpaid caregiving. In addition, the committee explained that the aging of the population meant that working adults increasingly had to care not only for their young children but also for their elderly parents. Finally, the right to unpaid, job-protected family and medical leave was desperately needed to support the increasing number of single-parent households, often led by women, who struggled to remain above the poverty line and for whom an unexpected illness could mean disaster.

In describing these factors, the Senate Committee cited several sources of data and policy analysis, including a guide issued by the Families and Work Institute and a report by Columbia University's National Center for Children in Poverty. These references reveal that advocates had successfully connected lawmakers with the body of research justifying the law and ensured that courts would consider such research in later interpretations of the law.

While the report made clear that changes within American society required a federal policy response in the form of a new law, the committee's report also made the counterbalancing point that the law sat "squarely within the tradition of the labor standards laws that have preceded it" (Senate Report, 1993). In this way, the law was framed not as groundbreaking and thus potentially destabilizing, but rather as the next logical step in a series of well-tested federal responses to changes in the workplace, dating back to the New Deal. This framing was critical, not only for the senators who later would vote to pass the bill, but also for the executive branch charged with implementing the law and the judicial branch ultimately charged with resolving its ambiguities.

Floor Debate, Amendments, and Voting

If a bill is approved by the relevant committee, it goes to the full chamber for debate and consideration, but its scheduling is at the discretion of the chamber's leader, who is chosen by the majority party. In 1993 both the House and the Senate were controlled by Democrats, who had pushed family and medical leave legislation for years and considered it a priority. Thus, the bill approved by the Senate Labor and Human Resources Committee on January 27, 1993 had a great deal of momentum. That momentum carried it to the floor of the Senate a short 6 days after its approval by the committee. Not surprisingly, the FMLA had seen very different treatment at other points in its long history.

In the House of Representatives, almost no bill is given access to the House floor without first receiving a "rule" from the House Rules Committee. The House Rules Committee is effectively governed by the leadership of the party in control of the House. This committee decides when, how, and for how long any bill will be considered on the floor, giving it an extraordinary power over the outcome of the debate. Thus, as a veteran Hill watcher has often observed: "The Rules Committee can do anything."

For instance, in 1990, when the FMLA got its first floor vote in the House, the Democratic leadership was so determined not to have the bill derailed by floor amendments that it placed the bill on the calendar with remarkably short notice to members, giving them little time to draft and propose amendments or to gather forces for debate. During debate itself, the committee allowed only a bipartisan substitute (agreed to by the bill's sponsors) and four carefully selected Republican amendments. In refusing to allow a number of other amendments, specifically those seen as most threatening to the bill, the Rules Committee exercised its absolute power with little more than a nod to its malcontents. One disgruntled representative described both parties in the debate as "straightjacketed" by the rule, but ultimately the tactic was successful: The bill passed by a vote of 237 to 187.

There is no comparable rules committee in the Senate; the majority leader in the Senate sets the calendar and virtually all business in the Senate is conducted by "unanimous consent." Under this procedure, Senate business may proceed according to the decisions of the leadership in control, in negotiation with the minority leadership. However, because there is no requirement in the Senate, like that in the House, that an amendment be "germane" (that is, related in subject matter) to the underlying bill, a Senator whose bill has not been approved for consideration by the Majority Leader may decide to offer her bill as an amendment to an unrelated bill that is on the floor. This is not, however, the best circumstance under which to offer a bill if one hopes for passage.

For instance, in March 2004, advocates seeking to broaden the FMLA to cover leave for those dealing with domestic violence tried to achieve this goal by amending the Unborn Victims of Violence Act. These advocates (and the members of Congress with whom they worked) had met with resistance from the Republican leadership in the past and had not been able to get floor consideration for such an expansion of the FMLA. Because the underlying bill concerned the issue of family violence and had considerable momentum, advocates hoped that they could end the stalemate on their proposal by attaching it to that bill.

During floor debate, Republicans and Democrats spoke adamantly on the amendment, raising the same vehement arguments for and against the FMLA that emerge whenever changes to the Act are proposed. The amendment failed by a vote of 53 to 46, but its near passage confirms the potential for using the amendment process to achieve one's goals.

If a bill does reach the floor, it is an opportunity for both opponents and advocates of the bill to build the record in favor of their position. Consequently, members of Congress may use the opportunity to present many of the arguments that they made behind the scenes at earlier stages or publicly at hearings.

Floor debate on the final FMLA demonstrates this point. During the nearly 10 years in which it had considered different forms of family and medical leave legislation, the Senate had heard arguments for and against such legislation many times. Nonetheless, the floor debate that occurred on February 2, 1993 was rich and extended; the official record of the debate spans over 90 pages. To a large extent, this debate was more show than substance—few Senators' minds were likely to change in response to their colleagues' statements. Yet the content of the debate was critically important, since it would stand as prominent evidence of congressional intent once the bill passed.

For instance, several senators described the medical leave that would be allowed under the law as a way for workers to deal with "critical illness" in themselves or a family member, providing a necessary safeguard for situations of "crisis" created by a sick child or parent. The urgency in the senators' language suggests that they understood the FMLA to cover only severe and extreme medical needs, not routine health care or something as common as an everyday cold. At the same time, the debate did not clearly resolve the meaning of the statute's term "serious health condition." In this way, the debate left open the precise scope of the term to be articulated by the Department of Labor in its regulations.

The lesson for the advocate to take from this illustration is that this moment in the legislative process—when senators take the floor to voice their opinions not only on the wisdom of the bill at issue but also on the very *meaning* of that bill—can be used as a critical chance to influence the making of law.

Congressional statements are also likely to be used in implementation of the law. As described below, executive agency officials often will look at these statements to guide their interpretations of the law in regulations and those interpretations will be enforced by the courts as long as they are "reasonable" interpretations of the law (*Chevron*, 1984). What this means is that members of Congress from each party often will make statements that display their particular (and often differing) interpretations of the bill's provisions.

Another critical aspect of floor debate is the potential for amendments. As noted above, bills frequently are subject to a number of amendments at this stage. The rules for debate and voting on these amendments are complex and detailed; suffice it to say that amendments can be used to clarify a bill, to change a bill, to "kill" a bill, or (in the Senate) to use the bill purely as a vehicle for attaching an unrelated bill. Thus, advocates must be in constant contact with key congressional staff, working to introduce and promote or to fend off and defeat amendments as necessary.

For instance, during final Senate debate of the FMLA, 22 separate amendments were offered, of which four passed. Amendments that sought to change the bill radically—for example, by providing only tax credit incentives for businesses instead of mandated leave—tended to fail on party-line votes. Other amendments—such as one to prohibit the new President Clinton from lifting the ban on the service of openly gay service members for 6 months while the Senate held hearings on the issue—passed.

Debate on most of these amendments served primarily to reinforce the arguments for and against the FMLA previously articulated in the hearings and in the committee reports. While the FMLA was not significantly changed by these amendments, it is important to note that the outcome of votes on such amendments, both germane and nongermane, often is not clear until the votes are cast and counted. Thus, while a bill is "on the floor," advocates must remain vigilant and ready to adjust to a potentially derailing amendment at any time.

Both legislative houses must approve a bill if it is to become law. Sometimes bills will proceed relatively simultaneously in both the House and the Senate. In many cases, however, advocates of a bill will not have the resources to tend to active movement of the bill in both houses. When those circumstances occur, advocates will make a strategic decision as to which house offers a better chance for the bill to progress. Advocates then will focus their active attention on that house, while simply trying to garner additional cosponsors for the bill in the other house.

Once a bill makes it through the first house, the process then begins all over again in the other house. As changes to the bill are almost inevitably made in the second chamber, advocates try to keep the bill's sponsors in the first chamber apprised of the changes and comfortable with them. If and when the bill finally makes its way through the second chamber's full consideration, it usually will look somewhat different from how it looked when it emerged from the first chamber. At this point, the two bills will be sent to a "conference committee."

Conference Committees and Final Voting

To reconcile two different versions of a bill, each house appoints several members to the conference committee, who will revise the bill and return it to the full bodies for approval or rejection. In the case of the final version of the FMLA, both houses passed identical forms of the bill, such that a conference was not necessary. Again, this efficiency reflected the fact that the bill had passed twice before; legislators had reached agreement on the bill and now were intent on advancing the FMLA without further delay.

In its passage the previous year, however, the FMLA had gone through a conference committee. In that process, members of the two bodies had negotiated their differences in the bill's provisions, each receding on certain provisions and prevailing on others. For instance, the Senate bill had provided that an employer could recover health insurance premiums paid for employees who never returned to work after taking FMLA leave, while the House bill had no such provision. During conference, the House version prevailed. By contrast, the Senate won out in the definition of "serious health condition." While the two versions shared the basic definition, the House had prefaced the definition with the word "disabling," thus narrowing the range of conditions covered. On this point, the Senate carried the day.

After the conference committee reaches a successful compromise, it will issue a "conference report" containing the new text of the bill and send that report back to each chamber for final approval.[1] This report and its accompanying explanation usually offer great insight into the negotiations and compromises that took place in conference. Thus, for example, the 1992 report is a key tool for understanding the compromises that paved the way for passage of the FMLA, even though it is not controlling legislative history, since the final bill was passed into law as a new piece of legislation in the next Congress.

If a conference report fails to pass either chamber, the bill is dead. In that event, the bill must be reintroduced and must undergo the process all over again.

Presidential Signature or Veto

If a bill successfully passes both houses of Congress, there is one final step before it can become law: presidential signature. The president has 10 days in which he may sign or veto a congressionally approved bill; he also can do nothing at all, which is tantamount to a veto and thus is referred to as a "pocket veto." If he signs the bill, it becomes law. If he vetoes the bill or does nothing, it goes back to Congress.

In such a case, Congress has one final option for enacting its will through passage—a two thirds majority vote in both houses will override a presidential veto. Such overwhelming consensus in Congress is difficult to achieve but not impossible; there have been several veto overrides in the past 2 decades.[2] As noted above, the FMLA was subject to two presidential vetoes before its signature by President Clinton in 1993. In neither case was the Congress able to override the veto, making amply clear the critical power of the White House at this stage.

Of course, the president and others in the executive branch are usually active in the development of legislation well before the moment of action noted in the Constitution. Indeed, President Clinton's commitment to the FMLA was the very reason for its swift passage in

1993—Congress acted quickly in order to ensure that the FMLA would be the first law signed by the president at the beginning of his term. Thus, advocates need to seek support from the administration well before a bill is passed—either to help pass a bill or to stop the passage of an unwanted bill.

This last point reinforces a key principle that applies throughout our story of the legislative process: *It is much easier to stop a bill than to pass a bill.* As we explore the roles of the other two branches of the federal government and the states, bear in mind that this principle informs legislative advocacy and ultimately the entire legal system, serving to motivate both the executive and the judiciary as they act in relationship with Congress.

THE EXECUTIVE BRANCH: AGENCIES AND THE FMLA

Background: Administrative Agencies

The executive branch is established by Article 2 of the Constitution. Its power is invested in the sole person of the president, who is also the commander-in-chief of the Armed Forces. The president's cabinet, whose members (appointed by the president) correspond to the various departments that work under the auspices of the executive branch, helps the president in the vast undertaking of executing the laws passed by Congress. For example, the Secretary of Labor heads the Department of Labor and advises the president on issues related to labor, including implementation of the FMLA. Thus, the executive's most powerful role in the lawmaking process (aside from signature or veto, of course) is in implementation and enforcement of the laws.

All agencies are created by congressional mandate to carry out specific statutes, and while agencies often play an advisory role to Congress (and sometimes a leading role) in the formulation of law, the bulk of the agencies' work takes place after a bill becomes law. Because Article 1 of the Constitution vests all legislative power in Congress, the Secretary of Labor cannot issue regulations without "enabling legislation" from Congress. Similarly, Congress does not have the Article 2 enforcement powers that the Constitution provides the executive branch. Thus, the meaning of a statute often depends on the separate but mutually influenced efforts of both branches, while the precise role of an agency varies depending on the statute that it is implementing. As discussed below, that role has been extremely significant in the case of the FMLA.

Rules issued by agencies are known as *regulations*. Agencies are required to follow a specific procedure when they develop and issue these regulations, known as "notice and comment." As its name suggests, the notice and comment period provides a key opportunity for advocates to influence the rulemaking process. This influence is critical, because once regulations have been promulgated under this procedure, they carry the full force of law and constitute a central mechanism by which many laws are applied and implemented. Moreover, if an individual brings a lawsuit to enforce some aspect of a law, the courts will defer to an agency regulation interpreting that law as long as the regulation is a *reasonable* interpretation of the law (*Chevron*, 1984).

Agencies are subject to two significant checks on their power to apply and enforce the law—one judicial and one legislative. In the case of many controversial regulations, parties affected by the regulations will challenge the validity of the regulations in court as soon as the final regulations are published. The courts then must decide whether the regulations were *substantively* within the statutory authority Congress gave the agency when it passed the law. The courts also will decide whether the agency followed all the necessary *procedural* rules in promulgating the regulations. Even if agency regulations are not challenged immediately, parties subsequently affected by the regulations can challenge the regulations on both substantive and procedural grounds when the regulations are applied against them in a specific case.

The role of the legislature in checking agencies' power is more blunt and straightforward: Because Congress is the author and originator of the laws, it has the authority to restrict or revise actions taken by the agencies in enforcing those laws. Such legislative interference is, however, predictably uncommon. Congress has neither the time nor the political will to micromanage agency action on a regular basis. Such reprimands do happen, however, and this exercise of legislative power serves as an important reminder that agencies are charged to apply and enforce laws only within the bounds of the laws as written by Congress. Thus, advocates should be aware of this option and should pressure Congress to monitor and respond to agency action as necessary.

The Department of Labor and the FMLA

Like other labor laws to which it was compared during consideration, the FMLA contains a provision empowering the Secretary of Labor to set forth regulations necessary for its enforcement. As we have discussed, Congress can direct the manner in which the executive branch applies the law, but the executive necessarily enjoys some degree of power in the regulatory process. In the case of the FMLA, Congress gave the implementing agency, the Department of Labor, some guidance for its enforcement. For example, Congress explicitly placed the new law within the preexisting legal and regulatory framework of other labor laws, such as the Fair Labor Standards Act (FLSA), stating that the FMLA "relies on the time-tested FLSA procedures already established by the Department of Labor" (Senate Report, 1993). In making this reference, Congress signaled that the Department should adopt many of the definitions and enforcement mechanisms already used to enforce the FLSA. Of course, the FMLA also introduced a number of new terms and standards that the Department would have to interpret without reliance on preexisting law.

To implement the FMLA, the Department of Labor in 1995 set forth regulations on a wide array of issues under the Act, explaining in specific terms which employers were covered, what constituted a "serious health condition" that would justify leave, and whether or not FMLA leave could be taken in increments. As is the normal procedure for significant regulations, the Department published proposed regulations first (in this case called "Interim Regulations"), to which interested groups and parties responded by submitting comments within a certain time period. After consideration of those comments, the Department issued final regulations. Needless to say, advocates' comments were critical at this stage, both to influence the content of the regulations and simply to ensure that all arguments were considered and recorded by the Department of Labor. The preamble to the final regulations recounts and responds to many of these arguments, forming a major part of the regulatory history on which courts may rely in interpreting the regulations.

In the case of the FMLA, the regulations did not change substantially between the proposed and final versions, but it is important to note that this is not always the case. The requirement of public notice and comment is meant to ensure public influence on the drafting of regulations, and many times the final version is significantly changed from the proposed version.[3]

The impact of the FMLA regulations has been extremely significant. In particular, the definitions of "serious health condition" and "treatment" under the 1995 regulations have invoked tremendous opposition in the business community and extensive litigation, even resulting in legislative proposals to change these definitions by statutory amendment. As this example demonstrates, agency regulations can be extremely important and advocates should carefully craft comments on proposed regulations to exert the greatest influence.

THE JUDICIAL BRANCH AND THE FMLA

Background: The Judicial Branch

Article 3 of the Constitution establishes the judicial branch of the federal government. Judges on the federal bench are nominated by the president and confirmed by the Senate and have life tenure. In both federal and state judiciaries, the courts operate at three levels: a trial court, an intermediate court of appeals, and a final court of appeals.

Federal trial courts are called United States District Courts. Each state, as well as Puerto Rico, the District of Columbia, and several other U.S. territories, has at least one federal district in the state; some states have several districts. Each district has a number of federal trial judges.

The intermediate courts in the federal system are called United States Courts of Appeals. Currently there are 13 such courts, each of which is responsible for a designated geographic region called a "circuit." (This is what people mean when they refer to "a decision from the First Circuit" or "an appeal to the Ninth Circuit.") Any party that loses a case in a district court has an automatic right of appeal to a court of appeals. The decisions from the court of appeals of a particular circuit are binding on the trial courts of that circuit.

The United States Supreme Court, which consists of nine Justices, is the court of last resort. It agrees to hear only a fraction of the cases that are appealed to it each year; the few cases heard each year are chosen based on a number of factors, including the importance of the issue, whether the courts of appeals have split on a question of law, and whether the Solicitor General of the United States (the top lawyer in the Department of Justice) advises the Court to take the case. Once the Supreme Court takes a case and decides it, that decision is binding on all federal and state courts.

The main task of courts today is to interpret and enforce statutory law, that is, the laws passed by state or federal legislatures. In this endeavor, the most critical factor is the *text*—the actual words passed by the legislature. Thus, for example, to apply and interpret the FMLA, courts turn first and foremost to the words of the statute itself.

Of course, the meaning of the words in a law is not always apparent. Sometimes words are ambiguous; sometimes the text is too general to answer the specific issue that the court has been asked to resolve; and sometimes the text is clear but seems to be contrary to the underlying purpose of the statute. Hence, the job of the court is to engage in "statutory interpretation"— that is, to determine what a legislature actually *meant* when it used certain words in a statute. There are a number of different methods of interpretation, but most judges rely to some extent on legislative intent, as evidenced through the legislative history and context of the statute, in order to interpret text that is not clear or is quite broad.

There are some basic restrictions on the power of the courts to interpret a statute. Courts cannot interpret a statute in a manner that is clearly inconsistent with the plain meaning of the text of the statute. (In rare cases, a judge faced with a "plain meaning" that seems clearly inconsistent with the intent of Congress will interpret a statute consistent with its understood purpose, rather than its text, but such cases are unusual.) But, the constraints of the text are less forceful than one might think—in the FMLA, as in most other statutes, there are plenty of terms and provisions that are general and that can be narrowed or expanded through court interpretations.

Courts often consider a statute within the context of preexisting statutes and regulations. For example, the FMLA explicitly adopts the definition of "employee" found in the FLSA. When courts determine whether or not a specific person is eligible for the protections afforded by the FMLA they can rely on extensive case law interpreting the FLSA definition of employee. This makes it easier for judges to reach decisions and provides for consistency in how statutory terms are interpreted and enforced. Courts also may look at preexisting laws even if there is no explicit adoption of terms. Because the FMLA is so similar in its terms and enforcement mechanisms to the FLSA, courts tend to look at FLSA precedent even in areas where the laws are not identical. For example, the FMLA does not explicitly provide a plaintiff with the right to a jury trial. Yet when faced with this question, courts have relied on cases finding such a right under the FLSA to find a similar right under the FMLA.

The task of interpretation is somewhat different if a federal agency has interpreted a statutory term in its regulations. In such a case, regardless of the judge's preferred methodology, the court first will determine whether Congress has "spoken clearly" on the issue. If it has, the court will apply that clear interpretation, regardless of what the regulations say. (Of course, deciding whether a word is sufficiently "clear" itself requires a judicial determination. Some judges have less difficulty discerning the "clear" meaning of words than do others.) If the court determines that Congress has not been clear, the court then will defer to the agency regulation as long as it is a *reasonable interpretation* of the statutory term. Courts will do this even if the legislative history of the law indicates that most members of Congress probably would *not* have intended that particular result. This is called *Chevron* deference, after a 1984 case, *Chevron, U.S.A. v. Natural Resources Defense Council*, in which the Supreme Court announced this rule.

In any case in which a court has engaged in statutory interpretation, including cases in which courts have deferred to agency interpretations, the legislature always has the final word. Congress may overrule the court simply by revising its laws to make its original intent clear; in effect, the legislature says: "You, the court (and/or the agency) got what we meant by this law wrong." State legislatures can do the same with regard to decisions from state courts.

Of course, the realities of the legislative process—including the constraints of time, political will, and the fact that "it is always easier to stop a bill than to pass a bill"—will prevent such revision in most cases.[4] Thus, the judiciary has a powerful role in deciding the practical meaning and impact of laws. Advocates should seek to influence this judicial stage of lawmaking just as they have influenced the legislative and administrative stages.

The FMLA in the Courts

Whole treatises could be written on judicial interpretations of the FMLA and related regulations, and these case decisions tell a fascinating story. For our purposes, it is sufficient to note the most prominent theme of these decisions, that is, that employers and employees have litigated the meaning of the FMLA down to the last word. For instance, employers have used court challenges to argue that the definition of a "serious health condition" is very narrow; to debate the nuances of adequate "notice" by employees taking leave; and even to belabor what it means to be an employer that "employs" over 50 workers. As of July 2004, a search of a legal database uncovered 942 published cases concerning the FMLA in federal district courts and 290 published cases in federal courts of appeals; there were another 69 published cases concerning the FMLA in state courts.

The volume and tenacity of employer challenges to the FMLA in court may be due to the fact that many in the business community view the mandates of the statute as unfair and burdensome. By narrowing the reach of the statute through interpretations by courts, employers have sought to minimize the impact of the statute on their businesses. Similarly, advocates for workers and families view the statute as a vital protection against employer abuse and thus fight to ensure that it applies to as many workers as possible and in as many situations as possible.

THE STATES

As noted earlier, the legal systems of the 50 states are microcosms of the federal system. Each state has its own legislative, executive, and judicial branches that perform the same essential functions as their counterparts in the federal system and exhibit similar features of dynamism and fluidly balanced powers. Thus, states may be a powerful force for change. Indeed, advocates for the FMLA relied on state family and medical leave laws as evidence of public support for such policies as well as their practical feasibility and affordability for businesses (Lenhoff & Bell, 2002). More recently, states have been critical in working toward paid leave, where California has led the way with a system of wage replacement for leave purposes, instituted in 2004.

When the federal government does act within proscribed bounds, the Constitution provides for preemption of state law by federal law, meaning that when federal law speaks to a certain matter, the states may not contradict that law through their own action. However, in many areas of civil rights and employment law, Congress explicitly allows states to legislate in the same area and to provide broader protection than provided by federal law.

BACK TO THE BEGINNING: LEGISLATIVE MODIFICATION

Finally, another force in lawmaking, and another point for influence by stakeholders and advocates, occurs when the process returns to where it began, in Congress. Whether it is to correct an enforcing regulation, to overrule a judicial interpretation or to repeal a law entirely, Congress always has the option to revisit its actions.

With respect to the FMLA, proposals to modify the law have been introduced virtually since the day of its passage, with some seeking to extend its guarantees (for example, ensuring paid leave for covered workers, rather than unpaid leave) and others seeking to restrict them severely (for example, limiting the law's application to businesses with over 500 employees, rather than 50). In the 108th Congress, such proposals numbered over 30 in total, including the Family and Medical Leave Expansion Act, the Family and Medical Leave Clarification Act, the Family and Medical Leave Inclusion Act, and the Family and Medical Leave Enhancement Act. While this proliferation of bills speaks primarily to the rancor surrounding the FMLA, it speaks also to the importance of continued advocacy in the legislative realm, long after a bill is enacted. Ultimately, this is both the beauty and the burden of lawmaking—the story is never finished.

LAWMAKING, THE THREE BRANCHES, AND THE ROLE OF THE LEGAL ADVOCATE

As the story of the FMLA demonstrates, there are multiple sources and types of legal authority that govern our society. The complex system in which these forces interact is both dynamic and knowable. Legislatures draft laws within what they perceive to be the bounds of their authority, relying on the courts to correct them if they go too far and on the executive to give specific meaning to the policies announced in statutes. The president and other executive actors apply and enforce the laws as written, subject to overruling by both the legislative and the judicial branches. And, courts interpret and apply all kinds of law, providing the final word on matters of constitutional interpretation, deferring to the executive on regulatory matters, and facing outright reversal by the legislature on matters of statutory interpretation.

Against this backdrop, a legal advocate can influence the drafting, passage, application, interpretation, and modification of law on issues relevant to her goals. Advocates can do this by using any and all points of entry into the process of lawmaking—legislative, executive, and judicial. Thus, in order to achieve broad-based policy change through law, an effective advocacy campaign must engage with lawmaking in all of its dimensions.

FINDING AND USING LEGAL MATERIALS IN RESEARCH

With the structure and dynamics of the legal system as background, this section now provides a basic sense of how to find and use the materials that are created through the lawmaking process. We cover five types of legal authority, roughly in descending order of their superiority: constitutional law, statutory law, administrative law, case law, and legislative history. For a general overview of doing legal research, see *The Legal Research Manual: A Game Plan for Legal Research and Analysis* (Wren & Wren, 1986).

Constitutional Law

The United States Constitution is available in printed form through a number of sources, but is perhaps most readily accessed on the Internet. Numerous Web sites post the text of the federal constitution, including the U.S. House of Representatives, at www.house.gov/Constitution/Constitution.html. State constitutions are indexed at www.findlaw.com/11stategov/indexconst.html. FindLaw is a legal research Web site with search tools available to the general public.

The practical meaning of the federal and state constitutions, of course, is determined on a continuing basis by the courts through their judicial opinions. These opinions form a body of constitutional "case law." Information on how to find and use case law is described below.

Statutory Law

Statutory law consists of the statutes passed (and not repealed) by a federal or state legislature and signed by the president or by a governor of a state. Statutory law is found in two kinds of collections: (a) *session laws*, which catalogue the statutes in the chronological order of their enactment (and are found in the series called *Statutes at Large*, abbreviated as "Stat."), and (b) *statutory codes*, which place all statutes according to subject matter in an overall code. Thus, for example, all criminal laws are grouped together regardless of the date on which individual criminal statutes were passed.

Most lawyers research and cite statutes through the codified version of the law. When you see a citation that reads: **29 U.S.C. §2601** you know you are dealing with a citation to a *federal statute*. U.S.C. stands for *United States Code*, the official compilation of the federal code.

Thus, for example, the citation **29 U.S.C. §2601** refers to volume 29 of the United States Code, which deals with all labor and employment issues. Section 2601 of volume 29 is where the first provision of the Family and Medical Leave Act is codified. The citation **29 U.S.C. §2601 et. seq.** refers to the entire FMLA as codified in volume 29.

By the way, you may also see the same cite listed as **29 U.S.C.A. §2601**, or more rarely, as **29 U.S.C.S. §2601**. These simply refer to two commercially published editions of the federal code: U.S.C.A. stands for *United States Code Annotated* and U.S.C.S. stands for *United States Code Service*.

Watch out for any citation that gives only a section number and the popular name of a law. That citation, often used as an informal reference among those familiar with a particular law, will not give you sufficient information to find the provision in question. If given such a citation, search around in the paragraph where that section number appears. Find out whether the author is referring to the section of a bill, as passed by *Congress*, or the section of the federal code where the enacted bill has been *codified*. You will need to know that information in order to find the right provision.

For example, Section **504** of the Rehabilitation Act (which prohibits discrimination based on disability by entities receiving federal funds) is codified at Section **794** of Chapter 29 of the U.S. Code (abbreviated as 29 U.S.C. §794). If you try to find "section 504" by looking at Section 504 of Chapter 29 in the code, you will come to something wholly unrelated to disability discrimination. Thus, in general, if the nature of a section number reference is not clear from its context, you may want to check both possibilities—the relevant section of the law itself and the relevant section of the code where the law is codified—to be sure that you have the right provision.

The Office of the Law Revision Counsel of the U.S. House of Representatives, which prepares and publishes the U.S. Code, hosts a Web site through which researchers may search and download the entire U.S. Code: http://uscode.house.gov/uscode.htm. Researchers also should check out (and bookmark) the Legal Information Institute hosted at Cornell University. This site has been a favorite one among lawyers for many years due to its easy-to-use online source of statutory law; researchers may access both state and federal statutes at http://www.law.cornell.edu/statutes.html.

Finally, statutory law can be searched through several commercial electronic databases. The most prominent ones are Westlaw (www.westlaw.com) and LexisNexis (http://lexis-nexis.com/). These are available both online and in CD-ROM form. But, users of these commercial databases must register and pay fees, although discounted rates may be available through academic institutions.

States maintain copies of their laws both in session law compilations and in statutory codes but vary in their practice in organizing and publishing these. The Cornell site, http://www.law.cornell.edu/statutes.html, provides a helpful way to navigate state statutes, organizing them both by topic areas and by state.

Agency Regulations (Administrative Law)

As described above, much of "the law" actually exists in the form of regulations and decisions issued by the president (or a governor) and by various national (or state) executive agencies interpreting or enforcing the statutes that have been passed by the legislature. These regulations, like statutes, are catalogued in two ways: in *administrative registers*, which are organized chronologically, and in *administrative codes*, which are organized according to subject matter.

Regulations from all federal agencies are collected chronologically in the *Federal Register* (abbreviated as "Fed. Reg."). The *Federal Register* is published daily in hard copy. It also can be accessed electronically at http://www.gpoaccess.gov/executive.html.

All regulations are also gathered in a federal regulatory code, organized by subject area. When you see the citation **42 C.F.R. §213(a)**, you know that you are dealing with a **federal regulation**. C.F.R. stands for the *Code of Federal Regulations*.

The CFR is available online at the same site as the *Federal Register*: http://www.gpoaccess.gov/executive.html. Numerous other executive rules, decisions, and publications—including the federal budget—can be accessed here as well. In addition, in 2003, all agencies began to post proposed regulations (known as NPRMs, for Notice of Proposed Rulemaking) and a heads-up that a NPRM would be coming (known as an ANPRM, for Advanced Notice of Proposed Rulemaking) on this Government Printing Office Web site.

State regulations are more difficult to find; many states do not regularly publish their administrative rules. In some states, a commercial publisher has stepped in to provide copies of regulations, but where no publication is available, researchers can contact the state agencies directly. In those states that do publish their regulations, the format and quality of publication vary widely.

Administrative law also includes the rulings of administrative law judges, arbitrators, and other agency officials who decide specific disputes. These officials are not federal or state judges, but instead are employees of an executive or independent agency such as the National

Labor Relations Board (NLRB). The easiest way to find these decisions is through the Web site of each agency. For example, the NLRB's website, www.nlrb.gov, contains a searchable database of the Board's decisions as well as lower rulings by the agency's administrative law judges and regional directors. Most administrative rulings also can be accessed through commercial databases, such as Westlaw and LexisNexis. In addition, hard copies of such decisions are available in many law libraries, often in official reporters published by the agency itself.

Case Law

Case law consists of the decisions issued in specific cases by courts throughout the federal and state systems. Case law determines much of the practical impact of both constitutional and statutory law. We doubt that researchers in nonlaw fields will want to spend very much time reading through opinions. Nevertheless, a basic knowledge in recognizing what case law citations refer to, and how to find specific cases, may be helpful.

Not all opinions are published or even available in written form. Many rulings, particularly those by the lower state courts, are delivered orally and without extensive explanation, while those issued in writing are too numerous to publish automatically. Decisions with any public or legal significance, however, are published in collections known as case reporters, in which court decisions are compiled chronologically by date of issuance.[5]

For every court opinion, the case name, the date of the opinion and its location in a case reporter are the official "citation," usually in this basic format: case name, volume and page in the reporter, court (unless the case is a Supreme Court opinion, which will be clear from the name of the reporter), and date of issuance.

One important note about case names: As a case moves from the initial (trial) court to the first appellate court and to the final appellate court, you may notice that the order of the parties' names reverses. This is because the party seeking relief from the court *at each particular stage* is always named first. Thus, at the initial stage of a case, the party that brought the suit is listed first. But, if that party wins and the other side then files an appeal asking the next level of the court system for relief, then that other party will be listed first for the appellate court purposes.

For example, in the *Hibbs* case, William Hibbs originally sued the Nevada Department of Human Resources. So the initial case name was *Hibbs v. Nevada Department of Human Resources*. Because Hibbs lost at the first stage and sought appeal from the court above, the case name stayed the same at the next level. When Hibbs won in the court of appeals, however, it meant that the Nevada Department of Human Resources had to appeal to the Supreme Court for relief. So, in the Supreme Court's decision in the case, the names in the title were reversed and the case is cited as *Nevada Department of Human Resources v. Hibbs*.

Each level of the federal courts has one or more case reporters that publish its decisions. Decisions issued by the Supreme Court are collected in *United States Reports* (abbreviated as "U.S."), which is the official, government-approved reporter of these decisions. When you see the citation *Nevada Department of Human Resources v. Hibbs,* 538 U.S. 721 (2003), it means that this 2003 decision of the Supreme Court is published beginning on page 721 of volume 538 of the *United States Reports*.

There are also 2 commercial reporters of Supreme Court decisions. These are extremely useful, given that the official reporter in print tends to lag 2 or more years behind real time in its publication. The West Publishing Company publishes the *Supreme Court Reporter* ("S. Ct."), and the Lawyers Cooperative Publishing Company publishes the *United States Supreme Court Reports, Lawyers' Edition* ("L.Ed." and "L.Ed.2d"). So, one Supreme Court case will have three different citations. For example, the cite for *Hibbs* is: 538 U.S. 721, 123 S. Ct. 1972, and 155 L.Ed.2d 953.

Decisions from all 13 U.S. Courts of Appeals (the "Circuit Courts") are collected in a commercial reporter, published by West. This is called the *Federal Reporter*. The Reporter is abbreviated as "F.," "F.2d," and "F.3d," depending on when the case was decided. The *Federal Reporter* is currently in its third series (hence F.3d), with 999 volumes in each series. The cite for the *Hibbs* case is 273 F.3d 844 (9th Cir., 2001). That means that the Ninth Circuit Court of Appeals issued an opinion in this case in 2001 that begins on page 844 of the 273rd volume of the third series of the *Federal Reporter*.[6]

Opinions from the federal trial courts, the U.S. District Courts, also are collected in a commercial reporter. This reporter is called the *Federal Supplement* and is abbreviated as "F.Supp." and "F.Supp.2d". So, for example, 296 F.Supp.2d 946 (E.D. Wis., Dec. 23, 2003) refers to a decision by the Eastern District of Wisconsin published beginning at page 946 of the 296th volume of the second series of the *Federal Supplement*.

Decisions of state courts are collected in state case reporters. Each state has at least one official reporter for its highest court. Some have separate reporters for their intermediate appellate courts and only a few have reporters for trial level courts.

How easy it is for nonlawyers to access cases usually will depend on how recently the case has been decided. When a high-profile case is decided, newspapers such as the *New York Times* and the *Washington Post* often will provide links to the case itself. The Supreme Court now posts its opinions relatively quickly on its Web site, http://www.supremecourtus.gov. In addition, you can access many recent federal (and some state) court decisions through Web sites hosted by the courts. These websites are listed on the Cornell site, http://www.law.cornell.edu/. And, finally, organizational parties involved in high-profile cases often provide copies of case decisions and briefs (written arguments presented to the court) on their Web sites.

Doing research on (and getting access to) cases that have been decided over time, however, is more difficult. In the print world, case law is collected according to subject matter in multi-volume collections known as *case digests*. These effectively function as indexes to the case reporters. Researchers would do well to consult a law library in finding and using such digests.

As with statutory and administrative law, the published collections of case law are available in all legal libraries. With the advent of electronic media, however, many legal researchers no longer use the books themselves but rely instead on electronic databases such as Westlaw and LexisNexis. These systems provide far more timely reporting of opinions (it often takes less than a week for decisions to be added to the databases, as opposed to the months or years that it takes for publication of reporters) and also provide ready access to a number of decisions that are never included in the published reporters. These benefits move many lawyers to rely solely on electronic case reporting, but, as stated above, these databases require user registration and charge large fees for their use.

Pending Bills and Legislative History: Reports, Debates, and Amendments

As discussed above, courts and agencies often rely on recorded legislative history as evidence of congressional intent as they interpret and apply a statute. Therefore, advocates and researchers should have some understanding of how legislative history is organized and where to find this history with respect to a particular statute or issue.

Committee reports are a key form of legislative history and are designated according to the year and order in which they were produced. For example, when you see the citation S. Rep. 104-351, it means that this conference report was the 351st report issued by *any* Senate committee during the 104th Congress, which ran from 1995 through 1996. When you look at the report itself, you will find more information about the report, such as the name of the committee issuing the report and the number of the related bill.

An excellent source of committee reports is http://thomas.loc.gov/, maintained by the Library of Congress and affectionately known as "Thomas." This is an excellent site for following every public piece of legislative action on a bill; the site covers bills introduced from the 93rd Congress (1973–1974) through the present. Committee reports also are available through the Web site of the Government Printing Office, http://www.gpoaccess.gov/legislative.html.

Committee hearings, which comprise another important piece of legislative history, are not as easily accessible as committee reports. Hearings usually are not published until at least several months after they occur and are not made available on the Internet. Only hearings that are released by the committees are available through the Government Printing Office Web site at http://www.gpoaccess.gov/legislative.html.

Another significant form of legislative history, congressional debates, are recorded in chronological order in the Congressional Record, which is the official record of each day's proceedings and debates within Congress. (The Constitution actually mandates that an official record be kept of these daily proceedings.) The Record relating to a particular bill (or Records, if debate occurs on more than one day) includes not only a transcript of what is said on the floor of the chamber but also any documents introduced into the Record by members during the course of debate.

Congressional Records for the current and preceding seven Congresses (1989 through the present) are publicly available and easily searchable through the Library of Congress Web site at http://thomas.loc.gov/.

The text of all amendments to a bill that are proposed in the full chamber of either house, together with their outcomes, is included in the Congressional Record. These amendments are available on the Library of Congress' Thomas Web site, starting from 1977. Amendments offered during committee markup (or at any time before a bill reaches the full chamber) are not available on the Thomas Web site.

State legislative action is far more difficult to track but can be followed in some states through state-hosted Web sites. For instance, California's Legislative Counsel provides extensive information on pending and recent bills through its Web site, http://www.leginfo.ca.gov/bilinfo.html.

At the state level, legislative history is extremely difficult to find. Tracking down the content of debates, amendments, and other significant actions is painstaking work and often impossible. While many states host Web sites devoted to tracking the legislative process (such as the California site mentioned above), these sites are usually far less comprehensive than the federal tracking system, making it all the more critical that advocates be present to inform and record the history of a bill. In the case of the FMLA, advocates and scholars have retold the 9-year saga of its passage (including some of the most important state legislative action), in hopes that the lessons of the story will not be lost (Lenhoff & Bell, 2002; Elving, 1995).

CONCLUSION

As the continuing story of the FMLA demonstrates, our legal system is complex, dynamic, and open to influence on a number of levels. Legal advocates are active in identifying, analyzing and informing all relevant sources of law within a particular area, working equally in legislatures, agencies, and courts. Properly understood, no source of law is untouched by the others, and in order to be effective, advocates see and use the key points of entry into all three arenas. It is precisely because of this complexity that the cross-disciplinary approach envisioned by this handbook is so crucial. Bringing together the insights of scholarly research, focused legal analysis and targeted public campaigns, work-family advocates can have—indeed, already have had—a real and lasting impact on the laws and policies that shape the everyday lives of Americans.

NOTES

[1] In most cases, a legislative "report" refers to the background legislative history and explanation provided by a committee. See section 5 on legal research. However, the text of the bill that comes out of the conference committee action is called a "conference report." Any legislative history, explanation, or background to that text is called the conferees' "joint explanatory statement."

[2] For example, the Civil Rights Restoration Act of 1987 was enacted over President Ronald Reagan's veto. See 134 Cong. Rec. H1037-03 (1988) and 134 Cong. Rec. S2730-02 (1988). The Civil Rights Act of 1866 and the 1947 Taft-Hartley Act (amending the National Labor Relations Act) also were enacted over presidential veto.

[3] For example, the revised regulations governing exemptions to the overtime provisions of the Fair Labor Standards Act changed substantially between their proposal in March of 2003 and their final issuance in March of 2004. Although the precise implications of the changes are subject to continued debate, it is undisputed that the Department of Labor significantly changed its revisions as a result of public and congressional response to the proposed regulations.

[4] The fact that a reaction by the Congress is rare does not mean that it never occurs. For example, the Pregnancy Discrimination Act, amending Title VII of the Civil Rights Act, was a response to the Supreme Court's interpretation of sex discrimination under Title VII; the Civil Rights Restoration Act of 1997 was a reaction to the Supreme Court's interpretation of Title IX of the Education Amendments of 1973; and the Civil Rights Act of 1991 was a response to several Supreme Court decisions interpreting Title VII and several other civil rights laws in a narrow fashion.

[5] The suitability of an opinion for publication is determined either by the judge, who may forward an opinion directly to the publisher, or by the publisher, who reviews opinions regularly for significance.

[6] The inevitable delay in publication necessitates a temporary form of citation, in which cases are cited without the precise reporter volume and page number. For example, a recent appellate decision might be cited as *Smith v. Jones*, __ F.3d __ (D.C. Cir., 2006). Whenever such a citation is given, the opinion is likely to be available on an electronic database (as described below) until its publication in the printed reporter.

REFERENCES

Chevron, U.S.A., Inc. v. Natural Res. Def. Council, Inc., 467 U.S. 837 (1984).

Lenhoff, D. R., & Bell, L. "Government Support for Working Families and for Communities: Family and Medical Leave as a Case Study," in C. Beem & J. Heymann, eds., *Learning from the Past–Looking to the Future*, Work, Family and Democracy Project, 2002 *available at* http://www.johnsonfdn.org/images/work_family_democracy.pdf.

Elving, R. D. (1995). *Conflict and compromise: How congress makes the law*. Simon & Schuster, New York.

Feldblum, C. R. (2003). The art of legislative lawyering and the six circles theory of advocacy. *McGeorge Law Review*, *34*, 785.

Final Rule on the Family and Medical Leave Act of 1993, 29 C.F.R. § 825.114.

Oleszick, W. J., *Congressional Procedures and the Policy Process*, 6th ed. 22 (2004); Dove, R. B. *Enactment of a law* (1997) (describing Senate procedure); and Johnson, C. W. *How our laws are made* (2003) (describing House procedure), available through the Library of Congress Web site at http://thomas.loc.gov/home/thomas.html.

Department of Labor. (2003). Regulatory Plan 2003, available at: http://www.dol.gov/asp/regs/unifiedagenda/plan03.htm.

S. Rep. No. 103-3 (1993), reprinted in U.S.C.C.A.N. 3.

The Family and Medical Leave Act of 1993, 29 U.S.C.A. §§ 2601–2654.

The Fair Labor Standards Act of 1938, 29 USCA § 201–219.

Wren, C. J., & Wren, J. R. (1986). *The legal research manual: A game plan for legal research and analysis* (2nd ed.). Madison, Wisconsin: Ambrose and Adams Pub.

137 Cong. Rec. S. 14154 (1991).

136 Cong. Rec. S. 7906 (1990).

31

Work-Family Interventions and Experiments: Workplaces, Communities, and Society[1]

Lotte Bailyn
Ann Bookman
Mona Harrington
Thomas A. Kochan
Massachusetts Institute of Technology

Addressing the challenges working families face today will require fundamental changes in how and where people work and in the organizational practices, institutions, and public policies that govern employment relationships. Making these changes happen will take time, experimentation and testing of new approaches at multiple levels, collaborative interactions and negotiations among multiple stakeholders, and will require an ongoing learning process. To understand these issues, the MIT Workplace Center was created to bring about changes in the connection between employment and family life by engaging in an innovative combination of research and action. Our approach involves work on three interrelated levels: experiments at the workplace level, public education at the associational level, and cross-sector organizations to convene stakeholder at the state level.

On the workplace level, we have conducted research–action projects in a number of specific sites, starting initially in the health care industry and more recently exploring sites in legal services and high-tech firms. We have adapted and modified the methodology of Collaborative Interactive Action Research (CIAR), as developed by Lotte Bailyn and her colleagues (Rapoport, Bailyn, Fletcher, & Pruitt, 2002), to address the particular workforce needs and the particular workplace conditions we have found. We begin by examining existing assumptions about work practices and, through dialogue with workers and managers about our findings, lay the groundwork for collaborations that can stimulate new workplace policies, practices, and work designs.

On the associational level, we have brought empirically grounded data from our workplace research into public education activities with unions, professional associations, industry and trade associations, and other organizations representing workers, employers, and community groups. Our purposes are twofold: to create greater public understanding that the issues faced by working families are social, not individual, problems requiring broad social responsibility and public solutions; and to engage the interest and support of these associations and institutions in diffusing flexible work practices and other work-family supports across the occupations and industries in which they work. We have also brought individual work unit findings into the training of professional managers by integrating work-family case studies into the business school curriculum of MIT.

Finally, on the state level, we have convened multiple private, nonprofit, and public sector stakeholders, including many of the associations mentioned above, to define and develop coordinated approaches to work-family issues in the state of Massachusetts. We are experimenting with new organizational forms that can combine private sector initiatives, public education, and public policy development. We are bringing together parties who often do not work together— and may even hold opposing views—to identify common ground and cross-sector solutions. We seek to make Massachusetts a model for other states and to demonstrate how work-family policies can contribute to a vibrant economy and to healthy families and communities.

Taken together, work on all three levels constitutes a *model for change* that reinforces and amplifies change efforts at each level through ongoing interchanges of information among them. While projects differ on the three levels, all are grounded in research and based on collaboration with the full set of stakeholders that need to be engaged to achieve changes in workplace practices and policies. At the heart of each lies the concept of the "dual agenda" and the belief that it is possible to devise new workplace policies and practices that enhance both the performance of work organizations and the well-being of employees, their families, and communities.

These organizing approaches and principles represent a fundamental shift in the paradigms and research traditions that have traditionally dominated the study of both employment relations and work-family integration. Work and family experts need to better understand the employment relations system and the links between work and family issues, human resource practices, organizational policies, and the external labor market institutions and public policies in which they are all embedded. Work and employment researchers and policymakers in turn need to broaden the outcomes or dependent variables they traditionally consider to make the dual agenda explicit in their analysis and policy evaluations (Kochan, 2005). Both need to make explicit the value base for the importance of needed supports for work-family integration—family care, equal economic opportunity for women and men, fair business competition for pro-family employers, and national economic strength based on the well-being of the workforce.

We are in the very early stages of developing and testing this three-pronged approach. In what follows, we will first describe a research–action methodology that has been developed for use on the workplace level and has had a major influence on our approach. Second, we will review some of the things we have learned to date from our work at the Workplace Center, with a focus on the types of experiments and interventions that are both possible and need to be encouraged to move forward.

DESIGNING WORKPLACE EXPERIMENTS: THE CIAR METHOD

In *Beyond Work-Family Balance: Advancing Gender Equity and Workplace Performance*, Rapoport et al. (2002) describe a method they call Collaborative Interactive Action Research (CIAR) that they have used in a number of organizations to redesign work practices to help employees integrate work with their personal lives *and* to enhance the effectiveness of the work unit—and to do this with an eye to equity between men and women. Their method is geared to bringing to the surface for questioning and analysis deeply held assumptions—often gendered—about work and its separation from family and personal life, and to identify the work practices embedded in these assumptions.

A key finding of this work is that practices that make life difficult for employees are often also detractors from effective work functioning—especially in today's complicated and competitive economic environment. The change efforts of CIAR practitioners bring work-personal life integration and equity together with work effectiveness, even though these "dual-agenda" goals are often seen as adversarial. To do so, they have found, requires continuous close collaboration and interaction between researchers and data analysts on the one hand, and workplace-based organizational partners with full understanding of their work structures and culture on the other. It is a joint effort to create change, and their book describes both their successes and the problems they have encountered.

The role of the outside researchers in this joint effort is to bring into the site the dual-agenda framework and to collect and analyze the data necessary to understand and explicate the cultural assumptions and practices embedded in them that create difficulties for employees' lives as well as for organizational effectiveness.

The sources of data used for this analysis are multifaceted. Though surveys can be used, a survey before going into a site is mainly only useful to convince management that these are important issues for men as well as women. These early surveys are not as helpful for diagnostic purposes. More useful for analysis are surveys conducted after a fair amount about a site is known and an instrument can be designed that deals with the practices that have emerged from this site-specific knowledge. But, the primary data come from one-on-one interviews about the work that people do, the culture behind it, and their personal and family situations.

During these interviews the researchers are not just passive receptors, but engage in what CIAR researchers call "micro-interventions." For example, if talking to a male manager who is describing how his career has evolved, instead of just asking more questions about his career, the following question could be asked: "I'd be curious to know, do you think your career could have evolved in this way if you had a wife who had a full career?" Or, if a manager says that he is very understanding when his women managers have to leave at 5:30 in the middle of a meeting and that it certainly would not affect how he thinks about them, a researcher could suggest that the only answer to people having to leave the meeting is not understanding, but to stop the meeting. These micro-interventions can prompt workers to reflect on their current work practices and the consequences of these practices both for equity issues among employees and for the effectiveness of the work.

CIAR researchers also use group sessions, what they call "roundtables." These are not like the standard focus groups held at the beginning of a project. Roundtables take place after much is known about the site and some analysis of data has occurred. These roundtables, which start by feeding back the themes that the researchers think are important for that particular workplace, serve as a way to begin to get shared understanding. Because of the traditional separation of work and family life, most workers think work-family issues are their own individual problems. In these roundtables, people begin to realize that they are shared problems and that there are systemic issues involved. This can lead to a collective understanding and a beginning point for subsequent intervention.

CIAR researchers also do work observations, shadowing, following people around, and asking them questions about their jobs and workplace norms. For example, at one site, Perlow (1997) had people carry timers and made them write down what they were doing whenever they beeped, which she could then follow up with questions to understand what was behind their actions. At another site, Fletcher (1999) shadowed engineers all day and then interviewed them the next day in detail about what they had done and why. Intensive participation and observation are critical both to gaining credibility needed for collaborative research and for gathering data needed to generate feasible alternatives for redesigning work processes and designing experiments to test them.

A final important source of data is the CIAR researchers themselves. If they on occasion take over the norms of the organization, then self-reflection on this experience can deepen their understanding of what the people at the worksite are facing. At one site, for example, the researchers agreed to expand the project beyond their original intent, which created increased pressure on them. On reflection, they realized they had agreed to this in order to appear committed, which is exactly the way the organization was putting pressure on its employees (Rapoport et al., 2002, p. 135).

The analysis of all these data consists of taking all the interviews, the field notes, the reports of the roundtables, the researchers' reflections on themselves, and asking questions like the following (Bailyn & Fletcher, 2003):

- What does the "ideal worker" look like in this setting?
- What is recognized as competence in this workplace?
- What work is seen as real work?
- How is time used in this workplace?
- How is commitment gauged?
- What is the differential impact on men and women?

The answers to these questions allow CIAR researchers to identify assumptions underlying the work practices that impede gender equity and work-personal life integration. Once these assumptions are identified, the team asks, "How are they affecting effectiveness? What is the relationship?" The analysis then proceeds through a number of steps. The first is to figure out why these practices exist, a type of functional analysis. There usually is a historical answer, but since times change what once was functional may no longer be so. Often, in fact, these practices are seen as problematic by the organization, for example command and control management, but people within the organization have not been able to change them. So the CIAR researchers ask: What is keeping them in place? There is also a cultural analysis that seeks to tease out key norms, rituals, and beliefs that serve to reinforce rather than challenge the status quo. Finally, the analysis concludes with an outline of the unintended negative consequences for equity and work-personal life integration on the one hand, and for work effectiveness on the other. Feedback of the analysis to the organization—ideally to the whole group in a particular company or work unit at the same time—starts the dialogue that hopefully will lead to successful change (Bailyn & Fletcher, 2003).

Designing the interventions and the indicators necessary to evaluate them—the action part of the process—is again very collaborative and interactive and involves *mutual inquiry and fluid expertise* (Fletcher, 1999). This recognizes the fact that organizational members have the expertise about the everyday workings of their work unit and what is really going on in the organization, as well as the experience of what their personal lives are like. Researchers bring expertise on the importance of making these unexpected connections between work, family, and personal life and how dual-agenda experiments have worked in other organizations. Previous CIAR experiments have been most successful when researchers' outside experience is interactively combined with their organization partners' knowledge of the specific setting and its work processes. Out of this collaboration emerge alternatives that organizational members believe will work for them and the organizational unit.

One other element of the CIAR process that should be mentioned concerns how to deal with the inevitable resistance to any kind of change. The goal is to *honor this resistance*. For example, if there is initial resistance to even trying to make the connection between the design of work and people's personal lives explicit, this is *not* something that has to be immediately overcome. Rather, such resistance provides important data that need to be dealt with in the collaborative process. Finally, *keeping the dual agenda on the table* is a key job of CIAR researchers. Neither the personal goal nor the organizational goal can be ignored if an intervention is to be successful and sustainable.

The CIAR method, the authors concluded, "is still emerging as a method, still 'under development' " and it, "like the Dual Agenda concept, needs to move out of the academic, 'experimental' realm.... To accomplish this task, many more people need to try it, work with the CIAR method, build on it, and improve it" (Rapoport et al., 2002).[2] At the MIT Workplace Center, we have been doing just that.

CIAR EXPERIMENTS IN HEALTH CARE: THE WORKPLACE LEVEL

Our experience at the MIT Workplace Center has led us to adopt certain parts of the CIAR method while modifying or changing other parts. To begin with, our research–action efforts have been based in the health care industry—an industry that has *not* been a locus of CIAR projects to date—and we have found that health care is a very challenging industry in which to use the CIAR method. For one thing, health care clinicians work in a time-squeezed environment. Primary care doctors are often required to see patients every 15 minutes. The length of patient stays in hospitals and nursing homes is constantly being shortened, which means that doctors and nurses are trying to provide the same amount and quality of care in much less time. This reality makes it difficult to build the kind of "collaborative, interactive" relationships between researchers and workers so essential to CIAR. Health care workers do not have time to sit down for 2-hour meetings and discuss the "underlying cultural assumptions" shaping their workplace. They are running from patient to patient, chasing down information about which patient is being covered by which insurance company, and making sure to document every "billable encounter."

So we have had to search for other ways to build collaborative relationships and develop the trust necessary for creating change. When we go into a health care workplace—thus far we have worked in teaching hospitals, nursing homes, and a large, multi-specialty practice organization—we begin by collecting baseline data on the work unit where we are hoping to conduct a research–action project. As in CIAR, our primary data come from two sources: one-on-one interviews and work observations. We conduct open-ended interviews in which we ask about the work people do, how people feel about their work, their routines outside of work in their families and communities, and the way work may spill over into family life and vice versa. We try through our questions to have interviewees consider whether current work practices enhance or impede quality patient care, and also how these work practices are affecting their personal and family lives outside of work. We have found that the term "work-family" is not much used—and certainly not well understood—in the health care industry. Thus, the request for an interview on work-family issues, and engaged participation in an interview, may in and of itself create some degree of change in people's thinking and lay the foundation for "action" in the future. Our questions help people to connect domains that are not usually connected, and in this way our baseline interviews become what CIAR practitioners call "micro-interventions."

Even when health care workers reject these connections, or signal their lack of interest in collabration, this in itself becomes data that enhance our understanding of the work unit. In one of our projects, where the health care clinicians have allowed us to sit in on many meetings, they occasionally say things like, "Well, I don't think there are going to be enough chairs in that room," or "The room is really not big enough to hold [x number] of people." This is either a sign that they do not want us in that meeting or a general reductance to engage in change or both— again, useful data. These kinds of actions might be termed "resistance," but by honoring this resistance (a basic tenet of CIAR) they also lead to a much deeper understanding of problems in that work unit and impediments to change in that organization. We find ourselves constantly challenged to find new ways of raising the dual agenda and keeping it on the table.

When we conduct work observations, health care workers seem fairly comfortable having us follow them around while they do what they need to do, and in this way we are able to interject additional questions about work processes and learn more about day-to-day work practices.

These observations have also led us to understand how much change in a health care workplace is, at its best, a cross-institutional exercise. For example, the high level of stress experienced by clinicians we observed in a nursing home was actually caused by problems in the hospitals that send patients to the nursing home and deficiencies in available community-based services when patients are discharged. Thus, redesign of the admission and discharge practices in the nursing home will not be sufficient to decrease the stress of nursing home workers.

Once we have analyzed and synthesized the interview and work observation data—the research part of CIAR—we are ready to feed back the themes we think are important in that particular workplace and ask whether our conclusions reflect the experience of the clinicians involved. Again, finding an opportunity for this kind of session is very difficult in the health care industry. We have found that the "roundtables" and full-group feedback sessions used by other CIAR researchers are often not possible. We have instead asked for half an hour in a regularly scheduled meeting that people are already expecting to go to, or presented thematic findings piecemeal to individual clinicians when we can grab them. These constraints make it more difficult to develop the "shared understandings" necessary for true collaboration.

In one of our projects, we actually were able to organize a meeting to feed data from one-on-one interviews back to physicians in a large medical specialty group. We provided a forum for these professionals to acknowledge for the first time that the long hours were causing severe problems for both men and women and, most importantly, were issues for older as well as younger physicians and their families. The group indicated that this was the first time these concerns were discussed openly in a staff meeting. The outcome of the meeting was a shared commitment to hold a retreat to explore options for addressing these issues. Without the one-on-one data to feed back to the physicians in a group setting, the norms of "patients first"—and therefore "family and personal life last"—that dominate medical care in general and this group of physicians in particular, would have kept them from acknowledging their individual work and family pressures as legitimate concerns at work.

We have been able to participate in "retreats" planned by the clinicians themselves in two of our projects. In these less time-pressured settings, participants can see that they have shared problems with systemic causes, and this leads to some level of collective understanding. In the case of the doctors described above, the retreat allowed discussion of the belief that the "ideal physician" is one who has a large clinical practice, does research, and teaches and trains interns and/or residents. Our role was to pose questions such as: Is this ideal still possible or relevant today? Is it changing? Is it shared by younger as well as older physicians? By men and women? Does it in fact reflect the way people work here? How do efforts to realize this ideal affect your ability to get your work done and your personal and family life? Reflections on these questions can lead to an intervention that challenges both underlying beliefs and work practices.

Our version of CIAR is part emergent ethnography and part orchestrated ethnography. In other words, in the early stages of the project, we are observing what goes on and not participating in the natural flow of workplace events; our understanding is emerging. In the later part of the projects we are carefully documenting how the collaboration and intervention are taking place, but it is orchestrated in the sense that we are playing a major role in what is occurring in the workplace and guiding it in a dual-agenda direction. The former is key in the early stages of our projects, while the latter grows in importance as the collaboration between researchers and workers at a workplace develops over time.

We do not come with particular intervention or solutions in mind; these must be developed collaboratively and reflect the issues that are most pressing in each work unit. We do not assume that all existing work practices are negative or dysfunctional. In one of our projects, based on collaboration with two dispersed teams of geriatric and palliative care workers, we found that many of their work practices supported both their work and family lives. They have a high level of flexibility and control of their time that allows them to spend significant time with individual patients *and* attend to their family responsibilities. Thus, when they attempted to expand their services without adding additional staff, they were in jeopardy of losing something valuable. Our role was to talk about "protecting what works well" and then identifying which existing problems might be addressed in this expansion process. We were also able to give voice to the concerns of some team members about anticipated overwork by conducting a special set of "reorganization interviews" and feeding back the results to the team leadership.

In working on solutions, our interaction is based on what Fletcher (1999) called "fluid expertise"—a major tenet of CIAR. This recognizes the fact that health care workers have special expertise on everyday work practices in their work unit as well as about what is really going on in different parts of their particular health care institution. They understand much better than we do the latest issues with health care costs, Medicare and Medicaid requirements and reimbursement rates, and how all these may affect and constrain the possibilities for change. We bring expertise on the myriad ways that work, family, and community are interconnected and the lessons of CIAR and dual-agenda experiments in other industries. Our working hypothesis, reflecting previous CIAR research and practice, is that both kinds of expertise are needed to suggest work design alternatives that health care workers believe will work for them and that they think are feasible in the current health care environment.

To date, our experience with redesigning work in health care is limited. One example of an ongoing intervention effort is located on one floor of a teaching hospital. It is an experimental attempt to bring self-scheduling into the allocation of nursing shifts. Because of the difficulties already alluded to, we were not able to do as in-depth an analysis as is usual in CIAR projects. We did discover that nurses, who have much flexibility in the number of hours worked per shift and per week but not in the scheduling of those hours, would like more control of their time. But, it was only in the process of putting the experiment into place that we discovered that the necessary responsibility for the group as a whole–the only thing that makes self-scheduling work—was not as firmly in place as necessary. In the initial attempts, only the personal side of the dual agenda was being considered, not the work side. And, the experiment had to be called off by the nurse manager before a group of nurses took the responsibility to make sure that both the unit's needs and the nurses' desires were taken into account during the self-scheduling process. Had a fuller buildup to this intervention been possible—as recommended by CIAR—this problem would have been anticipated (Bailyn, Collins, & Soug, 2005).

One piece of our approach that is an addition to previous CIAR experiments is a more systematic inclusion of community and an examination of its relationship to the domains of work and family. In the framework we are using, workers and workplaces are not free-floating entities but rather are embedded in communities of varying types (Bookman, 2004). Workers and their families leave from and return to homes in specific communities with particular characteristics and services that affect their ability to integrate their work and family lives. They may also participate in social networks of extended family members, neighbors, parents in their local school, congregants in their faith-based institution, or people from other organizations outside of their residential community that provide critical support for work-family needs. Workplaces are located in particular communities where access to transportation or family care services may be important to the ability of local employers to recruit and retain their workforce.

In our health care project on geriatric and palliative care, community issues have emerged as critically important. Our initial interviews with the health care professionals caring for elderly patients revealed the importance of family caregivers, both when patients are in institutional settings *and* when they are at home. Our initial work observations provided further evidence of the importance of family caregivers and the extent to which elderly patients are being cared for mainly in their homes, not in hospitals or nursing homes. In interviews with family caregivers, their reliance on a variety of uncoordinated medical and personal care services to support home care, and their problems with accessing and paying for these services, highlighted the role of community-based agencies. All these findings have led us to understand that any intervention in the provision of geriatric and palliative care must necessarily consider three workforces: health care workers, community service providers, and family caregivers. What began as a project to address the work and family issues of health care workers in a discrete set of health care workplaces has developed into-a project that necessarily broadens our understanding of the "health care workplace" to include communities and homes and broadens the "health care workforce" to include family caregivers (Bookman and Harrington, 2005).

Both our projects and our own adaptation of CIAR are "works in progress." Health care does present special challenges. In particular, the industry is heavily shaped by public polices that are beyond the reach of individual health care institutions to change. In addition, the time pressures on workers across health care occupations demand innovative approaches to collaboration and a multi-year commitment to each project. However, given the growing importance of service sector jobs in our economy and the importance of high-quality health care to our society as a whole, we believe that experiments in this industry are important to pursue. In fact, health care is a particularly important laboratory for CIAR experiments because women still compose the majority of the workforce and the need to achieve both sides of the dual agenda is particularly pressing.

MOVING BEYOND THE WORK UNIT: PUBLIC EDUCATION AND THE ASSOCIATIONAL LEVEL

Experience with CIAR has demonstrated that although it can be successful in achieving positive dual-agenda results in specific work units, it is difficult to diffuse to other parts of the organization in which the units are embedded. Evidence from other organizational interventions suggests that the inability to diffuse such innovations may lead them to atrophy, even in the specific units in which they demonstrate positive outcomes. Given this, an active organizational and broader professional learning and dissemination component needs to be built into these types of interventions and experiments.

The traditional organizational and action research approach to this challenge is to design an intra-organizational learning and diffusion process into the experiment or intervention. This can be done by paying attention to and engaging the powerful stakeholders who are outside the unit but whose support will be needed if the changes introduced are to be accepted as worthy of consideration and experimentation in other parts of the organization. We see this as a necessary but not sufficient step for producing change. Stakeholders, such as professional associations, outside the boundaries of any single organization need to be engaged as well.

Our work in the legal services industry to date has focused on professional associations and publicizing innovative practices in Boston-area law firms. In particular, we have focused on supporting and expanding the work of the Task Force on Professional Challenges and Family Needs of the Boston Bar Association, and the recommendations of its pioneering study, "Facing the Grail: Confronting the Costs of Work-Life Imbalance (1999)." This study made visible some of the difficulties facing women lawyers in securing part-time positions and securing other policies that would support "work-life balance." We are building on the findings from this study by working with women leaders of the Women's Bar Association of Massachusetts and participating in its Equality Commission newly formed to address the increasing attrition of women lawyers. Through a joint inquiry, we are documenting the extent to which women are leaving the practice of law, and specifying the conditions needed in law firms to ensure women's retention, advancement, and leadership.

We have also documented an interesting work-family experiment in a local law firm, and have used this case study in educating our students at the Sloan School of Management about critical issues they will face working in the private sector. This law firm in Boston was designed to attract lawyers who want flexible working arrangements. To date, it has been successful in doing so and serves as an interesting learning case for our efforts, which we have tried to disseminate through teaching the case to business students. A brief summary of this case follows:[3]

Sullivan Weinstein and McQuay (SWM) is a firm of 17 lawyers founded in 1995. The goal was to create a new type of law firm focused on providing better value to clients and more responsibility and flexibility for their attorneys. Eight years later, there is widespread belief at SWM that this is exactly what they have achieved. Bob Sullivan, the founding partner, describes the firm's strategy and culture: "We don't have many rules here. Our only rule is that you must be responsible in meeting your obligations to your clients and your coworkers." Attorneys can control their work schedule, work from home, negotiate a part-time position, and take leaves of absence. SWM also provides a home for lawyers in a variety of places in their professional careers with a variety of goals.

Eleven of the firm's lawyers are women, and six of them are on part-time schedules. All but one anticipates staying at the firm into the foreseeable future, though some were considering increasing or decreasing their workload. SWM relies heavily on information technologies to increase productivity and keep costs low. The firm relies exclusively on the Westlaw online legal library, which, through a secure virtual private network, can be accessed from home offices. A traditional firm might have as many as 23 support staff for 17 attorneys. SWM has only 3.5 nonlawyers on their payroll, helping to reduce labor and associated space and management costs to approximately 50% of the costs in a traditional firm.

In one SWM lawyer's words:

"What I saw at SWM when I was applying was a group of professionals all of whom were respected and treated like professionals by each other, with people responsible for their own work and their own time. It's a supportive group of people: we help each other out when someone's in a pinch and there's support for getting and handling cases on your own. [Lawyers at SWM get 10% of gross revenues received from clients they bring in.] No one has ever said anything about what hours I was in the office or not in the four years I have worked here. What I was told up front was: 'you need to be responsive to your clients and as long as you are doing that, you know best what you need to do.' And that's the way it's been."

The organizational practice that the attorneys in the firm cite as particularly valuable is an approach to flexible work arrangements that is responsive to individual and changing needs, not reliant on a prescribed system of benefits. Furthermore, responsiveness is the rule, not an exception to the rule or an unusual accommodation.

Case studies of innovative organizations like the law firm described above are a critical part of the research and learning process. They serve as "ideal types," not to be replicated exactly, but to be debated to see whether or not the features that make them successful can be adapted to different settings (Westney, 1987; Cole, 1989). We have used this case to structure a debate among management students on the question of whether or not the organizational features of this small law firm can or will be replicated in other firms in the industry.

By working with associations in law and other professions, we put what we have learned from individual work unit experiments into a broader social and cultural context. Overall, we see disseminating a rich *mix* of hard data and experimental results, as well as personal narratives and organizational stories, as critical to challenging norms that persistently deflect attention to work-family issues.

ENGAGING ALL THE STAKEHOLDERS: THE STATE LEVEL

Rethinking and reframing the links between work and family will not be successful if each of the stakeholders involved goes it alone. This requires going beyond the boundaries of individual workplaces and organizations to bring employee representatives, professional associations, local business groups, and community and public policy leaders into discussion of these issues. In the past, solutions to work-family problems have been piecemeal and fragmented, with concerned parties working alone or even at cross-purposes. The aim of the MIT Workplace Center is to encourage all the groups that share responsibilities for integrating work and family life to work together and bring their collective energies to bear on work and family issues. Doing so requires overcoming some ideological blinders that, if not shed, risk growing into insurmountable barriers. For example, American business leaders tend to guard their autonomy and power to control decisions affecting work and employment relations from influence of any group they consider "outside or third-party" influences. In actuality, their needs will also be served by encouraging researchers concerned with work-family issues to identify new approaches to the conflicts involved and to develop solutions that meet the interests of all of the parties.

Seeking to create a structure for such efforts, the Workplace Center is engaged in establishing a Massachusetts Work-Family Council.[4] The purpose of the Council is to promote understanding of work-family issues as matters of public concern and importance, to define the issues as requiring coordinated responses from multiple stakeholders, and to provide an instrument for constructing solutions by bringing together the full range of stakeholders involved in particular conflicts. Depending on need, the Council could discuss issues and proposals under consideration in the political process, propose both private sector and public policy initiatives, sponsor educational projects, and disseminate findings from academic research.

As there is no model for such an institution, the process of creation has been experimental at each step. Approximately 100 people are active participants in Council events. They are associated with a wide range of employers and institutions and form a multi-stakeholder constituency for an ultimate operation of a publicly influential, policy-initiating, problem-solving Council.[5] Once the council is established, it will be a successor organization to the Workplace Center, carrying on the Center's mission when its work is completed.

The process for constructing the base for a multi-stakeholder Council included the following steps:

- **Step 1:** Formation of a consortium of regional academic centers engaged in work and family issues for various populations to complete the following tasks: define salient issues, identify major stakeholding groups, outline a general Council mission, propose a range of potential Council projects, and organize steps for the creation of a Council.
- **Step 2:** Broad-scale collection of names of people active in six stakeholder sectors—business, government, labor, professional associations, community organizations, and low-income advocacy and service groups—and invitations through letters and e-mail to those identified to participate in the development of the Council.
- **Step 3:** Series of separate sector meetings—to learn the particular work-family issues, outcomes of attempted solutions, and present positions of stakeholders in each.
- **Step 4:** Experiment with cross-sector dialogue in a meeting of representatives from all six sectors. *Format:* 6 tables of 7–10 people, at least one from each sector, with discussion facilitated by a consortium member. *Subject:* identifying issues of greatest concern and potential grounds for solution acceptable to the diverse stakeholders involved. *Aim:* Test

possibility for people with conflicting interests in work-family issues to recognize benefits of coordinated solutions. *Outcome:* expression of clear differences but also common concerns about basic issues—workplace flexibility, family care, and job and income security.

- **Step 5:** Joint meeting for a "Solution-Seeking Workshop," with an academic presentation on the state of the Massachusetts workforce, followed by cross-sector solution-seeking dialogues in the same format as Step 4—resulting in the formation of working groups on family care and flexible work arrangements.
- **Step 6:** Joint meeting on work-family and public policy cosponsored by the Boston College State Legislators Network Project. Presentation by a panel of state legislators on committees dealing with work-family issues, followed by cross-sector dialogue exploring potential policies relating to family care and workplace flexibility.
- **Step 7:** Meetings with state legislators concerning the development of a legislative work-family agenda and exploration of the establishment of the Work-Family Council by legislation.
- **Step 8:** A bill, An Act to Establish a Massachusetts Work-Family council, is filed: by the majority whip of the House of Representatives in the Massachisetts state legislature with 32 co-sponsors.

Step 4, the testing of cross-sector dialogue, is a key element in the development of a Council. It prefigures the mode of operation of an established Council, the basic premises of which are an ultimate common interest of employers, employees, governments, and communities in resolving work-family conflict and the possibility of doing so on positive terms for contesting parties. The dialogues do not deny deep differences. Rather, by bringing a wide range of parties to the table, they demonstrate the complexity of the issues and the need for multi-party negotiation for stable solutions to be reached. And, they open up the possibility of identifying mutual benefits to solutions reached in this way.

Although, these steps would have to be modified and adapted to local conditions, if, similar Councils were established in a number of states, work and family policies could rise to the same level of discourse and concrete analysis that produced innovations in other employment and social policy domains in the past. This is an essential task if we are eventually to have an impact on the overall workforce and economy.

THE TASKS AHEAD

Developing a methodology that is both rigorous and that can be implemented in actual workplaces and in multi-stakeholder community and policy settings is a complex task. Standard principles of experimental design and policy analysis and evaluation need to be blended with action research, participant observation, education, and negotiations. The task is particularly difficult in the work-family arena because many of the parties who hold power over public policy and organizational decisions and practices have not yet defined these issues as critical problems and therefore need first to see the connections between these two traditionally separate domains of social and economic activity.

While researchers need to go into these projects with clear knowledge of and commitment to following experimental and quasi-experimental design principles, in practice, workplace interventions are negotiated at every step of the design, data collection, and evaluation process. The intervention process itself has to be one of collaboration between researchers and practitioners. Qualitative and quantitative data are both important for reaching valid conclusions; indeed, our experience is that it is the triangulation of qualitative and quantitative data from interviews, observations and collaborative interactions, and measurable outcomes that provide the necessary base for both understanding and learning among members of the research team and the organizations involved. These features, therefore, need to be incorporated into future research programs in the work-family field if the goal of having an impact on policy and practice is to be achieved.

Our efforts to design such a research and action strategy are still in an early, developmental stage. By discussing what we are learning as we go along, we hope to encourage others to test similar approaches and propositions. This will be a long-run effort. To be successful will require investments in institution-building to create centers like ours in diverse regions of the U.S., sustained commitment of researchers to build relationships and local institutional knowledge within key industries and specific workplaces in their regions, and comparison of lessons learned from the multiple experiments that would follow from this type of investment. We hope others will follow to strengthen and adapt this approach.

APPENDIX

Publications of Interest on Collaborative Interactive Action Research

Bailyn, L. (1997). The impact of corporate culture on work-family integration. In S. Parasuraman & J. H. Greenhaus (Eds.), *Work and family in a changing world: A multiple stakeholder perspective*. Westport, CT: Greenwood Publishing Group.

Bailyn, L., Bengtsen, D., Carré, F., & Tierney, M. (2000). The Radcliffe-Fleet work and life integration project. In J. Casner-Lotto (Ed.), *Holding a job, having a life: Strategies for change*. Scarsdale, NY: Work in America Institute.

Bailyn, L., Fletcher, J. K., & Kolb, D. (1997). Unexpected connections: Considering employees' personal lives can revitalize your business. *Sloan Management Review, 38*(4), 11–19.

Bailyn, L., Rapoport, R., Kolb, D., Fletcher, J. K., Friedman, D. E., Eaton, S., Harvey, M., & Miller, B. (1999). Re-linking work and family: A catalyst for organizational change. In M. Pina e Cunha & C. Alves (Eds.), *Readings in organizations science: Organizational change in a changing context*. Portugal: Instituto Superior de Psicologia Aplicada.

Bailyn, L., Rapoport, R., & Fletcher, J. K. (2000). Moving corporations in the U.S. toward gender equity: A cautionary tale. In L. Haas (Ed.), *Organizational change and gender equity: International perspectives on fathers and mothers at the workplace*. Newbury Park, CA: Sage.

Bailyn, L., Rayman, P., Harvey, M., Krim, R., Read, R., Carré, F., Dickert, J., Joshi, P., & Martinez, A. (1998). *Creating work and life integration solutions: The Radcliffe-Fleet project*. Cambridge, MA: Radcliffe Public Policy Institute.

Coleman, G., & Rippin, A. (2000). Putting feminist theory to work: Collaboration as a means toward organizational change. *Organization, 7*(4), 573–588.

Costello, C., (with Johnson, N., & Kolb, S. C.) (2002). *Designing work for life: A report on three work redesign projects in the U.S. department of health and human services*. Washington, DC: U.S. Department of Health and Human Services.

Ely, R. J., & Debra, E. M. (2000). Advancing gender equity in organizations: The challenge and importance of maintaining a gender narrative. *Organization, 7*(4), 589–608.

Fletcher, J. K., & Bailyn, L. (1996). Challenging the last boundary: Reconnecting work and family. In M. B. Arthur & D. M. Rousseau (Eds.), *The Boundaryless career: A new employment principle for a new organizational era*. Oxford, UK: Oxford University Press.

Fletcher, J. K., & Rapoport, R. (1996). Work-Family issues as a catalyst for change. In S. Lewis & J. Lewis (Eds.), *Rethinking employment: The work family challenge*. London: Sage.

Harvey, M. A. (2001). *Work-Life redesign at DTE energy*. Scarsdale, NY: Work in America Institute.

Johnson, R. D. (1994). Where's the power in empowerment? Definition, differences, and dilemmas of empowerment in the context of work-family boundary management. PhD dissertation, Harvard University.

Kolb, D. M., & Merrill-Sands, D. (1999). Waiting for outcomes: Anchoring a dual agenda for change to cultural assumptions. *Women in management review, 14*, 194–202.

Kolb, D. M., & Debra, E. M. (1999). Keeping gender in the plot: A case study of the body shop. In A. Rao, R. Stuart & D. Kelleher (Eds.), *Gender at work: Organizational change for equality*. West Hartford, CT: Kumarian Press.

Merrill-Sands, D., Fletcher, J. K., & Acosta, A. (1999). Engendering organizational change: A case study of strengthening gender-equity and organizational effectiveness in an international agricultural research institute. In A. Rao, R. Stuart, & D. Kelleher (Eds.), *Gender at work: Organizational change for equality*. West Hartford, CT: Kumarian Press.

Meyerson, D. E., & Kolb, D. M. (2000). Moving out of the armchair: Developing a framework to bridge the gap between feminist theory and practice. *Organization, 7*(4), 553–572.

Miller, B., & Cashman, J. (2000). Hewlett-Packard/Agilent technologies: Linking business challenges and work/life needs through "Reinventing Work." In J. Casner-Lotto (Ed.), *Holding a job, having a life: Strategies for change*. Scarsdale, NY: Work in America Institute.

Perlow, L. (1997). *Finding time: How corporations, individuals and families can benefit from new work practices*. Ithaca, NY: Cornell University Press.

Perlow, L. (1998). Boundary control: The social ordering of work and family time in a high-tech corporation. *Administrative Science Quarterly, 43*, 328–357.

Perlow, L. (1999). The time famine: Towards a sociology of work time. *Administrative Science Quarterly, 44*, 57–81.

Rapoport, R., Bailyn, L., Kolb, D., Fletcher, J. K., Friedman, D. E., Eaton, S., Harvey, M., & Miller, B. (1996). *Relinking life and work: Toward a better future*. New York: Ford Foundation.

Rapoport, R., Bailyn, L., Kolb, D., Fletcher, J. K., Friedman, D. E., Eaton, S., Harvey, M., & Miller, B. (1998). *Relinking life and work: Toward a better future*. Innovations in management series. Waltham, MA: Pegasus Communications.

Rayman, P., Bailyn, L., Dickert, J., & Carré, F. (with the assistance of H. Maureen, K. Rrobert, & R. Robert). (1999). Designing organizational solutions to integrate work and life. *Women in Management Review, 14*, 164–176.

Sindell, S. M., & Christensen, P. (2000). Bank of America's dual agenda: Improving both business and work/life balance through work redesign. In J. Casner-Lotto (Ed.), *Holding a job, having a life: Strategies for change*. Scarsdale, NY: Work in America Institute.

Young, M. B. (2000). The work group action planning process at Merck & Company. In J. Casner-Lotto (Ed.), *Holding a job, having a life: Strategies for change*. Scarsdale, NY: Work in America Institute.

NOTES

[1] A version of this paper was presented at the National Institute for Child Health and Development Conference on Workplace Strategies for Health and Well-being, Baltimore, Maryland, April 14, 2004.

[2] See appendix for a list of publications on dual-agenda CIAR projects. A number of these are also explored in Rapoport et al. (2002). There are also currently a number of projects underway in the UK, the Netherlands, Australia, and Greece.

[3] Source: B. Miller, T. Kochan, & M. Harrington, *Beyond the part time partner: A part time law firm?* MIT Workplace Center Working Paper # 100, 2003.

[4] The idea of establishing state or regional Work-Family Councils was first proposed in a report of the Sloan Work Family Policy Network by Lotte Bailyn, Robert Drago, and Thomas A. Kochan (2001).

[5] At the time of publication, a bill to establish the council has been filed in the Massachusetts Legislature (House, No. 3727) and assigned to the Joint Committee on Economic Development and Emerging Technologies for a hearing.

REFERENCES

Bailyn, L., Collins, R., & Soug, Y. (2005). Implementation of a self—scheduling system for hospital nurses: Guideline and pitfills. Cambridge, MA: MIT Workplace Center, Waking Paper Series No. 19.

Bailyn, L., Drago, R., & Kochan, T. A. (September, 2001). *Integrating work and family: A holistic approach*. A Report of the Sloan Work-Family Policy Network. Cambridge, MA: MIT Sloan School of Management.

Bailyn, L., & Fletcher, J. K. (2003). *The equity imperative: Reaching effectiveness through the dual agenda*. Boston: Center for Gender and Organizations (CGO) Insight # 18.

Bookman, A. (2004). *Starting in our own backyards: How working families can build community and survive the new economy*. New York: Routledge.

Bookman, A., & Harrington, M. (2005). A Shadow Workforce in the Healthcare Industry? Rethinking the job of the family Caregiver. Cambridge, MA: MIT Workplace Center, Working Paper Series, No. 22.

Cole, R. (1989). *Strategies for learning*. Berkeley: University of California Press.

Fletcher, J. K. (1999). *Disappearing acts: Gender, power and relational practice at work*. Cambridge, MA: MIT Press.

Kochan, T. A. (2005). *Restroring the American dream: A working families' agenda for America*. Cambridge, MA: MIT Press.

Boston Bar Association Task Force on Professional Challenges and Family Needs (1999). *Facing the grail: Confronting the cost of work-family imbalance*. Boston, MA: Boston Bar Association.

Perlow, L. A. (1997). *Finding time: How corporations, individuals, and families can benefit from new work practices*. Ithaca, NY: Cornell University Press.

Rapoport, R., Bailyn, L., Fletcher, J. K., & Pruitt, B. H. (2002). *Beyond work-family balance: Advancing gender equity and workplace performance*. San Francisco: Jossey-Bass.

Westney, D. E. (1987). *Imitation and innovation: The transfer of Western organizational patterns to Meiji Japan*. Cambridge, MA: Harvard University Press.

32

The Standards of Excellence in Work-Life Integration: From Changing Policies to Changing Organizations

Brad Harrington
Jacquelyn B. James
Boston College

Over the past 20 years, work/life issues have become an increasingly pervasive concern for employers and employees. As changes have continued in the composition of working families and as women have found their place in traditionally male-dominated occupations, employers have developed innovative practices that allow employees to find greater balance between their work and home lives (Friedman, Christensen, & DeGroot, 1998). Most often these practices are changes in human resource policies, such as:

- Extension of employee services: The addition of services such as onsite child care, employee health and fitness centers, and concierge services have provided greater convenience for employees and alleviated the need for employees to create their own solutions to some work/life challenges.
- Changes in employee benefits: New benefits programs have been added or modified in the HR portfolio including paid parental leave, resource and referral programs, adoption benefits, domestic partner benefits, and so on.
- Job restructuring initiatives: Greater use of alternative work schedules and loosening of requirements around part-time positions.
- Increased number of initiatives aimed at human resource and organization development including diversity programs, women's initiatives, leadership development, and cultural change efforts. (For a full review of these kinds of efforts, see Ichniowski, Levine, Kochan, Olson, & Strauss, 1996.)

Despite the many practices that have been implemented, their impact on the work/life climate of organizations is as yet unclear. Few organizations have undertaken a comprehensive assessment of their work/life culture (Lobel & Faught, 1996). As a result, after all these years, questions remain as to how much progress has actually been made in this area. The questions include: Have changes to human resource policies and practices translated into a fundamentally different corporate culture? (see, for example, Lewis, 2001; Berg, Kalleberg, & Appelbaum, 2003). How comfortable are employees in accessing these new work arrangements? (Eaton, 2000, 2003). Is there really a greater number of organizations today that provide not just policies, but environments that support working people in their pursuit of achieving greater balance and integration between their work and nonwork lives? Or, is it the case that these changes are mainly cosmetic in nature, creating the perception that organizations are more supportive of the whole person while maintaining outdated assumptions and approaches to managing people?

It is not difficult to imagine in the current challenging economic climate that has existed since the year 2000, that a concept such as work/life remains at the margins of corporate concerns. Skeptical corporate leaders are not known for embracing strategies that do not directly translate into enhanced business performance and financial results, especially under the economic conditions of recent years. The purpose of this chapter is to: (a) outline the challenges presented in moving from work/life policies to cultural change, (b) describe the development of a Standards of Excellence Index as a tool for organizations to use as a model for making progress toward organizational change that has staying power, and (c) review what we are learning from early results from organizations that have completed the Standards of Excellence Index (SEI).

THE CHALLENGES OF CULTURAL CHANGE INITIATIVES

The potential disconnect that exists between an organization's stated policies and the actual practices employed by line managers is hardly unique to the work/life field. Examples abound. Undoubtedly, organizations such as Enron and Worldcom had accounting and fiscal policies in place that claimed to ensure the integrity of their financial statements through mechanisms such as management review processes and internal audits. But, the financial scandals at these and other organizations in recent years illustrate the point that there is often a large gap between what an organization claims to do in its written policies and how it in fact behaves.

Organizational learning experts, most notably Argyris and Schon (1977, 1996), have framed this disconnect between one's stated intent and one's actions. These authors differentiate espoused theory, the theory of action to which an individual or organization gives allegiance and that which is communicated to others, from one's theory-in-use, the theory that actually governs the behavior of an individual or an organization.

For a host of reasons, it has been difficult for organizations to assess whether new work/life policies and programs have in fact become part of a new management paradigm. Organizational work/life literature and research more often focuses on assessing the efficacy of individual human resource (HR) policies and programs in creating more flexible workplaces (see, for example, Edelman, 1996; Lankau & Scandura, 1997; Martinez, 1997; Perlow, 1998). Such research, while highly useful and enlightening, can fail to grasp the "big picture" questions regarding changing organizational paradigms and management belief systems. The research may not answer the questions articulated above regarding policies and their impact on cultural change or whether employees feel inclined to seek out and use flexible work arrangements based on their perception of the acceptance of such programs in their organizations. Eaton (2003), for example, has shown that perceived usability of flexible work-family policies is more important to employees' commitment and productivity than the presence of formal or informal policies alone (see also Batt & Valeur, 2003).

To some extent, the media and its "Best Lists" (i.e., the 100 Best Places to Work, the Best 100 Companies for Working Mothers, etc.) may have also unintentionally exacerbated the problem of developing policies without changing the culture in which they are embedded. While recognition from such awards has done much to foster interest in and support for organizational work/life efforts, it has, for the most part, maintained the focus on HR policies, which are easier to measure, rather than tackling the more difficult and amorphous goal of changing the culture in a way that has lasting effects.

What is involved in changing a culture? Indeed, how do we define culture within an organization? Cultures exist in every organization. Sometimes they are strong and cohesive, at other times not. But whether strong or weak, culture can be a powerful influence on organizations and their members (see, for example, Peters & Waterman, 1982; Ouchi, 1981; Deal & Kennedy, 1982; Schein, 1985, 1992; Collins & Porras, 1994).

Schein (1985), for example, defined culture as:

> a pattern of basic assumptions—invented, discovered, or developed by a given group as it learns to cope with its problems of external adaptation and internal integration—that has worked well enough to be considered valid and, therefore, to be taught to new members as the correct way to perceive, think, and feel in relation to those problems. (p. 9)

As Schein makes clear, organizational cultures are quite durable and difficult to change. To clarify the difficulty in creating real cultural change versus more surface forms, Schien (1985) distinguished among three levels of culture:

Level 1: Artifacts. The most visible level would include physical space, social environment, written and spoken language, overt behavior, and work output. Work/life policies developed largely within HR might be placed in this category.

Level 2: Values. This refers to ideas of what the culture ought to be as distinguished from what it is. Values that cannot be tested and proved may become guiding principles, but may never become underlying assumptions. As such, they are more espoused values than they are values in use. Advocates of work/life integration policies may be placed in this category along with researchers and practitioners. Some companies may have elaborate values statements about the importance of employees as whole people and people with needs outside of work, but these values may grind against a stubborn culture with a very different view of workers.

Level 3: Basic underlying assumptions. Basic assumptions are those beliefs that are so taken for granted that one finds little variation within a cultural unit. Members in the unit would find behavior based on any other premise inconceivable. As Jacobs and Gerson (2004) pointed out, such beliefs about the value of face time and long hours, especially for the professional class, are deeply resistant to change.

Schein argued that the term "culture" should be reserved for the deeper level of "*basic assumptions and beliefs*" [italics added] that are shared by members of an organization. He suggested that, too often, what operates at a surface level is construed as *the* organizational culture; when in fact it is merely an artifact which may or may not accurately represent the essential culture of the organization. The assumptions and beliefs that Schein referred to are actually the learned responses of a group to its problems of survival in its external environment and its problems of internal integration. If we accept Schein's assertion that culture is really grounded in these basic underlying assumptions, it is easy to understand how difficult it is to succeed in a cultural change effort in an organization of any size. Leaders, not to mention the rest of us, are probably not frequently in the mode of rethinking their underlying assumptions. Schein saw culture and leadership as inseparable: One cannot separate the process of leadership from the process of building a culture. One might go as far as to say that a unique function of leadership, as contrasted with management or administration, is the creation and management of culture (Schein, 1985).

Finally, Schein also discussed how leaders can shape culture through what he called embedding mechanisms: what leaders pay attention to, measure, and control; how they role model, teach, and coach; how they react to critical incidents; and how they allocate rewards. Given our knowledge of the difficulties in changing culture and the relationship between culture and leadership, it follows then that leadership must play a key role when one thinks about how to move an organizational culture toward supporting work/life integration initiatives.

THE STANDARDS OF EXCELLENCE WORK/LIFE
INTEGRATION PROJECT

What spurs leaders to deeper commitment to work/life initiatives? Surely such programs as *Fortune Magazine's* list of "100 Best Companies to Work For" and *Working Mother Magazine's,* "Best Companies for Working Mothers" have inspired the development of benefits and policies that get visible and proactive companies on these lists. But, as we have said, these programs and policies do not necessarily translate into deeper organizational commitment to "family-friendly" environments. Therefore, there is a great need in the field for moving the conversation within organizations beyond programs and policies to a broader assessment of the organizational culture. In our view, companies needed a concrete and specific method for evaluating their progress in creating a family-friendly environment. Therefore, we convened a group of experts to develop criteria for standards of excellence for work/life integration.

At the outset, we drew from organizational learning theorists who suggest important prerequisites for learning to take place and for increasing the likelihood that substantive change will occur. These include, but are not limited to, ownership of the problem by top management, the availability of a structured model, the provision of assessment methods and measurement, and the possibility for benchmarking. While the existence of each of these elements does not ensure success, the absence of any of these will jeopardize the chances of making difficult cultural change efforts "stick" (Argyris & Schon, 1977, 1996; Senge, 1990; Shiba, Graham, & Walden, 1993). We will use each of these prerequisites for organizational change to show the ways that they informed the development of the Standards Index.

Placing Ownership with Senior Management

As we have seen with Schein's (1985, 1992, 1993, 1999) research on organizational culture and leadership, organization-wide cultural change is not likely to occur if the learning is focused on one segment of the organization. Too often, we discuss cultural change initiatives with regard to staff functions, such as the professional human resources community, focusing on the things they need to know and learn in order to be effective change agents. At best, these approaches represent artifacts of change or change in values statements and fall into the familiar category of "necessary but not sufficient." While HR professionals (whether they be diversity coordinators, work/life directors, organization development specialists, or human resource directors) are key enablers of change efforts, the key to making cultural change is conveying that ownership of the program belongs to line managers. While some specialist activities and policy formulation can be delegated, ownership of the culture cannot.

Therefore, the first step in fostering change from a process perspective is to ask the question, "Who owns this change process?" If the answer is "the HR department," it is unlikely that organization-wide change will occur (Fandray, 2000). In designing the standards, one of the critical considerations from a process perspective was, "Will our list of standards and the accompanying assessment tool help transfer responsibility for creating a supportive work/life culture from human resources (a staff function) to line management?" If so, the likelihood of fostering a cultural change is greatly increased.

The Importance of a Structured Model

Once ownership by line management and specifically senior leaders is made clear, the next challenge for senior managers might be posed as: "Now that I realize I own responsibility for creating the work/life culture, what should I do differently?" Lobel and Faught (1996) have shown that a concept such as work/life is likely doomed to failure if it is not seen as clear, understandable, and relevant. Indeed, leaders in all types of organizations (e.g., in business, health care, government, etc.) are not inclined to seek opportunities to champion issues that do not seem highly related to their organization's success and ongoing viability. For many managers, initiatives that are not focused on increasing their ability to satisfy customers, control costs, or make their products and services more highly differentiated are going to have difficulty competing for air time. Work/life, at face value, may seem at best as indirectly related to gaining strategic advantage and, at worst, unrelated. Showing relevance is part of the struggle that we frequently refer to as "making the business case" (see, for example, Scheibl & Dex, 1999).

Professional advocates of successful work/life integration must make the case that satisfied, loyal, healthy and balanced employees are more like to positively affect customers, costs, and efficiency than employees who are not any of these things. While this argument has some face validity and has been supported by a number of studies (Bailyn, Fletcher, & Kolb, 1997; DeCotiis & Summers, 1987; Rucci, Kirn, & Quinn, 1998), we must concede that the "business case" rationale is based on an indirect (i.e., if you satisfy employees, then they will deliver higher levels of service that will result in greater customer loyalty) rather than a direct (i.e., if you cut costs, you will increase profits) relationship. Clearly, the absence of direct effects makes our case for changing the culture of the workplace to one that is more congenial to the needs of workers outside of work more difficult to sell.

Beyond the fact that work/life is an indirect means to an end, an even more fundamental challenge might be that the notion is abstract. Business leaders are not typically social scientists. They deal with concrete, results-oriented outcomes (e.g., customers, products, bottom-line financial results). Do we believe that most business leaders could clearly articulate what constitutes work/life balance? Furthermore, do many executives even have any personal experience in being balanced? The evidence would suggest not. As Friedman and Lobel (2003) pointed out in "The Happy Workaholics," many senior executives operate in ways that others would see as imbalanced, such as working very long hours, and yet are happy to do so (see also Jacobs & Gerson, 2004). This does not mean that they cannot be role models or champions for work/life. In fact, Friedman and Lobel indicated that they can promote work/life balance by being authentic, respecting other's choices, and creating an environment that supports effective balance for their employees rather than cutting back their hours to meet someone else's definition of balance.

Most business leaders will be reluctant to champion an idea that seems controversial or unrelated, or not directly related, to business success. Supporting work/life balance can clearly be perceived as counterintuitive (i.e., how can having employees working less help companies be more profitable?). Leaders will also be slow to champion issues they do not understand or feel any personal empathy for. It seems virtually certain they will not champion an idea that lacks definition and structure. When it comes to quality, ethics, humanistic corporate cultures, and, yes, work/life, as we developed the Standards of Excellence we knew that we needed to provide leaders with a template that helps them understand and operationalize what constitutes work/life integration in their organization.

This is exactly what the national quality standards that were the basis of the Baldrige Award did for the quality movement. Created in 1987, the Malcolm Baldrige National Quality Award began setting forth guidelines and criteria that organizations can use to assess their ongoing quality improvement initiatives in a standardized manner. Indeed, many organizations use the Baldrige criteria to conduct a comprehensive organizational self-assessment and benchmark their organizations' performance. The seven key elements of the Baldrige criteria are leadership; strategic planning; customer and market focus; measurement, analysis, and knowledge management; human resources; process management; and business results.

While the Baldrige Award stimulated significant interest in and response from many sectors of the economy (i.e., business, government, health care, education), many would suggest that the award *criteria* have been more important than the award itself in helping organizations make a cultural change toward total quality management. While only a relative handful of U.S.

companies win or even apply for the Baldrige Award, the award criteria are widely used across many organizations as a means of self-assessment. Just 4 years after its creation, Garvin (1991) argued that the Baldrige Award and its criteria had "become *the* most important catalyst for transforming American business. More than any other public or private initiative, this award has reshaped managers' thinking and behavior" (p. 80). Therefore, the Baldrige model was a good one to emulate in developing the Standards of Excellence, a similar assessment not so much of organizational quality and strength, but rather an assessment of the work/life culture within an organization.

One reason the Baldrige Award became so popular among businesses is that the criteria are neither too specific (e.g., just product or service oriented) nor so broad that only a few organizations can relate to them. Just as the Baldrige Award makes tangible those abstract concepts (e.g., leadership and organizational culture) that affect quality management, the intent of the standards criteria is to make tangible those abstract concepts that are critical to work/life excellence. As will be seen, both the Standards of Excellence in Work/Life Integration and the Baldrige criteria provide tools for assessing organizations from a comprehensive organizational perspective that makes senior management buy-in and participation extremely important. Both measures also provide leaders with a tool to assess their own performance.

The value of such structured models for inspiring organizational change cannot be understated. To illustrate, in a study of organizational learning in a high-tech company in the 1990s, Harrington (2000) found that organizationwide adoption of quality improvement methods was facilitated by just such a model. Quality improvement, or Total Quality Management (TQM) as it is widely known, has some of the same characteristics as work/life initiatives and suffered some of the same barriers to implementation: Quality was an abstract notion; quality improvement presented the promise of better business results without a clear connection to the "bottom line"; and quality was a nonmainstream issue that required significant management attention, commitment, and involvement in order for successful implementation to occur. Participants in the study indicated that successful implementation of TQM in their organization was strongly facilitated by the use of a structured model, in this case a problem-solving model, which was concrete, clearly defined, and measurable. Using the model not only allowed managers to operationalize "quality" in an actionable way, but also allowed the leaders to measure and monitor progress in the implementation of their quality program. Such monitoring would not have been possible if it were not for the use of a structured model that clearly outlined observable steps and progress in the implementation of the quality program.

The Importance of Assessment Methods and Measures

If the term work/life is an abstraction, its implementation will be dramatically stalled. But, even making the concept more concrete through a structured model does not eliminate the uphill challenge to its implementation. In a corporate world that is increasingly measured (and often punished) by Wall Street for "bottom-line" financial performance indicators, giving careful consideration to other important business indicators can prove difficult. This is especially true of initiatives where current status or progress cannot be measured. As the old business cliché goes, "What gets measured gets done," and for better or worse, the one business metric that trumps all others is financial. In recent years, however, the quality movement has had a positive impact on encouraging the use of a broader set of business measures to calibrate the "health and well-being" of the business. One manifestation of this has been in the rise of the use of the "balanced scorecard" in many businesses. As Kaplan and Norton (1993) pointed out in "Putting the Balanced Scorecard to Work":

> Executives may introduce new strategies and innovative operating processes intended to achieve breakthrough performance, then continue to use the same, short-term financial indicators they have

used for decades, measures like return-on-investment, sales growth, and operating income. These managers fail not only to introduce new measures to monitor new goals and processes but also to question whether or not their new measures are relevant to the new initiatives. (p. 2)

It is worth noting that without a means to: (a) get work/life on the radar screen of senior management and (b) develop tangible measures of progress, it is unlikely that work/life initiatives (or other similar initiatives that do not show a clear or obvious connection to the "bottom line") will garner much management attention. Furthermore, without appropriate measures available, it is likely that senior managers will feel that measuring progress in this area is not even possible. As a result, the lack of a rigorous measurement may increase their tendency to simply choose not to address this issue as other more tangible and measurable concerns will continue to attract management attention (Davidson, 1998).

Benchmarking: Sharing and Seeing Best Practices

Since Xerox Corporation first began benchmarking against its Japanese competitors in 1979, businesses have increasingly turned to benchmarking to improve organizational performance and gain an edge over competitors (Gordon, 1999). At a basic level, benchmarking is a formal process used to gather information on other organizations' practices.

Fedor, Parsons, and Shalley (1996) defined four types of benchmarking: internal, industry, competitive, and best-in-class. As its name suggests, internal benchmarking occurs between departments or business units within the same organization. Industry benchmarking, on the other hand, takes place between organizations that are in the same industry but do not necessarily compete directly with one another. With competitive benchmarking, companies compare themselves against other organizations that compete with them for products or services. Finally, with best-in-class benchmarking, companies gather intelligence on organizations that are known to be superb in specific business areas. Southwest Airlines, for example, has often been considered a best practice company in the areas of employee recruitment and customer service (Stoughton, 2001) and is a popular company for firms to benchmark against that have no affiliation to the airline or transportation industries.

The type of benchmarking that companies choose ultimately depends on what they are interested in measuring and the benchmarking resources that are available to them. Regardless of the type of benchmarking chosen, the process will usually follow four distinct phases (Fedor et al., 1996). In Phase 1, the primary self-assessment takes place and the organization determines which functions or processes to measure. In Phase 2, the organization identifies partners to benchmark against and establishes those relationships. The third phase of benchmarking involves gathering data and analyzing significant gaps in performance. The fourth phase involves designing and implementing a program to deal with gaps. Organizational culture plays a strong role in this last phase, as the adaptiveness and openness of the culture will significantly influence the degree to which the organization accepts the proposed changes.

Benchmarking does have its limitations, and time and cost are at the top of this list. Thus, companies need to carefully consider the type of benchmarking that they choose. The results from best-in-class benchmarking may offer significant performance gaps that companies can strive to achieve, but having an understanding of these gaps may prove fruitless and countermotivational if the company lacks the resources to implement them. Moreover, if the company's culture or strategy does not fit with the strategies proposed in the benchmarking implementation, the entire process will be of no use.

With its acknowledged limitations, benchmarking can provide an effective way to identify both areas needing improvement and potential methods for doing so. In this way, it can serve as a catalyst for learning and progress. But, a key challenge in any cultural change initiative is to find ways to maintain momentum over time. As Kotter (1995) has observed, a mortal yet common sin in striving for cultural change is to assume it can be done quickly and, therefore, declare victory too early. Organizations must find ways to keep the change project going.

Taken together, the evidence presented above guided the development of the Standards of Excellence in Work/Life Integration as a strategy for catalyzing organizational change toward greater understanding and appreciation of the importance of work, family, and other personal concerns in the lives of workers. Using the Baldrige criteria as a guide and organizational learning concepts as theoretical underpinning, it was important to make ownership of the change process clear, use a structured model to make the learning more concrete, utilize measurement to facilitate the ability to see progress, and make benchmarking possible in order to accelerate progress.

To realize these lofty aims, we assembled a team of leading work/life practitioners from American corporations, leading academics in the field of work-family research, organizational development experts, and Boston College Center for Work and Family staff to develop the Standards of Excellence criteria. Seven elements were identified: leadership, strategy, infrastructure, accountability, relationships, communication, and measurement, all of which will be described in more detail below. Then, over the course of 2 years, a smaller group representing the experts mentioned above developed concrete indicators of each element. This aspect of the project was designated the Standards of Excellence Index (SEI), a measure that makes it possible for an organization to conduct a comprehensive assessment of its work/life culture. In short, the SEI is a measure of the extent to which an organization realizes the Standards of Excellence criteria. At the outset, the entire project was designed to shape the national dialogue on work/life integration (on a macro-level) and to ensure that organizational work/life policies were being translated into action and becoming an integral part of the way that leaders manage.

THE STANDARDS OF EXCELLENCE INDEX
AS AN ASSESSMENT TOOL

As we have said, the Standards of Excellence are comprised of seven components. The seven components, their definition, and supporting logic include the following:

(1) Leadership: Organizational leaders recognize the complementary importance of work and life priorities for the success of the business, and integrate this approach to build a supportive work environment.

During a change process, as Schein (1985, 1992) has pointed out, leaders are role models for all organization members. Employees look to leaders for information, guidance, and cues regarding the changes that are occurring. It is important that leaders have a clear sense of direction regarding the pending organizational change and align their communication and behavior to be consistent with the change initiative's desired result. In times of change, leaders' behavior will be scrutinized by employees to see if they "practice what they preach." While many leaders may make different personal choices for themselves (i.e., they may work very long hours and not see this as an inherent conflict due to their strong career identity), it is important that they convey respect and support for the choices and priorities of their employees (Friedman & Lobel, 2003).

Thus, the Standards Index was designed to assess leadership, that is, the extent to which leaders understand and communicate the importance of work/life integration and create an atmosphere of support for employees' work/life choices. Using sixteen-item scale, raters are asked to assess the extent to which leaders are working to build a culture where work/life integration is valued (Table 32.1 presents all elements and items).

TABLE 32.1
Standards of Excellence Index

Leadership

1.1 Leaders are working to build a culture where work/life integration[1] is valued.

1.2 Leaders communicate the importance of work/life[2] for the organizations' to other managers and employees.

1.3 Leaders communicate the importance of work/life to other organizations by promoting its "best practices."

1.4 Leaders reward those within the organization who support work/life needs and initiatives.

1.5 Through their behaviors (e.g., role modeling, sharing their own work/life experiences, listening, showing empathy), leaders create an environment conducive to work/life integration.

1.6 Leaders support work/life strategies and programs as a means of enhancing work productivity and effectiveness.

1.7 Leaders include work/life in an organizational recruitment and retention plan.

1.8 Leaders represent diverse groups, including those from different ethnic and gender groups.

1.9 Leaders include those who work a variety of schedules.

1.10 Leaders consider employee workloads in making business decisions.

1.11 The leadership development process considers both organizational and individual needs.

1.12 Leaders trust and respect their employees as the foundation for an effective organization.

1.13 Managers[3] discuss the integration between career and life goals with employees.

1.14 Managers evaluate employee performance on results, regardless of work schedule or work location (e.g., telecommuting).

1.15 Managers are empowered to use work/life policies and programs to meet both organizational and individual needs.

1.16 Managers are rewarded for using work/life policies and programs to meet both.

Strategy

2.1 The organization has a separate work/life vision and mission.

2.2 The organization has a separate work/life strategic plan.

2.3 The business case for work/life is included in the organization's vision and mission.

2.4 Organization identifies important work/life issues for the business, the employees, and the communities in which it operates.

2.5 Work/life strategies are applied throughout the organization (regardless of geographic location or section of the organization, if applicable).

2.6 Organization's work/life strategy is directed at the broadest spectrum of employees possible.

2.7 Strategic plans take into account changing workforce needs (e.g., societal demographic trends, business trends, other changes).

2.8 Organization creates long-term strategies to address the work/life needs of the next generation of workers.

2.9 The organization uses its understanding of community resources to develop its own work/life benefits (e.g., day-care centers, after-school programs, etc.).

2.10 Organization uses its resources (financial, human, etc.) to have a positive impact on the communities where it is located.

2.11 The overall culture of the organization is consistent with work/life practices.

2.12 Strategies are designed to create or sustain an organizational culture that supports work/life integration.

2.13 Work/life strategy contains the elements of a good strategic plan (i.e., makes the business case, addresses potential barriers, has measurable goals, etc.).

2.14 Work/life strategies and programs are developed using appropriate data sources (e.g., employee surveys, external benchmarking, research).

Infrastructure

3.1 New work/life initiatives (programs, policies, and services) are integrated with existing programs and policies (as appropriate).

3.2 Sufficient resources are allocated to work/life programs (either budget or time or staff).

3.3 Managers receive training about work/life strategies.

3.4 Managers are trained to help employees work through work/life issues and conflicts.

3.5 Employees are educated about the availability of work/life programs and benefits.

3.6 Policies and guidelines to support work/life strategies are developed (as needed).

3.7 The organization has a set of programs and policies tailored to the needs of its employees.

3.8 The organization provides tools and opportunities (e.g., education, training, interpretation) for departments to implement work/life programs and policies.

Accountability

4.1 Leaders are held accountable for balancing business goals with work/life initiatives.

4.2 Leaders encourage employees to use a range of work/life programs, services, and policies to achieve better work/life integration and meet business goals.

(continued)

TABLE 32.1
(Continued)

4.3 Managers are held accountable for implementing work/life programs and policies (consistent with organizational goals).

4.4 Managers and employees are responsible for working together to achieve work/life integration (consistent with organizational objectives).

4.5 Employees in the organization understand that some jobs, opportunities, and assignments are less conducive to better work/life integration.

4.6 The performance management system for managers is linked to work/life efforts and effectiveness.

4.7 The informal systems at the organization support work/life integration (e.g., promotions, new opportunities, etc.).

Relationship Building

5.1 Work/life professionals work with those in other departments to integrate the work/life function into the culture of the organization.

5.2 Organization collaborates with external organizations to provide effective work/life solutions (e.g., child care, elder care, after-school programs).

5.3 Organization contributes to the work/life field through collaboration and support for professional organizations (e.g., work/life associations, research organizations, etc.).

5.4 Organization communicates the importance of employee involvement in communities.

5.5 Organization establishes programs to facilitate employee involvement in communities.

5.6 Organization works with public policymakers to strengthen policies that benefit both employers and individuals.

Communication

6.1 The business case for work/life has been clearly communicated throughout the organization.

6.2 Employees receive regular communications about work/life strategies.

6.3 Employees feel free to openly discuss work/life issues in the workplace.

6.4 Direct communication with work/life professionals is available to employees throughout the organization.

6.5 The organization shares its work/life policies, programs, and strategy with other organizations.

6.6 The organization acts as an advocate for work/life issues (e.g., serving on community boards, etc.).

6.7 The organization communicates with other practitioners through professional work/life organizations.

6.8 Managers communicate and listen to their employees regarding work/life issues.

6.9 Work/life is publicly communicated as one component of organizational identity.

Measurement

7.1 Work/life strategy has measurable goals and objectives.

7.2 The organization collects work/life information (e.g., demographics, future trends, etc.) from its employees on a regular basis.

7.3 The organization uses the information collected from its employees to plan new programs and policies.

7.4 The organization measures the work/life needs of its employees.

7.5 The organization tracks the utilization of its work/life initiatives.

7.6 The organization tracks the effectiveness of its work/life initiatives.

7.7 The organization tracks satisfaction as part of its work/life efforts.

7.8 The organization tracks information related to the workload of its employees.

7.9 The organization examines the relationship between work/life programs and outcome measures (e.g., productivity, quality of work, etc.).

7.10 Cost benefit ratios or other "return-on-investment" analyses are conducted to examine the impact of work/life programs.

7.11 Measurement data are used to identify obstacles to implementing work/life programs and policies.

7.12 Research findings are used to develop and improve work/life programs.

7.13 Regular benchmarking is conducted to compare the organization's work/life practices with other organizations.

[1] "Work/life integration" is defined as: "the complementary pursuit of work and nonwork goals and activities."

[2] "Work/life" is defined as: "Actions taken by employers and employees to help the workforce effectively handle the pressures and responsibilities of work and personal lives as a means toward, meeting the organization's business goals."

[3] The term "manager" is used throughout the Index to refer to an individual who supervises at least one other employee. In some organizations, the term "supervisor" or another term may be used for this individual.

(2) Strategy: The work/life strategic plan supports the vision, goals, and priorities of the organization and its employees.

Research has shown that managers' ability to seek, respond to, and utilize feedback is critical to strategic planning (Argyris, 1990). However, managers' perceptions of current organizational conditions can often be inaccurate. This can generate a false sense of effectiveness and/or performance within the organization and can subsequently create resistance to any organizational change among managers (Mezias & Starbuck, 2003).

A coherent framework developed from a comprehensive assessment of the organization and its environment should guide organizational strategic planning. The Excellence Index is designed to assist managers in conducting this comprehensive internal assessment by rating the existing work/life culture in their organizations. Establishing a good fit between organizational activities and both the mission and culture of the organization is also critical to the development and implementation of a strategic work/life plan. As we have seen, the same work/life integration efforts will not work for every business—there is no one right path to achieving excellence in this area (Kelly, 1999). Success in work/life integration is directly tied to the specific needs of the business and its employees.

An effective work/life strategy should make the business case for work/life integration and address potential barriers to achieving work/life integration for both the organization and its employees and identify explicit, measurable goals that stem from the vision and priorities of the organization and its employees (Bailyn et al., 1997; Kelly, 1999). Work/life strategy should be based on data gathered from an internal assessment of the organization (i.e., employees' needs, current culture, existing work/life policies, organizational structure and business challenges, and an external assessment of other organizations' best practices, community needs, and resources available). The SEI is designed to facilitate dialogue within an organization that considers the individual needs of the organization and its employees.

(3) Infrastructure: The organization actively supports work/life strategies through a systemic (proactive, integrated, and ongoing) rather than programmatic approach.

Infrastructure serves as the basic framework necessary for an organization to function. Organizations seeking to establish or to further enhance their work/life strategy must have the appropriate infrastructure in place to support the development and implementation of their efforts. Infrastructure elements need to support work/life strategies by: dedicating the necessary financial, technological, and human resources (i.e., funding, time, and staff); providing education and training opportunities; and developing and implementing congruent policies and procedures.

Without appropriate resources, even the most developed initiatives will have difficulty thriving. Infrastructure serves as the foundation for work/life integration within an organization. It includes having the tools and opportunities to provide education and training to departments and/or individuals (i.e., managers and employees) on how to implement work/life programs and policies.

(4) Accountability: Management of work and personal life effectiveness is a shared responsibility between the employer and the employee, for which both are held accountable.

If cultural change is to take place within an organization, the management of work and personal life should be a shared responsibility among managers and employees. Leaders must be able to balance business goals with the work/life needs of employees. At the same time, managers need to achieve business results while creating a "people-friendly" work environment and employees must understand their roles and responsibilities in both the implementation of work/life initiatives as well as the attainment of business success. Achieving work/life integration that fits with the culture of an organization will ultimately involve choice and compromise for both employees and employers. Here, it is also important that managerial performance assessment reflects the organizational accountability system.

(5) Relationship building: The organization promotes a culture built on relationships of respect and mutual prosperity with its employee and community partners.

Organizations skilled at relationship building promote a culture built on respect and mutual prosperity (Mirvis, Pitt-Catsouphes, Lewis, & Litchfield, 1997). They strive to obtain the confidence, support, and trust of all stakeholder groups including investors, customers, employees, and the communities in which they reside. In an effective work/life program, the employer works in concert with the employees, and the community in order to develop a comprehensive and effective support system. This three-way partnership (or relationship) is a fundamental building block of success in the work/life arena (Pitt-Catsouphes, Fassler, & Googins, 1998). No one group working in isolation can be effective without the active engagement and commitment of the others. Thus, it is critical that the organization assess and develop its competencies in relationship building and use these to outline, plan, and deploy comprehensive and effective work/life solutions. Such efforts benefit not only the employees and employers, but also foster an effective community in which the organization operates. Six items comprise this scale.

(6) Communication: The organization's work/life strategy and resources are consistently and effectively promoted in communications, both internal and external.

Communication plays a critical role in the functioning of any organization. Organizational communication conveys information and ideas through the transfer and understanding of meaning, fosters motivation among employees by clarifying job tasks and providing performance feedback, and acts as a vehicle for the emotional expression of feelings and fulfillment of social needs. At no time is organizational communication more important than during times of change (Kanter, 1983; Shiba et al., 1993; Kotter, 1995).

Although effective and genuine communication is instrumental to the success of an organization, "silence" is pervasive in organizations, as many employees feel that keeping quiet about their needs, desires, and differences is the best way to accomplish tasks and preserve relationships with others. Organizational silence can be extremely costly to both the organization and the individual as it often leads to increased negative emotions within the organization (Perlow & Williams, 2003). Such negative emotions often decrease employees' satisfaction, productivity, and commitment to the organization.

The issues surrounding work and family are an example of an organizational issue about which employees often remain silent. Worried that they will appear uncommitted or denied promotional opportunities, employees frequently hesitate to express their needs or offer suggestions that might help the organization assist them in achieving a greater balance. In this silence, anxiety and resentment can develop and negatively affect employee satisfaction, productivity, and retention. To prevent these negative repercussions, it is critical that an organization's work/life strategy and resources are well communicated and are based in a thorough understanding of employees' needs. This also drives home the point that management needs to own the process.

Although emphasis is often placed on the internal communication of work/life culture, external communication is equally important. Through external communication of work/life efforts, organizations can share best practices with one another, attract talented candidates for employment, and impact the communities where their employees live and work by influencing policymakers and civic leaders. This influence can result in local social programs and services that complement the efforts of organizations. These programs, such as after school care and elder care, may eventually reduce the demand placed on the organization to be the sole provider of employee services.

(7) Measurement: The organization strives for continuous improvement of work/life integration through ongoing measurement of its work/life strategies, including evaluation, assessment, feedback, and response.

Most organizations view measurement as the primary means of gauging the effectiveness of policies, programs, or strategies. As mentioned, what gets measured in organizations is often what receives the most attention from leaders. Likewise, in addition to the need for financial metrics, it is important to assess the overall health of an organization in terms of employee productivity, satisfaction, retention, and utilization rates of various policies and benefits. Measurement data can be used to identify areas of organizational strength and weakness as well as to benchmark the organization's practices and performance with other organizations.

The Excellence Index can facilitate effective measurement of work/life integration efforts by dividing organizational performance into discrete and observable criteria. Focusing attention on tangible metrics adds credibility to these efforts and provides organizations with a catalyst for discussion and the basis for action to create sustainable change. Measurement of work/life strategies can help to justify the expenditure of resources for related efforts, including both financial and human capital.

Since its development in 2002, the SEI has been used by 57 mostly Fortune 100 companies where two or three professionals representing work/life advocacy (predominantly members of the human resources function) within the organization were invited by senior leaders or senior HR vice presidents to rate the company in the seven elements. These have been used to build a national database of scores that can be used for comparison purposes (total $n = 113$). (In several instances, 25 to 30 professionals across the organization have used the SEI to assess differences in success in different divisions of the company; these sets of scores are not included in the national database.) As it stands, the scores from the national database can be said to be representative of mostly HR representatives from large corporate entities in the United States Even so, an organization's ratings on the SEI have been assigned by subjective raters and therefore are limited by the knowledge and experience of the raters and their sometimes differing views of the organization's strengths and weaknesses.

Each scale in the Standards Index involves rating the item on a Likert scale indicating the extent to which the indicator has been established within an organization, from 1 (*not at all*) to 5 (*a great deal*). Scores are then summed for each of the seven elements and standardized for comparison across scales of differing lengths. Thus, a score is established for how the organization is currently performing on each of the essential elements. Cronbach's alpha for reliability for six of the seven scales were highly acceptable ranging from .70 to .91.

Table 32.2 presents descriptive results from the national database as it exists today and the correlations among items. As the table shows, the scales are highly correlated with each other. This should not be surprising given the fact that all scales measure some aspect of work/life culture. We maintain, however, that they are conceptually distinct, especially given the important differences that scores on the different scales reveal.

Figure 32.1 presents average scores on the SEI by each element. There are striking similarities across organizations in terms of organizational strengths and areas that need focus and attention. As can be seen, organizations are reporting generally high scores in the elements of relationship building and communications, while ratings on issues of leadership, measurement, and accountability are quite low. These results suggest that the element of relationship building is the area where the greatest work/life progress has been made, with an average score of 60 (out of a possible 100). In general, our participating organizations exhibit a strong commitment to community involvement, establish programs to facilitate employee involvement in communities, and use their resources (financial, human, etc.) to have a positive impact on the communities where they are located. The national database organizations also demonstrate their interest in being a part of the work/life field through communicating with other practitioners and supporting professional organizations. In addition, they develop work/life programs and policies geared to the needs of employees. These include direct communication with work/life professionals and the integration of new work/life programs with existing ones

TABLE 32.2
Standards of Excellence Scales

	L	S	I	A	R.B.	C	M
Leadership (16 items) $M = 46.5$ $SD = 17.6$ $\alpha = .91$	—	.65**	.70**	.82**	.54**	.70**	.56**
Strategy (14 items) $M = 50.8$ $SD = 23.7$ $\alpha = .91$		—	.81**	.63**	.68**	.78**	.75**
Infrastructure (8 items) $M = 50.5$ $SD = 21.2$ $\alpha = .87$			—	.72**	.66**	.84**	.74**
Accountability (7 items) $M = 35.5$ $SD = 18.7$ $\alpha = .85$				—	.53**	.70**	.60**
Relationship Building (6 items) $M = 60.0$ $SD = 20.8$ $\alpha = .70$					—	.75**	.61**
Communication (9 items) $M = 54.7$ $SD = 23.4$ $\alpha = .88$						—	.69**
Measurement (13 items) $M = 40.6$ $SD = 22.5$ $\alpha = .91$							—

$**p < .01$
L = Leadership   S = Strategy   I = Infrastructure   A = Accountability
R.B. = Relationship Building   C = Communication   M = Measurement

as well as tailoring them to the needs of employees. Finally, the organizations in the national database feel positively about the way they convey respect for employees. Over two thirds of respondents felt that this was true either "quite a bit" or "a great deal." Of course, it stands to reason that a company interested in taking the risk of assessing work/life culture (volunteering to submit to this kind of scrutiny), and HR personnel in general, would have strengths that bias the sample in some ways.

Still, considerable weaknesses were reported. The element of accountability is rated lowest ($M = 28.6$) across all organizations. Spokespersons for the organizations using the SEI do not feel that senior leaders or managers are held accountable for the implementation of work/life

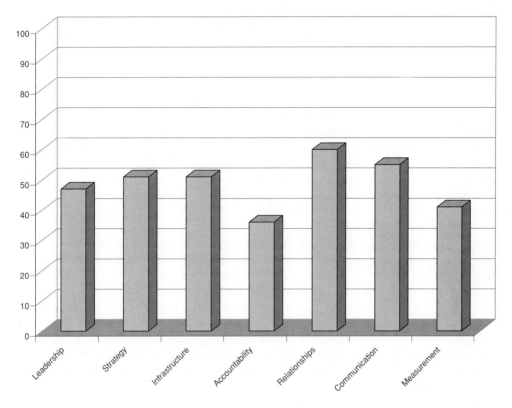

FIG. 32.1.   Average scores on the SEI by element.

initiatives or that the performance management system for managers is linked to work/life. Performance indicators that scored particularly low suggest that performance management systems for managers are not linked to work/life efforts and effectiveness, leaders are not held accountable for balancing business goals with work/life initiatives, and managers are not held accountable for implementing work/life programs and policies (consistent with organizational goals).

Results from our participating organizations also suggest that rewards for work/life are lacking in their organizations and that many measurement issues are not being addressed. Half of the lowest rated indicators for the national database organizations are in the area of measurement. These indicators suggest a failure to relate work/life with outcomes, to collect work/life information on a regular basis, or to use data in identifying obstacles to implementing work/life programs.

USEFULNESS OF THE STANDARDS OF EXCELLENCE INDEX

We must emphasize that the SEI is designed primarily as a self-assessment tool that can be useful to organizations regardless of their size or sector. Moreover, it was developed as a tool for learning and improvement, not for organizational rankings or awards systems. Indeed, benchmarking comparison scores are used in their aggregate form and convey no identifying information about the companies in the database. This means that the ultimate measure of the effectiveness of the SEI lies in its usefulness to practitioners in evaluating the state of organizational work/life efforts and in planning future interventions and initiatives. Although it was not originally intended for academic research purposes, its usefulness could only be expanded by systematic uses in noncorporate settings.

In general, company representatives can use results from the SEI to assess the current level of work/life integration for a particular subset of an organization (e.g., functional department, business unit, or geographic region) or for the organization as a whole. For purposes of conversation, and recognizing the limitations of cross-company comparisons, company representatives are usually interested in benchmarking against the national database even though there are differences in the kinds of businesses and sectors of the economy represented (pharmaceutical, high-tech, banking, insurance, automotive/transportation, and so on).

For some organizations, use of the SEI may be the first step in developing a work/life integration strategy, potentially representing a major organizational change process. For other organizations that are more advanced in their work/life initiatives, the Excellence Index can be used to gauge the effectiveness of work/life efforts in driving organizational culture. Subsequently, for these organizations modification of their current work/life integration strategy may involve more minor changes aimed at issues of sustainability or ongoing improvement.

The SEI can be used in different ways by different companies. The national database described above was created with responses from work/life directors from different companies. Other companies have conducted larger surveys of a business unit or the organization as a whole. This more comprehensive view of the current work/life culture can highlight areas of strength and weakness across units. At least three organizations have taken this approach with the instrument so far, an insufficient number for reporting results at this point. We hope, too, that some organizations will follow up with a new survey after some additional change efforts have been made to assess the impact of their efforts.

How are the results used in an organization? As one begins to develop an action plan for enhancing work/life integration, he or she may want to consider the following:

1. Who else should view these results and be involved in developing the organization's plan for work/life integration?
2. What are the organization's strengths (areas of excellence) and weaknesses (or areas of improvement) in work/life integration?
3. What areas of work/life integration are of highest priority for the organization? Where should the focus be?
4. What are the organization's objectives for work/life integration?
5. How should one start?

When used in these ways, the SEI can be a catalyst for change. As with any business activity or function, having a plan is critical. In order to develop a working hypothesis for how to make work/life an integral part of the organization, a strategic plan is key and the SEI can become a critical ingredient in the planning process. Especially if a cross-section of managers has helped to develop this snapshot of the current situation, they have provided powerful information for the purposes of planning. These same managers may also have a vested interest in becoming engaged in the planning process and their involvement can be critical to the success of the implementation.

An effective strategy also includes a vision of the future state an organization is hoping to achieve. The Standards Index helps facilitate this by laying out indicators that, in effect, describe what a world-class organization would look like in this arena. Strategic plans that are too general or too abstract are not likely to enable effective implementation. The standards provide a high degree of granularity and specificity in describing areas of focus as well as organizational strengths and weaknesses. This will allow an organization to pinpoint and plan precisely around the areas that need to be improved in the future and in what sequence. Using the SEI results in the context of a strategy formulation process will allow an organization's management team to discuss and decide what elements might be most critical to address first in order to gain the greatest leverage from their efforts.

During meetings to formulate a strategic plan and determine a course of action, the results from an SEI can provide a common vocabulary and be a useful reference document for developing a comprehensive plan that addresses an organization's priorities and areas of focus.

The Standards Project team members also developed some companion tools intended to help an organization move forward. Most notably, they developed an *E-Handbook*, an online database of company best practices, resources, and tools that have been used successfully by organizations in advancing their work-life initiatives.

DISCUSSION

The Standards of Excellence in Work/Life Integration were developed to respond to a pressing need felt by many corporate human resource practitioners. Their intent is to move the work/life dialogue away from HR policies toward measures of the degree to which the work/life has become integrated into the fabric of the organization. The question the Standards Index tries to address is, "To what degree does an organization integrate a work/life perspective in the way it manages its people?" The SEI was developed by a team of scholars and leading practitioners as a self-assessment tool to measure this cultural change. It incorporates ideas derived from both organizational change literature (i.e., what does it take to mobilize change in an organization) and organizational learning literature (what factors will help to facilitate organizational learning and lasting change?).

The index is a learning tool, not a ranking system. The intent is to help HR practitioners better understand and communicate the state of their organization's work/life culture to management and to transfer responsibility for the cultural transformation to the senior leadership team—ultimately, the only ones who can make this change a reality.

The Standards Index, which has now been used by more than 60 organizations for the purposes of calibrating their work/life efforts, has begun to surface patterns of strengths and weaknesses in this pursuit of work/life excellence. In terms of strengths, it is clear that organizations feel they are effective at communicating with employees about their programs, working in partnership with communities and external service providers, and providing policies and programs that are tailored to their employees' needs. Work/life practitioners also feel good about their willingness to share their learning and successes with others in the field. In terms of weaknesses, there seems to be a consensus that accountability, leadership, and measurement are areas that need significant focus and attention. It would seem that line managers and senior leaders have not yet stepped up to the challenge of driving a new mindset toward work/life throughout their organizations. Performance management systems do not set expectations or reward performance of managers in this area. Finally, important measures of work/life are not maintained and monitored. Specifically lacking are ones that look at the impact of management decisions on employees' workload. It is clear that among those organizations that have utilized the index, there is still much room for improvement in terms of leadership owning the cultural change process. Of course, the use of the SEI is just a first step to spur organizational change; time will tell whether such change occurs on the basis of the dialogues it inspires.

The SEI has been used primarily as a self-assessment tool, but it also offers opportunities to be used in more formal research. The SEI could provide a template and measurement instrument for any researcher interested in diagnosing, measuring, and monitoring cultural change initiatives relevant to work/life. Used in this context, much could be learned about what variables (i.e., elements or indicators) are most important in driving organizational change efforts.

While the SEI is still in the early stages of its development, it will hopefully help the field move forward and create lasting organizational change. In 2004, the Standards of Excellence in Work/Life Integration was selected by the Conference Board to receive its *Moving Into the Future Award* as a significant innovation developed by academics and practitioners to facilitate progress in the work/life field. We believe that it has potential for results in broader contexts as well.

ACKNOWLEDGMENTS

We gratefully acknowledge the following people who made a significant contribution to the Standards project and this chapter: Kathy Lynch, Standards Project Director; Leon Litchfield, the Standards of Excellence Advisory Committee; and Judi Casey and other staff members at the Boston College Center for Work & Family.

REFERENCES

Argyris, C. (1990). *Overcoming organizational defenses*. Boston: Allyn & Bacon.

Argyris, C., & Schon, D. A. (1977). *Organizational learning: A theory of action perspective*. Reading, MA: Addison-Wesley.

Argyris, C., & Schon, D. A. (1996). *Organizational learning II: Theory, method, and practice*. Reading, MA: Addison-Wesley.

Bailyn, L., Fletcher, J. K., & Kolb, D. (1997). Unexpected connections: Considering employees' personal lives can revitalize your business. *Sloan Management Review, 38*(4) 11–19.

Batt, R., & Valeur, M. (2003). Human resource practices as predictors of work-family outcomes and employee turnover. *Industrial Relations, 42*(2), 189–220.

Berg, P., Kalleberg, A. L., & Appelbaum, E. (2003). Balancing work and family: The role of high-commitment environments. *Industrial Relations, 42*(2), 168–188.

Collins, J. C., & Porras, J. I. (1994). *Built to last*. New York: Harper Collins.

Davidson, L. (1998, September). Measure what you bring to the bottom line. *Workforce*, 34–40.

Deal, T. E., & Kennedy, A. (1982). *Corporate cultures*. Reading, MA: Addison-Wesley.

DeCotiis, T. A., & Summers, T. P. (1987). A path analysis model of the antecedents and consequences of organizational commitment. *Human Relations, 40*, 445–470.

Eaton, S. (2000). Work-family integration in biotechnology: Implications for firms and employees. Unpublished doctoral dissertation, Massachusetts Institute of Technology, Cambridge, Massachusetts.

Eaton, S. (2003). If you can use them: Flexibility policies, organizational commitment, and perceived performance. *Industrial Relations, 42*(2), 145–167.

Edelman, K. A. (1996). *Building the business case for workplace flexibility*. Edited by the Conference Board. New York: the Conference Board.

Fandray, D. (2000, May). What is work/life worth? *Workforce*, 17(5), 64–71. Available online at *http://www.workforce.com/archive/article/001/11/76.xci*, accessed September 17, 2001.

Fedor, D. B., Parsons, C. K., & Shalley, C. E. (1996). Organizational comparison processes: Investigating the adoption and impact of benchmarking-related activities. *Journal of Quality Management, 1*, 161–192.

Friedman, S. D., Christensen, P., & DeGroot, J. (1998, November–December). Work and life: The end of the zero-sum game. *Harvard Business Review*, 119–129.

Friedman, S. D., & Lobel, S. (2003, August). The happy workaholics. *Academy of Management Executives, 17*(3), 87–98.

Garvin, D. (1991, November–December). How the Baldrige Award really works. *Harvard Business Review*, 80–93.

Gordon, J. (1999). Benchmarking: Striving for quality. *Metrics Manual*. Boston College Center for Work and Family.

Harrington, B. (2000). *Organizational learning: A theoretical overview and case study*. Unpublished dissertation for Boston University, Boston, Massachusetts.

Ichniowski, C., Kochan, T., Levine, D., Olson, C., & Strauss, G. (1996). What works at work: Overview and assessment. *Industrial Relations, 35*(3), 299–333.

Jacobs, J. A., & Gerson, K. (2004). *The time divide: Work, family, and gender inequality*. Cambridge, MA: Harvard University Press.

Kanter, R. M. (1983). *The change masters*. New York: Simon & Schuster.

Kaplan, R. S., & Norton, D. P. (1993, September–October). Putting the balanced scorecard to work. *Harvard Business Review*, 2–15.

Kelly, E. L. (1999). Theorizing corporate family policies: How advocates built "the business case" for "family-friendly programs." In Toby L. Parzel (Ed.), *Research in the sociology of work: Work and family* (vol. 8, pp. 169–202). Greenwich CT: JAI press.

Kotter, J. P. (1995, March–April). Leading change: Why transformation efforts fail. *Harvard Business Review*, 59–67.

Lankau, M. J., & Scandura, T. (1997). Relationships of gender, family responsibility, and flexible work hours to organizational commitment and job satisfaction. *Journal of Organizational Behavior, 83*(2), 139–149.

Lewis, S. (2001). Restructuring workplace cultures: The ultimate work-family challenge? *Women in Management Review, 16*(1), 21–29.

Lobel, S., & Faught, L. (1996). Four methods for proving value of work/life initiatives. *Compensation and Benefits Review, 28*(6), 50–57.

Martinez, M. N. (1997, June). Work-life programs reap business benefits. *Human Relations Magazine,* 110–114.

Mezias, J. M., & Starbuck, W. H. (2003). What do managers know, anyway? *Harvard Business Review, 81*(5), 16–18.

Mirvis, P., Pitt-Catsouphes, M., Lewis, S., & Lichtfield, L. (1997). Participation in change: Work-family groups in corporations. Work-Family Policy Paper Series.

Mohrman, S. A., & Mohrman, A. M. (1993). Organizational change and learning. In D. A. Nadler & M. L. Tushman (Eds.) (1989), *Organizational frame bending: Principles for managing reorientation. Academy of Management Executives, 3*(3), 194–204.

Ouchi, William G. (1981). *Theory Z*. Reading, MA: Addison-Wesley.

Perlow, L. A. (1998, June). Boundary control: The social ordering of work and family time in a high-tech corporation. *Administrative Science Quarterly, 43*(2), 328–357.

Perlow, L., & Williams, S. (2003). Is silence killing your company? *Harvard Business Review, 81*(5), 52–59.

Peters, T., & Waterman, R. H. Jr. (1982). *In search of excellence: Lessons from America's best run companies*. New York: Harper & Row.

Pitt-Catsouphes, M., Fassler, I., & Googins, B. (1997). Enhancing strategic value: Becoming a company of choice. Work-Family Policy Paper Series.

Pitt-Catsouphes, M., Fassler, I., & Googins, B. (1998). The web of stakeholder group relationships: Enhancing strategic value. Work-family Policy Paper Series.

Rucci, A. J., Kirn, S. P., & Quinn, R. T. (1998, January–February). The employee–customer–profit chain at Sears. *Harvard Business Review, 76*(1), 82–97.

Scheibl, F., & Dex, S. (1999). Business performance and family-friendly policies. *Journal of General Management, 24*(4), 22–37.

Schein, E. H. (1985). *Organizational culture and leadership*. San Francisco: Jossey-Bass.

Schein, E. H. (1992). *Organizational culture and leadership* (2nd ed.). San Francisco: Jossey-Bass.

Schein, E. H. (1993, August). On dialogue, culture and organizational learning. *Organizational Dynamics*, 40–51.

Schein, E. H. (1999). *The corporate culture survival guide*. San Francisco: Jossey-Bass.

Senge, P. M. (1990). *The fifth discipline*. New York: Doubleday.

Shiba, S., Graham, A., & Walden, D. (1993). *A new American TQM: Four practical revolutions in management*. Portland, OR: Productivity Press.

Stoughton, S. (2001, December 23). Southwest Airlines finds a patch of blue in troubled skies. *The Boston Globe,* pp. E1, E5.

33

The Arbitration of Work and Family Conflicts

Benjamin W. Wolkinson
Russell Ormiston
Michigan State University

As of March 2002, the American workforce included 49.9 million employees with children under the age of 18 (BLS, 2002). Considering the growing percentage of two-wage earner and single-parent families, it is apparent that the employment obligations of millions of workers must be balanced against their family responsibilities. In many cases, employees will be able to successfully harmonize and satisfy these competing constraints. Yet in other situations, workers may be confronted with circumstances where they must choose between two difficult options: subordinating the welfare of their family to that of the workplace or conversely the interests of the workplace to that of their family. At the same time, employers are placed in the precarious position of responding to employee requests for the accommodation of family needs while maintaining workplace efficiency. Within the framework of grievance arbitration, these issues materialize where firms discipline employees who have refused management directives in order to address and respond to family obligations.

To illustrate, consider a situation where a single mother awakens to find that her 6-year-old son has developed a fever, thus preventing him from attending school that day. The mother is currently one point away from discipline on the basis of her employer's attendance policy. Unable to find a babysitter on short notice, she is faced with a "Hobson's choice": Does she stay home and take care of her ill child and risk discipline, or abandon her child and keep her job? Alternatively, assume a father is responsible for picking up his 7-year-old daughter from school following the completion of his regular work day. Ten minutes prior to the end of his shift, the foreman tells the employee that he is being forced to work overtime. Unable to locate an alternate means of transportation for his daughter, the employee fails to work overtime in order to pick her up. The employee is then suspended for refusing to work overtime. Should the employee have done anything differently? Or, should the employer have taken his family concerns into account when disciplining the worker?

To alleviate this work-family burden of many employees, the Family and Medical Leave Act (FMLA) was enacted in 1993 to provide employees with unpaid leave for child-care issues involving births, adoptions, and serious health conditions. As a result, employees unfairly denied leave or disciplined for being absent from work for such purposes may sue for relief.

Yet despite the FMLA, many employees with pressing child-care needs may remain outside the scope of the Act's protection. For example, some employees may lack the employment hours to qualify, others may need leave to provide care for a child's illness that does not meet the "serious" health condition definition under FMLA regulations, while still other employees may be covered but find themselves unprotected by the statute because of their failure to invoke coverage. As a result, conflicts between workers and management in unionized settings over efforts to balance work-family obligations will often result in arbitrators having to determine whether the employer had proper or just cause to discipline employees for refusing management directives because of child-care obligations or whether the employer should have accommodated its employees in these situations.

Our examination is confined to reviewing how arbitrators in unionized settings adjudicate cases involving the discipline of employees who failed to report to work, were tardy, refused to work overtime, or left work early because of child-care concerns. Our work is based on all such discipline cases published by both the Bureau of National Affairs and the Commerce Clearing House between 1985 and 2004 in which concepts of just cause serve as the basis of the arbitrator's decision. Through this analysis, we can ascertain how arbitrators seek to reconcile the competing demands of work and family confronting the American worker.

To provide the reader with an institutional context within which these issues are determined, we commence this discussion with an examination of the settings in which arbitrators intervene. We then examine the role of arbitration in resolving labor–management disputes, how arbitrators are selected, sources of arbitral authority, and the criteria by which arbitrators determine whether there is just cause for discipline. This institutional overview concludes with a review of prior studies related to the arbitration of work-family conflicts.

SETTINGS IN WHICH ARBITRATORS INTERVENE

The influence of organized labor on the conditions of employment within American society has undoubtedly declined, as the unionized portion of wage and salary workers in private nonagricultural industries has declined from a high of 35% in 1955 to the current level of less than 9% (Carrell & Heavrin, 2004, p. 53; Hirsch & McPherson, 2004). Nevertheless, labor unions still vitally affect the working conditions of millions of workers, as over 17 million workers were covered by collective bargaining agreements in 2003. Studies conducted by the U.S. Bureau of Labor Statistics and the Bureau of National Affairs have indicated that at least 95% of such agreements provide for binding arbitration as the final step in the adjudication of grievances that arise over their interpretation and administration (Rubin, 2003, p. 10; BNA, 1995, p. 33).

In their role as collective bargaining representatives, unions are strategically based to address the child-care needs of their members. A 1998 study found that approximately 1.6 million unionized employees were contractually provided with some type of child-care benefits (Grundy, Bell, & Firestein, 1999, p. 11). These included receipt of funds for child care, child-care referral centers, onsite and near-site care centers, and extended child-care and emergency leave. Some unions have been particularly successful in negotiating these benefits. An AFSCME survey found that 648,000 of its members were eligible for some form of child-care benefits. Similarly, contracts between the United Auto Workers and the big three automotive companies (Ford, General Motors, and Daimler Chrysler) covering approximately 400,000 workers contain extensive child-care provisions.

At the same time, most agreements do not explicitly provide for child-care or family leave. More typically, contracts will provide for a leave of absence for good or sufficient reason subject to the approval of the employer, with such provisions found in 76% of contracts surveyed (BNA, 1995, p. 71). In the absence of specifically negotiated child-care or family leave provisions, the effort of the employees to take off from work because of child-care concerns may be challenged by management, who may discipline workers for absenting themselves from the workplace regardless of the reasons triggering the absence. Where unionized workers take advantage of their contractual right to grieve allegedly unjust discipline through the grievance arbitration process, arbitrators become the neutral intermediaries with the responsibility to adjudicate conflicts between employers and workers over family-work disputes.

It should be noted that the use of grievance arbitration to uphold a contractual right is traditionally confined to unionized settings; while arbitration processes in nonunion facilities are growing, most nonunion employees do not have access to the grievance machinery. Furthermore, where access to arbitration is granted to nonunion employees, the protection afforded workers is substantially reduced by the absence of requirements in these firms that discipline be for just cause (GAO, 1995). The potential relevance of these nonunion arbitration procedures for the resolution of work-family disputes is discussed in the concluding section of this chapter.

ROLE OF GRIEVANCE ARBITRATION

Formal grievance arbitration procedures constitute a cornerstone of the American industrial relations system and provide many critical benefits to employers, unions, and workers. Foremost, these mechanisms allow the parties to avoid conflict and economic loss by providing an orderly and rational mechanism for resolving disputes. Rather than resorting to strikes and lockouts, parties can resolve disputes through the settlement of grievances or the issuance of an arbitrator's award. Additionally, arbitration affords workers due process by enabling them to challenge and obtain redress from arbitrary management treatment.

Yet the significance of this process is not limited to resolving the instant dispute. Resolution of grievances helps develop a common law of the plant. By clarifying, addressing, and resolving day-to-day issues, the parties establish guidelines and/or precedents for resolving similar and related issues in the future. The arbitration process is also favored by both parties as a less costly and more expeditious forum for dispute resolution than formal litigation in the courts involving breach of contract claims. Finally, by requiring the active engagement of and communication between union and management representatives, grievance–arbitration procedures help employers and unions to develop a better understanding of each other's problems and perspectives.

SELECTION OF ARBITRATORS

Some contracts will identify the arbitrator authorized to resolve disputes that arise during the term of the contract, whereas others identify more than one permanent arbitrator. In such cases, the parties rotate cases among the listed adjudicators. Alternatively, the contract may require the parties to select an arbitrator from a roster of arbitrators provided by the American Arbitration Association or the U.S. Federal Mediation and Conciliation Service. Additionally, some parties may directly appoint and contact an arbitrator based on his or her reputation and credentials. The majority of arbitration is performed by those engaged in this activity full-time; however, there are numerous part-time arbitrators who serve as professors of law, economics, or industrial relations.

In terms of demographics, arbitrators do not represent a diverse group, with women representing approximately 6% of the arbitrators certified by the American Arbitration Association. Similarly, a survey of members of the National Academy of Arbitrators, an organization of the most experienced arbitrators in the United States, indicates that women represent less than 10% of this body (Eddy, 2001, pp. 771, 777; Bogananno & Coleman, 1992, pp. 44–46). While most arbitrators are male, current research is divided over the impact of the arbitrator's gender on the outcome of the case (see Knight & Latreille, 2001; Bemmels, 1998a, 1998b; Scott & Shadoan, 1989; Zirkel & Breslin, 1995).

SOURCES OF AN ARBITRATOR'S AUTHORITY

The Contract

The collective bargaining agreement is the primary source of the arbitrator's authority. The typical contract will confine such authority to the resolution of grievances or disputes that arise over "the interpretation or application of the agreement" or over an alleged "violation of the agreement." The arbitrator's acceptance of the agreement as the linchpin of their juridical authority is reinforced by contractual provisions often stating that the arbitrator has no power to "add to, subtract from, or modify any provision of the agreement." The Supreme Court has similarly upheld the primacy of the contract as the source of the arbitrator's decision-making powers by specifying that an arbitrator's award is "legitimate only so long as it draws its essence from the collective bargaining agreement" (*United Steelworkers v. Enterprise Wheel Car Corp.*, 1960). Within this framework, courts have not hesitated to overturn arbitration awards that violate the clearly expressed terms of the parties' agreement (for example, see *Trailways Lines vs. Trailways Joint Council*, 1986; *Operating Engineer Local 9 vs. Shank Artukovich*, 1985; *Morgan Services vs. Amalgamated Clothing and Textile Workers Local 323*, 1984).

Past Practice

It is generally well-accepted that the parties' contract includes not only the written provisions, but also mutually acceptable practices and understandings that have been developed over the years and which have consistently been implemented and accepted by the parties (Mittenthal, 1961). If the parties have not repudiated a practice when the contract is being negotiated, it is assumed that the parties intended to continue it in force following execution of a new agreement. Significantly, the Supreme Court has suggested that as implied terms of the agreement, past practices or the industrial common law also serve as an independent source of the arbitrator's authority in defining the scope and nature of a party's contractual rights (*United Steelworkers vs. Warrior Gulf Navigation Company*, 1960).

External Law

Beginning in the 1960s, Congress expanded the role of government in regulating the employment relationship by enacting such statutes as the Civil Rights Act of 1964, the Equal Pay Act of 1963, the Occupational Safety and Health Act, and the Age Discrimination in Employment Act (ADEA). As a result, an extensive debate among arbitrators has evolved regarding the role of law in labor arbitration. In essence, the question is whether arbitrators should apply external law in adjudicating the contractual rights of parties. Over the last several decades, arbitrators have not followed a uniform approach in resolving this matter.

Some arbitrators have endorsed the position of the late and well-respected arbitrator Robert Howlett that "every agreement incorporates all applicable law," and that arbitrators "should render decisions based on contract language and the law" (Howlett, 1967, pp. 67, 83, 85). Underlying this principle is the notion that the parties to a labor agreement cannot be presumed to intend that any of its provisions shall be contrary to law.

Other arbitrators have followed the approach advocated by Bernard Meltzer that arbitrators "are proctors of the agreement and not of the statutes," and therefore "they should respect the agreement and ignore the law" (Meltzer, pp. 16, 19, 1967). Under this view, decisions regarding violations of external law that are outside of the contract should be left in the hands of other tribunals, such as the Equal Employment Opportunity Commission. Accordingly, arbitrators should limit their role to determining whether or not a specific provision of the contract has been breached.

At the same time, there appears to be increased recognition by both schools of thought that where the contract incorporates the law either explicitly or implicitly, the arbitrator may have authority to apply the law. For example, the presence of a contractual provision prohibiting the parties from discriminating on the basis of race, religion, sex, national origin, or handicapped status implicitly affords the arbitrator the authority to rely on Title VII of the Civil Rights Act of 1964 or the Americans with Disabilities Act (ADA) in determining whether a worker's rights have been violated. Similarly, contractual reference to, or incorporation of, the FMLA will afford the arbitrator a basis to utilize FMLA law in determining whether the discipline of workers for taking leave because of child-care concerns was just or proper.

THE APPLICATION OF JUST CAUSE CRITERIA

Nearly all collective bargaining agreements contain a provision that the "employer has the right to discipline employees for just cause." When an employee files a grievance after having have been disciplined for failure to report to work, tardiness, refusal to work overtime, or leaving work because of family constraints, the issue before the arbitrator is whether the employer had just cause to impose discipline. No single formulation of just cause has received universal acceptance; yet for many arbitrators it remains an effort to determine whether the discipline is fair and just under all relevant circumstances. Arbitrator Harry Platt's statement is fairly typical of this approach:

> It is ordinarily the function of an arbitrator in interpreting a contract provision which requires "sufficient cause" as a condition precedent to discharge not only to determine whether the employee involved is guilty of wrongdoing and, if so, to confirm the employer's right to discipline where its exercise is essential to the objective of efficiency, but also [to] safeguard the interests of the discharged employee by making reasonably sure that the causes of discharge were just and equitable and as such discharge would appeal to reasonable and fair-minded persons as warranting discharge. To be sure, no standards exist to aid an arbitrator in finding a conclusive answer to such a question and, therefore, perhaps the best we can do is to decide what reasonable men, mindful of the habits and customs of industrial life and other standards of justice and fair dealing prevalent in the community, ought to have done under similar circumstances and in that light to decide whether the conduct of the discharged employee was defensible and the disciplinary penalty just. (Riley Stoker Corp., 1947, p. 767)

The obligation to view just cause within the framework of what "reasonable men . . . might have done under similar circumstances" arguably sets into motion a juridical inquiry as to whether employees responding to family constraints are only responding in a manner that would have been followed by most responsible parents. Therefore, child-care constraints should arguably operate as a mitigating factor in determining the propriety of any discipline assessed against a worker for rejecting management work directives in such situations. On the other hand, the notion that the employer may exercise authority to promote efficiency may call for limitations on employee absences regardless of the circumstances. How arbitrators identify and weigh these conflicting concerns may also determine arbitral outcomes. To address this consideration, we will examine the effect of the following situational factors on the arbitrator's determination whether or not to uphold discipline where employees were absent from work because of child-care concerns: (a) the duty of employers and employees to act responsibly, (b) an employee's overall attendance and work record, (c) emergency medical situations, and (d) the operational needs of the employer.

Additionally, it is well-established that past practice, or what the Supreme Court has identified as "common law of the shop" (*United Steelworkers vs. Warrior Gulf Navigation Company*, 1960), is not only a benchmark for determining rights and obligations, but also an indispensable component of just cause. This adjudicatory criterion most often comes into play when there are concerns over disparate treatment, specifically when one particular employee has been treated more harshly than others for the same conduct. For this reason, we will examine whether arbitrators might eliminate or reduce discipline because it conflicts with disciplinary practices an employer has previously adopted. Conversely, we will also determine whether arbitrators uphold discipline because of a prevailing company practice not to accommodate employees unable to work because of their child-care responsibilities.

Standards of just cause also have been held to require employers to afford due process to employees subject to discipline (Brand, 1998, pp. 37–43). This responsibility entails providing employees an opportunity to explain their behavior, conducting a thorough and objective examination, and giving employees notice of company rules and policies, the violation of which may lead to discipline. The effect of an employer's breach of these due process requirements on discipline imposed on employees absent from work because of child-care responsibilities will consequently be noted.

At the same, time, it is generally well-accepted that the arbitrator's own notions of just cause must be set aside if the parties have negotiated their own standards governing a particular situation. Underlying this recognition is the understanding that the arbitrator's role is to interpret the agreement and not to legislate new terms and conditions of employment. This doctrine is clearly represented in the following award by arbitrator Jonathan Dworkin:

> It is broadly recognized that contractual disciplinary rules, coupled with stated penalties, usually override broader just cause requirements. This is an entirely proper way for arbitrators to interpret contracts. Just cause is an amorphous term which lacks a concrete definition. When its principles control the outcome of the dispute, an arbitrator is invested with broader authority—much broader than in any other kind of "rights" grievance. Rulings on just cause cases routinely call for the application of an arbitrator's concepts of fairness, justice, and equity. By negotiating rules and penalties, parties express their intent to circumscribe arbitral authority. In effect, their agreement to find what is just cause for disciplining a breach of employment responsibilities and narrows the issue. It does away with the more speculative decision making implicitly licensed by the just cause standard. (*Northern Ohio Red Cross Blood Services*, 1988, p. 397)

Given the arbitrator's traditional deferral to considerations of contract language, we will examine the effect of this factor on the arbitrator's determination of just cause where employees refuse work directives because of child-care concerns. Finally, as noted earlier, statutory considerations may influence the arbitrator's determination whether or not an employee's contractual rights have been violated. A worker's right to leave is now governed statutorily by the FMLA. Where the grievant has asserted not only a violation of contractual rights but of the FMLA as well, we will examine the reliance of arbitrators on the FMLA in determining whether the employer had just cause to discipline employees who absented themselves from work because of their need to care for their children.

PRIOR RESEARCH

Prior research addressing the arbitral determination of work-family conflicts is scant and dated. Two earlier studies were conducted by Glass (1991) and Marmo (1991). Glass noted the effects of an employee's record, seniority, and knowledge of company rules and practices on the discipline of workers absent from work because of work-family conflicts. Where these factors prove relevant, they will be incorporated into our analysis of arbitral outcomes. Additionally, this chapter builds on Glass' work by considering such important factors as contract language, past practice, the FMLA, and a more comprehensive range of extenuating or aggravating circumstances surrounding an employee's absenteeism.

The bulk of Marmo's examination centers around work-family conflicts that are nondisciplinary in nature and thus outside the intended scope of this chapter. These include the right of employees to obtain shift reassignments and paid personal and unpaid leave to care for family members or attend funerals. Only a small number of cases dealt with the discipline of employees who refused to work overtime or report to work because of child-care responsibilities. Like Glass, his study is limited by its failure to identify the database supporting the conclusions drawn. At the same time, his work is useful in identifying the critical roles that contract language and past practice play in arbitral determinations.

What distinguishes the current review is its reliance on a more complete set of factors to identify the basis underlying arbitral determinations of work-family conflicts that precipitated employee discipline. By utilizing all arbitration awards reported over the last 20 years, the case data will establish a more reliable basis to identify prevailing trends in the development of arbitration thought and practice in regards to work-family conflict involving child-care concerns.

ARBITRATION CASES INVOLVING CHILD-CARE CONCERNS

Contract Language

Arbitrators afford critical weight to specific contract language when addressing work-family conflict situations and determining whether some accommodation is required. *Iron Workers Local 473* (1999) is illustrative. Here an employee had previously been reprimanded and suspended as a result of her poor attendance record. One evening, her 3-year-old child was taken to the emergency room, diagnosed with gastroenteritis, and sent home in her mother's care. Despite being on the brink of discharge under the company's no-fault work policy work, the grievant advised management that as a result of her child-care facility's policy not to accept a sick child, she would have to stay home. The company's human resources director subsequently denied the grievant's request for a leave of absence and terminated her for a further breach of the attendance policy.

In upholding the grievance, the arbitrator concluded that a leave of absence should have been granted in light of the contractual requirement that the company grant leaves to any employee for "reasonable cause." Finding that having a sick child was indeed a reasonable basis for a leave, the arbitrator ruled that the absence should not have counted against the no-fault attendance policy and ordered the grievant to be reinstated with back pay. Additionally, in determining whether a leave to provide care for a sick child was reasonable, the arbitrator rejected the notion that coverage of the illness under the FMLA was a qualifying criterion. Rather, the arbitrator found controlling the consideration that a child was ill and that no one but the employee was available to provide needed care.

At the same time, a contractual right to receive a leave of absence when "reasonable cause" is present may not afford an employee with child-care problems the right to have leave of indefinite duration, particularly where the collective bargaining agreement also affords the company the discretion to set limits on the amount of leave extended. In *Witte Hardware Corporation* (1990), an employee had been given 50 days of leave over a 2-year period, the maximum amount of unpaid leave the company traditionally extended to employees, to visit her son at the hospital and convalescent center where he was recovering from a serious motorcycle accident. When the employee was unable to provide the company with a definite date for returning to work, the company refused to grant her additional leave and terminated her.

The arbitrator noted that the employee did have reasonable cause to request a leave—the continuing need to assist her son in his recuperation. Yet he also indicated that the contract afforded the company the authority to terminate employees "for absences in excess of leave of absence without reasonable cause acceptable to the company." Ruling that this provision reserved to the company the right to designate the "acceptable" duration of a leave of absence, the arbitrator found that the company was not required to deviate from its existing policy of limiting leaves to not more than 50 days over a 2-year period, especially when the leave sought by the employee was for an indefinite duration.

In some cases, an employee's failure to satisfy contractual mandates relating to the extension of leave for child care will result in the denial of such leave and the employee's subsequent discipline. In *City of Columbus* (1990), the grievant was suspended for 20 days for refusing an overtime assignment in order to pick up his first-grade son from school. While the contract between the city and the union allowed for an employee to be excused from overtime "when a valid reasonable request is made by an employee," the employee never articulated his reasons for refusing overtime or requested to be excused from the overtime assignment before punching out for the day. Given these omissions, the arbitrator sustained the discipline. At the same time, the arbitrator noted that because another employee had been excused from mandatory overtime on that same day to pick up his wife, the grievant's excuse of having to pick up his young son from school would likely have been considered a reasonable excuse under the parties' contract.

Past Practice

Discipline that conflicts with standards and norms enforced by the company in similar situations is typically overturned. In *Jones Operation & Maintenance Co.* (1989), an employee returning from maternity leave was directed to work from 7:30 A.M. until 4:00 P.M. However, the employee advised management that this schedule prevented her from finding a suitable child-care center at which she could drop off her infant child prior to her shift. Although the employer had previously altered the grievant's schedule to facilitate her use of child-care facilities and had accommodated other employees' schedules for the same reason, it denied the employee's request for a schedule change. The company then terminated the employee following her failure to return to work after her leave date had passed.

Reversing the discharge, the arbitrator indicated that the grievant's need for a schedule change was "real" and "important." He also noted that accommodation of employees in such situations had been routine and that the employer could have easily accommodated her as well. Under these circumstances, he found the company's rejection of her request for a schedule change and her termination both puzzling and in breach of just cause.

In *V.A. Medical Center* (1992), the hospital suspended a nursing assistant for failure to report to the midnight shift following its denial of her request to take unpaid leave to care for her granddaughter, for whom she had recently been granted custody. Finding that the employer had granted child-care leave to other employees, the arbitrator found its suspension of the grievant discriminatory. Additionally, while noting that the grievant was not entitled to an indefinite excuse from working midnights, she was entitled to "some latitude" in seeking to deal with this problem before being considered AWOL. Similarly, in *Menasha Corporation* (1987), the arbitrator voided the dismissal of an employee, absent for a week because of severe family problems, because of the company's failure to discipline employees who previously had accumulated 10 absences within a year.

An established practice to leniently treat absences due to legitimate family problems and illness may be used to reduce the discipline of employees with exceptionally poor attendance records. In *Darling Store Fixtures* (1997), a 7-year employee maintained a 19% absence rate in the 12 months leading up to her discharge. The grievant's final absence was due to irritable bowel syndrome, which later resulted in a complete hysterectomy. Under the company's attendance and progressive disciplinary policies, the grievant was reprimanded and then issued a 5-day suspension, at which time her entire attendance record was reviewed. Following this review, she was terminated.

The arbitrator sympathized with the company's concern over the employee's poor attendance, calling such employees part-time workers. At the same time, he noted management's obligation not to ignore its own practice of excusing absences caused by an employee having a sick child at home. Finding that earlier discipline had been issued following an absence triggered by the employee's need to care for a sick child, the arbitrator found her dismissal excessive and reinstated her without back pay.

At the same time, past practice may be used to defend an employer's decision to discipline. In *SOS Leveling Company, Inc.* (2000), management discharged an employee who had received progressive discipline, including two suspensions, for poor attendance. The absence that triggered his termination was caused by the employee's need to stay home with his son who had been diagnosed with strep throat, a diagnosis accompanied by a doctor's note. In denying the grievance, the arbitrator noted that attendance points and discipline were assessed in other cases involving absences caused by a sick child.

BREACH OF DUE PROCESS REQUIREMENTS

The failure to advise employees of the consequences of absenteeism, the absence of clearly communicated policies, or the failure to conduct an objective investigation may serve to mitigate or void discipline. In *Harbor Furniture Manufacturing Co.* (1985), an employee with a lengthy history of attendance problems was fired after leaving work early to pick up his daughter at school. Nevertheless, the arbitrator reduced the discharge to a written warning notice and required the employer to reimburse the employee for 85% of his back-pay losses, because management had failed to warn the employee that his continued absenteeism would be viewed as a dischargeable. In *Cutler Hammer/Eaton Corp.* (1999), an employee was dismissed for leaving the worksite without permission from the human resources department after being advised of his son's automobile accident. The arbitrator reversed the discharge and ordered the employee reinstated with full back pay, as the employee had received permission to leave the plant from his immediate supervisor and employees had never been advised that their immediate supervisors lacked the authority to excuse employees from work. Similarly, in *Jefferson Partners* (1997), an employee who refused to accept a driving assignment, because of his need to pick up his children for the holiday, was ordered reinstated with back pay because of management's failure to offer the employee an opportunity to explain his circumstances prior to its decision to dismiss him.

External Law—FMLA

Employee grievances claiming a breach of the FMLA will result in arbitrators applying statutory considerations if the agreement incorporates this statute or otherwise requires the parties to interpret the agreement within the framework of their responsibilities under state or federal law. The arbitrator's award in *Tennneco Packaging* (1999) is illustrative. Here the agreement provided that "where any provision here shall conflict with any state or federal law operative, the latter shall take precedence." Given this legal supremacy clause, the arbitrator found that whether the employer could discharge an employee for breaching the company's no-fault absenteeism policy requires consideration of the employee's rights under Wisconsin's Family and Medical Leave Act. Relying on this statute, the arbitrator ruled that the employer should have permitted the employee to substitute vacation days for unpaid leave to take care of her mentally handicapped child when the caregiver was unable to report to work. Furthermore, the arbitrator discounted the employee's failure on her return to work to present proof for the reasons for her absenteeism because of the employer's violation of Wisconsin law to post information on an employee's statutory rights and duties regarding family leave. As a result, the employee was reinstated with full back pay.

What happens when an employee's assertion of statutory protection is misplaced? In *B.F. Goodrich* (1998), the employee, in good faith, believed that her absences from work to care for her son who had mental and emotional problems was protected under the FMLA. However, the arbitrator found that the grievant's absences were not protected, as she had failed to provide any documentation that her son suffered from a serious health condition. Nevertheless, the arbitrator found that discharge was an excessive penalty given the grievant's good faith belief that her son's condition qualified her for leave under the FMLA, ordering her reinstated but without back pay.

Yet other arbitrators are inclined to uphold discipline where the evidence demonstrates that the employee's absenteeism was not protected under the FMLA. In *Budget Rent-a-Car System* (2001), the arbitrator held that the employer's adoption of the handbook referring to the FMLA afforded employees rights under this statute. Nonetheless, he upheld the dismissal of an employee for excessive absenteeism under the no-fault system because the employee was unable to demonstrate through appropriate certification that her son's illness was within the scope of the serious health condition, or even that she had taken her son to see a physician on the 3 days she was absent. Similarly, in *Darling Store Fixtures* (1997), the arbitrator, in dismissing the claim to FMLA protection, noted that the grievant had not worked an adequate number of hours to qualify for FMLA benefits. Even had she qualified, no protection was available since her son's stomach flu failed to qualify as a serious health condition.

Situational Factors

While specific contract language, external law, or past practice may often control arbitral outcomes, such juridical criteria are not always present. In their absence, arbitrators give significant weight to various mitigating or aggravating factors, including the duty of employers and employees to act responsibly, an employee's work and/or attendance record, emergency medical situations, and the operational needs of the employer.

Duty to Act Responsibly

Where an employee's child-care arrangements have fallen through, questions arise as to the nature of any evidentiary burden that might be placed on employees to demonstrate that they have exhausted all means to locate and exploit alternative arrangements. For some arbitrators, the failure to satisfy this burden will support the imposition of discipline. For example, in *U.S. Steel Corp.-Fairfield* (1990),[1] an employee's babysitter called at 10:00 P.M. the night before the grievant's shift to advise the employee that she could not provide babysitting care the next day. Without secondary arrangements, the grievant stayed home to tend to his child while his wife went to work. The arbitration panel did not find the lack of a babysitter a justifiable excuse, because of the grievant's failure to examine other options that might have facilitated his ability to work:

> Grievant did absolutely nothing to try to make other arrangements either for another babysitter or to swap shifts so that he could be at home when his wife was at work. No doubt, it is not easy at 10:00 P.M. to find another babysitter. But it is not good enough, particularly in light of his record, for Grievant to wash his hands of the entire matter by simply saying, as he in effect did, that he is too busy to exercise any responsibility for arranging child-care and that his wife's employer was stricter on absenteeism than the Company, so it was left to him to report off work. (p. 613)

A similar outcome was reached in *Southern Champion Tray Company* (1991). Here the employer had dismissed a mechanic for insubordination following his refusal to work overtime in order to pick up his son from school. Influencing the arbitrator's decision to uphold the dismissal was the grievant's failure to make alternative arrangements for his son and the evidence that had he called the school and explained the situation, a teacher would have watched his son until the employee had completed his assignment. On the other hand, the arbitrator suggested that had he requested the school's assistance and been denied, the employer would have been required to accommodate the employee:

> It does not follow that every familial problem justifies disobeying direct orders. At the very least, the employee must *try* to satisfy his or her parental obligations without interfering with the employer's business. If all attempts fail, the family must come first as most employers would readily agree. On other hand, if the employee indicates from the start that he does not intend to obey the order and makes no effort to resolve the problem short of disobedience, he may not then stand behind the shield of his family. (p. 637)

Yet other arbitrators may treat employees more sympathetically when confronted with the sudden unavailability of child-care help. In *Tenneco Packaging* (1999), an employee was advised the previous evening that her son's regular caretaker would not be available to work on Saturday due to her own child's illness. As a result, the employee did not report for a Saturday overtime shift in order to care for her physically and mentally handicapped son. Her absence placed her at the termination level under the company's no-fault attendance policy.

In reversing her dismissal and making the grievant whole, the arbitrator asserted that the employer should have exhibited greater tolerance for the long-term employee who is a single parent of a disabled and handicapped child. Additionally, he indicated that the employer should have given greater consideration to the difficulties of obtaining substitute care on a weekend and the unforeseeable unavailability of the employee's caregiver that interfered with the employee's capacity to work overtime:

> The burden of caring for such a child would obviously be the central condition of her life.... The efforts necessary to take care of a 17-year-old disabled and retarded child would be a great strain for both the care giver and the custodial parent.... When the parent is required to work on Saturday, a day not normally considered a work day, obtaining a qualified care giver can be difficult.... The six-day, ten-hour daily work week, and the unforeseeable circumstance of the care giver's child's illness all support a more flexible application of the excessive absenteeism provision of the Absenteeism policy. (pp. 716, 718)

Cumulative Attendance Record

A good attendance record or long record of service will likely contribute to an arbitrator's willingness to sympathetically consider as a mitigating factor an employee's need to provide child care. For example, in *Marion Composites* (2000), the grievant, who was described as "an excellent employee" who consistently worked overtime, told his supervisor that he would only be available to work 8 hours of the 12-hour shift because of his need to care for his children. Subsequently, after leaving early that day, the grievant was given a 3-day suspension. While faulting him for leaving work without permission, the arbitrator noted that the grievant had an excellent work record and that his absence had no negative economic impact on the company. Because the grievant was dealing with extenuating family matters, the arbitrator reduced the suspension to a written warning:

> Nowadays, employers must give some consideration to the personal problems of employees. This is not to say that they should coddle them. In today's world, working families are often under a high degree of stress, and it may not be possible for an employee to leave his or her problems "at the gate." (p. 96)

On the other hand, arbitrators frequently stress a cumulatively poor record of attendance in justifying the imposition of serious penalties for tardiness or failure to report to work, even when the latest infraction leading to discipline results from an employee's effort to care for young children. In *Library of Congress* (1990), the grievant was absent from work 60% of the available working time during her 3 years of employment and was summarily discharged. Periods of her absenteeism were primarily attributable to the employee's inability to pay for child care for her two young children. The arbitrator dismissed this factor in finding just cause for discharge:

> The issue is that Grievant's absences were not excused and Grievant was not available to perform duties for which she was hired and retained on the payroll. . . . That Grievant's absences were caused by child-care problems is most unfortunate. We have no law or regulation which requires any employer to retain an employee who is unable to work because of child-care problems involving a 2 year old. (p. 4679)

Similarly, in *Supermarket Acquisitions Corp.* (1990), the arbitrator dismissed child-care issues as a factor mitigating or exonerating an employee's poor record of tardiness. While reducing the discharge to a disciplinary suspension without back pay because of other considerations, the arbitrator noted:

> The fact that the grievant had family problems . . . cannot excuse his repeated failure to report to work on time. To successfully compete in today's economy, the employer must have a workforce comprising members who report to work regularly and on a timely basis, and who perform their jobs well. There is hardly a working individual who does not have to cope with personal problems. But, the vast bulk of them refuse to allow such problems to interfere with the performance of their basic job responsibilities, as the grievant has done here. (p. 794)

Arbitrators may be more inclined to uphold the discipline of employees confronted with child-care or family problems when these workers previously accumulated a record of absenteeism unrelated to child-care needs. In *Pacific Northwest Bell Telephone Company* (1983), the grievant was discharged for more than 20 incidents of tardiness over a 2-year period. While many of these were the result of the grievant's involvement in court proceedings to obtain custody of her daughter, the arbitrator was unsympathetic to the grievant's circumstances and denied the grievance, as her absenteeism had commenced before the onset of her child-care problems and the subsequent tardiness incidents were not all related to child-care issues.

On the other hand, evidence that an employee has resolved the child-care problem triggering attendance failures may result in the mitigation of discipline. In *Internal Revenue Service*

(1987), an employee was discharged for accumulating 14 incidents of tardiness during a 6-week period. Underlying this poor record was the employee's inability to place her non-toilet-trained children in day-care. Noting that at the time of the arbitration the grievant's children were now toilet-trained and could be placed in a day-care facility, the arbitrator concluded that the grievant deserved a last chance. He ordered her reinstated without back pay, but indicated that more than four incidents of tardiness during the next year would justify her dismissal.

Although uncommon, an arbitrator may view an employee's need to care for a permanently ill or injured child as a factor mitigating an unusually poor attendance or tardiness record. In *N.Y. Department of Correctional Services* (1987), an employee was served with a notice of intent to discharge due to excessive absenteeism, as he was absent 16% and tardy 19% of the days within a 7-and-a-half month span. However, all his absences were documented, and many of these were due to the shooting and subsequent paralysis of his stepson. This circumstance was viewed in part as a basis for reversing the dismissal:

> The second factor influencing the Arbitrator in determining the penalty is that he believes that the tragedy of (grievant's) step-son's shooting and confinement to a wheel-chair is a mitigating factor which should be considered.
>
> [Grievant], who has to live with this tragedy, will be hit with a second heavy blow if his discharge is upheld. The Arbitrator believes (grievant) should, therefore, be given one more chance to show that he can further improve his attendance record. (p. 125)

Emergency Medical Conditions

Arbitrators may view an emergency medical situation involving an employee's child as an exonerating or mitigating factor even when an employee's previous attendance record has been deficient. In *Overhead Door Co.* (1978), an employee was absent or tardy to work eight times as result of child-care needs, for which she had been given verbal and written reprimands. When she reported to work late another time after visiting her child in a hospital, she was suspended for 3 days. In reviewing the discipline, the arbitrator maintained that considerations of just cause requires evidence that the final act leading to discipline stand by itself as a justifiable basis for discipline. Finding that her child's hospitalization was a justifiable and excusable reason for her tardiness, the arbitrator overturned the discipline.

The sudden onset of medical or family emergencies has also been the basis of arbitral judgments overturning discipline of employees for leaving work early and/or refusing to work overtime. In *Cutler Hammer/Eaton Corp.* (1999), a 12-year employee had been disciplined on several occasions for excessive absenteeism under the company's no-fault absenteeism policy. Directly prior to the incident in question, the grievant knew that his next absence could lead to his termination. Although scheduled for voluntary overtime commencing at 11:00 P.M., the employee left work after being advised that he needed to pick up his son who had been in an accident and who was waiting for him at a police station. Relying in part on this emergency occurrence, the arbitrator ruled that the grievant's dismissal would produce an "unconscionable result" and ordered the grievant to be reinstated with full back pay and no loss of seniority or benefits.

Operational Needs of the Employer

In examining the legitimacy of an employee's refusal to work overtime because of child-care needs, an arbitrator may balance the employer's production constraints against the exigencies of the employee's child-care requirements. In *Ashland Oil* (1998), the employer had asked the employee to remain at work after 5:00 P.M. in order to complete a critically important scaffolding job. However, the grievant had previously arranged with his wife, who also worked, that he would pick up his preschool-aged children from day care by 5:30 P.M. When the grievant clocked out at 5:17 P.M., he was suspended for 3 days for walking off the job without permission and for not completing his assigned work.

The arbitrator found that the scaffolding work had to be completed. Moreover, he noted that the day-care facility could have continued to watch the employee's children after normal closing hours. As a result, the arbitrator ruled that the company's need for his services was greater than the employee's need to leave. At the same time, the arbitrator found present other mitigating factors. These included the availability of other employees to complete the assignment, the short notice (30 minutes) management gave to the employee of his need to work overtime, and the employee's previous commitment to pick up his children from the day-care center. Weighing these considerations, the arbitrator reduced the discipline from a 3- to a 1-day suspension.

Other arbitrators have held that while employers may require employees to work overtime unless prohibited by contract, they must exercise this right in a reasonable manner (*A.O. Smith Corp.*, 1967; *Robert Brass Manufacturer*, 1969). This limitation has been interpreted to require management to not discipline employees for refusing overtime if they have reasonable excuses. Furthermore, the need to care for young children has been viewed as a valid reason or basis for rejecting overtime. Thus, in *Keebler Co.* (2003), the arbitrator reversed the discipline of an employee who had refused to work overtime because of his need to take his young daughter to a doctor's appointment.

Arbitrators may be less sensitive to an employee's need for accommodation where an employer may be viewed as confronting serious operational constraints, particularly those experienced by public safety organizations. In *Town of Stratford* (1991), a female police officer was ordered to report to work 4 hours prior to her regularly scheduled shift in order to fulfill the daily manpower requirement. However, the grievant could not locate a babysitter for her three children for the 4-hour period required by this "order back" and, following her failure to report as ordered, she was suspended for 5 days.

The police department argued that an officer's personal and family needs are separate matters from one's work responsibilities, and that a failure to report as ordered is insubordination regardless of the underlying reason. Furthermore, the police department contended that its paramilitary nature requires that employees secure their personal affairs in order to attend to their professional responsibilities. In opposition, the union contended that the grievant's situation should have been treated as that of an officer who fails to report because of illness. In addition, the union noted that the strict adherence to paramilitary strategy without accommodation makes it more difficult for women to work in the profession.

In denying the grievance and dismissing the grievant's child-care concerns, the arbitration board emphasized the employer's operational needs and the obligation of officers in a quasi-military organization to carry out orders:

> Even more important is the structure and function of the Department itself. It has a definite military like command and function. To erode even further than has been the case to date the traditional standards of police work, to attempt to make egalitarian social experiments, unnecessarily hampers the purpose and function of these critically important organizations. (p. 514)

Arbitrators will also be sensitive to an employer's operational and production constraints when employees fail to provide adequate notice of their family or child-care needs. In *Los Angeles County Social Services Department* (1989), the employee gave her supervisor just one day notice of her desire for leave to see off her non-English-speaking mother and grandchildren who were visiting from Mexico. The employer denied her request for leave and suspended her following her failure to report to work the following day. In upholding the discipline, the arbitrator cited the employee's failure to give management more than 24 hours' notice of her need for leave despite her knowledge for at least several days of her family's impending departure. In addition, the arbitrator noted the employer's reliance on a skeletal work crew the day the grievant failed to report to work and the resulting negative effects her sudden absence had on the facility's capacity to provide food and medical care to clients.

RECONCILING WORK-FAMILY CONFLICTS: A CRITICAL OVERVIEW

Arbitrators give substantial weight to specific contract language in determining whether or not an employer had just cause to discipline employees in work-family conflict situations. Thus, where the leave is protected by the parties' agreement, an employee's discipline for absenteeism is typically reversed. Conversely, absences in conflict with contractual leave policies will render the employee vulnerable to discipline. Past practice also plays a pivotal role in arbitral outcomes, as arbitrators will usually overturn or reduce the discipline imposed on employees absent because of child-care issues where the employer has condoned or leniently treated such absences in the past. In doing so, arbitrators are upholding the just cause standard that all employees merit equal treatment. An employer's failure to satisfy procedural due process requirements will often lead to mitigation or negation of employee discipline. These rulings affording deference to contract language, past practice, and due process requirements are consistent with patterns of arbitral behavior identified by Glass and Marmo in earlier studies of work-family disputes.

Arbitrators are also more likely to uphold discipline where an employee has chronic child-care issues leading to unacceptable levels of absenteeism. In such situations, many arbitrators will uphold the employee's dismissal where the latest absence triggering the discharge has been precipitated by an employee's response to family or child-care needs. In these cases, arbitrators are applying fairly well-established principles that chronic absenteeism, regardless of the cause, may result in discharge or discipline where the absences create a serious impediment to the operation of the facility and the capacity of other employees to perform their duties and services. At the same time, even in cases involving employees with poor attendance records, some arbitrators may reduce or at times completely overturn discipline where the employee was responding to emergency medical situations involving their children. Conversely, arbitrators will view a record of good performance or long service as a mitigating factor when assessing the degree of discipline to be imposed on employees.

Where employees refuse to work overtime, arbitrators have become more sensitive to the needs of employees who respond to family and child-care needs. Many arbitrators have implicitly imposed on firms a limited duty to accommodate by recognizing that the need to care for young children may constitute a reasonable excuse for leaving work early and/or refusing an overtime assignment, especially where the work to be performed is not urgent and where other personnel may be available to complete the assignment. Through carefully balancing the needs of management and the individual worker in determining whether an employee's refusal to work overtime merits discipline, arbitrators are adopting a standard of reasonableness inherent in the principle of just cause.

In cases where employees have been late or failed to report because of child-care responsibilities, arbitrators also have shown some sensitivity to employee needs and constraints. Thus, it is not uncommon for arbitrators to view absences resulting from a child's unexpected illness or the unavailability of a babysitter as justification for a more flexible and tolerant application of an employer's absenteeism policy.

At the same time, arbitrators have imposed on employees an obligation to act responsibly when seeking time off to care for their children. Arbitrators expect employees to give supervisors sufficient notice of their request for time off or a work schedule modification when the need for accommodation is foreseeable. Additionally, some arbitrators will impose on employees the added responsibility to seek alternative child-care arrangements if their customary child-care giver becomes unavailable. Employees may also be expected to document the illness of a child when leave is sought for an extensive time period. The failure of employees to act affirmatively to harmonize their family constraints with the employer's production concerns will frequently be cited by arbitrators as a basis for supporting employer discipline.

On the other hand, for a limited number of arbitrators, an employee's child-care needs will not be accepted as a valid basis for excusing the employee's absence from work, even when the employee's overall attendance record is satisfactory. The case of *Town of Stratford* (1991) is illustrative. Here the arbitrator upheld a female police officer's suspension for refusing to return to work early, despite her inability to find someone to watch her three young children during the 4-hour period for which she had been called back to duty. In so doing, he disregarded the well-established principle that work directives may be justifiably ignored when compliance would require the employee to perform an illegal act or engage in actions that might create an imminent threat to one's health or safety. Thus, the arbitrator ignored the reality that the police officer's return to work and abandonment of her small children would have resulted in her unlawfully jeopardizing the safety of her small children. Additionally, he failed to address whether the availability of other officers to report to work early or to remain on their shifts rendered the grievant's presence at work essential. Consequently, it is difficult to harmonize this award with concepts of just cause requiring a balanced consideration of all mitigating factors.

Similarly, some arbitrators may be responsible for unreasonable or harsh outcomes when they rigidly adhere to notions of past practice. Where the employer has routinely refused to accommodate employees with compelling child-care problems, even when the neglect of their children could imperil their safety, some arbitrators will nonetheless rely on company precedent to sustain discipline. In *SOS Leveling Co.* (2000), the arbitrator sustained the discipline by referring to the company's consistent practice of assessing attendance points where the employee's absence was the result of an employee's need to provide care to a sick child, even where the child's illness was confirmed by a doctor's note. Such an approach ignores the discretionary authority arbitrators possess to rule that adherence to company precedent does not relieve management of the responsibility to demonstrate that the attendance policy is reasonable and that excessive rigidity in the application of a fault policy breaches just cause standards. (For the application of this approach, see, for example, *Greater Baltimore Medical Center*, 1993; *Webster Electric Company,* 1984; *Park Poultry*, 1978; *S&S Corp.,* 1973.)

In some cases, arbitrators may interpret the contract so narrowly as to emasculate an employee's capacity to take leave because of child-care needs. In *Margaretta School District* (2000), the arbitrator sustained the discipline of a teacher absent from work to provide care for her pregnant daughter. In so doing, the ruling failed to even consider the legitimacy of the employee's request for leave or the school district's capacity to readily replace her as mitigating factors. Instead, the arbitrator narrowly interpreted the leave of absence provision allowing for leaves for "sufficient reason" to apply only to cases of illness and disability affecting the school district's employees. With this rigidly narrow interpretation, no employee would ever have the right to take leave regardless of the emergency nature of a child's medical situation. A more reasoned approach would have involved the arbitrator's recognition that whether a "sufficient reason" for a leave exists under the agreement requires the employer to assess all relevant factors including the gravity of the child-care issue confronting the employee, the availability of alternative child-care arrangements, and the costs imposed on the organization as a result of the employee's absence.

Yet these last three decisions are not reflective of prevailing arbitral opinion. On balance, most arbitrators have made it easier for employees to harmonize their work and family responsibilities by recognizing that principles of just cause require firms to respond reasonably to an employee's needs to care for their children. At the same time, unions could do more to protect employees who must not only work but also care for their children. The incorporation of the FMLA into the agreement will serve as an independent contractual basis for asserting an employee's rights to family leave. Yet the broadest protection of employees with child-care constraints would entail union efforts to negotiate contractual provisions offering employees on- or off-site care centers to care for children who are ill or whose usual child-care arrangements are unavailable. Alternatively, unions could negotiate for the extension of family leave rights to encompass legitimate child-care situations not satisfying the threshold requirements of the FMLA. The presence of such contractual provisions combined with vigorous union pursuit of just cause claims would afford the arbitrator a stronger foundation for accommodating an employee's efforts to harmonize the competing demands of work and family.

Finally, within the past decade, nonunion employers, in large part motivated by the desire to reduce their costs in terms of time, manpower, and legal fees, have been utilizing alternative dispute resolution (ADR) mechanisms as a means by which to resolve claims of discrimination that would otherwise require litigation in court under Title VII of the Civil Rights Act of 1964, the ADEA, and the ADA. ADR methods include ombudsmen, mediation, peer panels, management reviews, and arbitration. According to the General Accounting Office (1995), approximately 10% of firms with at least 100 employee have established for their nonunion workforce some form of arbitration process to handle discrimination complaints.

Nonunion employers may also be willing to use alternative dispute procedures, including arbitration, to resolve work-family conflicts resulting in the discipline and discharge of employees that would otherwise be litigated under the FMLA. Where such arbitrations occur, employees may benefit from the cost savings and reduced litigation time inherent in arbitration. At the same time, arbitration in the nonunion sector will not likely provide workers with the same degree of protection available to unionized employees who initiate grievances pursuant to their rights under a collective bargaining agreement. Cooper, Nolan, and Mellon (2000) have concluded from their review of published employment arbitration cases in the nonunion sector that a striking proportion of them are employer victories. They note that one possible cause is a nonunion employee's lack of legal counsel in arbitration. Another factor is the more narrow grounds available to a nonunion worker to establish a claim. As noted earlier, nonunion firms rarely limit their disciplinary authority by incorporating within their personnel policies just cause disciplinary standards. Nonunion workers subject to and benefiting from just cause standards are generally limited to the public sector (Wallihan, 2003, p. 625). As a result, the test of the legitimacy of the employer's conduct in the private sector will be compliance with the law and not standards of reasonableness and fairness. The application of these jurisprudential criteria inherent in just cause standards generally protects all unionized employees in work-family disputes, including those not otherwise covered by the FMLA. This outcome represents a significant achievement of the American labor movement.

TABLE OF CASES

A.O. Smith Corp., 67 ARB 8115 (1967)
Ashland Oil, 91 LA 1101 (1998)
B.F. Goodrich, 111 LA 603 (1998)
Budget Rent-a-Car System, 115 LA 1745 (2001)
City of Columbus, 96 LA 32 (1990)
Cutler Hammer/Eaton Corp., 113 LA 409 (1999)

Darling Store Fixtures, 108 LA 183 (1997)
Greater Baltimore Medical Center, 92-2 ARB 3566 (1993)
Harbor Furniture Co., 85 LA 359, 364 (1985)
Internal Revenue Service, 89 LA 59 (1987)
Iron Workers Local 473, 99-1 ARB 5533 (1999)
Jefferson Partners, 109 LA 335 (1997)
Jones Operation & Maintenance Co., 93 LA 239 (1989)
Keebler Co., 6-2003 ARB 3481 (2003)
Library of Congress, 91-2 ARB 8337 (1990)
Los Angeles County Social Svcs. Dept., 93 LA 1079 (1989)
Margaretta School District, 114 LA 1057 (2000)
Marion Composites, 115 LA 94 (2000)
Menasha Corporation, 90 LA 427 (1987)
Morgan Services vs. Amalgamated Clothing and Textile Workers Local 323, 724 F. 2nd 1217 (6th Cir. 1984))
Northern Ohio Red Cross Blood Services, 90 LA 393 (1988)
N.Y. Dept. of Correctional Svcs., 89 LA 122 (1987)
Operating Engineer Local 9 vs. Shank Artukovich, 751 F. 2nd 364 (10 Cir. 1985)
Overhead Door Co., 70 LA 1299 (1978)
Pacific Northwest Bell Telephone Company, 81 LA 97 (1983)
Park Poultry, 71 LA 1 (1978)
Riley Stoker Corp., 7 LA 764 (1947)
Robert Brass Mfg., 53 LA 703 (1969)
S&S Corp., 62 LA 882 (1973)
S.O.S. Leveling Company, Inc., 01-1 ARB 3778 (2000)
Southern Champion Tray Company, 96 LA 633 (1991)
Supermarket Acquisitions Corp., 101 LA 792 (1993)
Tennneco Packaging, 112 LA 760 (1999)
Town of Stratford, 97 LA 513 (1991)
Trailways Lines vs. Trailways Joint Council, 807 F. 2nd 1416 (8th Cir. 1986)
United Steelworkers v. Enterprise Wheel Car Corp, 46 LRRM 2423 (1960)
United Steelworkers vs. Warrior Gulf Navigation Company, 363 U.S. 574 (1960)
U.S. Steel Corp.-Fairfield, 95 LA 610 (1990)
V.A. Medical Center, 100 LA 233 (1992)
Webster Electric Company, 83 LA 141 (1984)
Witte Hardware Corporation, 94 LA 1161 (1990)

NOTE

[1] Yet see *Overhead Door Co.* (1978), where the arbitrator accepted as justifiable an employee's failure to report to work because of a sudden unavailability of a child-care helper, although no evidence was presented that the employee sought alternative arrangements.

REFERENCES

Bemmels, B. (1988a). Gender effects in discharge arbitration. *Industrial and Labor Relations Review, 42*(1), 63–76.

Bemmels, B. (1988b). The effect of grievants' gender on arbitrators' decisions. *Industrial and Labor Relations Review, 41*(2), 251–262.

Bognanno, M., & Coleman, C. (1992). *Labor arbitration in America: The profession and practice,* New York: Praeger.

Brand, N. (Ed.) (1998). *Discipline and discharge in arbitration* (pp. 37–43). Washington, DC: Bureau of National Affairs.

Bureau of Labor Statistics (2002). Current Population Survey, March 2002.

Bureau of National Affairs (1995). *Basic patterns in union contracts.* Washington, DC: Author.

Carrell, M., & Heavrin, C. (2004). *Labor relations and collective bargaining.* Englewood Cliffs, NJ: Prentice-Hall.

Cooper, L., Nolan, D., & Mellon, R. (2000). *ADR in the workplace.* St. Paul, MN: West Group, p. 605.

Eddy, K. (2001). To every remedy a wrong: The confounding of civil liberties through mandatory arbitration clauses in employment contracts. *Hastings Law Journal, 52*, 771–793.

General Accounting Office (1995). Employment discrimination: Most private sector employers use alternative dispute resolution. (GAO/HEHS-95-150), July.

Glass, J. (1991–1992). Rethinking the work-family conflict in the labor arbitration context. *Review of Law and Social Change, 19*, 867–889.

Grundy, L., Bell, L., & Firestein, N. (1999). Labor's role in addressing the child care crisis. The Foundation for Child Development, Working Paper Series, December, p. 11.

Hirsch, B., & McPherson, D. (2004). *Union membership, density, coverage, and employment among private non agricultural workers, 1977–2003*. Retrieved May 15, 2004, from www.unionstats.com.

Howett, R. (1967). The arbitrator, the NLRB, and the courts. In Dallas L. Jones (Ed.), *The arbitrator, the NLRB, and the courts, Proceedings of the 20th Annual Meeting, National Academy of Arbitrators* (pp. 64–74). Washington, DC: BNA.

Knight, K. G., & Latreille, P. L. (2001). Gender effects in British unfair dismissal tribunal hearings. *Industrial and Labor Relations Review, 54*(4), 816–834.

Marmo, M. (1991). Work versus family obligations: An arbitral perspective. *Arbitration Journal, 46*(3), 14–28.

Meltzer, B. (1967). Ruminations about ideology, law, and labor arbitration. In Dallas L. Jones (Ed.), *The arbitrator, the NLRB, and the courts, Proceedings of the 20th Annual Meeting, National Academy of Arbitrators* (pp. 1–20). Washington, DC: BNA.

Mittenthal, R. (1961). *Past practice and the administration of collective bargaining agreements* (pp. 44–56). Proceedings of the Fourteenth Annual Meeting of the National Academy of Arbitrators, BNA.

Rubin, A. M. (Ed.). (2003). *How arbitration works*. Washington, DC: Bureau of National Affairs.

Scott, C., & Shadoan, E. (1989). The effect of gender on arbitration decisions. *Journal of Labor Research, 10*(4), 429–436.

Wallihan, J. (2003). The politics of employee discharge: Triggering, representation, and venue. *Policy Studies Journal, 31*(4), 625–642.

Zirkel, P. A., & Breslin, P. H. (1995). Correlates of grievance arbitration awards. *Journal of Collective Negotiations in the Public Sector, 24*(1), 45–53.

34

Leadership in Action: A Work and Family Agenda for the Future

Kathleen Christensen
Alfred P. Sloan Foundation

How did the "field" of work-family research develop so quickly and richly over the last 10 to 15 years? After all, it was only a little over 25 years ago that sociologist Rosabeth Moss Kanter (1977) bemoaned the scholarly separation of work and family; and as recently as 20 years ago that the average number of peer-reviewed articles produced by scholars each year on the topic of work and family totaled just 20 (Estes, 2003). As the chapters in this handbook attest, however, a vibrant work-family field now exists. Beyond a greater number of peer-reviewed articles, we have seen increasingly more conferences, conference panels, special issues of journals, and books devoted to working families and the changing workplace. What accounts for the rapid growth of this field?

The most obvious and direct answer is that the issues were "in the air," ready to be studied and that, in effect, a critical mass of scholars undertook this important work. But, there is another answer. In this chapter, I examine how strategic thinking helped to shape and develop the work-family field. Specifically, I address how the Alfred P. Sloan Foundation, a nonprofit philanthropic organization, created a vision for the field of work-family in 1994 and moved that field forward through strategic grant making and the continued reshaping of its vision according to developing research in the field. Though it may seem strange to discuss strategic thinking vis-à-vis the development of an academic field, I intend to explain how and why I think strategic thinking influenced and enabled the development of the work-family field.

Strategic thinking occurs all the time, in all sorts of endeavors. We think about it naturally in politics and in business. But it is everywhere, even in the academy. Universities study their rankings on the *U.S. News and World Report* "Lists of Best Universities and Colleges" and determine how strategically to advance. Graduate departments examine how they rank according to the National Research Council and plan steps to improve their performance. Academic departments monitor students' decisions about course offerings and establish plans of action for improving curriculums. Individual professors set out strategically to achieve the goals identified in their syllabi. As these examples illustrate, strategic thinking involves *setting goals* based on a thorough assessment of what has and has not been accomplished to date and

705

then *articulating a plan of action* that cultivates the key people and resources needed to ensure not only that the goals are achieved, but also that they are sustained.

The grant-making program that the Sloan Foundation developed was grounded in the notion that we as a society are living through a major social and economic sea change. The foundation focused on the rise of two-income and single-parent households, thus charting a dramatically new direction for scholarship. At its core, this scholarship sought to understand what was happening within American families in which all primary caretakers work and, simultaneously, what was happening within workplaces in which employees no longer have spouses at home to nurture their families or tend to the house. The foundation chose to develop this field of scholarship because we believed that our funding strategies could make a profound difference in how society would ultimately navigate the social and economic sea change that was taking place.

This chapter tells the story of how the Sloan Foundation established its vision in 1994 and created a strategy to systematically develop the field of work and family. It concludes with a discussion of the critical next steps required to ensure that the field continues its rapid growth. As mentioned, we do not usually view the development of research in strategic terms, much less step back and examine the elements of that strategy. But, in the next sections of this chapter, we will look back on how the Sloan Foundation established its vision, how it developed and pursued its strategy, and how it continues to revise and redirect its strategy as required.

I should note that strategic planning in the development of an academic field, particularly a field that may potentially have profound impacts on people's lives, is not about controlling the outcome of the data. Attempting to achieve a particular outcome would undermine the integrity of the academic enterprise. To the contrary, strategic planning in the development of an academic field is about setting the vision, creating the conditions, and providing the resources that enable creative, valid, and exciting research to flourish. Strategic planning in these cases is also about forging partnerships. In the early years of the Sloan program, the foundation primarily formed partnerships with researchers. In subsequent years, however, the partnerships have extended to include those formed between researchers and practitioners, researchers and government, foundation and media, and researchers and law.

GETTING STARTED

Looking back to the beginning of Sloan's program on work and family, I should point out that it was quite unusual that this foundation would choose to take on the issue of work and family. Founded in 1934, by then General Motors CEO, Alfred P. Sloan, Jr.,[1] the Sloan Foundation traditionally focused its grant making on issues related to science, technology, and industry. Ralph Gomory, Sloan's president, was responsible for the foundation's new direction toward issues faced by working families. He recognized that the United States was incurring a major loss of human capital. With few quality part-time career opportunities available, many highly educated and professionally trained women were leaving the labor force completely once they had children. To achieve an understanding of the implications of this situation, Dr. Gomory asked me to launch a program on part-time careers in the professions and management.

This was 1994, and at the time, I was a professor of psychology at the Graduate School and University Center of City University of New York. My research focused on the ways in which the workplace was not meeting the needs of working women, particularly those with children and those facing retirement, and how these women circumvented the rigidity of full-time careers in conventional workplaces by structuring flexible forms of work, often at great financial and career costs to themselves, by either working at home or by working contingently (Christensen, 1988a, 1988b, 1989, 1996, 1998; Christensen & Staines, 1990). Although a small cadre of dedicated scholars had begun to pursue relevant research on women, children and family, a genuine, established community of work-family scholars had not yet emerged in the early 1990s. As such, I turned not only to scholars to create my community of peers, but also to the worlds of human resources managers and nonprofits concerned with developing family-friendly workplaces.

Though I was reluctant to suspend my own research program, I recognized that Sloan was offering me a unique opportunity to build an academic field of work-family scholarship. I also recognized that a foundation, when guided by a clear vision, could make a profound difference. The Ford Foundation had had a significant impact in the 1960s when it supported the development of regional theater in the United States and again in the 1970s when it developed women's studies by funding women's studies programs at universities across the country. The Sloan Foundation had had impacts of its own, by providing support in the 1980s that developed the field of molecular evolution and in the 1990s that led to the development of computational molecular biology and bioinformatics. Indeed, if a foundation is strategic in its grant making, it has the ability to propel a field far beyond where it might otherwise have gone.

I accepted the challenge of working with Sloan to build the field of work-family research on the condition that the program would not be limited to an examination of part-time careers. Part-time careers would certainly be a part of our research program, but the research would also include an examination of several other facets that constituted the broader relationship between work and family. My first step in crafting a vision for the foundation's funding strategy involved scanning existing research to determine its strengths and weaknesses and to set the directions for the next stage.

SCANNING THE RESEARCH IN THE EARLY 1990s

During the 1980s, the language of work-family was adopted primarily by pioneering corporate and nonprofit leaders who were focused on social change; it was not a language that the academic world had yet fully embraced. Through the 1980s, a number of nonprofit organizations launched initiatives designed expressly to work with corporate human resources managers to ensure the development of policies and practices that would help employees meet their family needs (http://www.bc.edu/bc_org/avp/wfnetwork/timelines). These nonprofit organizations, and the progressive corporations with which they worked, ushered in what we have come to refer to as the work-family movement for family-friendly policies. Also, unbeknownst to many in the academic world, they produced quality research. Unfortunately, this research remains largely unknown, for two reasons: (a) much of it was conducted for firms and remains proprietary and (b) since the goal was to advance social change, not to build a scholarly field, much of the written work was never published in peer-reviewed articles. But, if we are honestly to address the emergence of an interdisciplinary academic field, we would be seriously remiss if we did not include the initiatives of these pioneering organizations and leaders.

Dedicated to the advancement of women in business, *Catalyst* established its Career and Family Center in 1980. *The Conference Board*, a business membership organization, began its Work-Family Research Council in 1983. *Work/Family Directions*, with start-up funds from IBM, in 1983 established the first information and referral service for child care. In 1983, Ellen Galinsky at Bank Street College conducted the *Corporate Work and Family Life Study*. That same year, Eleanor Guggenheim laid the groundwork for what would evolve into the *Child Care Action Campaign*. Two years later, *Working Mother Magazine* launched its first "Best Companies for Mothers" Award. In 1988, the Conference Board, AT&T, Exxon Corporation, Dupont, and IBM cosponsored the *National Research Symposium on Workplace Research and the Family* at Arden House, which drew together researchers from academia and corporations and represented one of the first, if not the first, interdisciplinary research gatherings on working families and corporate responses.

In 1989, two events occurred that gave further shape to what we began to think of as the work-family movement. Felice Schwartz, the president of *Catalyst*, published an article in the *Harvard Business Review* (1989), which the press immediately positioned as a call for two career tracks for women: a slower, and potentially marginalized, "mommy track," and a fast track for those undistracted by caregiving responsibilities. Although never having used those words herself, her views were branded as such and instigated a very public debate about how the workplace should 'accommodate' working mothers. In the same year, Dana Friedman and Ellen Galinsky cofounded *Families and Work Institute*, a New York city-based research and consulting nonprofit that, in the early days, worked closely with large firms, including Johnson & Johnson and Corning Glass, to develop programs and policies that would meet the family needs of their employees. Throughout its history, *Families and Work* has also conducted research on the changing workforce and work-life practices of firms (Bond, Thompson, Galinsky, & Prottas, 2003; Friedman & Johnson, 1997; Galinsky & Bond, 1998; Galinsky, Bond, & Friedman, 1993; Galinsky, Friedman, & Hernandez, 1991).

The following year, Brad Googins created the *Center on Work and Family* at Boston University, which was the first university-based research-oriented center. He was shortly joined by Marcie Pitt-Catsouphes, who subsequently became the director of the center, and together they shepherded its move from Boston University to Boston College. They developed the Work Family Roundtable, made up of corporate HR executives who welcomed learning about relevant academic research as they were trying to craft their policies and practices.

The examples I have provided do not begin to include the many people who were instrumental in making changes within the firms themselves. These first-generation leaders included, but certainly were not limited to, Faith Wohl from Dupont, Chris Kjeldsen and Michael Carey at Johnson & Johnson, Ted Childs at IBM, and Donna Klein, formerly of Marriott, now president of *Corporate Voices for Working Families*. I mention these leaders and their pioneering organizations and initiatives, because it would be a mistake if we examined the development of the work-family field only on the basis of academic research. Yet, parallel to these pioneering social change efforts, a vital body of scholarly research on working women, particularly working mothers, was developing throughout the 1970s and 1980s. It was this research that I also wanted to scan to determine what should be the next steps in an academic research agenda on working families.

Scholarly research through the 1980s focused almost exclusively on women and work, paralleling the issues women faced as they entered and stayed in the workplace in record numbers throughout the 1970s and 1980s. The research can be grouped into three general categories: (a) trends and consequences of women in the paid labor force, with the focus on the individual woman; (b) changes in the social structure of the family and its division of labor, as the result of the woman supplementing or supplanting her traditional homemaking role with wage-earning roles; and (c) the demand for and consequences of employer-provided child care and alternate work schedules.

Research on women and work during the 1970s tended to provide broad overviews of women in the economy (Blaxall & Reagan, 1976; Kreps, 1976; Yohalem, 1979) and often focused on working mothers (Hoffman & Nye, 1974). During the 1980s, researchers refined this general focus to emphasize two core sets of issues: maternal employment and its effects on an individual woman's psychological well-being (Barnett & Baruch, 1985; Barnett & Baruch, 1987; Gerson, 1985; Greenhaus & Beutell, 1985; Repetti, Matthews, & Waldron, 1989; Repetti & Crosby, 1984); and occupational segregation and pay equity (Reskin, 1984; Roos & Reskin, 1984). In 1986, the National Academy of Science's National Research Council's Committee on Women's Employment and Social Issues Panel published *Work and Family Policy* (Ferber et al., 1991). It called for more family-friendly benefits in the workplace, but it did not provide an analysis of the conditions for creating a field of research.

Although the language of the "dual-career family" appears to have been introduced into the research literature in the late 1960s by two British psychologists (Rapoport & Rapoport, 1969), research on what happens when both parents work did not fully materialize until the 1970s and 1980s. This research continued to focus primarily on the changes in the family brought about by maternal employment and particularly on the effects of that employment on the well-being of their children, and whether those effects varied by the sex of the child (Hoffman & Nye, 1974; Greenstein, 1993; Parcel & Menaghan, 1994). Growing attention was also directed to how the demands of the mother's paid work role spilled over into the family, and to a lesser extent how the demands of family spilled over into her work (Greenhaus & Beutell, 1985; Greenhaus, 1988; Pleck & Staines, 1980; Crouter, 1984). Finally, the research had a political subtext of achieving a more equitable division of household labor between husband and wife (Oakley, 1974; Gershuny & Robinson, 1988; Hochschild & Machung, 1989).

Much less developed was the third category of research, which dealt with how the conditions of work, including the scheduling of work, affect the well-being of families (Bohen & Viveros-Long, 1981; Staines & Pleck, 1983, 1984; Christensen, 1988a, 1989). This third area of research also examined the need for better child care, whether provided by the state or by the employer (Kamerman & Kahn, 1978). Child care in the early research typically included only infant and preschool-aged children, as adolescent care had not yet shown up on the research radar screen.

My scan of the existing scholarly research led me to several conclusions. First, the topics were heavily weighted to one gender and one stage in life—working mothers and their children, particularly those of preschool age. Second, the studies were largely discipline-bound. Although individual researchers came from a number of different disciplines, including sociology, economics, psychology, social work, human development, and organizational development, research rarely crossed disciplines. Just as importantly, few forums existed to bring scholars from different disciplines together to discuss their work. With the exception of one invitation-only meeting hosted at Drexel University in 1994, the academy organized no significant interdisciplinary research conferences on issues related to work and family during the 1970s and 1980s (Parasuraman & Greenhaus, 1997). Scholars gathered at professional meetings and presented papers at disciplinary conferences, but attendance at these forums was usually limited to members of the hosting discipline. As a result, issues related to families in the workplace did not receive the multidisciplinary consideration necessary to propel forward a new field of research. Without a multidisciplinary infrastructure in place, questions as basic as what was known and what needed further study went unanswered.

My third conclusion was that the majority of the research was mono-methodological, with each study relying on one type of methodology. Fourth, the research received strikingly little attention from the media. Even as it provided to the public a vital mirror of changing social and economic trends in American families, research examining issues facing working families generated little interest from the major print, radio, and television outlets. Only the *Wall Street Journal's* weekly "Work Family" column by Sue Schellenbarger covered these issues regularly. Lastly, I concluded that the academic work underway was not being effectively translated to business or other vital institutions, including government and law. A major disconnect existed between scholars and the vibrant nonprofit, research, and advocacy communities who were concerned with work-family issues, such as *Families and Work Institute, Catalyst,* and *New Ways to Work.*

Compounding these issues was that, while Kanter's seminal 1977 piece had raised several provocative challenges for research, few other researchers had called scholars to arms to take their research in new and necessary directions. Menaghan and Parcel (1990) were an exception to this trend, inviting scholars to examine several compelling, unstudied areas of the relationship between work and family. They called for an enhanced understanding of values and norms within working families; greater attention to the variations of work conditions in specific jobs, such as work complexity, total work hours, and scheduling of work time, and their effects on family time; and an examination of the sequencing of jobs and time out of the labor force. In a subsequent article, futurist Joseph Coates (1996) issued additional challenges, arguing that researchers needed to devote greater attention to stresses on family functions, nontraditional families, and the implications of aging for the family and work. Based on this thorough examination of existing research, I believed that Sloan was now positioned to lay out several goals and principles for further development of the field.

DEVELOPING GOALS AND PRINCIPLES FOR RESEARCH ON WORKING FAMILIES

Let me first stress that I was not interested in micromanaging and defining small details of individual research projects. I was interested in setting a strategic course of action that would make conditions ripe for the creation of a vibrant field of research, a vital community of scholars, and a culture of generativity that would outlive the support of any one funder. I decided that it was not possible to build a field around a hyphen, such as work-hyphen-family. Rather, the research would have to focus on one side of the hyphen in a way that incorporated the other. It would have to focus either on working families or on family-oriented workplaces. Because research to date had produced a body of useful information on the family, and because corporations had begun to adopt family-friendly policies without a clear understanding of what families actually needed or wanted, I believed that Sloan's first area of emphasis ought to be the family, particularly the two-earner middle-class family because the middle class was the unmarked referent group to which other classes were compared and families in that class were not being studied explicitly. The program that I developed would examine the "working family," which was a term that had neither the popularity nor the resonance that it does today.

We established three meta-principles that would guide Sloan's grant making in the area of working families. Our grants would support: (a) *multidisciplinary research* focused on relationships, not individuals, over the life course; (b) *the creation of a community* of scholars, including the next generation of scholars, who would develop this field; and (c) *the communication of scholarly findings* beyond the academy to the public, business, and government where it could be put to practical use and make a difference.

Multidisciplinary Research on Relationships Across the Life Course

As mentioned above, research in the early 1990s primarily emphasized the impacts of work on mothers and was conducted from a single discipline's point of view. When we launched Sloan's new program in 1994, I advocated a different approach, with very real consequences that I will spell out later in the chapter. First, in contrast to research to date that had emphasized the individual, I believed that the next stage of research should emphasize the relationship. In other words, research in this stage should be designed to look at the couple as a unit or the employee and employer as a unit, rather than as two individuals making separate decisions. A relational approach clearly would increase the complexity of the research design and data analyses, but it would also provide a more realistic and nuanced understanding of the lives of working families.

Second, I specified that the research should be dynamic, looking at relationships over time rather than at an isolated point in time. This research would need to define time over the course of the day, the week, the year, or the life course.

Third, I prescribed that research should be genuinely multidisciplinary, drawing from a diverse and rich number of fields, including psychology, sociology, anthropology, geography, economics, management, industrial relations, and law. While the traditional approach to multidisciplinary research involved using an a priori disciplinary lens to frame and analyze the research and to compare research findings, I believed Sloan could take interdisciplinary research to another level. By creating vehicles that would nurture and promote the development of partnerships or communities of scholars from different disciplines, Sloan could facilitate an integration of theories and methods that would begin prior even to the development of the research design.

Finally, I believed firmly in the value of using mixed methods, and I specified that an array of quantitative and qualitative methods should be integrated into each study and into each disciplinary framework.

Creating a Community of Scholars

If Sloan intended to build a community of scholars from a number of different disciplines, we would need to create the infrastructure though which scholars could come together to learn about one another and the different areas of research underway. As discussed above, the existing framework of academic conferences aligned with specific disciplines did not nurture research that cut across different disciplines. To create this infrastructure, I developed a strategy through which Sloan would fund networks that would enable scholars to get to know one another and that would provide them with the resources they needed to nurture relationships. Sloan would also fund conferences to give scholars a platform to present their work. Our efforts to create a community of scholars assumed a variety of forms, including organizing face-to-face meetings in which scholars learned of one another's work and were given access to needed research resources; providing funding for print and online journals and newsletters; and supporting the creation of a body of scholarship through books and peer-reviewed articles. In addition, I sought out ways that Sloan could train young scholars at the pre- and postdoctoral levels and position them for tenure-track position, so that they, in turn, could carry on their research and training with subsequent generations.

Communicating Scholarly Findings

Admittedly, the first priority for scholarly research is to ensure that it reaches the academic community through the peer-review process, as this functions as a quality control and certifies the intellectual integrity of the work. But, if it is to have impact beyond the academy, research on pressing social problems must reach beyond the academic community to the general public and influential members of business, government, and other critical sectors; and I believed that Sloan had a responsibility to ensure that the research we funded reached these audiences. To accomplish this goal, Sloan would have to create avenues to ensure that information about the issues facing today's working families would be covered by the media. Over the years, we have achieved this goal in different ways, which we will discuss in greater detail throughout the course of this chapter. At the beginning, we created a receptive context for issues facing working families by funding media coverage of the research. In more recent years, based on the research findings showing a strong need for more flexibility, we launched a national campaign for workplace flexibility.

Based on these three meta-principles (multidisciplinary research, creating a community of scholars, and communicating scholarly findings), Sloan began to fund research in earnest in 1994.

A word about the organization of the chapter: Though I have divided the sections roughly by time, into early years, middle years, recent years, and looking forward, it is important to note that the issues of one time period typically carried over into another, and that issues emphasized in a later time were often presaged by grants in the early one. As a result, the time frames are somewhat artificial in terms of how the thinking and strategy in fact developed.

EARLY YEARS 1994–1999: BASIC RESEARCH
ON WORKING FAMILIES

To achieve *multidisciplinary research* in those early years required its own strategy and to that end, Sloan pursued three distinct tactics, some of which proved more fruitful than others. Our first tactic was to fund separate, stand-alone projects, led by top scholars in each discipline and then to fund meetings where the scholars would share their results with one another. Our second tactic was to fund a network to convene meetings to bring together scholars from disciplines who had not worked together with the intent of spawning interdisciplinary research partnerships. Our third tactic was to fund projects or centers that delegated to a lead scholar responsibility to assemble a community of multidisciplinary scholars. Although each achieved differing degrees of success, the last model yielded the most long-lasting interdisciplinary partnerships because it required the greatest level of commitment over time on the part of the researchers. Let me explain how we arrived at our ultimate approach to multidisciplinary research.

From 1994 to 1996, the Foundation supported 10 separate projects to study one general topic—part-time careers in professions and in management. Each project designed its own study that focused on one profession or on management. Some projects were led by an interdisciplinary team, and others by a same-discipline team. For example, an economist and a psychologist led the study on part-time careers in accounting; a psychologist and a social worker codirected the study on physician couples in which one partner worked part-time. On the same-discipline side, two sociologists directed a study of part-time careers in law (Epstein & Seron et al., 1998); two psychologists, one social psychologist and one in human development, examined part-time careers in management (MacDermid et al., 2001); and two sociologists focused on part-time careers in computer programming and technical writing (Meiksins & Whalley, 2002).

In addition, Sloan made several grants to researchers working on analytic overviews. In one such study, a labor economist examined how the organizational structure and sector of the workplace affected the success of part-time careers, revealing quite strikingly that organizational structure mattered. It was much more difficult to achieve a successful part-time career in a partnership firm, which billed by the hour, than it was in government or corporate settings, which paid on salary. In another study, a different labor economist analyzed which part-time careers provided the best compensation packages. In this approach, we intended for the multidisciplinary dimension to be incorporated at the end of the projects, when the principal investigators shared their findings. Unfortunately, by the end of the projects, the investigators were so wedded to their single-discipline framework that they could not speak easily with one another across disciplines. Although it was valuable to fund examinations of the same topic—part-time careers—by different disciplinary experts and to bring them together to share their findings, we discovered that this tactic provided too few incentives for scholars to cross disciplinary bounds and was not the most effective way to spawn interdisciplinary research.

Sloan's second model involved bringing an interdisciplinary team together to form relationships with one another and then providing the team with seed grants to develop projects together. In 1995, I asked three scholars—labor economist Eileen Appelbaum, industrial relations scholar Rose Batt, and social worker Brad Googins—to build a multidisciplinary team of researchers. With funding from the Sloan Foundation, these scholars formed the "Network on Work Restructuring and Work/Family Research," a face-to-face network of 29 labor economists and social scientists. The express goal of the network was to examine "how work organization and human resource practices can be restructured to improve firm performance and employee well being," and these scholars' work with one another represents the first time that economists teamed with sociologists and psychologists to do research on work and family issues.

The network's meetings yielded results that were at times fascinating and at other times frustrating. On the positive side, several economists, including Appelbaum and Robert Drago, who today are known for their research on work-family issues, engaged these issues for the first time through the network. In addition, a few very fruitful partnerships developed out of the network's seed grants. Perhaps the most notable involved Drago's 1996 partnership with psychologist Robert Caplan on an examination of the work-family demands on elementary school teachers. When an interdisciplinary partnership such as Drago's and Caplan's blossomed, we saw how different theories and methods yielded a study that was tremendously more complex and nuanced than anything either discipline could have achieved on its own.

More commonly however, the meetings were not so productive and usually consisted of people sitting for hours talking at or past each other. At their worst, the meetings actually impeded progress toward interdisciplinary research, with participants showing limited respect for different points of view, as happened in the first network meeting. As a result, despite one or two interdisciplinary partnerships, I concluded that forced marriages of disciplines yielded few fruits.

The third model for achieving a multidisciplinary approach—establishing the Sloan Centers on Working Families—proved ultimately to be the most successful. I developed the concept of the Centers on Working Families in 1995 because I felt that a center could achieve several of our goals simultaneously. Indeed, it could promote multidisciplinary research, focus on relationships within the family and between the family and workplace, create a micro-community within each center and a larger community across centers, and provide the means for training the next generation of scholars. My plan was that each center would be geographically based at a major research university, and that each would be directed by a leading scholar, who in turn would be responsible for drawing core faculty from diverse fields. The primary goals of the center would be twofold: to create the next generation of scholarship and the next generation of scholars.

The foundation decided that the centers should not be formulaic. Instead, each center would be directed by a leader in his or her respective field whose responsibility it would be to assemble an interdisciplinary community of scholars who would develop research that built on the collective intellectual strength of the center's members. As a result, each center developed its own distinctive approach to the study of middle-class working families. Since 1996, six Sloan Centers have been established: the *Employment and Family Careers Institute* at Cornell University; *the Center on Parents, Children, and Work* at the University of Chicago; *Center on Working Families* at the University of California, Berkeley; *The Center on the Ethnography of Everyday Life* (CEEL) at University of Michigan; *The Center on Myth and Ritual in American Life* (MARIAL) at Emory University; and the *Center on the Ethnography of Everyday Life of Families* (CELF) at the University of California, Los Angeles.

The foundation chose sociologists to lead the first three centers, but felt that American scholarship would also benefit from engaging anthropologists in the study of mainstream U.S. culture. However, finding American anthropologists who were willing to study mainstream domestic culture was no easy task. I brought the National Science Foundation on board as a cosponsor, and together we funded the American Anthropological Association to convene a series of meetings and publish essays in their newsletter about the role that anthropology could play in studies of mainstream U.S. culture. But, their tradition did not easily legitimize this direction. Sufficiently stymied in my effort to draw American anthropologists to this study, I traveled to Norway in the mid-1990s to try to find a leading Norwegian anthropologist who would come to the United States and study American working families. Eventually however, interest in U.S. mainstream culture took enough hold in the anthropological community that the foundation was able to establish three Centers on Working Families led by world-recognized anthropologists.

As anticipated, each center created its own internal community that was a distinct interdisciplinary community unto itself, and was also part of the larger interdisciplinary community formed by the Centers collectively. Today, this larger community meets annually at a centers' conference, which is hosted by one of the centers on a rotating basis. To illustrate how the Centers have operated, I would like to describe the Cornell *Careers Institute*.

Established in 1996 and directed by Phyllis Moen, the *Careers Institute* drew its faculty from the fields of sociology, geography, urban planning, psychology, home economics, and industrial and labor relations. Working collaborative, Institute faculty members and postdoctoral students developed a research design and survey instruments for a regional sample of married couples in upstate New York. The Institute collected data on nearly 5,000 working adults, 4,000 of whom were in dual-earner marriages.

The Institute's studies yielded a detailed understanding of how *couples* make decisions *over time* about work and retirement, particularly when they are between the ages of 50 and 72, a period often referred to as "late midlife." What Moen and her team found is that the timing of retirement is influenced, in part, by responsibilities for caregiving. Their findings showed that if one member of a couple becomes ill or disabled, a wife with caretaking responsibilities is more likely than a husband with caretaking responsibilities to retire earlier than expected. A husband who is in the position of caring for his wife will be more likely to continue working and to pay for help for his wife. Because he is, on average, likely to earn more than his working wife, his reluctance to retire seems much more tied to financial reasons than to a desire to escape family life. The Institute's focus on the health and well-being of couples as they approach and experience retirement was viewed in 1996 as an extremely important topic, particularly in light of the aging baby boom generation. Eight years later, the Institute's research has proved even more relevant as the first wave of baby boomers has now begun to retire.

In its focus on the couple, Institute research has also revealed that the passage from paid employment to retirement creates a high degree of marital stress among this first cohort of dual-earner couples facing joint retirement decisions. This stress is felt more acutely by retirees whose spouse continues to work, with the highest stress incurred by men who retire before their wives. The studies also found that men in their early 70s who stop work entirely experience more depression than men the same age who phase into retirement. Yet, if couples make it through the first 2 years of the transition into retirement, they report that the intensity of their experience of marital satisfaction outstrips the intensity of the depression experienced immediately following retirement.

In addition to establishing the Centers in those early years, Sloan continued to make project grants. In fact from 1995 to 1999, the Foundation approved over *70* nonCenter grants that advanced our goals of shaping research that focused on relational units of study, promoting the development of a community of scholars, and communicating the findings of the scholarly research beyond the academy.

Relational Focus

In the mid-1990s, public concern about long work hours and the pressure on dual-earner families was growing, due in part to Juliet Schor's 1991 book, *The Overworked American: The Unexpected Decline of Leisure*. It may seem surprising now, but common thinking at the time failed to factor family responsibilities into considerations of why Americans had less time for leisure. Instead, the argument was simply that individuals worked longer hours. To bring family back into the equation, Ralph Gomory and I developed the counter argument that the time squeeze experienced by the middle-class American family was more the result of the changing arithmetic of the American family than it was the result of an increase in the number of hours that individual adults were working for pay (Christensen & Gomory, 1999). We coined the notion of the "3/2 family." Our premise was that while the traditional family had two jobs—breadwinner and homemaker—and two adults, the same family in the 1990s was shouldering three jobs—two breadwinning and one homemaking—with no one person taking full responsibility for the domestic care work. The demands on these adults in the "3jobs/2adults" families outstrip their resources. Even if the three jobs are split evenly between the adults, both are overloaded, with 1.5 jobs per adult. In other words, while the number of adults has stayed constant, the amount of work has grown dramatically for the professional whose breadwinning job demands long hours and who must shoulder some amount of the homemaker job as well. The situation is even worse for the single parent who has at least two jobs and only one adult.

The Sloan Foundation's grant making in the mid-1990s was guided by this notion of a "3/2 family" and the conviction that the couple, not the individual, must be the unit of analysis regarding work hours. In 1997, we funded Jerry Jacobs and Kathleen Gerson to research hours worked in dual-earner families, with the stipulation that total couple work hours be included in the analyses. Their seminal research resulted in their groundbreaking book, *The Time Divide: Work, Family, and Gender Inequality* (2004). Also in 1997, the foundation awarded a research grant to Suzanne Bianchi and John Robinson, who designed a study that used time diaries to assess "a week in the life of dual earner families." Although quite complex methodologically, the study nonetheless yielded rich insights into the web of overlaid activities that compete for family members' time.

Creating Community

In 1994, virtually no infrastructure existed to support what we hoped would develop into a vibrant, interdisciplinary community of scholars focused on working families. To develop this infrastructure, the foundation pursued a threefold strategy of building networks that cut across disciplines, supporting face-to-face conferences that brought scholars together from around the world, and providing resources to train the next generation of scholars.

From 1995–1997, Sloan funded four networks. One of these was the Network on Work Restructuring and Work/Family Research, which, as I described earlier in this chapter, brought labor economists together with social scientists. The foundation also provided support to Purdue University so that it could establish the Midwestern Work Family Resource Center and Families and Work Institute to launch a network of small and medium-sized firms concerned with work-family issues. Probably our most significant contribution to network building arose from support that we provided to Marcie Pitt-Catsouphes in 1997 to launch the Sloan Work-Family Electronic Research Network. This Network is now 8 years old, and in the years since it was launched, it has been renamed the Sloan Work and Family Research Network and has gained recognition in the United States and Europe as a one-of-a-kind source for the resources, research, and teaching tools needed by scholars who are engaged in work-family research. The Network has produced an extensive database with over 6,000 annotated citations as well as a series of resources for faculty members teaching in the area of work and family. These teaching resources include the *Work-Family Encyclopedia,* Suggestions for Teaching, Lists of Recommended Readings, and the *Work Family Glossary*. The Network also produces several Newsletters each year on the newest work-family research, and it convenes research forums on specific themes, including flexibility and healthy aging and work. The director of the Sloan Network, Marcie Pitt-Catsouphes of Boston College, is co-editing this *Handbook.*

Nearly 900 scholars are currently affiliated with the Network. Two hundred fifty of these scholars actively contribute information to the Network's Web site—a clear indication of the Web site's relevance and value to the Network's scholars and to their colleagues. There have been 24,000 unique visitors to the home page, with evidence showing that many users pass information along to others. No other network, either in the United States or abroad, provides the infrastructure or services that the Sloan Network provides to its interdisciplinary community of scholars.

In addition to the Network, which operates largely in virtual space, face-to-face conferences organized by the foundation provided much-needed venues that enabled scholars from different disciplines to build relationships and share their work with one another. Over 10 years of funding, the Sloan Foundation has supported more than 20 conferences. We established our strategy for supporting conferences in those first few years. I wanted Sloan to support several types of conferences, including conferences exclusively for Sloan grantees, where they could learn from one another's work in an in-depth manner, conferences that were peer-reviewed and attracted scholars from around the world, and conferences that were more thematically focused.

The Center Conferences have been held annually since the Cornell Institute hosted the first one in New York City in 1998. These conferences for Sloan grantees provide opportunities for faculty and students at the pre- and postdoctoral levels and the undergraduate level to present their work and to get to know the researchers in their field. Because each of Sloan's Centers possesses its own unique focus, I decided early on that the location of the center conferences should rotate annually among the centers, so that each would have an opportunity to showcase its particular theoretical and methodological strengths. This has been particularly important since the latter three centers have been directed by anthropologists and have adopted approaches quite different from, albeit complementary to, those used at Sloan's first three centers, which are directed by sociologists.

In addition to nurturing the community of Sloan grantees through Center conferences, I recognized that we needed to communicate our research beyond our immediate community through peer-reviewed conferences open to the broader community of researchers across the world. To that end, in 1998, Sloan funded Wellesley College and together we cosponsored with the Business and Professional Women's Foundation (BPW) a peer-reviewed conference in Boston that was attended by over 200 researchers. In 2000 and 2002, Sloan cosponsored two more peer-reviewed international conferences with BPW and made successive grants to two different academic partners: the University of California-Berkeley in 2000 and Purdue University in 2002. The papers from the first two of what became known as the Sloan–BPW conferences resulted in well-received edited volumes covering existing research to date: *Working Families: The Transformation of the American Home* (Hertz & Marshall, 2001) and *Families at Work: Expanding the Boundaries* (Gerstel, Clawson, & Zussman, 2002).

During this period, Sloan sponsored over 10 additional conferences, including the annual meetings of the Eastern Sociological Society in 2002 and 2003, which focused on working families; two working conferences on part-time careers; an international symposium in France, which was organized as a means toward further developing a global work-life community; and a research conference with the National Institute for Child Health and Human Development (NICHD). The conference with NICHD adopted the Sloan Foundation framework of the Workplace-Workforce Mismatch, which as we will discuss later in this chapter, we developed based on an analysis of Sloan's work to date (Christensen, 2002). Furthermore, Jerry Jacobs and Janice Fanning Manning convened a working conference in 2003 at the University of Pennsylvania, which resulted in a special issue of *The Annals of the American Academy of Political and Social Science*, entitled, "Mommies and Daddies on the Fast Track: Success of Parent in Demanding Professions" (November 2004).

Beyond organizing conferences to build and nurture community among scholars, Sloan set a direction of ensuring that the community would outlast the current generation of scholars. To that end, a key goal of our centers and for many of our larger research grants has been to train the next generation of scholars and to place them in tenure-track positions, no small task given the restructuring of the career path in the academy away from tenure lines. Still, the centers' and related projects' efforts to train and place scholars have met with success. Over 50 PhDs have been completed as well as 40 postdoctoral fellowships. Even in this tight academic labor market, a significant percentage of the postdoctoral fellows have taken tenure-track positions at top research universities, and many are teaching courses that did not exist a decade ago. In addition, 111 predoctoral fellows and 18 postdoctoral fellows are currently supported by our Sloan Centers and projects.

These work-family scholars have produced more than 20 books, published by top university presses, and more than 80 peer-reviewed articles. Work-family is now a recognized academic field, and it has the resources and support it needs to ensure its continued existence.

Communicating Scholarship Beyond the Academy

In 1995, I recognized that Sloan could not focus the entirety of its resources on efforts to build a research community; it needed to reach beyond that academic community to the public. Indeed, in order for our research to have the kind of impact that we envisioned, we needed to ensure that issues facing working families became as much a part of our public and civil discourse as were issues related to the economy, the environment, or politics. Toward this objective, I approached National Public Radio in 1995 to discuss possible Sloan support for a work-family desk on NPR's *Morning Edition*. NPR was amenable to this idea, and David Molpus became the work-family correspondent. Subsequently, Sloan funded New York City's public radio station, WNYC, as well as a PBS documentary, the *Juggling Act,* and a nationally syndicated PBS show, *To the Contrary*. That first grant to NPR in 1995 spawned a Sloan tradition of support to public television and radio for coverage of working families, a tradition that has carried over to the present with a recent grant to American Public Media's leading business radio show, *Marketplace,* to air stories on workplace flexibility.

The early years of Sloan's work-family grant making were productive and informative. The Sloan Centers and the foundation's research grants on working families contributed to the growing scholarship and the public discourse about the social and cultural changes that were taking place as a result of mothers' sustained participation in the labor force and the aging of the workforce. But, it had also become clear that studying working families was insufficient. After all, this research alone could not provide insights into the full range of work conditions that affect the dynamics within the family. Those work conditions were set by the norms and practices of the professions, industries, and sectors in which people lived and worked for much of their days. To begin to explore these facets of the work-family equation, Sloan began in earnest in the late 1990s to fund workplace-oriented research that was industry and profession specific. Although we had done this in the early years in our studies of part-time, this new focus would be both broader and deeper.

MIDDLE YEARS 1998–2001: WORKPLACE

In 1990, Menaghan and Parcel called for research that addressed the specifics of work and its consequences for employees and their families. In the middle years, the Sloan Foundation focused its grant making on developing a detailed understanding of how the demands of work and the structure of career paths in selected industries, including the academy, health care, law, and financial services, affect parents' abilities to manage their work and family responsibilities. I started off those middle years with a *traditional approach to studying the workplace*, in which the researcher adopts a privileged position outside of the worksite and observes and analyzes the patterns therein. Because we wanted our research to bring about social change within the workplace, I developed a subsequent funding strategy that represented much more of a *researcher/practitioner partnership approach.* Both the traditional and partnership approaches to research have their advantages. But, what distinguished our approaches from others was our focus on the details of the work contexts. Research until that point had often treated work as a generic phenomenon. Through our funding, Sloan specifically contextualized the studies in particular industries or professions as a way to understand specific work conditions and expectations.

TRADITIONAL APPROACH TO WORKPLACE RESEARCH

The traditional approach provides important insights into the conditions under which people work as well as the norms that dominate their work culture. We studied two critical and complementary sets of conditions across different industries and professions: career advancement and work hours. Conditions surrounding both career advancement and work hours have direct and profound consequences on how employees handle their work and family responsibilities. Studies of these conditions constituted a major focus of our funding program during the middle years.

Career advancement in certain professions such as law, accounting, and the academy depends on a protracted probationary period that coincides with the childbearing years for many women. This conflict between career and family is dramatically clear in the academy, which is why the academy was the target of some of our earliest industry-specific research.

Tenure became the professional norm for the academy in 1940 when the professoriate consisted mainly of men married to full-time homemakers. Today, however, women are receiving doctorates at virtually the same rate as men, and we must ask ourselves how well this extended probationary period of tenure meshes with a woman's ability to bear children and achieve career success. With the average age of completion of the doctorate now at 34, the tenure-track years conflict directly with the final years for childbirth. Robert Drago and Carol Colbeck (2003) of the Pennsylvania State University conducted an extensive study of faculty at 600 colleges and universities in an attempt to understand how faculty at various types of institutions of higher education manage their work and family decision making and responsibilities. The faculty members selected to participate in the study were from two disciplines—chemistry and English. Drago and Colbeck selected these disciplines because of the vastly different cultures each presented for women. These disciplines were also selected because each had a significant gender imbalance. Less than 20% of chemistry faculty is female, while women conprise more than 60% of English faculty. Drago and Colbeck also wanted to sample a wide array of types of colleges and universities because they felt that that the climate at a research institution of higher education would likely differ from that at a comprehensive teaching institution.

Their findings are provocative. Within both disciplines, women raised fewer children than their male counterparts, and they perceived that they were receiving less organizational and supervisor support for family and personal needs. Interestingly enough, women in chemistry were more likely to have children than women in English, suggesting that the fact that a discipline is dominated by males does not mean that it will be less conducive to family formation. Women are also more apt than men to engage in "bias avoidance behavior." Examples of these bias avoidance behaviors include staying single for career purposes, not having children, having fewer children than the individual would have liked, and neglecting to request family-related leave when desired.

The legal profession, like the academy, has an up-or-out model of career advancement. Unlike the academy, however, organizational structure in the legal profession is assumed to affect work hours: Corporate counsel offices are generally perceived to provide a more conducive environment for lawyers who want to work shorter hours than provided by partnership firms. To determine whether these assumptions were correct, Joan Williams of the Washington Law School of American University conducted studies of law firms and corporate legal departments. According to her findings, part-time work in corporate legal departments is, in fact, frequently just as stigmatized as part-time work in law firms (Williams & Calvert, 2001). Indeed, part-time corporate counsels are often perceived as being less committed to their jobs than full-time counsels. They are criticized by business-side "clients" who want them to be full-time even when there is no problem with their availability. And, they are not promoted as readily as full-time attorneys.

However, there are exceptions to these patterns. Anecdotal evidence reveals that when corporate legal departments are predominantly female or headed by female attorneys, there is a more open climate in which personal needs can be discussed and there are more opportunities for creative scheduling. Significantly, they also found that some attorneys who would likely work part-time if they were at a partnership firm could work full-time in corporate legal departments because these department offered greater control over their caseload and the possibility periodically to shift portions of their work to an outside counsel.

In the next sections I discuss studies of other industries, including health care and financial services, which similarly sought to identify conditions under which it would be possible for employees to work shorter hours within the dominant long-hour cultures.

In 2001, Lotte Bailyn and Tom Kochan established the MIT Workplace Center, which, among its different activities, supported several research projects examining work hours and conditions in the health care industry and how these conditions affect employees and their personal lives. Health care is a particularly critical industry to the Boston metropolitan region, employing over 450,000 workers in a wide variety of professional, paraprofessional, and low-skilled occupations. Employers include acute care hospitals, sub-acute facilities such as rehabilitation centers and nursing homes, home-based health agencies, and outpatient clinics. But the health care industry in Boston, as elsewhere, is experiencing a fair degree of turbulence with the increasing number of health maintenance organizations (HMOs) and the severe nursing shortage. Employees in occupations across health care firms are putting in excess hours, with the most extreme cases involving some "part-time" physicians who are working as many as 50 hours per week. As a result of this situation, many professionals, including nurses and doctors, are reporting frustration at their loss of job autonomy, job continuity, and patient contact and a desire for greater flexibility. To determine the impacts of this situation, MIT faculty and doctoral students examined flexibility—in the scheduling of work hours, in the amount of time working, and in career flexibility—in different areas of health care delivery.

Issues of flexibility proved more complex than the MIT group had imagined. For example, surgical residents actually opposed a reduction of working hours from 120 to 80 hours per week because cultural norms in their profession idealize long hours to the point where long hours are part of their profession's identity. Meanwhile, physicians in large HMOs found more opportunities for flexibility than they had expected. In fact, in a finding that paralleled the legal profession studies described earlier, physicians in large HMOs reported more opportunities for flexibility in these larger bureaucracies than did their colleagues in smaller private practices that have partnership structures. These projects uncovered a range of subtleties that needed to be considered in any attempt to bring flexibility and choice into the health care workplace.

Within financial services, increased pressure to globalize services and markets has produced a 24-hour/7-day workweek and not surprisingly has increased the stresses on directors, managers, and brokers in the industry who are parents. According to Mary Blair-Loy of the

Washington State University and Jerry Jacobs (2003) of the University of Pennsylvania (2003) the principal investigators of a study of extended stock market hours, scheduling flexibility in this industry can be a liability rather than a benefit. Indeed, in the context of a 24-hour economy in which the work is never finished, flexibility appears to lead to more rather than less work-family conflict. Without limits to a workday, time is completely expandable, and flexibility enables work to be shifted to all hours of the day and night.

These studies of the academy, law, health care, and financial services yielded valuable insights into the conditions under which employees work and the points at which an intervention could and/or should occur to change the conditions. However, the studies themselves will not create that intervention, nor will they bring about the kinds of changes that many employees want. Academics are not trained to be agents of social change. But, I believe that if research could be structured in a less traditional way—one that brought the employer and, where appropriate, the union into the research process—then a linkage to action would become much more feasible. To that end, we developed an approach to research in which social change is an intended outcome. In this approach, the researcher plays a role, but not the only role, and a true partnership between the researcher and the practitioner is forged.

RESEARCHER/PRACTITIONER PARTNERSHIPS

In order for business leaders and policymakers to consider our research evidence as part of their decision making, dialogue and discussion about work-family research must extend beyond the academy. A straight model of the researcher studying the site will not produce this dialogue. Rather, successful research in the workplace requires a partnership model of research. And, despite the challenges implicit in establishing meaningful and productive partnerships between researchers and practitioners in the private, public, and civil sectors of our society, the results are often worth the effort. Indeed, these collaborations have resulted in important new insights and even breakthrough thinking about today's work-family challenges, and, properly executed, they can leverage new resources and generating opportunities for work-family studies. For these reasons, Sloan has actively pursued the development of research partnerships between scholars and employers, unions, nonprofits, and government agencies in its grant-making activities.

There are, however, several important factors that must be carefully considered before any partnership will work. First and foremost, researchers and their partnering organizations need to understand and respect the different, although hopefully aligned, motivations and goals for collaborating with one another. A partnership cannot be effective if it engenders a one-way, nonreciprocal relationship. From the very beginning, each partner must ask, "What does each side contribute?" Partnerships in which one or both parties focus exclusively on what the other brings to the table—rather than on how what each offers complements the other—are bound to fail.

As researchers in the field of work-life, we frequently speak of contributing to the "common good." We publish our findings, disseminate our data, and expand our knowledge base, all toward the ultimate goal of improving people's lives. But, to accomplish that goal requires that we work closely with decision makers from the outset of a project and continue that partnership through the project's end. To contribute to the common good, we must find common ground with practitioners, and that calls for effective research-practitioner partnerships.

Business leaders often observe that they become interested in engaging in action-research partnership if they identify a seemingly intractable issue that needs further research. For the business, which is after all the agent of change, the research will yield evidence-based information that will allow it to make the adjustments that will address the issues at a problem's core. In these situations, business leaders view researchers as possessing expertise that can serve the company. Researchers, meanwhile, gain access to the workplace where they can expand their understanding about selected work-family issues. In this fashion, a symbiotic relationship is formed and the common good is served.

Of course, all of this is easier said than done. Business organizations tend to have very different goals for work-family research than we do in academia. They tend even to adopt different language, identifying work-family experiences as part of a broader set of work-life issues. A company engaged in research will, in many cases, want to keep that information in-house because it gives them a certain competitive advantage. In fact, sharing details about workforce policies and programs seems counterintuitive to the corporate imperative.

But, there are examples of nonproprietary research in the work-family field. These include projects that have identified for individual firms areas for improvement while at the same time contributing to the overall work-family knowledge base. What these projects tend to have in common is a partnership approach to research. The firm sees the research as providing a service to both the company and the community. It has asked the question, "How will this project be of mutual benefit to both the researchers and the firm?" This does not mean the research has to be compromised, but it does mean that all members of the partnership must be clear from the outset what each party will gain from participating in the study.

The exciting news is that there are several important examples of successful partnerships. Two ongoing examples of the partnering research model are the Sloan Foundation's partnerships with the University of California-Berkeley and the University of Wisconsin System as part of Sloan's career flexibility program. The primary goal of the career flexibility program is to create flexible and fair career paths in the academy for both men and women who want to have families, by reforming tenure so that it allows for a more flexible career path, including options for part-time arrangements, pre- or post-tenure.

Researchers on the University of California-Berkeley and the University of Washington projects are working in direct partnership with their respective universities' administrations to design the projects. In all of our research, the workplace or industry first identifies a set of problems that is salient to its own situation. In these two projects, the universities identified the inherent conflict that exists in academia between family responsibilities and career advancement. In both projects, researchers and the institutions themselves recognized that nothing short of an institutional change with regard to academic career paths would address the problem.

The challenges inherent in these new forms of partnerships are significant, but it is absolutely critical that we begin these types of conversations between those engaged in research and those engaged in action. The conversation has to go both ways; we have so much to learn from one another. Ultimately, it is the nature of the partnership that may really matter. A true partnership is a relationship where "research" and "action" come together; it is not an artificial bridging of one to the other.

We have learned several lessons from our research on the workplace. Traditional research will not lead to social change. Even in a partnership approach, academics are not agents of change, except in their own industry, the academy. Yet both the traditional and partnership approach to research provide important insights that are needed for social change.

The most significant lesson we have learned from the research that the Sloan Foundation has sponsored on the work-family problem is that this problem is larger than any one individual, occupation, profession, or industry. The problem is not an individual's personal problem. And, the solution to the work-family problem cannot be found by individuals acting alone. Nor can it be found simply by accumulating insights from a number of different professions or industries. Indeed, if we are to understand this problem, we must broaden our framing of the issue to reach beyond the individual; and if we are to solve this problem, we must adopt a broader societal approach to change. Based on this analytic review of the research, it is evident that a structural workplace/workforce mismatch exists in which the workplace itself no longer fits the needs of increasing numbers of workers (Christensen, 2002).

RECENT YEARS 2000–2002: WORKPLACE/WORKFORCE MISMATCH

For most of the 20th century, the American workplace fit the needs of most of its workers. At mid-century, the typical American worker was a male breadwinner who earned a family wage while his wife stayed home to care for the family and home. His job required full-time, full-year work. It offered little to no time off from work and provided maximum opportunities for overtime, thus enabling the male breadwinner to earn a family wage and to support his stay-at-home wife and children. Federal laws, particularly the Fair Labor Standards Act (FLSA) passed in the late 1930s, codified this workplace structure. It set the standard workweek at 40 hours and made provisions for overtime compensation.

But by the beginning of this new 21st century, this workplace that once so well fulfilled the needs of the America worker has become profoundly mismatched to the needs of an increasingly diverse and varied workforce. In 2005, the typical worker is just as likely to be female as male. He or she is likely a member of a dual-earner household and is likely unable to earn a family wage on his or her own. Today, over 70% of married couples are dual earners, and that has resulted in a profound change in the arithmetic of the family.

As noted earlier, the traditional American family had two adults and two jobs—breadwinner and homemaker. But in most families today, the same two adults share three jobs—two bread-winner and one homemaker. In other words, while the number of adults has stayed constant or even declined with the growth in single-parent families, the overall workload has grown dramatically, with the demands of work outstripping the resources. This is particularly true for professionals, for whom paying jobs are demanding longer and longer hours. It is also true for low-wage workers, who often work overtime or take on another job to earn a living wage.

For many "three jobs–two adults" and "two jobs–one adult" single-parent families, the solution to the family work overload has been to purchase or rely on *care replacement* services. These include child-care and elder care services as well as sick-child-care back-up systems. Typically, families have to locate these services on their own; occasionally an employer will provide them. The basic reasoning behind these care replacement services is that they will free workers to work longer and harder. And, while these services constitute a legitimate solution to the "three jobs–two adults" work overload, they are not the only solution. Another type of solution can be found by rethinking the structure of work in America.

The current rigid structure of full-time, full-year work, with minimal-to-no-flexibility subverts the needs of today's "three–two family" and "two–one" families. Few opportunities exist for high-quality, flexible work arrangements—including flexibility for full-time workers, flexibility for reduced hours, and career flexibility—and those that do often carry wage and advancement penalties. For many workers for whom flexibility is not an option, there is a profound mismatch between the structure of the workplace and their needs. While the family does its best to accommodate this explosion of work, the costs of the workplace/workforce mismatch are revealed in many of the findings of the Sloan supported research.

- Working mothers lose approximately one night's worth of sleep per week, due to the combined demands of work and family (Bianchi, 2000).
- Husbands whose wives work 40 or more hours per week are in poorer health than husbands whose wives work shorter hours (Stolzenberg, 2001).

- Men over the age of 70 who retire abruptly from full-time employment incur greater health risks than men who phase into retirement (Moen, 2003).
- American firms that would like to offer older workers the possibility of phased retirement often face unintended obstacles to this objective from decades-old regulations and laws governing pension plans (Hutchens, 1994).
- Data gathered at the Sloan Center at the University of Chicago indicate that America is incurring a major loss of human and intellectual capital as educated, talented mothers leave the workforce because they cannot find career-continuous part-time arrangements (Schneider & Waite, 2005).

This research makes a compelling case that the "one size fits all" workplace of the last century needs to be rethought in light of the changing workforce. American workers want more choice over the hours they work. While the majority of Americans want and need to work full-time for most of their careers, many report that they also would like the opportunity to adjust their hours downward at certain points in their lives, without incurring the kinds of penalties and stigmas that now exist. It is not surprising that our research shows that a statistically significant percentage of working Americans, across age, income, and stage in life, want more flexibility at work. Flexibility becomes a vital means of correcting the workplace/workforce mismatch and realigning the workplace to the needs of its workforce.

Yet, while the demand for flexibility exists, the structure of the workplace does not currently match supply to demand. In an analysis of federal statistics, Lonnie Golden of the Pennsylvania State University found that the percentage of workers with flexible work schedules—the ability to control their start and stop times—has remained almost constant in recent years (Golden, 2001). The percentage of wage and salaried workers with flexible schedules in the United States nearly doubled in the years between 1991 and 1997—increasing from 15 to 28%. But more recently, this growth has stagnated. Indeed, in the years between 1997 and 2001, the percentage of workers in the United States with flexible schedules rose by only one percentage point, to 29%.

Among workers with young children, the pattern is similar: The proportion with flexibility more than doubled between 1991 and 1997, but then grew only one percentage point to 31.1% between 1997 and 2001. Notably, despite all of our research that shows that mothers want this flexibility, fathers are more likely than mothers to have access to flexible hours. In terms of occupations, lawyers and judges are most likely to have flexible schedules, and K-12 teachers are the least likely to have them. This is ironic as many women seek teaching careers specifically because they are purported to offer greater flexibility for managing work and family responsibilities.

Like options for flextime, opportunities for shorter work hours are limited. According to Eileen Appelbaum, of Rutgers University, part-time employment stabilized in 1979 at 18% of the workforce and has changed little since then. Furthermore, opportunities for part-time employment remain concentrated in lower-wage occupations, such as retail sales, that typically do not provide health benefits. According to these figures, therefore, the supply of part-time arrangements is limited both in terms of number and in terms of occupational distribution, despite the growing demand for such arrangements. For example, research by Cornell University's Sloan Employment and Families Careers' Institute reveals that many older Americans intend to work beyond what typically would be considered retirement age (Han & Moen, 1999). However, these Americans do not necessarily want to work full-time or year-round. Many report, instead, that they would like to phase into retirement, by stepping down initially from full-time to part-time schedules that move them more gradually toward full retirement. Yet, U.S. firms provide minimal opportunities for phased retirement.

With Sloan support, Cornell University and the Urban Institute undertook projects to identify the possible organizational and legal obstacles to phased retirement. In a study of 950 firms, Cornell University found that 73% of the firms answered yes to the question as to whether a "secure full time employee who is 55 or over could shift to a part time schedule" (Hutchens & Dentinger, 2003). Only one third of these firms, however, had formal policies regarding phased retirement, while the majority allowed for informal phasing into part-time work. Furthermore this research identified three intriguing patterns regarding which firms allowed phased retirement of any sort. First, firms are not likely to permit phased retirement if their employees, regardless of age, have limited opportunities to adjust their hours. Second, although firm size is not closely linked to opportunities for phased retirement, the size of the parent organization does matter. Small parent organizations are more likely to offer phased retirement than are large parent organizations. Third, a firm is less likely to permit phased retirement when a large percentage of the white-collar workforce is unionized. The latter two findings may be tied to the fact that most phased retirement is negotiated on informal bases and both large bureaucracies and unions often discourage informal arrangements and prefer the consistency of formal policies. Additional research on the legal obstacles to phased retirement was conducted by the Urban Institute.

According to the Urban Institute, legal impediments to phased retirement are unintended consequences of a number of regulations designed to protect employees—the Internal Revenue Services (IRS) rules governing employee benefit plans, ERISA's attempts to secure the benefits promised employees, and the Age Discrimination Employment Act that prevents discrimination against older workers (Penner, Perun, & Steuerle, 2002). These rules are complex and ambiguous, and they limit employers' ability to negotiate special arrangements. It is oftentimes easier for employers to hire older workers from the outside than it is for them to retain longtime employees. And, while many employers indicate an interest in developing plans for phased retirement, very few actually do so. Based on his findings, Penner recommended that the federal government provide more precise regulatory guidance on crucial points such as the definition of the "termination of employment" and the calculation of the "final average pay" for part-time workers; and he recommended the adoption of a statute explicitly authorizing phased retirement programs.

From the patterns regarding phased retirement, it is clear that many organizational and legal obstacles prevent widespread utilization of part-time work. A significant obstacle from the employee's perspective is the lack of employer-provided health insurance for part-time wage and salaried employees in America. For example, the Economic Policy Institute found that while 76% of part-time employees have health insurance—compared to 88% of full-time workers—these workers are not, for the most part, receiving this insurance from their employers (Wenger, 2001). Indeed, only 13.7% of part-time employees have employer-provided health insurance, compared to 66.3% of full-time workers. Instead, the primary source of health insurance for part-time employees is from a spouse or other member of the family. Twenty-four percent of all part-time workers make do with no health insurance.

Another organizational obstacle to part-time opportunities rests in the system used by most U.S. companies' human resources departments to determine how many people can be hired. In this system—the head count system—one person equals one head, regardless of the number of hours that person works. The alternative is the full-time equivalent (FTE) system. This system allows one or more people whose hours total 40 to account for one head, and provides firms with much greater flexibility to hire people who work shorter than 40-hour weeks (Appelbaum & Firpo, 2003).

Based on our findings, it is fair to conclude that standard full-time workweeks and rigid career paths dominate the American workplace, not because alternatives cannot be worked out, but rather because these conditions of work are so firmly established in our habits and attitudes that we lack creativity about nonstandard hours or variable career paths—if we think of them at all. And, in the occasions that more flexible conditions are arranged, we look down upon them as less serious. This rigid full-time structure is clearly at odds with the flexible way that many Americans want and need to work.

This workplace/workforce mismatch framework has proved to be a fruitful way of framing the structural dilemma facing our country. As noted earlier, Sloan cosponsored with NICHD a 2003 conference that adopted this framework and out of those conference papers has come a book, in which a number of the papers are framed in terms of the mismatch thesis (Bianchi, Casper, & King, 2005).

NEXT STAGE: LAUNCHING NATIONAL INITIATIVE ON WORKPLACE FLEXIBILITY

In 2000, the foundation began laying the groundwork for a national campaign to rectify the workplace/workforce mismatch and to create a workplace that provides greater flexibility to its workers. Early on, I attempted to gauge key players' interest in this endeavor as I met with congressional staff members, labor leaders, think tank researchers from both the liberal and conservative sides, and executives from advocacy groups such as AARP. In early 2002, Sloan contracted Peter Hart Associates, a Washington-based polling firm, to assess how the American public framed work-family issues and work time (Hart Associates, 2003). And in the spring of 2002, I assembled a kitchen cabinet of four leading thinkers—Ellen Galinsky, Chai Felblum, Michael Levine, and Ann Harrison Clark—to advise the foundation on the development of a campaign. With the Sloan Board of Trustees' approval, the foundation launched the National Workplace Flexibility Initiative in the fall of 2003.

The National Workplace Flexibility Initiative is a collaborative campaign consisting of a number of organizations that share a common goal: making workplace flexibility the standard way of working in the United States. The initiative's objectives are threefold: (a) make workplace flexibility a compelling national issue, (b) eliminate the legal and logistical barriers to its use and (c) produce cases where it works. Workplace flexibility provides employees with genuine choice and control over several facets of their work life, including:

- Scheduling of full-time work hours, including flextime.
- Amount of time spent working, including part-time, part-year, or job-sharing.
- Career flexibility with multiple points for entry, exit, and re-entry over the course of a career, including formal leaves and sabbaticals, as well as taking time out of the paid labor market, with the ability to re-enter.

The foundation is funding projects at the national, state, and local levels with business, labor, government and advocacy organizations, all aiming at making workplace flexibility the standard way of working in the United States. Each project is engaged in a variety of independent efforts, although all are driven by a shared set of principles. Making workplace flexibility a standard of the American workplace requires a combination of voluntary efforts by employers and employees and public policy efforts at the local, state, and federal levels. Research is critical for advancing action and research needs to be drawn from a range of academic disciplines. Workplace flexibility must effectively serve the needs of both employers and employees. Workplace flexibility must take into account people at different life stages and across personal and family situations.

At the center of this campaign are three projects—*When Work Works* at Families and Work Institute, *Workplace Flexibility 2010 (WF2010)* at Georgetown University Law Center, and the

State Legislators' Initiative at Boston College, as part of the Sloan Work and Family Research Network at Boston College. All three projects are committed to bringing the best in research, policy, and legal analysis to the public and business discourse on workplace flexibility.

When Work Works of the Families and Work Institute is designed to share research from their nationally representative studies of the U.S. workforce that reveal that workplace flexibility is a critical and missing ingredient of effective workplaces. *When Work Works*, partnering with the Center for Workforce Preparation, an affiliate of the U.S. Chamber of Commerce, and the Center for Emerging Futures, held forums in eight parts of the country with local chambers to present this research and to launch the Sloan Awards for Business Excellence in Workplace Flexibility in these same communities. The awards are designed to recognize and honor companies that successfully use flexibility to meet both business and employee goals. As part of the awards process, *When Work Works* has been providing technical assistance to companies wishing to enhance their workplace flexibility programs. Their efforts are helping to create a grassroots movement around flexibility among small and medium-sized businesses across the United States. Additional information is available at www.whenworkworks.org.

Workplace Flexibility 2010, an Alfred P. Sloan Foundation Initiative at Georgetown University Law Center, is an educational, research, and outreach effort designed to develop a comprehensive national policy on workplace flexibility at the federal, state, and local levels. Toward this goal, the initiative provides objective, legal analyses of existing laws and practices—in areas such as labor, employment, antidiscrimination, tax, health, and benefits—and explains how the existence or absence of laws and practices hinder or support workplace flexibility. Analyses by *Workplace Flexibility 2010* will include, for example, the legal and practical operation of laws such as the Family and Medical Leave Act (and selected state leave laws), the Employee Retirement Income Security Act (ERISA), the Fair Labor Standards Act and selected state wage and hour laws, Title VII of the Civil Rights Act of 1964 and selected state employment civil rights laws, and tax and benefits laws. *Workplace Flexibility 2010* brings together skilled lawyers, policy experts, and legislative experts to develop nonpartisan and nonideological documents on law and policy. For more information, visit www.workplaceflexibility2010.org.

The purpose of the *State Legislators' Initiative* of the Sloan Work and Family Research Network is to provide research-based information about working families to state legislators so that they can better understand the importance of work-family issues, consider work-family issues as a compelling policy concern, and make informed policy decisions that promote the well-being of working families and the productivity of businesses. As part of this initiative, the network will undertake four activities directed at all 50 states: (a) map current state statutes that focus directly on different groups of working families, including older workers, workforce entrants, and dual-earner couple families; (b) track bills introduced to state legislatures relevant to the well-being of working families; (c) track bills introduced to state legislatures relevant to the options for flexible work available to working families; and (d) prepare and disseminate briefs and other information about selected work-family issues to state legislators and their staffs. For more information, visit www.bc.edu/wfnetwork.

In addition to these three core projects, Sloan is funding a number of related projects. With Sloan support, public radio's leading business show, *Marketplace*, is developing extensive coverage of workplace flexibility. Corporate Voices for Working Families is producing case studies of what firms see as the business costs and benefits of workplace flexibility. The BOLD Initiative is working with 10 major U.S. corporations to develop demonstration projects that will examine how, and under what conditions, advancing flexibility can improve performance and productivity. The University of Iowa, under the direction of Jennifer Glass, is conducting a study that addresses the question of whether wage penalties, due to working flexibly, are distributed evenly over all employees working all types of flexible arrangements or whether there are variations by type of worker, type of arrangement, and type of firm. It will provide early and crucial insights into whether flexible employment practices, including full-time and part-time, produce disproportionate discriminatory wage penalties against only working mothers, which we know that they do, or all employees working these flexible arrangements.

We feel that we have assembled a powerful group of people in academia, business, government, and labor who can work as partners to drive the issue of workplace flexibility at the local and national levels, and in both the public and private sectors. Most importantly, this campaign is designed to promote workplace flexibility for people at all stages of life, from childbearing to childrearing and up to and through retirement.

CALL TO ARMS

Over the 10 years that the Sloan Foundation has engaged in grant making through its Workplace, Workforce, and Working Families Program, the work-family field has matured in size, in scope, and in influence. Work-family scholarship has grown, not just as a result of the resources that Sloan has provided, but also because of the foundation's intellectual vision and leadership and the remarkable efforts shown by the grantees whose work we have supported. Furthermore, at each stage of the program's grant making, research has been like an arrowhead, cutting through openings for new change-oriented initiatives: change in career paths in the academy; change in media coverage of working families; change in the framing of work-family problems away from individuals' problems to problems arising from a profound structural workplace/workforce mismatch; and change in public consciousness and workplace practices through the National Workplace Flexibility Initiative. But, just as much has been accomplished, much remains to be done.

Entirely new topics and approaches to research have been introduced since the early 1990s. As a result of Sloan's initiative, a critical mass of cultural anthropologists now study mainstream middle-class working families in terms of their day-to-day lives and how myths and rituals structure those lives. The research foci have expanded well beyond impacts on children at the preschool age to include children at all stages of development, as well as couples at all stages of their lives. Perhaps most importantly, research is now genuinely multidisciplinary and examines families as they move across their life courses. But, significant areas of research remain largely unexamined, particularly in the areas of older workers, career paths, and flexibility. Out of this research will emerge new opportunities for action.

As the baby boom generation ages, surveys indicate that large percentages of its members expect to work beyond the conventional age of retirement, yet do not want to work full-time or full-year. This projected pattern of the labor force raises many important research questions regarding aging and work: What role does work play in healthy aging? What are the mental and physical health outcomes of protracted work for older Americans? Are there optimal numbers of work hours for optimal health? How do culture, caregiving and work intersect, and what are their outcomes on the well-being of Americans as they age? For example, do the norms in one ethnic group in our country differ from another with respect to the types of care provided to the elderly, and how does that affect an aging population's ability to remain in the workforce? Does one culture support "buying" elder care, while another believes that care for sick or aging family members should be provided by a healthier spouse or by children? We know from earlier work conducted at the University of California-Berkeley that in a small study of Asian working families, there was minimal support for paying for elder care and strong support for providing direct, personal care. This research poses a seminal question of what the consequences are for an aging workforce that is caught between a need or desire to work and a comparably strong need or desire to provide direct personal care for sick or aging family members. What are the consequences on marriages of people working longer into what has been conventionally thought of as retirement years? How do we now think about retirement and geographic relocation? In the prior generation, middle-class retirees often moved to different climates when they retired, but if people continue to work, will they remain in their primary homes? Or, will sustained work tenure push a movement to part-year work, where individuals take part of the year off from work rather than part of the week, so that they have the option to relocate for part of the year?

Over the course of the last 10 years, we have funded research regarding career advancement in a number of fields, including law, medicine, and academia. Research reveals that the dominant career path is linear, often in the form of a probationary period with a sharp up-or-out progression, and that this model does not meet the needs of many working women for whom the years of career advancement conflict with the peak or, in some cases, the final years of childbearing. Additional research and action are required on new career advancement models that better mesh with the way that people live now. Is there evidence of career paths that allow for delayed entry into a career path, beyond the conventional entry point of one's twenties or early thirties, and how does the delayed entry model affect productivity? Can someone start a career at the age of 45 and have a meaningful career from the dual standpoints of the firm and the individual? Is there evidence of career paths with multiple peaks, whereby one enters at the conventional age, progresses at a normal rate, is allowed the option to slow or plateau, and then pushes again for another peak in his or her late forties or early fifties? The development of a less standard career model option could make eminent sense in a work world where people are working for a much longer portion of their lives than they have historically. Finally, what do we know about the effects of phased retirement models of careers on the health and well-being of the employee and the performance of the firm? In this model, an individual works a conventional pattern and continues to work longer than anticipated, but does this by phasing into retirement by progressively reducing the number of hours worked over the course of several years. What are the consequences of these elongated, variegated career paths on productivity, retention, and health costs for the employer? What are the consequences on the mental and physical health of the employees, and on well-being of the community as older workers are freed up and may have more time to invest in community activities? The research that we have seen from the Cornell Careers Institute indicates, as noted earlier, is that there are positive health consequences for men over the age of 70 who phase into retirement versus abruptly terminating employment and moving into retirement.

Much of our research shows a high demand for flexibility, in a variety of forms, including flexibility when working full-time hours, flexibility in working shorter hours, and flexibility in careers as noted above. But flexibility conflates control and hours, and research is needed to separate the two to learn how one impacts the other. Also, research is needed on flexibility in work cultures that demand long hours. We have seen in the case of the MIT part-time physicians' study that part-time gets perverted in a long-work-hours culture. In that study, part-time physicians worked 40 to 50 hours a week, a schedule that would clearly be defined as a full-time, rather than a part-time, schedule in a normal-work-hours culture. Intervention studies that identify flexibility as the independent variable and carefully define outcome measures are also needed. The best study of this type was done in the 1970s and was conducted at sites within the U.S. Department of Labor (Bohen & Viveros-Long, 1981). The multiple forms of flexibility—which include flextime; compressed workweeks; part-time; job sharing; part-year; and flex careers with multiple points of entry, exit, and re-entry, including leaves—must be included in this research. Moreover, the outcome measures must take into account outcomes to the employer, the employee, and the employee's family. Such research designs will be very complicated and, most importantly, will require partnerships with the employers. Because of these factors, I think it would be wise to pursue a research design similar to the one used successfully by Bohen and Viveros-Long in the late 1970s, which involved targeting government worksites as study sites. I believe that government worksites are excellent targets for intervention studies for a number of reasons. First, access is not as difficult to negotiate within the government as it can be within the private sector. Second, the federal government has implemented widely some of the most progressive forms of flexible work arrangements and would likely be interested in partnering in these studies. Third, there is variability of use of these arrangements within and across agencies, yet comparability in job descriptions. Finally, and perhaps most importantly, there is minimal turnover of staff. Government employees tend to stay in positions long enough to participate in a study.

Research must continue to draw on the talents and wisdom of people from many disciplines, it must continue to reach beyond the walls of the academy to the broader public, and it can and must continue to be forged into arrowheads cutting paths for action by business and government. Only through these partnerships will the work that academics have so painstakingly pursued over the last 10 years begin to bear witness to the changes that the American family has experienced and to the ways that the American workplaces must change to accommodate their needs.

ACKNOWLEDGMENTS

Chai Feldblum, Marcie Pitt-Catsouphes, and Patricia Raskin provided critical suggestions on this chapter and I am very grateful to them. I also appreciate the comments of Stephen Sweet, Ellen Kossek, and the two anonymous reviewers. Any errors in fact or interpretation remain solely my own.

NOTES

[1] Alfred P. Sloan Jr. was considered a brilliant manager and the father of modern management practices. By the time he had become president of General Motors in 1923, Mr. Sloan had developed his system of disciplined, professional management that provided for decentralized operations with coordinated centralized policy control. Applying it to General Motors, he set GM on its course of industrial leadership. For many years Mr. Sloan devoted the largest share of his time and energy to philanthropic activities, both as a private donor to many causes and organizations and through the Alfred P. Sloan Foundation, which he established in 1934. A MIT Sloan Foundation grant later established the MIT School of Industrial Management in 1952 with the charge of educating the "ideal manager."

REFERENCES

Adams, S. M. (1995). Part-time work: Models that work. *Women in Management Review, 10*(7), 21–31.

Appelbaum, E. (1981). *Back to work: Determinants of women's successful re-entry.* Boston: Auburn.

Appelbaum, E. (1997). *Managing work and family: Nonstandard work arrangements among managers and professionals* (Monograph). Washington, DC: Economic Policy Institute.

Appelbaum, E., & Firpo, K. (2003) *Headcount—A barrier to part-time employment.* Final report to the Alfred P. Sloan Foundation. New Brunswick, NJ: Center for Women and Work, Rutgers University. Published December 22. [Electronic version] Retrieved June 2, 2005. www.rci.rutgers.edu/~cww/dataPages/FINALREPORT12-22-03.pdf

Apter, T. (1993). *Working women don't have wives: Professional success in the 1990's.* New York: St. Martin's Press.

Bailyn, L. (1978) Accommodation of world family. In R. Rapoport & N. Rapoport (Eds) Working Couples, London: & Routledge & Kegen Paul.

Baltes, B. B., Briggs, T. E., Huff, J. W., Wright, J. A., & Neuman, G. A. (1999). Flexible and compressed workweek schedules: A meta-analysis of their effects on work-related criteria. *Journal of Applied Psychology, 84*, 496–513.

Barker, K., & Christensen, K. (Eds.). (1998). *Contingent work: American employment relations in transition.* Ithaca, NY: Cornell University Press.

Barnett, R. (1987). Multiple roles, gender, and psychological distress. In R. C. Barnett, L. Biener, & G. K. Baruch (Eds.), *Gender and stress* (pp. 427–445). New York: Free Press.

Barnett, R. C. (1998). Toward a review and reconceptualization of the work/ family literature. *Genetic, Social and General Psychology Monographs, 124*, 125–182.

Barnett, R., & Baruch, G. (1985). Women's involvement in multiple roles and psychological distress. *Journal of Personality and Social Psychology, 49*(1), 135–145.

Barnett, R. C., & Baruch. G. K. (1987). Social roles, gender and psychological distress. In R. C. Barnett, L. Biener, & G. K. Baruch (Eds.), *Gender and stress* (pp. 122–143). New York: Free Press.

Barnett, R. C., & Gareis, K. (2000, May). Reduced-hours employment: The relationships between difficulty of trade-offs and quality of life. *Work and Occupations, 27*(2), 168–187.

Barnett, R. C., & Hall, D. T. (2001). How to use reduced hours to win the war for talent. *Organizational Dynamics, 29*, 192–210.

Becker, P. E., & Moen, P. (1999). Scaling back: Dual-career couples' work-family strategies. *Journal of Marriage and the Family, 61*, 995–1007.

Bianchi, S. M. (2000). Maternal employment and time with children: Dramatic change or surprising continuity? *Demography, 37*(4), 401–414.

Bianchi, S. M., Casper, L. M., & King, R. S. (Eds.). (2005). *Work, family, health and well-Being*. Mahwah, NJ: Lawrence Erlbaum Associates.

Bianchi, S., & Robinson, J. (1997). What did you do today? Children's use of time, family composition, and the acquisition of social capital. *Journal of Marriage and the Family, 59*(2), 332–344.

Blair-Loy, M., & Jacobs, J. A. (2003). Globalization, work hours, and the care deficit among stockbrokers. *Gender and Society, 17*, 230–249.

Blaxall, M., & Reagan, B. (Eds.). (1976). *Women and the workplace: The implications of occupational segregation*. Chicago: University of Chicago Press.

Bohen, H. H., & Viveros-Long, A. (1981). *Balancing jobs and family life: Do flexible work schedules help?* Philadelphia: Temple University Press.

Bond, J. T., Galinsky, E., & Swanberg, J. (1998). *The national study of the changing workforce* (Report). New York: Families and Work Institute.

Bond, J. T., Thompson, C., Galinsky, E., & Prottas, D. (2003). Work-life supports on the job. *Highlights of the 2002 national study of the changing workforce* (pp. 29–45). New York: Families and Work Institute.

Bronfenbrenner, U., & Crouter, A. (1982). Work and family through time and space. In S. Kammerman & C. Hayes (Eds.), *Families that work: Children in a changing world* (pp. 39–83). Washington, DC: National Academy of Sciences.

Bureau of National Affairs. (1986). *Work and family: A changing dynamic*. Washington, DC: Bureau of National Affairs.

Carr, P., Gareis, K., & Barnett, R. (2003). Characteristics and outcomes for women physicians who work reduced hours. *Journal of Women's Health, 12*(4), 399–405.

Catalyst. (1993). *Flexible work arrangements II: Succeeding with part-time options*. New York: Catalyst.

Catalyst. (1997). *A new approach to flexibility: Managing the work/ time equation*. New York: Catalyst.

Christensen, K. (1988a). *Women and home-based work: The unspoken contract*. New York: Holt.

Christensen, K (1988b). Prepared testimony on the "Causes and Consequences of Contingent Work," before Subcommittee on Employment and Housing, U.S. House of Representatives (May, 1988).

Christensen, K. (1989). *Flexible staffing and scheduling in U.S. corporations* (Research Bulletin No. 240). New York: The Conference Board.

Christensen, K. (1996). Contingent work arrangements in family-sensitive corporations in the United States. In H. Holt & I. Thaulow (Eds.), *Reconciling work and family: An international perspective on the role of companies, 96:12* (pp. 105–143). Copenhagen: The Danish National Institute of Social Research.

Christensen, K (with K. Barker). (Eds.). (1998). *Contingent Work: American Employment Relations in Transition*. Ithaca, NY: Cornell University Press.

Christensen K. (2002). The Workplace-Workforce Mismatch. New York: Alfred P. Sloan Foundation. Unpublished paper.

Christensen, K., & Murphree, M. (Eds.). (1988). *Flexible work styles: A look at contingent labor*. Washington, DC: U.S. Department of Labor.

Christensen, K. E., & Gomory, R. E. (1999, June 2), Three jobs, two people. *The Washington Post*, p. A13.

Christensen, K. E., & Staines, G. L. (1990). Flextime: A viable solution to work/family conflict? *Journal of Family Issues, 11*, 455–476.

Coates, J. (September 1996). What's ahead for families: Five major forces of change. *The Futurist, 30*(5), pp. 1+.

Crosby, F. (1991). *Juggling: The unexpected advantages of balancing career and home for women and their families*. New York: Free Press.

Crouter, A. (1984). Spillover from family to work: The neglected side of the work-family interface. *Human Relations, 37*(6), 425–441.

Drago, R., & Colbeck, C. (2003). *The Mapping Project: Exploring the Terrain of U.S. Colleges and Universities for Faculty and Families*, Final Report to the Alfred P. Sloan Foundation. University Park, PA: Penn State University.

Epstein, C., Seron, C., Oglensky, B., & Saute, R. (1998). *The part-time paradox: Time norms, professional life, family and gender*. London: Routledge.

Estes, S. B. (2003). Growing pains and progress in the study of working families. *Work and Occupations: An International Sociological Journal, 30*(4), 479–493.

Ferber, A., O'Farrell, B., & Allen. L. (1991). *Work and family: Policies for a changing work force*. Washington, DC: National Academy Press.

Fogarty, M. P., Rapoport, R., & Rapoport, R. N. (1971). *Sex, career and family: Including an international review of women's roles*. Beverly Hills, CA: Sage.

Friedman, D., & Johnson, A. (1997). Moving from programs to culture change: The next stage for the corporate work-family agenda. In S. Parasuraman & J. Greenhaus (Eds.), *Integrating work and family: Challenges and choices for a changing world* (pp. 192–208). Westport, CT: Quorum Books.

Frone, M., & Rice, R. (1987). Work-family conflict: The effect of job and family involvement. *Journal of Occupational Behavior, 8*, 45–53.

Galinsky, E. (1999). *Ask the children: What America's children really think about working parents*. New York: Morrow.

Galinsky, E., & Bond, J. T. (1998). *The 1998 business work-life study*. New York: Families and Work Institute.

Galinsky, E., Bond, J.T., & Friedman, D. E. (1993) *The changing workforce: Highlights of the national study*. New York: Families and Work Institute.

Galinsky, E., Friedman, D., & Hernandez, C. (1991). *The corporate reference guide to work-family programs*. New York: Families and Work Institute.

Gershuny, J., & Robinson, J. (1988). Historical change in the household division of labor. *Demography, 25*(4), 537–552.

Gerson, K. (1985). *Hard choices: How women decide about work, career, and motherhood*. Berkeley: University of California Press.

Gerson, K. (1993). *No man's land: Men's changing commitments to family and work*. New York: Basic Books.

Gerstel, N. Clawson, D., & Zussman, R. (Eds.). (2002). *Families at work: Expanding the boundaries*. Nashville, TN: Vanderbilt University Press.

Gerstel, N. & Gross, H. (1989). Women and the American family: Continuity and change. In J. Freeman (Ed.), *Women: A feminist perspective* (4th ed., part 2). Mountain View, CA: Mayfield.

Golden, L. (2001, March). Flexible work schedules: What are we trading off to get them? *Monthly Labor Review, 124*(3), 50–67.

Greenhaus, J., & Beutell, N. (1985). Sources of conflict between work and family roles. *Academy of Management Review, 10*(1), 76–88.

Greenhaus, J., & Parasuraman, S. (1986). A work-nonwork interactive perspective of stress and its consequences. *Journal of Organizational Behavior Management, 8*(2), 37–60.

Greenhaus, J. H. (1988). The intersection of work and family roles: Individual, interpersonal, and organizational issues. *Journal of Personality and Social Psychology* 3(4: Special issue), 23–44.

Greenstein, T. (1993, September). Maternal employment and child behavioral outcomes: A household economics analysis. *Journal of Family Issues, 14*(3), 323–355.

Haas, L. (1990). Gender equality and social policy: Implications of a study of parental leave in Sweden. *Journal of Family Issues, 11*(4), 401–423.

Hall, D. T., & Associates (1986). *Career development in organizations*. San Francisco: Jossey-Bass.

Hall, F. S., & Hall, D. T. (1979). *The two career couple*. Reading, Ma: Addison-Wesley.

Han, S. K., & Moen, P. (1999). Clocking-out: Temporal patterning of retirement. *American Journal of Sociology, 105*(1), 191–236.

Hart, P. (2003 February). *Imagining the future of work: A strategic research study conducted for the Alfred P. Sloan Foundation*. Washington, DC: Peter D. Hart Research Associates.

Hartmann, H. (Ed.). (1985). *Comparable worth: New directions for research*. Washington, DC: National Academy Press.

Hartmann, H., Yoon, Y.-H., & Zuckerman, D. (2000). *Part-time opportunities for professionals and managers: Where are they, who uses them and why*. Washington, DC: Institute for Women's Policy Research.

Hertz, R., & Marshall, N. L. (Eds.). (2001). *The transformation of the American home*. Berkeley: University of California Press.

Hochschild, A. (1997). *The time bind: When work becomes home and home becomes work*. New York: Metropolitan Books.

Hochschild, A., & Machung, A. (1989). *The second shift: Working parents and the revolution at home*. New York: Viking.

Hoffman, L., & Nye, F. J. (1974). *Working mothers*. San Francisco: Jossey-Bass.

Hutchens, D. (1994). The United States: Employer policies for discouraging work by older people: In F. Naschold & B. de Vroom (Eds.), *Regulating employment and welfare: Company and national policies of labour force participation at the end of worklife in industrial countries*. Berlin: DeGruyter.

Hutchens, R. (1994). 'The United States: Employer policies for discouraging work by older people' In F. Naschold & B. de Vroom (Eds.), *Regulating Employment and Welfare. Company and National Policies of Labour Force Participation End of Worklife in Industrial Countries.* Berlin: Walter DeGruyter.

Hutchens, R., & Dentinger, E. (2003). Moving toward retirement: Employers, older workers, and reduced work schedules. In *It's about time: Couples and careers,* P. Moen (Ed.). Ithaca, NY: Cornell University Press.

Jacobs, J., & Gerson, K. (1998a). Toward a family-friendly, gender-equitable workweek. *University of Pennsylvania Journal of Labor and Employment Law, 1*(2), 457–472.

Jacobs, J., & Gerson, K. (1998b, Winter). Who are the overworked Americans? *Review of Social Economy, 56*(4), 442–459.

Jacobs, J. A., & Gerson, K. (2004). *The time divide: Work, family, and gender inequality (the family and public policy).* Boston: Harvard University Press.

Kahn, A. J., & Kamerman, S. (1976). *Childcare programs in nine countries: A report prepared for the OECD working party on the role of women in the economy.* Washington, DC: Social and Rehabilitation Service (Department of Health, Education, and Welfare).

Kamerman, S., & Kahn, A. J. (Eds.). (1978). *Family policy: Government and families in fourteen countries.* New York: Columbia University Press.

Kanter, R. (1977). *Work and family in the United States: A critical review and agenda for research and policy.* New York: Russell Sage Foundation.

Kelly, E., & Dobbin, F. (1999). Civil rights law at work: Sex discrimination and the rise of maternity leave policies. *American Journal of Sociology, 105*(2), 455–492.

Kreps, J. (1976). *Women and the American economy: A look to the 1980s.* Englewood Cliffs, NJ: Prentice-Hall.

Kropf, M. B. (2001). Part-time work arrangements and the corporation. In R. Hertz & N. L. Marshall (Eds.), *Working families: The transformation of the American home* (pp. 152–168). Berkeley: University of California Press.

Lee, M. D., Engler, L., & Wright, L. (2002). Exploring the boundaries in professional careers: Reduced-load work arrangements in law, medicine, and accounting. In R. J. Burke & D. L. Nelson (Eds.). *Advancing women's careers: Research and practice* (pp. 174–205). Oxford, UK: Blackwell.

Lee, M. D., MacDermid, S. D., Williams, M., Buck, M., & Leiba-O'Sullivan, S. (2002). Contextual factors in the success of reduced-load work arrangements among managers and professionals. *Human Resource Management, 41*(2), 209–223.

Lewis, S. (1998). *European perspectives of work and family* (Work-Family Policy Paper Series). Chestnut Hill, MA: Boston College Center for Work & Family.

Lewis, S., Izraeli, D., & Hootsmans, H. (1992). *Dual earner families: International perspectives.* London: Sage.

MacDermid, S., Lees, M., Buck, M., & Williams, M. (2001). Alternative work arrangements among professionals and managers: Rethinking career development and success. *Journal of Management Development, 20*(4), 305–317.

Marks, S. R. (1977). Multiple roles and role strain: Some notes on human energy, time, and commitment. *American Sociological Review, 42,* 921–936.

Meiksins, P., & Whalley, P. (2002). *Putting work in its place: A quiet revolution.* Ithaca, NY: ILR Press.

Menaghan, E., & Parcel, T. (1990). Parental employment and family life: Research in the 1980s. *Journal of Marriage and the Family, 52*(4), 1079–1098.

Moen, P. (2003). *It's about time: Couples and careers.* Ithaca, NY: Cornell University Press.

Moen, P., Elder, G., & Luscher, K. (with Quick, H.) (Eds.). (1995). *Examining lives in context: Perspectives on the ecology of human development.* Washington, DC: American Psychological Association.

Moen, P., & Han, S.-K. (2001a). Reframing careers: Work, family, and gender. In V. Marshall, W. Heinz, H. Krueger, & A. Verma (Eds.), *Restructuring work and life course* (pp. 424–445). Toronto: University of Toronto Press.

Moen, P., & Han, S.-K. (2001b). Gendered careers: A life course perspective. In R. Hertz & N. Marshall (Eds.), *Families and work: Today's realities and tomorrow's possibilities* (pp. 42–57). Berkeley: University of California Press.

Moen, P., Robertson, J., & Fields, V. (1994). Women's work and care giving roles: A life course approach. *Journal of Gerontology, 49*(4), S176–S186.

Moen, P., & Yu, Y. (2000). Effective work/ life strategies: Working couples, work conditions, gender and life quality. *Social Problems, 47,* 291–144.

Myrdal, G. (1969). *An American dilemma: The Negro problem and modern democracy.* New York: Harper & Row.

Nye, F., & Hoffman, L. (1963). *The employed mother in America.* Chicago: Rand McNally.

Oakley, A. (1974). *The sociology of housework.* New York: Pantheon Books.

O Sullivan, S. L., Macdermid, S. M., Lee, M. D., & Williams, M. (2002). *Direct Reports' Perceptions of Reduced-load Managers' Effectiveness: When does Absence Matter?* [Electronic version] Retrieved June 2, 2005, from http://www.msu.edu/user/kossek/flexwork/work-study.pdf.

Parasuraman S. & Greenhaus, J. (1997). *Integrating work and family: Challenges and choices for a changing world.* Wesport, CT: Quorum Books.

Parcel, T. L., & Menaghan, E. G. (1994). *Parents' jobs and children's lives*. New York: DeGruyter.

Penner, R., Perun, P., & Steuerle, E. (2002). Legal and institutional impediments to partial retirement and part-time work by older workers. [Electronic version] Published: November 20, Retrieved June 2, 2005, from http://www.urban.org/url.cfm?ID=410587

Pitt-Catsouphes, M. (2000). A coming of age: Work/ life flexibility. In E. Appelbaum (Ed.), *Balancing acts: Easing the burdens and improving options for working families* (pp. 139–149). Washington, DC: Economic Policy Institute.

Pleck, J. (1986). Employment and fatherhood: Issues and innovative policies. In M. Lamb (Ed.), *The father's role: Applied perspectives* (pp. 385–412). New York: Wiley.

Pleck, J. H., Staines, G. L., & Lang, L. (1980). Conflicts between work and family life. *Monthly Labor Review 103*(3), 29–32.

Rapoport, R. (1980). Balancing work, family, and leisure: A triple helix model. In C. Brooklyn Dorr (Ed.), *Work, family and the career: New frontiers in theory and research*. New York: Praeger.

Rapoport, R., & Bailyn, L. (with Kolb, D., Fletcher, J., Friedman, D., Eaton, S., Harvey, M., & Miller, B.). (1996). *Relinking life and work: Toward a better future* (Report). New York: Ford Foundation.

Rapoport, R., & Rapoport, R. (1969). The dual-career family: A variant pattern and social change. *Human Relations, 22*(1), 3–30.

Rapoport, R., & Rapoport, R. (1971). *Dual-career families*. Harmondsworth and Baltimore, MD: Penguin Pelican.

Rapoport, R., & Rapoport, R. (1977). *Dual-career families re-examined: New integrations of work and family*. New York: Harper & Row.

Rapoport, R., & Rapoport, R. N. (with Bumstead, J. M.). (Eds.). (1978). *Working couples*. London: Routledge & Kegan Paul.

Repetti, R., & Crosby, F. (1984). Gender and depression: Exploring the adult-role explanation. *Journal of Social and Clinical Psychology, 2*(1), 57–70.

Repetti, R., Matthews, K. A., & Waldron, I. (1989). Employment and women's health: Effects of paid employment on women's mental and physical health. *American Psychologist, 44*(11), 1394–1401.

Reskin, Barbara F. (1984). *Sex segregation in the workplace: Trends, explanations, remedies*. Washington, DC: National Academy Press.

Roos, P., & Reskin, B. (Eds.). (1984). *Institutional factors contributing to sex segregation in the workplace*. Washington, DC: National Academy Press.

Schaffer, R. H., & Thomson, H. A. (1992). Successful change programs begin with results. *Harvard Business Review. 70*(1), 80–89.

Schneider, B., & Waite, L. (Eds.). (2005). *Being together, working apart: Dual career familes and the work-life balance*. New York: Cambridge University Press.

Schein, E. (1978). *Career dynamics: Matching individual and organizational needs*. Reading, MA: Addison-Wesley.

Schor, J. (1991). *The overworked American: The unexpected decline of leisure*. New York: Basic Books.

Schwartz, F. (1989). Management women and the new facts of life. *Harvard Business Review, 67*(1), 65–76.

Sloan workplace, workforce and working families program (2004). *Family/work: Creating family friendly work*. New York: Alfred P. Sloan Foundation.

Staines, G., & Pleck, J. (1983). *The impact of work schedules on the family*. Ann Arbor, MI: Survey Research Center and Institute for Social Research.

Staines, G., & Pleck, J. (1984). Nonstandard work schedules and family life. *Journal of Applied Psychology, 69*(3), 515–523.

Stolzenberg, R. (2001, July). It's about time and gender; spousal employment and health. *AJS, 107*(1), 61–100.

Swiss, D. J., & Walker, J. P. (1993). *Women and the work/family dilemma: How today's professional women are finding solutions*. New York: Wiley.

Voydanoff, P. (1988). Work and family: A review and expanded conceptualization. *Journal of Social Behavior and Personality, 3*(4), 1–22.

Waite, L. J., & Nielsen, M. (2001). The rise of the dual-earner family, 1963–1997. In R. Hertz & N. L. Marshall (Eds.), *Working families: The transformation of the American home* (pp. 23–41). Los Angeles: University of California Press.

Wenger, J. (2001). *The continuing problems with part-time jobs*. Issue brief #155, Washington, DC: Economic Policy Institute. Published April 24. [Electronic version] Retrieved June 2, 2005, from www.uic.edu/cuppa/uicued/tempwork/RESEARCH/LitReviews/Wenger-Problems.pdf.

Williams, J. C. & Segal, N. (2003). Beyond the maternal wall: Relief for family caregivers who are discriminated against on the job. *Harvard Women's Law Journal*, 26, 77–161.

Wiliams, J., & Calvert, C. T. (2001). *Effective part-time policies for Washington Law firms*. Washington, DC: Project for Attorney Retention, Program on Gender Work and Family, American University, Washington College of Law. [Electronic version] Retrieved June 2, 2005, from http://pardc.org/FinalReport-secondedition.pdf.

Yohalem, A. (1979). *Careers of professional women*. Rowman & Littlefield.

Author Index

Italic numbers refer to bibliographical entries.

735

Subject Index